European Axis Signal Intelligence in World War II

As Revealed by "TICOM" Investigations and by Other Prisoner of War Interrogations and Captured Material, Principally German

National Security Agency

Republished by Nimble Books LLC

Nimble Books LLC
1521 Martha Avenue
Ann Arbor, MI, USA 48103
http://www.NimbleBooks.com
wfz@nimblebooks.com
+1.734-330-2593

Version 1.0; last saved 2010-10-26.

Printed in the United States of America

ISBN-13: 978-1-60888-008-9

The paper used in this publication meets the minimum requirements of the American National Standard for Information Sciences—Permanence of Paper for Printed Library Materials, ANSI Z39.48-1992. The paper is acid-free and lignin-free.

Contents

ARMY SECURITY AGENCY

Washington, D. C.

EUROPEAN AXIS SIGNAL INTELLIGENCE IN WORLD WAR II AS REVEALED BY "TICOM" INVESTIGATIONS AND BY OTHER PRISONER OF WAR INTERROGATIONS AND CAPTURED MATERIAL, PRINCIPALLY GERMAN

In Nine Volumes

VOL. 1

Prepared under the direction of the

CHIEF, ARMY SECURITY AGENCY

1 May 1946

WDGAS-14

DOCID: 3560861

~~TOP SECRET CREAM~~

~~TOP SECRET CREAM~~

VOLUME 1--SYNOPSIS

DOCID: 3560861

VOLUME 1 SYNOPSIS

Paragraph

1. Origin of "TICOM".-- The word "TICOM" served as a cover name for a special project and for an organization, the "Target Intelligence Committee." The project, which was originally conceived by Colonel George A. Bicher, Director of the Signal Intelligence Division, ETOUSA, in the summer of 1944, aimed at the investigation and possible exploitation of German cryptologic organizations, operations, installations, and personnel, as soon as possible after the impending collapse of the German armed forces. Colonel Bicher elicited and secured the support of the U. S. Navy and of the British, and accordingly a joint and combined "Target Intelligence Committee" was established in England in October 1944, by the authority of the Chief of Staff, United States Army; the Commander-in-Chief, United States Fleet; and the Chairman, London Sigint Board.

2

DOCID: 3560861

The Target Intelligence Committee originally planned airborne operations, even before the German collapse, to seize important German signal intelligence targets, known from Ultra material and prisoner of war interrogations. There were four objectives:

a. To learn the extent of the German cryptanalytic effort against England and America;

b. To prevent the results of such German cryptanalysis against England and America from falling into unauthorized hands as the German Armies retreated;

c. To exploit German cryptologic techniques and inventions before they could be destroyed by the Germans; and

d. To uncover items of signal intelligence value in prosecuting the war against Japan.

The TICOM mission was of highest importance. American cryptographers did not then know with certainty the extent to which United States communications were secure or ~~unsecure~~, insecure, nor did they know the extent of the enemy's cryptanalytic abilities, strength, and material, except by conjecture, by inference from Anglo-American cryptanalysis of German systems and from prisoner of war interrogations. German cryptanalytic successes were obviously unpublicized. They were reflected instead in higher casualty lists and lessened success on the part of Allied tactics and strategy.

In the Spring of 1945, however, conditions for the proposed operations became rapidly unsatisfactory. The known German signal intelligence agencies were dispersing or retreating to other localities in greatest disorder. Pinpoint locations could not be established. The possibility was remote that Anglo-American parachute units could seize worthwhile personnel and material and hold them through the confusion of major battles. Therefore, in March, 1945, TICOM decided instead to alert six United States-British target exploitation teams in England, these teams to be sent into enemy territory as either United States or British troops overran it, where they were to take over and exploit known or newly discovered targets of signal intelligence interest and to search for other signal intelligence targets and personnel.

3

The first exploitation team was dispatched in April 1945 to the Neumuenster-Flensburg area, and other teams were quickly dispatched to other areas as soon as overrun. The odyssies of the TICOM teams striving to locate and exploit signal intelligence targets during the confused days before and after the German capitulation, make entertaining as well as instructive reading. They are fully recorded in the TICOM publications.[1] A short summary of these operations is given in Volume 8, Chapter X, of this report.

The results obtained from these TICOM efforts were impressive. Approximately 4000 separate German documents were captured.[2] This material weighed 5 tons. Many cryptographic devices and machines were captured. One hundred and ninety six reports, based on interrogation of German signal intelligence personnel, together with other miscellaneous reports and translations were issued by TICOM.

The true value of the TICOM effort is not measurable in such statistics. Its importance lies rather in what the TICOM effort revealed to American cryptologists concerning German signal intelligence, with particular reference to American systems. The TICOM prisoner of war interrogations and captured documents, with the interrogations conducted by other Anglo-American agencies (notably the Combined Services Detailed Interrogation Centre, or "CSDIC") have given Anglo-American investigators a reasonably complete picture of German signal intelligence. The United States Army Security Agency has obtained from these interrogations and documents information useful in assessing its own cryptanalytic and cryptographic achievements, especially its own development of rapid analytic machinery, the state of its research in cryptography, and the cryptographic security of American systems.

1. See IF 15, IF 40, IF 51, IF 101, IF 165, IF 166, IF 167, and I-1.

2. By "document" is meant either one or a collection of papers, books, files of correspondence, messages, films, worksheets or other items of intelligence value, to which a TICOM document number was assigned for convenience in classification and handling.

4

2. The European Axis cryptanalytic effort against United States communications.--From TICOM sources it is learned that European cryptanalysts were unable to read any U. S. Army or Navy high-level cryptographic systems. The Army Converter M134C (SIGABA), the Army Teletypewriter Cipher Attachment known as the Converter M-228 (SIGCUM), the Army Teletypewriter Privacy Set (SIGIBS), the Army High Security Teletypewriter Cipher System (SIGTOT), the Army Speech Equipment RC-220-T1 (SIGSALY), the Combined Cipher Machine (CCM), the Navy Electric Cipher Machine Mark III (ECM, identical with SIGABA), and the Navy Teletypewriter Cryptographic Attachment (C. S. P. 1515, identical with the Army Converter M-228) were completely secure. One Army Strip system (System No. 47 or 67) and one Navy strip system (probably C. S. P. 1404) were read for short intervals until the principle of strip elimination was introduced. The low-grade ciphony device (Speech Equipment AN/GSQ-1, or SIGJIP) was not read, although theoretical solutions were worked out.

Both of the unenciphered War Department Telegraph Codes (SIGRIM and SIGARM) were read by the Germans. Hungary received photostatic copies of War Department Confidential Code Number 2, probably from the Bulgarians, together with at least one set of cipher tables, and the Italians reconstructed subsequent editions of the enciphering tables. The compromise appears to have been shared with other Axis powers, notably Germany, Finland and Japan. Military Intelligence Code No. 11 (physically compromised), used by the Military Attache in Cairo, was read throughout the summer of 1942. The Germans read messages in several versions of the Division Field Codes.

German cryptanalysts solved from 10 per cent to 30 per cent of intercepted U. S. Army M-209 messages. Save where keys were captured, it was usually read too late to be of tactical value. Messages sent by the U. S. Army in Slidex, Codex, Bomber Code, Assault Code, Aircraft Movement Code, Map Coordinate Codes, and Cipher Device M-94 where employed, were read regularly and almost 100 per cent.

Combined Naval Cypher No. 3, used by the U. S. Navy and the Royal Navy for Atlantic Convoy operations, was read almost 100 per cent by the Germans from the end of 1941 through the middle of 1943. The solution of this system was perhaps for the allies the most disastrous signal intelligence success achieved by the Germans. Allied convoy shipping losses suffered during this period were six times as great as during any other comparable period.

The Germans engaged in intensive and successful traffic analysis activities against United States Army and Army Air Force radio communications. This included direction-finding, analysis of call sign and frequency allocation systems, analysis of plain text and operator's chat, as well as more complex operations, such as air-borne radar route tracking, and monitoring of transmitter zero beat tuning.

The U. S. Army Converter M-134A (SIGMYC), and the U. S. Navy Cipher Machine (HCM), furnished by the Navy to the State Department, were not read by the Germans. The State Department Strip systems O-1 and O-2 were solved, the former probably through a compromise, and the latter through cryptanalysis. Several State Department codes, including the Brown Code (unenciphered) and Code A-1 (enciphered), were compromised and read, probably from 1938 and 1939, respectively.

From an intelligence standpoint the results obtained by the German cryptanalytic successes were important, but not decisive. American Army and Navy strategy was secure as long as high level systems were employed. Tactical operations, however, did suffer. The Anglo-American convoy shipping losses during 1942 and early 1943 were huge, largely because of German successes with Combined Naval Cypher No. 3. German traffic analysis and cryptanalysis provided a comprehensive order of battle for the U. S. Army and Army Air Forces in the United Kingdom, in the Mediterranean, and on the continent. According to a German air force officer, "no attack of the Eighth Air Force came as a surprise." The value of the intelligence which the Germans got from State Department codes and strip ciphers is not accurately known. The strip systems were probably read too late to be of any great value. The compromise of Military Intelligence Code No. 11 did provide intelligence of unquestioned tactical value, particularly in the summer of 1942 during Rommel's advance to Egypt.

The German cryptanalytic effort against Russian military communications was even greater than that made against the United States. The German successes in solution of medium and low grade English military and naval communications systems were considerable. The cryptanalysis of the diplomatic communications of Italy, Japan, France, Turkey, Bulgaria, Greece, Portugal, Spain, Switzerland, and other smaller nations also achieved important results.

A tabulation of the results of German and other European Axis cryptanalysis, country by country, is given in Chart 1-2, at the end of this Volume. These results will be discussed also in the subsequent volumes on the separate German agencies.

3. <u>Organization of German Signal Intelligence Agencies</u>.-- Germany possessed six main cryptologic organizations during World War II, with a total strength, including field units and overhead, of approximately 30,000 persons. Italy possessed two main signal intelligence organizations; Finland, Austria, and Hungary each had one. The grand total of European Axis personnel engaged in signal intelligence in World War II is estimated as 36,000.

This number is small when compared with the numbers engaged in the Anglo-American effort. The grand total of Anglo-American signal intelligence personnel at the end of the War, including all services and including field and overhead personnel, was in excess of 60,000 persons. Out of this total, the United States Army employed approximately 28,000 persons.

Of the six main German cryptologic organizations, four were military, and two were civilian.

The four military organizations were:

a. The Signal Intelligence Agency of the Army High Command (OKH/GdNA), which dealt with enemy Army traffic.

b. The Signal Intelligence Agency of the Navy High Command (OKM/4SKL III), which dealt with enemy naval traffic.

c. The Signal Intelligence Agency of the Air Force High Command OKL/LN Abt 350), which dealt with enemy Air Force traffic.

d. The Signal Intelligence Agency of the Supreme Command Armed Forces (OKW/Chi), which dealt with enemy, neutral or friendly diplomatic traffic, commercial traffic and news broadcasts

7

The two civilian organizations were:

a. The Foreign Office Cryptanalytic Section (Pers Z S) which also dealt with diplomatic traffic, enemy, neutral, or friendly.

b. Goering's "Research" Bureau (FA), a Nazi party agency which also dealt with diplomatic traffic, news releases, broadcast monitoring, telephone monitoring, and other types of communications intelligence, enemy, neutral, or friendly.

Chart number 1-1 at the end of this volume shows how the above six agencies were related. Brief descriptions of these agencies and their work follow.

4. The Signal Intelligence Agency of the Army High Command.-- The Signal Intelligence Agency of the Army High Command (Oberkommando des Heeres, General der Nachrichten Aufklaerung, abbreviated OKH/GdNA) was located at Jueterbog, about 60 miles southwest of Berlin. Its mission included cryptanalysis and evaluation of Allied army traffic, at any level, whether strategic or operational. It also did a small amount of radio broadcast monitoring.

This Agency was the main unit of the German Army signal intelligence service in 1945. Other units were:

a. Two intercept stations operating directly under the Signal Intelligence Agency, and supplying it with intercepts of Allied high-level traffic.

b. Nine field Signal Intelligence Regiments assigned to various Army Groups for the purpose of interception, traffic analysis, cryptanalysis, and evaluation of Allied Army low-level tactical traffic in the Army Group areas. These Regiments were independent of the Central Signal Intelligence Agency, but supplied the latter with intercepts and reports.

c. A small Signal Intelligence Section, assigned to the Army Commander in Chief, West, which acted as a coordinating section for the two Signal Intelligence Regiments on the Western front.

An estimated total of 12,000 persons was employed in the Army signal intelligence effort described above.

The main successes of the German Army signal intelligence organization from its formation to the end of the war included the following:

a. Before 1939 it was able to establish French, Dutch, and British order of battle. This was done by cryptanalysis of French codes and Dutch Army double-transposition ciphers, and through direction-finding and traffic-analysis directed against British Army communications systems.[3]

b. During the 1940 French campaign it established French mobile order of battle. This was done by cryptanalysis of French codes (unnamed).[4]

c. It established Russian army order of battle and location of strategic reserves, from early in the war through 1943. This was accomplished through traffic analysis and cryptanalysis of Russian 2, 3, 4, and 5-figure codes (both Army and Peoples Commissariat (NKVD)).[5]

d. It gave Rommel intelligence of great operational value during the fighting around Tobruk. This was done by solving the super-encipherment of a compromised British code (unidentified).[6]

e. Information on operations undertaken by the American Army in North Africa, and thereafter through the war, was obtained through solution of Converter M-209 traffic.[7] During the fighting in Sicily the Germans captured two weeks after it went into effect, a key list valid for one month[8] and were enabled thereby to read the system completely for the remaining two weeks.[9] On other nets when sufficient depth

[3] I 78

[4] I 78

[5] I 78; I 26; I 21; I 19

[6] IF 107; I 113. Germans called this "the British War Office Code."

[7] I 154; IF 107; I 60; I 113

[8] IF 107

[9] I 60

was available, from 10%[10] to 30%[11] of M-209 traffic was readable, though most of the traffic was read too late to be of tactical value.[12]

f. Information concerning U. S. Army activities in Iceland, England, Central America, and North Africa, was obtained by reading the U. S. Army Division Field Codes (DFC 15, 16, 17, 21, 25, and 28, and possibly others).[13]

g. Tactical information concerning Allied bombing and artillery targets,[14] weather reports,[15] and reports on the size and location of Allied units passing Military Police control points in France,[16] were obtained from solutions of "Slidex," a British device for protecting operational low-level traffic. This device was used by both British and American forces and various versions of it were solved, usually in from one to three hours.[17]

h. Solution of traffic passed on Hungarian internal networks in 1941 gave evidence that transportation of German troops over Hungarian railroads could be safely undertaken.[18]

i. Successful cryptanalysis was carried out against the traffic of Yugoslav partisans, Greek partisans, Czech agents, Russian agents, and the Polish resistance movement.[19]

The Signal Intelligence Agency of the Army High Command issued three daily reports. These were sent to the Army High Command, Navy High Command, Air Force High Command, and to the Supreme Command, Armed Forces; to Himmler as chief of the Elite guard; and probably to the Reich Security Office (RSHA).

[10] I 60

[11] I 113

[12] I 142

[13] IF 120 and IF 107

[14] IF 107 p 8

[15] I 74

[16] I 80

[17] I 74, I 76, I 80, I 109, IF 107

[18] IF 126 p 10

[19] I 115, I 76, D 60, I 170, I 58, and others.

10

Each of the nine Signal Intelligence Regiments in the field supplied intelligence directly to commanders at Army Group, Army, and Corps levels, looking to them for primary directives on missions and priorities. They cooperated closely with the local Air Force Signals Regiments.

The Signal Security Agency of the Army High Command (Inspektion 7/IV, abbreviated In 7/IV) issued Army Codes and Ciphers until 1944, when this function was taken over by the Signal Intelligence Agency of the Supreme Command, Armed Forces (OKW/Chi).

Volume 4 is a detailed account of the German Army Signal Intelligence Agency, its field units, and their activities.

5. The Signal Intelligence Agency of the Air Force High Command-- The Signal Intelligence Agency of the Air Force High Command (Oberkommando der Luftwaffe, Luftnachrichten Abteilung 350, abbreviated OKL/LN Abt 350, previously Chi Stelle, O B d L), was the principal unit of the German Air Force Signal Intelligence Service in 1945. Field units were:

a. Three autonomous Signal Intelligence Regiments with a total of eight battalions.

b. Five autonomous Signal Intelligence Battalions. Thirteen thousand people, including overhead, were employed in all the above units.

The German Air Force Signal Intelligence Service successes against the Royal Air Force and the United States Army Air Forces were outstanding.

a. The Service furnished a comprehensive and continuous picture of the battle order and deployment of United States Army Air Force and Royal Air Force units in the United Kingdom, in the Mediterranean Theater, and, after D-day, on the continent. This information came mainly from traffic analysis, radio-telephone monitoring, and monitoring of air-borne radar devices. The solution of Royal Air Force 4-figure codes (from March 1940 until 1 November 1942) gave basic data which was enlarged upon and used until the end of the war.[20]

[20] I 70, IF 182, IF 175 p 19

11

b. It gave prompt and accurate warning of United States Army Air Force and Royal Air Force heavy bomber missions. This resulted from advanced methods of traffic analysis, from radio-telephone monitoring, and from radar monitoring.[21]

c. It gave immediate warning to German ground forces and fighter squadrons of tactical operations by Allied ground support aircraft.[22]

d. In connection with its western front activities, the solution of the Bomber code, Slidex, Syko, and Rekoh (used by the Royal Air Force and, for a short time, by the United States Army Air Force), both by capture and cryptanalysis, was important throughout the war.[23]

The German Air Force Signal Intelligence Service successes against the Russian Air Force were also great.

a. Its cryptanalysis of Russian Air Force ground-to-ground 2-figure, 3-figure, and 4-figure administrative and operational codes, and some 5-figure codes, provided a complete order of battle for the Russian Air Forces from 1937 until the end of the war. A large amount of intelligence on Russian Army battle order was also obtained from a study of air networks.[24]

b. From partial decipherment of air-ground traffic, from plane-to-ground radio-telephone monitoring, and from radio-direction finding of bombers when airborne, it was able to give accurate warnings of all Russian long-range strategic bombing raids.[25]

c. From cryptanalysis of each Russian Air Army's 2-figure, 3-figure, and 4-figure traffic, from traffic analysis, from plane-to-plane radio-telephone monitoring, and from radio direction-finding of planes in flight, it was able to warn German ground forces and fighter squadrons of impending operations by Russian fighters and fighter bombers.[26]

[21] I 70

[22] IF 182

[23] IF 175

[24] I 120

[25] IF 187

[26] IF 187

Intelligence from both Western and Russian fronts, in the form of daily, weekly, or monthly reports, was furnished by the Signal Intelligence Agency (OKL/LN Abt 350) to the Air Force High Command and to the local Air Forces (Luftflotten). Daily and monthly reports were also sent to the local Army Signal Intelligence Regiments. Monthly reports were sent to the Army Commander in Chief West, to the Signal Intelligence Agency of the Army High Command (OKH/GdNA), to the Signal Intelligence Agency of the Navy High Command (OKM/4 SKL/III), to the Signal Intelligence Agency of the Supreme Command Armed Forces (OKW/Chi), and also to the Air Force Signal Intelligence units in the field.[27]

Field units, charged with the responsibility for warnings on allied air raids, telephoned their warnings and reports directly to fighter squadrons, anti-aircraft batteries, and the local Gauleiters in charge of civilian air raid warnings.[28]

Group IV of Division II in the Office of the Chief Air Force Signal Officer (Oberkommando der Luftwaffe/Generalnachrichtenfuehrer II, Gruppe IV, abbreviated OKL/Gen Nafue II/IV) issued codes and ciphers for the Air Force. Group IV of Division III (OKL/Gen Nafue III/IV) checked them for cryptographic security.

A detailed description of the Signal Intelligence Service of the Air Force is given in Volume 5 of this report.

6. The Signal Intelligence Agency of the Navy High Command-- The Signal Intelligence Agency of the Navy High Command (Oberkommando der Kriegsmarine, 4 Seekriegsleitung III, abbreviated OKM/4 SKL/III) was responsible for traffic analysis, cryptanalysis, and evaluation of British, American, Russian, French, and Swedish naval traffic. It had a strength of approximately 1,000 persons. It also had operational control over a field organization of approximately 2,500 persons. The field units were as follows:

a. Four detachments in Flanders, Brittany, Wilhemshaven and Pomerania engaged in cryptanalysis on low-level systems, interception and direction-finding. Each detachment had a total complement of 200 men, including 100 intercept operators and 10 cryptanalysts.

[27] IF 180 p 31 a

[28] IF 181

13

b. Eighteen "primary direction-finding stations", whose main duties were interception rather than direction finding. Each station had a strength of 100, including 60 intercept operators, and 5 cryptanalysts.

c. Twenty five "secondary direction-finding stations", whose duties were direction finding and traffic analysis. Each station had a strength of 26 persons.

d. Small detachments were occasionally set up for special missions.

The main successes of the Signal Intelligence Agency of the Navy High Command (OKM/4 SKL/III) included the following:

a. In 1939 it was able to establish the war-time organization and disposition of the British Fleet, through solution of British Naval Code No. 2.

b. In the spring of 1940 it obtained complete information concerning the proposed British and French Norway expedition ("Operation Stratford"). This was done by solution of British Naval Cypher No. 4.[29] The German invasion of Norway followed immediately. During the subsequent Norwegian campaign, solution of traffic sent in British Naval Cypher No. 4. gave detailed information on Allied counter-measures, such as proposed British landing fields, transport arrival schedules, and the disposition of British and French surface forces.[30]

c. Throughout 1942 and part of 1943 it provided important intelligence on Atlantic convoys by a current (and nearly 100%) solution of Combined Cypher No. 3 used by British and U. S. North Atlantic Convoys.[31] The average monthly allied shipping losses in the Atlantic during this period were approximately six times the average monthly losses in later periods.

Minor successes of the Signal Intelligence Agency of the Navy High Command (OKM/4 SKL/III) included the solution of the British Interdepartmental Cypher;[32] solution in 1943 of a Royal Air Force torpedo-bomber transposition cipher used for practice exercises in the English Channel;[33] and solution of various minor Navy and Merchant Navy codes and ciphers.

[29] T-517

[30] T-517

[31] I 12

[32] Performed jointly with Goering's "Research" Bureau (FA), the Signal Intelligence Agency of the Supreme Command Armed Forces (OKW/Chi), and with the Signal Intelligence Agency of the Commander in Chief German Air Force (Chi Stelle, OBdL) I 147.

[33] D 6 D 15 D 41

p.14

The Naval Signal Intelligence field units described above carried out direction-finding activities against Allied naval and merchant ships, plotted their positions and movements, and passed the information to local commanders. Detachment Flanders, at Bruges, assisted in the 1942 "escape" of the pocket battleships Scharnhorst and Gneisenau when they made their dash from Brest through the English Channel to Kiel. This same detachment read British naval traffic to advantage during the Dieppe raid.

The Signal Security Agency of the Navy High Command (OKM/4 SKL/II), as opposed to the Signal Intelligence Agency(OKM/4 SKL/III), issued German naval codes and ciphers, and made cryptographic security studies of these systems. Its exact strength is unknown.

The detailed organization and history of the two signal agencies of the Naval High Command (OKM/4 SKL/III and OKM/4 SKL/II) are not discussed further in this report. Their use of punch-card book-keeping machinery ("I. B. M."), their security studies, and their chief cryptanalytic methods, however, are discussed in Volume 2.

7. The Signal Intelligence Agency of the Supreme Command Armed Forces.- The Signal Intelligence Agency of the Supreme Command Armed Forces (Oberkommando der Wehrmacht, Chiffrierabteilung, abbreviated OKW/Chi) had three main functions:

a. It intercepted, studied, and evaluated diplomatic, military attache, and "agent" traffic.

b. It monitored, and evaluated commercial radio traffic and news broadcasts.

c. It made security studies of the codes and ciphers used by the Supreme Command, Armed Forces, the Army, the Air Force and the Navy, and many government departments, vetoing (after 1944) the use of those it deemed insecure.

The Signal Intelligence Agency of the Supreme Command Armed Forces (OKW/Chi) operated at least thirteen radio intercept stations of its own, and received radio traffic from other agencies as well (notably Goering's "Research" Bureau (FA)). It also received land-line traffic from sources not stated.[34]

[34] DF 9, p 3

DOCID: 3560861

With the exception of military attache systems, it did not work on enemy Army, Navy or Air Force traffic. Documentary evidence as to its cryptanalytic successes is limited. The following summary covers its most important known cryptanalytic achievements:

a. The most extensive 1939-1944 successes seem to have been achieved with French systems. The electrical Hagelin Cipher Machine B-211 (adopted by the French - now obsolete) was solved, and limited success was also achieved in the solution of the French Hagelin Machine BC-38.[35] An important military attache code (ASA trigraph FVD) was solved at the beginning of the war.[36] After 1940 all Vichy-French systems were automatically compromised when filed with the German Armistice Commission in Wiesbaden.

b. At least four Japanese diplomatic codes (including those designated by ASA trigraphs JAE, JAH and JBA) were solved. In 1938 and 1939 the Agency collaborated with the Cryptanalytic Section of the Foreign Office (Pers Z S) in a current solution of daily keys for the Japanese "Red" Machine.[37]

c. Precise details on solution of U.S. systems are not available. The agency had compromised copies of at least two U.S. State Department codes, namely "Brown" and "Al". Work was also done on the U.S. State Department Strip Ciphers 0-1 and 0-2, the lead in 0-2 solution being taken by the Foreign Office Cryptanalytic Section.[38]

d. Croatian Enigma traffic was solved through compromised machine wirings.[39]

[35] I 45 p 7; I 160 p 6

[36] I 31 p 8

[37] I 31 p 11

[38] I 89

[39] I 58 p 3; I 92 p 2

16

e. Little information is available on successes in solution of English systems. Polish, Turkish, Greek and Latin American systems were solved extensively. Prior to 1943, appreciable success was achieved in the solution of Italian diplomatic codes.

During the first half of the year 1944 important decodes designated as "VN's" (*Verlaessliche Nachrichten*) totaled 3,000 per month.[40] Selected decodes were sent to Field Marshal Keitel, Chief of Armed Forces; to Hitler; and by Keitel to General Jodl, Chief of the Armed Forces Operations Staff. They were also sent to the Army, Navy and Air Force High Commands,[41] and probably to the Signal Intelligence Agencies of these commands.[42] In addition, approximately 45 special reports were sent each day to special recipients, such as the Field Economic Office, the Department of Armed Forces Propaganda, the Western Armies Branch and Joint Intelligence.[43]

After 1944 the Signal Intelligence Agency of the Supreme Command Armed Forces issued cryptographic systems for the Army and interservice communications. One of its most important responsibilities by the end of the war was the evaluating of the cryptographic systems of other services. A file belonging to Dr. Erich Huettenhain, its chief cryptanalyst, indicated that cryptographic studies were made on cipher teleprinters, Enigma machines, specially designed Hagelin machines, small cipher devices and hand systems.[44]

[40] DF 9

[41] I 143, p 9

[42] I 13, p 3

[43] DF 9 p 2

[44] D 59

17

In connection with its security commitments, the Signal Intelligence Agency of the Supreme Command Armed Forces (OKW/Chi) was responsible for the two most serious German cryptographic mistakes of the war: the continued use in high level German military communications of the plugboard Enigma machine and the teleprinter cipher attachment SZ 42 in their insecure forms. OKW/Chi rejected the 1943 proposals of the Army Signal Security Agency (IN 7/IV) that the (insecure) SZ 42 be replaced by the cipher teleprinter T52d, a secure device.[45] It also frowned on suggestions that the insecure plugboard Enigma be used with pluggable reflector wheels, a change which would have made it secure.[46]

Approximately 800 persons were employed in all duties except intercept.

Volume 3 of this Report gives a more detailed account of this agency.

8. The German Foreign Office Cryptanalytic Section.--The German Foreign Office had two cryptologic sections, the Cryptanalytic Section (Personal Z Sonderdienst des Auswaertigen Amtes, abbreviated Pers Z S) and the Cryptographic Section (Personal Z Chiffrierdienst des Auswaertigen Amtes, abbreviated Pers Z Chi).

The Cryptanalytic Section of the Foreign Office (Pers Z S) was the senior German cryptanalytic agency. It was organized in 1919 or before. At its greatest strength it employed approximately 200 persons. Its mission was the solution of foreign diplomatic codes and ciphers. The Section had one small intercept station at Dahlem.[47] For the rest of its intercept it was dependent upon the Signal Intelligence Agency of the Supreme Command Armed Forces (OKW/Chi), Goering's "Research" Bureau (FA) and the German Postoffice.

[45] D59, p 17

[46] D 59, p 10; see also I 31

[47] I 22, para 103

[48] I 22, para 103

The Cryptanalytic Section achieved its greatest successes with diplomatic codes, both one-part and two-part, enciphered and unenciphered.

a. From 1935 until 1942 it achieved practically 100 per cent success in the solution of Italian diplomatic codes.[49]

b. It read the United States State Department Grey, Brown and A-1 Codes.[50] It also succeeded in solving the American Diplomatic Strip Ciphers O-1 and O-2, the former in partial fashion based upon a compromise.[51]

c. The Section solved two British Foreign Office "R" Codes and the British Government Telegraph Codes.[52]

d. In 1940 success in solution of French diplomatic codes was estimated at seventy five per cent.[53]

e. A number of major Japanese diplomatic codes were read, and there is some evidence that at least one major Chinese system was solved.[54]

f. The Section also solved two machine ciphers. The Japanese Red Machine was solved in 1938 and read currently until February, 1939.[55] The Section collaborated with the Signal Intelligence Agency of the Supreme Command Armed Forces (OKW/Chi) in this solution, and it is not known which agency deserves credit for the original solution.[56] In 1941, after a partial solution by Goering's "Research" Bureau (FA), the Swiss diplomatic Enigma traffic was solved.[57]

Little information is available on the Section's achievements in terms of intelligence. The distribution it gave its decodes is unknown. The Section's personnel seem to have thought primarily in terms of cryptanalysis as a science, rather than in terms of what their intelligence contribution meant to a successful German diplomacy.[58] The Section seems to have been badly neglected by higher Foreign Office authorities, both with respect to needed personnel, and with regard to interest in its work.

[49] I 22, para 25

[50] I 22

[51] I 22, para 54; DF 15, p 4, 5; I 89

[52] D 16, Reports 2, 3, 4

[53] D 54, p 13

[54] I 22, para. 176

[55] I 22, para 19

[56] I 22, para. 19

[57] D 54, p 18

[58] See Vol. VI. Ch. 5

19

Some of the Section's senior personnel acted in an advisory capacity to the Foreign Office Cryptographic Section (Pers Z Chi).59 The latter section was responsible for the preparation, compilation, distribution and security of Foreign Office codes and ciphers. Few details are available concerning its security studies or its personnel. It was presumably responsible for the use in German diplomatic correspondence of the code systems known as the "Deutsches Satzbuch", the Deutsches Satzbuch enciphered by "Floradora" (Army Security Agency trigraph GEC), and the "one-time pad" (Army Security Agency trigraph GEE), all of which were read by Anglo-American cryptanalysts. Volume 6 of this paper gives an account of the cryptologic Sections of the German Foreign Office.

9. Goering's "Research" Bureau. -- Goering's "Research" Bureau (Reichsluftfahrtministerium Forschungsamt, abbreviated as FA) was formed in 1933. According to Goering, it supplied the new Nazi government with a signal intelligence organization of its own which had "no political axe to grind nor ideology to follow". 60

In addition to non-military cryptanalysis, the "Research" Bureau had the following functions:

a. As a Nazi censorship organization in peace-time it monitored telephone conversations in all large German cities at first only in the Reich but later extending into Austria, Denmark, and "German" Poland.61. It had access to messages sent over all German commercial teletype and telegraph facilities, 62 and maintained investigators in all main postal censorship offices.63

b. In war-time it liaised closely in the censorship of all communications as directed first by the Abwehr and later by Himmler's Reich Main Security Office. It is known to have served the latter agency as a cryptanalytic agency for Russian Agent messages. (As no cryptanalytic organization within the Reich Main Security Office is known to TICOM it is probable that the "Research" Bureau filled this function). 64

59 I 172; I 22

60 I 143

61 TF 29; T 240

62 I 143; IF 15

63 IF 132

64 TF 29; T 240

20

c. It monitored world-wide radio news broadcasts, in particular the British Broadcasting Company (London) broadcasts.[65]

d. It operated six wireless intercept stations of its own, for intercepting foreign diplomatic and commercial traffic. In addition, it exchanged copies of wireless intercepts with the Signal Intelligence Agency of the Supreme Command Armed Forces (OKW/Chi), the Signal Intelligence Agency of the Navy High Command (OKM/4 SKL/III), and probably with the Signal Intelligence Agency of the Commander in Chief German Air Force (Chi Stelle OBdL).

As can be seen from the functions outlined above, the "Research" Bureau was not primarily concerned with cryptanalysis. No documentary evidence bearing on its cryptanalytic successes was found by TICOM. Based upon secondary evidence and scattered TICOM interrogations, the bureau's chief cryptanalytic achievements seem to have been as follows:

a. In 1941 the agency collaborated with the Cryptanalytic Section of the German Foreign Office (Pers Z S) in solving the Swiss Enigma.[66] Personnel from the Bureau claimed to have broken Finnish (or Swedish) Hagelin traffic.[67]

b. According to newspaper reports, 1938 decodes of French traffic revealed that, lacking English support, the French Government did not intend to oppose the Austrian Anschluss with force.[68]

c. In 1938, during the Munich Conference, the "Research" Bureau is said to have solved the British system which carried Chamberlain's messages to London. Hitler once delayed a conference with Chamberlain for several hours in order to get such decodes.[69]

d. Solution of Russian internal wireless messages revealed bottlenecks in the Russian military supply system. The dates of this solution are unknown.[70]

[65] IF 132

[66] I 25; I 54; D 54 Report 8

[67] I 25 p 6

[68] IF 188

[69] IF 132

[70] I 25

The "Research" Bureau circulated its intelligence in the following forms:

a. Decode bulletins were sent regularly to Hitler, Goering, Field Marshal Keitel and General Jodl of the Supreme Command Armed Forces (OKW), Foreign Minister Ribbentrop, and Admiral Doenitz of the Navy High Command.

b. Individual items of current interest, collected items on single subject, and consolidated special reports were sent to interested ministries.

c. Special liaison officers were assigned to the Foreign Office, the Supreme Command of the Armed Forces, the Reich Security Office, the Economic Ministry and Ministry for War Production, and the Propaganda Ministry.[71]

Goering's "Research" Bureau had over 2,000 personnel. Less than one per cent of these were apprehended by TICOM for interrogation.

Volume 7 of this report is a detailed account of this agency.

10. Collaboration between German Signal Intelligence Agencies in Cryptographic Matters-- It seems probable that, prior to 1943, there was some sort of collaboration between the various branches of the German Armed Forces in cryptographic matters. The widespread usage of the Enigma machine, the universality of the teleprinter systems used, the allocation of similiar hand cipher systems to army, air force and police units, all point either to an excellent cooperation in the cryptographic field, or to the existence of some shadowy interservice agency or higher authority whose responsibility it was to study, test and recommend the introduction of such devices and systems. There is no reference in the TICOM material to such an agency, other than a passing 1942 reference to "the big executive committee," a group which apparently had some responsibility for cryptographic changes and improvements in a cipher type teleprinter.[72] From the headings

[71] IF 135

[72] D 59, p 6

on various memos belonging to Dr. Huettenhain (chief cryptanalyst for the Signal Intelligence Agency of the Supreme Command Armed Forces (OKW/Chi)), it could be assumed that the Chief Armed Forces Signal Communications Group (OKW/Chef Ag WNV) acted as a senior military cryptographic authority, approving or disapproving the introduction of various systems, and using the facilities of the Signal Intelligence Agency of the Supreme Command Armed Forces (OKW/Chi) and the army agencies (Inspectorate 7/VI (In 7/VI) and the Army Ordnance Development and Testing Group Signal Branch (Wa Pruef 7)) as its staff or advisory agencies.[73]

An order from Field Marshal Keitel, Chief of Staff of the Supreme Command Armed Forces (OKW), dated October 1943, made the introduction of new ciphers for branches of the Armed Forces contingent upon the agreement of the Supreme Command Armed Forces (OKW), and probably upon the agreement of the Signal Intelligence Agency of the Supreme Command Armed Forces (OKW/Chi).[74]

In 1944 General Praun, who was both Chief Signal Officer of the Supreme Command Armed Forces (OKW/WFSt/Chef WNV) and the Chief Signal Officer of the Army (OKH/Chef HNW), made the Signal Intelligence Agency of the Supreme Command Armed Forces (OKW/Chi) a central clearing house for all German cipher development and security scrutiny work. This was easily done with reference to the Army. On September 5, 1944, General Praun signed an order directing that the cryptographic development and testing functions of the Army be turned over to the Signal Intelligence Agency of the Supreme Command Armed Forces (OKW/Chi). Personnel from the Army Security Agency (In 7/IV),

[73] D 59, various letters and memos. From the headings of cryptographic manuals, it could be assumed that Ag WNV/Fu I, as issuing authority, was responsible until 1944, when OKW/Chi apparently replaced it. See OKW/Ag WNV/Fu I "Schluesselanleitung zum RS 44" dated March 27, 1944 and OKW/Chef WFSt/Ag WNV/Chi "Rasterersatzverfahren" of Dec. 7, 1944, TF 31 and TF 32 respectively.

[74] D 68, p 11; D 57 p 14

including Technician Dr. Fricke, and the personnel of Inspectorate 7/VI (In 7/VI) who were engaged in cryptographic work, were transferred into the Signal Intelligence Agency of the Supreme Command Armed Forces (OKW/Chi).[75] Thereafter, while the actual production of keys was left as an Army responsibility, the Signal Intelligence Agency of the Supreme Command Armed Forces (OKW/Chi) devised the cipher systems and provided the material for Army key production.[76]

With the Navy and the Air Force the picture was somewhat different. They were permitted to continue their cryptographic development work, and retained the right to say which of their systems was to be used in what place--so long as the Signal Intelligence Agency of the Supreme Command Armed Forces (OKW/Chi) concurred from a security standpoint in the original introduction of the systems. As Admiral Krause of the Signal Intelligence Agency of the Naval High Command (OKM/4 SKL/III) pointed out, "OKW/Chi recommendations could only lay down the (security) limits within which it was possible to use a system." The responsibility for whether and where a Navy system was to be used lay with the Navy.[77]

With regard to ciphers used by the Waffen SS, the Signal Intelligence Agency of the Supreme Command Armed Forces (OKW/Chi) had consultative powers only. While General Gimmler, successor to General Praun as Chief Signal Officer, publicly characterized the cooperation between the two services as "perfect",[78] Col Mettig, chief of the cryptographic division in OKW/Chi, indicated that an effective supervision was never introduced.[79]

[75] D 68 p 3

[76] D 55, p 43 ?

[77] D 68, p 14

[78] D 68, p 13

[79] I 96, p 19

24

The preeminence of the Signal Intelligence Agency of the Supreme Command Armed Forces (OKW/Chi) in cryptographic matters and security was apparently official only with the military services. In his speech of ~~December 20~~ 29 November, 1944, General Gimmler pointed out that primacy in the civilian field was dependent upon voluntary concurrence from the agencies affected. He could only plead that "OKW was prepared to take the lead in this matter, providing that the Party and State concurred" and requested that "the Party and Reichs authorities" cooperate.[80] Goering's "Research" Bureau (FA) developed its own codes and ciphers,[81] although the Bureau did use cipher teleprinters adopted by the military services.[82] Evidence is available that in 1945 administrative hand ciphers (Behoerdenhandschluessel) were issued to Senior Specialist Wenzel of the "Research" Bureau (FA).[83] A similiar situation prevailed with the German Foreign Office. The Signal Intelligence Agency of the Supreme Command Armed Forces (OKW/Chi) was never allowed to know the details of the ciphers used by the Foreign Office.[84] The Foreign Office, however, did use cipher teleprinters and Enigma machines.[85]

11. Collaboration between German Signal Intelligence Agencies in Cryptanalytic Matters.-- The collaboration between Agencies in cryptanalytic matters varied. In general relationship between Goering's "Research" Bureau (FA) and the Signal Intelligence Agency of the Supreme Command Armed Forces (OKW/Chi) were not overly cordial. The Signal Intelligence Agency of the Naval High Command (OKM/4 SKL/III) maintained a traditional

[80] D 68 p 14

[81] IF 132

[82] I 25, page 9

[83] T 240

[84] I 31, page 15

[85] I 22, para 115

navy reserve in dealing with other agencies. There was no high-level signal intelligence coordination, and there was frequent overlapping and duplication of effort between the agencies dealing with diplomatic cryptanalysis. But, with the exceptions noted above, there seems to have been as much liaison and as much cooperation as were necessary. This was especially true in the case of the military field organizations, the Army Signal Intelligence Regiments ("KONAs") and their Air Force equivalents, the Air Signal Regiments (LN Rgts).

a. Relationships between Foreign Office Cryptanalytic Section, Goering's "Research" Bureau, and the Signal Intelligence Agency of the Supreme Command Armed Forces.-- The Cryptanalytic Section of the Foreign Office (Pers Z S) enjoyed reasonably good working relationships with both Goering's "Research" Bureau (FA) and the Signal Intelligence Agency of the Supreme Command Armed Forces (OKW/Chi). As stated, however, the relationships between the latter two agencies do not appear to have been cordial.

The Foreign Office (Pers Z S) received the bulk of its intercept from Goering's "Research" Bureau (FA) and the Signal Intelligence Agency of the Supreme Command Armed Forces (OKW/Chi).[86] It received numerous compromised codebooks and keys from both agencies.[87] Cooperative attacks on difficult problems were not uncommon. In the case of an unspecified U. S. Strip System, the Signal Intelligence Agency of the Supreme Command Armed Forces (OKW/Chi) worked on the point-to-point traffic, while the Foreign Office (Pers Z S) worked on the circular traffic,[88] with a complete exchange of results. In the case of the Japanese Red machine, the Foreign Office (Pers Z S) attempted to solve messages sent on even days, while the Signal Intelligence Agency of the Supreme Command Armed Forces (OKW/Chi) attempted to solve messages sent on odd days, a "practical arrangement" reached also between the U. S. Army and the U. S. Navy prior to the Pearl Harbor disaster. Results

[86] I 22, para 103

[87] T2038; D16, pages 3, 5; DF 15, pages 4, 5

[88] I 31, page 10

26

were exchanged.[89] Goering's "Research" Bureau (FA) and the Foreign Office Cryptanalytic Section (Pers Z S) cooperated on the solution of the Swiss Enigma.[90] Exchange of code group identifications, additives and enciphering keys between these two agencies were frequent, especially on English, Italian and Vatican systems.[91] Personnel were exchanged between the Foreign Office Cryptanalytic Section (Pers Z S) and the Signal Intelligence Agency of the Supreme Command Armed Forces (OKW/Chi).[92]

Goering's "Research" Bureau (FA) was formed by a small group of cryptanalysts who left the Cipher Department of the Reich Defense Ministry (Reichswehrministerium), the predecessor agency of the Signal Intelligence Agency of the Supreme Command Armed Forces (OKW/Chi). This defection may account for the bad feeling between the two agencies.[93] There are no known examples of direct cryptanalytic exchanges between the two agencies, nor were there subsequent exchanges of personnel. Goering's "Research" Bureau (FA) was not given access to the special cryptanalytic machinery developed by the Signal Intelligence Agency of the Supreme Armed Forces (OKW/Chi),[94] although this machinery was made available to other agencies. Relationships could probably have been improved had not Goering's "Research" Bureau (FA) sought to take over the Signal Intelligence Agency of the Supreme Command Armed Forces (OKW/Chi).[95]

[89] I 31, para 53

[90] D 54, page 18

[91] D16, pages 1, 2; I 172, paras. 11, 13, 14; T2252, various reports

[92] I 22, paras. 20, 84

[93] I 21, p 1; I 131, p 3

[94] DF 9 p 3

[95] I 131, p 3; I 78 p 4

With reference to the exchange of traffic, however, collaboration was apparently complete. It is known that in early 1944 approximately one third of the intercept received by the Signal Intelligence Agency of the Supreme Command Armed Forces (OKW/Chi) came from Goering's "Research" Bureau (FA).[96] The latter always received copies of all the traffic intercepted by Signal Intelligence Agency of the Supreme Command Armed Forces (OKW/Chi) stations.[97]

b. Military Agency Relationships-- exchanges of cryptanalytic information.-- Collaboration between the Army Signal Intelligence agencies (OKH/GdNA and its predecessors, In 7/VI and HLS Ost) and the Signal Intelligence Agency of the Supreme Command Armed Forces (OKW/Chi) was excellent. The Chief Signal Officer of the Supreme Command Armed Forces (OKW/Chef WNV) was also the Chief Signal Officer of the Army (OKH/Chef HNW)[98] However, since the Supreme Command agency's commitment was diplomatic and military attache traffic, no broad basis for cryptanalytic liaison existed.

The Army and Air Force Signal Intelligence Agencies maintained permanent liaison on English Naval and Air systems (SYKO, M209).[99] In 1943 the Army Agency (OKH/In 7/VI) had discovered how to recover true M-209 settings from relative settings, and they had passed the technique on to the Navy and Air Force agencies.[100] According to Senior Specialist Tranow of the Naval Agency, however, the Army-Navy cooperation was given up in early 1944 since "no results of value were obtained."[101] In 1943 the Signal Intelligence Agency of the Supreme Command Armed Forces (OKW/Chi), the Cryptanalytic Section of the German Foreign Office (Pers Z S), and the Signal Intelligence Agency of the Commander in Chief German Air Forces (Chi-Stelle OBdL) collaborated on solution of an unidentified US strip system.[102]

[96] DF 9, p 3

[97] I 85 , p 3

[98] IF 108

[99] I 93, p 3, 4

[100] I 144, p 2

[101] I 93, p 3

[102] D60, p 5

28

The Army-Navy- Air Force field collaboration was usually excellent.[103] It embraced on occasion exchange of personnel and equipment, a complete exchange of reports, and a close cryptanalytic liaison on operative systems.[104] Eastern front reports show a detailed operational collaboration between Air Force Signal Regiment 353 (LN Regt 353), the Army Signal Intelligence Regiment 1, (KONA 1), and the Naval units dealing with Russian Black Sea Fleet traffic.[105] Army Signal Intelligence Regiment 5 (KONA 5) worked closely with the Air Force Signal Intelligence organizations in the West (at Paris and Noisy).[106]

During the period 1940-1942 the Signal Intelligence Agencies of the Navy (OKM/4 SKL III) and the Air Forces (Chi-Stelle OBdL), and the Signal Intelligence Agency of the Supreme Command Armed Forces (OKW/Chi), and also Goering's "Research" Bureau (FA), all collaborated on solution of the English Interdepartmental Cipher.[107] There was "Research" Bureau (FA)-Naval (OKM/4 SKL/III) cooperation on the solution of the British Government Telegraph Code (South Africa) and Bentley's Code.[108] The Army Agency, Inspectorate 7/VI (In 7/VI) actually worked on Turkish diplomatic traffic, by agreement with Goering's "Research" Bureau[109] and had Army Signal Intelligence Regiment 4 (KONA 4) intercept this traffic for them. This work probably duplicated efforts of the Signal Intelligence Agency of the Supreme Command Armed Forces (OKW/Chi) however.

[103] I 26, p 2

[104] US M-94, M-209, Slidex, Russian codes, etc.

[105] I 130, p 15

[106] I 113, p 8

[107] I 93, p 4; I 147, p 11, 12

[108] I 93, p 3

[109] IF 126, p 8

c. Military Agency Relationships--exchange of personnel.--In 1942 Prof. Nowopaschenny of the Signal Intelligence Agency of the Supreme Command Armed Forces (OKW/Chi) and a group of his cryptanalysts were transferred to Intercept Control Station East (HLS), one of the predecessors of the Signal Intelligence Agency of the Army High Command (OKH/GdNA) for work on the main Russian army five-figure code.[110] At one time the Naval commander in the Aegean area placed his radar intercept personnel and equipment under the command of Air Signal Regiment (LN Rgt) 352.[111] On one occasion personnel from Air Signal Regiment (LN Rgt) 353 went aboard the cruiser "Prinz Eugen" to monitor traffic from the Air Arm of the Russian Baltic Fleet.[112] In the spring of 1942 the Signal Intelligence Agency of the Naval High Command (OKM/4 SKL III) exchanged personnel with the Army and Air Force in order to get trained Hollerith operators.[113] In 1939 Dr. Huettenhain of the Signal Intelligence Agency of the Supreme Command Armed Forces (OKW/Chi) was detailed to the Army agency to work on solution of French military systems.[114]

d. Military Agency Relationships--Cooperation with regard to IBM and Rapid Analytic Machinery.-- The Army Signal Security Agency (Inspektion 7/IV abbreviated In 7/IV) pioneered in the use of IBM (Hollerith) equipment. Its installations were set up in the winter of 1939 and 1940, and later transferred to Army Inspectorate 7/VI (In 7/VI), one of the predecessors of the Signal Intelligence Agency of the Army High Command (OKH/GdNA).[115]

110 IF 123 p 3
111 I 126 p 14
112 I 163 p 3
113 I 146 p 17
114 D 60 p 4, 5
115 I 67 p 2

30

In March, 1942, representatives of Goering's "Research" Bureau (FA), and of the Signal Intelligence Agencies of the Commander in Chief Air Forces (Chi Stelle OBdL) and the Navy High Command (OKM/4 SKL/III) visited the Army installations and obtained valuable information as to the possibilities of IBM in cryptanalysis.[116] The Signal Intelligence Agency of the Supreme Command Armed Forces (OKW/Chi) never owned its own Hollerith machinery and used the Army installations.[117]

In 1944 the Signal Intelligence Agency of the Supreme Command Armed Forces (OKW/Chi) developed a number of "decoding devices," some of which were handed over to the Army, Navy and Foreign Office agencies.[118] The Digraph Weight Recorder (Bigrammsuchgeraet) was made available to the German Weather Service (WENUEB).[119]

e. <u>Military Agency Relationships--cooperation with regard to interception.</u>-- Goering's "Research" Bureau (FA) occasionally furnished the Signal Intelligence Agency of the Commander in Chief of the Air Force (Chi Stelle, OBdL) with traffic.[120] The amount of this traffic is not known. Goering's "Research" Bureau (FA) also passed some intercepted commercial traffic of naval interest to the Signal Intelligence Agency of the Naval High Command (OKM/4 SKL/III).[121] The German Navy passed its weather intercept to the Air Force, who had some interservice responsibility for the solution of weather traffic.[122] On operational fronts, when army search receivers found air force frequencies, information concerning these frequencies was supplied to the appropriate air force field intercept units.[123] The Signal Intelligence Agency of the Supreme Command Armed Forces (OKW/Chi) controlled a naval direction finding station in Spain.[124]

[116] I 146, p 17
[117] I 67, p 2, 3
[118] DF 9, p 3
[119] I 31, p 4
[120] I 29, p 3
[121] I 93, p 12, 18
[122] I 93, p 4
[123] I 130, p 15
[124] I 96, p 7

f. Cooperation between Military and Civilian Agencies on solution of Agents' systems.-- The extensive German effort against agent-partisan systems warrants separate discussion. This effort was shared by at least three organizations, and perhaps a fourth. The organizations were: the Signal Intelligence Agency of the Supreme Command Armed Forces (OKW/Chi), Army Inspectorate 7/VI (OKH/In 7/VI), perhaps Goering's "Research" Bureau (FA), and a small organization which did little or no cryptanalysis, the Radio Defense Corps of the Supreme Command Armed Forces (OKW/WNV/FU III). The relationship between these agencies illustrates collaboration in both intercept and cryptanalysis, and an allocation of primary responsibility which varied from problem to problem.

At the beginning of the war, responsibility for monitoring clandestine transmissions in Germany and the occupied territories was borne by the Radio Defense Corps (OKW/WNV/FU III).[125] In the spring of 1942 the Radio Defense Corps pressed for the establishment of its own cryptanalytic section. Neither the Army nor the Supreme Command signal intelligence agencies were anxious to see the establishment of a new cryptanalytic agency for agent traffic. Accordingly, a section for cryptanalysis on agent transmissions was established in the Army Inspectorate 7/VI (In 7/VI).[126] This section was known (from its chief) as "Referat Vauck".

Originally located in Berlin, Referat Vauck moved in the fall of 1943 with the Radio Defense Corps (FU III) to Dorf Zinna, near Jueterbog. It was transferred in the fall of 1944 from Inspectorate 7/VI (In 7/VI) to the newly formed Signal Intelligence Agency of the Army High Command (OKH/GdNA) and was transferred again in early 1945 to the Signal Intelligence Agency of the Supreme Command Armed Forces (OKW/Chi/Gr. IV). Both these latter changes were administrative only, since the section remained with the Radio Defense Corps at Jueterbog.[127]

[125] I 115, p 2

[126] I 115, para 15

[127] I 115, paras 12, 31

Referat Vauck did not enjoy a monopoly on agent cryptanalysis. Most of its and the Radio Defense Corps' (FU III) effort was concentrated on western agent networks (France, Belgium). In the eastern and Balkan theaters, other agencies handled the bulk of agent intercept and cryptanalysis, as follows:

(1) Russian Partisan Traffic-- The work done by Referat Vauck on this problem covered only the period mid-1942 to mid-1943. Its work was then taken over by a section under Lt. Schubert of Army Signal Intelligence Regiment (KONA) 6.[128] Schubert was ultimately transferred to the Signal Intelligence Agency of the Army High Command (OKH/GdNA), where he took over "eastern" cryptanalysis on the NKVD-partisan networks.[129]

(2) Yugoslav systems-- Most of the interception and cryptanalysis on Yugoslav systems was done, not by the Radio Defense Corps (FU III), but by a special detachment of Army Signal Intelligence Regiment (KONA) 4, stationed in Belgrade.[130] Cryptanalytic work on the more difficult Balkan systems was done in Berlin by Balkan Section (Referat Bailovic) of Army Inspectorate 7/VI (In 7/VI), who thus complemented the activities of Referat Vauck.[131]

(3) Polish Resistance Movement Systems-- In 1943 Referat Vauck solved the principal system used by the Polish Government in Exile (London) for communication with the Polish Resistance Movement (Warsaw). So important was this traffic that, in the fall of 1943, eight members of Vauck's Section were transferred to the Polish Section in the Signal Intelligence Agency of the Supreme Command Armed Forces (OKW/Chi, Gr. V). The intercept work done by the Radio Defense Corps (FU III) was augmented by the Signal Intelligence Agency of the Supreme Command Armed Forces (OKW/Chi) intercept station at Lauf,[132] and I.B.M. assistance was given by Army Inspectorate 7/VI (In 7/VI).

[128] I 115, p 7
[129] I 26, p 1
[130] I 115, p 8
[131] I 115, p 8
[132] I 115, p 9

There is one reference (by Lt. Schubert) to "Research" Bureau (FA) participation in this work. In Janauary, 1945, Senior Specialist (ORR) Wenzel of Goering's "Research" Bureau (FA) was sent by the Radio Defense Corps (OKW/WNV/FU III) to the Signal Intelligence Agency of the Army High Command (OKH/GdNA) to work on resistance movement systems.[133]

(4) Other Agent Traffic-- Duplicates of all Radio Defense Corps intercept were forwarded to the Signal Intelligence Agency of the Supreme Command Armed Forces (OKW/Chi), who, on occasion, helped Referat Vauck with more difficult problems.[134]

12. Other European Axis Cryptanalytic Agencies--

a. Italian Cryptanalytic Agencies-- Until the September, 1943, armistice, there were four Italian cryptologic agencies, the two most important being the Cryptanalytic Section of the Army Intelligence Service (Servizio Informazioni Militari, abbreviated SIM) and the Cryptanalytic Section of the Navy Intelligence Service (Servizio Informazioni Speciali, abbreviated SIS). These two agencies had both cryptanalytic and cryptographic functions. The Ministry of Foreign Affairs maintained a small cryptographic office (Ufficio Crittografico) to compile Italian diplomatic codes and ciphers.[135] The Inspector General of Political Police in the Ministry of the Interior (Publica Sicurezza) also maintained a cryptanalytic section to deal with "Communist" and "foreign agent" codes and ciphers.[136] The Italian Air Force Intelligence Service (Servizio Informazioni Aeronautica, abbreviated SIA) maintained its own intercept organization, but no cryptanalytic personnel. The Cryptanalytic Section of the Navy Intelligence Service (SIS) acted for the Air Force in this matter.[137]

[133] I.26 p 27

[134] For example, their work on the Russian agent traffic called "Rote 3" - D60, page 16.

[135] IF 1500

[136] IF 1502

[137] IF 209

34

After September, 1943, the functions of the Cryptanalytic Section of the Army Intelligence Service (SIM) were taken over by a neo-Fascist organization, the Defense Intelligence Service (Servizio Informazioni Difesa, abbreviated SID), which confined its activities to commercial and broadcast monitoring and solution of systems read by its predecessor agency.[138] No TICOM information is available concerning the post-1943 activities of the other agencies mentioned above.

The Cryptanalytic Section of the Army Intelligence Service (SIM) maintained four fixed intercept stations in Italy, and a field organization whose precise strength is unknown.[139] After June, 1943, each field army probably disposed of both a cryptanalytic party (Nucleo) and intercept facilities.[140] The Cryptanalytic Section of the Naval Intelligence Service (SIS) maintained seven fixed intercept stations in Italy and its possessions. It also controlled intercept groups located on the flagships of all naval commands.[141]

Italian cryptanalytic successes seem to have been limited. The Army Cryptanalytic Section worked on diplomatic, military attache, commercial and army systems.[142] The Naval Section concentrated its efforts on British Naval and Air operational codes.[143] Both sections were small,[144] trained cryptanalysts were at a premium,[145] and IBM equipment was difficult to procure. The Army Cryptanalytic Section read the U. S. State Department "Brown" Code (through compromise) and solved (or purchased) several other U. S. systems including the Military Intelligence Code No. 11.[146] According to General Gamba, head

[138] IF 1517, 1524, 1526

[139] IF 1517

[140] IF 1520, IF 1523

[141] IF 209

[142] IF 1517

[143] IF 209

[144] IF 209

[145] IF 1518

[146] IF 1517, IF 1524

35

of the Section, they also read a British diplomatic five-figure code, and an unenciphered four-figure, two-part British diplomatic code (Foreign Office "R" Code ?), as well as French, Turkish and Rumanian systems.[147] The Naval Section read British naval tactical codes, the daily-changing air code enciphering tables, and an unidentified four-figure "Anglo-American Naval code".[148] A four-figure British Naval code was read from 1941 until the North African landings in November, 1942.[149]

The Germans held a low opinion of Italian cryptanalytic capabilities, and considered their cryptographic procedures to be highly insecure. As a result, good cooperation was never achieved. What formal liaison existed, ended with the 1943 Armistice. The Germans then took over the remnants of the Italian organization (SID), dissolving it in February, 1944.[150]

For a more detailed discussion of the Italian cryptanalytic organization see Volume 8.

b. <u>The Hungarian Cryptanalytic Agency</u>-- The Hungarian Cryptanalytic Bureau (Section X of the General Staff-Hungarian name unknown) was subordinated to the Ministry of Defense. It had a strength of approximately fifty persons.[151] Its principal cryptanalytic work was done on Turkish codes and ciphers, as well as Italian, Polish and Russian systems. TICOM recovered approximately 90 code books from the agency, covering work on codes from 16 countries.[152] The organization was evacuated in 1945 to German territory, and later dispersed into Hungarian collecting camps.

147 IF 1518

148 IF 209, IF 1527

149 IF 1527

150 IF 1527

151 I 193 p 3

152 A 27

36

The Hungarian Bureau was said to have had an excellent relationship with the German Signal Intelligence Agency of the Supreme Command Armed Forces (OKW/Chi), and the Finnish cryptanalytic organization.

For further discussion on the Hungarian Cryptanalytic Agency, see Volume 8.

c. The Austrian Cryptanalytic Agency-- A small Austrian Cipher Bureau (subordination and Austrian name unknown) had been in existence for some years prior to 1934. It had a staff of at least five key cryptanalysts, who worked principally on Italian, French, Swiss, Yugoslav, Spanish, U. S. and English systems. Before 1934, and during the critical period prior to the annexation its personnel made a regular "black market" exchange of cryptanalytic results with the Signal Intelligence Agency of the German War Ministry (Reichskriegsministerium) dealing with Senior Specialist (ORR) Fenner and Captain (later Major and Colonel) Boetzel. After annexation, its principle cryptanalysts went to work for various German Signal Intelligence Agencies including the Signal Intelligence Agency of the Supreme Command Armed Forces (OKW/Chi), and Goering's "Research" Bureau (FA).

d. The Finnish Cryptanalytic Agency-- The Finnish Signal Intelligence Agency (Finnish name unknown) was subordinated to the military intelligence organization of the Finnish General Staff. Of approximately battalion strength, it was subdivided into intercept, cryptanalytic and evaluation units.[153]

Highly regarded by German cryptanalysts, with whom excellent liaison existed, it worked on military, naval and diplomatic traffic. First priority was given to Russian traffic, followed by Polish, Swedish and U. S. traffic.[154] They succeeded in solving the five-figure Russian military code used at the time of the first Russo-Finnish war. In 1943 they also solved an unspecified U. S. Strip cipher.[155]

See Volume 8 for a further discussion of the Finnish Cryptanalytic Agency.

[153] I 106 p 3

[154] I 111 p 4

[155] I 31 p 9

e. The Bulgarian Cryptanalytic Agency-- TICOM sources make only one reference to Bulgarian cryptanalytic work. In 1944 the Signal Intelligence Agency of the Supreme Command Armed Forces (OKW/Chi) gave a training course to certain Bulgarian cryptanalytic personnel.[156]

13. Liaison between German Signal Intelligence Agencies and other Axis cryptanalytic Agencies.-- The four German military cryptanalytic agencies appear to have engaged in active liaison with allied (Axis) cryptanalytic agencies. There is no evidence (from TICOM sources) that any foreign liaison was undertaken by Goering's "Research" Bureau (FA) or the Cryptanalytic Section of the German Foreign Office (Pers Z S). The Signal Intelligence Agency of the Supreme Command Armed Forces (OKW/Chi) appears to have had some primacy, especially in the field of relationships with Japan.[157]

a. Liaison with Japan.-- The Signal Intelligence Agency of the Naval High Command (OKM/4 SKL III) attempted to give the Japanese data on the British Naval Cipher No. 3, receiving in return some strips and settings for the U. S. Strip Cipher "DUPYH".[158] There was a formal liaison between the Signal Intelligence Agency of the Supreme Command Forces (OKW/Chi) and the Japanese military attache in Berlin. Some data on American systems was given to the Japanese, but no intelligence was exchanged.[159] In January, 1945, a German interservice cryptanalytic delegation was to be sent to Japan by submarine, but the plan never materialized.[160]

[156] I 96, p 5

[157] I 119, p 6; I 29, p 6

[158] I 93, pages 8, 9; I 12, p 19

[159] I 21, p 3

[160] I 105, p 5; I 48, p 3

b. Liaison with Italy.--There was little practical cryptanalytic collaboration with the Italians. Code book groups were exchanged.[161] The Germans had no confidence in the security of Italian cryptographic systems.[162] Liaison was terminated at the end of 1943.[163]

c. Liaison with Hungary.--According to Colonel Kettler of the Signal Intelligence Agency of the Supreme Command Armed Forces (OKW/Chi), liaison with the Hungarians had existed since the 1920's.[164] In the spring of 1944 one-eighth of the intercept used by the Signal Intelligence Agency of the Supreme Command Armed Forces (OKW/Chi) came from Hungarian sources.[165] From April, 1944, until January, 1945, a Hungarian intercept company was attached to III/Air Signals Regiment 353.[166] The Hungarian agency also sent Italian, Rumanian and Polish traffic to the Signal Intelligence Agency of the Supreme Command Armed Forces (OKW/Chi), who returned solution methods on this traffic to the Hungarian agency.[167]

d. Liaison with Finland.--The liaison with the Finns on Russian traffic seems to have been the most satisfactory cooperation undertaken by the Germans. Detachments of Air-force Signal Intelligengg personnel worked with the Finns at Mikkeli and Sortavala.[168] There were permanently assigned liaison officers, both Finnish and German, at the Finnish agency and the Army Signal Intelligence Agency East (HLS/Ost).[169]

161 I 21, p 1

162 I 78, p 11

163 I 21, p 3

164 I 21, p 2

165 DF 9, p 3

166 I 130, p 15

167 I 21, p 2

168 I 120, p 3

169 I 21, p 2; I 116, p 10

DOCID: 3560861

The cooperation embraced exchange of intercepted traffic, work on keys and systems (including non-Russian systems, such as an unspecified U. S. Strip System[170]) and exchanges of equipment. There is, however, some evidence that the Finns did not provide the Germans with all the cryptanalytic material available.[171]

e. Liaison with Spain and Bulgaria-- Cryptanalytic liaison between these two countries and the Germans appeared to be unimportant.

14. Chart summarizing results of European Axis cryptanalysis-- Chart 1-2 summarizes the results of the European Axis cryptanalytic effort against the cryptographic systems of other nations, as learned from TICOM sources, and as annotated with Army Security Agency material.

For purposes of brevity, the following abbreviations have been used in this chart:

- FA- represents Goering's "Research" Bureau (FA).
- OKH- represents the Signal Intelligence Agency of the Army High Command (OKH/GdNA), its predecessors and/or field units.
- OKL- represents the Signal Intelligence Agency of the Air Force High Command (OKL/LN Abt 350), its predecessors and/or field units.
- OKM- represents the Signal Intelligence Agency of the Navy High Command (OKM/4 SKL/III and/or its field units.
- OKW- represents the Signal Intelligence Agency of the Supreme Command Armed Forces.
- Pers Z S- represents the Foreign Office Cryptanalytic Section (Pers Z S).
- SID- represents Italian Defense Intelligence Service (SID). (see Volume 8, Page 15).
- SIM- represents Italian Army Intelligence Service (SIM) and/or its field units.

In many cases, positive system identifications could not be made. Where doubt existed, the systems were therefore entered separately. Thus, many systems may have been entered more than once in the chart.

170 I 31, p 9

171 I 84, p 5

40

Volume 1

Tab A

A 27. "List of Documents Received from Hungarian Crypt. Unit Eggenfelden." A TICOM Publication.
Abwehr.-- Military Intelligence.
Agents Section of In 7/VI.-- Referat Vauck (Vauck's Section, named for its chief, First Lt. Vauck).
Ag WNV/Fu (Amtsgruppe Wehrmachtnachrichtenverbindungen/Funkueberwachung).-- Armed Forces Radio Monitoring Service.
Air Signal Regiment.-- Luftnachrichtenregiment (LN Regt).
Amtsgruppe Wehrmachtnachrichtenverbindungen/Funkueberwachung (Ag WNV/Fu).-- Armed Forces Radio Monitoring Service.
Armed Forces Radio Monitoring Service.-- Amtsgruppe Wehrmachtnachrichtenverbindungen/Funkueberwachung (Ag WNV/Fu).
Army Ordnance, Development and Testing Group, Signal Branch.-- Chef der Heeresruestung und Befehlshaber des Ersatzheeres, Amtsgruppe fuer Entwicklung und Pruefung des Heereswaffenamts, Waffenpruefung, Abteilung 7 (Wa Pruef 7).
Army Signal Intelligence Regiment.-- Kommandeur der Nachrichtenaufklaerung (KONA).
Boetzel, ____, Col. Chief of Code and Cipher Section of German War Ministry, 1934 - 1939. Chief of the Signal Intelligence Agency of the Army High Command. (OKH/GdNA).
Chief Armed Forces Signal Communications Group.--Oberkommando der Wehrmacht/Chef Amtsgruppe Wehrmachtnachrichtenverbindungen (OKW/Chef Ag WNV).
Chief Signal Officer of the Army.--Oberkommando des Heeres/Chef des Heeresnachrichtenwesens (OKH/Chef HNW).
Chief Signal Officer of the Supreme Command Armed Forces.--Oberkommando der Wehrmacht/Waffenfuehrungsstab/Chef der Wehrmachtnachrichtenverbindungen (OKW/WFst/Chef WNV).
Chiffrierdienst des Referats Z in der Personalabteilung des Auswaertigen Amtes (Pers Z Chi).--Foreign Office Cryptographic Section.
Chiffrierstelle, Oberkommando der Luftwaffe (Chi-Stelle Ob d L).-- Signal Intelligence Agency of the Air Force High Command.
Chi-Stelle Ob d L (Chiffrierstelle, Oberbefehlshaber der Luftwaffe).--Signal Intelligence Agency of the Commander in Chief of the Air Force.
Cryptanalytic Section of the Italian Army Intelligence Service.--Servizio Informazioni Militari (SIM).

Cryptanalytic Section of the Italian Navy Intelligence Service.--Servizio Informazioni Speciali (SIS).

CSDIC. Combined Services Detailed Interrogation Center.

D 6. "List of German Cover-names with equivalents and descriptions of British cipher systems worked on by OKM/4 SKL/III." Translation documents T 515 - T 520. A TICOM document.

D 15. "Translation of ten cryptanalytical reports by OKM/4 SKL/III on British Naval systems from folder entitled "Research Progress 30/11/44-21/3/45", in T 520.

D 16. Translation of Annual Progress Reports by Pers Z S covering 1927, 1941, 1942. A TICOM publication.

D 41. Translation of Cryptanalytic Reports by OKM/4 SKL/III on British Naval Systems, from Folder entitled "Research Progress 1/12/43-1/11/44." TICOM 519.

D 54. Translation of Eight Pers Z S Reports on Cipher Systems of Various Countries.

D 57. "Notes and Minutes of High-Level Meetings held at OKW/Chi." Translation of T 1650. A TICOM publication.

D 59. Notes on Cipher Security and Minutes of Meetings held at OKW/Chi.

D 60. Miscellaneous Papers from a file of RR Dr. Huettenhain of OKW/Chi.

D 68. Further Misc. Papers from a File of Huettenhain.

DF 9. Captured Wehrmacht Sigint Document: Translation of Activity Report of OKW/Chi for the Period 1st January, 1944 to 25th June, 1944.

Doenitz, Karl, Grand Admiral. Commander in Chief, German Navy; Reich Chancellor after Hitler's death.

ETOUSA. European Theater of Operations, United States Army.

FA (Forschungsamt).--Goering's Research Bureau.

Fenner, Wilhelm, Senior Specialist. Chief of Division B of OKW/Chi (cryptanalysis).

Foreign Office Cryptanalytic Section.--Sonderdienst des Referats Z in der Personalabteilung des Auswaertigen Amtes (Pers Z S).

Foreign Office Cryptographic Section.--Chiffrierdienst des Referats Z in der Personalabteilung des Auswaertigen Amtes (Pers Z Chi).

Forschungsamt (FA).--Goering's Research Bureau.

Fricke, Walther, Technician (Lt. Grade), Dr. Chief of Section IIb of OKW/Chi (development of German systems).

DOCID: 3560861

Gamba, Vittorio, General. Commander of Italian Cryptanalytic Section from World War I to Armistice of World War II.

German War Ministry.--Reichskriegsministerium.

Gimmler, _____, Maj. Gen. Chief of Army Ordnance, Development and Testing Group, Signal Branch (Wa Pruef 7), 1939-1943. Chief Signal Officer to Commander in Chief West, 1943 - 1945. Chief of Armed Forces Communications Group (Chef Ag WNV).

Goering's Research Bureau.--Forschungsamt (FA).

Group IV of Division II in the Office of the Chief Air Force Signal Officer.--Oberkommando der Luftwaffe/General-nachrichtenfuehrer II, Gruppe IV (OKL/Gen Nafue II/IV).

Himmler, Heinrich. Reichsfuehrer SS, Minister of Interior, Chief of German Police.

HLS Ost (Horchleitstelle Ost).--Intercept Control Station East.

Horchleitstelle Ost (HLS Ost).--Intercept Control Station East.

Huettenhain, Erich, Specialist Dr. Chief cryptanalyst of OKW/Chi from 1937 to end of war. Chief of Group IV (cryptanalytic research); also chief of Section IVd (training).

I 1. "Final Report on TICOM Team 3 on Final Exploitation on Burgscheidungen." A TICOM publication.

I 12. "Translation of the Preliminary Interrogation of O.R.R. Tranow of 4/SKL III/OKM, carried out at Flensburg on 24-25 May 1945 by TICOM Team 6." A TICOM publication.

I 13. "Composite Report on Two Interrogations of Oberstlt. Friedrich, Chief of the G.A.F. Sigint Service, 18/5/45 and 9/6/45." A TICOM publication.

I 19. Report on Interrogation of KONA 1 at Revin France June 1945.

I 21. "Preliminary Interrogation of Oberst Mettler, R.R. Dr. Huettenhain, Sdf. Dr. Fricke and Oblt. Schubert (OKH/Chi), 15 June 1945." A TICOM publication.

I 22. "Interrogation of German Cryptographers of Pers Z S Department of the Auswaertiges Amt." A TICOM publication.

I 25. "Interrogation of RLM/Forschungsamt Members: Dr. Paetzel R. R. Fingerhut, R. R. Oden, Dr. Klautsche and Min. Rat. Seifert, at Schloss Gluecksburg on 15, 21 June 1945." A TICOM publication.

I 26. "Interrogation of Oblt. Schubert (OKH/Chef HNW/Gen.d.NA) on Russian Military and Agents' Systems." A TICOM publication.

43

I 29. "Third Interrogation of Oberstltn. Friedrich, Chief of the G. A. F. Signals Intelligence Service." A TICOM publication.

I 31. "Detailed Interrogations of Dr. Huettenhain, formerly head of research section of OKW/Chi, 18th-21st June 1945." A TICOM publication.

I 45. "OKW/Chi Cryptanalytic Research on Enigma, Hagelin and Cipher Teleprinter Machines." A TICOM publication.

I 48. "Report on Special Interrogation of Drs. Huettenhain and Fricke, Oberst Mettig, and Lt. Morgenroth carried out on 29th July 1945." A TICOM publication.

I 54. "Second Interrogation of Five Members of the RLM/Forschungsamt." A TICOM publication.

I 58. "Interrogation of Dr. Otto Buggisch of OKW/Chi." A TICOM publication.

I 60. "Further Interrogation of Oblt. Schubert of OKH/GdNA." A TICOM publication.

I 67. "Paper by Dr. Otto Buggisch of OKH/ In 7/VI and OKW/Chi on Cryptanalytic Machines." A TICOM publication.

I 70. "Paper on the German Sigint Service by Oberstltn. Friedrich." A TICOM publication.

I 74. "Interrogation Report on Obgefr. Koller, formerly Auswertestelle 4 and Nachrichten Aufklaerungskompanie 611." A TICOM publication.

I 76. "Interrogation Reports on Lehwald, Haupts, Klett and Lauerbach. Also I 76 Supplement (Diagrams)." A TICOM publication.

I 78. "Interrogation of Oberstlt. Mettig on the History and Achievements of OKH/AHA/In 7/VI.

I 80. "P.O.W. Interrogation Report--Obgefr. Clement Schuck Insp. VII/6 (OKH)." A TICOM publication.

I 84. "Further Interrogation of R. R. Dr. Huettenhain and Sdf. Dr. Fricke of OKW/Chi." A TICOM publication.

I 85. "P.O.W. Interrogation Report on Reg. Rat Flicke, Techn, Insp. Pokojewski, Stabsintendant Hatz of OKW/Chi." A TICOM publication.

I 89. "Report by Prof. Dr. H. Rohrbach of Pers. Z. S. on American Strip Cipher." A TICOM publication.

I 93. "Detailed Interrogation of Members of OKM 4 SKL III at Flensburg." A TICOM publication.

I 96. "Interrogation of Oberstlt. Mettig on the Organization and Activities of OKW/Chi." A TICOM publication.

DOCID: 3560861

I 105. "Interrogation Report on Frau von Nida (Wife of Major Wolfgang von Nida, one-time Deputy Head of OKW/Chi)." A TICOM publication.
I 106. "Final Interrogation Report on the Norway Party (NAA 11)." A TICOM publication.
I 109. "Translation of a Report by Lt. Ludwig of Chi Stelle Obd.L. (Ref.B) based on questions set for him at A.D.I.-(K)." A TICOM publication.
I 111. "Further Interrogation of Oberstlt. Mettig of OKW/Chi on [illegible]th September 1945." A TICOM publication.
I 113. "Interrogation of Major Dr. Rudolf Hentze, Head of Gruppe IV (Cryptanalysis) General der Nachrichtenaufklaerung." A TICOM publication.
I 115. "Further Interrogation of Oberstlt. Mettig of OKW/Chi on the German Wireless Security Service (Funküberwachung). A TICOM publication.
I 116. "Report of Interrogation of Ltn. Alex Dettmann and Oberwachtmeister Sergius Samsonow of OKH (Gen.d.NA) at Oberursel, Germany, during August 1945." A TICOM publication.
I 120. "Translation of Homework by Obltn. W. Werther, Company Commander of 7/LN Rgt. 353, written on 12th August 1945 at A.D.I. (K)." A TICOM publication.
I 126. "Homework by Major Feichtner." A TICOM publication.
I 130. "Homework by Hauptmann Herold, O.C. Ln. Regt. III/353." A TICOM publication.
I 131. "Obstlt. Mettig of OKW/Chi on WA Pruef 7 and RLM/Forschungsamt." A TICOM publication.
I 135. "Homework by Lt. Ludwig of Chi-Stelle Ob.d.L. (Ref.B)." A TICOM publication.
I 142. "P/W Barthel's Account of German Work on British, American, Swedish, and French Machine Ciphers." A TICOM publication.
I 143. "Report on the Interrogation of Five Leading Germans at Nuerenberg on 27th September 1945." A TICOM publication.
I 144. "Further Interrogation of Lt. Muentz of 4 SKL III.
I 146. "Detailed Interrogation of Members of OKM 4 SKL III at Flensburg." A TICOM publication.
I 147. "Detailed Interrogation of Members of OKM 4 SKL III at Flensburg." A TICOM publication.
I 154. "Interrogation of Uffz. Rudolph Schneider of In 7/VI." A TICOM publication.

45

I 160. "Homework by Sonderfuehreer Kuehn of Gen. D. N. A. on General Organisation and Work of French Referat." A TICOM publication.
I 163. "Report on Interrogation of Hptm. Scheidl, Ltn. Sann and Ltn. Smolin, all of I/LN Rgt. 353 (East), on German Sigint Activity Against Russian Air Forces." A TICOM publication.
I 170. "Report on French and Greek Systems by Oberwachtmeister Dr. Otto Karl Winkler of OKH/FNAST 4." A TICOM publication.
I 172. "Interrogations of Hagen and Paschke of Pers Z S." A TICOM publication.
I 193. "Interrogation of SS Obersturmbahnfuehrer Urban, Liaison Officer of RSHA/VI with the Crypto Bureau of Hungarian General Staff." A TICOM publication.
IF 15. "Final Report of TICOM Team 1 on the Exploitation of Kaufbeuren and the Berchtesgaden area." From TICOM.
IF 40. "Final Report of TICOM Team 2." From TICOM.
IF 51. "Report of TICOM Team 4--visit to Southern Germany and Austria, 14th June to 12th July 1945." From TICOM.
IF 101. "Narrative and report of proceedings of TICOM Team 6, 11 April-6 July 1945." From TICOM.
IF 107. Interrogation of POW Werner K. H. Graupe regarding German cryptographic organization and solution of allied codes.
IF 108. Interrogation of Oblt. Arntz. CSDIC (U.K.) SIR 1606.
IF 120. First detailed interrogation report on Thomas Barthel. CSDIC/CMF/Y 40.
IF 123. "Consolidated report on information obtained from the following: Erdmann, Grubler, Hempel, Karrenberg, Schmitz, Suschowk. CSDIC (U.K.) SIR 1717.
IF 126. "Interrogation report on Kotschy and Boscheinen." CSDIC (U.K.) SIR 1335.
IF 132. "Notes by Huettenhain and Fricke on OKW/Chi and the German I. S." A TICOM publication.
IF 165. Special report by Kirby, on TICOM Team 6's relation with OKW/Chi personnel.
IF 166. Special report by Kirby on Sdf. Dr. Fricke.
IF 167. Final report on the visit of TICOM Team 5 to the Schliersee area.
IF 175. Seabourne report, Vol. XIII. "Cryptanalysis within the Luftwaffe SIS." From Commanding General, 9th Air Force.
IF 180. Seabourne Report, Vol. V. "The Chi-Stelle." From Commanding General, 9th Air Force.

46

IF 181. Seabourne Report, Vol. VI. "Origins of the Luftwaffe SIS and History of its Operations in the West." From Commanding General, 9th Air Force.
IF 182. Seabourne Report, Vol. VII. "Technical Operations in the West." From Commanding General, 9th Air Force.
IF 187. Seabourne Report, Vol. XII. "Technical Operations in the East." From Commanding General, 9th Air Force.
IF 188. Four Newspaper Articles. Subject: Goering's conversations concerning Austrian Anschluss. Associated Press. 4,5,6,7, November 1945.
IF 209. "Italian Communication Intelligence." Report by Admiral Maugin with U. S. Navy Introduction.
IF 1500. "Italian Intelligence Service: Report on "Organization and Working of the Servizio Informazioni Esercito (S.I.E.) within the Period 1/11/41--15/6/43." A TICOM Publication.
IF 1502. "First Detailed Interrogation Report of Guiseppe Samarughi." CSDIC/CMF/Y 29.
IF 1517. "First Detailed Interrogation of Augusto Bigi, who worked in the Cryptographic Section of SIM before the armistice and in SID afterward." CSDIC/CMF/Y 4.
IF 1518. "First Detailed Interrogation of Vittorio Gamba, director of SIM Cryptographic Section until Armistice." CSDIC/CMF/Y 7.
IF 1520. "First Detailed Interrogation of Guido Emer." CSDIC/CMF/Y 10.
IF 1523. "First Detailed Interrogation of Giovanni Gramola, pertaining to Turkish, French, British, and USA traffic." CSDIC (MAIN)/Y 24.
IF 1524. "First Detailed Interrogation Report on Three SID Cryptographers: de Witt, Biagi, Carlini." CSDIC/CMF/Y 32.
IF 1526. "Second Detailed Interrogation Report on Five Italian SID Cryptographers: de Witt, Biagi, Ulieni, Carlini, and Barbagallo." CSDIC/CMF/Y 35.
IF 1527. "First Detailed Interrogation Report of Alberto Barbagallo, Italian Naval Cryptographer." CSDIC/CMF/Y 34.

In 7/IV (Inspektion 7/IV).--Signal Security Agency of th Army High Command.
In 7/VI. (Oberkommando des Heeres, Inspektion 7/VI).--Inspectorate 7/VI.
Inspectorate 7/VI.--Oberkommando des Heeres, Inspektion 7/VI (OKH/In 7/VI, or simply In 7/VI). A predecessor of the Signal Intelligence Agency of the Army High Command (OKH/GdNA).
Inspektion 7/IV (In 7/IV).--Signal Security Agency of the Army High Command.
Intercept Control Station East.-- Horchleitstelle Ost (HLS Ost).--A predecessor of the Signal Intelligence Agency of the Army High Command (OKH/GdNA).
Italian Air Force Intelligence Service.--Servizio Informazioni Aeronautica (SIA).

Italian Defense Intelligence Service.--Servizio Informazioni Difesa (SID).

Jodl, Alfred, General. Chief of Operations Staff, Armed Forces High Command (Chef OKW/Ia).

Keitel, Wilhelm, Field Marshal. Chief of Armed Forces High Command (Chef OKW).

Kettler, Hugo, Col. Chief of OKW/Chi 1943-1945.

Kommandeur der Nachrichtenaufklaerung (KONA).--Army Signal Intelligence Regiment.

KONA (Kommandeur der Nachrichtenaufklaerung).--Army Signal Intelligence Regiment.

Krauss, _____, Admiral. Chief of OKM/4 SKL/III.

LN Regt (Luftnachrichtenregiment).--Air Signal Regiment.

Luftnachrichtenregiment (LN Regt).--Air Signal Regiment.

Meteorological Intercept Control.--Wetternachrichtenueberwachung (WENUEB).

Mettig, _____, Lt. Col. Second in command of OKW/Chi, Dec 1943-1945. Chief of Division a (cryptography).

Military Intelligence.--Abwehr.

Narodni Kommissariat Vnutrinikh Del (NKVD).--Peoples' Commissariat for Internal Affairs. A Russian secret police organization.

NKVD (Narodni Kommissariat Vnutrinikh Del).--People's Commissariat for Internal Affairs. A Russian secret police organization.

Oberkommando des Heeres/Chef des Heeresnachrichtenwesens (OKH/Chef HNW.--Chief Signal Officer of the Army.

Oberkommando des Heeres/General der Nachrichten Aufklaerung (OKH/GdNA).--Signal Intelligence Agency of the Army High Command.

Oberkommando des Heeres/Inspektion 7/VI (OKH/In 7/VI).--Inspectorate 7/VI of the Army High Command.

Oberkommando der Luftwaffe/Generalnachrichtenfuehrer II, Gruppe IV (OKL/Gen Nafue II/IV).--Group IV of Division II in the Office of the Chief Air Force Signal Officer.

Oberkommando der Luftwaffe/Luftnachrichtenabteilung 350 (OKL/LN Abt 350).--Signal Intelligence Agency of the Air Force High Command.

Oberkommando der Marine/4 Seekriegsleitung III (OKM/4 SKL III).--Signal Intelligence Agency of the Navy High Command.

Oberkommando der Wehrmacht/Chef Amtsgruppe Wehrmachtnachrichtenverbindungen (OKW/Chef Ag WNV).--Chief, Armed Forces Signal Communications Group.

Oberkommando der Wehrmacht/Chiffrierabteilung (OKW/Chi).--Signal Intelligence Agency of the Supreme Command Armed Forces.

Oberkommando der Wehrmacht/Waffenfuehrungsstab/Chef der Wehrmachtnachrichtenverbindungen (OKW/WFSt/Chef WNV).--Chief Signal Officer of the Supreme Command Armed Forces.

Oberkommando der Wehrmacht/Wehrmachtnachrichtenverbindungen/Funkueberwachung III (OKW/WNV/Fu III).--Radio Defense Corps.

OKH/Chef HNW (Oberkommando des Heeres/Chef des Heeresnachrichtenwesens).--Chief Signal Officer of the Army.

OKH/GdNA (Oberkommando des Heeres/General der Nachrichten Aufklaerung).--Signal Intelligence Agency of the Army High Command.

OKH/In 7/VI (Oberkommando des Heeres/Inspektion 7/VI).--Inspectorate 7/VI of the Army High Command.

OKL/Gen Nafue II/IV (Oberkommando der Luftwaffe/Generalnachrichtenfuehrer II, Gruppe IV).--Group IV of Division II in the Office of the Chief Air Force Signal Officer.

OKL/LN Abt 350 (Oberkommando der Luftwaffe/Luftnachrichtenabteilung 350).--Signal Intelligence Agency of the Air Force High Command.

OKM/4 SKL II (Oberkommando der Marine/4 Seekriegsleitung II).--Signal Security Agency of the Navy High Command.

OKM/4 SKL III (Oberkommando der Marine/4 Seekriegsleitung III).--Signal Intelligence Agency of the Navy High Command.

OKW/Chef Ag WNV (Oberkommando der Wehrmacht/Chef Amtsgruppe Wehrmachtnachrichtenverbindungen).--Chief, Armed Forces Signal Communications Group.

OKW/Chi (Oberkommando der Wehrmacht/Chiffrierabteilung).--The Signal Intelligence Agency of the Supreme Command Armed Forces.

OKW/WFSt/Chef WNV (Oberkommando der Wehrmacht/Waffenfuehrungsstab/Chef der Wehrmachtnachrichtenverbindungen).--Chief Signal Officer of the Supreme Command Armed Forces.

OKW/WNV/Fu III (Oberkommando der Wehrmacht/Wehrmachtnachrichtenverbindungen/Funkueberwachung III).--Radio Defense Corps.

People's Commissariat for Internal Affairs.--Narodni Kommissariat Vnutrinikh Del (NKVD). A Russian secret police organization.

Pers Z Chi (Chiffrierdienst des Referats Z in der Personalabteilung des Auswaertigen Amtes).--Foreign Office Cryptographic Section.

Pers Z S (Sonderdienst des Referats Z in der Personalabteilung des Auswaertigen Amtes).--Foreign Office Cryptanalytic Section.
Praun, Albert, Maj. Gen. Succeeded Fellgiebel as Chief Signal Officer of Armed Forces, 1944.
Radio Defense Corps of the Supreme Command Armed Forces.--Oberkommando der Wehrmacht/Wehrmachtnachrichtenverbindungen/Funkueberwachung III (OKW/WNV/Fu III).
Referat Vauck (Vauck's Section, named for its chief, First Lt. Vauck).--Agents Section of In 7/VI.
Reich Defense Ministry.--Reichswehrministerium.
Reich Main Security Office.--Reichsicherheitshauptamt (RSHA).
Reichsicherheitshauptamt (RSHA).--Reich Main Security Office.
Reichskriegsministerium.--German War Ministry.
Reichswehrministerium.-- Reich Defense Ministry.
von Ribbentrop, Joachim. German Foreign Minister.
Rommel, Erwin, Field Marshall. Commander of the Panzer Army of Africa in 1942.
RSHA (Reichsicherheitshauptamt).--Reich Main Security Office.
Servizio Informazioni Aeronautica (SIA).--Italian Air Force Intelligence Service.
Servizio Informazioni Difesa (SID).--Italian Defense Intelligence Service.
Servizio Informazioni Militari (SIM).--Cryptanalytic Section of the Italian Army Intelligence Service.
Servizio Informazioni Speciali (SIS).--Cryptanalytic Section of the Italin Navy Intelligence Service.
Schubert, _____, 1st Lt. Cryptanalyst with the Signal Intelligence Agency of the Army High Command. (OKH/GdNA).
SIA (Servizio Informazioni Aeronautica).--Italian Air Force Intelligence Service.
SID (Servizio Informazioni Difesa).--Italian Defense Intelligence Service.
Signal Intelligence Agency of the Air Force High Command.--Oberkommando der Luftwaffe/Luftnachrichtenabteilung 350 (OKL/LN Abt 350).
Signal Intelligence Agency of the Army High Command.--Oberkommando des Heeres/General der Nachrichten Aufklaerung (OKH/GdNA).
Signal Intelligence Agency of the Commander in Chief of the Air Force.--Chiffrierstelle, Oberbefehlshaber der Luftwaffe (Chi-Stelle Ob d L).

Signal Intelligence Agency of the Navy High Command.--Oberkommando der Marine/4 Seekriegsleitung III (OKM/4 SKL III).

Signal Intelligence Agency of the Supreme Command Armed Forces.--Oberkommando der Wehrmacht/Chiffrierabteilung (OKW/Chi).

Signal Security Agency of the Army High Command.--Inspektion 7/IV (In 7/IV).

Signal Security Agency of the Navy High Command.--Oberkommando der Marine/4 Seekriegsleitung II (OKM/4 SKL/II).

SIM (Servizio Informazioni Militari).--Cryptanalytic Section of the Italian Army Intelligence Service.

SIS (Servizio Informazioni Speciali).--Cryptanalytic Section of the Italian Navy Intelligence Service.

Sonderdienst des Referats Z in der Personalabteilung des Auswaertigen Amtes (Pers Z S).--Foreign Office Cryptanalytic Section.

T 517. Stand der Arbeiten (Report of work done on British and American Naval Ciphers).

T 240. T 100 Serie 1726 (Recovered letter-figure Substitution Code).

T 2038. Berichte der Gruppen Polen, Finnland, Litauen, Lettland, Tscheckoslovakei, Jugoslavien, Bulgarien.

Target Intelligence Committee (TICOM). A joint combined committee organized in the fall of 1944 in England for the exploitation of European Axis signal intelligence centers of special interest.

TF 29. Die Ueberwachung des Nachrichtenverkehrs im Kriege (Supervision of Information Channels in War).

TF 31. "Schluesselanleitung zum Rosterschluessel 44 (RS 44)."

TF 32. "Rasterersatzverfahren."

TICOM (Target Intelligence Committee).--A joint combined committee organized in the fall of 1944 in England for the exploitation of European Axis signal intelligence centers of special interest.

Tranow, ____, Senior Specialist Dr. Head of Subsection IIIf (Britain and USA) of the Signal Intelligence Agency of the Navy High Command (OKM/4 SKL/III).

Verlaessliche Nachricht (VN).--"Reliable Report." Translation into German of decoded diplomatic message.

VN (Verlaessliche Nachricht).--"Reliable Report." Translation into German of decoded diplomatic message.

Waffenpruefung 7 (Wa Pruef 7).--Army Ordnance Development and Testing Group, Signal Branch.

Waffenschutzstaffel (Waffen-SS).--Armed Elite Guard. Components of Elite Guard serving at front.

Waffen-SS (Waffen-Schutzstaffel).--Armed Elite Guard. Components of Elite Guard serving at front.

Wa Pruef 7 (Waffenpruefung 7).--Army Ordnance Development and Testing Group, Signal Branch.

WENUEB (Wetternachrichtenueberwachung).--Meteorological Intercept Control.

Wenzel,_____, Senior Specialist. Head of Section 9 of the FA.

Wetternachrichtenueberwachung (WENUEB).--Meteorological Intercept Control.

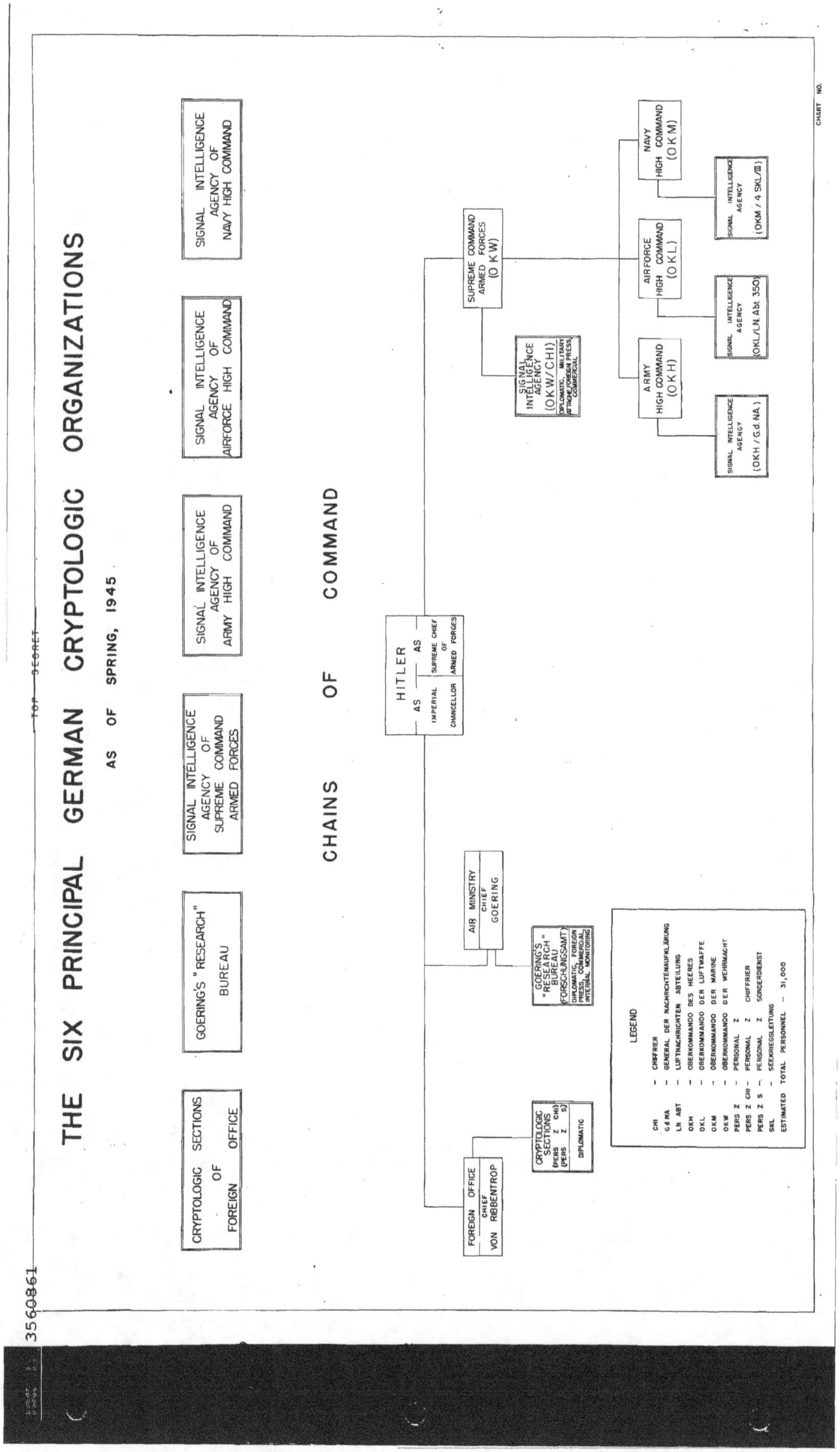
THE SIX PRINCIPAL GERMAN CRYPTOLOGIC ORGANIZATIONS
AS OF SPRING, 1945
CRYPTOLOGIC SECTIONS OF FOREIGN OFFICE
GOERING'S "RESEARCH" BUREAU
SIGNAL INTELLIGENCE AGENCY OF SUPREME COMMAND ARMED FORCES
SIGNAL INTELLIGENCE AGENCY OF ARMY HIGH COMMAND
SIGNAL INTELLIGENCE AGENCY OF AIRFORCE HIGH COMMAND
SIGNAL INTELLIGENCE AGENCY OF NAVY HIGH COMMAND
CHAINS OF COMMAND
HITLER
AS IMPERIAL CHANCELLOR
AS SUPREME CHIEF OF ARMED FORCES
FOREIGN OFFICE
CHIEF
VON RIBBENTROP
CRYPTOLOGIC SECTIONS
(PERS Z CHI)
(PERS Z S)
DIPLOMATIC
AIR MINISTRY
CHIEF
GOERING
GOERING'S "RESEARCH" BUREAU (FORSCHUNGSAMT)
DIPLOMATIC, FOREIGN PRESS, COMMERCIAL, INTERNAL MONITORING
SUPREME COMMAND ARMED FORCES (O K W)
SIGNAL INTELLIGENCE AGENCY (OKW/CHI)
DIPLOMATIC, MILITARY ATTACHE, FOREIGN PRESS, COMMERCIAL
ARMY HIGH COMMAND (OKH)
AIRFORCE HIGH COMMAND (OKL)
NAVY HIGH COMMAND (OKM)
SIGNAL INTELLIGENCE AGENCY (OKH / Gd. NA.)
SIGNAL INTELLIGENCE AGENCY (OKL/LN. Abt. 350)
SIGNAL INTELLIGENCE AGENCY (OKM / 4 SKL/III)
LEGEND
CHI - CHIFFRIER
Gd NA - GENERAL DER NACHRICHTENAUFKLÄRUNG
LN ABT - LUFTNACHRICHTEN ABTEILUNG
OKH - OBERKOMMANDO DES HEERES
OKL - OBERKOMMANDO DER LUFTWAFFE
OKM - OBERKOMMANDO DER MARINE
OKW - OBERKOMMANDO DER WEHRMACHT
PERS Z - PERSONAL Z
PERS Z CHI - PERSONAL Z CHIFFRIER
PERS Z S - PERSONAL Z SONDERDIENST
SKL - SEEKRIEGSLEITUNG
ESTIMATED TOTAL PERSONNEL - 31,000
CHART NO.
3560861

RESULTS OF EUROPEAN AXIS CRYPTANALYSIS AS LEARNED FROM TICOM SOURCES

(WITH ANNOTATIONS FROM ARMY SECURITY AGENCY SOURCES IN PARENTHESES)

COUNTRY OF ORIGIN	SERVICE	DESCRIPTION OF SYSTEM	NAME OF SYSTEM			DATES OF USE	WHEN ATTACKED AND BY WHOM	RESULTS	TICOM REFERENCE	STATUS OF THE SYSTEM AT ASA	REMARKS
			COUNTRY OF ORIGIN	AXIS	U.S.A.						
AFGHANISTAN 1	(ALL GOV'T AGENCIES, INCLUDING EMBASSIES, CONSULATES, FOREIGN OFFICE, PRIME MINISTER'S OFFICE, AND BANK.)	3-LETTER 1-PART CODE. (SOMETIMES ENCIPHERED WITH FIGURES, TWO FIGURES SUBSTITUTED FOR EACH LETTER, THEN SENT IN 1Ø-FIGURE GROUPS.)	?	AFGH. 1	(AFA)	1939 OR BEFORE-(CURRENT)	1942 PERS Z S	RECOVERED 1Ø% - 2Ø%	T 1Ø62 T 1Ø67 T 1Ø68 T 2Ø52	(ASA HAS RESULTS OF BRITISH PARTIAL RECOVERY, ABOUT 25% OF GROUPS, MAKING TRAFFIC PRACTICALLY 1ØØ% READABLE.)	--
ARGENTINA 1	DIPLOMATIC	5-LETTER 1-PART CODE. (1ØØ,ØØØ GROUPS.)	?	AB3	(ARA)	(1926-JANUARY 1946?)	? PERS Z S	RECOVERED LESS THAN 5%	T 3Ø15	(75% READABLE)	--
ARGENTINA 2	DIPLOMATIC	5-FIGURE 1-PART CODE. 95,ØØØ GROUPS IN MAIN VOCABULARY, TOTAL "11Ø,ØØØ." AFTER 1926 NUMBER 1ØØ ADDED TO EACH 5-PLACE GROUP.	?	?	(ARB)	(1926-1945)	1927 PERS Z S	SOLVED	D 16, REPORT 1, P 2 D 16, REPORT 2, P 3 I 172 P 5	(1ØØ% COMPROMISED)	--
ARGENTINA 3	DIPLOMATIC?	?-PART CODE. SOMETIMES ENCIPHERED BY MEANS OF AN EASY SYSTEM. IN MANY VOLUMES CONTAINING A LARGE NUMBER OF GROUPS.	?	?	?	? - ?	? SIM	?	IF 1518	(UNKNOWN)	--
ARGENTINA 4	DIPLOMATIC	?-PART CODE	?	?	?	?-194Ø-?	194Ø SIM	READ	IF 1524	(UNKNOWN)	--
BELGIUM 1	(COMMERCIAL AND DIPLOMATIC)	4-LETTER 1-PART CODE. SOMETIMES DIGRAPHICALLY ENCIPHERED WITH DAILY CHANGING TABLES.	?	?	(BEA) AND (BEB)	(BEA: 1939-CURRENT) (BEB: 1942-CURRENT)	194Ø PERS Z S 194Ø SIM PERHAPS ALSO FA	1ØØ% COMPROMISED BY SIM. READ BY PERS Z S.	I 22 P 19 I 25 P 2 D 54 P 12 P 18 IF 1517 P 3	(BEGAN BREAKING CODE 1943. COMPROMISED 1944. BEGAN BREAKING ENCIPHERMENT 1944. BOTH CURRENTLY READ.)	--
BELGIUM 2	DIPLOMATIC?	4-LETTER 1-PART CODE. ENCIPHERED DIGRAPHICALLY WITH SAME DAILY CHANGING TABLES AS BELGIUM 1. CODE GROUP "KAMI" = "FULL STOP."	?	?	?	?-1942. PERHAPS LATER.	194Ø PERS Z S	READ	I 22 P 19 D 54 P 12 P 18	(UNKNOWN)	--
BELGIUM 3	DIPLOMATIC	3-LETTER UNENCIPHERED CODE.	?	?	(BEC?)	(1943-CURRENT)	? ?	?	I 22 P 19	(BOOK 8Ø% BROKEN)	(BEC ONLY 3-LETTER UNENCIPHERED SYSTEM ASA KNOWS)
BELGIUM 4	COLONIAL	4-FIGURE ?-PART CODE. TRANSPOSED 1/2 OF GROUP AND USED DIGRAPHIC SUBSTITUTION FOR OTHER 1/2. COULD BE USED AS 5-FIGURE "IN WHICH CASE THE VALUE IN THE SECOND COLUMN HAD TO BE TAKEN."	?	?	?	? - ?	? PERS Z S	READ COMPLETELY	I 22 P 19	(UNKNOWN)	(NO FIGURE CODES KNOWN)
BELGIUM 5	DIPLOMATIC	4-FIGURE 4-LETTER 1-PART CODE ENCIPHERED BY 31 DAILY CHANGING TABLES, USED SAME DAY EACH MONTH.	?	?	?	? - 194Ø	? SIM	READ	IF 1522 P 3 P 8	(UNIDENTIFIED)	--
BELGIUM 6	DIPLOMATIC	4-FIGURE ?-PART CODE.	?	?	?	?-194Ø-?	194Ø SIM	READ	IF 1517 IF 1524	(UNIDENTIFIED)	--
BELGIUM 7	DIPLOMATIC?	?-FIGURE CODE OF 1Ø,ØØØ GROUPS ENCIPHERED WITH NUMBER AND LETTER TABLES OF 1ØØ PLACES.	?	?	?	? - 194Ø	194Ø PERS Z S	TABLES NEARLY SOLVED. MOST OF TRAFFIC READ BY 194Ø	D 54 P 12	(UNKNOWN)	(NO FIGURE CODES KNOWN)

CHART NO. 1-2

RESULTS OF EUROPEAN AXIS CRYPTANALYSIS AS LEARNED FROM TICOM SOURCES

(WITH ANNOTATIONS FROM ARMY SECURITY AGENCY SOURCES IN PARENTHESES)

COUNTRY OF ORIGIN	SERVICE	DESCRIPTION OF SYSTEM	NAME OF SYSTEM: COUNTRY OF ORIGIN	NAME OF SYSTEM: AXIS	NAME OF SYSTEM: U.S.A.	DATES OF USE	WHEN ATTACKED AND BY WHOM	RESULTS	TICOM REFERENCE	STATUS OF THE SYSTEM AT ASA	REMARKS
BELGIUM	5 MILITARY.	3-FIGURE SYSTEM ENCIPHERED WITH SUBSTITUTION TABLES IN SUCH A WAY THAT THE FIRST FIGURE OF EACH GROUP REMAINED UNCHANGED AND THE SECOND AND THIRD WERE EACH ENCIPHERED INDIVIDUALLY.	?	?	?	? - ?	? OKW/CHI	READ	I 31 P 6	(UNKNOWN)	(NO FIGURE CODES KNOWN)
BOLIVIA	1 DIPLOMATIC	5-LETTER 1-PART CODE	?	?	(BVD?)	? - ?	? PERS Z S	RECOVERED LESS THAN 3%	T 1311	(25% READABLE)	--
BOLIVIA	2 DIPLOMATIC	5-FIGURE 1-PART CODE WITH 73,000 GROUPS. ENCIPHERED WITH 1,000 AND 100-PLACE TABLES AND BY TRANSPOSING THE GROUP ELEMENTS.	?	?	(BVA) AND (BVB)	(1939-CURRENT)	? PERS Z S	?	D 16, REPORT 2, P 4 T 1585	(100% COMPROMISED)	--
BOLIVIA	3 DIPLOMATIC	POLYALPHABETIC SUBSTITUTION CIPHER USING 10 ALPHABETS.	?	?	?	?-1927-?	1927 PERS Z S	LONG TELEGRAMS SOLVED. SHORT ONES IMPOSSIBLE.	D 16, REPORT 1, P 3	(UNKNOWN)	--

CHART NO. 1-2

DOCID: 3560861

TOP SECRET

RESULTS OF EUROPEAN AXIS CRYPTANALYSIS
AS LEARNED FROM TICOM SOURCES
(WITH ANNOTATIONS FROM ARMY SECURITY AGENCY SOURCES IN PARENTHESES)

COUNTRY OF ORIGIN		SERVICE	DESCRIPTION OF SYSTEM	NAME OF SYSTEM: COUNTRY OF ORIGIN	NAME OF SYSTEM: AXIS	NAME OF SYSTEM: U.S.A.	DATES OF USE	WHEN ATTACKED AND BY WHOM	RESULTS	TICOM REFERENCE	STATUS OF THE SYSTEM AT ASA	REMARKS
BRAZIL	1	DIPLOMATIC	5-LETTER (2-PART) CODE WITH 32,ØØØ GROUPS.	?	BRAS B 2	(BZD)	(1937 OR BEFORE-CURRENT)	1941 OKW 1941 PERS Z S ? SIM	2,2ØØ GROUPS RECOVERED THEN 1ØØ% COMPROMISED BY OKW WHICH SENT COPY TO PERS Z S	D 16, 1941 REPORT, P 3 D 16, 1942 REPORT, P 4 T 3Ø16 IF 1518	(MORE THAN 5Ø% READABLE. STILL BEING RECOVERED.)	--
BRAZIL	2	DIPLOMATIC	5-LETTER 1-PART CODE WITH 165,625 GROUPS.	?	BRAS B 1	(BZC)	(1941-CURRENT)	1941 PERS Z S	2,2ØØ GROUPS RECOVERED BY 2Ø NOV. 1941. READ ALMOST WITHOUT GAP.	D 16, 1941 REPORT, P 3 D 16, 1942 REPORT, P 4 T 3Ø18	(MORE THAN 5Ø% READABLE. STILL BEING RECOVERED.)	--
BRAZIL	3	DIPLOMATIC	5-FIGURE (2-PART) CODE (REPAGINATED).	?	BRAS Z 3	(BZA)	(PRIOR TO 1941-CURRENT)	1942 PERS Z S	NOT READ	D 16, 1941 REPORT, P 3 D 16, 1942 REPORT, P 4 T 3Ø17	(MORE THAN 5Ø% READABLE; STILL BEING WORKED ON.)	--
BRAZIL	4	DIPLOMATIC	5-FIGURE 1-PART CODE WITH 1ØØ,ØØØ GROUPS.	?	BRAS Z 1	(BZ1)	(1937 OR BEFORE - ?)	1941 PERS Z S	READ ALMOST WITHOUT GAP	D 16, 1941 REPORT, P 3 D 16, 1942 REPORT, P 4	(OVER 5Ø% READABLE.)	--
BRAZIL	5	DIPLOMATIC	5-FIGURE ?-PART CODE WITH 1ØØ,ØØØ GROUPS. ENCIPHERED WITH A TABLE OF LETTERS.	?	?	?	?-1941-1942-?	1941 PERS Z S	NOT READ	D 16, 1941 REPORT, P 3 D 16, 1942 REPORT, P 2	(UNIDENTIFIED)	--
BRAZIL	6	DIPLOMATIC	TWO 5-FIGURE CODES, REPAGINATIONS OF ITEM 4.	?	BRAS Z 7 BRAS Z 8	(BZK?)	(BZK: ?-1943)	1941 PERS Z S	READ ALMOST WITHOUT GAP	D 16, 1941 REPORT, P 3 D 16, 1942 REPORT, P 1	(BZK OVER 5Ø% READABLE.)	--
BRAZIL	7	?	5-FIGURE ?-PART CODE.	?	ZAHLEN II	?	? - ?	? PERS Z S	RECOVERED ABOUT 1%	T 3115	(UNIDENTIFIED)	--
BRAZIL	8	?	4-FIGURE ?-PART CODE, REPAGINATED.	?	ZAHLEN I	?	? - ?	? PERS Z S	RECOVERED 15% - 2Ø%	T 3Ø19	(UNIDENTIFIED)	--
BRAZIL	9	?	4-FIGURE ?-PART CODE, REPAGINATED.	?	ZAHLEN IV	?	? - ?	? ?	RECOVERED 5%	T 311Ø	(UNIDENTIFIED)	--
BRAZIL	1Ø	?	4-FIGURE 1-PART CODE, REPAGINATED.	?	ZAHLEN V	?	? - ?	? ?	RECOVERED LESS THAN 1Ø%	T 3111	(UNIDENTIFIED)	--
BRAZIL	11	?	4-FIGURE ?-PART CODE, REPAGINATED.	?	ZAHLEN VI	?	? - ?	? ?	RECOVERED LESS THAN 3%	T 3112	(UNIDENTIFIED)	--

CHART NO. 1-2

TOP SECRET

DOCID: 3560861

TOP SECRET

RESULTS OF EUROPEAN AXIS CRYPTANALYSIS
AS LEARNED FROM TICOM SOURCES
(WITH ANNOTATIONS FROM ARMY SECURITY AGENCY SOURCES IN PARENTHESES)

COUNTRY OF ORIGIN		SERVICE	DESCRIPTION OF SYSTEM	NAME OF SYSTEM: COUNTRY OF ORIGIN	NAME OF SYSTEM: AXIS	NAME OF SYSTEM: U.S.A.	DATES OF USE	WHEN ATTACKED AND BY WHOM	RESULTS	TICOM REFERENCE	STATUS OF THE SYSTEM AT ASA	REMARKS
BULGARIA	1	DIPLOMATIC	5-FIGURE 1-PART CODE, TWO PAGINATIONS.	?	?	(BUE)	(? - DEC 1945)	? PERS Z S	RECOVERED ABOUT 50%	T 20	(CODE RECOVERED .5% BEFORE RECEIPT OF COPY FROM TICOM.)	--
BULGARIA	2	DIPLOMATIC	5-FIGURE 1-PART CODE, TWO PAGINATIONS. RANGE 36,400.	98844	BD 15	(BUO)	(1938-JAN 1946)	? PERS Z S ? SIM	RECOVERED 75%; LATER 100% COMPROMISED.	T 1192 T 2125 T 2339 IF 1525	(CODE RECOVERED ABOUT 2%; LATER 100% COMPROMISED.)	--
BULGARIA	3	DIPLOMATIC	5-FIGURE 1-PART CODE, REFAGINATED.	?	BD 30	(BUJ)	(? - 1945)	? PERS Z S	RECOVERED 30%-40%	T 24	(NOT WORKED ON BEFORE RECEIPT OF TICOM COPY.)	--
BULGARIA	4	DIPLOMATIC	5-FIGURE 1-PART CODE.	?	BD 19	?	? - ?	? PERS Z S	RECOVERED 5%	T 2335	(UNIDENTIFIED)	--
BULGARIA	5	DIPLOMATIC	5-FIGURE 1-PART CODE.	?	BD 25	?	? - 1944 - ?	? PERS Z S	RECOVERED 10%	T 2334	(UNIDENTIFIED)	--
BULGARIA	6	DIPLOMATIC	5-FIGURE 1-PART CODE.	?	BD 27	?	? - ?	? PERS Z S	40% - 50% RECOVERED	T 2353	(UNIDENTIFIED)	--
BULGARIA	7	DIPLOMATIC	5-FIGURE 1-PART CODE.	?	BD 28	?	? - ?	? PERS Z S	RECOVERED LESS THAN 5%	T 1176	(UNIDENTIFIED)	--
BULGARIA	8	DIPLOMATIC	5-FIGURE 1-PART CODE.	?	BD 33	?	? - ?	? PERS Z S	RECOVERED 5%	T 2333	(UNIDENTIFIED)	--
BULGARIA	9	DIPLOMATIC	5-FIGURE 1-PART CODE. INDICATOR: 33311.	?	BD 16	?	? - ?	? PERS Z S	RECOVERED 10% - 15%	T 12; T 13 T 1178 T 1177 T 1179 T 1181 T 2331 T 2332	(UNIDENTIFIED)	--
BULGARIA	10	DIPLOMATIC	5-FIGURE PROBABLY 1-PART CODE.	?	BD 1	?	? - ?	? PERS Z S	RECOVERED ABOUT 5%	T 2116	(UNIDENTIFIED)	--
BULGARIA	11	DIPLOMATIC	5-FIGURE PROBABLY 1-PART CODE.	?	BD 3	?	? - ?	? PERS Z S	RECOVERED 5% - 10%	T 2161	(UNIDENTIFIED)	--
BULGARIA	12	DIPLOMATIC	5-FIGURE PROBABLY 1-PART CODE.	?	BD 26	?	? - ?	? PERS Z S	RECOVERED ABOUT 10%	T 2147	(UNIDENTIFIED)	--

CHART NO. 1-2

TOP SECRET

RESULTS OF EUROPEAN AXIS CRYPTANALYSIS AS LEARNED FROM TICOM SOURCES

(WITH ANNOTATIONS FROM ARMY SECURITY AGENCY SOURCES IN PARENTHESES)

COUNTRY OF ORIGIN		SERVICE	DESCRIPTION OF SYSTEM	NAME OF SYSTEM: COUNTRY OF ORIGIN	NAME OF SYSTEM: AXIS	NAME OF SYSTEM: U.S.A.	DATES OF USE	WHEN ATTACKED AND BY WHOM	RESULTS	TICOM REFERENCE	STATUS OF THE SYSTEM AT ASA	REMARKS
BULGARIA	13	DIPLOMATIC	5-FIGURE PROBABLY 1-PART CODE.	?	BD 31	?	? - ?	? PERS Z S	RECOVERED LESS THAN 5%	T 2379	(UNIDENTIFIED)	--
BULGARIA	14	DIPLOMATIC	5-FIGURE PROBABLY 1-PART CODE.	?	BD 35	?	? - ?	? PERS Z S	VERY LITTLE SUCCESS	T 1185 T 1184	(UNIDENTIFIED)	--
BULGARIA	15	DIPLOMATIC	5-FIGURE PROBABLY 1-PART CODE.	?	"N.B.D. NEUER"	?	? - ?	? PERS Z S	RECOVERED 15% - 20%	T 2134	(UNIDENTIFIED)	--
BULGARIA	16	PROBABLY DIPLOMATIC	5-FIGURE PROBABLY 1-PART CODE.	?	BULG. 885	?	? - ?	? PERS Z S	VERY LITTLE SUCCESS	T 2135	(UNIDENTIFIED)	--
BULGARIA	17	DIPLOMATIC	5-FIGURE ?-PART CODE.	?	BD 14	?	? - ?	? PERS Z S	RECOVERED 2Ø% - 25%	T 213Ø	(UNIDENTIFIED)	--
BULGARIA	18	PROBABLY DIPLOMATIC	5-FIGURE ?-PART CODE.	?	"72Ø 1-15"	?	? - ?	? PERS Z S	?	T 2213	(UNIDENTIFIED)	--
BULGARIA	19	PROBABLY DIPLOMATIC	5-FIGURE ?-PART CODE.	?	"Ø62 925 1-15"	?	? - ?	? PERS Z S	?	T 2214	(UNIDENTIFIED)	--
BULGARIA	20	PROBABLY DIPLOMATIC	5-FIGURE ?-PART CODE.	?	"Ø95"	?	? - 1927 - ?	1927 PERS Z S	?	T 2127	(UNIDENTIFIED)	--
BULGARIA	21	PROBABLY DIPLOMATIC	5-FIGURE ?-PART CODE.	?	"5Ø7 16-21"	?	? - 1932 - ?	? PERS Z S	RECOVERED LESS THAN 1%	T 2174	(UNIDENTIFIED)	--
BULGARIA	22	PROBABLY DIPLOMATIC	5-FIGURE ?-PART CODE	?	"698"	?	? - ?	? PERS Z S	?	T 2157	(UNIDENTIFIED)	--
BULGARIA	23	MILITARY	5-FIGURE 1-PART CODE	?	BM 7	?	? - ?	? PERS Z S	RECOVERED 5% - 10%	T 2165	(UNKNOWN)	--
BULGARIA	24	MILITARY	5-FIGURE 1-PART CODE	?	BM C 5	?	? - ?	? PERS Z S	RECOVERED LESS THAN 10%	T 2169	(UNKNOWN)	--

CHART NO. 1-2

DOCID: 3560861

TOP SECRET

RESULTS OF EUROPEAN AXIS CRYPTANALYSIS
AS LEARNED FROM TICOM SOURCES
(WITH ANNOTATIONS FROM ARMY SECURITY AGENCY SOURCES IN PARENTHESES)

COUNTRY OF ORIGIN		SERVICE	DESCRIPTION OF SYSTEM	NAME OF SYSTEM: COUNTRY OF ORIGIN	NAME OF SYSTEM: AXIS	NAME OF SYSTEM: U.S.A.	DATES OF USE	WHEN ATTACKED AND BY WHOM	RESULTS	TICOM REFERENCE	STATUS OF THE SYSTEM AT ASA	REMARKS
BULGARIA	25	MILITARY	5-FIGURE ?-PART CODE.	?	BM C 1	?	? - ?	? PERS Z S	RECOVERED LESS THAN 1%	T 2167	(UNKNOWN)	--
BULGARIA	26	MILITARY	5-FIGURE ?-PART CODE WITH APPARENTLY FOUR DIFFERENT POSSIBILITIES FOR THE FIRST THREE FIGURES.	?	BM 11	?	? - ?	? PERS Z S	RECOVERED LESS THAN 10%	T 2169	(UNKNOWN)	--
BULGARIA	27	MILITARY	5-FIGURE ?-PART CODE.	?	BM 12	?	? - ?	? PERS Z S	RECOVERED LESS THAN 1%	T 2132	(UNKNOWN)	--
BULGARIA	28	?	5-FIGURE 1-PART CODE.	?	?	?	? - ?	? PERS Z S	RECOVERED 25%	T 1190	(UNKNOWN)	--
BULGARIA	29	?	5-FIGURE 1-PART CODE.	?	"430 16-31"	?	? - ?	? PERS Z S	RECOVERED LESS THAN 10%	T 1270	(UNKNOWN)	--
BULGARIA	30	?	5-FIGURE 1-PART CODE.	?	BG B 2	?	? - ?	? PERS Z S	RECOVERED 20%	T 2145	(UNKNOWN)	--
BULGARIA	31	?	5-FIGURE 1-PART CODE.	?	"088 ABD 1-15"	?	? - ?	? PERS Z S	RECOVERED LESS THAN 5%	T 2162 T 2163	(UNKNOWN)	--
BULGARIA	32	?	5-FIGURE 1-PART CODE	?	?	?	? - ?	? PERS Z S	RECOVERED LESS THAN 1%	T 2133	(UNKNOWN)	--
BULGARIA	33	?	5-FIGURE 1-PART CODE.	?	"BU 11"	?	? - ?	? PERS Z S	RECOVERED 5% - 10%	T 2149	(UNKNOWN)	--
BULGARIA	34	?	5-FIGURE ?-PART CODE. POSSIBLE 60,000 GROUPS.	?	"BU 4"	?	? - ?	? PERS Z S	RECOVERED ABOUT 10%	T 2159	(UNKNOWN)	--
BULGARIA	35	?	5-FIGURE ?-PART CODE. RECONSTRUCTED ON BASIS OF 100,000 VALUES.	?	36633 M8	?	? - ?	? PERS Z S	VERY LITTLE SUCCESS	T 2166	(UNKNOWN)	--
BULGARIA	36	?	5-FIGURE ?-PART CODE.	?	?	?	?-1936-1937-?	? PERS Z S	RECOVERED LESS THAN 1%	T 2172	(UNKNOWN)	--
BULGARIA	37	?	5-FIGURE ?-PART CODE.	?	"BULG HOF CODE 4C"	?	? - ?	? PERS Z S	VERY LITTLE SUCCESS	T 2121	(UNKNOWN)	--

CHART NO. 1-2

TOP SECRET

DOCID: 3560861

TOP SECRET

RESULTS OF EUROPEAN AXIS CRYPTANALYSIS
AS LEARNED FROM TICOM SOURCES
(WITH ANNOTATIONS FROM ARMY SECURITY AGENCY SOURCES IN PARENTHESES)

COUNTRY OF ORIGIN		SERVICE	DESCRIPTION OF SYSTEM	NAME OF SYSTEM: COUNTRY OF ORIGIN	NAME OF SYSTEM: AXIS	NAME OF SYSTEM: U.S.A.	DATES OF USE	WHEN ATTACKED AND BY WHOM	RESULTS	TICOM REFERENCE	STATUS OF THE SYSTEM AT ASA	REMARKS
BULGARIA	38	?	5-FIGURE ?-PART CODE	?	"36333-OHNE 5 16-21"	?	?-1929-?	1929 PERS Z S	VERY LITTLE SUCCESS	T 2128	(UNKNOWN)	--
BULGARIA	39	?	5-FIGURE ?-PART CODE	?	"NHC OR N4C"	?	? - ?	? PERS Z S	?	T 2178	(UNKNOWN)	--
BULGARIA	40	?	5-FIGURE ?-PART CODE	?	"A2 166 16-31"	?	? - ?	? PERS Z S	?	T 2160	(UNKNOWN)	--
BULGARIA	41	?	5-FIGURE ?-PART CODE	?	"Ø4C"	?	? - ?	? PERS Z S	?	T 2136	(UNKNOWN)	--
BULGARIA	42	DIPLOMATIC	4-FIGURE 1-PART CODE	?	BD 26	?	? - ?	? PERS Z S	RECOVERED 5%	T 2339	(UNKNOWN)	--
BULGARIA	43	DIPLOMATIC	4-FIGURE 1-PART CODE	?	"JZ.-C. REG. 1"	?	? - ?	? PERS Z S	RECOVERED 30%-40%	T 2131	(UNKNOWN)	--
BULGARIA	44	DIPLOMATIC	4-FIGURE ?-PART CODE	?	BD 27	?	? - ?	? PERS Z S	VERY LITTLE SUCCESS	T 2337	(UNKNOWN)	--
BULGARIA	45	?	4-FIGURE 1-PART CODE	?	"2 FRIED-RICHS"	?	? - ?	? PERS Z S	RECOVERED ABOUT 25%	T 2177	(UNKNOWN)	--
BULGARIA	46	MILITARY ATTACHE?	?-PART CODE. FIRST GROUP AFTER ADDRESS WAS BALKAN.	?	?	?	? - ?	? SIM	NOT READ	IF 1525	(UNKNOWN)	--

CHART NO. 1-2

TOP SECRET

DOCID: 3560861

TOP SECRET

RESULTS OF EUROPEAN AXIS CRYPTANALYSIS AS LEARNED FROM TICOM SOURCES

(WITH ANNOTATIONS FROM ARMY SECURITY AGENCY SOURCES IN PARENTHESES)

COUNTRY OF ORIGIN		SERVICE	DESCRIPTION OF SYSTEM	NAME OF SYSTEM: COUNTRY OF ORIGIN	NAME OF SYSTEM: AXIS	NAME OF SYSTEM: U.S.A.	DATES OF USE	WHEN ATTACKED AND BY WHOM	RESULTS	TICOM REFERENCE	STATUS OF THE SYSTEM AT ASA	REMARKS
CHILE	1	?	5-FIGURE 5-LETTER 2-PART CODE. 100,000 GROUPS. DIVIDED INTO THREE CONSECUTIVE BOOKS.	?	?	?	BEFORE 1941	? SIM	100% COMPROMISED.	IF 1517 IF 1518	(UNKNOWN)	--
CHILE	2	DIPLOMATIC	5-LETTER 1-PART CODE. 26,500 GROUPS. FIRST TWO AND LAST TWO LETTERS OF EACH GROUP ENCIPHERED WITH DIGRAPHIC SUBSTITUTION TABLE.	?	?	?	1924 - ?	1924 PERS Z S	SOLVED.	D 16, REPORT 1, P 2	(UNKNOWN)	--
CHILE	3	CONSULAR	5-LETTER ?-PART CODE.	?	CHILE KONSULAR CODE	?	? - ?	? PERS Z S	RECOVERED LESS THAN 5%	T 3026	(UNKNOWN)	--
CHILE	4	DIPLOMATIC	1-TO 4-LETTER 1-PART CODE. 42,000 GROUPS.	CLAVE SOLAR	?	(CLA)	(1936-CURRENT)	1940 PERS Z S	SOLVED. LATER 100% COMPROMISED.	D 16, REPORT #2, P 4 D 16, REPORT #4, P 4	(COMPROMISED 100% -- DATE OF EDITION 1936.)	--
CHILE	5	DIPLOMATIC	4-LETTER ?-PART CODE.	?	?	?	? - ?	? PERS Z S	RECOVERED LESS THAN 5%	T 1400 T 3025	(UNKNOWN)	--
CHILE	6	DIPLOMATIC	?-PART CODE WITH COMPLICATED ENCIPHERMENT.	?	?	?	1941-?	? SIM	?	IF 1517 IF 1518	(UNKNOWN)	--

CHART NO. 1-2

TOP SECRET

RESULTS OF EUROPEAN AXIS CRYPTANALYSIS AS LEARNED FROM TICOM SOURCES

(WITH ANNOTATIONS FROM ARMY SECURITY AGENCY SOURCES IN PARENTHESES)

COUNTRY OF ORIGIN		SERVICE	DESCRIPTION OF SYSTEM	NAME OF SYSTEM: COUNTRY OF ORIGIN	NAME OF SYSTEM: AXIS	NAME OF SYSTEM: U.S.A.	DATES OF USE	WHEN ATTACKED AND BY WHOM	RESULTS	TICOM REFERENCE	STATUS OF THE SYSTEM AT ASA	REMARKS
CHINA	1	?	5-LETTER ?-PART CODE.	?	?	?	?	? PERS Z S	RECOVERED LESS THAN 10%	T 1157	(UNKNOWN)	--
CHINA	2	(DIPLOMATIC)	4-LETTER (1-PART) CODE. THOUGHT TO HAVE BEEN ENCODED IN CHINESE CHARACTERS AND ENCIPHERED IN LATIN CHARACTERS.	?	?	(CNS) OR (CNF) OR (CNJ)	(CNS, 1944 - CURRENT) (CNF, 1942 - CURRENT) (CNJ, 1944 - CURRENT)	? SIM	NOT READ	IF 1518 P 5	(CNS, CNF, CNJ BROKEN AND READ BY ASA.)	--
CHINA	3	DIPLOMATIC AND CONSULAR	4-LETTER 1-PART CODE. SOMETIMES ENCIPHERED.	OJYJ	?	(CNS)	(1943-CURRENT)	? PERS Z S	RECOVERED SUBSTITUTION ALPHABETS	T 3	(RECOVERED BY BRITISH. BOOK GIVEN TO ASA. BEING READ.)	--
CHINA	4	DIPLOMATIC	4-LETTER ?-PART CODE, ALTERNATE CONSONANT AND VOWELS.	HUKO	?	?	?	? PERS Z S	PARTIALLY BROKEN	T 2297	(UNKNOWN)	--
CHINA	5	DIPLOMATIC	4-LETTER ?-PART CODE, OCCASIONALLY DIGRAPHICALLY ENCIPHERED.	?	?	?	1935-1937	? PERS Z S	CODE AND ENCIPHERMENT PARTIALLY BROKEN	T 2112 T 2113	(UNKNOWN)	--
CHINA	6	DIPLOMATIC	4-LETTER ?-PART CODE.	?	?	?	?	? PERS Z S	PROBABLY READ. PARTIALLY BROKEN.	T 2291	(UNKNOWN)	--
CHINA	7	DIPLOMATIC	4-LETTER ?-PART CODE, OCCASIONALLY DIGRAPHICALLY ENCIPHERED.	?	?	?	1926-1929	? PERS Z S	FAIRLY COMPLETE RECOVERY OF BOTH CODE AND ENCIPHERMENT	T 2111	(UNKNOWN)	--
CHINA	8	COMMERCIAL	4-LETTER ?-PART CODE, OCCASIONALLY ENCIPHERED DIGRAPHICALLY. USED BETWEEN CHINA AND A CHINESE COMMERCIAL MISSION IN GERMANY.	?	?	?	1937-1938	? PERS Z S	CODE AND ENCIPHERMENT PARTIALLY BROKEN	T 2010 T 2110	(UNKNOWN)	--
CHINA	9	(DIPLOMATIC)	3-LETTER 2-PART CODE. (USUALLY ENCIPHERED. HAD MANY ENCIPHERMENTS.)	HNM	?	(CNL)	(1943-CURRENT)	? PERS Z S	?	T 1159	(SOLVED BY ASA 1944)	--
CHINA	10	DIPLOMATIC	3-LETTER 1-PART CODE. SOMETIMES ENCIPHERED.	WIN	?	(CNC)	(1939-CURRENT)	? PERS Z S	PARTIALLY READ	T 4	(PARTIALLY RECONSTRUCTED COMPROMISED COPY RECEIVED. COMPLETED BREAKING. NOW BEING READ.)	--
CHINA	11	DIPLOMATIC	3-LETTER 1-PART CODE.	?	UTI	?	?	1941 PERS Z S	SOLVED	I 22 P 21 T 202 T 214 T 198 T 2296	(UNKNOWN)	
CHINA	12	(DIPLOMATIC)	3-LETTER 1-PART CODE. SOMETIMES ENCIPHERED. HAD MANY ENCIPHERMENTS.	?	DRYO	(CNB)	(? - 1940 - CURRENT)	? PERS Z S ? OKW	COMPLETELY READ	T 2 T 2292	(PLAIN CODE AND LETTER ENCIPHERMENTS NOT BEING WORKED ON -- LOW INTELLIGENCE VALUE. NUMBER ENCIPHERMENT BEING READ.)	--

CHART NO. 1-2

DOCID: 3560861

TOP SECRET

RESULTS OF EUROPEAN AXIS CRYPTANALYSIS
AS LEARNED FROM TICOM SOURCES
(WITH ANNOTATIONS FROM ARMY SECURITY AGENCY SOURCES IN PARENTHESES)

COUNTRY OF ORIGIN		SERVICE	DESCRIPTION OF SYSTEM	NAME OF SYSTEM: COUNTRY OF ORIGIN	AXIS	U.S.A.	DATES OF USE	WHEN ATTACKED AND BY WHOM	RESULTS	TICOM REFERENCE	STATUS OF THE SYSTEM AT ASA	REMARKS
CHINA	13	MILITARY ATTACHE	3-LETTER ?-PART CODE. ENCIPHERMENT CONSISTED OF TRANSPOSITION WITHIN THE CODE GROUPS. FIRST GROUPS OF TRAFFIC WERE EFR, SKW, OR JKW.	?	?	?	? - 1943	? PERS Z S	ENCIPHERMENT SOLVED. NOT READ.	I 22 P 8	(UNKNOWN)	--
CHINA	14	MILITARY	3-LETTER ?-PART CODE. UNENCIPHERED. DISCRIMINANT WAS NKDBN. CONTAINED MANY SPELLS, USING SIMPLE SUBSTITUTION.	?	?	?	?	? PERS Z S	INVESTIGATED	I 22 P 8	(UNIDENTIFIED)	--
CHINA	15	?	"POST CODE"	?	?	?	?	? OKW	?	I 15Ø P 9	(UNKNOWN)	--
CHINA	16	DIPLOMATIC	POLYALPHABETIC SUBSTITUTION. 26 ALPHABETS. (USED ON CODES CNF, CNL, CNS, CNU, AND CNW.)	SXS	?	(SXS)	(1944-CURRENT)	? PERS Z S	SOLVED	T 3	(ALPHABETS SENT BY BRITISH.)	--
CHINA	17	DIPLOMATIC	POLYALPHABETIC SUBSTITUTION. 1Ø ALPHABETS. (USED WITH CODES CNB, CNC, CNF, CNJ, CNL, CNS, CNU, AND CNW.)	AMC	?	(AMC)	(1943-CURRENT)	? PERS Z S	SOLVED	T 3	(ALPHABETS SENT BY BRITISH.)	--
CHINA	18	DIPLOMATIC	MONOALPHABETIC SUBSTITUTION. (USED WITH CNB, CNC, CND, CNF, CNJ, CNL, CNS, CNU, AND CNW.)	AMA	?	(AMA)	(1943-CURRENT)	? PERS Z S	SOLVED	T 3	(ALPHABETS SENT BY BRITISH.)	--
CHINA	19	DIPLOMATIC	MONOALPHABETIC SUBSTITUTION. DAILY CHANGING ALPHABETS. (USED ON CODES CNB, CNC, CND, CNF.)	ECTIA	?	(ECTIA)	(1943-1945)	? PERS Z S	SOLVED	T 3	(ALPHABETS SENT BY BRITISH.)	--
COLOMBIA	1	DIPLOMATIC	POLYALPHABETIC SUBSTITUTION CIPHER WITH 5 TO 15 ALPHABETS.	?	?	?	? - 1942 - ?	1941 PERS Z S	READ	D 16, REPORT 2, P 4	(UNKNOWN)	--
COLOMBIA	2	DIPLOMATIC	POLYALPHABETIC SUBSTITUTION CIPHER WITH 5 ALPHABETS.	?	?	(COA)	(1927-CURRENT)	1927 PERS Z S	READ	D 16, REPORT 1, P 3	(READABLE)	--
CZECHO-SLOVAKIA	1	AIR FORCE	TRANSPOSITION CIPHER.	?	?	?	? - 1937 - ?	1937 OKL	NOT BROKEN	I 121 P 7	(UNKNOWN)	--
CZECHO-SLOVAKIA	2	AIR FORCE	DOUBLE TRANSPOSITION CIPHER.	?	?	?	? - 1938 - ?	1938 OKL	SOLVED.	I 112 P 6	(UNKNOWN)	--
CZECHO-SLOVAKIA	3	?	DOUBLE TRANSPOSITION CIPHER.	?	?	?	? - 1938 - ?	1938 OKL	?	I 112 P 1Ø	(UNKNOWN)	--
CZECHO-SLOVAKIA	4	ARMY	VARIOUS POLYALPHABETIC SUBSTITUTION CIPHERS. USED IN 1925, 1926, AND 1927.	?	?	?	1925-1927	OKL	SOLVED	T 1794	(UNKNOWN)	--
CZECHO-SLOVAKIA	5	COMMERCIAL	CODE USED BY SKODA FIRM TO IRAN AND IRAQ CONCERNED WITH BRIDGE BUILDING PROJECTS.	?	?	?	? - 1935 - ?	1935 OKL	SOLVED	I 162 P 2	(UNKNOWN)	--

CHART NO. 1-2

TOP SECRET

DOCID: 3560861

TOP SECRET

RESULTS OF EUROPEAN AXIS CRYPTANALYSIS
AS LEARNED FROM TICOM SOURCES
(WITH ANNOTATIONS FROM ARMY SECURITY AGENCY SOURCES IN PARENTHESES)

COUNTRY OF ORIGIN		SERVICE	DESCRIPTION OF SYSTEM	NAME OF SYSTEM			DATES OF USE	WHEN ATTACKED AND BY WHOM	RESULTS	TICOM REFERENCE	STATUS OF THE SYSTEM AT ASA	REMARKS
				COUNTRY OF ORIGIN	AXIS	U.S.A.						
DENMARK	1	DIPLOMATIC	CODE	?	?	?	? - ?	BEFORE 1940 FA	50% OF TRAFFIC READ UP TO 1940	I 162 P 3	(UNIDENTIFIED)	--
DOMINICAN REPUBLIC	1	DIPLOMATIC	SUBSTITUTION CIPHER WITH 5 ALPHABETS.	?	?	(DOA)	?-(CURRENT)	1941 PERS Z S	COMPLETELY READ	D 16, REPORT 2, P 4 T 2507	(READABLE)	--
ECUADOR	1	DIPLOMATIC	2-LETTER 3-LETTER 4-LETTER 2-PART CODE. GROUPS IN FROM OF VC, VCC, OR VCCC. TRANSMITTED IN 10-LETTER GROUPS.	?	?	?	1923-?	1926 PERS Z S	COMPLETELY READ	D 16, REPORT 1, P 3	(UNKNOWN)	--
ECUADOR	2	DIPLOMATIC	2-LETTER 4-LETTER 1-PART CODE. 61,945 GROUPS. INTERSPERSED CLEAR TEXT.	?	?	(ECA)	(?-1941-CURRENT)	1941 PERS Z S ? SIM	SOLVED	D 16, REPORT 2, P 4 T 1592	(80% READABLE)	--
EGYPT	1	DIPLOMATIC?	TWO ?5-FIGURE ?-PART CODES, VALUES IN FRENCH. ENCIPHERED.	?	?	?	? - ?	? SIM	?	IF 1518	(UNIDENTIFIED)	--
ETHIOPIA	1	DIPLOMATIC	5-FIGURE 1-PART CODE. VALUES IN FRENCH.	?	"AETH.1"	(ETA)	(?-CURRENT)	? ?	RECOVERED LESS THAN 5%	T 1061	(ALMOST COMPLETELY READABLE.)	--
ETHIOPIA	2	DIPLOMATIC	DOUBLE TRANSPOSITION	?	?	(ETB)	(?-1944-CURRENT)	? OKH	NO SUCCESS	T 57	(CURRENTLY BEING ATTACKED; NOT YET BROKEN.)	--
FINLAND	1	DIPLOMATIC AND MILITARY ATTACHE	HAGELIN. (5-WHEEL AND 6-WHEEL MACHINES.)	?	?	(FIA-1) (FIA-2)	(1942-CURRENT)	? OKW ? FA	NOT READ BY OKW. READ OCCASIONALLY BY FA.	I 31 P 7 I 54 P 2 I 25 P 6	(SOLVED IN 1943. FIA-1 STILL BEING READ; FIA-2 NOT READABLE, SINCE TABLES CHANGED, BUT BEING WORKED ON.)	--

CHART NO. 1-2

TOP SECRET

DOCID: 3560861

TOP SECRET

RESULTS OF EUROPEAN AXIS CRYPTANALYSIS AS LEARNED FROM TICOM SOURCES

(WITH ANNOTATIONS FROM ARMY SECURITY AGENCY SOURCES IN PARENTHESES)

COUNTRY OF ORIGIN		SERVICE	DESCRIPTION OF SYSTEM	NAME OF SYSTEM			DATES OF USE	WHEN ATTACKED AND BY WHOM	RESULTS	TICOM REFERENCE	STATUS OF THE SYSTEM AT ASA	REMARKS
				COUNTRY OF ORIGIN	AXIS	U.S.A.						
FRANCE--VICHY, FREE FRANCE	1	(DIPLOMATIC)	CIPHER MACHINE, HAGELIN M-209. (6 WHEELS, VARIABLE PINS, VARIABLE LUGS, NO SLIDE, MAXIMUM KICK OF 27 OVERLAPPED.)	(M-209)	?	(FRENCH M-209)	DURING SAN FRANCISCO CONFERENCE, 1945	1943 OKW	PROBABLY READ	I 58 P 3 I 136 P 2	(READ FRENCH HAGELIN DURING SAN FRANCISCO CONFERENCE.)	--
FRANCE	2	DIPLOMATIC?	5-LETTER 1-PART COCE, APPROXIMATELY 20,000 GROUPS.	?	9	?	?-1940-?	1940 PERS Z S	?	D 54 P 12	(UNIDENTIFIED)	--
FRANCE--VICHY, FREE FRANCE	3	DIPLOMATIC	4-LETTER 2-PART CODE.	PC 148	6 VARIA 1-352; F 2	(FRG)	(1937-CURRENT)	1944 SID PRIOR TO 1941 PERS Z S	75% RECONSTRUCTED BY ITALIANS. COMPROMISED BY ITALIANS AND GERMANS. READABLE BUT NOT WORKED ON BY PERS Z S DUE TO LACK OF PERSONNEL.	T 1521 T 1504 T 3251 D 54 P 12	(RECOVERED AT ASA IN 1942.)	--
FRANCE	4	DIPLOMATIC?	4-LETTER 2-PART CODE. VCVV OR VCVC. (SIMILAR TO FRG.)	?	F.B. 1, VOL. 1	?	? - ?	? PERS Z S	RECOVERED 50%	T 2033 T 2034 T 2035	(UNKNOWN)	--
FRANCE	5	DIPLOMATIC	4-LETTER 2-PART CODE.	?	?	?	?-1937-?	? OKW	COMPLETELY READ	T 898	(UNKNOWN)	--
FRANCE	6	DIPLOMATIC	4-LETTER (?-PART) CODE, APPROXIMATELY 20,000 GROUPS. (UNENCIPHERED)	VESTA	?	(FCF)	1941-(1944)	AFTER 1941 PERS Z S	RECOVERED 15%	D 54 P 12 T 3256	(BEGAN WORK 1944. COMPROMISED CODE. READ. SCANT MATERIAL.)	--
FRANCE	7	DIPLOMATIC?	4-LETTER 4-FIGURE 1-PART CODE, NOT STRICTLY ALPHABETIC.	?	?	?	? - ?	? PERS Z S	RECOVERED 40%	T 2019	(UNIDENTIFIED)	--
FRANCE	8	DIPLOMATIC	5-FIGURE 2-PART CODE.	?	F 21	?	1920	? GERMANS	WORKED ON. KNEW SYSTEM.	T 3536 T 3539	(UNIDENTIFIED)	--
FRANCE--FREE FRANCE	9	DIPLOMATIC?	5-FIGURE 2-PART CODE ENCIPHERED BY SINGLE TRANSPOSITION KEY TAKEN FROM THE ENCODE. KEY VARIES FROM 12 TO 29 LETTERS, NONE DIVISIBLE BY 5.	"1918 TYPE C"	?	?	?-1939-?	? OKW	COMPROMISED	T 1728	(UNIDENTIFIED)	--
FRANCE	10	DIPLOMATIC	5-FIGURE 2-PART CODE.	?	R 2	?	? - ?	? GERMANS	RECONSTRUCTED 15%	T 3152	(UNKNOWN)	--
FRANCE	11	DIPLOMATIC?	5-FIGURE 2-PART CODE.	?	R 4. GEGEN-CODE	?	? - ?	? PERS Z S	PARTIALLY RECONSTRUCTED	T 3088	(UNKNOWN)	--
FRANCE--FREE FRANCE	12	DIPLOMATIC?	5-FIGURE ?-PART CODE, ENCIPHERED BY TRANSPOSITION.	?	?	?	?-1941-?	1941 OKW ? PERS Z S	NO SUCCESS.	I 58 P 6	(UNIDENTIFIED)	--
FRANCE--(VICHY)	13	(DIPLOMATIC)	4-FIGURE 2-PART CODE. (UNENCIPHERED)	PC 151	80. 7. BLN. 103 1-- VARI 601--	(FAF)	(1941-1944)	? GERMANS	RECOVERED 50%; COMPROMISED 100%	T 3246 T 3247 T 1505	(BROKEN WITH HELP FROM GCCS. 50% RECOVERED, 90% READABLE.)	--

CHART F.D. I-2

TOP SECRET

DOCID: 3560861

TOP SECRET

RESULTS OF EUROPEAN AXIS CRYPTANALYSIS
AS LEARNED FROM TICOM SOURCES
(WITH ANNOTATIONS FROM ARMY SECURITY AGENCY SOURCES IN PARENTHESES)

COUNTRY OF ORIGIN		SERVICE	DESCRIPTION OF SYSTEM	NAME OF SYSTEM: COUNTRY OF ORIGIN	NAME OF SYSTEM: AXIS	NAME OF SYSTEM: U.S.A.	DATES OF USE	WHEN ATTACKED AND BY WHOM	RESULTS	TICOM REFERENCE	STATUS OF THE SYSTEM AT ASA	REMARKS
FRANCE	14	DIPLOMATIC	4-FIGURE 2-PART CODE.	?	C 51	?	? - ?	? GERMANS	ABOUT 35% RE-COVERED	T 3149	(UNKNOWN)	--
FRANCE	15	DIPLOMATIC?	4-FIGURE 2-PART CODE.	?	?	?	?-1937?-?	? OKW	RECOVERED 40%; 85% READABLE.	T 929	(UNKNOWN)	--
FRANCE	16	DIPLOMATIC	4-FIGURE 2-PART CODE.	?	471 BER-LIN 1.A-300 E	?	? - ?	? GERMANS	ABOUT 65% RECOVERED	T 3147	(UNKNOWN)	--
FRANCE	17	DIPLOMATIC	4-FIGURE 2-PART CODE.	?	NA 5	?	? - ?	? GERMANS	ABOUT 25% RE-CONSTRUCTED	T 3148	(UNKNOWN)	--
FRANCE	18	DIPLOMATIC	4-FIGURE 2-PART CODE.	?	FC	?	? - ?	? GERMANS	READ.	T 2536	(UNKNOWN)	--
FRANCE	19	DIPLOMATIC	4-FIGURE 2-PART CODE. PERHAPS USED IN THE NEAR EAST.	?	34 VARIA 1-599	?	? - ?	? GERMANS	ABOUT 30% RE-COVERED	T 3155	(UNKNOWN)	--
FRANCE	20	DIPLOMATIC	4-FIGURE 2-PART CODE.	?	11 NAM. OSTEN	?	? - ?	1941 PERS Z S	RECOVERED 25%	T 3249 D 54 P 12	(UNKNOWN)	--
FRANCE-- (VICHY)	21	DIPLOMATIC	4-FIGURE 2-PART CODE. (ENCIPHERED WITH RUNNING ADDITIVE.)	(Z 4)	12 FERN-OST	(FAJ)	(1941)-1943	1943 PERS Z S	RECOVERED 20%	T 3250 D 54 P 12	(BOOK COMPROMISED 1942.)	--
FRANCE	22	DIPLOMATIC?	4-FIGURE 2-PART CODE.	?	FZC 18	?	? - ?	? OKW	RECONSTRUCTED 30%	T 885	(UNKNOWN)	--
FRANCE	23	(DIPLOMATIC)	4-FIGURE (2-PART) CODE. (5 ENCIPHERMENTS USED CONSISTING OF 1 SUBSTITUTION AND 4 ADDITIVE SYSTEMS.)	CTX	?	(FRB)	1944-(CURRENT)	1944 SID	PROBABLY NOT SOLVED	T 1522	(CODE BOOK COMPROMISED 1943. COMPROMISED SUBSTITUTION TABLES AFTER SOME WORK DONE. ADDITIVES BROKEN. ALMOST ALL TRAFFIC COMPLETELY READ.)	--
FRANCE	24	DIPLOMATIC	4-FIGURE 2-PART CODE, (UNENCIPHERED).	(PC 154)	17	(FAE)	(1941-1944)	? GERMANS	RECONSTRUCTED 75%	T 3241 T 3242 T 3243 T 3300 T 3301	(BROKEN WITH HELP OF GCCS. RECOVERED 65%.)	--
FRANCE	25	DIPLOMATIC	4-FIGURE 2-PART CODE, (UNENCIPHERED).	(PC 152)	14 BERLIN	(FAC)	(1941-1944)	? GERMANS	RECOVERED 50%	T 3235	(ENCODE. COMPROMISED 1943. REMAINDER LARGELY SOLVED.)	--
FRANCE	26	DIPLOMATIC	4-FIGURE 2-PART CODE.	?	?	?	? - ?	? PERS Z S	RECOVERED 10%	T 3101	(UNKNOWN)	--
FRANCE	27	DIPLOMATIC	4-FIGURE 2-PART CODE.	?	111 1-500	?	? - ?	? PERS Z S	RECOVERED 50%	T 3091	(UNKNOWN)	--
FRANCE	28	DIPLOMATIC	4-FIGURE 2-PART CODE.	?	?	?	? - ?	? GERMANS	COMPROMISED	T 2441	(UNIDENTIFIED)	--
FRANCE	29	DIPLOMATIC?	4-FIGURE 2-PART CODE.	?	15 VARIA	?	? - ?	? GERMANS	RECOVERED 35%	T 3236	(UNKNOWN)	--

CHART NO. 1-2

TOP SECRET

DOCID: 3560861

TOP SECRET

RESULTS OF EUROPEAN AXIS CRYPTANALYSIS
AS LEARNED FROM TICOM SOURCES
(WITH ANNOTATIONS FROM ARMY SECURITY AGENCY SOURCES IN PARENTHESES)

COUNTRY OF ORIGIN		SERVICE	DESCRIPTION OF SYSTEM	NAME OF SYSTEM: COUNTRY OF ORIGIN	NAME OF SYSTEM: AXIS	NAME OF SYSTEM: U.S.A.	DATES OF USE	WHEN ATTACKED AND BY WHOM	RESULTS	TICOM REFERENCE	STATUS OF THE SYSTEM AT ASA	REMARKS
FRANCE	30	DIPLOMATIC	4-FIGURE 2-PART CODE. UNENCIPHERED. DIGITS IN INDICATOR ADD TO 19.	PC 156; TNU	F 18	(FRH)	1945-(CURRENT)	1945 SID	RECONSTRUCTED 75% BY SID. READ.	T 733; T 745; T 735; T 1508; T 1511; T 1520; T 1524; T 1521; IF 1526 P 4	(COMPLETELY COMPROMISED BEFORE CODE WAS USED.)	--
FRANCE-- FREE FRANCE	31	DIPLOMATIC	4-FIGURE 2-PART CODE. (NOW UNENCIPHERED. HAD BEEN ENCIPHERED FOR A SHORT TIME.)	PC 146	5 BERLIN 1901; 5 VARIA 1-1900	(FRL)	(?-1941-CURRENT)	? SID ? PERS Z S	COMPROMISED 100% BY SID; CODE 75% RECOVERED BY PERS Z S	T 1509; T 2029; T 3299; T 3253; T 3254; T 360	(87% COMPROMISED NOV. 1942. REMAINDER PROVIDED THROUGH TICOM SOURCES SEPT. 1945.)	--
FRANCE	32	DIPLOMATIC	4-FIGURE 2-PART CODE.	?	19 RN	?	? - ?	? GERMANS	RECOVERED 35%	T 3245	(UNKNOWN)	--
FRANCE	33	DIPLOMATIC	4-FIGURE 2-PART CODE.	?	?	?	?-1930-?	? PERS Z S	RECONSTRUCTED	T 2018	(UNKNOWN)	--
FRANCE	34	DIPLOMATIC?	4-FIGURE 2-PART CODE.	?	33 BERLIN	?	? - ?	? PERS Z S	RECOVERED 20%	T 2032	(UNKNOWN)	--
FRANCE	35	DIPLOMATIC?	4-FIGURE 2-PART CODE.	?	F 4	?	? - ?	? PERS Z S	ABOUT 5% RECOVERED	T 2031	(UNKNOWN)	--
FRANCE	36	DIPLOMATIC?	4-FIGURE 2-PART CODE.	?	?	?	?-1930-?	? OKW	PARTIALLY RECONSTRUCTED	T 893	(UNKNOWN)	--
FRANCE	37	DIPLOMATIC?	4-FIGURE 2-PART CODE.	?	?	?	? - ?	? OKW	RECONSTRUCTED 35%	T 892	(UNKNOWN)	--
FRANCE	38	DIPLOMATIC	4-FIGURE 2-PART CODE.	?	358 BERLIN 1-1195; 358 VARIA 1-; 358 VARIA D-E 1-799	?	? - ?	? PERS Z S	APPROXIMATELY 70% RECOVERED	T 3096; T 3086; T 2021; T 2020; T 2022	(UNKNOWN)	--
FRANCE	39	DIPLOMATIC?	4-FIGURE 2-PART CODE.	?	?	?	? - ?	? OKW	RECOVERED 40%	T 883	(UNKNOWN)	--
FRANCE	40	DIPLOMATIC?	4-FIGURE 2-PART CODE.	?	111 1-482	?	? - ?	? GERMANS	RECONSTRUCTED 30%	T 2485 T 2489	(UNKNOWN)	--
FRANCE	41	DIPLOMATIC?	4-FIGURE 2-PART CODE.	?	?	?	? - ?	? PERS Z S	PARTIALLY RECOVERED	T 3099	(UNKNOWN)	--
FRANCE	42	(DIPLOMATIC)	4-FIGURE (2-PART) CODE. UNENCIPHERED. DIGITS IN 5-FIGURE INDICATOR ADD TO 20.	?	F 20	(FRJ)	(1945-CURRENT)	1945 SID	WORKED ON.	T 1521	(IN PROCESS OF RECOVERY. FAIRLY READABLE.)	--
FRANCE	43	DIPLOMATIC	4-FIGURE 2-PART CODE.	?	1 BERLIN 1; 1 VARIA 1-	?	? - ?	? PERS Z S	ABOUT 75% RECOVERED	T 3087 T 3150 T 2017	(UNKNOWN)	--
FRANCE	44	DIPLOMATIC	4-FIGURE 2-PART CODE.	?	2 BERLIN 1-500; 2 VARIA 1-	?	? - ?	? GERMANS	RECOVERED 75%	T 2486 T 3154	(UNKNOWN)	--
FRANCE	45	DIPLOMATIC?	4-FIGURE 2-PART CODE.	?	3 BERLIN 1-?; 3 VARIA 1	?	? - ?	? PERS Z S	ABOUT 75% RECOVERED	T 3157 T 3153 T 2488	(UNKNOWN)	--

CHART NO. 1-2

TOP SECRET

DOCID: 3560861

TOP SECRET

RESULTS OF EUROPEAN AXIS CRYPTANALYSIS AS LEARNED FROM TICOM SOURCES

(WITH ANNOTATIONS FROM ARMY SECURITY AGENCY SOURCES IN PARENTHESES)

COUNTRY OF ORIGIN		SERVICE	DESCRIPTION OF SYSTEM	NAME OF SYSTEM: COUNTRY OF ORIGIN	AXIS	U.S.A.	DATES OF USE	WHEN ATTACKED AND BY WHOM	RESULTS	TICOM REFERENCE	STATUS OF THE SYSTEM AT ASA	REMARKS
FRANCE-- VICHY, FREE FRANCE	46	DIPLOMATIC	4-FIGURE 2-PART CODE. (UNENCIPHERED.)	(PC 149)	FRANCIA F 149; 4 BERLIN 102	(FRO)	?-1935-(CURRENT)	? ITALIANS 1935 GERMANS	COMPROMISED 100% BY ITALIANS. 75% RECOVERED BY GERMANS.	T 1584 T 3252 T 3255	(APPROXIMATELY 98% READABLE; 55-60% RECOVERED. TICOM MATERIAL ELIMINATES THE NEED FOR FURTHER BOOKBREAKING.)	--
FRANCE-- VICHY	47	(DIPLOMATIC)	A SET OF EIGHT 4-FIGURE (2-PART) CODES, UNENCIPHERED.	"PC" SERIES	F 4, 5, 7, 10, 14, 15, 16, 17	(PROBABLY FAC THROUGH FAH, FMO, OR FAS)	?-(SOME CURRENT)	PRIOR TO 1941 PERS Z S	READ, SOME COMPROMISED, SOME BROKEN.	T 3239; T 3240 T 3300; T 3299 T 1504; T 1505 T 2029 D 54 P 12	(MAINLY COMPROMISED; SOME BREAKING DONE ON PORTIONS OF FAG AND OTHERS.)	--
FRANCE-- (VICHY, LATER FREE FRANCE)	48	DIPLOMATIC	4-FIGURE 2-PART CODE. (ENCIPHERED.)	PCN 9	19 AP	(FAT)	1941-(1944)	1941 FA	RECONSTRUCTED 40%	T 1093 T 3244	(COMPROMISED VICHY'S BOOK AND TABLES 1942. COMPROMISED 30 OUT OF 124 OF THE FREE FRENCH TABLES. BUILT UP MANY OTHERS READ.)	--
FRANCE-- (FREE FRANCE)	49	(DIPLOMATIC)	CIFHER TABLES--DIGRAPHIC SUBSTITUTION OF NUMBERS FOR LETTERS. (CHANGED QUARTERLY BUT REPEATED FROM YEAR TO YEAR.)	TABLES III AND IV	19 AP	(FAT TABLES)	(1940-1943)	? ?	COMPROMISED	T 2452	(COMPROMISED 1942. SEE ITEM 48.)	--
FRANCE-- (VICHY, LATER FREE FRANCE?)	50	(DIFLOMATIC)	4-FIGURE (2-PART) CODE WITH LETTER DIGRAPHIC SUBSTITUTION WITH LIMITATIONS OF 10 LETTERS. TABLES OF 100 DIGRAPHS CHANGED QUARTERLY. SAME TABLE USED ON DIFFERENT DATES IN SUCCESSIVE MONTHS OF QUARTER. DIGRAPHS TAKEN QUARTERLY. SEVERAL OF THIS TYPE.	(PCN-9)	?	(FAT?) OR (FAU?)	(FAU: 1941-1944) (FAT: 1943-1945)	? PERS Z S	COMPROMISED SOME MATERIAL. PROBABLY READ AFTER 1941.	I 22 P 19 D 54 P 13 T 3532	(IF FAU, WORK STARTED 1942, THEN COMPROMISED; READ. IF FAT, SEE ITEM 48.)	--
FRANCE-- VICHY, FREE FRANCE	51	DIFLOMATIC	4-FIGURE 2-PART CODE. ENCIFHERED--SOME BY TABLES. MANY OF THIS TYPE.	?	?	(FAM, FAN, FAO, FAP, FAL. FMH, OR FAU)	?-1940-?	1940 SIM	HAD COMPROMISED COPY OF ONE CODE AND ONE 1-TIME ENCIPHERING TABLE.	IF 1522 P 2	(COMPROMISED MOST CODES AND TABLES 1942. SOME BREAKING DONE ON FAU AND TABLES OF FMH.)	--
FRANCE	52	DIFLOMATIC	4-FIGURE 2-PART CODE.	PC 28	?	?	?-1925-?	1929 PERS Z S	PARTIALLY RECONSTRUCTED	T 2156	(UNKNOWN)	--
FRANCE	53	DIFLOMATIC	4-FIGURE 2-PART CODE.	(PC 155)	16-1-3600	(FAD)	?-1940-(1944)	? GERMANS ? ITALIANS	APPROXIMATELY 75% RECOVERED BY GERMANS AND ITALIANS.	T 3237 T 3238 T 3239 T 3240 T 1507 T 2306	(ASA HAS COMPROMISED COPY. READ FROM 1942-1944.)	--
FRANCE	54	DIFLOMATIC?	4-FIGURE 2-PART CODE.	?	F 36	?	1930 - ?	? OKW	RECONSTRUCTED 45%	T 879	(UNKNOWN)	--
FRANCE	55	DIFLOMATIC?	4-FIGURE 2-PART CODE.	?	F 49	?	?-1931-?	? OKW	RECONSTRUCTED 30%	T 881	(UNKNOWN)	--
FRANCE	56	DIPLOMATIC?	4-FIGURE 2-PART CODE.	?	F 50	?	?-1931-?	? OKW	RECONSTRUCTED 33%	T 880	(UNKNOWN)	--
FRANCE	57	DIFLOMATIC?	4-FIGURE 2-PART CODE. USED BETWEEN PARIS AND BEIRUT AND ADDIS-ABBABA.	?	?	?	?-1930-1937-?	? PERS Z S	PARTIALLY READ	T 2036	(UNKNOWN)	--

CHART NO. 1-2

TOP SECRET

DOCID: 3560861

RESULTS OF EUROPEAN AXIS CRYPTANALYSIS AS LEARNED FROM TICOM SOURCES

(WITH ANNOTATIONS FROM ARMY SECURITY AGENCY SOURCES IN PARENTHESES)

TOP SECRET

COUNTRY OF ORIGIN		SERVICE	DESCRIPTION OF SYSTEM	NAME OF SYSTEM: COUNTRY OF ORIGIN	NAME OF SYSTEM: AXIS	NAME OF SYSTEM: U.S.A	DATES OF USE	WHEN ATTACKED AND BY WHOM	RESULTS	TICOM REFERENCE	STATUS OF THE SYSTEM AT ASA	REMARKS
FRANCE--VICHY, FREE FRANCE	58	DIPLOMATIC	4-FIGURE 2-PART CODE. SOMETIMES ENCIPHERED WITH DAILY CHANGING REPEATING 5-DIGIT ADDITIVE. (UNENCIPHERED UNTIL JUNE 1944.)	PC 150	F J	(FRA; FRA-3)	?-(1943-CURRENT)	1944 SID PRIOR TO 1945 PERS Z S	READ BY PERS Z S. SID READ FREE FRENCH TRAFFIC 1944-1945. COMPROMISED DEC. 1944.	IF 1526 P 4; I 22 P 19; T 732; T 734; T 1506; T 1503; T 1521; T 792; T 1523; T 1525; T 1529	(TRAFFIC READABLE FROM 1942. BOOKBREAKING CONTINUED UNTIL SEPT. 1945 WHEN ITALIAN COMPROMISED CODE WAS RECEIVED. CURRENT FORMS BEING READ.)	--
FRANCE	59	DIPLOMATIC	4-FIGURE 1-PART CODE, NOT STRICTLY ALPHABETIC.	?	BE (ZAHLEN CODE)	?	? - ?	? GERMANS	RECOVERED 90%	I 359	(UNKNOWN)	--
FRANCE--FREE FRANCE	60	DIPLOMATIC	4-FIGURE 1-PART CODE, NOT STRICTLY ALPHABETIC.	PR 19	?	?	?-1927-?	? OKW	COMPROMISED	T 1723	(UNKNOWN)	--
FRANCE	61	DIPLOMATIC	4-FIGURE 1-PART CODE, NOT STRICTLY ALPHABETIC.	?	?	?	?-1937?-?	? OKW	RECOVERED 50%	T 1826	(UNKNOWN)	--
FRANCE	62	DIPLOMATIC	4-FIGURE 1-PART CODE, NOT STRICTLY ALPHABETIC. LESS THAN 1,300 GROUPS.	?	"CODE LEHE"	?	?-1937?-?	? OKW	RECOVERED 75%	T 1827 T 1828	(UNKNOWN)	--
FRANCE	62	DIPLOMATIC	4-FIGURE 1-PART CODE, NOT STRICTLY ALPHABETIC. "SMALL CODE."	?	?	?	?-1937-?	? OKW	RECOVERED 50%	T 1830	(UNKNOWN)	--
FRANCE	64	DIPLOMATIC	4-FIGURE 1-PART CODE, REPAGINATED. LESS THAN 2,000 GROUPS.	?	?	?	?-1937?-?	? OKW	RECONSTRUCTED 50%	T 1829	(UNKNOWN)	--
FRANCE	65	DIPLOMATIC?	4-FIGURE 1-PART CODE, REPAGINATED. "SUBSTITUTION ENCIPHERMENT BY TABLE #3."	?	?	?	?-1939-?	? PERS Z S	?	D 54 P 7	(UNKNOWN)	--
FRANCE--(FREE FRANCE)	66	DIPLOMATIC	4-FIGURE 1-PART CODE.	?	?	?	?-1927-?	? OKW	COMPROMISED	T 1721	(UNIDENTIFIED)	--
FRANCE--(FREE FRANCE)	67	DIPLOMATIC	4-FIGURE 1-PART CODE.	?	?	?	?-1940-?	? OKW	COMPROMISED	T 1719	(UNKNOWN)	--
FRANCE	68	DIPLOMATIC?	4-FIGURE 1-PART CODE.	H. D. 2	?	?	? - ?	? OKW	PARTIALLY RECONSTRUCTED	T 2496	(UNIDENTIFIED)	--
FRANCE--VICHY	69	DIPLOMATIC	4-FIGURE ?-PART CODE.	?	?	?	?-1939-?	? GERMANS	READ	T 2494	(UNKNOWN)	--
FRANCE	70	DIPLOMATIC?	4-FIGURE ?-PART CODE. USED TO TRANSMIT ENGLISH TEXT.	?	8	?	? - 1941	? PERS Z S	?	D 54 P 2	(UNKNOWN)	--
FRANCE	71	DIPLOMATIC?	4-FIGURE ?-PART CODE. "SUSPECTED THAT IT COMBINES AN ADDITIVE AND A SUBSTITUTION PROCESS."	?	?	?	?-1940-?	1940 PERS Z S	NOT READ BY PERS Z S PRIOR TO 1941	D 54 P 13	(UNIDENTIFIED)	--
FRANCE	72	DIPLOMATIC?	4-FIGURE ?-PART CODE. ENCIPHERED BY A 100-PLACE LETTER SUBSTITUTION TABLES.	?	19	?	?-1941-?-	PRIOR TO 1942 FA, PERS Z S	FIRST SOLUTION BY FA USING CAPTURED TABLES.	D 54 P 18	(UNIDENTIFIED)	--

CHART LH 1-2

TOP SECRET

DOCID: 3560861

TOP SECRET

RESULTS OF EUROPEAN AXIS CRYPTANALYSIS AS LEARNED FROM TICOM SOURCES

(WITH ANNOTATIONS FROM ARMY SECURITY AGENCY SOURCES IN PARENTHESES)

COUNTRY OF ORIGIN		SERVICE	DESCRIPTION OF SYSTEM	NAME OF SYSTEM			DATES OF USE	WHEN ATTACKED AND BY WHOM	RESULTS	TICOM REFERENCE	STATUS OF THE SYSTEM AT ASA	REMARKS
				COUNTRY OF ORIGIN	AXIS	U.S.A.						
FRANCE	73	DIPLOMATIC?	4-FIGURE ?-PART CODE.	?	FU 5, FU 4, FU 3, FU 2, FU 1	?	? - ?	? PERS Z S?	NO BOOKBREAKING DONE.	T 3146; T 3145 T 3144; T 3143 T 3142	(UNIDENTIFIED)	--
FRANCE	74	DIPLOMATIC	"CODE FOREIGN OFFICE OR HANOI MESSAGES."	?	?	?	?-1940-?	1940 SIM	READ	IF 1524	(UNIDENTIFIED)	--
FRANCE	76	DIPLOMATIC?	ADDITIVE ENCIPHERMENT SYSTEM.	CODE 1919 TYPE 2	?	?	?-1939-?	? OKW	COMPROMISED 100%	T 1624	(UNIDENTIFIED)	--
FRANCE	76	DIPLOMATIC?	"CIPHER TABLES #14." TRIGRAPHIC SUBSTITUTION.	DS-B 614	?	?	?-1940-?	? OKW	COMPROMISED	T 918	(UNKNOWN)	--
FRANCE	77	DIPLOMATIC, CONSULAR	4-FIGURE ?-PART CODE. INDICATOR 66666. USED BETWEEN PARIS AND DUBLIN.	?	F CONS DUBLWE	?	? - ?	? ITALIANS	?	T 1521	(UNKNOWN)	--
FRANCE	78	DIPLOMATIC, CONSULAR, COLONIAL	4-FIGURE 2-PART CODE. ALWAYS ENCIPHERED BY SIMPLE DIGIT FOR DIGIT SUBSTITUTION.	RD 12	?	?	1918 - ?	? ?	COMPROMISED 100%	T 3537	(UNKNOWN)	--
FRANCE	79	CONSULAR	4-FIGURE ?-PART CODE.	?	?	?	?-1940-?	? OKW	PROBABLY NOT READ	T 1704	(UNKNOWN)	--
FRANCE	80	COMMERCIAL	4-FIGURE 1-PART CODE, NOT STRICTLY ALPHABETIC.	DICTIONAIRE CHIFFRE HAVAS	?	?	?-1932-?	? OKW	COMPROMISED 100%	T 1681	(UNKNOWN)	--
FRANCE	81	MILITARY ATTACHE	5-LETTER 5-FIGURE ?-PART CODE. PERHAPS ENCIPHERED BY TRANSPOSITION.	?	F 152	?	1939 - ?	1941 GERMANS	?	T 3549	(UNKNOWN)	--
FRANCE	82	(MILITARY ATTACHE)	5-FIGURE (2-PART) CODE. HAD (10) ENCIPHERMENTS. (FVB-5 USES COLUMNAR TRANSPOSITION WITH NULL PATTERNS ON A KEY TAKEN FROM THE ENCODE.)	(CODE EMPIRE 1943)	?	(FVB; FVB-5; AND POSSIBLY FVB-2 OR FVB-3)	1943-1945	? OKH	PROBABLY NOT BROKEN	I 160 PP 7, 19-21 POSSIBLY I 58 P 2	(FVB-2, FVB-3, FVB-5 BROKEN BY ASA IN 1943-1944. FOUR OTHER ENCIPHERMENTS SOLVED. THREE OTHERS IN PROCESS OF SOLUTION. ONLY ONE IS CURRENT.)	--
FRANCE	83	(MILITARY ATTACHE)	5-FIGURE 2-PART CODE.	(JOCAM) OR (CODE EMPIRE)	?	(FNF?) OR (FVB?)	1941 - ?	? OKW	?	I 58 P 2	(IF FNF, BROKEN AND READ. IF FVB, SEE ITEM 82.)	--
FRANCE	84	MILITARY ATTACHE	4-FIGURE 2-PART CODE ENCIPHERED BY ONE-TIME TRANSPOSITION KEYS, 13-27 LETTERS IN LENGTH, TAKEN FROM THE ENCODE. KEYS ARE REVERSED BEFORE USED. FOR USE BY FRANCO POLISH MILITARY MISSION.	?	?	?	1940 - ?	? ?	COMPROMISED 100%	T 3553	(UNKNOWN)	--
FRANCE-- (FREE FRANCE)	85	(MILITARY ATTACHE)	4-FIGURE 1-PART CODE USING TRANSPOSITION ENCIPHERMENT. (SPECIAL PAGINATIONS ASSIGNED TO EACH STATION. ONE GENERAL PAGINATION.)	?	?	(FVD)	1940-(CURRENT)	? OKW	BROKEN AND READ	I 31 P 5	(BROKE 3 ENCIPHERMENTS. FVD-4 IN SOLUBLE STATE. FVD-5 BEING WORKED ON.)	--
FRANCE	86	MILITARY ATTACHE	ONE-TIME TRANSPOSITION KEYS OF VARYING LENGTHS. USED BETWEEN FRANCE AND ROME.	?	?	?	1940 - ?	? OKW	COMPROMISED 100%	T 1753	(UNKNOWN)	--
FRANCE	88	MILITARY ATTACHE	2-LETTER ENCIPHERING TABLES REPLACING THE SUDAMERI SYSTEM.	?	?	?	1925 - ?	? OKW	COMPROMISED	T 1819	(UNKNOWN)	--

CHART NO. 1-2

TOP SECRET

DOCID: 3560861

TOP SECRET

RESULTS OF EUROPEAN AXIS CRYPTANALYSIS
AS LEARNED FROM TICOM SOURCES
(WITH ANNOTATIONS FROM ARMY SECURITY AGENCY SOURCES IN PARENTHESES)

COUNTRY OF ORIGIN		SERVICE	DESCRIPTION OF SYSTEM	NAME OF SYSTEM: COUNTRY OF ORIGIN	NAME OF SYSTEM: AXIS	NAME OF SYSTEM: U.S.A.	DATES OF USE	WHEN ATTACKED AND BY WHOM	RESULTS	TICOM REFERENCE	STATUS OF THE SYSTEM AT ASA	REMARKS
FRANCE	89	COLONIAL	1-PART CODE, 5 OR MORE LETTERS PER GROUP.	?	?	?	?-1923-?	? ?	COMPROMISED	T 2453	(UNKNOWN)	--
FRANCE--VICHY AND FREE FRANCE	90	COLONIAL	5-LETTER 1-PART CODE.	(1926 B)	?	(FBT)	1926-(1944)	? GERMANS	PARTIALLY RE-CONSTRUCTED AND 100% COM-PROMISED	T 3137 T 3158	(COMPROMISED 1942 AFTER SOME WORK WAS DONE.)	(FBU BASIC BOOK; FBT REPAGINA-TION)
FRANCE	91	COLONIAL	ENCIPHERMENT TABLE FOR 1926 B.	MX	?	?	? - ?	? ?	WORKED ON	T 2457	(UNKNOWN)	(ASA KNOWS OF NO EN-CIPHERMENT ON FBT)
FRANCE	92	COLONIAL?	5-LETTER 1-PART CODE.	?	9 MARNE	?	? - ?	? GERMANS	RECOVERED 20%	T 3248	(UNKNOWN)	--
FRANCE	93	COLONIAL	?-LETTER ?-PART CODE, SOMETIMES ENCIPHERED.	?	?	?	? - 1941	1940 PERS Z S	NOT READ PRIOR TO 1941 FOR LACK OF HELP	D 54 P 13	(UNIDENTIFIED)	--
FRANCE	94	COLONIAL?	5-FIGURE 2-PART CODE	?	F 13	?	? - ?	? OKW	COMPROMISED 100%	T 1672	(UNKNOWN)	--
FRANCE	95	COLONIAL	5-FIGURE (1-PART) CODE. (APPROXIMATELY 8,000 GROUPS. SIMITATION ON FIRST DIGITS TO 0, 1, OR 2. FIRST UNENCIPHERED; LATER SOMETIMES ENCI-PHERED BY ADDITIVE ON 10 X 10 DAILY SQUARE WITH RANDOM COORDINATES.)	(1943)	F COL 29	(FNC)	?-1944-1945	? SID	KNEW INDICA-TORS	T 1521	(CODE BOOK COMPROMISED 1945 AFTER SOME BOOK BREAKING HAS DONE. ASA SOLVED ENCIPHER-MENT.)	--
FRANCE	96	COLONIAL?	5-FIGURE 1-PART CODE. BOOK HAS 3 SETS OF TRI-GRAPHIC PAGE DESIGNATIONS FOR EACH PAGE, ALL AT THE SAME INTERVAL AND PROGRESSING BY ONES.	?	?	?	?-1918?-?	? OKW	COMPROMISED 100%	T 1802	(UNKNOWN)	--
FRANCE	97	COLONIAL (NAVAL, MILI-TARY, DIPLO-MATIC ATTACHE)	4-FIGURE 2-PART CODE. (NOW UNENCIPHERED. HAS HAD 2 MAJOR ENCIPHERMENTS.)	(CODE V)	F COL 000	(FNB)	?-1943-(CUR-RENT)	? ITALIANS	?	T 1521	(COMPROMISED CODE BOOK. BROKE BOTH ENCIPHERMENTS. READ 100%.)	--
FRANCE	98	COLONIAL	4-FIGURE 1-PART CODE. SOME GROUPS SENT IN CLEAR. FOR USE IN ALGERIA. SPELL GROUPS BEGIN WITH 51 OR 53 AND END WITH 52 OR 54.	CHIFFRE 60	?	?	? - ?	? ?	COMPROMISED 100%	T 1621	(UNKNOWN)	--
FRANCE	99	COLONIAL	RUNNING ADDITIVE ENCIPHERING SYSTEM FOR COLONIAL 1923 CODE.	C.M.A.N.	?	?	?-1941-?	? ?	TABLES 100% COMPROMISED	T 2456	(UNKNOWN)	--
FRANCE	100	ARMY	HAGELIN CIPHER MACHINE. (6 WHEELS, VARIABLE PINS, VARIABLE LUGS, SLIDE, MAXIMUM KICK OF 27.)	BC 38	BC 38	(BC 38)	(1944-CURRENT)					
FRANCE--FREE FRANCE	101	(ARMY)	CIPHER MACHINE EMPLOYING FRACTIONATION, SUBSTITU-TION, AND RECOMBINATION. (USED 5 X 5 SQUARE. HAD 6 WHEELS AND 2 SETS OF PLUGS. "MODIFIED" VERSION HAD 10 WHEELS AND 4 SETS OF PLUGS.)	B-211	B-211 AND V-211 WITH SURCHIF-FREUR	(B-211 AND MODIFIED B-211)	(ABOUT 1938-CURRENT)	APPROXIMATELY 1941 OKH, OKW	ORIGINAL VER-SION READ. MODIFIED VER-SION NOT READ.	I 160 P 6 I 111 F 5 I 31 PP 1, 7 D 60 P 7	(NOT READ)	--

CHART NO. 1-2

TOP SECRET

DOCID: 3560861

TOP SECRET

RESULTS OF EUROPEAN AXIS CRYPTANALYSIS AS LEARNED FROM TICOM SOURCES

(WITH ANNOTATIONS FROM ARMY SECURITY AGENCY SOURCES IN PARENTHESES)

COUNTRY OF ORIGIN		SERVICE	DESCRIPTION OF SYSTEM	NAME OF SYSTEM: COUNTRY OF ORIGIN	NAME OF SYSTEM: AXIS	NAME OF SYSTEM: U.S.A.	DATES OF USE	WHEN ATTACKED AND BY WHOM	RESULTS	TICOM REFERENCE	STATUS OF THE SYSTEM AT ASA	REMARKS
FRANCE-- FREE FRANCE	102	(ARMY)	CIPHER MACHINE, HAGELIN TYPE. 5 WHEELS (FIXED LUGS, VARIABLE PINS.)	C-36	C-36	(C-36)	(APPROXIMATELY 1936-CURRENT)	1940 OKH 1940 OKW 1939 SIM	SOLVED AND FREQUENTLY READ BY OKH AND OKW. MAY HAVE BEEN READ BY SIM.	I 92 P 3 I 160 P 6 I 42 P 4 I 58 P 5 I 48 P 2 I 45 PP 6-7 I 79 PP 2-3 I 78 PP 4, 9 I 31 P 7 IF 107 P 5 IF 1518 IF 1524 T 1658 T 1673	(READ. CAN BE BROKEN BY STATISTICAL METHODS.)	--
FRANCE	103	MILITARY	MACHINE CIPHERS.	?	?	?	1939-1940	? SIM	NOT READ	IF 1522	(UNIDENTIFIED)	--
FRANCE	104	ARMY	5-LETTER ?-PART CODE ENCIPHERED BY DIAGONAL TRANSPOSITION BY MEANS OF A NUMERICAL KEY DERIVED FROM A KEY WORD. KEY WORD CHANGED MONTHLY, LATER EVERY TWO WEEKS. IN WEST AFRICA LETTER SUBSTITUTION TABLES WERE INTRODUCED WITH A MONTHLY CHANGE FOR THE INDICATOR GROUPS.	?	?	?	1943-1945	? OKH	READ	I 160 P 7	(UNIDENTIFIED)	--
FRANCE	105	ARMY	5-LETTER ?-PART CODE. FIRST 2 AND LAST GROUPS ARE 5-FIGURE. ENCIPHERED BY DIAGONAL TRANSPOSITION. USED IN EQUATORIAL AFRICA.	?	?	?	1943-APPROXIMATELY 1945	? OKH	READ	I 160 P 7, PP 12-14	(UNKNOWN)	--
FRANCE	106	ARMY	5-LETTER ?-PART CODE. ENCIPHERED BY SIMPLE TRANSPOSITION. "10 DAILY KEY CHANGE."	?	?	?	1943 - ?	? OKH	READ	I 160 P 6	(UNKNOWN)	--
FRANCE	107	ARMY	4-LETTER 2-PART CODE, UNENCIPHERED. COULD BE USED AS A 4-FIGURE 1-PART CODE ENCIPHERED BY "TABLES 3, 102, AND 103."	M.C.	?	?	1935-1940-?	? OKW	COMPROMISED 100%	T 1646	(UNKNOWN)	--
FRANCE	108	ARMY?	4-LETTER ?-PART CODE.	?	F 51	?	? - ?	? GERMANS	?	T 3615	(UNIDENTIFIED)	--
FRANCE-- FREE FRANCE	109	ARMY	3-LETTER 1-PART CODE. FIELD TYPE.	?	?	?	1942-1943	? GERMANS ? SIM	READ BY GERMANS AND SIM. PROBABLY FIRST BROKEN BY GERMANS.	IF 1517 P 5 IF 1523 P 7	(UNKNOWN)	--
FRANCE	110	(ARMY)	3-LETTER 1-PART CODE, THE MIDDLE LETTER BEING ONE OF THE 5 VOWELS. SEVERAL ENCIPHERMENTS WERE USED. LATER THE ENCIPHER KEY CHANGED MORE FREQUENTLY.	?	?	?	1941 - ?	? OKH	READ.	I 170 PP 2-3	(UNKNOWN)	--
FRANCE	111	ARMY	3-LETTER 1-PART SMALL CODE. KEY CHANGED EVERY 2 WEEKS.	?	?	?	1942-1944	? OKH	READ	I 160 PP 6, 8	(UNKNOWN)	--
FRANCE	112	ARMY	3-LETTER 1-PART SMALL CODE. IDENTICAL IN CONSTRUCTION TO ITEM 111, BUT VOCABULARY MORE ADAPTABLE TO WIRELESS TRAFFIC. KEY CHANGED EVERY 2 WEEKS.	?	?	?	APPROXIMATELY 1943-1944	? OKH	READ	I 160 PP 6, 9	(UNKNOWN)	--
FRANCE	113	ARMY, AIR, NAVY	MIXED 3-LETTER, 4-FIGURE, AND 3-FIGURE 2-PART CODE. EMERGENCY CODEBOOK FOR USE IN NORTH AFRICA. BOOK DIVIDED INTO SECTIONS FOR THE USE OF THE THREE SERVICES.	G.M.A.	?	?	1942 - ?	? ?	COMPROMISED 100%	T 1790	(UNKNOWN)	--

CHART NO. 1-2

TOP SECRET

DOCID: 3560861

TOP SECRET

RESULTS OF EUROPEAN AXIS CRYPTANALYSIS
AS LEARNED FROM TICOM SOURCES
(WITH ANNOTATIONS FROM ARMY SECURITY AGENCY SOURCES IN PARENTHESES)

COUNTRY OF ORIGIN	SERVICE	DESCRIPTION OF SYSTEM	NAME OF SYSTEM: COUNTRY OF ORIGIN	NAME OF SYSTEM: AXIS	NAME OF SYSTEM: U.S.A.	DATES OF USE	WHEN ATTACKED AND BY WHOM	RESULTS	TICOM REFERENCE	STATUS OF THE SYSTEM AT ASA	REMARKS
FRANCE--VICHY	114 ARMY	TWO 5-FIGURE 2-PART CODES WITH ABOUT 50,000 GROUPS. VARIOUS SYSTEMS OF ENCIPHERMENTS USED. USED BETWEEN FRANCE AND COLONIAL ARMIES.	?	?	?	? - ?	? SIM	READ AFTER BEING DEPOSITED WITH ARMISTICE COMMISSION	IF 1522 P 1, APPENDIX A	(UNIDENTIFIED)	--
FRANCE	115 (ARMY)	5-FIGURE 2-PART CODE.	?	?	?	1943 - ?	? OKH	BROKEN AND READ	I 170 P 4	(UNIDENTIFIED)	--
FRANCE	116 (ARMY)	(5-FIGURE 1-PART CODE. LATER REPAGINATED. 3 ENCIPHERMENTS IN USE SIMULTANEOUSLY.)	SYSTEME CRYPTOGRAPHIQUE MODELE 1923	?	--	1923 - ?	? OKW	COMPROMISED 100%	T 1605 T 1735 T 1814 T 1627	(COMPROMISED BOOK 1927 OR 1928. NO TRAFFIC. NO WORK DONE.)	--
FRANCE	117 MILITARY	TRANSPOSITION KEYS FOR SYSTEM 1923.	1933 D	F 1457; F 1377	--	1940 - ?	1940 GERMANS	COMPROMISED 100%	T 3613	(CODE BOOK COMPROMISED. SEE ITEM 116.)	--
FRANCE	118 ARMY	5-FIGURE 2-PART CODES. USED IN FRANCE, NORTH AFRICA, WEST AFRICA, AND ECUATORIAL AFRICA.	?	?	?	?-1943-1944?	? OKH	NOT READ BY FEBRUARY 1945	I 160 P 7	(UNIDENTIFIED)	--
FRANCE--FREE FRANCE	119 ARMY	4-FIGURE 5-FIGURE CODE SENT IN 5-FIGURE GROUPS. ENCIPHERED BY ADDITIVE SYSTEM.	?	?	?	? - ?	? SIM	NOT READ	IF 1522 P 2	(UNIDENTIFIED)	--
FRANCE	120 ARMY?	4-FIGURE 2-PART CODE. SHORT CODE. SOMETIMES ENCIPHERED BY DIGRAPHIC LETTER SUBSTITUTION.	CODE CHIFFRE NO. 3	?	?	? - ?	? OKW	COMPROMISED 100%	T 1640	(UNKNOWN)	--
FRANCE	121 ARMY	4-FIGURE 2-PART FIELD CODE. ENCIPHERED BY A 11 DIGIT REPEATING ADDITIVE. INDICATOR WAS 55555.	?	F 112 OR RA	?	1937-1939	1937 OKW	SOLVED AND READ. ENCIPHERING TABLES COMPROMISED 100%.	I 59 P 6 I 176 P 2 T 3684	(UNKNOWN)	--
FRANCE	122 ARMY	4-FIGURE 2-PART CODE. APPROXIMATELY 6,000 GROUPS. ENCIPHERED BY DIGRAPHIC LETTER SUBSTITUTION.	SERIE 67	?	?	?-1920-?	? OKW	COMPROMISED 100%	T 1793 T 1644	(UNKNOWN)	--
FRANCE	123 ARMY	4-FIGURE 2-PART CODE. APPROXIMATELY 55,000 GROUPS. DIGRAPHIC LETTER SUBSTITUTION. SIMILAR TO ITEM 122.	CONCORDANCE NO. 3	?	?	? - ?	? OKW	COMPROMISED 100%	T 1794	(UNKNOWN)	--
FRANCE	124 ARMY	4-FIGURE 2-PART CODE.	CODE CHIFFRE SERIE 68	?	?	? - ?	? OKW	COMPROMISED 100%	T 1666	(UNKNOWN)	--
FRANCE	125 ARMY	4-FIGURE 2-PART CODE. ENCIPHERED BY LETTER SUBSTITUTION WITH VARIANTS. NO GROUP BEGINS WITH 0.	SERIE 69	?	?	? - ?	? OKW	COMPROMISED 100%	T 1636	(UNKNOWN)	--
FRANCE	126 ARMY?	4-FIGURE 2-PART CODE.	SERIE 71	?	?	?-1940-?	? OKW	ALMOST COMPLETELY RECOVERED	T 877	(UNKNOWN)	--
FRANCE	127 ARMY	4-FIGURE 2-PART CODE. USED BETWEEN NORTH AFRICA AND CORSICA. REVERSED 4TH GROUP SUBTRACTED FROM THE 3RD GROUP ALWAYS GAVE SAME DIFFERENCE FOR ALL MESSAGES.	ATM43	?	?	1943-1945	1944 OKW	RECOVERED AND READ	I 160 PP 7, 14-19	(UNKNOWN)	--

CHART NO. 1-2

TOP SECRET

RESULTS OF EUROPEAN AXIS CRYPTANALYSIS AS LEARNED FROM TICOM SOURCES

(WITH ANNOTATIONS FROM ARMY SECURITY AGENCY SOURCES IN PARENTHESES)

COUNTRY OF ORIGIN		SERVICE	DESCRIPTION OF SYSTEM	NAME OF SYSTEM: COUNTRY OF ORIGIN	NAME OF SYSTEM: AXIS	NAME OF SYSTEM: U.S.A.	DATES OF USE	WHEN ATTACKED AND BY WHOM	RESULTS	TICOM REFERENCE	STATUS OF THE SYSTEM AT ASA	REMARKS
FRANCE	128	ARMY	4-FIGURE 2-PART CODE, ALWAYS ENCIPHERED.	AFR	?	?	?-1942-?	? GERMANS	COMPROMISED 100%	T 3683	(UNKNOWN)	--
FRANCE	129	ARMY	4-FIGURE ?-PART CODE WITH SHORT REPEATING ADDITIVE, WHICH MAY HAVE CHANGED WEEKLY. GROUP 1 WAS MESSAGE NUMBER; GROUP 2 GAVE NUMBER OF GROUPS; AND THE LAST GROUP WAS THE INDICATOR GROUP.	?	?	?	1944-1945	? OKH	CAPTURED AND READ	I 160 PP 7, 19	(UNKNOWN)	--
FRANCE	130	ARMY	4-FIGURE ?-PART CODE WITH SHORT REPEATING ADDITIVE. USED IN TRANSPORT NETWORKS IN NORTH AFRICA. EXTERNAL CHARACTERISTICS SAME AS THOSE OF ITEM 129. TRANSMITTED IN 3-FIGURE GROUPS.	?	?	?	1944-1945	? OKH	READ	I 160 PP 7, 19	(UNKNOWN)	--
FRANCE	131	ARMY	4-FIGURE ?-PART CODE CONSTRUCTED BY A CODE "TABLE" IN WHICH RANDOM 2-DIGIT COORDINATES FORMED THE 4-FIGURE GROUPS. ENCIPHERED BY DAILY CHANGING FIGURE SUBSTITUTION TABLES IN MONTHLY CYCLES.	?	?	?	1944-1945	? OKH	READ	I 160 PP 6, 8	(UNKNOWN)	--
FRANCE	132	ARMY	4-FIGURE ?-PART CODE ENCIPHERED BY "ORDINARY" TRANSPOSITION.	?	F 90	?	? - 1940	1937 OKW	SOLVED AND READ	T 3611 I 58 P 6 I 176 P 2	(UNKNOWN)	--
FRANCE-- FREE FRANCE	133	ARMY	(4-FIGURE 1-PART CODE NOT STRICTLY ALPHABETIC, ENCIPHERED BY SUBSTITUTION OF A TRIGRAPH FOR THE INITIAL DIGRAPH. SUPERENCIPHERED BY TRANSPOSITION KEY TAKEN FROM THE MAGAZINE "FRANCE LIBRE", VOL. IV, #23.) 5-FIGURE INDICATOR REPEATED AT THE BEGINNING IN REVERSED ORDER.	(GAMMA?)	?	(FRE 4)	(?-1942-CURRENT)	? GERMANS	NOT READ	T 312	(CODE BOOK ABOUT 80% RECOVERED BY GCCS AIDED BY ASA. ENCIPHERMENT SYSTEM ALMOST COMPLETELY COMPROMISED BY GCCS. READ AT ASA SINCE 1944.)	--
FRANCE	134	ARMY	4-FIGURE 1-PART CODE TRANSMITTED IN 5-FIGURE GROUPS. WAS ORIGINALLY A 3-LETTER 2-PART CODE. ENCIPHERMENT BY 10-DIGIT REPEATING ADDITIVE CONSTRUCTED FROM THE DATE.	ATM	?	?	BEFORE 1939-?	? GERMANS	COMPROMISED 100%	T 3551 T 3528 I 160 P 18	(UNKNOWN)	--
FRANCE	135	ARMY	4-FIGURE 1-PART CODE, REPAGINATED. VARIOUS ENCIPHERMENTS USED, SOMETIMES ONE-TIME TRANSPOSITION KEYS, SOMETIMES A REPEATING ADDITIVE.	G.N.1; G.C.1; G.F.1; G.R.1; CODE B.L.C CODE B.J; G.L.1; REPERTOIRE 1927	?	?	1927-1940-?	? OKW	COMPROMISED 100%	T 3541 T 1653 T 1652 T 3542 T 3545 T 3546 T 3552 T 3554 T 1751 T 1755	(UNKNOWN)	--
FRANCE-- VICHY	136	ARMY?	4-FIGURE 1-PART CODE, NOT STRICTLY ALPHABETIC. ENCIPHERED BY ADDITIVE TAKEN FROM A TABLE.	CARNET DE CHIFFREMENT "P.L."	?	?	1941 - ?	? OKW	COMPROMISED 100%	T 1647	(UNKNOWN)	NOT GIVEN TO ARMISTICE COMMISSION.
FRANCE	137	ARMY	4-FIGURE 1-PART CODE, NOT STRICTLY ALPHABETIC. VARIANTS USED ON MOST FREQUENT GROUPS. 2-DIGIT DIFFERENTIAL FOR GROUPS REPRESENTING PLAIN TEXT DIGITS. CODE TO BE USED ONLY WITH ENCIPHERMENT--LETTER OR FIGURE. TRANSPOSITION ONE-TIME KEY USED.	SERIE M	?	?	?-1940-?	? OKW	COMPROMISED 100%	T 1831 T 1725 T 1626 T 1633 T 1665	(UNKNOWN)	NOT TURNED OVER TO GERMANS OR ITALIANS AT ARMISTICE.
FRANCE	138	ARMY-COLONIAL	4-FIGURE 1-PART CODE WITH LETTER ENCIPHERMENT--2 OR 3 ALTERNATIVE LETTERS FOR EACH FIGURE.	?	?	?	? - 1939	? SIM	READ	IF 1519 P 2	(UNIDENTIFIED)	--

CHART NO. 1-2

DOCID: 3560861

TOP SECRET

RESULTS OF EUROPEAN AXIS CRYPTANALYSIS
AS LEARNED FROM TICOM SOURCES
(WITH ANNOTATIONS FROM ARMY SECURITY AGENCY SOURCES IN PARENTHESES)

COUNTRY OF ORIGIN		SERVICE	DESCRIPTION OF SYSTEM	NAME OF SYSTEM: COUNTRY OF ORIGIN	NAME OF SYSTEM: AXIS	NAME OF SYSTEM: U.S.A.	DATES OF USE	WHEN ATTACKED AND BY WHOM	RESULTS	TICOM REFERENCE	STATUS OF THE SYSTEM AT ASA	REMARKS
FRANCE	139	ARMY	4-FIGURE 1-PART CODE. USED FOR SMALL UNITS. USED UNENCIPHERED IF NO SECURITY REQUIRED. SOMETIMES ENCIPHERED BY 5-DIGIT REPEATING ADDITIVE WHICH FREQUENTLY CHANGED.	SERIE FC; CARNET DE CHIFFREMENT	?	?	?-1939-1939-?	? OKW	COMPROMISED 100%	T 1938 T 1629 T 1630	(UNKNOWN)	--
FRANCE-- (FREE FRANCE)	140	ARMY	4-FIGURE 1-PART CODE.	?	?	?	?-1938-?	? OKW	COMPROMISED	T 1629 T 1630	(UNKNOWN)	--
FRANCE	141	ARMY	4-FIGURE 1-PART CODE, TRANSPOSED.	?	?	?	PRIOR TO 1939	PRIOR TO 1939 SIM	READ	IF 1519 P 1	(UNIDENTIFIED)	--
FRANCE-- (FREE FRANCE)	142	ARMY	4-FIGURE 1-PART CODE, ENCIPHERED BY LETTER SUBSTITUTION TABLE. FIRST GROUP ALWAYS TTSF.	?	?	(FYB)	1944-(CURRENT)	? OKH	READ	I 160 PP 7, 11	(BROKEN AND BEING READ 100%)	--
FRANCE	143	ARMY, AIR	4-FIGURE 1-PART CODE, NOT STRICTLY ALPHABETIC.	J 2 CODE	?	?	?-1942-?	? OKW	COMPROMISED	T 904	(UNKNOWN)	--
FRANCE	144	ARMY	3-FIGURE 2-PART CODE. PROBABLY A FIELD CODE.	CARNET REDUIT: 222	?	?	1939?-1942-?	? OKW	COMPROMISED 100%	T 1736	(UNKNOWN)	--
FRANCE	145	ARMY?	3-FIGURE 1-PART CODE, NOT STRICTLY ALPHABETIC.	CODE DE SERVICE 1936	F 23	?	?-1926-?	? GERMANS	RECONSTRUCTED 63%; PERHAPS PARTIALLY COMPROMISED.	T 3559 T 3031?	(UNKNOWN)	--
FRANCE	146	ARMY	?-FIGURE ?-PART CODE. USED TRANSPOSITION ENCIPHERMENT.	?	F NIL	(FNG 112)	1945 ONLY	? SID	WORKED ON. PROBABLY NOT READ.	T 1521	(UNREADABLE. BEING WORKED ON.)	--
FRANCE	147	ARMY	2-FIGURE SUBSTITUTION TABLE WITH ALTERNATIVE EQUIVALENTS. USED IN SYRIA.	?	?	?	? - ?	? OKH	READ.	I 160 P 6	(UNKNOWN)	--
FRANCE-- FREE FRANCE	148	ARMY	CODE VALUES IN BLOCKS DESIGNATED BY FIGURE FOR BLOCK, LETTER FOR LINE. FIGURE COULD BE SUBSTITUTED BY DIGRAPH. USED IN SYRIA.	?	?	?	? - ?	? GERMANS ? SIM	READ PARTIALLY	IF 1523	(UNIDENTIFIED)	--
FRANCE	149	ARMY	SUBSTITUTION TABLES, 2 LETTERS PER NUMBER.	?	?	?	1943 - ?	? OKW	COMPROMISED	T 1749	(UNIDENTIFIED)	--
FRANCE	150	(ARMY)	CIPHER SYSTEM. SIMPLE LETTER SUBSTITUTION. SUBSTITUTION KEYS AND BOXES CHANGED EVERY 14 DAYS	?	?	?	?-1943-?	? OKH	READ	I 170 P 4	(UNIDENTIFIED)	--
FRANCE-- FREE FRANCE	151	ARMY	CIPHER?	"CONTROL BEDOUIN"	?	?	? - ?	? OKH	READ	I 74 P 2	(UNKNOWN)	--
FRANCE-- FREE FRANCE	152	ARMY	CIPHER?	"SERVICE POLITIQUE"	?	?	? - ?	? OKH	READ	I 74 P 2	(UNKNOWN)	--
FRANCE	153	ARMY	3 SETS OF ENCIPHERING KEYS--LETTER DIGRAPHS.	V.F.	?	?	APRIL 1940	? ?	COMPROMISED 100%	T 3557	(UNKNOWN)	--
FRANCE	154	ARMY?	TRANSPOSITION ENCIPHERMENT BASED ON A KEYWORD TAKEN FROM THE ENCODE.	MA	?	?	? - ?	? ?	ENCIPHERING DIRECTIONS COMPROMISED 100%	T 3543	(UNKNOWN)	--

CHART NO. 1-2

TOP SECRET

DOCID: 3560861

TOP SECRET

RESULTS OF EUROPEAN AXIS CRYPTANALYSIS
AS LEARNED FROM TICOM SOURCES
(WITH ANNOTATIONS FROM ARMY SECURITY AGENCY SOURCES IN PARENTHESES)

COUNTRY OF ORIGIN		SERVICE	DESCRIPTION OF SYSTEM	NAME OF SYSTEM: COUNTRY OF ORIGIN	NAME OF SYSTEM: AXIS	NAME OF SYSTEM: U.S.A.	DATES OF USE	WHEN ATTACKED AND BY WHOM	RESULTS	TICOM REFERENCE	STATUS OF THE SYSTEM AT ASA	REMARKS
FRANCE	155	(ARMY)	CIPHER SYSTEM USING SIMPLE LETTER TRANSPOSITION.	?	?	?	?-1943-?	? OKH	READ	I 170 P 4	(UNIDENTIFIED)	--
FRANCE	156	ARMY	SIMPLE TRANSPOSTION. USED IN SYRIA.	?	?	?	? - ?	? OKH	READ	I 160 P 6	(UNIDENTIFIED)	--
FRANCE	157	ARMY	21-LETTER REPEATING TRANSPOSITION KEY USED ON CODE RA. USED DURING MONTH OF SEPTEMBER, 1939. REPLACED BY CLEF ZERO B 2.	CLEF ZERO A 2	?	?	1939 ONLY	? OKW	COMPROMISED 100%	T 1736	(UNKNOWN)	--
FRANCE	158	ARMY	TRANSPOSITION ENCIPHERMENT BASED UPON A KEY, 14-25 LETTERS IN LENGTH, TAKEN FROM THE ENCODE FOR USE ON CODE RA. REPLACED BY CLEF ZERO C 2.	CLEF ZERO B 2	?	?	1939 ONLY	? OKW	COMPROMISED 100%	T 1736	(UNKNOWN)	--
FRANCE	159	ARMY	ENCIPHERMENT FOR USE ON CODE RA. REPLACED BY CLEF ZERO D 2.	CLEF ZERO C 2	?	?	1939-1940	? OKW	?	T 1736	(UNKNOWN)	--
FRANCE	160	ARMY	ENCIPHERMENT FOR USE ON CODE RA. REPLACED BY CLEF ZERO E 2.	CLEF ZERO D 2	?	?	1940 ONLY	? OKW	?	T 1736	(UNKNOWN)	--
FRANCE	161	ARMY	13-29 LETTER TRANSPOSITION KEY. LENGTH IS NEVER A MULTIPLE OF 4. FOR USE ON CODE RA.	CLEF ZERO E 2	?	?	1940 ONLY	? OKW	COMPROMISED 100%	T 1736	(UNKNOWN)	--
FRANCE	162	AIR	4-FIGURE 1-PART CODE, NOT STRICTLY ALPHABETIC. SOMETIMES ENCIPHERED.	?	?	?	1939-1942-?	? OKW	COMPROMISED 100%	T 1639	(UNKNOWN)	--
FRANCE	163	AIR	4-FIGURE 1-PART CODE, NOT STRICTLY ALPHABETIC.	?	FC 1; 42	?	?-1939-?	1939 GERMANS	PARTIALLY RE-CONSTRUCTED	T 3544	(UNKNOWN)	--
FRANCE	164	AIR	4-FIGURE 1-PART CODE, ENCIPHERED BY LETTERS.	?	?	?	?-1939-?	1939 OKL	READ	I 112 P 6	(UNKNOWN)	--
FRANCE	165	(AIR)	3-FIGURE 2-PART CODE, CAPTIONATED.	DICTIONNAIRE ET VOCABULAIRE GEOGRAPHIQUE DU CODE AERO; D.S. D 105	?	?	?-1936-?	? OKW	COMPROMISED 100%	T 1643	(UNKNOWN)	--
FRANCE	166	AIR	3-FIGURE 1-PART CODE. ENCIPHERED BY LETTERS WHICH CHANGED 2-5 TIMES A MONTH.	?	?	?	?-1935-?	? OKL	READ	I 112 P 6	(UNKNOWN)	--
FRANCE	167	AIR	WEATHER CODE. SINGLE DIGITS AND LETTERS. ENCIPHERED BY DAILY CHANGING ADDITIVE.	R.A.V.	?	?	? - ?	? OKW	COMPROMISED	T 1804	(UNIDENTIFIED)	--
FRANCE	168	AIR, NAVY	COMBINATION LETTER AND FIGURE CODE. PARTIALLY PLAIN TEXT. USED FOR LIAISON OF ARMY AND NAVY. LESS THAN 100 GROUPS.	LE CODE, AIR-MARINE, 1938	?	?	1938 - ?	? OKW	COMPROMISED	T 1733	(UNKNOWN)	--
FRANCE	169	AIR FORCE	CODE ENCIPHERED.	?	D. S. D 107	?	1940-1941	? SIS	READ. CAPTURED CODE INCLUDING KEYS FOR FEB., MAY, AND JUNE 1941	IF 1506	(UNIDENTIFIED)	--

TOP SECRET

DOCID: 3560861

TOP SECRET

RESULTS OF EUROPEAN AXIS CRYPTANALYSIS
AS LEARNED FROM TICOM SOURCES
(WITH ANNOTATIONS FROM ARMY SECURITY AGENCY SOURCES IN PARENTHESES)

COUNTRY OF ORIGIN		SERVICE	DESCRIPTION OF SYSTEM	NAME OF SYSTEM: COUNTRY OF ORIGIN	NAME OF SYSTEM: AXIS	NAME OF SYSTEM: U.S.A.	DATES OF USE	WHEN ATTACKED AND BY WHOM	RESULTS	TICOM REFERENCE	STATUS OF THE SYSTEM AT ASA	REMARKS
FRANCE	170	NAVY AIR	ADDITIVE ENCIPHERMENT SYSTEM FOR D.S.-D 107. DAILY CHANGING REPEATING ADDITIVE OF VARYING LENGTHS WHICH CHANGED ACCORDING TO DAY OF MONTH.	D.S.-D 109	?	?	?-1940-1941-?	? OKW ? SIS	COMPROMISED AND READ BY OKW AND SIS	T 1803 IF 1506	(UNKNOWN)	--
FRANCE	171	NAVY AIR	ADDITIVE ENCIPHERMENT (REPLACING?) D.S.-D 109. SIMILAR TO ITEM 170.	?	?	?	1941-?	? OKW	COMPROMISED	T 1806	(UNKNOWN)	--
FRANCE--VICHY, FREE FRANCE	172	NAVY	4-LETTER 2-PART CODE. 15 VARIANTS FOR EACH VALUE	D.S. 224 OR ISMC4	?	?	1940-?	? ?	COMPROMISED 100%	T 3555	(UNKNOWN)	--
FRANCE	173	NAVY	4-LETTER ?-PART CODE.	ISMC5; D.S.-D 225	?	?	1941-1942	? OKW	COMPROMISED	T 1805	(UNKNOWN)	--
FRANCE	174	NAVY?	4-LETTER CALL SIGN SYSTEM	?	ISMC1 (D.S.D 220) RENO	?	? - ?	? SIS	READ. CAPTURED.	IF 1506	(UNKNOWN)	--
FRANCE	175	NAVY?	3-LETTER CALL SIGNS.	?	N.S.4 (D.S.D244) VATI	?	? - ?	? SIS	READ. CAPTURED.	IF 1506	(UNKNOWN)	--
FRANCE	176	NAVY	COMBINATION LETTER AND FIGURE CODE. SIGNAL CODE.	D.S.-D 101	?	?	1936 - ?	? OKM	COMPROMISED 100%	T 573	(UNKNOWN)	--
FRANCE	177	NAVY	COMBINATION LETTER AND FIGURE CODE. SIGNAL CODE.	D.S.-D 102	?	?	1936 - ?	? OKM	COMPROMISED 100%	T 483	(UNKNOWN)	--
FRANCE	178	NAVY	5-FIGURE 2-PART CODE, WITH ENCIPHERING TABLES. ENCIPHERMENT SIMILAR TO THOSE MENTIONED IN ITEM 191.	T.B.M. 2	T.B.M. 2	?	1934 ONLY	1934 SIS	READ	IF 1506, 17B, P 3	(UNKNOWN)	--
FRANCE	179	NAVY	5-FIGURE 2-PART CODE WITH ENCIPHERING TABLES. ENCIPHERMENT SIMILAR TO THOSE MENTIONED IN ITEM 87.	T.B.M. 3	T.B.M. 3	?	1934-1935	1934 SIS	READ	IF 1506, 17B, P 5	(UNKNOWN)	--
FRANCE	180	NAVY	5-FIGURE 2-PART CODE.	T.B.M. 54; V.N. 2; D.S.B. 205; D.S.B. 301	F.Z. 21	?	1936-1939	1936 OKM	COMPROMISED 100%	T 589	(ASA HAS COMPROMISED COPY. NO TRAFFIC RECEIVED.)	--
FRANCE--FREE FRANCE, VICHY	181	NAVY	5-FIGURE 2-PART CODE. (USUALLY ENCIPHERED BY RUNNING ADDITIVE TAKEN FROM A CHART.)	T.B.M. 56; V.N. 3; A.R. 3; D.S.B. 302	F.Z.26; D.S.B.354 D.S.B.359 D.S.B.361	(FBX)	1939-(1943-?)	1939 SIS 1942 OKM	COMPROMISED AND READ BY OKM AND SIS.	T 586 IF 1504 PP 1, 20 IF 1506	(HAVE COMPROMISED COPY OF CODE AND ENCIPHERMENT. RECEIVED SOME TRAFFIC IN 1943. READ.)	--
FRANCE--(VICHY, FREE FRANCE)	182	NAVY	5-FIGURE 2-PART CODE.	C.A. 31; BDG 31; D.S.B 108	?	?	?-1939-?	1942 OKM	COMPROMISED	T 588	(UNKNOWN)	--
FRANCE	183	NAVY	5-FIGURE 2-PART CODE.	G.E. 58; D.S.B 209	?	?	?-1940-?	? OKM	COMPROMISED	T 590	(UNKNOWN)	--
FRANCE	184	NAVY	5-FIGURE 2-PART CODE.	B.D.G. 27; D.S.B 104	F.Z. 22	?	1935-1939	1935 OKM	COMPROMISED 100%	T 585	(UNKNOWN)	--

CHART NO. 1-2

TOP SECRET

DOCID: 3560861

TOP SECRET

RESULTS OF EUROPEAN AXIS CRYPTANALYSIS AS LEARNED FROM TICOM SOURCES

(WITH ANNOTATIONS FROM ARMY SECURITY AGENCY SOURCES IN PARENTHESES)

COUNTRY OF ORIGIN	SERVICE	DESCRIPTION OF SYSTEM	NAME OF SYSTEM			DATES OF USE	WHEN ATTACKED AND BY WHOM	RESULTS	TICOM REFERENCE	STATUS OF THE SYSTEM AT ASA	REMARKS
			COUNTRY OF ORIGIN	AXIS	U.S.A.						
FRANCE--VICHY, FREE FRANCE 185	NAVY	5-FIGURE 2-PART CODE.	B.D.G.3Ø1; C.A. 3Ø; D.S.B.1Ø7	B.D.G. 3Ø CIAK; DAMCUT	?	1939 - ?	? OKM ? SIS	COMPROMISED 1ØØ% BY SIS AND OKM. READ BY SIS.	T 587 IF 15Ø6	(UNKNOWN)	--
FRANCE 186	NAVY	5-FIGURE ?-PART CODE. 4Ø,ØØØ GROUPS, WITH ENCIPHERING TABLE AND 4,ØØØ APPENDIX GROUPS.	TBM 21	TBM 21	?	1938-1939	1938 SIS	SOLVED AND READ.	IF 15Ø6, 15 B, PP 1-25	(UNKNOWN)	--
FRANCE 187	NAVY	5-FIGURE ?-PART CODE WITH ENCIPHERING TABLE. 4Ø,ØØØ GROUPS.	TBM 22; POSSIBLY TBM 55; ENCIPHERMENT "A"	?	?	1939 - ?	? SIS	PERHAPS READ.	IF 15Ø6, 16B, PP 1-8	(UNKNOWN)	--
FRANCE 188	NAVAL, DIPLOMATIC, CONSULAR, COLONIAL	4-FIGURE 2-PART CODE. ADDITIVELY ENCIPHERED. ADDITIVES WERE CHOSEN FROM 6 SETS OF 31 ADDITIVE TABLES, EACH TABLE WITH 8ØØ DIGITS.	RD 37	?	(FBM)	194Ø-(1944)	? OKM	COMPROMISED 1ØØ%	T 1789 T 584	(CODE 1ØØ% COMPROMISED; ENCIPHERMENTS BROKEN 1942.)	--
FRANCE 189	NAVY	REVISION OF THE ENCIPHERING KEY #68 OF THE NAVAL ATTACHE IN BERNE. RUNNING ADDITIVE: TO BE USED WITH NAVAL CODE RD.	CLEF SPECIALE (#68 FOR BERNE)	?	?	1943 - ?	1943 PERS Z S	COMPROMISED 1ØØ%	T 245Ø	(UNKNOWN)	--
FRANCE 19Ø	NAVY	4-FIGURE 2-PART CODE. ALWAYS ENCIPHERED BY ADDITIVE TABLE. (USES SAME VOCABULARY AS RD 37)	DICTIONAIRE E.X. 36; FORMERLY RD 36	?	--	?-1939-?	1943 PERS Z S	COMPROMISED	T 2442 T 2443 D 3N-A	(NAVY HAS WORKED ON SYSTEM. ASA HAS NOT.)	--
FRANCE 191	NAVY	4-FIGURE 2-PART CODE. 5 SYSTEMS OF ENCIPHERMENT. USED 1ØØ ENCIPHERING TABLES.	TBM 1	TBM 1	?	1931-1934	1933 SIS	CODE AND ENCIPHERMENTS BROKEN AND READ.	IF 15Ø6	(UNKNOWN)	--
FRANCE 192	NAVY	TRIGRAPHIC SUBSTITUTION "TABLES # 13" TO BE USED ON B.D.G., T.B.M., AND V.N. 1.	D.S.-B 613	?	?	?-1939-?	? OKW	COMPROMISED	T 919	(UNKNOWN)	--
FRANCE 193	NAVY	4-FIGURE 1-PART CODE, NOT STRICTLY ALPHABETIC.	D.T.; D.S.B 81Ø	?	?	?-1939-1941-?	? OKW	COMPROMISED	T 9Ø3	(UNKNOWN)	--
FRANCE 194	NAVY?	ENCIPHERED CODE.	?	D.S.D 3Ø4	?	? - ?	? SIS	COMPROMISED; READ.	IF 15Ø6	(UNKNOWN)	--
FRANCE 195	NAVY	DIGRAPHIC SUBSTITUTION SYSTEM, 2 LETTERS FOR EACH FIGURE.	?	?	?	?-194Ø-?	? OKW	COMPROMISED	T 935	(UNKNOWN)	--
FRANCE 196	NAVY	DIGRAPHIC SUBSTITUTION ENCIPHERMENT SYSTEM REPLACING A MARCH 1929 ENCIPHERMENT. COMBINES LETTERS AND FIGURES.	C.C.S. NO. 1; D.S.D 142	?	?	194Ø - ?	? OKW	COMPROMISED INSTRUCTIONS	T 1734	(UNKNOWN)	--
FRANCE 197	NAVY	NAVAL KEY TABLES TO BE USED WITH CODE E.X.	EXZO 5Ø, 6Ø, 7Ø	?	?	1941 - ?	? ?	COMPROMISED 1ØØ%	T 3562	(UNKNOWN)	--
FRANCE 198	NAVY	TRANSPOSITION ENCIPHERMENT SYSTEM WITH DIGRAPHIC LETTER SUBSTITUTION. USED ON INTERNATIONAL CODE BETWEEN COMMERCIAL SHIPS AND THE NAVY.	D.S.-B 7Ø4	NACOM; D.S.-B 7Ø4; INTERNATIONAL CODE N.C. 4	?	1941 - ?	? OKW ? SIS	COMPROMISED 1ØØ% BY OKW AND SIS. READ BY SIS.	T 18Ø3 IF 15Ø6	(UNKNOWN)	--

CHART NO. 1-2

TOP SECRET

DOCID: 3560861

TOP SECRET

RESULTS OF EUROPEAN AXIS CRYPTANALYSIS AS LEARNED FROM TICOM SOURCES

(WITH ANNOTATIONS FROM ARMY SECURITY AGENCY SOURCES IN PARENTHESES)

COUNTRY OF ORIGIN	SERVICE	DESCRIPTION OF SYSTEM	NAME OF SYSTEM: COUNTRY OF ORIGIN	NAME OF SYSTEM: AXIS	NAME OF SYSTEM: U.S.A.	DATES OF USE	WHEN ATTACKED AND BY WHOM	RESULTS	TICOM REFERENCE	STATUS OF THE SYSTEM AT ASA	REMARKS
FRANCE 199	NAVY	ENCIPHERMENT SYSTEM TO REPLACE D.S.-B 704 AND IS SIMILAR TO IT.	N.C. NO.5	?	?	1941 - ?	? OKW	COMPROMISED 100%	T 1803	(UNKNOWN)	--
FRANCE 200	NAVY	TRANSPOSITION ENCIPHERING TABLES WITH HOURLY CHANGING KEY. REPLACES VAPETRA NO. 16.	D.S.D 120 VARETPA NO. 17	?	?	1940 - ?	? OKW	COMPROMISED 100%	T 1683	(UNKNOWN)	--
FRANCE--VICHY 201	POLICE	5-LETTER ?-PART CODE.	?	?	?	?-1940-1942-?	? OKW	READ	T 1708	(UNKNOWN)	--
FRANCE 202	POLICE	4-FIGURE OR 5-FIGURE ?-PART CODE.	?	?	?	?-1929-1938-?	? OKW	READ	T 2626	(UNKNOWN)	--
FRANCE 203	GENERAL PURPOSES	3-LETTER 1-PART CODE.	?	?	?	? - ?	? ?	COMPROMISED 100%	T 1840	(UNKNOWN)	--
FRANCE 204	GENERAL PURPOSES?	4-FIGURE 1-PART CODE. PAGINATION AND FIRST 2 DIGITS TO BE FILLED IN BY USERS.	CHIFFRE 13	?	?	? - ?	1920 PROBABLY GERMANS	PROBABLY 100% COMPROMISED	T 3548	(UNKNOWN)	(RESEMBLES SITTLER)
FRANCE 205	?	4-FIGURE-LETTER 1-PART CODE.	?	H.Z.B.	?	? - ?	? GERMANS	RECOVERED 8%	T 2484	(UNKNOWN)	--
FRANCE 206	?	4-FIGURE 2-PART CODE.	?	C 53 STAT. 1-279	?	? - ?	? GERMANS	RECOVERED 10%	T 3156	(UNIDENTIFIED)	--
FRANCE 207	?	4-FIGURE 2-PART CODE.	?	F 5	?	? - ?	? ?	RECOVERED 5%	T 2497	(UNIDENTIFIED)	--
FRANCE 208	?	4?-FIGURE 2-PART CODE.	CHIFFRE NO. 110	H 26 DAUTE	?	? - ?	? ITALIANS	RECONSTRUCTED 10%	T 9	(UNIDENTIFIED)	--
FRANCE 209	?	4-FIGURE 1-PART CODE. 9,900 GROUPS.	?	?	?	? - ?	? ?	COMPROMISED 100%	T 3553	(UNKNOWN)	--
FRANCE--FREE FRANCE 210	?	PROBABLY 4-FIGURE ?-PART CODE WITH ADDITIVE ENCIPHERMENT.	?	?	?	? - ?	? SIM	NOT READ	IF 1522	(UNIDENTIFIED)	--
FRANCE 211	?	4-FIGURE ?-PART CODE.	?	FRANZ	?	?-1925-?	? ?	READ	T 2536	(UNIDENTIFIED)	--

CHART NO. 1-2

TOP SECRET

RESULTS OF EUROPEAN AXIS CRYPTANALYSIS AS LEARNED FROM TICOM SOURCES

(WITH ANNOTATIONS FROM ARMY SECURITY AGENCY SOURCES IN PARENTHESES)

COUNTRY OF ORIGIN		SERVICE	DESCRIPTION OF SYSTEM	NAME OF SYSTEM: COUNTRY OF ORIGIN	NAME OF SYSTEM: AXIS	NAME OF SYSTEM: U.S.A.	DATES OF USE	WHEN ATTACKED AND BY WHOM	RESULTS	TICOM REFERENCE	STATUS OF THE SYSTEM AT ASA	REMARKS
GREECE	1	(CONSULAR AND SOME DIPLOMATIC)	4-LETTER (2-PART) CODE. UNENCIPHERED. ONLY 10 LETTERS USED TO FORM CODE GROUPS.	(ETA)	G7	(GRD)	(1940-CURRENT)	? OKW AND PERHAPS PERS Z S ? SIM	ALMOST COMPLETELY READ BY GERMANS. READ BY SIM.	T 1065 AND PERHAPS I 22 P 2 D 71	(HAD BRITISH COMPROMISED BOOK. CODE UNREADABLE. VALUES ADDED. TICOM GAVE SOLUTION)	--
GREECE	2	(MILITARY ATTACHE, DIPLOMATIC, AND CONSULAR)	4-LETTER (2-PART) CODE WITH 5TH LETTER ADDED FOR INFLECTION. (UNENCIPHERED)	(IOTA)	?	(GRB)	(1941-CURRENT)	? PERS Z S	READ	I 22 P 20 T 2253 T 2255 T 2257	(BEGAN TO READ IN 1944 WITH COMPROMISED BOOK. STILL READ.)	--
GREECE	3	CONSULAR	4-LETTER (2-PART) CODE WITH 5TH LETTER ADDED FOR INFLECTION. UNENCIPHERED. ONLY 10 LETTERS TO FORM CODE GROUPS.	BETA	T	(GRC)	(1938-CURRENT)	? PERHAPS PERS Z S	READ, PROBABLY COMPROMISED.	T 1063 AND PERHAPS I 22 P 20 T 2052	(BEING READ AS RESULT OF TICOM)	--
GREECE	4	CONSULAR	4-LETTER 2-PART CODE. UNENCIPHERED. ONLY 10 LETTERS USED TO FORM CODE GROUPS.	(PHI)	F	(GRH)	BEFORE 1939 - (CURRENT)	1939 PERS Z S	PARTIALLY RECONSTRUCTED	T 2052	(UNKNOWN UNTIL MADE READABLE AS RESULT OF TICOM)	--
GREECE	5	MILITARY ?	4-LETTER ?-PART CODE WITH 5TH LETTER ADDED FOR INFLECTION, ADDITIVELY ENCIPHERED -- PERIOD OF 35.	?	?	?	? - ?	1941 OKW	SOLVED	I 58 P 6	(UNKNOWN)	--
GREECE	6	?	5-FIGURE ?-PART TRANSPOSED CODE.	?	?	?	? - 1941 - ?	1941 OKW	?	I 58 P 2	(UNKNOWN)	--
GREECE	7	(DIPLOMATIC)	4-FIGURE 2-PART CODE. NUMBER DIGRAPHS ENCIPHERED BY LETTER DIGRAPHS. ENCIPHERING TABLE CHANGES WITH DAY OF MONTH.	(ALPHA)	?	(GRA)	(1942-CURRENT)	BEFORE 1940 SIM ? OKW ? PERS Z S	READ COMPLETELY BY OKW. PROBABLY READ BY SIM.	I 22 P 20 IF 1518 P 3 T 731	(IN PROCESS OF BOOK SOLUTION)	--
GREECE	8	(DIPLOMATIC)	4-FIGURE (?)-PART CODE REPAGINATED AND ENCIPHERED BY DIGRAPHIC LETTER SUBSTITUTION.	DELTA	?	(GRG)	? - 1938 - (CURRENT)	BEFORE 1940 SIM ? GERMANS	COMPROMISED BY GERMANS. READ BY SIM.	IF 1518 P 2 T 3267 T 3269 T 3050	(READABLE AS RESULT OF TICOM LIGHT TRAFFIC)	--
GREECE	9	?	4-FIGURE 1-PART CODE.	ELLENIKON KRYPTOGRAPHIKON LEXIKON	?	?	? - 1927 - ?	? PERHAPS PERS Z S	100% COMPROMISED.	T 3051	(ASA HAS COMPROMISED CODE BOOK. UNKNOWN SYSTEM).	--
GREECE	10	PROBABLY DIPLOMATIC	2 UNENCIPHERED CODES.	?	?	?	? - ?	? FA	READ	I 25 P 8	(UNIDENTIFIED)	--
GREECE	11	ARMY AND NAVY	CODES	?	?	?	? - ?	AFTER 1940 OKH	BROKEN BY OKH	I 170 P 2	(NO MILITARY SYSTEMS WORKED ON)	--
GREECE	12	AIR	UNENCIPHERED CODE. VERY ELEMENTARY.	?	?	?	? - 1941 - ?	? OKL	READ	I 65 P 3 I 121 P 9	(NO MILITARY SYSTEMS WORKED ON)	--

CHART NO. 1-2

DOCID: 3560861

TOP SECRET

RESULTS OF EUROPEAN AXIS CRYPTANALYSIS AS LEARNED FROM TICOM SOURCES

(WITH ANNOTATIONS FROM ARMY SECURITY AGENCY SOURCES IN PARENTHESES)

COUNTRY OF ORIGIN		SERVICE	DESCRIPTION OF SYSTEM	NAME OF SYSTEM: COUNTRY OF ORIGIN	AXIS	U.S.A.	DATES OF USE	WHEN ATTACKED AND BY WHOM	RESULTS	TICOM REFERENCE	STATUS OF THE SYSTEM AT ASA	REMARKS
GREECE	13	MILITARY	2-FIGURE SUBSTITUTION CIPHER WITH VARIANTS.	?	?	?	? - 1944 ?	PRIOR TO 1944 OKH	READ	I 17Ø P 5	(NO MILITARY SYSTEMS WORKED ON)	--
GREECE	14	AIR	SINGLE TRANSPOSITION CIPHER.	?	?	?	? - 1941 - ?	1941 OKH	BROKEN AND ALMOST COMPLETELY READ	I 17Ø P 2	(NO MILITARY SYSTEMS WORKED ON)	--
GREECE ELAS	15	ARMY	DOUBLE TRANSPOSITION CIPHER.	?	?	?	1944? - 1945?	APPROX. 1944 OKH	5Ø% - 6Ø% OF THE TRAFFIC READ	I 17Ø P 5	(NO MILITARY SYSTEMS WORKED ON)	--
GREECE	16	DIPLOMATIC	4 LETTER 4 FIGURE 1-PART CODE ENCIPHERED BY TABLES INTO LETTERS. PAGE DIGRAPH COULD PRECEDE OR FOLLOW GROUP DIGRAPH.	?	?	?	? - ?	? SIM	READ?	IF 1518	(UNIDENTIFIED)	--

CHART NO. 1-2

TOP SECRET

RESULTS OF EUROPEAN AXIS CRYPTANALYSIS AS LEARNED FROM TICOM SOURCES

(WITH ANNOTATIONS FROM ARMY SECURITY AGENCY SOURCES IN PARENTHESES)

COUNTRY OF ORIGIN		SERVICE	DESCRIPTION OF SYSTEM	NAME OF SYSTEM			DATES OF USE	WHEN ATTACKED AND BY WHOM	RESULTS	TICOM REFERENCE	STATUS OF THE SYSTEM AT ASA	REMARKS
				COUNTRY OF ORIGIN	AXIS	U.S.A.						
HUNGARY	1	?	ENIGMA CIPHER MACHINE.	?	ENIGMA	?	?-1941-?	? OKH ? SIM	GERMANS BUILT MACHINES BUT COULD NOT COMPROMISE WHEEL WIRINGS BECAUSE HUNGARIANS CHANGED THEM AT NIGHT. NOT READ BY SIM.	I 84 P 3 IF 1518	(UNKNOWN)	--
HUNGARY	2	DIPLOMATIC	5-FIGURE (2)-PART CODE. ORIGINALLY UNENCIPHERED, BUT LATER ENCIPHERED. 500 PAGE RANGE. INDICATOR WAS LAST GROUP OF MESSAGE CONSISTING OF 5 ODD NUMBERS. (USED ON TOKYO-BUDAPEST CIRCUIT ONLY.)	?	"U.1"	(HUA)	(1938-1945)	1940 OKW	SOLVED UNENCIPHERED; UNABLE TO SOLVE ENCIPHERED.	T 2248	(READ FROM SEPTEMBER 1944 TO END OF WAR. 1932 VII CODE BOOK COMPROMISED.	(HUC, CIRCULAR SYSTEM, USED SAME SYSTEM AND BOOK. READABLE ONLY WITH KEYS DERIVED FROM HUA.)
HUNGARY	3	DIPLOMATIC	5-FIGURE (2)-PART CODE. 300 PAGE RANGE. ASSUMED TO BE ENCIPHERED BY DIGIT-FOR-DIGIT SUBSTITUTION.	?	"U.3"	(HUE?)	1938-1940-?	1940 OKW	NO SUCCESS	T 2248	(NOT READABLE. 1935 VIII CODE BOOK COMPROMISED.)	--
HUNGARY	4	DIPLOMATIC	5-FIGURE (2)-PART CODE. 300 PAGE RANGE. ENCIPHERED BY DIGIT-FOR-DIGIT SUBSTITUTION. INDICATOR WAS LAST GROUP WITH 2 ODD AND 3 EVEN NUMBERS.	?	"U.2"	(HUD)	1938-1940-?	1940 OKW	NO SUCCESS	T 2248	(PARTLY READABLE WITH KEYS DERIVED FROM HUA AND HUC. 1936 IX CODE BOOK COMPROMISED.)	--
HUNGARY	5	?	TRANSPOSITION CIPHER USING REVERSIBLE REVOLVING GRILLE. USED BY HUNGARIAN RAILWAYS ADMINISTRATION.	?	?	?	? - 1941 - ?	1941 OKH	SOLVED	I 58; I 100 IF 126 P 9	(UNKNOWN)	--
IRAN	1	DIPLOMATIC	3-LETTER 1-PART CODE WITH VARIOUS ENCIPHERMENT SYSTEMS.	?	?	(IRA)	(1939-CURRENT)	? PERS Z S	SOLVED	I 22 P 20	(100% COMPROMISED. MOST KEYS READ.)	--
IRAN?	2	COMMERCIAL	CODE USED BY CZECHOSLOVAKIA SKODA FIRM TO IRAN AND IRAQ CONCERNING BRIDGE BUILDING PROJECTS.	?	?	?	? - 1935 - ?	1935 OKL	SOLVED	I 162 P 2	(UNKNOWN)	--
IRAQ?		COMMERCIAL	CODE USED BY CZECHOSLOVAKIA SKODA FIRM TO IRAN AND IRAQ CONCERNING BRIDGE BUILDING PROJECTS.	?	?	?	? - 1935 - ?	1935 OKL	SOLVED	I 162 P 2	(UNKNOWN)	--
IRELAND EIRE	1	DIPLOMATIC AND CONSULAR	5-LETTER 1-PART CODE. 84,000 GROUPS. USED UNENCIPHERED AND ENCIPHERED WITH SUBSTITUTION AND WITH REPEATING ADDITIVE WITH A PERIOD OF 330.	GOVERNMENT TELEGRAPH CODE	B 22	(IEB, IEC, AND IEA)	(IEA, IEB: 1942-CURRENT. IEC: 1942-1945)	1939 PERS Z S 1944 FA	BROKE CODE. LATER RECEIVED COMPROMISED COPY. IN 1941 SUBSTITUTION ENCIPHERMENT SOLVED. ADDITIVE NOT WORKED ON IN 1941	D 16, 1941 REPORT P 1 D 16, 1942 REPORT PP 2, 3 I 172 PP 3,4 ALSO SEE I 54 P 3	(PARTIALLY BROKEN IN 1944 WHEN COMPROMISED BOOK WAS OBTAINED. STILL BEING READ. SUBSTITUTION ENCIPHERMENT SOLVED IN 1945. ADDITIVE SYSTEM BEING READ ON DEPTHS. STILL BEING WORKED ON.)	--

CHART NO. 1-2

DOCID: 3560861

TOP SECRET

RESULTS OF EUROPEAN AXIS CRYPTANALYSIS AS LEARNED FROM TICOM SOURCES

(WITH ANNOTATIONS FROM ARMY SECURITY AGENCY SOURCES IN PARENTHESES)

COUNTRY OF ORIGIN		SERVICE	DESCRIPTION OF SYSTEM	NAME OF SYSTEM: COUNTRY OF ORIGIN	NAME OF SYSTEM: AXIS	NAME OF SYSTEM: U.S.A.	DATES OF USE	WHEN ATTACKED AND BY WHOM	RESULTS	TICOM REFERENCE	STATUS OF THE SYSTEM AT ASA	REMARKS
ITALY	1	(FOREIGN MINISTRY)	(5-LETTER) 2-PART CODE. ABOUT 3Ø,ØØØ GROUPS. NO ENCIPHERMENT.	AR 38	R 19	(ITF) (ITX-6)	194Ø - ?	? PERS Z S	3,Ø25 GROUPS SOLVED	T 2252	(1Ø,25Ø GROUPS RECOVERED. COMPROMISED COPY RECEIVED 1944.)	--
ITALY	2	FOREIGN MINISTRY	5-LETTER 2-PART CODE. PAGE RANGE ABA-OFU. NO INDICATOR, NO ENCIPHERMENT.	(AR 4Ø)	ITALIAN CODE-BOOK 21	(ITG)	1942 - ?	1942 PERS Z S	RECOVERED ? PERCENT	T 2194	(4,ØØØ GROUPS RECOVERED. COMPROMISED COPY RECEIVED 1944.)	--
ITALY	3	?	5-LETTER 2-PART CODE.	?	P 1Ø	?	1937 - ?	? ?	RECOVERED 2Ø%	T 92	(UNIDENTIFIED)	--
ITALY	4	(FOREIGN MINISTRY)	5-FIGURE 1-PART CODE. PAGE RANGE 1ØØ-3Ø2. VALUES IN FRENCH.	H 25	H 26	?	BEFORE 1914 - ?	? PERS Z S	ABOUT 3,ØØØ GROUPS RE-COVERED	T 2252	(UNKNOWN IN ASA BEFORE RE-CEIPT OF COMPROMISED COPY, 1944.)	--
ITALY	5	FOREIGN MINISTRY	5-FIGURE 1-PART CODE. 18,5ØØ OR 19,5ØØ GROUPS. FIRST GROUP WAS INDICATOR.	RA 1 CIFRARIO TASCABILE	R 15	?	1937 - ?	? PERS Z S	RECOVERED 5Ø%	T 88 T 2252 T 3Ø36 T 3Ø37	(COMPLETELY RECONSTRUCTED IN ASA. COMPROMISED COPY RECEIVED 1944.)	--
ITALY	6	FOREIGN MINISTRY	5-FIGURE 1-PART CODE. PAGE RANGE ØØ3-186. 18,4ØØ GROUPS. ENCIPHERED WITH "TABELLA LM" AND 1Ø-PLACE TABLE.	RA	R 11	(ITH)	?	1935-194Ø PERS Z S	RECOVERED 7Ø%	T 2252 T 3Ø35	(COMPLETELY RECONSTRUCTED IN ASA. COMPROMISED COPY RECEIVED 1944.)	--
ITALY	7	FOREIGN MINISTRY	5-FIGURE 2-PART CODE. PAGE RANGE 1ØØ-544. NO ENCIPHERMENT. 13,4ØØ GROUPS.	Y-1	R 4 ZILLI II OR R 7	(ITP)	193Ø-1933	? PERS Z S	5,5ØØ GROUPS SOLVED	T 94 T 2249 T 2252 T 3Ø33	(COMPROMISED COPY RECEIVED IN ASA FROM GCCS IN 1943.)	--
ITALY	8	FOREIGN MINISTRY	5-FIGURE 2-PART CODE. 27,7ØØ GROUPS.	AR 25	R 8	(ITB) (ITX-2)	1933 - ?	? PERS Z S	9,5ØØ GROUPS SOLVED	T 2252 T 3Ø45	(8,1ØØ GROUPS RECOVERED IN ASA. COMPROMISED COPY RE-CEIVED 1944.)	--
ITALY	9	FOREIGN MINISTRY	5-FIGURE 2-PART CODE. 26,5ØØ GROUPS. EN-CIPHERED WITH "TABELLA LM".	AR 29	R 12	(ITC)	1936-1938	? PERS Z S	RECOVERED ABOUT 5Ø%	T 2252 T 3Ø46	(3,75Ø GROUPS RECOVERED.)	--
ITALY	1Ø	FOREIGN MINISTRY	5-FIGURE 2-PART CODE. 26,1ØØ GROUPS. PAGE RANGE 2Ø1-6Ø5.	AR 15	R 13	?	1936 - ?	? PERS Z S	RECOVERED 2Ø%	T 2252 T 3Ø44	(PAGINATION SENT TO ASA BY GCCS, WHERE SYSTEM IS KNOWN AS AR-Y. TRAFFIC NOT SEEN IN ASA.)	(3,ØØØ GROUPS IDENTI-FIED IN GCCS.)
ITALY	11	FOREIGN MINISTRY	5-LETTER 2-PART CODE. 29,Ø64 GROUPS. NO EN-CIPHERMENT.	AR 3Ø	R 14	(ITD) (ITX-3)	? - ?	1938 PERS Z S	1Ø,125 GROUPS SOLVED	T 2252	(12,4ØØ GROUPS RECOVERED IN ASA. COMPROMISED COPY RE-CEIVED 1944.)	--
ITALY	12	FOREIGN MINISTRY	5-FIGURE 2-PART CODE. 27,6ØØ GROUPS. PAGE RANGE 2Ø1-652. ENCIPHERED WITH 1ØØ-PLACE TABLE. INDICATOR: Ø BEFORE THE DATE.	AR 17	R 16	?	1937 - ?	1938 PERS Z S	4,442 GROUPS RECOVERED	T 2252 T 3Ø43	(PAGINATION AND ABOUT 2ØØ IDENTIFICATIONS SENT BY GCCS TO ASA. TRAFFIC NOT SEEN IN ASA.)	(KNOWN TO GCCS AS AR-Z.)
ITALY	13	(FOREIGN MINISTRY)	5-FIGURE 2-PART CODE. 26,7ØØ GROUPS.	IMPERO	R 18	(ITA) (ITX-4)	1937 - ? (1939 - ?)	? PERS Z S	6,ØØ6 GROUPS SOLVED; "READ" BY PERS Z S. WORKBOOK: 4Ø% RECOVERED	T 97 T 2252 T 2314 T 3Ø4Ø T 3Ø47 T 1117 I-22 P 3 P 8	(8,5ØØ GROUPS RECOVERED. COMPROMISED COPY RECEIVED, 1944.)	--

CHART NO. 1-2

TOP SECRET

DOCID: 3560861

TOP SECRET

RESULTS OF EUROPEAN AXIS CRYPTANALYSIS AS LEARNED FROM TICOM SOURCES

(WITH ANNOTATIONS FROM ARMY SECURITY AGENCY SOURCES IN PARENTHESES)

COUNTRY OF ORIGIN	SERVICE	DESCRIPTION OF SYSTEM	NAME OF SYSTEM: COUNTRY OF ORIGIN	NAME OF SYSTEM: AXIS	NAME OF SYSTEM: U.S.A.	DATES OF USE	WHEN ATTACKED AND BY WHOM	RESULTS	TICOM REFERENCE	STATUS OF THE SYSTEM AT ASA	REMARKS
ITALY 14	(FOREIGN MINISTRY)	5-FIGURE 2-PART CODE. 251 PAGES.	(AQUILA)	R 22	(ITX-7)	(PUBLICATION DATE 1942)	? ?	RECOVERED 20%-25%	T 96 T 1120	(UNKNOWN IN ASA BEFORE RECEIPT OF COMPROMISED COPY IN 1944.)	--
ITALY 15	(FOREIGN MINISTRY)	5-FIGURE (2-PART) CODE. (17,775 GROUPS.)	(ASSE)	I.T.B. 20	?	(PUBLICATION DATE 1941)	? ?	RECOVERED 7%	T 2196	(COMPROMISED COPY RECEIVED 1944. UNKNOWN IN ASA BEFORE THEN EXCEPT FOR PAGINATION SUPPLIED BY GCCS.)	--
ITALY 16	?	5-FIGURE 2-PART CODE.	?	K 16	?	?	? ?	RECOVERED 20%	T 2093	(UNKNOWN)	--
ITALY 17	?	5-FIGURE 2-PART CODE.	?	K 18	?	1917 - ?	? ?	RECOVERED ABOUT 40%	T 2095	(UNKNOWN)	--
ITALY 18	?	5-FIGURE 2-PART CODE.	?	K 19	?	?	? ?	RECOVERED 50%	T 1040 T 2090	(UNKNOWN)	--
ITALY 19	?	5-FIGURE 2-PART CODE.	?	K 20	?	?	? ?	RECOVERED 20%	T 2094 T 3039	(UNKNOWN)	--
ITALY 20	?	5-FIGURE 2-PART CODE.	P 1	P 1	?	1919 - ?	? ?	RECOVERED LESS THAN 5%	T 3042	(KNOWN IN ASA BY NAME ONLY, THROUGH GCCS.)	--
ITALY 21	?	5-FIGURE 2-PART CODE.	P 2	P 2	?	1919-1920	? ?	RECOVERED 50%	T 3041	(KNOWN IN ASA BY NAME ONLY, THROUGH GCCS.)	--
ITALY 22	?	5-FIGURE 2-PART CODE.	P 3	P 3	?	BEFORE 1931	? ?	RECOVERED 15%-20%	T 89	(PAGINATION KNOWN IN ASA, SENT BY GCCS.)	(ENCODE WAS SOURCE OF LMB AND LMC ADDITIVE)
ITALY 23	?	5-FIGURE 2-PART CODE.	P 4	P 4	?	1924 - ?	? ?	RECOVERED 40%-50%	T 90	(KNOWN IN ASA BY NAME ONLY, THROUGH GCCS.)	--
ITALY 24	?	5-FIGURE 2-PART CODE. PAGE RANGE 100-598.	?	S 1	?	?	? ?	RECOVERED 10%-15%	T 2197	(UNKNOWN)	--
ITALY 25	?	5-FIGURE 2-PART CODE. PAGE RANGE 000-211.	?	F.Z. 2 CHIFFRIER-CODE	?	? - 1918 - ?	? ?	RECOVERED 20%	T 2092 T 2097	(UNKNOWN)	--
ITALY 26	?	5-FIGURE POSSIBLY 1-PART CODE.	?	K 14	?	?	? ?	RECOVERED 15%	T 3038	(UNKNOWN)	--
ITALY 27	?	5-FIGURE 2-PART CODE.	?	R 3	?	?	? PERS Z S	RECOVERED 50%-60%	T 91	(UNKNOWN)	--
ITALY 28	?	4-FIGURE ?-PART CODE.	?	K 15 3 R 14	?	?	? ?	RECOVERED 30%-40%	T 3040	(UNKNOWN)	--

CHART NO. 1-2

TOP SECRET

DOCID: 3560861

TOP SECRET

RESULTS OF EUROPEAN AXIS CRYPTANALYSIS
AS LEARNED FROM TICOM SOURCES
(WITH ANNOTATIONS FROM ARMY SECURITY AGENCY SOURCES IN PARENTHESES)

COUNTRY OF ORIGIN		SERVICE	DESCRIPTION OF SYSTEM	NAME OF SYSTEM			DATES OF USE	WHEN ATTACKED AND BY WHOM	RESULTS	TICOM REFERENCE	STATUS OF THE SYSTEM AT ASA	REMARKS
				COUNTRY OF ORIGIN	AXIS	U.S.A.						
ITALY	29	EMBASSY, MADRID	GERMAN DESCRIPTION: "1943. 4-PLACE ITALIAN FIGURE CODE COMPILED ON THE BASIS OF CAPTURED MATERIAL. TRAFFIC: ITALIAN EMBASSY MADRID AND THE ITALIAN REPRESENTATIONS IN SPAIN." PAGE RANGE ØØ-99.	?	?	?	? - 1943 - ?	?	RECOVERED 5%-7%	T 3Ø48 T 3Ø49	(UNKNOWN)	--
ITALY	3Ø	FOREIGN MINISTRY	2-PART CODE. 21,4ØØ GROUPS.	AR 1	?	?	1931 - ? USED IN 1939	1939 PERS Z S	?	T 2252	(UNIDENTIFIED)	--
ITALY	31	FOREIGN MINISTRY	2-PART CODE. ABOUT 3Ø,ØØØ GROUPS. USUALLY UNENCIPHERED.	RA 18	?	?	1938 - ?	194Ø PERS Z S	?	T 2252	(UNIDENTIFIED)	--
ITALY	32	?	2-PART CODE. ABOUT 22,ØØØ GROUPS. ENCIPHERED WITH 1ØØ-PLACE TABLE.	?	TB OHNE BEZEICHNUNG	?	1938 - ?	194[illegible] PERS Z S	RECOVERED ABOUT 3,ØØØ GROUPS	T 2252	(UNIDENTIFIED)	--
ITALY	33	POLICE	4-FIGURE 2-PART CODE.	CIFRARIO "S.P."	?	?	?	1942 PERS Z S	1ØØ% COMPROMISED	T 87	(UNKNOWN IN ASA BEFORE RECEIPT OF COMPROMISED COPY)	SENT BY SCHAUFFLER OF PERS Z S TO PASCHKE OF PERS Z S, 12 SEPT. 1942.
ITALY	34	FOREIGN MINISTRY	CODE-ENCIPHERMENT SYSTEM: ADDITIVE TABLES RUNNING FROM 1 - 3 DAYS.	TABELLA LM	TABELLA LM	(ITA) (ITB) (ITC) (ITP)	1938 - ?	194Ø PERS Z S	BROKEN	T 2252	(ADDITIVE TABLES LARGELY RECOVERED)	--
ITALY	35	?	CODE-ENCIPHERMENT SYSTEM: 1ØØ-PLACE FIGURE-LETTER SUBSTITUTION TABLES.	?	?	?	?	? PERS Z S	?	T 2252	(UNIDENTIFIED)	--

TOP SECRET

CHART NO. 1-2

RESULTS OF EUROPEAN AXIS CRYPTANALYSIS AS LEARNED FROM TICOM SOURCES

(WITH ANNOTATIONS FROM ARMY SECURITY AGENCY SOURCES IN PARENTHESES)

COUNTRY OF ORIGIN		SERVICE	DESCRIPTION OF SYSTEM	NAME OF SYSTEM			DATES OF USE	WHEN ATTACKED AND BY WHOM	RESULTS	TICOM REFERENCE	STATUS OF THE SYSTEM AT ASA	REMARKS
				COUNTRY OF ORIGIN	AXIS	U.S.A.						
JAPAN	1	DIPLOMATIC	MACHINE CIPHER	"TACHI-BANA" OR "ANGOOKI TAIPU A"	JB 48	("RED" MACHINE)	1935-1941	BEFORE 1939 PERS Z S	READ REGULARLY	I 64 P 3 I 9Ø P 2 P 4 D 5Ø P 33 I 118 PP 7-8 I 22 P 2 P 7 P 16	(SOLVED BY 1936)	--
JAPAN	2	DIPLOMATIC	MACHINE CIPHER, NOT RECOGNIZED BY GERMANS AS DIFFERENT FROM "RED" MACHINE.	"HINOKI" OR "ANGOOKI TAIPU B"	JB 48	("PURPLE" MACHINE) (JAA)	1939-1945	? PERS Z S	NOT READ	D 5Ø PP 22-31, 33 I 64 P 3 I 9Ø PP 2-4 I 118 PP 7-8 I 22 PP 2, 7, 16	(BROKEN 2Ø FEBRUARY 194Ø)	--
JAPAN	3		A SERIES OF LETTER CODES USED BEFORE 1934; GERMAN DESIGNATIONS RUN FROM JB 3 TO JB 28, PLUS JB 3Ø AND JB 31.					? PERS Z S		D 5Ø		--
JAPAN	4	DIPLOMATIC	5-LETTER CODE, GROUPS IN FORM CVCCV. 1Ø,ØØØ VALUES.	?	JB 55	?	194Ø - ?	1941 PERS Z S	NOT SOLVED	D 5Ø P 34	(UNIDENTIFIED)	--
JAPAN	5	?	4-LETTER CODE MADE FROM CO-ORDINATES.	?	JB 51	?	? - ?	?	COMPLETELY RECOVERED WITHIN LIMITS OF AVAILABLE DIAGRAM	T 335	(UNIDENTIFIED)	--
JAPAN	6	DIPLOMATIC	4-LETTER CODE, PRONOUNCEABLE GROUPS.	?	JB 59	?		1941 PERS Z S	NOT READ	D 5Ø P 35	(UNIDENTIFIED)	--
JAPAN	7	?	4-LETTER CODE.	?	KIMI	?	? - ?	?	RECOVERED 1Ø%	T 2ØØØ T 2ØØ1 T 2ØØ2 T 23ØØ	(UNIDENTIFIED)	--
JAPAN	8	(DIPLOMATIC)	2-LETTER 4-LETTER CODE; INDICATOR WAS "LA".	?	JB 29 OR "LA"-CODE	(JAH) OR ("LA")	1925-1945	? OKW ? PERS Z S	OKW: FULLY RECOVERED. PERS Z S: GREATER PART OF TEXTS READ.	D 5Ø P 14 P 16 I 9Ø PP 2-4 I 118 PP 7-8 I 15Ø P 8	(BROKEN IN 1927. 1925 COPY OF CODE CAPTURED. SLIGHTLY CHANGED IN 1934. READ 1ØØ%.)	--
JAPAN	9	DIPLOMATIC	2-LETTER 4-LETTER CODE; 2-LETTER GROUPS CV OR VC; 4-LETTER GROUPS PRONOUNCEABLE. INDICATOR: "IJ". (OTHER INDICATORS: IP, AN, PA, KA)	?	JB 44	(JAI?)	(1941-1945)	? PERS Z S	?	D 5Ø P 33	(SOLVED 1941)	
JAPAN	1Ø	DIPLOMATIC	2-LETTER 4-LETTER CODE. 2-LETTER GROUPS VC OR CV; 4-LETTER GROUPS VVCC. INDICATOR: "HE". USED AS SPELLER.	?	JB 47	("HE")	? - ?	? PERS Z S	?	D 5Ø P 33	(READ)	--
JAPAN	11	?	2-LETTER 4-LETTER CODE. TRANSPOSED ON KEY OF LENGTH 7, 1Ø, 14, OR 15. FIRST CIPHER GROUP OF TEXT TRANSPOSED ACCORDING TO UNIT OF DATE AND PLACED AT END OF MESSAGE. ENCIPHERMENT CHANGED 1 JUNE 194Ø AND 3 NEW 7-PLACE KEYS WERE FOUND.	?	JB 5Ø	("PA-KI")	(1939-194Ø)	? PERS Z S	?	D 5Ø P 34	(READ)	--

CHART NO. 1-2

DOCID: 3560861

54

TOP SECRET

RESULTS OF EUROPEAN AXIS CRYPTANALYSIS AS LEARNED FROM TICOM SOURCES

(WITH ANNOTATIONS FROM ARMY SECURITY AGENCY SOURCES IN PARENTHESES)

COUNTRY OF ORIGIN		SERVICE	DESCRIPTION OF SYSTEM	NAME OF SYSTEM: COUNTRY OF ORIGIN	NAME OF SYSTEM: AXIS	NAME OF SYSTEM: U.S.A.	DATES OF USE	WHEN ATTACKED AND BY WHOM	RESULTS	TICOM REFERENCE	STATUS OF THE SYSTEM AT ASA	REMARKS
JAPAN	12	DIPLOMATIC	2-LETTER 4-LETTER CODE. 2-LETTER GROUPS, ANY EXCEPT "PAIRS;" 4-LETTER GROUPS PRONOUNCEABLE.	?	JB 52	("J-12")	1 JAN 1940 - 31 MAY 1940	? PERS Z S	SOME RECOVERED	D 50 P 34 T 336	(READ)	--
JAPAN	13	DIPLOMATIC	2-LETTER 4-LETTER CODE WITH INDICATOR IN FORM CVCCV. ENCIPHERED BY TRANSPOSITION; RECTANGLE HAD BLANK CELLS.	?	JB 57	("J-16 K-5")	1940-1942	? PERS Z S ? RLM/FA	READ BY PERS Z S VIRTUALLY THE ENTIRE TIME	D 50 P 34 PP 42-43 T 380 I 22 P 21 I 54	(READ)	--
JAPAN	14	(FOREIGN OFFICE)	2-LETTER 4-LETTER CODE. 4-LETTER GROUPS HAD FORM CCVC OR VCCC. INDICATOR GROUP: "IP".	?	JB 50	(JAI?)	(1941-1945)	? OKW ? PERS Z S	?	D 50 P 42 I 150 P 8	(SOLVED IN 1941)	--
JAPAN	15	(FOREIGN OFFICE)	2-LETTER 4-LETTER CODE ENCIPHERED BY TRANSPOSITION. RECTANGLE HAD BLANK CELLS.	?	J-13 "FUJI"	(JAE) OR ("J-19")	(1941-1943)	? OKW	SOLVED	I 31 PP 4-5, 8 I 118 PP 7-8 I 84 P 5 I 124 P 3	(SOLVED AUGUST 1941)	--
JAPAN	16	DIPLOMATIC	2-LETTER 4-LETTER CODE, TRANSPOSED ON BASIS OF A REPEATING 19-PLACE KEYWORD. "KOKOK", "GAGAG", ETC., WERE INDICATOR GROUPS.	?	"KOKOK"	?	? - 1942	1941 OKW	READ	I 31 P 5 P 8 I 90 PP 2-4 I 118 PP 7-8 I 84 P 5 I 150 P 8	(UNIDENTIFIED)	--
JAPAN	17	DIPLOMATIC	2-LETTER 4-LETTER CODE. 2-LETTER GROUPS OF FORM VC OR CV AND 4-LETTER GROUPS PRONOUNCEABLE. INDICATOR GROUP: "KO".	?	?	(JAW)	? - 1940 - ?	1940 PERS Z S	?	D 50 P 35	(COMPROMISED)	--
JAPAN	18	DIPLOMATIC	2-LETTER 4-LETTER CODE ENCIPHERED BY DOUBLE ? TRANSPOSITION.	?	?	?	1942-1943	1942 PERS Z S	READ FROM MIDDLE OF 1942 TO JUNE OR JULY 1943	I 22 P 8	(UNIDENTIFIED)	--
JAPAN	19	DIPLOMATIC	2-LETTER 3-LETTER 4-LETTER CODE. 2-LETTER GROUPS ANY, EXCEPT "PAIRS AND DOUBLE VOWELS;" 3-LETTER GROUPS VOWELS; 4-LETTERGROUPS PRONOUNCEABLE.	?	JB 53	("J-14")	1 JAN 1940 - 15 AUG 1940	? PERS Z S	?	D 50 P 34	(READ)	--
JAPAN	20	DIPLOMATIC	2-LETTER 3-LETTER 4-LETTER CODE. 2-LETTER GROUPS ANY, EXCEPT "PAIRS AND DOUBLE VOWELS;" 3-LETTER GROUPS VOWELS, TAKEN FROM "J-14"; 4-LETTER GROUPS PRONOUNCEABLE.	?	JB 54	("J-15"?)	15 AUG 1940 - 31 OCT 1940	? PERS Z S	?	D 50 P 34	(READ)	--
JAPAN	21	DIPLOMATIC	SUCCESSOR TO PA-K 1. 2-LETTER 3-LETTER 4-LETTER CODE. 2-LETTER ANY, EXCEPT "PAIRS AND DOUBLE VOWELS;" 3-LETTER VOWELS, TAKEN FROM J-14; 4-LETTER PRONOUNCEABLE.	?	JB 58	("K-3")	1 JUL 1940 - 1 DEC 1940	? PERS Z S	?	D 50 P 34 P 35	(READ)	--

CHART NO. T-2

TOP SECRET

DOCID: 3560861

TOP SECRET

RESULTS OF EUROPEAN AXIS CRYPTANALYSIS
AS LEARNED FROM TICOM SOURCES
(WITH ANNOTATIONS FROM ARMY SECURITY AGENCY SOURCES IN PARENTHESES)

COUNTRY OF ORIGIN		SERVICE	DESCRIPTION OF SYSTEM	NAME OF SYSTEM: COUNTRY OF ORIGIN	NAME OF SYSTEM: AXIS	NAME OF SYSTEM: U.S.A.	DATES OF USE	WHEN ATTACKED AND BY WHOM	RESULTS	TICOM REFERENCE	STATUS OF THE SYSTEM AT ASA	REMARKS
JAPAN	22	?	3-LETTER CODE, 12ØØ VALUES IN BOX 1ØX12Ø.	?	JB 35	("XA")	1934 - ?	1934 PERS Z S	BROKEN	T 1124	(READ)	--
JAPAN	23	?	3-LETTER CODE, SIMILAR TO JAPAN 22.	?	JB 37	("XB")	1934 - ?	1934? PERS Z S	BROKEN	T 1124 T 5Ø	(READ)	--
JAPAN	24	DIPLOMATIC	2-LETTER 3-LETTER CODE, TRANSPOSED. RECTANGLE WAS 25X1Ø. ORIGINALLY USED "SIGNATURE" NULLS, (LATER ADOPTED BLANK CELLS INSTEAD.)	?	JB 54	(JBA)	(1943-1945)	? PERS Z S	BROKEN	I 22 P 17 T 346 T 345	(5Ø% - 1ØØ% READABLE TILL MARCH 1945; 25% - 5Ø% IN APRIL 1945; UNDER 25% AFTER APRIL 1945.)	--
JAPAN	25	DIPLOMATIC	2-LETTER 4 (?)-LETTER CODE, TRANSPOSED. RECTANGLE HAD WIDTH OF 25, DEPTH OF 1Ø, WITH BLANK CELLS. IN JAN 1944, BLANK CELLS RAN VERTICALLY AND HORIZONTALLY.	?	?	(JBA)	(1943-1945)	? OKW	BROKEN	I 9Ø PP 2-4	(5Ø% - 1ØØ% READABLE TILL MARCH 1945; 25% - 5Ø% IN APRIL 1945; UNDER 25% AFTER APRIL 1945.)	(JBA IS A 2-LETTER 3-LETTER CODE BUT CHANGE IN NULLS DESCRIBED TOOK PLACE IN JBA IN DEC 1944)
JAPAN	26	DIPLOMATIC	2-LETTER CODE: INDICATOR GROUP: "CA".	?	JB 56	(JAJ)	1936-1945	194Ø PERS Z S	READ SMALL AMOUNT	D 5Ø P 34 T 3179	(BROKEN, FALL 194Ø)	(OFTEN ENCIPHERED BY JAA, JBB, JBC, OR JBD)
JAPAN	27	DIPLOMATIC	2-LETTER 1-PART CODE, CV, ENCIPHERED BY SINGLE TRANSPOSITION WITH RECTANGLE 6 WIDE, 5 OR 1Ø DEEP WITH BLANKS DISTRIBUTED EVENLY THROUGHOUT. THREE KEYS. USED BETWEEN JAPAN AND BURMA, PHILLIPINES, ETC.	?	ABABA, BCBCB, CDCDC, ETC.	?	1942-1943	1942 PERS Z S ? OKW	PERS Z S: ? OKW: READ UNTIL 1944	I 9Ø PP 2-4 I 22 P 17	(UNIDENTIFIED)	--
JAPAN	28	DIPLOMATIC	?-LETTER ?-PART CODE, TRANSPOSED. RECTANGLE HAD BLANK CELLS. DAILY KEY.	?	?	?	? - 1943	? OKW	?	I 9Ø PP 2-4	(UNIDENTIFIED)	--
JAPAN	29	DIPLOMATIC	4-FIGURE 12ØØ-VALUE CODE ENCIPHERED BY BOOK ADDITIVE. ADDITIVE BOOK HAD 4ØØ,ØØØ ADDITIVE VALUES, EACH PAGE OF BOOK BEING DRAWN UP 2Ø X 25. THE POINT AT WHICH THE ENCIPHERER STARTED TO USE THE ADDITIVE WAS INDICATED BY AN INDICATOR GROUP, E.G. TLUSR. AFTER THE ADDITIVE PROCEDURE WAS COMPLETED, THE FIGURES WERE CONVERTED TO LETTERS, THE SAME LETTERS ALWAYS REPRESENTING THE SAME NUMBERS.	?	?	(JAM)	(1942-1944)	? OKW	?	I 9Ø PP 2-4	(BROKEN JAN 1945, 25% - 5Ø% READABLE; WORK DISCONTINUED APR 1945)	--

CHART NO. 1-2

TOP SECRET

DOCID: 3560861

TOP SECRET

RESULTS OF EUROPEAN AXIS CRYPTANALYSIS
AS LEARNED FROM TICOM SOURCES
(WITH ANNOTATIONS FROM ARMY SECURITY AGENCY SOURCES IN PARENTHESES)

COUNTRY OF ORIGIN		SERVICE	DESCRIPTION OF SYSTEM	NAME OF SYSTEM: COUNTRY OF ORIGIN	NAME OF SYSTEM: AXIS	NAME OF SYSTEM: U.S.A.	DATES OF USE	WHEN ATTACKED AND BY WHOM	RESULTS	TICOM REFERENCE	STATUS OF THE SYSTEM AT ASA	REMARKS
JAPAN	30	(FOREIGN OFFICE)	4-FIGURE CODE WITH ONLY 2,500 GROUPS. ENCIPHERED BY BOOK ADDITIVE AND SIMPLE LETTER SUBSTITUTION USING THE LETTERS CFGKLNORSY.	?	JB 62	(JBC)	(1943-1945)	? PERS Z S	ADDITIVE STRIPPED AND BOOK-BREAKING BEGUN	I 22 P 17	(BROKEN JAN 1944; 2 ADDITIVE BOOKS USED, SECOND EFFECTIVE 1 FEB 1944, BOTH RECOVERED. 100 % READABLE.)	--
JAPAN	31	DIPLOMATIC-COMMERCIAL	DIGRAPHIC SUBSTITUTION AND TRANSPOSITION APPLIED TO 4 CODES, DESIGNATED AHSAJ, ETGAV, AMNUM, ILNIM. AHSAJ WAS A 3, 4, 5-LETTER CODE; ETGAV WAS 2-LETTER; AMNUM WAS 5-LETTER; ILNIM WAS UNKNOWN. EACH CODE HAD 10,000 VALUES. 2 ENCIPHERING TABLES: CIFOL USED ON EVEN DAYS, VEVAZ ON ODD DAYS.	?	"CIFOL-VEVAZ"	("CIFOL-VEVAZ")	(1940 - ?)	? OKW	40% - 50% RECOVERED	I 31 P 8 I 90 PP 2-4 I 118 PP 7-8 I 150 P 8	--	
JAPAN	32	DIPLOMATIC	MONOALPHABETIC SUBSTITUTION CIPHER WITH 2-LETTER GROUPS FOR PUNCTUATION; INDICATOR GROUP: "YUG".	?	JB 41	("YUG")	1936-1941	? PERS Z S	?	D 50 P 33	(READ)	
JAPAN	33	COMMERCIAL	MONOALPHABETIC SUBSTITUTION ACCORDING TO THE DAY OF THE MONTH. INDICATOR: "IPADE".	?	?	?	? - 1940 - ?	? OKW	?	D 50 P 35 P 42	--	--
JAPAN	34	DIPLOMATIC	TRANSPOSITION CIPHER WITH 5-FIGURE INDICATOR GROUP.	?	?	?	? - 1940 - ?	? PERS Z S	?	D 50 P 35	(UNIDENTIFIED)	--

CHART NO. T-2

TOP SECRET

RESULTS OF EUROPEAN AXIS CRYPTANALYSIS AS LEARNED FROM TICOM SOURCES

(WITH ANNOTATIONS FROM ARMY SECURITY AGENCY SOURCES IN PARENTHESES)

COUNTRY OF ORIGIN	SERVICE	DESCRIPTION OF SYSTEM	NAME OF SYSTEM: COUNTRY OF ORIGIN	NAME OF SYSTEM: AXIS	NAME OF SYSTEM: U.S.A.	DATES OF USE	WHEN ATTACKED AND BY WHOM	RESULTS	TICOM REFERENCE	STATUS OF THE SYSTEM AT ASA	REMARKS
LATVIA 1	DIPLOMATIC	TRANSPOSITION CIPHER, BOTH SINGLE AND DOUBLE, SOMETIMES SUPERENCIPHERED WITH VIGENERE SUBSTITUTION.	?	?	?	? - ?	? PERS Z S	?	I 22 P 10	(UNKNOWN. ONLY PLAIN TEXT MESSAGES RECEIVED AT ASA.)	--
LITHUANIA 1	DIPLOMATIC	TRANSPOSITION CIPHER, BOTH DOUBLE AND SINGLE, SOMETIMES SUPERENCIPHERED WITH VIGENERE SUBSTITUTION.	?	?	?	? - ?	? PERS Z S	?	I 22 P 10	(LITHUANIAN TRAFFIC NOT WORKED ON BY ASA.)	--
LITHUANIA 2	AIR FORCE	TRANSPOSITION CIPHER WITH REVOLVING GRILLE.	?	?	?	1938-1939	1938 OKL	READ CURRENTLY	I 121 P 4	(LITHUANIAN TRAFFIC NOT WORKED ON AT ASA.)	--
MANCHURIA 1	DIPLOMATIC	5-FIGURE 2-PART CODE.	?	?	(MAA)	1942-1945	? ?		T 1	(NOT WORKED ON AT ASA.)	--
MANCHURIA 2	?	5-LETTER ?-PART CODE.	?	?	?	1938 - ?	? PERS Z S	?	T 76 P 36	(UNKNOWN)	--
MANCHURIA 3	?	5-LETTER ?-PART CODE. INDICATOR ABXYZ.	?	?	?	1940 - ?	? PERS Z S	?	T 76 P 36	(UNKNOWN)	--
MANCHURIA 4	?	4-LETTER ?-PART CODE OF FORM CVCV. USED BETWEEN BERLIN AND ROME.	?	?	?	USED ONLY IN MARCH 1945	? PERS Z S	?	T 75 P 37	(UNKNOWN)	--
MANCHURIA 5	?	4-FIGURE 2-PART CODE. ALL MESSAGES STARTED WITH GROUP 00011.	?	?	?	? - ?	? OKW	COMPROMISED.	I 177 P 3	(UNKNOWN)	--
MANCHURIA 6	DIPLOMATIC	TRANSPOSITION CIPHER WITH BLANK CELLS IN RECTANGLE AND DAILY CHANGING KEY. USED JAPANESE LANGUAGE.	?	?	?	1936 - ?	1940 PERS Z S	SOLVED.	T 76 P 36, PP 39-41	(UNKNOWN)	--
MANCHURIA 7	PROBABLY COMMERCIAL	TRANSPOSITION CIPHER WITH CHANGING ENCIPHERMENTS GOVERNED BY DATE AND NUMBER.	?	?	?	1935 - ?	? PERS Z S	?	I 76 P 35	(UNKNOWN)	--
MANCHURIA 9	?	TRANSPOSITION ENCIPHERMENTS OF A BASIC JAPANESE 3-LETTER BOOK.	?	?	?	? - ?	? PERS Z S	?	I 22 P 21	(UNKNOWN)	--

CHART NO. 1-2

DOCID: 3560861

TOP SECRET

RESULTS OF EUROPEAN AXIS CRYPTANALYSIS AS LEARNED FROM TICOM SOURCES

(WITH ANNOTATIONS FROM ARMY SECURITY AGENCY SOURCES IN PARENTHESES)

COUNTRY OF ORIGIN	SERVICE	DESCRIPTION OF SYSTEM	NAME OF SYSTEM: COUNTRY OF ORIGIN	AXIS	U.S.A.	DATES OF USE	WHEN ATTACKED AND BY WHOM	RESULTS	TICOM REFERENCE	STATUS OF THE SYSTEM AT ASA	REMARKS
MEXICO 1	DIPLOMATIC	5-LETTER 1-PART CODE, WITH 20,000 PRONOUNCEABLE GROUPS. USED WITH A DAILY ENCIPHER TABLE AND WORKED ON SLIDING SCALE PRINCIPLE.	?	?	?	?-1940-?	? SIM	READ	IF 1517	(UNKNOWN)	--
MEXICO 2	DIPLOMATIC	5-LETTER 1-PART CODE. 100 DIFFERENT ENCIPHERMENTS: EACH GROUP ENCIPHERED BY A GROUP IN BASIC CODE OF FROM 1 TO ABOUT 150 PLACES LATER.	?	"POMOS"	(MXA)	(?-1941-1945)	1941 PERS Z S	SOLVED	D 16	(80% READABLE)	--
MEXICO 3	DIPLOMATIC	5-LETTER 1-PART CODE.	?	"MEXIKO ÜBER P"	(MXB)	(? - 1945)	? ?	RECOVERED LESS THAN 5%	T 2519	(75% - 80% READABLE)	(USED IN 1945 BY ONLY PORT-AU-PRINCE LEGATION)
MEXICO 4	DIPLOMATIC	5-LETTER 1-PART CODE, 20,000 PRONOUNCEABLE GROUPS. DAILY ENCIPHERING TABLE. CODE MIXED WITH CLEAR.	?	?	?	? - ?	? SIM	READ	IF 1517	(UNIDENTIFIED)	--
MEXICO 5	DIPLOMATIC	5-LETTER ?-PART CODE.	?	"XEPIT"	?	1941 - ?	1942 PERS Z S	READ. 100% COMPROMISED.	D 16	(ASA STATES THIS SYSTEM MAY BE A PART OF MXA OR MXB)	--
MEXICO 6	DIPLOMATIC	POLYALPHABETIC SUBSTITUTION CIPHER WITH 26 ALPHABETS, 5 OF WHICH WERE USED AT A TIME. KEY LASTED SEVERAL DAYS. STARTING IN 1927, KEY CHANGED WITH EACH MESSAGE. SEPARATE SUBSTITUTION ALPHABETS FOR ENCIPHERMENT OF INDICATOR GROUP.	?	?	?	1926 - ?	1926 PERS Z S	READ	D 16	(UNKNOWN)	--
MEXICO 7	DIPLOMATIC	POLYALPHABETIC SUBSTITUTION CIPHER WITH 20 ALPHABETS.	?	?	(MXC)	(?-CURRENT)	1942 PERS Z S 1942 SIM	READ BY SIM.	D 16 IF 1517	(100% READABLE)	--
NETHERLANDS 1	DIPLOMATIC, MILITARY, AND NAVAL ATTACHES	4-LETTER 4-FIGURE 1-PART CODE. (USED WITH AND WITHOUT ENCIPHERMENT. 220 GROUP REPEATING ADDITIVE USED IN ENCIPHERMENT.)	?	?	(NEB) AND (NEB-1)	1939, PERHAPS EARLIER-(CURRENT)	1939 PERS Z S	PARTIALLY BROKEN	D 54, REPORT 3, P 6 T 2490 T 2491 T 2493 T 2495	(CODE BROKEN. ENCIPHERMENT IN READABLE STATE.)	--
NETHERLANDS 2	?	FRENCH FIGURE CODE, 1-PART REPAGINATED. ENCIPHERMENT BY DIGRAPHIC SUBSTITUTION AND TRANSPOSITION WITHIN THE GROUP.	?	?	?	?-1939-?	1939 PERS Z S	PARTIALLY RECOVERED	D 54, REPORT 3, P 7 T 2045 T 2047 T 2049	(UNKNOWN)	--
NETHERLANDS 3	?	MESSAGES TO AND FROM THE ROME LEGATION.	?	?	?	? - ?	? SIM	A SMALL NUMBER OF MESSAGES READ	IF 1518 P 3	(UNIDENTIFIED)	--
NORWAY 1	DIPLOMATIC	5-LETTER ?-PART UNENCIPHERED CODE.	?	?	?	? - 1940?	BEFORE 1940 FA	READ COMPLETELY TO 1940. NOT AFTER 1940.	I 162 P 3	(UNIDENTIFIED)	--

CHART NO. 1-2

TOP SECRET

DOCID: 3560861

TOP SECRET

RESULTS OF EUROPEAN AXIS CRYPTANALYSIS AS LEARNED FROM TICOM SOURCES

(WITH ANNOTATIONS FROM ARMY SECURITY AGENCY SOURCES IN PARENTHESES)

COUNTRY OF ORIGIN		SERVICE	DESCRIPTION OF SYSTEM	NAME OF SYSTEM: COUNTRY OF ORIGIN	NAME OF SYSTEM: AXIS	NAME OF SYSTEM: U.S.A.	DATES OF USE	WHEN ATTACKED AND BY WHOM	RESULTS	TICOM REFERENCE	STATUS OF THE SYSTEM AT ASA	REMARKS
PERU	1	DIPLOMATIC	5-LETTER 1-PART CODE. INTIAL DIGRAPHS SUBSTITUTED BY DIGRAPHIC TABLES AND FINAL TRIGRAPH SUBSTITUTED BY TRIGRAPHIC TABLES.	?	?	(PEA)	(1924-CURRENT)	? PERS Z S ? SIM	?	T 1585 D 15	(COMPROMISED)	--
PERU	2	DIPLOMATIC	5-LETTER 2-PART CODE WITH 10,000 TO 20,000 PRONOUNCEABLE GROUPS.	?	?	?	1920-1927-?	? PERS Z S	NOT READ	D 16	(UNKNOWN)	--
PERU	3	DIPLOMATIC	5-LETTER 2-PART CODE. (ENCIPHERMENT MAYBE "PEA" OR PREDECESSOR.)	?	"PERU: LIMA-GENF"	?	? - ?	? ?	RECOVERED LESS THAN 1%	T 1391	-	--
PERU	4	DIPLOMATIC	5-LETTER 2-PART CODE. (ENCIPHERMENT MAY BE "PEA" OR PREDECESSOR.)	?	"PERU: LIMA-GENF"	?	? - ?	? ?	RECOVERED LESS THAN 5%	T 1397	-	--

CHART NO. 1-2

TOP SECRET

DOCID: 3560861

TOP SECRET

RESULTS OF EUROPEAN AXIS CRYPTANALYSIS AS LEARNED FROM TICOM SOURCES

(WITH ANNOTATIONS FROM ARMY SECURITY AGENCY SOURCES IN PARENTHESES)

COUNTRY OF ORIGIN		SERVICE	DESCRIPTION OF SYSTEM	NAME OF SYSTEM			DATES OF USE	WHEN ATTACKED AND BY WHOM	RESULTS	TICOM REFERENCE	STATUS OF THE SYSTEM AT ASA	REMARKS
				COUNTRY OF ORIGIN	AXIS	U.S.A.						
POLAND	1	NAVY	5-FIGURE 1-PART CODE	SZYFR ZA-SADNICZY "MAR 2"	?	?	(1924-1926)	1939 OKW	100% COMPRO-MISED	T 477	(UNKNOWN)	NOTE AC-COMPANY-ING THIS DOCUMENT SAYS THERE WERE THREE CODEBOOKS IN ALL.
POLAND	2	NAVY	5-FIGURE 1-PART CODE	SZYFR ZA-SADNICZY "MAR 3"	?	?	(1924-1926)	1939 OKW	100% COMPRO-MISED	T 478	(UNKNOWN)	NOTE AC-COMPANY-ING THIS DOCUMENT SAYS THERE WERE 3 CODES IN ALL.
POLAND	3	NAVY	1-PART CODE, PERHAPS 5-FIGURE.	SZYFR "1937"	?	?	? - ?	? OKW	100% COMPRO-MISED	T 476	(UNIDENTIFIED)	--
POLAND	4	DIPLOMATIC	4-FIGURE (2-PART) CODE ENCIPHERED BY ADDITIVE.	?	PD 1?	(FLO)	? - 1944 - ?	1940 FA 1944 OKW 1941 PERS Z S	FA READ UNTIL 1943; OKW READ REGU-LARLY.	I 124 P 3 I 162 P 4 T 2030	(NO GROUPS RECOVERED. 1942-1943, 40% OF LONDON-NEW YORK TRAFFIC DECIPHERED. 1943-1944, VERY LITTLE DECIPHERED)	--
POLAND	5	DIPLOMATIC	4-FIGURE ?-PART CODE	?	N P D	?	? - ?	? - ?	RECOVERED ABOUT 40%	T 2155	(UNIDENTIFIED)	--
POLAND	6	DIPLOMATIC	4-FIGURE ?-PART CODE	?	O F D	?	? - ?	? - ?	RECOVERED 30% - 40%	T 2152	(UNIDENTIFIED)	--
POLAND	7	DIPLOMATIC	4-FIGURE 2-PART CODE	?	P P D 5	?	? - ?	? - ?	RECOVERED 40% - 50%	T 2150 T 2154	(UNIDENTIFIED)	--
POLAND	8	DIPLOMATIC	4-FIGURE 2-PART CODE	?	C P D	?	? - ?	? - ?	RECOVERED ABOUT 40%	T 2137 T 2151 T 2176	(UNIDENTIFIED)	--
POLAND	9	DIPLOMATIC	4-FIGURE ?-PART CODE WITH 10,000 GROUPS. ENCI-PHERED WITH ADDITIVE TABLE 24 X 26.	?	?	?	? - 1943	? OKW	MOST OF TRAFFIC READ	I 31 PP 20 - 21	(UNIDENTIFIED)	--
POLAND	10	DIPLOMATIC	4-FIGURE ?-PART CODE WITH 10,000 GROUPS. ENCI-PHERED WITH ADDITIVE TABLES 80 X 100.	?	?	?	1943 - ?	? OKW	MOST OF TRAFFIC READ	I 31 PP 20 - 21	(UNIDENTIFIED)	--
POLAND	11	DIPLOMATIC	4-FIGURE ?-PART CODE, VALUES IN FRENCH.	?	FRANZ. CODE DER POLN. DIP-LOMATIE?	?	? - ?	? - ?	RECOVERED ABOUT 10%	T 2144	(UNIDENTIFIED)	--
POLAND	12	?	4-FIGURE 2-PART CODE	?	?	?	? - ?	? - ?	RECOVERED ABOUT 25%	T 2153	(UNIDENTIFIED)	--

CHART NO. 1-2

TOP SECRET

DOCID: 3560861

TOP SECRET

RESULTS OF EUROPEAN AXIS CRYPTANALYSIS
AS LEARNED FROM TICOM SOURCES
(WITH ANNOTATIONS FROM ARMY SECURITY AGENCY SOURCES IN PARENTHESES)

COUNTRY OF ORIGIN		SERVICE	DESCRIPTION OF SYSTEM	NAME OF SYSTEM			DATES OF USE	WHEN ATTACKED AND BY WHOM	RESULTS	TICOM REFERENCE	STATUS OF THE SYSTEM AT ASA	REMARKS
				COUNTRY OF ORIGIN	AXIS	U.S.A.						
POLAND	13	FOREIGN OFFICE	4-FIGURE 2-PART CODE. ENCIPHERED ON KEY TAKEN FROM BOOK. PAIR OF ENCIPHERMENT TABLES USED FOR EACH OUTSTATION. INDICATORS: TWO 5-FIGURE GROUPS AT BEGINNING OF MESSAGE.	?	PD 1	?	1934-1942	1939 PERS Z S 1939 FA? ? OKH	1941-1942 ALL MESSAGES READ, MOST OF THEM CURRENTLY	I 63 PP 2-4 I 111 P 2 D 3N, ITEM 1, P 5 T 2Ø38	(UNIDENTIFIED)	--
POLAND	14	MILITARY ATTACHE	4-FIGURE (2-PART) CODE ENCIPHERED BY ADDITIVE.	?	?	(PLF)	? - 1942 - ?	1945 OKW	READ	I 118 PP 8-9	(ABOUT 6Ø GROUPS RECOVERED. 1942-1943, 6Ø% OF WASHINGTON-LONDON TRAFFIC DECIPHERED. 1943-1944, 1Ø% OF WASHINGTON-LONDON TRAFFIC DECIPHERED.)	--
POLAND	15	?	3-FIGURE ?-PART CODE	?	POLNISCHER DREI-STELLER-CODE I	?	? - ?	? - ?	RECOVERED ABOUT 9Ø%	T 2148	(UNIDENTIFIED)	--
POLAND	16	?	3-FIGURE ?-PART CODE	?	POLNISCHER DREI-STELLER-CODE II	?	? - ?	? - ?	RECOVERED ABOUT 9Ø%	T 2148	(UNIDENTIFIED)	--
POLAND	17	?	3-FIGURE ?-PART CODE	?	?	?	? - ?	? - ?	RECOVERED ABOUT 9Ø%	T 2148	(UNIDENTIFIED)	--
POLAND	18	AIR FORCE	2-PART CODE, 2,ØØØ VALUES. ENCIPHERED.	?	?	?	? - ?	? OKL	1ØØ% COMPROMISED	I 121 P 6 P 7	(UNIDENTIFIED)	--
POLAND	19	NATIONAL RESISTANCE MOVEMENT	TRANSPOSITION-SUBSTITUTION CIPHER: CLEAR TEXT WRITTEN INTO 1Ø x 12 SQUARE, TAKEN OUT IN COLUMNS IN ORDER, CONVERTED TO FIGURES BY 2-FIGURE SUBSTITUTION. TRANSMITTED IN 3-FIGURE GROUPS.	?	Ø66	?	? - ?	? OKH,	READ	I 26 P 6 P 14	(UNIDENTIFIED)	--
POLAND	2Ø	NATIONAL RESISTANCE MOVEMENT	TRANSPOSITION-SUBSTITUTION CIPHER.	?	Ø98	?	? - ?	? OKH,	READ	I 26 PP 14-15	(UNIDENTIFIED)	--
POLAND	21	NATIONAL RESISTANCE MOVEMENT	TRANSPOSITION-SUBSTITUTION CIPHER.	?	117	?	? - ?	? OKH,	READ	I 26 P 6 PP 14-15	(UNIDENTIFIED)	--
POLAND	22	NATIONAL RESISTANCE MOVEMENT	TRANSPOSITION-SUBSTITUTION CIPHER	?	118	?	? - ?	? OKH,	READ	I 26 P 6 PP 14-15	(UNIDENTIFIED)	--
POLAND	23	NATIONAL RESISTANCE MOVEMENT	TRANSPOSITION-SUBSTITUTION CIPHER.	?	181	?	? - ?	? OKH	READ	I 26 P 6 PP 14-15	(UNIDENTIFIED)	--
POLAND	24	NATIONAL RESISTANCE MOVEMENT	SIMPLE TRANSPOSITION CIPHER.	?	?	?	? - 1944 - ?	1944 OKH	BROKEN	I 26 P 14	(UNIDENTIFIED)	--

TOP SECRET

RESULTS OF EUROPEAN AXIS CRYPTANALYSIS AS LEARNED FROM TICOM SOURCES

(WITH ANNOTATIONS FROM ARMY SECURITY AGENCY SOURCES IN PARENTHESES)

COUNTRY OF ORIGIN		SERVICE	DESCRIPTION OF SYSTEM	NAME OF SYSTEM: COUNTRY OF ORIGIN	NAME OF SYSTEM: AXIS	NAME OF SYSTEM: U.S.A.	DATES OF USE	WHEN ATTACKED AND BY WHOM	RESULTS	TICOM REFERENCE	STATUS OF THE SYSTEM AT ASA	REMARKS
PORTUGAL	1	DIPLOMATIC	5-FIGURE 1-PART CODE WITH 50,000 GROUPS. ENCIPHERED DIFFERENTLY ON DIFFERENT CIRCUITS: ADDITIVE FOR CIRCUIT APPLIED TO LINE NUMBER; TRANSPOSITION OF GROUP ELEMENTS; 1,000-PLACE SUBSTITUTION TABLES APPLIED TO PAGE NUMBERS.	?	?	(POC?) (POD?) (POE?)	(POC: 1941-CURRENT) (POD: 1939-CURRENT) (POE: ?-1945)	1941 PERS Z S	?	D 16, 1941 REPORT, P 2	(POC, POD, POE ALL 100% COMPROMISED; ALL HAVE THE SAME BASIC BOOK.)	--
PORTUGAL	2	DIPLOMATIC	5-FIGURE 1-PART CODE, WITH 61,500 GROUPS. ENCIPHERED.	?	329	(POJ)	(1941-CURRENT)	1942 PERS Z S	READ	D 16, 1942 REPORT, P 3 T 3020 T 3024 T 3022	(100% COMPROMISED)	--
PORTUGAL	3	DIPLOMATIC	5-FIGURE 1-PART CODE WITH 50,000 GROUPS. ENCIPHERED WITH 1,000-PLACE SUBSTITUTION TABLES.	?	302	(POL)	(1942-CURRENT)	1942 PERS Z S	READ	D 16, 1942 REPORT, P 3	(100% COMPROMISED)	--
PORTUGAL	4	DIPLOMATIC	5-FIGURE 1-PART CODE (WITH 50,000 GROUPS. ENCIPHERED WITH TABLES.)	?	352	(POU)	(1943-CURRENT)	? ?	LARGELY RECOVERED	T 3022	(90% RECOVERED; COMPLETELY READABLE.)	--
PORTUGAL	5	DIPLOMATIC	5-FIGURE 1-PART CODE, 61,500 GROUPS. ENCIPHERED.	?	299	?	?-1942-?	1942 PERS Z S	READ	D 16, 1942 REPORT, P 3	(UNIDENTIFIED)	--
PORTUGAL	6	DIPLOMATIC	5-FIGURE 1-PART CODE: BASIC BOOK OF WHICH "299" AND "329" WERE REPAGINATIONS. 2½ SUBSTITUTION TABLES USED WITH IT.	?	205	?	?-1942-?	1942 OKW 1942 PERS Z S	100% COMPROMISED; LOANED BY OKW TO PERS Z S FOR PHOTOSTATING INCLUDING 9 TABLES; REST OF TABLES BROKEN. READ 100%.	D 16, 1942 REPORT, P 3	(REPAGINATION "328" IS ASA'S POJ.)	--
PORTUGAL	7	DIPLOMATIC	5-FIGURE 1-PART CODE WITH 61,500 GROUPS. ENCIPHERED WITH TWENTY 100-PLACE SUBSTITUTION TABLES FOR LINE NUMBERS AND ON SOME CIRCUITS ALSO WITH 1,000-PLACE TABLE FOR PAGES. DIFFERENT TRANSPOSITION OF GROUP ELEMENTS FOR EACH CIRCUIT.	?	?	?	?-1941-?	1941 PERS Z S	LARGE PART OF MESSAGES READ WITH SOME GAPS. BERLIN-LISBON TRAFFIC NOT READ; TRAFFIC SMALL AND KEYS CHANGED RAPIDLY.	D 16, 1941 REPORT, P 2	(UNIDENTIFIED)	--
PORTUGAL	8	DIPLOMATIC	5-FIGURE 1-PART CODE WITH 61,900 GROUPS. ENCIPHERED WITH TWENTY 100-PLACE SUBSTITUTION TABLES FOR LINE NUMBERS AND ON SOME CIRCUITS ALSO WITH 1,000-PLACE TABLE FOR PAGES. DIFFERENT TRANSPOSITION OF GROUP ELEMENTS FOR EACH CIRCUIT.	?	?	?	?-1941-?	1941 PERS Z S	ENCIPHERMENTS BROKEN, BEGINNINGS MADE ON CODE, BUT NOT READ.	D 16, 1941 REPORT, P 2	(UNIDENTIFIED)	--

CHART NO. 1-2

DOC ID: 3560861

TOP SECRET

RESULTS OF EUROPEAN AXIS CRYPTANALYSIS
AS LEARNED FROM TICOM SOURCES
(WITH ANNOTATIONS FROM ARMY SECURITY AGENCY SOURCES IN PARENTHESES)

COUNTRY OF ORIGIN		SERVICE	DESCRIPTION OF SYSTEM.	NAME OF SYSTEM: COUNTRY OF ORIGIN	NAME OF SYSTEM: AXIS	NAME OF SYSTEM: U.S.A.	DATES OF USE	WHEN ATTACKED AND BY WHOM	RESULTS	TICOM REFERENCE	STATUS OF THE SYSTEM AT ASA	REMARKS
PORTUGAL	9	?	5-FIGURE ?-PART CODE.	?	?	?	? - ?	? ?	RECOVERED LESS THAN 1%	T 3127	(UNIDENTIFIED)	--
PORTUGAL	10	?	5-FIGURE ?-PART CODE.	?	?	?	? - ?	? ?	RECOVERED LESS THAN 10%	T 3023	(UNIDENTIFIED)	--
PORTUGAL	11	DIPLOMATIC	4-FIGURE 1-PART CODE, REPAGINATED.	?	62 146	?	?-1936-?	? ?	RECOVERED 30%	T 1336	(UNIDENTIFIED)	--
PORTUGAL	12	?	4-FIGURE 1-PART CODE, REPAGINATED.	?	?	?	? - ?	? ?	RECOVERED 30% - 50%	T 1332	(UNIDENTIFIED)	--
PORTUGAL	13	?	4-FIGURE 1-PART CODE, REPAGINATED.	?	502	?	? - ?	? ?	RECOVERED 20% - 30%	T 1333	(UNIDENTIFIED)	--
PORTUGAL	14	?	4-FIGURE 1-PART CODE, REPAGINATED.	?	611	?	? - ?	? ?	RECOVERED 20% - 30%	T 1334	(UNIDENTIFIED)	--
PORTUGAL	15	?	4-FIGURE ?-PART CODE.	?	?	?	? - ?	? ?	RECOVERED LESS THAN 5%	T 1335	(UNIDENTIFIED)	--
PORTUGAL	16	?	4-FIGURE ?-PART CODE.	?	?	?	? - ?	? ?	RECOVERED LESS THAN 1%	T 1337	(UNIDENTIFIED)	--
PORTUGAL	17	?	4-FIGURE ?-PART CODE.	?	?	?	? - ?	? ?	RECOVERED LESS THAN 5%	T 1338	(UNIDENTIFIED)	--
PORTUGAL	18	?	4-FIGURE ?-PART CODE.	?	557 93	?	? - ?	? ?	RECOVERED LESS THAN 3%	T 1340	(UNIDENTIFIED)	--
PORTUGAL	19	DIPLOMATIC	4-FIGURE ?-PART CODE.	?	55 141	?	? - ?	? ?	RECOVERED LESS THAN 1%	T 1386	(UNIDENTIFIED)	--
PORTUGAL	20	DIPLOMATIC	MONOALPHABETIC SUBSTITUTION CIPHER.	?	?	?	?-1942-?	1942 PERS Z S	READ	D 16, 1942 REPORT, P 3	(UNKNOWN)	--
PORTUGAL	21	DIPLOMATIC	5-LETTER ?-PART CODE.	?	?	?	?-1937-?	? SIM	READ. COMPROMISED.	T 1590	(UNIDENTIFIED)	--
PORTUGAL	22	DIPLOMATIC	5-LETTER 5-FIGURE CODE, 60,000 GROUPS. ENCIPHERED BY ESTIMATED 200 TABLES.	?	?	?	? - ?	? SIM, SID	READ	IF 1526	(UNIDENTIFIED)	--

CHART NO. 1-2

TOP SECRET

DOCID: 3560861

~~TOP SECRET~~

RESULTS OF EUROPEAN AXIS CRYPTANALYSIS
AS LEARNED FROM TICOM SOURCES
(WITH ANNOTATIONS FROM ARMY SECURITY AGENCY SOURCES IN PARENTHESES)

COUNTRY OF ORIGIN		SERVICE	DESCRIPTION OF SYSTEM	NAME OF SYSTEM: COUNTRY OF ORIGIN	NAME OF SYSTEM: AXIS	NAME OF SYSTEM: U.S.A.	DATES OF USE	WHEN ATTACKED AND BY WHOM	RESULTS	TICOM REFERENCE	STATUS OF THE SYSTEM AT ASA	REMARKS
PORTUGAL	23	DIPLOMATIC	5-FIGURE 1-PART CODE. LINE DIGRAPHS ON PAGE IN EITHER ASCENDING OR DESCENDING ORDER. USED LISBON-ANKARA-BERN.	?	?	?	? - 1945	1945 SID	READ	IF 1517 IF 1526	(UNIDENTIFIED)	--
PORTUGAL	24	DIPLOMATIC	5-FIGURE AND 2-FIGURE ?-PART CODE REPAGINATED FOR DIFFERENT LINKS. UNENCIPHERED. TRAFFIC GENERALLY OF MARITIME NATURE.	?	?	?	?-1944-?	? SID	READ	IF 1526	(UNIDENTIFIED)	--

~~TOP SECRET~~

CHART NO. 1-2

DOCID: 3560861

RESULTS OF EUROPEAN AXIS CRYPTANALYSIS AS LEARNED FROM TICOM SOURCES

(WITH ANNOTATIONS FROM ARMY SECURITY AGENCY SOURCES IN PARENTHESES)

COUNTRY OF ORIGIN		SERVICE	DESCRIPTION OF SYSTEM	NAME OF SYSTEM: COUNTRY OF ORIGIN	NAME OF SYSTEM: AXIS	NAME OF SYSTEM: U.S.A.	DATES OF USE	WHEN ATTACKED AND BY WHOM	RESULTS	TICOM REFERENCE	STATUS OF THE SYSTEM AT ASA	REMARKS
RUMANIA	1	DIPLOMATIC	5-FIGURE 2-PART CODE (ENCIPHERED WITH MONO-ALPHABET)	?	R 18	(ROD)	(?-1945-?)	? - ?	100% COMPROMISED	T 752 T 1097 T 1096 T 1095	(WORKED ON INTERMITTENTLY DURING 1942, 1943, 1944, AND 1945. ENCIPHERMENT STILL BEING ATTACKED, END 1945.)	--
RUMANIA	2	DIPLOMATIC	5-FIGURE 2-PART CODE (ENCIPHERED WITH BOOK ADDITIVE)	?	?	(ROF)	(?-1945-?)	? - ?	100% COMPROMISED	T 751	(WORKED ON INTERMITTENTLY DURING 1942, 1943, 1944, AND 1945. ADDITIVES STILL BEING ATTACKED, END 1945.)	--
RUMANIA	3	DIPLOMATIC	5-FIGURE 2-PART CODE (ENCIPHERED WITH REPEATING ADDITIVE)	?	?	(ROH)	(?-1945-?)	? - ?	100% COMPROMISED	T 746	(WORKED ON INTERMITTENTLY DURING 1942, 1943, 1944, AND 1945. ADDITIVES STILL BEING ATTACKED, END 1945.)	--
RUMANIA	4	DIPLOMATIC	5-FIGURE 2-PART CODE, 70,000 GROUPS. ENCIPHERED WITH 10-PLACE TABLE.	?	R 11	?	? - ?	? PERS Z S	RECOVERED 5% - 10%	T 2220 D 54 P 15	(UNIDENTIFIED)	--
RUMANIA	5	DIPLOMATIC	5-FIGURE 2-PART CODE, 70,000 GROUPS. ENCIPHERED WITH 10-PLACE TABLE.	?	R 12	?	? - ?	? PERS Z S	RECOVERED 5% - 10%	T 2221 D 54 P 15	(UNIDENTIFIED)	--
RUMANIA	6	DIPLOMATIC	5-FIGURE 2-PART CODE, 70,000 GROUPS. ENCIPHERED WITH 10-PLACE TABLE.	?	R 13	?	? - ?	? PERS Z S	RECOVERED ABOUT 5%	T 2216 T 2222 D 54 P 15	(UNIDENTIFIED)	--
RUMANIA	7	DIPLOMATIC	5-FIGURE 2-PART CODE, 100,000 GROUPS. ENCIPHERED WITH 10-PLACE TABLE.	?	14	?	? - ?	? PERS Z S	RECOVERED LESS THAN 5%	T 2219 D 54 P 15	(UNIDENTIFIED)	--
RUMANIA	8	DIPLOMATIC	5-FIGURE 2-PART CODE, 100,000 GROUPS. ENCIPHERED WITH 10-PLACE TABLE.	CIFRU GRIGORCEA	15	?	? - ?	? PERS Z S	RECOVERED LESS THAN 5%	T 1095 D 54 P 15	(UNIDENTIFIED)	--
RUMANIA	9	DIPLOMATIC	5-FIGURE 2-PART CODE, 100,000 GROUPS. ENCIPHERED WITH 10-PLACE TABLE.	?	R 16	?	? - ?	? PERS Z S	RECOVERED 5% - 10%	T 2217 T 2225 D 54 P 15	(UNIDENTIFIED)	--
RUMANIA	10	DIPLOMATIC	5-FIGURE 2-PART CODE, 100,000 GROUPS. ENCIPHERED WITH 10-PLACE TABLE.	?	17	?	1940 - ?	? PERS Z S	RECOVERED LESS THAN 5%	T 2224 D 54 P 15	(UNIDENTIFIED)	--
RUMANIA	11	DIPLOMATIC	5-FIGURE ?-PART CODE WITH 50,000 - 60,000 GROUPS. ENCIPHERED BY FIGURE SUBSTITUTION TABLE.	?	?	?	? - ?	? SIM, SIC	CODE 100% COMPROMISED; ENCIPHERMENT BROKEN.	IF 1517 P 3 IF 1526 P 6	(UNIDENTIFIED)	--
RUMANIA	12	?	5-FIGURE 2-PART CODE.	?	R 6	?	? - ?	? - ?	RECOVERED 5% - 10%	T 1006	(UNIDENTIFIED)	--
RUMANIA	13	?	5-FIGURE 2-PART CODE.	?	R 7	?	? - ?	? - ?	RECOVERED LESS THAN 5%	T 1007	(UNIDENTIFIED)	--
RUMANIA	14	?	5-FIGURE 2-PART CODE	?	R 8	?	? - ?	? - ?	RECOVERED 5% - 15%	T 2223	(UNIDENTIFIED)	--
RUMANIA	15	?	5-FIGURE 2-PART CODE.	?	9	?	? - ?	? - ?	RECOVERED 5% - 10%	T 2215	(UNIDENTIFIED)	--

CHART NO. 1-2

DOCID: 3560861

TOP SECRET

RESULTS OF EUROPEAN AXIS CRYPTANALYSIS AS LEARNED FROM TICOM SOURCES

(WITH ANNOTATIONS FROM ARMY SECURITY AGENCY SOURCES IN PARENTHESES)

COUNTRY OF ORIGIN		SERVICE	DESCRIPTION OF SYSTEM	NAME OF SYSTEM: COUNTRY OF ORIGIN	NAME OF SYSTEM: AXIS	NAME OF SYSTEM: U.S.A.	DATES OF USE	WHEN ATTACKED AND BY WHOM	RESULTS	TICOM REFERENCE	STATUS OF THE SYSTEM AT ASA	REMARKS
RUMANIA	16	?	5-FIGURE 2-PART CODE	?	10	?	? - ?	? ?	RECOVERED LESS THAN 5%	T 2219	(UNIDENTIFIED)	--
RUMANIA	17	?	5-FIGURE 2-PART CODE.	?	?	?	? - ?	? ?	RECOVERED ABOUT 10%	T 1139	(UNIDENTIFIED)	--
RUMANIA	18	DIPLOMATIC	5-FIGURE 2-PART CODE. FIGURE SUBSTITUTION ENCIPHERMENT. SEVERAL BOOKS USED SIMULTANEOUSLY.	?	?	?	? - ?	? SIM	100% COMPROMISED.	IF 1521	(UNIDENTIFIED)	--
RUMANIA	19	DIPLOMATIC	5-FIGURE 2-PART CODE. 50,000 - 60,000 GROUPS. ENCIPHERED WHEN HIGH SECURITY WAS DESIRED. KEYS WERE 49 X 5 AND 58 X 5 LONG.	?	?	?	? - ?	? SIM, SID	100% COMPROMISED.	IF 1526	(UNIDENTIFIED)	--
RUMANIA	20	MILITARY ATTACHE	5-FIGURE 2-PART CODE. EACH PAGE NUMBERED BY ONE OF FOUR 3-FIGURE GROUPS PRINTED AT TOP. PAGE DIVIDED INTO TWO PARTS, EACH PART CONTAINING 5 BLOCKS OF 10 GROUPS EACH. ENCIPHERED WITH A SYSTEM CALLED BY ROMANIANS "FISE."	?	?	?	1942-1943	? SIM	READ	IF 1521	(UNIDENTIFIED)	--
RUMANIA	21	MILITARY ATTACHE	TRANSPOSITION CIPHER. RECTANGLE DIVIDED INTO 4 SMALLER ONES, EACH 7 X 10 OR 7 X 7. SOME BLANK CELLS. CLEAR TEXT WRITTEN IN ON A PATTERN.	AMG 1943	?	?	?-1943-?	? SIM	READ	IF 1521 IF 1515 T 1536	(UNIDENTIFIED)	--
RUMANIA	22	MILITARY ATTACHE	TRANSPOSITION CIPHER. 6 RECTANGLES, 6 X 5; CLEAR TEXT WRITTEN IN ON PATTERN.	CIFRUL DE MEMORIE	?	?	?-1943-?	1943 SIM ? SID	READ	IF 1517 IF 1521	(UNIDENTIFIED)	--
RUMANIA	23	AIR FORCE	TRANSPOSITION CIPHER.	?	?	?	?-1939-?	? OKL	NOT READ	I 121 P 8	(UNKNOWN)	--
RUMANIA	24	POLICE	CIPHER, DESCRIBED AS "ELEMENTARY", BUT NO DETAILS AVAILABLE.	?	?	?	? - ?	? OKL	READ CURRENTLY	I 121 P 9	(UNKNOWN)	--

CHART NO. 1-2

TOP SECRET

DOCID: 3560861

TOP SECRET

RESULTS OF EUROPEAN AXIS CRYPTANALYSIS
AS LEARNED FROM TICOM SOURCES
(WITH ANNOTATIONS FROM ARMY SECURITY AGENCY SOURCES IN PARENTHESES)

COUNTRY OF ORIGIN		SERVICE	DESCRIPTION OF SYSTEM	NAME OF SYSTEM			DATES OF USE	WHEN ATTACKED AND BY WHOM	RESULTS	TICOM REFERENCE	STATUS OF THE SYSTEM AT ASA	REMARKS
				COUNTRY OF ORIGIN	AXIS	U.S.A.						
RUSSIA	1	ARMY	HAGELIN B-211 MACHINE, OLD STYLE, EMPLOYING FRANCTIONATION, SUBSTITUTION, AND RECOMBINATION.	K 37	K 37	--	? - ?	1941 OKH	ACCOMPLISHED THEORETICAL SOLUTION ON 10-LETTER CRIB. AUTUMN 1941, MODEL OF MACHINE CAPTURED.	I 136 P 2 I 58 P 5 I 92 P 4	--	--
RUSSIA	2	ARMY	SPEECH ENCIPHERER, TIME SCRAMBLING TYPE.	?	X^2	--	1939-1945	1939 OKH/GDNA, WA PRUEF 7	NOT BROKEN.	I 73 I 31 P 12 IF 123 P 13	--	--
RUSSIA	3	ARMY	TELETYPE ENCIPHERER, KEY GENERATOR TYPE.	?	Z	--	? - ?	1943 OKH	NOT READ	I 31 P 12	--	--
RUSSIA	4	ARMY	5-FIGURE 2-PART CODE ENCIPHERED WITH ONE-TIME PAD.	?	?	--	? - 1945	? OKH	?	I 19 C I 116	--	--
RUSSIA	5	ARMY: BRIGADE, DIVISION STAFFS UPWARD TO GENERAL STAFF	5-FIGURE 2-PART CODE	Ø11-A	?	--	194Ø-1941?	? OKH	?	T 8Ø5	--	--
RUSSIA	6	ARMY: BRIGADE, DIVISION STAFFS UPWARD TO GENERAL STAFF	5-FIGURE 2-PART CODE	Ø23-A	?	--	194Ø?- ?	? OKH	?	T 8Ø5	--	--
RUSSIA	7	ARMY: BRIGADE, DIVISION STAFFS UPWARD TO GENERAL STAFF	5-FIGURE 2-PART CODE	Ø45-A	?	--	194Ø - ?	? OKH	?	T 8Ø5	--	--
RUSSIA	8	ARMY: BRIGADE, DIVISION STAFFS UPWARD TO GENERAL STAFF	5-FIGURE 2-PART CODE	Ø62-A	?	--	194Ø - ?	? OKH	?	T 8Ø5	--	--
RUSSIA	9	ARMY: BRIGADE, DIVISION STAFFS UPWARD TO GENERAL STAFF	5-FIGURE 2-PART CODE	Ø91-A	?	--	? - 1945	? OKH	?	T 8Ø5	--	--
RUSSIA	1Ø	ARMY: TANK	4-FIGURE 2-PART CODE ENCIPHERED BY SUBSTITUTION.	PT-B	?	--	? - 1945	? OKH	1ØØ% COMPROMISED, MARCH 1945	I 19 C I 19 E	--	--

CHART NO. 1-2

TOP SECRET

DOCID: 3560861

TOP SECRET

RESULTS OF EUROPEAN AXIS CRYPTANALYSIS AS LEARNED FROM TICOM SOURCES

(WITH ANNOTATIONS FROM ARMY SECURITY AGENCY SOURCES IN PARENTHESES)

COUNTRY OF ORIGIN		SERVICE	DESCRIPTION OF SYSTEM	NAME OF SYSTEM: COUNTRY OF ORIGIN	NAME OF SYSTEM: AXIS	NAME OF SYSTEM: U.S.A.	DATES OF USE	WHEN ATTACKED AND BY WHOM	RESULTS	TICOM REFERENCE	STATUS OF THE SYSTEM AT ASA	REMARKS
RUSSIA	11	ARMY: GUARDS TANK	4-FIGURE ?-PART CODE ENCIPHERED BY SUBSTITUTION.	?	?	--	? - 1945	? OKH	?	I 19 C I 19 E	--	--
RUSSIA	12	ARMY: TANK	4-FIGURE ?-PART CODE ENCIPHERED BY SUBSTITUTION.	?	?	--	? - 1945	? OKH	?	I 19 C I 19 E	--	--
RUSSIA	13	ARMY: GUARDS TANK	4-FIGURE ?-PART CODE ENCIPHERED BY SUBSTITUTION.	?	?	--	? - 1945	? OKH	?	I 19 C I 19 E	--	--
RUSSIA	14	ARMY	4-FIGURE ?-PART CODE	?	?	--	? - 1945	? OKH	PARTLY READ	I 19 C I 19 E	--	--
RUSSIA	15	ARMY	4-FIGURE ?-PART CODE	?	?	--	1941-1945?	? OKH	?	I 26	--	--
RUSSIA	16	ARMY	4-FIGURE ?-PART CODE	?	?	--	1945 - ?	? OKH	?	I 19 C I 19 E	--	--
RUSSIA	17	ARMY	3-FIGURE ?-PART CODE	?	?	--	1941-1945	? OKH	?	I 19 C I 26	--	--
RUSSIA	18	ARMY	2-FIGURE SUBSTITUTION CIPHER USING A 10 x 10 SQUARE CONTAINING ALPHABET, FIGURES, ETC. DAILY CHANGING KEY.	?	?	--	1940-1943	? SIM	?	IF 1517	--	--
RUSSIA	19	ARMY	2-FIGURE SUBSTITUTION CIPHER	PT 41	?	--	1941-1945	? OKH	?	I 26 T 805	--	--
RUSSIA	20	ARMY	2-FIGURE SUBSTITUTION CIPHER	PT 41 N	?	--	1941-1945?	? OKH	?	I 26	--	--
RUSSIA	21	ARMY GROUPS, ARMIES, CORPS	2-FIGURE SUBSTITUTION CIPHER	PT 42	?	--	1942 - ?	? OKH	?	I 19 C I 19 D	--	--
RUSSIA	22	ARMY	TRANSPOSITION CIPHER USING REVOLVING GRILLE	?	?	--	1944 - ?	? OKH	?	I 19 C	--	--
RUSSIA	23	ARMY	TRANSPOSITION CIPHER	?	?	--	1944 - ?	? OKH	?	I 19 C	--	--
RUSSIA	24	ARMY, AIR FORCE	4-FIGURE ?-PART CODE	OKK 5-8	?	--	1939-1941?	? OKH	?	I 116 T 305	--	--
RUSSIA	25	ARMY, AIR FORCE	2-FIGURE SUBSTITUTION CIPHER	PT 35	?	--	1935-1939	? OKH	?	T 805	--	--

CHART NO. 1-2

TOP SECRET

RESULTS OF EUROPEAN AXIS CRYPTANALYSIS AS LEARNED FROM TICOM SOURCES

(WITH ANNOTATIONS FROM ARMY SECURITY AGENCY SOURCES IN PARENTHESES)

COUNTRY OF ORIGIN		SERVICE	DESCRIPTION OF SYSTEM	NAME OF SYSTEM			DATES OF USE	WHEN ATTACKED AND BY WHOM	RESULTS	TICOM REFERENCE	STATUS OF THE SYSTEM AT ASA	REMARKS
				COUNTRY OF ORIGIN	AXIS	U.S.A.						
RUSSIA	26	ARMY GROUPS, ARMIES, CORPS, DIVISIONS, AIR FORCE	2-FIGURE SUBSTITUTION CIPHER	PT 39	?	--	1939-1942	? OKH	?	I 19 C I 19 D I 26 T 805	--	--
RUSSIA	27	ARMY: DIVISIONS, REGIMENTS. AIR FORCE	2-FIGURE SUBSTITUTION CIPHER	PT 42 N	R 27 C 731	--	1942-1944	? OKH	?	I 19 C I 19 D T 3349	--	--
RUSSIA	28	AIR FORCE	4-FIGURE 2-PART CODE	VAK 39	?	--	1935 - ?	? OKH	?	F 305 I 116	--	--
RUSSIA	29	AIR FORCE	4-FIGURE 2-PART CODE	?	?	--	1944-1945	? OKH	?	I 19 C I 19 E	--	--
RUSSIA	30	AIR, CIVILIAN	3-FIGURE 2-PART CODE, UNENCIPHERED	?	?	--	1943-1944	? OKH	READ	I 116	--	--
RUSSIA	31	AIR FORCE	2-FIGURE SUBSTITUTION CIPHER	PT 43	?	--	? - 1945	? OKH	NOT BROKEN	I 19 C I 106	--	--
RUSSIA	32	NKVD*	5-FIGURE 1-PART CODE	?	N5/529/5 R 57 C 1500	--	? - 1945	? OKH	?	I 55 T 2534	--	--
RUSSIA	33	NKVD	5-FIGURE 2-PART CODE ENCIPHERED WITH ONE-TIME PAD ADDITIVE.	?	CH ?	--	1944 - ?	? OKM	?	T 564	--	--
RUSSIA	34	NKVD	5-FIGURE 2-PART CODE ENCIPHERED WITH ONE-TIME PAD ADDITIVE	?	?	--	1944 - ?	? OKM	?	T 542 T 564	--	--
RUSSIA	35	NKVD	5-FIGURE 2-PART CODE ENCIPHERED BY DIGRAPHIC SUBSTITUTION.	?	?	--	? - 1945	? OKH	?	I 26 I 116 T 805	--	--
RUSSIA	36	NKVD, DIVISION OF REGIMENT TO DIVISION OF BATTALION SIZE	4-FIGURE 2-PART CODE ENCIPHERED WITH ADDITIVE	WHITE SEA	?	--	1943-1944	1944 OKH	10% OF TRAFFIC READ	I 106	--	--
RUSSIA	37	NKVD	4-FIGURE 2-PART CODE	049	R 47 1102	--	? - 1944	? OKH	?	I 55 I 106 T 2577	--	--

*PEOPLE'S COMMISSARIAT FOR INTERNAL AFFAIRS

DOCID: 3560861

TOP SECRET

RESULTS OF EUROPEAN AXIS CRYPTANALYSIS
AS LEARNED FROM TICOM SOURCES
(WITH ANNOTATIONS FROM ARMY SECURITY AGENCY SOURCES IN PARENTHESES)

COUNTRY OF ORIGIN		SERVICE	DESCRIPTION OF SYSTEM	NAME OF SYSTEM: COUNTRY OF ORIGIN	NAME OF SYSTEM: AXIS	NAME OF SYSTEM: U.S.A.	DATES OF USE	WHEN ATTACKED AND BY WHOM	RESULTS	TICOM REFERENCE	STATUS OF THE SYSTEM AT ASA	REMARKS
RUSSIA	38	NKVD--REGIMENTS, BATTALIONS	4-FIGURE 1-PART CODE ENCIPHERED BY SUBSTITUTION.	ZERNO	P 47 1200	--	1943-1945	? OKH	?	I 19 C I [illegible]7; I 106 I 55; T [illegible]	--	--
RUSSIA	39	NKVD	4-FIGURE 1-PART CODE	?	?	--	1941?-1945	? OKH	?	I 26	--	--
RUSSIA	40	NKVD	4-FIGURE 2-PART CODE ENCIPHERED WITH ADDITIVE.	?	?	--	1939 - ?	? OKH	?	T 805	--	--
RUSSIA	41	NKVD	4-FIGURE 2-PART CODE ENCIPHERED WITH ADDITIVE.	?	?	--	1941?-1945	? OKH	?	I 26	--	--
RUSSIA	42	NKVD	4-FIGURE 2-PART CODE ENCIPHERED BY SUBSTITUTION.	VIZA	?	--	? - 1945	? OKH	?	T 5[illegible]5	--	--
RUSSIA	43	NKVD	4-FIGURE 2-PART CODE ENCIPHERED BY DIGRAPHIC SUBSTITUTION.	NIVA	?	--	? - 1945	? OKH	?	I 116 T 805	--	--
RUSSIA	44	NKVD	4-FIGURE 2-PART CODE	?	R 47 1600	--	? - ?	? OKH	?	I 106	--	--
RUSSIA	45	NAVY	5-FIGURE 2-PART CODE ENCIPHERED WITH ONE-TIME PAD ADDITIVE.	?	KLAGENFURT I, II	--	1941-1942	? OKM	NOT SOLVED	T 564 T 541	--	--
RUSSIA	46	NAVY	5-FIGURE 2-PART CODE ENCIPHERED WITH DOUBLE ADDITIVE.	?	KOENIGSBERG	--	1942-1943	? OKM	NOT SOLVED	T 564	--	--
RUSSIA	47	NAVY	5-FIGURE 2-PART CODE ENCIPHERED WITH PERMUTED ADDITIVE.	?	FASAN	--	? - ?	? OKM	?	I 40	--	--
RUSSIA	48	NAVY	5-FIGURE 2-PART CODE ENCIPHERED WITH ADDITIVE.	?	KOMMANDEUR	--	1936-1941	? OKM	NOT SOLVED	I 16 T 564	--	--
RUSSIA	49	NAVY	5-FIGURE 2-PART CODE ENCIPHERED WITH ADDITIVE.	?	TROMSOE	--	1942-1943?	? OKM	NOT SOLVED	I 40 T 564	--	--
RUSSIA	50	NAVY	4-FIGURE 2-PART CODE ENCIPHERED WITH ADDITIVE.	?	GAMVIK	--	1943-1944	? OKM	NOT SOLVED	T 542 T 564 D 39	--	--
RUSSIA	51	NAVY	4-FIGURE 2-PART CODE ENCIPHERED WITH ADDITIVE.	?	GRAZ	--	? - ?	? OKM	READ AT TIMES	T 564 I 40	--	--
RUSSIA	52	NAVY	4-FIGURE 2-PART CODE ENCIPHERED WITH ADDITIVE.	?	M 4/374/S NAMSOS	--	1942?-1943	? OKM	AT TIMES ABOUT 50% READABLE	I 40 T 542; T 561 T 562; T 564	--	--

*PEOPLE'S COMMISSARIAT FOR INTERNAL AFFAIRS

CHART NO. 1-2

TOP SECRET

RESULTS OF EUROPEAN AXIS CRYPTANALYSIS AS LEARNED FROM TICOM SOURCES

(WITH ANNOTATIONS FROM ARMY SECURITY AGENCY SOURCES IN PARENTHESES)

COUNTRY OF ORIGIN		SERVICE	DESCRIPTION OF SYSTEM	NAME OF SYSTEM: COUNTRY OF ORIGIN	NAME OF SYSTEM: AXIS	NAME OF SYSTEM: U.S.A.	DATES OF USE	WHEN ATTACKED AND BY WHOM	RESULTS	TICOM REFERENCE	STATUS OF THE SYSTEM AT ASA	REMARKS
RUSSIA	53	NAVY	4-FIGURE 2-PART CODE ENCIPHERED WITH ADDITIVE.	?	?	--	1941-1942?	? OKM	50% READABLE	I 16 T 564	--	--
RUSSIA	54	NAVY	4-FIGURE 2-PART CODE ENCIPHERED BY SUBSTITUTION TO MARCH 1941, WITH ADDITIVE THEREAFTER.	?	R 47 C KKF	--	1939-1941?	? OKM	VARIED AT DIFFERENT TIMES	T 564 I 15 I 40	--	--
RUSSIA	55	NAVY	4-FIGURE 1-PART CODE ENCIPHERED WITH ADDITIVE.	?	M 5/4/493/S ELEING	--	1943-1945	? OKM	NOT SOLVED	I 40 T 542 T 564 D 39	--	--
RUSSIA	56	NAVY	4-FIGURE 1-PART CODE ENCIPHERED WITH ADDITIVE.	?	NARVIK	--	1942-1943	? OKM	AT TIMES ABOUT 50% READABLE	I 40 T 542; T 562 T 564	--	--
RUSSIA	57	NAVY	4-FIGURE 1-PART CODE ENCIPHERED WITH ADDITIVE.	?	WIEN	--	? - ?	? OKM	READ AT TIMES	I 40 T 564 T 1932	--	--
RUSSIA	58	NAVY; SIGNAL STATIONS	4-FIGURE 1-PART CODE ENCIPHERED BY SUBSTITUTION.	DF 9 DF 26	M 4/490/S ALLENSTEIN I; M 4/559/S ALLENSTEIN II; M 4/637/S ALLENSTEIN III	--	1943-1945	? OKM	SOLVED	T 542 T 564	--	--
RUSSIA	59	NAVY	4-FIGURE 1-PART CODE ENCIPHERED BY SUBSTITUTION.	?	HARSTAD	--	1943 - ?	? OKM	?	T 562	--	--
RUSSIA	60	NAVY	4-FIGURE 1-PART CODE ENCIPHERED BY SUBSTITUTION.	?	OSLO	--	1942-1944	? OKM	READ ALMOST 100% AT TIMES	I 40; I 55 T 542; T 562 T 564; T 2591	--	--
RUSSIA	61	NAVY	4-FIGURE 2-PART CODE ENCIPHERED WITH ADDITIVE.	?	BERGEN	--	1942-1943	? OKM	NOT SOLVED	T 562; T 564	--	--
RUSSIA	62	NAVY	4-FIGURE 2-PART CODE ENCIPHERED WITH ADDITIVE.	?	GASTEIN	--	1942-1944	? OKM	NOT SOLVED	T 564	--	--
RUSSIA	63	NAVY	4-FIGURE 2-PART CODE ENCIPHERED WITH ADDITIVE.	?	RIGA SUBSTITUTE	--	1942 - ?	? OKM	NOT SOLVED	T 564	--	--

CHART NO. 1-2

DOCID: 3560861

TOP SECRET

RESULTS OF EUROPEAN AXIS CRYPTANALYSIS AS LEARNED FROM TICOM SOURCES

(WITH ANNOTATIONS FROM ARMY SECURITY AGENCY SOURCES IN PARENTHESES)

COUNTRY OF ORIGIN		SERVICE	DESCRIPTION OF SYSTEM	NAME OF SYSTEM: COUNTRY OF ORIGIN	AXIS	U.S.A.	DATES OF USE	WHEN ATTACKED AND BY WHOM	RESULTS	TICOM REFERENCE	STATUS OF THE SYSTEM AT ASA	REMARKS
RUSSIA	64	NAVY	4-FIGURE 2-PART CODE ENCIPHERED WITH ADDITIVE.	?	THORN	--	1943-1943	? OKM	READ CURRENTLY PART OF TIME	T 564	--	--
RUSSIA	65	NAVY	4-FIGURE 2-PART CODE ENCIPHERED WITH ADDITIVE.	?	TILSIT	--	? - 1942	? OKM	NOT READ	T 564	--	--
RUSSIA	66	NAVY	4-FIGURE 2-PART CODE ENCIPHERED WITH ADDITIVE.	?	M 5-4561 S	--	1944 - ?	? OKM	NOT SOLVED	T 542 T 564	--	--
RUSSIA	67	NAVY	4-FIGURE 2-PART CODE ENCIPHERED WITH ADDITIVE.	?	?	--	1944 - ?	? OKM	NOT SOLVED	T 564; T 542 D 39	--	--
RUSSIA	68	NAVY	4-FIGURE 2-PART CODE ENCIPHERED BY SUBSTITUTION.	?	ALTA	--	1943 - ?	? OKM	FAIRLY READ	T 562	--	--
RUSSIA	69	NAVY	4-FIGURE 2-PART CODE ENCIPHERED BY SUBSTITUTION.	?	GOLDAP	--	1944 - ?	? OKM	?	T 564	--	--
RUSSIA	70	NAVY	4-FIGURE 2-PART CODE ENCIPHERED BY SUBSTITUTION.	?	GRAUDENZ	--	1943-1945	? OKM	READ TO DIFFERENT EXTENTS AT VARIOUS TIMES.	I 16; I 48 T 542; T 545 T 564 D 39	--	--
RUSSIA	71	NAVY	4-FIGURE 2-PART CODE ENCIPHERED BY SUBSTITUTION.	?	KYBERG	--	1943 - ?	? OKM	?	T 562 I 40	--	--
RUSSIA	72	NAVY	4-FIGURE 2-PART CODE ENCIPHERED BY SUBSTITUTION.	?	SPITTAL	--	1944 ONLY	? OKM	READ	T 564	--	--
RUSSIA	73	NAVY	4-FIGURE 2-PART CODE ENCIPHERED BY SUBSTITUTION.	?	M 4/485/S TANNENBERG	--	1943 - ?	? OKM	?	T 564; T 542	--	--
RUSSIA	74	NAVY	4-FIGURE 2-PART CODE ENCIPHERED BY SUBSTITUTION.	?	VILLACH	--	1942 - ?	1942 OKM	READ	T 564 I 48	--	--
RUSSIA	75	NAVY	4-FIGURE 2-PART CODE ENCIPHERED BY SUBSTITUTION.	?	WERA	--	1943 - ?	? OKM	?	T 564	--	--
RUSSIA	76	NAVY	4-FIGURE 2-PART CODE ENCIPHERED BY SUBSTITUTION.	?	WINDAU	--	JAN 1945 - ?	? OKM	?	I 48 D 39 T 563 T 564	--	--

CHART NO. 1-2

TOP SECRET

DOCID: 3560861

TOP SECRET

RESULTS OF EUROPEAN AXIS CRYPTANALYSIS AS LEARNED FROM TICOM SOURCES

(WITH ANNOTATIONS FROM ARMY SECURITY AGENCY SOURCES IN PARENTHESES)

COUNTRY OF ORIGIN		SERVICE	DESCRIPTION OF SYSTEM	NAME OF SYSTEM: COUNTRY OF ORIGIN	NAME OF SYSTEM: AXIS	NAME OF SYSTEM: U.S.A.	DATES OF USE	WHEN ATTACKED AND BY WHOM	RESULTS	TICOM REFERENCE	STATUS OF THE SYSTEM AT ASA	REMARKS
RUSSIA	77	NAVY	4-FIGURE 2-PART CODE ENCIPHERED BY SUBSTITUTION.	?	M 4/542/S M 4/590/S	--	1943-1944	? OKM	SOLVED	T 542; T 564	--	--
RUSSIA	78	NAVY	4-FIGURE 2-PART CODE ENCIPHERED BY SUBSTITUTION.	?	M 4/544/S	--	1943-1944	? OKM	NOT SOLVED	T 564; T 542	--	--
RUSSIA	79	NAVY	2-FIGURE 3-FIGURE 4-FIGURE 2-PART CODE ENCIPHERED BY SUBSTITUTION.	?	DRONTHEIM	--	1942 - ?	1942 OKM	SOLVED	T 564	--	--
RUSSIA	80	NAVY	3-FIGURE 2-PART CODE ENCIPHERED BY SUBSTITUTION.	?	M 3/333/S	--	1942 - ?	? OKM	?	T 542	--	--
RUSSIA	81	NAVY	3-FIGURE 2-PART CODE ENCIPHERED BY SUBSTITUTION.	T-10-1025	M 3/533/S	--	1943 - ?	? OKM	NOT SOLVED	T 542	--	--
RUSSIA	82	NAVY	3-FIGURE 2-PART CODE ENCIPHERED BY SUBSTITUTION.	?	M 3/533/S	--	1943 - ?	? OKM	NOT SOLVED	T 542	--	--
RUSSIA	83	NAVY	3-FIGURE 2-PART CODE ENCIPHERED BY SUBSTITUTION.	?	M 3/612/S	--	1944 - ?	? OKM	ABOUT 70% READ	T 542	--	--
RUSSIA	84	NAVY	3-FIGURE 1-PART CODE ENCIPHERED BY SUBSTITUTION.	PT 3	BODO	--	1943-1944?	? OKM	SOLVED	I 40 T 564; T 562 T 542; T 544	--	--
RUSSIA	85	NAVY	3-FIGURE 1-PART CODE ENCIPHERED BY SUBSTITUTION.	?	LIBAU	--	1944-1945	? OKM	READ	I 40 D 39 T 563; T 564	--	--
RUSSIA	86	NAVY	3-FIGURE 1-PART CODE ENCIPHERED BY SUBSTITUTION.	PT 13	NORDKAP	--	1943 - ?	? OKM	NORDKAP I PARTIALLY SOLVED; NORDKAP II NOT SOLVED.	T 561; T 562 T 564	--	--
RUSSIA	87	NAVY	3-FIGURE 1-PART CODE ENCIPHERED BY DIGRAPHIC SUBSTITUTION.	?	STOLP	--	1944 - ?	? OKM	?	I 40 T 564 D 39	--	--
RUSSIA	88	NAVY	3-FIGURE 1-PART CODE ENCIPHERED BY SUBSTITUTION.	?	TAUROGGEN	--	1944-1945	? OKM	?	T [illegible] I 40	--	--

CHART NO. [illegible]

TOP SECRET

DOCID: 3560861

~~TOP SECRET~~

RESULTS OF EUROPEAN AXIS CRYPTANALYSIS
AS LEARNED FROM TICOM SOURCES

(WITH ANNOTATIONS FROM ARMY SECURITY AGENCY SOURCES IN PARENTHESES)

COUNTRY OF ORIGIN		SERVICE	DESCRIPTION OF SYSTEM	NAME OF SYSTEM: COUNTRY OF ORIGIN	NAME OF SYSTEM: AXIS	NAME OF SYSTEM: U.S.A.	DATES OF USE	WHEN ATTACKED AND BY WHOM	RESULTS	TICOM REFERENCE	STATUS OF THE SYSTEM AT ASA	REMARKS
RUSSIA	89	NAVY	3-FIGURE 1-PART CODE ENCIPHERED BY SUBSTITUTION.	BTSVVS	M 3/51Ø/S VARDÖ	--	1942-1943	? OKM	READ	I 16; I 4Ø T 542; T 562 T 564	--	--
RUSSIA	9Ø	NAVY: ARTILLERY BATTERIES, GULF OF FINLAND	3-FIGURE 1-PART CODE ENCIPHERED BY SUBSTITUTION.	T-19-SN	M 3/5ØØ/S	--	1943 - ?	? OKM	PARTLY READ	T 542	--	--
RUSSIA	91	NAVY	3-FIGURE 1-PART CODE ENCIPHERED BY SUBSTITUTION OR BY SUBSTITUTION PLUS ADDITIVE.	?	M 3/4ØØ/S	--	APRIL-MAY 1943	? OKM	4Ø% OF VALUES KNOWN	T 542	--	--
RUSSIA	92	NAVY	3-FIGURE 1-PART CODE ENCIPHERED WITH GENERATED ADDITIVE AND SUBSTITUTION.	?	M 3/6Ø2/S	--	1944 - ?	? OKM	NOT SOLVED	T 542	--	--
RUSSIA	93	NAVY	3-FIGURE 1-PART CODE, ENCIPHERED BY SUBSTITUTION TO 15 AUGUST 1942. BY ADDITIVE THEREAFTER.	?	MASUREN	--	1941-1943	1942 FINNS 1942 OKM	READ PRACTICALLY 1ØØ%	T 564 I 12; I 16	--	--
RUSSIA	94	NAVY	3-FIGURE 2-PART CODE ENCIPHERED BY SUBSTITUTION AND ADDITIVE.	?	DANZIG	--	1942-1944	? OKM	NOT SOLVED	T 564	--	--
RUSSIA	95	NAVY	3-FIGURE 2-PART CODE ENCIPHERED WITH ADDITIVE.	?	LYBERG	--	1943 - ?	? OKM	?	T 564	--	--
RUSSIA	96	NAVY	3-FIGURE 2-PART CODE ENCIPHERED BY SUBSTITUTION.	?	BUKET	--	MAY-DEC 1943	? OKM	?	T 564	--	--
RUSSIA	97	NAVY	3-FIGURE 2-PART CODE ENCIPHERED BY SUBSTITUTION.	?	INSTERBURG	--	1942 - ?	? OKM	READ WHEN TRAFFIC WAS SUFFICIENT	T 564	--	--
RUSSIA	98	NAVY	3-FIGURE 2-PART CODE ENCIPHERED BY SUBSTITUTION.	?	VUK MARBURG	--	1942-1943	1942 OKM	READ CURRENTLY PART OF TIME	T 564	--	--
RUSSIA	99	NAVY	3-FIGURE 2-PART CODE ENCIPHERED BY SUBSTITUTION.	?	RIGA	--	6 JULY 1942-25 JULY 1942	1942 OKM	READ CURRENTLY	T 564	--	--
RUSSIA	1ØØ	NAVY	3-FIGURE 2-PART CODE ENCIPHERED BY SUBSTITUTION.	?	SALZBURG	--	1941-1942	1942 OKM	READ CURRENTLY PART OF TIME	T 564 I 4Ø	--	--

CHART NO. 1-2

~~TOP SECRET~~

RESULTS OF EUROPEAN AXIS CRYPTANALYSIS AS LEARNED FROM TICOM SOURCES

(WITH ANNOTATIONS FROM ARMY SECURITY AGENCY SOURCES IN PARENTHESES)

COUNTRY OF ORIGIN		SERVICE	DESCRIPTION OF SYSTEM	NAME OF SYSTEM			DATES OF USE	WHEN ATTACKED AND BY WHOM	RESULTS	TICOM REFERENCE	STATUS OF THE SYSTEM AT ASA	REMARKS
				COUNTRY OF ORIGIN	AXIS	U.S.A.						
RUSSIA	1Ø1	NAVY	3-FIGURE ?-PART CODE ENCIPHERED BY SUBSTITUTION.	?	SEELAND	--	1943-1945	? OKM	?	I 4Ø; I 16 I 55	--	--
RUSSIA	1Ø2	NAVY	3-FIGURE ?-PART CODE ENCIPHERED BY SUBSTITUTION.	PT 4	SSS	--	8 OCTOBER 1943 -16 OCTOBER 1943	? OKM	NOT SOLVED	T 562; T 564	--	--
RUSSIA	1Ø3	NAVY	3-FIGURE ?-PART CODE ENCIPHERED BY SUBSTITUTION.	?	STAVANGER	--	1943 - ?	? OKM	?	T 562	--	--
RUSSIA	1Ø4	NAVY	3-FIGURE ?-PART CODE ENCIPHERED BY SUBSTITUTION.	?	M 3/468/S	--	1942-1943	? OKM	READ	T 542	--	--
RUSSIA	1Ø5	NAVY	3-FIGURE ?-PART CODE ENCIPHERED BY SUBSTITUTION.	?	M 3/519/S	--	1943 - ?	? OKM	?	T 542	--	--
RUSSIA	1Ø6	NAVY	3-FIGURE ?-PART CODE ENCIPHERED BY SUBSTITUTION.	D.S. 17	M 3/524/S	--	AUGUST-NOVEMBER 1943	? OKM	NOT SOLVED	T 542	--	--
RUSSIA	1Ø7	NAVY	3-FIGURE ?-PART CODE ENCIPHERED BY SUBSTITUTION.	?	M 3/563/S	--	1943-1944	? OKM	READ ALMOST 1ØØ%	T 542	--	--
RUSSIA	1Ø8	NAVY	3-FIGURE ?-PART CODE ENCIPHERED BY SUBSTITUTION.	?	?	--	MARCH-JUNE 1941	? OKM	SOLVED	T 564	--	--
RUSSIA	1Ø9	NAVY: COASTAL AND RAILWAY BATTERIES ON GULF OF FINLAND	3-FIGURE ?-PART CODE ENCIPHERED BY SUBSTITUTION.	?	?	--	1942-1943	1942 OKM	READ	T 564	--	--
RUSSIA	11Ø	NAVY: BATTERIES OF 4Ø2 AND 435 DIVISIONS AND BRIGADE COMMUNICATIONS OFFICERS	3-FIGURE ?-PART CODE ENCIPHERED BY SUBSTITUTION.	?	?	--	1943 - ?	1943 OKM	SOLVED	T 564	--	--
RUSSIA	111	NAVY	3-FIGURE ?-PART CODE ENCIPHERED BY SUBSTITUTION.	?	?	--	1944 - ?	? OKM	NOT READ	T 564	--	--
RUSSIA	112	NAVY	3-FIGURE ?-PART CODE ENCIPHERED BY SUBSTITUTION.	?	?	--	1944 - ?	? OKM	READ	T 564	--	--

CHART NO. 1-2

DOCID: 3560861

TOP SECRET

RESULTS OF EUROPEAN AXIS CRYPTANALYSIS
AS LEARNED FROM TICOM SOURCES
(WITH ANNOTATIONS FROM ARMY SECURITY AGENCY SOURCES IN PARENTHESES)

COUNTRY OF ORIGIN		SERVICE	DESCRIPTION OF SYSTEM	NAME OF SYSTEM: COUNTRY OF ORIGIN	AXIS	U.S.A.	DATES OF USE	WHEN ATTACKED AND BY WHOM	RESULTS	TICOM REFERENCE	STATUS OF THE SYSTEM AT ASA	REMARKS
RUSSIA	113	NAVY	3-FIGURE ?-PART CODE	?	FUVA	--	1941-1942	? OKM	NOT READ	T 564	--	--
RUSSIA	114	NAVY	2-FIGURE ?-PART CODE ENCIPHERED BY SUBSTITUTION.	?	TANA	--	1943 - ?	? OKM	?	T 562	--	--
RUSSIA	115	NAVY	2-FIGURE ?-PART CODE ENCIPHERED BY SUBSTITUTION.	?	M 2/249/S	--	NOV-DEC 1942	1942 OKM	SOLVED	T 564; T 542	--	--
RUSSIA	116	NAVY	?-PART CODE	?	M 5/500/S	--	1943 - ?	? OKM	?	T 542	--	--
RUSSIA	117	ARMY	2-FIGURE ?-PART FIELD CODE. MADE IN 10 X 10 SQUARES. DAILY CHANGING KEY.	?	?	--	? - ?	? SIM	READ	IF 1517	--	--
~~RUSSIA~~	~~118~~	~~?~~	~~?-PART CODE.~~	?	?	--	? - ?	? SIS	100% COMPROMISED.	IF 1506	--	--
SAUDI ARABIA	1	DIPLOMATIC	?-PART CODE TRANSMITTED IN 5-FIGURE GROUPS.	?	?	?	?-1944-1945	? GERMANS	NOT SOLVED	T 430	(UNKNOWN)	--
SAUDI ARABIA	2	DIPLOMATIC	SUBSTITUTION CIPHER--2 DIGITS PER LETTER. TRAFFIC WAS SMALL.	?	?	(ABD) OR (ABB)	(ABD: 1943-CURRENT) (ABB: ?-1945-CURRENT)	? SIM	READ	IF 1519 P 4	(ABD: BROKEN IN 1945. 100% READABLE. ABB: BROKEN IN 1944. 100% READABLE.)	--
SAUDI ARABIA	3	DIPLOMATIC	SUBSTITUTION CIPHER--2 DIGITS PER LETTER. SEE ITEM 2.	?	?	(ABD)	(?-1943-CURRENT)	1942 PERS Z S	READ	T 2052	(BROKEN IN 1945. NOW 100% READABLE.)	--

CHART NO. 1-2

TOP SECRET

RESULTS OF EUROPEAN AXIS CRYPTANALYSIS AS LEARNED FROM TICOM SOURCES

(WITH ANNOTATIONS FROM ARMY SECURITY AGENCY SOURCES IN PARENTHESES)

COUNTRY OF ORIGIN		SERVICE	DESCRIPTION OF SYSTEM	NAME OF SYSTEM			DATES OF USE	WHEN ATTACKED AND BY WHOM	RESULTS	TICOM REFERENCE	STATUS OF THE SYSTEM AT ASA	REMARKS
				COUNTRY OF ORIGIN	AXIS	U.S.A.						
SPAIN	1	DIPLOMATIC	4-FIGURE 2-PART CODE, ENCIPHERED BY MEANS OF A 1ØØ-GROUP-LONG ENCIPHER KEY.	(CLAVE 1537 OR CLAVE 1539)	?	(SPA?) OR (SPE?)	(1938-CURRENT)	1939 SIM	BROKEN	IF 1517 IF 1518	(BOTH COMPROMISED)	--
SPAIN	2	DIPLOMATIC	4-FIGURE 2-PART CODE.	?	SP. 234	?	? - ?	? PERS Z S	RECOVERED 5%	T 1358	(UNKNOWN)	--
SPAIN	3	DIPLOMATIC	4-FIGURE 2-PART CODE.	?	SP. 1339	?	? - ?	? PERS Z S	RECOVERED 2Ø%-25%	T 1383 T 2534	(UNKNOWN)	--
SPAIN	4	DIPLOMATIC	4-FIGURE 2-PART CODE.	?	?	?	? - ?	? ?	RECOVERED LESS THAN 1%	T 1361	(UNKNOWN)	--
SPAIN	5	DIPLOMATIC	4-FIGURE (1-PART CODE REPAGINATED.) 1Ø,ØØØ GROUPS. LAST TWO PLACES OF EACH GROUP ARE READ FIRST.	(Ø4)	"Ø4"	(SPB)	(1915-CURRENT)	1927, 1942 PERS Z S	RECOVERED 3Ø% - 4Ø%	T 1382 D 16, REPORT 2, P 3	(COMPROMISED. BEING READ.)	--
SPAIN	6	DIPLOMATIC	4-FIGURE 1-PART CODE, RANDOMIZED ON PAGES. 1Ø,ØØØ GROUPS.	?	"3Ø1"	?	?-1927-?	1927 PERS Z S	RECOVERED 5Ø% - 6Ø%	T 1373 D 16, REPORT 1, P 2	(UNKNOWN)	--
SPAIN	7	CONSULAR	4-FIGURE 1-PART CODE, RANDOMIZED ON PAGES. 1Ø,ØØØ GROUPS.	?	"311"	?	?-1927-?	1927 PERS Z S	RECOVERED 5Ø% - 6Ø%	T 1377 T 1378 T 1382 D 16, REPORT 1, P 2	(UNKNOWN)	--
SPAIN	8	CONSULAR	4-FIGURE 1-PART CODE, RANDOMIZED ON PAGES.	?	"156"	?	?-1938-?	? ?	RECOVERED 15% - 2Ø%	T 125Ø T 1251	(UNKNOWN)	--
SPAIN	9	?	4-FIGURE 1-PART CODE, RANDOMIZED ON PAGES.	?	"CODE 1Ø7"	?	? - ?	? ?	RECOVERED 8Ø% - 85%	T 1344	(UNKNOWN)	--
SPAIN	1Ø	?	4-FIGURE 1-PART CODE.	?	"1Ø8"	?	? - ?	? PERS Z S	RECOVERED LESS THAN 1%	T 1211 T 3Ø11	(UNKNOWN)	--
SPAIN	11	?	4-FIGURE 1-PART CODE, RANDOMIZED ON PAGES.	?	"CODE 1Ø9"	?	? - ?	? PERS Z S	RECOVERED 5Ø% - 6Ø%	T 1212 T 1213	(UNKNOWN)	--

CHART NO. 1-2

DOCID: 3560861

TOP SECRET

RESULTS OF EUROPEAN AXIS CRYPTANALYSIS AS LEARNED FROM TICOM SOURCES

(WITH ANNOTATIONS FROM ARMY SECURITY AGENCY SOURCES IN PARENTHESES)

COUNTRY OF ORIGIN	SERVICE	DESCRIPTION OF SYSTEM	NAME OF SYSTEM: COUNTRY OF ORIGIN	NAME OF SYSTEM: AXIS	NAME OF SYSTEM: U.S.A.	DATES OF USE	WHEN ATTACKED AND BY WHOM	RESULTS	TICOM REFERENCE	STATUS OF THE SYSTEM AT ASA	REMARKS
SPAIN 12	?	4-FIGURE 1-PART CODE, RANDOMIZED ON PAGES.	?	CODE 111	?	? - ?	? PERS Z S	RECOVERED 40% - 50%	T 1214	(UNKNOWN)	--
SPAIN 13	?	4-FIGURE 1-PART CODE, RANDOMIZED ON PAGES.	?	"119"	?	? - ?	? PERS Z S	RECOVERED 50% - 60%	T 1224	(UNKNOWN)	--
SPAIN 14	?	4-FIGURE 1-PART CODE.	?	"124"	?	? - ?	? PERS Z S	RECOVERED 20%	T 1226	(UNKNOWN)	--
SPAIN 15	?	4-FIGURE 1-PART CODE, RANDOMIZED ON PAGES.	?	"127"	?	? - ?	? PERS Z S	RECOVERED 10% - 20%	T 1345	(UNKNOWN)	--
SPAIN 16	?	4-FIGURE 1-PART CODE, RANDOMIZED ON PAGES.	?	SP. 134	?	? - ?	? PERS Z S	RECOVERED LESS THAN 1%	T 1346	(UNKNOWN)	--
SPAIN 17	?	4-FIGURE 1-PART CODE, RANDOMIZED ON PAGES.	?	"152"	?	? - ?	? PERS Z S	RECOVERED LESS THAN 5%	T 1256	(UNKNOWN)	--
SPAIN 18	?	4-FIGURE 1-PART CODE.	?	"157"	?	? - ?	? PERS Z S	RECOVERED 50% - 60%	T 1242 T 1243	(UNKNOWN)	--
SPAIN 19	?	4-FIGURE 1-PART CODE, RANDOMIZED ON PAGES.	?	"166"	?	? - ?	? PERS Z S	RECOVERED 5%	T 1239 T 1255	(UNKNOWN)	--
SPAIN 20	?	4-FIGURE 1-PART CODE, RANDOMIZED ON PAGES.	?	"167"	?	?-1932-?	? PERS Z S	RECOVERED 50% - 60%	T 1244 T 1245 T 1246	(UNKNOWN)	--
SPAIN 21	?	4-FIGURE 1-PART CODE, RANDOMIZED ON PAGES.	?	"169"	?	? - ?	? PERS Z S	RECOVERED 25%	T 1240	(UNKNOWN)	--
~~SPAIN 22~~	?	4-FIGURE 1-PART CODE.	?	"SP. 172"	?	? - ?	? PERS Z S	RECOVERED 40%	T 1234 T 1233 T 1347	(UNKNOWN)	--
SPAIN 23	?	4-FIGURE 1-PART CODE, RANDOMIZED ON PAGES.	?	"SP. 175"	?	? - ?	? PERS Z S	RECOVERED 10%	T 1348	(UNKNOWN)	--

CHART NO. [illegible]

TOP SECRET

RESULTS OF EUROPEAN AXIS CRYPTANALYSIS
AS LEARNED FROM TICOM SOURCES
(WITH ANNOTATIONS FROM ARMY SECURITY AGENCY SOURCES IN PARENTHESES)

COUNTRY OF ORIGIN		SERVICE	DESCRIPTION OF SYSTEM	NAME OF SYSTEM			DATES OF USE	WHEN ATTACKED AND BY WHOM	RESULTS	TICOM REFERENCE	STATUS OF THE SYSTEM AT ASA	REMARKS
				COUNTRY OF ORIGIN	AXIS	U.S.A.						
SPAIN	24	?	4-FIGURE 1-PART CODE, RANDOMIZED ON PAGES.	?	"SP. 179"	?	? - ?	? ?	RECOVERED LESS THAN 10%	T 1349	(UNKNOWN)	--
SPAIN	25	?	4-FIGURE 1-PART CODE, RANDOMIZED ON PAGES.	?	"213"	?	? - ?	? ?	RECOVERED 5% - 10%	T 1352	(UNKNOWN)	--
SPAIN	26	?	4-FIGURE 1-PART CODE, RANDOMIZED ON PAGES.	?	"SP. 217"	?	? - ?	? ?	RECOVERED 60% - 75%	T 1353 T 1354	(UNKNOWN)	--
SPAIN	27	?	4-FIGURE 1-PART CODE.	?	"SP. 229"	?	? - ?	? ?	RECOVERED LESS THAN 1%	T 1357	(UNKNOWN)	--
SPAIN	28	?	4-FIGURE 1-PART CODE.	?	"239"	?	? - ?	? ?	RECOVERED 5%	T 1359	(UNKNOWN)	--
SPAIN	29	?	4-FIGURE 1-PART CODE, REPAGINATED.	?	"SP. 243"	?	? - ?	? ?	RECOVERED LESS THAN 5%	T 1360	(UNKNOWN)	--
SPAIN	30	?	4-FIGURE 1-PART CODE, REPAGINATED.	?	"SP. 249"	?	? - ?	? ?	RECOVERED 5%	T 1362	(UNKNOWN)	--
SPAIN	31	?	4-FIGURE 1-PART CODE, REPAGINATED.	?	"261"	?	? - ?	? ?	RECOVERED 60%	T 1370	(UNKNOWN)	--
SPAIN	32	?	4-FIGURE 1-PART CODE.	?	"271"	?	?-1937-?	? ?	RECOVERED LESS THAN 5%	T 1371	(UNKNOWN)	--
SPAIN	33	?	4-FIGURE 1-PART CODE, RANDOMIZED ON PAGES.	?	?	?	? - ?	? PERS Z S	RECOVERED 30% - 40%	T 1210	(UNKNOWN)	--
SPAIN	34	?	4-FIGURE 1-PART CODE.	?	?	?	? - ?	? ?	RECOVERED 70%	T 1329	(UNKNOWN)	--
SPAIN	35	?	4-FIGURE 1-PART CODE.	?	?	?	? - ?	? ?	RECOVERED 20% - 30%	T 1384	(UNKNOWN)	--
SPAIN	36	?	4-FIGURE 1-PART CODE.	?	?	?	? - ?	? ?	RECOVERED 65% - 70%	T 1343	(UNKNOWN)	--
SPAIN	37	?	4-FIGURE 1-PART CODE, RANDOMIZED ON PAGES.	?	?	?	? - ?	? ?	RECOVERED 50%	T 1372	(UNKNOWN)	--

DOCID: 3560861

TOP SECRET

RESULTS OF EUROPEAN AXIS CRYPTANALYSIS
AS LEARNED FROM TICOM SOURCES
(WITH ANNOTATIONS FROM ARMY SECURITY AGENCY SOURCES IN PARENTHESES)

COUNTRY OF ORIGIN		SERVICE	DESCRIPTION OF SYSTEM	NAME OF SYSTEM			DATES OF USE	WHEN ATTACKED AND BY WHOM	RESULTS	TICOM REFERENCE	STATUS OF THE SYSTEM AT ASA	REMARKS
				COUNTRY OF ORIGIN	AXIS	U.S.A.						
SPAIN	38	?	4-FIGURE 1-PART CODE, RANDOMIZED ON PAGES.	?	?	?	? - ?	? ?	RECOVERED 1Ø% - 15%	T 12Ø8	(UNKNOWN)	--
SPAIN	39	?	4-FIGURE 1-PART CODE.	?	"113"	?	? - ?	? ?	RECOVERED 5Ø%	T 1215; T 1216 T 1217; T 1218 T 1219; T 122Ø T 1221; T 1222	(UNKNOWN)	--
SPAIN	4Ø	?	4-FIGURE 1-PART CODE.	?	"SP. 121"	?	? - ?	? ?	RECOVERED 1Ø% - 15%	T 1225	(UNKNOWN)	--
SPAIN	41	?	4-FIGURE 1-PART CODE.	?	"14Ø"	?	? - ?	? ?	RECOVERED 2Ø% - 25%	T 1257	(UNKNOWN)	--
SPAIN	42	?	4-FIGURE 1-PART CODE.	?	"148"	?	? - ?	? ?	RECOVERED 1Ø%	T 1238	(UNKNOWN)	--
SPAIN	43	?	4-FIGURE 1-PART CODE.	?	"165"	?	? - ?	? ?	RECOVERED 1Ø% - 15%	T 126Ø	(UNKNOWN)	--
SPAIN	44	?	4-FIGURE 1-PART CODE.	?	"N.3Ø3 SP"	?	? - ?	? ?	RECOVERED 5Ø% - 6Ø%	T 1375	(UNKNOWN)	--
SPAIN	45	?	4-FIGURE ?-PART CODE.	?	"SP. 73"	?	? - ?	? ?	NO SUCCESS	T 1263	(UNKNOWN)	--
SPAIN	46	?	4-FIGURE ?-PART CODE.	?	"112"	?	? - ?	? ?	NO SUCCESS	T 1262	(UNKNOWN)	--
SPAIN	47	?	4-FIGURE ?-PART CODE.	?	"114"	?	? - ?	? ?	NO SUCCESS	T 1261	(UNKNOWN)	--
SPAIN	48	?	4-FIGURE ?-PART CODE.	?	"118"	?	? - ?	? ?	NO SUCCESS	T 1223	(UNKNOWN)	--
SPAIN	49	?	4-FIGURE ?-PART CODE.	?	"126"	?	? - ?	? ?	NO SUCCESS	T 1227	(UNKNOWN)	--
SPAIN	5Ø	?	4-FIGURE ?-PART CODE.	?	"SP. 128"	?	? - ?	? ?	NO SUCCESS	T 1236	(UNKNOWN)	--

CHART NO. 1-2

TOP SECRET

RESULTS OF EUROPEAN AXIS CRYPTANALYSIS AS LEARNED FROM TICOM SOURCES

(WITH ANNOTATIONS FROM ARMY SECURITY AGENCY SOURCES IN PARENTHESES)

COUNTRY OF ORIGIN		SERVICE	DESCRIPTION OF SYSTEM	NAME OF SYSTEM			DATES OF USE	WHEN ATTACKED AND BY WHOM	RESULTS	TICOM REFERENCE	STATUS OF THE SYSTEM AT ASA	REMARKS
				COUNTRY OF ORIGIN	AXIS	U.S.A.						
SPAIN	51	?	4-FIGURE ?-PART CODE.	?	"SP. 138"	?	? - ?	? ?	RECOVERED LESS THAN 5%	T 1252	(UNKNOWN)	--
SPAIN	52	?	4-FIGURE ?-PART CODE.	?	"SP. 142"	?	? - ?	? ?	RECOVERED LESS THAN 1%	T 1253	(UNKNOWN)	--
SPAIN	53	?	4-FIGURE ?-PART CODE.	?	"144"	?	? - ?	? ?	RECOVERED ABOUT 1%	T 1254	(UNKNOWN)	--
SPAIN	54	?	4-FIGURE ?-PART CODE.	?	"155"	?	1931-1936-?	? ?	NO SUCCESS	T 1249	(UNKNOWN)	--
SPAIN	55	?	4-FIGURE ?-PART CODE.	?	"161"	?	? - ?	? ?	RECOVERED LESS THAN 3%	T 1259	(UNKNOWN)	--
SPAIN	56	?	4-FIGURE ?-PART CODE.	?	"164"	?	? - ?	? ?	NO SUCCESS	T 1247	(UNKNOWN)	--
SPAIN	57	?	4-FIGURE ?-PART CODE.	?	"SP. 170"	?	? - ?	? ?	NO SUCCESS	T 1248	(UNKNOWN)	--
SPAIN	58	?	4-FIGURE ?-PART CODE.	?	"SP. 171"	?	? - ?	? ?	NO SUCCESS	T 1228	(UNKNOWN)	--
SPAIN	59	?	4-FIGURE ?-PART CODE.	?	"VALENCIA 174"	?	? - ?	? ?	RECOVERED 5% - 10%	T 1235	(UNKNOWN)	--
SPAIN	60	?	4-FIGURE ?-PART CODE.	?	"SP. 187"	?	? - ?	? ?	VERY LITTLE SUCCESS	T 1350	(UNKNOWN)	--
SPAIN	61	?	4-FIGURE ?-PART CODE.	?	"SP. 209"	?	? - ?	? ?	RECOVERED LESS THAN 1%	T 1351	(UNKNOWN)	--
SPAIN	62	?	4-FIGURE ?-PART CODE.	?	"253"	?	? - ?	? ?	RECOVERED 60% - 70%	T 1363 T 1364 T 1365 T 1366 T 1367 T 1368	(UNKNOWN)	--
SPAIN	63	?	4-FIGURE ?-PART CODE.	?	"302"	?	? - ?	? ?	RECOVERED LESS THAN 1%	T 1374	(UNKNOWN)	--

CHART NO. 1-2

DOCID: 3560861

TOP SECRET

RESULTS OF EUROPEAN AXIS CRYPTANALYSIS
AS LEARNED FROM TICOM SOURCES
(WITH ANNOTATIONS FROM ARMY SECURITY AGENCY SOURCES IN PARENTHESES)

COUNTRY OF ORIGIN	SERVICE	DESCRIPTION OF SYSTEM	NAME OF SYSTEM: COUNTRY OF ORIGIN	NAME OF SYSTEM: AXIS	NAME OF SYSTEM: U.S.A.	DATES OF USE	WHEN ATTACKED AND BY WHOM	RESULTS	TICOM REFERENCE	STATUS OF THE SYSTEM AT ASA	REMARKS
SPAIN 64	?	4-FIGURE ?-PART CODE.	?	"SP. 3Ø6"	?	? - ?	? ?	RECOVERED LESS THAN 1%	T 1376	(UNKNOWN)	--
SPAIN 65	?	4-FIGURE ?-PART CODE.	?	"SP. 345"	?	? - ?	? ?	RECOVERED LESS THAN 3%	T 1379	(UNKNOWN)	--
SPAIN 66	?	4-FIGURE ?-PART CODE.	?	"4Ø2"	?	? - ?	? ?	RECOVERED LESS THAN 1%	T 138Ø	(UNKNOWN)	--
SPAIN 67	?	4-FIGURE ?-PART CODE.	?	"754 41"	?	? - ?	? ?	NO SUCCESS	T 1381	(UNKNOWN)	--
SPAIN 68	?	4-FIGURE ?-PART CODE.	?	?	?	? - ?	? ?	?	T 1265	(UNKNOWN)	--
SPAIN 69	?	4-FIGURE ?-PART CODE.	?	?	?	? - ?	? ?	RECOVERED LESS THAN 1%	T 12Ø9	(UNKNOWN)	--
SPAIN 7Ø	DIPLOMATIC	2-PART CODE ENCIPHERED BY 1ØØ-GROUP KEY.	?	?	?	1939 - ?	? SIM	NOT READ	IF 1518	(UNIDENTIFIED)	--
SPAIN 71	NAVAL	CIPHER	?	CIPHER NO. 13	?	? - ?	? SIS	1ØØ% COMPROMISED	IF 15Ø6	(UNKNOWN)	--
SPAIN 72	?	4-FIGURE ?-PART CODE.	?	?	?	1941-1942?	1941 SIM	NOT READ	IF 1524	(UNIDENTIFIED)	--
SPAIN REPUBLICAN		GENERAL REMARKS ON SPAIN REPUBLICAN: DESPITE BASIC SIMILARITIES THE SYSTEMS DIFFERED IN INDICATOR AND APPARENTLY IN TYPE OF TEXT.									
SPAIN REPUBLICAN 73	MILITARY	SUBSTITUTION USING DIGRAPHS ØØ TO 99 ARRANGED IN COLUMNS AGAINST AN ALPHABET STRIP CONTAINING 3 NULLS.	?	R. 5	?	? - 1938	1938 SIS	READ	IF 15Ø4	(UNKNOWN)	--
SPAIN REPUBLICAN 74	MILITARY	DIGRAPHIC SUBSTITUTION USING SLIDING STRIPS.	?	N.	?	?-1938-?	1938 SIS	READ	IF 15Ø4	(UNKNOWN)	--
SPAIN REPUBLICAN 75	MILITARY	DIGRAPHIC SUBSTITUTION USING SLIDING STRIPS.	?	S.N	?	?-1938-?	1938 SIS	READ	IF 15Ø4	(UNKNOWN)	--
SPAIN REPUBLICAN 76	MILITARY	DIGRAPHIC SUBSTITUTION USING SLIDING STRIPS.	?	5 C.R	?	?-1938-?	1938 SIS	READ	IF 15Ø4	(UNKNOWN)	--
SPAIN REPUBLICAN 77	MILITARY	DIGRAPHIC SUBSTITUTION, 1Ø X 1Ø SQUARE AND COORDINATE SLIDING STRIPS 17 VALUES LONG. SUBSTITUTION BY BOTH LETTERS AND DIGITS.	?	S.N.D	?	?-1938-?	1938 SIS	READ	IF 15Ø4	(UNKNOWN)	--
SPAIN REPUBLICAN 78	MILITARY	SUBSTITUTION BY DIGRAPHS ØØ-99. ONE HUNDRED DIFFERENT KEYS WERE USED IN ARRANGING THE SUBSTITUTION.	?	S.O.	?	?-1938-?	1938 SIS	READ	IF 15Ø4	(UNKNOWN)	--

TOP SECRET

DOCID: 3560861

~~TOP SECRET~~

RESULTS OF EUROPEAN AXIS CRYPTANALYSIS
AS LEARNED FROM TICOM SOURCES
(WITH ANNOTATIONS FROM ARMY SECURITY AGENCY SOURCES IN PARENTHESES)

COUNTRY OF ORIGIN	SERVICE	DESCRIPTION OF SYSTEM	NAME OF SYSTEM: COUNTRY OF ORIGIN	NAME OF SYSTEM: AXIS	NAME OF SYSTEM: U.S.A.	DATES OF USE	WHEN ATTACKED AND BY WHOM	RESULTS	TICOM REFERENCE	STATUS OF THE SYSTEM AT ASA	REMARKS
SPAIN REPUBLICAN 79	MILITARY	DIGRAPHIC SUBSTITUTION USING 10 X 10 SQUARE AND COORDINATE SLIDING STRIPS. SUBSTITUTION BY BOTH LETTERS AND FIGURES.	?	S. MARZO	?	?-1938-?	1938 SIS	READ	IF 1504	(UNKNOWN)	--
SPAIN REPUBLICAN 80	MILITARY	DIGRAPHIC SUBSTITUTION USING 13 X 13 SQUARE AND COORDINATE SLIDING STRIPS. SUBSTITUTION BY MIXED ALPHABETS AND FIGURES.	?	"AIR ALARM"	?	?-1938-?	1938 SIS	READ	IF 1504	(UNKNOWN)	--

CHART NO. 1-?

~~TOP SECRET~~

DOCID: 3560861

TOP SECRET

RESULTS OF EUROPEAN AXIS CRYPTANALYSIS AS LEARNED FROM TICOM SOURCES

(WITH ANNOTATIONS FROM ARMY SECURITY AGENCY SOURCES IN PARENTHESES)

COUNTRY OF ORIGIN		SERVICE	DESCRIPTION OF SYSTEM	NAME OF SYSTEM			DATES OF USE	WHEN ATTACKED AND BY WHOM	RESULTS	TICOM REFERENCE	STATUS OF THE SYSTEM AT ASA	REMARKS
				COUNTRY OF ORIGIN	AXIS	U.S.A.						
SWEDEN	1	(DIPLOMATIC)	HAGELIN -- SMALL MACHINE, SIMILAR TO M-2Ø9. 6 WHEELS.	?	SMI	(SWA)	? - ?	AFTER SPRING 1944 OKH ? OKW	NOT BROKEN BUT MESSAGES IN DEPTH COULD BE READ	I 142 P 4	(NOT READABLE -- NOT BEING WORKED ON)	--
SWEDEN	2	CONSULAR	MACHINE THOUGHT TO HAVE 15-NUMBERED WHEELS. CALLED BY PW THE KRYTAA BUT MAY HAVE MEANT THE KRYHA OR HAGELIN.	?	?	?	? - ?	? FA	NO SUCCESS	I 162 P 3	(UNKNOWN IF IT HAD 15 NUMBERED WHEELS.)	THOUGHT BY FA TO BE 1ØØ% SECURE
SWEDEN	3	?	TRAFFIC THOUGHT TO HAVE BEEN HAGELIN. 1ST MONTH 25-LETTER ALPHABET USED; 2ND MONTH 26-LETTER ALPHABET USED.	?	?	?	? - ?	1941, AGAIN IN 1944 PERS Z S	NOT READ	I 22 P 7	(TRAFFIC USING 25-LETTER ALPHABET KNOWN AS SWC.)	--
SWEDEN	4	ARMY	HAGELIN -- LARGE MACHINE. THOUGHT BY GERMANS TO HAVE BEEN SIMILAR TO ENIGMA.	?	?	?	? - ?	? OKH	NOT READ BY OKH	I 142 P 4	(UNKNOWN)	--
SWEDEN	5	NAVY	APPARENTLY A MACHINE CIPHER. 4-LETTER SYSTEM.	?	"4-LETTER SYSTEM"	?	? - 1944 - ?	1944 OKM	PROBABLY NO SUCCESS -- SCANT MATERIAL	D 38 P 3, 4	(UNKNOWN)	--
SWEDEN	6	NAVY	MACHINE CIPHER.	?	KARL	?	? - 1944 - ?	1944 OKM	NO SUCCESS	D 38 P 3	(UNKNOWN)	--
SWEDEN	7	NAVY	MACHINE CIPHER.	?	PAUL	?	? - 1944 - ?	1944 OKM	NO SUCCESS	D 38 P 3	(UNKNOWN)	--
SWEDEN	8	NAVY	MACHINE CIPHER	?	RICHARD	?	? - 1944 - ?	1944 OKM	NO SUCCESS	D 38 P 3	(UNKNOWN)	--
SWEDEN	9	NAVY	MACHINE CIPHER	?	OTTO	?	? - 1944 - ?	1944 OKM	MONITORED 1944, 1945. PROBABLY NO SUCCESS	D 38 PP 2,3	(UNKNOWN)	--
SWEDEN	1Ø	NAVY	MACHINE CIPHER	?	SOFHIE	?	? - 1945 - ?	1945 OKM	PROBABLY NO SUCCESS -- SCANT MATERIAL	D 38 P 3	(UNKNOWN)	--
SWEDEN	11	NAVY	5-LETTER ?-PART CODE CVCCV. PROBABLY A COVER-NAME SYSTEM.	?	MORSE	?	? - 1944 - ?	1944 OKM	PROBABLY NO SUCCESS	D 38 P 5	(UNKNOWN)	--
SWEDEN	12	NAVY	5-LETTER ? CODE. CVCVC.	?	SEDER	?	? - 1944 - ?	1945 OKM	?	D 38 P 4	(UNKNOWN)	--

CHART NO. 1-2

TOP SECRET

DOCID: 3560861

TOP SECRET

RESULTS OF EUROPEAN AXIS CRYPTANALYSIS AS LEARNED FROM TICOM SOURCES

(WITH ANNOTATIONS FROM ARMY SECURITY AGENCY SOURCES IN PARENTHESES)

COUNTRY OF ORIGIN		SERVICE	DESCRIPTION OF SYSTEM	NAME OF SYSTEM: COUNTRY OF ORIGIN	NAME OF SYSTEM: AXIS	NAME OF SYSTEM: U.S.A.	DATES OF USE	WHEN ATTACKED AND BY WHOM	RESULTS	TICOM REFERENCE	STATUS OF THE SYSTEM AT ASA	REMARKS
SWEDEN	13	?	3-LETTER ?-PART CODE.	?	SASSNITZ	?	? - 1944 - ?	1945 OKM	BROKEN	D 38 P 4	(UNKNOWN)	--
SWEDEN	14	ARMY	3-LETTER ?-PART FIELD CODE.	?	SC2	?	? - ?	1943 OKH	READ	IF 12Ø P 5	(NO MILITARY SYSTEMS WORKED ON)	--
SWEDEN	15	ARMY	3-LETTER PARTIALLY 1-PART UNENCIPHERED FIELD CODE.	?	SC3	?	? - ?	1943 OKH	READ	IF 12Ø P 5	(NO MILITARY TRAFFIC WORKED ON)	--
SWEDEN	16	ARMY	3-LETTER 1-PART CODE.	?	SC4	?	? - ?	1943 OKH	READ	IF 12Ø P 5	(NO MILITARY TRAFFIC WORKED ON)	--
SWEDEN	17	MILITARY	2-LETTER AND 3-LETTER CODES.	?	?	?	? - ?	AFTER 1944 OKH	READ	I 55 P 11	(NO MILITARY SYSTEMS WORKED ON)	--
SWEDEN	18	?	1-FIGURE 2-LETTER CODE, ?-PART, 475 GROUPS.	?	"FIGURE-LETTER-LETTER"	?	? - 1945 - ?	1945 OKM	INVESTIGATED	D 38 P 5	(UNKNOWN)	--
SWEDEN	19	(DIPLOMATIC)	5-FIGURE 2-PART UNENCIPHERED CODE. NO 5-FIGURE GROUP CONTAINED THE SAME DIGIT TWICE.	?	?	(POSSIBLY SWB-1 OR SWB-2)	? - 1939	1943 PERS Z S 1940 SIM	?	IF 1518 P 3 I 22 P 21	(IF SWB-1, PARTIALLY COMPROMISED. BEING WORKED ON. IF SWB-2, BEING WORKED ON.)	(TRAFFIC IN SWB-1 AND SWB-2 CONTINUED LATER THAN THE CLOSING DATE GIVEN BY PW FOR THIS CODE)
SWEDEN	20	CONSULAR	5-FIGURE AND 4-FIGURE 2-PART UNENCIPHERED CODE. IN 1939 ALMOST ALL LINKS EXCEPT STOCKHOLM - TOKYO WENT OVER TO A MACHINE.	?	?	?	? - 1939, ON MOST LINKS	BEFORE 1939 FA	READ	I 162 P 3	(UNIDENTIFIED)	--
SWEDEN	21	DIPLOMATIC	4-FIGURE ?-PART CODE.	?	?	?	AFTER 1939 - ?	AFTER 1939 SIM	?	IF 1518 P 3	(UNIDENTIFIED)	--
SWEDEN	22	MILITARY	SIMPLE RECIPROCAL SUBSTITUTION.	?	?	?	? - ?	AFTER SEPT 1944 OKH	READ	I 55 P 11	(NO MILITARY TRAFFIC WORKED ON)	--
SWEDEN	23	ARMY	REVOLVING GRILLE TRANSPOSITION CIPHERS.	?	SRA-1 SRA-5	?	? - ?	1943 OKH	READ	IF 12Ø P 5	(NO MILITARY TRAFFIC WORKED ON)	--

CHART NO 1-

TOP SECRET

DOCID: 3560861

TOP SECRET

RESULTS OF EUROPEAN AXIS CRYPTANALYSIS AS LEARNED FROM TICOM SOURCES

(WITH ANNOTATIONS FROM ARMY SECURITY AGENCY SOURCES IN PARENTHESES)

COUNTRY OF ORIGIN		SERVICE	DESCRIPTION OF SYSTEM	NAME OF SYSTEM: COUNTRY OF ORIGIN	AXIS	U.S.A.	DATES OF USE	WHEN ATTACKED AND BY WHOM	RESULTS	TICOM REFERENCE	STATUS OF THE SYSTEM AT ASA	REMARKS
SWEDEN	24	ARMY	TRANSPOSITION SYSTEM. "HARDER THAN REVOLVING GRILLE."	?	HGA	?	? - 1944 - ?	1944 PERS Z S 1944 OKH 1944 OKM	PROBABLY NOT BROKEN	IF 120 P 5 D 38 P 4	(NO MILITARY TRAFFIC WORKED ON)	--
SWEDEN	25	MILITARY	ELEMENTARY TYPE TRANSPOSITION.	?	?	?	? - ?	AFTER SEPT 1944 OKH	READ	I 55 P 11	(NO MILITARY SYSTEMS WORKED ON)	--
SWEDEN	26	?	?	?	FFFF	?	? - 1944 - ?	1944 OKM	?	D 38 P 5	(UNKNOWN)	--
SWEDEN	27	?	?	?	FFF	?	? - 1944 - ?	1944 OKM	?	D 38 P 5	(UNKNOWN)	--
SWEDEN	28	DIPLOMATIC	MACHINE CIPHER	?	?	?	1939 - ?	? SIM	NOT READ	IF 1518	(UNIDENTIFIED)	--
SWEDEN	29	DIPLOMATIC	MACHINE	?	?	?	1939 - ?	? SIM	NOT READ	IF 1518	(UNIDENTIFIED)	--
SWEDEN	30	DIPLOMATIC?	5-FIGURE 2-PART CODE. NO DIGIT REPEATED IN A GROUP. UNENCIPHERED.	?	?	?	? - 1939	? SIM	?	IF 1518	(UNIDENTIFIED)	--
SWEDEN	31	DIPLOMATIC	4-FIGURE ?-PART CODE.	?	?	?	1939 - ?	? SIM	?	IF 1518	(UNIDENTIFIED)	--

TOP SECRET

RESULTS OF EUROPEAN AXIS CRYPTANALYSIS AS LEARNED FROM TICOM SOURCES

(WITH ANNOTATIONS FROM ARMY SECURITY AGENCY SOURCES IN PARENTHESES)

COUNTRY OF ORIGIN		SERVICE	DESCRIPTION OF SYSTEM	NAME OF SYSTEM			DATES OF USE	WHEN ATTACKED AND BY WHOM	RESULTS	TICOM REFERENCE	STATUS OF THE SYSTEM AT ASA	REMARKS
				COUNTRY OF ORIGIN	AXIS	U.S.A.						
SYRIA	1	ARMY	FRENCH LANGUAGE CODE: TABLE OF 17 LINES AND 8Ø COLUMNS, 3-LETTER GROUPS OF WHICH MIDDLE ONE IS A VOWEL. KEY WORD CHANGED ABOUT ONCE A MONTH. APPROXIMATELY 1,7ØØ WORDS.	?	?	?	?-1941-?	1941 SIM	READ	IF 118C P 3 IF 118G P 4	(UNKNOWN)	--
SYRIA	2	POLICE	4-FIGURE ?-PART CODE. ENCIPHERED BY SIMPLE SUBSTITUTION.	?	?	?	?-1943	? OKH	READ	I 17Ø P 3	(UNKNOWN)	--
SYRIA	3	POLICE	CIPHER SYSTEM. SIMPLE FIGURE SUBSTITUTION.	?	?	?	?-1943	? OKH	READ	I 17Ø P 3	(UNKNOWN)	--
SYRIA	4	POLICE	"1Ø X 1Ø MULTIALPHABETICAL TABLE WITH OMOPHONES." (??) "KEY" CHANGED MONTHLY.	?	?	?	? - ?	? ITALIANS	READ	IF 118G P 5	(UNKNOWN)	--
SYRIA	5	?	3-LETTER "CIPHER."	?	?	?	?-1941-?	1941 SIM	"PROBABLY" READ	IF 118C P 3	(UNKNOWN)	--
SYRIA	6	?	3-FIGURE "CIPHER."	?	?	?	?-1941-?	1941 SIM	PROBABLY READ	IF 118C P 3	(UNKNOWN)	--
SYRIA	7	POLICE	"CODE". TABLE OF 1Ø X 1Ø.	?	?	?	?-1941-?	1941 SIM	READ	IF 118C P 3	(UNKNOWN)	--

CHART NO. 1-?

DOCID: 3560861

TOP SECRET

RESULTS OF EUROPEAN AXIS CRYPTANALYSIS AS LEARNED FROM TICOM SOURCES

(WITH ANNOTATIONS FROM ARMY SECURITY AGENCY SOURCES IN PARENTHESES)

COUNTRY OF ORIGIN	SERVICE	DESCRIPTION OF SYSTEM	NAME OF SYSTEM: COUNTRY OF ORIGIN	NAME OF SYSTEM: AXIS	NAME OF SYSTEM: U.S.A.	DATES OF USE	WHEN ATTACKED AND BY WHOM	RESULTS	TICOM REFERENCE	STATUS OF THE SYSTEM AT ASA	REMARKS
SWITZERLAND 1	DIPLOMATIC	ENIGMA CIPHER MACHINE.	(ENIGMA)	?	(SZD)	(?-1942-CURRENT)	? PERS Z S ? SIM	READ AT DIFFERENT TIMES. SIM DID NOT READ.	I 22 P 14 P 19 I 54 P 2 IF 1526	(THREE TYPES OF TRAFFIC PRESUMED TO BE ENIGMA--SZD-1, SZD-2, AND SZD-3. SZD-1 READ OVER 50%, OTHERS NOT READ.)	--
SWITZERLAND 2	DIPLOMATIC	4-LETTER ?-PART CODE IN FORM VCVC. (BOTH 1-PART AND 2-PART.)	(I.E. 1, 2 3, 4)	?	(SZA FR.) (SZB GER.) (SZC ENG) (SZR FR.)	(?-1939-CURRENT)	? SID, SIM	NO SUCCESS	IF 1526 P 6	(ALL READABLE.)	--
SWITZERLAND 3	DIPLOMATIC	3-LETTER 1-PART CODE. 3,000 GROUPS. FIRST LETTER OF GROUP INDICATED PAGE, SECOND LETTER THE COLUMN, AND THIRD THE LINE. INDICATOR: 5-LETTER GROUP AT BEGINNING. (TWO BOOKS: FRENCH AND GERMAN)	(CODE K)	"S.V. 1"	(SZG)	(1942-CURRENT)	1944 SID ? SIM	75% OF FRENCH BOOK READ; GERMAN BOOK PARTIALLY READ	IF 1526 PP 6-9 T 1537 T 1502 T 1603 IF 1522	(100% READABLE THROUGH RECOVERY.)	--
SWITZERLAND 4	CONSULAR	3-LETTER 1-PART CODE. VALUES IN FRENCH AND GERMAN. FIRST LETTER INDICATED PAGE, SECOND LETTER COLUMN, AND THIRD LETTER THE LINE. INDICATOR: FIFTH LETTER OF FIRST GROUP AND FIRST AND FIFTH LETTERS OF SECOND GROUP.	(CODE G)	CONSOLARE G2X	(SZG FR.) (SZH GER.)	(?-1941-CURRENT)	1944 SID	RECOVERED ABOUT 25% OF FRENCH BOOK	IF 1526 PP 9-11 T 1532 T 1537	(100% READABLE THROUGH RECOVERY.)	--
SWITZERLAND 5	?	3-LETTER 1-PART CODE. VALUES IN GERMAN.	?	?	?	? - ?	? ?	RECOVERED 15% - 20%	T 1533	(UNIDENTIFIED)	--
SWITZERLAND 6	?	?-PART CODE, VALUES IN FRENCH.	?	?	?	? - 1941	? SIM	READ	IF 1517 P 3	(UNIDENTIFIED)	--
THAILAND 1	DIPLOMATIC ?	5-LETTER ?-PART CODE. USED BETWEEN BERNE, STOCKHOLM, AND BANGKOK. (LANGUAGE UNKNOWN, ENCIPHERED WITH ONE OF THREE DIFFERENT FORMS OF SUBSTITUTION.)	?	?	(THB)	(1944-CURRENT)	? GERMANS	PROBABLY NOT SOLVED.	T 2364	(ENCIPHERMENT SOLVED 1945. CODE NOT WORKED ON.)	--
THAILAND 2	DIPLOMATIC	5-FIGURE 1-PART CODE. ENGLISH LANGUAGE USED. USED WITH AND WITHOUT ENCIPHERMENT. SOMETIMES USED REPEATING 5-FIGURE ADDITIVE. (WHICH CHANGED EVERY FEW MONTHS, OR MONOALPHABETIC, OR POLYALPHABETIC SUBSTITUTION USED.)	?	?	(THA)	(?-1941-CURRENT)	1941 PERS Z S 1942 FA	ALMOST COMPLETELY READ	D 16, REPORT 2, P 2 D 16, REPORT 3, P 3 T 2375 T 2378 T 2368 T 2376	(BROKEN AND READ IN 1943. NOW 100% READABLE.)	--
THAILAND 3	(COMMERCIAL ?)	5-LETTER ?-PART CODE. USED BY MINISTER OF FINANCE.	?	?	?	?-1941-1943-?	? GERMANS	PROBABLY NOT READ	T 2364	(UNKNOWN)	--
THAILAND 4	(COMMERCIAL ?)	?-PART CODE USED BETWEEN BANGKOK AND BREMEN.	?	?	?	? - 1945	? GERMANS	PROBABLY NOT READ	T 2364	(UNKNOWN)	--

CHART NO. 1-.

TOP SECRET

DOCID: 3560861

TOP SECRET

RESULTS OF EUROPEAN AXIS CRYPTANALYSIS
AS LEARNED FROM TICOM SOURCES
(WITH ANNOTATIONS FROM ARMY SECURITY AGENCY SOURCES IN PARENTHESES)

COUNTRY OF ORIGIN		SERVICE	DESCRIPTION OF SYSTEM	NAME OF SYSTEM: COUNTRY OF ORIGIN	NAME OF SYSTEM: AXIS	NAME OF SYSTEM: U.S.A.	DATES OF USE	WHEN ATTACKED AND BY WHOM	RESULTS	TICOM REFERENCE	STATUS OF THE SYSTEM AT ASA	REMARKS
TURKEY	1	DIPLOMATIC	2-PART CODE. ENCIPHERED ABOUT 1/2 THE TIME WITH A REPEATING 5-FIGURE ADDITIVE WHICH CHANGED DAILY BUT WAS SOMETIMES REPEATED FROM YEAR TO YEAR. USED ON RATHER UNIMPORTANT TRAFFIC.	?	?	?	1934-1935	1934? PERS Z S	SOLVED.	I 103 P 2	(UNIDENTIFIED)	--
TURKEY	2	DIPLOMATIC	4-FIGURE 2-PART CODE. LATER GIVEN THREE REPAGINATIONS. SEE ITEMS 3, 4, AND 5.	INKILAP	?	-	?-1930-1940	? SIM	COMPROMISED. READ.	IF 1517 P 3, IF 1523 PP 2, 3, PERHAPS IF 115	(UNKNOWN UNTIL INFORMATION WAS RECEIVED FROM BRITISH. NO WORK DONE. NO TRAFFIC RECEIVED.)	--
TURKEY	3	DIPLOMATIC	REPAGINATION OF ITEM 2. USED IN MONTHLY ROTATION WITH ITEMS 4 AND 5. AFTER 1940 SOMETIMES ENCIPHERED BY 40-FIGURE REPEATING ADDITIVE WHICH FREQUENTLY CHANGED.	ZAFER	?	(TUB)	1935-(1944)	1935 PERS Z S, 1940 SIM	BROKEN AND READ BY SIM AND PERS Z S	IF 1517 P 3, IF 1523 PP 2, 3, I 103 PP 2, 3	(WORK HAD BEGUN WHEN PHOTOSTAT COPY WAS RECEIVED FROM THE BRITISH IN 1943.)	NOT KNOWN BY ASA TO HAVE BEEN USED IN MONTHLY ROTATION
TURKEY	4	DIPLOMATIC	REPAGINATION OF ITEM 2. USED IN MONTHLY ROTATION WITH ITEMS 3 AND 5. AFTER 1940 SOMETIMES ENCIPHERED BY 40-FIGURE REPEATING ADDITIVE WHICH FREQUENTLY CHANGED.	SAKARIA	?	(TUD)	1935-(CURRENT)	1935 PERS Z S, 1940 SIM	BROKEN AND READ BY SIM AND PERS Z S	IF 1517 P 3, IF 1523 PP 2, 3, I 103 PP 2, 3	(SOLVED IN 1943 AND 1944.)	
TURKEY	5	DIPLOMATIC	REPAGINATION OF ITEM 2. USED IN MONTHLY ROTATION WITH ITEMS 3 AND 4. AFTER 1940 SOMETIMES ENCIPHERED BY 40-FIGURE REPEATING ADDITIVE WHICH FREQUENTLY CHANGED.	?	?	(TUJ)	1935-(1945)	1935 PERS Z S, 1940 SIM	BROKEN AND READ BY SIM AND PERS Z S	IF 1523 PP 2, 3, I 103 PP 2, 3	(SOLVED IN 1943 AND 1944.)	
TURKEY	6	DIPLOMATIC	4-FIGURE 2-PART CODE. SOMETIMES ENCIPHERED BY A 40-FIGURE REPEATING ADDITIVE WHICH FREQUENTLY CHANGED. USED BY THE TURKISH EMBASSIES IN BERLIN AND VICHY?.	CANKAYA	?	(TUE)	1940-(CURRENT)	1941? SIM	RECOVERED 5,000 GROUPS	IF 1517 PP 3, 9, APPENDIX F; IF 1523 P 3	(BROKEN AND AIDED BY BRITISH. READ IN 1943. NOW BEING ALMOST COMPLETELY READ.)	--
TURKEY	7	DIPLOMATIC	4-FIGURE (2)-PART CODE. ENCIPHERED BY A 40-FIGURE REPEATING ADDITIVE. USED BETWEEN ANKARA AND THE ROME EMBASSY.	INEUNU (INÖNU)	ROMA	(TUF)	1940-(1945)	1941 SIM	RECOVERED 5,000 GROUPS	IF 1517 P 3, IF 1523 P 3	(PARTIALLY BROKEN BY BRITISH IN 1943. NO FURTHER SOLUTION DONE BY BRITISH OR ASA. TRAFFIC RECEIVED AND SOME DECODED AND TRANSLATED.)	--
TURKEY	8	DIPLOMATIC, CONSULAR	SET OF THREE 4-FIGURE PARTIALLY 1-PART CODES IN ARABIC SCRIPT. USED IN MONTHLY ROTATION. SOMETIMES ENCIPHERED BY A 40-FIGURE OR A 5-FIGURE REPEATING ADDITIVE.	(CUMHURIET)	?	(TUK)	1934-(1944)	1934 PERS Z S, ? SIM	SOLVED AND READ BY PERS Z S. COMPROMISED BY SIM.	I 103 P 2, IF 1517 P 3, IF 1523 P 4	(COMPROMISED BOOK RECEIVED FROM THE BRITISH IN 1944.)	--
TURKEY	9	DIPLOMATIC	4-FIGURE 1-PART CODE. ENCIPHERED BY 40-FIGURE REPEATING ADDITIVE (WHICH FREQUENTLY CHANGED).	?	?	(TUH)	(?-1943-CURRENT)	1943 SIM, 1944 PERS Z S	BROKEN AND READ BY SIM. READ BY PERS Z S.	IF 1517 P 3, SEE ALSO I 63 P 2	(BRITISH AND ASA EXCHANGED VALUES AND BROKE BOOK AND ENCIPHERMENT. READ IN 1944)	--
TURKEY	10	MILITARY ATTACHE	5-FIGURE ?-PART CODE. ALL GROUPS BEGAN WITH DIGIT 1. IN 1942 REPLACED BY CODE DESCRIBED IN ITEM 11.	?	?	?	?-1940-1942	? SIM	BROKEN AND READ	IF 1517 P 3, IF 1523 P 4	(UNKNOWN)	--

CHART NO

TOP SECRET

DOCID: 3560861

TOP SECRET

RESULTS OF EUROPEAN AXIS CRYPTANALYSIS AS LEARNED FROM TICOM SOURCES

(WITH ANNOTATIONS FROM ARMY SECURITY AGENCY SOURCES IN PARENTHESES)

COUNTRY OF ORIGIN		SERVICE	DESCRIPTION OF SYSTEM	NAME OF SYSTEM: COUNTRY OF ORIGIN	AXIS	U.S.A.	DATES OF USE	WHEN ATTACKED AND BY WHOM	RESULTS	TICOM REFERENCE	STATUS OF THE SYSTEM AT ASA	REMARKS
TURKEY	11	MILITARY ATTACHE	5-FIGURE 1-PART CODE. (AT FIRST) FREQUENTLY ENCIPHERED BY A 5-FIGURE (REPEATING) ADDITIVE. (NOW UNENCIPHERED OR ENCIPHERED BY 40-FIGURE REPEATING ADDITIVE.) USED BY ALL TURKISH MILITARY ATTACHES.	?	?	(TUA)	(1940-CURRENT)	1943 SIM PERHAPS PERS Z S	BROKEN AND COMPLETELY READ. ALSO COMPROMISED.	IF 1517 P 8, APPENDIX E SEE ALSO I 63 P 2	(PARTIALLY BROKEN AND AIDED BY BRITISH. LATER 100% COMPROMISED. NOW COMPLETELY READ.)	--
TURKEY	12	DIPLOMATIC, MILITARY ATTACHE	?-FIGURE ?-PART CODE WITH LETTER SUBSTITUTION. USED IN TRAFFIC FROM RUSSIA, BULGARIA, AND ITALY.	?	?	?	? - 1944 - ?	1944 FA 1944 OKH	READ.	IF 126 P 12	(UNKNOWN)	--
TURKEY	13	ARMY, AIR	POLYALPHABETIC SUBSTITUTION CIPHER. USUALLY HAD 5-13 ALPHABETS. MONTHLY KEY CHANGE; GEOGRAPHICAL NAMES USED FOR CODEWORDS. J, W, X ARE USED AS NULLS.	?	?	?	?-1940-1943-?	1940 OKH 1941 SIM	READ BY SIM. BROKEN AND READ BY OKH.	IF 1523 P 4, APPENDIX A IF 1517 P 6 IF 126 PP 10, 11 IF 118C P 3 IF 115G P 2,3	(UNKNOWN)	--
TURKEY	14	MILITARY	?-PART CODE. SOMETIMES ENCIPHERED BY A METHOD WHICH ENCIPHERED ONLY ONE OR TWO FIGURES OF EACH GROUP.	?	5 Z	?	?-1936-1939-?	1936, 1939 PERS Z S	SOLVED	I 103 P 3	(UNKNOWN--NO MILITARY TRAFFIC WORKED ON.)	--
TURKEY	15	MILITARY	?-PART CODE.	?	?	?	1939 - ?	AFTER 1939 OKW, PERS Z S	PROBABLY "SPASMODIC SUCCESS ACHIEVED"	I 103 P 3	(UNKNOWN)	--
TURKEY	16	MILITARY	?-PART CODE. "A TURKISH PROCEDURE CODE."	?	?	?	?-1941-1943-?	1941 SIM	?	IF 1523 P 5	(UNKNOWN)	--
TURKEY	17	MILITARY	?-PART CODE. ALL TRIGRAMS BEGAN WITH THE LETTER S.	G	?	?	?-1941-1943-?	1941 SIM	?	IF 1523 P 5	(UNKNOWN)	--
TURKEY	18	POLICE	?-PART CODE, LOW GRADE. ONLY 100 GROUPS. OF THE FIELD-CODE TYPE, A SQUARE OF 10X10, WITH COLUMNS AND LINES NUMBERED 1 TO 10, IN ASCENDING ORDER. THE ARRANGEMENT WITHIN THE SQUARE WAS CHANGED PERIODICALLY.	?	?	?	?-1941-1943-?	1941 SIM	READ.	IF 1523 P 6	(UNKNOWN)	--
TURKEY	19	AIR	1-PART CODE. UNENCIPHERED.	?	?	?	? - ?	? OKL	EASILY READ	I 119 P 5	(UNKNOWN)	--
TURKEY	20	AIR	PERIODIC POLYALPHABETIC SUBSTITUTION CIPHER USING SLIDING STRIPS. CHANGED MONTHLY.	?	?	?	? - ?	? OKL	EASILY READ	I 119 P 5	(UNKNOWN)	--
TURKEY	21	AIR	SINGLE TRANSPOSITION CIPHER FOR WEATHER REPORTS.	?	?	?	? - ?	? OKL	EASILY READ	I 119 P 5	(UNKNOWN)	--
TURKEY	22	NAVY	POLYALPHABETIC SUBSTITUTION CIPHER. KEY LENGTH VARIED FROM 5 TO 13; NO KEY WORD USED. KEY CHANGED EVERY 2 OR 3 MONTHS. SIMILAR TO ITEM 13.	?	?	?	?-1941-1943-?	1941 SIM	BROKEN AND READ	IF 1523 P 5 IF 115C P 3 IF 115G P 3	(UNKNOWN)	--
TURKEY	23	NAVY		-	-	-	-	-	PROBABLY NO WORK DONE BY OKM ON ANY NAVY SYSTEMS	I 83 P 2		--

CHART NO. 1-2

TOP SECRET

DOCID: 3560861

RESULTS OF EUROPEAN AXIS CRYPTANALYSIS
AS LEARNED FROM TICOM SOURCES
(WITH ANNOTATIONS FROM ARMY SECURITY AGENCY SOURCES IN PARENTHESES)

COUNTRY OF ORIGIN		SERVICE	DESCRIPTION OF SYSTEM	NAME OF SYSTEM: COUNTRY OF ORIGIN	NAME OF SYSTEM: AXIS	NAME OF SYSTEM: U.S.A.	DATES OF USE	WHEN ATTACKED AND BY WHOM	RESULTS	TICOM REFERENCE	STATUS OF THE SYSTE[M] AT ASA
TURKEY	24	POLICE	SUBSTITUTION CIPHER SYSTEM USING 2 FIGURES FOR EACH LETTER OR NUMBER. MOST FREQUENT LETTERS USED VARIABLES.	?	?	?	?-1941-1943-PERHAPS CURRENT	1941 OKH	READ	IF 126 PP 12, 13	(UNKNOWN)
TURKEY	25	POLICE	SUBSTITUTION CIPHER SYSTEM USING TWO OR THREE FIGURES FOR EACH LETTER. TWO DIFFERENT SUBSTITUTION TABLES USED.	?	?	?	1942-1943-PERHAPS CURRENT	1942? OKH	PROBABLY READ	IF 126 P 13	(UNKNOWN)
TURKEY	26	POLICE	SUBSTITUTION CIPHER SYSTEM USING 2 OR 3 FIGURES PER LETTER. WEEKLY OR MONTHLY KEY CHANGE. TRANSMITTED IN 4, 5, OR 6 FIGURES.	?	?	?	?-1941-1943-?	1941 SIM	READ	IF 1523 P 6	(UNKNOWN)
TURKEY	27	POLICE	MONOALPHABETIC SUBSTITUTION CIPHER. NORMAL ALPHABET SLID AGAINST ITSELF WITH DAILY CHANGING STARTING POINT. THE LETTERS C, X, AND W WERE ONLY USED TO SEPARATE WORDS.	?	?	?	1941-1943-?	1941 SIM 1941 OKH	READ	IF 1523 P 6 IF 126 P 12	(UNKNOWN)
TURKEY	28	?	?-PART CODE.	?	?	?	? - ?	1943 OKW	SOLVED CRYPTANALYTICALLY. LATER COMPROMISED.	I 132 P 2	(UNIDENTIFIED)
TURKEY	29	?	"NUMBER CODE". USED ONLY BY THE TURKISH PRESIDENT ON THE STATE-YACHT "SAVARONA" ON HIS TRIP TO IZMIR.	?	?	?	1943 ONLY	? OKH	BROKEN	IF 126 P 12	(UNKNOWN)
TURKEY	30	DIPLOMATIC	SMALL SUPPLEMENTARY CODE IN FRENCH. APPROXIMATELY 1,000 GROUPS.	?	"FRENCH" CODE	(FRENCH SUPPLEMENT TO TUK)?	"VERY OLD"	1940, 1941 SIM	NOT READ	IF 1523 P 3	(COMPROMISED COPY RECEIVED FROM BRITISH WITH TUK)
TURKEY	31	DIPLOMATIC	?-PART CODE FOR USE ON BERLIN-ANKARA LINK.	?	?	?	? - ?	? SIM	?	D 71	(UNIDENTIFIED)
TURKEY	32	MILITARY, AIR, AND NAVAL ATTACHES	?-PART CODE OF 261 PAGES.	?	?	?	? - ?	? SIS	READ. COMPROMISED.	IF 1506	(UNIDENTIFIED)
TURKEY	33	POLICE	4-FIGURE 2-PART CODE, UNENCIPHERED.	?	?	?	?-1943-?	1943 SIM	READABLE SINCE JUNE 1943	IF 118C P 4 IF 118F IF 118F P 2	(UNIDENTIFIED)
TURKEY	34	POLICE	SIMPLE TRANSPOSITION CIPHER USING 29-LETTER ALPHABET; DAILY-CHANGING KEY. J, W, AND X ARE NULLS.	?	?	?	?-1941-?	1941 SIM	?	IF 118C P 3 IF 118F IF 118G	(UNIDENTIFIED)
TURKEY	35	?	"METEOROLOGICAL CODE."	?	?	?	? - ?	1942 OKL	"DECIPHERED"	IF 118B P 17	(UNIDENTIFIED)

TOP SECRET

CHART NO. 1-2

DOCID: 3560861

TOP SECRET

RESULTS OF EUROPEAN AXIS CRYPTANALYSIS
AS LEARNED FROM TICOM SOURCES
(WITH ANNOTATIONS FROM ARMY SECURITY AGENCY SOURCES IN PARENTHESES)

COUNTRY OF ORIGIN		SERVICE	DESCRIPTION OF SYSTEM	NAME OF SYSTEM			DATES OF USE	WHEN ATTACKED AND BY WHOM	RESULTS	TICOM REFERENCE	STATUS OF THE SYSTEM AT ASA	REMARKS
				COUNTRY OF ORIGIN	AXIS	U.S.A.						
UNITED KINGDOM	1	DIPLOMATIC	CIPHER MACHINE OF SWEDISH ORIGIN, PERHAPS HAGELIN, USED FOR MESSAGES FROM ITALIAN THEATER.	?	?	--	?-1944-?	1944 OKW	OKW POSSESSED MACHINE; READ ALL TRAFFIC FROM ITALIAN THEATER.	I 76 P 12	--	--
UNITED KINGDOM	2	DIPLOMATIC	5-LETTER 1-PART CODE WITH 84,000 GROUPS.	GOVERNMENT TELEGRAPH CODE	B 22	--	?-1939-1942-?	1939 PERS Z S	READ SINCE 1939. SUMMER 1940, CAPTURED ORIGINAL GIVEN TO PERS Z S.	D 16, REPORT 2, P 1 D 16, REPORT 4, P 1	--	--
UNITED KINGDOM	3	DIPLOMATIC	5-LETTER 1-PART CODE WITH ABOUT 84,000 GROUPS.	GOVERNMENT TELEGRAPH CODE, AFRICA	B 23	--	?-1941-1942-?	1941 PERS Z S	READ ALMOST WITHOUT GAP	D 16, REPORT 2, P 1 D 16, REPORT 4, P 2	--	--
UNITED KINGDOM	4	DIPLOMATIC	5-LETTER ?-PART CODE, UNENCIPHERED.	?	?	--	? - ?	? PERS Z S	BOOK ONLY PARTLY BUILT	I 22 P 12	--	--
UNITED KINGDOM	5	DIPLOMATIC FOREIGN OFFICE	4-LETTER 2-PART CODE WITH 16, 224 GROUPS.	R CODE 1935	B 25;	--	1935-1942-?	PRIOR TO 1940 PERS Z S	READ ALMOST COMPLETELY. CAPTURED AT BERGEN, 1940	D 16, REPORT 2, P 1 D 16, REPORT 4, P 1 I 172 P 3	--	--
UNITED KINGDOM	6	DIPLOMATIC	4-LETTER 2-PART CODE USED IN NEAR, MIDDLE, AND FAR EAST.	R CODE 1941?	B 30	--	?-1941-1942-?	1941 PERS Z S	AT END OF 1942 ABOUT 1,000 GROUPS WERE RECOVERED	D 16, REPORT 2, P 1 D 16, REPORT 4, P 1	--	--
UNITED KINGDOM	7	DIPLOMATIC	4-LETTER 2-PART CODE WITH 16,000 GROUPS.	?	B 31	--	1942 - ?	1942 PERS Z S	AT END OF 1942 2,500 GROUPS RECOVERED. FIRST TELEGRAMS READ IN OCTOBER 1942.	D 16 REPORT 4, P 1	--	--
UNITED KINGDOM	8	DIPLOMATIC	4-LETTER ?-PART CODE, UNENCIPHERED.	?	?	--	?-1940-?	? PERS Z S	BOOK CAPTURED IN NORWAY; ALREADY READ BEFORE THIS.	I 22 PP 11-12	--	--
UNITED KINGDOM	9	DIPLOMATIC	2-PART CODE USED MAINLY FOR TRAINING IN 1942 AND 1943. ENCIPHERED BY ADDITIVE. INDICATOR WAS SECOND GROUP.	?	?	--	1942-1943	1942 OKW	SMALL PART OF TRAFFIC READ BEFORE 1943.	I 76 P 14	--	--

CHART NO. I-2

TOP SECRET

RESULTS OF EUROPEAN AXIS CRYPTANALYSIS AS LEARNED FROM TICOM SOURCES

(WITH ANNOTATIONS FROM ARMY SECURITY AGENCY SOURCES IN PARENTHESES)

COUNTRY OF ORIGIN		SERVICE	DESCRIPTION OF SYSTEM	NAME OF SYSTEM: COUNTRY OF ORIGIN	NAME OF SYSTEM: AXIS	NAME OF SYSTEM: U.S.A.	DATES OF USE	WHEN ATTACKED AND BY WHOM	RESULTS	TICOM REFERENCE	STATUS OF THE SYSTEM AT ASA	REMARKS
UNITED KINGDOM	1Ø	DIPLOMATIC	?-FIGURE ?-PART CODE.	INTERDEPARTMENTAL CODE	?	--	?-1941-?	1941 PERS Z S 1941 OKW 1941 OKL	BOOK 1ØØ% COMPROMISED 1941. ADDITIVE PARTLY BROKEN BY OKW, OKL. WORK STOPPED 1942.	D 16, REPORT 2, P 1	--	--
UNITED KINGDOM	11	DIPLOMATIC	ADDITIVE ENCIPHERMENT SYSTEM WITH KEYS CHANGING EVERY TWO OR THREE MONTHS. TRAFFIC PREFIXED "PRODROME". TOTAL LENGTH ESTIMATED BY PERS Z S AT 1Ø,ØØØ 4-FIGURE GROUPS.	?	?	--	?-194Ø-1941-?	194Ø PERS Z S ? OKW	PERS Z S RECOVERED 23% OF ADDITIVE; DID NOT ATTACK BOOK. OKW DID NOT READ.	I 22 PP 17-18 I 31 P 6	--	--
UNITED KINGDOM	12	DIPLOMATIC	DOUBLE TRANSPOSITION WITH SAME KEY-LENGTH FOR BOTH RECTANGLES.	?	?	--	? - ?	? OKW	SOME READ	I 31 P 6	--	--
UNITED KINGDOM	13	ARMY	4-LETTER OR 5-LETTER ?-PART CODE ENCIPHERED WITH ADDITIVE.	EMPIRE CODE	?	--	?-1941-1942-?	1941 OKH	BOOK PARTLY BUILT	IF 126 P 13	--	--
UNITED KINGDOM	14	ARMY	3-LETTER ?-PART CODE. SECOND LETTER OF GROUP WAS ALWAYS A VOWEL (INCLUDING Y).	TIGER CODE	?	--	? - ?	? OKW	SOLVED IN SIX MONTHS.	I 76 P 13	--	--
UNITED KINGDOM	15	ARMY-CORPS-DIVISION	4-FIGURE 2-PART CODE ENCIPHERED WITH ADDITIVE WHICH WAS A TABLE WITH STARTING POINTS INDICATED BY 5-LETTER GROUPS. ADDITIVE CHANGED ABOUT EVERY TWO WEEKS. FROM SPRING 1943 ENCIPHERED WITH ONE-TIME PADS.	WAR OFFICE CODE	WOC	--	194Ø-1943	194Ø OKH ? SIM	RECONSTRUCTED AND READ UNTIL CODE COMPROMISED IN AFRICA, JULY 1942. COMPROMISED ALSO IN NORWAY, APRIL 194Ø, AND NEAR DUNKIRK JUNE 194Ø. NOT READ BY SIM.	I 51 I 113 P 4 IF 1Ø7 P 7 IF 1517 IF 1519	--	--
UNITED KINGDOM	16	ARMY	POLYALPHABETIC SUBSTITUTION SYSTEM EMPLOYING BOOK OF RANDOM ALPHABETS AND NOTCHED CARD FOR SELECTING CIPHER TEXT.	LINEX	LINEX	--	1945 - ?	1945 OKH	NOT READ	IF 144 PP 6-8	--	--
UNITED KINGDOM	17	ARMY, AIR FORCE	2-LETTER CODE WITH 2Ø4 VALUES ARRANGED IN RECTANGLE. CODE GROUPS FORMED FROM COORDINATES ON SLIDING STRIPS.	SLIDEX	BRITISH SIDE-SQUARE, EC PLUS A NUMBER	SLIDEX	?-1943-?	? OKH ? OKL	OKH READ CURRENTLY; OKL READ CURRENTLY.	I 76 P 4 I 1Ø9 P 38 IF 126 PP 13-14 IF 144 PP 2-3 P 6	--	--
UNITED KINGDOM	18	AIR FORCE COMMAND NETWORKS	CIPHER MACHINE: TRAFFIC SENT IN 5-LETTER GROUPS.	?	?	--	? - ?	? OKL	NOT BROKEN	I 1Ø9 P 35	--	--

DOCID: C3560861

TOP SECRET

RESULTS OF EUROPEAN AXIS CRYPTANALYSIS
AS LEARNED FROM TICOM SOURCES

(WITH ANNOTATIONS FROM ARMY SECURITY AGENCY SOURCES IN PARENTHESES)

COUNTRY OF ORIGIN		SERVICE	DESCRIPTION OF SYSTEM	NAME OF SYSTEM: COUNTRY OF ORIGIN	NAME OF SYSTEM: AXIS	NAME OF SYSTEM: U.S.A.	DATES OF USE	WHEN ATTACKED AND BY WHOM	RESULTS	TICOM REFERENCE	STATUS OF THE SYSTEM AT ASA	REMARKS
UNITED KINGDOM	19	AIR FORCE	CIPHER DEVICE	?	"32 COLUMN CAESAR CODING MACHINE"	--	?-1942-?	PRIOR TO 1942 OKH	OKH HAD CAPTURED DEVICE. TRAFFIC READ UNTIL 1942.	IF 126 P 13	--	--
UNITED KINGDOM	20	AIR FORCE	3-LETTER 2-PART CODE.	AIRCRAFT REPORTING CODE	?	--	? - ?	? OKL ? OKM	OKL BROKE REGULARLY TO AN EXPLOITABLE EXTENT. OKM READ WITH MANY GAPS.	I 112 P 3 I 147 P 17	--	--
UNITED KINGDOM	21	AIR FORCE	2-LETTER 2-PART CODE WITH DAILY CHANGE OF KEY.	BOMBER CODE	?	--	?-1942-?	1942 OKL	BROKEN WITH AID OF CAPTURED KEYS.	I 109 P 38 I 112 P 2	--	--
UNITED KINGDOM	22	AIR FORCE	4-FIGURE 2-PART CODE. FIRST TWO GROUPS REPEATED AT END. USED IN RAF GROUND-GROUND TRAFFIC.	?	?	--	?-1940-1943-?	1940 OKL	BROKEN IN MEDITERRANEAN AREA SPRING 1941 BUT NOT ON WESTERN FRONT. BOOK RECONSTRUCTED. READ WITH LAG OF 2-4 WEEKS. BECAME UNREADABLE NOV 1942.	I 109 P 35 I 152 PP 12-13	--	--
UNITED KINGDOM	23	AIR FORCE	4-FIGURE 2-PART CODE, ENCIPHERED WITH ADDITIVE.	?	?	--	?-1942-?	1942 OKL	NOT READ AFTER 1942	I 13 P 6	--	--
UNITED KINGDOM	24	AIR FORCE	TRANSPOSITION CIPHER WITH KEY LENGTH OF 10, USED BY TORPEDO BOMBERS ON EXERCISES IN NORTH CHANNEL.	?	SPESSART	--	? - 1944	1943 OKM	READ CURRENTLY	D 6 D 15 P 10 D 41 P 5	--	--
UNITED KINGDOM	25	ARMY, NAVY, AIR FORCE	4-FIGURE 2-PART CODE USED FOR TRAFFIC BETWEEN BRANCHES OF THE ARMED FORCES.	INTERSERVICE CIPHER	STRALSUND	--	? - ?	1944 OKM	NOT BROKEN	D 6 I 144 P 3	--	--
UNITED KINGDOM	26	ARMY, NAVY	CIPHER MACHINE WITH 5 WHEELS--2 OUTSIDE WHEELS FIXED.	TYPEX	TYPEX	--	?-1940-?	1943 OKL ? OKH 1940 OKW BEFORE 1939 OKM	NOT BROKEN. MACHINES WITHOUT WHEELS CAPTURED AT BREST, DUNKIRK, AND/OR NORTH AFRICA, 1940. KEYS WERE SOMETIMES CAPTURED.	D 15 P 4 D 40; D 49 I 2 P 3 I 31 P 11 I 49 P 3 I 59 P 5 I 78 P 9 I 93 PP 10,16 I 112 P 3 I 113 P 4 I 119 P 5 I 142 P 2 I 144 PP 2,4 I 161 P 2 PP 4-5 P 6 IF 142 P 9	--	--

CHART NO. I-2

TOP SECRET

DOCID: 3560861

TOP SECRET

RESULTS OF EUROPEAN AXIS CRYPTANALYSIS AS LEARNED FROM TICOM SOURCES

(WITH ANNOTATIONS FROM ARMY SECURITY AGENCY SOURCES IN PARENTHESES)

COUNTRY OF ORIGIN		SERVICE	DESCRIPTION OF SYSTEM	NAME OF SYSTEM: COUNTRY OF ORIGIN	NAME OF SYSTEM: AXIS	NAME OF SYSTEM: U.S.A.	DATES OF USE	WHEN ATTACKED AND BY WHOM	RESULTS	TICOM REFERENCE	STATUS OF THE SYSTEM AT ASA	REMARKS
UNITED KINGDOM	27	NAVY	ADDITIVE SUPERENCIPHERING SYSTEM, EMPLOYING GRILLE. 1Ø,ØØØ POSSIBLE DAILY STARTING POSITIONS USED TO SUPERENCIPHER VARIOUS NAVAL CODES.	STENCIL SUBTRACTOR FRAME	"S.S. FRAME"	--	1942 - ?	1943 OKM	OKM READ FOR ONE MONTH; THEN CODE BOOK CHANGED, AND OKM DEVELOPED THEORETICAL SOLUTION ONLY.	D 15 PP 1Ø-11 D 25; D 37 D 4Ø I 12 P 5 I 76 P 14 I 93 P 24 I 114 P 2	--	--
UNITED KINGDOM	28	NAVY	CIPHER MACHINE	COMBINED CIPHER MACHINE	ULM	--	1944-1945	1944 OKM	NOT BROKEN; WORK STOPPED ON 31 JAN 1945	D 6 D 15 P 6 D 18 P 7 D 41 P 5 D 43 P 2 P 4	--	--
UNITED KINGDOM	29	NAVY	CIPHER	NYKO	TAUNUS	--	?-1942-?	1942 OKM	NO SUCCESS REPORTED; WORKED ON UNTIL BEGINNING OF 1944.	D 6 D 15 P 9 D 18 P 9 I 147 P 17	--	--
UNITED KINGDOM	3Ø	NAVY	SUBSTITUTION CIPHER USING 37-PLACE ALPHABET: 26 LETTERS, FIGURES Ø-9, AND DASH. THERE ARE 32 COLUMNS.	SYKO	RHÖN	--	?-1939-?	1939 OKM 1943? OKL ? SIM	OKM BROKE EASILY. OKL READ ALMOST CURRENTLY. SIM READ.	D 6; D 15 D 18 I 1Ø9; I 147 IF 118 IF 15Ø6 IF 1517 IF 1523 IF 1519	--	--
UNITED KINGDOM	31	NAVY	4-LETTER ?-PART CODE WITH 32,ØØØ GROUPS; TWO VALUES TO EACH GROUP.	?	?	--	192?-1939	? OKM	READ CURRENTLY	I 147 P 3	--	--
UNITED KINGDOM	32	NAVY	4-LETTER ?-PART CODE WITH BOOK CHANGING THE 15TH OF EACH MONTH.	FLEET CODE	HAMBURG	--	?-1944-1945-?	1944 OKM ? SIS	READ FROM 15 NOV 1944 TO MAY 1945. READ BY SIS?	D 6; D 44 D 15 P 2 P 8 D 18 P 8 I 12 P 5 I 83 P 2 I 93 P 11 P 13 I 95 P 6 I 114 PP 2-3 IF 15Ø6	--	--
UNITED KINGDOM	33	NAVY	4-LETTER ?-PART CODE, ENCIPHERED.	ANGLO-FRENCH CODE	?	--	?-1944-?	1944 OKM ? SIS	NOT BROKEN BY OKM. ? SIS.	D 15 PP 4-5 IF 15Ø6	--	--
UNITED KINGDOM	34	NAVY	3-LETTER ?-PART CODE, USED BY CONVOYS OFF BRITISH EAST COAST AND IN IRISH SEA.	ECCO	HARZ	--	? - 1943	? OKM	?	D 6 D 41 P 5	--	--

CHART NO.

TOP SECRET

RESULTS OF EUROPEAN AXIS CRYPTANALYSIS
AS LEARNED FROM TICOM SOURCES
(WITH ANNOTATIONS FROM ARMY SECURITY AGENCY SOURCES IN PARENTHESES)

COUNTRY OF ORIGIN		SERVICE	DESCRIPTION OF SYSTEM	NAME OF SYSTEM: COUNTRY OF ORIGIN	NAME OF SYSTEM: AXIS	NAME OF SYSTEM: U.S.A.	DATES OF USE	WHEN ATTACKED AND BY WHOM	RESULTS	TICOM REFERENCE	STATUS OF THE SYSTEM AT ASA	REMARKS
UNITED KINGDOM	35	NAVY	3-LETTER ?-PART CODE, UNENCIPHERED. 4-LETTER, PRONOUNCEABLE INDICATORS: ADCO, AGOG, ALBA, AMID, AGUA. USED FOR INTER-ALLIED TRAFFIC IN LANDING OPERATIONS IN FRANCE.	COMBINED ASSAULT CODE	ALTONA "A"	--	1944 ONLY	1944 OKM	ALBA, AMID, AGUA READ EXTENSIVELY. AGOG COMPROMISED DURING INVASION OF FRANCE.	D 6 D 15 P 2 P 9 D 18 P 8 I 12 P 6 I 93 P 6	--	--
UNITED KINGDOM	36	NAVY	3-LETTER ?-PART CODE, UNENCIPHERED. 4-LETTER, PRONOUNCEABLE INDICATORS: BABY, BANK, BEEF, BIKE, BOLO. USED FOR INTER-ALLIED TRAFFIC IN LANDING OPERATIONS IN MEDITERRANEAN.	COMBINED ASSAULT CODE	ALTONA "B"	--	1944 ONLY	1944 OKM	BIKE, BOLO PARTLY BROKEN	D 6 D 15 P 2 P 9 D 18 P 8 D 44 P 5 I 12 P 6 I 93 P 6	--	--
UNITED KINGDOM	37	NAVY	?-PART CODE.	ODAM OR ØDAM	?	--	? - ?	? OKM	BROKEN, PARTLY THROUGH CAPTURED MATERIALS.	I 14Ø P 2	--	--
UNITED KINGDOM	38	NAVY	UNTIL 3Ø SEPT 1944, 2-LETTER ?-PART CODE CHANGING DAILY. FROM 1 OCT 1944, 3-FIGURE ?-PART CODE, CHANGING DAILY.	COFOX	HUNSRÜCK; SÖNTEL	--	?-1944-?	1944 OKM	READ CONTINUOUSLY.	D 6 D 15 PP 6-7 D 18 P 8 I 12 P 5 I 95 P 6	--	--
UNITED KINGDOM	39	NAVY	5-FIGURE CODE UNTIL 2Ø AUG 194Ø; 4-FIGURE CODE AFTER 2Ø AUG 194Ø. USED UNENCIPHERED UNTIL SPANISH WAR, THEN ENCIPHERED WITH ADDITIVE.	ADMINISTRATIVE CODE	?	--	1934 - ?	1934 OKM	READ AFTER 6 MONTHS OF WORK. ADDITIVE BROKEN DURING SPANISH WAR. BOOK CAPTURED AT BERGEN, BUT ALREADY RECOVERED.	I 12 P 2 I 147 P 3 P 1Ø T 47Ø	--	--
UNITED KINGDOM	4Ø	NAVY	4-FIGURE ?-PART CODE. FROM 1 DEC 1943 ENCIPHERED WITH STENCIL SUBTRACTOR.	NAVAL CODE NO.2	MÜNCHEN BRAUN--FOR PATROL VESSELS, ETC.; MÜNCHEN BLAU--PERSONNEL AND GENERAL.	--	1937-1945?	1938 OKM	BROKEN IN 1938. IN 1941 COMPROMISED BOOK AT TOBRUK. READ IN 1942, BUT NOT AFTER INTRODUCTION OF STENCIL SUBTRACTOR IN 1943.	D 6; D 4Ø D 25; D 41 D 18 PP 5-6 I 12 P 2 P 3 P 5 I 93 PP 6, 21, 22, 25 I 95 P 5 I 147 P 1Ø IF 118F P 1	--	--
UNITED KINGDOM	41	NAVY	4-FIGURE ?-PART CODE ENCIPHERED WITH BOOK ADDITIVE. USED BY BOTH THE UNITED KINGDOM AND THE UNITED STATES.	NAVAL CIPHER NO. 3	FRANKFURT	COMBINED CIPHER NO. 3	1941-1943	1941 OKM; PRIOR TO 1943 SIS	READ UNTIL JUNE 1943	D 6; D 41 I 12 PP 4-5 IF 118F F 1	--	--
UNITED KINGDOM	42	NAVY	4-FIGURE ?-PART CODE ENCIPHERED BY BOOK ADDITIVE.	NAVAL CIPHER NO. 4	KÖLN	--	PRIOR TO 1938 - 1945	1938 OKM	1938, BROKEN. 194Ø, READ. FROM 1943 ON, NOT READ.	D 6; D 4Ø D 41 D 18 PP 5-6 I 12 P 2 P 5 I 93 P 26 I 95 P 5 I 147 P 4 PP 15-16	--	--

CHART NO. 1-2

DOCID: 3560861

TOP SECRET

RESULTS OF EUROPEAN AXIS CRYPTANALYSIS AS LEARNED FROM TICOM SOURCES

(WITH ANNOTATIONS FROM ARMY SECURITY AGENCY SOURCES IN PARENTHESES)

COUNTRY OF ORIGIN		SERVICE	DESCRIPTION OF SYSTEM	NAME OF SYSTEM: COUNTRY OF ORIGIN	NAME OF SYSTEM: AXIS	NAME OF SYSTEM: U.S.A.	DATES OF USE	WHEN ATTACKED AND BY WHOM	RESULTS	TICOM REFERENCE	STATUS OF THE SYSTEM AT ASA	REMARKS
UNITED KINGDOM	43	NAVY	4-FIGURE 2-PART CODE UNTIL FEB 1944, THEN TWO 4-LETTER CODES, A AND B. ONE WAS USED FOR INDIVIDUAL DIRECTION-FINDING BEARINGS, CHANGED SEMI-MONTHLY. THE OTHER WAS USED FOR CONSOLIDATED DIRECTION-FINDING REPORTS, CHANGED MONTHLY.	?	KOLBERG A AND B	--	?-1944-?	1944 OKM	READ	D 6 D 15 P 9	--	--
UNITED KINGDOM	44	NAVY	1-PART CODE UNTIL 1 JULY 1944; 2-PART CODE THEREAFTER.	FOXO	HUNSRÜCK; SÜNTEL	--	?-1944-?	1944 OKM	READ UNTIL 1 JULY 1944 AND FROM NOV 1944 TO END OF YEAR.	D 6; D 44 D 15 P 2 P 8 D 18 P 9 I 12 P 5 I 14Ø P 2	--	--
UNITED KINGDOM	45	NAVY	1-PART CODE, CHANGING DAILY, UNTIL 1 APRIL 1944; 2-PART THEREAFTER, CHANGING DAILY.	LOXO	HUNSRÜCK; SÜNTEL	--	?-1944-?	1944 OKM	READ	D 6; D 44 D 15 PP 7-8 D 18 PP 8-9 I 12 P 5 I 14Ø P 2	--	--
UNITED KINGDOM	46	NAVY	1-PART CODE UNTIL APRIL 1944, 2-PART THEREAFTER VOCABULARY IDENTICAL WITH COFOX.	MEDOX	HUNSRÜCK; SÜNTEL	--	?-1944-?	1943 OKM	READ UNTIL AUTUMN 1944, WHEN WORK STOPPED. BOOK FOR MARCH-APRIL 1944 COMPROMISED. APRIL 1944. READ AGAIN 1945.	D 6 D 15 P 7 D 18 P 8 D 44 P 2 I 12 P 5 I 95 P 7	--	--
UNITED KINGDOM	47	NAVY	2-PART CODE	TRAXO	HUNSRÜCK; SÜNTEL	--	?-1944-?	1944 OKM	BROKEN CONTINUOUSLY,* READ UNTIL SUPERSEDED.	D 6; D 44 D 15 P 2 P 8 I 95 P 6	--	--
UNITED KINGDOM	48	NAVY	ONE-TIME PAD ENCIPHERMENT SYSTEM.	ONE-TIME PADS	ONE-TIME PADS	--	?-1944-?	1944 OKM ? OKW	NOT READ. PADS CAPTURED IN AEGEAN IN MARCH 1944.	D 15 P 4 I 31 P 6 I 93 P 6	--	--
UNITED KINGDOM	49	NAVY	ADDITIVE SYSTEM: CONTAINED 1ØØ PAGES OF 3Ø LINES OF ADDITIVE. HALF WAS FOR ADDRESSES, HALF FOR TEXT. VALID FOR ABOUT 1Ø DAYS.	LONG SUBTRACTOR	?	--	? - 1944	? OKM	?	D 4Ø PP 12-13	--	--
UNITED KINGDOM	5Ø	CONSULAR AND NAVAL	5-LETTER 2-PART CODE USED FOR ADDRESSES IN NAVAL SHORE CODE, ALSO USED FOR CONSULAR SERVICE. HAD A NAVAL SUPPLEMENT.	GOVERNMENT TELEGRAPH CODE	ALFEN		?-194Ø-1944-?	194Ø OKM	READ CURRENTLY IN 194Ø. BASIC BOOK COMPROMISED 194Ø. NAVAL SUPPLEMENT COMPROMISED BERGEN CONSULATE 194Ø.	D 6 D 15 P 1Ø D 18 P 9 I 93 PP 17-18 I 147 P 3	--	--

CHART NO. I-2

TOP SECRET

DOCID: 3560861

TOP SECRET

RESULTS OF EUROPEAN AXIS CRYPTANALYSIS
AS LEARNED FROM TICOM SOURCES

(WITH ANNOTATIONS FROM ARMY SECURITY AGENCY SOURCES IN PARENTHESES)

COUNTRY OF ORIGIN		SERVICE	DESCRIPTION OF SYSTEM	NAME OF SYSTEM: COUNTRY OF ORIGIN	NAME OF SYSTEM: AXIS	NAME OF SYSTEM: U.S.A.	DATES OF USE	WHEN ATTACKED AND BY WHOM	RESULTS	TICOM REFERENCE	STATUS OF THE SYSTEM AT ASA	REMARKS
UNITED KINGDOM	51	CONSULAR AND NAVAL	4-FIGURE ?-PART CODE USED IN TRAFFIC BETWEEN SHORE STATIONS INCLUDING CONSULATES.	NAVAL SHORE CODE	STETTIN	--	?-1944-?	1944 OKM	ABOUT 200 RELATIVE CODE-GROUPS OBTAINED NO ABSOLUTE VALUES.	D 6 D 15 P 10 D 41 PP 5-6 I 93 P 12	--	--
UNITED KINGDOM	52	NAVAL ATTACHE	4-FIGURE ?-PART CODE ENCIPHERED WITH ADDITIVE. DISCRIMINANTS VCVCV OR CVCVC.	INTERDEPARTMENTAL CIFHER	BREMEN	--	? - 1940-1942	1938 OKM 1940 OKL 1940 FA 1940 OKW	OKM HAD NOT RECOVERED BASIC BOOK; COMPROMISED 1940 IN NORWAY.	D 6 I 12 P 5 I 22 P 12 I 31 P 11 I 111 P 3 I 119 P 4 I 147 PP 10-11, 12 I 152 P 9 I 172 P 2 P 4 IF 118A P 9	--	--
UNITED KINGDOM	53	MERCHANT NAVY	5-FIGURE 5-LETTER CODE, ENCIPHERED BY SUBSTITUTION OR UNENCIPHERED. LATER ENCIPHERED WITH ONE-TIME PADS.	BENTLEY CODE	TATRA	--	? - 1944	1944 OKM 1944 OKL	OKM READ. OKL READ EASILY.	D 6 D 15 P 9 D 18 P 9 I 93 P 12 P 17 I 119 P 5 I 152 PP 9-10	--	--
UNITED KINGDOM	54	MERCHANT NAVY	4-LETTER OR 5-LETTER 2-PART CODE, UNENCIPHERED OR ENCIPHERED BY SUBSTITUTION.	MERCHANT NAVY CODE	MERCHANT NAVY CODE	--	1940 - ?	1940 OKM 1940 OKL	OKM CAPTURED SEVERAL COPIES IN NORWAY, READ TRAFFIC SOON THEREAFTER. OKL READ FROM EARLY IN WAR.	I 93 P 28 I 121 P 11 I 147 P 10 D 63	--	--
UNITED KINGDOM	55	MERCHANT NAVY	4-LETTER 4-FIGURE ?-PART CODE. ENCIPHERED WITH TABLES AND PADS.	MERCHANT SHIPS CODE; MERSIGS	GALLIEN	--	1942?-CURRENT	1942 OKM ? SIS	BOOK CAPTURED. OKM READ CURRENTLY 1 JAN 1944 TO END OF WAR. SIS READ. 2 TABLES RECONSTRUCTED.	D 6; D 43 D 15 P 5 D 18 P 7 D 41 P 5 I 12 P 5 P 7 I 95 P 5 IF 1506	--	--
UNITED KINGDOM	56	AIR FORCE	3-FIGURE ?-PART CODE, ABOUT 1,000 GROUPS. ENCIPHERED WITH "SYKO MACHINE.	AIR FORCE CODE	"AIR FORCE CODE"	--	? - ?	? SIS ? OKL	SIS READ; OKL READ "LIKE CLEAR TEXT"	I 109 P 40 IF 1513 P 2 IF 115F F 2	--	--
UNITED KINGDOM	57	DIPLOMATIC	?-PART CODE. INDICATOR ABABY OR ABABI.	?	?	--	?-1940-?	1940 SIM	READ	IF 1524	--	--
UNITED KINGDOM	58	DIPLOMATIC	?-PART CODE.	?	ENGLISH DIP CODE W. 1938	--	? - ?	? SIS	READ. 100% COMPROMISED.	IF 1506	--	--
UNITED KINGDOM	59	DIPLOMATIC	DETAILS OF SYSTEM UNKNOWN.	?	?	--	? - ?	? SIM	PARTLY RECONSTRUCTED	IF 1517	--	--

CHART NO. 1-2

TOP SECRET

DOCID: 3560861

TOP SECRET

RESULTS OF EUROPEAN AXIS CRYPTANALYSIS
AS LEARNED FROM TICOM SOURCES
(WITH ANNOTATIONS FROM ARMY SECURITY AGENCY SOURCES IN PARENTHESES)

COUNTRY OF ORIGIN		SERVICE	DESCRIPTION OF SYSTEM	NAME OF SYSTEM			DATES OF USE	WHEN ATTACKED AND BY WHOM	RESULTS	TICOM REFERENCE	STATUS OF THE SYSTEM AT ASA	REMARKS
				COUNTRY OF ORIGIN	AXIS	U.S.A.						
UNITED KINGDOM	6Ø	MILITARY	CIPHER. SAME TYPE AS SYKO. USED FOR TRAINING IN THE UNITED KINGDOM.	?	ANNA	--	? - ?	? SIM	READ	IF 1517	--	--
UNITED KINGDOM	61	MILITARY	5-LETTER ?-PART CODE OF ABOUT 1ØØ VALUES. PREARRANGED VOCABULARY. CODE VALUES SLIDE AGAINST VOCABULARY DEPENDING ON MESSAGE INDICATOR.	CODEX	CODEX	--	? - ?	1942 SIM 1944 OKH	READ ONLY INFREQUENTLY BY SIM. SOLVED BY OKH.	IF 1528 IF 5 P 8 IF 1Ø7 P 8	--	--
UNITED KINGDOM	62	MILITARY	2-LETTER CODE MADE OF COORDINATES OF A 676 SQUARE. DAILY CHANGING KEY.	?		--	? - ?	? SIM	READ	IF 1517	--	--
UNITED KINGDOM	64	MILITARY	4-FIGURE ?-PART CODE, ENCIPHERED.	?	?	--	? - ?	? SIM	READ	IF 1518	--	--
UNITED KINGDOM	65	AIR - LAND	3-LETTER ?-PART CODE USED FOR CROSS-CHANNEL TRAFFIC.	?	?	--	? - ?	1944 SID	?	IF 1527	--	--
UNITED KINGDOM	66	R A F	CODE FOR COMMUNICATION BETWEEN PLANES AND DROME-"ENCIPHERED BY SYKO."	?	"X"	--	? - ?	? SIS, SIM	READ	IF 1513 IF 1523	--	--
UNITED KINGDOM	67	AIR FORCE	CODE	?	AIRFORCE CODE C.O. 75 2	--	? - ?	? SIS	READ. COMPROMISED.	IF 15Ø6	--	--
UNITED KINGDOM	68	NAVY-AIR	TACTICAL CODE.	?	FOX	--	? - ?	? SIS	READ	IF 1527	--	--
UNITED KINGDOM	69	NAVY	TWO-LETTER THREE-LETTER ABBREVIATION CODE.	?	SELF EVIDENCE	--	? - ?	? SIM	READ. COMPROMISED.	IF 1523	--	--
UNITED KINGDOM	7Ø	NAVY	4-FIGURE ?-PART CODE WITH 1Ø,ØØØ GROUPS. KEY ENCIPHERMENT.	?	ANGLO-AMERICAN	--	? - ?	1942 SIS AND GERMANS	READ	IF 1527	--	--
UNITED KINGDOM	71	NAVY	4-FIGURE ?-PART CODE. USED NON-REPETITIVE CIPHER KEY.	?	?	--	1941-1943	1941 SIS	READ DEPTHS. NOT READ AFTER 1942 BECAUSE OF INDICATOR CHANGE.	IF 1527	--	--
UNITED KINGDOM	72	NAVY	ENCIPHERED CODE. 3Ø,ØØØ OR 1ØØ,ØØØ GROUPS. ENCIPHERMENT BY VOLUME 1ØØ PAGES WITH 3Ø LINES OF 5 DIGITS. GOOD FOR 3 MONTHS.	?	?	--	? - ?	? SIS	READ	IF 15Ø6	--	--
UNITED KINGDOM	73	NAVY	TACTICAL CODES WITH DAILY-CHANGING ENCIPHERING TABLES.	?	?	--	? - ?	? SIS	READ	IF 2Ø9	--	--
UNITED KINGDOM	74	NAVAL AIR-CRAFT	CODE	?	NAVAL AIR CRAFT CODE NO. 2 S.P. Ø2192 2	--	? - ?	? SIS	READ. COMPROMISED.	IF 15Ø6	--	--

CHART NO. 1-2

TOP SECRET

DOCID: 3560861

TOP SECRET

RESULTS OF EUROPEAN AXIS CRYPTANALYSIS AS LEARNED FROM TICOM SOURCES

(WITH ANNOTATIONS FROM ARMY SECURITY AGENCY SOURCES IN PARENTHESES)

COUNTRY OF ORIGIN		SERVICE	DESCRIPTION OF SYSTEM	NAME OF SYSTEM			DATES OF USE	WHEN ATTACKED AND BY WHOM	RESULTS	TICOM REFERENCE	STATUS OF THE SYSTEM AT ASA	REMARKS
				COUNTRY OF ORIGIN	AXIS	U.S.A.						
UNITED KINGDOM	75	NAVAL INTELLIGENCE	CIPHER	?	NAVAL INTELLIGENCE NO. 1 S.P. Ø23Ø7; PBLOK	--	? - ?	? SIS	READ. 1ØØ% COMPROMISED.	IF 15Ø6	--	--
UNITED KINGDOM	76	?	5-FIGURE 1-PART CODE. SIMILAR TO U.S. GREY.	?	?	--	? - ?	? SIM	READ	IF 1518	--	--
UNITED KINGDOM	77	?	4-LETTER 2-PART CODE, UNENCIPHERED.	?	?	--	? - ?	? SIM	READ	IF 1518	--	--
UNITED KINGDOM	78	DIPLOMATIC	1-PART CODE.	?	"INDIAN WORD CODE"	--	1939-194Ø	? FA	READ	I 172 P 3	--	--
UNITED KINGDOM	79	DIPLOMATIC	SUBSTITUTION TABLES FOR ENCIPHERING GOVERNMENT TELEGRAPH CODE IN EIRE TRAFFIC. 26 RANDOM ALPHABETS.	?	?	--	?-1942-?	1942 PERS Z S 1943 FA	PERS Z S READ UNTIL 1943. FA READ BERLIN AND MADRID LINKS.	I 172 PP 3-4	--	--
UNITED KINGDOM	8Ø	FOREIGN OFFICE	?-PART CODE	R CODE 1941	?	--	? - ?	? PERS Z S	BROKEN IN 6 MONTHS, 6,ØØØ GROUPS IDENTIFIED.	I 172 P 3	--	--
UNITED KINGDOM	81	AIR FORCE	AIR-GROUND CODE	"CONFIDENTIAL AIR CODE"	?	--	? - ?	? GERMANS	COMPROMISED	IF 118G PP 3-4	--	--
UNITED KINGDOM	82	?	METEOROLOGICAL "CIPHER FORMED OF 5-FIGURE GROUPS. LETTERS BEING ENCIPHERED IN THE RECOGNITION GROUP. TWO TYPES: WITH A VOWEL AT THE BEGINNING, AND WITH A CONSONANT."	?	?	--	?-1942-?	1942 OKL	8Ø% DECIPHERED	IF 118A P 5 F 1Ø	--	--
UNITED KINGDOM	83	?	DETAILS OF SYSTEM UNKNOWN.	?	AIRCRAFT MOVEMENT CODE	--	?-1942-?	1942 OKL 1943 SIS?	READ 9Ø%	IF 118A P 5 PP 9-1Ø IF 118F P 2	--	--

TOP SECRET

CHART NO. 1-2

DOCID: 3560861

TOP SECRET

RESULTS OF EUROPEAN AXIS CRYPTANALYSIS
AS LEARNED FROM TICOM SOURCES
(WITH ANNOTATIONS FROM ARMY SECURITY AGENCY SOURCES IN PARENTHESES)

COUNTRY OF ORIGIN		SERVICE	DESCRIPTION OF SYSTEM	NAME OF SYSTEM: COUNTRY OF ORIGIN	NAME OF SYSTEM: AXIS	NAME OF SYSTEM: U.S.A.	DATES OF USE	WHEN ATTACKED AND BY WHOM	RESULTS	TICOM REFERENCE	STATUS OF THE SYSTEM AT ASA	REMARKS
UNITED STATES	1	DIPLOMATIC	5-LETTER 1-PART CODE OF ABOUT 72,000 GROUPS OF CVCVC PATTERN. UNENCIPHERED.	--	B-1; GREEN	--	? - ?	1916 PERS Z S	READ. ORIGINALLY SOLVED BY "SUSSEX NOTE" WHICH PROVIDED ABOUT 1,000 GROUP CRIB. SOME 20,000 GROUPS RECOVERED BY 1919	DF 15	--	--
UNITED STATES	2	DIPLOMATIC	5-LETTER CODE. USED BY COL. HOUSE IN TRAFFIC TO WASHINGTON.	--	B-2; COL. HOUSE'S GREEN & BLUE CODE	--	1916-1920	? PERS Z S	NOT READ.	DF 15	--	--
UNITED STATES	3	DIPLOMATIC	5-LETTER 1-PART CODE OF ABOUT 59,000 GROUPS. UNENCIPHERED. STILL IN USE IN 1942.	--	B-3; GRAY CODE	--	1918-1943	1919 PERS Z S 1919 SIM	READ CURRENTLY AFTER 1919. SOLVED ON BASIS OF PLAIN TEXT OBTAINED FROM EMBASSY IN STOCKHOLM.	DF 15; IF 1518	--	--
UNITED STATES	4	DIPLOMATIC	5-LETTER 1-PART CODE WITH GROUP PATTERN CVCCV. ABOUT 14,400 GROUPS.	--	B-5	--	1919 - ?	1919 PERS Z S	READ BY CRYPTANALYTIC COMPROMISE.	DF 15	--	--
UNITED STATES	5	DIPLOMATIC	5-LETTER 2-PART CODE, ENCIPHERED.	--	B-6A; A-1; AC1	--	1920-1944	1924 PERS Z S 1941 OKW	80% RECONSTRUCTED IN 1939. 100% COMPROMISED IN 1941.	I 22; DF 15	--	--
UNITED STATES	6	DIPLOMATIC	5-LETTER 2-PART CODE, ENCIPHERED.	--	B-6B; B-1	--	1920-1942-1944?	1940 PERS Z S	PRESUMABLY NOT READ	I 22; DF 15	--	--
UNITED STATES	7	DIPLOMATIC	5-LETTER 2-PART CODE, UNENCIPHERED.	--	B-7; C-1	--	1920-1942?	1937 PERS Z S	READ	DF 15; I 22 T 371; T 372 D 3C	--	--
UNITED STATES	8	DIPLOMATIC	5-LETTER 2-PART CODE OF "ABOUT 125,053 GROUPS."	--	B-8; AM-9; BROWN	--	? - 1938?	1938 PERS Z S 1941 OKW ? FA?	READ CURRENTLY AFTER 1938. 100% COMPROMISED IN 1941.	DF 15; I 22 TF 10; IF 15 I 143:	--	--
UNITED STATES	9	DIPLOMATIC	5-LETTER CODE IN 3 VOLUMES. "MESSAGES WERE ENCODED IN 3 PARTS, ONE PART FROM EACH VOLUME."	--	BROWN	--	? - ?	? SIM	READ. COMPROMISED.	IF 1518 IF 1524	--	--
UNITED STATES	10	DIPLOMATIC	5-FIGURE 1-PART CODE OF ABOUT 8,000 GROUPS. UNENCIPHERED.	--	Z-1; BLUE CODE	--	?-(1916)-?	1916 PERS Z S	READ. COMPROMISED BY "SUSSEX NOTE"	DF 15	--	--
UNITED STATES	11	DIPLOMATIC	5-FIGURE 1-PART CODE OF ABOUT 72,000 GROUPS. UNENCIPHERED. USED MAINLY BY CHARGE D'AFFAIRES AT CONSTANTINOPLE WITH WASHINGTON, BERLIN, VIENNA, ETC.	--	Z-2	--	? - ?	? PERS Z S	READ. SOLVED BY NOTING STATISTICAL RESEMBLANCE TO B-1 WHICH WAS READ.	DF 15	--	--

CHART NO. 1-2

TOP SECRET

DOCID: 3560861

TOP SECRET

RESULTS OF EUROPEAN AXIS CRYPTANALYSIS
AS LEARNED FROM TICOM SOURCES
(WITH ANNOTATIONS FROM ARMY SECURITY AGENCY SOURCES IN PARENTHESES)

COUNTRY OF ORIGIN	SERVICE	DESCRIPTION OF SYSTEM	NAME OF SYSTEM: COUNTRY OF ORIGIN	NAME OF SYSTEM: AXIS	NAME OF SYSTEM: U.S.A.	DATES OF USE	WHEN ATTACKED AND BY WHOM	RESULTS	TICOM REFERENCE	STATUS OF THE SYSTEM AT ASA	REMARKS
UNITED STATES 12	DIPLOMATIC	5-FIGURE 1-PART CODE OF ABOUT 47,ØØØ GROUPS. UNENCIPHERED.	--	Z-3; RED	--	? - ?	? PERS Z S	READ. LATER COMPROMISED AND PHOTOGRAPHED AT FRANKFORT AM MAIN	DF 15	--	--
UNITED STATES 13	DIPLOMATIC	5-FIGURE 1-PART CODE OF ABOUT 24,ØØØ GROUPS. UNENCIPHERED.	--	Z-7	--	1918 - ?	1919 PERS Z S	PARTIALLY SOLVED	DF 15	--	--
UNITED STATES 14	DIPLOMATIC	STRIP CIPHER, NO STRIP ELIMINATION, GENERATRIX SPLIT 15-15.	--	Ø-2	--	1942-1944?	1942 PERS Z S 1942 OKW, POSSIBLY OKH ? FA	READ CURRENTLY 1943-1944	I 2; I 22 I 25; I 31 I 54; I 94 I 89; I 176 I 76; I 13 I 39; I 46 I 53; IF 51 IF 175; TF 1Ø I 25; I 54	--	--
UNITED STATES 15	DIPLOMATIC	DOUBLE TRANSPOSITION SYSTEM USED BY "COORDINATOR OF INFORMATION, WASHINGTON."	--	DOUBLE TRANSPOSITION	--	? - ?	? PERS Z S	PRESUMABLY NOT READ.	I 22	--	--
UNITED STATES 16	MILITARY ATTACHE	5-LETTER CODE, ENCIPHERED WITH 1Ø TABLES OF 2Ø RANDOM ALPHABETS, VOWEL FOR VOWEL, CONSONANT FOR CONSONANT.	--	?	--	?-1942-?	1942 SIM	READ. PHOTOSTAT COPIES OF CODE BOOK RECEIVED FROM HUNGARY. TABLES RECONSTRUCTED BY SIM.	IF 1524	--	--
UNITED STATES 17	MILITARY ATTACHE	5-LETTER CODE, ENCIPHERED.		MI-3; WAR DEPARTMENT CONFIDENTIAL CODE NO. 2	--	?-1942-?	1942 PERS Z S	1ØØ% COMPROMISED	DF 15	--	--
UNITED STATES 18	MILITARY ATTACHE	5-LETTER CODE, UNENCIPHERED.	--	MI-1	--	?-1942-?	1942 PERS Z S	1ØØ% COMPROMISED	DF 15	--	--
UNITED STATES 19	MILITARY ATTACHE	DOUBLE TRANSPOSITION, USING INCOMPLETE RECTANGLES.	--	MILITARY ATTACHE'S EMERGENCY CIPHER	--	?-1942-?	1942 SIM	READ	IF 1519 I 31	--	(PROBABLY RECOVERED BY ANAGRAMMING)
UNITED STATES 2Ø	ARMY	CIPHER MACHINE	--	AM 2; AMERICAN "BIG" MACHINE	--	1941 - ?	? OKL ? OKH? ? OKM?	NOT READ	I 74; I 112 I 113; I 1Ø9 I 119; D 7	--	--
UNITED STATES 21	ARMY	HAGELIN CIPHER MACHINE.	--	AM-1; M-2Ø9	--	1942 - ?	1943 OKH 1943 OKM 1944 OKL? ? OKW ? PERS Z S	1Ø%-2Ø% OF ARMY TRAFFIC INTERCEPTED WAS READ	I 23; I 46 I 45; I 6Ø I 76; I 85 I 142; I 175 I 31; I 35 I 93; I 93 I 6; I 1Ø9 I 119; IF 127 IF 127; I 112 I 22; I 5Ø I 95; I 147	--	--

CHART NO. I-2

TOP SECRET

RESULTS OF EUROPEAN AXIS CRYPTANALYSIS AS LEARNED FROM TICOM SOURCES

(WITH ANNOTATIONS FROM ARMY SECURITY AGENCY SOURCES IN PARENTHESES)

COUNTRY OF ORIGIN		SERVICE	DESCRIPTION OF SYSTEM	NAME OF SYSTEM			DATES OF USE	WHEN ATTACKED AND BY WHOM	RESULTS	TICOM REFERENCE	STATUS OF THE SYSTEM AT ASA	REMARKS
				COUNTRY OF ORIGIN	AXIS	U.S.A.						
UNITED STATES	22	ARMY	5-LETTER 1-PART CODE, UNENCIPHERED.	--	WAR TELEGRAPH CODE 1919	--	? - ?	1942? PERS Z S	READ: COMPROMISED BY PHOTOSTAT COPY	DF 15 P 3	--	--
UNITED STATES	23	ARMY	5-LETTER 2-PART CODE OF ABOUT 14Ø,ØØØ GROUPS. UNENCIPHERED.	--	TELWA	--	1943 - ?	1944 OKL	READ 1Ø% IN 1944, CURRENTLY IN 1945	I 112; IF 175	--	--
UNITED STATES	24	ARMY	4-LETTER OR 4-FIGURE 2-PART CODE.	--	D.F.C.	--	194Ø-1944?	1944 OKH	READ OCCASIONALLY. COMPROMISED.	I 76; IF 1Ø7 IF 127	--	--
UNITED STATES	25	ARMY	DOUBLE TRANSPOSITION.	--	DOUBLE TRANSPOSITION	--	?-1945-?	1945 OKH	READ OCCASIONALLY.	I 8Ø; IF 1Ø7 I 22; IF 175	--	--
UNITED STATES	26	ARMY-AIR	STRIP CIPHER, NO STRIP ELIMINATION.	--	"CENEB"	--	? - ?	1942 OKL	READ UNTIL STRIP ELIMINATION WAS INTRODUCED IN 1943.	I 112; I 119 IF 175	--	--
UNITED STATES	27	ARMY-AIR	POLYALPHABETIC SUBSTITUTION USING 25 DISCS.	--	"STRIP"; "URSAL"; "COAC"	--	?-1942-?	1942 OKH 1943 OKL	READ	I 112; I 113 I 142; I 119 IF 1Ø7; IF 175	--	--
UNITED STATES	28	ARMY-AIR	DIGRAPHIC CODE CHART WITH CHANGEABLE COORDINATES.	--	SLIDEX	--	? - 1945	? OKH ? OKL	READ CURRENTLY WITH 1-3 HOURS LAG.	I 76; I 8Ø I 1Ø9; I 174 IF 1Ø7; IF 127	--	--
UNITED STATES	29	AIR	ENCIPHERED SPEECH DEVICE.	--	"MUSTANG TIGERSTEDT"	--	? - ?	1945 OKW	DEVICE CAPTURED FROM MUSTANG PLANE. THEORETICAL SOLUTION ONLY.	I 17; I 31 I 44; I 92 I 96; I 1Ø4 I 127; D 68 I 57; I 2Ø I 71; I 88 I 186; I 19Ø	--	--
UNITED STATES	3Ø	AIR	CIPHER MACHINE.	--	AM 2; AMERICAN "BIG" MACHINE	--	? - ?	? OKL ? OKH? ? OKM?	NOT READ.	I 74; I 1Ø9 I 112; I 113 I 119; D 7	--	--
UNITED STATES	31	AIR	HAGELIN CIPHER DEVICE	--	AM-1; M 2Ø9	--	1942 - ?	SEE UNITED STATES 21	1Ø%-2Ø%			
UNITED STATES	32	AIR	2-LETTER CODE. DAILY CHANGE OF CODE.	--	BOMBER CODE	--	?-1944-?	1944 OKL	READ CURRENTLY	I 1Ø9	--	--
UNITED STATES	33	COMBINED UNITED STATES-GREAT BRITAIN JOINT ARMY-AIR-NAVY	CIPHER MACHINE.	--	"COMBINED CIPHER MACHINE"	--	1944 - ?	1944 OKM	NOT READ	DF 3; D 15 D 17; D 18 D 43; I 93	--	--

CHART NO. 1-2

DOCID: 3560861

~~TOP SECRET~~

RESULTS OF EUROPEAN AXIS CRYPTANALYSIS
AS LEARNED FROM TICOM SOURCES
(WITH ANNOTATIONS FROM ARMY SECURITY AGENCY SOURCES IN PARENTHESES)

COUNTRY OF ORIGIN		SERVICE	DESCRIPTION OF SYSTEM	NAME OF SYSTEM: COUNTRY OF ORIGIN	NAME OF SYSTEM: AXIS	NAME OF SYSTEM: U.S.A.	DATES OF USE	WHEN ATTACKED AND BY WHOM	RESULTS	TICOM REFERENCE	STATUS OF THE SYSTEM AT ASA	REMARKS
UNITED STATES	34	ARMY-AIR-NAVY	HAGELIN CIPHER MACHINE.	--	AM-1; M-209	--	1942 - ?	(SEE UNITED STATES 21)	READ	I 23; I 46 I 48; I 60 I 76; I 80 I 142; I 175 I 31; I 35 I 83; I 93 I 5; I 109 I 119; I 112 IF 107; IF 127	--	--
UNITED STATES	35	ARMY-NAVY	3-LETTER 2-PART CODE, UNENCIPHERED. FOR JOINT ARMY-NAVY ASSAULT OPERATIONS. 4-LETTER PRONOUNCEABLE INDICATOR.	--	"COMBINED" ASSAULT CODE	--	1944 - ?	1944 OKM	READ "EXTENSIVELY." ALSO COMPROMISED BY CAPTURE.	D 15; D 18 D 44	--	--
UNITED STATES	36	NAVY	CIPHER MACHINE.	--	AM-2?; "BIG" MACHINE	--	? - ?	? OKL ? OKH? ? OKM?	NOT READ	I 74; I 109 I 112; I 113 I 119; D 7	--	--
UNITED STATES	37	NAVY	HAGELIN CIPHER MACHINE	--	AM-1; M-209	--	1942 - ?	(SEE UNITED STATES 21)	READ--ONLY A FEW DAY'S TRAFFIC, DUE TO LACK OF DEPTH	I 5; I 35 I 92; I 95	--	--
UNITED STATES	38	NAVY	STRIP CIPHER	--	"DUPYH"	--	?-1942-?	1942 OKM	READ. COMPROMISED STRIPS AND SETTINGS RECEIVED FROM JAPANESE.	I 12; I 93	--	--

CHART NO. 1-2

~~TOP SECRET~~

DOCID: 3560861

72

TOP SECRET

RESULTS OF EUROPEAN AXIS CRYPTANALYSIS
AS LEARNED FROM TICOM SOURCES

(WITH ANNOTATIONS FROM ARMY SECURITY AGENCY SOURCES IN PARENTHESES)

COUNTRY OF ORIGIN	SERVICE	DESCRIPTION OF SYSTEM	NAME OF SYSTEM: COUNTRY OF ORIGIN	NAME OF SYSTEM: AXIS	NAME OF SYSTEM: U.S.A.	DATES OF USE	WHEN ATTACKED AND BY WHOM	RESULTS	TICOM REFERENCE	STATUS OF THE SYSTEM AT ASA	REMARKS
URUGUAY 1	DIPLOMATIC	4-LETTER 1-PART CODE WITH 2,142 GROUPS. INTERSPERSED PLAIN TEXT AND PLAIN TEXT ENCIPHERMENT. 1ØØ-PLACE TABLES USED TO SUBSTITUTE 2-FIGURE GROUPS FOR LETTERS OR SYLLABLES.	?	?	(URA)	(? - CURRENT)	? PERS Z S	COMPLETELY READ	D 16, REPORT 2, P 5	(ALMOST COMPLETELY READABLE.)	--
URUGUAY 2	DIPLOMATIC	5-FIGURE OR 4-FIGURE CODE.	?	?	?	? - ?	? SIM	1ØØ% COMPROMISED	IF 1517	(UNIDENTIFIED)	--
URUGUAY 3	DIPLOMATIC	?-PART CODE WITH DIGRAPHIC FIGURE ENCIPHERMENT.	?	?	?	? - 1927 - ?	? PERS Z S	?	D 16, REPORT 1, P 4	(UNKNOWN)	--

TOP SECRET

DOCID: 3560861

TOP SECRET

RESULTS OF EUROPEAN AXIS CRYPTANALYSIS AS LEARNED FROM TICOM SOURCES

(WITH ANNOTATIONS FROM ARMY SECURITY AGENCY SOURCES IN PARENTHESES)

COUNTRY OF ORIGIN		SERVICE	DESCRIPTION OF SYSTEM	NAME OF SYSTEM			DATES OF USE	WHEN ATTACKED AND BY WHOM	RESULTS	TICOM REFERENCE	STATUS OF THE SYSTEM AT ASA	REMARKS
				COUNTRY OF ORIGIN	AXIS	U.S.A.						
VATICAN	1	?	4-FIGURE ?-PART CODE ENCIPHERED WITH A TABLE.	?	VAT. T. E. 2	--	?-1938-1939-?	1939 PERS Z S 1939 RLM/FA	TABLES SOLVED. RECOVERED ABOUT 15% OF VALUES.	T 93	--	--
VATICAN	2	?	3-LETTER 1-PART CODE. FIRST TWO ELEMENTS INDICATE PAGE AND LAST ELEMENT INDICATES GROUP. LETTERS "Y" AND "Z" USED AS DUDS OR AS SPELLER INDICATORS.	?	"NULLE YZ"	--	?-1943-?	1943 SIM	400-500 GROUPS RECOVERED.	IF 1517 P 5 IF 1526 P 11	--	--
VATICAN	3	?	3-LETTER 1-PART CODE. FIRST TWO ELEMENTS INDICATE PAGE AND LAST ELEMENT INDICATES GROUP. LETTER "E" USED AS DUD OR AS SPELLER INDICATOR.	?	"NULLA E"	--	?-1944-?	1944 SID, SIM	READ	IF 1526 P 10 IF 1517	--	--
VATICAN	4	?	3-LETTER ?-PART CODE.	?	VATIKAN CODE 11 441	--	? - ?	? ?	RECOVERED 30%-50%	T 2195	--	--
VENEZUELA	1	DIPLOMATIC	4-LETTER 1-PART CODE. 12,000 GROUPS. INTERSPERSED ENCIPHERED PLAIN TEXT.	?	?	(VZB)	(?-1941-CURRENT)	1941 PERS Z S	?	D 16, REPORT 2, P 5 T 3010	(95% READABLE)	--
VENEZUELA	2	?	4-FIGURE ?-PART CODE.	?	?	?	? - ?	? ?	RECOVERED LESS THAN 3%	T 3014	(UNKNOWN)	--
VENEZUELA	3	DIPLOMATIC	POLYALPHABETIC SUBSTITUTION CIPHER WITH 5 TO 10 ALPHABETS.	?	?	(VZA)	(?-1941-CURRENT)	1941 PERS Z S	READ	D 16, REPORT 2, P 5	(100% READABLE)	--

CHART NO. 1-2

TOP SECRET

DOCID: 3560861

TOP SECRET

RESULTS OF EUROPEAN AXIS CRYPTANALYSIS
AS LEARNED FROM TICOM SOURCES
(WITH ANNOTATIONS FROM ARMY SECURITY AGENCY SOURCES IN PARENTHESES)

COUNTRY OF ORIGIN	SERVICE	DESCRIPTION OF SYSTEM	NAME OF SYSTEM: COUNTRY OF ORIGIN	NAME OF SYSTEM: AXIS	NAME OF SYSTEM: U.S.A.	DATES OF USE	WHEN ATTACKED AND BY WHOM	RESULTS	TICOM REFERENCE	STATUS OF THE SYSTEM AT ASA	REMARKS
YUGOSLAVIA- 1 CROATIA	DIPLOMATIC	5-LETTER 1-PART CODE ENCIPHERED BY SUBSTITUTION. USED BY THE FOREIGN OFFICE. DATE GIVEN AT END OF MESSAGE PRECEDED BY S OR SVT.	?	C I	?	?-1944-?	1944 SID	ENCIPHERMENT SYSTEM KNOWN. PERHAPS READ.	T 16Ø4	(UNKNOWN)	--
YUGOSLAVIA 2	(DIPLOMATIC)	(4-LETTER 2-PART CODE UNENCIPHERED.)	?	?	(YOA)	(1935-CURRENT)	1944 OKW	READ	T 797	(GCCS BROKE CODE. ASA NOW READING 1ØØ%. VERY LIGHT TRAFFIC.)	--
YUGOSLAVIA- 3 CROATIA	DIPLOMATIC	5-FIGURE 1-PART CODE. APPROXIMATELY 3Ø,ØØØ GROUPS. CODE GROUPS SPLIT INTO SINGLE DIGITS AND DIGRAPHS, EACH SEPARATELY ENCIPHERED.	?	?	?	?-1943-1944-?	1943 SIM	COMPROMISED. READ JUNE 1944 --SEPT 1944.	IF 1525 PP 5-6	(UNKNOWN)	--
YUGOSLAVIA- 4 MICHAILOVITCH AND TITO	DIPLOMATIC AND CONSULAR	5-FIGURE ?-PART CODE. ABOUT 3Ø,ØØØ-4Ø,ØØØ GROUPS. LATER REPAGINATED. ENCIPHER TABLES USED IN TWO DIFFERENT WAYS. (SIMILAR TO ITEM 2. VARIATION OF YOA ENCIPHERMENT.)	?	?	?	1934-1944-?	1944 SIM AND PREDECESSOR	PLAIN CODE COMPROMISED. ENCIPHERMENTS NOT READ.	IF 1525 PP 2, 5, 6	(UNKNOWN)	--
YUGOSLAVIA 5	DIPLOMATIC AND MILITARY ATTACHE	5-FIGURE PARTIALLY 1-PART CODE. APPROXIMATELY 3Ø,ØØØ GROUPS. PAGES RENUMBERED PERIODICALLY. CLEAR TEXT IN SERBIAN. ENCIPHERED AFTER 1921.	?	?	?	1918-1934	? SIM AND PREDECESSOR	PROBABLY READ.	IF 1525 PP 2, 3	(UNKNOWN)	--
YUGOSLAVIA- 6 SERBIA	DIPLOMATIC?	5-FIGURE ?-PART CODE. ENCIPHERED BY SUBSTITUTION	?	?	?	193Ø - ?	1929 OR 193Ø PERS Z S	?	I 22 P 2	(UNKNOWN)	--
YUGOSLAVIA 7	DIPLOMATIC?	5-FIGURE ?-PART CODE. ENCIPHERED BY DIGRAPHIC SUBSTITUTION WITH TABLES CONSISTING OF 1ØØ DIGRAPHS.	?	?	?	1938-1943-?	1935, 1943 PERS Z S	READ	I 22 P 9	(UNKNOWN)	--
YUGOSLAVIA 8	DIPLOMATIC?	5-FIGURE, PROBABLY 1-PART CODE.	?	STOCKHOLM ØØ1-249	?	? - ?	? PERS Z S	APPROXIMATELY 15% RECOVERED	T 2138	(UNKNOWN)	--
YUGOSLAVIA 9	DIPLOMATIC?	5-FIGURE 1-PART CODE.	?	S D III	?	? - ?	? PERS Z S	RECOVERED LESS THAN 3%	T 2119	(UNKNOWN)	--
YUGOSLAVIA 1Ø	DIPLOMATIC	5-FIGURE 1-PART CODE.	?	37 IX D LESART: 345-12	?	? - ?	? PERS Z S	APPROXIMATELY 35% RECOVERED	T 2238	(UNKNOWN)	--
YUGOSLAVIA 11	DIPLOMATIC	4-FIGURE ?-PART CODE. PROBABLY REPAGINATED TO 5-FIGURE.	?	SERBIEN I	?	?-1924-?	? PERS Z S	WORKED ON	T 2117	(UNIDENTIFIED)	--
YUGOSLAVIA 12 CROATIA	DIPLOMATIC	?-FIGURE ?-PART CODE. "CHILDISH" ENCIPHERMENT.	?	?	?	? - ?	PRIOR TO 1941 SIM	COMPROMISED	IF 1517 P 4	(UNIDENTIFIED)	--
YUGOSLAVIA 13 CROATIA	DIPLOMATIC?	PROBABLY CONSISTED OF A SQUARE 1Ø x 1Ø WITH KEYS FOR EVERY MESSAGE.	?	?	?	? - ?	1942 SIM	READ	IF 1524 P 4	(UNKNOWN)	--
YUGOSLAVIA 14	MILITARY ATTACHE	2-PART CODE.	?	22? AM BOOK	?	1921-1927	1923? SIM	READ FOR 5 YEARS.	IF 1525 P 4	(UNKNOWN)	--
YUGOSLAVIA 15	MILITARY ATTACHE	SIMILAR TO ITEM 12, BUT MORE COMPLICATED PAGE NUMBERING WHICH CHANGED YEARLY. ENCIPHERMENT SIMILAR TO LATER SYSTEM OF FOREIGN OFFICE AND DIPLOMATIC MISSIONS BUT OF SIMPLER CONSTRUCTION.	?	?	?	1927 - ?	? SIM	?	IF 1525 P 4	(UNKNOWN)	--

CHART NO. 1-2

TOP SECRET

DOCID: 3560861

TOP SECRET

RESULTS OF EUROPEAN AXIS CRYPTANALYSIS
AS LEARNED FROM TICOM SOURCES
(WITH ANNOTATIONS FROM ARMY SECURITY AGENCY SOURCES IN PARENTHESES)

COUNTRY OF ORIGIN	SERVICE	DESCRIPTION OF SYSTEM	NAME OF SYSTEM: COUNTRY OF ORIGIN	NAME OF SYSTEM: AXIS	NAME OF SYSTEM: U.S.A.	DATES OF USE	WHEN ATTACKED AND BY WHOM	RESULTS	TICOM REFERENCE	STATUS OF THE SYSTEM AT ASA	REMARKS
YUGOSLAVIA- 16 CROATIA	ARMY	ENIGMA K -- 3 WHEELS AND NO STECKER.	?	?	?	1941-1942-?	1941 OR 1942 OKW	WIRINGS COMPROMISED 1941 OR 1942. READ 100%.	I 92 P 2 I 58 P 3	(NOT KNOWN TO HAVE BEEN USED.)	--
YUGOSLAVIA- 17 TITO	ARMY	FIELD CODE OF THE 26 X 26 SQUARE TYPE. CHANGEABLE ALPHABET COORDINATES.	?	?	?	? - ?	AFTER APRIL 1941 SIM	BROKEN AND RECONSTRUCTED	IF 1517 P 5	(UNKNOWN)	--
YUGOSLAVIA 18	ARMY	CODE OF THE 26 X 26 SQUARE TYPE. SIMILAR TO ITEM 17. TABLES CHANGED EVERY TWO OR THREE MONTHS.	?	?	?	?-1941-?	BEFORE 1941 SIM	READ	IF 1519 P 3	(UNKNOWN)	--
YUGOSLAVIA 19	ARMY	FIELD CODES OF THE 10 X 10 SQUARE TYPE.	?	?	?	? - ?	? SIM	?	IF 1525 P 6	(UNKNOWN)	--
YUGOSLAVIA- 20 CROATIA	ARMY	DIGRAPHIC SUBSTITUTION, 2-SQUARE CHECKERBOARD. USED IN THE FIELD.	?	?	?	1941-1943	AFTER APRIL 1941 SIM	EASILY READ	IF 1517 P 4 IF 1520 P 5 IF 1512 P 4?	(UNKNOWN)	--
YUGOSLAVIA 21	ARMY	DOUBLE PLAYFAIR.	?	?	?	? - ?	? SIM	?	IF 1525 P 6	(UNKNOWN)	--
YUGOSLAVIA- 22 CROATIA	AIR	REVERSED PLAIN TEXT IN UNALTERED SEQUENCE.	?	?	?	?-1940-1943-?	? SIM	?	IF 1525 P 6	(UNKNOWN)	--
YUGOSLAVIA- 23 MICHAILOVITCH	MILITARY	?-LETTER CODE OF THE 26 X 26 SQUARE TYPE. SPACES CONTAINED DIGRAPHS, TRIGRAPHS, AND WORDS IN FULL.	?	?	?	? - ?	AFTER JUNE 1943 SIM	READ	IF 1520 P 4	(UNKNOWN)	--
YUGOSLAVIA 24	ARMY-NAVY	4-FIGURE 1-PART CODE.	?	?	?	? - ?	? OKW	COMPROMISED 100%	T 962	(UNKNOWN)	--
YUGOSLAVIA- 25 MICHAILOVITCH	MILITARY	DOUBLE TRANSPOSITION CIPHER SYSTEM WITH SAME KEY FOR BOTH RECTANGLES. RECTANGLE WIDTH USUALLY 12 OR 13. NO CALL SIGNS USED. KEYS WERE ANNOUNCED THEN FOLLOWED COVER NAMES OF ADDRESSES.	?	JRC	(YOB)	(1943-1944)	? OKH ? SIM ? PERS Z S	READ BY GERMANS AND ITALIANS	I 69 P 23 D 30 PP 1-11 IF 1520 P 4 IF 1525 P 6	(TRAFFIC RECEIVED. WORKED ON FOR 1-2 MONTHS 1944. NO SUCCESS.)	--
YUGOSLAVIA- 26 TITO	MILITARY	DOUBLE TRANSPOSITION.	?	?	?	? - ?	? OKH	READ	I 113 P 5	(UNKNOWN)	--
YUGOSLAVIA- 27 MICHAILOVITCH	MILITARY	SIMPLE TRANSPOSITION CIPHER ON A PATTERN OF AN INCOMPLETE RECTANGLE, WITH KEY VARYING FROM 13-21. USED IN THE FIELD.	?	?	?	? - ?	1944 SID	PROBABLY READ	IF 1525 P 6	(UNKNOWN)	--
YUGOSLAVIA- 28 MICHAILOVITCH	MILITARY	POLYALPHABETIC SUBSTITUTION CIPHER WITH 5? ALPHABETS.	?	?	?	? - ?	? SIM	READ	IF 1520 P 4	(UNKNOWN)	--
YUGOSLAVIA- 29 TITO	MILITARY	POLYALPHABETIC SUBSTITUTION, 1 OR 2 DIGITS PER LETTER, WITH 3, 4, 5, 6, 9, 11, OR 19 ALPHABETS. KEY CHANGED EVERY 5 DAYS. USED BY DIVISIONS AND BRIGADES.	?	?	?	?-1944-?	? OKH	?	I 69 P 5 I 52 P 5	(UNKNOWN)	--
YUGOSLAVIA- 30 TITO	MILITARY	2-DIGIT SUBSTITUTION BY MEANS OF 10 X 10 ENCIPHERING SQUARE FORMED FROM A 10-LETTER KEYWORD WRITTEN IN VERTICALLY.	?	?	?	? - ?	? OKH	?	I 69 PP 22,23	(UNKNOWN)	--

TOP SECRET

DOCID: 3560861

TOP SECRET

RESULTS OF EUROPEAN AXIS CRYPTANALYSIS AS LEARNED FROM TICOM SOURCES

(WITH ANNOTATIONS FROM ARMY SECURITY AGENCY SOURCES IN PARENTHESES)

COUNTRY OF ORIGIN	SERVICE	DESCRIPTION OF SYSTEM	NAME OF SYSTEM: COUNTRY OF ORIGIN	NAME OF SYSTEM: AXIS	NAME OF SYSTEM: U.S.A.	DATES OF USE	WHEN ATTACKED AND BY WHOM	RESULTS	TICOM REFERENCE	STATUS OF THE SYSTEM AT ASA	REMARKS
YUGOSLAVIA- 31 TITO	MILITARY	2-DIGIT SUBSTITUTION BY MEANS OF 8 x 8 ENCIPHERING SQUARE WITH 8-LETTER KEYWORD WRITTEN IN HORIZONTALLY. PROBABLY USED BY 11TH DIVISION OF 5TH CORPS.	?	?	?	? - ?	? OKH	?	I 69 P 23	(UNKNOWN)	--
YUGOSLAVIA- 32 TITO	MILITARY AND (DIPLOMATIC)	MONOALPHABETIC SUBSTITUTION, 2 DIGITS PER LETTER, AND ALSO AUXILIARY 3-DIGIT CODE, ALL SUPERENCIPHERED WITH NUMERICAL RUNNING ADDITIVE CONVERTED FROM THE TEXT OF A BOOK. USED ABOVE DIVISION.	NOVA SIFRA	?	?	1944-1945	? OKH	NOT BROKEN BUT COULD HAVE BEEN WITH MORE TRAFFIC	I 69 PP 16-20	(IN EFFECT THIS IS A NON-RANDOM ONE-TIME PAD ENCIPHERMENT AND BECAUSE IT IS NON-RANDOM IT IS THEORETICALLY SOLVABLE. ASA IS NOT WORKING ON THIS PROBLEM.)	--
YUGOSLAVIA- 33 TITO	MILITARY?	BELIEVED TO BE SIMILAR TO ITEM 32. MESSAGES TO MOSCOW HAD A SPECIAL GROUP 66666, SOMETIMES 11111 66666 EITHER AT THE BEGINNING OR AT THE END OF THE MESSAGE. FIRST GROUP OF THE ACTUAL MESSAGE USUALLY REPEATED AFTER ADDITION OF A CERTAIN NUMBER.	?	?	?	?-1944-?	? OKH	NOT SOLVED	I 69 P 30	(UNKNOWN)	--
YUGOSLAVIA- 34 TITO	MILITARY	MONOALPHABETIC SUBSTITUTION--LETTER FOR LETTER OR 2 DIGITS PER LETTER. USED BY BRIGADE AND UNITS.	?	?	?	?-1944-?	? OKH	READ	I 69 P 2 I 52 P 5	(UNKNOWN)	--
YUGOSLAVIA- 35 TITO	MILITARY	MONOALPHABETIC SUBSTITUTION, 2 DIGITS WITH 5-DIGIT REPEATING ADDITIVE. USED BELOW DIVISION LEVEL.	?	?	?	?-1944-?	? OKH	?	I 69 PP 2-3	(UNKNOWN)	--
YUGOSLAVIA- 36 TITO	MILITARY	MONOALPHABETIC SUBSTITUTION, 2 DIGITS PER LETTER, WITH NULLS INSERTED IN EVERY 5TH AND 6TH GROUPS AND MULTIPLES THEREOF, AND WITH 15-DIGIT REPEATING ADDITIVE. KEY CHANGED EVERY 7 TO 14 DAYS. USED BELOW DIVISION.	?	?	?	?-1944-?	? OKH	?	I 69 PP 4-5	(UNKNOWN)	--
YUGOSLAVIA- 37 MICHAILOVITCH	MILITARY	MONOALPHABETIC SUBSTITUTION, 1 OR 2 DIGITS FOR SINGLE LETTERS, WITH SHORT REPEATING ADDITIVE. BASED ON A KEYWORD.	?	?	?	?-1943-1944-?	? OKH	READ	I 51 P 3 I 52 P 5	(UNKNOWN)	--
YUGOSLAVIA- 38 TITO	MILITARY	MONOALPHABETIC SUBSTITUTION, 2 DIGITS PER LETTER, ENCIPHERED WITH REPEATING ADDITIVE FORMED MATHEMATICALLY FROM AN ADDITIVE SQUARE OF 300 DIGITS.	?	?	?	?-1944-?	? OKH	?	I 69 P 20	(UNKNOWN)	--
YUGOSLAVIA- 39 TITO	MILITARY	MIXED SUBSTITUTION ENCIPHERED BY MEANS OF ADDITIVESFROM A FIGURE TABLE.	?	?	?	? - ?	? OKH	?	I 52 P 5	(UNKNOWN)	--
YUGOSLAVIA- 40 TITO	MILITARY	VARIABLE SUBSTITUTION WITH SHORT REPEATING ADDITIVE. CIPHER CHANGED EVERY MONTH. USED ABOVE DIVISION, LATER BY UNITS.	?	?	?	?-1944-?	? OKH	READ	I 58 PP 3-15	(UNKNOWN)	--
YUGOSLAVIA- 41 TITO	MILITARY	VARIABLE SUBSTITUTION WITH ENCIPHERING TABLE.	?	?	?	?-1944-?	? OKH	?	I 69, ITEM 13	(UNKNOWN)	--
YUGOSLAVIA-42 TITO	MILITARY	1800 GROUP CODE IN 30 x 60 RECTANGLE SUPERENCIPHERED BY "ENCIPHERING ROWS."	?	?	?	? - ?	? OKL	READ EXTENSIVELY	I 121 P 9	(UNKNOWN)	--
YUGOSLAVIA 43	?	5-LETTER ?-PART CODE.	?	?	?	? - ?	? GERMANS	?	T 2122	(UNKNOWN)	--

TOP SECRET

DOCID: 3560861

TOP SECRET

RESULTS OF EUROPEAN AXIS CRYPTANALYSIS
AS LEARNED FROM TICOM SOURCES
(WITH ANNOTATIONS FROM ARMY SECURITY AGENCY SOURCES IN PARENTHESES)

COUNTRY OF ORIGIN	SERVICE	DESCRIPTION OF SYSTEM	NAME OF SYSTEM: COUNTRY OF ORIGIN	AXIS	U.S.A.	DATES OF USE	WHEN ATTACKED AND BY WHOM	RESULTS	TICOM REFERENCE	STATUS OF THE SYSTEM AT ASA	REMARKS
YUGOSLAVIA 44	?	5-FIGURE PROBABLY 1-PART CODE.	?	STOCKHOLM 25Ø-499	?	? - ?	? GERMANS	APPROXIMATELY 2Ø% RECOVERED	T 2139	(UNKNOWN)	--
YUGOSLAVIA 45	?	5-FIGURE CODE PROBABLY 1-PART.	?	?	?	? - ?	? GERMANS	RECOVERED LESS THAN 2Ø%	T 2124	(UNKNOWN)	--
YUGOSLAVIA 46	?	5-FIGURE ?-PART CODE WITH ABOUT 3Ø,ØØØ-4Ø,ØØØ GROUPS. CLEAR TEXT IN SERBIAN.	?	?	?	1934 - ?	? SIM	COMPROMISED	IF 1525 P 2	(UNKNOWN)	--
YUGOSLAVIA-SERBIA 47	?	5-FIGURE PROBABLY 1-PART CODE.	?	S D IV	?	? - ?	? GERMANS	APPROXIMATELY 25% RECOVERED	T 2123	(UNKNOWN)	--
YUGOSLAVIA 48	?	5-FIGURE 1-PART CODE.	?	?	?	1941 - ?	? ?	1ØØ% COMPROMISED	T 2576	(UNKNOWN)	--
YUGOSLAVIA 49	?	4-FIGURE PROBABLY 1-PART CODE.	?	?	?	? - ?	? GERMANS	APPROXIMATELY 15% RECOVERED	T 2126	(UNKNOWN)	--
YUGOSLAVIA 5Ø	?	4-FIGURE PROBABLY 1-PART CODE.	?	S D V. II	?	? - ?	? GERMANS	APPROXIMATELY 15% RECOVERED	T 2118	(UNKNOWN)	--
YUGOSLAVIA 51	?	DETAILS OF SYSTEM UNKNOWN.	?	S D V. I	?	? - ?	? GERMANS	WORKED ON	T 2123	(UNKNOWN)	--
YUGOSLAVIA 52	?	DETAILS OF SYSTEM UNKNOWN.	?	HOF CODE	?	? - ?	? GERMANS	?	T 2123	(UNKNOWN)	--
YUGOSLAVIA-SERBIA 53	?	DETAILS OF SYSTEM UNKNOWN.	?	S D VI	?	?-1933-?	? GERMANS	WORKED ON	T 2123	(UNKNOWN)	--
YUGOSLAVIA-CROATIA 54	?	CIPHER TRANSPOSITION WITH INCOMPLETE RECTANGLES.	?	?	?	? - ?	AFTER APRIL 1941 SIM	RECONSTRUCTED	IF 1517 P 4	(UNKNOWN)	--
YUGOSLAVIA-SERBIA 55	MILITARY	"TABLE OF 28 x 28, ABOUT 5ØØ WORDS. TRANSMITTED IN 5-LETTER GROUPS. DAILY KEY."	?	?	?	? - ?	? SIM	"HAS BEEN RECONSTRUCTED."	IF 118C, P 4	(UNKNOWN)	--
YUGOSLAVIA-SERBIA 56	MILITARY	SIMPLE TRANSPOSITION WITH VARIABLE LENGTH NUMERICAL KEY. ALL MESSAGES BEGAN WITH BRX CITIRI. INCOMPLETE RECTANGLES.	?	?	?	? - ?	? SIM	READABLE	IF 118C, P 4	(UNKNOWN)	--

CHART NO. 1-2

TOP SECRET

TOP SECRET CREAM

TOP SECRET CREAM

ARMY SECURITY AGENCY

Washington, D. C.

EUROPEAN AXIS SIGNAL INTELLIGENCE IN WORLD WAR II AS REVEALED BY "TICOM" INVESTIGATIONS AND BY OTHER PRISONER OF WAR INTERROGATIONS AND CAPTURED MATERIAL, PRINCIPALLY GERMAN

COMMENTS

VOLUME 2--NOTES ON GERMAN HIGH LEVEL CRYPTOGRAPHY AND CRYPTANALYSIS

Prepared under the direction of the

CHIEF, ARMY SECURITY AGENCY

1 May 1946

WDGAS-14

Volume 2

NOTES ON GERMAN HIGH LEVEL CRYPTOGRAPHY AND CRYPTANALYSIS

Volume 2

Chapter I The Paradox of German High-Level Cryptography

Paragraph

1. German high-level cryptographic systems were insecure, although brilliantly conceived-- German high-level cryptography was brilliantly conceived (as will be shown in this volume) but more brilliantly conceived cryptanalytic procedures and large expenditures in manpower and machinery by the United States and Brisish Governments, in one of the most dramatic chapters of World War II, accomplished daily solutions of German high-level systems that cost Germany heavily, if they did not, as some believe, bring about actual defeat. For instance:

a. The German Air Force lost the Battle of England in 1940, partly because it entrusted bomber-target information to the insecure Air Force Enigma.[1] Unknown to and even unsuspected by the Germans, their operations from this date on were constantly embarrassed by the cryptographic insecurity of this machine.

b. The German Army suffered terrific casualties and losses of materiel in Africa and on the continent because of blind faith in two of its high level military cryptographic machines: the Army Enigma, and the teleprinter cipher attachment "SZ-42." Both were insecure.[2]

[1] The great debt England owes its cryptanalysts is to be recorded in a history of the Government Code and Cypher School, London, to be available in the fall of 1946. The statement here is based on verbal information from intelligence officers and cryptanalysts of the School, and awaits proper documentation. This history will also include data regarding the German Army and Navy Enigmas.

[2] A written report by Brigadier E. T. Williams, chief intelligence officer to Field Marshall Montgomery, 5 October 1945, to be included in the Government Code and Cypher School history, gives specific examples bearing out this statement.

DOCID: 3560816

c. The German Navy lost a staggering number of submarines for a similar reason: insecurity of the Enigma, Navy version.[3]

d. The German Foreign Office employed three main systems, all insecure. Two of them (the Deutsches Satzbuch unenciphered, and the Deutsches Satzbuch enciphered by "Floradora,") were read during the war; the third system (a "one time pad," Army Security Agency trigraph "GEE") was read only in the last six months of war, but gave information of much military value against the Japanese.

2. German military cryptographers had secure cipher devices under development-- It is a paradox that German high-level cryptography was a "practical" failure and at the same time German military cryptographers had so many secure devices in various stages of development.

a. One simple item alone, a "variable-notch" rotor, would probably have prevented Anglo-American attempts at reading the Enigma after 1942, if it had been produced in quantity and installed. This rotor was called "Lueckenfuellerwalze."[4]

[3]The real truth behind these losses has been and still is at this writing (May 1946) so carefully concealed that the following statement by Admiral Doenitz in the Nuremberg trial is of considerable interest: "The Battle of the Atlantic was nearly won prior to July 1942, when German losses were within reasonable limits. But they jumped 300 per cent when Allied aircraft, aided by radar, which came like an epileptic stroke, were used in the fight." He reported 640 to 670 submarines and 30,000 men lost as a result of British and American action. (See IF 259). A captured, unsigned, naval report dated 1944, evidently sent to the Navy High Command regarding cipher security, stated: "... . the high degree of efficiency of the enemy's aircraft Radar, so often surprising, has received remarkable and decisive assistance from directions based on the results of the direction finding service." (See IF 142). It was never realized that cryptanalysis, rather than radar and direction finding, disclosed the positions and intentions of the German submarines.

[4]M 11; I 104 pp 2,3

b. An irregular-drive Enigma that would have defied all presently known methods of solution, was being developed. This was called "Cipher Device 39" ("Schluesselgeraet 39," abbreviated "SG-39").[5]

c. An improved "cipher teleprinter" had been built, installed on several circuits, and used, which prevented easy reading of teleprinter messages in depth; and even if this reading in depth was accomplished, the machine remained secure against known methods of attack as far as all other messages enciphered by it were concerned. This was called "cipher teleprinter T-52e" ("Schluesselfernschreibmaschine T-52e," abbreviated "SFM T-52e").[6]

d. Apparatus was being developed for "cryptizing" a radio teleprinter circuit--that is, for applying a basic cryptographic process to the circuit itself even before any intelligence is superimposed on the emissions. This was called "cipher attachment 42c" ("Schluesselzusatz 42c," abbreviated "SZ-42c"), which was to be used with a continuously operating, crystal-controlled, synchronized teleprinter.[7]

e. A mechanical, portable, keyboard-operated cipher machine, employing an interacting wheel-motion principle applied to Hagelin-type wheels, had been developed and built and partially distributed, which would have been completely secure against reconstruction even if messages were read in depth. This was called "Cipher Device 41" ("Schluesselgeraet 41," abbreviated "SG-41").[8] It was cryptographically superior to its much smaller U.S. Army equivalent device, Converter M-209.

f. Other devices were also in varying stages of development; these included the "Cipher Box" ("Schluesselkasten"), and the "Cipher Disk" ("Schluesselscheibe"), which were two miniature enciphering devices intended for use by secret agents and by the Army.[9]

[5] I 53

[6] I 20, I 31. In this document the term "cipher teleprinter" will be employed consistently to designate a teleprinter in which the cryptographic mechanism is an integral part of and is contained within the machine itself; the term "teleprinter cipher attachment," to designate an auxiliary cryptographic mechanism associated with the teleprinter but not an integral part thereof.

[7] I 57 E 14

[8] I 72

[9] I 20 I 96

The foregoing devices have been studied and are being studied by cryptographers and cryptanalysts at the Army Security Agency, and the general opinion is that the Germans were making rapid strides toward greatly improving their communications security.

The very least that can be said is that they had something different. Their teleprinter devices employed mechanical cipher wheels, as opposed to the U.S. Army and U.S. Navy use of electrically-wired cipher wheels ("rotors"); furthermore, the mechanical wheel arrangements, in their new devices, were highly developed and secure. They also employed interacting wheel motions (wheels mutually controlling one another) for several of their cipher-teleprinters, as well as for their SG-41 (Hagelin-type machine). Mechanical wheels and interacting wheel motions for teleprinter enciphering devices have long been considered by United States cryptographers; our development along other lines has been from choice. None of our present devices uses interacting motion, and the excellent developments of the Germans not only furnish us greater insight into such possibilities, but also increase greatly our store of knowledge.

3. German security studies revealed only theoretical weaknesses of their cryptography-- German military cryptographers failed to realize that their existing Enigmas and teleprinter cryptographic apparatus were insecure. This was because they were unable, in their security studies, to put forth the costly practical effort required to solve them. Their security studies were theoretical only,[10] since actual traffic was never obtained for such studies.[11] They were completely without practical knowledge of how successfully a careful and determined attempt at traffic analysis can provide daily "cribs" and other data for cryptanalytic attack; and they had not advanced sufficiently in applied cryptanalysis to realize that determined engineering staffs can produce items like the Polish (later French, later English, later American) "bombe," the U.S. Navy "duenna," the Army Security Agency "autoscritcher," or the British "colossus." The flashes of intuition and inspiration that come from doing, as well as theorizing, were denied them.

[10] I 45 pp 4,5

[11] I 31

4

A report on naval ciphers dated 10 July 1944, apparently written by the Signal Security Agency of the Navy High Command (OKM/4 SKL/II), stated that solution of the naval Enigma was conceivable, based on "the assumption of extraordinary mechanical outlay on the part of the enemy for cryptographic activities.... though we [OKM/4 SKL/II] can conceive of a machine which would be suitable for this kind of work, we have none available or under consideration, since the whole question does not yet appear to justify undertaking such a difficult special constructional problem."[12] The British did undertake this problem, and were rewarded with astounding success.

4. Interrogation of Anglo-American prisoners failed to disclose German cryptographic weaknesses-- Furthermore, TICOM reveals that Germany never became aware of the Anglo-American solution of German high grade systems. Not even a hint of this fact came to them through their agents, their interrogations of Anglo-American prisoners of war, or their cryptanalysis.

It may be said that Germany lost the cryptologic war even before 1939, in Poland. The Poles invented the "bombe," a device which later, in improved form in England and in America, provided daily solutions of the German plugboard Enigma. The "bombe" secret was almost revealed when three deciphered German messages were found by the Germans in Poland in 1939. The Germans became alarmed and conducted many interrogations;[13] the case was re-opened in 1942 and 1943; but at no time did the Germans learn the real secret of the Poles' success. The Germans became convinced that probably the Enigma indicator system had been at fault (as it partly had been) and since it had already been changed in 1940, they were no longer concerned with the suspected solutions.

Also, there were intelligence officers who feared that Enigma traffic was insecure, but their fears were based only on inference and not on direct proof. Thus, when the Navy High Command became alarmed at mounting submarine losses, the increasing effectiveness of Anglo-American airplane radar was blamed, and the Enigma was exonerated.[14]

[12] IF 142

[13] I 127

[14] See footnote number 3 of this volume.

An intelligence officer attached to the Air Force High Command at the time of the landings in North Africa expressed his suspicions to the Chief Signal Officer of the Air Force, a General Martini, and caused him to reduce "his earlier belief in the 100% security to 80% security,"[15] but his evidence was insufficient to cause the Air Force to discontinue use of the Enigma.

Germany was unable to cryptanalyze British and American high-grade systems carrying cryptanalytic operational information and other ULTRA matters between England and America. As a result she had no hint from cryptanalysis that her own high-grade systems were insecure.

It is absolutely clear that United States and British security regulations applicable to ULTRA were so good and so closely adhered to by all concerned that knowledge of our Enigma-solving and teleprinter-solving operations was kept from the Germans. An interrogation of two of the leading German cryptanalysts, Drs. Huettenhain and Fricke of the Signal Intelligance Agency of the Supreme Command Armed Forces (OKW/Chi), revealed only that:[16]

> "One Allied PW in North Africa had said the United States and British operated with a very large joint 'park' of I.B.M. machinery, but this interrogation was never followed up. No personalities whatever were known."

[15] IF 5
[16] I 84 p 6

6

Volume 2

Chapter II The Enigma Cipher Machine

Paragraph

5. <u>Enigma cipher machine was the backbone of German high-level cryptography</u>-- The Enigma cipher machine, in five different forms, was used by German commercial firms, by the Post Office, the Railways, and miscellaneous other German government departments; by the Supreme Command of the Armed Forces; by the High Command of the Army, and in Army communications down through division; by the High Command of the Air Force, and in Air Force communications down through group and sometimes squadron; by the High Command of the Navy and in Naval communications down through submarine; by Military Intelligence (Abwehr), by the Reich Security Office (Reichssicherheitshauptamt, abbreviated "RSHA"); and by Military Attachés.

The five main forms in which it appeared were called the commercial (or "K") Enigma; the "counter" (or "Zaehlwerk") Enigma, sometimes called the "Abwehr" Enigma or the "G" Enigma; the plugboard ("Stecker") Enigma; the plugboard with (pluggable) reflector-D ("Stecker mit Umkehrwalze D") Enigma; and the Navy Enigma. The plugboard Enigma with "variable-notch" rotors ("Stecker mit Lueckenfuellerwalzen") was to have appeared soon. Another model, Cipher Device 39 ("Schluesselgeraet 39") was under study. See Chart No. 2-1 herewith.

DOCID: 3560816

Enigma Model	Used by	Number of rotors	Number of notches per rotor	Type of reflector	Type of end plate	How machine would be solved
Commercial ("K")	Commercial firms Reichspost Reichsbahn. Misc. govt. depts.	3	1	Rotor, not pluggable	Not pluggable	4 or 5 letter crib and catalogue; or rapid analytic machinery. (Bombe, duenna or scritcher not needed.)
Counter ("Zaehlwerk")	Military attaché until 1943; then Reich Security Office	3	Multiple but fixed	Rotor. Not pluggable	Not pluggable	10 letter crib and catalogue; or rapid analytic machinery. (Bombe, duenna, or scritcher not needed.)
Plugboard ("Stecker")	Supreme Command Army. Air Force	3 from set of 5	1	Fixed plate Not pluggable	PLUGGABLE	Bombe (duenna or scritcher not needed).
Navy Plugboard	Navy standard machine	3 from set of 8 & 1 from 2	5 with 1 3 with 2 2 with Ø	Fixed plate Not pluggable	PLUGGABLE	Bombe, duenna, or scritcher
Plugboard with pluggable reflector (Umkehrwalze D)	Just beginning to be used by Air Force. Proposed for Armed Forces and for Army	3 from set of 5	1	Fixed plate PLUGGABLE	PLUGGABLE	Duenna or scritcher. VERY DIFFICULT.
Plugboard with variable notch rotors (Lueckenfuellerwalzen)	Proposed for Armed Forces, Army, Navy, Air	3 from set of 5 ?	Multiple, CHANGEABLE and therefore non-predictable	Fixed plate PLUGGABLE or not pluggable	PLUGGABLE	Bombe, duenna, or scritcher (if at all possible)
Cipher Device 39 (Schluesselgeraet 39)	Proposed for Armed Forces, Army, Navy, Air	4 variable notch rotors from set of ?	Multiple, changeable; plus Hagelin type drive	Fixed plate PLUGGABLE	PLUGGABLE	Bombe, duenna, or scritcher (if at all possible).

PROGRESSIVE CHANGES IN GERMAN ENIGMA

Chart No. 2-1

8

6. "Commercial" Enigma was known to be insecure-- It was well known by the Germans that the commercial Enigma was not difficult to solve. They suggested hand methods of "stripping off the fast-moving rotor," which were almost identical with our methods and which involved small prepared catalogues.[20] They suggested statistical methods using rapid analytic machinery.[21] They had also investigated the machine mathematically, from a "group theory" standpoint.[22] The commercial machine had been, until about 1934, sold on the commercial market by the German firm which owned the patents and developed them; but soon after the Nazi accession into power the machine was withdrawn from the market. The Germans furnished these machines to the Croat puppet government.[23] The Germans themselves used it for their post office, their railroads, and other government agencies. Because of its insecurity, every message enciphered by it was supposed to be re-enciphered at a second setting,[24] a procedure which if adopted would have made the messages quite secure. It is doubtful if such procedure was generally carried out, because of the difficulties involved.[25]

7. "Counter" Enigma was known to be insecure-- The "counter" Enigma (so called because it incorporated a letter counter in its machanism) was important because it introduced multiple-notch rotors. In general, the more often enciphering rotors in machines of the Enigma class step, the more difficult solution becomes, and multiple-notch rotors bring about this desirable motion. Even so, the "counter" machine was known to be solvable by short cribs.[26] Regulations were also issued with this machine to double-encipher each message.[27] Only about 100 of the "counter" machines were made in all; they were issued to German military attachés, withdrawn in 1943, and issued to Military Intelligence (Abwehr). Some were also sold to the Dutch government.[28]

[20] I 47

[21] I 45

[22] T 372

[23] I 92

[24] I 92

[25] I 92

[26] I 77

[27] I 77

[28] I 104

8. Plugboard Enigma was believed safe if used properly--Plugboard Enigma was used by the Supreme Command Armed Forces, by the Army, by the Air Force, and, with an additional rotor, by the Navy, as the ubiquitous and "secure" cipher device, able to carry highest-level traffic "if used properly." It was also supplied to the Hungarians, Rumanians, Finns, and Italians.[29] Investigations by Dr. Pietsch, of the Signal Intelligence Agency of the Army High Command (OKH/G d NA), showed the safety margin to be 20,000 letters a day.[30] Dr. Fricke believed that if the instructions on maximum length of messages were followed, "everything would be all right."[31] Yet it was traffic in this Enigma, even when "used properly," which was regularly solved day-by-day by the tremendous Anglo-American cryptanalytic effort.

9. Plugboard Enigma was known to be solvable with "cribs."-- It is an astonishing fact that although German cryptographers knew, at least as early as 1943, that it was theoretically possible to solve the German Army plugboard Enigma whenever a proper crib was available,[32] they seemed little concerned about this possibility and failed to realize that a practical solution might be based upon it. This knowledge should have aroused their most vivid apprehensions but did not, because of lack of imagination regarding the possibilities presented by the invention, development, and use of specially designed high-speed analytic machinery.

In 1944, Lt. R. Hans-Joachim Frowein of the Signal Security Agency of the Navy High Command (OKM/4 SKL/II) suggested an International Business Machine (I.B.M.) method of solving the plugboard Enigma, given a twenty-five letter crib.[33] This suggestion was based on a hand method which employed sequential testing, or "scritching," a method which was mechanized by the Army Security Agency and incorporated in the "auto-scritcher." After describing this hand process, Lt. Frowein made the following suggestions:[34]

[29] I 92 p 2
[30] I 78
[31] I 20
[32] D 58 p 18
[33] I 38 pp 3-4
[34] I 38 p 4

"In practice, Hollerith [I.B.M.] machinery would be used... . With a 3-wheel (Army) Enigma, only 70,000 cards are required... . The enemy could have produced the 70,000 cards at the beginning of the war and this catalogue would have been valid throughout the life of the three-wheel Enigma. The first Hollerith card sorting process would take 200 machine-hours, the second only 8 machine-hours, and so on."

Thus a total of approximately 220 I.B.M. sorter-hours would have been sufficient to test the "crib" to see if it could break the plugboard machine. Another way of stating this, is that 10 sorters could test one crib in one day. This is not rapid, but it is within practical limits. And this suggestion is only the first theoretical answer, not the climax of a comprehensive, practical attempt at solution.

Perhaps the cryptographers of the Signal Intelligence Agency of the Supreme Command Armed Forces (OKW/Chi) believed that it would be too difficult for an ememy to obtain the cribs necessary for solution by Lt. Frowein's methods. Possibly they were too busy designing improved apparatus which they would put into effect "someday." Certainly there is no indication in the TICOM interrogations or documents that cryptographers of either the Armed Forces or the Army worried about Lt. Frowein's results when the results were shown to them. The Navy, with a four-rotor, more nearly secure Enigma, did take his results somewhat seriously. Lt. Frowein stated:[35]

"The official reaction to the findings of the investigation was the immediate decision [by the Navy] that only rotors with two turn-overs should be allowed to be used in the right-hand ["fast"] position. This [action] was introduced at the beginning of December, 1944... . The view of the German Army was that their Enigma was theoretically solvable. The four-rotor [Naval] Enigma was not considered theoretically solvable and the Army were astonished at the Navy's view based on this investigation."

The action taken by the Navy, as indicated above, was so ineffective an answer to the problem raised by Lt. Frowein, that it almost might as well not have been taken. Nevertheless, for his excellent work, Lt. Frowein was awarded the War Merit Cross.

[35] I 38 p 5

10. Theoretical weaknesses of plugboard Enigma were understood.-- We may not conclude from the lack of all-out practical efforts to make a worthwhile security study of the plugboard Enigma that the German military cryptographers were in any way mentally inferior to the British and American cryptanalysts who succeeded against this Enigma. Despite that fact that the Germans discovered every weakness the Enigma had, their theoretical studies and conclusions apparently did not impress them. According to Dr. Buggisch of the Signal Intelligence Agency of the Army High Command (OKH/G d NA), the weaknesses of the plugboard Enigma were:[36]

a. Rotor I (the "fast" rotor) moved uniformly.

b. Rotors II and III moved too seldom.

c. The machine needed more than three rotors to be inserted in it at once. That is, the period $26^2 \times 25$ was too short.

d. The machine needed more than five rotors to be issued with it. That is, the number of rotor orders, the permutations of 5 rotors taken 3 at a time (= 60), was too small.

e. The reflector was not pluggable, and the "enemy" could set up the $60 \times 26^2 \times 25$ alphabets of the machine in its unplugged form, possibly proceeding to a solution from there.

Dr. Buggisch was so right! Improvement in any one of the foregoing particulars could easily have pushed the plugboard Enigma beyond the reach of already-straining Anglo-American cryptanalytic fingers, and possibly altered the course of the war. If the multiple turn-over rotors of the "counter" machine had been inserted in the plugboard Enigma, if ten rotors had been issued instead of five, if five rotors simultaneously could have been used in the machine instead of three, if the rotors already in it had been kept more active by suitable motions, or if a pluggable reflector had been universally adopted, regular, day-by-day solution would hardly have been possible.[37]

[36] I 37

[37] Another effective security measure would have been to issue new rotors at regular intervals, or whenever compromise of those in use was suspected. This procedure was evidently not considered favorably by the Germans, who had so many Enigmas in the field and in use elsewhere, that the chance of capture was great, and the number of rotors to be replaced in case of compromise prohibitive. Newly wired rotors were issued at the outset of the war, but these wirings were kept throughout the war without change, on the theory that the Enigma was secure regardless of rotor compromise.

12

How close the Anglo-Americans came to losing out in their solution of the German Army Enigma is a matter to give cryptanalysts pause.

British and American cryptanalysts recall with a shudder how drastic an increase in difficulty resulted from the introduction by the German Air Force of the pluggable reflector ("Umkehrwalze D," called "Uncle Dick" by the British) in the Spring of 1945. It made completely obsolete the "bombe" machinery which had been designed and installed at so great an expense for standard, plugboard-Enigma solution. It necessitated the development by the U.S. Navy of a new, more complex machine called the "duenna," and by the U.S. Army of a radically new electrical solver called the "autoscritcher." Each of these had to make millions of tests to establish simultaneously the unknown (end-plate) plugboard and the unknown reflector plugging. Only a trickle of solutions would have resulted if the pluggable reflector had been adopted universally; and this trickle of solutions would not have contained enough intelligence to furnish the data for cribs needed in subsequent solutions. Thus even the trickle would have eventually vanished.

Credit must be given to the unknown German Air Force cryptographer, possibly a member of the Security Group of the Signal Intelligence Service (OKL/Gen Nafue/III, Gruppe IV), who brought about the use of "Uncle Dick" throughout the German Air Force in the spring of 1945. It is indeed lucky for the Allies that the cryptographers of the Signal Intelligence Agency of the Supreme Command Armed Forces (OKW/Chi) did not agree with his belief in the pressing need for additional security. Dr. Fricke said:[38] "It was not considered important, as the plugboard was the real safeguard." Dr. Huettenhain said in effect:[39] "The G.A.F. had introduced the pluggable reflector, but the Army said it was too much trouble."

11. <u>"Variable-notch" rotors would probably have made plugboard Enigma secure</u>-- Daily solution of the plugboard Enigma would probably have been prevented if the Germans had introduced the variable-notch rotor ("Lueckenfuellerwalze") in 1943 as planned.

This rotor was designed to "hold the security line" until the introduction of Cipher Device 39, a Hagelin-type-drive Enigma designed in 1939 (as its name implies) and already past the blueprint stage.

[38] I 20

[39] I 31

13

The effect of variable-notch rotors in an Enigma would have been to make impossible the foretelling of exact successive rotor settings, when preparing to "bombe" a crib. Assumptions would have to be made as to the presence or absence of turn-overs of the "medium speed" and "slow speed" rotors, at each successive element of text. This would have multiplied the number of trials necessary to test cribs, and thereby reduced the number of solutions to the small trickle which has already been characterized as not being, in all probability, self-sustaining.

The following excerpts from minutes of conferences held by the Signal Intelligence Agency of the Supreme Command, Armed Forces (OKW/Chi) on 1[illegible] December 1943 and 18 March 1944, are interesting sidelights:[40]

a. "Concerning improvement of the Enigma, Wa Pruef 7 /Army Ordnance, Development and Testing Group, Signal Branch/ stated that the replacement of all rotors by variable-notch rotors required reconstruction and time for development. It was however possible to exchange one rotor; the necessary variable-notch rotors could be delivered within a reasonable time."

b. "In collaboration with Wa Pruef 7, in view of the introduction of the variable-notch rotor, the keying pressure /required to encipher on the Enigma/ was reduced by about 1000 gr. at the firm of Heimsoeth & Rinke."

Mechanical drawings of the variable-notch rotor are now in the files of the Army Security Agency.[41] Several such rotors have been captured and are available.

12. Cipher Device 39 would have been secure against present attack-- Cipher Device 39 was to be the epitome of Enigma perfection. It was to have everything--end-plate plugboard, pluggable reflector, 4 variable-notch rotors, 3 added Hagelin-type irregular drive wheels, and a simple inter-acting motion. It was to have a keyboard; and it was to print both plain and cipher texts, at a rate of 85 words per minute.

A note in Dr. Huettenhain's files dated 30 May 1944 stated:[42]

[40] D 59 p 1[illegible] p 2[illegible]

[41] M 11

[42] D 59 p 26

"The model built by the Telefonbau u. Normalzeit Company, Frankfurt a. Main is being demonstrated in operation. The machine essentially satisfies all the requirements laid down for it. Wa Pruef 7 /Army Ordnance, Development and Testing, Signal Branch/ has settled what features of the machine require improvement. F.A.N. (?) in Frankfurt a. Main has been completely destroyed. The machine cannot therefore be expected to go into large scale production there for some considerable time. It is therefore intended to get an additional production center at once. The Wanderer Company, which already has wide experience of large scale production, is proposed for this additional production. Dr. Fess of Wanderer's is awaited in Planken for detailed negotiations on the subject of this production.

"According to Wa Pruef 7 /Army Ordnance, Development and Testing Group, Signal Branch/ small scale production is approved.

"OKW/Chi sees at the moment no possibility of a break-in, but exhaustive investigations are still in progress.

"On completion of plant at Wanderer it is planned to arrange a final conference there with the units requiring the machines and the special committee. The aim is to begin large scale production by the end of 1944."

None of the test models of Cipher Device 39 has ever been received at Army Security Agency.[43] Excellent descriptions

[43]Two test models of Cipher Device 39 were packed in boxes at Telefonbau u. Normalzeit, Frankfurt, and the boxes "picked up by an Army Corporal on March 22, 1945, for movement to a military depot at Tauberbischofsheim." See I-53 p 3. These were never found. A third, incomplete, machine however was captured and is now at London Signal Intelligence Centre. Captured German Army plugboard Enigmas, commercial Enigmas, counter Enigmas, variable-notch rotors, and pluggable reflector wheels are available at the Army Security Agency museum, however.

DOCID: 3560816

exist, however.[44] The main elements of this device may be represented by the following skeleton schematic diagram:

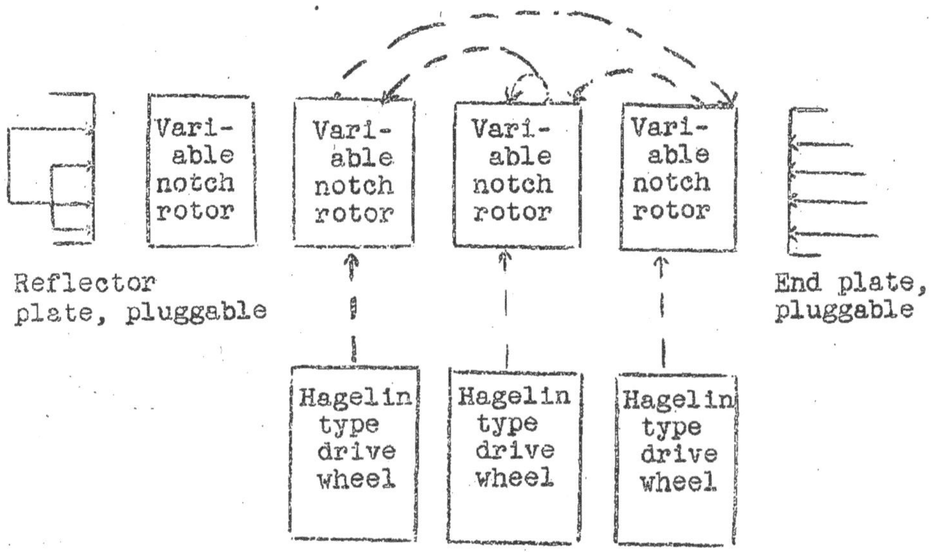

[44] I-53, I-57. It is interesting to note that Cipher Device 39 was originally planned to have been issued in 1939, as its name implies. A TICOM report on an interrogation of Dr. Otto Buggisch of the Signal Intelligence Agency of the Supreme Command Armed Forces (OKW/Chi) stated: "Geraete 39 and 41 were both in development for years and still had not come out at the end. B [Buggisch] has the almost inevitable comments about the military non-technicians who blocked things." According to a writing by Dr. Liebknecht, of the Army Ordnance, Developing and Testing, Signal Branch, "This delay was due in part to lack of clarity in the operational requirements, in part due to changes following mathematical researches, but in large part due to pure technical difficulties."

16

Motion controls of the variable-notch rotors are indicated by broken lines in the diagram. Solid lines to the "end plate" indicate wires from keyboard and tape printers. Note that the first variable-notch rotor never moves during encipherment. Better cryptographic procedure would be not to allow any completely stationary rotor.

13. Enigma development is worthy of study-- To recapitulate, German cryptographers throughout the war used a cryptographic device known as the "plugboard Enigma," which had a high degree of security, but was insecure against determined and costly Anglo-American cryptanalysis. This device was on the threshold of almost complete security, through the introduction of pluggable reflectors and/or the variable-notch rotors. The pinnacle of German Enigma development was reached with the completion of plans for Cipher Device 39 and the building of a very small number of test models. The four rotors and three Hagelin wheels, irregular interacting motions, and dual end plate pluggings of Cipher Device 39 would have produced a machine that, if used properly, would probably have ranked along with our own SIGABA for security.[45]

[45] Cryptanalysts Schauffler and Hauthal of the Foreign Office Cryptanalytic Section (Pers Z S) discussed the construction of a proposed new cipher machine with Willi Korn, engineer of the Enigma firm Heimsoeth and Rincke, Berlin, in February 1942. It was to be called "Machine 42" ("Maschine 42") and was to be, in effect, an Army plugboard Enigma with three additional rotors inserted in front of the plugboard--that is, between the plugboard and the key-and-light bank. The first of these three additional rotors was to step each time a letter was enciphered, and the second and third were to be stepped by notches in the customary Enigma manner. Traffic in such a machine could not have been solved by normal bombe methods, although a special autoscritcher can be conceived of for such reading. The practical difficulties would be tremendous, so that for practical purposes Machine 42 would have been secure. Machine 42 never passed the stage of theoretical development because of engineering and procurement difficulties. See T-5 for details.

Volume 2

Chapter III Teleprinter Cryptographic Apparatus

Paragraph

14. <u>German teleprinter cryptographic apparatus was of two main types.</u>- German cryptographers developed two main types of teleprinter cryptographic apparatus. They were:

a. Cipher attachments, which could be associated with or attached to any teleprinter.
b. Cipher teleprinters, in which the cryptographic mechanisms were integral parts of the teleprinters.

The cipher attachments were called "Schluesselzusaetze." Of these, model SZ-40 (later discarded), and models SZ-42a and SZ-42b were insecure against Anglo-American cryptanalysis. Model SZ-42c, which was designed to "cryptize" the radio circuit as a whole, would probably have been completely secure.
The cipher teleprinters were called "Schluesselfernschreibmaschinen." Of these, models T-52a, T-52b, T-52c (first model), and T-52c (second model) were insecure against Anglo-American cryptanalysis, and were eventually discarded by the Germans as a result of their own security studies; models T-52d and T-52e could not have been solved by any presently-known methods of attack. The T-43 was a "one-time tape" cipher teleprinter and likewise secure if proper tapes were inserted, and if certain electrical elements in the apparatus were properly adjusted.

18

Various models of all the above machines carried high-level communications for the Foreign Office, the Air Force, the Navy, the Reich Security Office, and miscellaneous government departments; and practically all models were used at some time or other by the Army down through division.

Land-lines carried most of the teleprinter traffic, and land-line traffic was, of course, not interceptible by the Anglo-Americans. Radio links were "beamed transmissions" which were difficult to intercept, yet certain important Army radio links employing such transmissions were intercepted. They included, among others, circuits between Berlin and each of the following: Athems, Salonika, Rome, Bucharest, Belgrade, French ports, Paris, Rotterdam, and Oslo; they also included circuits among corps areas (Wehrkreis) in Germany itself.

From Ultra sources, it is known that solved German teleprinter messages gave information in detail concerning supplies shipped, troop movements, police data, and agent information. Important battle order information was often obtained, and important orders from Hitler.

The information transmitted by German teleprinter cryptographic apparatus was therefore of utmost importance to the Anglo-American government and field forces during the war from an intelligence standpoint. The various machines themselves are still important, as a result of TICOM investigations, for the cryptographic features they involve.

British cryptanalysts gave the generic cover name "fish" to any German teleprinter cryptographic machine, the cover name "tunny" to the cipher attachments of the first type mentioned in paragraph 14, and the cover name "sturgeon" to the cipher teleprinters, the machines of the second type.[49]

15. <u>German teleprinter cryptographic apparatus enciphered individual teleprinter impulses.</u>-- A standard teleprinter of the so-called "start-stop" type transmits seven impulses for each letter or character sent, as follows: a start impulse, a set of five distinguishing impulses or "bauds," and a stop impulse. Each of the five bauds is either "plus" or "minus" depending on the character being sent. (Thus, the set of bauds for "e" is plus minus minus minus minus, and the following sequence of impulses is sent: start, plus minus minus minus minus, stop.) German teleprinter cryptographic apparatus, just as

[49] Captured T-52d/e and SZ-42b apparatus are available in the Army Security Agency Museum.

19

similar machines of other origin, enciphered such teleprinter transmissions by enciphering these five individual bauds. The apparatus did this by generating a key made up of a lengthy sequence of teleprinter characters, and causing the sets of bauds corresponding to the successive keying characters to be combined, baud by baud, with the sets of bauds corresponding to the successive plain text characters. Combining was done according to a principle invented in 1918 by an American engineer named Vernam, who originated the so-called "Vernam Rule" that a combination of like signs produced a "plus" impulse, and a combination of unlike signs produced a "minus" impulse. The result was, of course, a succession of sets of five bauds corresponding to the <u>cipher</u> characters. In the German teleprinter cipher attachments, these cipher characters were transmitted without further encipherment; in the cipher teleprinters, they underwent transposition of bauds within characters as further encipherment before they were transmitted.

16. <u>German teletype cryptographic apparatus used mechanical wheels.</u>- Mechanical cipher wheels were used in all German teleprinter cryptographic apparatus, except in the one-time-tape cipher teleprinter. Around its periphery, each of these mechanical wheels had small pins which operated a switch (or switches) as the wheels rotated. Operation of the switches gave in effect the "plus" or "minus" impulses needed to form key characters. In the teleprinter cipher attachments SZ-40, -42a, and-42b, the "pin patterns" of each of the wheels, i.e. the sequence of pins with respect to their being in operable or inoperable positions, was changeable simply by manually setting the individual pins into effective or ineffective positions. In the SZ-40 (original model) and in the cipher teleprinters (T series except for T-43) the pin patterns were not variable, and were fixed at the time of their manufacture. The T-43 used tape and no cipher wheels.

17. <u>"Cipher attachments" were insecure.</u>- The German teleprinter cipher attachments, or "tunny" machines, are of importance to Anglo-American cryptographers in showing them what not to do. All of the actually built models of these machines were insecure. Dr. Huettenhain, of the Signal Intelligence Agency of the Supreme Command Armed Forces (OKW/Chi), told Dr. Vierling that their "security was good for about two years,"[50] but he evidently had a rather high opinion of the SZ-42a and SZ-42b as used with beamed radio, because he permitted their use past the two-year mark.

[50] E 14 p 6

The SZ-40 (original model) had ten mechanical cipher wheels, with fixed peg patterns. The ten elements produced by these wheels combined in pairs to form one set of 5 elements, and the set was then used as the keying character for the plain text character to be enciphered.[51] Only 40 of these machines were built. Dr. Fricke said that since it had been ascertained that single messages of 1,000 letters sent on the SZ-40 (original model) could be solved, it was decided to introduce a machine with an irregular element in the wheel motion.[52] This was done by introducing the SZ-40 (regular), which consisted of 12 wheels with changeable patterns, divided as follows: 5 "springcaesar" wheels, all of which stepped in unison but irregularly, being driven by a pair of "vorgelege" (control) wheels; and 5 "spaltencaesar" wheels, all of which stepped in unison and regularly, once for each character enciphered. Anglo-American solutions of messages sent on this machine were accomplished by statistical recovery of the pin patterns of the regularly-stepping wheels and the removal of their effects from the cipher texts; this was then followed by recovery of the pin patterns of the irregularly-stepping wheels and the removal of their effects. Dr. Huettenhain believed that solution could be obtained by attacking the motion of the five irregular ("springcaesar") wheels first[53] and therefore suggested the SZ-42a, which gave an additional irregular control to these irregular wheels. This further irregular motion came from two sources: one source was the pattern on the first of the five irregular wheels itself, another was the variation in the fifth baud of the plain-text character "two letters back" in the plain text, i.e., two characters before the character actually being enciphered at the moment. This plain text autokey control was optional; and because it gave rise to many errors it was not used often. The SZ-42b was next developed with a third element contributing to the irregularity, namely, a control by the second regular ("spaltencaesar") wheel.[54] None of these ruses succeeded in preventing Anglo-American cryptanalysis, since the attack was to ignore temporarily the irregularly-moving wheels, and to remove the effects of the

[51] In this respect this machine was identical with that developed by the International Telephone and Telegraph Company in the United States in 1931, employing 10 mechanical wheels and the property of pairing.

[52] I 45

[53] I 31

[54] I 45 p 19

regularly-moving wheels first. This made attack on the irregularly-moving wheels possible. The Germans had evolved elaborate protection for the wrong end of their machine.

18. Proposed SZ-42c with synchronization would have "cryptized" a whole radio circuit.-- The SZ-42c was being designed to "cryptize" a whole radio teleprinter circuit.[55] Teleprinters on this circuit were to operate at all times, transmitting a stream of characters forming an entirely unintelligible "message" whenever bonafide enciphered messages were not being sent. An interceptor would not be able to distinguish any signals representing real messages from those corresponding to unintelligible or random sequences of characters. Therefore the number, length, precedence, classification, and timing of messages would not be known to enemy intercept, and the circuit would be secure against traffic analysis. Dr. Vierling of the Feuerstein Laboratory was developing the crystal controlled synchronizing apparatus, called "gleichlauf," which was to keep the teleprinters synchronized, regardless of radio fading and interference.[56]

The nonsense to be transmitted on the air whenever messages were not being sent would actually be "pure key" generated by the SZ-42c. An enemy would therefore have a great advantage in trying to cryptanalyze the SZ-42c. No one can state accurately what results could have been obtained by an enemy given possession of tens of thousands of consecutive characters of pure key, but the design for the SZ-42c appeared to be secure for normal operation. The five regularly-moving wheels (spaltencaesars) of the earlier models no longer were to move regularly or even together; this would have prevented the methods of cryptanalytic attack theretofore used by the Anglo-Americans. Dr. Huettenhain was probably right in his report as follows:[57]

> "Wa Pruef 7 are at the moment carrying out a reconstruction in which the five righthand wheels are driven separately irregularly. This eliminates a cardinal weakness of the SZ 40 and 42, the regular movement of the Spaltencaesar, and makes methods of reconstructing the pin arrangements impossible."

[55] E 14

[56] E 13

[57] D 59 p 18

A full description of the interacting motions involved in the SZ-42c can be found in TICOM reports.[58] Briefly there were to be 10 wheels. These moved constantly unless interrupted. Interruption of motion of wheels 1, 2, 3, 4, and 5, (which were the springcaesars and which moved in unison) was accomplished by action of wheels 9 and 10; interruption of wheel 6 was accomplished by wheels 8 and 2; of 7 by 9 and 3; of 8 by 10 and 4; of 9 by 6 and 5; of 10 by 7 and 1. If it happened that all wheels became stationary (thus resulting in monoalphabetic encipherment), the machine counted to three, and then wheels 1 through 5 stepped automatically.

The firm of Lorenz, which was developing SZ-42c with electromagnetic drive rather than mechanical, called their model of the SZ-42c machine "SK-44." They also planned SK-45, which was to be identical with SK-44 except for an eleventh wheel; the eleventh wheel was to step the machine past "dead spots," so that the counting device used in SZ-42c for that purpose would not be needed.

19. <u>Some "cipher teleprinters" were secure.</u>-- There were five main types of cipher teleprinters developed by German cryptographers: T-52 a/b, T-52c (first model), T-52c (regular), T-52d, and T-52e. The T-52d (probably) and T-52e (certainly) were secure against known methods of attack, but were not actually much in use on radio circuits.

All five of the foregoing cipher teleprinters were important because they introduced a new principle into teleprinter cryptography: that of positionally transposing, as a form of superencipherment, the five separate bauds constituting the set corresponding to each cipher character, after the normal or basic encipherment had been accomplished.[59]

[58] I 57, E 14

[59] A similar principle is the subject of a U.S. patant by Mr. William F. Friedman of the Army Security Agency. The German cryptographers, however, brought into actual use the first secret teleprinters to employ these principles in practice.

A schematic diagram demonstrating the principles involved in the two processes of encipherment, substitution and transposition, is shown below:

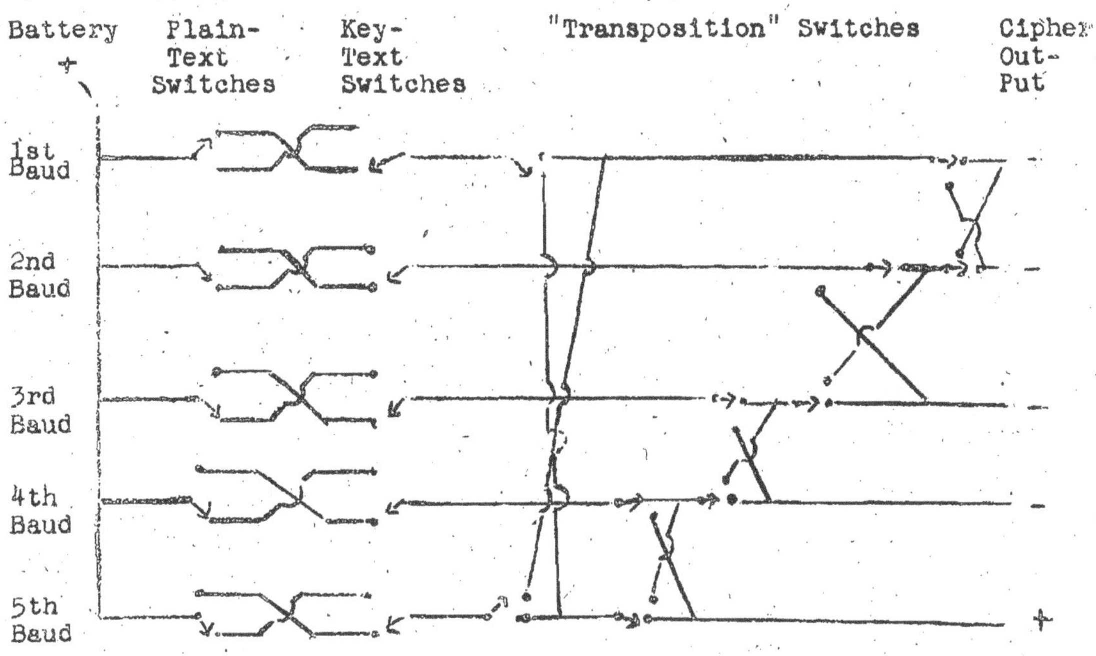

The foregoing diagram is not electrically accurate, but it is accurate in principle. It indicates, for example, the result of enciphering the plain-text character "e" (plus minus minus minus minus) by the key-text character "blank" (minus minus minus minus minus) and passing the result through a transposition network as shown, with a transposition taking place between the first and fifth bauds. The result is the character "t."

It can be demonstrated that the security of any cipher teleprinter employing the foregoing principles depends upon the manner of generating the key-text characters, the manner of controlling the transposition switches, and in addition whether or not the order of the transposition switches may be changed.

All of the T-52 series of cipher teleprinters had ten mechanical cipher wheels, and the pegs on each of these wheels were set into permanent peg patterns. In the T-52 a/b model, each of the five key-text switches and the five transposition switches was operated by one of the ten mechanical wheels. The ten wheels moved regularly. The transposition switches themselves could not be interchanged. The machine was insecure because the settings of the wheels could be attacked independently of one another and statistically. In the T-52c (first) model, each of the five key-text switches was controlled by a given combination of four of the ten mechanical wheels; each of three of the transposition switches was controlled by a given combination of four of ten mechanical wheels; each of the remaining two transposition switches was controlled by a given combination of six of the ten mechanical wheels. The ten wheels moved regularly, and it is believed that the order of the transposition switches was not changeable. Furthermore, the particular choice the Germans made for the sets of four wheels to be used in controlling the key-text switches resulted in a limited number of substitution permutation combinations, which made solution possible. This effect was partially eliminated in the T-52c (regular model) and for this reason the regular T-52c was harder to solve.[60]

Model T-52d made the order of the transposition switches changeable, and while each key-text switch and each transposition switch was controlled by only one wheel, the wheels themselves stepped irregularly. The movement of each wheel was controlled by the patterns of two other wheels, and interacting controls resulted. Provision was also made for the optional use of an additional plain-text control of the irregular motion. It is seriously doubted if this machine could have been solved, even if pure key was available from reading messages in depth, solely because of the interacting, irregular motion of the wheels.[61]

[60] Inspectorate 7/VI (In 7/VI) discovered that the T-52c was breakable in 1942, and suggested alterations that led to the T-52d. I 78 p 11.

[61] Single messages might have been partially read by a crib matching method suggested by Inspectorate 7/VI (In 7/VI). I 78 p 12.

Model T-52e had wheel motion identical with that in model T-52d. Its order of transposition switches was not changeable, but each of the transposition switches and the key-text switches was operated by the combined pattern of a set of four wheels chosen for it from the ten wheels. The T-52e was therefore also probably secure.

Full details concerning the interacting and irregular wheel motions, the transposition of bauds, and the manner in which wheel patterns were combined to get replication of controls, are given in TICOM publications.[62]

20. Cipher teleprinter model T-43 used one-time tape.-- The T-43 used a one-time key tape to supply the sequence of keying characters, instead of mechanical cipher wheels as in the other T-series models. The T-43 was just as secure against cryptanalysis, therefore, since the key tapes employed consisted of "random characters."

In practice the key tape was generated by the running of a fifty-meter-long loop of random tape over and over through a T-52d machine, with the T-52d punching out the key tape as long as desired. The key tape was not random in a true sense, but it was unpredictable for practical purposes, and secure.

A serious electrical defect in the T-43 was discovered by radio engineers and corrected. This defect actually had rendered the T-43 insecure. It resulted from the fact that at the instant of encipherment the keying character was electrically slightly out of phase with the plain-text character. As a result, minute inspection of the cipher characters on an oscilloscope permitted separation of the composite cipher characters into their plain-text and key-text elements--resulting in a "solution" without cryptanalysis.[63] The moral from the above story is plain: there are more ways than one to read a message.

21. Conclusion: German teleprinter cryptographic apparatus is worthy of detailed study.-- To recapitulate, although the Anglo-Americans were able to read German teleprinter traffic sent on important Army and Air Force links as a daily procedure, because of the insecurity of the SZ-42a and SZ-42b cipher attachments and the willingness of the Anglo-Americans to build the expensive machinery necessary for solution, (such as the British "colossus"), nevertheless the more recently developed German cipher-teleprinters (T- series) were completely secure.

[62] I 45, I 20, I 31

[63] I 45, p 15

The latter units were designed along different lines from any lines taken by Anglo-American development of teleprinter cryptographic apparatus. They therefore make definite contributions to our knowledge. Their main features were:

a. Irregular and interacting wheel motions.
b. Use of baud transposition as an additional protection, superimposing this on the basic substitution process.

Furthermore, the attempted development of a cipher attachment (SZ-42c) for cryptizing a radio circuit, thus protecting it against traffic analysis as well as cryptanalysis, indicated that the Germans were giving serious thought to all phases of the cryptographic problem.

Volume 2

Chapter IV - Cipher Device 41, the Cipher Box, the Cipher Disk, and the "Number Printer."

Paragraph

22. <u>German Cipher Device 41 was a secure Hagelin-type machine</u>-- Cipher Device 41 ("Schluesselgeraet 41") was a mechanical cipher device (Hagelin type) similar to the U. S. Army converter M-209 and was originally intended for use forward of division.[70] The German Army, Air Force, Weather Bureau, and probably others, had ordered a total of eleven thousand machines,[71] but only a small (unknown) quantity had been manufactured and put in use. Cipher Device 41 was remarkable for two reasons:

a. Although it required no electrical power, being operated by a hand crank, it was compact, portable, printed both plain and cipher tapes, and was provided with a typewriter keyboard.

b. The daily wheel settings and pin patterns were protected against reconstruction by cryptanalysis even when "pure key" was available. This was because even though the plain texts of identically-keyed messages could readily be obtained by well-established procedures and the corresponding portion of the keying sequence reconstructed, nevertheless this reconstructed sequence ("pure key") did not provide data whereby the wheel settings and pin patterns could

[70] I 72. The Army Security Agency has a captured Cipher Device 41 in its museum.

[71] D 59 p 23

28

also be reconstructed. As a consequence, no other messages on the same day could be read. This is not usually the case in other Hagelin type machines, including the U. S. Army converter M-209.

23. Security of Cipher Device 41 lay in interacting, irregular, cipher-wheel motions-- The security of Cipher Device 41 came from the interacting and irregular movements of its cipher wheels.

Here again is demonstrated the German capacity to make secure in practice an otherwise not too secure machine, by employing the principles of interacting and irregular movements of wheels.

The enciphering principles of Cipher Device 41 may be described as follows:

a. It had 6 mechanical Hagelin-type "pin" wheels, "prime" to each other. In cryptographic parlance, the first five of these wheels had "kicks" of 1,2,4,8, and 10 respectively. Wheel 6 made these "kicks" positive or negative.

b. The enciphering cycle (one turn of the hand crank) consisted of three elements, as follows:

"Element 1." This element of the cycle took place if and only if wheel 6 had an active peg in the "motion index position." If wheel 6 had such an active peg, then all the following events occurred: Wheel 1 moved one step. Each of the remaining four wheels moved one step, unless the wheel to its left had an active pin in its "motion index position," in which case each such wheel moved two steps.

"Element 2." A key "kick" was generated, which was the sum of all the kicks of wheels which had active pegs in the "kick index positions." This was so unless wheel 6 had an inactive peg in the "kick index position," in which case the key kick which resulted was equal to "25 minus the sum of the kicks" of the wheels with active pegs. This key kick was in effect the "key text" or "key character" which was "added" to the plain text character in encipherment. Encipherment took place at this point.

"Element 3." This element of the cycle was identical in principle to Element 1, except that it occurred whether or not wheel 6 had an active peg in the "motion index position." The purpose of this element was to insure some change in the wheel positions before the encipherment of the next letter of text, if any.

When one compares the foregoing irregular and interacting motions of the wheels, and the use of occasional negative kicks, with the simple regular motion and simple regular kick addition of the usual Hagelin-type machine, the reason for the far higher order of security of Cipher Device 41 is indeed apparent.

In 1945 the British had intercepted certain traffic enciphered by German agents with Cipher Device 41. Several messages were read because of improper mechanical working of one of the machines. The machine itself, however, was not solved thereby, and remained a mystery until capture revealed its construction.

It is believed by investigators that the mechanical designs of the Cipher Device 41 was poor but that its faults could probably be corrected by improved engineering. Mechanical problems in all likelihood prevented its wider and earlier use by the Germans.

Cipher Device "41-Z" was a modification of the standard model 41. It was designed to encipher ten figures instead of twenty-five letters, for use by the German Weather Bureau.[72]

A model of Cipher Device 41 which would be more compact and would eliminate the typewriter keyboard was also under consideration, for use by front line troops.

24. "Cipher Box" was to replace Enigma-- A mechanical device, made out of aluminum and weighing 1-3/4 pounds, was being developed, which involved cryptographic principles entirely new to German cryptography. It was hoped to use this device to replace the Enigma in the German Army above the level of division![73] It was called the "Cipher Box" ("Schluesselkasten") and made use of the cryptographic principle of sliding strips.[74]

Lt. Col. Mettig, of the Signal Intelligence Agency of the Supreme Command, Armed Forces (OKW/Chi) reported as follows:[75] "Field tests...had been so successful and had brought out the handiness and speed of operation of the machine so clearly, that its introduction into the field army was ordered. As the RSHA (Reich Security Office) had already got in ahead with the order for 70,000 items, mass production was introduced." The mass production was scheduled to have produced at least one thousand devices by October 1945 and to reach a rate of 10,000 per month by January 1946.

[72] D 59 p 25
[73] I 96
[74] I 20
[75] I 96

30

No Cipher Box has ever been captured, and the descriptions are not sufficiently detailed to do more than reveal the cryptographic principles involved, leaving the mechanics for the imagination. Fricke stated[76] that "it consisted of a small box in the top of which was inserted a slide rule." He described the slide rule as consisting of two mixed alphabets which were written in by pencil with each key change.

Half of the first mixed alphabet was written on the upper base part of the slide rule, the remaining half of the alphabet on the upper slide part of the slide rule. Half of the second mixed alphabet was written on the lower base part of the slide rule, the remaining half of the alphabet on the lower slide part of the slide rule. The two alphabets were so written in that when the halves of the first (upper) alphabet were in phase with each other, the halves of the second (lower) alphabet were out of phase, and vice-versa.

The drawing below illustrates with sample alphabets the way this may have been done:

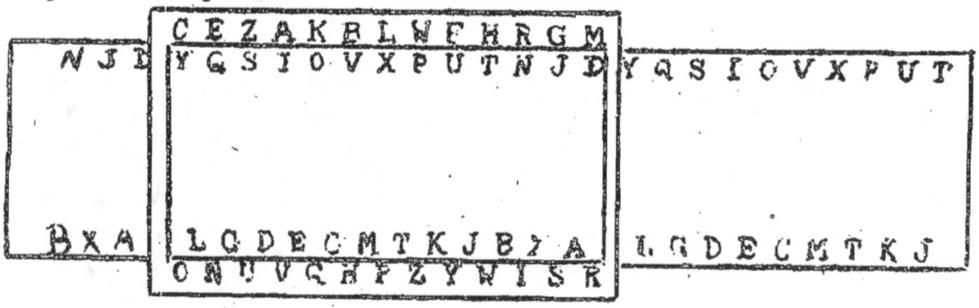

Encipherment of a letter was accomplished by reading off the letter opposite it on the slide rule. This was to be chosen from whichever alphabet was "in phase" at the time of encipherment. In the foregoing drawing, the cipher equivalent of plain text "I" at the setting shown would be "A" and the cipher equivalent of plain text "A" would be "I." Thus there resulted exactly 26 possible reciprocal enciphering alphabets.

Any sliding-strip device is secure if the successive settings of the sliding strip are unpredictable. Security of the Cipher Box therefore had to rest primarily in the manner of successively setting the slide. Dr. Fricke said this was done as follows:

> "Under the slide were three Hagelin type wheels on separate axes, in a plane perpendicular to that of

[76] I 20

the slide. Each had a different period, around 26. (The pin settings were changeable). The slide was pulled to the right against the action of a spring, and upon release drove the wheels. It did not come to rest until at a reading position of the wheels on one side the pins were all active, or until at another reading position on the other side they were all inactive. There were 26 stopping places possible, but no step zero."[77]

Dr. Liebknecht of the Army Ordnance, Development and Testing Group, Signal Branch (Wa Pruef 7) stated:[78]

> "The tongue (slide) of the instrument was shoved by hand to the right as far as it would go, thereby putting a spring inside the Cipher Box under tension. By means of pressing a blocking notch on the top of the Cipher Box, one causes the sliding tongue to move back varying step lengths into the Cipher Box."

[77] I 20. A cryptograph called the M-40, invented by Inspector Menzer of the Signal Intelligence Agency of the Supreme Command Armed Forces (OKW/Chi), also employed three Hagelin-type wheels for alphabet selection. This device was considered reasonably secure but was never adopted. It consisted of a cylinder with 39 horizontal bars arranged around its periphery; the cylinder rotated in steps equal to one plus the sum of the kicks given it by the three Hagelin-type wheels. The Hagelin-type wheels had changeable pins. Normal alphabetic sequences, each starting however with a different letter of the normal alphabet, were permanently inscribed on 26 of the 29 bars; the remaining 3 bars contained "dummy positions." These bars represented the plain components of enciphering alphabets of which the common cipher component was one mixed sequence written in by pencil on a fixed strip, so fastened on the base of the device that the bars of the cylinder could rotate into juxtaposition with it. The device was cryptographically equivalent to a pair of sliding strips, with the plain component a normal alphabet, with the cipher component a mixed alphabet, with the stepping controlled irregularly by Hagelin-type wheels, and with dummy letters thrown into the cipher text whenever a "dummy bar" came into position. See I-118 for fuller details. The Cipher Box was an improvement over the M-40, in that the small slide-rule construction accomplished nearly the same results as the large cylinder construction, the Cipher Box had two "reading positions" for the Hagelin-type wheels instead of just one, and there was provision for two mixed alphabets to be inscribed instead of just one.

[78] I 57 p 9

Nowhere in TICOM was it recorded whether or not the slide was pulled to the right after each encipherment, or only when necessary.

Serious study of this device has not been undertaken as yet at the Army Security Agency. However, the Germans felt that it was most secure. Lt. Col. Mettig stated as follows:[79]

> "The cryptographic security of this machine is very high and was considered superior to that of the Enigma. The safety margin for the daily cipher was calculated in the neighborhood of 40,000 to 50,000 letters, whereas with the Enigma this margin was 20,000 letters."[80]

25. "Cipher Disk" was to be a simplification of the "Cipher Box."-- The Cipher Box, small as it was, was the larger of two miniature cipher devices. The smaller device was called the Cipher Disk ("Schluesselscheibe.") Dr. Liebknecht gave TICOM its best description of this device.[81] He said:

> "Oberinspektor Menzer designed this machine for agents. The machine was not to exceed in size a shoe polish can. The encoding principle was similar to that of the Cipher Box. The equipment (consisted) of a rotatable inner disk and a stationary frame. The disk and frame had to be provided with scrambled alphabets similar to the Cipher Box. In operation the inner disk was rotated against the frame, and thereby in a manner similar to the Cipher Box, put a spring under tension. By means of a pressure and blocking notch, the disk is returned in various step lengths back toward its original position. In contrast to the Cipher Box, in this machine only control (wheels) with fixed notches were to be used. In the design, three control wheels to be set from the outside were to be included. The number of notches was to be determined once and for all for each pair of devices (one for the agent and one for central office). For this, a hand punch was thought of for punching the notches."

[79] I 96

[80] See also D 57 p 4.

[81] I 57 p 9.

According to Mettig:[82]

"The security investigations on this machine by Dr. Huettenhain and Lt. Dr. Stein proved so successful that it was decided to employ the Cipher Disk as enciphering equipment for forward (Army) units and indeed for forward of Regt HQ."

In Dr. Huettenhain's records was found the following, dated 21 April 1944:[83]

"The Chiffrier department requires.... 10,000 Cipher Disks and 20,000 sets each of 3 pin disc blanks."

The Army Security Agency has as yet made no serious study of this device, but it is believed that it has only limited security.

26. Foreign Office "Number Printer" produced non-random one-time pads-- A report on German cryptographic machines would not be complete unless it mentioned the "Number Printer" ("Numerierwerk") of the Foreign Office Cryptographic Section (Pers Z Chi). This device printed "one-time pads." These were used to encipher the Diplomatic Code Book (Deutsches Satzbuch); the system was called "GEE" at the Army Security Agency and was solved in the winter of 1944-45.

Cryptanalysts believe that a "one-time pad" is cryptographically 100% secure, if it is made up of random additive or key. The emphasis must be on the "random" as well as on the "one-time." The German Foreign Office Cryptographic Section (Pers Z Chi) overlooked the "random" when they made use of the Number Printer.

The Number Printer looked almost exactly like a large printing "job press." The type bed carried 240 small wheels, similar to the wheels on a rubber date stamp. Each wheel carried a sequence of ten digits around its periphery. The wheels were individually removable and interchangeable, as well as interchangeable in groups. Each time the press operated, it printed a sheet of paper with 240 numbers on it (8 lines of 6 groups of 5 digits). The press could be adjusted to print up to thirty sheets of paper identically, but was usually adjusted to print two sheets identically, one sheet of which became a page in a one-time "send" pad, while the duplicate became a page in the corresponding one-time "receive" pad. Before printing the next set of two

[82] I 96

[83] D 59 p 25

34

sheets, the machine proceeded to turn all the 240 wheels up one notch except such wheels as were at the moment kept from turning by special mechanical means. The cryptographic laws governing exactly which wheels paused in their movements, when and how often, were extremely simple. In principle, this was accomplished by what might be termed "non-turnover notches." These laws were discoverable by cryptanalysis. The result was that, while each page contained numbers that were random so far as that page alone was concerned, any given position on such a page was related to the same position on all the succeeding pages, and this non-random property permitted reconstructing sequences involved on the printing wheels. Shuffling of the sheets before binding into pad forms, of course, added to the cryptanalysts' difficulties, but did not prevent recovery and almost 100% reading of messages.

No Number Printer has ever been captured, but TICOM documents contain descriptions of early models.[84]

[84] T-1282. Captured files of the Foreign Office show that Number Printer apparatus was purchased from the German firms Maschinenfabrik Otto Krebs, and Clemens Mueller, in 1925, 1927, and 1933. See D-51 p 4. Similar number printer apparatus was offered for sale to the British Government on 14 June 1932 by the English firm Loranco Ltd., Engineers, by a Mr. Lorant, who described the apparatus, showed photographs, and stated that his firm (Loranco Ltd.) had supplied Number Printers to the German Government in 1925, 1928, and 1932. According to Mr. Lorant, the apparatus was for printing given numbers of copies of cipher telegrams, although it became immediately apparent to the British Government representatives that its real purpose was the generating of pages of random additives. Mr. Lorant stated that German Government had printed 2,000,000 pages without a breakdown, and that they kept an additional set of 250 spare wheels from which to choose. The British Government asked Mr. Lorant to submit prices, but apparently subsequently lost interest in his apparatus. The connection between the British firm Loranco Ltd., Engineers, and the German firms, is not known at this time.

VOLUME 2

Chapter V German Ciphony

27. German enciphered speech apparatus was unsuccessful.--Telephone or radiophone transmission of intelligence, swiftly, accurately, and securely, has been a goal of cryptanalysts for many years. Such speech encipherment is called "ciphony."

German experiments with ciphony were singularly unsuccessful. No satisfactory ciphony method was developed at any time.[90]

Dr. Werner Liebknecht, of the Army Ordnance, Development and Testing Group, Signal Branch ("Wa Pruef 7"), where ciphony experiments were undertaken, stated:[91]

> "If a process giving unintelligible speech was arrived at, then unfortunately it always happened that the speech quality after unscrambling was no longer acceptable; and the process of scrambling was therefore unacceptable."

Speech encipherment experiments were carried out by the following seven German commercial firms from 1937 to 1940:

[90] I 57
[91] I 57

36

1. Siemens and Halske, Berlin.
2. Deutsche Telefon und Kabelwerke, Berlin.
3. Sueddeutsche Apparate Fabriken, Berlin.
4. A. E. G., Berlin. ("Allgemeine Elektrische Gesellschaft")
5. Telefunken, Berlin.
6. Dr. Vierling, Technische Hochschule, Hanover.
7. Fabrik C. Lorenz Aktiengesellschaft, Berlin, Muelhausen, Thuer.

In 1943 only Telefunken and Dr. Vierling worked on speech enciphering, and from 1944 on, only Dr. Vierling, at his Laboratorium Feuerstein ("Firestone Laboratory") at Ebermannstadt, Germany.

Dr. Vierling's laboratory was captured almost intact by TICOM, because of Dr. Vierling's orders on the eve of surrender that none of his expensive equipment was to be destroyed. Ciphony and other varied electronic researches were in progress at the time of surrender. Two Army Security Agency ciphony engineers were dispatched to Ebermannstadt to exploit the German ciphony research, in conjunction with U. S. Navy and British engineers. As a result of this exploitation, plus interrogations of other German engineers elsewhere, it is believed the German ciphony picture is fully known at least as far as concerns their latest experiments.

Six main ciphony methods had been developed by German engineers. These methods were called:

a. Frequency inversion.
b. Noise superimposition.
c. Time scrambling.
d. "Little Building Block."
e. "Big Building Block."
f. Triple wobbling.

Each method in turn promised to prove less unsuccessful than its predecessor.

28. Experiments showed frequency inversion insecure.--Methods of frequency inversion usually require that speech frequencies (from 250 cycles per second to 2,750 cycles) be beat against a "carrier" frequency of about 3,000 cycles. The resultant frequencies are the differences in frequencies; these differences are transmitted. Thus, a low speech frequency of say 300

37

cycles would be transmitted as a high frequency of 2,700 cycles (or 3,000 cycles minus 300 cycles) whereas a high speech frequency would be sent as a low one.

The German inverter apparatus, which evidently worked along such lines, was "a large equipment of the size of a field telephone (installation) used in the field since the outbreak of the war. This set was considered safe and encouraged careless and insecure conversation. In reality it was possible with an ordinary receiver to re-establish the impulses normally. The equipment was, therefore withdrawn from units in 1942."[92]

There are no other important references to frequency inversion, and as it is considered insecure by most engineers everywhere, it is likely that no further experiments were carried out by the Germans along simple inversion lines.

29. Noise superimposition gave bad quality.--Methods of noise superimposition require that the superimposed noise frequencies cover the speech frequency band width, so that the noise can mask out the speech. At the receiving end a noise is applied exactly equal to that applied at the sending end,, exactly 180 degrees out of phase, so that the noise component is cancelled and clear speech remains.

C. Lorenz, Berlin, experimented with this method from 1937 to 1939, and found that frequency distortion over transmission lines was too great, as well as that faulty noise cancellation gave poor speech quality.[93]

From 1939 to 1943, after exhaustive experimentation, Telefunken (Berlin) determined that it would be impossible to cancel the noise correctly, and the speech quality would never become acceptable.

In spite of this, an ultra-high-frequency radio link between Athens, Crete, and Derna continued noise superimposition tests. Results from these tests were also disappointing.[94]

No further details of the experiments are available.

[92] I-96

[93] I-57

[94] I-57

38

30. "Time scrambling" was insecure.-- Methods of time scrambling require that the speech at the sending end be recorded immediately (usually magnetically on a steel tape) as a means of storing it for encipherment; encipherment results from breaking up the stored speech into small elements (of 60 milliseconds duration in the case of the German devices) and transposing them. The transposed elements are then transmitted by radio or wire to the receiving station which stores them, retransposes them, and puts them into the receiving telephone as speech. These principles, for instance, formed the basis for the U. S. Army's AN/GSQ-1, or SIGJIP.

The first German experiments in "time scrambling" required a long "time-delay" in order to store sufficient speech for transposition, and still did not result in completely enciphered (unintelligible) speech.[95]

In order to reduce the amount of time-delay needed to accomplish complex enough transpositions to result in unintelligibility, Siemens (Berlin) attempted to divide the speech into three frequency bands, and scramble each band separately. Dr. Liebknecht said as follows: "Despite the large bulk of this equipment (each station weighed about 100-150 kilograms) this process did not deliver completely unintelligible speech. The device was never manufactured."[96]

Possibilities of time-scrambling were brought to the fore again in late 1944, when an American Mustang airplane was shot down and found to include in its equipment an American time-scrambling radio-telephone apparatus (SIGJIP). According to Lt. Col. Mettig of the Signal Intelligence Agency of the Supreme Command Armed Forces (OKW/Chi):[97]

> "The technical experts believed that with the availability of necessary equipment, it would be possible to solve this apparatus in 10 minutes. The traffic was picked up on a sound track, photographed and through the regular division of the track it was possible for an expert to read the conversation. As a result, there was

[95] I-57
[96] I-57
[97] I-96

39

a controversy over the development of a German version of the Mustang apparatus. Forward units were of the opinion that it was impossible to carry out any tactical interception of such traffic since they would require a large quantity of special equipment. Consequently they felt the Mustang type could safely be used until a more practical machine was developed. The decision on this matter was never taken."

Time-scrambling devices were called "Tigerstedt" devices by German cryptographers (after a Swedish inventor named Tigerstedt). Dr. Fricke, of the Signal Intelligence Agency of the Supreme Command Armed Forces (OKW/Chi), offered the following information concerning the American Mustang device:[98]

> "He had seen an American machine on the Tigerstedt principle taken from a Mustang. It had a magnetophone band which revolved between nine heads which scrambled the speech horizontally (i.e. in time). This type of machine was rejected in Germany because you had to wait in between utterances for the machine to act. He himself did not think 750 milliseconds was very long to wait, but he supposed if a German major was talking to a general, the latter would find it desirable to cut him off abruptly with a reply."

There is no indication in the interrogations that Tigerstedt devices were ever adopted and used by the Germans.

31. "Big Building Block" proved too difficult to control. -- Since German ciphony experiments indicated that too much time would be required to develop secure ciphony apparatus, plans were developed for the independent construction of a machine which could be built quickly as a "stop-gap." The first of these attempts resulted in the "Building Block" ("Baustein"), later renamed the "Big Building Block" ("Der Grosse Baustein") after it was discovered that a second and still simpler device (called the "Little Building Block") would be needed.

The "Big Building Block" used the principle of "ring wobbling." "Ring wobbling" was the name given to a process

[98] I-20

by which the voice frequencies were shifted up and down the frequency scale. When they were shifted up, the frequencies at the top were electrically taken out of the spectrum and put back in at the bottom of the scale; when they were shifted down, the frequencies at the bottom were electrically taken out of the spectrum and put back in at the top of the scale. The process was called "ring," because what went off at the top came back around to the bottom, and vice versa. It was called "wobbling" because the frequencies wobbled or shifted, by being modulated on a "wobble frequency" "carrier." American engineers call the process "re-entrant wobbling."

Obviously such a system needed a wobbler--an agent to control the amount of the wobbling of the wobble frequency. In the case of the "Big Building Block" the wobbler was to have resulted from an autokey. The enciphered voice itself, operating through a time delay circuit, 100 to 200 milliseconds later, provided the key for enciphering the following voice.

We have on record the following epitaph:[99]

> "The experiment resulted in such difficulties in control of the receiving equipment that the experiment up to the present has led to no conclusions."

32. "Little Building Block" combined noise superimposition and frequency inversion.-- The "Little Building Block" ("Der Kleine Baustein") was intended to be a low-security speech scrambler for land-line use only.[100] It was to be secure against the human ear only. It combined noise superimposition and frequency inversion. Speech frequencies of from 300 cycles per second to 1,300 cycles per second were accepted by the filter system. These were inverted alternately by a 1,700 cycles per second carrier resulting in a frequency band from 1,400 cycles to 400 cycles; and by a 2,700 cycles per second carrier, resulting in a frequency band from 2,400 cycles to 1,400 cycles. The alternations in choice of carrier for inversion occurred about three to six times per second, depending upon the volume level of the speech. Into whichever of the frequency bands the speech was not inverted, noise was superimposed. Thus if inverted

[99] I-57
[100] I-57; E-9

DOCID: 3560816

speech occurred in the 400-1400 cycle band, noise occured in the 1400-2400 cycle band; and vice versa. Note that the noise was not superimposed at the same frequencies as the speech, as in the noise superimposition method described first; therefore, it could be eliminated by simply being electrically ignored at the receiving end, provided, of course, the receiver had the appropriate apparatus. The receiver then would proceed to re-invert the speech, rendering it intelligible.

This apparatus was under test by Dr. Vierling at the close of the war; but only a single one-way circuit had been constructed for the tests.[101] Evidently switching imperfections, bad filter networks, and scarcity of electrical parts, prevented its development. The apparatus was not complete when captured, but diagrams are available.[102]

33. Hopes centered on synthetic speech enciphered by "triple wobbling."--German engineers recognized as early as 1939 that synthetic speech might prove easier to encipher than actual speech. Experiments were begun which resulted in the development of a synthetic speech apparatus called "Anna" by the German engineers, and patterned closely after the American "Vocoder," patented by Homer Dudley of Bell Telephone Laboratories. The German apparatus, "Anna," divided actual speech into eight separate frequency bands, by means of filter networks. It produced eight carrier frequencies, to correspond to the eight speech bands; and when the energy level of any speech band varied, the amplitude of the corresponding carrier frequency varied in proportion. These carrier frequencies, plus two more carriers each of which represented variations in the pitch of the speech fundamental and whether or not the speech was "voiced" or "whispered," formed the set of ten carriers which was then to be enciphered.

"Triple wobbling" was the method proposed for the encipherment. By this process, the composite set of carriers (ranging in frequency from 450 to 2110 cycles per second) was passed through a single stage of ring wobbling much as in the "Big Building Block;" the output from this stage of wobbling

101 E-9

102 E-9

was split by filters into halves, and each was separately ring-wobbled; these two outputs were combined and passed through a third stage of ring wobbling. The signal was then passed through a fixed carrier modulator which restored the scrambled signal to a transmittable frequency range.

The following are important to note: Wobbling was to have been done three separate times; wobbling was to have been controlled by a specially built cipher machine, and not by an autokey system as in the "Big Building Block."

Dr. Liebknecht said:[103]

> "A triple wobbling project is still under way at the Feuerstein Laboratory, but it is also very complicated. Through this system, condensers were to be turned under the influence of teletype impulses from the SZ-42 enciphering device, and thus the wobbling is to be brought about. Until now the results from triple wobbling have not been very satisfactory. The speech quality after dewobbling was very bad."

Excellent descriptions of the speech filters etcetera appear in the TICOM reports.[104] It is believed by Allied investigators that "triple wobbling" would not have proved satisfactory unless much research could have been carried out, especially in filter designs. Nevertheless, German hopes of successful ciphony apparently centered on synthetic speech enciphered by "triple wobbling."

34. Conclusions: Germans had no usable ciphony machines.--Unless new evidence is unearthed the conclusions are: Germany had no usable ciphony machines; and Germany probably would not have had any usable ciphony machines even if the war had gone on several more years.

[103] I-57

[104] E-9, E-10, E-11

43

VOLUME 2

Chapter VI - German "I.B.M." and Rapid Analytic Machinery

Paragraph

35. <u>German "I.B.M." equipment paralleled ours.</u>-- Electric accounting machines using punch cards, called "Hollerith" throughout Europe and simply "I.B.M." (after International Business Machines Corporation) in America, are a primary yardstick of cryptanalytic progress. By this yardstick the Germans measured up well.

A chart comparing the I.B.M. equipment of the principal German cryptologic bureaus with that of the Army Security Agency (U.S. Army) is shown herewith as Chart No. 2-2. (See next page.)

From the chart it may be seen that the estimated total number of I.B.M. machines used by the German non-Navy bureaus was less than the total employed at Army Security Agency; but if the Army Security Agency machines devoted exclusively to the attack on Japanese Army systems are not counted, than the German non-Navy machines in general probably exceed the Army Security Agency machines.

Four key punches, 2 sorters, 1 collator, 2 reproducers, 1 multiplier, and 1 tabulator, represent

DOCID: 3560816

I.B.M. PUNCH CARD ("HOLLERITH") EQUIPMENT OF THE SIX PRINCIPAL GERMAN CRYPTOLOGIC ORGANIZATIONS COMPARED WITH THAT AT ARMY SECURITY AGENCY

	OKM/4 SKL/III (Navy)	Pers ZS and Chi (Foreign Office)	FORSCHUNGS-AMT (Goering's Research Bureau)	OKW/Chi and OKH (Supreme Command and Army)	OKL (Air)	German Non-Navy	ARMY SECURITY AGENCY (U.S. Army)		
	Cryptanalysis Cryptography	Cryptanalysis Cryptography ?	Cryptanalysis	Cryptanalysis Cryptography	Cryptanalysis Cryptography	TOTAL at least	TOTAL	General c.anals. Cryptography	Jap Army Code Solution only
Punches and verifiers	30	20	10*	40	20	90	109	35	74
Reproducers	6	2	1	8*	2*	13	52	10	42
Sorters	7	10	4	30*	5	49	85	27	58
Collators	1	2	0	4*	?	6	39	13	26
Multipliers	3	1	0	0	?	1	4	1	3
Interpreters	0	0	0	0*	?	0	7	1	6
Tabulators, all types	7	6	3	2	3*	14	47	10	37
Special Equipment	2 tape-to-card readers	1 comparator counter. 1 selective	?	?	? tape-to-card readers	-	-	11 card operated type-writers 2 presensing gang-punches	4 tape-to card readers. 4 presensing-gang-punches. Also special attachments**
Personnel	80	45*	15*	150*	50*	260	1100	300	800
References	I-146 I-158	I-1 I-22	I-25 I-58 I-96 I-113 I-67	I-20 I-127 I-152	I-119	-	-	-	-

*Estimated
**See Chart No. 2-3, following page 50.

Chart No. 2-2

45

the total of captured I.B.M. equipment belonging to the German signal intelligence organizations; these were captured at Zschepplin; they belonged to the Foreign Office Cryptanalytic Section (Pers Z S). Their wires were all ripped out and plugboards missing. They were studied briefly by TICOM Team 1 and then destroyed by dynamite.[109] Therefore, practically all our knowledge of German use of I.B.M. must come from the TICOM interrogation reports, and these discuss I.B.M. but scantily. Nevertheless, scattered remarks indicate the used to which the I.B.M. machines were put by the Germans, and under what conditions. These technical uses were almost identical with those at Army Security Agency. The important excerpts from the interrogations are given below:

a. Dr. Buggisch, of the Signal Intelligence Agency of the Army High Command (OKH/G. d NA), stated as follows concerning the use of I.B.M. by his agency:[110]

> "Some of the bigger I.B.M. machines were always being provided with special new wirings for special cryptanalytic purposes, as for non-carrying addition and subtraction in code work. Most of the tasks, however, consisted of the usual statistics (digraphs, trigraphs, "chain" statistics, "column" statistics, and of simple figure calculations, e.g. in work on Hagelin Machines). But, as a rule, no tasks were undertaken which could not have been carried out by hand by perhaps 100 people in a reasonable time."[111]

b. Evidently Army code problems (usually problems of finding messages in depth) were turned directly over to the I.B.M. section. An interrogation report stated:[112]

> "A new (Russian) code came in October 1941, and depths were less thereafter. Buggisch and other mathematicians were withdrawn from this work in November 1941, and he states that the problem was handed over largely to the I.B. M. section."

[109] I-1
[110] I-67
[111] At the Government Code and Cypher School the basis was 20 to 25 persons.
[112] I-58

46

c. A complaint by Dr. Buggisch on the way I.B.M. mishandled some of its more specialized statistics was recorded in one report as follows:[113]

> "The breaking of cipher texts (without crib) is possible when the pin arrangement of the pin wheels can be discovered from column statistics of the cipher text....The calculation is carried out with an I.B.M. machine provided with special wiring. As mistakes were frequent and the time required was considerable, the construction of special calculating machines for this purpose was proposed."

(It so happens that I.B.M. is not well adapted to solution of the Hagelin machine, as the Army Security Agency, U. S. Army, has itself found out. The number of operations required to furnish all necessary statistics by the I.B.M. method allows for too many handling errors.)

d. A further reference to the German Army use of I.B.M. is made with reference to a double transposition used by the Allies in Italy in February 1945. Such messages included times of origin in their plain text, with such times of origin first enciphered by digraphs involving infrequent letters. (These enciphering alphabets never changed.) The whole messages were then subjected to the double transposition encipherments. The times of origin were seldom more than half an hour before the times of sending, so the Germans had information they could "crib into" the cipher text, once they had broken the digraphic substitution. These cribs were at least four letters long, and in short messages could almost always be placed accurately. Corporal Clemens Schuck of Inspectorate 7/VI (In 7/VI) stated as follows:[114]

> "A four letter entry would thus be obtained. Such a combination would be run through all the possible widths on the I.B.M. machines. The time required to break these messages was one to five days, depending on the number of men and machines available."

[113] I-137

[114] I-80

e. Some of the I.B.M. machines the Army had were evidently not working too well. The following was learned from Dr. Fricke, when he discussed the making up by the German Army of some of its own keys and tables:[115]

> "Daily changing trigraphic substitution tables were introduced (by the German Army). They were made at first by I.B.M.....The section moved to Weimar late in the war, and there the machines were so old and out of repair that they made too many mistakes in the tables."

As a result, Fricke had the tables handset by a printer. This later method proved more efficient.

f. Specialist Voegele, discussing the use of I.B.M. by the Signal Intelligence Agency of the Commander in Chief of the Air Forces (Chi Stelle Ob d L), stated as follows concerning June 1942 Allied air traffic:[116]

> "The breaking of strip traffic was subject to time lags of two months before the receipt of I.B.M. machinery, but only two to four weeks afterwards."

According to another report by him I.B.M. was used in "brute-forcing," or the discovery of depths by double repeats.[117]

g. I.B.M. was used in a "brute force" method applied to the British Naval Cypher "to find double repeats at intervals up to 10," by the Signal Intelligence Agency of the Navy High Command (OKM/4 SKL/III), according to Oberregierungsrat Tranow and Graduate Engineer Schmalz.[118] I.B.M. was also used by them to provide "a catalogue of differences, repeats, and double repeats," and most interestingly, "reciphering of captured subtractor groups." By this last was meant that captured additive was applied to known high-frequency unenciphered code groups, to obtain a catalogue of likely enciphered code groups against which messages could be tested--a key finding technique often used at Army Security Agency.

[115] I-20

[116] I-119

[117] I-152

[118] I-146

48

h. A "baby brute force" (index of single hits between messages known to be from approximately the same part of the additive tables) was also carried out by I.B.M. in connection with British codes.

i. Senior Specialist Tranow and Graduate Engineer Schmalz stated as follows:[119]

> "Five per cent of our I.B.M. capacity was devoted to producing our own cipher systems. We constructed reciphering tables, substitution tables, and the Signal-Tafeln, e.g., reciprocal 2-letter tables, 3- and 4-digit figure tables. The number of cards needed for each substitution table was one set, for 2-letter tables was 26 x 26, and for the 3- and 4-figure tables was 1,000 and 10,000 respectively."

36. Rapid Analytic Machines were built on simple and effective Lines.--Just as in the United States, cryptanalysts in Germany felt the need in special cases for more rapid means of searching, comparing, and otherwise statistically treating code and cipher texts than hand and I.B.M. methods could offer. They developed a series of teleprinter tape devices, employing photocell readers, which accomplished these tasks speedily, inexpensively, and very practically. Such machines may be called "rapid analytic machinery." They differed from rapid analytic machinery developed in the United States in that in general they employed teleprinter (paper) tapes, rather than celluloid film. However, it is true that the first German film device was in process of construction; it was almost identical to our "Tetra-Tester," and had an estimated speed of search of 10,000 letters per second, as against the actual speed of the Tetra-Tester of 5,000 per second.

In comparing the states of development of German rapid analytic machinery with American, it might be said (loosely) that the German scientists were a year and a half behind the Americans. Development of rapid analytic machinery was done almost entirely by the Signal Intelligence Agency of the Supreme Command Armed Forces (OKW/Chi), and this mainly as a result of security studies. The special Cipher Security Section was formed

[119] I-146

within OKW/Chi in 1940, later being put under control of Dr. Huettenhain. Interrogation of Dr. Huettenhain revealed:[120]

"By 1941 it had become clear that machines would be necessary for the dual - offensive and defensive - task of research, but engineers were not obtained until 1942, when the following were appointed: Two graduate engineers: ROTSCHEIDT (formerly with Siemens) and JENSEN (who came directly from school), both telecommunications experts. (These are now thought to be in the South); three working engineers, TODT, SCHAEFFER, and KRACHEL (with a Technical High School Training), who were decidedly subordinate to Rotscheidt and Jensen; and twenty-five mechanics.

"They decided to use I.B.M. wherever possible, but it was found that I.B.M. machinery was not suitable for all problems, and auxiliary deciphering machines were developed as the occasion arose. Special problems were laid before the engineers, and they were told 'This is what I want to do, how would you do it?' The machines which resulted were built in a more generalized way than the immediate problem demanded so that they could be of use again."

As a result the following special machines were developed:

a. Digraph "weight" recorder.
b. Polygraphic coincidence counter.
c. Statistical "depth increaser."
d. Differencing calculator (non-recording).
e. Differencing calculator (recording).
f. Likely additive selector.
g. Simple counting apparatus.
h. Proposed repeat finder.

Chart No. 2-3 herewith, compares these rapid analytic machines, developed by the Signal Intelligence Agency of the Supreme Command Armed Forces (OKW/Chi), with those owned by the Army Security Agency.

[120] I-31

37. Rapid analytic machines developed by Armed Forces cryptanalysts described.--The main features of the rapid analytic machines developed by the Signal Intelligence Agency of the Supreme Command Armed Forces (OKW/Chi) were as follows:

a. Digraph "weight" recorder.--The "Bigramm Suchgeraet," or "digraph search apparatus," was a device for making frequency evaluations of digraphs and recording the evaluations. It cost approximately $5,800.00[121] and was the most expensive rapid analytic machine owned by the Signal Intelligence Agency of the Supreme Command Armed Forces (OKW/Chi).

It was used to solve the Japanese two-letter transposed code (J-19, or "Fuji") "and the machine would find a solution in less than two hours."[122] It did the work of twenty people, according to Dr. Huettenhain.[123] "The machine was once used for work on an English meteorological cipher, figure traffic employing a stencil, when Huettenhain liaised with the Air Force Weather Service. They were allowed to use the machine."[124]

The digraph "weight" recorder consisted of: two teleprinter tape "reading heads," a relay-bank interpreter circuit, a plugboard "weight" assignor, and a recording pen and drum.[125]

Each head read its tape photoelectrically, at a speed of 75 positions per second.

The interpreter took the two impulses from the reading heads at any given moment, and translated them from two separate letter impulses into one digraphic impulse, which it sent to the plugboard.

The plugboard contained 676 jacks on its left side, representing digraphs; these could be wired at will to any jack in any one of five different sets of jacks on the right side of the plugboard, these sets representing "weights." Thus on the plugboard, any digraph could

[121] D-60

[122] I-31

[123] D-60

[124] I-31

[125] I-37

be assigned any integral weight from 1 to 5 by simply plugging the digraph to the weight; unplugged digraphs had the value zero. A sketch of the plugboard follows:

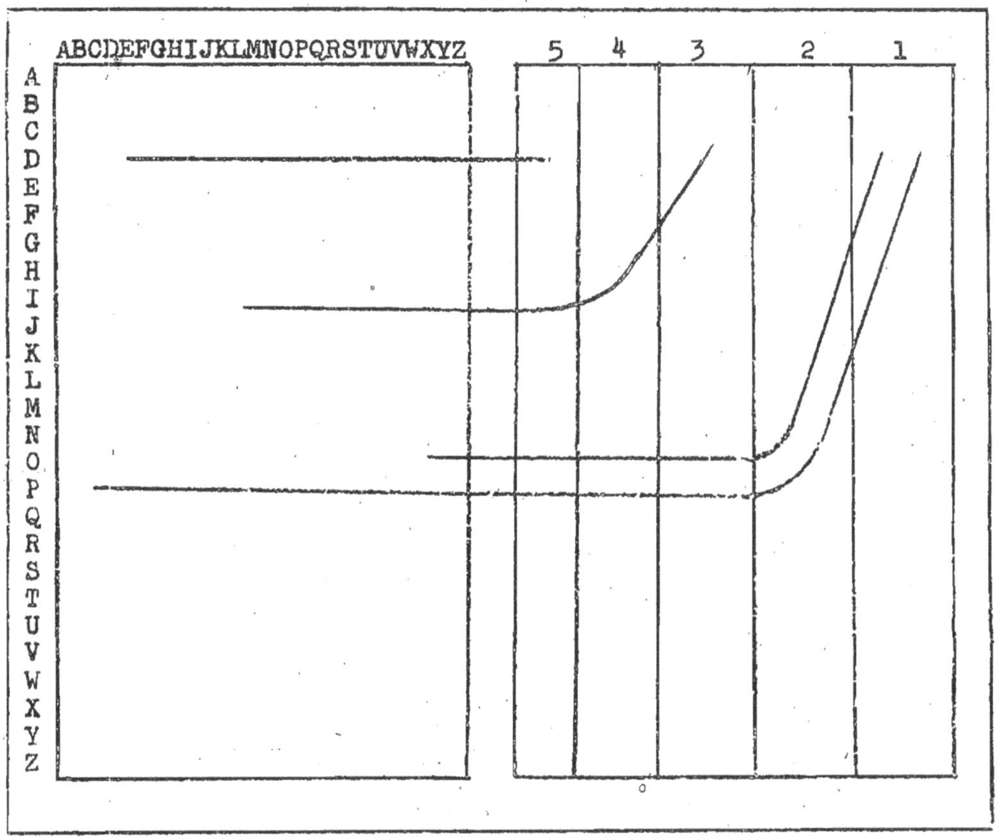

In the foregoing sketch, for illustration, the digraph DE was given the weight 5, the digraph IL the weight 3, the digraphs PC and OX were each given the weight 1. All other digraphs had the weight 0.

The recording device was in effect an undulator. It consisted of a paper drum revolving at an even rate under a pen which in turn moved on a spindle across the drum. As a result the line traced by the pen was a cylindrical spiral. Undulations occurred in this spiral however, wherever a digraph occurred with a weight other than 0. The heights of the undulations varied directly with the weights assigned the corresponding digraphs.

This device was said to have made solution of a single transposition easy. Such solution is a familiar process to most cryptanalysts, requiring much trial and error. A message under study must, in effect, be broken into likely columns and these matched against each other, with the resulting digraphs being examined for their "goodness" to determine whether or not such matches are probable. If, for instance, the message is broken into sixteen columns, there are 1,307,674,368,000 (factorial 15) possible matches, but these are attacked of course by successive steps: that is, one column is tried against each of the other fourteen and the most probable combination selected before proceeding further; with this pair as a basis, another of the remaining thirteen columns is selected to add to the left or right of the initial pair, and so on.

It is assumed that the German digraphic weight recorder was used in the following manner to solve such single-transposition problems:

Two duplicate teleprinter tapes were punched, corresponding to the message to be solved, each tape then being formed into a loop and one loop being made one space (or more) longer than the other, so that as they revolved through the tape reading heads they would "slide" relative to each other. Digraphic weights, probably logarithmic in nature, were then plugged up on the plugboard and the machine started. The result would be an undulatory graph indicating, digraph by digraph, for every possible juxtaposition of the whole message against itself, the probability of a "good match" at each point along its length. Careful investigation of this graph would thus show visually (by dense areas of tall undulations) those positions where "good" matches occurred, and the limits in length of each such good match--that is, the length of the columns involved.

The German digraph weight recorder was therefore quite different from the Army Security Agency's "electromechanagrammer," which also was designed specifically to solve the Japanese J-19 code. The American machine ran a deck of I.B.M. cards representing the message under study through an I.B.M. tabulator, with a specifically chosen section of the message (representing a definite column) wired up on the plugboard; digraphs were weighted with ten logarithmic probability values (ranging from 0 through 9) and totals were printed, rather than individual weights being recorded separately as in the German digraphic weight recorder. The American machine took about four minutes per section to calculate and print the results. If the sections of text chosen from any given message were well chosen from a cryptanalytic viewpoint, the American machine proved much faster than the German machine, because the print of totals was easier for the cryptanalyst to analyze than just the individual values listed by the German machine; but if the sections of text were not well chosen and no true columns were included in the choice, then the German machine had the advantage, since it recorded all possible juxtapositions quickly, and all true matches were included in the data.

The German digraph weight recorder could also be used to advantage to locate coincidences between messages. The digraphs aa, bb, cc, ... zz, could be plugged up to the value 1 and all other digraphs left unplugged. Then when two message tapes would be run against each other, coincidences would be shown by the undulator. Such an arrangement would be especially valuable in revealing interrupted repetitions.

b. Polygraph coincidence counter.--The "Saegebock," or "Sawbuck," was a machine for recording the frequency of polygraphs occurring within one message, or for counting polygraphic coincidences between messages.[126] It was especially useful for work on periodic substitutions. Polygraphs could be of any size up to and including decagraphs. The machine cost approximately $1,200.00.[127]

The apparatus consisted of two teleprinter-tape "reading heads," a "calculator" (not described), and ten different "recorders."

Each head read its tape photoelectrically and had a speed of 75 positions per second. Each recorder comprised a pen which recorded dashes on a paper strip 20 inches wide, making a short dash whenever the recorder received an impulse from the calculator. The short dashes combined to form dashes of varying lengths. One recorder was assigned to "count" single letters, another to "count" digraphs, another to "count" trigraphs, and so on, up to ten.

[126] I-37, I-31. The Germans adopted cover names for many of these devices, and these names were apparently not selected at random, but like ours, were derived from characteristics of the devices. The cover name "Saegebock" was probably so derived.

[127] D-60

DOCID: 3560816

The machine worked as follows: if it was desired to record the number of polygraphic coincidences occurring within one message, two duplicate tapes corresponding to the message, were prepared as described above in connection with the digraph weight recorder, the looped tapes then being inserted in the two reading heads and the machine started. During the first revolution of the loops, each recorder would make a short vertical stroke every time a coincidence of the length assigned to that recorder occurred between the tapes. Thus, if there were ten digraphic coincidences between the tapes during the first revolution, then recorder number two made ten small strokes, each above the other, so that a line ten units high resulted; if there were four trigraphic coincidences, then recorder number three made four strokes, and so on.

All the recording pens then returned to the zero position and the paper in all the recorders moved along one step automatically, to be set for the next revolution of the tapes, wherein the tapes were of course at a different juxtaposition.

A polyalphabetic substitution of period seven being studied might therefore have given a chart of single letter coincidences at the different justapositions of the tapes, much as follows:

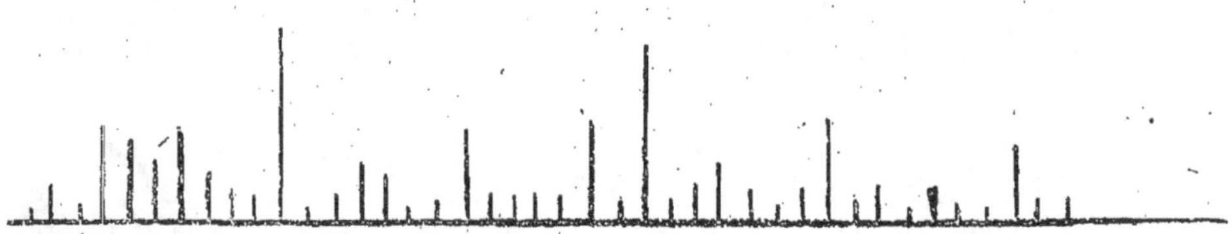

Highest single letter coincidences in this sample are indicated at intervals of seven, the causal interval.

To record the number of polygraphic coincidences between two different messages, a tape would be punched for each message, and similar procedure followed with these two different rather than duplicate tapes, as in the first case.

Drs. Huettenhain and Fricke did not identify the specific cryptographic systems the polygraphic coincidence counter was designed to attack. Dr. Huettenhain stated, however:[128]

[128] I-31

55

DOCID: 3560816

> "The problem was to determine the periods in short periodic substitutions by finding the distances between repeats in a message....It (the counter) could also be used to find two enigma messages in depth."

The foregoing machine was one of a class called "Fasen Suchgeraet (Perioden)," or "Phase search apparatus (Periods)."

c. Statistical "depth-increaser."--The "Turmuhr," or "Tower clock," was a device for testing a sequence of thirty consecutive cipher letters statistically against a given "depth" of similar sequences, to determine whether the former belonged to the given depth.[129] It was used "primarily for work on the U.S. strip cipher, when cribbing which was generally employed was impossible."[130] It cost approximately $1,000.00.[131]

The apparatus consisted of a single teleprinter tape reading head (speed 1 1/2 symbols per second); a storage means, by which any one of five different scores could be assigned, on a basis of frequency, to each of the letters in the 30 separate monoalphabets that resulted from the 30 columns of depth; a distributor that rotated in synchronism with the tape stepping, and selected which set of 30 scores was to be used as basis for evaluating the successive cipher letters; and a pen recording device.

The machine was used somewhat as follows:

First, several sections of cipher text, believed from statistical study to be enciphered with the same set of strips and on the same generatrix, were superimposed properly. As a result, the letters within columns fell into successive and separate monoalphabets with characteristic frequencies. A new section of 30 letters of cipher text would have to "match" these alphabets, that is, show a greater than random number of coincidences with them, before it could be added to this depth. The machine was used to test the goodness of such a match. Weights were assigned each letter in each of the basic thirty alphabets, depending on the frequencies therein, and these weights were "stored" in the machine. A message under study was punched on tape; the tape was run through the

[129] I-20, I-37

[130] I-31

[131] D-60

machine; the machine read the cipher text in sequences of thirty; for each sequence it applied the proper weights to each of the letters by choosing the weights from the thirty alphabets in succession; it recorded the total weight for each sequence by strokes of the recording pen. A long resultant stroke meant a great total weight; a sequence giving a long resultant stroke probably therefore belonged to the basic set of superimposed sequences.

Dr. Huettenhain and Dr. Fricke, of the Signal Intelligence Agency of the Supreme Command Armed Forces (OKW/Chi), in describing the statistical depth-increaser stated that it had a photoelectric reading head.[132] In view of the also-stated speed of 1 1/2 symbols per second, which is reasonable considering the probable slowness of the distributor, a photoelectric head hardly seems likely, and it is believed that actually a standard teleprinter reading head was used. They stated that "provision is made for 5 different scores," which seems reasonable, although a written description of the machine found in Dr. Huettenhain's papers indicated that 20 scores were possible. which seems unreasonable.[133] Drs. Huettenhain and Fricke also stated:

> "The cipher text passages already recognized as on the same key are stored in the calculating apparatus of the 'tower clock' as a basis on which to start; and in such a way that for each of the substitution alphabets the elements receive different scores according to the frequency of the cipher texts.."

It is believed this storage was done by hand after collection and examination of the cipher text, rather than mechanically by a huge and unnecessary bank of relays, as might be inferred from their statement.

The machine was named "Tower clock" because it ticked after each set of calculations. Presumably it could be operated by the cryptanalyst himself.

d. Differencing calculator (non-recording) and additive tester.--This machine (German name not known) was a manually-operated device designed to assist additive recovery in superenciphered code problems, by speeding the differencing of depths of super-enciphered code groups

[132] I-37

[133] D-60

and the trial of likely additives thereon.[134] It cost approximately $40.00.[135] It was identical in its function to the U.S. Navy "CXDG-CNN-10ADW." often called the "N.C.R. differencing calculator." The German version had a capacity of thirty 5-figure groups, as against the N.C.R. capacity of twenty. The German device was much slower to operate, though far simpler in construction.[136]

The German differencing calculator consisted of five small metal rods arranged vertically and side by side. Down each rod were 31 small metal "rollers," each roller carrying on its periphery the sequence of figures 0, 1, 2, 3, ... 9. A skeleton sketch of the machine, with its cover removed, is shown, on the following page, just as drawn by Dr. Huettenhain.[137]

The top roller of each rod was fastened permanently to its rod; each of the lower thirty rollers was rotatable independently on its rod so that it could be set at will to any of its ten possible positions. Each of the five rods revolved at will, carrying all of its thirty-one rollers around with it simultaneously. The apparatus had a lid which when closed revealed only the one figure at the center of each roller. (In the sketch, if the lid had been closed, the five rollers across the top would have indicated the five-figure group "00000," the next row of five rollers would have indicated the group "13870," the next row, "44651," and so on.)

Differencing a depth of 5-figure enciphered codegroups was a simple process with this machine. The five rods were locked into position with the top (fixed) row of rollers reading "00000." Then the first enciphered code group in the depth was set up on the next row of rollers (marked row "1" in the sketch) then the second enciphered code group was set up on row "2;" the third enciphered code group on row "3," etc., until all the enciphered code groups were set up. Then the five rods were unlocked.

To subtract the first enciphered code group (appearing in row "1") from all the others, all one now had to

[134] I-37

[135] D-60

[136] Army Security Agency constructed a differencing calculator in 1943 identical in principle to the German device. It was a rough model and was not perfected because the N.C.R. devices were made available. It is now in the Army Security Agency museum.

[137] I-37

DOCID: 3560816

<u>German Differencing Calculator, Non-Recording</u>

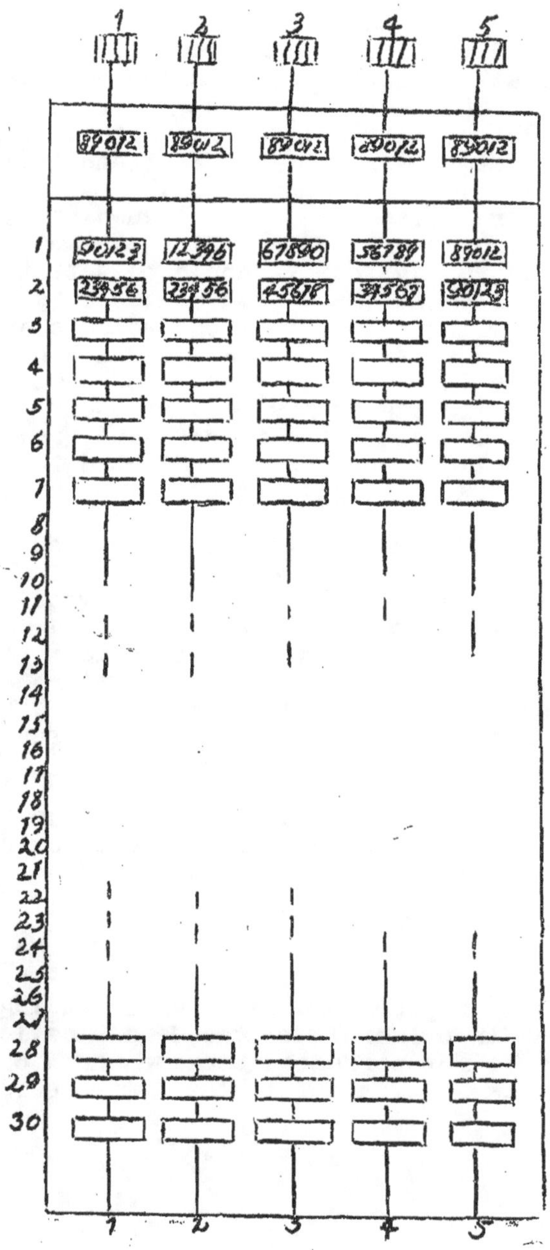

do was to rotate each of the five rods until the rollers in row "1" read "00000." The numbers appearing in all the lower rows now represented "differences." These differences could now be looked up in "difference tables," and the most probable unenciphered pairs of code groups they represented be noted down for trial--an analytic process familiar to all cryptanalysts. To "try" one of these likely unenciphered groups with the aid of the machine, all one had to do was to rotate the five rods until it appeared in the window instead of the enciphered code group supposed to be representing it; immediately all other rows represented the consequences of the assumption, and the very top row (above the row marked "1") represented the enciphering "additive."

This device could be operated by the cryptanalyst himself at his own desk.

e. Differencing Calculator (recording).--This machine which the Germans probably called the "Differenzen Rechengeraet," or "Difference Calculating Apparatus," was designed to compute a "flag of differences" for a set of enciphered code groups and to record this flag.[138] It consisted of two teleprinter tape photoelectric reading heads, a set of calculating relays, and a recording electric typewriter. The speed of the whole machine was limited to 7 symbols a second by the typewriter speed, with time out for carriage return and line feed. It cost approximately $800.00.[139]

This machine worked as follows: the figure groups between which differences were to be made were punched onto a tape. A duplicate of the tape was made, with one blank group additional. The two tapes were formed into loops and placed into the reading heads, so that the first group of the duplicate tape and the second group of the original tape were ready to be read at the same time. The machine was then started. The calculating relays computed the difference (modulo 10) between the two groups and the typewriter recorded it; the two tapes then stepped simultaneously, and the difference between the second and third was computed and recorded; then between the third and fourth; and so on. On the second time around, since the duplicate tape was one group longer than the original, the "offset" was automatically changed so that the first group was now differenced with the third group, the second with the fourth, and so on. In this way every group was

[138] I-37

[139] D-60

60

eventually differenced with all other groups. The "flag" actually came out as a rectangle (rather than as a triangle). That is, the difference between the first group and the second was recorded, as also was the difference between the second and the first (a complementary difference). This gave an opportunity to ignore all "minor" differences and consider only "major" ones.

A second version of this machine was built, in which one tape was left in strip form and one tape used as a loop. The strip tape moved through the reading head for one group only; this group was read and stored in the computor; the loop tape revolved; the computor subtracted the stored group from each group in turn of the revolving tape; when the revolving tape made one complete revolution the strip tape moved up to its second group; this second group was stored in the computor and subtracted from every group of the revolving tape; and so on until each group had been subtracted from every other one.

f. Likely-additive selector.--The "Witzkiste," or "Brainbox," was an exceptionally simple device for removing additive from a column of super-enciphered code groups arranged in depth. It could be used with any four-digit (or smaller) enciphered code, the frequency of whose unenciphered code groups had been discovered from previous removal of additives.[140] Five-digit codes had to rely on the differencing calculators previously described. The cost of the "Witzkiste" is unknown, but believed less than $50.00.

Suppose, for example, a four-digit code was under study, and that the following three unenciphered code groups were known to be high-frequency groups, from the removal of additive from previous depths: 0032, 0033, and 6748. Then if enciphered code group "0000" appeared in a new depth, it very likely resulted from additive 0078, 0077, or 4362. Similarly, if enciphered code group "0001" appeared in the same depth, it very likely resulted from additive 0079, 0078, or 4363. (Note that additive 0078 has been indicated twice.) Any other enciphered code group in the depth would also have a set of three likely additives associated with it. A tally of these additives would show highest frequency for the most likely additive for that depth.

[140] I-37

61

The "Witzkiste" was a device for tallying such likely additives photographically. In essence it consisted of a "lattice-frame," with each cell therein representing one of the different possible additives from 0000 to 9999; a black-enameled glass plate which fitted under the lattice-frame and was removable; a light source behind both; and a camera in front. For the specific code used in the example in the preceding paragraph, the glass plate would have had the black enamel scratched off at positions 0078, 0077, 4362 (the likely additives for "0000"). Whenever enciphered code group "0000" appeared in a depth, the glass plate would be placed between the lattice and the light source, and the lattice photographed. Only additive positions 0078, 0077, and 4362 would be photographed because only in those spots could light appear. In case enciphered code group "0001" appeared in the depth, the same glass plate would be placed between the lattice and the light source, but <u>moved one position</u> over, and the lattice would be <u>photographed</u> -- on the same piece of film. Only additive positions 0079, 0078, and 4363 would be photographed this time. But since 0078 would now have been photographed twice, it would appear darker when the film was developed. Thus the one glass plate could be slid around and made to tally likely additive for any one of the ten-thousand possible enciphered code groups that might be encountered in a depth; and the additive whose position was darkest, after development of the film, was the most probable one; that is, statistically, it was likely to be correct.

The "Witzkiste" was complicated slightly by the fact that additive-encipherment addition is non-carrying (that is, modulo 10). In order to make the same glass plate and lattice do for all enciphered code groups, in view of the non-carrying addition, the glass plate had to be sixteen times as large as it would have been with normal addition (each additive scratch having to be entered in 2x2x2x2 different positions instead of one) and the lattice frame had to be four times as large. This can be explained to a mathematician by saying that to accomplish four-digit addition modulo 10, the lattice-frame was spread out double size in two dimensions to eliminate carry over, and the scratches on the glass were doubled in each of four ways to make the system re-entrant. Such a glass plate for one additive would have looked as follows:

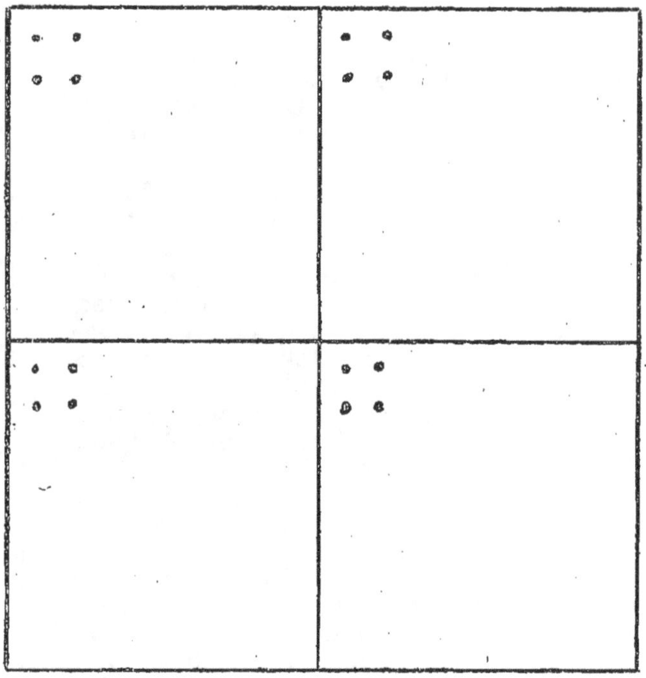

instead of
as follows:

In the two drawings the black spots represent holes scratched in the black enamel of the glass plate to represent just one additive. In actual practice, many additives of course would be represented.

With the "Witzkiste" made as above, testing for most likely additive was rapid and simple and as described. Final photographs could be printed out on print paper, or projected onto a screen for study.

g. Simple counting apparatus.--This is best described in the words of Dr. Huettenhain as follows:[141]

"By means of simple counting apparatus it is possible quickly to work our statistics, when there are not more than 100 different elements.

"100 counting machines (Post Office counters) are put side by side. The text for which statistics

[141] I-37

are to be worked out is punched on a tape. The perforated strip is read and the symbol in each case put on the corresponding counter. The counters are read off and their position photographically recorded.

"In practice this apparatus was used with success within the scope of the investigations into the security of our own systems."

Cost was approximately $600.00.[142]

h. Proposed "repeat finder."--This ultra-high-speed machine, planned and in production but not yet finished, was designed to study from 20 to 25 messages for repetitions of five or more characters. Each message could be 500 letters (or figures) in length. Thus study of approximately 10,000 letters of cipher text could be undertaken at any one time.

Dr. Huettenhain stated as follows:[143]

"The 10,000 letters were recorded one after another as 5-unit alphabetical symbols onto an ordinary film. A duplicate was made. Both strips were now to pass at high speed in front of a reader working without inertia [i.e., a photocell reader]. In the event of the two strips being completely identical for at least 5 letters, this passage would be likewise registered without inertia.

"The strips were to pass before the reading device at a speed of 10,000 symbols per second. Accordingly, not quite three hours would have been required to work through 10,000 letters. (10,000 x 10,000 = 100,000,000 comparisons.)

"It was also intended at first to record repeats that occurred thus, not yet how the passages read and exactly when (sic) they were ...."

The American rapid analytic machine most nearly comparable to the foregoing proposed device, is the "Tetragraph Tester," developed by Eastman Kodak Company

[142] D-60

[143] I-37

64

for OP-20-G, and manufactured for both OP-20-G and the Army Security Agency. This American device uses film; the speed past the film gate is 5,000 letters per second; and photocells ("readers working without inertia") are used.

It is unfortunate that more technical data are not available on the German device. Information concerning drive mechanisms, photocell operation, electronic counters, provision for accurate registration, and means to prevent film shrinkage while drying, all of which are of utmost importance in the building of any modern photo-electronic analytic machine, would be useful. Even the dark room procedures to be used would have been of extreme interest.

38. German Army and Foreign office experimented with rapid analytic machinery.--Dr. Buggisch gave an interesting comment on the ill-fated attempt of Inspectorate 7/VI (OKH/In 7/VI) to build rapid analytic machinery, to-wit:[144]

> "The limited width of the I.B.M. card was soon found to be inconvenient, particularly in counting out of repeats for the purpose of lining-up 2 cipher texts. The obvious solution appeared to be in this case to work with perforated strips and 5-unit alphabet. Orders were given at the beginning of '43 (?) for the construction of such a machine. As, however, Section VI only had a completely inadequate workshop at its disposal, and by that time it was already impossible to get any more tools, etc., an agreement was made with the Hollerith [I.B.M.] firm that a few rooms, together with workshop machines, tools, etc., in factory buildings at Lichterfelde Ost should be placed at the disposal of Section VI. An engineer of the name of Schiessler of the Hollerith firm was placed in charge of this newly set-up workshop; he was dressed up as a technician(Lieutenant grade), and was given a special section of his own. He was, in my opinion, pretty unsuitable for solving the problems set and, anyway, as far as his specialist knowledge was concerned, not even remotely comparable to the undermentioned gentlemen of OKW/Chi. The repeat counting machine

[144] I-67

was ready in the autumn of '43 (or winter 43/44). It worked on a mechanical-electrical principle, the speed was not very high (I think a maximum of 40 pairs of letters a second), and there was somehow an 'idling period' (Leerlauf) which was very inconvenient. It is worth noting that, when this apparatus was completed, none of the specialist department doing practical cryptanalysis had any use for it, so that the question was justifiably raised why such an apparatus had been built at all. I do not think that it was ever used for practical tasks.

"In the winter of '43/44, the workshop becan to be engaged on the construction of various mechanical aids, but they cannot be described as cryptanalytic machines. Thus, for example, a machine was made which automatically punched on Hollerith cards the Russian T/P traffic taken on perforated strips with 5-unit alphabet. Plans were made, too, in the spring of '44 for machines which were to perform certain calculation tasks such as arose during work on Hagelin Machines; but those were not cryptanalytic machines either, but special calculating machines. I do not know whether work was ever started on the construction of these machines -- the order was probably issued -- because I went to an entirely different department in June '44 and was given quite different tasks. In short, Ag N/NA had until June '44, and in all probability subsequently, no cryptanalytic machine which could be used for the practical solution of any codes or ciphers.

"Things were different at OKW/Chi. There was no I.B.M. department there (as far as I know), and perhaps for that very reason they felt, more than in Ag N/NA, the necessity of developing and constructing special devices..."

Dr. Buggisch stated later that the machines developed at the Signal Intelligence Agency of the Supreme Command Armed Forces (OKW/Chi) were very satisfactory, however.

At the Foreign Office Cryptanalytic Section (Pers ZS) the "Automaton" was successfully developed for mass deciphering of American strip cipher messages. This was not properly a rapid analytic machine (though it used a statistical principle) but was actually a rapid deciphering machine. Dr. Rohrbach, of the Foreign Office Cryptanalytic Section (Pers Z S) gave the following information concerning it:[145]

"As was to be foreseen at the outset, the total material [American State Department messages sent in the strip cipher "O-2"] could not be deciphered by hand on account of its immense size. The number of available qualified workers with sufficient knowledge of English was too small for that. Deciphering...through moving the strips by hand required 6 - 7 minutes on an average, so that the work...would have taken a whole year, provided that 4 collaborators had worked on it 8 hours daily. It was, therefore, of the utmost importance that the automaton should be available for the decipherment of the material at the time when all keys had been worked out. It is not possible to describe the machine more explicitly within the scope of this report, but we should like to say briefly the following about the method of its working:

"The decipherment...consists of two operations: (1) arranging the strips so that the cipher text letters are made to lie in a row, (2) selecting the line containing the true reading out of 25 parallel lines. The adjustment of the strips that move up and down, so that the true reading can be read horizontally, is accomplished by the machine quite automatically, as the cipher text is touched by hand on the keyboard of a typewriter, or taken by means of a sensing device from the I.B.M. cards that had already been punched. Finding the true reading is simplified by the fact that...the most frequent letters in the English language (about 80% of true reading) are printed in a heavy tone, the others in a light tone. A line consisting of 15 letters chosen at random would contain 6 bold ones on an average, while the true reading line of 15 letters with 12 bold ones on an average stands out distinctly...The 30 strips necessary for the decipherment of a double line are arranged side by side in two groups of 15 each for the line;

[145] I-89

if the left-hand group is in the first movement, the right-hand one is in the second movement and vice versa. During the time when the clerk copies the true reading from the indicated line on the typewriter, the machine prepares automatically the adjustment of strips for the next line and performs it at the touch of a key. In this way the decipherment of a double line requires barely half a minute on average. By means of this machine the total material could be deciphered within a month."

Volume 2

Chapter VII. German Cryptanalytic Methods

35. <u>German cryptanalysis was generally against "medium grade" systems.</u>--Germany's cryptanalytic successes were in what might be termed "medium grade" or "medium security" systems.[149] These systems consisted for the most part of codes, either enciphered or unenciphered, the solving of some of which required perserverance, intelligence, and linquistic ability, but certainly very little of what might be called "higher cryptanalysis." And in their solution of these relatively easier systems, they developed no important cryptanalytic methods not already used by the Anglo-Americans.

[149] See Chart No. 1-2, Vol. 1 of this report.

In higher cryptanalysis, and especially in the field of high-grade machine ciphers, the record of what German cryptanalysts did not accomplish is a long one. Although they were successful with the Japanese "red" machine, they did not solve its successor, the "purple" machine. They did not solve the United States Army Converter M-134c (SIGABA), Converter M-228 (SIGCUM), the Teleprinter Cipher System using double-tapes (SIGIBS) nor, of course, its successor, the One-time Tape System (SIGTOT), nor the United States Navy equivalents thereof, nor the joint Army-Navy-British Combined Cipher Machine (CCM). If they were even aware of the existence of the Anglo-American highsecurity ciphony system (SIGSALY) is very doubtful, as not a single reference to it is to be found in any TICOM document. They did not solve the British Typex machine. They apparently did not read traffic sent in the Russian B-211, nor the French modified B-211. In their security studies they certainly did not develop and probably were not aware of practical methods of solving their own plugboard Enigma, or their teleprinter cipher attachments.

It cannot be said that this failing was necessarily due to inability or ignorance. Perhaps, Japan being Germany's ally, Germany felt it was not worth while to expend the great energy necessary to solve the difficult Japanese "purple" machine.[150]

[150]The German cryptanalytic failure in the case of this machine and the fact that this failure probably led higher authority to conclude that the machine was secure against cryptanalysis had immeasurably disastrous consequences upon the German war effort. Since the machine was regarded as secure, very important information was constantly being given Japanese representatives in Europe without reservation, and this information was promptly forwarded to Tokyo by the Japanese, using the machine. Thus, from approximately February 1941, when the United States gave the British the solution to the "purple" system, until the very end of the war in both hemispheres, Anglo-American intelligence had the benefit of authentic, accurate, and timely information about conditions within Germany and the occupied countries, German intentions, results of bombing, war potential, etc. This fact was the central fact in the reluctance of the American high command to have any public investigation and disclosure of the secret facts and events preceding the Japanese attack on Pearl Harbor.

70

Perhaps German inability to read Anglo-American high-grade systems should be credited to our successful cryptography rather than to their cryptanalytic incompetence, for certainly our security studies showed these systems to be secure. Had these studies proved otherwise the systems would either have been modified or discarded. But in order to make valid studies of cryptographic security there must be cryptanalytic competence; and had the Germans been competent in this respect they would have realized the extent and significance of their cryptographic insecurity. However, this, too, must be added: as regard the German security studies on the German plugboard Enigma, which revealed to them no practical method of solving it, who can say that either British or American cryptanalysts would have thought of the "bombe" as a practical answer, if Polish cryptanalysts had not invented or devised the first crude apparatus from which the final "bombe" was developed?

Whether the Germans deserve praise or censure, the fact remains that their cryptanalytic methods had no very bright highlights. Their ciphony breaking was not advanced. Enciphered teleprinter messages were solved only by finding "depths" and processing them by long known procedures. Only the easiest (commercial type) Enigma was solved in actual attempts to solve enemy traffic. Solutions of messages enciphered by Hagelin machines of the M-209 type were accomplished only where messages in depth were found as a precondition. Additively superenciphered codes were solved the way additive codes usually are solved in America, but the U. S. Army and the U. S. Navy highly specialized machinery, specifically designed for the purpose of expediting the processing of Japanese military, naval, and air secret communications (all superenciphered codes) had no counterparts in German cryptanalytic organizations. The cryptanalytic highlights, such as they are, are discussed in the paragraphs to follow, in order to make them a matter of record.

36. Washington-London commercial radiotelephone network conversations were solved by analysis of Spectrograms.-- Conversations over the commercial radiotelephone circuits between London and Washington were monitored, solved, and recorded by the German Post Office Research Laboratories in Eindthoven, Holland, and also by the press monitoring group (Gruppe VI) of

DOCID: 3560816

the Signal Intelligence Agency of the Supreme Command, Armed Forces (OKW/Chi) located at Ludwigsfelde, about 25 miles south of Berlin.[151] Some of the participants in these conversations are worth noting: Prime Minister Churchill and Anthony Eden when the latter was in Washington; the Minister of War Transport, and his representative; the same Minister and the British Shipping Mission; the Foreign Office and the British Embassy; the Dutch government representatives in both cities; the Russian embassies; the United States Embassy and the State Department. These radiotelephone circuits were enciphered by a "frequency scrambling" principle, according to Mr. K. Vetterlein, of the German Post Office.[152] The speech*frequencies 450 cycles wide and the small blocks were rearranged in positions within the speech frequency spectrum, to give the finally enciphered speech.

Simple frequency scrambling of speech can usually be solved by examining the spectrographic records of the enciphered speech, cutting out the "blocks" of frequencies with scissors, rearranging them by sight into proper order, and pasting them back together. This reveals the "pattern" or key used. Simpler yet, if the scrambling pattern has a sufficiently long duration, the rearranging can be done electrically, with the ear for a guide. On the Washington-London commercial radiotelephone circuit, scrambling and recombining of frequencies was by a pattern that remained fixed for 20 seconds, and then changed into another such pattern. There were only 36 such patterns in all, and then the whole procedure repeated. Thus the grand cycle was twelve minutes. The German Post Office had no apparent difficulty in solving this system. They built a five-bank rotary switch with 36 positions, drove it with a synchronous motor so as to step every 20 seconds, repeating every 12 minutes, and controlled this operation accurately over 24 hour periods with a quartz-crystal-controlled oscillator. Once the German engineer wired this switch correctly to match the patterns, they were able to monitor transmissions 100% and receive the speech instantaneously in the clear, so that they could record the

[151] I 84, I 88, I 118, I 190

[152] I 88 p 2

72

* FREQUENCY SPECTRUM WAS BROKEN INTO FIVE SMALL BLOCKS OF

speech traffic magnetically on steel tapes. The pattern cycle was rearranged by the American Telephone and Telegraph Company (that is, the enciphering keys changed) only several times between April 1942 and April 1945; after each change it took German Post Office engineers "only a few hours" to reconstruct the new patterns and their sequence.[153] Oscillographs, spectrographs, magnetophone recorders, and quartz-crystal oscillators for time control were available for this work, but well trained ears were said to have played the most important role in the solution. While this commercial ciphony system was known to be insecure by the United States and British authorities, and therefore secret matters were normally kept in other channels, it is nevertheless important to our cryptographers and engineers alike to know that the Germans did solve it. Their total ignorance of even the existence of SIGSALY transmissions has already been mentioned.

37. <u>Early Russian ciphony was solved by analysis of spectrograms</u>.--Radio telephone conversations between Moscow, Leningrad, Irkutsk, Alma Ata, and Tscheljabinks, involving Russian Army and People's Commisariats, up until 1943, were enciphered by two simple methods which were said to be easily solvable by German engineers at the Army Ordnance, Development and Testing Group, Signal Branch (Wa Pruef 7), according to Corporal Karrenberg, of the Signal Intelligence Agency of the Army High Command (OKH/G d NA).[154] These two methods of Russian enciphering were:

a. Inversion, employing superimposed modulation of several audio frequencies; and,

b. Distortion, by artificial raising of amplitudes of speech harmonics.

German scientists were able to solve these two simple enciphering methods by recording the enciphered speech, making spectrograms from the recordings, and analyzing them. Evidently the voice engineers could see the results of the inversion and distortion, on careful inspection, and could readily identify the frequencies and methods used for encipherment. They tried it only a few times, according to Karrenberg, but were successful at will. At the beginning of 1944, however, the

[153] I 88 p 2

[154] I 173 p 18

simple enciphering methods were dropped by the Russians, radio telephone traffic networks themselves were changed, and no further entry was gained by the Germans.

Dr. Buggisch of the Signal Intelligence Agency of the Supreme Command, Armed Forces (OKW/Chi) studied spectrograms of this later unsolved Moscow-Madrid radiophone traffic at the Army Ordnance, Development and Testing Group, Signal Branch Laboratories (Wa Pruef 7) where he became convinced that Russian ciphony then involved time scrambling, with the length of the individual time segments being 10 milliseconds each, and a synchronizing pulse occurring every .6 second.[155] The number of "pickup heads" used by the Russians to obtain this time scrambling was reported in one interrogation to be three[156] and in another to be four.[157] German engineers were unable to learn any more than this from the spectrograms. They could reconstruct fragments of speech, they thought, but "the validity of the solution did not satisfy Dr. Huettenhain's critical sense," when shown to him.[158] Dr. Huettenhain, who consulted with Dr. Buggisch, believed that some form of one-time strip might have been used to key the time transposition, as he could find no period whatever in the encipherments.

38. Some Anglo-American teleprinter messages were read.--How much Anglo-American teleprinter traffic was read by the Germans is not too clear from the TICOM reports, but it is doubtful if they ever solved any teleprinter enciphering machines themselves.

a. Dr. Huettenhain denied that his agency, the Signal Intelligence Agency of the Supreme Command Armed Forces (OKW/Chi) did any work at all on the United States teleprinter traffic, although he admitted that the German Army Ordnance, Development and Testing group, Signal Branch (Wa Pruef 7) passed intercepts to his agency.[159]

[155] I 73

[156] I 73

[157] I 31

[158] I 31

[159] I 31, p 19

74

b. Dr. Voegele stated that from April to October 1944 his agency, the Signal Intelligence Agency of the Commander in Chief of the Air Force (Chi Stelle, Ob d L) intercepted plain-text American teleprinter messages which concerned aircraft movements between American and North Africa, but he mentioned no other non-Morse.[160]

c. Corporal Karrenberg stated that his agency, the Signal Intelligence Agency of the Army High Command (OKH/G d NA), had a section (Gruppe VI, Referate 2A) which "undertook preliminary evaluation of British and American wireless teleprinter and automatic Morse traffic," and another section (Gruppe VI, Referate 2 B) which "picked up the traffic evaluated in Referate 2A," [161] and that another section (Referate I B) charged with cryptanalysis of Russian secret teleprinters also "worked on British and United States (non-Morse) systems."[162] But he made no references to any actual reconstruction of American or British teleprinter cryptographic apparatus.

d. Russian teleprinter cryptographic apparatus may have been solved by Goering's "Research" Bureau in 1943, according to Dr. Buggisch of the Signal Intelligence Agency of the Army High Command (OKH/G d NA).[163] Dr. Buggisch knew no more details. Traffic was supposed to have stopped soon after, and the machine evidently went out of use. He reported that the Army did some work on a Russian teleprinter cryptographic machine, read a few depths, obtained about 1400 letters of pure key, but went no farther. Corporal Karrenberg, mentioned above, said that Russian enciphered teleprinter messages, when sent in depth, were read by anagramming, and the corresponding keying characters recovered, but the machine itself was not solved.[164] Russian teleprinter links of which he had any knowledge were from Moscow to the Russian armies, and there were about eight in all. Reading of the depths indicated the messages contained operational and reconnaissance information. Examination of the sections of key obtained from the readings in depth led Karrenberg to the conclusion that the Russian enciphering device was similar in construction to the German teleprinter cipher attachment SZ-42 with

[160] I 112 p 5

[161] IF 123 p 11

[162] I 149 p 2

[163] I 64 p 2

[164] I 169

a "motor" wheel or "motor" wheels arranged somehow to give a cycle of 43. None of his surmises was investigated to ascertain its validity, it being claimed that the traffic was too scanty to effect a solution.[165]

39. Swiss Enigma rotor wirings were solved by cribs; other Enigmas were compromised.--The Swiss diplomatic Enigma ("K" type) was read regularly, probably by the Signal Intelligence Agency of the Supreme Command Armed Forces (OKW/Chi), although Dr. Huettenhain, who revealed this solution, did not state definitely that it was his agency which accomplished it. The Swiss changed their Enigma rotor wirings every three months, but the changes were not effected on the Berne-Washington link at the time they were made on the Berne-London link. As a result, duplicate messages sent by the Swiss to Washington and to London during the periods of changeover provided the "break" necessary to learn the new wirings.[166] The Croat enigma, used for both diplomatic and military traffic, was read regularly by Inspectorate 7/VI (IN 7/VI). This was no credit to the cryptanalysts involved, however, as their problem was particularly easy: (1) they had obtained the rotor wirings from Konski and Krueger (Berlin) who made the rotors; (2) there was no end-plate plugging involved; (3) the rotor orders were not changed by the Croats; (4) the "ringstellungen" (devices enabling the notches and alignment indicator letters to be "slid" in relation to the rotors) remained fixed; and (5) there were only 100 initial rotor alignments used by the Croats each month.[167]

An excellent treatise on Enigma ("K" type) solution was found in the files of the Foreign Office Cryptanalytic Section (Pers Z S). It involved obtaining many messages in depth, reading these messages by solving the successive (monoalphabetic) columns of superimposed text, and then applying the resultant cribs to recovering the wirings of the rotors. These methods are well-known to Anglo-American cryptanalysts.[168]

[165] I 169

[166] I 31

[167] I 84 p 3

[168] T 372

British Typex was the object of study by Dr. Buggisch, of the Signal Intelligence Agency of the Supreme Command, Armed Forces (OKW/Chi). He showed British Typex to be an Enigma type machine, by statistical study of 10,000 letters of cipher text, but was unable to go further.[169] No German cryptanalytic agency was able to solve it.

40. Traffic in Converter M-209 was solved only by depths.--Traffic in U. S. Army Converter M 209, used by our field forces (including the Air Forces) and the U. S. Navy, was under study more or less constantly by the Signal Intelligence Agency of the Supreme Command Armed Forces (OKW/Chi) by the Signal Intelligence Agency of the Army High Command (OKH/G d NA), by the Signal Intelligence Agency of the Air Force High Command (OKL/Ln abt 350 and its predecessor Chi Stelle Ob d L), and by the Signal Intelligence Agency of the Navy High Command (OKM/4 SKL/III). Many theories were developed for statistical solution of M-209 messages, though none was successful. Solutions depended entirely upon reading messages in depth, recovery of key therefrom, then obtaining absolute settings, and reading the remaining messages in the same day's traffic. Items of interest throughout the TICOM reports concerning these solutions are as follows:

a. Dr. Huettenhain of the Signal Intelligence Agency of the Supreme Command, Armed Forces (OKW/Chi) stated that M-209 depths were found by using "Fasensuchgeraet," a rapid analytic machine, probably the "digraphic weight recorder" described in Chapter VI of this volume.[170]

b. Dr. Buggisch of the Signal Intelligence Agency of the Army High Command (OKH/G d NA) gave a statistical formula to be used with I.B.M. machines for aiding in finding M-209 pin patterns.[171] This consisted of writing the cipher text out "on the width" of one of the wheels, and applying a form of "phi" test to the resulting alphabets. Alphabets having distributions which showed the least randomness were supposed to be indicative of inactive pins. Dr. Buggisch did not state that he was ever able to make the test work, and it is believed at the Army Security Agency from long experience with similar tests that this particular one certainly would not have worked.

[169] I 66

[170] I 31

[171] I 137

c. Lt. Muentz, of the Signal Intelligence Agency of the Navy High Command (OKM/4 SKL/III) developed a statistical theory for solving Converter M-209 as used by the U. S. Navy, based on the frequent use of "Z" as a word separator.[172] This never worked on actual traffic.[173] Amtsrat Schultze, of the same Agency, developed a theory on how to guess plain text from a statistical study of the cipher text, but he was never able to make it work.[174]

41. B-211 machines were solved in theory only.--German successes with the French (modified) B-211 Hagelin and the Russian B-211 were practically non-existent. Dr. Huettenhain said a French (modified) B-211 was captured, and believed that an 8 to 10 letter crib could solve the wheel settings, pin settings, and pluggings, if the cipher wheel wirings were known. A Russian B-211 was also captured and a theoretical solution devised, but since no traffic was received this solution was never tested in practice.[175]

42. Additive super-enciphered codes were solved in the "usual" way.--No great new cryptanalytic methods were developed by German cryptanalysts to assist in solving additive super-enciphered codes. They were solved as such codes usually are: by superimposing identically-keyed texts (by virtue of identical indicators and by means of repetitions), removing the additive from the depths, and reconstructing, from the resultant relative code values, the basic code--unless the code book is already known.

a. An example of the foregoing type of solution by the Germans is noted in the case of their cryptanalysis of the British War Office Cypher, a 4-figure super-enciphered code used between Army, Corps, and Division, which was read during the campaign in North Africa in 1940.[176]

[172] I 50

[173] I 6

[174] I 147

[175] I 58

[176] I 51

78

b. Another example is the Turkish 4-figure diplomatic code enciphered by repeating additives,[177] which was solved without regard to indicators simply by superimposing sections of messages at the period of the additive (in this case a period of 20) thereby obtaining enough depth to eliminate the additives and reconstruct the code.[178]

c. The German Navy's solutions of British naval codes (including "British Naval Cypher No. 3") are perhaps the most completely described solutions of the foregoing type in TICOM publications.[179] These solutions extended from before 1939 to the end of the war. Before 20 August 1941, when the indicator groups were not super-enciphered, messages were lined up in depth by indicators, and additives were eliminated therefrom by the use of "difference tables" or by guessing stereotyped texts. Some of the codes themselves were solved by cryptanalytic reconstruction, and some were captured. When the Merchant Marine code indicator systems became difficult, in 1942, messages were lined up in depth by other methods. One such method was that colloquially called "brute force," that is, pairs of messages were sought wherein at least two code groups in one message, separated by a definite interval, coincided with at least two code groups in the other message, separated by the same interval. Such messages were likely to have been enciphered with the same sections of additive, especially if the interval was not over 10, according to the Germans. However, they considered "brute force" unreliable and used it as little as possible. Whenever sections of additive were already known, messages were set against these sections by a technique quite familiar to the Army Security Agency. This consisted of applying all of the individual additive groups of a known section to 15 or 20 of the usually most frequently occurring unenciphered code groups, and obtaining thereby a set of enciphered code groups most likely to occur in messages enciphered with the known additive section. If two or more such likely enciphered code groups occurred in a message, at an

177 Army Security Agency trigraph, "TUK"

178 I 103

179 I 93, I 146, I 147

interval matching the interval between the groups of additive from which they were derived, then it was very likely that the rest of the message could be deciphered from that point on in the section of known additive. The ordinary cryptanalytic aids, such as difference tables (made by German cryptanalysts usually from the 300 highest-frequency code groups), known and frequently-used addresses, spelling groups, figure groups, and place names, as well as stereotyped texts, aided them in aligning messages and eliminating additives. By such means, depths of only two were often read-- in fact, if the two messages were routine reports, "they were read without exception."[180]

When the British Navy introduced the "S.S. Frame" in December 1943,[181] German cryptanalysts were able to analyze correctly the new cryptographic system being employed, and were able to read messages superenciphered in this new system for one month. The German cryptanalysts were able to superimpose a few messages in depth, which permitted them to recover several sequences of additive; they discovered that parts of one sequence of additive at times overlapped parts of other sequences, albeit out-of-phase and very irregularly; by using this knowledge to test new assumptions, and after much trial and error, they were able to recover and reconstruct a complete set of number tables; they also solved the weak December 1943 indicator system, which relied only on random co-ordinates to indicate the stencil position; and as a result of these activities they obtained a fair understanding of the British "S.S. Frame". They complained:[182]

[180] I 93 p 2

[181] In one type of Stencil Subtractor Frame, a stencil of 100 irregularly located apertures, each aperture 4-digits wide, is placed on a card of randomly chosen numbers, 48 by 68 digits in size, at any one of 100 settings determined by a specific key, and the 4-digit groups that appear in the apertures of the stencil provide additive. Parts of additive obtained at any one setting of the stencil will not properly "overlap" additive obtained at another adjacent setting, because of the irregular spacing of the stencil apertures. Thus satisfactory depths that can be found in such a system are obtained only from identically keyed messages.

[182] I 93 p 25

"We discovered that we had formerly had on the long subtractor system 1,500 starting points over a 10 day period; whereas we now had 10,000 different starting points on one daily table."

On 1 January 1944 the British changed their basic codes as well, and soon thereafter began to use "doubly enciphered indicators" for the "S. S. Frame". The Germans, with almost no depths possible, and with the basic code book unknown to them, could no longer read the traffic. Senior Specialist Tranow, of the Signal Intelligence Agency of the Navy High Command (OKM/4 SKL/III) stated:[183]

"We came to the conclusion that we could not recover a system of this kind within six months, without having the basic book. However it was clear to us that if we were able to capture the book, we should then be able to break this system in a very short time. We provided our own proof for this.... We constructed synthetic messages of our own on the pattern of the British originals. We began the first trial with 200 messages a day and broke all of them within three weeks.... We then carried out a second trial with 100 messages. The staff was much more practiced and succeeded with a smaller number of messages in a shorter time."

So far as is known, however, they did not "capture the book" or continue solving the system.

d. The Polish government in London used an additive super-enciphered code for Military Attaché messages, which was read regularly by the Signal Intelligence Agency of the Supreme Command Armed Forces (OKW/Chi) until about 1943 when the Poles changed their methods of obtaining the additives. The Poles had introduced their version of the British "S.S. Frame," at the suggestion of the British Government; their stencils had from 28 to 40 randomly placed apertures, rather than 100 as in the British version. The German cryptanalysts, having the Polish code book from their previous solutions, were able, with it and with depths obtained by I.B.M. searches for repeats, to reconstruct additives, discover the irregular positions of the stencil apertures, and reconstruct the stencils, and read the messages.[184]

[183] I 93 p 25. Even with the indicators amply enciphered, much headway was made by German cryptanalysts in recovering relative starting points. See D 25.

[184] I 118, I 31

43. Mihajlovic double-transpositions were solved by anagramming.--Yugoslavian double-transpositions (Draza Mihajlovic traffic) were solved by Corporal Herzfeld of Inspectorate 7/VI (In 7/VI), in from one to three days.[185] In each message, the same key was used for the two transposition matrices, and the matrices were usually incompletely filled. The width of the transposition matrices were assumed by Corporal Herzfeld each time"with some degree of accuracy," based on his previous experience with messages of the same length and on the same networks. This was of course a great advantage, since it permitted a marking off in the cipher text of the approximate columns of the second transposition matrix. The words "GENERAL DRAZA MIHAJLOVIC" which nearly always appeared as a signature, made an excellent crib because several of the letters were infrequent, and because these words could be written in as the final rows of the first transposition matrix. With the dimensions of the matrices chosen by good guessing, and with both the complete columns of the second transposition matrix and the final rows of the first transposition matrix delineated, the German corporal then tried to match elements of his cipher text with elements of his crib, and by anagramming recover plain text and the key. The methods used were not unusual.

44. Solutions of American Strip ciphers involved statistical analysis.-- Cryptanalytic successes against American strip ciphers were obtained by at least three German agencies. Dr. Rohrbach, cryptanalyst of the Foreign Office Cryptanalytic Section (Pers Z S), who claimed that his group of six cryptanalysts solved the United States State Department strip cipher ("0-2") in 1943 without any previous knowledge concerning the general system, required over a year for solution. The State Department strip cipher "0-2" which he solved did not employ strip elimination, but it did make use of the principle of "split generatrices"--that is, 30 strips were chosen out of a possible 50 strips each day and arranged in a channel board according to the daily key, and messages were then enciphered by successively setting up 30 letters of plain text across one line of the strips, each time reading off 15 letters of resultant cipher text from the first half of another line, chosen at random,

[185] I 69 p 23; I 52

and the remaining 15 letters of cipher-text from the last half of a third line, chosen at random. Dr. Rohrbach's methods of solution were recorded in a detailed paper written by him at the request of TICOM interrogators,[186] and they were similar to the statistical methods suggested as a general solution by United States Army cryptanalysts in 1934. Messages were punched on I.B.M. cards, repeats were found which indicated that intervals of 15 and 30 were significant, the material was sorted into "families" (Dr. Rohrbach defined a "family" as a collection of homogeneous cipher material based on use of the same generatrix in the enciphering process) and the larger "families" were solved, as similarly-keyed polyalphabetic cipher sequences, by analyzing the material "column by column." The alphabets recovered permitted reconstruction of many of the strips, and with their aid the remaining "families" and strips were solved. Although Dr. Rohrbach indicated in his writing that he had had no previous knowledge of the general system when he started his solution activities in November 1942, it is a fact that the Foreign Office Cryptanalytic Section (Pers Z S) had received photographic copies in 1941 from the Signal Intelligence Agency of the Supreme Command Armed Forces (OKW/Chi) of a set of instructions for an earlier American strip cipher ("O-1") and "4 series of strips by means of which a number of messages could be deciphered."[187] Files of the Foreign Office Cryptanalytic Section (Pers ZS) captured in 1945 also contained photographs of two Tables of Numerical Keys for the same earlier State Department strip cipher ("O-1"). The advance knowledge of the general system given by this compromise, and the stereotyped beginnings that Dr. Rohrbach indicated in his paper were present in State Department traffic ("O-2") (such as "Strictly confidential from Murphy.... ") together with the State Department's reuse of each daily key an average of 9 times throughout the year (only 40 different strip arrangements were provided for 365 days traffic) should have made the solution much easier for Dr. Rohrbach than he found it.

[186] I 89

[187] DF 15 p 5.

Dr. Huettenhain of the Signal Intelligence Agency of the Supreme Command, Armed Forces (OKW/Chi) stated that his agency worked on American diplomatic strip systems, and that they were not aided in their work by any captures, but succeeded through cryptanalysis only.[188] This statement is also at variance with the record, already mentioned, of compromised strips being handed over from the Signal Intelligence Agency of the Supreme Command Armed Forces (OKW/Chi) to the Foreign Office Cryptanalytic Section (Pers Z S). The techniques used by Dr. Huettenhain are not recorded, but his Agency considered American strip ciphers of sufficient importance to build a special rapid analytic machine (the "statistical depth-increaser") for facilitating statistical solutions.[189]

According to Dr. Ferdinand Voegele, Chief Section B, of the Signal Intelligence Agency of the Air Force High Command (OKL/LN abt 350), a strip cipher of the United States Army Air Force South Atlantic Ferry Command was solved before 1943. He wrote:[190]

> It was quite evident from the cipher text that there was a break after each 15 letters.... Accordingly an analysis was made on the basis of groups of 15 letters with the assistance of I. B. M. machines. A depth of 80 passages of parallel construction was needed to reconstruct the 100 strips, 30 of which were valid in any one day.... The system was read as long as it was used.
>
> "In 1943 a new difficulty presented itself. While 30 strips were still valid on any one day, the encipherer could arbitrarily remove any five of the strips to encipher any one message... . After about six weeks, some of these messages were also deciphered. However, at the same time the volume of this type of traffic began to decline, so that finally the analysis work had to be discontinued."

Techniques employed by Voegele and his assistants are not known. Decipherment "after about six weeks" of some of the later messages, when strip elimination was employed, may have been accomplished by the skilful use of cribs. It is interesting to note that soon after strip elimination had been introduced, "the analysis work had to be discontinued."

[188] I 84

[189] See Chapter VI of this volume. It will be recalled that another device, the "automaton", was also developed by the Foreign Office Cryptanalytic Section (Pers Z S) for rapid deciphering of a large backlog of strip traffic.

[190] IF 175 p 15.

Major Dr. Rudolph Henze, head of the cryptanalysis group of the Signal Intelligence Agency of the Army High Command (OKH/G d NA) reported solution of an American "strip" cipher the intelligence of which was "mixed military and diplomatic," and which, from the description of the system, and its indicators, was actually enciphered by Army cipher device Type M-94 rather than by any of the strip cipher devices.[191]

This was technically not a mistake in terminology by Dr. Henze, since the aluminum disks of the M-94 may be considered to be strips from a cryptanalytic viewpoint.[192] A soldier, Werner K. H. Graupe (rank unknown) reported that he cryptanalyzed an American "strip" cipher (actually the M-94) carrying Iceland and Carribean area traffic, while he was presumably in Inspectorate 7/VI (In 7/VI) in Berlin.[193] He used cribs, with the help of synoptic tables, to determine the "strip" (disk) orders, and stated that he later believed I. B. M. methods were developed to eliminate impossible keys. According to the interrogator, Graupe "knew of what he called a 30-strip system, but stated very definitely that it had never been solved." Lt. Col. Mettig, who was the commanding officer of Inspectorate 7/VI (In 7/VI) from November 1941 through June 1943, stated[194] "..it was eventually recognized that the main cipher procedure used by the Americans was the strip method whereby 25 variously arranged alphabets were vertically laid out one alongside the other. In the workshop of In 7/VI mechanical aids were constructed and with the help of the I. B. M. section and by noting the addresses and signatures, the various alphabets were recreated."

[191] I 113

[192] Dr. Voegele, the Air Force cryptanalyst, considered North Atlantic Air Force M-94 traffic as being "strip." See I-112.

[193] IF-107. Inspectorate 7/VI was a predecessor of the Signal Intelligence Agency of the Army High Command (OKH/G d NA).

[194] I 78 p 10

To summarize: German cryptanalysis of both the strip cipher and the M-94 apparently developed no exceptional methods, although it did result in the construction of two special rapid cryptanalytic machines, the "statistical depth-increaser" and the "automaton," described in chapter VI.

45. Conclusion.--German cryptanalysis was very successful on low grade systems, not only because the German cryptanalysts were sufficiently skilled to take advantage of the presence of low security traffic, but also because of the failure on the part of Anglo-American commanders to realize the extent to which the Germans were able to go in taking advantage of insecure practices.

German medium-grade cryptanalysis was extensive and worthwhile, as can be seen from the Cryptanalytic Successes chart, Chart No. 1-2, Volume 1 of this report; but no outstandingly different or unusual cryptanalytic methods were developed by the Germans in their medium grade solutions.

German cryptanalysis was not outstandingly successful against systems of high-security. This may have been not only because Anglo-American high-security systems were actually of high-security, and were to some extent insolvable to Anglo-American cryptanalysts as well, but also because the German cryptanalysts never became technically proficient enough to undertake even the solution of the less difficult of the high-security systems.

TAB A

Volume 2

Tab A

General Information and References

Abwehr - See "Military Intelligence."

Army Ordnance, Development and Testing Group, Signal Branch (Wa Pruef 7). This organization developed, engineered and tested Signal Corps equipment. It also did some non-morse interception. It is described in Volume 8 of this paper.

A.E.G., Berlin. ("Allgemeine Elektrische Gesellschaft"). German commercial firm which worked on speech encipherment.

Air Force Weather Service (Wetterdienst der Luftwaffe). This service was charged with cryptanalysis of enemy meteorological ciphers.

Allgemeine Elektrische Gesellschaft. German Commercial firm which worked on speech encipherment.

Buggisch, Staff Sgt. Dr. Otto. Cryptanalyst of Inspectorate 7/VI (In 7/VI). Expert on German cryptographic apparatus, and on ciphony matters.

D-25. "S.S. Frame Indicator System." A TICOM publication.

D-51. "Translation of Miscellaneous Documents from Pers Z S Archives." A TICOM publication.

D-57. "Notes and Minutes of High-Level Mettings held at OKW/Chi-- Cryptographic and Administrative." A TICOM publication.

D-58. "Description of Facsimile Intercept Recorder." A TICOM publication.

D-59. "Notes on Cipher Security and Minutes of Meetings held at OKW/Chi." A TICOM publication.

D-60. "Miscellaneous Papers from a File of RR Dr. Huettenhain of OKW/Chi." A TICOM publication.

Deutsche Telefon und Kabelwerke, Berlin. German Commercial firm which worked on speech encipherment.

DF-15. IF 20 "A Group" Reports (American Systems).

E-9. "Detailed Feuerstein Technical Project Report Ref. No. 2 Little Baustein." A TICOM publication.

E-10. "Detailed Feuerstein Technical Project Report. Ref. No. 3: Artificial Speech and Encoding." A TICOM publication.

87

E-11. "Detailed Feuerstein Technical Project Report, Ref. No. 4: Three-Fold Wobbulation and Mechanical Wobbulator Generators." A TICOM publication.

E-13. "Detailed Feuerstein Technical Project Report Ref. No. 6: Synchronous cipher system for teletypewriters--Gleichlauf." A TICOM publication.

E-14. "Detailed Feuerstein Technical Project Report, Ref. No. 7: Investigation of SZ Cipher Machines at Feuerstein Laboratory." A TICOM publication.

FA. See: Goering's "Research" Bureau.

Fabrik C. Lorenz Aktiengesellschaft, Berlin, Muelhausen, Thuer. Firm which worked on speech encipherment and developed teleprinter enciphering devices.

Fess, Dr. ..... Member of Wanderer Co.

Feuerstein Laboratory .... Electronic research laboratory owned and managed by a Dr. Oskar Vierling. This is described in Volume 8 of this paper.

Fricke, Dr. Walter, Technician, grade of Lieutenant. Head of Section IIb of the Signal Intelligence Agency of the Supreme Command Armed Forces (OKW/Chi). Specialized in the production of codes and ciphers.

Foreign Office, Cryptanalytic Section (Pers Z S) and Foreign Office Cryptographic Section (Pers Z Chi). These made up one of the six principal German cryptologic organizations. These are described in Volumes 1 and 6 of this paper.

Frowein, Lt. R. Hans-Joachim. Assigned temporarily to the Signal Security Agency of the Navy High Command (OKM/4 SKL/II) in 1944 to make security studies on the Enigma. He had no previous experience with this machine and yet developed a workable solution.

German Weather Bureau (Reichswetterdienst). This service was charged with cryptanalysis of enemy meteorological ciphers. It was part of the German Air Force, and maintained close liaison with the Signal Intelligence Agency of the Commander in Chief of the Air Force (Chi-Stelle, Ob d L).

Goering's Research Bureau (Reichsluftfahrtministerium Forschungsamt, abbreviated FA). This was one of the six principal German cryptologic organizations, and is described in Volumes 1 and 7 of this paper.

88

Heimsoeth & Rinke. German firm engaged in manufacture of Enigma rotors and parts.

Herzfeld, Corporal Heintz Wolfgang. Member of Gruppe IV, Signal Intelligence Agency of Army High Command (OKH/GdNA); formerly member of British, Italian, and Balkan sections of Inspectorate 7/VI (In 7/VI).

Huettenhain, Specialist Dr. Erich. Principal cryptanalyst of the Signal Intelligence Agency of the Supreme Command Armed Forces (OKW/Chi) from 1939 to end of war.

I-1. "Report of TICOM Reporting Team No. 3. A TICOM publication.

I-6. "Interrogation of Lt. D.R. Muentz of the OKM 4/III." A TICOM publication.

I-20. "Interrogation of Sonderfuehrer Dr. Fricke of the Signal Intelligence Agancy of the Supreme Command Armed Forces (OKW/Chi)." A TICOM publication.

I-31. "Detailed Interrogations of Dr. Huettenhain, Formerly Head of Research Section of OKW/Chi, 18th-21st June 1945." A TICOM publication.

I-37. "Translation of Paper Written by Reg. Rat. Dr. Huettenhain of OKW/Chi on Special Apparatus Used as Aids to Cryptanalysis." A TICOM publication.

I-38. "Report on Interrogation of Lt. Frowein of OKM/4 SKL/III, on His Work on the Security of the German Naval Four-wheel Enigma." A TICOM publication.

I-45. "OKW/Chi Cryptanalytic Research on Enigma, Hagelin, and Cipher Teleprinter Machines." A TICOM publication.

I-47. "P/W Situation Report." A TICOM publication.

I-50. "Paper Written by Lt. Muentz of OKM/4 SKL/III on Statistical Solution of the M-209 Hagelin Machine." A TICOM publicatinn.

I-51. "Interrogation Report on Uffz. Herzfeld, Heintz Worfgang, and Translation of a Paper He Wrote on the British War Office Code." A TICOM publication.

I-52. "Papers Written by Uffz. Herzfeld on Mihailovic and Tito Ciphers." A TICOM publication.

I-53. "Construction of Schluesselgeraet 39." A TICOM publication.

I-57. "Enciphering Devices Worked on by Dr. Liebknecht at Wa Pruef 7." A TICOM publication.

I-58. "Interrogation of Dr. Otto Buggisch of OKW/Chi." A TICOM publication.

I-64. "Answers by Wm. Buggisch of OKH/Chi to Questions sent by TICOM." A TICOM publication.

I-66. "Paper by Dr. Otto Buggisch of OKH/In 7/VI and OKW/Chi on Typex." A TICOM publication.

I-67. "Paper by Dr. Otto Buggisch of OKH/In 7/VI and OKW/Chi on Cryptanalytic Machines." A TICOM publication.

I-69. "Summary of Cipher Information on Jugoslav Traffic Provided byUffz. Herzfeld (Appendices to TICOM/ I-52)" A TICOM publication.

I-72. "First Part of the Report by Wm. Buggisch on S.G. 41." A TICOM publication.

I-73. "Translated Version of Homework done by Wm. Buggisch." A TICOM publication.

I-77. "Translations of Joint Report made by Drs. Huettenhain and Fricke on the "Zaehlwerk" Enigma Machine." A TICOM publication.

I-78. "Interrogation of Oberstlt. Mettig on the History and Achievements of OKH/AHA/In 7/VI." A TICOM publication.

I-80. "P.O.W. Interrogation Report--Obgefr. Clement Schuck Insp. VII/6 (OKH)." A TICOM publication.

I-84. "Further Interrogation of R.R. Dr. Huettenhain and Sdf. Dr. Fricke of OKW/Chi." A TICOM publication.

I-88. "Report on Interrogation of ME. K. Vetterlein of the Reichspost Laboratorium on German Interception of Transatlantic Speech Circuits." A TICOM publication.

I-89. "Report by Prof. Dr. H. Rohrbach of Pers Z S on American Strip Cipher." A TICOM publication.

I-92. "Final Interrogation of the Wachtmeister Otto Buggisch (OKH/In 7/VI and OKW/Chi)" A TICOM publication.

I-93. "Detailed Interrogation of Members of OKM/4 SKL/III At Flensburg." A TICOM publication.

I-96. "Interrogation of Oberstlt. Mettig on the Organisation and Activities of OKW/Chi." A TICOM publication.

I-103. "Second Interrogation of Reg. Rat Hermann Scherschmidt of Pers Z S Auswaertiges Amt. on Turkish and Bulgarian Systems." A TICOM publication.

I-104. "Report on Berlin Targets by Major Heller of G.S.I.(S) 21 A.G., B.A.O.R." A TICOM publication.

I-112. "Preliminary Interrogation of Reg. Rat. Dr. Ferdinand Voegele (Chi Stelle, Ob d. L) and Major Ferdinand Feichtner (O.C. of LN Regt. 352, Etc.)" A TICOM publication.

I-113. "Interrogation of Major Dr. Rudolph Hentze, Head of Gruppe IV (Cryptanalysis), General der Nachrichtenaufklaerung." A TICOM publication.

I-118. "Joint Reports by Reg. Rat. Dr. Huettenhain and Sdf. Dr. Fricke, Written at C.S.D.I.C. on or about 28th August 1945." A TICOM publication.

I-119. "Further Interrogation of Reg. Rat. Voegele and Major Feichtner on G.A.F. Sigint." A TICOM publication.

I-127. "Interrogation of Oberstlt. Mettig of OKW/Chi." A TICOM publication.

I-137. "Final Report Written by Wachtmeister Otto Buggisch of OKH/Chi and OKW/Chi." A TICOM publication.

I-146. "Detailed Interrogation of Members of OKM/4 SKL/III At Flensburg." A TICOM publication.

I-147. "Detailed Interrogation of Members of OKM/4 SKL/III At Flensburg." A TICOM publication.

I-149. "Report by Uffz. Karrenberg and Colleagues on Allied Cypher Machines." A TICOM publication.

I-152. "Second Homework and Report on Further Interrogation of RR Voegele." A TICOM publication.

I-169. "Report by Uffz. Karrenberg on the Bandwurm." A TICOM publication.

I-173. "Report by the Karrenberg Party on Russian W/T." A TICOM publication.

I-190. "Extracts from Report on Interrogation of Dr. Hans Wilhelm Thost." A TICOM publication.

IF-107. "Interrogation of P.O.W. Werner Graupe by interrogators of Signal Intelligence Division, ETOUSA.

IF-123. "Consolidated Report on Information Obtained from the Following: Erdmann, Grubler, Hempel, Karrenberg, Schmitz, and Suschowk." A publication of the Combined Services Detailed Interrogation Centre, number CSDIC (UK) SIR 1717.

IF-142. "Naval Cipher and W/T Procedures. Marineschluesseldienst und Marinefunkverfahren." A British Naval Intelligence Division publication, number TR/PG/17626/NID.

IF-175. "Seabourne report, Volume XIII. "Cryptanalysis Within the Luftwaffe SIS." 24 November 1945.

IF-259. "Radar Most Decisive Weapon, Won Ocean Fight Says Doenitz." United Press Article in the Washington Post 10 May 1946.

In 7/VI. See Inspectorate 7/VI.

Inspectorate 7/VI (OKH/In 7/VI). Central Cryptanalytic Agency of the Army High Command for Non-Russian Traffic 1942-1943.

Jensen, Graduate Engineer. Member of Section IVb of the Signal Intelligence Agency of the Supreme Command Armed Forces (OKW/Chi) which dealt with the development of cryptanalytic machinery.

Karrenberg, Corporal Erich. Cryptanalyst of Signal Intelligence Agency of Army High Command (OKH/GdNA) who studied Baudot traffic.

Konski and Krueger, Berlin. Firm which manufactured rotors for the Enigma.

Krachel, ... Working engineer who came to Signal Intelligence Agency of the Supreme Command of the Armed Forces (OKW/Chi) in 1941 to help Rotscheidt and Jensen in research on cipher machines.

Kunze, Dr. Werner. Head of mathematical cryptographic subsection of Pers Z S.

Liebknecht, Graduate Engineer Dr. Werner. Chief of section IIIh of Army Ordnance, Development and Testing Group, Signal Branch (Wa Pruef 7). Maintained technical liaison with Dr. Huettenhain of the Signal Intelligence Agency of the Supreme Command Armed Forces (OKW/Chi).

M-11. Five drawings of the Lueckenfuellerwalze.

Martini, Lt. General Hermann. Chief Signal Officer, German Air Force.

Menzer, Senior Inspector. Chief of Section IIc of Signal Intelligence Agency of the Supreme Command of the Armed Forces (OKW/Chi) which dealt with the development and production of special ciphers for government departments, industry, and the Main Reich Security Office (RSHA), developing of deciphering aids for agents.

Mettig, Lt. Col. Head of Inspectorate 7/VI (In 7/VI) from Nov. 1941 to June 1943; second in command of Signal Intelligence Agency of the Supreme Command Armed Forces (OKW/Chi) from Dec. 1943 to April 1945.

Military Intelligence (Abwehr). Military intelligence and counter espionage section of the Supreme Command of the Armed Forces (OKW). After 20 July 1944, this section was taken over by RSHA.

Muentz, Lt. ..... Member of the Signal Intelligence Agency of the Navy High Command (OKM/4 SKL/III) who worked on the Navy Hagelin Machine--M-209.

OKH/GdNA. See Signal Intelligence Agency of the Army High Command.

OKL/LN Abt 350. See Signal Intelligence Agency of the Air Force High Command.

OKW/Chi. See Signal Intelligence Agency of the Supreme Command Armed Forces.

OKM/4 SKL/II See Signal Security Agency of the Navy High Command.

OKM-4 SKL/III See Signal Intelligence Agency of the Navy High Command.

Pers Z Chi. See Foreign Office Cryptographic Section.
Pers Z S. See Foreign Office Cryptanalytic Section.
Pietsch, Specialist Dr. ..... Head of mathematical section of Inspectorate 7/VI (In 7/VI)
Rohrbach, Dr. Hans. Group head in Mathematical and cryptanalytic subsection (Kunze) of Foreign Office Cryptanalytic Section (Pers Z S). Also Math Professor at University of Prague.
Rotscheidt, Graduate Engineer. Appointed in 1941 to Signal Intelligence Agency of the Supreme Command Armed Forces (OKW/Chi) for Research in offensive and defensive warfare in cipher machines. Telecommunication expert.
Reich Security Office. Reichssicherheitshauptamt, abbreviated RSHA.
Reichsluftfahrtministerium Forschungsamt. See Goering's "Research" Bureau.
Reichswetterdienst. See German Weather Bureau.
Schaeffer ..... Engineer who came to Signal Intelligence Agency of the Supreme Command Armed Forces (OKW/Chi) in 1941 to help Rotscheidt and Jensen in research on cipher machines.
Schmalz, Graduate Engineer. Head of Hollerith section of Signal Intelligence Agency of the Navy High Command (OKM/4 SKL/III).
Schuessler. Engineer of I.B.M. Firm in charge of section workshop at Erfurt (section 4 of Gruppe IV, GdNA)
Schuck, Corporal Clemens. Cryptanalyst of Inspectorate 7/VI who worked on SLIDEX and M-209.
Schultze, Amtsrat. Cryptographer of OKM/4 SKL/III. An expert on the Hagelin machine.
Security Group of the Signal Intelligence Service (OKH/Gen Nafue/III, Gruppe IV). This service did security studies on German Air Force traffic.
Siemens & Halske, Berlin. German commercial firm which worked on speech encipherment.
Signal Intelligence Agency of the Air Force High Command (OKL/LN Abt 350). This was one of the six principal German cryptologic organizations. This agency is described in Volume 5 of this paper.
Signal Intelligence Agency of the Army High Command (OKH/GdNA). This was one of the six principal German cryptologic organizations. It is described in Volume 4 of this paper.

Signal Intelligence Agency of the Supreme Command Armed Forces (OKW/Chi). This made up one of the six principal German cryptologic organizations. It is described in Volume 3 of this paper.

Signal Security Agency of the Navy High Command (OKM/4 SKL/II) and Signal Intelligence Agency of the Navy High Command (OKM/4 SKL/III). These made up one of the six principal German cryptologic organizations.

Sueddeutsche Apparate Fabriken, Berlin. German Commercial firm which worked on speech encipherment.

Stein, Lt. Dr. Head of the section of Gruppe IV of OKW/Chi which concerned itself with security investigations for new procedures and all investigations on inventions.

T-372. "The Enigma by Dr. Rudolf Kochendoerffer, from Scientific Writings of Foreign Office Cryptanalytic Section 8 Dec. 1941." A captured German document in possession of TICOM.

T-1282. A set of miscellaneous Foreign Office papers, in possession of TICOM.

Telefonbau U. Normalzeit Co., Frankfurt am Main. Firm which built test models of Cipher Device 39.

Telefunken, Berlin. German commercial firm which worked on speech encipherment.

Todt, ... Engineer who came to OKW/Chi in 1941 to help Rotscheidt and Jensen in research on cipher machines.

Tranow, Specialist ..... Head of English Cryptographic section in OKM-4 SKL/III.

Vetterlein, Mr. K. Supervised the monitoring service in Holland for trans-Atlantic monitoring of telephone conversations.

Vierling, Dr. Oskar. Specialized in communications equipment reaearch. Was owner and chief engineer of the Feuerstein Laboratory.

Voegele, Specialist Dr. Ferdinand. Chief of Section E of the Signal Intelligence Agency of the Commander in Chief of The Air Force (Chi-Stelle Ob d L) and principal cryptanalyst in the German Air Force.

Wa Pruef 7. See Army Ordnance, Development and Testing Group, Signal Branch.

Wanderer Co. This firm was to have manufactured Cipher Device 39 on large scale production.

Wetterdienst der Luftwaffe. See Air Force Weather Service.

Pho[illegible]graph of German Plugboard Enigma, described in Chapter II, at present in Army Security Agency Museum.

Photograph of German Pluggable Reflector Plate, (Umkehrwalze D), for use in the Enigma. It is described in Chapter II. Item at left is rear view of plate showing plugs inserted in jacks; item in center is the metal cover; item at right is face view of the complete assembly. This is at present in Army Security Agency Museum.

Photograph of a German changeable notch rotor, or Lueckenfuellerwalze, for use in the Enigma. This is described in Chapter III. Item at left is complete assembly. Item in center is rim, showing changeable notches. Item at right is rotor core. This is at present in Army Security Agency Museum.

Ein
Aus

[illegible] of [illegible]-52d/e, a German cipher teleprinter, [illegible] in [illegible] III, at present in Army Security [illegible] Museum

Photograph of German Cipher Device 41, described in Chapter IV, at present in Army Security Agency Museum.

COMPARISON OF RAPID ANALYTIC MACHINERY - OKW/CHI AND A.S.A.

GERMAN (OKW/CHI) RAPID ANALYTIC MACHINERY					AMERICAN (A.S.A.) RAPID ANALYTIC MACHINERY				
NAME	PURPOSE	MAKEREADY REQUIRED	SPEED	DATE ACQUIRED	NAME	PURPOSE	MAKEREADY REQUIRED	SPEED	DATE ACQUIRED
DIGRAPHIC WEIGHT RECORDER ("BIGRAMMSUCHGERAET")	SLIDING WHOLE MESSAGE AGAINST ITSELF; LISTING THE WEIGHTS OF THE RESULTANT DIGRAPHS. (ESPECIALLY DESIGNED TO SOLVE JAPANESE TRANSPOSITION "JAE.") SLIDING MESSAGE AGAINST ANOTHER TO RECORD LOCATIONS OF COINCIDENCES.	PUNCHING TELETYPEWRITER TAPES. (DIGRAPHIC WEIGHTS ALREADY PLUGGED ON PLUGBOARD.)	75 LETTERS PER SECOND USING TAPES OF ANY LENGTH.	1943?	ELECTROMECHANAGRAMMER (ATTACHMENT TO I.B.M. TABULATOR.)	SLIDING PART OF MESSAGE AGAINST WHOLE, LISTING TOTALS OF WEIGHTS OF RESULTANT DIGRAPHS. (ESPECIALLY DESIGNED TO SOLVE JAE.)	PULLING I.B.M. CARDS BY HAND; WIRING PLUGBOARD FOR EACH TEST. (DIGRAPHIC WEIGHTS ALREADY PUNCHED IN CARDS.)	2 POSITIONS TESTED PER SECOND, USING CARD DECK OF ANY LENGTH.	1941
POLYGRAPHIC COINCIDENCE COUNTER ("SAEGEBOCK")	SEPARATE COUNTING OF MONOGRAPHS, TRIGRAPHS, ETC., UP TO DECAGRAPHS, COINCIDENT BETWEEN MESSAGES, OR REPEATING WITHIN A MESSAGE; AND A RECORDING OF THE SEPARATE TOTALS THEREOF.	PUNCHING TELETYPEWRITER TAPES.	75 LETTERS PER SECOND USING TAPES OF ANY LENGTH.	1942	HAWKINS' RESISTOR BOARD AND COUNTER.	RECORDING TOTAL OF COINCIDENCES BETWEEN MESSAGES OR OF REPEATS WITHIN A MESSAGE. (NO SEPARATE POLYGRAPHIC COUNT.)	PUNCHING TELETYPEWRITER TAPES.	7 LETTERS TESTED PER SECOND, USING TAPE OF ANY LENGTH.	194Ø (NOW OBSOLETE)
					JOOS' TYPEWRITER	RECORDING TOTAL OF COINCIDENCES BETWEEN MESSAGES OR OF REPEATS WITHIN A MESSAGE. (NO SEPARATE POLYGRAPHIC COUNT.)	PUNCHING TELETYPEWRITER TAPES.	7 LETTERS TESTED PER SECOND, USING TAPE OF ANY LENGTH.	1943
					INDEX OF COINCIDENCE MACHINE	INDICATING (BUT NOT EVALUATING OR RECORDING) TOTAL OF COINCIDENCES BETWEEN MESSAGES, OR OF REPEATS WITHIN A MESSAGE. (ACTUAL COUNT MUST BE DONE BY EYE AFTER HIGH VALUED POINTS ARE FOUND.)	PUNCHING TELETYPEWRITER TAPES; PHOTOGRAPHING AND DEVELOPING PLATES.	INSTANTANEOUS OVER SPAN OF 6ØØ LETTERS ONLY.	1943
					7Ø-MM. COMPARATOR	RECORDING SEPARATE TOTALS FOR ANY 5 PATTERNS UP TO TEN LETTERS IN LENGTH, COINCIDING BETWEEN MESSAGES OR REPEATING WITHIN A MESSAGE. (A "PATTERN" MAY BE, FOR EXAMPLE, A DIGRAPH-SPACE-TRIGRAPH.)	PUNCHING 7Ø-MM. TAPES.	3ØØ LETTERS EXAMINED PER SECOND USING TAPES OF ANY LENGTH.	1944
STATISTICAL DEPTH-INCREASER ("TURMUHR")	RAPID TESTING OF MESSAGES TO SEE IF ANY OF THEIR PARTS BELONG TO A GIVEN DEPTH OF STRIP-SYSTEM GENERATRICES. (ESPECIALLY DESIGNED TO SOLVE AMERICAN STRIP SYSTEM.)	PUNCHING TELETYPEWRITER TAPE. (SINGLE LETTER WEIGHTS ALREADY PLUGGED ON PLUGBOARD.)	1 LETTER PER SECOND USING TAPE OF ANY LENGTH.	1943?	(NONE COMPARABLE; WOULD PROBABLY ADAPT REGULAR I.B.M. PROCEDURES.)				
SIMPLE COUNTING APPARATUS	COUNTING OCCURRENCES OF FIGURE DIGRAPHS WITHIN A MESSAGE OR SET OF MESSAGES. (1ØX1Ø CLASSES OF DIGRAPHS.)	PUNCHING TELETYPEWRITER TAPE. (NECESSARY TO COPY OFF OR PHOTOGRAPH ANSWER.)	7 DIGRAPHS PER SECOND USING TAPE OF ANY LENGTH.	1943?	DIGRAPHIC FREQUENCY COUNTER OR "FREAK" (BEING BUILT.)	COUNTING OCCURRENCES OF LETTER OR FIGURE DIGRAPHS WITHIN A MESSAGE OR SET OF MESSAGES. (~~32X32 CLASSES OF DIGRAPHS.~~)	PUNCHING TAPES.	(ESTIMATED: 7 DIGRAPHS PER SECOND)	DUE IN 1946
DIFFERENCING CALCULATOR, NON RECORDING	COMPUTING UNENCIPHERED CODE GROUPS RESULTING FROM APPLYING TRIAL ADDITIVES TO A DEPTH OF ENCIPHERED CODE GROUPS; DIFFERENCING A DEPTH OF ENCIPHERED CODE GROUPS. DEPTH LIMITED TO 3Ø GROUPS.	SETTING UP OF DEPTH MANUALLY. (PROBABLY 5 MINUTES.)	RAPID MANUAL.	1943?	NATIONAL CASH REGISTER DIFFERENCING CALCULATOR	COMPUTING UNENCIPHERED CODE GROUPS RESULTING FROM APPLYING TRIAL ADDITIVES TO A DEPTH OF ENCIPHERED CODE GROUPS; DIFFERENCING A DEPTH OF ENCIPHERED CODE GROUPS. DEPTH LIMITED TO 2Ø GROUPS.	SETTING UP OF DEPTHS ELECTRICALLY. (ABOUT 1 MINUTE.)	RAPID MANUAL.	1944
DIFFERENCING CALCULATOR, RECORDING	FLAGGING DIFFERENCES IN A DEPTH OF ENCIPHERED CODE GROUPS. NO LIMIT TO DEPTH.	PUNCHING TELETYPEWRITER TAPES.	7 NUMBERS PER SECOND USING TAPE OF ANY LENGTH.	1943?	(NONE COMPARABLE; WOULD USE REGULAR I.B.M. PROCEDURES, PROBABLY WITH PRE-SENSING GANG PUNCH.)				
LIKELY ADDITIVE SELECTOR ("WITZKISTE")	RECORDING SCORES SHOWING STATISTICAL LIKELIHOOD OF EACH POSSIBLE ADDITIVE, IF APPLIED TO A GIVEN DEPTH OF ENCIPHERED CODE GROUPS. PRACTICAL LIMITS OF DEPTH, 5 TO 2Ø. (ADAPTABLE TO NON-NORMAL ARITHMETIC IF SUFFICIENTLY LARGE DECK OF SPECIAL PLATES HAS BEEN PREPARED.)	(NO MAKEREADY AS USED PREMADE PHOTOGRAPHIC PLATE.) (PHOTOGRAPHING OF ANSWER REQUIRED.)	ABOUT 1 TO 5 MINUTES PER AVERAGE DEPTH.	1943?	LIKELY ADDITIVE SELECTOR. (PROPOSED AND TESTED BUT NEVER USED.)	RECORDING TALLIES SHOWING STATISTICAL LIKELIHOOD OF EACH POSSIBLE ADDITIVE, IF APPLIED TO A GIVEN DEPTH OF ENCIPHERED CODE GROUPS. PRACTICAL LIMITS OF DEPTH, 5 TO 2Ø. (ADAPTABLE TO NON-NORMAL ARITHMETIC IF SUFFICIENTLY LARGE DECK OF SPECIAL CARDS OR PHOTOGRAPHIC PLATES HAS BEEN PREPARED.)	(NO MAKEREADY AS USED PREMADE PUNCHED CARDS OR PHOTOGRAPHIC PLATE.) (PHOTOGRAPHING OF ANSWER REQUIRED.)	ABOUT 1 TO 5 MINUTES PER AVERAGE DEPTH.	TESTED IN 1943
					KEY FINDER. (ATTACHMENT TO I.B.M. TABULATOR.)	RECORDING MOST LIKELY ADDITIVES AND RESULTANT UNENCIPHERED CODE GROUPS, WHEN TESTING DEPTHS OF UP TO 2Ø ENCIPHERED CODE GROUPS. (ADAPTABLE EQUALLY WELL TO NORMAL OR NON-NORMAL ARITHMETIC.)	PUNCHING OF I.B.M. CARDS FOR GROUPS IN DEPTH. (PLUGBOARDS ALREADY WIRED FOR SCORES INVOLVED.)	3 MINUTES PER DEPTH OF 2Ø.	1943?
(NONE COMPARABLE; GERMAN NAVY ADAPTED REGULAR I.B.M. PROCEDURES TO ACCOMPLISH (I-146).)					SLIDE RUN MACHINE. (ATTACHMENT TO I.B.M. MACHINE.)	DETERMINING AN ENCIPHERED CODE MESSAGE'S ENCIPHERMENT-STARTING-POINT IN A BOOK OF KNOWN ADDITIVES. THIS IS DONE BY TESTING 8 CONSECUTIVE ENCIPHERED CODE GROUPS AGAINST A DECK OF ADDITIVE "CARDS", AND SCORING TRIAL DECIPHERMENTS. (ADAPTABLE EQUALLY WELL TO NORMAL OR NON-NORMAL ARITHMETIC.)	PUNCHING OF CIPHER CARDS. (PLUGBOARD ALREADY WIRED; CARD DECK OF ADDITIVES ALREADY PUNCHED.)	25 COMPLETE TESTS PER SECOND.	1943
(NONE COMPARABLE; PROBLEM DID NOT ARISE.)					"CAMEL" (ATTACHMENT TO I.B.M. MACHINE)	PERMITS DISCOVERY OF MESSAGES (IN CERTAIN JAPANESE ARMY CODE SYSTEMS) LIKELY TO CONTAIN CERTAIN SPECIFIED CLASSES OF PLAIN TEXT.	PUNCHING I.B.M. CARDS FOR MESSAGES.	3 OR 4 MESSAGES TESTED PER MINUTE	1945
(NONE EXACTLY COMPARABLE; ACTUALLY USED REGULAR I.B.M. PROCEDURES OR COULD ADOPT "POLYGRAPHIC COINCIDENCE COUNTER", "DIGRAPHIC WEIGHT RECORDER", OR PROPOSED "REPEAT FINDER.")					BRUTE FORCE (ATTACHMENT TO I.B.M. MACHINE)	INDEXING IN-PHASE BUT NOT NECESSARILY CONSECUTIVE, REPEATS BETWEEN MESSAGES. (REPEATS NO MORE THAN 18 GROUPS APART.)	PUNCHING I.B.M. CARDS FOR MESSAGES AND EXPANDING DECK TO ONE CARD PER CIPHER GROUP.	?	1942
REPEAT FINDER (WAS BEING BUILT)	SEARCHING MASS OF MESSAGES FOR REPEATS OF 5 LETTERS OR MORE BETWEEN THEM.	PUNCHING TELETYPEWRITER TAPES; PHOTOGRAPHING AND DEVELOPING FILMS.	1Ø,ØØØ PER SECOND USING ANY LENGTH FILM.	WAS STILL TO BE DELIVERED.	TETRA-TESTER	FINDING REPEATS OF ANY GIVEN TYPE PATTERN, BETWEEN MESSAGES.	PUNCHING TELETYPEWRITER TAPES; PHOTOGRAPHING AND DEVELOPING FILMS. (PHOTOGRAPHING OF ANSWERS REQUIRED.)	5,ØØØ POSITIONS PER SECOND USING FILM OF ANY LENGTH.	1944
(NONE COMPARABLE.)					52Ø2	ESPECIALLY ADAPTED TO BREAKING 5 PERIODIC WHEELS OF GERMAN TELETYPE ENCIPHERING DEVICES, FROM A GIVEN MESSAGE.	PUNCHING TELETYPEWRITER TAPES; PHOTOGRAPHING AND DEVELOPING FILMS.	5,ØØØ POSITIONS PER SECOND USING FILM OF ANY LENGTH.	1945
					DRAGON	ESPECIALLY ADAPTED TO SETTING A CRIB AGAINST PARTIALLY SOLVED GERMAN TELETYPE ENCIPHERED MESSAGE, SO AS TO AID FINAL SOLUTION.	PUNCHING TELETYPEWRITER TAPES.	5 MINUTES PER MESSAGE PER CRIB, USING TAPE OF ANY LENGTH.	1945
(NONE COMPARABLE.)					"ØØ3" OR "MADAME X" ("BOMBE") SINGLE FRAME DUD-BUSTER ATTACHMENT	ESPECIALLY DESIGNED TO SOLVE END PLATE STECKER, WHEEL ORDER AND WHEEL SETTINGS, OF A GERMAN ARMY ENIGMA, FROM A GIVEN CIPHER MESSAGE AND CRIB. ESPECIALLY DESIGNED TO SOLVE WHEEL SETTINGS WHEN STECKER AND WHEEL ORDER ARE KNOWN.	PLUGGING UP PLUGBOARD.	4Ø PER SECOND	1943
					SCRITCHER	ESPECIALLY DESIGNED TO SOLVE END PLATE STECKER, WHEEL ORDER, WHEEL SETTINGS, AND REVERSING WHEEL WIRING, OF A GERMAN ARMY ENIGMA, FROM A GIVEN CIPHER MESSAGE AND CRIB.	PLUGGING UP PLUGBOARD.	25 PER SECOND ("SUPER" STILL TO COME WILL HAVE SPEED OF 1,ØØØ TO 1Ø,ØØØ PER SECOND.)	1945

CHART NO. 2-3

ARMY SECURITY AGENCY

Washington, D. C.

(EUROPEAN AXIS SIGNAL INTELLIGENCE IN WORLD WAR II)

AS REVEALED BY "TICOM" INVESTIGATIONS AND BY OTHER PRISONER OF WAR INTERROGATIONS AND CAPTURED MATERIAL, PRINCIPALLY GERMAN

(VOLUME 3--THE SIGNAL INTELLIGENCE AGENCY OF THE SUPREME COMMAND, ARMED FORCES)

Prepared under the direction of the

CHIEF, ARMY SECURITY AGENCY

1 May 1946

WDGAS-14

VOLUME 3

The Signal Intelligence Agency of the Supreme Command, Armed Forces (Oberkommando der Wehrmacht/Chiffrierabteilung, abbreviated OKW/Chi)

VOLUME 3: OKW/Chi

1. Sources of Information. Before the TICOM teams began their investigation in Germany, it was known that the Supreme Command of the German Armed Forces (Oberkommando der Wehrmacht, abbreviated OKW) contained a signal intelligence section (Chiffrierabteilung, abbreviated Chi, hence OKW/Chi).[1] Pre-TICOM knowledge of the activities of OKW/Chi was very limited, but it was assumed that, as the highest echelon signal intelligence service, it would coordinate and perhaps direct the signal intelligence work of the Army, Navy and Air Force and would probably assemble the ablest cryptanalysts for attacks on systems with which the signal intelligence services of the separate branches were unable to cope. Consequently, OKW/Chi was given first priority among the TICOM targets.

By the time the TICOM teams began operations, OKW/Chi had left Berlin and had separated, as was learned later, into a northern and southern group. Shortly afterwards, most of their documents had been disposed of and most of the personnel had been swallowed up by one or another of the large prison camps hastily set up to receive the defeated German armed forces. Thence they were released into civilian life, often without leaving a trace in the records of the camps.[2]

[1]Within the organization of the OKW, the Signal Intelligence Section was subordinated to the Armed Forces Group (Amtsgruppe Wehrmachtnachrichtenverbindungen, abbreviated Ag. WNV). This department was in turn under the Armed Forces Operations Staff (Wehrmachtfuehrungsstab, abbreviated WFSt). The full abbreviation for the Signal Intelligence Section of the Supreme Command of the Armed Forces is, therefore, OKW/WFSt./Ag. WNV/Chi. The Germans ordinarily used the short form, OKW/Chi. For the sake of brevity, this form is used throughout the present paper.

[2]On TICOM's attempt to find some of these people in August 1945, see IF 167, p. 8.

There was no question, therefore, of capturing OKW/Chi as a group. A number of individual prisoners were taken who had once belonged to the organization or who knew something about its activities. Of these, three proved to be of outstanding importance:[3]

a. Col. Hugo Kettler was chief of OKW/Chi (Chef OKW/Chi) from the late summer of 1943 until the evacuation of Berlin by the unit in March 1945. Kettler impressed interrogators as an alert, intelligent officer. He had persuaded himself that, in view of the complete collapse of German arms, he could best serve his country by cooperating with the Western allies in an effort to rebuild Germany on a different basis. He was, therefore, willing to give any information desired, as far as he was able. His task at OKW/Chi was purely administrative. As a consequence, he was well informed on matters of charter, organization, number of personnel engaged, channels for commands and directives, liaison with allies and other German cryptological agencies. He was almost completely ignorant of the technical side of his unit's cryptological operations.[4]

b. Lt. Col. Mettig was second in command of OKW/Chi from December 1943 until immediately before the end of the war, when, as nominal head of the organization, he accompanied the German surrender party first to Flensburg and then to SHAEF Headquarters at Rheims. There he was taken into custody. Like Kettler, Mettig was a regular signal officer, who had occupied important posts in command of intercept and cryptological units. From November 1941 until June 1943 he commanded Inspectorate 7/VI of the Army High Command (OKH/In 7/VI). Between June 1943 and his arrival as second in command of OKW/Chi in December 1943, he had commanded the signal battalion of an armored corps on the eastern front (Armored Corps Signal Battalion 448). In addition to his duties as second in command,

[3]The most complete account of the finding of Kettler and Mettig and their reaction to interrogation will be found in Lt. Kirby's supplement to the report of Ticom Team 6, IF-165.

[4]Col. Kettler was interrogated 15 June 1945 and released(I-47).

Mettig had served in OKW/Chi as officer in charge of intercept. After the re-organization in November 1944, he became head of the cryptographic division. In general, Mettig's knowledge of the work of his organization was, like that of Kettler, the knowledge of an administrative officer. The interrogations of Mettig, however, were more numerous and more thorough than those of Kettler. Unlike Kettler, he was brought to the United Kingdom for detailed interrogation. Besides confirming what had already been obtained from Kettler, therefore, Mettig supplied, on matters of organization and of specific tasks accomplished or attempted, a great many details omitted by Kettler. His knowledge, however, like Kettler's, was principally of a non-technical sort. Mettig was truthful in so far as his statements could be verified, and many of them could be,[5] but he seemed to feel that his dignity as an officer would be compromised by over-eagerness to volunteer information.[6]

c. Specialist Dr. Erich Huettenhain was the chief cryptanalyst of OKW/Chi. Huettenhain had been with the organization from 1937 and had himself built up the section which he headed, personally selecting most of those employed in it. Huettenhain's section may be described as the cryptanalytic research section of the organization. It had a dual task. First, it attacked the more difficult enemy and neutral systems, those which were beyond the capacity of the routine breaking section which consisted mainly of linguists whose primary tasks were the breaking of unenciphered codes and translation. Second, it investigated the security of German systems and made suggestions to the cryptographers. Huettenhain was primarily not an administrator but a working cryptanalyst who had a detailed technical knowledge of the work of his section. He was, therefore, a valuable source of information on cryptanalytic techniques both manual and machine

[5]Below some instances are pointed out where Mettig's account fails to agree in minor details with certain information from other sources. Here it is a question of Mettig's memory rather than his veracity.

[6]Estimate of interrogators in I-78 and I-127; life history in I-78, details on OKW/Chi in I-96.

known to the organization. His position also makes his negative testimony of considerable value, since it is inconceivable that he should not have known of any considerable cryptanalytic accomplishment of the organization. Huettenhain was captured with Kettler, had discussed with him the ethical aspects of the question of revealing information to the western allies, and was in agreement with him that Germany could best be served by an attitude of complete co-operation. The interrogators considered him an honorable and truthful man. In addition, they came to have a high regard for his technical ability.[7] Before he was employed by OKW/Chi, Huettenhain was an academic mathematician whose interest in the problems of Mayan chronology led to an interest in cryptography and finally to OKW/Chi.

In answering the interrogators and in writing papers for them, Huettenhain was always assisted by Technician (Lieutenant Grade) Dr. Walther Fricke. Fricke was a mathematician of some distinction who had been drafted into the Signal Corps and assigned to the Signal Intelligence Service of the Army. Here he came to specialize in the development of German Army ciphers. With his unit, Inspectorate 7/VI of the Army High Command, (OKH/In 7/VI) he was taken into OKW/Chi in November 1944 where he continued his former work on German Army ciphers, but added to it the broader task of assisting Huettenhain and others in the work of revising the security of the German Armed Forces -- a work which had become the primary task of OKW/Chi.[8] In many of the interrogation reports it is impossible to distinguish between the contribution of Fricke and that of Huettenhain. It is a pretty safe assumption however, that in regard to the work of OKW/Chi, Fricke contributed little or nothing that Huettenhain could not have supplied.

[7] This estimate is based on oral statements of the interrogators. Important interrogations are report and "homework" translated in I-2, I-31, I-84.

[8] Fricke's career is described in I-20, 2. His capture and a view of his personality is reported in IF 166.

Compared to Kettler, Mettig, and Huettenhain, the other prisoners taken were of secondary importance, although in some cases they were able to fill out the picture obtained from the principal informants. Mrs. von Nida, the wife of one Major Wolfgang von Nida, officer in charge of the OKW/Chi intercept network in Spain from January 1940 until April 1942 and second in command of OKW/Chi from that date until his death in November 1943, supplied a considerable amount of picturesque detail and some information on the intercept picture in Spain, where she had lived during part of her husband's tour of duty. She also supplied a few shrewd details that throw some light on the relation between officers and civilians and on the general efficiency of the Berlin section of the unit.[9] A considerable amount of information about the intercept station at Lauf near Nuremberg was supplied by three prisoners who were intimately associated with it: Specialist Flicke, in charge of the technical side of the work previous to the autumn of 1944, Technical Inspector Kurt Pokojewski, Flicke's subordinate and later his successor, and [Staff Director] Heinrich Hatz, in charge of administration.[10] The work of at least one of the language desks, the Japanese, is well known because a number of prisoners who formerly worked there were interrogated: Messrs. Grosse, Hierer, Rave, and Schroeder had been detached from OKW/Chi to the Foreign Office Cryptanalytic Section (Pers ZS) and were captured with the members of this section.[11] Cpl. Heinz W. Beyreuther, who was in the Japanese sub-section of OKW/Chi since 1941, supplied a written account of his work and associates. He also gave some valuable details on the later history of the organization.[12] Acting Cpl. Reinhard Wagner, who had worked at the Japanese desk since 1941, was made the subject of a special interrogation.[13] Dr. Werner Weber, one of the mathematicians assigned to Huettenhain's section, but working in close collaboration with the Japanese desk, supplied some

[9]I-49 is a paper by Mrs. von Nida which reached TICOM through intelligence channels. I-105 is a later TICOM interrogation aimed at clarifying the paper.

[10]I-85.

[11]I-22, 8. and I-1,11 *et passim*.

[12]I-150.

[13]I-90.

details about his work as well as a few things about the research section which Huettenhain had forgotten to mention.[14] On the special problem of OKW/Chi work on ciphony some information was given by S/Sgt. Dr. Otto Buggisch, who was one of the leading Army cryptanalysts. He had been transferred to OKW from the Army in November, 1944 and his work with OKW/Chi was simply an extension of his work with the Army.[15] Dr. Werner Liebknecht, an employee of Army Ordnance Development and Testing Group, Signal Branch (WA Pruef 7), had worked with Huettenhain and Fricke on the practical engineering problems involved in the production of cipher devices. He substantiated the information supplied by Huettenhain and Fricke and supplied a few details omitted by them.[16] Col. Randewig furnished the information on the signal intelligence activity of Armed Forces Signal Officer for Special Employment, Number 700 (Wehrmachtnachrichtenfuehrer z. b. V. 700).[17] This activity was connected with the OKW but had no relation to the activity of OKW/Chi. Rudolf Trappe and the dim light he shed on the obscure problem of the pre-war activity of OKW/Chi is discussed below.

The picture obtained from prisoners can be supplemented and verified, at least in part, by a number of documents now available. Of these documents, three are of the first importance for questions regarding the charter, organization, and history of the organization. They were found in the Chasseurs' Barracks (Jaegerkaserne) in Strub near Berchtesgaden and formed part of the personal files of General Staff Major Nielsen, operations officer on the staff of the Chief Signal Officer, Supreme Command of the Armed Forces (OKW/WFSt./ Chef WNV, Ia.). The documents are:

d) An unsigned document with the heading "Order of Battle of OKW/Chi." This is a brief description of the organization of the unit with the names of the heads of sections. It is undated, but its position in the files is stated

[14] I-124.

[15] I-46, 2.

[16] I-46, 2. and I-57.

[17] I-68.

DOCID: 3560827

to indicate a date of approximately April 1945. Translated at Government Code and Cypher School, it was first published as one of their publications.[18] Later the document was discussed with Kettler, and a revised version issued by TICOM.[19]

e) A document with the title "Activity Report of OKW/Chi, 1/1/ 44--25/ 6/44," dated 27 June 1944 and signed Kettler. This is a brief outline of the unit's charter and activities during the Spring of 1944.[20] It was evidently prepared for presenting to Kettler's superiors, probably the Chief, Armed Forces Communications Group (Chef Ag. WNV) and the Chief Signal Officer, Armed Forces Supreme Command (Chef WNV). It is referred to henceforth as the "Kettler report".

f)An order dated 5 September 1944, signed Praun, subject, "Coordination and Allocation of Cryptanalytic and Cryptographic Work." Praun was the Chief Signal Officer, Armed Forces Supreme Command (Chef WNV). The document was translated and published as TICOM D-55. The German original was (fortunately) also published.[21]

In addition, there is available a group of captured documents of uncertain provenance assigned the TICOM No. T 1620. The character of these documents suggests that they are from the personal file of a section head in OKW/Chi, in all probability Huettenhain. There are various official bulletins and directives on personnel matters, air-raid precautions, etc., minutes of meetings, correspondence and other documents on security matters. The material throws a considerable amount of light on the cryptographic and security activities of the organization during the winter 1944-1945.[22]

[18] DF-8.

[19] I-29.

[20] TICOMMA file number DF-9.

[21] Filed with D-55. Original TICOM Number is T-4503.

[22] Some of the documents have been translated in D-57 (where the TICOM number is erroneously said to be 1650). The documents are stated to have been received by TICOM in October 1945 from C.I.C. via S.I.D. USFET.

7

The great bulk of the OKW/Chi documents, the archives of the unit, which consisted principally of broken messages and reports based on broadcast interception, are known to have been moved from Berlin to Lauf near Nuremberg in the spring of 1945. From there, they were brought to the Schliersee south of Munich and, when it became evident that high level signal intelligence work was no longer possible, they were boxed and dumped into the lake. A waterproof box with some of these documents was recovered in July 1945 by accident and eventually taken over by TICOM. It contained a number of translations of decoded messages and some miscellaneous material,[23] among which the most important was a file of correspondence between OKW/Chi and its intercept stations covering the years 1939 to 1945.[24] Other boxes were recovered in September 1945 by American divers operating under the direction of TICOM,[25] but the material therein was not of such nature as to expand our understanding of the workings of OKW/Chi.

From the material available, a fairly clear general outline can be extracted of the charter, organization, and major cryptanalytic and cryptographic operations of OKW/Chi during the war and particularly during the last two years of the war. For charter and organization, the Chief of OKW/Chi and his second in command were available for questioning and their statements could be verified by the Nielsen documents. For operations, the chief witness was Huettenhain, whose position was very central. As head of the section composed of the organization's outstanding cryptanalysts, he was personally concerned with all the more difficult cryptanalytic problems faced, both in attacks on enemy systems and in security scrutiny of German systems. It is almost certain that no major cryptanalytic successes were achieved without his knowledge. Of the low-grade successes achieved by the unaided efforts of the language desks, however, --even when these had considerable intelligence value-- he knew little and seems to have cared less. Consequently, our information on minor successes and the intelligence obtained from them is scanty. Fenner, who was head of the routine breaking and translation; von Kalkstein, who had

[23] A-13 contains a complete list of the contents.

[24] T-804.

[25] IF-167.

DOCID: 3560827

charge of the evaluation and routing of broken messages; and Schädel, who was head of the archives and in touch with the intelligence picture; could, if found and interrogated, supply considerable valuable information on such details.

2. Notes on OKW/Chi before the War. The pre-war history of OKW/Chi (and its shadowy predecessor) cannot be reconstructed from TICOM material. Of the important prisoners interrogated, only Huettenhain, who joined the service in 1937, was connected with it before the war. Principal Specialist Fenner was with Chi from the beginning and wrote a "History of the Cipher Section" (Geschichte der Chiffrierabteilung) in the winter of 1944-1945. Unless Fenner can be found and interrogated or his history picked up, any treatment of Chi before the war must be confined to a few brief notes developing hints supplied by Huettenhain and Mettig.

According to Mettig, the germ of what later became OKW/Chi is to be found in a "section" of the German Defense Ministry (Reichswehrministerium) formed in 1920 and staffed by cryptological personnel from World War I.[26] This section was organizationally part of Military Intelligence (the Abwehr).[27] Presumably when OKW was formed, it took over Military Intelligence (the Abwehr) from the German Defense Ministry, now called German War Ministry (Kriegsministerium) and with it the cryptologic "section". With the setting up of the Armed Forces Communications Group (Ag/WNV) within the OKW, however, the "section" was taken from Military Intelligence (the Abwehr) and transferred to the Armed Forces Communications Group (Ag/WNV).[28] As will appear later, traces of the old connection with the Abwehr remained.

Huettenhain stated that when he entered OKW/Chi in 1937 he found 40 cryptanalysts headed by Fenner who were known as the "cipher party" and organized as Referat G.[29] Referat is the word used for the smallest unit in the German administrative hierarchy, roughly equivalent to our "sub-section" or "desk". It is unlikely, therefore, that Fenner's Referat G

[26] I-96, 2.

[27] I-86, 2.

[28] I-96, 2.

[29] I-36, 3.

9

was co-extensive with the cryptological "section" mentioned by Mettig. It was only part of it, but probably the most important part.

We know by name only a few of the earlier members of Referat G. The head of the Referat, Principal Specialist Fenner, later emerges as one of the most important figures in OKW/Chi during the war. Of the early Fenner little is known. That he was primarily interested in the linguistic rather than the mathematical side of cryptanalysis is suggested by his later position as head of the language sections as well as by the fact that Huettenhain was charged with developing the mathematical side of the work. He was, according to Cpl. Beyreuther, born in Petersburg and was thoroughly acquainted with Russian.[30] An early interest in cryptography as well as cryptanalysis is suggested by the fact that in the Nineteen-twenties he assisted one Willi Korn in developing the Enigma.[31] Fenner was apparently valued for his long experience in signal intelligence work and the valuable connections he had made for the organization. He is never praised as a cryptanalyst. One of his directives is found in the TICOM 1620 collection. It lays down grammatical rules to be followed by translators. Perhaps this evidence is too slight to warrant the suggestion that he was a somewhat pedantic type of person.

In any case, the low opinion of the work of Fenner and his colleagues expressed by the second known member of the organization need not be taken too seriously. This member was Principal Specialist Schapper, who later fell into TICOM hands as the head of Goering's "Research" Bureau. According to Mettig, Schapper had once been Fenner's subordinate.[32] Schapper had a somewhat different story. In the Autobiography which he wrote out for the benefit of his interrogators Schapper stated that from 1927 to 1933 he had been in Berlin as "Administration Officer and head of department in the Cryptographic Bureau of the Reichswehr Ministry." He resigned in 1933 "as I could not agree with the thoroughly incompetent methods of the Cryptographic Bureau."[33] Earlier

[30] I-150, 2.

[31] I-84, 2.

[32] I-131, 3.

[33] IF-15, (Report of TICOM Team 1), p. 23.

Schapper had made it clear to the interrogators that not only he but several colleagues had left the Bureau to propose to Goering the establishment of a new intelligence agency. "Head of department" seems a rather elaborate description of Schapper's position if he was really subordinate to Fenner whose sub-section contained in 1937 only 40 people. On a matter involving his vanity, Schapper is perhaps not a reliable witness. On the other hand, Mettig may very well be mistaken, and it is possible that Schapper was not a subordinate of Fenner, but his equal and head of another Referat in the section.

In 1935 Senior InspectorMenzer joined the organization. He is described as an old Regular Army man with little formal education. He had a natural aptitude for cryptologic work, however, and previous to 1940--41, he was wholly responsible for security.[34] His interest seemed to lie in developing cryptographic and later cryptanalytic devices.[35]

Huettenhain appeared in 1937. He spent about a year in training and then was ordered to expand the mathematical side of the cryptologic work. Huettenhain believes that Fenner was responsible for this policy.[36] It was, in any case, a good if somewhat obvious one. Huettenhain evidently used his acquaintance with German mathematical circles to advantage. He introduced into the organization five academic mathematicians, Professors Aumann, Witt, Franz, Weber, and Schultze, and a mathematically interested physician, Dr. Aigner.[37] These men remained with the organization until the end, and formed the backbone of its cryptanalytic work, both in attacks on enemy systems and in security scrutiny.[38]

[34] I-31, 3.

[35] I-31, 16.

[36] I-31, 2.

[37] I-31, 2. Weber later told interrogators that at first he worked at Chi as a Private First Class (Gefreiter). Witt and Aigner were also enlisted men as appears from a note from Huettenhain to Kempf complaining that these key cryptanalysts were overburdened with company duties. (T 1620).

[38] I-123.

A few things can be surmised about the early charter of operations of Chi, or at least of that part of it subordinate to Fenner. Some strictly cryptographic work was done, particularly in the development of systems for Military Intelligence (the Abwehr) and, perhaps, for the army. Fenner's early interest in the Enigma may be one instance of this. Huettenhain states that for some years previous to 1939 there had been a section where "our own codes and cyphers were developed and tested."[39] This section was in all probability under Menzer who was solely responsible for security[40] previous to 1940--41. Huettenhain himself made his acquaintance with OKW/Chi as an amateur cryptographer. His studies in Mayan chronology had inspired him to devise a cryptographic system which he submitted to the "local military authorities". Huettenhain's system was forwarded through channels and eventually found its way to OKW/Chi.[41] This happened in 1937, and is a clear indication that Chi was regarded as the chief authority on security matters at that time.

It is pretty certain, however, that Chi's early mission was primarily to attack the cryptographic systems of foreign nations. The 40 cryptanalysts whom Huettenhain found working under Fenner in 1937 were apparently mainly linguists organized into language desks and getting along without the assistance of professional mathematicians. Between 1937 and 1939 systems of the following countries were under attack: England, U.S.A., France, Holland, Belgium, Switzerland, Russia, Rumania, Bulgaria, Italy, Poland, Czechoslovakia, and Yugoslavia.[42] OKW/Chi's charter is said to have been originally confined to the Armed Forces systems of foreign countries. The Foreign Office Cryptanalytic Section (Pers ZS) handled diplomatic material. On the plea that it needed more material to train

[39] I-36, 3. The context makes it almost certain that this "section" was a part of Fenner's Referat G. In 1940--41 security scrutiny was made the work of a separate section.

[40] I-31, 3. See also I-161, 4.

[41] I-31, 2.

[42] I-36, 3.

cryptanalysts, OKW/Chi took over diplomatic systems also,[43] thus duplicating the work of the Foreign Office. Once having taken these systems over, Chi refused to abandon them.[44] Just when this extension of OKW/Chi's charter took place is unknown.[45] Chi was definitely committed to diplomatic material by 1937.[46] In 1939, the Army intercept stations at Lauf and Treuenbrietzen were given the task of intercepting diplomatic traffic exclusively and were subordinated directly to OKW/Chi.[47]

At the beginning of the war, then, Fenner's section, Referat G, seems to have had at its disposal the following personnel:

A group of linguists with some cryptanalytic experience.

A group of mathematicians who had been spending the past year familiarizing themselves with cryptologic problems. In 1939, the mathematicians were given a status apart from the linguists and put to tasks such as stripping encipherments from codes.[48]

[43]It is perhaps a safe guess that the dearth of material for training purposes in OKW/Chi was caused (1) by expansion of the service incident to increased militarization and preparation for war and (2) by the assignment of cryptanalytic work on enemy service systems to the separate Branches of the Armed Forces. See Tab "B" below on early relations between the cryptanalytic effort of OKW and of the Army (OKH).

[44]This information came from Karstien, a member of the Foreign Office Cryptanalytic Section (Pers ZS) who felt very strongly against OKW/Chi. (I-22, 9.)

[45]According to one informant (I-62, 5--6) the intercept station at Treuenbrietzen, which was already operating in 1933, in the days of the Reichswehr, specialized in intercepting diplomatic traffic. It is possible that not all this traffic was routed to the Foreign Office and that the Reichswehr predecessor of OKW/Chi had worked on such traffic. In adding diplomatic material to its official commitments, therefore, OKW/Chi was merely expanding a foothold it already had in the cryptanalytic domain of the Foreign Office.

[46]I-31, 10.

[47]I-85, 2 and 3.

[48]I-36, 3.

Menzer, who now had about four years experience in devising cryptographic procedures and devices. He probably had some assistants.

There is no information on the total number of personnel at this time. There had probably been considerable expansion since 1937 when the Referat numbered only about 40.

In 1939 there seem to have been some organizational changes within OKW/Chi. Referat G was upgraded to a section and called Section IV.[49] This implies the existence of sections I, II, and III, but what they did can only be conjectured on the basis of what we know about their later tasks. In general, it is probable that OKW/Chi already had in 1939 the organizational structure and tasks which were to characterize it until the changes of the summer of 1944.

[49] I-36, 3.

Chapter II. Organization

3. Organization from 1939 until the summer of 1944. A solid basis for an understanding of the charter and organization of OKW/Chi in the years from 1939 to 1944 is afforded by Kettler's activity report for the period 1 January to 25 June 1944. From this report the bifurcated character of the organization, reflecting a two-fold mission, is clearly evident. Kettler starts his report by stating that Chi's mission is to intercept and interpret two classes of traffic:

International wireless traffic of enemy and neutral states (enciphered and unenciphered telegraphic communications of diplomats, military attaches, government authorities, economic authorities, etc.)

Radio-telephone transmissions of enemy and neutral states; enemy and neutral commercial wireless transmissions of the major wireless stations and of the wireless news service.[56]

The first part of the mission was high-level signal intelligence work as it is understood in the United States. The second part was essentially the work of a broadcast or news monitoring service.

The organization set up to accomplish this two-fold mission, as it may be deduced from the remarks in the Kettler report, is outlined in chart No. 3-1 . The main work of the service was divided among four sections. Chi I controlled the intercept of class 1 traffic. The job was principally one of liaison. The head of the section was briefed by the head of OKW/Chi who was aware of intelligence requirements. He was also in contact with the cryptanalysts, who knew what they could break. On the basis of this information he gave instructions to the intercept stations. The section was evidently considered important since it was headed by an important officer. Lt. Col. Andrae, who later became second-in-command of the Army Signal Intelligence Agency, was head of Group I

[56] DF-9, 1.

15

until he was replaced by Major von Nida, who was recalled from his position as head of OKW intercept in Spain for the purpose.[57] Mettig, who had formerly been chief of the Army Cryptanalytic Service, replaced von Nida in December 1943.[58] The Head of Section I (Gruppenleiter I) was also operational head of the service.[59]

The raw material from Chi I's intercept stations was passed on to Chi IV for breaking and translation. This was Fenner's section, the descendant of Referat G, and the most important section of the service from an operational point of view. Kettler's report mentions no sub-sections, but something about the internal organization and division of labor within the section is known from other sources.

The bulk of the personnel in the section were linguists, engaged on code-breaking, removal of simple encipherments, and translation. The linguists were organized into small groups or desks.[60] In 1942 all the desks were lumped together in a subsection called IVb[61] and the desks were given arabic numbers, e.g. IV b 1, etc. The total number of desks increased to 22 in the course of the war but they were never all occupied simultaneously.[62] A desk was, of course, kept in existence only so long as the material was being read and the linguists could be kept usefully occupied.

[57]In I-49, 3, this is said to have been in April 1943; in I-105, 2, in April 1942. Since both publications are reporting statements of Mrs. von Nida, there is no criterion for preferring one or the other date.

[58]I-96, 2.

[59]This at least was Mrs. von Nida's opinion (I-105, 4). Mettig describes himself as "deputy to the Chief OKW/Chi" (I-96, 3).

[60]Called Laendergruppen by Trappe (I-123,3), Referate by Beyreuther (I-150,2).

[61]I-36, 3.

[62]The number is mentioned independently by Huettenhain (I-36, 3) and Mettig (I-96, 3).

Huettenhain and his mathematicians occupied a special position within Section IV from 1939. They were apparently organized into a desk on the same structural level as the individual language desks. In 1942, Huettenhain's people were upgraded to a sub-section and called IVc. This change was doubtless a recognition of the growing importance of their work. Mathematical work and linguistic work were now organizationally on a level. The mathematicians were a research group. Their job was to make the initial break into more difficult ciphers. When the breaking became routine, the work was handed over to the appropriate language desk. If continued expert cryptanalytic assistance was necessary, one or more members of IVc might be permanently detailed to assist a language desk, as Weber seems to have been in the case of the German attack on Japanese transposition systems.[63]

In addition, section IV contained a sub-section devoted to cipher development and security scrutiny. After 1941, Huettenhain was in charge of this sub-section and Menzer, who had formerly been in sole charge of development and security, was attached to it.[64] Just what the organizational status of this sub-section was is not clear. It may have been a desk subordinate to Chi IVb or it may have been a wholly independent subsection perhaps known as IVa, the existence of which is implied by the existence of IVb and IVc.

In connection with security scrutiny, a sub-section for developing cryptanalytic machinery was introduced in 1942 when two graduate engineers, Rotscheidt and Jensen, three working engineers and twenty-five mechanics had been hired. Where this group fitted into the organizational structure is also unknown. Almost certainly, it was ultimately subordinate to

[63] I-124, 3.

[64] The precise historical development is obscure. For some years previous to 1939, Fenner's Referat had contained a "section where our own codes and cyphers were developed and tested". (I-36, 3). Menzer was apparently in charge of this section (I-31, 3; I-161,4). In 1940, a special section was formed for security scrutiny (apparently without development) "to test new service systems and check on old ones." (I-31, 3). This section was "later" under Huettenhain. (I-31,3). Before the reorganization of 1944, however, Menzer was attached to Huettenhain (I-21, 4), so that at some time his security section must have taken over development as well.

Huettenhain and worked in close collaboration with the research sub-section in attacks on enemy systems. After the re-organization in 1944 it emerges as a separate sub-section in Huettenhain's research section.

Whatever the organizational details may have been, it is certain that attacks on more elaborate enemy cipher systems, security scrutiny of German ciphers, and development of cryptanalytic devices were carried on in very close connection with each other and were all under the supervision of Huettenhain. Kettler's report also mentions some training activity, and it is likely that this too was carried on in Chi IV and that Huettenhain had a hand in it.

After messages were broken and translated by Chi IV they were passed on to a section called in Kettler's report Chi "X". Its task was to evaluate the material from an intelligence point of view. Unimportant items were rejected and the others routed to the proper recipients. This work was done by a single officer, Lt. Col. von Kalkstein, and a few assistants.

In the handling of news and broadcast monitoring, Chi II occupied a position analogous to Chi I's position in the intercept of government traffic. But it was somewhat differently organized. Whereas Chi I was primarily a liaison organization maintaining contact between headquarters and the intercept stations which had their own organizational existence, Chi II actually was the intercept organization. It controlled directly the personnel of the main intercept station at Ludwigsfelde and of the subsidiary stations.[65] This difference was probably the result of the difference in the intercept technique involved. The broadcasts picked up at Ludwigsfelde and the outstations were carried by line to Berlin and recorded there, usually by typewriter. They were then translated immediately. The material thus gathered was processed by Chi VI, which was staffed principally by personnel with newspaper experience.[66] On the basis of the foreign broadcasts, a daily news summary was prepared. In addition special reports on various subjects were sent periodically to departments which had regular use for them. Chi III originally did its own distribution. On the broadcast side of the

[65] DF-9, 1.

[66] I-96, 16.

organization, there was no department equivalent to Chi "X", which, as Kettler's report makes clear, sorted only material from Chi IV.

The only operational connection between the two sides of the organization was afforded by the Archives. Here copies of the broken and translated messages and of the broadcast reports were filed and presumably indexed. The accumulated material was available to the code-breakers and others in Chi IV. Later on, the Archives with its chief, S/SGT. Dr. Schaedel, seems to have been subordinated to von Kalkstein's distribution section. At an earlier date, it was under Fenner.[67] The Kettler report of June 1944 does not make it clear what the situation was at that time.

It is probable that this dual nature of OKW/Chi characterized the organization since the outbreak of the war. Already in 1939, Fenner's group had been named section IV. This implies the existence of sections II and III. It is probable that they were engaged in broadcast monitoring and news analysis from the beginning. Whether the pre-war Chi had a similar service is unknown. If Fenner's Referat before the war was Referat G, Referate A--F must have existed. Perhaps some of these Referate were engaged in news and broadcast monitoring.

Besides OKW/Chi's split personality, another fact emerges clearly from the Kettler report, namely that, in so far as its activity is expressed in its organizational structure, OKW/Chi is primarily an agency for gathering intelligence. It is true that a certain amount of development and security work had always been done. The original charter for security and development is obscure, but since the Army, Navy, and Air Force was each responsible for its own security and development, the only definite commitment of OKW/Chi seems to have been to develop ciphers for the agents of Military Intelligence (the Abwehr) and for some government agencies. No special interservice systems seem to have been used. The separate branches were free to submit their systems to OKW for security scrutiny, but originally there was no obligation to do so. This situation was partly changed by an order of Keitel, as Chief of OKW, issued in October 1943 to the effect that no new ciphers could be introduced by any branch of the Armed Forces or

[67]I-96, 16.

government agency "without the prior consent of OKW/Chi".[68] Chi obviously made some efforts to meet the increasing demands for security work, as is evident from the setting up of the security sub-section within Chi IV and the introduction of the machine development group, largely for security purposes, but this work was buried organizationally and perhaps operationally within Chi IV whose principal mission remained that of producing intelligence. The organization as a whole remained an intelligence organization. The pre-war connection with Military Intelligence (the Abwehr) was still apparent in its structure.

It was apparent in other ways too. The regular chain of command was through the OKW signal authority, Hitler -- Keitel (Chief, OKW) -- Jodl (Chief of the Operations staff) -- Thiele (Chief, Armed Forces Communications Group (Chef Ag WNV)-- Kettler (Chief of OKW/Chi). In practice this channel was little used for passing on operational directives. Ordinarily, Fellgiebel was by-passed, and Kettler received his briefing and directives not from the Signal authorities but from the Chief of Military Intelligence (the Abwehr). The briefing seems ordinarily to have consisted of a general outline of the intelligence picture and some suggestions as to the part OKW/Chi was intended to play.

[68]The wording of the original order may have been ambiguous. At a conference held 27 October 1944, the navy representative, Krauss, said, "The Navy refused to allow OKW/Chi .... to forbid the use of a system in a certain place. OKW/Chi's recommendations can only lay down the limits within which it is possible to use a system. The responsibility for whether and where the system will be used must remain with the Navy." Gimmler replied, "According to the order of the Chef OKW 2000/43 Top Secret of 21/10/43, the approval of OKW/Chi is required." (D-57, 14). By the following meeting, however, held on 15/11/44, Gimmler seems to have consulted the order and stated that "according to the Keitel order, the consent of Chi must be asked for before the introduction of a new code or cipher. The decision on the introduction rests with the sections of the Wehrmacht." (D-57, 5). It is odd that the Praun order of 5 September 1944 was not mentioned in this connection.

A further testimony to the strength of the old connection with Military Intelligence (the Abwehr) was the fact that Chi V, which was in charge of the teleprinter connections between Chi I and the Intercept Stations, had the additional (and apparently larger) commitment of providing and maintaining a teleprinter system for the Military Intelligence (the Abwehr).

4. Organization from the summer of 1944 until March 1945. Events during the summer of 1944 resulted in a fundamental change in the official interpretation of OKW/Chi's mission and a corresponding change in the organizational structure. These events centered around the attempt on Hitler's life on 20 July 1944. General of Signal Troops (Lt. Gen.) Erich Fellgiebel, Chief Signal Officer of the Armed Forces and also of the Army was deeply involved in the plot. He was dismissed in disgrace from the Armed Forces on the following day and was later executed. Some of the leading figures in Military Intelligence (the Abwehr) were also involved. As a result, Military Intelligence (the Abwehr) was taken away from the Supreme Command of the Armed Forces and transferred to Himmler's Main Reich Security Office (RSHA). Here it became the "Military Department" ("Mil. Amt") and was subordinated to SS Brigadier Gen. Walter Schellenberg who was already head of the Foreign Security Service (SD Ausland) which was Department VI of the Main Reich Security Office (RSHA).[71]

OKW/Chi became a prize for various National Socialist leaders whose ambition was whetted by the opportunities afforded by the rescrambling. Goering's "Research" Bureau, a safe party organization whose activities duplicated almost completely those of OKW/Chi, made an effort to asorb its rival.[72] Goering's people could point to the political unreliability of OKW/Chi which had been under the traitor Fellgiebel and closely associated with the abolished Military Intelligence (the Abwehr) as well as to the desirability of combining activities and thus

[71]See I-86, 2; I-96, 4; and IF-164, 1. (If-164 is an interrogation report on Schellenberg, without title page but, to judge by the language, of British origin.)

[72]Thus Mettig in I-96, 4, and I-86, 2. In I-131, 3, Mettig says it was only the broadcast and news-monitoring activities of OKW/Chi that the Research Bureau wanted to take over.

conserving manpower, a commodity in increasingly short supply. The ambitions of the "Research" Bureau, however, were defeated by Schellenberg, whose grandiose schemes for a central German intelligence agency called for control of all high-level cryptanalytic work including both OKW/Chi and the Research Bureau (FA).[73]

The immediate reaction of the leaders of OKW/Chi is somewhat obscure. Fellgiebel's second in command, Brig. Gen. Thiele, took over the assignment of Chief Signal Officer of the Armed Forces and the Army. Thiele's old position as second in command and head of the Armed Forces Communications Group (Ag/WNV) was filled with Maj. Gen. Gimmler, who had been Chief of Army Ordnance Development and Testing Group, Signal Branch (Wa Prüf 7) in the Army Ordnance Department (HWA). Kettler continued as chief of OKW/Chi with Mettig as his second in command. According to Schellenberg's story, most of these officers were in accord with his schemes. Thiele was an old friend of his. They had at one time both been on the Board of Directors of the Standard Electric Company. Thiele was completely sympathetic with Schellenberg's schemes to unite all high-level cryptanalytic services and put them at the disposal of Schellenberg. After Thiele was arrested for his part in the July plot, Kettler continued to seek close contact with Schellenberg. When OKW/Chi evacuated Berlin, Kettler modeled his evacuation measures on those of Schellenberg "because he had always thought, just as Gimmler had done, that Schellenberg by taking over the Forschungsamt [Goering's Research Bureau] would acquire decisive influence over the deciphering department."[74]

Now Schellenberg is not a reliable source of information on the affairs of OKW/Chi. Cryptanalysis was, of course, only a very small corner of his vast field of interest. Besides, he tends to confuse his magnificent schemes with actual accomplishments. There is, for example, no evidence that Kettler modeled his evacuation plans on those of Schellenberg, but the core of truth in Schellenberg's remarks on the subject is perhaps to be found in Mettig's statement, made of course quite independently and in an entirely different connection, that there was a plan to accomodate some of the OKW/Chi personnel,

[73] IF-164, 7. See also the proposed organization at the end of the report.

[74] IF-164, 7.

those directly concerned with ciphers of the Reich Main Security Office (RSHA), in one of the latter organization's headquarters. This plan was not adopted because the Reich Main Security Office (RSHA) could not furnish the transport to move the Chi personnel when Berlin was evacuated.[75] It is likely too that there was similar exaggeration in Schellenberg's claim to enthusiastic support from the heads of OKW/Chi for his plans to absorb the organization. The chief result of the disappearance of the old Military Intelligence (Abwehr), indeed, seems to have been a marked loosening of OKW/Chi's ties with military intelligence. Huettenhain and Fricke stated that Kettler never saw Schellenberg after 20 July, the date of the attempt on Hitler's life.[76] Mettig, who was in a better position to know, said Kettler saw Schellenberg only five or six times--presumably for briefing on intelligence matters.[77] It may be true that when Thiele was arrested and the plans of Goering's Research Bureau (FA) to take over OKW/Chi reached a climax in the early autumn of 1944, Kettler and Mettig welcomed the protection of Schellenberg as the less of two evils.

Meanwhile, the development of OKW/Chi was in quite a different direction -- away from intelligence and towards cipher security as the main task of the agency. Doubtless the moving spirit in this change was Major General Gimmler. The Army Ordnance Development and Testing Group, Signal Branch (Wa Prüf 7) which Gimmler had formerly headed included a section for directing the production of cipher devices. He is known to have had very marked opinions on the purpose of a signal intelligence service. Huettenhain and Fricke give what is obviously an unsympathetic account of these opinions:

> He [Gimmler] gave a sort of standard lecture to various groups at various times. His approach was that of the Officer-layman. He had no technical knowledge and no one could tell him anything. His speech began something like this: "I will make Chi an orderly organization.

[75] I-96, 22.

[76] I-84, 3.

[77] I-86, 2. Compare I-96, 4.

> Before this, it has not been so. We must have three pillars in our work: Development, Security, Cryptanalysis." Then he would expound his views on the relation between these three. The head of the first branch must be an Officer, who would know what the troops need. The second could be left to a civil servant. It is the most important of the three, and the other two exist primarily to fertilize it. He considered cryptanalysis very unimportant in itself.[78]

While Thiele was still Chief Signal Officer, Gimmler made plans to put his ideas into operation. Huettenhain and his mathematicians were upgraded to a separate section and a series of monthly conferences under Huettenhain was inaugurated. These conferences were to be attended by representatives of all the branches of the Armed Forces and the SS. Their purpose was to co-ordinate all work on cipher security in Germany.[79]

Meanwhile, Thiele himself was relieved of his command and imprisoned. He was replaced by Maj. Gen. Albert Praun. Praun had been a divisional commander, and Gimmler's ideas on a signal intelligence service whose primary mission would be to furnish practical and secure ciphers for the use of troops in the field probably appealed to him. Also, he seems to have had no connection with Schellenberg, who now represented the intelligence, and hence, cryptanalytic point of view.[80] Finally, the whole cryptographic service of the Army had fallen under political suspicion. Gimmler seized his opportunity to push his theories into action. The old orientation of OKW/Chi was towards intelligence. The new was to be towards security. The new orientation is most clearly apparent in an order dated 5 September 1944 and signed by Praun.[81] Concerning cryptanalysis there is little change. Army, Navy, and Air Force are to attack the systems of their enemy counterparts as heretofore. This leaves diplomatic and military attaché traffic as

[78] I-84, 2.

[79] I-96, 13. I-84, 4.

[80] IF-164, 7. Schellenberg could not recall his name.

[81] D-55.

the cryptanalytic sphere of OKW/Chi.[82] It is emphasized, however, that the separate branches are to adhere strictly to material within their competence and to pass on to OKW/Chi all other material. They are further ordered to acquaint OKW/Chi with all cryptographic systems under study or solved. In short, the old cryptanalytic charter is restated. In addition, OKW/Chi is made a sort of clearing house for cryptanalytic information obtained by the separate branches of the armed forces.

With regard to cipher development and security scrutiny, however, the charter and authority of OKW/Chi is enlarged. In so far as Praun could accomplish it, OKW/Chi was turned into a central authority for these matters. For the Army, this could be done thoroughly. The Army had no influential party members like Goering or Doenitz to protect its operations, and besides, Army cryptographers had been deeply involved in the 20 July plot. Originally, the Army had a section devoted to cipher production and development (Inspectorate 7/IV (In 7/IV) and, in addition, some personnel in Inspectorate 7/VI (In 7/VI) were employed on security scrutiny. All of Inspectorate 7/IV (In 7/IV)and the personnel in Inspectorate 7/VI (In 7/VI) who were engaged on security scrutiny were moved into OKW/Chi, which was made directly responsible for the scrutiny of Army systems, and, in collaboration with the Chief Signal Officer of the Army (Chef HNW), for their development. The actual production of keys is left as a responsibility of the Army, but OKW/Chi will devise key systems and supply material for Army key production.[83]

[82]Although there is no mention of the matter, the order, in effect, removes the attack on enemy agents' systems from the Army and puts it officially under OKW/Chi. This made no practical difference in the structure for attacks on enemy agents' ciphers. See below.

[83]The German text is clear here, but the translation in D-55, p. 43, is misleading. The distinction is between the devising of methods of key production and preparation of the necessary material (Aufstellung von Schluesseln) and the actual production (printing, manufacture of grids, etc.) (Herstellung). On this subject, see Fricke's description of his duties (clearly Aufstellung von Schluesseln) in I-2. Section IV of the order should be translated:

IV

Devising and Producing Keys.

The Air Force and the Navy, both of them under reliable Nazis and never really subordinate to OKW as the Army was, had to be handled more carefully. They were requested to keep OKW/Chi informed on their work in development. In return, OKW/Chi would keep them in the general picture regarding German cryptography. The agreement of OKW/Chi had to be obtained, however, before any new system could be introduced by any of the separate branches. This is, of course, merely a restatement of Keitel's order of October 1943, and it is perhaps significant that it needed to be restated.[84] All separate branches were requested to submit material for security scrutiny to OKW/Chi which was in this matter the central authority. Finally, OKW/Chi was to furnish guidance in devising keys to the separate branches. The Waffen-SS, over which OKW had not even a shadow authority, was put in a third category. OKW/Chi was ordered to maintain close liaison with it on all matters relating to cryptanalysis, development, security scrutiny, and devising of keys.

By 1 November 1944, a wholly new structure was on paper and partly in operation.[85] This is the structure outlined in Chart No. 3-1. Our evidence for its genuineness is good. A rough draft of the organization was found in the same personal file with the two documents already discussed. It is undated and unsigned. The document was made the basis of an interrogation of Kettler after he was captured. He suggested a few changes, mainly in the names of section heads, and added the statistics on the numbers employed in each of the sections. Mettig supplied independently an almost identical picture of the new structure.[86]

OKW/Ag. WNV will furnish guidance for the branches of the Armed Forces in devising keys and will act for the Army in devising keys. The production of keys is the affair of the separate branches of the Armed Forces, in the case of the Army, the affair of the Chief of Army Equipment and Commander of the Replacement Army/General Army Office/Signal Department.

[84] cf. note 73.

[85] Fricke refers to the re-organization 1 November 1944 (I-20, pp. 6-7.) and it is very likely that Chi started to operate according to the new structure at about that time.

[86] Original document is DF-8. Revised document with Kettler's corrections is I-39. Mettig's testimony is in I-96.

The new emphasis on cryptography is evident in the separation of the main work of OKW/Chi into two divisions (Hauptgruppen), Division A devoted to cryptography and Division B for cryptanalysis. It is worth noting that the second in command (Mettig definitely describes himself as such)[87] is no longer head of Section I, but of Division A, which was evidently intended to be the more important division. From other sources too, we know that it was intended that the activities of the organization should reach their climax in Division A.[88] The cryptanalytic sections of Division B were to serve directly or indirectly the purposes of German security. Consequently, the research section of Division B (Chi B IV, Huettenhain's section) had a divided mission. Part of its resources were devoted to initial breaks into more difficult enemy cipher systems, part to security scrutiny of German systems. Of the 46 experts available to the section, 10 spent their time wholly on security and 10 on enemy systems. The 26 experts in the machine section evidently divided their time between the two.

In general, the work of Chi seems much better articulated in the new organization. The heterogeneous character of the old Section IV in which the most diverse activities were incorporated has been rectified. The following comments on the details of the new organization may be made:

Section Z.

Section Z dealt with details of payroll and other purely administrative matters. It also exercised a political scrutiny over all the members of the organization.[89] Some such section doubtless existed in the old organization, but no mention would be made of it in the purely operational report which is our chief source of information on that organization.

Section I.

After the second-in-command became head of Division A rather than Section I, Section I probably lost much of its

[87] I-96, 3.

[88] I-84, p. 2.

[89] All enlisted personnel working in the organization were organized into the Operational Comapny (Einsatzkompanie) OKW/Chi under Major Hein. This was formerly called First Company of those Detached to OKW/Chi (1. Kommandiertenkompanie OKW/Chi). Previous commanding officers had been Captain Krüger, Major Walter. See I-150, 5.

old importance. Logically, it should have been subordinate to Division B, since all its intercept was routed there. It was probably kept directly under the Chief in order to keep it in entirely military control. Division B was under civilian control. The new head of Section I, Capt. Grotz, was formerly commanding officer of the intercept station at Sofia.[90] Subsection Ib, whose mission was to study call signs and frequencies used in world diplomatic traffic as a guide to the intercept stations, seems seriously understaffed. The fact that the head of the sub-section was originally to have been a captain suggests that a larger group was originally planned. The T/Sgt. Schnueckel, who according to Kettler was head of the sub-section, is probably identical with the T/Sgt. Suenkel who was said to have been in charge of call sign and frequency study in the intercept station at Lauf.[91]

Sub-sectionIc was identical with the Chi V of the old organization, which, it will be recalled, had charge of the teleprinter network of Military Intelligence (the Abwehr) as well as of OKW/Chi. When the work (and probably many of the personnel) of Military Intelligence (Abwehr) was taken over into the Main Reich Security Office (RSHA), Chi continued to service its network until early in 1945, when Himmler's people took over this task for themselves, thus severing the last link between OKW/Chi and the old military intelligence organization. The work of section Ic then became appreciably lighter and Senior Inspector Buck, formerly in charge, left in April 1945.[92] The name of his successor is not known.

Division A was staffed almost entirely with personnel taken over from the Army. The chief exception to this was Senior Inspector Menzer and perhaps some of his assistants in sub-section II c. In complete charge of security and development at first, and then attached to Huettenhain's security section, Menzer had always acted more or less as a free lance, specialising in agents' ciphers and ciphers for government services. He had only occasionally consulted Huettenhain on security problems "when questions of probability were involved".[93]

[90] I-105, 4.

[91] I-85, 4.

[92] I-96, 7.

[93] I-31, 3.

The new structure recognized his independent status. His section is large and it is not unlikely that some of the personnel came from the Army.

There were elaborate plans for sub-section II a. Here the closer contact with the needs of the troops in the field, in cryptographic matters -- obviously one of the leading ideas behind the re-organization of OKW/Chi -- was to become a reality. The function of the section was to allocate keys and cipher systems. To carry out this task, the sub-section was to maintain intimate liaison with field units through skilled signal personnel from the services who were to be assigned to the sub-section and then detached back to the field where they were to observe the reaction of the troops to various systems and thus to advise II a on allocation. They would also be in a position to give on-the-spot instruction to the troops in the use and security of ciphers. The head of the sub-section was to be Capt. Bernsdorff, whom Mettig describes as "an experienced tank signaller....peculiarly suited for this job."[94] Fricke, who may only have been revealing an academic lack of sympathy with the practical turn being given to the work of OKW/Chi, told interrogators that Bernsdorff was a tank captain who "had no knowledge of cryptography".[95] Whatever Bernsdorff's personal qualifications may have been, he did not arrive until January 1945 and never really had an opportunity to get the section operating. He apparently did succeed in assembling First Lt. Eckert of the Air Force, Senior Specialist Franke of the Navy, and SS First Lt. Fricke of the Main Reich Security Office (RSHA) to represent their services in his sub-section. He himself was to represent the Army and the SS. No one was ever sent into the field. However sound the basic idea of the section may have been, Mettig and Fricke agree that it accomplished nothing. Bernsdorff had to be assigned to more urgent work very shortly after his arrival.[96]

Despite the relatively few people allotted to it, Fricke's sub-section (IIb) seems to have been very active. According to the plan, IIb was to carry out the details of cipher and key composition in close conjunction with IIa, which was presumably

[94] I-96, 8.

[95] I-20, pp. 6-7.

[96] I-96, 8.

29

thoroughly acquainted with the needs, usages, and desire of the field. Since IIa never really functioned, Fricke apparently simply carried out the same tasks of key and cipher development that had been his mission while he and his section had been attached to the Army.[97] In addition, he personally worked in close collaboration with Huettenhain on security problems.

Section III was originally subordinate to the Army. The main body of the Section was located in Dresden and remained there after the change in subordination. The mission of Section III was the compilation of keys and of codes in so far as this could be accomplished by mechanical processes of randomization, the printing of this material, and its distribution. The basic material for the compilation was supplied by Fricke and his sub-section. The work of printing was mostly farmed out to about thirty printing firms, most of which were located in Saxony. Printed ciphers were packed in Dresden and sent by truck to the OKW Distribution Office (Kurierstelle) at Zossen, whence they were forwarded. Field units notified Section III of compromises and alternative keys were then brought into operation. There was a sub-section (IIIb) in Berlin under S/Sgt. Mertz (5 soldiers, 20 women) who kept up liaison with the Field Economic Office (Feldwirtschaftsamt) and other agencies on procuring paper. There were also small liaison groups with the printing firms.[98] It is doubtful that the work of this section was changed appreciably when it came under OKW/Chi in November 1944. Liaison with the Army through the Army Chief Signal Officer (Chef/HNW) continued. The head of the section, Major Metzger, was injured early in 1945 and was replaced by Bernsdorff.[99]

Division B was the old Chi IV. All strictly cryptographic work had been removed and the organization revised to reflect more perfectly the actual tasks performed. The old mathematical sub-section, IVc, was upgraded to new section IV.[100] Some of the subsections of the new section IV were further subdivided

[97]Described in I-2.

[98]Such groups existed at Halle, Zwickau, Chemnitz, Leipzig, Frankfurt/Oder, Bischofswerda, Magdeburg, and Reichenbach (Vogtland) according to Kettler (I-39, 4.)

[99]On Section III se I-36, 2, and I-96, 13 and 17.

[100]It will be recalled that this had been done in August 1944 prior to the reorganization. See above.

into desks. We hear of a desk B IV c1,[101] headed by Dr. Weber who was one of the mathematicians brought in by Huettenhain before the war. No further details of this subdivision are known.

The old linguistic sub-section, IV b, became Section V. The designation of the language desks of the new section V is anomalous for historical reasons. Originally, the language desks had been IV b 1--22. When sub-section IVb became section V, strict logic would have demanded that the language desks be upgraded to subsections and lettered. Actually, they kept their arabic numerals. Doubtless, the small size of most of the language desks and the ephemeral character of some of them contributed to this result.

Technician Koehler's sub-section (Va) was brought into OKW/Chi from the Army Cryptanalytic Service in November 1944. All we know about it is what Mettig tells us:[102] "It was contemplated that this department would not only advise the cryptographers on linguistic problems but would also direct all matters that concerned foreign languages for the OKW. ..... This co-ordination was desirable owing to the number of independent agencies concerned."[103] The plan for co-ordination was never actually put into operation.

Section VII.

Section VII is the old Chi "X". The organizational plan called for the subordination of the section with its task of evaluating and distributing broken and translated messages (VII a) and maintenance of the Archives (VII b) to Fenner's Division B. Since VII a handled only the output of Division B and VII b served mostly the personnel of Division B, this seems to have been a logical arrangement. The Section, however, was left directly subordinate to the Chief of Service out of

[101] I-124, 2.

[102] I-96, 15.

[103] For instance, Interpreter Training Battalion (Dolmetscher Lehrabteilung), Berlin, Newspaper Section (Nachrichtenabteilung), Berlin, General of Signal Intelligence (General der Nachrichtenaufklärung, the final German designation of the Army Signal Intelligence Agency), Signal Interpreter Replacement and Training Battalion (Nachrichtendolmetschherersatz und Ausbauabteilung), etc.

regard to the feelings of Lt. Col. von Kalkstein who would presumably have considered subordination to Fenner a humiliation. According to an order of the Fuehrer, von Kalkstein was to be dismissed from the forces anyway "because he had friendly relations with people outside Germany." After his departure Section VII was to be subordinated to Division B.[104] He never departed.

The broadcast monitoring sections, old Chi II and Chi III, were combined into a single section, Section VI. Operations were continued in the same location and were probably little affected by the change. The new orientation of the whole service towards security rather than intelligence has altered the relative importance of the activities of this section, however. In the earlier structure, the activities of Chi II and Chi III form an important part of the activities of the whole organization, if not quite half as Chart 3-1 suggests. In the later structure, when Division A was the supremely important unit and Division B existed primarily to assist the security work of A, Section VI appears as a vestigial irrelevance. It could have ceased operations without noticeable effect on the rest of the work of OKW/Chi.

The history of the charter and organization of OKW/Chi during the war illustrates the development of the German idea of the purpose of a signal intelligence organization at the highest command level. OKW/Chi began the war as a purely intelligence organization, born within the Military Intelligence Department and incorporating news and broadcast monitoring as important parts of its operations. It ended as a high level security organization where even the cryptanalysis of enemy traffic was intended primarily to assist in assuring German security among all branches of the Armed Forces and government agencies. This change was accelerated by changes in command caused by events wholly unrelated to signal intelligence, but it would be a mistake to regard it as caused solely by the replacement of Fellgiebel and Thiele by Praun and Gimmler. It reflects a more general trend of thought on the part of the German High Command and of the leading signal intelligence personnel.

[104] I-96, 17.

5. The Disintegration of OKW/Chi. The plan put partly into effect in November 1944 is the final organizational expression of German ideas on high-level signal intelligence. Later organizational changes were ad hoc, forced by the pressure of Germany's impending defeat. The local movements towards the end are clearer than the changes in organization and command. They may be mentioned first. In February 1945, plans were made to move OKW/Chi out of Berlin. In March, the move actually took place and most of the personnel were moved to Halle along with the cryptanalytic machinery. Operations were started at the Army Signal School (Heeresnachrichtenschule) there.[105] The archives were probably moved to Lauf at this time. In any case, they were there before 10 April.[106] Section III moved from Dresden to Halle but did not begin operations in the new location.[107] On 10 April[108] most of the unit moved to Ammersdorf and there entrained on the 12th for South Germany under Major Hein as Commander of Transport (Transportfuehrer). The train was routed to the Chiemsee via Falkenberg, Dresden, Prague, Pilsen.[109] Part of the shipment (sections II, IV, V, VI) was at one time reported stuck between Prague and Pilsen.[110] Most of the personnel, however, got through to Werfen near Salzburg.[111] Some of the people from the intercept station at Treuenbrietzen also reached Werfen.[112]

[105] I-150, 6; I-36, 2.

[106] I-39, 4.

[107] I-36, 2.

[108] I-150, 6, from Beyreuther who was on the spot. Mettig (I-96, 22) says 9 April.

[109] I-96, 22.

[110] I-39, 4.

[111] Trappe arrived there 3 May (I-123, 2).

[112] I-85, 5. Kettler says, probably speaking broadly, Salzburg, (I-39, 4).

The Lauf station with the archives set out for the Schliersee south of Munich on 10 April, arrived on 19 April, set up, and operated for three days. On the thirtieth orders were received for some of the personnel to proceed with one-tenth of the intercept equipment to Werfen. Those who remained disposed of the rest of the equipment and the archives in the lake.[113] The others joined the remnants of OKW/Chi at Werfen.[114] There the Chi personnel were incorporated into an ad hoc unit called Corps Group (Korpsgruppe) Bork, which was apparently picking up stragglers, whether for a last stand or an orderly surrender we do not know. The Chi personnel were finally captured by American units under Colonel Clifton.[116] Some of them worked for the Americans until the end of May. They were then moved to Heufeld near Bad Aibling whence they were released.

Kettler, Huettenhain, and Fricke, on the other hand, ended the war in the North. They had, according to an unreliable authority, left Berlin for the intercept station at Husum.[117] Kettler was captured in the town of Ausacker, near Flensburg, Huettenhain and Fricke in the vicinity of Ausacker. They were accompanied by First Lt. Schubert, one of the leading Army cryptanalysts.[118] Mettig went with the OKW mission to the allies, first to Flensburg and then to the SHAEF headquarters at Rheims, where he was taken into custody.[119]

No one obtained from the prisoners a consistent account of the organizational changes accompanying the collapse of German arms, but from occasional remarks recorded in the reports and our knowledge of the movements of the personnel a fairly consistent picture can be reconstructed. When Chi evacuated Berlin and arrived in Halle, a mysterious Col. Hoepfner seems to have taken

[113] Their account in I-85,5, is substantiated by the Team 5 report (IF-167, p. 6).

[114] I-85, 5.

[116] I-150, 6.

[117] From Beyreuther (I-150, 11) who was not in a position to know Kettler's plans.

[118] See Kirby's supplement to the report of Team 6. (IF-165)

[119] I-78, 2; I-17, 4.

command.[120] Kettler and Mettig remained behind in Berlin, perhaps to assist in high-level decisions being made regarding splitting the Supreme Command of the Armed Forces into a northern and southern group. The head of the Army Signal Intelligence Service, Col. Boetzel, and his immediate staff also were in Berlin at the time, and remained there until April.[121] It was apparently decided to amalgamate the signal intelligence forces of the OKW and the Army (OKH) into a single Army Signal Intelligence Service. Boetzel was to command the combined forces in the South and Kettler in the North. The plan was put into operation on 14 April.[122] Boetzel took over the elements of OKW/Chi in the south. Just when Kettler left to take charge in the North is not known, but in its initial report on him, the SHAEF control party at Flensburg describes him as the northern counterpart of Boetzel, head of the Army Signal Intelligence service in the South.[123] Mettig, himself, perhaps with a skeleton staff, seems to have remained as the sole representative of OKW/Chi. Mettig told his first TICOM interrogators that Boetzel was head of Army Signal Intelligence in the south and Kettler in the north.[124] As such, he accompanied the OKW surrender mission to SHAEF. He told his interrogators that he was "in charge of OKW/Chi in the closing stages."[125]

120The Foreign Office people, who knew the Chi situation in Halle, mentioned him as titular head of Chi, although none of them was quite certain of the name (I-1, 19). Quite independently, Trappe mentions Colonel Hoepfner as head of OKW/Chi in March 1945 (I-123, 4). Nothing else is known about him. He does not seem to have accompanied the Chi-train to the south. Major Hein, the CO of Troops, and Lt. Col. Kaehler, the head of Section VI, seem to have been in charge here. At least they are mentioned as having lists of the personnel who made the trip. (I-150, 11).

121I-17, 4.

122The date is Weber's (I-124, 2). Trappe says OKH took over late in April (I-123, 4). Grube, a high ranking signal officer, told interrogators that the final split of OKW did not take place until 22 April 1945 (I-17, 2).

123I-5.

124I-17, 4.

125I-78, 2.

35

Chapter III. Intercept

6. OKW/Chi had two wholly distinct intercept systems. The dual character of OKW/Chi's operations, reflected particularly in the earlier organization, is also apparent in the intercept structure (See Chart No. 3-1). One intercept system concentrated on diplomatic Morse networks of enemy and neutral countries. Secondary commitments were nets of other government agencies (military attachés, economic authorities, etc.). This system consequently took mostly encrypted traffic. The material picked up was passed on to the breaking sections of OKW/Chi. The second system concentrated on monitoring foreign broadcasts, principally news broadcasts. A second important task was monitoring the correspondents' reports of news agencies such as Reuter and Domei. In addition, the second system seems to have had the mission of taking material requiring special apparatus, such as multiple Morse and commercial radio telephone. Some agents' traffic was apparently also covered, but most of traffic picked up by the second system was in clear.[131]

The core of the first intercept system was constituted by two large intercept stations, one at Treuenbrietzen, near Berlin, and the other at Lauf near Nuremberg.[132] Treuenbrietzen was one of the old intercept stations.[133] It was apparently already in existence by 1933 and is said to have specialized in intercepting diplomatic traffic.[134] It was definitely subordinated to OKW/Chi for the interception of

[131]See DF-9, 2 (Kettler's report). In his report, Kettler also mentions Hellsendungen as picked up by the second system. This probably means transmissions with the Hellschreiber, rather than picture transmissions as it is translated.

[132]Called Feste Horchstellen up to 1941, after that Feste Nachrichtenaufklärungsstellen (I-85, 2-3).

[133]It was originally situated at Frankfurt/Oder and moved to Treuenbrietzen at an unspecified date (I-85, 2-3).

[134]I-62, 5-6. This information, from an army intercept operator named Raatz, cannot be considered wholly reliable.

diplomatic traffic in 1939. Although the personnel of the station got to Werfen at the end of the war, none of them was interrogated. Little is known about the station except that its commanding officer was a captain, Dr. Rust.[135] Apparently it controlled no subsidiary stations, at least towards the end of the war.[136] Some of the personnel were despersed to Tennenlohe, a subsidiary station of Lauf, because of danger of air attack in the spring of 1944.[137]

Lauf was developed after the army was ordered to expand its intercept system in 1933. The original location was at Hersbruck.[138] It was intended primarily to operate against Czech traffic. By 1939, the necessity for intercepting Czech traffic had passed and the station was turned over to OKW/Chi for diplomatic traffic.[139] Lauf had three small intercept stations subordinate to it. The one at Loerrach near the Swiss border was set up in order to pick up traffic from Switzerland on the ground wave. This traffic could be heard at Lauf only with difficulty. Loerrach had eight or nine sets. While Lauf was being completed, there had been a temporary station at Tennenlohe. This was left equipped with four or five sets and retained for emergencies. Finally,

[135] I-96, 6.

[136] Mettig mentions none although he does mention the outstations of L auf. Dettmann and Samsonow, two reliable informants on Army matters, mention an Army intercept station (Feste Horch-stelle) which operated at Treuenbrietzen in 1939 and had subsidiary stations at Meserik, Fraustadt, Schneidemuehl, and Schlochau. The relation of this station to the OKW station is obscure. (I-116, 12).

[137] DF-9, 2.

[138] I-85, 3. See also Mettig, I-96, 6, who makes it clear that Tennenlohe, Lorrach, and Libourne were subordinateto Lauf. Kettler's report(DF-9, 2) says Flicke was in charge at Libourne until June, 1944.

[139] Operations were begun at Tennenlohe pending the completion of Lauf. The statement in I-85, 3 that Lauf itself did not become operational until December 1944 must be an error, perhaps a typists's error, since the informant Flicke, in charge of operations at Lauf, was certainly in a position to know. Kettler speaks of Lauf as well as Tennenlohe as operating in the spring of 1944. (DF-9).

37

there was a subsidiary station at Libourne near Bordeaux in France. This operated eight or nine sets from autumn 1943 until the spring of 1944. It was used principally for the interception of Swedish and Turkish traffic.[140]

The total establishment at Lauf, apparently including the outstations, was 200-250 persons. After January 1944 about eighty of these were women. The operators were apparently mostly soldiers organized in a military unit.[141] The total number of sets in operation, including those in the outstations, was eighty to ninety.[142] Specialist Flicke, our principal informant on the activity of the station, states that up to the beginning of 1943, the station attempted to cover "all diplomatic traffic" and the traffic of the Polish underground. After this time, Berlin assumed closer control and sent priority directives as a result of which the total intercept dropped from 25,000 to 10,000 messages per month. The station carried on no cryptanalytic work, but hada sergeant, perhaps with some assistants, who was an expert in traffic identification.[143] Flicke was in general charge on the technical side. The commanding officer from 1 December 1939 until the end was Reserve Major Wend.[144]

Intercept stations in foreign countries had a special status. They are called "special outstations" by Mettig.[145] They were not large or elaborate enough to be called Fixed Intercept Stations, but unlike the smaller stations at home (and in occupied territory) they were subordinated directly to Group I of OKW/Chi rather than to a larger station .

[140]I-85, 5. See also Mettig (I-96, 6) who makes it clear that Tennenlohe, Lörrach and Libourne were subordinate to Lauf. Kettler's report (DF-9, 2) is liable to misinterpretation on this point.

[141]I-85, 6. The head of this unit was Staff Director Hatz.

[142]I-85, 6-7 has a list of equipment. 60 Hellschreiber are also mentioned. What these were used for is obscure.

[143]His name was said to be Suenkel, but see above note 91.

[144]I-85, 4. Wenden according to Mettig (I-96, 6) whose memory for names was not entirely accurate. I-49, 3 says Wendt.

[145]I-96, 6.

They were administered by Military Intelligence (Abwehr) through its organization in foreign countries. Two such special out stations are known to have existed, one in Spain and one in Sofia.[146] Of the latter, little is known beyond the fact that it existed. It specialized in intercepting short-wave traffic from England.[147] Its communications with Berlin were probably poor, although teleprinter lines existed.[148] One informant stated that the messages he had handled from Sofia were always delayed.[149] Fenner visited the station several times.[150] The commanding officer was Capt. Grotz who was replaced by First Lt. Thielen[151] when Grotz became head of Chi I.

Considerable information is available, on the other hand, about the German intercept system in Spain. The OKW conducted a small network there which in 1941 employed, according to Mrs. von Nida, about fifty men.[152] It was established in 1940 in order to intercept Mediterranean traffic and also short-wave traffic from Sweden.[153] The original plan seems to have been that it should also supervise the Spanish stations of the other branches of the Armed Forces.[154] The commanding officer was Major (at that time Capt.) von Nida, who served from the winter of 1940 until April 1943.[155] Von Nida was succeeded by

[146] I-96, 6. Df. DF-9.

[147] I-96, 6.

[148] DF-9, 2.

[149] I-150, 6.

[150] I-150, 11.

[151] I-96, 6.

[152] I-105.

[153] I-96, 7.

[154] This supervision was not maintained. See below. Ltn. August Schroeder (I-75, 203), who was in intercept work in Spain in 1949 considered that he was working for a joint OKW-Army organization.

[155] See note 57. Mettig's statement (I-96, 7) that Major Marquardt was in charge is almost certainly an error. Mrs von Nida states positively that her husband was CO until relieved by Plankert.

First Lt. Plankert.[156] Communication between stations and to Berlin was by courier and wireless, for which the unit had a powerful transmitter.[157] There were also teleprinter communications to Berlin.[158] All intercepts were sent back to Berlin; no cryptanalytic work was carried on by the unit.[159]

The controlling station was in Madrid, originally situated in the German consulate (10 Ayala).[160] Because of interference from the nearby broadcasting station EFE, and perhaps for security reasons, the outfit was moved to the northeast section of the city (Castillana). After 1942, perhaps as a result of expansion, the unit took over the Florida, a large night club in the vicinity.

The largest outstation was on a German owned cattle ranch north of Seville.[161] Second Lt. Eichner was in charge.[162] Apparently on the same site but under separate navy control was a naval D/F station under Lt. Comdr. Zeimer.[163] Previous to 1944, there had been some wireless operators, probably intercept people, in Tangiers.[164] Whether they were subordinate to the Madrid unit is not entirely clear. On the Canary Islands, there was a single intercept operator, Jeschol by name, a former

156 From Mrs. von Nida (I-49,3) Mettig (I096,7) also mentions Plankert as finally in command. The "Planhart" on the previous page is probably a mistake.

157 I-105, 3.

158 I-105, 3 and DF-9, 2.

159 I-105, 2.

160 I-49, 4. The "embassy" of the text is probably a mistranslation See I-105, 3.

161 I-105, 4; I-96, 7; DF-9, 2.

162 I-96, 6. He is probably identical with the Eichsner mentioned in I-105, 4, as an outstanding enlisted man brought from Seville to Madrid and commissioned.

163 I-93, 7. This information is from the chief cryptanalyst of the Navy cryptanalytic agency and is probably reliable. Mettig's statement that "the naval D/F station was controlled by the OKW/Chi" (I-96, 7) is, therefore, not wholly accurate.

164 DF-9, 2.

Lufthansa man. He was in contact with the Madrid station by wireless.[165] The air intercept station at Barcelona came under exclusive Air Force control in 1942.[166] Mrs. von Nida also mentions a sub-station in the Balearic Islands and a large one at Bordeaux (at first at Arcachon).[167] The Balearic station, if it existed, was probably very small. The fact that the large Bordeaux station is not mentioned in the Kettler report makes it almost certain that Mrs. von Nida was mistaken about its being subordinate to Madrid, or to the OKW. The station was almost certainly under the Army.[168]

The Spanish network was apparently conducted without the official approval of the Spanish government. Very elaborate security precautions were taken to keep the work secret. The personnel were encouraged to keep to themselves in small groups and to avoid contact even with other Germans in Spain.[169] Married men might not be accompanied by their wives, and single men were strictly forbidden to marry Spanish women. In January 1944, the Seville station was betrayed to the Spanish police and had to be closed to avoid being raided.[170] About the same time the intercept operators in Tangiers were expelled.[171] Mettig believes that the personnel of the Madrid unit were interned in April 1945.

A clandestine relationship did, however, exist with certain individual Spaniards, some of them highly placed in

[165]I-105, 3-4.

[166]I-49, 4. Cf. I-96, 7.

[167]I-105, 4.

[168]See I-76, 5 where the Army intercept operator Werner Klett mentions his being assigned to Arcachon.

[169]This exclusiveness was well observed. Friedhelm Baechle, a wireless operator for the Abwehr in Spain, had only the vaguest information on German intercept activity there (I-61, 3).

[170]DF-9, 2; I-96, 7.

[171]DF-9, 2.

the Spanish Army.[172] It was the job of two Military Intelligence (Abwehr) officials, Amberg and Friedemann, to contact such Spaniards as well as to take care of the economic side of the unit, doubtless as representatives of the War Organization (Kriegsorganisation). The only known case of Spanish military cooperation with the Madrid intercept unit did not turn out happily for the Germans.[173] According to Mettig, contact was made with the Spanish General Staff regarding the equipment of the naval D/F station at Seville which had been closed in January 1944. Colonel Sarmiento, Chief Signal Officer of the Spanish Army, was persuaded to agree to let the equipment be set up by Spaniards on Spanish military ground. Some of it was then to be operated by Germans for German purposes; the rest was to become Spanish property. The equipment was delivered to the Spaniards, but was never set up and never operated. Apparently, it remained in Spanish hands, tactfully expropriated.[174]

It is likely that around 1940 there was a plan to set up a number of interservice networks in neutral and Allied countries under the control of OKW/Chi. Capt. Wadim Herold, an Air Force officer, told interrogators that he was detached to OKW/Chi in January 1940 and given a tour of the establishment preparatory to being sent into the field as an intercept officer, because OKW was at this time interested in establishing stations in Bulgaria for the Army, Navy, and Air Force. The Navy refused to come in on the project. By the time Herold arrived in the field at Varna (cover name Kommando Nordland), the Air Force had evidently already taken over the station. But Herold said that it was "formerly part of the OKW complex".

[172]Mrs. von Nida's assumption (I-105, 3) that, because the von Nidas enjoyed "friendly personal contact with the head of the Spanish intelligence service" the Spanish authorities, as a whole, knew "what was going on" is too sweeping and inconsistent with the strictly enforced security measures, and with the threatened of the Spanish police against the Seville station once it was betrayed.

[173]Traffic obtained from the Spaniards seems to have been passed via military intelligence (the Abwehr) rather than through the Madrid station. On this traffic see below, p. 45 .

[174]Mettig's story in I-96, 7.

The station consisted of 22 men, who wore civilian clothes. There were five receivers. They covered air force traffic in Syria, Greece, Rumania, and some ferry flights in the Mediterranean. Plain language was dealt with on the spot. Cipher messages were sent back to Berlin; Herold thinks to OKW/Chi.[175] If true, this may be a vestige of former OKW control of the station.

Mrs. von Nida speaks of other OKW outstations at Belgrade, at Budapest, at Vienna, and at Rome.[176] One may reasonably doubt that these were actually OKW stations. It has already been noted that Mrs. von Nida was probably mistaken about the subordination of the station at Bordeaux. Foreign Office cryptanalytic workers told interrogators that OKW had an intercept station in Greece.[177] One may doubt this also. It is clear from documents[178] that the firm and permanent part of OKW's intercept structure consisted of the Treuenbrietzen station, the Lauf station with its subsidiary stations, Sofia, and the Spanish network.[179]

Control of Intercept was in the hands of the head of Group I. The method of control is described by Mettig who held this position from December 1943 until November 1944.[180] The Chief of OKW/Chi prepared a monthly report on the most interesting links as he appreciated them from his knowledge of the military and political situation. Doubtless, the regular briefings he received from Military Intelligence (the Abwehr) were the basis for these evaluations. A report from the cryptanalytic point of view was prepared by Section IV (later SectionV). On the basis of these reports, the head of Group I

[175]I-65, 2-3.

[176]I-105, 4; I-49.

[177]I-22, 13. They also mention one in France (probably Libourne) and in the Balkans (probably Sofia).

[178]Particularly DF-9 and the Kempf list of intercept stations in T 1620.

[179]See also the account of the cryptanalytic worker Beyreuther (I-150, 6) who said he worked on signals from Lauf, Treuenbrietzen, and "one place in Bulgaria". He also knew of an intercept system in Spain which had been visited by Fenner and the head of the Archives, S/Sgt. Schaedel (I-150, 11).

[180]I-96, 6.

made his decisions as to what links were to be covered and then passed on orders to the intercept stations. A persistent difficulty was created by the heads of the language sections who demanded that only traffic being currently solved should be intercepted, "in order that the results of their work would appear more effective." If we can believe Flicke, it must be assumed that this careful system of intercept control must have been introduced around the beginning of 1943.[181] Before that time, the stations seem to have had more choice of what they were to cover although it is hard to believe that the situation was as chaotic as Flicke implies.

Various outside organizations contributed traffic to the OKW/Chi cryptanalysts. Of these, the most closely related to OKW/Chi from an organizational point of view was the German Radio Defense Corps (Funküberwachung, abbreviated Fu) which was also part of the OKW and was subordinated, like OKW/Chi, to the Armed Forces Communications Group (Ag. WNV) hence the abbreviation OKW/ Ag. WNV/Fu.[182] Mettig describes the work of the Service as follows:

"In conjunction with the Reichspost, OKW/Fu gave permission for transmission, distributed frequencies and call signs to Army agencies, Government agencies and industries, and was responsible for the distribution of codes. These matters were the concern of Gruppe I (Organization and Tactical employment) and Gruppe II (Supply). Gruppe III was responsible for WT security and as such controlled the agencies that enforced it."[183] Part of the work of Gruppe III was the interception of agents' traffic. For this purpose it controlled units of its own and also gave operational directives to the intercept units of the Regular Police (Ordnungspolizei), who passed the intercepted traffic back to Fu III.[184] There was a special unit attached

[181]See above, page 15 .

[182]See above, note 1.

[183]I-115, 2.

[184]For further details on the intercept facilities and methods of Fu III see I-115. For the division of labor with the police, see I-91, an interrogation report of Robert K. H. Schlake, Brigadier General of the Regular Police and Chief of Communications in the Main Office.

to Fu III for cryptanalysis of agents' traffic,[185] but some of the agents' traffic picked up found its way into OKW/Chi. Military Intelligence (Abwehr) organizations in foreign countries conducted line tapping operations in Bordeaux, Lisbon, Madrid, Sofia, and Ankara.[186] The heads of OKW/Chi's special outstations in Madrid and Sofia had some liaison with Military Intelligence (the Abwehr) on the matter, but actual operations were entirely in the hands of Military Intelligence (the Abwehr). The material was passed directly to the head of OKW/Chi or to Fenner as head of cryptanalytic work. It did not go, like ordinary intercepts, through Section I. Line intercepts, according to Mettig, formed about one-third of the traffic dealt with by OKW/Chi.[187] This agrees with the Kettler report of Spring 1944 according to which a monthly average of 36,480 wireless messages (both plain and enciphered) and 12,330 line messages were taken from January to June 1944. It is surprising that Kettler includes the line messages in his report of the regular intercept from facilities "centrally controlled by Chi." He must have included the Military Intelligence (Abwehr) line intercept service in this category, because there is no evidence for line intercept work on the part of any of the stations directly subordinate to OKW/Chi.[188]

Of the other German signal intelligence agencies, Goering's "Research" Bureau seems to have made the largest contribution to OKW/Chi's raw traffic. According to the Kettler report, "rather more than a third" of the total traffic handled by his cryptanalytic section in the period January to June 1944

[185]This unit (Referat Vauck) finally became a part of OKW/Chi. See below, chapter III.

[186]Military Intelligence (the Abwehr) also procured cryptographic material through agents (I-127, 5). See the case of the code purchased from the Hungarians (Section V C).

[187]I-96, 5.

[188]DF-9, 2. Morgenroth (I-114, 2) stated that postoffice intercepts had gone to OKW/Chi. This may mean that copies of messages handed over to the postoffice (which controlled cables and telegraphs) were passed on to OKW/Chi. There is, however, no other mention of traffic from this source.

was intercepted and handed over by the "Research" Bureau.[189] No mention is made of any other German signal intelligence service. In a list of sources of traffic dated 28 April 1943, however, Kettler's predecessor, Kempf,[190] mentions the Foreign Office as well as Goering's service. Of the signal intelligence services of allied and neutral countries the Kettler report mentions only Hungary. Budapest, he says, contributed about one-eighth of his cryptanalysts' total raw material.[191] In the 1943 lists, however, Kempf mentions traffic from Bulgaria, Italy, Finland, Rumania, and Spain.[192] The Bulgarian material seems to have been passed on from the German station at Sofia. Rumanian material was apparently handled by Military Intelligence (the Abwehr) although it was to be separately handled, or at least separately marked, after April 1943. Spanish material had likewise been handled previously by Military Intelligence (the Abwehr), but was now to be separately handled or at least separately marked. The suggested source for this material is the Spanish Signal Intelligence Service whose head was Rafael Sarmiento. This Spanish officer is almost certainly to be identified with the Sarmiento whom Mettig mentions as the one with whom the deal on the D/F equipment was made. He was apparently one of the leading Abwehr contacts in Spain.[193]

The total personnel engaged in intercept for Group I was according to Kettler "about 420".[194] The personnel in Spain and Bulgaria are not included in this figure. Perhaps about 500 is a maximum estimate for the number of people directly engaged on intercept for OKW/Chi's cryptanalysts. For the total accomplishment of the intercept organization, we have the statistics for the period January to June 1944 in the Kettler report: in that period, the monthly average was about

[189] DF-9, 3.

[190] T 1620.

[191] DF-9, 3.

[192] He also mentions the German Armistice Commission at Wiesbaden, which doubtless monitored Vichy traffic, and Military Intelligence (the Abwehr) as German sources of traffic.

[193] See above p. 42

[194] I-39, 4.

36,500 messages. It must be remembered, however, that at this time the effect of the Allied bombings was making itself felt. It had been necessary to organize an emergency plan whereby intercept of important traffic could be switched from one station to another in case of local disturbances or air attack. The emergency plan was controlled by wireless from the Fehrbellinerplatz, Berlin, (where Section VI was located).[195] In addition, Kettler complains of breakdown of teleprinter communications with Libourne, Madrid, and Sofia, "especially since the beginning of the invasion".[196]

Less is known about the second intercept system, which had its main station at Ludwigsfelde, and branch stations at Koenigsberg, Gleiwitz, Muenster, and Husum.[197] The material intercepted was conveyed from both Ludwigsfelde and the branch stations to the Fehrbellinerplatz in Berlin. The technician in charge of intercept equipment was Graduate Engineer Salzbrunn. Mettig says that, as a result of his efficiency, Ludwigsfelde was particularly well equipped. There were 80 receivers here. Ludwigsfelde was completely destroyed by air attack on 2 January 1944 and was not back in operation until autumn of that year. It was, therefore, out of operation for the entire period covered by the Kettler report of June 1944. Despite the fact that the main station was not operating, Kettler states that the broadcast intercept system kept up a monthly average of 7,280 press reports and 7,340 radio telephone transmissions (average duration 20 minutes) during the period from January to June 1944.[198]

The general impression derived from the Kettler report and the remarks of the informants is that the great bulk of the material picked up by the whole intercept system of OKW/Chi was either ordinary Morse or ordinary radio telephone. To be sure, the commitment of Ludwigsfelde and its associated stations included "enemy multiple Morse transmissions", but in general

[195] I-96, 6; DF-9, 2.

[196] DF-9, 2.

[197] DF-9, 2; I-9C, 15.

[198] DF-9, 2.

47

it is clear that the signal officers who controlled OKW/Chi were interested in efficient administration rather than in experiments or attempts to expand into new fields. This is doubtless what Huettenhain meant when he said "OKW/Chi itself was not concerned with intercept problems."[199]

OKW/Chi had, apparently, no facilities for intercepting Baudot. Huettenhain had seen some Baudot traffic, and this had come from the intercept station at Staats. This station was conducted by the Reserve Army and was subordinate to a section of the Army Ordnance Testing Department whose work was the development of Signal Equipment. Staats also picked up Multiplex, Duplex, and Verdun transmissions and passed them to OKW/Chi.[200] It was in operation since before the war, but its subordination indicates that the chief mission of the station was the development of equipment rather than operational intercept. It does not seem to have passed on any considerable amount of material to OKW/Chi. It is mentioned neither in the Kempf list nor in the Kettler report as a source of traffic.

The only elaborate attempts to develop intercept facilities for special kinds of transmission were made late in the war. They were not directed by OKW/Chi and, as far as can be discovered, OKW/Chi had no particular interest in them. The moving spirit behind these attempts was Col. Randewig, an officer who had been engaged in signal intelligence work for the Army on the western front in 1940.[201] He was impressed with the need for a large, centrally controlled intercept organization, staffed with at least 3000 technicians. For two years (1940-1942), he addressed a series of memoranda on the subject to the Chief Signal Officer of the Armed Forces.[202] He held various signal assignments but never had a chance to put his ideas into operation. In August 1944, he was made responsible for all questions concerning wireless in connection with rockets.[203] Since retaliation was feared, this mission

[199] I-31, 19.

[200] I-31, 19.

[201] See I-68. Other activities of Randewig are mentioned in I-47 and I-98.

[202] I-68, 4.

[203] I-68, 5.

included keeping a watch for enemy transmissions which might be control beams or signals for rockets. In November 1944, Randewig was given the title: Armed Forces Signal Commander for Special Employment No. 700 (Wehrmachtnachrichtenfuehrer Zu Besonderer Verwendung 700).[204] As such, he was chief of a unit consisting of a staff of technical specialists and liaison officer from the Army, Navy, Air Force, Waffen SS, and about 300 men. The unit was directly subordinate to the Chief Signal Officer of the Armed Forces. Its original mission was to study remote control and remote jamming and to devise counter-measures for enemy attempts in this field. Since this mission involved work along all wave lengths, the unit acquired the additional task of covering all gaps in the German intercept scheme, including particularly the centimeter and decimeter wave lengths, which had been completely ignored by all German intercept organizations. To accomplish this the unit had at its disposal the following three intercept stations:[205]

Husum, midway between Schobüll and Husum town. By means of an intercept receiver coupled to a sound film recorder (Tonschreiber) this station picked up a considerable volume of unidentified traffic ranging between 30 and 60 kcs. It was hoped that further study of this traffic would reveal its nature and origin. Radar impulses were also picked up which Randewig believed would be useful in developing radar counter-measures.

Kahle Asten (on a hill near Winterberg overlooking the Ruhr). This station specialized in attempts to pick up Allied decimeter traffic. Electrical disturbances during the brief period the station was in operation made it impossible to obtain any positive information.

Feldberg in the Black Forest. Nothing is known about the activity of this station.

Randewig's intercept activities came too late to be of any practical importance.

[204]That this is the correct title is established by a find of some German monitoring pro-formas addressed to Wehrmachtnachrichtenfuehrer 700. T 3366). In I-68, Randewig is called Heeresnachrichtenfuehrer ZBV 700 on p. 4 (although he operated for the Wehrmacht rather than the army alone), Wehrmachtnachrichtenfuehrer on p. 5, Hoeherer Wehrmachtnachtrichtenfuehrer on page 1.

[205]I-68, 5.

1. Practical cryptanalysis. In a sense, Fenner's linguists were the core of OKW/Chi. This unit operated in much the same way from the beginning. It seems to have represented the original German idea of a highlevel signal intelligence organization. The guiding principle behind its operations seems to have been to supply a steady stream of intelligence by breaking codes and ciphers which did not offer a very high degree of resistence to cryptanalysis and by furnishing translations of clear texts so obtained and of signals originally sent in the clear text. Innovations such as the introduction of a mathematical research section and the late attempt to reorient the whole organization towards cryptographic security rather than intelligence seem to have had little effect on this group. Fenner appears, in fact, to have been hostile to Gimmler's innovations.[211]

a. "VN's": The final product of the linguistic section was the translation of decoded traffic. These translations were called "VN's", or "Verlässliche Nachrichten", "reliable reports". A large number of these VN's have fallen into TICOM hands. They are all typed on form sheets headed by a large VN and classified "Geheime Kommandosache," the German classification for "Top Secret" material. Missing groups and garbles are indicated by dots, doubtful groups by dots underneath the translation. We are told that dubious translations were enclosed in parentheses and marked with question marks and that free translations were sometimes accompanied by a literal translation in brackets if necessary.[213] The date of the message and the date of publication are indicated. No evaluation was done by the sections and no reports were written. As we have seen above,[214] the

[212] IF-167, 7.

[213] I-84, 6.

[214] p. 18

50

completed product was passed on to von Kalkstein's evaluation section. Here material judged to be of no importance was put aside and the rest routed to authorized recipients. The principal recipients were, of course, Jodl, the Chief of the Operations Staff of the Supreme Command of the Armed Forces (Chef OKW/WFST.); Keitel, the Chief of the Supreme Command of the Armed Forces (Chef OKW); and Hitler. We know that Friedrich, the head of the Air Force Signal Intelligence Service, received the VN's[215] and it is likely that this courtesy was extended to the heads of the Navy and the Army Signal Intelligence Services also. Within OKW/Chi itself one copy went to the Archives where it was available to the members of the research section and one copy to the language sub-section which had produced it. Here it was used in compiling lists of cribs and for similar purposes. The total number of copies ordinarily distributed is indicated by the fact that, "for a long time," thirteen copies were prepared, "later on," more copies were prepared and for this purpose stencils were cut. The recipients are said to have kept the VN's and handled them in the same way as any other "Top Secret" document.[216]

Captured VN's in the possession of TICOM represent the traffic of twentynine countries. Most of the messages were from the Foreign Ministry of the country in question to its representatives in the various national capitals, or vice versa. In some cases the correspondents were two such representatives away from home. Some of the messages were signed with the name of the originator; some were signed "Foreign Ministry"; and many were unsigned.

With respect to content, the captured VN's can be roughly classified as follows:

Diplomatic household affairs such as personnel moves, exchange of stranded personnel through neutral countries, requests for jobs, moves of embassies into new quarters;

Requests for passports and visas;

Press reports;

Non-press reports;

Commercial and shipping arrangements.

[215] I-13, 6.

[216] I-84, 5.

DOCID: 3560827

It can be assumed that the German High Command had little interest in such housekeeping problems of the diplomatic establishments as are represented by the journey of one Leon Lévy from Algiers to Paris to fetch the archives, 2 empty mail-bags, and the typewriter.

The requests for passports and visas, which take up much VN space, were probably likewise of little interest to the OKW, unless it happened that the request came from a person of international importance.

The press reports are merely résumés of what the Germans could very well read for themselves in the papers.

The non-press reports, on the other hand, could conceivably have borne some interest for the Germans. Topics included formation of new cabinets, situation on the battle and home fronts, morale, and impending or accomplished political moves. A few examples of non-press reports from captured VN's follow.

Brazil No. 1514[217]
Ankara-Rio
19.9.44

The Vice-president of the National Party has been appointed new Foreign Minister. This appointment is, it seems to me, significant of a striving toward a closer approach to Russia, whose advance in Bulgaria is growing into a threat to Turkey.

Brazil No. 2006[218]
Ankara-Rio
29.9.44

The sudden departure of the Anglo-American Military Mission from Sofia upon the demand of the Russians has caused animated perturbation here. This appears to be the first conflict of interests betwixt the Russians and the Anglo-Americans. In Turkey, public opinion is disturbed by the attempt of the Russians to proceed in the Balkans without any control and to exclude any influence, no matter from what quarter or in what form.

Brazil No. 1703[219]
Stockholm-Rio
22.8.44

The arrival of Keitel in Helsingfors, concerning which silence was kept up to now, was announced today for the first time. It is certain that this third visit of Nazis brought

[217] T 791.

[218] T 791.

[219] T 791.

52

a result quite opposite to that of the other two; for Mannerheim did not allow himself to be impressed either by the usual threats or by any kind of promises. Many believe that this firm attitude strengthens the prestige of the Finnish President with the Soviets in connection with the peace negotiations reported in my telegram of yesterday. However, the first impression in Moscow of Keitel's journey was very bad.

Brazil No. 309 or 319[220]
Ankara-Rio
5.10.44

The new Thrace-statute imposed by Russia without previous announcement and (discussion) negotiations has called forth in Greek circles deep indignation and among the Allies great suspicion and not groundless fears. It is not known here what the English reaction will turn out to be. However, Turkey sees its European frontier seriously menaced by the Russian troops.

Chungking-China No. 1300[221]
. . . - Chungking
13.9.44

The reason for the visit of the Vice-minister of the Interior to consul Hou was . . . and the meeting at Quebec. This time he informed Consul Hou as follows:

The reason for the discussions of the two statesmen Churchill and Roosevelt concerning problems of English-American conduct of the war is said to lie in the necessity for sending new contigents of troops to . . . Churchill and . . . will confer on the preparation of further contingents of troops for landing in the Netherlands Indies or the Bonin Islands. The fleet movements are to be accelerated, even though it appears as if the European war were more pressing than the war in the Pacific.

One Japanese message in which the Germans would undoubtedly have been interested was, unfortunately for them, solved just 10 months late. Intercepted on 10 December 1943, it was marked "Solved after delay" and issued as a VN under date 11 October 1944. It was sent from Moscow to Tokyo and contains over five pages of annual report for the year 1943 on the situation of the Soviet Union. Such topics as the German-Russian front, Russian home-front morale, and Russian foreign policy are treated in some detail.[222]

220 T 7[illegible]

221 T 788.

222 T 803.

53

DOCID: 3560827

Among the messages dealing with shipping and other commercial matters, ones such as the following may have interested the Germans:

Brazil 1704[223]
Rio-London
23.8.44

The Economic Office for Sugar and Alcohol approves the extension of the international agreement for two years and deems it suitable to ask for an increase of the quota, which of course could not be used at once, but would afford greater assurance in planning; for . . . increased during the effectiveness of the London agreement by 25% . . .

France No. ? [224]
Washington-Paris
19.10.44

Sodium Cyanide. For Import and Production.

The situation here is very critical. Before the war the United States was the principal customer for French sodium cyanide. The War Production Board inquires whether France is at this time in a position to supply a certain amount to the United States. Please answer by telegram.

DeGaulle-France No. 740[225]
Madrid-Algiers
4.9.44

The steamer "Sac II" sailed this morning, 4 September, from Huelva bound for Port Lyautey with a cargo of 4,601 tons of pyrites.

The following messages are presented as miscellaneous material which may have interested the Germans:

Brazil 324[226]
Lisbon-Rio
20.9.44

On the basis of the instructions issued by Minister Aranha in the telegram of 28 July I yesterday gave Dino Grandi as remuneration for his work the sum of 24,600 escudos, equals 1,000 dollars. I had received this sum from our clearing-house for this purpose. Dino Grandi hailed the Brazilian Government in words of acknowledgement. The text, which was handed out to me, I shall send air-mail.

[223] T-791

[224] T-782

[225] T-782

[226] T-791

54

Chile No. ? [227]
Washington-Santiago
7.10.44

The Government of the United States has granted to the Military Mission the following war material: 12 howitzers . . . with 9,000 . . ., 24 machine guns caliber 30 with 50,000 rounds, 48 anti-tank cannon with 9,000 rounds, 500 gasoline tanks . . .

Directives as to what systems were to be attacked came to Fenner from the head of OKW/Chi (Kempf, and later, Kettler). The head of the service was in turn, as we have seen, briefed by Military Intelligence (the Abwehr). From what little we know, liaison was, at least from the cryptanalysts' point of view, not very satisfactory. Neither Military Intelligence (the Abwehr) nor-oddly enough - the heads of OKW/Chi seem to have had an adequate idea of the difficulties faced by the cryptanalysts. As a result, directives always came too late.[228] Huettenhain remarks that Kempf had requested that an American strip system be broken by a particular Sunday. By a great stroke of luck the system was broken to meet the deadline. This caused the operational personnel some concern, "because", as Huettenhain said, "they were always afraid after that he (Kempf) would expect systems to be broken to order."[229]

When Mettig was asked point blank what was the greatest cryptanalytic achievement of OKW/Chi, he hesitated.[230] It became apparent that OKW/Chi had not achieved any outstanding cryptanalytic success. Nevertheless, Fenner's group, aided by the research section, did achieve a series of minor successes and kept a steady stream of intelligence flowing to their superiors. During the period from January to June 1944, as we are informed by Kettler's report, Fenner's linguists produced a monthly average of about 3,000 VN's.[231] It may be noted in

[227] T-789.

[228] I-84, 3.

[229] I-84, 5.

[230] I-111, 2.

[231] DF-9, 3.

passing that during the same period SSA reported a number of completed diplomatic messages which averaged 3,700 per month. Earlier, it may well be that OKW/Chi's output of VN's was greater, because during the period for which we have the report the effects of the Allied air raids on the German cities were beginning to be felt. OKW/Chi had been bombed out of its regular quarters in the Tirpitzufer section in Berlin in November 1943.[232] During the period covered by the report, Kettler's crypto-linguists were working in temporary quarters, unheated, and in many cases without doors and windows.[233] In 1944 the number of crypto-linguists engaged was about 320. It is probable that this number had declined from a peak reached about 1941. Kettler in his report refers to a combing out of able-bodied personnel for active service.[234]

Fenner's linguists, it will be recalled, were organized into desks according to the language used in the material attacked. What we know about their work in detail can best be arranged according to the language in question. When Mettig was asked the embarrassing question about OKW/Chi's outstanding cryptanalytic achievement, he was able to point out that from an intelligence point of view the Turkish section perhaps made the most important contribution. He also mentions Polish traffic as having proved important for intelligence.[235] This was confirmed by Kettler's report, where Turkey and the Polish Government in exile were mentioned as fruitful sources of information. To these he adds the United States of America.[236]

b. Turkey:

The Turkish desk in OKW/Chi consisted of about ten people[237]

[232] I-105, 2.

[233] DF-9, 4.

[234] DF-9, 4.

[235] I-128, 3.

[236] DF-9, p. 3.

[237] I-1, 20.

and seems to have been headed by Specialist Dr. Locker.[238] Beyond the fact that the achievements of this desk were very valuable, we have no information about what systems were broken. Scherschmidt, who was in charge of Turkish cryptanalysis in the Foreign Office Cryptanalytic Section (Pers ZS) said that the bulk of the work on Turkish Military Systems was done by OKW/Chi. Despite the fact that he had a low estimate of their ability as linguists, Scherschmidt believed OKW/Chi had considerable success, particularly with Turkish military systems.[239]

c. Poland:

The Polish desk had twenty people and was one of the largest language desks.[240] It was headed by a civil servant named Berndt.[241] The main success of OKW/Chi in the polish field was attained against an enciphered four-figure code used by the London Government in Exile. This system was first attacked and solved by Huettenhain's research section toward the end of 1942 or the beginning of 1943.[242] It was worked on continually and changes in the system were followed. Weber mentions having worked on the material in the spring of 1944.[243] Kettler in his report of spring '44 mentions the solution of a Polish cipher as one of the outstanding cryptanalytic achievements of his organization. This cipher was probably one of the variations in the system under consideration. By 1945, twelve different stencils and a large number of enciphering tables had been recovered.[244] In the attack

[238]Thus Beyreuther (I-150, 3). Mettig (I-96, 3) says a Lt. Dr. Kern was head of the desk and Locker his subordinate. Trappe (I-123,3) puts Turkey, Greece, and Persia at a desk under Min. Rat Seifert and Dr. Locker. Scherschmidt of the Foreign Office Cryptanalytic Section (Pers ZS) (I-103, 3) said Locker was head of the OKW/Chi Turkish desk.

[239]I-103, 3.

[240]I-150, 3.

[241]I-96, 3; I-150, 3; I-1, 20.

[242]See I-31, 20-21.

[243]I-124, 3.

[244]I-118, 9.

on the system, Huettenhain's people used a specially developed cryptanalytic device called the Witzkiste ("Brainbox") and also ordinary IBM machinery.[245] The system was referred to by some informants as "Military Attaché",[246] by others as "Diplomatic".[247]

The most valuable intelligence results from Polish traffic, however, were obtained through the breaking of the traffic between the underground organization in Poland and its government in London. This traffic was said to have been particularly valuable during the period immediately preceding the Normandy invasion. All wireless traffic from England was banned, but the traffic of Polish agents to England continued and was read.[248] Most of this traffic seems to have been in a five-figure system. The original break was apparently made not by OKW/Chi but by the Agents Section of Inspectorate 7/VI (In 7/VI).[250] Once the break had been made, however, the traffic proved to be so valuable that in the autumn of 1943 a group from The Agents Section of In 7/VI was transferred to the Polish desk of OKW/Chi where it worked as part of the organization. The translated clear texts were published as regular VN's and given an extremely limited distribution. The traffic itself was intercepted by the OKW/Chi intercept station at Lauf.[251]

d. U.S.A. and Great Britain:

The precise organization of the attack on the traffic of the English-Speaking Allies is not quite clear. Mettig stated that there was a special desk for U.S.A. and that this desk was headed by Senior Specialist Rohen. British traffic was separately handled by a desk under Senior Specialist Rotter.[252] All the other informants, however, put both Great Britain and the U.S.A. in a single desk headed by Rohen.[253]

245 I-31, 21.

246 By Huettenhain in I-118.

247 By Weber in I-124.

248 I-115, 9.

250 See below under "Agents' Systems".

251 I-115, 9.

252 I-96, 3.

253 So Beyreuther (I-150, 2). Trappe (I-123, 3) and the Foreign Office people (I-1, 20).

This was a large section containing forty to fifty people.[254] Rotter was apparently a cryptanalyst of some experience. He had once headed the Czechoslovakian desk[255] and later the Bulgarian desk.[256] It may be suggested that there was actually one desk for England and the U.S.A. and that Rohen was the head of it. Since success with U.S.A. traffic was much greater than success with English traffic, most of the personnel were probably employed against the U.S.A. It is possible that Rotter headed a small research group engaged, perhaps unsuccessfully, on some of the English systems.

With high grade American machine ciphers, OKW/Chi had no success and seems to have made very little effort. Huettenhain knew nothing of the "big American machine".[257] He apparently had never concerned himself with American diplomatic machine ciphers. No work was done on American enciphered teleprinter traffic. Huettenhain stated that he had never seen any such traffic.[258] OKW/Chi's work on the American Hagelin is mentioned below.[259] Hagelin was, of course, never a practical problem for OKW/Chi since it was never employed for diplomatic traffic.

The leading German success in the American diplomatic field was the reading of the American strip systems. We know that the American strip system (O-2) was read by the Foreign Office Cryptanalytic Section (Pers ZS).[260] Whether this is the same system mentioned by Huettenhain as having been broken at OKW/Chi is not known. The story told by Huettenhain - that Kempf had ordered the section to break an American strip system before a certain Sunday and that this was done, much to the consternation of the personnel who feared that after that he would expect systems to be broken to order - does not state

[254] I-1, 30.

[255] I-123, 3. From Trappe, who knew the situation in 1938.

[256] I-1, 20.

[257] I-84, 6.

[258] I-31, 19-20; I-84, 6.

[259] See Chapter IV.

[260] I-89.

specifically which American strip system was meant.[261] In any case, OKW/Chi deserves credit for the development of a cryptanalytic machine which facilitated the regular breaking of the traffic once the initial break-in had been made.[262] Huettenhain says the break-in was obtained through mistakes in the use of the system and that there was no physical compromise.[263] No German agency read American strip systems after the introduction of channel elimination.

For a short time, some sort of American military attaché traffic seems to have been read. Huettenhain says this was emergency double transposition but he was not sure, on thinking it over, whether this was British or American.[264] Mettig had a vague recollection of the matter. He described the system as a military attaché system although the sender was not a military attaché. The traffic was between Washington and North Africa. He thought the system was M-209.[265] Rave, who, it will be recalled, was a minor light in the Japanese section and who cannot therefore be taken seriously as the other two witnesses, had heard some vague rumors of the breaking of American military attaché traffic. He thought the system in question was a book with encipherment.[268] The most likely conclusion from these confused remarks is that an American military attaché double transposition used in Cairo sometime during Rommel's campaign was read by anagramming two messages of identical length. The evidence is so contradictory and confused, however, that the matter must remain very doubtful. It is a case where the prisoners' memory failed.

In addition, an unenciphered code of about 100,000 groups in use since 1926 was read.[269]

[261] I-84, 5.

[262] I-31, 4.

[263] I-2, p 2; I-84, 5.

[264] I-31, 9. See below note.

[265] I-111, p 2.

[268] I-22, 8.

[269] I-31, 9.

The U.S.A. desk of OKW/Chi also broke a code encipherment system employing twenty-letter alphabets.[271] Weber said that in June or July of 1941 he and a crypto-linguist named Teischmueller worked on a United States diplomatic five-letter system to which an encipherment using seven to ten alphabets was applied. Different alphabets were used for the odd and even groups. Weber did not read the system and whether it was read later we do not know.[272]

There is no evidence for high-level success against British systems. A Typex machine captured at Dunkerque was on display at OKW/Chi. This machine was without rotors and no rotors were ever obtained.[273] The OKW/Chi prisoners could give a reasonable accurate description of the machine but they were not sure how many rotors were actually used.[274] Carefully questioned on the subject, they were emphatic in their statements that it had never been solved, either by OKW/Chi or any other German cryptanalytic agency.[275]

There is considerable evidence for successful work on the British Interdepartmental Cypher. The book was captured in Bergen, Norway, and OKW/Chi collaborated with the Navy and Air Forces in solving the encipherment and reading the traffic.[276] The rest of the evidence is largely negative. Miss Hagen, head of the English desk in the Foreign Office Cryptanalytic Section

271 I 31, 9

272 I 124, 3

273 See I 161, 4; I 31, 11; I 66, p 3

274 I 31, 11

275 An unsuccessful effort was made to trap Huettenhain and Mettig on this point. At the conclusion of the interrogation, even the most skeptical of the interrogators was convinced that they were telling the truth. See I 161.

276 See I 22, p. 12; I 119, 4; I 93, 4. Mettig (I 111) is probably mistaken in his statement that OKW/Chi did not work on the Interdepartmental Cypher. Huettenhain (I 31; 11) simply said he knew nothing about it, so that it had not been referred to the research section. The linguists may have worked on it unaided.

61

(Pers ZS), said she believed that OKW/Chi was not successful with British diplomatic ciphers although they were attempted.[277] No work was done by OKW/Chi on India-Office traffic, British Commercial or Bank of England systems. Huettenhain said that no English systems had been read since 1943.[278]

e. France, Belgium, Netherlands:

At the beginning of the war OKW/Chi detached Huettenhain to the armies on the Western Front for the purpose of working on French high-level military traffic. This traffic was probably passed between the Ministry of War and the Southern District, later between the Ministry and all important commands.[279] The personal file in T-1620 contains two letters written by Huettenhain to Fenner during the time of his detachment. From these letters it is clear that Huettenhain was wholly successful. The traffic was read up to the end of October 1939 and leads were apparently given for continued reading. The military authorities were pleased with Huettenhain's work but Huettenhain made it clear that he could not have been successful without preliminary work in reconstructing French books done by Trappe and others at OKW/Chi before the outbreak of the war. Towards the end of the war the French desk was headed by Senior Specialist Mueller and consisted of about twenty people.[280] Huettenhain's interest in the primitive French form of the Hagelin, the C-36, and in the more complicated French cipher device, the B-211,[281] was an indication that some of the traffic in these systems was perhaps dealt with by this desk. This desk may have assisted with the supervision of the Vichy French traffic which was under the direct control of the French Armistice Commission at Wiesbaden, but we know no details of this work.

[277] I-27.

[278] I-31, 6. Huettenhain adds as an exception: except "a Double Transposition system... where the same key length was used on both cages". This may be a confusion with the American military attaché system discussed above.

[279] I-31, 5.

[280] I-96, 3; I-150, 2; I-123, 3; I-1, 20.

[281] See below, Chapter IV.

Of successes against the other western allies, we can say only that prior to the fall of Belgium a Belgian desk existed in OKW/Chi.[282] Since the division of labor with the Army does not seem to have been so rigorously carried out in the early days of the war as it was later, it is possible that this desk had something to do with the reading of the Belgian military three-figure code enciphered by substitution tables. In any case, this system was read. No Belgian attaché systems were studied.[283]

At the outbreak of the war there was a desk for Netherlands traffic.[284] Of the work of this desk we know nothing.

f. Russia.

The Russian desk was under Professor Nowopaschenny.[285] Wendland,[286] the head of the practical cryptanalysis section, (Section V) was also interested in Russian. It is known that, as early as 1934, Nowopaschenny was connected with the Cipher Section, and was interested at that early date in Russian problems. At that time, Russian military traffic was being worked on. During the war, the Russian section was small, and it seems to have been able to accomplish nothing. Mettig stated definitely that Russian diplomatic traffic was enciphered with a one-time pad and was never read. Traffic was intercepted from time to time and tested, but the desk never had any luck.[287] The Foreign Office People said that up to the time of Stalingrad the Army had read a Russian diplomatic system based on a one-time pad.[288] They were probably mistaken. The system read was almost certainly a military system. We know that such a system was read. A diplomatic system would not have been handled by the Army.

282 I-36, 3.

283 I-31, 6.

284 I-36, 3.

285 I-96, 3; I-123, 3.

286 Beyreuther was, however, wrong in considering him head of the Russian desk (I-150, 3).

287 I-96, 14.

288 I-22, 15.

63

g. Yugoslavia:

The Yugoslavian desk was headed by Principal Specialist Wendland, who seems for a time to have been assisted by Senior Specialist Bailovic.[289] The desk is said to have been small,[290] and we do not know precisely what it attempted or accomplished. Buggisch stated that OKW/Chi attacked the systems of Mihailovic and Tito.[291] However this may be, it is known that the Army also worked on these systems.[292] What the division of labor was we do not know.

h. Japan, China, Manchukuo:

The Japanese Desk was headed by First Lt. Adler and seems to have consisted of about fifteen people.[293] Five members of this section were interrogated, and we have a fairly complete picture of its accomplishments. The following Japanese systems were read:[294]

(1.) A two and four-digit code unenciphered, known as the LA Code. Another informant adds the CA and IP Codes.[295]

(2.) The KOKOK Code.[296] This was a two and four-letter code transposed on the basis of a repeating nineteen digit keyword. This system was solved up until the time it was dropped on 1 January, 1942.

[289] I-96, 3; I-123, 3.

[290] I-1, 20.

[291] I-58, 7.

[292] I-69.

[293] I-96, 4; I-123, 3. Beyreuther, who was a member of the section, mentions 14 names (I-150, 4). This is, therefore, a minimum number. The Foreign Office people simply refer to a "largish group". (I-1, 20).

[294] The following list is based on that given by Reinhard Wagner, a member of the desk in I-90.

[295] Beyreuther (I-150, 8.).

[296] Called KAKAK by Beyreuther (I-150, 8). The system was worked on by the Research Section (I-31, 8; I-31, 5; I-118, 7).

(3.) FUJI, a transposition by means of a transposition square with nulls applied to a two and four letter code.[297] This system was read until it ended in August, 1943. It was broken in a very short time by the use of special apparatus designed by the research section and operated by Weber.[298] New traffic could be read in less than two hours with the aid of this machine.

(4.) The slightly more complicated system which succeeded FUJI in January, 1944 was also read.[299]

(5.) A four-figure basic code with 1,200 values enciphered by an additive book of 400,000 values.

(6.) Various commercial codes, each of about 10,000 values, enciphered by transposition. For example: A[illegible]AJ, a three, four, six-letter code; ETGAV, a six-letter code; AMNUM, a five-letter code. The enciphering processes were indicated by letters CIFOL or VEVAZ.[300]

(7.) ABABA BCBCB CDCDC. This system was exclusively employed in the Far East and consisted of a very primitive basic code enciphered by transposition. It was not read after New Year, 1944, because interception became impossible.

(8.) A system used by Satō, Oshima's counter-intelligence man, to pass messages which Satō did not wish to come to the attention of the Ambassador. For each letter of the alphabet two digits were substituted. The resulting text was then enciphered by a repeating additive of ten figures which never changed.

(9.) A machine which apparently consisted of two enciphering wheels, one with six letters of the alphabet, the other with the remaining twenty. This system was read until February, 1939.

[297] See also I-31, 8; I-84, 5. This is probably identical with the Kennwort (indicator) code mentioned by Rave (I-22, 8) and Beyreuther (I-150, 8).

[298] The apparatus was called the Bigrammsuchgeraet "the bigram-searching machine" (I-31, 4). Weber himself says traffic three to four days old was read (I-124, 3).

[299] Weber denies that any success was obtained with "new Jap systems" after August 1943. Weber may not be a reliable informant.

[300] I-31, 8; I-150, 8.

It was originally broken, however, by the Foreign Office Cryptanalytic Section (Pers ZS).[301] After 1939, the machine was replaced by another machine, and this second machine was never broken by any German cryptanalytic agency. When the Army cryptanalyst, Steinberg, who had worked on American machine systems, was transferred to OKW/Chi in November 1944, he was assigned the mission of attacking the Japanese machine. To assist him, Steinberg had only one or two enlisted men.[302] It was determined that, like the old machine, the new machine enciphered letters in two groups, a group of six and a group of twenty. The work, however, was interrupted by theend of the war, and no traffic in this system was ever read.[303]

No Japanese Military Attaché systems, either Rikugun or Kaigun, were ever read, although they were attacked at various times.[304] Huettenhain himself investigated them in 1943. In 1942, a very favorable opportunity offered itself when the Germans passed the details of certain book recoveries to the Japanese. These details were passed by Hayashi to Tokyo in the Military Attaché system. Despite the wealth of cribs offered by this process, the Germans did not succeed in solving the system.[305]

Adler's section also worked with Chinese, although not many people were engaged on this. No Chinese systems were ever referred to the research section.[306] The only clear success we are certain of was with the Chinese Military Attaché system which was discontinued in April or May, 1943. This was a three-letter code, and the first groups were always EFR SKW JKW. The encipherment consisted of transposition within the code groups.

[301] From Huettenhain, I-118, 7.

[302] I-150, 5.

[303] I-31, 8; I-118, 7-8, from Huettenhain. Buggisch's idea (I-64,3) that Steinberg solved the machine is certainly wrong.

[304] I-84, 5; I-118, 7; I-31, 8.

[305] I-31, 9.

[306] I-31, 9.

The encipherment was solved, but no messages were ever read.[307] Chinese traffic with the discriminant NKDBN was also "investigated", with what success we do not know. It consisted of three-letter groups, unenciphered, with many spells. Apparently enough traffic was read to show that it was of a purely military character.[308] Some Manchurian material was also worked on, but no details are known.[309]

i. Italy:

Senior Specialist Raffel was head of the Italian desk.[310] The section contained thirty-five to forty people and apparently had considerable success. Senior Specialist Paschke, of the Foreign Office Cryptanalytic Section (Pers ZS) said that between 1935 and 1942 his people had "read everything" in Italian, and it is likely that their results were passed on to OKW/Chi. We know that OKW/Chi read a diplomatic system called AR 22, and the Impero Code. Between 1942 and 1943, the Italians increased their additive material and employed digraphic substitution. After the surrender of the Italian Government, the Impero Code continued to be read by the Foreign Office Cryptanalytic Section (Pers ZS) for a while. Later, there was no longer sufficient depth to do this, and it was suspected that a double transposition was being employed. The systems of the Neofascist Italian Republic were also read by the Foreign Office Cryptanalytic Section (Pers ZS). They used a 5,000-figure additive; during the last three months, they also used unenciphered books and an alphabetical book with a short additive called RA 1.[311]

j. Bulgaria, Rumania, Hungary, Finland:

At an early date a desk existed for attack on Bulgarian traffic.[312] At one time after its establishment this desk was headed by Rotter.[313] There was a Rumanian section headed by

[307] I-22, 8.

[308] I-22, 8.

[309] I-150, 9.

[310] I-96, 4; I-150, 3; I-123, 3; I-1, 20.

[311] I-22, 5; 8.

[312] I-36, 3.

[313] I-1, 20.

Major Lenschau, which also had existed for a long time and which at the end of the war contained six people.[314] A desk for Hungary also existed.[315] Finnish may have been worked on in the Scandinavian section. We know, however, no details of German successes against Germany's smaller allies.

k. Scandinavia:

In 1940, Scandinavia became a place of great military importance, and all Scandinavian work was transferred to OKW/Chi.[316] The Scandinavian Desk was headed by Senior Specialist Wevering and contained about six people.[317] The desk read only Swedish unenciphered codes for which the books had been captured.[318] In view of Huettenhain's interest in the Hagelin, it is likely that the research section devoted some attention to the Swedish diplomatic use of this device. He was able to recall a message of more than 5,000 letters sent by the Swedish Attaché in Moscow.[319] No Swedish Hagelin traffic, however, was ever read.

l. Switzerland:

There was apparently a separate desk for Swiss traffic headed by First Lt. Kunze.[320] Traffic enciphered on the Swiss Enigma was regularly read. Huettenhain said that the wiring was changed every three months, but the changes at Washington were not made at the same time as those in London. Cribs thus provided by the Washington Traffic for the London traffic made it possible to solve the London wirings.[321]

[314] I-150, 3; I-123, 3; I-36, 3; I-1, 20.

[315] I-150, 3.

[316] I-22, 21.

[317] I-150, 3; I-123, 3; I-36, 3; I-1, 20.

[318] I-31, 9.

[319] I-31, 7.

[320] From Mettig. The Foreign Office people said a Herr Jung-Fischer was head of desk; Beyreuther, a Studienrat Dr. Peters. Trappe (I-123, 3) says work on Swiss was carried on by Mueller's French desk.

[321] I-31, 14.

m. Vatican, Greece:

Around the beginning of the war, a desk was established for attacks on Vatican traffic. Seifert, a former member of the Austrian Cryptanalytic Bureau, joined OKW/Chi at the time of the Anschluss and broke a Vatican book.[322] A small Greek desk existed under Cpl. Dr. Poetsgens.[323] Seifert also seems to have concerned himself with Greek systems, and is said to have broken one or more Greek books.

n. Spain, Portugal, Latin America:

We do not know what was accomplished by the small desk for Latin America, Spain, and Portugal, headed by Specialist Dr. Kiefer.[324]

o. Agents' Traffic:

Codes and ciphers of enemy and neutral agents were not a regular commitment of OKW/Chi. They were handled by the Agents' Section of In 7/VI, sometimes called Vauck's Section from its head, first Lt. Vauck. Nominally attached to In 7/VI, actually it was detached to Group III of the Radio Defense Corps (Fu III), which, it will be recalled,[325] was concerned with the interception of agents' traffic. Located at Dorf Zinna, near Jueterbog, the group acted more or less independently.[326] It is not clear whether the 6,000 agents' messages, which, deciphered and translated, formed a portion of the production claimed for OKW/Chi in the Kettler report of June, 1944, were actually turned out by OKW/Chi or by Vauck.[327] It is much more likely, however, that Vauck had nothing to do with these messages and that they were actually part of the work of Kettler's own organization. Occasionally more difficult problems were

[322] I-118, 3. He is also stated to have broken Polish, Turkish, and Greek books.

[323] I-150, 3. The Foreign Office informants said Seifert was head of the Greek Desk and that Poestgen, Bruckmann and Ruesing were "also active on a more or less independent footing".

[324] I-150, 3; I-123, 3; I-1, 20.

[325] See above, Chapter III.

[326] I-115, 6.

[327] DF-9, 3.

turned over by Vauck to OKW/Chi. One example of this is the case of the signals from the so-called Rote 3 (Red 3) Network, a Russian agents' network operating from Switzerland. Signals from this source were dealt with by Professor Nowopaschenny, Trappe and Schmidt of OKW/Chi early in 1943. Schmidt succeeded in solving ten of these messages, and Vauck's people then discovered that the encipherment was based on a book. Apparently, however, this was not enough to solve all the traffic passed by the network.[328]

The transfer of work on London-Warsaw traffic from the Agents' Section of In 7/VI to OKW/Chi in the autumn of 1943 has already been mentioned. This transfer was apparently a result of an appreciation of the importance of the traffic and of a desire to give work on it the limited distribution of the regular OKW/Chi VN's.[329] In the autumn of 1944, the whole of the Agents' Section of In 7/VI was subordinated to OKW/Chi. The group remained with Fu III, however, and its work was not affected by this paper change.[330]

8. Cryptanalytic Research, Security, and Development. While the crypto-linguists had a steady and unified mission, the research cryptanalysts of Huettenhain's section in OKW/Chi were pulled in two directions - towards the cryptolinguists whom they could assist in the solution of enemy systems and towards the cryptographers who were interested in security scrutiny of German systems. Research cryptanalytic work in the first field has already been mentioned. In some cases, it was merely a matter of detaching a few people to assist a language section, as for example Weber and his "Digraphic Weight Recorder" Rapid Analytic machine assisted in the solution of the Japanese transposition system. Only a few people seem to have been employed in the unsuccessful attack on the United States enciphered code. Not more than three participated in the study of the later Japanese diplomatic machine.

[328] I-132, 2. See also I-115, 7. T 1620 contains material relating to the "Rote 3" affair.

[329] See above under Poland.

[330] I-115, 6.

How many were employed regularly on the Polish diplomatic stencil we do not know-probably not many. The attack on the United States strip system was perhaps originally a larger effort. The research cryptanalysts seem, in addition, to have made a detailed study of the various Hagelin machines and to have obtained plain text for the linguists, at least in the case of the simplest type, the French C-36. Huettenhain outlined the various methods by which the C-36 could be solved:[331]

from messages in depth

from stereotyped beginnings, where a crib of five or six letters could be confirmed if the cipher text contained more than 323 letters

by statistical means without any cribs when the text was sufficiently long

Their investigations also extended to the more difficult later Hagelin development, the BC-38,[332] and here the general principles of solution were also understood:

solution of messages in depth

solution made possible by errors in wheel setting and consequent retransmission

general statistical solution employing Pearson's X^2 test.

For this last method an artificial message of five thousand letters was used.[333] Results could be checked step by step and the work was brought to a stage where it was apparent that final solution would have been possible. No actual traffic was ever solved by this method, however, despite the fact that a Swedish message of more than five thousand letters was available.[334] The Finnish Hagelin seems never to have been attacked.[335] So far as is known, OKW/Chi did not concern

[331] I-45, 6.

[332] I-45, 7-8.

[333] I-48, 2; I-31, 7.

[334] I-31, 7; I-31, 9.

[335] I-31, 7.

itself officially with the solution of any United States Hagelin traffic. The French B-211, both in the original and in the modified form, and the Russian B-211 were also studied. The section had time for a small amount of purely theoretical work, as for example, Dr. Schulze's study of the X^2 test.[336] Huettenhain was thinking of suggesting "A general theory for the solution of Double Transposition" as a doctoral dissertation. Such work could be kept secret by arrangement with the university authorities.[337]

Probably one of the outstanding achievements of the OKW/Chi cryptanalytic section was the development of various types of rapid cryptanalytic machinery.[338] We have already had occasion to notice the use of this machinery in attacks on cryptographic systems such as the Japanese transposition, the Polish stencil, and the American strip. The section also did a small amount of work in assisting in the development of cipher devices. We hear of a relay mechanism for changing teleprinter letters to digits and thus producing an additive for the use of the Navy.[339] The machinery was extensively used, too, in the security scrutiny of German cipher systems. The machines were shown, as developed, to the other German cryptologic agencies, which could, if they wished, order models for their own use.[340]

Cryptanalytic machinery was first introduced into German signal intelligence work with the adoption of IBM machinery by the Army in 1941.[341] OKW/Chi did not have any IBM machinery[342]

[336] I-84, 2.

[337] I-31, 6.

[338] A detailed discussion of this machinery as well as a more technical treatment of the various cryptographic devices mentioned in this chapter will be found in volume 2 of this report.

[339] I-20, p. 5.

[340] I-31, 10.

[341] I-93, 5.

[342] I-67, 2-3; I-96, 13. Despite this, Huettenhain speaks of using IBM equipment. This must have been the Army's equipment. The Army cryptanalytic agency and OKW/Chi were neighbors. (See below ChapterV.)

and may have made use of the Army's equipment for this purpose. Instead of acquiring IBM machinery for themselves, OKW/Chi established its machine section for the development of special equipment. This equipment was to be used in the first place for security scrutiny of German systems.[343] Huettenhain explained that IBM machinery can be used only for processes which can be reduced to sorting.[344] For processes which could not be so reduced, it was necessary to develop special apparatus. In general, the aim of the section was to build reading and recording apparatus in all conceivable forms in order to put together suitable equipment as soon as a practical problem arose.[345] The machine section was one of the show places of OKW/Chi. Capt. Bigi of the Italian Army saw it in 1942 and was impressed.[346] Certain Army cryptanalysts such as Buggisch made use of the machinery on some occasions.[347] Toward the end of the war, OKW/Chi was empowered to take over the IBM machinery of the Army, but because of the chaotic condition of affairs at that time, this was never actually done.[348]

The energy spent on developing cryptanalytic devices could be used for either cryptanalysis or security scrutiny. An increasing amount of the available expert manpower of the research section, however, was spent on security research and on the resulting problems in the development of cipher devices. The organizational changes expressive of this general tendency have already been traced. The overlapping of security and development work in the Army and OKW/Chi was remedied only at the end of the war when OKW/Chi took over the security and development personnel from the Army. Throughout most of the war there was considerable duplication of effort and a very intimate liaison between Huettenhain and the Army security

[343] I-31, 3.

[344] I-37, p. 2.

[345] I-37, 9.

[346] I-78, 11.

[347] I-58, 7.

[348] D-55, 4.

people.[349] Most security problems were presented to TICOM in the form of joint reports by Huettenhain and Fricke. Fricke, it will be recalled, spent most of the war in Army security research. As a result, it is often difficult to determine what work was done by the Army and what by OKW/Chi.

The chief German cryptographic device was the Enigma. It is possible that OKW/Chi - or rather its predecessor, the Reichswehr Cryptologic Section - was responsible for its adoption. In any case, Fenner had a hand in developing the device.[350] Once adopted, the device was privately produced.[351] The Enigma was produced in three principal models and OKW/Chi had apparently worked on all of them. The simplest form of the machine known as the Commercial Enigma had three wheels with a uniform motion and a fixed end-plate. Huettenhain's research section knew very well that this machine could be solved:[352]

with a depth of twenty to twenty-five messages.

with a short crib.

without a crib by running the cipher text against a catalogue of the results obtained by enciphering the letter E, the most common German letter, in all possible positions of the machine (the so-called E-strip).

The Commercial Enigma was used by the German railways and as a result of OKW/Chi's investigations, new instructions for its use were introduced which required the double encipherment of every message.[353]

A second form of the Enigma, known as the "counter" Enigma, had three wheels with an irregular motion and a movable reflector wheel. This machine was used by military attachés until around the middle of 1943. At that time it was shown that the device could be broken on a ten-letter crib. The machines were withdrawn from the military attachés and replaced by the military type of Enigma. The "counter" Enigmas

[349] See I-67, 2-3.

[350] I-84, 2.

[351] I-84, 3.

[352] I-45.

[353] I-92, 4-5.

were collected by the Radio Defense Corps for use by Military Intelligence (Abwehr). Menzer worked on a new set of instructions for the use of the machine by the Abwehr people.[355]

The most common variety of Enigma, the one used in the field by the Army and Air Force, was the Plugboard Enigma. This was identical with the Commercial Enigma mentioned above except that an additional monoalphabetic substitution was applied to the letters as they entered the wheel-maze and another as they came out, by means of plugs connecting one entry position with another. This plugging was known as the "Stecker". This device was the keystone of the German cipher security structure during most of the war.

Shortly after the beginning of the war, in October 1939, the Germans learned from a captured Polish Officer named Ružek that the Enigma had been worked on in conjunction with the French.[356] Ružek did not say the Enigma had been read. In the remnants of the Polish cryptanalytic bureau files, the plain texts of three German messages known to have been transmitted from a German cruiser in Spanish waters during the Spanish Civil War were found.[357] It is said that there were many interrogations at the time, but the interrogators "drew a blank".[358] They did not find out whether the messages were obtained by cryptanalysis or by physical compromise. At the interrogations in Warsaw in 1942, one of the Poles interrogated was a lieutenant colonel, the head of the Polish cryptanalytic bureau. A second series of interrogations was held in Berlin later in 1942.[359] In 1943 the case was reopened and

[355] I-77; I-92, 4-5.

[356] I-31, 3. This incident became known as the "Fall Wicher" or Wicher Case, from the fact that the Polish cryptanalytic bureau was located at Wicher, Poland. (I-78, p 7). Buggisch, however, (I-92, p 5) thought that Wicher was the Polish cover name for the solution operation.

[357] I-127, 5.

[358] Hentze of the Army Signal Intelligence Service states (I-113, 4); "They had learned from a Polish officer that the Poles had read it [the Enigma] before Stecker was introduced and that Stecker had been brought in in consequence."

[359] The exact date of the interrogations is not stated.

75

the prisoners interrogated again. No information was obtained. Mettig attributed this lack of success to the stupidity of the Abwehr, which left the prisoners together before the interrogations so that they had an opportunity to agree on a consistent story. Present at the interrogations besides Mettig, who probably attended as Chief of Inspectorate 7/VI (In 7/VI), were Steinberg and Pietsch, two Army cryptanalysts, and a Captain Singer, who represented the Navy.[360] Mettig did not recall whether Huettenhain was present or not.[360]

In the West, the Germans had no better luck. They were able to discover nothing in Belgium that threw any light on the vulnerability of their cryptographic systems. When Paris was captured, the French cryptanalytic agency, the Deuxième Bureau, was visited but it had been moved to Vichy. When Vichy was occupied, no search was made.[361] From interrogations and visits to the cryptanalytic agencies of conquered countries, therefore, the Germans got no conclusive evidence that the Enigma was being broken, but enough was found to arouse their suspicions.

In the interrogations and investigations consequent to the Polish discovery, the Army was primarily concerned. It is quite certain, however, that the doubts which were raised about German security had repercussions in OKW/Chi and that Huettenhain's research people did some work on the Enigma. Their precise responsibility for the change in the indicator technique, which was one of the results of the Polish incident, is not certain. Huettenhain, at least, mentions the possibility of a solution resulting from faulty indicator procedure. He also thought that a general solution might be theoretically possible by the use of an E-strip as in the case of the Commercial Enigma.[362] Such a solution, however, would be slow and would take an enormous assembly of equipment and personnel. It was never actually attempted in Germany. OKW/Chi's final general judgment on the Plugboard Enigma seems to have been that the device was secure if used according to regulations. They

[360] I-127, 5.

[361] I-31, 3.

[362] I-45, 4.

were aware that solution might be possible by means of stereotyped beginnings, stereotyped messages, or a number of messages in depth. No texts of messages actually transmitted in the field were ever made available to OKW/Chi by any branch of the armed forces. The enforcement of cryptographic regulations in the field, however indirectly, was no part of the duty of OKW/-Chi. It is worth noting that early in 1944 the German Navy became concerned about their cryptographic security as a result of heavy U-boat losses in 1943 and early 1944. A naval lieutenant named Frowein was detached from the Signal Intelligence Agency of the Navy High Command (OKM/4 SKL/III) to the Signal Security Agency of the Navy High Command (OKM/4 SKL/II),[363] to study the Naval Enigma. The Naval Enigma was like the army and airforce machines, but it had four wheels instead of three and, therefore, a higher degree of theoretical security. Frowein broke the naval machine with known wheels on a crib of twenty-five letters.[364]

OKW/Chi's cryptanalysts had a generally uneasy feeling about the security of the chief German ciphers. In a lecture given as part of the Chi conferences in the autumn of 1944, Lt. Dr. Stein told the assembled cryptographers that no German system was secure if the cryptographic regulations were violated. Without any authority to monitor actual traffic with a view to finding out how well the regulations were observed, all German cryptographic agencies, including OKW/Chi, were driven from security scrutiny to an attempt to develop cryptographic devices that would have a higher degree of theoretical invulnerability. OKW/Chi's contribution to increased security for the Enigma was a suggestion that the wheels be redesigned so that they could be given an irregular motion. This device, the "Changeable Turnover Rotor" (Lueckenfuellerwalze), was developed by OKW/Chi in conjunction with the Army cryptographers.[366] It meant that every Enigma machine in operation would have to be supplied with

[363] I-38, 2.

[364] I-38, 2. Cf. also I-95, 7 in which Morgenroth of OKM 4/SKL III states that Frowein investigated the Naval Enigma in the summer of 1944.

[366] I-104, p 2-3. It may be noted that the Russians visited the part of the firm of Heimsoeth and Rincke in Russian occupied Territory and removed from it a complete set of drawings for the Lueckenfuellerwalze but did not get a model, according to the members of the firm.

a new set of wheels. The wheels were never produced in great enough quantity so that the system could be changed. Side by side with the attempt to increase the security of the Enigma went an effort to develop entirely new cryptographic devices with the intention of replacing the Enigma entirely. One of the most interesting of these devices, the SG-39, a kind of combination of Enigma and Hagelin principles, was scheduled for production in the year 1939, but because of technical difficulties, lack of clarity in the operational requirements and, finally, the bombing out of factories capable of producing the device, the first experimental models were not ready for delivery before February or March 1945, and they never reached their destination in Berlin.[367] This device seems to have been mainly developed by the Army. The former Army cryptanalyst, Buggisch, was a specialist in the machine.[368] On the part of OKW/Chi, Menzer seems to have had the most fertile mind in the development of cryptographic devices. Between 1937 and 1939 he produced a purely mechanical machine called the M-40 and about thirty models were built. The machine was tested by the Army security people and found "moderately secure", but was actually never used.[369] One variety was to have been adopted for automatic Morse sending.[370] An invention of Menzer's of great practical significance was the SG-41,[371] this was a purely mechanical machine wherein the wheels had an irregular interlocking motion. The machine received the approval of the OKW/Chi cryptanalysts who considered that a fundamental weakness of the Hagelin had been overcome.[372] Like all machines of the Hagelin type, the SG-41 can be read in depth, but the setting of the

[367] I-57, 8. Major Barlow of the United States Army visited the firm which was building the SG 39, Telefonbau und Normalzeit. He reported it completely bombed out (I-52, p 2.)

[368] I-58, 6.

[369] I-118, 5; I-58, 5.

[370] I-84, 5.

[371] I-58, 5.

[372] I-31, 7.

machine cannot be recovered even from a very considerable length of key. The SG-41 was built, and used by German Agents, but it was never finally authorized for the army, largely because of interdepartmental differences of opinion, which seem to have been typical of the German signal intelligence set-up where the link leading from the cryptologic experts to the troops in the field seems to have been unusually long and tenuous. The technical development was in the hands of a Dr. Pupp of Army Ordnance Development and Testing Group, Signal Branch (Wa Pruef 7), and a few engineers from the Wanderer Works at Chemnitz were also concerned. The cryptographers spent a great deal of time in discussion as to whether the order of the letters on the printing wheel should be alphabetical. Gen. Fellgiebel decided that he wanted a machine with a keyboard. Consequently, the alphabetical arrangement on the printing wheel was not required; a mixed alphabet was used instead as adding some slight additional security. Production was started on this basis and a thousand machines were actually built. Then all the officers in the Army Signals Department decided that they wanted a smaller machine without a key board for use below the regiment. On such a machine an alphabetic arrangement of letters on the printing wheel was necessary; if such a machine was to be used with the key board machines, they too would have to have a regular alphabetical arrangement on the printing wheel. As a result of the change-over delay, the machine was never turned out in sufficient quantity for wide use. But a model with ten digits rather than letters was produced for the use of the weather services.[373]

Medium grade and low grade field systems were no concern of OKW/Chi until it took over all Army cryptographic work in the autumn of 1944. Fricke, who joined OKW/Chi along with other cryptographic experts, had, during his career with army security research,[374] shown the weaknesses of the Double Playfair system, which had been the Army medium-grade system at the outbreak of the war. He had been partly responsible for the development of the "Raster" transposition system which replaced it. The transposition system proved awkward for field use because the original metal grilles could not be turned

[373] I-72, 8ff.

[374] I-20, p 2.

out owing to a shortage of material, and paper grilles requiring constant replacement were used. OKW/Chi turned again to Menzer and became interested in a little device he had developed for agents called the "Schluesselkasten" (Literally "key box").[375] This was a device that looked like a slide rule with wheels. T-1620 contains the results of OKW/Chi's security investigation of this device and it was found to be very satisfactory for medium grade use.[376]

The OKW/Chi research section gave considerable attention to the security scrutiny and development of German teleprinting security devices. The Germans produced two series of such devices. The first series, distinguished by the letters SZ, were cryptographic devices separate from the teleprinter and attachable. Encipherment was effected by twelve mechanical (pin) wheels. The second series of devices were actually built into the teleprinter. The teleprinter and the device were designated by a number prefixed by the letter T. Encipherment was obtained by the use of ten wheels with fixed pin patterns.

The SZ series began to be developed in the year 1937 by the Army Ordnance Development and Testing Group Signal Branch (WA Pruef 7) in conjunction with the Lorenz Firm.[377] Originally, no expert cryptologic assistance was sought. In 1937, Menzer and Huettenhain visited Liebknecht, the representative of Army Ordnance Development and Testing Group Signal Branch (WA Pruef 7), and examined the first model, the SZ-40. It was shown that the cipher produced by this machine could be broken on a thousand letters of text without cribs or other assistance.[378] Only about a hundred of the

[375] I-57, 9.

[376] To some extent OKW/Chi concerned itself with the development of ciphers for German commercial firms as Huettenhain states (I-84, 4). The Military Intelligence (Abwehr) Office (possibly III-F) was responsible for the security of commercial firms' ciphers but when there were difficulties, Menzer of OKW/-Chi sometimes helped. Huettenhain himself had advised that when there was little traffic, the firms should use a one-time pad on a commercial book, such as ABC Code or Mosse.

[377] I-45, 16.

[378] I-31, 17.

machines were consequently produced, and, apparently in consultation with Menzer, a new model, the SZ-42, was designed.[379] This model, in turn, proved to be by no means impervious to cryptanalytic attack, and variations, designated SZ-42 A, B, and C, were developed on consultation with Huettenhain and his assistant, Dr. Stein.

The original models of the T series, the T-52 A and B, were produced by the firm of Siemens. These devices were examined by Huettenhain in 1939, and he showed that they had an extraordinarily low degree of security and could be broken on a hundred letters of cipher text without a crib. Changes in design were suggested to Siemens, including means of producing a non-uniform turning of the wheels, but for engineering reasons Siemens refused to accept these suggestions.[380] Instead, the T-52 was produced, which overcame some of the more obvious disadvantages of the earlier models. There were no short sub-periods in its keying sequence.[381] The T-52 C was studied by the Army cryptanalyst, Doering, in 1942, and he showed that it could be broken on a text of 1,000 letters.[382] In these studies OKW/Chi evidently had a hand because it is known that special cryptanalytic machinery, such as OKW/Chi had and the Army did not have, was used in the solution.[383] These investigations led to the production of the T-52 D. Security work, mainly by Doering, continued, and early in 1943 he

[379] I-31, 16. See I-57 for a paper by Liebknecht on his work at Wa Pruef 7 on the SZ 40, SZ 42, SFM T52 etc.

[380] I-31, 14.

[381] I-45, p 12.

[382] I-58, 6.

[383] I-45, 13 ff. On page 13 Huettenhain states: "Meanwhile the different deciphering machines (Entzifferungs hilfsgeraete) had shown their worth in solving cryptographic problems. Experiences had been gained particularly about the good work of these deciphering aids even at high speeds. With these prerequisites it was possible to give a method with which T 52 C could be solved by employing deciphering machines."

showed that the T-52 D was not secure either, and as a result, the T-52 E was produced.[384] It is likely that Huettenhain's section had some part in these researches, or at least that Huettenhain kept abreast of developments. He knew, for example, that T-52 D and E messages could be read on a depth of ten without a crib.[385] There follows the familiar story about difficulties in getting the Army to introduce and use the improved devices. The original Army position was that security did not make any difference with the teleprinter anyway because the signals went over lines and could not be intercepted. In the summer of 1942, for example, the T-52 A and B, shown to be woefully insecure three years earlier, were still being used, and the T-52 C, with all its faults, was being distributed. Evidence of line tapping found in Paris in the years 1942 and 1943 did something to arouse the Army signal authorities to the necessity for teleprinter security.[386] But again, the Germans were too late with their cipher development. The newly developed machines could not be generally introduced.

Throughout the war there was considerable interest in Germany in ciphony. The authority chiefly interested during most of the war was the war was the Army Ordnance Development and Testing Group, Signal Branch (Wa Pruef 7), which was in these matters represented by Liebknecht, whom we have already met in connection with teleprinter security devices. Liebknecht kept abreast of the experiments being conducted for the Army at the Vierling Laboratories. Various other German firms and individuals, for example, Siemens, which were also concerned with teleprinter security, worked more or less independently on the problem. OKW/Chi was not directly concerned, although Huettenhain and perhaps some of his associates were interested spectators.[387] The first effort at co-ordination was made in the summer of 1943 when all authorities and firms engaged in the development of speech encipherment were called together by Fellgiebel.[388] The aim of the meeting was to eliminate

[384] I-78, 11-12.

[385] I-31, p 14.

[386] I-78, 11 ff.

[387] I-20, par. 30 ff.

[388] I-44, 2.

overlapping work and to make it clear just what the Armed Forces wanted. They wanted: (1) As an immediate development, an improvement in their present ciphony methods. Here they would be willing to accept something very imperfect, if it could be got out quickly - and if interception were difficult; (2) as a long-term project, an absolutely secure system of special encipherment. The Army Ordnance Development and Testing Group, Signal Branch (Wa Pruef 7) had a representative at these meetings, but apparently OKW/Chi did not. Finally, in November 1944, Praun, the new Chief Signal Officer of the Armed Forces (Chef WNV), commissioned OKW/Chi to check developments in ciphony. This move was obviously a part of the program of Praun and Gimmler, whereby OKW/Chi was to be the central authority for all cryptographic materials in Germany. One of the Chi-conferences was devoted to ciphony, but again Chi was too late. "Owing to the general war situation", said Huettenhain and Fricke, "it was no longer possible to do this in such a way that technical details could be reliably reconstructed."[389]

Any arrangement for assuring a high degree of cryptographic security necessarily involves three steps:

the systems actually in use must be put into the hands of skilled cryptanalysts who are able to judge their effectiveness;

they must be thoroughly examined by these cryptanalysts, and if they are accepted as usable, the regulations for their use must be produced by the experts;

the recommendations of the cryptanalysts regarding acceptance or rejection of systems and regarding the use of systems finally accepted must be adequately enforced.

One can arrive at some conclusion regarding the success or failure of the German security effort by examining what they accomplished under these three points:

With regard to point one, the Germans were largely a failure. When the war began, the administration of German cryptographic systems was in a chaotic state. The signal authority of each branch of the armed forces did pretty much as it pleased, at times without regard to the recommendation of the cryptanalytic authorities. It will be recalled that prior to October, 1943, OKW/Chi, the highest-level German

[389] I-44, 2.

cryptologic agency, had no authority whatever to examine systems used by the branches of the armed forces. The Keitel order of October, 1943, which required at least the opinion of OKW/Chi before any system was adopted by any of the separate branches, was apparently very incompletely observed. Huettenhain states as a general truth, apparently valid for the entire course of the war, that "no compulsion was put on anyone to apply to OKW/Chi for security tests, except where the Army was concerned(to Fricke), and many organizations never thought of doing so."[390] After his accession to office in the summer of 1944, Gimmler seems to have made a real effort to establish OKW/Chi as a security authority for the separate branches. This effort came too late. Conditions were too chaotic for a complete examination of existing German systems, the constant air attacks made the mass production of any new cipher device almost impossible.

In regard to the second point, despite the lack of any real authority in the matter, OKW/Chi did manage to examine fairly thoroughly at least the leading Army and Air Force systems. They appraised correctly the weaknesses of the commercial and "counter" models of the Enigma. They at least saw that the plugboard Enigma was not invulnerable to attack. Huettenhain's early remark to interrogators to the effect that they knew the Enigma to be secure should not perhaps be taken too seriously.[391] One might even suggest that he was trying to trap his captors into some kind of an admission. Huettenhain's later statement, however, is to be taken at its face value: the official judgment of OKW/Chi was that the plugboard Enigma was secure if the instructions were observed. The development of such devices as the changeable turnover rotor, and the Enigma plugboard permuter, as well as the consideration of the various substitutes for the Enigma, such as the SG-39 and the SG-41, was not due to any immediate concern that they felt for the security of the cipher systems, but was intended to provide against future possibilities.

[390] I-31, 16. The translation of the document: "Never thought of doing so" is probably a faulty translation of the German idiom: "Hachten gar nichtdaran."

[391] I-2, p 4.

84

In his final decision on the Enigma, Huettenhain betrays a certain academic aloofness and, one is tempted to say, smugness, which may have been his leading flaw as a cryptographer. The standard mathematical tests had been applied to the device and regulations laid down on the basis of these tests. The possibility of other attacks not arising from a standard application of well-known mathematical procedures, but based on new discoveries, never seems to have been seriously considered by him. Allied to this academic attitude is the curious lack of interest which Huettenhain and the other German cryptographers seemed to have shown in the actual size of the Allied cryptanalytic effort against the German systems. The Germans knew of the Deuxième Bureau. They knew nothing, however, of English cryptanalysis - "the English, of course are notoriously stupid." - All they knew about American cryptanalysis they had learned from Yardley's Black Chamber.[392] One prisoner-of-war captured by the Germans in North Africa mentioned a very large park of IBM Machines operated jointly by the British and Americans. This hint was never followed up.[393]

This academic aloofness of OKW/Chi was probably only partly responsible for the almost complete German failure with regard to point three. It was only with the greatest difficulty that devices demonstrably insecure like the T-52 A and B were actually withdrawn from use, or new and secure devices introduced. The regulations for the use of cipher devices, once they had left the hands of OKW/Chi, were entirely outside their competence.[394] The Army refused to submit live traffic to the cryptanalysts for analysis or monitoring from a security point of view. Gimmler's insistence on a more vital connection between the security center and the troops in the field, a connection, it will be recalled, that was to be carried out through Capt. Bernsdorff's sub-section, was amply justified. But the scheme, though good, was too late. By January, 1945, conditions were too chaotic to put it into effect. The chance for effective security control had passed.

[392] I-48, 2.

[393] I-84, 6.

[394] I-20, par. 11. Fricke (I-20 par. 28) states that Oberpostrat Halder in the office of the Military Attaché at Stockholm astonished OKW/Chi by asking that T 52 keys be sent in clear !

9. Miscellaneous Operations. a. Broadcast Monitoring: The department located at the Fehrbelliner Platz, in Berlin, (finally called Section VI) put out its findings in a daily newspaper called the "Chi Nachrichten" ("Chi Reports").[395] These reports were divided into sections devoted to military affairs, economic affairs, and so on, with one section given over to comments. The material for the reports came from the news broadcasts and other plain-language material picked up by the broadcast intercepting system. Originally, these reports had a fairly wide distribution. Every section in OKW/Chi got a copy, and probably many of the higher ups. After Stalingrad, when the news became less favorable from the German point of view, the Chi Reports received increasingly narrow distribution until finally Keitel's approval had to be obtained before anyone could receive a copy. In effect, Keitel became the distribution agency for the Reports. One copy, however, continued to go to the OKW/Chi Archives, and the head of the Archives, Dr. Schaedel, gave Gimmler a daily briefing on the news.

Besides the Chi Reports the monitoring section published special reports which it sent regularly to interested authorities. Russian news, for example, was regularly passed on to the Department of Armed Forces Propaganda which used it as material for its newspaper for the anti-Soviet Russian troops fighting on the German side. For some time, previous to 6 June 1944, all references to the coming invasion were compiled into a single report which was sent daily to the "Department of Foreign Armies West" (Abteilung Fremde Heere West). References to German prisoners-of-war in Allied hands were also included in a special report for separate distribution. The information was probably passed on eventually to the relatives of the prisoners, and thus the effectiveness of the PW broadcasts as bait to the German public to listen to Allied propaganda broadcasts was probably destroyed.

b. Attacks on Ciphony Devices: One of the most interesting items to appear in the Chi Reports was doubtless political conversations between Churchill and Roosevelt, carried on over a radio telephone link between London and Washington. The German informants state that this link was evidently not intended to have any very high degree of security, since an

[395] I-150, 11. For a discussion of the Chi-Nachrichlon see also I-96, 16.

operator warned the conversing parties whenever the talk approached highly secret matters. The transmission, however, was not in clear, but scrambled. The intercept took place at the broadcast monitoring station at Ludwigsfelde by means of a descrambling apparatus developed by the Army Ordnance Development and Testing Group, Signal Branch (Wa Pruef 7). This apparatus is said to have been completely effective, and changes in the key of the scrambler could be easily followed by turning a few knobs.[396]

In June, 1944, the Army cryptanalyst, Buggisch, was assigned to the experimental intercept station at Staats, conducted by the Army Ordnance Development and Testing Group, Signal Branch (Wa Pruef 7). Here his mission was to study the Russian scrambler known as X^2.[397] Apparently at the time of the organizational changes of November, 1944, Buggisch became a member of OKW/Chi. With the exception of a six-weeks stay in Berlin, he continued his work at Staats.[398] He was not successful in solving the scrambler. Some interest at OKW/Chi was aroused by a ciphony device recovered intact from a crashed American Mustang plane. This device was kept on an airfield for six months before it finally was identified as being a cipher device, and it reached OKW/Chi in the spring of 1945. There it was handed over to the Army Ordnance Department (HWA) where it was worked on by Buggisch and a Dr. Lotze.[399] Their investigations are said to have been inconclusive. It was possible to reconstruct the key setting from

[396] I-84, 6; I-118, 4. In I-88 Mr. K. Vetterlein of Abt IIIc of the Research Institute of the Reichspost Ministry revealed that the Germans had constructed apparatus which was used to restore the "scrambled" radio circuits in use between Britain and the United States to complete intelligibility. Vetterlein started work in 1940, by 1942 the equipment was working on a 24-hour basis at Kelheim in the Munich area. The records of the speech were sent to the Propaganda Minister at Berlin. By April 1945 they had also succeeded in deciphering to some extent teletype messages sent over the same circuit. The work of Vetterlein and the Reichspost evidently had no connection with the OKW effort at Ludwigsfelde.

[397] I-73, 2.

[398] I-31, 12. I-58, 4.

[399] I-31, 12; I-118, 4.

intercepted oscillograms. But it was doubtful whether solution could have been rapid enough to be of any use during an actual fighting operation.

c. Training: Training was a regular part of the operations of OKW/Chi. Occasionally, special courses were given. Herold's training tour in 1941 may be recalled in this connection. Kettler's report mentions that, in the Spring of 1944, some Bulgarian officers were given a special course in elementary cryptology, and some German Air Force officers, a special advanced course.[400] Most of the training, however, was for the benefit of OKW/Chi's own personnel. Huettenhain mentions that when he first came to the cipher section, in 1937, he was allocated to a training section for the first six months. There he worked on low-grade Spanish government military systems for practice.[401] For members of the language sections the training procedure, which had been followed since as early as 1930, was somewhat different.[402] These members came to OKW/Chi trained in the language in which they were to work, and it is likely that during the war the military personnel was drawn from such special Army language training units as the Interpreters' Replacement and Training Battalion, in Berlin. Once in OKW/Chi, they were introduced to cryptanalysis gradually, concurrently with their work as linguists. A course was conducted for two days per week during the six winter months. Each new member was expected to attend this course for two winters. During the first winter, substitution ciphers were studied; during the second, transposition. Originally, the course was conducted by Fenner, than by Fenner and Wendland. During the war, it was conducted by Wendland and Huettenhain. Attendance at these courses was about three to twelve persons per winter. This indicates that only the more prominent personnel in the language sections were given the courses. Candidates received into the research cryptanalytic section got two to four months continuous training, at the end of which they were supposed to be able to tackle unsolved problems. In the summer of 1943, Huettenhain started an advanced cryptanalytic course for which eight of the most able cryptanalysts were detached from the language sections.[403]

[400] DF-9, 3.

[401] I-31, 2.

[402] I-118, 2, 3.

[403] Cf. Beyreuther's statement (I-150, 9) that he had heard about Dr. Huettenhain giving lectures about decoding work.

Those who were admitted were expected to be able to break systems independently in the language sections. The scheme was perhaps to relieve pressure on the research section, which was becoming increasingly involved with security problems. The course met for three two-hour periods each week but the total duration was not fixed. The syllabus included mathematical bases for cryptanalytic work, related cryptanalytic problems, machine ciphers, IBM and other cryptanalytic machines, German ciphers, practical work. Members of the course were expected to do a considerable amount of independent research. In November, 1944, because of the general situation, the course was dropped.

10. OKW/Chi's relations with the Signal Intelligence Services of Army, Navy, and Air Force. These varied with the field of effort. In the matter of Intercept, and in Security Scrutiny, OKW/Chi actually exercised some control over the other three agencies; but in the field of cryptanalysis the material was divided so that each agency had its own logical assignment. Army cryptanalysts attacked enemy army systems; Navy cryptanalysts attacked enemy naval systems; Air Force cryptanalysts attacked enemy air force systems. OKW/Chi left the Army, Navy, and Air Force systems almost completely alone and worked on diplomatic and military attaché traffic. This is not to say that there was no liaison among the four agencies in cryptanalytic matters; there was both liaison and cooperation. But OKW/Chi did not control the activities of the other Signal Intelligence Services in this field.

In general, no material was passed from the branches to OKW/Chi. Kettler was emphatic on this point.[411] This arrangement seems to have held throughout the war with some apparent exceptions. Dettmann, for instance, told the interrogators that in the years 1942 and 1943 his army unit had passed considerable Russian five-letter traffic to OKW/Chi.[412] The traffic in question was probably diplomatic or at least was suspected of being diplomatic. Capt. Herold, it will be recalled, stated that his air intercept unit at Varna passed material back to Berlin, to OKW/Chi.[413] If Herold was not mistaken,

[411] I-21, p 1.

[412] I-116, 2.

[413] I-130, 13.

this was wholly exceptional. The special direction to the separate branches in the Praun order of 5 September 1944 to pass on diplomatic material to OKW suggests that there may have been some difficulty in keeping the cryptological services of the individual branches from poaching on OKW/Chi's own preserves.

Occasionally Huettenhain seems to have been consulted about the cryptanalytic difficulties of the separate branches. This was, however, a purely informal matter. Even in the case of the M-209 of the United States of America, British Typex, and the "big American Machine", OKW/Chi was not called in by the Agencies working on them. The German Army, Navy, and Air Force worked independently on the M-209 of the U.S. Army, Navy, and Air Force, and constantly exchanged among themselves all technical data, but OKW/Chi took up the study of the M-209 only in passing and because it might be used for diplomatic traffic sometime in the future.

An attempt of OKW/Chi to achieve a certain amount of coordination seems to have been made in the field of intercept. It has already been pointed out that the original plan seems to have been to subordinate all intercept stations in neutral countries to OKW. Herold's experiences at Varna have already been mentioned.[414] Even when that plan was in its early stages, the German Navy refused to participate, and we must assume that OKW/Chi had no real authority to compel its cooperation. The plan was a failure. By the end of the war, only remnants of the original scheme, such as the existence of an OKW and Navy intercept station on the same site near Seville, remained. However, according to Keitel, OKW/Chi was the intercept clearing house, when needed, for all the Services. The intercept systems of the separate branches were apparently never an important source of traffic in OKW's own field. We have already seen that Col. Randewig had a scheme very early in the war for an extensive interservice intercept structure. Randewig's plan remained a dream. His memoranda to the Chief Signal Officer of OKW seem to have been considered a nuisance. No such extensive plan as his was ever even considered by OKW/Chi.

The development of cryptographic devices for use by the troops was originally left entirely to the individual branches. It has already been noted that development was partly taken over from the Army in the autumn of 1944. The other branches kept their right to originate until the end, although OKW/Chi had the right of review.

[414] I-130, 13.

OKW/Chi's greatest effort to assert its authority as a coordinating agency was made in the field of security scrutiny. The development of this effort is a basic element in the history of the organization of OKW/Chi and has been traced. It is worthy of note that despite Keitel's order of October 1943, little real effort was made by OKW/Chi to assume effective supervision of the security of all branches until Gimmler took office almost a year later.[415] In August 1944, the representatives of the separate branches met those of OKW/Chi at Chi-conferences. After August 1944, there was insufficient time left to overcome the difficulties caused by the neglect of five years. The minutes of some of the Chi-conferences are available, and it is apparent that not very much was accomplished. The first meeting of which we have a record was largely devoted to a discussion of OKW/Chi's authority in matters of security scrutiny. The other meetings were filled with talks of a more or less general nature by OKW/Chi's leading cryptanalysts. No new devices were submitted to OKW/Chi by the separate branches for security testing during this period, because the deterioration of German production made it impossible to introduce any new devices. In the security scrutiny of cryptographic systems already employed by the separate branches nothing seems to have been accomplished. As we have seen, the theoretical limitations of these systems were increasingly apparent to OKW/Chi. The Chi-conferences never succeeded in producing any actual traffic for examination, and apparently left the adherence of the German troops to the cryptographic regulations a matter of pious hope.

We now turn to a separate examination of OKW/Chi's relations to the Signal Intelligence Services of each of the separate branches.

Relations were closest with the Signal Intelligence Service of the Army. This is to be expected in view of the fact that the whole OKW structure was more intimately associated with the Army than with the Navy or the Air Force. The Chief Signal Officer of the Supreme Command of the Armed Forces (Chef WNV) also acted as Chief Signal Officer of the Army (Chef HNW). The officers who controlled OKW/Chi and the Signal Intelligence Service of the Army were drawn from the same set of regular German signal officers. Boetzel, who ended the war as head of the Army Signal Intelligence Service, had once been second in

[415] See I-84, 4.

command of OKW/Chi. Before he became head of OKW/Chi, Kettler had been associated with an Army Signal Intelligence Unit. For a while, he had been head of the principal Army intercept unit in the east. Mettig, who ended the war as second in command of OKW/Chi, had previously been head of the Army cryptanalytic agency. Furthermore, OKW/Chi and the highest echelon Army cryptanalytic agency were originally located very close to each other in Berlin, in the Tirpitzufer section. So close was the liaison between Army and OKW on command level that an Italian captain, Bigi, who visited the German Signal Intelligence Services in December 1942, seems to have thought that OKW/Chi and the Army cryptanalytic agency were actually one unit. When he was captured much later, this Italian told interrogators that German signal intelligence was under Colonel Kempf, and that subordinate to Kempf was Fenner who was in charge of diplomatic material and Major Mang who was in charge of military material.[416] We now know that Bigi was quite wrong. Kempf was head of OKW/Chi in December 1942; Fenner was subordinate to him, and in charge of cryptanalysis. Mang was head of the Army cryptanalytic agency and in no way subordinate to Kempf. But the fact that Bigi could have made this mistake indicates that the actual cooperation between these two agencies was extremely close. The officers seemed to have been well satisfied with the relations between the Army cryptanalytic agency and OKW/Chi. Huettenhain, on the other hand, who represented the civilian specialist point of view, was not so well satisfied. He told interrogators that "liaison with OKH was not such as the younger men would have wished, nor such as would be natural in scientific work. But the"Higher-ups" had a private war on and liaison among specialists was discouraged."[417] One may perhaps doubt that this statement means much more than that the organizational lines were held and indiscriminate contact between the two services prevented. Actually Huettenhain himself seems to have worked most intimately with the Army cryptanalysts. He knew a great deal about special Army problems, such as the work on Typex, which were no official concern whatever of OKW/Chi. Buggisch, one of the leading Army cryptanalysts, seems likewise to have had a very good knowledge of what went on at OKW/Chi. He mentions conferences with the OKW/Chi specialists on the security of German cryptographic devices and on the

[416] IF-1517 is Captain Bigi's report on German signal intelligence.

[417] I-31, p 10.

93

Hagelin machine in the summer of 1943, long before the official Chi-conferences were started.[418] He also speaks of a visit which he paid to the cryptanalytic machine section of OKW/Chi.[419] For a while, Army cryptographic devices seem to have been submitted to a double security check, one by the Army and one by OKW/Chi.[420] This duplication of effort was eliminated when the Army security people were incorporated into OKW/Chi in November 1944. The intimate liaison between the Army and OKW/Chi seems to have existed only on a higher level, particularly with regard to security. OKW/Chi specialists were never permitted to know precisely what was going on in the field. The Army cryptanalysts, moreover, apparently labored under the same difficulties. Fricke says that the Army had been using an amazingly insecure system, (the socalled <u>Barbaraschluessel</u> or "Barbara Keys") for weather traffic from 1939 to 1944. It was not until that late date (1944) that OKW/Chi heard about it.[421] Presumably, the Army cryptanalysts had not heard about it either.

Contact with the Air Force was more lax. The head of the Air Force Signal Intelligence Service, Lt. Col. Friedrich, a prisoner of TICOM, was asked about his relations with OKW/Chi. Although he was an extraordinarily communicative prisoner, on the subject of OKW he could give very little information. Apparently this was because he knew very little about the organization and was rather bored by it. He remembered that decoded traffic had been sent to him by OKW/Chi but said it was of no use whatever to him and he stopped reading it.[422] His cryptanalysts, he said, "got nothing from OKW."[423]

418 I-58, 3; I-72, 6.

419 I-58, 3.

420 Buggisch states (I-72, 6), "The types of small Hagelin known in the year 41 (C 36 and BC 38) did not satisfy the security demands set by OKW/Chi and OKH/In 7."

421 I-20, p 7.

422 I-13, 6.

423 I-13, 1.

(Friedrich made it very clear that he did not think very much in general of cryptanalysts or of cryptanalysis). There was a little more contact than he implies. Mettig told his first interrogator that he had had some liaison with Dr. Voegele, chief cryptanalyst of the German Air Force.[424] Voegele himself was interrogated later and gave some details of what this liaison actually amounted to. He had worked in the early part of the war on the British Government Telegraph Code and later got a photo copy of it from OKW.[425] In 1940 and 1942, he had exchanged traffic in the Interdepartmental Cypher, results of the reconstruction of the recipher book used with it with OKW as well as with the Navy.[426] In 1945, messages and items in a United States code were exchanged with OKW and the Army.[427] He also had on order from OKW a cryptanalytic machine employed for an attack on the American strip cipher.[428] Apparently he never received the machine; but he was rather dubious about its efficiency in any case. He said he could get along well enough on American strip with IBM machinery. Voegele showed OKW as well as the Foreign Office the method of attack on the American strip cipher which his organization had developed.[429] He did not know what use, if any, OKW/Chi had made of this method. Huettenhain says that he gave some assistance to the GAF weather service in their attack on an English meteorological system.[430] This assistance consisted in putting at their disposal a cryptanalytic device which Huettenhain called the Bigrammsuchgeraet (digraph "weight" recorder). Even with the assistance of Huettenhain and his machine, however, the weather service failed to solve

[424] I-17, 2.

[425] I-112, 6.

[426] I-119, 4.

[427] I-112, 9.

[428] I-112, 4.

[429] I-119, 3.

[430] I-31, 4; I-84, p 2, p 7.

the cipher. One cryptographic achievement of the German Air Force was the development of the Enigma plugboard permuter. This device seems to have been developed entirely by the Air Force and initial research on the mathematical aspects of the machine was carried out by them. Later on, however, OKW/Chi did give some help in mathematical research on the device.[431]

The Navy was the most aloof of the services. It had worked on the Interdepartmental Cypher and sent representatives to the Chi-conferences, but otherwise, it had little connection with OKW/Chi. The chief cryptanalyst of the Navy, Tranow, stated that OKW/Chi was kept informed of the cryptanalytic work carried out by the Navy cryptanalytic agency.[432] This was required, it will be recalled, by the Praun order of 5 September 1944. Tranow is emphatic, however, in his statement that no naval research problems were referred to OKW/Chi.[433] The Navy received some raw traffic intercepted by OKW, which had been passed over commercial circuits. They had adopted at least one of the cryptanalytic devices developed by OKW/Chi, the so-called Roller apparatus.[434] One of the Navy ratings had devised some improvements for the apparatus and was ordered to cooperate with OKW/Chi in developing these.[435] Otherwise, contact seems to have consisted of informal conversation between Tranow and Huettenhain. It was in one of these conversations that Tranow learned from Huettenhain that the exiled Polish Government in London used a stencil system somewhat similar to the British Naval System.[436]

[431] I-57, 8.

[432] I-93, 4.

[433] I-93, 4.

[434] I-37, 3.

[435] D-45, 5. From a report of 4/SKL, dated 6/3/44. "FK. Gfr. Zimmermann, of Section III Fq, submitted within the last few weeks a proposal for a printing synthetic producing machine [Rollmaschine]. Zimmermann was instructed by OKW/Chi, where new developments are worked out for the branches of the armed forces, to have a prototype ready within 3 weeks in order to fix the final model."

[436] I-93, 25.

DOCID: 3560827

11. OKW/Chi and other German High-Level Signal Intelligence Agencies. When attacks on enemy service systems were assigned to the separate branches and OKW/Chi assumed responsibility for enemy and neutral diplomatic systems, OKW/Chi definitely became the competitor of two other German high-level signal intelligence agencies, Goering's Research Bureau (hereafter indicated by FA, the abbreviation for Forschungsamt), and the Foreign Office Cryptanalytic Section (Pers ZS).

Since 1933, Goering's Research Bureau (the FA) had apparently given some attention to diplomatic material as well as dabbled in a great many other things. Since World War I, the German Foreign Office had maintained a cryptanalytic bureau whose main commitment was attack on diplomatic traffic. One of the problems of OKW/Chi was, consequently, to establish its position in the face of these agencies which had been longer in the field.

Goering's Research Bureau (the FA) had started in a fashion likely to prejudice its relations with OKW/Chi. It will be recalled that the FA owed its existence to the fact that Schapper and other members of the Abwehr Cipher Section had gone to Goering and proposed a new intelligence organization. They said at the time that the older organization was inefficient and involved in departmental politics.[437] They apparently kept this opinion until the end of the war. Schapper's remarks on OKW/Chi have already been noted. His colleague, Seifert, had an equally low opinion of OKW/Chi and told the interrogators that Goering's Research Bureau (the FA) had been established "to provide diplomatic and commercial intelligence of an absolutely reliable kind... and to insure..the elimination of all bias which might have resulted from association with the old established ministries.[438] Hermann Goering expressed particular scorn for OKW/Chi "the most junior member of the family".[439] The personnel of OKW/Chi, on the other hand, seem to have returned scorn for scorn. Mettig stated that Fenner, who seems to have been in charge of liaison with other cryptologic agencies,

437 IF-15, p 20.

438 I-54, 3.

439 I-143, 15.

97

felt particularly strongly on the subject of Goering's Research Bureau (the FA), probably because it had been established by his former subordinate, Schapper.[440] Huettenhain also refers to Fenner's particularly violent "prejudice". He further said that some personnel of OKW/Chi had gone over to Goering's Research Bureau (the FA) and that they were regarded in OKW/Chi as people who had "deserted the ship". He knew Paetzel and had discussed cryptanalytic work with him. His personal impression was that Goering's people knew little in the field of cryptanalysis. "They employed no mathematicians".[441] Fricke denied that he had ever known any of the personnel of Goering's Research Bureau (the FA) until he was brought together with them as a prisoner at the end of the war. They had a bad name, he said, at OKW/Chi. His personal opinion was that they were a big name with nothing behind it. The interrogators told Fricke that Goering's Research Bureau (the FA) employed twenty-five hundred people. He replied, "For their deciphering they should have needed a handful. They must have had other work to do, but what the devil could they have been doing with twenty-five hundred people?".[442]

The chiefs of both services professed a willingness to cooperate, but each accused the other of failing to do so. Schapper told his interrogators that at the beginning of the war he wished his work to become a general intelligence bureau but that his competitors, the Foreign Office and OKW/Chi, refused.[443] He was quite willing, he said, to work with Col. Kettler, but this willingness was not reciprocated. Kettler, on the other hand, said, "the Forschungsamt monitored Press traffic. It carried out cryptographic work but I do not know what it was. We tried to work together but the Forschungsamt refused for reasons unknown to me.[444]

[440] I-131, 3.

[441] I-31, 10.

[442] I-20, p 8.

[443] IF-15, p 17.

[444] I-21, p 1.

In view of this mutual feeling, it is surprising to find that there actually was considerable cooperation with Goering's Research Bureau (the FA). The most conclusive evidence of this is that, according to Kettler's report, one-third of the raw traffic reaching OKW/Chi in the Spring of 1944 came from Goering's Research Bureau (the FA). It is probable that a similar proportion came during the other periods for which we have no record. Goering's Research Bureau (the FA) was probably not interested in cryptographic development but, despite this fact, it was represented at Gimmler's Chi-conferences. Their representative was Kroeger, a leading machine specialist,[445] who had, according to Paetzel, broken the Finnish Hagelin.[446] In cryptanalysis, however, cooperation was non-existent.[446] On the other hand, the cryptanalytic machines developed by OKW/Chi were made available to all German cryptanalytic agencies except the FA.[447] Intelligence obtained by Goering's Research Bureau (the FA) from cryptanalytic and other activity[448] was passed on to the OKW directly by the liaison officer.[448] OKW/Chi was by-passed.

The Foreign Office Cryptanalytic Section (Pers ZS) was senior to OKW/Chi. There is no doubt that OKW/Chi had intruded on its domain when it took over diplomatic traffic. This aspect of the relations between the two organizations is particularly stressed by Specialist Karstien, who of all the Foreign Office Cryptanalytic Section (Pers ZS) personnel seems to have felt most strongly against OKW/Chi.[449] The attitude of the other members of the Foreign Office Cryptanalytic Section (Pers ZS) was one of mild contempt. They definitely felt that they were an older organization, that they had a greater number of able people, and that they were in general more competent. This feeling of superiority was tinged with a certain bitterness because they felt that their efforts were unappreciated in higher quarters and that they were discriminated against in such matters as

[445] I-54, 2.

[446] I-54, 4.

[447] I-31, p 10.

[448] Klautschke, liaison officer to OKW, OKM, OKL, OKH was concerned solely with passing intelligence and intelligence requests. There was no liaison on cryptanalytic matters as far as he knew (I-54, 4).

[449] I-22, 9.

procurement of additional personnel. Prof. Rohrbach, who was the principal spokesman for the captured Foreign Office Cryptanalytic Section (Pers ZS) people, was at great pains to point out that Rave, Hierer, Grosse, and Schroeder, who were OKW/Chi personnel working with the Foreign Office Cryptanalytic Section (Pers ZS) and captured with them, were people of an inferior type who had been sent to the Foreign Office Cryptanalytic Section (Pers ZS) for training. "He spoke of them", the interrogator remarked, "with obvious distaste."[450] Rohrbach was careful to point out that when Zastrow, the expert on U.S.A. systems, was detached from the Foreign Office Cryptanalytic Section (Pers ZS) to OKW/Chi his status was entirely different. He had gone to OKW/Chi not for training but to lend his expert assistance to the junior organization. It is noteworthy that this mild contempt was not reciprocated by OKW/Chi. As spokesman for the OKW/Chi party detached to the Foreign Office Cryptanalytic Section (pers ZS), Rave spoke in the most flattering terms of his hosts. OKW/Chi, he said, had neither the long experience nor the "expertise" which the Foreign Office Cryptanalytic Section (Pers ZS) possessed although Fenner and a small party had been engaged on this work in time of peace.[451] Huettenhain had seen the papers which Schauffler of the Foreign Office Cryptanalytic Section (Pers ZS) had written on the mathematical aspects of cryptanalysis.[452] Although he did not speak of them with a high regard, he at least does not hold them in contempt. At one time Huettenhain seems to have considered contributing papers on cryptologic subjects to the Foreign Office Cryptanalytic Section (Pers ZS) publication. Nothing came of this, however, because Fenner discouraged it for reasons of security.

Kettler stated that he considered the relations of OKW/-Chi with the Foreign Office Cryptanalytic Section (Pers ZS) good,[453] and there is considerable evidence that a high degree of cooperation was achieved and the delicate problems arising

[450] I-22, 7, 11.

[451] I-22, 8.

[452] I-31, 11.

[453] I-21, p 2.

from the fact that both organizations were committed to the same material were partly met. In the case of the American strip system, for example, the Foreign Office Cryptanalytic Section (Pers ZS) worked on circular traffic, OKW/Chi on point to point traffic.[454] When both organizations were breaking the older Japanese cipher machine, OKW/Chi worked on odd days, the Foreign Office Cryptanalytic Section (Pers ZS) on even.[455] Results were exchanged. There was also a division of labor among the language sections on some book-breaking problems and there were occasionally some exchanges of personnel. Huettenhain and his mathematicians had worked with the Foreign Office Cryptanalytic Section (Pers ZS) research party. He felt that a satisfactory division of labor had been achieved.[456] Fenner directed liaison for OKW/Chi and Senior Specialist Paschke for the Foreign Office.[457] The head of the Foreign Office Cryptanalytic Section (Pers ZS), Minister Selchow, is said to have been opposed to too intimate a relationship.[458] It is known that he refused to permit the cryptographic system developed by his department for Foreign Office use to be turned over to OKW/Chi for security scrutiny. The actual debt of OKW/Chi to the Foreign Office Cryptanalytic Section (Pers ZS) cryptanalysts is hard to assess, particularly in view of the fact that the leading members of the OKW/Chi language sections, Fenner, Wendland, and Nowopaschenny, were not captured and interrogated. On the basis of the material available, however, it seems that that debt is considerable. The Foreign Office Cryptanalytic Section (Pers Z S) gives the impression of being old, conservative, slow-moving but able. It was a cipher party of the old type such as Fenner's had been previous to the outbreak of the war. It had never been subject to the dynamic and somewhat feverish expansion that had been the lot of OKW/Chi, where emphasis had been changed from intelligence to security, and

[454] I-31, 10.

[455] I-31, p 11.

[456] I-31, 10.

[457] I-22, 8.

[458] I-22, 8.

101

where a great many of the leading cryptanalytic personnel had been taken into purely cryptographic research. In the Foreign Office Cryptanalytic Section (Pers Z S), the mathematicians existed solely to assist the crypto-linguists. The linguists themselves were apparently more carefully selected, older, and better trained than those of OKW/Chi. It is very likely that in the exchange of results, OKW/Chi received more than it gave. It is known that the initial break into the older Japanese machine was made by the Foreign Office Cryptanalytic Section (Pers ZS).[459] It is possible that they also were the first to break the American strip system, as Rohrbach so emphatically claims.[460] Two South African codes were worked on jointly by OKW/Chi and the Foreign Office Cryptanalytic Section (Pers Z S), with the latter taking the lead. On the other side of the ledger is the loan by OKW/Chi to the Foreign Office Cryptanalytic Section (Pers Z S) of a Brazilian, a Mexican, and a Portuguese compromised code for photographing. Prior to the compromise of the Portuguese code, the two agencies had regularly exchanged group meanings.[461] Where quality and expertness were primary considerations as in initial attacks on cipher systems, and in more difficult book breaking problems, the Foreign Office Cryptanalytic Section (Pers Z S) was superior to its military colleague. When a problem had reached the mass production stage, however, OKW/Chi was able to profit by the comparative ease with which it could obtain partly trained, medium-grade personnel.[462]

12. Liaison with Foreign Signal Intelligence Agencies. In the matter of liaison with the signal intelligence agencies of Germany's allies, the authority of OKW/Chi seems to have been partly recognized. Fenner had been working for a number of years previous to the outbreak of the war to establish

[459] I-22, p 2, 7, 16.

[460] I-89.

[461] D 16 Report 2 P 3; Report 4 P 3, 5.

[462] Cf. Also the statement (I-22, 13) "If when a new system was broken, it was discovered that traffic dealt mainly with matters outside the diplomatic field, it was handed over to OKW for exploitation."

Y02

DOCID: 3560827

firm relationship between OKW/Chi and Germany's probable future allies. There is some evidence that the signal intelligence agencies of the Army, Navy, and Air Force were expected to approach their allied counterparts through OKW/Chi. Thus Friedrich, head of the Air Force signal intelligence, told interrogators that he had no liaison with the Japanese authorities and that such liaison took place only through OKW/Chi.[463] Voegele, the chief cryptanalyst of the Air Force, stated that he visited Berlin once in January and again in February 1942 for cryptographic discussions with Hayashi, the Japanese representative, but that the meeting never actually took place. Voegele believed that the discussions were prevented by Kempf, who was the head of OKW/Chi at the time.[464] To be sure, the Army had independent relations with the more reliable axis allies, the Italians and particularly the Finns. It is clear from the case of Bigi, however, that insofar as these relations were conducted on a high level, OKW/Chi had a hand in them. Bigi, it will be recalled, was never clear as to whether his relations were with OKW/Chi or the Army.[465] It is noteworthy, too, that the members of OKW/Chi were well acquainted with the Finnish liaison officers stationed with the army cryptanalytic agency.

a. Austria:

Before the annexation, Austria is said to have had a small but efficient cryptologic office. This was located in Vienna and headed by a Mr. Seifert. It had a small staff which dealt with the traffic of Italy, Rumania, Greece, Jugoslavia, Bulgaria, Turkey, Poland, and Czechoslovakia.[466] It is said that these organizations had close contact with OKW/-Chi even during the period of tension preceding the Anschluss. Huettenhain, from whom this information is derived, does not know precisely what this contact amounted to. At the time of the Anschluss, Gen. Fellgiebel and Fenner paid a visit to the

[463] I-29, 3.

[464] I-119, 6.

[465] See above, page ___.

[466] I-118, 3.

Austrian cipher office and brought the best personnel to Berlin where they were incorporated into OKW/Chi. Seifert became a high ranking civil servant (principal specialist, Ministerialrat) and specialist in book-breaking.[467]

b. Japan:

With representatives of the Japanese signal intelligence, a more or less astute sparring went on from the time of Japan's entry into the war. In 1942, one of the leading Japanese cryptanalysts, Colonel (later General) Hayashi, happened to be in Berlin. Unable to return home, he became Japanese Military Attaché in Budapest. During his stay in Berlin, he arranged for an exchange of material with OKW/Chi and a relationship was started between the head of OKW/Chi and the Japanese representative in Berlin which lasted throughout the war.[468] From cream sources, we know that Kempf was a favorite of the Japanese and that a proposal was made that he be decorated by Japan. What became of this proposal is unknown. Kettler maintained the relationships established during Kempf's regime. He admitted that he knew Japanese officers in Berlin well. Rave says that he remembered a Japanese naval attaché paying a visit to Col. Kettler.[469] There was, however, no regular Japanese liaison officer at OKW/Chi, and no Japanese worked there. Just what the Japanese got out of the relationship is difficult to say. Kettler stated that various book recoveries were passed on to them. Some of these were probably American,[470] although Huettenhain said that he was convinced that no United States strip material had ever been passed to the Japanese by OKW.[471] Some unworked traffic was exchanged, but there was never any exchange, so far as is known, of information on cryptologic procedures. In short, the Germans

[467] Cf I-118, 3. I-84, 4 in which it is stated that "Sieffert" head of the bureau, came to work at OKW/Chi with other members of the Austrian bureau: Dr. Mauler, Dr. Locker ORR Bailovic. This is not the man of the same name who headed the evaluation section of Goering's Research Bureau.

[468] I-21, p 2-3. I-31, 9.

[469] I-22, 8.

[470] I-21, p 3.

[471] I-31, 10. Cf. also Buggisch's statement (I-64, 3) that he had never heard of any Japanese cryptanalytic relations with OKW/Chi.

gave the Japanese very little cryptanalytic assistance and got nothing in return. In the cryptographic field, the Germans were apparently even more reticent. "We did not tell the Japanese," says Kettler, "that we considered their systems bad".[472] Huettenhain, however, knew of a proposal to sell to the Japanese some Enigmas, probably for naval use in the far east. He says that when the cryptanalysts of OKW/Chi found that the non-plugboard Enigma was readable, it was suggested to Fellgiebel that the Japanese should have plugboard machines. Fellgiebel vacillated. Huettenhain does not know what was finally done about the matter.[473]

There was to have been a last minute attempt to improve cryptologic relations with Japan. A plan existed to send a cryptographic delegation by submarine from Germany to Japan in the winter of 1944-45.[474] This delegation was to include Capt. Opitz and First Lt. Schubert, Army signal intelligence personnel, and Lt. Morgenroth, one of the Navy cryptanalysts. So little was known about Japanese cryptanalytic activity that the delegation did not know where they were to go in Japan or to whom they should announce their arrival. The first contact was to be with the German Military Intelligence (Abwehr) in the far east. The Military Intelligence (Abwehr) presumably would have further contacts.[475] According to Mrs. von Nida, only one of the delegates was able to speak Japanese[476] and it is perhaps true, as Mettig said, that the delegation did not plan to reveal or hope to get much. Mettig added that, in general, German liaison with the Japanese was not considered good, and that the German officers who visited Japan had to wear civilian clothes so that they would not embarrass their Axis partners.

[472] I-21, p 3.

[473] I-84, 7.

[474] I-105, 5.

[475] From Mettig I-127, 2, I-48, 3.

[476] I-49, p 2.

[477] I-127, 2.

c. Italy:

Despite the fact that cryptologic liaison with Italy had gone on for some time, and is said to have been started by General Gamba at the time of the Abyssinian war, it does not seem to have been much closer than liaison with the Japanese.[478] Bigi's visit to OKW/Chi in 1942 has already been mentioned.[479] An Italian proposal for a similar visit in December of that year was refused by the Germans.[480] A deal, however, was made and carried out whereby certain Italian IBM equipment was exchanged for German IBM equipment in order to enable the Italians to use IBM machinery in their cryptanalytic work. Huettenhain mentions exchanges of book groups. He also tells a story of how the Germans broke an Italian cipher and told the Italians, who refused to believe it. "To prove it to them we finally sent a cryptographer to Rome and he was locked in a room until he had done so!"[481] After the surrender of the Italian government, the Italian Fascist Republic set up a new signal intelligence service. With this service Kettler refused to have any dealings whatever, "since we did not know what they would do with it".[482] Kettler was instrumental in obtaining a German order that the Fascist Republic cryptologic bureau be dissolved. This occurred on 25 February 1944.

d. Hungary:

Liaison with the Hungarian cryptanalysts had existed since the early twenties, and there was a regular exchange of material throughout the war.[483] In the report of June 1944, Kettler stated that, during the Spring of '44, he received one-eighth of his raw traffic from the Hungarians. The exchange took place through the Hungarian embassy. There was no

[478] I-21, p 3, from Huettenhain.

[479] IF-1517 Appendix A. See above p 73. Cf. also I-78, 11.

[480] I-21, p 3.

[481] I-21, p 3.

[482] I-21, p 3.

[483] I-21, p 2.

regular exchange of liaison officers although Wendland, Fenner's under-study, was sent to Hungary.[484] A few weeks before the entrance of Hungary into the war, Hungarian General Petrikovic visited OKW/Chi when he passed through Berlin, probably on his way to Helsinki. This was during Kempf's term of office.[485] Kettler, moreover, made two good-will visits to Hungary. In return for the traffic which they received, the Germans gave the Hungarians methods of solution for Italian, Rumanian, and Polish systems, the only countries whose systems were of interest to the Hungarians.[486] Huettenhain tells an odd story which indicates that relations were not always quite so happy as the above details suggest. In the summer of 1944, OKW/Chi broke a Turkish code and gave it to the Hungarians. The Hungarians sold the code to Himmler's Security Service, the RSHA, which brought it proudly back to OKW/Chi.[487] At the beginning of 1945, liaison with the Hungarians was terminated. Kettler sent a liaison officer to the German border at Steinamanger but he returned after having exchanged courtesies with the Hungarians. Nothing further is heard.[488]

e. Finland:

Liaison with the Finnish cryptanalysts began around the year 1938 and was intensified just after the first Russo-Finnish war.[489] In 1942, a Lieutenant Mikkoja arrived to act as liaison officer at army headquarters. He may also have had some contact with OKW/Chi. In any case, OKW/Chi had liaison with a Colonel Hallimaa from the beginning of the second Russo-Finnish war.[490] Traffic was exchanged in both the military and diplomatic fields. The Finns were said to have been interested

[484] p 2 Ibid.

[485] p 2 Ibid.

[486] p 2 Ibid.

[487] I-132, 2.

[488] I-21, p 1.

[489] I-96, p 5; I-29, p 3.

[490] I-111, 4.

principally in the traffic of Russia, Poland, Rumania, and Sweden.[491] There was close liaison with the Finns on the solution of an American strip system, but no exchange was made on any other system since OKW/Chi had nothing to offer. It is probable that the Finns were given to driving sharp bargains with their allies. We know that the German solution of the American strip system depended partly on the traffic for March 1943, and that it was not broken by them before that date.[492] We know, too, that on the tenth of March 1943, the Finns gave their solution of the American cipher system to the Japanese. It seems that the Finns had broken the American cipher system previous to March 1943, and withheld this information from their German allies. They started to exchange only when the Germans had something to offer. What the Finns got from the Japanese in return for the information on the American strip, we do not know from TICOM.

In his report for Spring 1944, Kettler states that German relations with the Hungarian and Finnish cryptanalytic organizations were of great assistance to the Germans in restoring the Archives of OKW/Chi which had been destroyed by the air raid of November 1943.

f. Bulgaria:

The only evidence of any connection of OKW/Chi with Bulgarian signal intelligence is the statement in the Kettler report for Spring 1944: that several Bulgarians were given a course in elementary cryptography at OKW/Chi.[494]

g. Spain:

The extent of OKW/Chi's relations with the Spanish Signal Intelligence has been covered in the discussion of the intercept systems of OKW/Chi in Spain. There is no doubt that the head of the Spanish signal intelligence service, Colonel Sarmiento, cooperated with the Germans. He received French traffic and military traffic in general sent to North Africa. In return, he gave the cablegrams about ship movements probably originating

[491] I-31, 9.

[492] I-89.

[494] DF-9, 3.

with commercial attachés.[495] About cryptanalytic materials, he told the Germans nothing. Mettig believes that this was because he knew nothing.[496]

[495] I-111, 4. It is not clear whether these cablegrams were given, however, to OKW or to OKH.

[496] I-111, 4.

TAB
A

VOLUME 3

Tab A

A-13. "Consolidated List of Documents received from: I. A.F.H.Q., Italy; II. Feuerstein; III. Japanese Embassy, Berlin; IV. Lisbon; V. M.I.8; VI. N.S.VI; VII.OSS, Wiesbaden." A TICOM publication.
Abwehr.-- Military Intelligence.
Adler, Walter, First Lt. Dr. Member of Subsection of OKW/Chi working on China, Japan.
Agents' Section.-- "Referat Vauck," named for its head, Lt. Vauck.
Ag/WNV (Amtsgruppe Wehrmachtnachrichtenverbindung).-- Armed Forces Communications Group.
Aigner, ____, Dr. (of Medicine). Member of Section IVc of OKW/Chi (initial breaking of more difficult systems; cryptanalytic theory).
Amberg, Hans Contact man for OKW/Chi in Spain.
Amtsgruppe Wehrmachtnachrichtenverbindung (Ag/WNV).-- Armed Forces Communications Group.
Andrae, ____, Lt. Col. Chief of Group I of OKW/Chi (intercept) until replaced by von NIDA. Chief of Staff of the Signal Intelligence Agency of the Army High Command (OKH/G d NA).
Armed Forces Communications Group.-- Amtsgruppe Wehrmachtnachrichtenverbindung (Ag/WNV).
Armed Forces High Command.-- Oberkommando der Wehrmacht (OKW).
Armed Forces Signal Communications.-- Wehrmachtnachrichtenverbindung (WNV).
Armed Forces Signal Officer for Special Employment # 700.-- Wehrmachtnachrichtenfuehrer zu besonderer Verwendung 700 (Wehrmachtnachrichtenfuehrer z. b. V. 700).
Armed Schutzstaffel (Waffen-SS).-- Components of Elite Guard serving at front.
Army Ordnance, Development and Testing Group, Signal Branch.-- Waffenpruefung 7 (Wa Pruef 7).
Army Ordnance Office.-- Heereswaffenamt (HWA).
Aumann, ____, Prof. Dr. Member of Section IVc of OKW/Chi (initial breaking of more difficult systems; cryptanalytic theory).

DOCID: 3560827

Baechle, Friedhelm. Radio operator with Military Intelligence (Abwehr), Department I-1 in Madrid, Spain, Jul 1940 - Nov 1944. This department was responsible for radio operation, telegraphy, teletype, and cryptography of Military Intelligence (Abwehr).

Bailovic, _____, Senior Specialist. Former member of Austrian cryptanalytic bureau, transferred at the time of Germany's annexation of Austria to Goering's Research Bureau (FA). After a short time, went to the Signal Intelligence Agency of the Army High Command (OKH/G d NA) and in Oct 1944 joined Balkan Section of Group V of OKW/Chi.

Barlow, _____, Maj. U.S. Army officer who tried to trace personnel and plant of the firm of Telefonbau und Normalzeit of Frankfurt/Main, which was responsible for the development of SG 39.

Berndt, _____ Mr. Chief of Polish part of Subsection V 6 of OKW/Chi.

Bernsdorff, _____ Capt. Chief of Section IIa of OKW/Chi (liaison between OKW/Chi and field units); in 1945 replaced Metzger as chief of Group III.

Beyreuther, Heinz W., Cpl. Member of Subsection of OKW/Chi working on China, Japan.

Boetzel, _____, Col. Chief of Code and Cipher Section of German War Ministry, 1934 - 1939. Chief of the Signal Intelligence Agency of the Army High Command (OKH/G d NA).

Bruckmann, _____. Mentioned (I-1, p. 20) as being "active on more or less independent footing" in OKW/Chi. Specialty: Greek.

Buck, _____, Senior Inspector. Chief of Section Ic of OKW/Chi (telecommunications).

Buggisch, Otto, S/Sgt. Dr. Cryptanalyst in Inspectorate 7/VI (In 7/VI). Expert on Russian ciphony.

Buschenhagen, _____, First Lt. Chief of the Defense Ministry Cipher Section, predecessor to OKW/Chi (1919).

Chi (Chiffrierabteilung).-- Cipher section.

Chiffrierabteilung (Chi).-- Cipher section.

Chiffrierstelle des Oberbefehlshabers der Luftwaffe (Chi-Stelle Ob d L).-- Signal Intelligence Agency of the Commander in Chief of the Air Force.

Chi-Stelle Ob d L (Chiffrierstelle des Oberbefehlshabers der Luftwaffe).-- Signal Intelligence Agency of the Commander in Chief of the Air Force.

Clifton, _____, Col. USA officer in command of units which captured some of the OKW/Chi personnel.

111

Cryptanalytic Section of the German Foreign Office.-- Sonderdienst des Referats Z in der Personalabteilung des Auswaertigen Amtes (Pers Z S).

D-16. "Translation of Annual Progress Reports by Pers Z S S covering 1927, 1941, and 1942." A TICOM Publication.

D-55. "Translation of Order concerning Cryptanalytic and Cypher Production Work promulgated by OKW/WFS /Chef WNV, taken from Papers of Major Nielson." A TICOM publication.

D-57. "Notes and Minutes of High-Level Meetings held at OKW/Chi." A TICOM publication.

Defense Ministry.-- Reichswehrministerium.

Dettmann, Alex, Lt. Head of cryptanalysis at Intercept Control Station East (HLS Ost); later head of Section 3, Group IV of the Signal Intelligence Agency of the Army High Command (OKH/G d NA). Specialty: machine cipher and research.

DF-8. Captured Wehrmacht Sigint Document: Statement of Order of Battle of OKW/Chi based on document dated April 1945. A TICOM publication.

DF-9. Captured Wehrmacht Sigint Document: Translation of Activity Report of OKW/Chi for the period 1st January, 1944 to 25th June, 1944. A TICOM publication.

Doenitz, Karl, Grand Admiral. Commander in Chief, German Navy; Reich Chancellor after Hitler's death.

Doering, _____, S/Sgt. Dr. Mathematician of Inspectorate 7/VI (In 7/VI); later with the Signal Intelligence Agency of the Army High Command (OKH/G d NA). Specialty: machine cipher and research.

Eckert, _____, First Lt. Liaison Officer from OKW/Chi to the Signal Intelligence Agency of the Commander in Chief of the Air Force (Chi-Stelle Ob d L).

Eichner, _____, Second Lt. Officer in charge of OKW/Chi's "Section Spain" office in Sevilla, Spain.

Elite Guard of the Nazi Party.-- Schutzstaffel (SS).

Fellgiebel, Erich, Lt. Gen. Chief Signal Officer of Army and Armed Forces High Commands from beginning of war until he was executed in 1944.

Fenner, Wilhelm, Principal Specialist. Chief of Division B of OKW/Chi (Cryptanalysis).

Flicke, _____, Specialist. In charge of technical matters at OKW Intercept station at Lauf.

Foreign Security Service.-- Sicherheitsdienst Ausland (SD Ausland).

112

DOCID: 3560827

Franke, _____, Senior Specialist. In charge of work on Swedish BC 38 in OKW/Chi, 1940.

Franz, _____, Prof. Dr. Chief of Section IVc of OKW/Chi (initial breaking of more difficult systems; cryptanalytic theory).

Fricke, _____, SS First Lt. Liaison Officer from the Reich Main Security Office (RSHA) to OKW.

Fricke, Walter, Technician (Lt. Grade) Dr. Chief of Section IIb of OKW/Chi (development of German systems).

Friedemann, _____. One of chief members of Joint Intelligence (Abwehr) in Spain.

Friedrich, _____, Lt. Col. Chief of Division III of Chief Signal Office (Gen NaFue III) and of the Signal Intelligence Agency of the Commander in Chief of the Air Force (Chi-Stelle Ob d L).

Frowein, _____, Lt. (Navy). Member of the Signal Intelligence Agency of the Navy High Command (OKM/4 SKL/III).

Fu (Funkueberwachung).-- Radio Defense Corps.

Funkueberwachung (Fu).-- Radio Defense Corps.

Gamba, Vittorio, Gen. Head of Italian Cryptanalytic Department.

Gimmler, _____, Maj. Gen. Chief of Army Ordnance Development and Testing Group, Signal Branch (Wa Pruef 7), 1939 - 1943. Chief Signal Officer to Commander in Chief West, 1943 - 1945. Chief of Armed Forces Communications Group (Chef Ag WNV).

Goering, Herrmann, Reichsmarschall. Commander in Chief of German Air Force, German Air Minister, etc.

Grosse, Arthur, Mr. OKW/Chi employee detached to Foreign Office Cryptanalytic Section (Pers Z S) for training. Specialized in Chinese and Japanese.

Grotz, _____ Capt. Chief of Group I of OKW/Chi (control of intercept stations).

Hagen, Ursula, Miss. Head of the group in the Foreign Office Cryptanalytic Section (Pers Z S) which worked on English and British Empire, Spanish, Portuguese, and Latin-American Systems.

Hallimaa, _____, Col. Head of Finnish Cipher Section. Had liaison with OKW/Chi.

Hatz, Heinrich, Staff Director, in charge of administration of OKW intercept station at Lauf.

Hayashi, _____, Col. (later Gen.). Head of Japanese military cryptographic organization, caught in Germany at outbreak of war; became Japanese Military Attaché at Budapest. Had some liaison with OKW/Chi.

113

Heereswaffenamt (HWA).-- Army Ordnance Office.
Heimsoeth & Rincke. Firm which made the changeable turnover rotor (Lueckenfuellerwalze) for the Enigma cipher machine. Address of the firm: Uhlandstrasse 138, Berlin-Wilmersdorf.
Hein, _____, Maj. Commander of Transport in move of part of OKW/Chi to South Germany, 1945.
Hentze, Rudolf, Maj. Dr. Head of Group IV, Signal Intelligence Agency of the Army High Command (OKH/GdNA).
Herold, Wadim, Capt. German Air Force Officer detached to OKW/Chi in Jan 1940 to be intercept officer in the field.
Hierer, _____, Mr. OKW/Chi employee detached to Foreign Office Cryptanalytic Section (Pers Z S) for training.
Himmler, Heinrich. Reichsfuehrer SS, Minister of Interior, Chief of German Police.
Hoepfner, _____, Col. Took command of OKW/Chi after it moved to Halle, 1945.
Huettenhain, Erich, Specialist Dr. Chief cryptanalyst of OKW/Chi from 1937 to end of war. Chief of Group IV (cryptanalytic research); also chief of Section IVd (training).
HWA (Heereswaffenamt).-- Army Ordnance Office.
I-1. "Report of TICOM reporting team number three, which uncovered the Foreign Office Cryptanalytic Section (Pers Z S)." A TICOM publication.
I-2. "Interrogation of Dr. Huettenhain and Dr. Fricke at Flensburg, 21 May 1945." A TICOM publication.
I-13. "Composite Report on Two Interrogations of Oberstlt. Friedrich, Chief of the G.A.F. Sigint Service, 18/5/45 and 9/6/45." A TICOM publication.
I-17. "Extracts of SHAEF Interrogations of Maj. Gen. Boner, Colonel Grube, Lt. Col. Mettig, and Major Rottler." A TICOM publication.
I-20. "Interrogation of Sonderfuehrer Dr. Fricke of OKW/Chi (Formerly of OKH/Chi)." A TICOM publication.
I-21. "Preliminary Interrogation of Oberst Kettler, R.R.Dr. Huettenhain, Sdf. Dr. Fricke and Oblt. Schubert (OKH/Chi), 15 June 1945." A TICOM publication.
I-22. "Interrogation of German Cryptographers of Pers Z S Department of the Auswaertiges Amt." A TICOM publication.
I-27. "Preliminary Interrogation of Fraeulein Hagen, Head of English Section of Pers. Z S, Auswaertiges Amt." A TICOM publication.
I-29. "Third Interrogation of Oberstltn. Friedrich, Chief of the G.A.F. Signals Intelligence Service." A TICOM publication.

DOCID: 3560827

I-31. "Detailed Interrogations of Dr. Huettenhain, formerly head of research section of OKW/Chi, 18th-21st June 1945." A TICOM publication.

I-36. "Translation of Paper Written by Reg.Rat.Dr. Huettenhain and Sonderfuehrer Dr. Fricke on the Development of OKW/Chi, Sections A.III and B.V." A TICOM publication.

I-37. "Translation of Paper Written by Reg.Rat.Dr. Huettenhain of OKW/Chi on Special Apparatus used as aids to cryptanalysis." A TICOM publication.

I-38. "Report on Interrogation of Lt. Frowein of OKM/4 SKL/III, on his work on the Security of the German Naval Four-Wheel Enigma." A TICOM publication.

I-39. "Organization of OKW/Chi." A TICOM publication.

I-44. "Memorandum on Speech Encipherment Apparatus by O.R.R. Huettenhain and Sdf. Dr. Fricke." A TICOM publication.

I-45. "OKW/Chi Cryptanalytic Research on Enigma, Hagelin and Cipher Teleprinter Machines." A TICOM publication.

I-46. "Preliminary Report on Interrogation of Dr. Otto Buggisch (of OKH/Gen.d.NA) and Dr. Werner Liebknecht (employed by OKH and OKW as tester of cryptographic equipment) 23 June 1945." A TICOM publication.

I-47. "P/W Situation Report." A TICOM publication.

I-48. "Report on Special Interrogation of Drs. Huettenhain and Fricke, Oberst Mettig, and Lt. Morgenroth carried out on 29th July 1945." A TICOM publication.

I-49. "Notes on OKW/Chi and on Intercept Organization under K.O. Spain." A TICOM publication.

I-53. " Construction of "Schluesselgeraet 39." A TICOM publication.

I-54. "Second Interrogation of Five Members of the RLM/Forschung amt." A TICOM publication.

I-57. "Enciphering Devices worked on by Dr. Liebknecht at Wa Pruef 7." A TICOM publication.

I-58. "Interrogation of Dr. Otto Buggisch of OKW/Chi." A TICOM publication.

I-61. "Interrogation Report on Friedhelm Baechle, W/T Operator with KO Spain." A TICOM publication.

I-62. "Field Interrogation of Paul Ratz of the German Army Signals Intelligence (1933-1945)." A TICOM publication.

I-64. "Answers by Wm. Buggisch of OKH/Chi to Questions sent by TICOM." A TICOM publication.

I-65. "Interrogation Report on Four Members of the G.A.F. Sigint Service." A TICOM publication.

115

DOCID: 3560827

I-66. "Paper by Dr. Otto Buggisch of OKH/In 7/VI and OKW/Chi on TYPEX." A TICOM publication.
I-67. "Paper by Dr. Otto Buggisch of OKH/In 7/VI and OKW/Chi on Cryptanalytic Machines." A TICOM publication.
I-68. "Consolidated Report Based on Two Interrogations of Oberst Randewig, of Hoeh. Wehrmachts Nafue z.b.V. 700, carried out at CSDIC on approx. 1 Aug. and 10 Aug. 1945."
I-69. "Summary of Cipher Information on Jugoslav Traffic Provided by Uffz. Herzfeld (Appendices to TICOM I-52)." A TICOM publication.
I-72. "First part of the Report by Wm. Buggisch on S.G. 41." A TICOM publication.
I-73. "Translated Version of Homework done by Wm. Buggisch." A TICOM publication.
I-75. "Interrogation Reports on German Field Sigint Personnel carried out at BUFFER - Ltn. August Schroeder, Ltn. Starke, Obgefr. Heudorf, and Hptm. Holetzke." A TICOM publication.
I-76. "Interrogation Reports on Lehwald, Haupts, Klett and Lauerbach. Also I/76 Supplement (Diagrams).." A TICOM publication.
I-77. "Translations of Joint Report made by Drs. Huettenhain and Fricke on the "Zaehlwerk" Enigma Machine." A TICOM publication.
I-78. "Interrogation of Oberstlt. Mettig on the History and Achievements of OKH/AHA/In 7/VI." A TICOM publication.
I-79. "Supplementary Paper by Drs. Huettenhain and Fricke on the Solution of the Hagelin Machine." A TICOM publication.
I-84. "Further Interrogation of R.R. Dr. Huettenhain and Sdf. Dr. Fricke of OKW/Chi." A TICOM publication.
I-85. "P.W. Interrogation Report on Reg. Rat Flicke, Techn. Insp. Pokojewski, Stabsintendant Hatz of OKW/Chi." A TICOM publication.
I-86. "Interrogation of Oberstlt. Mettig of OKH and OKW/Chi on the higher direction of German cryptanalytic work." A TICOM publication.
I-88. "Report on Interrogation of Mr. K. Vetterlein of the Reichspost Laboratorium on German Interception of Transatlantic Speech Circuits." A TICOM publication.
I-89. "Report by Prof. Dr. H. Rohrbach of Pers Z S on American Strip Cipher." A TICOM publication.
I-90. "Interrogation of Herr Reinhard Wagner (OKW/Chi) on Japanese Systems." A TICOM publication.
I-91. "P.O.W. Interrogation Report - General Major Robert K.H. Schlake, Chief of Communications in the Main Office of the Ordungspolizei, Ministry of the Interior." A TICOM publication.

DOCID: 3560827

I-92. "Final Interrogation of Wachtmeister Otto Buggisch (OKH/In 7/VI and OKW/Chi)." A TICOM publication.
I-93. "Detailed Interrogation of Membersof OKM/4 SKL/III at Flensburg." A TICOM publication.
I-95. "Interrogation of Lt. Morgenroth on organization of OKM/4 SKL/III." A TICOM publication.
I-96. "Interrogation of Oberstlt. Mettig on the Organization and Activities of OKW/Chi." A TICOM publication.
I-98. "Interrogationof Oberst Randewig on German Deception Plans." A TICOM publication.
I-103. "Second Interrogation ofReg.Rat Hermann Scherschmidt of Pers Z S Auswaertiges Amt, on Turkish and Bulgarian Systems." A TICOM publication.
I-104. "Report on Berlin Targets by Major Heller of G.S.I.(s), 21 A.G., B.A.O.R." A TICOM publication.
I-105. "Interrogation Report on Frau von Nida (wife of Major Wolfgang von Nida, one-time Deputy Head of OKW/Chi)." A TICOM publication.
I-111. "Further Interrogation of Oberstlt. Mettig of OKW/Chi on 14th September 1945." A TICOM publication.
I-112. "Preliminary Interrogation of Reg.Rat. Dr. Ferdinand Voegele (Chi Stelle, Ob.d.L) and Major Ferdinand Feichtner (O.C. of LN Regt. 352, etc.)" A TICOM publication.
I-113. "Interrogation of Major Dr. Rudolf Hentze, Head of Gruppe IV (Cryptanalysis) General der Nachrichtenaufklaerung." A TICOM publication.
I-115. "Further Interrogation of Oberstlt. Mettig of OKW/Chi on the German Wireless Security Service (Funküberwachung)." A TICOM publication.
I-116. "Report of Interrogation of Ltn. Alex Dettmann and Oberwachtmeister Sergius Samsonow of OKH (Gen.d.NA) at Oberursel, Germany, during August 1945." A TICOM publication.
I-118. "Joint Reports by Reg.Rat. Dr. Huettenhain and Sdf. Dr. Fricke, written at CSDIC on or about 28th August 1945." A TICOM publication.
I-119. "Further Interrogation of Reg.Rat Voegele and Major Feichtner on G.A.F. Sigint." A TICOM publication.
I-123. "Interrogation Report on Rudolf Trappe (Civilian) of OKW/Chi." A TICOM publication.
I-124. "Interrogation Report on Dr. Werner Weber of OKW/Chi." A TICOM publication.
I-127. "Interrogation of Oberstlt. Mettig of OKW/Chi." A TICOM publication.

117

I-128. "Deciphering Achievements of In 7/VI and OKW/Chi." A TICOM publication.
I-130. "Homework by Hauptmann Herold, O.C. Ln. Regt. III/353." A TICOM publication.
I-143. "Report on the Interrogation of Five Leading Germans at " remberg on 27th September 1945." A TICOM publication.
I-150. "Report by Uffz. Heinz W. Beyreuther on the Organization of OKW/Chi." A TICOM publication.
I-161. "Further Statements on Typex by Huettenhain, Fricke, and Mettig." A TICOM publication.
IF-15 "Final Report of TICOM Team 1 on the exploitation of Kaufbeuren and the Berchtesgaden area." From TICOM.
IF-130. Copy of MIS dossier on Fellgiebel. From Captured German Army Official Dossier, now in MIS files in Pentagon.
IF-164. "Report on Interrogation of Walter Schellenberg."
IF-165. Special report by Kirby, on TICOM Team 6's relation with OKW/Chi personnel. Original.
IF-166. Special report by Kirby on Sdf. Dr. Fricke. Nov 23, 1946. Original.
IF-167. "Final report on the visit of TICOM Team 5 to the Schliersee area." TICOM, but not registered.
IF-1517. "First detailed Interrogation of Augusto Bigi, who worked in the Cryptographic Section of SIM before the Armistice and in SID afterward." CSDIC/CMF/Y 4.
Inspectorate 7/VI of the Army High Command.-- Oberkommando des Heeres/Inspektion 7/VI (OKH/In 7/VI)
Jensen, _____, Graduate Engineer. Member of Section IVb of OKW/Chi (development of cryptanalytic machinery).
Jeschol, _____. Intercept operator in OKW Section Spain substation on Canary Islands.
Jodl, Alfred, Gen. Chief of Operations Staff, Armed Forces High Command (Chef OKW/Ia).
Jung-Fischer, _____, Mr. According to I-1, p. 20, chief of Swiss subsection of OKW/Chi.
Kaehler, _____, Lt. Col. Chief of Group VI of OKW/Chi (broadcast and press monitoring).
von Kalkstein, _____, Lt. Col. Chief of Group VII of OKW/Chi (intercept reports and their distribution; evaluation).
Karstien, Hans, Specialist Dr. Cryptanalyst with Foreign Office Cryptanalytic Section (Pers Z S). Specialist in Slavonic Languages. Headed the group which worked on Yugoslav, Bulgarian, Croatian, and Polish systems, as well as systems originating from the Baltic States. During the evacuation period (Dec 1943 - Mar 1945) headed that portion of the Section which was located in Hirschberg in the Riesengebirge. Also worked on Chinese problems 1930-1938.

DOCID: 3560827

Keitel, Wilhelm, Field Marshal. Chief of Armed Forces High Command (Chef OKW).

Kempf, _____, Col. Chief of OKW/Chi prior to 1943.

Kern, _____, Lt. Dr. Chief of Turkish Subsection of OKW/Chi.

Kettler, Hugo, Col. Chief of OKW/Chi, 1943 - 1945.

Kiefer, _____, Specialist Dr. Chief of subsection of OKW/Chi working on Spain, South America, Mexico.

Klautschke, Heinz, Specialist Dr. Liaison Officer with the Supreme Command of the Armed Forces (OKW not just OKW/Chi). Stated that he had "university training in economics and politics." Gives examples of information he supplied in the OKW and mentions offices he had dealings with. (I 25, IF 135, D 22, especially I 54).

Klett, Werner, Cpl. Member of Control Station Signal Intelligence West, located in Berlin.

Klinger, _____, Mr. Chief of Section Ia of OKW/Chi (liaison with intercept stations).

Koehler, _____, Technician (Lt. Grade). Head of linguistics at Inspectorate 7/VI (In 7/VI); later member of Signal Intelligence Agency of Army High Command (OKH/G d NA); finally (from Nov 1944) chief of Section Va of OKW/Chi (technical assistance for language work).

Korn, Willi, Graduate Engineer. Employee of firm of Heimsoeth & Rincke, who manufactured the Enigma. Collaborated with Fenner in developing the Enigma.

Krause, _____, Mr. Chief of Section VIc of OKW/Chi (foreign broadcasts).

Kriegsministerium.-- War Ministry.

Kroeger, _____, Specialist. The "cipher machine" specialist of Goering's Research Bureau (FA). Was said to have broken Finnish Hagelin. Was the representative of his organization in Huettenhain's Cipher Security Committee.

Kunze, _____, First Lt. Chief of Swiss Subsection of OKW/Chi.

Lenschau, _____, Maj. Dr. Chief of Subsection V 3 of OKW/Chi (Rumania). Worked with Mueller of French Subsection.

Liebknecht, Werner, Graduate Engineer Dr. Chief of Section IIIh of Army Ordnance Development and Testing Group, Signal Branch (Wa Pruef 7), research agency for developing voice scramblers.

Lober, _____, Maj. Chief of Group Z of OKW/Chi (personnel).

119

Locker, _____, Specialist Dr. Formerly member of Austrian cipher bureau; later chief of subsection on Turkish military systems of OKW/Chi.

Lotze, H., Graduate Engineer. Member of Army Ordnance Development and Testing Group, Signal Branch (Wa Pruef 7), Section e. Specialty: ciphony.

Lufthansa.-- German commercial airline.

Mang, _____, Maj. Chief of Inspectorate 7/VI (In 7/VI), 1941-1942.

Mauler, _____, Dr. Former member of the Austrian cryptanalytic bureau transferred at time of annexation to OKW/Chi, where he was deputy chief of Italian Subsection.

Menzer, _____, Senior Inspector. Chief of Section IIc of OKW/Chi (development and production of special ciphers for government departments, industry, and the Reich Main Security Office ((RSHA)), developing of deciphering aids for agents).

Mettig, _____, Lt. Col. Second in command of OKW/Chi, Dec 1943 - 1945. Chief of Division A (cryptography).

Mertz, _____, S/Sgt. Chief of Section IIIb of OKW/Chi (paper supply).

Metzger, _____, Maj. Chief of Group III of OKW/Chi (production and distribution of keys) until injured (early in 1945) and replaced by Bernsdorff.

Mihailovic, Draha. Yugoslav patriot leader.

Mikkoja, _____, Lt. Finnish liaison officer to OKW/Chi, 1942 - ?

Military Intelligence.-- Abwehr.

Morgenroth, _____, Lt. (Navy). A Navy cryptanalyst.

Mueller, _____, Senior Specialist. Chief of Subsection V5 (France, Switzerland) of OKW/Chi toward end of war.

von Nida, Wolfgang, Maj. Officer in charge of OKW intercept network in Spain, Jan 1940 to Apr 1942. From Apr 1942 to his death, Nov 1943, second in command of OKW/Chi.

von Nida, Mrs. Wife of Maj. Wolfgang von Nida.

Nielsen, _____, Maj. (Gen Staff) Operations Officer on staff of Chief Signal Officer of the Armed Forces.

Novopaschenny, _____, Professor. Chief of Russian subsection of OKW/Chi.

Oberkommando des Heeres/General der Nachrichten Aufklaerung (OKH/G d NA).-- Signal Intelligence Agency of the Army High Command.

Oberkommando des Heeres/Inspektion 7/VI (OKH/In 7/VI)-- Inspectorate 7/VI of the Army High Command.

Oberkommando der Marine/4 Seekriegsleitung II(OKM/4 SKL II).-- Signal Security Agency of the Navy High Command.

Oberkommando der Marine/4 Seekriegsleitung III (OKM/4 SKL III).-- Signal Intelligence Agency of the Navy High Command.

Oberkommando der Wehrmacht (OKW).-- The German Armed Forces High Command.

OKH/G d NA (Oberkommando des Heeres/General der Nachrichten Aufklaerung).-- Signal Intelligence Agency of the Army High Command.

OKH/In 7/VI (Oberkommando des Heeres/Inspektion 7/VI).-- Inspectorate 7/VI of the Army High Command.

OKM/4 SKL II (Oberkommando der Marine/4 Seekriegsleitung II).-- Signal Security Agency of the Navy High Command.

OKM/4 SKL III (Oberkommando der Marine/4 Seekriegsleitung III).-- Signal Intelligence Agency of the Navy High Command.

OKW (Oberkommando der Wehrmacht).-- The German Armed Forces High Command.

OKW/Chi (Oberkommando der Wehrmacht/Chiffrierabteilung).-- Signal Intelligence Agency of the Supreme Command, Armed Forces.

Operations Staff.-- Waffenfuehrungsstab, (WFSt).

Opitz, Carl Heinz, Capt. An Army Signal Intelligence Officer, member of a cryptographic delegation which was supposed to go from Germany to Japan by submarine in the winter of 1944-1945.

Ordnungspolizei (Orpo).-- Regular Police.

Orpo (Ordnungspolizei).-- Regular Police.

Oschmann, Maj. Chief of the Defense Ministry Cipher Section, predecessor to OKW/Chi (1932).

Oshima. Japanese Ambassador to Germany, 1943.

Paetzel, Martin, Senior Specialist Dr. Head of the research section, section 6, of Goering's Research Bureau (FA).

Paschke, Adolf, Senior Specialist Dr. Co-head of the Foreign Office Cryptanalytic Section (Pers Z S). Also headed the Linguistic-Cryptanalytic Subsection, his language specialties being Italian, Greek, and Russian. Was principally responsible for the Section's successes with Italian diplomatic codes 1935 to 1943.

Pers Z S (Sonderdienst des Referats Z in der Personalabteilung des Auswaertigen Amtes).-- Cryptanalytic Section of the German Foreign Office.
Peter or Peters, -----, Assistant Schoolmaster Dr. According to Beyreuther (I-150, p. 2), chief of Swiss Subsection of OKW/Chi.
Petrikóvic, _____, Gen. Head of Hungarian cryptanalytic bureau.
Pietsch, _____, Specialist. Head of mathematical section of Inspectorate 7/VI (In 7/VI).
Plankert, _____, First Lt. In April 1943, succeeded Major von Nida as officer in charge of German intercept system in Spain, which was conducted by OKW.
Poetsgens, _____, Cpl. Dr. Chief of Greek subsection of OKW/Chi.
Pokojewski, Kurt, Technical Inspector. Subordinate to Flicke, civilian in charge of OKW intercept station at Lauf; later became civilian in charge.
Praun, Albert, Maj. Gen. Succeeded Fellgiebel as Chief Signal Officer of Armed Forces, 1944.
Pupp, _____, Dr. Member of Army Ordnance Development and Testing Group, Signal Branch (Wa Pruef 7), Section IV.
Raatz, Paul, Non-commissioned Officer. Member of various German Army Radio Intelligence Units.
Radio Defense Corps.-- Funkueberwachung (Fu).
Raffel, _____, Senior Specialist. Chief of Subsection V 6 (Italy) of OKW/Chi.
Randewig, _____, Col. Chief of Western intercept stations in 1939. In 1944, Armed Forces Signals Officer for Special Employment # 700 (Hoeherer W NaFue z. b. V. 700).
Rave, Kurt, Mr. OKW/Chi employee detached to the Foreign Office Cryptanalytic Section (Pers Z S) for training.
"Referat Vauck". Agents' Section, named for its head, Lt. Vauck.
Regular Police.-- Ordnungspolizei (Orpo).
Reichswehrministerium.-- Defense Ministry.
Rohen, _____, Senior Specialist. Chief of USA subsection of OKW/Chi.
Rohrbach, Hans, Prof. Dr. Member of Foreign Office Cryptanalytic Section (Pers Z S). Mathematician, and professor at the Charles University in Prague. Worked in Dr. Kunze's Mathematical-Cryptanalytic Subsection. Awarded the War Service Cross Grade 2 (KVK II) in September 1944, probably for his achievements in solution of the US Diplomatic Strip Cipher 0-2.

Rotscheidt, _____, Graduate Engineer. Chief of Section IVb of OKW/Chi (development of cryptanalytic machinery).

Rotter, _____, Senior Specialist. Chief of Czechoslovak Subsection of OKW/Chi; later chief of Bulgarian Subsection.

Ruesing, _____. Mentioned (I-1, p. 20) as being "active on more or less independent footing" in OKW/Chi. Specialty: Greek.

Rust, _____, Capt. Dr. Commanding Officer of OKW intercept station at Treuenbrietzen.

Ružek, _____. Captured Polish officer interrogated by Germans late in 1939 with regard to Polish work on German Enigma.

Salzbrunn, _____, Specialist Graduate Engineer. Chief of Section VIa of OKW/Chi (interception and recording equipment). In charge of Ludwigsfelde outstation.

Sarmiento, Rafael, Col. Chief Signal Officer of the Spanish Army.

Sato, _____. Counterintelligence man for Oshima, Japanese Ambassador to Germany.

Schaedel, _____, S/Sgt. Dr. Chief of Section VIIb of OKW/Chi (archives).

Schapper, Gottfried, Ministerial Director. A captain in Signals Intelligence in World War I. A member of the cipher section of the Defense Ministry, he resigned and joined Schimpf and others in forming Goering's Research Bureau (FA) for Goering in 1933. He was the third (and last) head of this organization and claims to have held a rank equivalent to that of a Generalleutnant in the Air Force.

Schauffler, Rudolf, Senior Specialist. Cryptanalyst, Co-head of the Foreign Office Cryptanalytic Section (Pers Z S) with Dr. Paschke. Head of the Research Subsection, head of the Japanese-Chinese cryptanalytic group, and adviser on cipher and code security to the Foreign Office Cryptographic Section.

Schellenberg, Walter, SS Brig. Gen. Head of Amt VI of the Reich Main Security Office (RSHA) which took over Joint Intelligence (the Abwehr) in Spring 1944. Schellenberg claimed to have arranged to take over Goering's Research Bureau and to have reached an understanding with Kettler to control OKW/Chi.

Scherschmidt, Hermann, Senior Specialist. Cryptanalyst, who headed at various times the work on Bulgarian, Turkish, and Polish systems in the Foreign Office Cryptanalytic Section (Pers Z S). Turkish was his language specialty, and this was the section which he headed in 1945.

DOCID: 3560827

Schlake, Robert K. H., Brig. Gen. Chief of radio and communications in the ministry of the Interior, 1933 - 1945.
Schmidt, _____, Maj. Chief of the Defense Ministry Cipher Section, predecessor to OKW/Chi (1927).
Schmidt, _____, First Lt. Chief of Section VIb of OKW/Chi (news agency transmissions, including pictures; international commercial radio traffic; multiplex).
Schnueckel, _____, T/Sgt. Chief of Section Ib of OKW/Chi (call sign and frequency study).
Schroeder, _____. OKW/Chi employee detached to the Foreign Office Cryptanalytic Section (Pers Z S) for training.
Schubert, _____, First Lt. Cryptanalyst with the Signal Intelligence Agency of the Army High Command (OKH/G d NA).
Schultze, _____, Dr. Member of Section IVc of OKW/Chi (initial brea..ing of more difficult systems; cryptanalytic theory).
Schutzstaffel (SS).-- Elite guard of the Nazi Party.
SD Ausland (Sicherheitsdienst Ausland).-- Foreign Security Service.
Seifert, _____, Principal Specialist. Formerly a member of the Austrian Cryptanalytic Bureau, joined OKW/Chi upon annexation of Austria, 1938.
Selchow, _____, Minister. Head of Z Branch (Referat Z), the Foreign Office Branch which handled cryptography, cryptanalysis, and Foreign Office Communications.
Seyfarth, _____, First Lt. Dr. Chief of Section VId of OKW/Chi (evaluation of Group VI's material; publication of reports).
SHAEF.-- Supreme Headquarters Allied Expeditionary Forces.
Sicherheitsdienst Ausland (SD Ausland).-- Foreign Security Service.
Signal Intelligence Agency of the Army High Command.-- Oberkommando des Heeres/General der Nachrichten Aufklaerung (OKH/G d NA).
Signal Intelligence Agency of the Commander in Chief of the Air Force.-- Chiffrierstelle des Oberbefehlshabers der Luftwaffe (Chi-Stelle Ob d L).
Signal Intelligence Agency of the Navy High Command.-- Oberkommando der Marine/4 Seekriegsleitung III (OKM/4 SKL/III).
Signal Security Agency of the Navy High Command.-- Oberkommando der Marine/4 Seekriegsleitung II, (OKM/4 SKL II).
Signal Intelligence Agency of the Supreme Command, Armed Forces.- Oberkommando der Wehrmacht/Chiffrierabteilung (OKW/Chi).

124

DOCID: 3560827

Singer, _____, Capt. German naval officer who attended interrogations of captured Polish cryptanalytic personnel, 1942.

Sonderdienst Des Referats Z in Der Personalabteilung Des Auswaertigen Amtes (Pers Z S).-- Cryptanalytic Section of the German Foreign Office.

SS (Schutzstaffel).-- Elite guard of the Nazi Party.

Stein, _____, Lt. Dr. Chief of Section IVa of OKW/Chi (security investigation of new systems, new inventions). Machine specialist.

Steinberg, _____, Technician Dr. Member of mathematical section of Inspectorate 7/VI (In 7/VI), later in Section 1, Group IV of the Signal Intelligence Agency of the Army High Command (OKH/G d NA). Transferred in Nov 1944 to OKW/Chi. Worked on Japanese machine. Expert on solution of M-94 and M-209.

Supreme Headquarters Allied Expeditionary Forces. Abbreviated SHAEF.

T 782. Frankreich [German translations of decodes of French diplomatic traffic, dated Aug - Oct 1944.]

T 788. Chungking-China [German translations of decodes of Chinese diplomatic traffic, dated Aug - Oct 1944].

T 789. Chile [German translations of decodes of Chilean diplomatic traffic, dated Aug - Oct 1944].

T 791. Brasilien [German translations of decodes of Brazilian diplomatic traffic, dated Aug - Oct 1944].

T 803. Japan [German translations of decodes of Japanese diplomatic traffic, dated Aug - Oct 1944].

Target Intelligence Committee (abbreviated TICOM).-- A joint combined committee organized in the fall of 1944 in England for the exploitation of European Axis signal intelligence centers of special interest.

Telefonbau & Normalzeit. Firm in Frankfurt/Main which was constructing the SG 39 at the end of the war.

Teischmueller, _____. Member of Section IVc of OKW/Chi (initial breaking of more difficult systems; cryptanalytic theory). Worked with Weber in 1941 on a USA system.

Thiele, _____, Grig. Gen. Chief of Staff to Chief Signal Officer of Army.

Thielen, _____, First Lt. Succeeded Capt. Grotz as head of OKW intercept station at Sofia.

TICOM.-- Target Intelligence Committee. A joint combined committee organized in the fall of 1944 in England for the exploitation of European Axis signal intelligence centers of special interest.

TICOMMA. TICOM Materials.
Tito. Yugoslav Patriot leader.
Tranow, ____, Senior Specialist Dr. Head of Subsection IIIf (Britain and USA) of the Signal Intelligence Agency of the Navy High Command (OKM/ 4 SKL III).
Trappe, Rudolf, Mr. Member of OKW/Chi. Translated French and English military manuals, news items, etc.
Vauck, ____, First Lt. Dr. Member of Inspectorate 7/VI (In 7/VI); later member of Section IV, Signal Intelligence Agency of the Army High Command (OKH/G d NA); still later member of Section V of OKW/Chi. Chief of Subsection dealing with agents' traffic, called "Referat Vauck."
Verlaessliche Nachricht (VN).-- Translation into German of decoded diplomatic message. "Reliable Report"
VN (Verlaessliche Nachricht).-- Translation into German of decoded diplomatic message. "Reliable Report"
Voegele, Ferdinand, Specialist Dr. Chief of Section E (Referat E) of the Signal Intelligence Agency of the Commander in Chief of the Air Force (Chi-Stelle Ob d L) and principal cryptanalyst in the German Air Force.
Waffenfuehrungsstab (WFSt.).-- Operations Staff.
Waffenpruefung 7 (WA Pruef 7).-- Army Ordnance, Development and Testing Group, Signal Branch.
Waffen-SS (Waffen-Schutzstaffel).-- Armed Elite Guard. Components of Elite Guard serving at front.
Wagner, Reinhard, Acting Cpl. Member of Japan-China Subsection of OKW/Chi. Specialty: Japanese. Cryptanalyst as well as linguist.
Wa Pruef 7 (Waffenpruefung 7).-- Army Ordnance, Development and Testing Group, Signal Branch.
War Ministry.-- Kriegsministerium.
Weber, Werner, Prof. Dr. Member of Section IVc of OKW/Chi (initial breaking of more difficult systems; cryptanalytic theory).
Wehrmachtnachrichtenfuehrer z. b. V. 700 (Wehrmachtnachrichtenfuehrer zu besonderer Verwendung 700).-- Armed Forces Signal Officer for Special Employment #700.
Wehrmachtnachrichtenfuehrer Zu Besonderer Verwendung 700 (Wehrmachtnachrichtenfuehrer z. b. V. 700).-- Armed Forces Signal Officer for Special Employment #700.

DOCID: 3560827

Wehrmachtnachrichtenverbindung (WNV).-- Armed Forces Signal Communications.

WFSt. (Waffenfuehrungsstab).-- Operations Staff.

Wend, _____, Reserve Maj. Dr. Commanding officer of OKW intercept station at Lauf from 1 Dec 1939 to end of war.

Wendland, _____, Principal Specialist. Chief of Group V of OKW/Chi (routine breaking and translation); also chief of Balkan Subsection of Group V. Interested in Russian.

Wevering, _____, Senior Specialist. Chief of Scandinavian Subsection of OKW/Chi.

Witt, _____, Prof. Dr. Member of Section IVc of OKW/Chi (initial breaking of more difficult systems; cryptanalytic theory).

WNV (Wehrmachtnachrichtenverbindung).-- Armed Forces Signal Communications.

Yardley, Herbert Osborne. Author of book: The American Black Chamber (Indianapolis, the Bobbs-Merrill Co., 1931) which dealt with cryptanalysis in USA Military Intelligence Department.

Zastrow, Karl. Cryptanalyst in the Foreign Office Cryptanalytic Section (Pers Z S); specialist on USA systems. Lent to OKW as visiting specialist.

Zeimer, _____, Lt. Cmdr. Head of D/F station of Signal Intelligence Agency of the Navy High Command (OKM/4 SKL III) in Spain.

127

TAB
B

TAB "B"

OKW/Chi and the beginning of Cryptologic Work in the German Army.

The pre-war relation between OKW/Chi and the Army's early signal intelligence agency called the Intercept Control Station (Horchleitstelle) is very obscure and into this obscurity the following remark of Mettig throws only a little light: "Before the war, cryptography in the German Army was carried out by OKH/In 7 Horchleitstelle.[1] This organization originated in the cipher section of the German War Ministry, and grew up parallel with the cipher section of the OKW (OKW/-Chi). Before the war, In 7 Horchleitstelle was merely a small department."[2] Now the War Ministry (Kriegsministerium) is simply the name the Defense Ministry (Reichswehrministerium) acquired after 1934. The organizations are identical. Since it is unlikely that this ministry had two cipher sections, one in Military Intelligence and one elsewhere, it is probable that the cipher section mentioned here as the parent of the Intercept Control Station (Horchleitstelle) is identical with the cipher section of the Defense Ministry which Mettig said elsewhere was the parent of OKW/Chi.

It may be suggested further that the officer in charge of the cipher section also controlled the fairly extensive intercept network which it is known that the Defense Ministry and later the War Ministry operated.[3] This suggestion is based on the remarks of Mr. Trappe who stated:

[1]An early designation of the Army Cryptanalytic Service. See Chapter II

[2]I-78, 2.

[3]See Chapter II

(1) That he was "employed by the Chiffrierstelle[4] office [sic]... at first of the Reichswehr Ministerium and later OKW from 1919" until he was captured by the Americans.

(2) That from 1919 to 1933, presumably while employed by the Chiffrierstelle, he served at intercept stations in Munich, Kassel (Niederzwehren), and Stuttgart before coming to the Reichswehr Ministerium in Berlin.[5]

The fact that an employee of the Cipher Section was physically located at the intercept stations implies a unified control of the two organizations.

Further, Trappe gives the following list of "Chiefs of the Chiffrierstelle":

1919: 1st Lt. Buschenhagen
1927: Major Schmidt
1931: Major Fellgeibel [sic]
1932: Major Oschmann
1934: Major Boetzel
1939: Major Kempff [sic]
1943: Major Kettler.[6]

Fellgeibel is probably identical with the Fellgiebel who was Chief Signal Officer both of the OKW (Chef WNV) and of the OKH (Chief of Army Signals), (Chef HNW) from the beginning of the war until he was dismissed in disgrace and executed for his part in the attempt on Hitler's life in July 1944. The German official file on Fellgiebel is available, and he is known to

[4] There is other evidence that the cryptologic section of the Reichswehr and later the OKW was known as the Chiffrierstelle. (Cipher Office). According to A-22 B, 7 a folder stamped Reichswehrministerium, Heeresleitung (Army Directorate), Chiffrierstelle, has been found among the Schliersee documents. A collection of correspondence of the German Navy signal intelligence service (TICOM Document 514 in film 49) contains a letter dated 23/9/36 and headed "Chiffrierstelle/Abw. II" (Abw. is probably for Abwehr). In a report from Huettenhain to Fenner dated November 1939, a reference is also made to the Chiffrierstelle of OKW. (Letter in T-1620).

[5] I-123, 2.

[6] I-123, 4.

have been a major in 1932.[7] Major (later Col.) Boetzel is well known as an expert in intercept. He ended the war as chief of the Signal Intelligence Agency of the Army High Command (OKH/ G d NA). It is very unlikely that these signal officers would have been in charge of the Cipher Section if the Cipher Section had been organized wholly separately from the intercept network.

Trappe is not a wholly trustworthy witness. That he was connected with Chi from an early date is undoubtedly true. He is mentioned in a letter from Huettenhain to Fenner as one who had worked on French codes in 1939, before the outbreak of the war.[8] Later on he seems to have worked on agents' ciphers,[9] and it may be in this connection that he made the trips abroad mentioned by Beyreuther. Beyreuther was unquestionably wrong when he stated that "Mr. Trappe .. has nothing to do with OKW/Chi.[10] He was, however, too far down in the organization to be a wholly reliable witness as to the niceties of organization at the top. His list of chiefs of the Cipher Section of the Defense Ministry (Chiffrierstelle) may be nothing more than a list of individuals whom at one time or another Trappe had considered the "big boss".

On the basis of the above material, the following development may be suggested, with the caution that the evidence is scanty and uncertain. The Cipher Section of the Defense Ministry (later the War Ministry) was subordinate to a signal officer who also controlled the Ministry's intercept network. When the War Ministry was replaced by the Supreme Command of the Armed Forces (OKW) and a separate Army High Command (OKH) set up to control the Army, the intercept organization was subordinated to the Army High Command. At the same time the Army drew on the Ministry's Cipher Section for a few trained

[7] IF-130, p 3. In 1932, the file declares Major Fellgiebel was Commander of Signal Battalion 2 (Kdr. Nach. Abt. 2). If Trappe is right, then this battalion must have controlled intercept operations.

[8] T 1620 (Film ES)

[9] I-132, 2.

[10] I-150, 9.

cryptanalysts and used them to work on foreign military traffic, which now became the exclusive sphere of the Army. Meanwhile, the main body of the Cipher Section came under the OKW, took over diplomatic traffic as a definite commitment, and remained for a while without an intercept organization of its own. Finally in 1939 the two Army intercept stations at Lauf and Treuenbrietzen were subordinated to the OKW and commissioned to intercept diplomatic traffic for OKW/Chi. The split between Army and Armed Forces signal intelligence services was then complete.[11]

[11] OKW/Chi's intercept operators, however, continued to be trained in the Army Signal School at Halle, according to Mrs. von Nida. (I-105, 5).

DOCID: 3560827

TOP SECRET

SIGNAL INTELLIGENCE AGENCY OF SUPREME COMMAND ARMED FORCES (OKW/CHI)

OPERATIONS CHART AS OF SPRING 1944

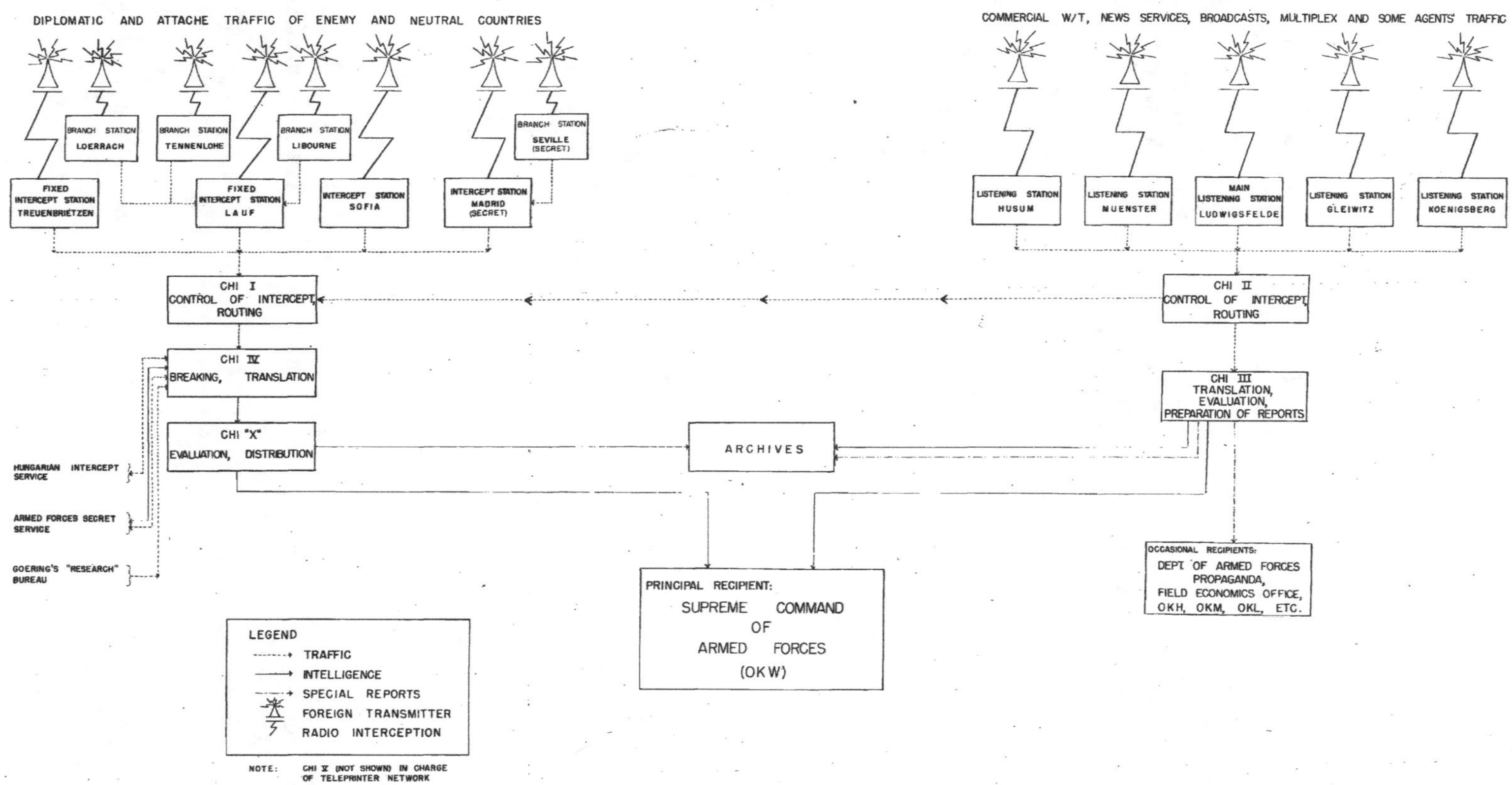

CHART NO. 3-2

TOP SECRET CREAM

TOP SECRET CREAM

TOP SECRET

SIGNAL INTELLIGENCE AGENCY OF SUPREME COMMAND ARMED FORCES

(OKW/WFST./AG. WNV/CHI)

ORGANIZATION AS OF APRIL 1945

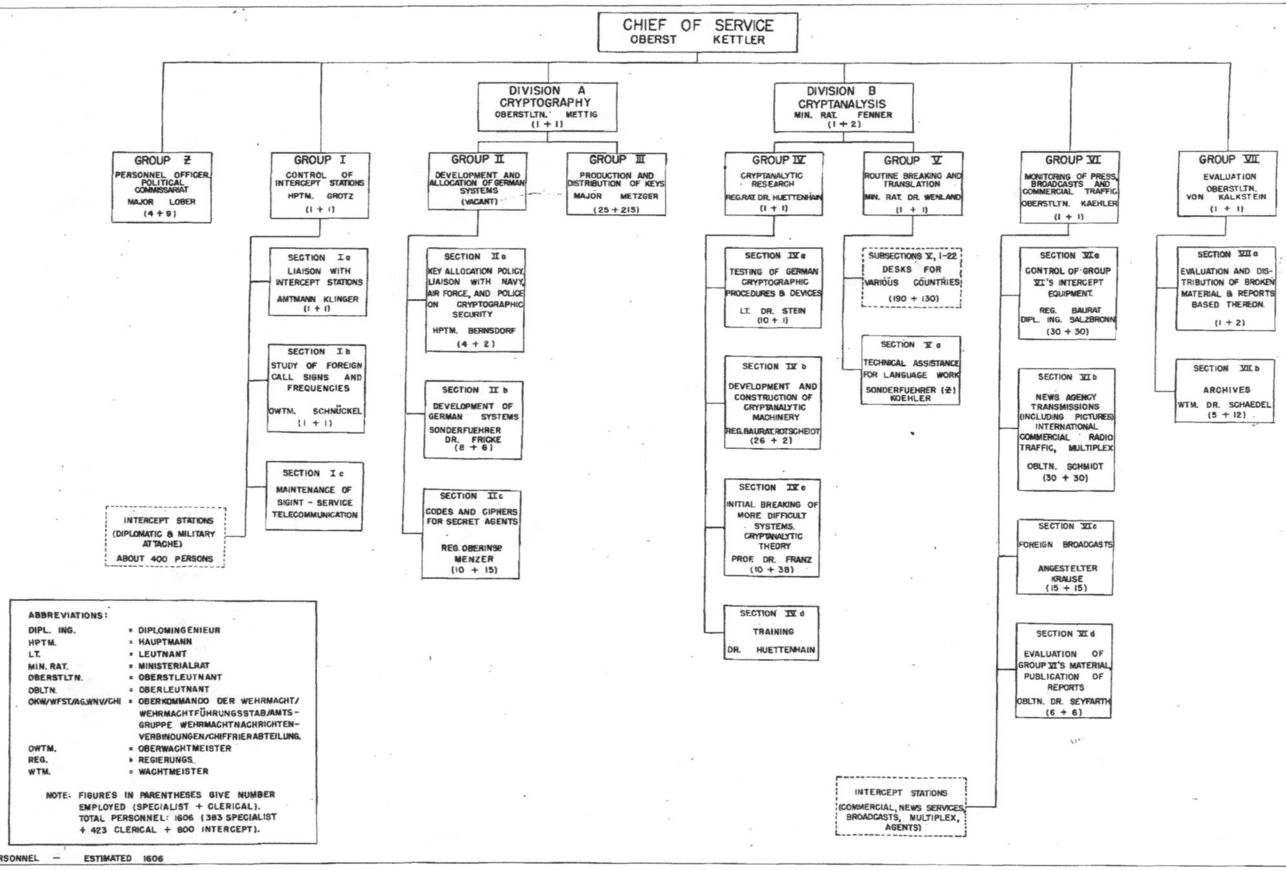

CHART NO. 3-1

ARMY SECURITY AGENCY

Washington, D. C.

EUROPEAN AXIS SIGNAL INTELLIGENCE IN WORLD WAR II AS REVEALED BY "TICOM" INVESTIGATIONS AND BY OTHER PRISONER OF WAR INTERROGATIONS AND CAPTURED MATERIAL, PRINCIPALLY GERMAN

VOLUME 4--SIGNAL INTELLIGENCE SERVICE OF THE ARMY HIGH COMMAND

Prepared under the direction of the

CHIEF, ARMY SECURITY AGENCY

1 May 1946

WDGAS-14

 14251

TOP SECRET CREAM

VOLUME 4

The Signal Intelligence Service
of the Army High Command

TOP SECRET CREAM

DOCID: 3486746

VOLUME 4

Chapter I: The History of the German Army Signal Intelligence Service.

1. The pre-Hitler Period(1919-1933)-- The pre-Hitler period of signal intelligence in the German Army is very obscure. From the scanty and uncertain evidence, however, the following organization may be suggested. A Codes and Ciphers Section of the German Defense Ministry (Reichswehrministerium Chiffrierabteilung), subordinated to an Army Signal Officer, had been maintained in skeleton force from the end of the first World War.[1] The Chiefs were:[2]

Lt. Buschenhagen	1919-1927
Major Schmidt	1927-1931
Major Fellgiebel	1931-1932
Major Oschmann	1932-1934
Major Boetzel	1934-1939

The head of the Codes and Ciphers Section of the German Defense Ministry also controlled the Ministry's intercept network. This network dated from 1923/4 when the first fixed intercept stations (Feste Horchstelle, abbreviated Feste) were established.[3] There is evidence of at least seven such stations operating before 1933.[4] Six of these were devoted primarily to the interception of foreign military traffic; and one to the interception of foreign diplomatic traffic. The six for military traffic were located at Stuttgart, Munich, Muenster, Koenigsberg, Liegnitz, and Breslau; the one for diplomatic traffic, at Treuenbrietzen.[5]

1 I 96 p 2

2 I 123 p 4

3 I 62 p 5; IF 181 p 1

4 I 85 p 2

5 I 62 p 6

2. The pre-World War II Period (1933-1939)-- In 1933/34, the German Defense Ministry set up three more intercept stations: one at Hersbruck (later moved to Lauf); the other two, at Striegau and Chemnitz.[6] With these ten intercept stations, the German Defense Ministry intercepted foreign Army, Air Force, and diplomatic traffic. The German Defense Ministry also set up in 1933/4 in Berlin its own military code and cipher section called the Intercept Control Station (Horchleitstelle, abbreviated HLS).[7] For this it drew a few trained cryptanalysts from the Codes and Cipher Section of the German War Ministry (Reichskriegsministerium).[8] Foreign Army traffic intercepted by the German Defense Ministry was sent to the Intercept Control Station (Horchleitstelle); Air Force traffic, to the Signal Intelligence Agency of the Commander-in-Chief of the Air Force (Chiffrierstelle des Oberbefehlshabers der Luftwaffe, abbreviated Chi-Stelle OBdL) established in 1937.[9] Diplomatic traffic was sent to both the Codes and Ciphers Section of the German Defense Ministry (called after 1934 the German War Ministry (Kriegsministerium) and the Foreign Office Cryptanalytic Section (Sonderdienst des Referats Z in der Personalabteilung des Auswaertigen Amts, abbreviated Pers ZS).[10]

3. The early World War II Period (1939-1941)-- During the early years of the war, the main developments within the German Army signal intelligence service were the following:

a. The narrowing of the mission of the intercept service to include only Army traffic. In 1939 a newly formed Signal Intelligence Agency of the Supreme Command of the Armed Forces (Oberkommando der Wehrmacht/Chiffrier-Stelle, abbreviated OKW/Chi) took over the interception of all foreign diplomatic traffic from the German Army Signal Intelligence Service, and for that purpose the Army gave it two of its own intercept stations, at Lauf and Treuenbrietzen.[11]

6 I 85 p 3

7 I 78 p 2

8 The German Defense Ministry was renamed the German War Ministry after 1935.

9 IF 181 p 15

10 I 85 p 2

11 I 85 p 3

2

b. The expansion of intercept service. In 1939, the Army established two new branch stations for the intercept of foreign Army traffic emanating from the east, one at Graz and the other at Tullin.[12]

c. The establishment of five Signal Intelligence Regiments (Kommandeur der Nachrichten Aufklaerung, abbreviated "KONA"). These regiments were sent into the field as complete intercept and evaluation units, attached to Army Groups.[13] The KONA were given the numbers one through five. KONA 1, 2, 3 were assigned to German Armies on the eastern front: KONA 1 to the Army Group on the southern front, KONA 2 to the Army Group on the central front, and KONA 3 to the Army Group on the Northern front. KONA 4 was not attached to any Army Group but was subordinated to the Commanding Officer who controlled the German Armies in the Balkans (Befehlshaber Suedost).[14] KONA 5 was assigned to the Army Group on the Western front.[15]

d. The introduction of mathematicians and linguists. To cope with the increased amount of enemy Army traffic on all levels, and the increasingly difficult problems of solution, mathematicians and linguists were drafted into the Army in 1939 and were assigned either to the various field units or to the Intercept Control Station.[16]

e. An increased interest on the part of the Army in the security of its own systems. This new interest gave rise to the establishment of an Army Signal Security Agency designated as Group IV of Inspectorate 7 (Inspektion 7 Gruppe IV, abbreviated In 7/IV) which was subordinated to the Chief of Army Equipment and Commander of the Replacement Army (Chef der Heeresruestung und Befehlshaber des Ersatzheeres, abbreviated "Chef H Ruest u. BdE"). In 7/IV was composed

[12] I 85 p 3

[13] I 78 p 4

[14] IF 171 p 1

[15] IF 127

[16] I 78 p 4

3

of mathematicians and former actuaries whose function was the examination of cryptographic systems used by the German Army, and the preparation, printing and distribution of codes and ciphers.[17]

The German Army signal intelligence service in 1939 consisted of the following parts:

(1) at least 10 intercept stations for the interception of foreign Army traffic called Feste Horchstellen, abbreviated Feste
(2) five Signal Intelligence Regiments attached to Army Groups (each called Kommandeur der Nachrichten Aufklaerung, or "KONA")
(3) an Intercept Control Station (Horchleitstelle, or HLS) for the analysis and evaluation of foreign Army traffic;
(4) an Army Signal Security Agency (Inspectorate 7/IV, or In 7/IV) for testing and issuing codes and ciphers for the Army.

4. The Middle World War II Period (1941-1944)-- When, in 1941, the small staff at the Horchleitstelle was found to be inadequate to cope with the large amount of traffic which had resulted from the increasing pressure of the war, two central agencies were established to replace the station: a central cryptanalytic agency at Berlin designated as Inspectorate 7/VI of the Chief of Army Equipment and Commander of the Replacement Army (Chef der Heeresruestung und Befehlashaber des Ersatzheeres Inspektion 7 Gruppe VI, abbreviated Chef H Ruest u BdE/ In 7/VI or more simply In 7/VI); and a central evaluation agency at Zossen designated as Control Station for Signal Intelligence (Leitstelle der Nachrichten Aufklaerung, abbreviated LNA).

In 7/VI was organized by Major Mang of the German Army, whose aim was not only to increase the cryptanalytic staff of the new agency but also to provide reserves of cryptanalysts to work in key areas in the field. In order to acquire personnel easily, Major Mang subordinated In 7/VI in matters of personnel and administration to the Chief of Army Equipment and Commander of the Replacement Army (Chef H Ruest u BdE)[18]

[17] I 92 p 6

[18] I 78 p 5

4

In matters of policy, however, In 7/VI was subordinated to the Field Army. This curious form of organization is said to have enabled the cryptanalytic service to recruit sufficient personnel without serious interference while maintaining close operational contact with field units.[19]

During the first few months of the existence of In 7/VI, Russian cryptanalysis was included in the cryptanalytic work done at In 7/VI, and Russian evaluation was included in the evaluation done by LNA. Both these organizations, however, soon felt that the cryptanalysis and evaluation of Russian traffic should be carried on closer to the forward echelon of the German Field Army in East Prussia. In late 1941, therefore, some cryptanalysts and evaluators skilled in Russian traffic were detached from In 7/VI and from LNA respectively, and were sent to Loetzen to work.[20] These cryptanalysts and evaluators became the nucleus of the organization which later became the chief cryptanalytic and evaluation agency for Russian traffic, named Intercept Control Station East (Horchleitstelle Ost, abbreviated HLS Ost). From this point until November 1944 signal intelligence activities were sharply divided into Russian signal intelligence, carried on by HLS Ost, and non-Russian signal intelligence, carried on by In 7/VI and LNA.

In 1942, the responsibility for security testing of existing German Army cryptographic systems had been transferred from In 7/IV to In 7/VI.[21] From that time, the Army Signal Security Agency, In 7/IV, had been confined to the development of new systems for the Army and to the production, printing and distribution of current keys and systems.[22]

[19] I 78 p 5

[20] I 78 p 5

[21] I 78 p 6

[22] I 36 p 2

5

In the fall of 1943, In 7/VI had been transferred to the newly created Department of Signals of the General Army Office and renamed Signal Intelligence, Department of Signals, General Army Office, Army High Command (Oberkommando des Heeres/Allgemeines Heeres Amt/Amtsgruppe Nachrichten/Nachrichten Aufklaerung, abbreviated OKH/AHA/AgN/NA) Minor changes in internal organization were effected, but the function and operation of the agency was not changed.[23]

Although there was no essential change in the organization of the field units of the German Army Signal Intelligence Service from 1941 to 1944, additional units were placed in the field. In 1942 the eastern KONA (1, 2, and 3) were supplemented by the addition of KONA 6 which was formed to cover the German campaign in the Caucasus.[24] This KONA was not subordinated to any Army Group but was directly under HLS Ost. KONA 7 was established in February 1943 and was subordinated to the Commander-in-Chief South (Oberbefehlshaber Sued) who controlled Army Group C and the German forces in Italy.[25]

The organization of the German Army Signal Intelligence Service in 1944 consisted of:

1) a central cryptanalytic agency for non-Russian traffic, In 7/VI (latterly AgN/NA)
2) a central evaluation agency for non-Russian traffic, LNA;
3) a central cryptanalytic and evaluation agency for Russian traffic, HLS Ost;
4) seven Signal Intelligence Regiments (KONAs);
5) an Army Signal Security Agency for the distribution and development of Army systems (In 7/IV).

5. The Late World War II Period (1944-1945).-- In October 1944, the organization of the German Army signal intelligence service was completely changed through the amalgamation of the three central agencies, In 7/VI (latterly AgN/NA), LNA, and HLS Ost, into one central cryptanalytic and evaluation agency, (the Signal Intelligence Agency of the Army High Command, the Oberkommando des Heeres/General der Nachrichten Aufklaerung, abbreviated OKH/GdNA). This amalgamation was the logical result of the retreat of HLS Ost together with the German Army, from East Prussia to Zossen, where In 7/VI and LNA were situated.[26]

[23] IF 190 B p 4

[24] DF 18 p 81

[25] IF 172 p 2

[26] IF 123 p 5

6

The Signal Intelligence Regiments (KONAs) were not greatly affected by the amalgamation of the central agencies into the GdNA, although the KONAs did come "under closer centralized control in matters of administration and signal intelligence policy."[27]

The main changes in the Army's signal intelligence field organization in 1944-1945 were necessitated by the Allied invasion of France in June 1944. To cope with this situation, KONA 6 was moved from the eastern front to the western;[28] and a Senior Commander of Signal Intelligence (Hoeherer Kommandeur der Nachrichten Aufklaerung, abbreviated Hoeh Kdr d NA) was set up to coordinate and control KONA 5 and 6.[29] In late 1944 and early 1945, two additional KONAs were formed in the east, KONA 8 and KONA Nord,[30] but it is noteworthy that these KONAs were largely composed of units borrowed from other eastern front Signal Intelligence Regiments, and the creation of these last two KONA was thus not so much a mark of expansion as of redeployment to areas under stress.[31]

Colonel Boetzel, chief of the Signal Intelligence Agency of the Army High Command (OKH/GdNA) stated that KONA 4 was transferred to the West at the end of the war.[32] A captured document[33] indicated that KONA 4 had been succeeded by a signal battalion Nachrichten Aufklaerung Abteilung, abbreviated NAA) 16, in February 1945 but did not mention its transfer to the West. It is probable that the KONA disintegrated and that various parts were sent to the different fronts.

The organization of the German Army signal intelligence service at the end of the war consisted of:

1) the Signal Intelligence Agency of the Army High Command(OKH/GdNA) a central cryptanalytic and evaluation agency for all traffic.
2) a Senior Commander of Signal Intelligence,(Hoeh Kdr d NA) with control over the KONA stationed in the west and responsibility for all signal intelligence activities of the German Army in the West;
3) nine Signal Intelligence Regiments (KONAs) which were attached to Army Groups or Commanders in the field.

27 IF 123 p 5

28 I 76 Appendix, Chart I

29 IF 123 p 5

30 T 1402

31 See below Chapter IV

32 I 76 p 7

33 T 1402

7

VOLUME 4

Chapter II: Organization of Central Agencies of the German Army Signal Intelligence Service.

Paragraph

6. Organization of the Intercept Control Station 1933-1941.-- Not much is known of the organization of the Intercept Control Station (Horchleitstelle, abbreviated HLS), before 1941. The existence of sections for the cryptanalysis and evaluation[35] of Belgian, Polish, Russian, and British traffic may be surmised from Mettig's account of its activities.[36] Nothing specific, however, is known from TICOM sources. The small staff was commanded by Major Dr. Jung.[37]

7. Organization of In 7/VI.--

a. Inspectorate 7/VI (Inspektion 7/VI, abbreviated In 7/VI) in the autumn of 1941 was headed by Major Mang, and was divided into the following sections with heads as shown:[38]

Personnel Section	Captain Herbrueggen
British Section	Senior Inspectors Zillman and Liedtke
French Section	Senior Inspector Kuehn
Italian Section	Captain Fiala

[35] Evaluation is a free translation of the German word "auswertung" which to the Germans meant traffic analysis, the interpretation of news broadcast and plain text transmissions, the interpretation of radio telephone intercept, and the interpretation of the results of successful cryptanalysis. All these things taken together resulted in fully evaluated intelligence.

[36] I 78 p 3

[37] I 78 p 2

[38] IF 190 B App. 3

8

DOCID: 3486746

Balkan Section..............	Senior Specialist Bailovic
Mathematical Section........	1st Lt. Lueders and Technician Dr. Pietsch
Russian Section.............	1st Lt. Dettman
Linguistic Section..........	Technician Koehler
Training Section............	Senior Inspector Kuehn

Between 1941 and 1943 the following changes in the Organization of In 7/VI took place:

a) the Russian section was sent to Loetzen, East Prussia[39]

b) a section for cryptanalysis of USA systems was formed with the entry of the USA into the war[40]

c) a section for cryptanalysis of traffic of agents (foreign and internal) was added in 1942[41]

d) the investigation of the security of current German Army systems was transferred from In 7/VI, the former Army Signal Security Agency, to the mathematical section of In 7/VI[42]

e) an IBM section together with its machinery from In 7/IV was added[43]

b. In 7/VI in the spring of 1943 was divided into the following sections:[44]

Chief.......................	Major Mettig
British Section..........	Senior Inspector Zillmann
USA Section..............	Technician Dr. Steinberg
Balkan Section...........	Senior Specialist Bailovic
French Section...........	Technician Kuehn
Italian Section..........	Corporal Manaigo
Mathematical Section......	Technician Dr. Pietsch
Linguistic Section........	Technician Koehler
Training Section.........	Senior Inspector Kuehn
Agents Section...........	1st Lt. Vauck
IBM Section..............	Specialist Schenke

[39] I 78 p 8

[40] I 78 p 10

[41] I 115 p 3

[42] I 78 p 6

[43] I 78 p 6

[44] IF 190 B App 4

9

DOCID: 3486746

The sections of In 7/VI were housed during this period in buildings near the Bendlerstrasse in Berlin. The headquarters Training Section and sections for USA, French and Agents' traffic were located at Matthaekirchplatz 4;[45] the British and Balkan section, at Schellingstrasse 9; the IBM section, on Viktoriastrasse. Location of the Mathematical section is not known.[46]

In November 1943, the first large RAF raid on Berlin destroyed a great part of the offices of the Army High Command on Bendlerstrasse in Berlin, among which were those of In 7/VI. In 7/VI was thereupon moved to Jueterbog, where it was located until its amalgamation in November 1944 into GdNA.[47]

No estimate is given of the number of people employed in In 7/VI.

c. Organization of AgN/NA. When In 7/VI was reorganized as the Signal Intelligence Section of the Department of Signals of the General Army Office, of the Army High Command, the internal organization was somewhat changed. The previously independent sections were organized into a main section (Hauptreferat) for mathematics, and a main section for languages. The IBM section retained its autonomy.

The Main Section for Languages, with the exception that one section was added for Swedish traffic, covered the same field as had been covered by the individual language sections of In 7/VI. The organization of AgN/NA is outlined thus:[48]

Chief	Major Lechner
Main Section A for Mathematics	1st Lt. Lueders
Main Section B for Languages	Senior Specialist Bailovic
British Section	Senior Inspector Zillmann
USA Section	Technician Steinberg
French Section	Technician Kuehn
Balkan Section	Senior Specialist Bailovic
Swedish Section	Pfc. Rohden

[45] I 58 p 2

[46] IF 126 pp 6-7

[47] IF 126 p 6

[48] IF 190 B App 5

10

Linguistic Section..........	Technician Koehler
Training Section............	Senior Inspector Kuehn
IBM Section.....................	Specialist Schenke

8. Organization of the Control Station for Signal Intelligence (LNA).-- The organization of the central evaluation agency for non-Russian traffic, the Control Station for Signal Intelligence (Leitstelle der Nachrichten Aufklaerung, abbreviated LNA) is obscure.

According to Krause, a member of LNA, there were sections for evaluating British, USA, Italian, Balkan, Greek, Turkish, Tunisian, Near Eastern, Portuguese, and Spanish traffic. Evaluation was made both of traffic and of the contents of decoded messages passed to these sections from In 7/VI. The staff of LNA was comparatively small, consisting of about seventy-five persons who were housed in one building for which the ground plan is given in a CSDIC publication.[49]

9. Organization of HLS Ost.-- The Intercept Control Station East (Horchleitstelle Ost, abbreviated HLS Ost) was the central cryptanalytic and evaluation center for Russian traffic located at Loetzen, East Prussia from late 1941 to late 1944. The exact size of the station is not known, but the organization is outlined as follows:[50]

Section "Z"................	Personnel problems
Section 1..................	Supply, maintenance, evaluation of captured documents and general research into wireless procedures.
Section 2..................	Evaluation, compilation of intercept situation report
Section 3..................	Russian cryptanalytic section.
Section 4..................	Monitoring of inter-Soviet State traffic; Russian radio broadcasts and Reuter and Tass News Agency broadcasts.

[49] IF 111 Annexes 1 and 2

[50] IF 123 p 4

In the winter of 1942-43, the Baudot Reception Station was moved from Minsk to Loetzen and subordinated to HLS/Ost, Section 4.

HLS Ost was first directed by Col. Kettler, who later became chief of the Signal Intelligence Agency of the Supreme Command of the Armed Forces (OKW/Chi). In the summer of 1942, Kettler was succeeded by Baron Col. von der Osten-Sacken, who remained its chief until July 1944, when he was implicated in the plot on Hitler's life and committed suicide.[51]

10. Organization of Signal Intelligence Agency.--The three agencies, In 7/VI (latterly AgN/NA), HLS Ost and LNA were amalgamated in November, 1944, into the Signal Intelligence Agency of the Army High Command (Oberkommando des Heeres General der Nachrichten Aufklaerung, abbreviated OKH/GdNA) almost intact.[52] In 7/VI (latterly AgN/NA), with some slight depletion of personnel, became Group IV of GdNA, which was assigned the responsibility for all cryptanalysis on foreign military traffic. LNA was transferred as a unit to Group II of OKH/GdNA, except for those sections which had been dealing with wireless and news agency traffic. These sections were assigned to Group I at OKH/GdNA. The various sections of HLS Ost were absorbed into the appropriate sections of OKH/GdNA as follows:

Section Z........................ into Group Z
Section 1........................ into Group V
Section 2........................ into Group III
Section 3........................ into Group IV
Section 4........................ into Group VI (except the wireless and news agency which went to Group I)

The organization of the OKH/GdNA which is explained in the following pages is outlined on Chart 4-2. It was in effect from November 1944 to the capitulation. Approximately 700 people were employed by the OKH/GdNA.[53]

[51] IF 123 p 4

[52] IF 123 pp 5-6

[53] All material concerning the organization of the GdNA is derived either from IF 123 pp 6-14 or I 113 pp 5-12, the account by Major Hentze, head of Group IV of the GdNA.

a. Headquarters unit. The Headquarters unit of OKH/GdNA consisted of the Chief, Signal Intelligence Service (Chef, General der Nachrichten Aufklaerung, abbreviated Chef/GdNA), Colonal Boetzel; his Chief of Staff, Lt. Col. Andrae; the Adjutant, Lt. Moravec, and the Chief of the Understaff, Lt. Koebe.

The staff controlled the signal intelligence work of all units of the GdNA, Groups I through VI. It also controlled two intercept stations, Feste 6 and Feste 11. These had been subordinated to HLS Ost before being attached to the GdNA. They specialized in intercepting high frequency traffic of the Red Army and NKVD.[54]

The Understaff of the OKH/GdNA supervised the intercept coverage of the Signal Intelligence Regiments (Kommandeure der Nachrichten Aufklaerung, abbreviated KONA) and their subordinate units: directly, in the case of KONA 1,2,3,7, and 8; and through the Senior Commander of Signal Intelligence (Hoeherer Kommandeur der Nachrichten Aufklaerung, abbreviated Hoeh, Kdr. d NA) for KONA 5 and 6.[55]

b. Group I. Group I was under the supervision of Bodenmueller. It had two main tasks:

1) the maintenance of communications between the units of the GdNA;
2) press monitoring.

For internal communications, teleprinter was used until the final debacle, when it became necessary to resort to radio. To carry out the second task of Group I, press monitoring, there were four subsections: the monitoring of eastern wireless, western wireless, plain text monitoring, and evaluation. The evaluation sub-section (4) was responsible for collating all information from the other three sub-sections and consolidating it into reports. The collated reports were divided into separate parts for political, economic, or military news. They were circulated within the departments of the Army High Command, sometimes with the classification SECRET (Geheimkommandosache, abbreviated GKdoS). Because of the personnel shortage, the BBC London Service and the Reuter Agency were the only news agencies monitored for western traffic.

[54] IF 123 p 6

[55] IF 123 p 6

c. Group II. Group II which had cannibalized LNA and consisted of about 50 people, produced radio situation reports correlating the information from KONAs 5, 6, and 7. Capt. Thiel, who was head of this group, had been with LNA for a long time and was said by Hentze to have been thoroughly familiar with the problems of western evaluation.

d. Group III. This group, under the supervision of Capt. Gorzolle, was responsible for the evaluation of traffic and cryptanalytic work emanating from the Russian front. The department was divided into the following sections:

Traffic Sorting Office
Northern Sector Evaluation
Central Sector Evaluation
Southern Sector Evaluation
Russian Special Police (NKVD) Evaluation
Partisan traffic evaluation
Swedish traffic evaluation

e. Groups IV. Group IV, under Major Hentze, was responsible for all cryptanalytic work done at GdNA. It was one of the largest groups of the OKH/GdNA, having been built up from parts of three former agencies, In 7/VI, LNA and HLS Ost. The group was divided into separate sections according to the origin of the material.

Section I, headed by the mathematician, Dr. Pietsch, was the former Mathematical Section of In 7/VI. It was responsible for the security of German Army Systems. Sub-section 1a, headed by Marquardt, was engaged in research on German Army hand systems; sub-section 1b, under Dr. Pietsch handled research on German Army machine systems.

Section 2, headed by Kneschke, dealt with the cryptanalysis and deciphering of non-Russian traffic. There were three sub-sections:

2a: British and USA systems;
2b: French systems;
2c: Balkan systems

Section 3, headed by Lt. Dettmann, was composed of the cryptanalytic sections of HLS Ost. It dealt with Russian systems and had four sub-sections:

3a: Russian Special Police traffic (NKVD);
3b: Russian Army traffic;

14

3c: Russian Partisan traffic;
3d: Research on Russian systems.

Section 4 was the former IBM section of In 7/VI. According to Major Hentze, this section performed mainly statistical work. Most of the members were women used to run the machines. The section maintained its own repair shop for the machines.

Section 5 was the training department of the GdNA, where cryptographic and cryptanalytic courses were given under the direction of Inspector Kuehn, who had headed the Training Section of In 7/VI. During the last months of the war, the once flourishing section dwindled to a group of forty students every three months.

f. Group V. Group V was a mixed group containing three sections all of which carried out unrelated activities.

Section 1. This section headed by Inspector Zipper, was engaged in reconstructing Russian, British, and USA call signs and call signs systems, and deducing units therefrom. It covered various procedures of enemy wireless and the allocation of wave lengths.

Section 2. This section under Specialist Block was responsible for the exploitation of captured Russian documents of signals interest. Captured manuals were translated and descriptions of Russian equipment examined.

Section 3. This section was engaged in supplying the KONAs with necessary intercept equipment and in maintaining a workshop to service the needs of the OKH/GdNA itself.

g. Group VI. Group VI, located at Potsdam under Capt. Roeder, was responsible for intercepting and evaluating special high-grade machine systems, Russian systems were handled by Section 1, with three sub-sections:

1a: interception and evaluation of Inter-Soviet State traffic;
1b: intercepting and evaluation of Russian Baudot;
1c: intercepting and evaluation of Russian Army traffic.

Western teleprinter and automatic morse traffic was handled by Section 2. (Interception was done in sub-section 2b, evaluation in sub-section 2a).

h. Group Z. Group Z (which is not shown on the chart) was responsible for general administrative control of all departments within the OKH/GdNA. The work was divided into four types: personnel, communications, pay, and drawing. A central card index was kept of all personnel employed in the OKH/GdNA and the personnel section was responsible for all transfers, either inter-departmental or outside the OKH/GdNA. The section for communications registered all incoming and outgoing correspondence and was responsible for all courier communications between the OKH/GdNA and its subordinate units. For local communications, this section had its own runners; but for long distances, the courier services of the Army High Command were used. All personnel of OKH/GdNA were paid by the "pay" section. In the drawing section, all situation maps and radio networks were reproduced. A certain amount of photostat and book-binding activity was also carried on here.

Because of the lack of detailed information concerning German signal intelligence at the end of the war, it is difficult to appraise the effectiveness of the final reorganization of November 1944. In large measure, the logical simplicity of outline was disrupted in the last months. The full organization existed as an integrated unit only from November, 1944 to February, 1945. From that time until the surrender, the OKH/GdNA was almost continously on the move seeking refuge in southern Germany. Most of the groups moved from Zossen to Bad Reichenhall either directly or by way of Erfurt. Somewhere between Erfurt and Bad Reichenhall in the Weimar area, the IBM section was lost. Group VI which had been located at Potsdam went first to Stuttgart and then to Rosenheim.[56]

[56] IF 123 p 6-13

VOLUME 4

Chapter III: Organization of the German Army Field Signal Intelligence Service

Paragraph

11. The organization of the typical Signal Intelligence Regiment.-- The basic element of the field organization of the German Army signal intelligence service was the Signal Intelligence Regiment (Kommandeur der Nachrichten Aufklaerung, abbreviated KONA). Each Army Group was provided with a Signal Intelligence Regiment (KONA), which had control over all signal intelligence units in the area governed by the Army Group. If, as was the case with KONA 4 and KONA 7, the Signal Intelligence Regiment was attached to a Commander of the German Armies stationed in an area, the Signal Intelligence Regiment had control of all signal intelligence units within the area of that command.

There were, of course, variations in the organization and manner of operation of the various Signal Intelligence Regiments corresponding to differences in personnel, equipment, and operational responsibilities. The typical component parts of a Signal Intelligence Regiment, however, were: [60]

[60] I 190 p 5

One Signal Intelligence Evaluation Center (Nachrichten Aufklaerung Auswertestelle, abbreviated NAAS), designed to work with KONA headquarters at Army Group level; usually one Stationary Intercept Company (Feste Nachrichten Aufklaerungsstelle, abbreviated Feste), designed to work at Army level; usually two Long Range Signal Intelligence Companies (Nachrichten Fernaufklaerung Kompanie, abbreviated FAK), designed to work at Army level; usually two Close Range Signal Intelligence Companies (Nachrichten Nahaufklaerung Kompanie, abbreviated NAK), designed to work at Army Corps level; each Close Range Company usually had two or three Close Range Signal Intelligence Platoons (Nachrichten Nahaufklaerungszug, abbreviated NAZ), designed to work below the NAK but still at Army Corps level.

In 1944, the Signal Intelligence Battalion (Nachrichten Aufklaerung Abteilung, abbreviated NAA) was introduced into the organization of the KONA. These battalions were small administrative units, which acted as coordinating units at Army level.

Major Hertzer, CO of KONA 1, stated that the NAA commanders were generally elderly supervisors whose chief duty was to make the rounds of the units forming the NAA gathering opinions and effecting small adjustments in the use of close range signal intelligence platoons. Colonel Boetzel, head of OKH/GdNA, stated that the NAA was not considered an effective improvement.[61]

This chapter will deal with each Signal Intelligence Regiment separately and will give in some detail the organization and history of the components of each.

[61] I 19g p 5

12. Organization of KONA 1.-- KONA 1 was organized in the following way. To KONA headquarters were subordinated:[62]

1 Signal Intelligence Evaluation Center, NAAS 1
1 Stationary Intercept Company, Feste 10
1 Close Range Signal Intelligence Company, NAK Preuss
2 Signal Intelligence Battalions, NAA 3 and NAA 4

To NAA 3 were subordinated:

1 Long Range Signal Intelligence Company, FAK 623
1 Close Range Signal Intelligence Company, NAK 953 (later NAK Benold)

To NAA 4 were subordinated:

1 Long Range Signal Intelligence Company FAK 617
1 Close Range Signal Intelligence Company, NAK 954

a. Headquarters Unit. The headquarters units of KONA 1, which worked at Army Group headquarters, consisted of the commandant of the KONA, his Adjutant, a Chief of Operations (S-3), a paymaster, a technical inspector, clerks, and truck drivers. The following statistics show the breakdown of the headquarters unit.[63]

	Officers	Enlisted Men	Women
Co	1	-	-
Adj.	1	-	-
S-3	1	-	-
Paymaster	1	-	-
Technical Inspector	1	-	-
Clerks	-	4	2
Truck drivers	-	9	-
	5	13	2

[62] I 198 p 5

[63] IF 40 p 12

b. NAAS 1. The NAAS of KONA 1 had two major operational subdivisions: a section engaged in evaluation and traffic analysis, and a section for cryptanalytic activities. There were also a headquarters section, a communication line section, and a section of truck drivers. The personnel, totalling eight officers, one hundred sixty enlisted men, and fifty enlisted women were thus divided among the section: 64

Section	Officers	Enlisted Men	Women
Headquarters	1	18	2
Evaluation	6	66	25
Cryptanalysis	1	42	-
Communication	-	21	23
Truck Drivers	-	13	-
	8	160	50

c. Feste 10 and the Long Range Intercept Companies. The Stationary Intercept Company, Feste 10, and the Long Range Signal Intelligence Companies, FAK 617 and FAK 623, were similar in their organization and operation. Each had a headquarters section, monitoring platoons, an evaluation section, a cryptanalytic section, and a communication line platoon. The differences between Feste 10 and the FAK were minor. Feste 10 was less mobile than the FAK, having eight truck drivers instead of the twelve and sixteen assigned to FAK 617 and FAK 623 respectively.

64 IF 40 p 12

The following lists show the subsections and strength of Feste 10, FAK 617, and FAK 623:[65]

Feste 10

Section	Officers	Enlisted Men	Women
Headquarters	1	18	2
Monitoring Plt.	-	32	61
Evaluation	1	25	8
Cryptanalysis	1	15	2
Communication Ln. Plt.	-	10	-
Truck Drivers	-	8	-
Enemy Radio Station Locators	-	50	-
	3	158	73

FAK 617

Section	Officers	Enlisted Men	Women
Headquarters	1	15	3
Monitoring Plts.	1	91	-
Evaluation	1	33	-
Cryptanalysis	-	20	-
Communication Ln. Plt.	-	23	-
Truck Drivers	-	16	-
	3	198	3

65 IF 40 p 13

FAK 623

Section	Officers	Enlisted Men	Women
Headquarters	1	14	4
Monitoring Plts.	1	83	-
Evaluation	1	34	-
Cryptanalysis	-	16	-
Communication Ln. Plt.	1	17	-
Truck Drivers	-	12	-
	4	176	4

d. NAK 954. The Close Range Signal Intelligence Company, NAK 954, was divided into sections comparable to those of Feste 10 and the long-range intercept companies, as the following chart indicates:[66]

Section	Officers	Enlisted Men	Women
Headquarters	1	41	-
Evaluation	-	30	-
Radio Receiving	-	25	-
Communication Ln. Plt.	-	18	-
4 Monitoring Plts.	4	112	-
	5	226	-

The NAK operated by platoons, one platoon attached to each Army Corps.[67] The strength of a platoon was from twenty to thirty men, of which approximately twelve were engaged in radio telephone intercept, two in radio intercept, five in direction finding, and three in evaluation. The rest of the platoon comprised clerks, drivers, cooks, etc.

[66] IF 40 p 13

[67] I 19b p 2

e. NAK 953. Up to September, 1944 NAK 953 was subordinated to NAA 3 of KONA 1; but at that time it was moved to the west, leaving behind only its interpreters and cryptanalysts, who continued to serve on the eastern front.[68]

f. NAK Benold. NAK Benold, named after its CO, was composed of specialists of various kinds who had been drawn from the signal intelligence companies subordinate to KONA 1. As a company it formed part of NAA 3.

g. NAK Preuss. NAK Preuss, taking its name as did NAK Benold, from its CO, was formed from forces withdrawn from other units of KONA 1. This close range signal company was, in contrast to the other companies, subordinated directly to KONA Headquarters.

13. Organization of KONA 2. -- The organization of KONA 2 is not known in detail. As far as can be determined from TICOM sources, there were subordinated to this KONA in 1944:[69]

1 Signal Intelligence Evaluation Center, NAAS 2
3 Signal Intelligence Battalions, NAA 6, 7, and 8
1 Stationary Intercept Company, Feste 7
3 Long Range Signal Intelligence Companies, FAK 610, 619, 622
3 Close Range Signal Intelligence Companies, NAK 951, 955, 958

In February 1945, these components of KONA 2 were split: part of them remained with KONA 2, which was reassigned from Army Group North to Army Group Weichsel; part of them were attached to KONA Nord, which took the place of KONA 2 with Army Group North. The original components were divided between the two KONA in the following way:[70]

KONA 2:

2 Long Range Signal Intelligence Companies, FAK 610, 622
1 Close Range Signal Intelligence Company, NAK 958
1 Stationary Intercept Company, Feste 7

68 I 19b p 1

69 DF 9; I 76 Appendix

70 DF 9

KONA Nord:

1 Long Range Intercept Company, FAK 619
1 Close Range Signal Intelligence Platoon, NAZ Brutus
2 Close Range Signal Intelligence Company NAK 951, 955
1 Signal Intelligence Evaluation Center, NAAS 2

This remained the general organization until 28 March, 1945, when by order of General Praun, Chief Signal Officer, Armed Forces (Chef Wehrmacht Nachrichtenverbindungen, abbreviated Chef WNV) and Chief Signal Officer, Army (Chef Heeres Nachrichtenverbindung's wesen, abbreviated Chef HNW.) KONA Nord returned to KONA 2 all its units except the Close Range Signal Intelligence Companies, NAK 951 and 955. [71]

14. Organization of KONA 3.-- KONA 3 was composed, insofar as is known, of one NAA (10),[72] one FAK, one NAK and one Feste. (The FAK may have been Number 611, which was transferred to the west under KONA 6 in October 1944) [73] Nothing further isknown about KONA 3, which was caught by the Russians in a pocket in Kurland at the end of the war.[74]

15. Organization of KONA 4.-- KONA 4, was subordinated to the Commanding Officer Southeast (Befehlshaber Suedost), who controlled the German Armies in the Balkans.[75] The responsibility of these armies appears to have been essentially that of and occupational force; and KONA 4, therefore, added to its normal task of intercepting long range traffic emanating from the Middle East and Africa that of monitoring the traffic of the occupied Balkan countries. This circumstance may account for the fact that the organization of KONA 4 included no mobile Long Range Signal Intelligence Companies and only two mobile Close Range Signal Intelligence Platoons. The other units of KONA 4 were the Signal Intelligence Evaluation Center NAAS 4, and two Stationary Intercept Companies (Feste 5 and 6)[76]

71 DF 9

72 I 76 Appendix

73 I 76 Appendix

74 I 116 p 8

75 IF 171 p 1

76 IF 171

24

a. NAAS 4. The code name for NAAS 4 was the abbreviation HASSO, which stood for Horchauswertestelle Suedost, Intercept Evaluation Station Southeast.[77] NAAS 4 was divided into a cryptanalytic section, a direction finding section, a tactical evaluation section, and a final evaluation section.[78] The strength of NAAS 4 was about 80-100 men, including interpreters, decoders, cryptanalysts, evaluating personnel, draughtmen, drivers and switchboard operators.[79]

b. Feste 5. Feste 5 was the former Army Fixed Intercept Station at Graz. It had the following sections:

1) headquarters
2) radio intercept section
3) radio operation and maintenance section, operating a radio transmitter
4) decoding and cryptanalytic section
5) evaluation section for direction finding.

Feste 5 had a strength of 150-170 men and operated fifty radio intercept sets. Its personnel was composed of radio intercept operators, code clerks, cryptanalysts, interpreters, drivers, radio operators, typists, and switchboard operators.[80]

c. Feste 6. Feste 6 was the former Army Fixed Intercept Station at Tulln. It had the same subordinate sections as Feste 5, with a strength of about 130 men:[81]

1) headquarters
2) radio intercept section
3) radio operations and maintenance section, operating a radio transmitter
4) decoding and cryptanalytic section
5) evaluation section for direction finding

[77] IF 171 p 1

[78] IF 171 p 2

[79] IF 171 p 2

[80] IF 171 p 3

[81] IF 171 p 3

d. NAZ T. The Close Range Signal Intelligence Platoon, NAZ T, consisted of about forty-two men; among these were Turkish decoders who also acted as interpreters. Its organization was as follows:[82]

1) platoon headquarters
2) radio intercept station with 10 sets
3) radio operation and maintenance section
4) direction finding platoon
5) decoding section for Turkish only
6) final evaluation section for direction finding

e. NAZ W. The signal intelligence platoon, NAZ W, consisted of about eighty men who specialized in monitoring internal Balkan radio traffic. Its organization was as follows:[83]

1) platoon headquarters
2) radio intercept station
3) radio operation and maintenance section
4) direction finding platoon
5) decoding section
6) final evaluation section

f. Radio Control Station. The Radio Control Station (Rundfunkueberwachungstelle) which had been part of the organization of KONA 4 was dissolved in 1942.[84]

16. Organization of KONA 5.--
a. Organization through 1944. KONA 5 was the only Signal Intelligence Regiment on the western front until the establishment of KONA 7 in February 1943. It remained throughout the war preeminent on this front.

[82] IF 171 p 3

[83] IF 171 p 3

[84] IF 171 p 3

DOCID: 3486746

Before February 1944, the organization KONA 5 consisted of a Signal Intelligence Evaluation Center, NAAS 5, four Stationary Intercept Companies, Feste 2, 3, 9, and 12; and two Long Range Signal Intelligence Companies, FAK 613 and 624.[85]

Some time after February 1944, the organization of KONA 5 was changed.[86] The reorganization of KONA 5 parallels changes in the German order of battle which took place on the western front in early 1944. Prior to this time the western armies had been under the command of Army Group D, to which KONA 5 was attached as the Signal Intelligence Regiment of the West. In early 1944, however, Army Group D was absorbed into the Commander-in-Chief West (Oberbefehlshaber West), who took control of three newly formed Army Groups on the western front, Army Groups B, H, and G. KONA 5 therefore modeled its organization so that it controlled three Signal Intelligence Battalions, NAA 12, 13, and 14. Each battalion was attached to a separate Army Group: NAA 12 to Army Group D, NAA 13 to Army Group B, and NAA 14 to Army Group G.[87]

In regard to the subordination of the six component parts of KONA 5 to the three Signal Intelligence Battalions, there is disagreement between a Combined Services Detailed Interrogation Centre publication[88] and a TICOM interrogation report.[89-90]

[85] IF 127

[86] IF 127 p 2

[87] I 76 Appendix

[88] IF 127

[89] I 76

[90] The CSDIC report describing the grouping of the six component parts indicate that FAK 624 combined with signal intelligence platoon 12 to form NAA 12; Feste 2 and 12 combined to form NAA 13; Feste 613 combined with a short range intercept company, NAK 965, to form NAA 14. Feste 3 and 9 were left as independent units administered by the Kommandeur.

Chart 4-3 shows the distribution of the six elements according to the TICOM report. Feste 12 combined with Feste 3 to form NAA 12; Feste 2 and 9 combined with FAK 613 to form NAA 13. There is no indication whether FAK 624 combined with other companies when it formed NAA 14.

b. After 1944. The organization of KONA 5 as outlined above remained constant throughout most of 1944. In late 1944, however, an attempt was made to centralize and to strengthen the western field organization. Accordingly, a senior Commander of Signal Intelligence (Hoeherer Kommandeur der Nachrichten Aufklaerung, abbreviated Hoeh Kdr d NA) was established. This Senior Commander, Col. Kopp, was attached to the Commander-in-Chief West (Oberbefehlshaber West) and was made responsible for all signal intelligence activities in the west.[91] The strengthening of the western field signal intelligence was effected by moving KONA 6 from the eastern front to the western front to join KONA 5. Both KONAs were subordinated to the Senior Commander: KONA 5 was assigned to Army Group D, which controlled the German armies on the southern end of the western front; and KONA 6 was attached to Army Group B, which controlled the German armies on the northern end of the western front.[92]

With the move of KONA 6 to the west, the organization of KONA 5 was modified. The Signal Intelligence Battalions of KONA 5 were reduced to two, NAA 12 and NAA 14. NAA 13, which had been composed of two Stationary Intercept Companies (Feste 2 and 9) and one Long Range Signal Intelligence Company (FAK 613), was taken from KONA 5, broken up, and its components reassigned. Feste 2 was placed under the direct supervision of the Hoeh Kdr d NA; Feste 9 was shifted from Norway to Italy, where it fell under KONA 7; and NAA 13 with FAK 613 was assigned to KONA 6. KONA 5 was compensated for the loss of FAK 613 by the addition of FAK 626, which was taken from one of the eastern KONA (perhaps KONA 8) and brought to the western front.[93]

[91] IF 123 p 6

[92] I 76 Appendix

[93] I 76; IF 127

28

c. Organization of component parts: The organization of KONA 5, therefore, in the spring of 1945 was, as Chart 4-3 indicates: one evaluation center (NAAS 5) with two battalions (NAA 12 and 14); subordinated to NAA 12, one Stationary Intercept Company (Feste 12), and one Long Range Signal Intelligence Company (FAK 624); subordinated to NAA 14, one Signal Intelligence Company (FAK 626). This was the organization of KONA 5 until the capitulation.

1) NAAS 5. NAAS 5, the Signal Intelligence Evaluation Center of KONA 5, was located near Paris at St. Germaine-en-Laye. The strength of the organization was about 150 men, consisting of interpreters, cryptanalysts, evaluators, draughtsmen, switchboard operators, drivers, etc. In addition, some women auxiliaries were available, particularly for switchboard work. The internal organization of NAAS 5 is not known.[94]

2) Feste 12. Feste 12 was the Stationary Intercept Company which was subordinated to NAAS 5 until early 1944, when it joined with Feste 3 to form NAA 12.

The organization of Feste 12 consisted of a radio intercept platoon, and a telephone communications unit. When it was attached to NAAS 5, Feste 12 had no cryptanalytic or evaluation personnel since this work was being done at NAAS 5, it is probable that this type of personnel was added. The strength of Feste 12 was estimated at 120 men and 30 women auxiliaries.[95]

3) Feste 2. According to a prisoner's account,[96] the organization of Feste 2, the former Army intercept station at Muenster, closely approximated that of Feste 3. It had a radio intercept platoon, a direction finding platoon, and an evaluation platoon consisting of two sections: one for the evaluation of content of messages (Inhaltsauswertung) and one for the evaluation of traffic. (Verkehrsauswertung).

[94] IF 127 p 2

[95] IF 127 p 4

[96] IF 127 p 4

In 1944, Feste 2 combined with Feste 9 and FAK 613 to form NAA 13. When NAA 13 was broken up in November 1944, Feste 2 was subordinated directly to the Senior Commander of Signal Intelligence in the West.

4) Feste 3. Feste 3 was the original Army intercept station at Euskirchen. Early in the war it had been subordinated to KONA 5. At first administered independently, in 1944 it combined with Feste 12 to form NAA 12. When KONA 5 was reorganized in the fall of 1944, Feste 3 was combined with the Long Range Signal Intelligence Company, FAK 626, which had been brought from the eastern front to form NAA 14. This organization was valid until the end of the war.[97]

The internal organization of Feste 3 is described by a liaison officer, Lt. Hans Lehwald, attached to it as consisting of a radio reception platoon of approximately 70 receivers, and an evaluation platoon of 25-30 men. The evaluation platoon was broken down into sections for traffic analysis, cryptanalysis, evaluation, direction finding, and filing section for diagrams of the nets, call signs, personalities, code names, and direction finding results.[98]

5) Feste 9. Feste 9 was a Stationary Intercept Company formed in Frankfurt/Main in the spring of 1942 and sent to Norway in July of that year. It was first stationed at Trondhiem, later at Bergen, and in the spring of 1944 at Ski near Oslo. (Between the summer of 1944 and the following winter, most of the personnel were moved to Italy; by Christmas of 1944, there was nothing left of the unit in Norway.)[99]

[97] IF 127 p 3

[98] I 76 p 2

[99] IF 120 p 6

While in Norway Feste 9 was organized along the lines of a Long Range Signal Intelligence Company, with a headquarters platoon, an intercept platoon of 80-120 men, a direction finding, a radio platoon of about 20 men, and an evaluation section of about 30 men. The evaluation section had one subsection for the evaluation of message contents, one for traffic, and one for cryptanalysis.[100]

When in Norway, Feste 9 was subordinated to KONA 5. It can be surmised, however, that its connection with KONA 5 was always more flexible than that of the other units because of its geographical position in Norway. When NAA 13 was broken up, Feste 5 remained under the supervision of KONA 5 until, it was shifted to Italy under KONA 7.[101]

6) FAK 624. FAK 624 was formed at Montpellier on 16 April 1943 and attached to KONA 5.[102] In February 1944, FAK 624 was subordinated to NAA 14 of KONA 5, and in late fall of that year it combined with Feste 3 to form the reorganized NAA 14.[103]

The company was composed of an intercept platoon with an advanced listening post, a communications platoon, and an evaluation platoon. For transport, FAK 624 is said to have had approximately 85 vehicles with six special French radio trucks and trailers with direction finding equipment. The strength of the company was approximately 250 men including interpreters, code clerks, cryptanalysts, radio intercept operators and ninety drivers.[104]

[100] IF 120 p 6

[101] IF 144 p 2

[102] IF 127 p 3

[103] I 76 Appendix

[104] IF 127 p 3

7) FAK 613. FAK 613 belonged to KONA 5, in so far as is known, from its inception. In February 1944, FAK 613 combined with Feste 2 and 9 to form NAA 13. When this battalion was broken up in late 1944, FAK 613 was reassigned to KONA 6, with which it remained until the end of the war.[105]

Very little is known of the organization of FAK 613; according to IF 127, its organization paralleled that of FAK 624.[106]

8) FAK 626. FAK 626 was established in August 1943, trained until January 1944 and formally activated at that time at Winniza. It was subordinated to one of the eastern KONA (perhaps KONA 8) and was stationed in the Ukraine area. In October 1944, FAK 626 was sent to Landau where it was schooled in western traffic and reorganized. In November 1944, it met FAK 624 at Landau; and both units were sent west to KONA 5 with which they remained until the end of the war.[107]

The original strength of FAK 626 on the Russian front is said to have been 250-300 men of whom 80-100 were intercept operators, 10-15 direction finding operators, 10-15 cryptanalysts, 5-7 translators, 10 traffic analysts. The unit, however, was greatly under strength on the western front.[108]

17. <u>Organization of KONA 6</u>.-- KONA 6 was activated as an eastern KONA at Frankfurt/Main in 1941 and stationed in the Crimea to[109] work in the Caucasian campaign.[110] After that campaign, its assignment was the interception of Russian partisan traffic.[111] This remained its task until the KONA was detached in early 1944 and reassigned to work on the western front.[112]

[105] I 76 Appendix

[106] IF 127 p 4

[107] I 76 p 3

[108] I 76 p 4

[109] IF 195

[110] DF 18 p 81

[111] DF 18 p 81

[112] I 76 Appendix

There is no statement in TICOM documents about the organization of KONA 6 while it was in the east. The organization after it was assigned to the west, however, is clear from I 76 Appendix. As a western KONA, KONA 6 had two Signal Intelligence Battalions: NAA 9 and NAA 13. NAA 9 had been brought from the east in November 1944. Subordinated to it were the Close Range Signal Intelligence Company, NAK 956, which was established in October 1944, and the Long Range Signal Intelligence Company, FAK 611, which had been brought from the east at that time. NAA 13, it will be recalled, had been given to KONA 6 by KONA 5 with the Long Range Signal Intelligence Company, FAK 613. Subordinated to NAA 13 were also FAK 610, which had been brought from the east in November, 1944; and NAK 953, which had been brought from the east in October, 1944.[113]

a. FAK 613. FAK 613 was given by KONA 5 to KONA 6 in late 1944. As has been stated under the material on KONA 5, nothing is known of the organization of FAK 613. It was probably parallel to that of other Long Range Signal Intelligence Companies such as FAK 624.[114]

b. FAK 611. FAK 611 was active on the eastern front during the Russian campaign from June 1941. It was also stationed in Poland, where it was attached to Army Group Center.[115] In November 1944, FAK 611 was moved to the western front and subordinated to KONA 6, NAA 9.[116]

Nothing is known of the size of FAK 611 on the eastern front. On the western front it was small enough to occupy a house in Zutphen, Holland, near the Vandyk church, and consisted of 30-40 radio and radio telephone operators, 10 decoders and cryptanalysts, and 25 evaluators.[117]

[113] I 76 Appendix

[114] IF 127 p 4

[115] I 55 p 4

[116] I 76 Appendix

[117] I 74 p 2

c. FAK 610. FAK 610 was activated in 1940 for operations on the eastern front.[118] Subordinated to KONA 2, it worked at Tilsit in September 1940 and later settled at Volkhov, where it intercepted Russian traffic. In November 1944 it was transferred to the western front. Nothing is known of FAK 610 on the western front except that it was subordinated to NAA 13 of KONA 6.[119]

18. Organization of KONA 7.-- KONA 7 was established in February 1943 as the Signal Intelligence Regiment subordinated to the Commander-in-Chief South (Oberbefehlshaber Sued) who controlled the German Armies in Italy. In 1944, the component parts of KONA 7 were: [120]

Headquarters unit
1 Signal Intelligence Evaluation Center, NAA 7, with covername Krimhilde
2 Stationary Intercept Companies, Feste 1 and 9, with covernames Monika and Astrid
1 Long Range Signal Intelligence Company, FAK 621, with covername Erika

a. NAAS 7. NAAS 7 was organized into sections for cryptography, cryptanalysis, and evaluation. The evaluation sections included immediate, tactical, Direction Finding, traffic, content, and final evaluation. The strength of the evaluation center was about 150 men.[121]

b. Feste 1. Feste 1, the former Army intercept station at Stuttgart, which had been stationed at Strasbourg in 1940, Brittany in 1941, and later that year at Montpellier, moved to Italy and was attached to KONA 7 in 1943.[122]

The main task of Feste 1, was interception. No evaluation was done by the personnel who consisted of radio intercept operators, telegraph and telephone operators, and direction finding operators.[123]

[118] I 62 p 3

[119] I 76 Appendix

[120] IF 172

[121] IF 172 p 2

[122] IF 172 p 2

[123] IF 172

34

c. Feste 9. The origin and organization of Feste 9 has been described under KONA 5.

d. FAK 621. FAK 621 was organized in 1942 from the former intercept (Horch) company 3 (H) NA 56.[124] Its original commander was Seebohm, who was captured with most of FAK 621 in the African campaign on 10 July, 1942. The remnants of this company continued to work on Allied systems under Captain Habel until May 1943, when the Allies completed the capture of the unit at Tunisia.[125] Nothing is known of the organization of the company and interrogations of the prisoners are not available for this report.

19. Organization of KONA 8.-- KONA 8, which was formed in October 1944 and assigned to the Eastern front, Army Group South, had one Signal Intelligence Evaluation Center, NAAS 8; two Signal Intelligence Battalions, NAA 1 and 2;[126] one Long Range Signal Intelligence Company, FAK 620; one Close Range Signal Intelligence Company whose identity is unknown; and one Stationary Intercept Company (either 4 or 8). It is known that Feste 8 attempted in the winter of 1942-3 to intercept Russian radio telephone traffic at Koenigsberg; but it is not certain to what eastern KONA this Feste was assigned.[127] FAK 620 had monitored western traffic on the Norderney Island from August 1939 until it was sent to the eastern front and subordinated to KONA 8.[128] Nothing more is known of the units.

[124] IF 126 p 10 See I 55 p 4 for a list of the seven intercept companies (Horchkompanie) in the German Army.

[125] I 78 p 9

[126] I 76 Appendix

[127] IF 123 p 3

[128] I 76 p 3

35

20. Organization of KONA Nord.-- KONA Nord was organized in February 1945 to serve Army Group North when KONA 2, which had been attached to that group, was transferred to Army Group Weichsel. From KONA 2, KONA Nord received NAAS 2, FAK 619, NAK 951 and 955, and NAZ Brutus. This organization was valid only until 28 March, when by order of General Praun, KONA Nord was ordered to return to Army Group Weichsel all its components except the two Close Range Signal Intelligence companies, NAK 951 and 955. These probably remained with KONA Nord until the capitulation.[129]

21. Organization of NAA 11.-- NAA 11 was a field unit unique in the German Army Signal Intelligence organization. Although it was assigned to the 20th Mountain Army (XX Gebirgsarmee), in matters of signal intelligence it was an independent unit subordinated directly to HLS Ost acting in all respects like a Signal Intelligence Regiment.[130]

The original core of NAA 11 was the Long Range Signal Intelligence Platoon designated North (Nachrichten Fernaufklaerungszug Nord, abbreviated FAZ Nord) which operated in Finland after 1941. On 1 March 1944, FAZ Nord was merged with the Close Range Signal Intelligence Company, NAK 961, to form NAA 11. In the fall of 1944, after Finland's capitulation, NAA 11 retreated to Norway.[131] In May 1945, when it was at Gjovik, Norway, it was ordered to turn over all documents and papers to the 20th Mountain Army and to organize a group which would incorporate the experience and knowledge of the unit.[132] The interrogations of this group which became known as the "The Norway Party" are published as I 55 and I 106.

[129] DF 9

[130] I 55 p 5

[131] I 55 p 5

[132] I 55 p 3

The major function of NAA 11 was interception, although it was also responsible for direction finding, evaluation, cryptanalysis, and communications. The division of personnel gives an estimate of the comparative importance of these functions. Of the 475 men, from 200 to 250 were assigned to intercept and operated seventy-five sets; thirty men were assigned to direction finding, forty to evaluation, twenty-five to cryptanalysis, and thirty to communications. One hundred men were needed for driving, cooking, etc.[133]

22. Feste Loekken.-- The Feste Loekken was the Stationary Intercept Company attached to the German military commander in Denmark. Nothing is known of its organization.

133 I 55 p 8

VOLUME 4

Chapter IV: German Army Intercept Operations

Paragraph

23. Intercept operations, 1923-1933-- Assignment of intercept coverage from 1923-1933 was made by the Codes and Ciphers Section of the Defense Ministry, (Reichwehrministerium Chiffrierabteilung). The division of intercept tasks was established on a geographical basis. Munich monitored Italy (including her colonies), Yugoslavia, Greece, Turkey, Bulgaria, Rumania, Hungary, Austria, and Czechoslovakia. Stuttgart monitored France (including her colonies), Belgium, Holland, and Spain. Munster monitored England (including her colonies) and Dominions. (There is no record in TICOM sources of intercept of United States traffic before 1941. With the entry of the United States into the war, a USA section was formed within In 7 VI.) The station in Koenigsberg intercepted Russian traffic, and that at Breslau monitored Polish, Czechoslovakian (and Russian) communications. The station at Liegnitz had twice the personnel of the other stations, and its cover was directed by the Codes and Ciphers Section of the German Defense Ministry.[140]

The personnel of each intercept station consisted of one officer (chief of the station), one radio mechanic, eighteen or twenty enlisted men, and six or eight civilian employees used as clerks, interpreters, etc. In 1933,

[140] IF 181 p 2

38

five technicians were added to the personnel. Major Feichtner of the German Air Force, Air Signals Regiment 352 (LN Regt. 352) stated that these units had no tables of organization, their personnel being detached from signal battalions and signal platoons of the Infantry, Cavalry, etc. Not until 1932 did the Fixed Intercept Stations (Feste Horchstelle, abbreviated Feste) receive their tables of organization. The quality of the personnel of the Fixed Intercept Stations was certain to be of best because the stations received the direct support of the German Defense Ministry.[141]

The material intercepted daily was studied by the traffic analysis section of the Feste, and the results were incorporated into a daily traffic analysis report. The deciphered radio messages were then evaluated. All radio messages which could not be decoded by the intercept stations were sent daily to the Codes-Ciphers Section of the German Defense Ministry. On one occasion, when the maneuvers of one of the large foreign powers were being monitored, Feichtner stated that the head of the Sub-section dealing with the country in question was sent from the Codes and Ciphers Section to the appropriate intercept station for the duration of the maneuvers.[142]

The first real military activity was the monitoring of the Riff War in the middle 1920's (Feichtner said 1930). The deployment and operational tactics of the Spanish and French were learned in detail through the decoding of radio messages, and the German HQ was regularly serviced with reports. In recognition of the fine performance of the Munich intercept station, its chief was given leave to pursue technical studies at the expense of the state.[143]

Major Feichtner made it clear that the period prior to 1933 was one of training for the German intercept units.

24. Intercept operation, 1933-1939-- In 1933, the Army High Command (OKH) assumed general control of the

[141] IF 181 p 3

[142] IF 181 p 4

[143] IF 181 p 5

intercept organization[144] and the Intercept Control Station[145] (HLS) directed intercept coverage. A program of expansion and improvement was instituted, with establishment of three new Fixed Intercept Stations at Striegau, Hersbruck, and Chemnitz.[146] All Army intercept stations were improved. By 1934, for instance, each had its own building outside the city limits where it was free from electrical interference, and each was equipped with the latest technical improvements.[147] In 1935, the first mobile Signal Intelligence Companies were activated, for the greater part from Signal Corps recruits. Officers, non-commissioned officers, and privates from the Fixed Intercept Stations acted as instructors.[148]

At this time the Army was intercepting all Army, diplomatic, and Air Force traffic. The Army traffic was sent for analysis to the Army cryptanalytic and evaluation agency[149] the Intercept Control Station (HLS) at Berlin. Diplomatic traffic was passed either to the Codes and Ciphers Section of the German Defense Ministry or to the Foreign Office.[150] Sergeant Jering of the Signal Intelligence Agency of the Air Force High Command (OKL/LN Abt 350) noted that during this period the Army intercepted and evaluated foreign Air Force traffic but did not give it so much attention as it gave the ground force traffic.[151] The Air Force was becoming increasingly dissatisfied with the Army intercept work and in 1935 began to organize its own Signal Intelligence Service. For three years however (1935-1938), the Air Force maintained close relations with the Army. Air Force employees underwent familiarization training at Army Fixed Intercept Stations and the Air Force radio intercept stations, Wetterfunkenpfangstelle, (W-stellen) were set up according to the Army prototypes.[152] By 1939, the break between the Signal Intelligence Service of the Army High Command and that of the Air Force High Command was complete.

144 I 78 p 2
145 See Chapter II, Volume IV
146 I 85 p 3
147 IF 181 p 9
148 IF 181 p 10
149 I 78 p 2
150 I 85 p 2
151 IF 181 p 13
152 IF 181 p 14

At this time the Supreme Command of the Armed Forces also set up its own intercept service for diplomatic traffic. The Army gave to the Armed Forces two of its intercept stations, Lauf (formerly at Hersbruck) and Treuenbrietzen, for the interception of this traffic.[153] From this period on, the Army intercept service confined itself exclusively to the interception of foreign Army traffic.

The activities of the Army intercept service from 1933 to 1939 centered around the various crises of the international situation. In 1934, at the time of the Austrian revolt, Munich was given the task of monitoring all Austrian traffic including internal communications.[154] At the same time it monitored Italians communications and through its discovery that the Italians were massing troops at the Brenner pass brought about the timely withdrawal of Germany from the affair.[155] In 1935, Munich was monitoring French traffic at the time of the occupation of the Rhineland; and, as a result of the intelligence derived German troops marched in without fear of reprisal.[156] From 1933 to 1936, the period of the Abyssinian War, intercept stations of the Army High Command monitored Italian traffic without cessation.[157] From 1936 to 1939, Munich and Stuttgart monitored the traffic of both factions in the Spanish Civil War.[158] During this period, the first mobile signal intelligence company went into the field attached to the Legion Condor. Feichtner stated that, in spite of the opposition of some of the regular Army officers to a mobile organization of this type, this company quickly assumed its role as a most important instrument of intelligence to the Legion Command.[159]

[153] I 85 p 3

[154] IF 181 p 6

[155] IF 181 p 6

[156] IF 181 pp 6-7

[157] IF 181 p 7

[158] IF 181 p 8

[159] IF 181 p 8

25. Intercept operations 1939-1944-- Before 1939, the German General Staff had placed very little emphasis upon intercept in the field. Nearly all intercept had been carried on by the Fixed Intercept Stations (Feste). With the approach of mobile warfare, however, German Army intercept operations also became mobile. The new emphasis on field intercept resulted in the establishment of Signal Intelligence Regiments (KONA) whose mobile component parts were designed to work with units of the Army from Army Group to Army Corps level. The adaptation of the Signal Intelligence Regiments to meet the needs of the Field Army is one of the chief accomplishments of the Army signal intelligence service.

a. Control of Intercept Coverage 1939-1944-- Control of intercept coverage during the war stemmed from the Intelligence Officers of the Eastern Armies Branch and the Western Armies Branch[160] As Jodl stated, these officers were thoroughly familiar with the general signal intelligence picture.[161] The chain of command is very clear during the last year of the war. The Intelligence officers of the Eastern Armies Branch and the Western Armies Branch briefed the chief of the Understaff of OKH/GdNA, who had control over all the Signal Intelligence Regiments (KONA) and who issued to them their directives for intercept coverage.[162] In the west, the Understaff worked through the Senior Commander of Signal Intelligence (Hoeh Kdr d NA) whose function it was to coordinate the intercept coverage of KONAs 5 and 6.[163] With the other KONA, the chain of command from the Understaff was direct. The Signal Intelligence Evaluation Centers (NAAS) of the KONAs issued the directives for intercept coverage to all units subordinate to the KONA.

In 1941-1944, previous to the establishment of the GdNA, the chain of command appears to have been the following: non-Russian intercept coverage was directed by the Western Armies Branch through the Control Station of Signal Intelligence of the Army High Command (OKH/LNA);[164] Russian

[160] I 86 p 2

[161] I 143 p

[162] IF 123 p 6

[163] IF 123 p 6

[164] I 196 p 10

intercept coverage was directed by the Eastern Armies Branch through the Intercept Control Station East of the Army High Command (OKH/HLS Ost).[165]

b. Assignment of intercept-- Assignment of intercept was established on the geographical basis: eastern, southeastern, western, southwestern. From the beginning of the war eastern interception was given high priority and KONA 1, 2, 3, were assigned to eastern coverage. In 1942 KONA 6 and in 1944/45 two other KONAs, 8 and Nord were formed also for the interception of eastern traffic.[166] In addition, eastern interception was carried on by three independent Stationary Intercept Companies, Feste 7, 8, 11, and one Long Range Signal Intelligence Platoon, FAZ Nord. After 1942, new monitoring of eastern traffic was also done by the Intercept Control Station East (HLS Ost.)[167] In contrast, southeastern, western, and southwestern interception were covered by one KONA apiece, with one central monitoring agency for all three area, the Control Station for Signal Intelligence (LNA).

1. Eastern intercept.-- The mission of all eastern KONA was the interception and evaluation of Russian Army, Air Force, and Partisan (guerrilla troops) traffic. Their intercept coverage differed only in respect to the geographical origin of the traffic. KONA 1, which was attached during the period 1939-1944 to Army Group South Ukraine, covered the southern part of the Russian front. It moved in the vicinities of Lemberg, Winniza, Poltava, Reichshof, and Novy Jicin in Czechoslovakia.[168] KONA 2, which was attached to Army Group Center and covered traffic on the central Russian front, moved in the vicinity of Warsaw, Borisov, Orscha, Vitebsk, Smolensk, Minsk, and Grodno.[169] KONA 3, which was attached to Army Group North, covered

[165] IF 123 p 4

[166] I 19g p 1

[167] IF 123 p 5

[168] I 116 p 8

[169] I 116 p 8

traffic on the northern part of the Russian front and in the Baltic states. It was variously at Riga/Dueneberg, Pskov, and Kurland, where in 1945 it was caught in a pocket by the Russians and captured intact.[170] KONA 6 was formed in 1942 to cover the traffic of the campaign in Caucasus.[171] While in the east the unit was located at Rostov on the Don, Novocherkassy, and Minsk.[172] After that campaign, it was assigned to the interception of Russian Partisan traffic and kept this as its intercept coverage until November 1944, when it was withdrawn from the east and reassigned to the western front.[173]

The four independent Stationary Intercept Companies assigned to work on the eastern front had the following assignments. To Feste 11 was assigned coverage of high-frequency traffic on the Red Army and the NKVD. Originally, this Feste was located at Winniza, latterly at Kiev.[174] The other two Feste, 7 and 8, concentrated on special Russian traffic. Feste 7 was the Russian Baudot reception station at Minsk. In 1942-43 it was moved to Loetzen where it became part of Section 4 of the HLS Ost and continued to intercept Russian Baudot traffic.[175] Feste 8 was the former Army intercept station at Koenigsberg. After 1942, this station concentrated on Russian wireless telephone traffic called by the Germans Russian X-traffic. Attempts were made to pick up this traffic by equipment developed by Army Ordnance, Signal Equipment Testing Laboratory (Waffenpruefung, abbreviated Wa Pruef 7). The channels monitored ran east of Moscow; the traffic was mainly economic. From 1942 to 1944, this traffic was successfully recorded; but after 1944 the Russians scrambled their wireless telephone traffic, and after unsuccessful efforts to intercept this scrambled type had been made, the monitoring was dropped.[176]

[170] I 116 p 8

[171] DF 18 p 81

[172] I 116 p 8

[173] I 116 p 8

[174] IF 123 p 12

[175] IF 123 p 5

[176] IF 123 p 14

The Long Range Signal Intelligence Platoon, FAZ Nord, operated in Finland after 1941. The mission of this unit (which was attached to the 20th German Mountain Army) was the interception of Russian Army traffic.[177] All Russian Army systems were handled by FAZ Nord except five-figure traffic which was sent in an unprocessed state to HLS.[178]

Section 4 of HLS Ost monitored NKVD Inter-Soviet State traffic, and radio broadcasts of the Tass News Agency from Moscow.[179] (Mention has already been made, Chapter II, of the acquisition by the section of the Baudot reception station in 1942-43, when Feste 7 was moved from Minsk).

2. <u>Southeastern intercept</u>-- Southeastern intercept was the task of KONA 4, which was the only Signal Intelligence Regiment in the Balkans during the war. For the task of intercepting traffic in this area, the component parts of the KONA were located in strategic places: NAAS 4, the Signal Intelligence Evaluation Center, was moved in the summer of 1941 to Neon Phaleron near Athens;[180] it remained there until February 1944, when it retreated to Belgrade.[181] From Belgrade it moved to Graz whence it had departed some four years before.[182] Feste 5, the former Army intercept station at Graz, was moved to Epanome, 30 km south of Salonika in the Chalcidice.[183] Feste 6, the former Army intercept station at Tulln, was stationed during this period in Athens, from which it returned to Tulln in 1944.[184] The Close Range Signal Intelligence Platoon NAZ T was located at Kavalla on the Thracian Sea; NAZ W, at Belgrade.[185]

The traffic intercepted by KONA 4 and its component parts was divided into two types:

a) long range traffic emanating from the Middle East and Africa:

b) traffic of the occupied Balkan countries.

Long range traffic of the Middle East emanated from Turkey, from the British Ninth Army in Palestine and the Tenth Army in Iraq, and from the French Armies in Syria.

177 I 55 p 5
178 I 55 p 9
179 IF 123 p 5
180 IF 171 p 2
181 IF 171 p 2
182 IF 171 p 3
183 IF 171 p 3
184 IF 171 p 3
185 IF 171 p 3

45

Interception of Turkish traffic was carried on from 1941-1944 partly by the NAAS 4 at Neon Phaleron,[186] but chiefly by the close Range Signal Intelligence Platoon, NAZ T, stationed at Kavalla, whose sole mission was the interception and decoding of Turkish traffic.[187] Traffic from the British and French troops in Palestine and Syria was intercepted by NAAS 4 at Neon Phaleron.[188]

Traffic of the occupied countries was covered before 1944 mainly by NAZ W, operating from Belgrade. This platoon covered the traffic of the Croatian terrorists, the Serbian partisans, and Tito.[189] Feste 5 aided by covering Greek partisan traffic.[190] Feste 6 added Hungarian traffic to its intercept coverage in 1943 by sending a plainclothes detail to Slovakia near Pressburg, Hungary to monitor this traffic.[191] When NAAS 4 was moved to Belgrade, it concentrated on the traffic of the occupied countries and covered Yugoslav, Rumanian, Bulgarian, and Hungarian traffic.[192]

3. <u>Western intercept</u>.-- The traffics assigned to western intercept emanated from:

a) The British Isles;
b) USA (including Iceland and American troops in the British Isles), after the entry of the USA into the war; and
c) Spain, Portugal, Brazil.
d) Miscellaneous.

The coverage of these traffics was the task of KONA 5 which, until November 1944, was the only Signal Intelligence Regiment in the western area.

a) Traffic from the British Isles was considered the most important of the western traffics. It had been monitored intensively since August 1939, when a Long Range Signal Intelligence Company, FAK 620, was sent to the Atlantic coast near Norderney Island to monitor British

186 IF 171 p 2
187 IF 171 p 3
188 IF 171 p 3
189 IF 171 p 3
190 IF 171 p 3
191 IF 126 p 10
192 I 74 p 2

Army maneuvre traffic.[193] Although FAK 620 was sent at a later date to the eastern area,[194] British traffic continued to be monitored by the following units of KONA 5 from 1939 to 1944:

1) Long Range Signal Intelligence Company, FAK 613. This unit stationed at St. Malo monitored exclusively radio traffic from the British Isles:[195]
2) Feste 2, a Stationary Intercept Company located until November 1943 at Husum in Holland, after that at Lille. This unit monitored exclusively traffic of the British Isles:[196]
3) Feste 9, formed in June 1942, at Frankfurt/Main and sent to Norway to monitor British traffic. At first the unit was stationed at Trondhjem; later, at Bergen, where it remained until the spring of 1944 when it moved to Ski near Oslo. The task of the unit was to intercept traffic originated by the British Army in Northern England, Scotland, and Faroes.[197]
4) Feste 12, a Stationary Intercept Company attached to the Evaluation Center of KONA 5 and located at Louveciennes. Until January 1944 this station monitored exclusively traffic from the British Isles.[198]

b) Traffic emanating from the United States and Iceland, and from American troops in the British Isles was monitored chiefly by Feste 3 at Euskirchen and Feste 9 at Bergen, Norway. Feste 3 concentrated on traffic from the USA.[199] After the autumn of 1943, Feste 3 had a special intercept unit for USA non-Morse radio teletype traffic, designated by the Germans as FF5 (Funk Fernschreib 5)[200] From Feste 9 in Bergen, USA traffic from Iceland was monitored. This unit watched for short wave radio traffic from London to Washington via Ireland, but without success.[201]

[193] I 76 p 3

[194] I 76 p 3

[195] IF 127 p 5

[196] IF 127 p 5

[197] IF 120 p 6

[198] IF 127 p 4

[199] IF 127 p 3

[200] I 149 p 2

[201] I 78 p 10

DOCID: 3486746

c) The traffic of Spain, Portugal, and the Brazilian Army in Italy was monitored from 1939 to 1942 by Feste 3 at Euskirchen. In early 1943, however, the Long Range Signal Intelligence Company, FAK 624, was formed at Montpellier on the southern coast of France for the interception of this traffic.[202] In January 1944, the interception of Spanish, Portuguese, and Brazilian traffic was shared with FAK 624 by Feste 12.[203]

d) In addition to the three main commitments of the western intercept units, two other minor traffics were monitored: Swedish Army traffic, and French police traffic originating in Corsica. The Swedish Army traffic was intercepted by a subordinate unit of Feste 9 in Norway. This unit, known as out-station Halden (Aussenstelle Halden) was stationed at Halden, Norway, and was attached for administrative purposes to the Halden Police Battalion.[204] The French police traffic from Corsica was monitored by FAK at Montpellier.[205]

4. Southwestern intercept.-- Before 1943, the German Army appears to have had no signal intelligence unit in Italy. In February of that year, however, KONA 7 was established with the task of intercepting traffic from Italy and from North Africa.[206] The traffics consisted of British, American, Polish, French, and Brazilian Army traffic in Italy and North Africa.[207] So far as can be determined, there was no specific division of tasks among the various units of KONA 7: all units intercepted all Army traffic from these countries.

The most southerly location of NAAS 7, the Signal Intelligence Evaluation Center of KONA 7, was Rocca di Papa, 25 km south of Rome.[208] In September 1943, it moved into the neighborhood of Rome, establishing itself at Vallerano. Later it moved to Vicenza in northern Italy.[209] Feste 1, the former Army intercept station at Stuttgart, after sundry moves in France from 1940 to 1943 was ultimately stationed in Italy at Genzano near L'Aquila.[210] Feste 9,

[202] IF 127 p 3
[203] IF 127 p 3
[204] IF 120 p 6
[205] IF 127 p 3
[206] IF 172 p 3
[207] IF 172 p 3
[208] IF 172 p 1
[209] IF 172 p 1
[210] IF 172 p 1

48

which came to Italy from Norway in November 1944, was located at Breganze and remained there until shortly before the collapse.[211]

The Long Range Signal Intelligence Company, FAK 621, which was attached to KONA 7, had been originally designated as the Army Signal Company 3 (Horch Nachrichten Aufklrg. H NA 56).[212] This unit, which was particularly active in North Africa during the campaigns there, was captured (in part) in July 1942. In May 1943, the entire company was captured at Tunisia.[213] Until the time of its final capture, this unit intercepted traffic of the British, French, and American troops in North Africa and of the Egyptian Army and Camel Corps.[214]

26. Intercept service 1944-1945--

a. Intercept operations of OKH/GdNA. The years 1944-1945 saw the centralization of the German Army Signal Intelligence Service and its catastrophic dissolution in the months prior to the capitulation. As part of the movement to centralize the service, OKH/GdNA assumed responsibility for the intercept and evaluation of the following types of traffic:

1) foreign press;
2) special high grade machine ciphers;
3) wireless photography.

1. Intercept and evaluation of the foreign press was done by Section 2 of Group I, OKH/GdNA. This section was divided into four subsections:[215]

a) monitoring of eastern wireless (Rundueberwachung Ost);
b) monitoring of western wireless (Rundueberwachung West);
c) monitoring of clear text (Helldienst); and
d) evaluation.

Owing to the personnel shortage during the years 1944-1945, Section 2 was not able to cover its commitments to any

211 IF 144 p 2

212 IF 126 p 10

213 I 78 p 9

214 I 74 p 2

215 IF 123 pp 7-8

large extent. Eastern monitoring was confined for the most part to the Moscow wireless, although in the later months a certain amount of Balkan monitoring was instituted for Turkey and Rumania. Western monitoring was confined to the BBC London Service. News monitoring was confined to the Reuter and Tass Agencies. From these sources the evaluation center collected and collated material for its reports.

2. The interception and evaluation of special high grade machine ciphers of Russia, Britain, and the USA were assigned to Group VI of OKH/GdNA which was located at Potsdam. Section 1, dealing with Russian traffic, had three subsections:[216]

1a) Interception of Inter-Soviet State traffic,
1b) Interception of Russian Baudot traffic,
1c) Interception of Russian Army traffic.

The interception of Russian Baudot traffic (called by the Russians Z-traffic) was carried on by the same personnel who had manned the Russian Baudot station at Minsk in 1942/43. In 1943, the Russian Baudot station was moved to HLS Ost at Loetzen, where it was absorbed by Section 4 of HLS Ost. When HLS Ost was absorbed by the OKH/GdNA, the Baudot station became Section 1b of the OKH/GdNA.[217]

Section 2 of Group VI was employed with the interception (2b) and the evaluation (2a) of British and American high grade machine ciphers.[218] The interception of this traffic has been carried on by Feste 3 at Euskirchen until the establishment of the OKH/GdNA, when the responsibility for interception was transferred to the central agency.[219]

The interception of wireless photography, called by the Germans Y-traffic, was carried on by a special unit of Section I of Group VI. This unit intercepted traffic from all over the world but the non-Russian channels are said not to have yielded any valuable information. Photos intercepted from internal Russian traffic, however, often contained technical diagrams and charts.[220]

[216] IF 123 p 9

[217] IF 123 p 11

[218] IF 123 p 11

[219] IF 123 p 5

[220] IF 123 p 13

b. Intercept service in the field.-- The intercept service in the field during the last year of the war maintained its geographical distribution: eastern, southeastern, western, southwestern. Paralleling the changes in the war situation, there was an increasing emphasis on western intercept and a corresponding decreasing emphasis on southeastern intercept in the war situation.

With the pressure of the Allied invasion, western intercept assumed of necessity a position of greater importance. It will be recalled that KONA 6 was reassigned at this time from eastern to western intercept and that the western Signal Intelligence Regiments, KONAs 5 and 6, were subordinated to a Senior Commander of Signal Intelligence (Hoeh Kdr d NA) who was responsible for all signal intelligence operations in the west.[221] Upon these two KONAs fell the task of intercepting the traffic of the invading Armies.

KONA 6 monitored traffic for Army Groups H and B which were stationed in the northern part of the western front; KONA 5 monitored the traffic of Army Group G which was stationed in the southern half of the western front.[222] One member of the Long Range Signal Intelligence Company, FAK 626 (Haupts), states that his unit's original mission was the interception of traffic of the First French Army and of the Seventh USA Army. Later it intercepted traffic of the USA First, Third, and Ninth Armies.

The decreasing emphasis on southeastern interception was manifested by the disbandment of KONA 4. The component parts were apparently reassigned to various fronts. Southeastern intercept and evaluation was carried on by KONA 4's successor, the newly formed Signal Intelligence Battalion, NAA 16.[223]

The situation on the eastern and southwestern fronts remained, for the most part, much as it had been in the previous year. To the eastern front were assigned two new KONAs, KONA 8 and KONA Nord;[224] and to KONA 7 in Italy,

[221] I 76 Appendices

[222] I 76 Appendices

[223] DF 9

[224] DF 9

51

one new intercept unit, Feste 9, which was moved to Italy from Norway.[225]

A German Army Report on the intercept situation about January, 1945 gives the following picture of the units and their coverage:[226]

Eastern Front:
- Units:
  - KONA 8 for Army Group South
  - KONA 1 for Army Group Center
  - KONA 2 for Army Group Weichsel
  - KONA Nord for Army Group North
  - KONA 3 for Army Group Kurland
  - NAA 11 for 20th Mountain Army
- Coverage:
  - Russian front traffic
  - Radio nets of NKVD
  - Rumania
  - Roving bands in Poland and Ukraine
  - Espionage units in operational areas

Southeastern front:
- Unit: NAA 16 for Army Group E
- Coverage:
  - Allied troops and communications staffs in Balkans
  - Soviet front traffic
  - TITO traffic (Jugoslavian)
  - ELAS traffic (Greek)
  - Bulgarian traffic
  - Mihailovic traffic (Jugoslavian)

Western front:
- Units:
  - Senior Commander of Signal Intelligence
  - KONA 6 for Army Groups H and B
  - KONA 5 for Army Groups G and Oberrhein
- Coverage:
  - English, American French front traffic
  - British traffic from British Isles
  - USA traffic from United States
  - French traffic from France

Southwestern front:
- Unit: KONA 7
- Coverage:
  - English, American, French front traffic
  - Allied traffic from western Mediterranean and North Africa
  - Italian bands in upper Italy

[225] DF 9

[226] DF 9

52

c. Disintegration of Intercept Operations-- It may be safely assumed that the constant movement of the German Armies and their intercept units during the last months of the war prevented continuous and orderly interception of enemy traffic. A brief resume of the movements of the various Signal Intelligence Regiments will illustrate the confusion of these last months.[227] KONA 1 withdrew from the eastern front into Czechoslovakia and was found by the invading forces at Novy Jicin (Neutitschein); KONA 2 retreated from the vicinity of Grodno to Ortelburg in Prussia, Danzig, Holstein, and finally the Wismar area; KONA 3 was caught by the Russians in a pocket at Kurland and captured; KONA 8 withdrew first into Rumania, then Croatia, and finally to Lenz. KONA 5 in the west withdrew from Louveciennes in mid-August, 1944 and went first to Viggingen near Metz. At the beginning of September, it moved to krofdorf near Giessen, where it stayed until March; from there it went to the Rhoen and finally to Dischingen in the Donauwoerth area.[228] Of the component parts of KONA 6 less is known. One of its units, FAK 611, moved in the spring of 1945 from Holland to Flensbrug;[229] Feste 3 moved from Euskirchen into the Black Forest.[230]

The southwestern unit, KONA 7 and its subordinates retreated into northern Italy. Concerning southeastern intercept in the last months of the war, it is known only that NAA 16 remained as the only unit in that area.[231]

The constant shiftings of the KONAs, and in the late months of the war, the disruption of internal communications between the various parts of the KONAs and between the KONAs and the GdNA had a disastrous effect on the whole problem of enemy intercept.

[227] I 116 p 8

[228] I 113 p 2

[229] I 74 p 2

[230] I 76 p 11

[231] DF 9

During the last months of the war, the internal intercept units of the GdNA were also disrupted. The units of Groups I and V moved with the other Groups of the GdNA to Erfurt and then to Bad Reichenhall.[232] The intercept unit of Group VI which had been covering high grade machine traffic at Potsdam was moved to Stuttgart and from there to Rosenheim.[233] The equipment was buried in the cellar in the surrounding neighborhood of a house, the Pioneer-Kaserne, in Rosenheim where it was later found by TICOM interrogators.[234]

[232] IF 123 p 12

[233] IF 123 p 12

[234] IF 15

VOLUME 4

Chapter V: Operations of a Typical Signal Intelligence Regiment on the Eastern Front

Section A. Introduction

27. Sources for this chapter.--The materials describing Signal Intelligence Regiment 1 (Kommandeur der Nachrichten Aufklaerung, abbreviated KONA) provided a rather complete account of that unit, and were generally more thorough than reports available for other field signal intelligence formations; therefore, KONA 1 is discussed in this chapter as a typical Signal Intelligence Regiment. This completeness resulted from the availability of a substantial portion of this unit's personnel for interrogation. The circumstances under which the remnants of KONA 1 were found are not without interest:

> "The full facts of the surrender of this unit were explained by the Commandant, Major Ernst Hertzer. The remnant of the regiment -- approximately 700 officers, enlisted men and women, first contacted American troops on 9 May 1945 in the vicinity of Tausing, where they were directed to a PW enclosure at Stift Tepl. They had destroyed almost all of their papers except those that they considered most essential for reconstruction of their records. These documents were kept in three brief cases plus one book. In the afternoon of the 9 May, while rumors circulating in the PW enclosure to the effect that the Russians were moving into the area, the contents of the three brief cases were burned. The book, however, remained in one of the vehicles but a minute search of that car failed to produce it."[240]

Three hundred and fifty prisoners were screened at a town near Pilsen between 23 May and 28 May. All operational personnel were interviewed; and of these 41 were chosen for

[240] IF 40 p 10

further questioning. A few reports were written near Pilsen, but the bulk of documents which formed the basis for later interrogations were written between 30 May and 2 June, at Oberursel, near Frankfort-am-Main, where the unit had been moved. More specific information was given and further documents written after the group was moved to Revin, in the Ardennes.[241] The material produced consisted of 31 reports,[242] supported by supplementary "Annexes" giving information on traffic analysis, organization, etc.

Interrogations of Prisoners of War from units other than KONA 1 were relied upon in this chapter to fill out the picture. The outstanding of these was the Karrenberg Party report on "Russian Radio." Corporal (Unteroffizier) Karrenberg was an "exceedingly brilliant" man with a "phenomenal memory."[243] The report was written by him and his colleagues. All were members of the Signal Intelligence Agency of the Army High Command (Oberkommando des Heeres, General der Nachrichten Aufklaerung, abbreviated OKH/GdNA).[244]

Since the Signal Intelligence Regiments were the important field units of the German Army signal intelligence service, and since information on one of these, KONA 1, was available, in this chapter an account will be given of the functions and operations of KONA 1, which may be considered typical of those of the other Signal Intelligence Regiments operating in the East. Because organization has already been treated in Volume 4, Chapter 11, organizational matters will be noted here only as some review of them appears necessary to a full understanding of the operations.

28. Successes of KONA 1.--KONA 1 operated in the southern sector of the Russian front from June 1941 until May 1945, intercepting and evaluating Russian Army, Army Air, and NKVD[245] in that traffic area. Elements of this unit appear to have succeeded in reconstructing the detailed Order of Battle of the Russian forces, and in predicting the locality and timing of the Russian offensives before they occurred.[246] Captain Roman Roessler, Chief Evaluator of KONA 1 and Commanding Officer of the Intelligence Evaluation Center (Nachrichten Aufklaerung

241 IF 40 p 4

242 I 19b

243 IF 123 p 2

244 I 173 p 1

245 NKVD is translated as "Peoples' Commissariat for internal affairs." During the war it maintained frontier troops which performed counter espionage and had many military police functions. See I 67 p 3.

246 I 19b, 1

56

Auswertungsstelle, Abbreviated NAAS) of the regiment, pointed out that even when identification of individual formations became impossible, the KONA was still successful in picturing the overall grouping and the number of formations. He conceded that in the case of Russian Rifle Corps and Divisions, German Intelligence units had to rely on means other than signal intelligence. However, he emphasized that the overall picture afforded, by signal intelligence units of the "movements of strategic reserves, of points of main efforts, chain of command, intentions to attack," etc., were of great value to German Intelligence units.[247]

It should be emphasized that Roessler's style was rather pompous, and his estimate of KONA 1 successes may have been overenthusiastic.[248]

29. Importance of Traffic Analysis on the Eastern Front.-- In general the successes noted above were due to traffic analysis rather than to cryptanalysis. While there seems to have been great disagreement among the persons interrogated on the relative merits of these two methods, the evidence indicated that the results achieved by the careful integration of all sources available from traffic analysis appeared to outweigh those achieved through reading of the Russian low grade codes and ciphers. This situation may be accounted for by two principal factors. In the first place: although the Germans were highly successful in reading Russian low grade systems (as described in Volume 4, Chapter VI), most of the Russian high grade codes employed by the army were one-time pad systems, and consequently defied attack by the KONA cryptanalysts.

Secondly: an enormous amount of information was available "from the Russian practice in the use of indicators, call-signs, and the generally low though improving standard of Russian wireless discipline."[249]

Because of this relative importance of cryptanalysis and traffic analysis the emphasis in this chapter will be upon the procedures through which intelligence was derived from a study of the aspects of Russian radio operations. The cryptanalysis performed by the field units will be discussed in another chapter and only its organizational relationship to the operations of the components will be noted here.

The functional relationship of the units of a KONA is pictured on Chart Number 4-4. Roughly, the KONA consisted of a Signal Intelligence Evaluation center (NAAS); of companies (FAK), subordinate to it in intelligence functions, which

247 I 19b pp 14-15
248 I 19g pp 3-4
249 I 19b p 1

intercepted enemy traffic and fed the traffic back to the Evaluation center; and close range companies (NAK), which intercepted enemy low level traffic, did some analysis of the simpler systems, and passed the results and intercept into the Signal Intelligence Evaluation Center. To pick up enemy traffic of higher formations, there were so-called Long Range Signal Intelligence Companies (FAK) and so-called Fixed companies (Feste). The first intercepted primarily traffic already identified; the second concentrated on networks carrying unidentified traffic. Both types of these long range companies did analysis on the traffic they intercepted, and passed the results and their traffic up to the Signal Intelligence Evaluation Center (NAAS).

VOLUME 4

Chapter V

Section B. Functions of the KONA Units

30. Introduction.--The purpose of the KONA was to supply intelligence from signal sources to the G-2's of the Army Corps, Armies, and Army Groups. A typical KONA consisted of one Regimental Evaluation center and of 5 or 6 intercept and intelligence companies. Chart Number 4-4 shows the layout of such a Signal Intelligence Regiment.

The chart gives the picture of a typical KONA as it actually operated, with its signal intelligence platoons operating near the front lines, with its companies situated back near army headquarters, and with its main regimental evaluation center in the rear at Army Group Headquarters.

Close Range Signal Intelligence platoons intercepted very low level traffic, evaluated what they could, kept the G-2 of their assigned Army Corps informed of all intelligence derived, and passed back to an evaluation platoon at company headquarters all their results and presumably their intercepts.

Long Range Signal Intelligence Companies intercepted higher level traffic; did some evaluation, the results of which were given to the G-2 of their assigned Army headquarters; and passed back evaluation reports and intercepts to the regimental Signal Intelligence Evaluation Centar (NAAS). The Stationary Intercept Companies operated in an almost identical manner, with primary emphasis on enemy unidentified traffic.

The regimental Evaluation Center (NAAS) evaluated the reports and the intercepts from all companies of the regiment and passed their results to G-2 of Army Group.

More detailed functions of the NAAS, of the companies, and of the platoons are discussed below. (The organization of these units has already been described in Volume 4, Chapter III).

31. Functions of the Signal Intelligence Evaluation Center (NAAS).[250]--The NAAS was situated close by Army Group Headquarters.[251] The functions of the NAAS included Evaluation and Traffic Analysis, Cryptanalysis, Dissemination of Intelligence, and Direction of intercept cover.

a. Evaluation and Traffic Analysis included four types of activity:[252]

(1) Evaluation, checking, and coordination of reports passed up to the NAAS by other elements of the KONA, and the synthesis of the results.

(2) Traffic Analysis (including the study of Direction Finding results) of identified traffic passed in to the NAAS by the Long Range Companies (FAK); and of NKVD and Russian Air traffic, passed in (presumably) by either the Long Range or Close Range Companies.

(3) Attempts to identify unidentified traffic passed in by the companies, chiefly by the Feste.

(4) Keeping of full files and card indexes in which all data of any possible significance was recorded.

b. Cryptanalysis in the NAAS primarily meant the solution of unknown systems, the study of developments in known systems, and work on NKVD code. The NAAS worked on Russian systems up to and including 4-figure systems. (The cryptanalytic operations are discussed in Volume 4, Chapter VI.)

c. The NAAS was responsible for the dissemination of intelligence; it passed its results to the Intelligence Officer of the Army Group to which the KONA was attached, and reported its findings to the Signal Intelligence Agency of the Army High Command (OKH/GdNA).[253]

250 For graphic representation of the functions of the NAAS see Chart Number 4-4. It should be emphasized that this chart portrays the main functions only, and does not represent the breakdown by table of organization sections, which is given in Chapter III.

251 I 19b p 1

252 I 19b p 6

253 I 19g p 7

d. The NAAS had a key position in the direction of intercept cover. It controlled the intercept coverage of all the lower elements of the KONA, following the overall coordination exercised by the OKH/GdNA.[254]

Certain items were passed, unprocessed, through the KONA to the GdNA. The main item treated thus was 5-figure (including NKVD) traffic, and NKVD traffic which fell outside of the area of the particular KONA by whose units it was intercepted.[255]

32. Functions of the Stationary Intercept Company (Feste).-- The Stationary Intercept Companies (Feste) were designed to work at the next lower level to the NAAS, that of Army. The Feste were pre-war Army intercept stations; and though they retained the traditional designation implying they were "fixed" (Feste Horchstelle), they actually were semi-motorized early in the Russian campaign. Feste 10, the "stationary" company of KONA 1 operated for, and near to, Army Headquarters.[256]

Feste 10[257] consisted of five functional sections, besides the Headquarters section. An intercept platoon (whose coverage was controlled by the NAAS)[258] covered unknown traffic in the 3500-5500 kilocycle band, fixed NKVD nets assigned by the NAAS, and nets of mobile formations[259] as directed by the NAAS.[260]

An evaluation section identified and reported unknown traffic. Apparently the interception and study of unidentified traffic were the main functions of the Feste.[261]

A cryptanalytic section contributed to the interpretation of unknown traffic by the identification of keys, also translated plain-text messages, and did some solution.[262]

The Feste had a Direction Finding platoon, which carried out the requests "of the Companies." Communications between the Direction Finding sites and the Regiment were carried out by a Communications platoon. This platoon passed the results of Evaluation by telegram or teleprinter to the NAAS.[263]

[254] DF 18 p 82
[255] I 19g p 8
[256] I 19g p 6
[257] See Volume 4, Chapter III
[258] DF 18 p 82
[259] These were also partly covered by the FAK's
[260] I 19b p 3
[261] I 19b pp 3-4; pp 19-20
[262] I 19b p 4
[263] I 19b p 4

33. Functions of the Long Range Signal Intelligence Company (FAK).--The Long Range Signal Intelligence Companies were distinguishable in function from the Feste, mainly that they were concerned to a much greater degree with identified traffic. Like Feste 10 (e.g.) they were semi-motorized and were designed to operate near Army Headquarters.[264] It was planned that one should work with each army staff covering an army sector. In actuality, however, the operations of these companies (and likewise those of Feste 10) took place further and further in the rear. The crush of work would become heaviest just at a time when safety precautions demanded a withdrawal; and it was thus found more practical to undertake the work in the rear echelon areas where it would be less frequently interrupted. Fak's 617 and 623 and Feste 10 ended up by operating in the immediate vicinity of the Evaluation Center (NAAS 1).[265]

In their interception of identified traffic, the coverage of the FAK's was directed, as was that of the Feste, by the cover control section of the Evaluation Center (NAAS).[266] The traffic intercepted by the FAK was studied by it as fully as resources would permit. Plain-text messages were translated, and traffic of known codes decoded by specialists assigned to the unit. A general section was devoted to card indexes and lists. (Raw traffic which defied analysis was sent to the cryptanalytic and traffic analysis sections of the NAAS.)

34. Functions of Close Range Signal Intelligence Company (NAK).--The Close Range Company (Nahaufkleerung Kompanie, abbreviated NAK) presumably worked at Army Corps level. Its main responsibility was to pick up and work on low-level (2-figure, 3-figure, and possibly some 4-figure) traffic.[267] It should be noted that, although the Close Range Company seemed to have been designed to work at Army Corps level, in practice such a company was apparently also stationed by the "Kommandeur" of the Regiment (KONA) with each Army as well.[268]

In contrast to the Long Range Companies, which were designed to operate in full company strength, the Close Range Companies operated by platoon.[269] The operations of each company was

264 I 19g p 6
265 I 19b p 1
266 DF 18 p 82
267 I 19h p 2
268 I 19g p 1
269 I 19g p 6

62

divided among four platoons: Intercept (Horchzug); Direction Finding (Peilzug); Evaluation (Auswertezug); and Communications (Sendezug).[270]

As in the case of the other units, intercept coverage was directed by the NAAS.[271] Although they were army units, in at least one case the NAK apparently covered not only enemy traffic, but also enemy air-ground, and air traffic as well. A normal program of intercept called for about twenty receivers.[272] The platoon usually had two or three intercept operators, while there were generally about twelve operators who knew Russian to pick up the radio talk.[273]

The organization of Direction Finding Platoon was rather elaborate. Normally for one company there were about eight outstations, separated from each other by 5 to 10 kilometers and parallel to the front at a distance of from one to several hundred kilometers.[274] Each section had about five men.[275]

With each platoon was a small evaluation section, consisting of two or three evaluators,[276] who worked usually in a room near the intercept station.[277] Presumably their results would be passed to the Evaluation platoon of the company. Only the simplest systems were worked on at the NAK level; most of the raw traffic was passed upwards to the NAAS, which studied it cryptanalytically as well as for tactical intelligence derivable through traffic analysis. Captain Roessler considered evaluation at NAK level a "dispersal of strength,"[278] but the NAK evaluation must not be brushed aside too lightly, for these NAK's did no evaluation and did pass the results to the Corps Intelligence Officer.[279]

270 I 62 p 4. The documents relied upon for the following account are not limited to those describing KONA 1 units. The account in I 62 is based upon one man's experience with Funkhorchkompanie 610 and 520 Nahauflklaerungkompanie on the Eastern Front.

271 DF 18 p 82

272 I 62 p 4

273 I 19b p 2

274 I 62 p 4

275 I 19b p 2

276 I 19b p 2

277 I 62 p 4

278 I 19g p 2

279 I 19b p 2

VOLUME 4

Chapter V

Section C. Features of Russian Radio Communications

Paragraph

35. Introduction.--The components of the KONA described in the preceding section were designed to provide the most effective overall attack upon Russian radio communications. Since unidentified traffic formed the great percentage of German intercept in the East, the identification and interpretation of unknown traffic was one of the most important functions of the KONA.[280] Thus it is pertinent here to survey briefly some of the characteristics facilitating German identification of Russian traffic. The operating data (such as networks and call signs) and the visible properties of the message text as transmitted formed the basic subject matter with which all units in varying degrees were concerned, and provided the clues leading to identification.

The reports available did not provide sufficient evidence to build a full picture of Russian communications. Russian nets were discussed for the most part only in terms of types of traffic they passed and their call sign practices. Details on such data as frequency systems, time of communication, and so on, were lacking. The discussion which follows is therefore limited by the sources available, and concentrates upon the distinguishing features of Russian Signal operations of value to the German signal intelligence field units.

36. Some identifying characteristics of Russian networks.--Since it was frequently possible to identify a station by its place in its network structure, the first objective of German traffic analysis was, broadly speaking, the identification of

280 I 19b p 14; I 19g p 4

networks of which any station might form a part. This process of identification was facilitated by the following characteristics of Russian network:

a. Radio teleprinter (Baudot) traffic was characteristic of the communications of the Russian General Staff to the Front Staffs (Army Group Staffs), and of that of the Front Staffs to the "Assault Armies." Russian General Staff radio teleprinter transmissions were 2-channel, as opposed to the "modulated" (i.e. probably multichannel) transmitters used from Front Staffs to Assault Armies. Also, these latter links used lower frequencies.[281] Automatic high-speed morse transmission was possible on all such higher links, but was seldom used.[282] (Three radio teleprinter links passing Air Force traffic from Moscow to higher Air Force headquarters were also identified.)[283]

b. Great radio activity was characteristic of the morse networks of Assault Armies, because of the mobility of these Armies and their lack of land lines.[284]

c. Radio silence marked Divisional and Regimental networks just preceding attacks.

d. In general, units below division used low frequencies (2,200 to 3,900 kilocycles).[285]

37. Some identifying characteristics of Russian Call Sign Practice.--Apparently the Germans put a great deal of effort into the study of Russian call signs, which were mentioned frequently throughout the reports. One reported stated that up to "July 1944 the Russian call sign system was well known to the Germans and predictions reliable. The 1944 summer offensives, however, brought a change of system."[286] In spite of the seemingly general Russian practice of enciphering their station call signs,[287] the Germans do appear to have had considerable success in their study

281 I 168 p 2; I 272 pp 5-7

282 I 173 p 6

283 I 173 p 11

284 I 173 pp 8-10

285 I 75 p 4

286 I 75 p 7

287 I 168 pp 3-4; I 173 p 21

of them as characteristics aiding in traffic identification. The prisoner quoted above stated that by the end of the hostilities the Germans had made good progress in solving the systems.[288]

Two reports indicated that most Army, Air Force, and NKVD call signs down to division level consisted, in their transmitted form, of three-figure calls, of which the first two figures were Roman letters with the third either a letter or a number.[289] Regimental networks could be distinguished from Army, Air Force, and NKVD networks, because, although they used three-figure calls, these were composed entirely of letters of the Russian alphabet.[290] Moreover, the calls of stations on the regimental networks were "usually composed of three letters of the cover name; they were either three consecutive letters or three consonants of the cover name."[291]

One Prisoner of War stated that, provided the formations took their call signs from a "Basic Book for Allotment of Call Signs (Hauptverteiler), it was possible to identify with considerable certainty Army or Air units as belonging on certain fronts.[292]

Call signs of a few higher NKVD networks, of the network of the "Artillery Reserve of the Supreme Command," and of the traffic passed on the networks of the Air Force ground stations were distinctive in that they used four-element calls.[293] One prisoner stated that the NKVD calls were mostly pronounceable,[294] and another witness went so far as to declare that the "only means of establishing the central NKVD authority" was the study of call sign usage.[295] The same reporter was of the opinion that Partisan traffic could be identified with certainty because of the consistent practice of using one call sign only.[296]

38. Some identifying characteristics of procedure.--NKVD traffic could be spotted with a high degree of probability because of the transmittal of "NK" to separate the preamble from the address(or text),[297] and because of the practice of tuning by sending a series of dots and dashes instead of by keying "v" as in other Russian traffic.[298] The absence in NKVD Administrative traffic of the group separation sign "r," common in Army

288 I 75 p 7
289 I 168 pp 3-4; I 173 p 21
290 I 173 p 21
291 I 173 p 11
292 I 19b p 36
293 I 173 p 11 and p 21
294 I 19b p 48
295 I 19b p 36
296 I 19b p 36
297 I 168 p 2
298 I 19b p 47

traffic, was a clue aiding identification.[299] The appearance of SMERSCH in the preamble characterized NKVD messages sometimes picked up on Army or Air nets which might be used by the Counter Espionage organization OKR SMERSCH.[300]

The appearance of "WZD" (air raid warning signal) in the preamble characterized Russian Air Force traffic. The use of "QCO" rather than "QTC" in the preamble also was some (though by no means the exclusive) indication that the traffic was Air Force,

Partisan procedure was characterized by its use of the international abbreviations of amateur radio, such as the use of "CK" for the group count. Furthermore, most of the traffic was sent blind.[301]

Army traffic could to some degree be characterized by the absence of the features noted above.[302]

30. Some Identifying Characteristics of Russian Message Text as Transmitted.--The message texts (cipher texts) transmitted by the various formations had recognizable features. Generally, high level traffic was sent in 5-figure groups while low level traffic tended to be sent in groups of 2, 3, and 4 figures. For instance, the traffic passed on the operational networks of the General Staff, the Front Staffs, and the Armies tended to be predominantly 5-figure.[303] One witness made the generalization that 4-figure systems were used "from corps to army and from army to army group."[304] The traffic passed from Division downwards tended to be 2- or 3-figure.[305]

The significance of the characteristics of 5-figure traffic in traffic identification was emphasized in one of the reports. Two of these characteristics, the "blocknot" indicator and the "Chi-number," were of particular importance.

According to one witness, a "Blocknot" consisted of fifty sheets of 5-figure random additive, 100 additive groups to a sheet. No sheet was used more than once; thus the blocknots were in effect one-time pads. Fifty of these additive sheets, numbered 1 to 50, were issued in a sealed envelope, which bore a 5-figure number. The additive sheets in any "pad" were always

[299] I 173 p 12

[300] I 19b p 48

[301] I 19b p 36

[302] I 19b pp 36-37

[303] I 173 pp 608

[304] I 191 p 8

[305] I 173 pp 10-11

67

designated by the same block number. The 5-figure group designating the block number was always transmitted within the first ten groups of the message. A further 5-figure group, usually in the first seven groups but always following the clock number contained, "as the last two figures, the number of the (additive) sheet (1 to 50) used. The middle figure of this group indicated the formation level, e.g. '6' might be Corps forward to Division, '5' might be Div to Div."[306] By a daily recording of all blocknot numbers, traffic enciphered in the same blocks could be segregated and identified as being transmitted by the same unit.

Another characteristic of this 5-figure traffic, actually a "message external" feature, was the serial numbering of all messages. Every 5-figure message was assigned a 5-figure serial number. This was called the Chi-number by the Germans. These Chi-numbers began at 00001 on 1 January and ran serially throughout the year. The number was sent always as the last group of the message.[307] "Newcomers of formations would start at 000001."[308] A study of the Chi-numbers assisted materially in traffic identification. Generally, a Corps sent ten messages a day, an Army twenty to thirty, and a "front" (roughly, Army Group) from sixty to one hundred. Since each message was serially numbered with a Chi-number, the progression of these numbers could be charted on a graph, and it was possible after a short time to determine the type of formation sending out the traffic from the individual curves on this graph.[309] The importance the Germans attributed to the Chi-number was great; in fact, one non-commissioned officer who recorded the time-of-origin as a Chi-number, was threatened with court-martial.[310]

The absence of blocknot and Chi-numbers distinguished 5-figure Russian Partisan traffic from 5-figure Army traffic.[311]

NKVD messages consisted of 4 or 5 figures was said to "be easily distinguished by their characteristics from Army and Air Force messages." This was probably due to the features of NKVD traffic reported as follows:

> "The first group is a discriminant which in most cases remains constant for one line of traffic. The

306 U 75 p 12
307 I 19b p 17
308 I 75 p 12
309 I 19b p 17
310 I 19g p 3
311 I 19b p 37

> penultimate group contains the date and a number representing the number of groups in the message less a variable number according to the number of indicator groups used. .....Exceptions to these rules are very rare. Two and three-figure messages usually contained technical 'wireless chat.'"[312]

Messages of the NKVD Frontier Troops were of both 4- and 5-figure types, and in regimental networks 2-figure codes appeared as well.[313] The 2-figure NKVD messages could usually be recognized as such because of the practice, in contrast to that of the army, of enciphering the same system for months. Moreover, 3- and 4-figure codes rarely changed in NKVD traffic; and once their characteristics had been ascertained, they were also fairly easily recognizable.[314]

On the whole a good deal of carelessness prevailed in the encoding of NKVD messages, at least in those appearing on the Frontier Troop networks.[315] Such a lack of security on the part of the Russians facilitated the work of the KONA's,

Air Force traffic, which might be picked up on search by the KONA units, could be distinguished from Army traffic by several external characteristics. For instance, meteorological messages usually carried an "X" or some other padding letter between the numerals. Special Air Force expressions often appeared in 2, 3, and 4-figure messages with an admixture of plain language. In plain language messages there were mentions of take-offs, and permission to land or to take-off. Such messages appeared frequently, and once picked up enabled the immediate spotting of the network as Air Force. "In general, very many more plain language messages were passed over air force networks than over army networks."[316] Air reconnaissance reports, for example, were sent mainly in the clear.[317]

[312] I 19b p 47

[313] I 173 p 13

[314] I 167 pp 5-6

[315] I 173 p 13

[316] I 173 p 11

[317] I 19b p 37

VOLUME 4

Chapter V

Section D. Direction Finding and Radio "Finger-Printing"

40. Direction Finding.--Direction finding was of the greatest importance in Signal Intelligence activities, and its importance increased as Russian radio discipline and code and cipher security were improved.[318] "A relatively large number of direction finding personnel was employed by the KONA, e.g., five with each forward platoon, 50 (as against 84 intercept operators) with Feste 10."[319]

The NAAS evaluation section was fed by the Direction Finding sections from both the FAK and the NAK. The FAK's sent requests not only to the long range but to the close range direction finding sites. FAK 617, for example, sent its orders both to three or four long-range direction find sites and to about twelve close range ones.[320]

Long-range direction finding sets were located 200-350 kilometers behind the front line. Two to three direction finding sets at one spot constituted a direction finding group.[321] The supervisor worked in the company intercept rooms, and sent requests to the direction finding operators over a command transmitter. Through this means simultaneous fixes could be taken by two, and frequently by three sites.[322]

The Close Range sets were located with the NAK platoons. The sets received requests not only from the Long Range Companies but also from the Close Range headquarters.[323]

> "The distance from company headquarters to the nearest outstation was generally twenty to thirty

318 I 19b p 38
319 I 19g p 5
320 I 19b p 38
321 I 19b p 2
322 I 173 p 34
323 I 19b p 2

70

kilometers. Each station was completely mobile, and moved with the sectors of heavy fighting. Wire communication was occasionally available, but for the most part W/T /wireless/ communication was employed between outstations and headquarters. There was no communication between outstations. Bearings were requested by and at the discretion of, the duty officer at the intercept station. The outstations, listening on a common frequency, were advised of active enemy frequencies by means of messages sent in simple substitution cipher. Bearings were then returned, enciphered by a daily additive. Thirty to sixty seconds were required to notify all outstations of bearings required."[324]

While generally Long Range direction finding operations could fix a station within fifteen kilometers, Close Range platoon direction-finding operations could narrow the possibility to two or three kilometers.[325]

The results were screened at company level, and the good bearings were selected, with all relevant information, and reported back to the NAAS, which passed final judgment on them.[326]

41. "Radio Finger-Printing."--To enable the identification of particular radio stations, a Corporal Arno-Graul working in the NAAS constructed an apparatus designed to "radio fingerprint" the Russian transmitters through a study of oscillograms. The method was

> "to register the incoming telegraphic traffic in the form of an image on a cathode ray tube and analyze the image. Analysis consists of a number of steps, so that all details and peculiarities of the transmitter are comprised. The apparatus is attached to a normal intercept set. The individual characteristics of the transmitter can be recorded graphically by means of tracings, or in the form of photostats, in a card index."[327]

Attempts to study the characteristics of particular radio operators, by the peculiarities of their sending habits, were evidently not undertaken by KONA 1 in any formal manner.

[324] I 62 p 4
[325] I 19b p 38
[326] I 19b p 38
[327] I 19b p 39

VOLUME 4

Chapter V

Section E. Some Aspects of Evaluation and Cryptanalysis in the KONA

Paragraph

42. Evaluation in the NAAS.--The main duty of the NAAS was to evaluate the enemy traffic intercepted and passed to it by the Long Range and Close Range Signal Intelligence Companies.

Captain Roessler, Chief Evaluator of KONA 1, and Commanding Officer of the NAAS, observed that "there were no prescribed rules for evaluation, and this fact...made the success or failure of the signal intelligence service a personal matter depending on the perspicacity and experience of a few specialists and persons operating in key positions."[328]

Evaluation in the NAAS was concerned with "the observation and interpretation of known (radio) nets," the study of unidentified traffic, and the results of cryptanalysis. Roessler emphasized that in the case of KONA 1, "the interpretation of unknown traffic was...from a long term intelligence point of view, the chief evaluation problem."[329]

Comprehensive research work was necessary to systematize the evidence available, and the basic instruments of this systematization were the Card Indexes. The Card Indexes were exhaustive in detail, thorough and methodical. The Germans believed that the tiniest detail, though utterly lacking in any apparent significance at the moment of interception, might form part of a significant picture when scrutinized in context with similar details. Thus the minutest phenomenon, irrespective of its momentary irrelevance was recorded.[330]

328 I 19b p 13

329 I 19b p 14

330 I 19b p 13; I 19g p 3

A special section in NAAS 1 kept up to date all card indexes.[331] These will be described below.

a. Personality Index. This index listed all officers and radio operators whose names were derived not only from radio but from all sources (interrogations, captured documents, etc.). All names were treated with caution because of the Russian propensity for using cover names. There was a special file for indexing these.

b. Unit Index. This file contained all information available from all sources on all Russian units. Each card was designed to list the following items: unit, commanding officer, chief of staff, components to which the unit was subordinate, subordinate units comprising the unit in question, location, date of first appearance, and sources of information.

c. Blocknot Index. Both Blocknots and Chi-numbers were contained in the same index. A careful recording and study of blocknots provided positive clues in the identification and the tracking of formations using 5-figure codes. This index was subdivided into two files: one, the search card index, contained all Blocknots and Chi-numbers whether or not they were known; the other, the unit card index, contained only known Block-and Chi-numbers. Inspector Berger observed that the two files formed "The most important and surest" instrument for identifying Russian radio nets known to him.[332]

d. Key (Schluessel) Index. This index contained all solved keys, irrespective of the areas in which they were used. They were arranged according to the German designation of the Russian keys. "The German system of key designation includes a self-evident description of the code plus an allotted number; e.g., R4ZC 1800: russischer 4-Zahlen Code 1800 /Russian 4-figure code 1800/."[333] The 2 and 3-figure keys especially were

331 The information on the Card Index down to but not including sub-paragraph h, follows very closely the detailed report made by Inspector Georg Berger, in charge of documents in KONA 1. This report is No. 8, I 19b pp 16-18.

332 I 19b p 16

333 I 19g p 10

"peculiar to definite formations," and thus certain inferences about the formation in question could sometimes be made on the basis of the key alone.[334]

e. Call Sign Index. All call signs picked up on the entire Eastern front, known or unknown, were listed in this index, which showed not only the call sign, but also the connection in which it previously might have appeared.[335] The index was fully cross-referenced and was relied upon not only for spot identification but for building new call sign blocks.[336]

f. Cover Name Index. The Russians used cover names abundantly, not only for units, but for "common military expressions and tactical measures as well." Some were so consistently used that all disguise was lost, and they became accepted "expressions." On the whole they presented no great difficulty and could usually be interpreted successfully.[337] All cover names obtained were scrupulously recorded by the Index Section. In many cases nearly complete cover tables were reconstructed for the various Russian fronts.[338]

g. Coordinates Index. The map coordinates derived by solution of Russian map reference systems were recorded in this index, the coordinates being arranged both by the system and by the unit making use of the system.[339] It is significant that, even though the coordinate system might not be understood, the method itself might be enough to furnish important clues facilitating the tracking of a particular formation.[340]

h. Direction Finding Bearings. This file consisted of a listing of the various bearings on each Russian radio station obtained through direction finding, and helped the NAAS to estimate the value and significance of the bearings.[341]

i. Air Traffic Index. Russian Air Traffic was frequently picked up by operators assigned to search missions. In order to spot this intercept as Air traffic, a cataloguing of its

334 I 19b p 17

335 I 19b p 17

336 I 19b p 36

337 I 173 p 25

338 I 19b p 18

339 I 19b p 18

340 I 19g p 10

341 I 19b p 38

74

characteristics was necessary; and to accomplish this a special index was set up in the NAAS. In this index were recorded not only the statistics derived from German Army interception of Air traffic, but also data supplied by units of the German Air Force (2nd and 3rd battalions of Air Signal Regiment 353, operating with Local Air Forces 4 and 6 respectively). The statistics gathered were passed on to the Long Range Signal Intelligence Companies (FAK), which were likely to pick up Air traffic. The companies did not have separate air data indexes, but kept the data in the Army card index.[342]

It should be pointed out that in order to insure the most comprehensive indexes possible, liaison was maintained laterally between the NAAS of KONA 1 and the other regiments on the Eastern front. Full collaboration was effected also with OKH/GdNA. A system for exchanging current information, new interpretations, corrections, etc., operated smoothly, the data being passed by telegraph or courier depending upon the urgency of the item in question.[343]

Below the level of the NAAS, card indexes were extensively used; but they were naturally less comprehensive, being only as complete as the company cover assignment permitted.[344] Of the card index in general, Roessler made a significant (and characteristic) observation, emphasizing that while "the card indexes formed the indispensable material basis for evaluation, memory, experience, and perspicacity of the individual evaluators lent the spark."[345]

43. Evaluation in a Feste.--Evaluation in the Feste was a matter of identifying and interpreting unknown traffic, the interception of which was its particular function.[346] Some characteristics of Russian communications facilitating identification have been discussed in the preceding section. The systematization of this work as carried on by the Feste Evaluation Section showed how the identifying elements were studied at this level.

The first task of the Traffic Evaluation Section[347] was to work up the information into a network diagram, which not only

342 I 19b p 52

343 I 19b p 16

344 I 19g p 10

345 I 19b p 13

346 I 19b p 4

347 The data on Traffic Evaluation in the Feste follows closely Report No. 9 I 19b pp 19-20.

represented the net structure but listed all pertinent informatio and formed the basic medium studied. The diagram contained:

a. The net number
b. The date
c. Traffic workings with call signs
d. The number and kind of messages (if any) sent
e. The "Direction finding number"
f. Block numbers and Chi-numbers on any 5-figure messages
g. Short plain text messages when available

In the case of 5-figure traffic, this diagram was turned over to a 5-figure section, where an attempt was made to identify the station from a study of the Blocknots and the Chi-numbers, which were checked against the previously indexed or charted data.

All diagrams passed through the Traffic Analysis Section, where the call sign composition was scrutinized, studied in relation to the "Basic Book for Allotment of Call Signs"(Hauptverteiler), and, if unidentified, recorded in the index. Network diagrams and messages were checked against the Card Indexes of names and cover-names[348] for interpretation in the light of the evidence accumulated there.

The network diagrams were passed to the Direction Finding Evaluation Section, which determined by the location of the "fixes" whether the intercept was likely to be, for example, Army (if in an area near the front) or Air Force; or Line of Communication traffic (if in a rear area).

The diagrams went finally to the final Evaluation[349] or Fusion Section, where the results entered on the diagram by the various sections were weighed and considered in the light of information passed to the Final Evaluation unit by the Cryptanalytic section. From here the traffic identified by the Final Evaluation unit was reported to the NAAS, together with the tactical information derived from the messages. The findings guided modification of the cover towards dropping the less important traffic and placing more sets on the "interesting" circuits.

44. <u>Evaluation in a FAK</u>.--The Evaluation Section in the FAK was apparently organized like that in the Feste, although the relative dearth of evidence available precluded drawing a close parallel. Presumably it differed in function from the

[348] The source did not make clear whether this function was performed in the Traffic Analysis Section.

[349] Endauswertung, I 19g p 3

Evaluation section in the FAK worked on identified traffic as well.[351]

As in the case of the Feste, the basic document of evaluation was the network diagram, prepared by the Traffic Evaluation section. This diagram included all evidence by which the station in question had been identified (in the case of 5-figure traffic, the Blocknots and Chi-numbers) and other significant data. Apparently, as in the case of the Feste, this diagram passed through various sections devoted to direction finding evaluation, traffic analysis, work on unidentified traffics, contents evaluation[352] and finally to fusion or final evaluation.[353]

45. Cryptanalysis in the KONA.--The details of cryptanalysis performed by the field units are discussed in Chapter VI of this volume. Because of the importance of cryptanalysis in the total evaluation, however, it is pertinent to note here the organization and function of the sections carrying out this work at KONA level.

Cryptanalysis in the NAAS was performed by a special section separate from the Evaluation and Traffic Analysis sections. The cryptanalytic section totalled less than 60 persons. It was divided into subsections, the most important of which was that devoted to "new developments." Other subsections were 2-figure, 3-figure, 4-figure, NKVD, bookbreaking, and plaintext examination. There was also a small subsection devoted to administration.[354]

The cryptanalytic section had the following tasks:[355]

a. To collect and work on the traffic which the companies could not deal with (whether because of lack of material or preoccupation with more important systems).

b. To test and check doubtful solutions passed up by the companies.

c. To establish whether keys broken by the companies were the first examples of their kind; to complete them and put them in a handy workable form (the so-called "basic form"), and to assign a number to each key appearing in the area of the regiment.

351 I 19b p 5

352 The section concerned with content evaluation "/worked/ on all readable messages, (identified) places, names and cover-names...and sees to the immediate forwarding of all important messages to the NAAS." (I 19b p 5)

353 I 19b p 5

354 I 19b pp 10-11

355 I 19b p 9

77

d. To pass back down all solved key systems to companies who might be concerned.

The function and organization of cryptanalysis in the long range companies (both Feste and FAK) appears to have been much the same in each. On paper, cryptanalysis at company level was a part of the evaluation platoon, in contrast to its independent position as a separate section in the NAAS;[356] it appears to have functioned in practice independently, however, because of the special nature of its work. The evidence indicated that there may have been 15 to 20 persons engaged in cryptanalytic work in the company evaluation platoons.[357]

> "It was the task of company cryptanalysis not only to solve systems, to recover ciphers, to decode already known procedures, and/or to translate all this material, but also to contribute to the identification and interpretation of traffics on the basis of keys employed... /The cryptanalytic section/ cooperated closely with cryptanalysis of the NAAS, but was so organized and equipped that it could work on most messages itself."[358]

The cryptanalytic group was divided into separate sections for plaintext message translation, 2-, 3-, and 4-figure traffic (one section for each), and a general section which kept card indexes and lists and performed certain administrative duties. These sections, besides being responsible for the solution of new systems, the recovery of additive, and the decoding of solved systems, played an important part in traffic identification through a study of the keys employed.[359] The key indicators, which the Russians placed at the beginning and often at the end of messages, were arranged by the numerical designation arbitrarily assigned by the Germans to Russian keys in an index file.[360]

The cryptanalysts relied heavily upon the card indexes in their work, and also had at hand graphic and statistical presentations of single letter, digraphic, and trigraphic frequencies, and lists of pattern words.[361]

356 I 19b p 6
357 I 19b p 11
358 I 19b pp 11-12
359 I 19b pp 11-12
360 I 19b p 41
361 I 19b p 41

They cooperated closely with the personnel engaged in the final evaluation section, often passing notes with the translated messages calling the attention of the evaluators to the key employed on the message or to peculiarities which might have a significance when viewed in relation to the total data. Moreover, the cryptanalysts kept in touch with those responsible for intercept, to the end of obtaining the best possible copy for solution of new systems.[362]

46. Reports.--The findings of the intelligence units were passed to the operating agencies in various reports, and the intelligence in them was made available by an efficient reporting system. Captain Roessler observed that "a smoothly functioning report system was the chief problem discussed at almost all meetings to consider organization."[363] In general, careful provision was made both on low and high levels for efficient reporting. The reports were passed either laterally to other field formations or upwards through signal intelligence channels to the higher agencies. "Hot" items were sent out in "Advance Reports,"[364] while other important but less urgent conclusions were sent in the daily "Situation Reports."[365]

The companies were required to provide highly detailed reports.[366] They had to exercise their own judgment, showing initiative and intelligence in selecting the items to be passed on. A great deal of material was never reported at all but simply went into the card indexes of the companies. The companies had to distinguish urgent from routine items, and the NAAS frequently rebuked the forward units for a failure to send back in a "flash" what they had allowed to get through only in a routine report.[367]

The NAK maintained an evaluation platoon at Company Headquarters which correlated and interpreted the materials from the other platoons, and reported the findings laterally to the Army Corps G-2 and upward to the NAAS.[368]

The basic technical report at company level was a "Day

[362] I 19b p 12

[363] I 19b p 13

[364] I 19g p 7

[365] I 19b p 14

[366] I 19b p 13

[367] I 19g p 7

[368] I 19g p 5; I 19b p 22

Report" made by the intercept operators, listing all traffic heard on the frequencies monitored. There were columns for recording the time of intercept, the frequency upon which the traffic was taken, the call signs to and from, the contents of the transmission, the intercept number and remarks. All intercept operators made similar logs, which gave a picture of the total traffic carried on a particular link or network.

These logs provided the company evaluation sections with the subject matter studied in drawing up their Situation Reports.[369] A typical Situation Report described the deployment and status of identified Russian units and reported any appearance of a new unit.[370]

The reports issued by the Feste and the FAK were much the same. These included:[371]

a. Twice-daily Network Reports (Netzmeldungen)

b. Advance Reports (Vorausmeldungen or Sofortmeldungen) for important tactical items

c. Daily Situation Reports (Tagesmeldungen) for a summary of the day's Advance Reports and all less important data

These reports were sent to the NAAS for further interpretation, and significant intelligence items were then passed laterally to the Armies.[372] A long range company needed an average of 16 typist hours to get out its daily report for the NAAS.[373]

The Feste on the Eastern front issued in addition to the reports listed above a type of report known as the "5-figure offer" for circulation by OKH/GdNA to the other KONA's. The purpose of the 5-figure offer was to assure the maximum exploitation of information available, and in effect constituted invitations to all KONA's to check the data in these reports with their own files. They listed all current data derivable from the external characteristics of messages consisting of 5-figure groups.[374]

The section at the NAAS for technical and tactical analysis, collated and combined the significant findings from all these

369 I 173 p 24
370 I 19b pp 21-23
371 I 19g p 8
372 I 19g p 8
373 I 19b p 13
374 I 19g p 8

reports with the data at hand, passed material not immediately exploitable to the various specialists in the NAAS for a further "squeeze" and passed its combined report to the Army Group.[375] Roessler referred to the daily Situation Reports issued by the NAAS as a "Lagemeldung."

Information furnished by members of In 7/VI showed that the Signal Intelligence Reports issued by the Evaluation Centers of some regiments were called "Funklagemeldungen."[376] These consisted of four component reports:

a. Direction finding reports (Peilmeldungen)

b. Radio traffic reports (Betriebsmeldungen)

c. Radio clear text reports (Funkmeldungen)

d. Radio code-text reports (Verkehrsnachrichten)

These reports went beyond In 7/VI and were passed to the "Army Group Commander as well as to the Army High Command and other echelons and commands on a distribution list of 14 ~~listing~~ listings."[379]

375 I 19g p 8

376 IF 105 p 4

377 These were the evaluated daily reports compiled on call signs (Rufzeichen) and radio traffic (Verstaendigungsverkehr) of enemy and neutral broadcasting stations (Funkstellen).

378 These contained the decoded and translated texts of enemy messages.

379 IF 105b p 4

VOLUME 4

Chapter VI. Russian Cryptanalysis

Section A. Organization of Cryptanalytic Effort against Russia

47. Review of Central Office Organization.-- Prior to 1939, an agency known as the Intercept Control Station (Horchleitstelle, abbreviated HLS) had a section for handling Russian traffic; but little is known in detail of its achievements.[385] In summarizing German activities before the outbreak of war with Russia, Lt. Col. Mettig (second in command of OKW/Chi) stated that the Germans were able during the first Russo-Finnish war to break a number of two-, three-, and four-figure codes.[386] In addition, a copy of the Russian five-figure code was obtained from the Finnish General Staff. (This particular code was used by the Russians in the first year of war with Germany.[387] The Intercept Control Station (HLS) was replaced in 1941 by two agencies, Inspectorate 7/VI (abbreviated In 7/VI)(serving as a cryptanalytic unit in Berlin), and the Control Station of Signal Intelligence (Leitstelle der Nachrichten Aufklaerung, abbreviated LNA) in Zossen.[388] The section for Russian cryptanalysis that had been part of HLS remained attached to In 7/VI during the first few months of its existence; Russian "evaluation" was done at LNA. Both organizations felt, however, that cryptanalysis and evaluation should be done further forward; and late in 1941, the Russian section of In 7/VI (including cryptanalysts and evaluators) was sent to Loetzen in East Prussia.[389] This section formed the nucleus for a third

[385] IF 181 p 4

[386] I 78 p 3

[387] I 78 p 8

[388] I 78 p 5

[389] I 78 p 8

82

central agency, the Intercept Control Station East (Horchleitstelle Ost, abbreviated HLS Ost). From this time until November, 1944, German Army Signal Intelligence activities were sharply divided into non-Russian (performed at In 7/VI)[390], and into Russian (performed at HLS Ost and LNA).

In October, 1944, HLS Ost and LNA were amalgamated, together with In 7/VI, into the Signal Intelligence Agency of the Army High Command (Oberkommando des Heeres, General der Nachrichten Aufklaerung, abbreviated OKH/GdNA), the one final central agency of the war.[391]

For the ultimate breakdown of OKH/GdNA in detail see Volume 4, Chapter II.[392] In brief, the assignment of Russian cryptanalytic functions were as follows:

Group III (under Capt. Gorzolla): evaluated traffic and cryptanalytic work from the Russian front

Group IV (under Major Hertze): did all the cryptanalytic at OKH/GdNA

Section 3 (under Lt. Dettmann): the former cryptanalytic section of HLS Ost, and handled

a. Russian NKVD traffic
b. Russian Army traffic
c. Russian Partisan traffic
d. Research on Russian Systems

390 Discussed in Volume 4, Chapter VII

391 The amalgamation was necessitated by the retreat of HLS Ost to Zossen, where In 7/VI and LNA were located. This move was one of operational rather than cryptanalytic expediency: the Russians were advancing; HLS Ost was retreating; and when the home office and the field cryptanalytic and evaluation offices were all close together, it was certainly more expedient to combine them. The result: GdNA.

392 Derived almost wholly from IF 123 pp 6-14

Group V Section 1 (under Specialist Block): reconstructed Russian call signs
Section 2 (under Specialist Block): exploited captured Russian documents of signals interest

Group VI (under Capt. Roeder at Potsdam):
Section 1: worked on high-grade machine systems
a. Intercept and evaluation of Inter-Soviet State Traffic
b. Intercept and evaluation of Russian Baudot traffic
c. Intercept and evaluation of Russian Army traffic

Section 3 of Group IV in the above chart was the Russian cryptanalytic section. It may be assumed that HLS Ost, although amalgamated into GdNA, continued very much as it had in its duties, and that the work performed earlier by HLS Ost was identical in nature to the work performed later in Section 3 of Group IV of GdNA.[393]

48. Review of Field Office Organization.-- While preparations were being made for the attack on Russia, it was found that there was an "acute shortage" of cryptanalysts available for field work.[394] Cryptanalysts were culled from the fixed intercept stations and trained for field work with the newly organized Signal Intelligence Regiments (Kommandeure der Nachrichten Aufklaerung, abbreviated KONA). Five of these regiments were sent into the field as complete low level intercept and evaluation units attached to Army Groups: two went to the western front; KONAs 1, 2, and 3 were assigned to the eastern front. These eastern KONAs were supplemented in 1942 by KONA 6, which was sent out to cover the German campaign in the Caucasus[395], and which was attached directly to HLS Ost. Low level cryptanalysis and evaluation was also done by KONA 8 and KONA Nord, which were made up from other Eastern front signal intelligence regiments, and activated in late 1944 and early 1945.

[393] Nothing is known from TICOM sources of the cryptanalytic activities of HLS Ost before its amalgamation into GdNA except a brief statement of Mettig in I 78 p 8

[394] I 78 pp 4, 7

[395] DF 18 p 81

84

The organization of field units for cryptanalysis has already been discussed in detail.[396] Since the information on Russian cryptanalysis used in this chapter, however, derives as much from interrogations of prisoners engaged in field operations as from the discussion of cryptanalysis of GdNA [397], the reader is referred for a brief review to the chart of organization of KONA 1 [398] about which we know more than any other as it was captured in toto.[399]

49. Assignment of cryptanalytic tasks to the central offices and the KONAs.-- In discussing the task of In 7/VI, Lt. Mettig said: [400]

> "Once the forward crypto-analytic units had been set up and attached to the various forward wireless units it was agreed to allot to them the investigation of forward and Line of Communication traffic which could be solved in the field. In 7/VI remained, however, responsible for all army crypto-analytic work and concentrated on the most difficult and unsolved procedures."

Of the assignments for HLS Ost and LNA as central offices, or for various KONAs in the field, there is no statement in TICOM interrogations. Of GdNA, there is only the statement of Dettmann and Samsonov [401] to the effect that "the solution of agent, guerilla, and Kundschafter traffic was the responsibility of Referat 3c [of Group IV]." The nature, extent, and assignment of cryptanalytic work to these units, both central and field, can only be inferred from the discussions of the Prisoners of War regarding solution and achievement.[402]

[396] Volume 4 Chapter III

[397] Dettmann and Samsonov, "A Report on Russian Decryption in the Former German Army", published as DF 18.

[398] Charts 4-1, 4-4

[399] See also Volume 4, Chapter V for discussion of the functions and duties of the various field units.

[400] I 78 p 8

[401] I 116 p 7

[402] DF-18 passim, for GdNA; all reports quoted in this chapter, passim, for the KONAs

It is clear, in all the interrogations, that actual cryptanalysis was done on all levels of field operations and the central offices almost interchangeably: from the lowest level (where it was considered merely a function of "evaluation") up through the highest level (where it involved pure mathematics and the assistance of IBM machinery). By inference from the interrogations, it can be said that, with one or two exceptions,[403] all types of problems were handled in all units. The flexibility of cryptanalytic assignment was determined mainly by the Russians' use of their own systems. Aside from machine traffic and five-figure codes (Army or NKVD), which it can be assumed contained the most important operational communications, the Russian tactical, strategic, and lower level operational communications were not carried in any set category of systems, determined by their relative importance. Two-, three-, four-, and even some five-figure traffic was used by the Russian Air Force, the NKVD, and the Army at all levels of operations. The German Army cryptanalytic effort, therefore, was oriented to fit the situation as determined by Russian usage. The discussion of cryptanalytic operations on the part of German Prisoners of War was invariably set forth in terms of types of encipherment and difficulty of solution, and took the form of two-figure, three-figure, four-figure, five-figure, NKVD, address, Agents' solution. As Lt. Loeffler pointed out, in discussing company cryptanalysis, "The strength of the various sections was modified to cope with developments on the Russian side--namely, the shifting of emphasis from 2-figure to 3-figure, and then later to 4-figure." Cryptanalytic sections were divided according to this scheme in the company (FAK), the battalion (NAA), and the central agency of the KONA (the NAAS). The same scheme was followed by Dettmann and Samsonov in discussing the whole problem of German Army cryptanalysis of Russian systems [404], and appears to be the underlying

[403] 5-figure codes and partisan and agents' codes are to be discussed later in this chapter.

[404] DF 18

basis for the organization of training the "Russian Cryptanalysis Course" given by Group IV of OKH/GdNA for field training.[405] In this course, more attention was given to two-figure tables and three-figure and four-figure codes because of their operational frequency and their importance for tactical and strategic intelligence.

In short, the various cryptanalytic assignments seem to have been determined for the most part by how the Russians used their own systems (operational area and importance) and by the amount of time and manpower the Germans needed to effect solution. A summary of the assignments follow:

two-figure codes were worked on mostly by the companies (where, it has been pointed out, it was considered part of "evaluation") because of the simple solution and the immediate need for the tactical intelligence involved; but it was also handled by the battalion (NAA), the central KONA agency (the NAAS), and even by the home office (GdNA): Lt. Dettmann says that solving the two-figure codes was "merely a form of crossword puzzle."[406]

three-figure codes were worked on in the companies, but were also handled by the NAA, the NAAS and HLS Ost.

[405] I 166, complete

[406] IF 5 p 6

four-figure codes offered more difficulty in solution, since a large amount of material was "absolutely necessary... the majority of unsolved four-figure codes were abandoned because of an insufficient number of messages"[407]; these were handled by the NAAS and GdNA, rather than on company level, because of the lack of men, machinery (IBM), and time necessary for solution on a forward level.

three-figure and four-figure signal codes were considered somewhat "special" and were handled in the company (FAK) by "chosen cryptanalysts, sometimes by the chief cryptanalyst"[408] and in the NAAS.[409]

five-figure codes, which were generally considered unbreakable, were handed by GdNA, though KONA 1 for a period did five-figure cryptanalysis independently[410]; Dettmann and Samsonov state that five-figure traffic was submitted for the exclusive processing of the [GdNA]."[411]

agents' codes, which had always been done in the central offices[412], were "the responsibility of Referat 3c"[413], mainly because solution "depended on captured material."[414] They were probably given to these central offices by other than Army sources.

[407] I 191 p 8

[408] I 19b p 11

[409] I 19b p 11

[410] I 19b p 43

[411] DF 18 p 83

[412] See Volume 4, Chapter VI and later in this Chapter

[413] I 116 p 7

[414] ibid.

NKVD systems formed a special group of wireless traffic from the Russian and the German points of view, and cryptanalysis of NKVD material was handled by the NAAS[415], LNA[416] and GdNA (through 4-figure) (five-figure)[417]

machine ciphers were considered on the same level of solution as five-figure code and were handled exclusively at GdNA

Whatever systems were solved, or could be easily solved and deciphered, were done as far forward and with as few men and as little time as possible. When more time, or manpower, or mechanical (IBM) or theoretical help was needed, the solution was removed as far to the rear as practicable or necessary. Because of the difficulty involved in solution of five-figure codes (Army or NKVD) and machine traffic, the GdNA was obviously the best agency for handling these; at the other extreme, the companies could almost always solve and process two-figure systems, because of their simple encipherment. All systems of intermediate difficulty, however, were assigned not only to these units but to the intermediate units, depending on state of solution, amount of material necessary, number of men required, etc. Rather than cutting across systems and thinking in terms of specific levels of operation and levels of intelligence priority, both the Russians and the Germans thought in terms of types of encipherment. In discussing the German Army cryptanalytic effort of Russian systems, therefore, the discussion will take the form of two-figure, three-figure, four-figure, five-figure, address, NKVD, etc.

415 I 96 pp. 46-47

416 _ibid._ pp 9-10

417 DF 18 p 63

VOLUME 4

Chapter VI. Russian Cryptanalysis

Section B. Cryptanalytic Achievements against Russia

50. 2-figure codes.-- 2-figure codes were used by the Russian Army, Air Force and NKVD. In the Army, they were used by Army Groups, Armies, Corps, Divisions, and Regiments; and by small independent special units such as Combat Engineer Brigades, Motor Regiments, and Artillery Brigades. In the NKVD, they were used on frontier regimental networks and from divisional level downwards.

Solution of 2-figure systems was done mostly on company level (FAK), but was also handled by NAA, the NAAS, and the GdNA.

a) The PT-39. The PT-39 (Peregovornaa Tablica, literally "conversation table"), a 2-figure code placed in a square 10 x 10 and then enciphered by substitution through a 2-figure, 10 x 10 Latin square[422], can be taken as the "mother" 2-figure code.[423]

[422] i.e. no figure was repeated in any row or column

[423] I 191 p 1;I 19c p 1

(Actually, according to the Dettmann and Samsonov[424], the first 2-figure operational system used over a long period by the Army and Air Force of the whole Soviet Union was PT-35, a code with 100 values, re-enciphered daily within the individual networks. In the last months of 1939, PT-35 was replaced by PT-39.) From 1940-1942, it was used far more than all other codes combined.[425] PT-39 was used by Army Groups, Armies, Corps, and Divisions. The identification of the latin square used for encipherment enabled the Germans to establish to which Russian front or army the wireless station using it belonged, or whether it was an Army or Air Force Station. Since the squares were often used for several months, the reconstruction of squares could be easily checked; this appears to have been hardly necessary, however, since the rows and columns could be solved (reconstructed) with a minimum of 15 to 20 groups. The messages were of a technical signal or tactical nature, the latter more especially after the beginning of the Russian campaign in June, 1941. This particular code (PT-39) was used from the extreme south to the extreme north of the eastern front, and in the back areas as far as the Caucasus, middle Asia, and North Persia.[426]

b) The PT-42 and PT 42N. The PT-39 was superseded in May 1942 by PT-42. There is a flat disagreement with this statement in the report of Dettmann and Samsonov, who say that "at the beginning of 1942, PT-41 came into use as the successor of PT-39."[427] Dettmann and Samsonov do not mention PT-42 at all, but their description of PT-41 corresponds to the description given of PT-42. They are very probably the same code and encipherment, misnamed by one or the other of the Prisoners of War. The PT-42 was similar to PT-39 in construction except that the distribution of

[424] DF 18 p 45

[425] I 19c p 1

[426] I 19c p 1

[427] DF 18 p 47

values in the basic square was made random, and variants for values (as many as four for common letters such as o, e, i, a) were introduced. The enciphering method was the same as for PT-39; but because of the random nature of value assignment in the basic square, the solution of a row (or column) of the enciphering square now required about 30 groups. PT-42 was restricted in use to Army Groups, Armies, or Corps. For divisions and regiments, PT-42N was used. It was smaller, with a square 7 x 10 instead of 10 x 10, but its construction was the same as PT-42. As in the case of PT-42, enciphermant was performed by rows, but these were rarely derived from a Latin square. It was used almost exclusively from division forwards and remained in force in some cases until 1944.[428] It produced much tactical information.

c) The PT-43. The PT-42 and PT-42N were superseded (no date given) by PT-43, which was the last general 2-figure code used and which remained in force up to the capitulation of the Germans. Unlike the basic square in PT-39, PT-42, and PT-42N, it contained no letters. PT-43, was used for addresses, particularly by the Air Force and the PWO (A. A. Defense).[429]

d) In addition to PT-39, PT-42, PT-42N, and PT-43, small independent special units, such as Combat Engineer Brigades, Motor Regiments and Artillery Brigades, had their own home-made 2-figure codes which were often in use for only short periods and which, besides the letters of the alphabet and numbers, contained specialized expressions appropriate to the unit concerned.[430]

[428] I 19c pp 1, 2

[429] I 19c p 2

[430] I 19c p 2

92

It is clear from all the interrogations that 2-figure codes were not always in use, but were being constantly read. Prisoners of War of NAA 11 said that the last known PT table was PT-43, but that they could not reconstruct it.[431] But their statement is the only contradictory one among many others according to which solution was not only easy but current. Capt. Noletzko, (of Ln. Reg. 353) though speaking mainly of air systems (ground/ground, etc.) said, for example, that 2-figure codes were used only by forward troops and were almost 100% readable;[432] he admitted that much assistance was gained through security breaches on the part of Russian operators, but insisted that 2-figure traffic was never very difficult to read.[433] For Lt. Dettmann, solving the PT codes was "merely a form of crossword puzzles."[434] Gerlich stated that one or two men were sufficient at NAAS 1 to cope with current decipherment of 2-figure messages, especially as the greater part of them were already being solved in the companies, but added that solution was made easier when plain text was interspersed.[435]

The Prisoners of War of KONA 1 stated categorically that the Russians practically ceased using 2-figure codes after 1943.[436] But other evidence would indicate that the Russians continued to use them up to the cessation of hostilities, although only for forward troops. Capt. Schmidt stated that the Army and NKVD used 2-figure codes up to the end of hostilities[437]; but Gerlich said, "In the last stages 2-figure systems only occurred where the units were engaged

[431] I 106 p 2

[432] I 75 p 10

[433] I 75 p 4

[434] IF 5 p 6

[435] I 191 pp 2, 3, 4

[436] I 19c p 1

[437] I 55 p 11

93

in fighting: Thus it is to be expected that they are still being used in the Red Army even if they are not appearing at the moment."[438]

51. 3-figure codes.- 3-figure codes were used by the Army, the Air Force and the NKVD. They were used first (1941-42) mainly by the Air Force; later, more widely by the Army. Every Army Group, Army, Corps, Division, Brigade, Regiment and Battalion had its own 3-figure code. The 3-figure codes were replaced by 3-figure Signal Codes in 1943 which were used by all units from Army downwards. In the NKVD, they were used by the Black Sea Fleet and from division downwards.

Solution of 3-figure codes was carried on mostly in the companies (FAK), but since the 3-figure codes offered more difficulty to solution than the 2-figure codes, they were also handled by the NAA, the NAAS, and HLS Ost.

Three-figure codes were first noticed in February, 1941. They were used increasingly from May, 1941 and the beginning of the Russian campaign. From then until the second half of 1942, the Air Force were the greatest users of this code and each Air Division had its own cipher. In 1942, the first Army unit (the 48th Army then in the Caucasus) started using a three-figure syllabic code.

"By the time of Stalingrad practically every Army engaged in the battle had its own 3-figure cipher."[439] Although they speak of specific 3-figure codes under various circumstances, Dettmann and Samsonov do not discuss any 3-figure codes as such; it can only be assumed that they considered the type of book and encipherment so similar to the 2-figure PT series that they did not warrant discussion as a special type.

Like the 2-figure system, the 3-figure system consisted of a code-book, and an enciphering table of some sort. The first 3-figure codes were simple in form, and were made up of several pages (at most 10) which contained common words arranged alphabetically. Originally the letters of the

[438] I 191 p 4; see also DF 18, p 47

[439] I 19c p 2

94

alphabet were placed at the end of the book (arranged alphabetically, semi-random, or random), but were soon afterwards put into the book in their alphabetic position. After some months, this total alphabeticity was replaced by a partial-alphabetic arrangement (alphabeticity maintained only within letters); and numbers were scattered at random through the book.[440] The book could have 1,000 groups, but 1st. Lt. Schubert stated that the average was 300-800, "in general small scope, but frequent change."[441] If the code were smaller than 1,000 groups, alternatives were given either to pages or first figures of the lines.[442] The methods of enciphering were extremely varied in details, but always involved encipherment of a single figure separately.[443] The substitutions could be constructed without any recognizable system or they could be made up from a Latin square; the square usually lasted about a month, although in the Air Force, it sometimes lasted longer.[444] Schubert stated that "Towards the end, there appeared quite isolated 4 to 7-figure substitution systems-- presumably private systems of the respective cypher departments. I imagine this to be so as they appeared very seldom."[445]

The only specific 3-figure code referred to in TICOM is what the Germans called R3ZC (Russian, 3-Zahlen [figure], Code) mentioned by Corporal A. Faure of NAA 11, the "Norway Party."[446] (It was a code with 10 pages of 100 positions each, 10 x 10, alphabetically arranged. Only the hundreds and tens figures of each group were enciphered.) In general, either the 3-figure code book itself or the method of encipherment were so varied that Prisoners of War were able to remember only general characteristics, no specific examples.

[440] I 19c pp 2, 3

[441] I 26 p 2

[442] I 19c p 3

[443] I 19c, p 3; I 26 p 2

[444] I 19c p 3

[445] I 26 p 3

[446] I 55 p 12

The 3-figure code, it is clear from all interrogations, was used mainly by the Army, but also by the Air Forces. According to the Karrenberg party, on regimental networks and for less important messages on the level of assault armies, mainly the 3-figure code (with a 2-figure latin square encipherment) was used.[447] But the Prisoners of War of KONA 1 stated that every Army Group, Army, Corps, Division, Brigade, Regiment, and Battalion had its own 3-figure code which it used to communicate with its subordinate units.[448]

It is curious to note that a good deal of plain text was inserted in the 3-figure enciphered code as transmitted.[449] Gerlich pointed out the advantages of plain-text insertion: "They often gave words and names not contained in the code ....."[450]; and continued, "3-figure systems were always solved when sufficient material on one encipherment was available."[451] This would appear to be the general viewpoint, since Capt. Holetzko stated that 3-figure traffic was only slightly more secure than 2-figure traffic and was 80% readable.[452] In this case, Holetzko was talking particularly of 3-figure codes as used by the Russian Air forces (ground/ground). It is known that Air Force codes were often current for much longer periods than those of the Army, sometimes lasting a year;[453] and would thus afford more opportunity to find depths and set up overlaps. Army 3-figure codes were nearly always changed after a big operation and were with few exceptions never current for more than a month or two, sometimes for only a week;[454] solution was thereby made more difficult. Nevertheless, Lt. Starke (who worked with 3-figure traffic in a NAK) stated that, given depth of traffic, all codes were readable;[455] and

[447] I 173 pp 10, 11

[448] I 19c p 4

[449] I 26 p 2

[450] I 191, p 7

[451] I 191 p 7

[452] I 75 p 10

[453] I 19c p 4; DF 18 p 5

[454] I 19c p 4; DF 18 p 5

[455] I 75 p 6

96

Lt. Col. Mettig said flatly that from the spring of 1943 to 1945, 2-figure and 3-figure traffic was regularly decoded.[456] It can be assumed that 3-figure traffic was being read currently enough and constantly enough, to provide a great amount of tactical intelligence.

The operational 3-figure codes were discontinued in 1943 and were superseded by 3-figure Signal Codes[457] which were different only in that they contained no letters, but only words or phrases of tactical importance, and were not alphabetic but had meanings grouped under various headings such as "attack," "defense", "enemy movements," "designation of units", "figures or numbers","signal connections", etc. Each meaning had two or three 3-figure groups allotted to it. As in the case of the former 3-figure codes, anything not contained in the book itself was sent in clear.[458] Every unit from Army downward had its own signal code for use with subordinate units. There is no evidence that solution of these 3-figure Signal Codes was more difficult than solution of the 3-figure codes; nor is there any record of success either in totality or currency of decipherment. Lt. Loeffler of Feste 10 did, however, state that they were considered "special procedures", and "were studied in the appropriate section by specially chosen cryptanalysts, for the most part also by the chief cryptanalyst."[459] The solution time varied according to

[456] I 78 p 8

[457] Dettmann and Samsonov spoke of 3-figure and 4-figure "signal codes" described by members of KONA; but there are discrepancies between the two descriptions, and again it is impossible to determine where the mistake lies. The discussion as given by KONA 1 members seems generally more reliable.

[458] I 19c p 4

[459] I 19b, report 6, p 11

security, amount of material for overlapping, etc.; and we can only assume that the Signal Codes were read as consistently and as fully as the 2-figure and 3-figure codes they superseded.

52. 4-figure codes.-- 4-figure codes were used by the Army, Air Force, and NKVD. They were used in the Army as General Army Codes (called General Commanders' Codes), and on lower operational levels by mobile formations such as Tank and Mechanized Corps, Tank Armies, and Tank Administration and Supply Units. In NKVD, they were used on Railway and Transport Nets.

Solution was handled partly by the companies (FAK) (There was a 4-figure section, as well as a 2-figure and a 3-figure section, in the organization of a typical company cryptanalytic setup[460], but in all probability mostly by the NAAS and GdNA.)

1st Lt. Schubert (of GdNA) stated that, "The Russian Army keys are 3- or 4-figure systems. The basis is the same."[461] Actually, the construction of 4-figure codes was in principle the same as in the case of 3-figure codes, except that the basic book had a possible 10,000 groups instead of 1,000.[462] Schubert stated that there were in the code perhaps only six or seven pages[463], each with a block of consecutive numbers; but the description given by the members of KONA 1 indicates books of from 5 to 100 pages. The latter seems more likely.[464] In any case, the number of pages could vary from 5 to 100 (the Air Force Codes usually had about 10,000 groups and the Army 5,000 or less), and each page could have variant page designation.[465]

[460] I 19b p 11

[461] I 26 p 2

[462] I 19c p 4

[463] I 26 p 2

[464] I 19c p 5

[465] I 19c p 5

98

The actual construction of pages varied in 4-figure code-books as much as it did in the 3-figure code books, in respect to alphabeticity and sequence of numbers, etc.. But the methods of enciphering the last two digits were still more varied than those used in 3-figure systems: substitution by row, digraph substitution (in comparison to single-letter substitution in the case of 3-figure codes), combinations of these two, abbreviated figures in the substitution, and others.[466] Karrenberg, in his discussion of the "Russian Cryptanalysis course", given for field training mentioned that "a 3-figure or 4-figure code can also be reciphered on an adder. For this purpose a text chosen at random is enciphered (likewise by the code) and the code text added to or subtracted from (non-carrying)."[467] But there is no other indication in interrogations that this method was met in actual practice. The general method seems to have been variant page designations for the book (2 figures), and encipherment of the last 2 digits by various means, including 2-figure Latin squares.[468]

From May, 1941, the Air Force began to use 4-figure codes in many different forms but often of the simplest construction. In the middle of 1943 many mobile formations, Tank and Mechanized Corps, Tank Armies, and Tank Administration and Supply units also started using 4-figure codes. They were also used by Railway and Transport Nets.[469]

Dettmann and Samsonov (of GdNA) described the "first general army and air force" code (4-figure with roughly 4,600 groups, enciphered with digraphic substitution), and its successors "OKK 5" to "OKK 8" (General Commanders' Codes) that rapidly replaced one another from 1939-41. OKK 5 was captured in the Russo-Finnish war; and OKK 6, 7, and 8 were captured in the Russo-German war. But Dettmann and Samsonov

[466] I 19c p 5

[467] I 166 p 7, 8

[468] I 173 pp 10, 11

[469] I 19c pp 5, 6

insisted that, "All these systems were, however, recovered by cryptanalysis before their capture and were made completely and currently readable."[470] Lt. Loeffler (of Feste 10) stated that "a general army 4-figure cipher was last observed in use in North Persia in the winter 1941-42. It had 50 pages, each designated by two alternative bigrams and 100 lines to each page."[471] There is no other indication in the interrogations that four-figure codes were no longer, or less frequently employed.[472] In 1944, however, four-figure Signal Codes (of the same form as the 3-figure Signal Codes) made their appearance in the Army, especially with the army groups,[473] and probably superseded in great part, if not wholly, the 4-figure codes just discussed.

Generally speaking, 4-figure codes were changed less frequently than other codes[474]; but even then, the change came too frequently to judge from Gerlich's statement that " a more frequent change of encipherment would have made decipherment impossible."[475] Certainly the 4-figure codes gave German cryptanalysts a certain amount of trouble; actually, a large amount of material was "absolutely necessary, and the majority of unsolved 4-figure codes were abandoned because of an insufficient number of messages."[476]

[470] DF 18, p 55

[471] I 19c p 5

[472] Lt. Loeffler said only that a four-figure code was used by the VI Guards Mech. Corps (1st Ukraine Front) from January 1945 to the end of hostilities. It was captured in January, 1945.

[473] I 19c pp5, 6

[474] I 19c p 8

[475] I 191 p 8

[476] I 191 p 8

Captain Holetzko (speaking mainly about 4-figure air force codes (ground/ground), said that they were "only 60% readable".[477] And Corporal Heudorf (of NAA 8) admitted that later 4-figure traffic on occasion provided some difficulty, but on the other hand recalled an [Engineer] Unit in March and April, 1945, whose 4-figure messages were read currently.[478]

In the interrogations of KONA 1 members, the following 4-figure codes were listed as solved:[479]

4-figure code of VI Guards Mech. Corps (1st Ukranian Front) from January, 1945 to end of hostilities

4 figure code of 152 Independent Tank Brigade (60th Army, 1st Ukranian Front)

4-figure Signal Code of VI Guards Tank Corps (1st Ukranian Front)

4-figure code of Tank Supply and Administration Authorities of 1st Ukranian Front

4-figure code of 76th Regional Air Base (Russian 76 RAB)

4-figure code of Supply Units of 13th Army (1st Ukranian Front)

4-figure code of 3rd Guards Tank Army.

1st. Lt. Schubert, of GdNA, said simply, "We broke Army three-and four-figure re-enciphered books. These were enciphered on a conversion table. Early in the war we read most of this traffic, but at the end only 40 to 50%.[480]

[477] I 75 p 10

[478] I 75 p 8

[479] I 19c pp 6-8

[480] I 15 p 1

53. 5-figure codes.-- 5-figure codes were used by the Army, Air Force, and NKVD. In the Army, they were used by the NKO (Defense Council), Army Groups, Armies, Corps, Divisions and Brigades. In the Air Force, they were used by Air Armies, Air Corps, Air Divisions, Regional Air Bases, Anti-Aircraft Defense, Anti-Aircraft Corps, and Anti-Aircraft Divisions. They contained strategic, tactical, personnel and supply matters, and political reports and directives.

With the exception of a short period in 1943, when KONA 1 did independent 5-figure cryptanalysis, solution of the 5-figure codes was handled exclusively by GdNA.

In discussing the achievements of In 7/VI (predecessor of GdNA),Lt. Col. Mettig said very glibly, "The breaking of the Russian 5-figure recyphered code... was the most outstanding cryptanalytic achievement of In 7/VI. The Russian 5-figure was broken chiefly by Dettmann."[481] And elsewhere, when rating the relative importance of cryptanalytic achievements contributing to total intelligence, he was "most impressed by the continuous breaking of the Russian 5-figure code despite the difficulties that were experienced after the Spring of 1943."[482] As the interrogator pointed out in reference to this last statement of Mettig, "Even in this case, however, there exists the danger that PW is laying more stress on organizational measures carried out to facilitate the breaking of the code than on actual cryptographic achievement."[483] It might be mentioned in passing that Dr. Otto Buggisch (of OKH/Chi and OKW/Chi) evaluated Mettig as follows: "Only a few fundamental ideas about cryptanalysis."[484]

[481] I 111, p 2

[482] I 128 p 2

[483] I 128 p 2

[484] I 176 p 6

Certainly the evidence from other Prisoner of War interrogations pointed conclusively and without a doubt to an almost complete failure on the part of German cryptanalysts to make any real progress with the solution of the 5-figure code. In the interrogations of members of KONA 1, Corporal Althans (of the NAAS) clearly stated that successful cryptanalysis of the 5-figure code was possible only if

1) there were a number of messages, at least three, which had had the same additive applied; or
2) the 5-figure code had been captured.[485]

Dettmann and Samsonov[486] talked at great length about the 5-figure codes used by the Russians. According to them, codes "011-A," "023-A," "045-A", "062-A", and "091-A", used successively from the beginning of the Russo-German war to the capitulation, did prove difficult for pure cryptanalytic solution; but they continued, "It is interesting to point out that during the course of the war all the newly appearing versions of the "cipher-code" were captured through fortunate circumstances, and always so soon that the originals were almost always in the hands of the cryptanalyst at the instant of their being put into use by the Russians."[487] Of course, this "continuous capture" was an aid in solution, under such circumstances because of the one-time pad encipherment. (See below for discussion of the encipherment itself) As they said, the "individual" tables "offer almost complete security against breaking."[488]

[485] I 19b, report 25 p 43

[486] DF 18 p 59

[487] DF 18 p 59

[488] DF 18 p 61

In the reports of personnel from NAA 11, Capt. Schmidt stated that "with regard to Russian traffic, the Abteilung /Battalion/ did everything up to and including 4-figure. 5-figure they considered insoluble and forwarded to GdNA."[489]

Corporal Karrenberg, (of GdNA) discussing 5-letter and 5-figure codes used for operational orders, said, "These were the so-called Blocknot codes, which were only used once and were therefore unbreakable."[490] Elsewhere, in his description of the "Russian Cryptanalysis course given at GdNA he stated flatly:

> "5-figure and 5-letter messages were not touched at all. In general very little work was done on decipherment of 5-group messages, although these contained the most important operational reports. They were only used to identify units and were only read if code books happened to have been captured.[491]

In 1943, KONA 1 for a period did 5-figure cryptanalysis independently of GdNA.[492] But the general practice was for all units to send 5-figure traffic directly to GdNA for possible decipherment.[493] And as Karrenberg pointed out, "even at the HQ of GdNA little attention was given to the 5-figure messages and very little enthusiasm displayed in working on it. Only the preambles were used to identify units, from Blocknots and indicator groups.[494]

[489] I 55, pp 9 and 11

[490] I 173 p 6

[491] I 166 p 78; see also I 75 p 10

[492] I 19b report 25 p 43

[493] see I 19b report 5 pp 9, 10

[494] I 166 p 79

Finally, Lt. Schubert, when questioned on possible success on five-figure codes, replied: "In the Finnish campaign the book was captured and the Russians used the one-time pads over again. Because of this we had considerable success. Recently the Russians used the pads correctly, and only very few messages were read, these through re-encodements."[495] This small measure of success was obviously due to the fulfilment of the two conditions set forth by Corporal Althans for successful cryptanalysis.[496]

Actually, the Finns had captured and turned over to the Germans a Russian 5-figure book which was used continually until the Russian-Finnish war. An additional copy had been captured by the Germans. And though the Russians introduced a new 5-figure code on 1 April, 1942, the change-over was faulty and it was possible to establish 2,000 groups of the new code within a week.[497] But it is clear that after this time, there was practically no success in 5-figure code solution, though the Germans were able to establish the nature of the book and the type of encipherment:

> The 5-figure code books contained about 25,000 out of the possible 100,000 groups, the pages being numbered 000999 with a hundred lines on each page. The Germans never broke a book and any examples they had were captures.[498]

Alphabetic at first, the 5-figure codebooks later became partially alphabetic; they contained letters, words, phrases, 2-figure numbers, types of units, specific units of the Red army, full stops and commas on every page, all designations of types of tanks, ammunition, etc.

[495] I 15 p 1

[496] see above, p 28; I 19b report 25 p 43

[497] I 78 p 8

[498] I 19c p 8

The encipherment was effected by applying additives taken from enciphering pads known as BLOCKNOTS (a variable number of sheets on which 50-100 5-figure groups appeared). Each pad had a 5-figure number, and each sheet had a 2-figure number running consecutively. There were five different types of Blocknots:

1) I - (individual): 50 pages, additive read off in one direction only
2) Z - (circular) - 30 pages, additive read off in
3) OS (?) either direction
4) Notblock (emergency)
5) Blocknot used for passing on traffic [499]

The distribution of Blocknots was carried out centrally from Moscow to Army Groups to Armies. The Army was responsible for their distribution throughout the lower levels. Occasionally the same Blocknot was distributed to two units on different parts of the front; and here the second condition for successful cryptanalytic success established by Corporal Althans was fulfilled: depth was established. "It seems that depths of up to 8 were established at the beginning of the Russian Campaign but that no 5-figure was broken after May 1943."[500]

54. Address Codes.-- Address Codes (2-figure, 3-figure, and 4-figure) were used by the Army for Army Groups, Armies, and Independent Corps. They were used more widely by the Air Force and the Anti-Aircraft Defense.

Solution of address codes was considered somewhat "special," to judge from the statements in KONA 1 interrogations describing cryptanalytic operations of the various units:

In the FAK: 15 to 20 people were adequate for company cryptanalysis. Special procedures such as Signal Codes (3-figure and 4-figure) and word codes and address codes (3-figure), were studied by chosen cryptanalysts, sometimes by the chief cryptanalyst.[501]

[499] I 190 p 9

[500] I 19c p 10

[501] I 19b report 6 p 11

106

In the NAAS: Section 4 /new developments/ did the real cryptanalysis: it normally concentrated on difficult systems which the companies had neither time nor manpower to deal with adequately. It consisted mainly of mathematicians and worked on, inter alia, addresses (2-F, 3-F, 4-F)[502]

Although mention was made in the KONA 1 interrogations of 2-figure address material, nothing was recorded in the interrogations on this subject except one statement in the final interrogation of NAA 11 personnel:

"Bigrams and Trigrams in Addresses

Blome knew of the two used separately, but could not recall any case of the two in conjunction. He suggested that this might accompany something he had seen, namely 3 Z code mixed into 2Z traffic."[503]

There was no record of extent or success of solution with regard to 2-figure address codes. Likewise there was no description of 4-figure address codes nor any statement regarding the extent or success of solution.

Schubert of GdNA stated that towards the close of hostilities, the Russians were using a 3-figure code for addresses. "In this code the clear position remained unchanged for periods, but the ciphers were changed daily. These ciphers were in some way related to the call signs."[504] The only description of 3-figure address codes was given in the KONA 1 reports.[505]

[502] I 196 p 11

[503] I 106 p 2

[504] I 60 p 2

[505] I 19c--"Annexe on Russian Codes and Ciphers"

Three-figure address codes were used in connection with 5-figure messages;[506] their construction was similar to that of the PT-39 or PT-42 codes,[507] but they contained only figures, unit designations, authorities, and words such as "for" or "from." A code of this type was first used at the beginning of 1944[508] on the 1st and 2nd Ukrainian and the 1st White Russian fronts for communications between Army Groups and their respective Armies, and Independent Corps. In the summer of 1944, Armies began to use similar codes with their subordinate units; and latterly the use of such codes increased still further. According to the members of KONA 1, the solution of these codes given a fair amount of material, was generally easy.[509] But members of NAA 11 stated the following:

> "Addresses to personal names rather than titles were common in all Russian traffic, and this suggested the use of initials. The vagueness of this answer surprised interrogator who asked if the addresses, being enciphered on the PT table, were not read currently. The answer was that unless the same address was used frequently and some outside hint was given they were usually unable to read the address. They supposed it used values which had special local meanings added to the table."[510]

[506] I 173 p 8

[507] "PT 42 was superseded by PT 43.. . It contained no letters and was used for addresses, particularly by the Air Force and PWO (AA Defense.") I 19c p 2

[508] Dettmann and Samsonov gave1943 in DF 18 p 5

[509] I 19c p 4

[510] I 106 p 2

/ 108

55. Miscellaneous.-- Most of the statements given here are taken from the interrogations of members of KONA 1. It is not the complete story, as the Prisoners of War themselves were aware:

> "In the above paper examples are given only of those ciphers whose basic construction was established. There were many types of cipher which were only partially broken and whose basic form could not be established, these are not mentioned... . The number of Russian ciphers of all sorts that were broken was about 3,000."[511]

a) Four-letter codes. Two forms of four-letter code first appeared in practice traffic between Army Groups and Armies and Independent Corps of the 1st Ukraine Front in November, 1944:

1) Revolving stencil: sheet of paper ruled off into 8 x 8 squares; a sheet with 16 holes superimposed and revolved at 90° turns around the central point; all 64 squares were filled; the text was enciphered horizontally in 1, 2, 3, 4 positions; the cipher text was read off horizontally.

2) Transposition: a keyword gave the key; the text was written in vertically according to the key, and upwards or downwards according to instructions; the cipher text was read off horizontally.

The contents were usually about tactical signal matters, through "recently [1944] units and positions were named."[512]

On the subject of transposition systems, Gerlich (of GdNA, Group IV, Section 3) said only this:

> "These were comparatively rarely used by the Russians... I do not know whether such transposition systems were solved at Sigint. Stn. 1, however, I know that transposition messages were being read that "stencils", etc. were used; however, I think they were solved at General of Sig. Int's."[513]

[511] I 19c p 11

[512] I 19c p 10

[513] I 191 p 10

109

b) Word-Code. From the middle of 1944 a word code was used in the area of the 2nd Ukranian Front. The book consisted of 2 halves each designated by a word such as SEVER ZAPAD /literally, North West/; clear groups were in 2 columns; each half of the code contained a number of columns with cover words. The words identified were only used by the Army and contained strategic and tactical reports and the names of units. They were small in size and contained only essential groups.[514] Schubert added that they were called TARNTAFELN.[515] There was no statement regarding extent of solution.

c) Periodic and Columnar Substitutions. Corporal Karrenberg stated, in discussing the "Russian Cryptanalysis Course," "/These/ rarely appear in Russian cipher systems... . Periodic and columnar substitutions concluded the sections on substitution systems in the course. Not so much time was spent on them as they are rarely encountered in practice."[516]

d) Coordinate systems. "These were very varied. Armies made up their own systems and arbitrary reference points and grids were used."[517]

e) Machine ciphers. The handling of teleprinter traffic has been mentioned earlier in this chapter in description of GdNA duties. It was processed exclusively at GdNA. Lt. Schubert stated that teleprinter traffic was worked on in the machine section /Group VI/; he thought that messages in depth had been read, but was uncertain whether the machine had been recovered. He himself never worked on machines, but knew that the Russians had a machine in use already at the beginning of the war, but not on military traffic.[518]

[514] I 19c pp 10, 11

[515] I 15 p 9

[516] I 166 pp 54, 62

[517] I 19c p 11 See also DF 18 pp 72-75 for details

[518] I 15 pp 8-9

Corporal Karrenberg(of GdNA) spoke of "Bandwurm," and defined it as Russian Baudot letter "strip," not to be confused with Russian 5-letter traffic also carried on Baudot lines. The Germans did not capture any of the apparatus used, but felt that it consisted of 2 parts: 1) a Baudot teleprinter and 2) a cipher attachment consisting of 5 small wheels driven by one large wheel.[519] Depths were frequent, but the Germans did not seem to have any attempt to reconstruct the wheel patterns. The system used by the Army and Air Force and to a lesser extent by NKVD.[520]

Dr. Otto Buggisch (of OKH/Chi) went into somewhat more historical detail and stated that:

1) In 1943 (He heard), Goering's Research Bureau Forschungsamt, abbreviated FA) had claimed some success on a Russian teletype machine and had recreated the action.[521]

2) Late in 1943 and early in 1944, OKH itself began to intercept non-morse, 5-impulse traffic (called "Hughes" by Buggisch). The Mathematics section of In 7/VI (see Vol. V, Chapter II, on organization) worked on it; at the end of 1943, there was a "Kompromiss," and a depth of 8 messages with the same setting was created. The section was able to recover 1400 letters of pure key, and to determine that the traffic was derived from a 5-figure code. The Germans postulated a machine like the German T 43, but was not able to prove any theories they had.

3) Hollerith machinery was devised to locate depths, but in actuality only three or four more depths were found and were of no long-termed value.

4) The traffic (Buggisch thought, since he left the section in June) slumped off in 1944, and LNA took steps to improve reception.[522]

[519] I 30 p 2

[520] I 30 p 2

[521] I 176 p 6; I 64 p 2

[522] I 64 p 2

111

"Buggisch stressed one fact which had surprised him, that they had never had information about either of these machines (he assumed that the one the FA broke was not the same because of the difference of cycles) from PW or agent sources."[523]

The number of links, according to Corporal Karrenberg, varied according to the number of armies, with a maximum of 8. One end of link was Moscow, the other mobile. After 1944, no work was done on the traffic except on the spot. No vital clues to the system were given away by the Russians, though their security precautions were not considered good.[524]

56. NKVD and Agents' Codes. NKVD Codes were simple mono-alphabetic substitution, 2-figure, 3-figure, 4-figure, 5-figure, and 5-letter types. They were used without any apparent reason on two large networks: 1) the networks of the NKVD Central Authorities (the networks were subdivided into those of Security Troops, Frontier Troops, and Railway and Convoy Troops); 2) the networks of NKVD Formation (communication between units attached to Army Front Staffs). 4-figure and 5-figure codes were used on the front lines: there was a 4-figure code, for example, used by the military police, and a general 4-figure code used on Staff-Regiment-Battalion links.

Solution of NKVD codes was handled by the NAAS and GdNA. "The traffic of the NKVD formed a special group of Russian wireless traffic. The distinction applied equally to the manner of conducting traffic and to the message themselves."[525] The German Army cryptanalysts reflected this Russian "distinction" in their own attacks on NKVD systems, allocating the work--again as in regular army and air force traffics--to levels of operation determined by difficulty of solution. Lt. Ed. Woellner (of KONA 1) stated that "NKVD traffic was always covered, but only by Long Range Sigint [the FAK]. Evaluation and cryptanalysis were done by NAAS."[526] On this same subject, Lt. Loeffler (of Feste 10) stated that "all NKVD signals originating in the regiment's area were worked on in the NAAS, others were sent on to LNA."[527] But in neither case was there specified what type of NKVD traffic was worked on, and what type was passed to higher echelons. Apparently, the distinction corresponded to that observed in the case of actual army traffic. All lower-level

[523] I 64 pp 2,3

[524] I 153 p 7

[525] I 19b, report 28, p 47

[526] I 19b, report 27 p 46

[527] I 19b, report 6, pp 9, 10

112

operational codes (up through 4-figure, e.g) could be handled by NAAS. The five-figure codes were not dealt with by the KONA, but handled by 40 to 50 men in LNA at Zossen[528] where Lt. Loeffler "thought that a good deal of success was obtained in the case of the Far Eastern traffic." Dettmann and Samsonov substantiated this point, in their discussion of the German army cryptanalytic effort:[529]

> "All the five-place message material from the Army or the Airforce, as well as the NKVD messages, was submitted for the exclusive processing of the General of Communications Intelligence" [GdNA]

They also gave full descriptions of NKVD systems.[530] (There was no discrepancy between the facts in their report and the facts given by Lt. Loeffler.) The details of description were scattered throughout the report according to types of encipherment. They mentioned the following:

a) Mono-alphabetic substitution systems common to all NKVD organizations
b) Conversion systems [substitution and additive]
- 1936: 4-figure code: 2500 values; used in district
- by 1939: three 4-figure conversion systems; codebooks of up to 5,000 values; enciphered by digraphic substitution or conversion tables
- 1939: first general NKVD 4-figure code; 10,000 book positions enciphered first by single digit substitution, later by additive

[528] I 19c p 12

[529] DF 18 p 83

[530] DF 18 pp 62-71

DOCID: 3486746

At time of capitulation: three 4-figure systems: (ZERNO, NEVA, VIZA, see infra) used respectively by
1) NKVD troops
2) NKVD border defense troops
3) NKVD security troops 531
(200 messages were read daily in all three)
last of larger systems: 5-figure railway code: 2500 groups; digraphic substitution encipherment few 3-figure smaller codes (read currently) letter transposition codes: never found in NKVD traffic number series:
1940:4-figure; single letter conversion encipherment (1941 - 1942): 4-figure; enciphered by text key (letters equalling numbers)
1942:4-figure enciphered by military technical manual (used by Interior troops) until end of 1944: general encipherment combining single digit conversion and Gama Tables (no description of these is given)

Private Huchting (of Feste 10)532, speaking primarily from a traffic analysis point of view, gave the breakdown of NKVD nets:

1) Networks of the Central Authority, subdivided into
   a) Central Authority of the Security Troops
   b) Central Authority of the Frontier Troops
   c) Central Authority of the Security Troops (Divisions and Brigades of the Back Areas)
   d) Central Authority of the Railway Troops
2) Networks of Formation, consisting of communications between commanders of the security troops at front Staffs and their regiments and between the latter and their battalions.533

531 cf. Schubert's report, I 26

532 I 19b report 28, p 47

533 I 19b p 48

114

A close watch was kept on the networks of 1a, because they carried communications between the central NKVD authority in Moscow and the commanders of Security troops working with the Army groups, the directing staffs North and South, and the "less interesting independent Company Headquarters Signals regiments." The messages were not readable.[534] Messages passed on formation networks, however, were "for the most part readable."[535] In addition to the monitoring of Central Authority NKVD--Front HQ. NKVD and Front Staffs (Frontier Regiments) traffic, close watch was kept on traffic from regiments to battalions, because "most of the messages could be read. They mentioned army units by name, etc."[536] ("Traffic of rear NKVD troops and of the Signals regiments were of no interest, and were not covered by KONA 1."[537]

Lt. Schubert (of GdNA) stated, "After my studies [winter of 1941], I was posted to a cryptanalytic course at OKH. Since I have functioned as a cryptanalyst. I worked on Russian Army till March, 1943. Then KONA 6 was given the commitment of covering Russian partisans, and I worked on that till September of that year. After that KONA 6 was dissolved... . and I went to GdNA... .and took over all Eastern Cryptanalysis [3 branches: Army, NKVD, and Partisans]."[538] Lt. Schubert was familiar with the same codes mentioned in Private Huchting's net breakdown (1a, 1b, 1d): Security Troops', Frontier Troops', and Railway and Convoy Troops' codes, but mentioned also "one or two ciphers of NKGB... .the 4th section of NKVD,"[539] concerned with measures against enemy agents and their own active espionage.

[534] I 19b, report 28 p 47

[535] I 19b p 48

[536] 19b, report 27 p 46

[537] I 19b p 46

[538] I 26 p 1

[539] I 26 p 3

Lt. Schubert spoke of two 5-figure codes: the SMERSCH /operations of Russian agents/ organization code (with an individual subtractor); and the Railways Troops Code (actually a 4-figure code, enciphered by substitution tables, the 5th digit representing the quadrant on the page in which the group appeared).[540] But he was much more familiar with 4-figure NKVD Codes, which were apparently much more exploitable than the 5-figure codes.

The Security Troops Codes were of two types. One was used forward of regiment, when a regiment was used in approximately an Army Group Sector ("it is a cipher, therefore, used forward of Army Group")[541] This particular code ran for a comparatively long period; "the last one which was still valid in the middle of February when I left OKH, had already been running 1 1/2 years." This code was alphabetical and contained 100 pages, 25 or 50 groups per page; it was enciphered by means of an enciphered indicator which provided for page and position substitution, the result of which was again enciphered by a substitution table. These substitution tables were also valid for a longer time and varied with the network.[542] The additives on the page did not change, only the substitution table.

The second type, a code used rearwards of regiment, was enciphered by a figure subtractor originally taken from tables (up to Sept. 1944). The same tables could appear on different networks, and since the subtractor was used very frequently, "it was not uncommon for 20 messages to have the same subtractor."[543] In October, 1945, 2 subtractors were used, taken from different tables; and the indicators for the 2nd subtractor were enciphered with the first one.[544] In spite of the potential difficulties involved in this method of encipherment, the system was solved by February 15, 1945, though mainly because of bad Russian usage of the system.

[540] I 26 p 4 ; see also DF 18 p 67

[541] I 26 p 3

[542] I 26 p 3

[543] I 26 p 3

[544] I 26 p 4

The Frontier Troops Code was exactly like the Security Troops Code rearwards of regiment, with a different basic book, at least in traffic out of Leningrad.[545] (Lt. Schubert made a statement on the Railways and Convoy Troops Code quoted above).

The four-figure NKVD codes exploited by KONA 1 were used by front line units (regiments and battalions) mainly employed as Military Police. "From 1933-42, R4ZC4 /Russian, 4-figure, Code 4/ was in use. It consisted of a 100 page alphabetic book each with a hundred lines. Recipher was carried out by means of 31 bigram tables. It was broken by the Germans in 1940."[546] "Only one code book (known to the Germans R4ZC 1800 and to the Russians as KODOWAA TABLICA "ZERNO") was used by the NKVD from October 1943 until the end of 1944. It was used from Battalion upwards to Front HQ's."[547]

The R4Z1800 code (which was captured in the summer of 1944)[548] was described by four different people: Corporal Thomas of NAAS 1 (as report no. 29, I 19b); Karl Exter, of NAA 11 (I 55); Lt. Loeffler of Feste 10 (as Annex I to I 19c) and the personnel of NAA 11.[549] It would seem to be the most important, if not the only 4-figure code solved and readable. "RZ 1800 was the general code of NKVD introduced in February, 1944, as successor to RZ 1100. The White Sea Code[550], broken by NAA 11, was an older /1942/ code used from 1943 to the fall of 1944. Then the White Sea Command adopted the RZ 1800

[545] I 26 p 4

[546] I 19c p 13

[547] I 19c p 12

[548] I 106 p 5

[549] I 166 p 5

[550] The White Sea Code was tackled by NAA 11 from April to July 1944, and about 60% of the traffic was solved, almost entirely on higher links. There was a different "key" for each KONA, and by them to their subordinate units, in all 6. Solution was only relative, never basic. I 166 p 6

itself... .It was used on the highest levels, Staff to Regiment and Regiment to Battalion. No addition was ever used with it. The code was still used in September 1944 and possibly in April 1945."[551] Although there were slight discrepancies in the accounts, it can be established that this particular code was alphabetic, and had 50 pages, each consisting of 50 lines-- a total of 2500 groups. The encipherment was carried out by 1) a "chiffrant" and 2) digraphic substitution tables. The "chiffrant" consisted of figures 0-9, in random order printed at the top of the page, (a different order for each page): one figure in this "chiffrant," determined by the 3rd figure of the indicator group, was added to the numbers of the lines on the page before they were enciphered by the digraphic tables.

Ten sets of 2 digraphic tables (each 10 x 10), the sets numbered 0-9, were used to encipher the 2 halves of the 4-figure group; the set number for enciphering the line was the 2nd digit of the indicator group; the set number for the page, the fourth. A series of substitution tables was current for a period of from 2 to 6 months.[552] The first digit of the indicator group was a dummy, and the indicator group itself was inserted in clear in one of the first ten groups of the message.[553]

[551] I 106 p 5

[552] I 19c p 12

[553] I 19c p 13

Though the emphasis was put by the Prisoners of War on 4-figure NKVD codes, it should be pointed out that a great variety of encipherments were worked on, though not all read. Karrenberg (of GdNA) gave the following breakdown of nets and types of codes used:

Administration networks: usually sent 5-figure messages and, less often, 4-figure and 5-letter messages.
Frontier networks: used 4-and 5-figure codes: on regimental networks, also 2-figure systems.
Black Sea Fleet: used 3-figure and 5-figure codes networks from divisional level downward: used 2-figure and 3-figure, plain language and figure messages with plain language.[554]

Corporal Exter (of NAA 11) stated[555] that he worked on 2-figure NKVD ("used up to end of hostilities"); and on 4-figure codes of the NKVD type described by him as RZ4C1800 and codebooks enciphered with an additive. "In this latter type, they had had considerable success with traffic of an NKVD net on the White Sea Front, controlled from the NKVD HQ at Archangel, but that was with a captured basic book and instructions for the system... .They could not cope with 5-figure; that was sent on to Berlin."[556]

In general, certain elements seemed to be constant in all NKVD codes: contrary to regular Army usage, NKVD messages were enciphered on the same system for many months[557] ; NKVD codes were always arranged alphabetically[558]; and all NKVD messages, whether 5-letter or 4-figure or 5-figure, had the date in the penultimate group.[559]

[554] I 173 pp 13-14

[555] I 55 p 11

[556] I 55 p 11

[557] I 167 p 5; I 26 p 4

[558] I 167 p 6

[559] I 173 p 35; I 19c p 13

119

b) Agents' Codes. Agents' Codes included codes used by agents, guerillas, and "Kundschafter."[560] All types of systems were used, from substitutions, double transpositions, grilles, and subtractors to one-time pads (tape). Solution was always done centrally in Berlin.

"The solution of agent, guerilla, and "Kundschafter" traffic was the responsibility of Referat 3c [of Group IV, GdNA]... .Solution depended mainly on captured material to accomplish solution. Some agent traffic was one-time tape and therefore unbreakable. By and large the Gruppe did not place much value on agent traffic and neglected it."[561]

It should be pointed out that Russian agent systems were not handled exclusively by OKH/GdNA/IV/3c, who really were processing the traffic from the viewpoint of military operations (countermeasures against the partisans, for example). The agent systems were also handled by:

1) The Radio Defense Corps, (Oberkommando der Wehrmacht, Wehrmacht Nachrichtenverbindungen, abbreviated (Amtsgruppe OKW/AgWNV/FU III) who were responsible for locating, eliminating, or neutralizing all enemy agents' radio activities.[562] Preliminary reading, especially when the code was captured, or the system recognized, was done by WNV/FU/III.[563] For more difficult cryptanalysis, traffic was turned over to OKW/Chi, and worked on in the Referat VAUCK.[564] "Dr Vauck and his section used to be with OKW/Chi but were transferred to WNV/FU/III. They continued to be controlled by OKW/Chi and passed their results to them. Vauck was then posted to OKH."[565]

[560] Defined by Dettmann and Samsonov as an agent dropped for a single specific mission, e.g., blowing up a bridge; a Kundschafter was more "localized" whereas the agent was mobile. I 116 p 7

[561] I 116 p 7

[562] IF 176, foreword

[563] IF 176 p 13

[564] See also I 115 p 2

[565] I 21, p 4; cf. also I 115 p 7, par 37-40 and D 60 p 16

120

2) Some agents' traffic was picked up independently of OKW/WNV/FU (III) by the regular police (Ordnungs-polizei, abbreviated ORPO) who sent their traffic to Kurt Sauerbier of Goering's Research Bureau (Forschungsamt, abbreviated FA), Hauptabteilung IV, Referat 9c;[566] this was an entirely independent, personal relationship between the ORPO and Sauerbier.[567] Sauerbier's superior in the FA, Specialist Wenzer, an expert in Agents' Systems, was sent from the FA by WNV/FU/III to assist Lt. Schubert of OKH/GdNA, in January, 1944[568] on Polish Resistance Movement Traffic.

There was, consequently, a certain duplication of effort and a certain amount of confusion as a result of this arrangement.[569] There were also conflicting opinions on the successes achieved. Schubert reported that "Russian agents' systems were tried by Vauck, who said they could not be solved. Later, he said that they were digit substitutions and P/L enciphered with a one-time running key derived from a book."[570] But, in another report, he stated that he could not remember enough about agents' codes to give details which were in many cases not known. In the middle of 1944, for example, the Russians had, he thought, about 3000 agents spread over all areas, and it was impossible to pick out one system and say that it was used in one area. Moreover, he pointed out that he himself had worked only on Partisan and Kundschafter traffic and knew of other systems only indirectly. Nevertheless, in his first interrogation, he stated that Agent's codes were of two types:

1. Double transpositions and grilles
2. Subtractors.

[566] See the whole report of the homework of Sauerbier, I 164

[567] IF 162

[568] I 26 p 7

[569] D 60, pp 19-20

[570] I 21 p 4

"Double transposition was only used by partisans and not by spies." The system was completely unbreakable.[571] He went into more detail about substitution systems.[572] They consist of three elements:

1. The basic cipher (code), i.e., the substitution of the plain text by a substitution system
2. The encipherment by figure subtractor
3. The encipherment of the indicators

<u>The basic cipher</u>: on certain links, a 3- or 4-figure code was used; in general, however, simple substitution systems were employed.[573]

<u>The subtractor</u>: these were of three different kinds:

a. They were printed on teleprinter rolls (the most frequently used and called "Blocknot rulon" by the Russians); the rolls had 5-figure numbers which were given in clear as indicators in Partisan traffic, not in Spy-traffic
b. They were taken from tables. There were 4 basic systems: a simple enciphering with a table of 100-300 groups, used especially in NKGB Leningrad traffic (solved); 100 enciphering pages, used especially in NKGB Leningrad traffic (solved); a double encipherment (table of 30 lines, each line, 10 groups) (solved); a special very complicated mixing procedure (not solved)
c. They were built up from an indicator: simple addition in columns, simple cross addition, addition in column with a key phrase, cross addition with a key phrase, substituted cross addition, subtractor boxes.

571 I 26 pp 3, 5

572 In the appendix to I 26, written as a single report on code-systems of the Russian Partisans and Spies (from which report the material given below is taken

573 For details, see I 26 p 8

122

The indicator: indicators based on a roll, were always inserted in plain. Apart from a very few exceptions, there were always two indicators. The encipherment could be broken under the following conditions:

a. when both indicators were enciphered in the same systems
b. when there were messages on the same key
c. when indicators consisted of 5 different figures
d. when indicator was known by virtue of the circumstances.[574]

Lt. Schubert also mentioned[575] a third type of encipherment, by occasional simple substitution systems; but he gave no details on the types of substitutions or methods of solution. In conclusion, the interrogator said:

> The above gives the most important cipher used by Russian Partisans and spies, as far as they are known from breaks, captured documents and POW statements. Systems used in the Balkans are not included by they are of a similar type. After the middle of 1944, W/T traffic of the partisans and spies dropped heavily, as they were constantly being overtaken by the advance of the Red Army."[576]

[574] I 26 p 13 Note: on p 5 of the original interrogation, Schubert said of subtractor systems:

> "One could talk a whole day describing these methods. There was in existence a report of over 50 typed pages.... There was rarely enough depth to break these tables."

[575] I 26 appendix

[576] I 26 p 14

VOLUME 4

Chapter VI

Section C. Liaison with other Agencies on Russian Cryptanalysis

57. Liaison with the Signal Intelligence Agency of the Supreme Command of the Armed Forces.-- The liaison between the Signal Intelligence Agency of the Army High Command (OKH/GdNA) and OKW/Chi was close because of the joint derivation of both offices from the Codes and Ciphers Section of the Defense Ministry, and because of the joint and simultaneous control of OKW and OKH signal activities in the person of the Chef HNW and Chef WNV (Chef des Heeresnachrichtenverbindungswesens and Chef des Wehrmachtnachrichtenverbindungsabteilung). A certain amount of jealousy existed on the top levels of signal intelligence operations, and "liaison between specialists was discouraged."[581] Nevertheless, there were specific cases of specialist inter-service cooperation on Russian cryptanalysis.

[581] I 30 p 10

The Russian Referat of In 7/VI, under Lt. Dettmann (and, for a time, under Professor Novopaschenny) which was detached to the Chief, Army Signals Communication Agency (Chef des Heeresnachrichtenverbindungwesen, abbreviated Chef HNW/(HLS)), in Loetzen, had had considerable initial success on a Russian 5-figure code until the spring of 1942. In 1942 [probably April 1, when the Russians introduced a new 5-figure code] OKW/Chi sent a special Russian "party" to HLS/Ost to collaborate with the OKH cryptanalysts there in the solution of a Russian 5-figure code. Professor Novopaschenny, head of that OKW/Chi party, returned to Berlin in 1943; but the cryptanalysts who had gone with him were absorbed into HLS/Ost and remained there. During 1942-43, Lt. Dettmann (of HLS/Ost) was also passing considerable Russian 5-letter traffic to OKW/Chi in Berlin for solution.[582]

In February 1943, the language department of the Radio Defense Corps (Oberkommando der Wehrmacht, Wehrmachtnachrichtenverbindung, Funkueberwachung, abbreviated OKW/WNV/FU) headed by Fenner, began collaboration on Agents' Codes with OKH/In 7/VI. By the end of March, In 7/VI had given to Fenner's section all agents' traffic intercepted since 1941. Solution was begun, and the results achieved by Fenner were passed on to In 7/VI. Somewhat later, liaison on this particular problem disintegrated, however, since In 7/VI was uncooperative about turning traffic over to Fenner.

There were no other specific examples in TICOM sources of cooperation by OKW/Chi with OKH/GdNA on Russian cryptanalysis. It is known only that OKW/Chi regularly used the IBM machinery of OKH in their cryptanalytic work.[583]

[582] I 116 p 2

[583] I 96 p 13; I 67 p 2

58. Liaison with the Signal Intelligence Agency of the Air Force High Command.-- Relations between the Signal Intelligence Service of the Air Force High Command (Oberkommando der Luftwaffe Generalnachrichtenfuehrer Abteilung III, abbreviated OKL/Gen Nafu/III) and OKH/GdNA were on the whole good. On a very high level, reports and information were exchanged, and periodic meetings were held to discuss techniques and experience.[584] On an operational level, the 3rd Battalion of Air Signals Regiment 353 (Luftnachrichten Regiment 353, abbreviated LN Regt 353) (on the southern sector of the Russian front) collaborated with KONAs 1 and 8 of the Army Liaison officers were exchanged and evaluation closely coordinated.[585] The German Air Force Signal Intelligence Service often helped fill in the gaps through their work on air armies when the Soviet land army observed radio silence.[586] It should be pointed out in review that the Signal Intelligence Regiments (KONAs) on the Eastern front intercepted and solved a great deal of Russian Air Force Traffic as well as Army and NKVD traffic; and Prisoners of War discussed the cryptanalytic work on Air Force systems not as a special task but as part of their general "army" assignment. Cooperation on cryptanalytic problems was good after 1943; and it can be assumed that the liaison on traffic analysis and evaluation was close and constant.

59. Liaison with the Signal Intelligence Agency of the Navy High Command.-- In its relations with other agencies, the Signal Intelligence Agency of the Navy High Command (Oberkommando der Marine, Seekriegsleitung IV, III, abbreviated OKM/SKL IV/III) maintained a traditional aloofness. There was no statement in TICOM sources of specific cooperation with

[584] I 126 p 14

[585] I 130 p 15

[586] IF 186

126

OKH/GdNA on Russian cryptanalysis. Lt. Schubert (of OKH/GdNA), who attempted to establish some sort of liaison with the Navy, stated simply:

"I endeavored to achieve cooperation between the Army and the Navy. This task was actually no concern of mine. A naval officer was detached for six weeks who looked at all Army systems originating in the West and the East and I went to him to attempt some settlement. I tried to achieve collaboration, but later events upset things. There are practically no points of contact between Army and Navy--as regards the Russians."[587]

60. Liaison with Goering's Research Bureau.-- Cryptanalysts of the Signal Intelligence Agency of the Army High Command (OKH/GdNA) were not too well informed on the organization or operations of the cryptanalytic unit of Goering's Research Bureau (Forschungsamt, abbreviated FA). Liaison did exist, however, between the two organizations, and took the form of actual division of tasks, sharing of personnel, and cooperation on IBM developments.[588] Dr. Buggisch stated that (he had heard in 1943) the FA was able to break and read Russian teletype traffic,[589] though he did not know know may details. On another occasion, however, he stated (revealing that there must have been at least a modicum of liaison,[590] "The FA had analysed a Russian cipher teleprinter system in 1943 and recognized that it must have been based on a machine having certain similarities with the German SZ 40. After a short time the Russians altered the system. The FA then communicated its results to my unit and was given as a kind of recompense a report on the solution of a German cipher teleprinter. This was one of the very rare cases where FA and In 7/VI exchanged results."

[587] I 26 p 2

[588] It should be pointed out that Col. Mettig objected to liaison with the FA, however, because of the "SS" taint, and that Dr. Buggisch of GdNA considered liaison with the FA "bad anyway" I 64 p 2

[589] for details see above, Volume 4, Chapter VI, section on machine ciphers

[590] I 176 p 6

The liaison between OKH/GdNA and the FA has already been discussed in this chapter, with reference to the visit of Specialist Wenzel of the FA to OKH/GdNA to help Lt. Schubert on Polish Resistance Movement traffic.

With regard to cooperation on IBM developments, there was no statement about specific Russian cryptanalytic problems in TICOM interrogations. It is known that the Signal Intelligence Agency of the Army High Command took the lead in the development and application of IBM machinery to cryptanalysis, however, and their machinery was made available to other agencies. Tranow (of the Signal Intelligence Agency of the Navy High Command, (OKM/SKL IV/III) stated:

> "About March 1942 we paid a visit, in conjunction with the GAF and the FA, to the OKH Hollerith/IBM/ department in Berlin... ."[591]

Since there was no evidence in TICOM sources of coordinated application of IBM machines to specific Russian cryptanalytic problems, it can only be assumed that such liaison existed.

61. Liaison with the Foreign Office Cryptanalytic Section.-- There was no statement in TICOM interrogations about any liaison between OKH/GdNA and Pers Z S on Russian cryptanalysis.

62. Liaison with the Japanese.-- When asked about liaison with the Japanese on cryptanalytic problems, Dr. Buggisch said he "did not know about OKW--but had never heard of any--and as for OKH he was sure that there had never been any Japs around in the flesh or any liaison he knew of."[592] Actually, it seems, there was a certain amount of alleged liaison with

[591] I 146 p 17

[592] I 64 p 3

128

Japan; for, as Dettmann and Samsonov pointed out, "the Russian Referat had been visited at Loetzen in 1942 by two Japanese officers.[593] The Japanese were given a polite reception but shown very little of anything, and no solution work: their tour lasted only three to four hours. The Japanese said they had solved the Russian OKK 6 and OKK 7, otherwise no Russian 5-figure traffic.[594] For all intents and purposes, there was liaison only on paper, certainly no collaboration on solution techniques or exchange of information.

63. Liaison with the Finns.-- Quite the contrary was true in the case of liaison with Finland. "Liaison on all cryptanalytic matters was excellent."[595] The Germans, to begin with, had a very high opinion of Finnish cryptanalysts:[596] "The Finnish crypt personnel were considered outstanding and the exchange was a great benefit to NAA 11."[597]

The main Finnish unit was RTK, "Radio Telegraf Kompanie." It was of battalion strength, with one motorized company and a fixed unit of about 200 men, located at Sortavala. RTK had about 70 cryptanalytic men, mostly officers, headed by Captain of the Reserve, Erkki Pale. It also had evaluation men.[598] The Finns worked largely on Army traffic and had no separate unit for Air Force Signal Intelligence operations.

[593] I 116 p 9

[594] I 116 p 9

[595] I 106 p 3

[596] I 116 p 10

[597] I 106 p 3

[598] I 116 p 10

Lt. Dettmann visited Finland in 1942 and exchanged technical letters from that time on. But the first German liaison officer with the Finns was Captain Marquardt (later head of Group I, GdNA, not a cryptanalyst); he was succeeded by 1st Lt. Riemerschmidt, who was stationed directly at RTK (the Air Force Liaison officer, 1st Lt. Vaatz, was stationed at Finnish HQ's in Mikkeli), and had a direct radio link to NAA 11. In return, the Finns had a liaison officer at Loetzen from 1942, 1st Lt. Mje-Koja (also not a cryptanalyst), who was succeeded by 1st Lt. Ohn; in addition, small Finnish parties visited NAA 11 from time to time.[599]

Results were exchanged between the Finns and NAA 11 every two or three days, and NAA 11 varied its cryptanalytic priorities to give full attention to any special links required by the Finns; in return, information and solution from LNA to Sortavala were sent to NAA 11: "On one occasion (the captured RZ 1800) this was faster than the direct transmission from LNA to NAA11.[600] The Finns solved 3-figure and 4-figure codes extensively, with emphasis on NKVD material. They had no success with 5-figure traffic and "never captured any copies of those codes as far as Schmidt knew."[601] This is, of course, not true: see the section on 5-figure solution (Volume IV, Chapter VI) for an account of Finnish capture and delivery and German exploitation of the Russian 5-figure code book.[602] The Germans sometimes used Finnish equipment and vice versa, but they "gave the Finns much advice..no physical help."[603] And Capt. Schmidt stated that, "NAA 11 never got straight intelligence from the Finns or vice versa. This was characteristic of the general German-Finnish understanding that Lapland was a German area for operations with South Finland allotted to the Finns."[604]

It should be pointed out, in passing, that there was no statement in TICOM interrogations about any liaison whatsoever with Hungary and Italy, German's other allies.

[599] I 116 p 10; I 106 p 3; I 21 p 2

[600] I 106 p 3

[601] I 106 p 3

[602] I 15 p 1

[603] I 106 p 3

VOLUME 4

Chapter VI. Russian Cryptanalysis

Section D. Successes and Failures

64. Successes and failures.-- In their criticism of the defects of the structure of the German Army Signal Intelligence Agency (OKH/GdNA) from the viewpoint of cryptanalysis, Lt. Dettmann and Sgt. Samsonov made five points:[608]

1) the administration, both of the central office and of the subdivisions, had no, or at most a very small specialized knowledge regarding the fields of work... Their effect was...mostly to hinder and not to forward the work.

2) Because the NAAS worked closely with Army Group commands, the NAAS and its technical direction tended to correspond more closely to the desires of the Army HQ's rather than to their own central office.

3) The division of cryptanalysts between the central office and the NAAS had as a result that in addition to an enormous amount of "paper warfare"....work of cryptanalysis and exploitation was carried on with almost complete duplication.

608 DF 18 part III

131

4) The multiplication of effort derived also from the erroneous ambition of administrators in individual stations, due to "competition."

5) The most serious interference with the actual work, both in the central office and in all its branches, however, was doubtless brought about by the purely military "manipulation" of this set-up, involving treatment according to rank, not skill or competence; military exercises, field maneuvers, and the like.

They were, of course, not concerned with specific details of the cryptanalytic set-up, but rather the overall organizational and administrative difficulties involved. The contents of their report and of the reports of other Prisoners of War on the technical aspects of cryptanalysis, however, belied any long-range serious effects on the actual functioning of the specific cryptanalytic units, either in the central office or in the field. The only major failure of the German Army vis-a-vis the Russian systems was the failure to solve and read currently the 5-figure codes. Maj. Dr. Rudolf Hentze (head of Group IV of GdNA) spoke of the accomplishments of Dettmann and Samsonov in Referat 3b: "[They] had good success, especially on the NIVA code, which did not change for a period of two years and therefore could be read almost entirely up to the end of 1944. This was a 5-figure code enciphered.. A new NIVA cane in at the end of 1944 and about 500 groups of this had been recovered by the end of the war."[609] Although he remarked in passing that Referat I of Group IV also "worked on 4- and 5-figure enciphered codes and had partial success working from depths,"[610] he was speaking there of only one specific code. And in spite of Lt. Col. Mettig's two glib statements on the "continuous breaking" of 5-figure codes;[611]

[609] I 113 p 6

[610] I 113 p 5

[611] I 128 p 2; I 111 p 2

132

and in spite of Dettmann and Samsonov's boast that they always captured the books and could read (although with difficulty), it seems apparent, judging from the total sum of reports from other Prisoners of War, that the 5-figure code was not read currently and that, even if the book had been captured, the encipherment by almost exclusively one-time pads rendered actual solution practically impossible.

On the operational level (i.e., outside of GdNA), it was generally agreed by all Prisoners of War that there was no trouble in reading 2-figure and 3-figure traffic of all sorts, and only a relative difficulty in the case of 4-figure traffic. The solution of the 2-figure and 3-figure codes was simple enough to be carried out on company level; and what was not finished there (either because of lack of time or lack of manpower) was completed on the level of the NAAS which did solution up to and including 4-figure material. A certain amount of difficulty was encountered in address material in agents' codes, but not enough to destroy continuity or to impede the derivation of enough intelligence of a tactical nature for current use.

In the case of NKVD codes, Dettmann and Samsonov claimed that from cryptanalysis they were able to determine the organization, deployment, and general significance of NKVD as a Russian organization; and were able to establish either direct or indirect knowledge of dispositions and changes in dispositions, enemy orders for deployment or attacks, preparations for major operations, supply, ammunition, losses, reinforcements, health and morale of troops, conditions rearwards of lines, the general traffic situation, production capacity of factories, partisan movements, and finally, information on the Polish Resistance Movement.[612]

This is certainly an impressive amount of information to have been derived solely from cryptanalysis, as is the chart made up by Dettmann and Samsonov detailing actual codes read.[613] By comparison to other interrogations, there seems to be a large amount of boasting in their report, giving a clear impression that all the informations was not strictly true as given, at least for cryptanalysis on central office level.

[612] DF 18 pp 16-33

[613] DF 18 p 75

If one can assume a truthful exposition in those cases where their statements agreed with the statement of other Prisoners of War, however, the amount of cryptanalytic achievement on the part of GdNA (and of HLS Ost) and of the small units on lower levels of operation and solution is still impressive. It must be remembered that other elements than pure cryptanalysis entered into the picture and played a large part in the production of total intelligence:

1) The great amount of Traffic Analysis, Direction Finding analysis carried on in the Eastern front area.[614] Statements of Prisoner's of War indicated that, although 5-figure traffic was not read, it produced, nevertheless, a great amount of intelligence from external characteristics, blocknot series numbers (for disposition of units using series numbers), etc.[615]

2) The generally "low, but improving calibre of Russian transmission," coupled with bad Russian security. As Lt. Starke stated in one place, "although 2-figure traffic was never very difficult to read, much assistance was gained from security breaches on the part of Russian operators.[616] There were scattered references throughout the interrogations to conversations of Russian operators which provided much real information on movements of all kinds. Besides, as Dettmann and Samsonov pointed out in the reference exclusively to NKVD, but by extension to ther systems," the fact alone that NKVD ciphers continued to be used often for more than two years at a time must indicate that the Russians did not believe it possible that the enemy was reading the traffic."[617]

[614] See Chapter V, Vol. V for details

[615] e.g., I 19b report 5 p 14

[616] I 75 p 4

[617] DF 18 p 71

134

3) Finally, the apparently large amount of capture of both codebooks and tables. The importance of this type of compromise in solution can not be over estimated.

In spite of these considerations, it is still true that the German Army read a tremendous amount of material purely cryptanalytically which, though only rarely of high level operational importance, produced a steady flow of tactical and strategic intelligence. As an example which may or may not be typical, Corporal (Uffz) Althans (of NAAS 1) drew up the following chart showing the estimated monthly average, for the year 1944, of traffic intercepted and solved:[618]

Survey of Successes in Cryptanalysis

Type of Message	Intercepted	Dealt with	%	Remarks
2-figure	140	125	90	
3-figure	6,000	2,600	43	
4-figure	5,000	1,900	38	
mixed	2,350	865	37	
Total	13,500	5,500	41	= degree of Cryptanalytic Success
Clear text	6,000	6,000	100	
Practice	500	500	100	
Grand total	20,000	12,000		
	Plus			
5-figure and NKVD 5-figure	8,000			(not studied at KONA 1)
NKVD	2,000			only partially studied at KONA 1
Grand total	30,000			

[618] I 19b report 25 p 44

135

Dettmann and Samsonov listed the following as systems worked on and solved:[619]

Army and Air Force:

1) Operation systems (carrying text concerning operations and traffic technique)
   PT-35, PT-39, PT-41: there was a large volume of messages in the PT systems, which were superseded by "small Codes" in 1944
2) Signal Codes: these were used in the second half of the war and were 3 and 4-figure codes, called CYB or "front" codes. They were partially solved, but completely worked out only in the rarest cases
3) Address Codes: these were used by any unit in the "front" commands; interpretations were hard to make, because of the Russian use of covernames, and it was difficult to solve the encipherments
4) "Conversion" systems: these included codes, code tables and extended substitutions. Among those specifically mentioned were:
   The Air Force General Code (1934-37), carrying information on landings, takeoffs, weather, etc.
   The BAK-38, the last general Air Force system used to the end of 1939
   The Army and Air Force "General Commanders' Code", OKK-5 to OKK-8 (1939-41), and OTSKK-7 ("General Central Commanders' Code"), used in rear areas
   All "conversion" systems were considered CYB, or "front" systems
5) Transpositions: pure transpositions were used in the Army and Air Force only for practice traffic
6) Number codes (called by the Germans "cipher-code"): these were 5-figure codes for relaying radio reports of operational or tactical content, direction of troops (on the highest networks). Specifically mentioned were 011-A (19,000 code values in 390 pages), 023-A, 045-A, 062-A, 091-A (23,000 code values in 430 pages), which was used until the capitulation.

[619] DF 18 p 45

136

All these books were captured; but the encipherment by Blocknots (one-time pads) made solution practically impossible: there was almost complete security in these systems.[620]

NKVD

1) Operational systems: these were used by individual units until 1939, when a general operational system (mono-alphabetic substitution, no description was given) was introduced

2) "Conversion systems": a 4-figure code was used in the Kasakhastan area; three 4-figure codes were in use by 1939; three 4-figure codes were in use at the time of capitulation: ZERNO, NIVA, VIZA; a 5-figure railway code was also in use

3) Transposition systems: these were not used by NKVD, with the exception of one 4-figure code (used in the Arctic Ocean district and on the Finnish-Russian border) which was enciphered by a transposition: it was read currently in part

4) Number series: from 1940 on, a 4-figure code was enciphered by various methods, monographic letter substitution, sliding number sequences, and Blocknots. These were read currently up to the end of the war.

Agents' and Partisans' Systems: these were transpositions (single and double), grilles, and keyword substitutions. (Though there was no statement of cryptanalytic achievement, apparently great difficulty was encountered in solution, and not much success was achieved)

[620] DF 18 p 61

Dettmann and Samsonov concluded their discussion with a chart of German cryptanalytic achievements on Russian systems.[621] The details of which are to be found on chart #1-2 (results of European axis cryptanalytic achievements)[622]

[621] DF 18 p 75

[622] It should be pointed out once again that though Dettmann and Samsonov gave a comprehensive picture of German achievements, they were not to be trusted in every detail. Throughout this chapter it has been shown that composite picture of German achievements in Russian cryptanalysis as derived from the interrogations of other Prisoners of War in many cases did not agree with Dettmann and Samsonov, but would seem to contain more truth.

138

VOLUME 4

Chapter VII. Miscellaneous Cryptanalysis

Section A. Period from 1919 to 1939

65. German Army Cryptanalytic Effort 1919-1933-- Before 1938, there was no Army High Command and consequently no separate German Army Signal Intelligence Service. The codes-cipher section of the German Defense Ministry which had been maintained in skeleton force since the end of World War I handled the cryptanalytic work on foreign Army systems and any security work done on German Army systems. There is no record of the work done by this section.

66. German Army Cryptanalytic Effort 1933-1939-- In 1933 the newly established Army High Command (Oberkommando des Heeres abbreviated "OKH") set up its own central agency to handle the Army traffic of foreign countries. This central agency known as the Intercept Control Station (Horchleitstelle) was staffed by a few trained cryptanalysts who had been drawn by the Army from the Cipher Section of the German Defense Ministry.[630] Although little is known about the organization of the Intercept Control Station, Major Feichtner of the German Air Force states that it was divided into geographical sections, each section dealing

[630] I 78 p 2

with an individual country.[631] We know that before 1939 there were sections for the traffic of Belguim, Holland, Switzerland, England, and Russia.

67. French systems 1933-1939-- Mettig stated that during the years 1937-1939, continuous and significant successes were obtained by the Intercept Control Station against French Army systems.[632] In the crises of 1937 and 1938, the Germans read the systems used by the French on the wireless net which radiated from Paris to the static French formations within France. These systems, designated by the Germans as F 90 and F 110[633] were described by Dr. Otto Buggisch, one of the leading Army cryptanalysts, as French Army systems based on a four-figure code.[634] In one case, the encipherment was by means of a periodic additive; in the other it was an ordinary transposition, the transposition key being obtained from a key word which itself was taken from the code. Solution, said Buggisch, was obtained by methods generally known in cryptanalytic circles.[635]

68. Belgian systems 1933-1939-- The complete Order of Battle of the Belgian Army was known to the Germans in 1939, at least partly through the reading of Belgian systems.[636] Huettenhain, one of the leading cryptanalysts of the Signal Intelligence Agency of the Supreme Command of the Armed Forces (OKW/Chi), described the Belgian Army system as a 3-figure code used with substitution tables in such a way that the first figure of each group remained unchanged and the second and third were each enciphered individually with types of substitutions that could be varied with each message.[637]

[631] IF 181 p 4

[632] I 78 p 3

[633] I 58 pp 2, 6

[634] I 176 p 2

[635] I 176 p 2

[636] I 78 p 3

[637] I 31 p 6

69. Dutch systems 1933-1939-- Mettig states that the Dutch Order of Battle was also available to the German Army at least partly from cryptanalytic achievements.[638] The maneuvers of the Dutch Army in 1937 were covered by the intercept stations of the Army.[639] Very simple techniques, principally double transposition ciphers; were used and these were read by the cryptanalysts of the Intercept Control Station without much difficulty. As a result, Dutch Order of Battle was established down to battalion level.

70. Swiss systems 1933-1939-- Switzerland, Mettig said, was only casually monitored.[640] Nothing is known from TICOM sources concerning the Swiss systems used in this period.

71. British systems 1933-1939-- During the period 1933-1939, the Intercept Control Station had very little success in reading British systems. Mettig attributed this to the very poor quality of the personnel employed on the task.[641] The Order of Battle of the British Army, however, was built up from direction-finding information and the evaluation of call-signs or other radio procedure.[642]

72. Summary of the 1933-1939-- The cryptanalytic effort of the Germans from 1933 to the beginning of the war, 1939, was fairly successful. The Order of Battle of the French, Belgian, and Dutch Armies up to that time was known from cryptanalytic achievements. Only in the case of Britain was cryptanalysis unsuccessful, and here traffic analysis indicated the Order of Battle. Against Germany's feebler opponents, such as Poland, little was necessary, if we may believe Mettig. Mettig stated that the speedy development and completion of the Polish campaign in 1939 made cryptanalytic effort unnecessary, particularly in view of the fact that the Poles, he believed, transmitted their radio traffic in the clear. It was with justifiable confidence in their Signal Intelligence Service that the Germans faced the early years of the war.

[638] I 78 p 3
[639] I 78 p 3
[640] I 78 p 3
[641] I 78 p 3
[642] I 78 p 3

VOLUME 4

Chapter VII. Miscellaneous Cryptanalysis

Section B. Period from 1939-1941

73. German Army Cryptanalytic Effort 1939-1941--
In the early years of the war, the cryptanalytic staff of the Intercept Control Station (Horchleitstelle) was unable to cope with the added burden of the wartime traffic. The British section of the Intercept Control Station was unable to solve British systems;[650] the French section was forced to call upon the Signal Intelligence Agency of the Supreme Command Armed Forces (Oberkommando der Wehrmacht Chiffrier Stelle, abbreviated OKW/Chi) to aid in the solution of French Army systems;[651] and there were not enough cryptanalysts to furnish the forward units with adequate staffs.[652]

The failure of the British section of the Intercept Control Station (Horchleitstelle) to achieve any success with British systems continued. In 1940 the six people comprising the section were moved to Bad Godesberg where no success was achieved despite an abundance of material with which to work.[653] Dr. Buggisch, who in 1942 looked over the files of the British section regarding work on the British high grade machine, Typex, characterized the work of Inspector Breede who worked in the winter of 1939/40 on the British "big machine" as complete nonsense.[654] He stated that Breede described an imaginary machine which had nothing whatever to do with Typex. No cryptanalytic success was recorded in this period. In April 1940, however,

[650] I 78 p 4

[651] D 60 p 4

[652] I 78 p 4

[653] I 78 p 4

[654] I 66 p 2

142

the British section received a copy of the British War Office Code captured in Norway. A second copy was obtained at Dunkirk.[655] Successes with this system were thereafter possible, since the British continued to use this system until 1943.[656]

The failure of the cryptanalysts of the Intercept Control Station to solve independently the French Army system succeeding the F 110 was another indication of their inadequacy. In early autumn 1939, the French replaced the peace-time systems, F 90 and F 110, with a new war-time system whose name is not known from TICOM sources.[657] The Army cryptanalysts found themselves unable to cope with the situation and called the cryptanalysts of the Signal Intelligence Agency of the Armed Forces, (OKW/Chi) to their aid. Huettenhain, one of the cryptanalysts of OKW/Chi, was sent to the Army Intercept Station at Frankfurt/Main to aid in the solution. Among his papers were two memoranda describing the work he did there.[658] In the memoranda, Huettenhain reported that the task was accomplished, with the aid of his own colleagues of OKW/Chi by October, (1939), so that all the September material could be read retrospectively. The system continued to be worked on successfully through October; and in November, Dr. Huettenhain returned to his own agency, the system solved. It may be noted that the head of the Army station requested Huettenhain to convey the thanks of the Army to the Signal Intelligence Agency of the Supreme Command of the Armed Forces (OKW/Chi) for the assistance given to the Army's cryptanalytic section and remarked that in his opinion such a large cryptanalytic task could not be done by the Army High Command either then or in the near future.

The system was decoded by the Intercept Control Station successfully until the German offensive of the spring of 1940. At this time the French began to use systems in the forward echelons which the cryptanalysts of the Horchleitstelle were unable to solve.[659] Mettig remarked that

[655] I 51 p 2

[656] I 51 p 6

[657] D 60 p 4

[658] D 60 pp 4-5

[659] I 78 p 4

DOCID: 3486746

the Army cryptanalysts both of the forward units and of the Intercept Control Station (Horchleitstelle) finally concentrated on two machine systems, the C-36 and the B-211.[660] Neither was solved, however, until after the cessation of hostilities with France. According to Mettig, the final solution of these two machines rated lower than that of the preceding system since it was not timely and was done only with the aid of captured material.[661]

In the winter of 1939, the dearth of field cryptanalysts became apparent to the German Army. When the Signal Intelligence Regiments (KONAs) were preparing to move into the field, the Army found that there were no trained cryptanalysts to send with them.[662] Col. Randewig, the commander of all intercept units in the west, was able to procure a number of cryptanalysts from intercept units around Berlin and filled out that number with mathematicians and linguists. As a result, when the German offensive started in 1940, the Signal Intelligence Regiments had a moderate supply of cryptanalytic personnel; but more were needed to cope with the field problems.

74. Summary of the 1939-1941 Period-- Although the cryptanalytic achievements of the Intercept Control Station (Horchleitstelle) during the years 1939-1941 were minor, their success in intercepting traffic and decoding solvable known systems was of great aid to the German Army. Mettig stated that all messages on the French system which succeeded the F110 were read from late 1939 until the spring of 1940 when the system changed; and that these messages, despite their administrative nature helped to fill in the tactical picture.[663] For example, the strength of units being set up on the training ground at Mourmelon was estimated by statistics of water bottles and blankets. It was possible to deduce facts about the shortage of armor-piercing ammunition with the French infantry units. Similarly, the conversion of the Second and Third French Cavalry Divisions to Armored Divisions in the area northeast of

660 I 78 p 4

661 I 128 p 2

662 I 78 p 4

663 I 78 p 3

Paris was ascertained in December 1939.[664] By the end of 1939, the complete Order of Battle of the French Army was available to the German Army from the reading of French traffic. The capture of a copy of the British War Office Code in Norway in 1940 (and of another copy at Dunkirk in June of that year) afforded the British section its first successes and furnished a constant and important source of information from that time until 1943, when the British discontinued use of the code.

In this period the Germans realized the inadequacy of their personnel and effort, and set about correcting them.

[664] I 78 p 4

VOLUME 4

Chapter VII. Miscellaneous Cryptanalysis

Section C. Period from 1941 to 1945

Paragraph

75. <u>German Army Cryptanalytic Effort 1941-1944</u>-- The experiences of 1940 showed that considerable expansion in the German Army cryptanalytic effort was desirable. As a result, in the spring of 1941, Major Mang of the German

146

Army, was ordered to establish a new German Army cryptanatytic and evaluation agency to replace the old Intercept Control Station.[670] The new agency was established as Group VI Inspectorate of 7 (Inspecktion 7 Gruppe VI, abbreviated In 7/VI). Its aim was to increase the cryptanalytic effort in the central office and to train cryptanalytic reserves for field work.[671] A large number of mathematicians and linguists were introduced into the organization and the number of countries covered greatly increased; detachments were sent from In 7/VI to key areas (the Russian section was dispatched to Loetzen to form there the nucleus of the (later) Intercept Control Station East (Horchleitstelle Ost); and cryptanalysts trained in British traffic were sent to Rommel's headquarters in North Africa to the evaluation center of Signal Intelligence Regiment 4 (KONA 4) in Athens, to KONA 5 in Paris, and to Feste 9 (Feste Horchstelle) in Bergen, Norway.

The cryptanalytic work of In 7/VI is described in the following pages according to geographical divisions: western and southwestern cryptanalysis; southeastern cryptanalysis; eastern cryptanalysis. Following these paragraphs the work of the Agents' Section, of the Research Section Linguistic and Mathematical, and of the IBM Section will be discussed.

76. Western and southwestern cryptanalysis, 1941-1944-- Western and southwestern cryptanalysis was handled at In 7/VI by the British section with outposts in North Africa, Athens, Paris, and Bergen, Norway; by the American section; by the French section with subsections for Swiss, Spanish, Portuguese, and Brazilian traffic; and by the Italian section. The field units which handled western and southwestern traffic were the western field units, KONAs 5 and 7. Swedish Army traffic was handled by a special unit of Feste 9 in Norway.

77. Work on British 1941-1944-- During the years 1941-1943, the main success of the British section was the reading of the British War Office Code (WOC), two copies of which had been captured in early 1940.[672] After the capture of these documents, the British section under Inspektor Liedtke was successful in reading messages from

[670] I 78 p 5
[671] I 78 p 5
[672] I 51 p 2

147

North Africa during the spring of 1941, encoded with WOC and superenciphered with additives.[673] British traffic in WOC was read constantly throughout 1941. In March of that year, a considerable volume of messages was read during the British Cyrenaic offensive of the British Eighth Army under Wavell. The organization of the base services and the Order of Battle of the Army were recognized. During the late summer of 1941, Rommel's counter-attack took place leading to the siege of Tobruk. The besieged fortress was solely dependent on radio for its signal communications to the Eighth Army and Cairo, and as it used the WOC with an enciphering table almost exclusively its traffic was read by the Germans. The British section of In 7/VI followed accurately the British Eighth Army's relief attempts in November 1941 which led to the cutting off of Rommel between Tobruk, Bir Omar and Sollum and, eventually, Rommel's famous break-out to the West at Sidi Rezegh.

As a result of the success with the WOC in Berlin, a special detachment of eight cryptanalysts was sent to the evaluation center of KONA 4 at Athens to solve traffic at that point and thereby reduce the time wasted in sending the traffic back to Berlin. Unfortunately for the Germans, about the time the party started (the middle of December 1941) certain difficulties were encountered in the solution of the War Office Code which prevented the solution of the WOC for the following eight or nine months.[674] During this period the British section suffered a further blow through the capture in July 1942 of the greater part of the Long Range Signal Intelligence Company, FAK 621, which had been operating in North Africa under Seebohm. Although the remnants of the unit continued to operate under a Captain Habel, information gained from the captured part of the unit gave evidence to the British that their code was being read and from that time on the British section had no success with the code.[675] Herzfeld said that after his return to Berlin in October 1942, there was a little WOC traffic but that its volume was too small for successful exploitation.[676] From December 1942 to March 1943, the British used enciphered indicators, and in March and April 1943 changed to one-time pads for enciphering tables.[677]

[673] I 51 pp 16-17

[674] I 51 p 17

[675] I 113 p 4; I 78 p 9

[676] I 51 p 20

[677] I 51 p 20

148

The British section had no success with these innovations although Liedtke worked for a year attempting to break into the new system.[678]

From 1942 to the end of the war, the only success attained was with British low-level traffic, particularly Slidex. Slidex was designated by the Germans as English Code (Englische Code abbreviated "EC") followed by a number to denote the variations of the basic system. Slidex was used by the British and later by the American and Canadian Army in front line units and in air support networks (tentacles). The variations of the EC system mentioned in TICOM sources are: EC 5, 12, 23, 24, 25, 30/3, and 30/20.[679]

EC 5 is described by Graupe of In 7/VI as a system in which the code values are written in alphabetical order in the columns of a rectangle 25 x 25.[680] The code groups are represented in the cipher text by the digraphic coordinates and sent in 5 letter groups. Intercepted Slidex was principally practice traffic in the United Kingdom during the period 1942-1943 [681] and was solved by the British section of In 7/VI which then forwarded the material to the training section of In 7/VI for instruction purposes.[682]

In EC 12, the successor of EC 5, the code group of two letters derived from the coordinates was enciphered by a group of four figures and sent in 5 figure groups. The traffic in this code appeared in North Africa in 1942-43 and was of tactical value for operations in that area.[683] It was solved at In 7/VI and was decoded easily in most of the field units of KONA 5 and 7.

[678] IF 107 p 7

[679] IF 120 p 3

[680] IF 107 p 3

[681] IF 120 p 3

[682] IF 107 p 3

[683] IF 120 p 3

149

EC 23, 24, 25 were developments of the basic EC series. The systems are not described in detail in TICOM sources. The traffic originated mainly from the United Kingdom and was used from November 1943 until the time of the invasion in June 1944. Traffic in these systems was intercepted by Feste 9 in Norway and units of KONA 5 in France. The evaluation center of KONA 5 at St. Germain is said to have succeeded in reconstructing all the cards used in systems 23 and 24. Feste 9 succeeded in this only once after two days' work, and then with the help of a message of 190 digraphs. System 25 was recognized but seldom intercepted.[684]

EC 30/3 was a variation of the EC series intended to be used specifically for the Invasion and thereafter.[685] It had, however, been used by air liaison links in the United Kingdom during May 1944, and had already been reconstructed by Feste 9 by the time the invasion occurred on 6 June, 1944. The reconstruction of this code allowed the Germans at once to discover the order of battle of the invading armies at Corps level. The evaluation center of KONA 5 at St. Germain took over the work of intercepting and decoding this traffic during the summer and fall of 1944; at which time the system was currently and easily solved by units of KONA 5 and later those of KONA 6 with the aid of captured tables. Traffic in this system is said to have been solved so quickly that it could be handled like plain text.[686]

EC 30/20 was a variation of the EC system reconstructed by KONA 7 in Italy. Traffic was originated by supply units of the British Eighth Army and was currently solved until the end of September, 1944 when the traffic was replaced by a four-figure type which was not broken.[687]

After D-day, Slidex was also used by the American Army.[688] When the Germans found that the American MP units were using Slidex to report all Army units which passed their control points, the deciphering of Slidex was given high priority.[689] Graupe stated that Slidex messages were also particularly valuable for identifying bombing and

[684] IF 144 p 2
[685] IF 120 p 3
[686] I 109 p 38
[687] IF 120 p 3
[688] I 113 p 3
[689] I 80 p 3

artillery objectives.[690] The time estimated for the solution of Slidex was one to three hours if the basic cards were at hand, five to six hours if they were not. Sixty-five percent of the work is said to have been done with the cards available.[691]

Not much material concerning other British low-grade systems solved can be found in TICOM sources. Hentze of KONA 5 said that Maplay was worked on throughout 1944, but that the volume was low and the Germans found this system harder to break than Slidex. They were successful only with a great deal of traffic or with a re-encodement from Slidex which had provided the original break.[692] Codex was solved by the Germans largely with the help of a captured specimen which had been in the possession of the Germans since the days of the Leros Invasion.[693] It was read by Feste 9 in 1944-45, when that unit was in Italy. A Tiger-code (so-called from its use during the "Tiger" pre-invasion exercises in England) was solved by the Germans after a half year of work.[694] Solution was made possible by a long report in a British paper giving the names of units, officers, etc. Another British system, the '999', which was used during the pre-invasion period,was solved by the Germans; but it was never used operationally.[695] KONA 5 is said to have had considerable success with the Tiger Code and to have achieved solution on the fourth or fifth day after its regular monthly changes.[696] Matin, another British Army system, was never solved. Hentze says that the Germans arrived at the decision that Matin was a small machine, but he does not say whether research on this system was carried on at In 7/VI or in KONA 5.[697]

[690] IF 107 p 8

[691] I 80 p 3

[692] I 113 p 4

[693] IF 120 p 4

[694] I 76 p 13

[695] I 113 p 4

[696] I 113 p 4

[697] I 113 p 4

The outstanding failure of the British section of In 7/VI, and of In 7/VI in general, was the failure to solve the British 'big machine', Typex. Mettig stated that had the Germans of In 7/VI had been able to solve this system, it would have been their outstanding achievement.[698] At a previous interrogation, Mettig had stated that Typex was read in 1942 in North Africa and that success continued until the autumn of 1942 from which time In 7/VI had no more success with the system.[699] This fact, coupled with some information from Ultra sources to the effect that FAK 621 in North Africa had been reading Typex at the time of its capture in North Africa in July and November 1942, brought about a thorough investigation of this subject by the interrogators.[700] The story in brief was that in June 1943 one of the prisoners of Bode claimed that he had worked on British machine methods from 1937 to 1940 and that messages which could not be decoded by FAK 621 in North Africa were sent to In 7/VI at Berlin. Two other prisoners from FAK 621, Haunhorst and Possel, stated that all high grade traffic was handled by a Warrant Officer Wagner, and that this man had at his disposal one or more British Typex machines captured at Tobruk. They described the machine as resembling a German Enigma machine with a special type of adjustable keyboard. They said also that certain documents were used in the solution of the settings, either captured British cipher documents or machine settings compiled by In 7/VI at Berlin from three or four years of traffic. No further information was gained concerning this incident during the war since other officers refused to give information and Warrant Officer Wagner was never identified. This 1943 evidence was contradicted by the statements made after the war by highly placed german cryptanalysts. Drs. Huettenhain and Fricke of the Signal Intelligence Service of the Armed Forces (OKW/Chi), and Mettig, emphatically denied having solved or heard of a solution of Typex. They had never seen a Typex machine

[698] I 128 p 2

[699] I 48 p 3

[700] I 161

with rotors although all admitted that a Typex machine without rotors had been captured at Dunkirk. The TICOM interrogators of Dr. Huettenhain and Fricke reported:

> "Should it turn out that some of the experts named above [i. e. Mettig] were in possession of a complete Typex machine and have achieved successes, both these POW's [Huettenhain and Fricke] would lose their last faith in their fellow beings."[701]

Mettig, moreover, stated categorically that a success of this nature would have been mentioned in the list of German cryptographic successes which was drawn up for him prior to his visit to Supreme Headquarters Allied Expeditionary Forces with the liaison commission of the Supreme Command of the Armed Forces (OKW).[702] Mettig's former statement that Typex was read in 1942 in North Africa and that success continued until the autumn of 1942 (from which time In 7/VI had no more success with the traffic) may have been a misstatement for Slidex. At least, the interrogators assumed that Huettenhain, Fricke, and Mettig in their last interrogation were speaking the truth.

Although it is almost certain that In 7/VI never solved Typex, a great deal of effort was expended on the project from 1940 to 1943. In January 1942 the files of the work on Typex done up to that time at In 7/VI were turned over to Buggisch who found work dating back to 1940,[703] when Inspector Breede of the British section had attempted to solve the system. Breede recognized the traffic as machine traffic but described a purely imaginary machine which Buggisch says had no relation to Typex, and was complete nonsense. In 1941 some mathematical studies were made on Typex; and in January 1942, Buggisch made a study of the system, from which he made the following conclusions:

a. the system was similar to that of the Enigma, according to single letter frequency counts based on 10,000 cipher letters
b. certain relationships between two message-settings frequently existed

701 I 161 p 6

702 I 161 p 7

703 I 66 p 2

There is no evidence that Buggisch proceeded further than this in his investigation. He stated that a Typex machine without rotors was captured during the French campaign near Dunkirk and that some documents taken from an English security officer pointed out frequent breaches in the strict regulation that rotors of the Typex machine should be turned at random after a message was enciphered.[704] There seems to have been no knowledge of how many rotors the Typex machine had; Buggisch vaguely remembered having read that there were twenty-five.[705] He also stated that casual consideration was given to whether or not, one might be able to tackle the problem of breaking (if one knew the inner wiring of the wheels). Since no one at In 7/VI knew neither the wiring of the wheels or how many wheels there were, the question was of no practical interest. The whole matter was evidently permanently abandoned sometime in 1943.

Mention should also be made of the solution in KONA 4 of British traffic emanating from the Transjordan Frontier Force which gave valuable information concerning British troop movements in the Middle East. An intercepted (and decoded) message from the Transjordan Frontier Force indicated which units of the Ninth Army were being moved to Egypt to counter Rommel's threat to Alexandria. Even when this code was changed in July 1942, solution proceeded regularly after a few hours' work.[706]

In summary, one may state that the British section was able to give intelligence concerning the movements of enemy forces from the solution and constant decoding of such low-level traffic as Slidex, Codex, Maplay, 999, and the Tiger Code. During the early part of the war the solution of the enciphering tables used to encipher the British War Office Code made possible current decoding which furnished an excellent source of information; during the later years Slidex decodes were the main source. With Typex, no success was attained, and all efforts at solution were abandoned in 1943.

[704] I 61 p 3

[705] I 61 p 3

[706] IF 190B p 7

154

78. Work on USA traffic 1941-1944-- The USA section of In 7/VI was created with the entry of the United States into the war in early December 1941.[707] The section, made up of personnel who had been drafted from the mathematical section of In 7/VI, was placed under the leadership of Steinberg, a leading mathematician. Initial attempts at breaking USA traffic were fraught with difficulties. Because of the size of the USA wireless network and the use of alternative frequencies by USA operators, considerable trouble was experienced in identifying the various links and sorting the different systems. After a few weeks, however, order was established through the reading of call signs and the sorting by discriminants.[708]

The first major success of the USA section was in the summer of 1942 when the M-94 was solved.[709] The Germans designated the M-94 variously as URSAL, CDAF, strip, and ACr2. URSAL was a name given to the system from the fact that traffic from the USA weather stations in Greenland which used URSAL as an indicator provided the first breaks into the system.[710] CDAF was found in the traffic emanating from the Caribbean Defense Area.[711] "Strip" and "ACr2" (Amerikanischer Caesar 2) stem from the fact that this system was long thought to be a strip system.[712] The solution of the M-94 was achieved by Steinberg and Luzius, mathematicians of the USA section, who are said to have written a twenty-five page report on their work. After the solution had been achieved cryptanalytically, a USA manual (FM 11-5) with a complete description of the M-94 was found in a Berlin library.[713]

Current solution of the M-94 from 1942 to 1943 was done both at In 7/VI and at the Signal Intelligence Evaluation Center of KONA 5 at St. Germain. The work consisted of finding the daily key. A set of 25 charts (synoptic tables) corresponding to the 25 discs of the machine was constructed, apparently similar to the "synoptic tables" used by American cryptanalysts. The daily key was found by assuming a beginning, and using the charts to discover possible disc arrangements. Later IBM was used to eliminate

[707] I 78 p 10

[708] I 78 p 10

[709] I 113 p 3

[710] I 142 p 2

[711] IF 107 p 4

[712] I 142 p 2

[713] I 142 p 2

"impossible" charts. Graupe of NAAS 5 stated that it usually took two days to recover the order of the discs and that only fifty groups were required for the system to be broken.[714] This solution time seems exceptionally long, as American security studies have shown. Solution of the M-94 usually takes only a few hours. Estimates on the amount of material solved range from 70% to 90%.

The M-94 was succeeded in 1943 by the M-209, which was first solved by the Germans in the autumn of 1943.[715] and continued to be solved with some success throughout the remaining years of the war. Solution was achieved in In 7/VI by Steinberg and Luzius, who were aided by the knowledge that the US government had bought the Hagelin machine which had once been offered to the German government.[716] At first only relative settings could be recovered,[717] but later the section refined its technique of recovering absolute settings so that not only paired messages but in a large number of cases a whole day's traffic could be read. The technique of achieving true settings was passed on by In 7/VI to the Navy and the Luftwaffe.[718]

Work on an operational level was carried on jointly by the USA section of In 7/VI and NAAS 5 at St. Germain. Early in 1944, NAAS 5 had been supplied with a group of cryptanalysts skilled in work on the M-209; and this small group headed by Engelhardt competed with the section at In 7/VI in the quick solution of M-209 traffic.[719] It is estimated that 10-20% of all M-209 messages intercepted were read by establishing the true settings of the wheels, and that about half of these settings were established at In 7/VI, half at NAAS 5.[720] To insure speedy

[714] IF 107 p 4; I 113 p 3
[715] IF 107 p 5
[716] I 80 p 3
[717] I 113 p 3; I 142 p 3
[718] I 144 p 2
[719] I 142 p 2
[720] IF 153 p 1

solution all units subordinated to KONA 5 were ordered to teleprint to NAAS 5 all messages on the smae setting or with indicators differing only in the first two letters.[721] In addition, copies of all intercepts were sent to In 7/VI as well as to NAAS 5 in an effort to obtain all possible solutions.[722] Under the most favorable circumstances two days were needed to solve a depth, and two more days to reconstruct the absolute settings.[723] There were times, however, when captured lists of keys or settings made possible a quick solution of the traffic. During the campaigns of Sicily and Italy, messages of great tactical value were decoded using captured booklets containing M-209 settings.[724] At the time of the invasion of Normandy, the M-209 keys of the 82nd and 101st Airborne Divisions which covered the critical days of June 6, 7, 8, 9, 10, 11 were captured and all traffic on those days was read.[725]

The Germans of In 7/VI knew of the existence of a 'big American machine' which was designated the AM 1 (Amerikanische Maschine 1); but it is quite clear that In 7/VI never solved this machine and had no idea about its construction.[726] Hentze of KONA 5 says that his unit never succeeded in getting a model of the machine.[727] Keller's remark that the American machine cipher was tackled in Berlin with approximately 2% success and that the conclusion that it was not worth the trouble is without doubt utter nonsense.[728]

The Germans were successful with American codes. One code of no strategic value, a United States Army Administrative Code, designated by the Germans as AC 1 (Amerikanischer Code 1) had been captured before 1939, and photostatic copies of the code had been distributed to all field cryptanalytic units.[729]

[721] I 113 pp 11-12

[722] IF 107 p 6

[723] IF 107 p 6

[724] IF 107 p 5; IF 153 p 1

[725] IF 153 p 1

[726] IF 153 p 2

[727] I 113 p 4

[728] I 74 p 3

[729] IF 153 p 2; IF 105 p 5

DOCID: 3486746

The code was a 5 letter code with 60,000 groups, each page containing 90 groups.[730] Feste 9, while it was in Norway, intercepted and read traffic passed in this code from the summer of 1942 to the autumn of 1943.[731] Although no traffic of strategic value was passed, the intelligence was valuable enough so that when AC 1 was succeeded by a simplified version designated as TELWA (USA: SIGARM) Feste 9 took pains to reconstruct the code with the help of AC 1.[732]

Feste 9, aided to some extent in more difficult solution by the USA section of In 7/VI, also broke the simple codes used by US Army units stationed in Iceland and the Caribbean. These were designated as Division Field Code (DFC) followed by a number indicating the variation of the system. The variations described in TICOM sources were: DFC 15, 16, 17, 21, 25, 28, and 29.[733]

a. DFC 15: a 4 letter code, two-part, with variants and nulls. The system was used by the US Army in Iceland during the autumn of 1942 and was solved in January 1943 by Feste 9 in Norway by assuming clear routine messages with a basis of encoded text such as Daily Shipping Report, Weather Forecast etc.

b. DFC 16: a 4 letter code enciphered by means of daily changing letter conversion tables. The system was used by stations inside Iceland and on the Iceland-Washington link for one month only, probably November 1942. DFC 16 was solved in January 1943 by In 7/VI. The solution was given to Feste 9 which thereafter succeeded in reading 80% of the traffic intercepted.

c. DFC 17: similar to DFC 16 but with different code equivalents for certain clear letters, words, abbreviations etc. The system was used in Iceland and also from USAAF links in Central America and in the Caribbean Area in February and March of 1943. With the aid of a captured DFC 16 code, Feste 9 broke and read nearly 100% of DFC 17 traffic.

730 IF 120 p 4

731 IF 120 p 4

732 IF 120 p 5

733 IF 120 p 4; IF 144 pp 3-5

158

d. DFC 18: Similar to DFC 17, and this system was current in April, May, and June of 1943 with a decline in the volume of traffic in Iceland. It was broken by Feste 9 with the aid of experience gathered in the solution of DFC 17.

e. DFC 21: Similar to DFC 17 and 18, this system was current in July 1943. It was broken and read by Feste 9 with the aid of routine administrative messages.

f. DFC 25: Current only in the Caribbean Sea Area from August to November 1943, this system was intercepted by Feste 3 at Euskirchen but the traffic was handed over to Feste 9 for solution. The system was read only in part because the letters and figures which presumably meant types and makes of aircraft made book reconstruction very difficult and the intelligence was not of interest to the Army.

g. DFC 28: A training code used in the south of England, from December 1943 to March 1944, was intercepted by Feste 9. A noticeable rise in the standard of encoding occurred in comparison with the messages intercepted from Iceland. Traffic in this code was of no intelligence interest.

h. DFC 29: a copy of this book was captured in the autumn of 1943 but it was never used.

Mention should also be made of the success of the USA section of In 7/VI with the Air Transport Code used for air cargo and passenger transport circuits to Africa and South America.[734] This code, consisting of two-figure elements from 00-99, was successfully decoded by In 7/VI from May 1942 until early 1943 when it was given to the German Air Force.

[734] IF 153 p 2

The work of In 7/VI, USA section, appears to have been successful in low-grade ciphers and in some medium grade ciphers such as M-94 and M-209. Mettig rated the solution of the M-209 as the outstanding achievement of this section and one of the best of In 7/VI. It is clear also from references concerning the work on this system made by members of other agencies such as Tranow, chief cryptanalyst of the Navy, and Voegele, chief cryptanalyst of the German Air Force, that the USA section of In 7/VI evolved the best techniques of solving the M-209 and led the other German Signal Intelligence Agencies in the work on this system.

79. Work on French traffic 1941-1944-- French traffic from 1941-1944 was of two main types, Vichy French and Free French. Vichy French traffic which was under the direct control of the French Armistice Commission at Wiesbaden was monitored by the French section of In 7/VI.[735] By agreement with the Vichy government, the French were to inform the Germans of their code and cipher procedures, but wary watch was kept on their traffic. The work on Free French traffic which emanated during this period from Free French troops in Syria and in North, West, and Equatorial Africa was carried on by In 7/VI and the Signal Intelligence Evaluation Center of KONA 4 at Athens where the traffic was easily intercepted.

In a list compiled by Juehn, head of the French section of In 7/VI, of the Free French systems worked on by In 7/VI and NAAS 4, the following systems are mentioned as being used in Syria:[736]

a. a 3-letter system: code table with fortnightly key change. This system appeared from about 1942 to the middle of 1944 in Syria but was not intercepted after this. Content is described as moderate to good.
b. a variant of the above code which passed technical details of wireless traffic.
c. police systems which appeared, according to Kuehn, rarely: either 2/F substitution tables or simple transpositions.

[735] I 78 p 9

[736] I 160 p 6

160

d. a 4/F code with daily key change. Appeared in 1944 in the Syrian coastal network. Content described ship movements in the coastal area.

From other sources may be added the de Gaullist systems, two of which are named: Control Bedouin and Service Politique.[737] The work on French systems used in Syria was summarized by Winkler and Loeckher, two members of KONA 4: "All Syrian traffic was read and a complete picture obtained of the French armed forces."[738]

Among the Free French systems from North Africa which were solved and read by In 7/VI and KONA 4, Kuehn listed:[739]

a. 5 letter messages from a diagonal transposition system, with monthly, later semi-monthly changes, used in West Africa from 1943 to 1945. It was later discovered from a captured document that this system had been used in World War I, and was resurrected evidently for use in West Africa.

b. TTSF code. A 4 latter code reciphered by letter substitution into 4 letter cipher text. The first group of the message is always TTSF; the last group the indicator. The code was used in North Africa from 1944-1945 for routine messages.

c. 5 letter messages from a diagonal transposition used in Equatorial Africa in 1943-1944.

d. 5 figure messages from a 4 figure hatted code, designated ATM 43. Kuehn of In 7/VI notes that ATM 43 derived its name from the fact that it was possible to use the vocabulary of the pre-war French Code, the ATM, in the reconstruction of this code.

e. 3 figure messages from a 4 figure code with subtractor. This system was used in North Africa in 1944 for transport work.

A 5 figure de Gaulle code was used in North, West, and Equatorial Africa, and later in France, which had not been solved by the end of the war despite efforts made by In 7/VI since

[737] I 74 p 2

[738] I 170 p 2

[739] I 160 p 6

1941/2.[740] Buggisch stated that in 1941/2 he worked on this code with Kunze, one of the chief cryptanalysts of the Foreign Office.[741] Despite these efforts, no success was attained until compromise revealed that the code was transposed with daily changing key. No further headway appears to have been made with this system.

The French section of In 7/VI, it will be recalled, had solved the C-36 and the B-211 after the French campaign in 1940. When, therefore, the de Gaullist troops in North Africa and Corsica began to use the C-36 machine for their traffic, the French section already had a solution and it was easily solved during 1943. Even when a new indicator system based on numbers was introduced in early 1944, a high percentage of the traffic continued to be solved through the use of cribs and statistics. The indicator system itself was broken in the autumn of 1944.[742]

At the end of his paper on the French systems treated by the French section of In 7/VI and KONA 4, Kuehn made it clear that the French section was greatly aided by certain fundamental weaknesses in French cryptography which led to easy solutions of most of their systems. These weaknesses, he described as:[743]

a. "the extraordinary conservatism of the French regarding the construction of their code systems or reciphering methods. Systems which must have been used in the first World War were, for instance, used in a slightly modified form up to 1945 in West Africa. Reciphering methods are regularly of two types: either subtraction with finite subtractors or transposition with keywords taken from the code."

b. "the habitual use by the French of stereotyped message beginnings and endings which facilitates breaking into the systems."

[740] I 160 p 7

[741] I 58 p 6

[742] I 92 p 3

[743] I 160 p 22

c. "the idiosyncrasy of the French of communicating cipher matters or key changes by radio. For instance, through the diagonal system in West Africa In 7/VI was able on several occasions to break the key for C 36 machine and once a key change for the ATM 43 code was announced."

With these weaknesses, it was possible for the French section to read all or most of Free French traffic during the years 1941-1944. Their previous experience with the C-36 and B-211 provided them with solutions to this machine traffic as it was used by de Gaulle. No high grade traffic appears to have been passed by the French during this period.

80. Work on Swiss, Spanish, Portuguese, Brazilian traffic-- From 1941-1944, the French section of In 7/VI had subsections for Swiss, Spanish, Portuguese, and Brazilian traffic. As Kuehn stated, however, the volume of traffic was always extremely small and unimportant.[744]

Buggisch, one of the chief cryptanalysts of In 7/VI, worked with Kunze of the Foreign Office on the solution of the Swiss Enigma (the Commercial Enigma);[745] although they worked out a theoretical solution of the machine, the theory was never applied at In 7/VI to Swiss traffic because the volume did not warrant the effort.[746] Moreover, easy solution of the traffic was precluded by the fact that the Swiss did their own wiring of the Enigma wheels and changed these frequently.[747]

Monitoring of Spanish, Portuguese, and Brazilian traffic was coordinated by the French section of In 7/VI [748] and was carried out by various field signal intelligence units: from 1939-1942, by Feste 3; from 1942 to 1944, by FAK 624, and from

[744] I 160 p 3

[745] I 58 p 5

[746] I 176 p 3

[747] I 84 p 3

[748] I 78 p 10

1944 by FAK 624 and Feste 12. The amount of traffic read in these units was evidently small enough to be handled satisfactorily by the personnel stationed there. Graupe stated that Spanish military transpositions and also a Spanish digit system with variants were read. Of seven Brazilian systems known, five were read. Most of the systems were used between Brazil and the United States and were signed by Ciudada.[749]

81. Work on Italian traffic 1941-1944-- From the beginning of the war, the security of Italian systems was a matter of constant concern to the Germans. An Italian section under Captain Dr. Fiala was set up in In 7/VI to check the security of Italian traffic, particularly from Italy to North Africa. The Germans feared that troop movements of the German Army to North Africa were being betrayed by the insecurity of the Italian systems.[750]

As early as 1941, Dr. Fiala paid a visit to Rome to notify the Italians of the weaknesses of their systems and to request greater security.[751] The visit, however, made little impression on the Italians who remained confident of their own systems.[752] An attempt to improve Italian security as well as to demonstrate the use of IBM machinery for cryptanalysis probably lay behind the German invitation in 1942 for an Italian cryptanalyst to visit the IBM section of In 7/VI.[753] Captain Bigi, one of the cryptanalysts of the Italian Army, was sent but his report did not result in any changes in Italian cryptography. Captain Bigi's next visit to Berlin met only with coldness on the part of In 7/VI.[754] By late 1942, the general impression among the Germans was that the Italians were incapable of improving their own systems, even with Germans monitoring them,[755] and the Italian section of In 7/VI was disbanded in 1942 by order of Hitler.[756]

[749] IF 107 p 3
[750] I 78 p 11
[751] I 78 p 11
[752] IF 1524; IF 1519
[753] I 78 p 11
[754] IF 1517
[755] I 78 p 11
[756] I 100 p 2

164

In June 1943, however, with Italy's defection (from German viewpoint) to the Allies, work on Italian traffic was again started at In 7/VI.[757] The section in 1943 consisted only of the section head, Manaigo, and a small number of assistants. Herzfeld, who was transferred to the section in July, gave an account of the work of this section until November 1943 when it was again dissolved, this time by Major Lechner, head of In 7/VI.[758] The decision to disband the section the second time was justified by the fact that after the fall of Leros, no more Italian wireless messages could be intercepted and there was no traffic with which to continue work. The Germans assumed that the Allies had prohibited further Italian wireless transmissions.

During its brief existence from July to November 1943, the Italian section worked on two codes, the Ellade and Piave, which were being used by the Italians in that period. Great help in the solution of these codes was given by an Italian enciphering table which had been captured by some German Officers in Athens under dramatic circumstances.[759] With the aid of this and other captured cipher material from northern Italy, two codes, Ellade and Piave, were identified and their reciphering tables reconstructed. Later the Piave code with enciphering table and many messages were captured from northern Italy. Traffic was read on the Piave code. The Ellade code was partly reconstructed when the section was dissolved from lack of current traffic.

757 I 100 p 2

758 I 100 pp 2-4

759 When the news of Mussolini's arrest and the Italian armistice was received at the headquarters of KONA 4 in Athens, two German officers drove to the headquarters of the Italians in Odos Amerikis, Athens, walked into the Italian code office, and began to collect the material lying on the tables and to pack it into a case in front of the bewildered Italians. In the midst of this, a number of Italian officers came in and began shouting rather excitedly. After some controversy, the Germans thought it preferable to disappear quietly since the attitude of the Italians became too threatening. They did, however, carry with them what they had collected from the tables and sent it to the Italian section in Berlin.

DOCID: 3486746

We know that at the end of the war, KONA 7 in Italy was ordered to cover the traffic of Italian bands in northern Italy, but how much traffic was read or of what the traffic consisted is not known.

82. Work on Swedish traffic 1941-1944-- Work on Swedish Army traffic from 1941 to 1944 was handled by a special detachment of Feste 9 called Out Station Halden (Aussenstelle Halden) from the fact that is located in Halden. For administrative purposes the station was attached to the Halden Police.[760] The best account of the systems worked on is found in a report by Bartel, a German cryptanalyst who had formerly worked on these systems.[761] According to Bartel the following Swedish Army systems were worked on:

a. SRA 1, SRA 5: a revolving grille system. Numerous cases of compromises occurred and the system was continuously read. First broken in the spring or summer of 1943.
b. HGA grille: a more difficult system not read by NAA 11 or Feste 9 in Norway. Worked on by the German Foreign Office but without success.
c. SC 2: read in May 1943. A simple field code like Slidex.
d. SC 3:read in April 1943. Simple, partly alphabetical, 3-letter field code without reciphering.
e. SC 4: read in June 1943. 3-letter alphabetical code without recipher.

The first Swedish cipher machine (Schwedische Maschine 1,abbreviated SM 1), was worked on in Norway in 1944 and was identified as a small Hagelin like the M-209.[762] Messages were read at Halden with crib, by errors in the cryptography, or by having two messages in the same key. The second machine (SM 2) was thought to be a "large Hagelin" machine. Two copies of the traffic on this machine were made, one for In 7/VI, one for the station at Halden.[763] Friedrich, a member of the station at Halden, thinks that some SM 2 traffic was read.[764] The intelligence gained from the breaking of traffic of SM 1 and the simple field codes allowed the Germans to build up a complete tactical picture of the Swedish Army

760 I 55 p 9

761 IF 120 p 5

762 I 142 p 4

763 IF 149 p 2

764 IF 149 p 2

during the late years of the war, but neither the high grade grille, HGA, nor the large Swedish machine was solved.[765]

83. Work on Southeastern traffic 1941-1944---Southeastern cryptanalysis was handled at In 7/VI by the Balkan section under the leadership of Bailovic and in the field by KONA 4. KONA 4 had been stationed in the Balkan area during the entire period of the war, and in addition to its regular task of intercepting the traffic emanating from Syria and North Africa, it had been given the task of monitoring the traffic of the occupied countries in the Balkan area. The Balkan countries whose systems were worked on by In 7/VI and KONA 4 were: Greece, Hungary, Romania, Yugoslavia, Albania, Turkey, and Bulgaria. The work done on the traffic of each of these countries is given below.

84. Work on Greek traffic 1941-1944-- Nearly all of our information concerning Greek systems comes from a report on Greek systems by Dr. Otto Karl Winkler who was a translator and cryptanalyst with KONA 4 from the spring of 1941 to May 1945.[766]

According to Dr. Winkler, work on Greek systems started in 1941 when KONA 4 was stationed in Bucharest. The first system broken was a Greek Air Force system which consisted of a single transposition sent in 3-letter groups. Dr. Winkler stated that nearly all messages were read by the use of stereotyped beginnings. Although the messages were of insignificant value, a continuous check on officer personalities, deliveries of stores and information concerning airfields contributed to tactical knowledge of the Greek forces.

KONA 4 worked at this time also on Greek Army and Navy messages, but without success until the conquest of Greece. At that time, Winkler stated, 'Codes' were captured which were used by the Greeks during the attack on Crete.[767]

[765] I 55 p 9

[766] I 70

[767] I 170 p 2

DOCID: 3486746

The only other Greek system mentioned as having been attacked in 1941 was a 5-letter code with a cyclic recipherment which Buggisch says he worked on at In 7/VI. Solutions were becoming rapid when the Greek campaign ended.[768]

After KONA 4 moved its Evaluation Center to Athens in May 1941, no more work was done by KONA 4 on Greek systems until the withdrawal of NAAS 4 from Athens in the autumn of 1943. At this time Greek Partisan traffic began to be intercepted. In the spring of 1944, KONA 4 gave Winkler the task of forming a small Greek unit to handle traffic of the Greek People's Army of Liberation ("ELAS"). The unit consisted of six persons, chief among whom were one Strobl, a cryptanalyst who worked on and solved a double transposition system of ELAS while Winkler concentrated on translating the traffic already readable. The work became more important and the unit, now increased to sixteen persons, was attached to a Close Range Signal Intelligence Platoon, NAZ G, newly formed in Salonika to cover wireless and line traffic of the Greek Partisans.

Winkler stated that in the beginning the Greeks sent their traffic in two figure substitution with alternative groups.[769] As few messages were sent on the same substitution, it took several days to break and read these substitutions. ELAS soon went over exclusively to letter traffic based on double transposition, which Strobl successfully solved largely through the aid given by the carelessness of the Greek cryptographers.

Winkler estimated that 50-60% of the traffic tackled by NAZ G was solved. From these messages, the unit was able to build up an almost complete picture of the organization and composition of the Greek People's Army of Liberation (ELAS) and the National Liberty Front ("EAM"). It also compiled lists of leading Greek personalities and officers and informed the competent German political and military authorities about many planned military and political actions, acts of sabotage, ambushes, dynamitings, etc. In addition, the messages provided information about the exact location of Allied airfields in

[768] I 58 p 6

[769] I 170 p 5

168

DOCID: 3486746

the Greek mountains, about the position, strength, and activity of the Allied military missions and various British commando troops, about Greek internal and inter-allied crises and struggles, about the British tactics for the occupation of Greece, etc.[770] Work on Greek systems ceased on 15 October 1944 when NAZ G was transferred to Sarajevo.[771]

85. Work on Hungarian traffic 1941-1944-- The Hungarians used the commercial model of the Enigma, and had the rotors for the machine made by the German firm of Konski and Krueger. This firm usually turned over the records of rotor wirings to the Armed Forces Radio Communications Branch (Ag WNV/Fu) which in turn gave them to In 7/VI. However, Hungarians connected with the firm took the rotors at night and changed the wirings enough to make the firm's records incorrect.[772] No effort appears to have been made on the part of the Germans to recover the wirings or to prevent the sabotage. It is difficult to suppose that the Germans could have been so easily duped had they wished to press the matter. Evidently, they did not consider the traffic worth causing embarrassment to the Hungarians.

With the onset of war, however, the Germans grew more cautious, particularly with the movement of German troops through Hungary.[773] During the spring and summer of 1941, the radio traffic of the Hungarian Railway Administration was monitored from the Fixed Intercept Station at Tulin. The code being used at that time by the railways was a turning grille (Raster Code) with permanent squares which could be turned in four different positions, and reversed to give four additional positions. The code was solved by Doering of the mathematical section of In 7/VI.[774] After the check on the railway authorities had proved that they were dependable, interception was stopped.[775]

[770] I 170 p 6

[771] I 170 p 7

[772] I 84 p 3

[773] IF 126 p 10

[774] I 58 p 7

[775] IF 126 p 10

Watch on Hungarian traffic was dropped from 1941 to 1943 because of the high priority given to Russian traffic.[776] In 1943, however, interest again developed and a detail was sent from Feste 6 (the former Fixed Intercept Station at Tulln) to Slovakia near Pressburg, Hungary to monitor Hungarian traffic.[777] Some tenseness in the relations of Germany and Hungary may be reflected by the fact that all members of the detail wore civilian clothing. At that time also, In 7/VI began to resume its work on Hungarian traffic. Count Esterhazy of the Balkan section began work on a Hungarian code and turning grille;[778] Teuchtler and Seper are said to have worked on Hungarian messages enciphered with a two figure substitution key.[779]

Work on Hungarian traffic was done by the Balkan section of In 7/VI only when the Army thought it necessary to check up on the Hungarian allies, but the attempts which were made were apparently successful. The solution in 1941 by Doering of the Hungarian grille, while not of great strategic or tactical importance, is characterized by Buggisch as 'brilliant'.[780]

86. Work on Rumanian traffic 1941-1944-- Very little is known of the work of the Balkan section on Rumanian traffic from 1941-1944. According to Mettig, the monitoring of Rumanian traffic ceased in 1941 because of high priority given to Russian traffic.[781] In 1941, however, monitoring appears to have resumed. Kotschy and Boscheinen of In 7/VI state that Rumanian traffic was completely monitored at that time, and that the Balkan section was reading a transposition system which was decoded with comparative ease.[782] Other references to Rumanian systems are found in Herzfeld's brief statement that Schmidt, Karl, and Wagner of the Balkan section were working on a Rumanian diplomatic code consisting of 5 or 6 figure groups;[783] and in

[776] I 78 p 11

[777] IF 126 p 10

[778] I 100 p 4

[779] I 100 p 5

[780] I 58 p 7

[781] I 78 p 11

[782] IF 126 p 4

[783] I 100 p 5

170

Keller's statement that KONA 4's Evaluation Center while at Belgrade from September to December 1944 worked on Rumanian messages.[784]

87. Work on Yugoslav traffic 1941-1944-- With the insistence of the German government that Yugoslavia align itself with Nazi policy in the spring of 1941, and the consequent wave of Yugoslav national resistance, the Balkan section of In 7/VI and KONA 4 undertook the heavy burden of monitoring the various types of Yugoslav traffic.
These types were:

a. the traffic of the friendly Croatian Regular Army (Domobrani) and the Secret Police of that Army (Ustashi), military units of the puppet government established by the Germans in 1941;
b. the traffic of the Chetniks under General Mihailovitch who were resisting German aggression;
c. the traffic of the Yugoslav Partisans under Marshal Tito;
d. the traffic of the Croatian Resistance Movement led by Dr. Matchek.

When the German government established the puppet government of Croatia in 1941, the Croats were given the commercial model of the Enigma for use by their Army and Secret Police.[785] The traffic of these units was read by the Balkan section currently without any delay. According to Buggisch, the solution of this traffic was not an outstanding cryptanalytic achievement for the following reasons:

a. the machine used was the K model with three wheels and no stecker;
b. the wheels of the machine were wired for the Croats by the firm of Konski and Krueger which habitually gave the wirings to the Armed Forces Radio Communications, which in turn gave them to In 7/VI;
c. A single key was used throughout the entire Croat Army and area, and this consisted of a list of 100 settings per month;
d. the ringstellung of the wheels remained at AAA;
e. the wheel order 1,2,3 was always used.

[784] I 74 p 2

[785] I 92 p 2

Just to make sure, however, adds Buggisch, "the Germans paid for one of the first keys used, and with this decoded traffic were able to establish stereotypes and solve almost 100% of the traffic from the first."[786] Although Buggisch did not recall the contents in detail, he stated that there were some interesting passages about actions against Tito. He also stated that the Germans had considered equipping the Croats with the plugboard Enigma, but that they decided against this since they believed the corrupt Croats would continue to sell the keys to British agents.[787] In that case, the Germans would have to pay for the keys used by the Croats instead of solving them as they could with the commercial Enigma.

Hentze of In 7/VI states that the Balkan section was successful with a double transposition used by the Croats but nothing more is known of this system.[788]

Herzfeld states that the Domobrani and Ustashi used a five figure code based on a former Yugoslav military code.[789] Evidence is lacking about the actual results obtained but it is probable that the system was solved since the former Yugoslav code was known.

Solution of the systems of General Mihailovitch and Marshall Tito was divided between a unit of KONA 4 in Belgrade and the Balkan section of In 7/VI. The breaking of easy guerilla techniques, particularly the solution of daily recipherings, was carried on at Belgrade by a special detachment which had served in 1941 under Wollny as an evaluation center for Section III Armed Forces Radio Communications Branch (Amtsgruppe Wehrmachtnachrichten Verbindungen, Abteilung Funkwesen, Gruppe III, abbreviated "AgWNV/Fu III" or "Fu III"). With the assumption by the unit of work against the enemies Tito and Mihailovitch, the detachment came under Army control and was attached to KONA 4 which had its Evaluation Center at that time in Belgrade.[790]

[786] I 92 p 2

[787] I 92 p 3

[788] I 113 p 5

[789] I 100 p 4

[790] I 115 p 8

172

DOCID: 3486746

The solution of the more difficult systems was carried on at In 7/VI by the Balkan section under the immediate supervision of Bailovic, a former employee of the Austrian cryptanalytic bureau and specialist in Slavic traffic. Bailovic is named throughout TICOM sources as the specialist in the systems of Tito and Mihailovitch.[791] Unfortunately, he was not interrogated personally.

Herzfeld, a member of the Balkan section of In 7/VI from 1941 to the capitulation, has written in two reports, I 52 and I 69, a full discussion of the Yugoslav systems worked on by that section. The traffic of Mihailovitch was entirely double transposition with fixed key length and key word.[792] These were regularly, if somewhat slowly, solved at In 7/VI with the aid of stereotyped phrases, frequency charts, and other well known cryptanalytic methods. Herzfeld states that it took one to three days to break a single message.

The systems of Tito were far more varied, most of them of Russian origin.[793] In I 69, Herzfeld lists among the Tito systems broken at In 7/VI:

a. a simple letter or two figure substitution system used for enciphering messages sent by brigades and partisan units to Tito divisions in 1944;
b. a simple substitution key with short reciphering set used below division level in 1944;
c. simple two figure substitution key with nulls and short reciphering set used below division in northern and western Yugoslavia and Bosnia in 1944, possibly also in Serbia and Macedonia;
d. multi-columnar substitution key used for traffic between divisions and brigades in Slovenia, western Croatia, western Bosnia in 1944;
e. an Albanian multiple substitution key used by Tito partisans of Albanian nationality;
f. variable substitution key with short reciphering set, the main cipher above division until June 1944.

[791] IF 126 Appendix 2; I 51 p 5; IF 120 p 8

[792] I 52 p 2

[793] I 52 p 5

173

The system which succeeded the variable substitution key with short reciphering set was called Tito's "Novo Sifra." It was used after June 1944 above division level and was not broken by In 7/VI. Herzfeld claims that it could have been broken with sufficient traffic and close scrutiny.

In the autumn of 1944, work on Tito traffic was increased. Besides the unit stationed in Belgrade under Wollny, the Evaluation Center of KONA 4 was moved from Athens to Belgrade and began work on Tito ciphers.[794] The Close Range Signal Intelligence Platoon, NAZ G, which had been working on Greek Partisan traffic was also moved from Saloniki to Sarajevo to cover Yugoslav traffic.[795]

The only reference to the work of the Balkan section of In 7/VI on Croatian Resistance Movement systems is the note by Kotschy and Boscheinen that this traffic was decoded mainly by KONA 4 and was rechecked by the Balkan section of In 7/VI.[796]

In general, it may be said that the work on Yugoslav systems was successful. The systems of Tito and Mihailovitch formed the most important part of the work of the Balkan section and received the personal attention of the head of the section, Bailovic.

88. Work on Turkish traffic 1941-1944-- Both the intercept and the decoding of Turkish traffic was handled largely by signal units subordinate to KONA 4. The Close Range Signal Intelligence Platoon, NAZ "T", which was stationed at Graz, worked only on Turkish traffic.[797] At first it had intercepted Turkish Navy and Merchant Marine traffic as well as Army and Police traffic, but certain disagreements arose with the German Navy over the interception of the Navy and Marine traffic and this was abandoned.[798]

794 I 170 p 7

795 I 170 p 7

796 IF 126 p 4

797 IF 171 p 4

798 IF 126 p 9

The police traffic of Turkey is described as:[799]

a. simple transposition used by the police departments of Ankara, Edirne, Istanbul, Izmir for police matters only;
b. two letter or figure code used for police counter-intelligence with police agents;
c. two or three letter code used for agent traffic.

The Turkish Army Codes were mainly transposition codes with a key word, sent in five letter groups preceded by a four figure number.[800] All of these systems were decoded by NAZ T, and were sent to In 7/VI simply for the purpose of checking all work.[801]

One special Turkish code is mentioned as having been read by the Germans either of In 7/VI or NAZ T -- the special code used by the President of Turkey while sailing on the State Yacht, the Savarona. This code was used in 1943 for radio messages while the President was on the yacht, and not thereafter.[802]

Sometime in 1942/43, In 7/VI received from the Research Bureau of Goering (the Forschungsamt, abbreviated "FA") the mission of solving certain Turkish diplomatic traffic. This the Balkan section did under the supervision of Bailovic, and the decoded traffic was sent to the Research Bureau. Kotschy and Boscheinen state that the traffic was used by military attaches for their reports from Russia, Bulgaria, and Italy, and that it was read continually by In 7/VI.[803] We know from other sources that this traffic proved to be a very valuable source of information concerning Russia. Mettig remembers a number of reports from the winter of 1943-44 on the Russian military situation and the preparations for an offensive.[804] Despite many warnings from British sources that the traffic was being read, Turkey failed to change the system, and the reading of Turkish diplomatic traffic remained a constant source of information.[805]

[799] IF 126 pp 12-13

[800] IF 126

[801] IF 126 p 9

[802] IF 126

[803] IF 126 p 9

[804] I 96 p 14

[805] I 96 p 14

89. Work on Bulgarian traffic 1941-1944-- There was very little work done on the traffic of Bulgaria during the war. According to Kotschy and Boscheinen, the traffic of the Bulgarian military attaches was decoded.[806] Herzfeld states that Thiele of the Balkan section worked on a Bulgarian cipher but no details are known.[807]

90. Work on Agents' traffic 1941-1944-- The Agents' section of In 7/VI was established in 1942. Before that time, the activities of this section which consisted of radio security inside Germany and monitoring of illegal transmissions had been carried on by Section III of the Armed Forces Radio Communication Branch (Amtsgruppe Wehrmacht Nachrichten Verbindungen, Funkwesen Gruppe III, abbreviated "AgWNV/Fu III" or "Fu III").[808] In 1942, however, it was seemed necessary to establish a deciphering section specializing in agents' ciphers. Fu III wanted it set up within itself, but the Supreme Command of the Armed Forces and the Army High Command opposed the establishment of another cryptanalytic agency. As a result of their opposition, it was agreed to set up a section for agents' traffic within an existing cryptanalytic organization. In 7/VI was chosen because the Armed Forces could not spare the personnel. The Agents' section was thus attached to In 7/VI although it appears to have maintained the close relation with Fu III, housing itself near Fu III and moving with it in November 1943 to Jueterbog.[809]

The most complete account of the work of the Agents' section, commonly called the Vauck section from its chief cryptanalyst, First Lt. Dr. Vauck, is found in a CSDIC report by Mettig (S. I. R. 1726) later re-published as I 115. Mettig gives great credit to the work of Dr. Vauck saying that this section achieved good results because of Vauck's leadership and his personal cryptanalytic successes. The section was not large, consisting of twenty people in the main section, ten at outposts in Paris and Brussels and other cities, and eight lent to the Polish section of the Signal Intelligence Agency of the Supreme Command, Armed Forces (OKW/Chi). Recognized traffic was decoded in the outstations; the rest was sent to Berlin. All traffic, moreover, was sent to Berlin in duplicate.[810]

806 IF 126 p4

807 I 100 p5

808 I 115 p 2

809 I 115 p3

810 I 111 p 5

176

The cryptanalytic methods employed by the Vauck section differed from normal methods of solution because of the peculiar nature of Agents' systems.[811] Some of the achievements of the Vauck section are outlined in the following pages.

91. Work on Czech Agents' Traffic-- The Vauck section worked on Agents' traffic of the Czechoslovak Resistance Movement.[812] Mettig believed that the breaking in 1942/43 of two links running to England made possible the arrest of British agents in Czechoslovakia. The greatest success was achieved by intercepting the wireless communications of the Czech Resistance Movement in London. This was the only case in which Mettig is certain that it was possible for the Vauck section to break into an agent network by purely cryptanalytic means, and this was largely through breaches of security on the part of the Czech chief. After the system had been broken, the book for enciphering was found and the key recovered. In September 1942, the Czechs were about to go over to a new system but were foolish enough to name in the old system the book to be used for enciphering in the new system. Contents of messages solved on this link were nearly always concerned with reports on the political situation and activities of the Czech Resistance Movement, and were so important that for a long time the W/T traffic was allowed to continue unhindered.

92. Work on Yugoslav Agents' traffic-- Work on Yugoslav Agents' traffic was carried on by a detachment in Belgrade under Lt. Wollny. This detachment had beeh under Group III of the Armed Forces Radio Communication Branch (Fu III) but was attached in 1942 to KONA 4 because all fighting against hostile organizations such as Mihailovitch and Tito was directed by the Army.[813] The work of this group has already been described under the Balkan section's work on Yugoslav traffic, where it properly belongs since the traffic which was not solved in the detachment was sent to the Balkan section of In 7/VI for solution.

93. Work on Agents' traffic in Southern Franca and Spain-- Agents' traffic in southern France and Spain emanated largely from USA, British and Spanish Republican agents who were in

811 I 115 pp 4-5

812 I 115 p 8

813 I 115 pp 8-9

radio contact with stations in Spain. To cope with this traffic, a camouflaged branch station was set up in Madrid and the intercepted traffic passed to Vauck's section. According to Mettig, the results of the traffic were very good although no details are known.[814]

94. Work on Russian Agents' traffic-- Mettig knew of three important Russian Agents' network: the "Red 3" (Rote 3), the Schulze-Boysen net operating in Berlin in 1942, and two links running from Brussels. The last named links were, as far as Mettig knew, not solved.[815]

The story of the work on the "Red 3" net is most interesting. In addition to Mettig's account, we have two memoranda written by Fenner, the chief cryptanalyst of the Signal Intelligence Agency of the Armed Forces.[816] Fenner reported that on 23 February 1943 his agency was asked by Vauck's section to collaborate in work on certain messages of Russian agents on the "Red 3" net. By the end of March, the Vauck section had furnished Fenner's cryptanalysts, Novopashni, Trappe, and Schmidt, with all the traffic in that system since September 1941 so that a start was made on solution. Fundamental findings were communicated to In 7/VI which enabled that organization to break into the system roughly at the time as did Fenner's group. After the initial break in, it was agreed that In 7/VI should continue to work on the system, and Mettig stated that from this help the Vauck section discovered that the system was based on a book text.[817] In the autumn of 1944, Vauck is said to have told Mettig that the exact sending position of this net had been determined in Switzerland. A raid was planned but had to be cancelled as Swiss authorities had forestalled the Germans. The station, according to Mettig, was evacuated and destroyed before the Germans could take action.[818]

[814] I 115 p 7

[815] I 115 p 7

[816] D 60 pp 16-20

[817] I 115 p 8

[818] I 115 p 10

The story of the second Russian net, the Schulze-Boysen net operating from Berlin in 1942, is equally dramatic.[819] This net received its name from First Lt. Dr. Schulze-Boysen whose house was the center of a Communist inspired espionage agency operating on a large scale. When the first inroad into this traffic was made by the Vauck section, Dr. Lenz, one of the members of the Vauck section, mentioned the name Schulze-Boysen to another member of the Vauck section named Haymann who frequented the Schulze-Boysen house. Haymann warned Mrs. Schulze-Boysen. Subsequently, both Haymann and Dr. Lenz were arrested, and Haymann condemned to death. Lenz was released and transferred to an out-station in Paris, since all that could be proved against him was that he mentioned the name Schulze-Boysen to Haymann. With the aid of knowledge obtained from decoded traffic, the Gestapo made arrests of from seventy-nine to eighty people of whom seventy were condemned to death. The case was kept strictly secret because some of the accused were employed in various war agencies and were betraying secrets to Russia.[820]

95. <u>Work on Polish Resistance Movement traffic</u>-- The most notable results in the Agents' section were achieved in the interception and solution of the systems used by the Polish Resistance Movement, particularly during the Polish uprising in Warsaw in 1944.[821] From information passed on this system, the dispositions of the Polish liberation troops as well as friction between them and the Russians could be established. It was possible, moreover, to solve all wireless traffic which the Polish government in London carried on with its organizations in Poland. In order to preserve secrecy and to insure quicker delivery of the decodes, eight members of the Vauck section were transferred in the autumn of 1943 to the Polish section of the Signal Intelligence Agency of the Supreme Command, Armed Forces (OKW/Chi)

[819] I 115 p 10

[820] See Volume 4, Chapter VI

[821] I 115 p 9

for work there. The clear text was published by the Armed Forces in their bulletins and was given extremely restricted distribution. To insure complete radio intercept coverage, the Armed Forces Agency (OKW/Chi) ordered its station at Lauf also to intercept the traffic. First Lt. Schubert, a cryptanalyst of GdNA, wrote a brief account of the systems used by the Polish National Resistance Movement in which he stated that systems 006, 117, 118, and 181 were broken and that others were worked on. Most of them were simple two figure substitutions used without an indicator, with some variations in development and the use of basic keys or key phrases.[822]

96. Work on German Traitors' Traffic-- Mettig stated that he once saw a report concerning a German who transmitted by wireless to England details of a newly constructed signals shelter in Berlin urgently requesting that it be bombed. No details of these systems are known.[823]

97. Linguistic Research 1941-1944-- Linguistic research during the years 1941-1944 was carried on at In 7/VI by a section designated as the Linguistic Research Section (Sprachforschungsreferat). Mettig listed this section as one of the twelve sections of In 7/VI in 1942 and named Koehler as its head.[824] Koehler remained head of this group throughout the war, and in November 1944 the section was transferred with Koehler from GdNA to the Signal Intelligence Agency of the Supreme Command of the Armed Forces (OKW/Chi).[825] Mettig claimed that it was contemplated that the members of the linguistic research section would advise the cryptanalysts on language problems and direct all matters of the Armed Forces concerning foreign languages. Although the plans were never realized, the nature of the work of the section can be inferred from these plans.

[822] I 26 pp 14-15
[823] I 115 p 10
[824] I 78 p 6
[825] I 96 p 15

98. Mathematical Research 1941-1944-- The Mathematical Research Section was headed by Dr. Pietsch, who, according to Mettig, collected in this section the best available mathematical brains.[826] The work of the section was twofold:

a. the investigation of all unsolved traffic from the various sections of In 7/VI so long as it was necessary to achieve an inroad by purely analytical means;

b. the investigation of the security of current German Army systems.

To achieve these purposes, three subsections were found necessary:

a. a subsection designated "F" for the German word for research, Forschung. This subsection was headed by von Denffer and handled research on foreign systems.[827]

b. a subsection designated "7". This subsection was headed by First Lt. Lueders and dealt with the security of German Army hand systems.

c. a subsection designated "13". This subsection was headed by Dr. Doering and dealt with the security of German Army machine systems.

99. Cryptanalytic work of subsection "F" 1941-1944-- Subsection "F" of the mathematical section appears to have done some excellent work in the solution of the more simple machine systems used by foreign countries. The following examples of solution may be cited:

a. The discovery of theoretical methods of solving traffic in the Russian "K-37" (a B-211 type cipher machine) after capture of a model in 1941.[828]

[826] I 78 p 6

[827] I 78 p 6

[828] I 58 p 5; I 176 p 3

b. Development of a technique for converting the relative settings, recovered for wheels of Converter M-209 on days when such solution was possible through reading of some of the traffic, into absolute settings, thus making it possible to read all the traffic sent on those days.[829]
c. The discovery in 1943 of theoretical methods of solving messages sent in the French B-211 cipher machine.[830]
d. The reading of de Gaulle traffic enciphered by the C-36.[831]
e. The solution in 1944 of the Swedish Hagelin, the BC 38, by Marquardt and Hilburg.[832]

Doering's solution in 1941 of the Hungarian grille should be counted as one of the achievements of this section. As has been pointed out, the section had no success whatever with the large cipher machines such as the British Typex, the USA SIGABA, and large Swedish Hagelin. Hentze of GdNA states that the mathematical section worked on Russian 4 and 5 figure enciphered code with partial success.[833]

The outstanding men of this section were named by Buggisch as Hilburg, Rinow, and Wuenoche.

Subsections "7" and "13" of the mathematical section were concerned with security studies of German Army hand and machine cipher systems. They will be treated in Chapter VIII, which deals with German Army cryptographic systems.

100. Use of IBM in Cryptanalysis, 1941-1944-- The IBM section of In 7/VI was derived from the IBM section set up in 1939/40 by the German Security Agency (In 7/IV), at the suggestion

[829] I 58 p 6; I 113 p 6

[830] I 160 p 6

[831] I 160 p 6; I 58 p 5. The C-36 had been solved previously in 1940 with the aid of the Signal Intelligence Agency of the Supreme Command Armed Forces, OKW/Chi.

[832] I 176 p 3; I 160 p 6; I 58 p 5

[833] I 113 pp 5-6

182

of the mathematicians and former actuaries of this section.[834] It was natural that in 1942, when the study of the security of German Army systems was transferred from In 7/IV to In 7/VI, the use of IBM machinery for security studies was transferred to In 7/VI and quickly adapted for cryptanalytic work on foreign systems. The machinery used by In 7/VI was mostly of German make, although a number of captured French IBM machines were included.[835] The section, headed by Schenke, consisted in 1943 of thirty or forty women key punchers, and twenty to thirty soldier mechanics.[836] We have no exact evidence as to the number or types of machines used although Hentze states that in 1944 there were 30 key punchers and 2 tabulators.[837] The special contribution of In 7/VI to IBM work was the adaptation of the machines to various tasks by special wirings.[838] In 1943, a special workshop for the development of improved wirings was set up with the IBM firm at Lichterfeld.[839] The major success obtained was the work on the Russian 5-figure traffic.[840] In the early stages of the Russian campaign, it was comparatively simple to establish depths in these messages without the use of IBM, but by 1943 IBM machinery was indispensable for locating depths.

Buggisch declared that no tasks were undertaken by the IBM section which could have been done by 100 people. He maintained that lack of IBM machinery spurred the analysts of the Signal Intelligence Service of the Armed Forces (OKW/Chi) to the development of new and better types of analytic devices while In 7/VI remained content with inferior adaptations of IBM machinery. The Army's general attitude concerning IBM machinery is hinted at in Buggisch's statement that the Enigma could probably be solved by a large enough array of IBM machinery,[841] but it never occurred to him, evidently, that such would be contemplated by the enemy.

[834] I 67 p 2

[835] I 78 p 6

[836] I 67 p 2

[837] I 113

[838] I 67 p 2

[839] I 67 p 2

[840] I 58 p 6

[841] I 92 p 5

It should be noted that the IBM section of In 7/VI was at least toward the last hampered by the fact that their machines were outworn, outmoded and irreplaceable. The factories which had been producing parts were bombed out and, as the machines wore out, their work became inaccurate. In some instances, work by machine was abandoned. An example of this is cited by Mettig in his discussion of the attempt in 1944/5 by the Signal Intelligence Service of the Armed Forces to provide units below regimental level with signal tables. The values were to be set up by the IBM section of GdNA (formerly of In 7/VI) but it transpired that the IBM machines had been overworked in the last years and were not functioning properly.[842] As a result the trigrams were not being reciprocally enciphered and other methods of producing them were developed. In early 1945, the IBM section of GdNA was offered to Signal Intelligence Agency of Supreme Command of the Armed Forces (OKW/Chi), but Mettig states that the matter was never clinched because of the confusion at the end of the war.[843]

101. German Army cryptanalytic effort 1945-- With the establishment of the GdNA in late 1944, all operational cryptanalysis was carried on by sections 2, 3, and 4 of Group IV of the GdNA. Section 2, headed by Kneschke, dealt with the deciphering of western European traffic and probably also with Hungarian, Rumanian, and Italian ciphers. There were three subsections:[844]

2a. headed by Dr. Werner Schulz, dealt with British, USA, and Swedish systems,
2b. headed by O/Insp Otto Kuehn, handled French systems
2c. headed by Kneschke, processed Balkan systems.

[842] I 96 p 12

[843] I 96 p 13

[844] I 160 p 2

184

Section 3 was headed by Dettman and dealt with Russian systems, with four subsections:[845]

3a for Russian NKVD (Special Police) traffic,
3b for Russian Army traffic,
3c for Russian Partisan traffic,
3d for research on Russian systems in general.

Section 4 was devoted principally to statistical IBM work.

There is no record of any new or difficult systems being solved after late 1944. The main effort of the GdNA was apparently directed to the deciphering of systems already solved and to the simple necessity of finding a place to operate. From February 1945 until the capitulation, Group IV of the GdNA was constantly on the move seeking refuge in the south from the Allied advance.

[845] IF 123 p 10

DOCID: 3486746

VOLUME 4

Chapter VIII. German Army Cryptographic Systems

102. German Army cryptographic systems.--The German Army used three main types of cryptographic machines in its communications down through division: the Enigma, the teleprinter cipher attachment ("Schluesselzusatze," abbreviated "SZ"), and the cipher teleprinter ("Schluesselfernschreibmaschine," abbreviated "SFM").

The commercial type Enigma was introduced probably in 1925.[850] It was replaced in 1939 by the plugboard Enigma.[851]

The first teleprinter cipher attachment, the SZ-40 "original model," was introduced into the Army probably in 1940[852] although Dr. Huettenhain of the Signal Intelligence Agency of the Supreme Command Armed Forces (OKW/Chi) said that the Army had been experimenting with this type of cryptographic apparatus as early as 1937.[853] It was replaced by the SZ-40 "regular model," and this was succeeded by the SZ-42a and the SZ-42b, developed by Dr. Liebknecht of the Army Ordnance Development and Testing Group Signal Branch (Wa Pruef 7) and by Inspector Menzer and Dr. Huettenhain of the Signal Intelligence Agency of the Supreme Command Armed Forces (OKW/Chi).[854] The SZ-42c was also developed and 30 or 40 test sets built, but the apparatus was evidently not used.[855]

The first cipher teleprinter, the SFM T-52a, was introduced in 1939; improved models were called the SFM T-52b, c, d, and e. By the end of the war only models T-52 c, d, and e were in use. A one-time tape cipher teleprinter designated the SFM T-43 was introduced in 1943.

[850] I 31 p 17
[851] I 78 p 7
[852] I 31 p 14
[853] I 31 p 7
[854] I 57 pp 5-6; I 45 p 19
[855] I 31 p 13

186

The German Army used hand ciphers below division. After World War I, and before 1942, some of the hand systems of the Army, as listed by Dr. Huettenhain of the Signal Intelligence Agency of the Supreme Command Armed Forces (OKW/Chi) were:[856]

a. A monoalphabetic type substitution using a keyword mixed alphabet in a 5 x 5 square.

b. A "comb-transposition" ("Kammwurfel").

c. A "book key" ("Heftschluessel").

d. A double transposition (DOPPEL WUERFEL, abbreviated "4-S-40"). This system was used until 1926 or 1927.

e. The "Single Playfair" (KASTE-SCHLUESSEL, abbreviated "TS-42").

f. The "Double Playfair" (DOPPEL-KASTE-SCHLUESSEL, abbreviated "NS-42").

In 1942, subsection 7 of the Mathematical Section of In 7/VI declared that all hand systems currently used by the German Army were insecure.[857] Since the Field Army had no reserve hand systems, In 7/VI was ordered to cooperate with In 7/IV in producing new systems.[858] The following hand systems were evolved and used by the German Army from 1942-1945:

a. Three letter field codes ("Signaltafeln") with or without enciphering tables ("Schluesseltafeln").[859]

b. Single transposition using grille ("Rasterschluessel 44," usually called "Raster").[860]

c. Double transposition ("Rasterersatzverfahren").

Under field conditions many makeshift systems were employed, such as monoalphabetic substitution, transposition consisting only of reversing the order of the letters of the plain text, and whatever the particular radio operators might adopt by agreement among themselves.

856 I 31 p 17
857 I 20 p 3
858 I 78 p 13
859 I 20 p 3
860 I 20 p 3

1587

For weather reporting, the Army used two types of systems until 1945:

a. The "Barbara Code" ("Barbaraschluessel") consisting of figure cards for encoding artillery meteorological reports for Army and anti-aircraft units.

b. Weather substitution tables, for enciphering meteorological reports in the Reich Weather Service (Reich Wetterdienst).

Lt. Col. Mettig stated that the Barbara Code was replaced in 1945 by the "Raster."[861]

103. Preparation and distribution of cryptographic keys.--The history of the preparation, printing, and distribution of cryptographic keys by the German Army was outlined by Fricke, a member of In 7/IV and latterly of the Signal Intelligence Agency of the Armed Forces (OKW/Chi).[862] According to Fricke, the keys for the Army were produced at the beginning of the war on In 7/IV's own press. The number of personnel required was small (about twenty people in all), since only enigma, weather and book keys (Heftschluessel) were printed.

With the introduction of the SZ 40/42 and other cryptographic systems which required keys, the amount of work entailed in the preparation, printing, and distribution of keys became too great for In 7/IV alone. In 1942, therefore, the production of key table manuscripts was transferred to the IBM section of In 7/VI, and the printing to the Reich press in Berlin; In 7/IV was confined to reading proof and distributing the finished product.

At the time of the bombing attacks on Berlin in November 1943, the printing press and all key material of In 7/IV were destroyed. The key producing section of In 7/IV was then moved from Berlin into emergency quarters prepared some weeks before in the Army Signal School (Heeres Nachrichten Schule) at Halle/Saale. During this period, private printing firms were increasingly drawn on for the production of keys; first, because the Reich printing press could not meet the requirements; and secondly, because decentralization was increasingly necessary to avoid bombing. About twenty firms in the central German area were given contracts for the printing of keys. The high number was largely attributable to the introduction in 1944 of the Stencil System 44 (Rasterschluessel 44).

861 I 96 p 12

862 I 36

In May 1944, the key producing section of In 7/IV was transferred to the Hindenburg barracks at Dresden, where Major Dr. Metzger assumed direction. This remained the situation until 1 November 1944 when all tasks of producing, printing, and distributing of keys for the Army were transferred from In 7/IV to Section IIIa of the Signal Intelligence Agency of the Armed Forces (OKW/Chi/IIIa). This section was established at Dresden in the headquarters which the key preparation section of In 7/IV had occupied. In March 1945, Section IIIa was transferred from Dresden to the Army Signal School at Halle/Saale because of the approach of the Russians. Work was never begun, however; and on 12 April, keys and material for producing them were loaded on trucks to be sent to southern Germany. Keys left at Halle were destroyed by the Germans at the approach of the United States Army.[863]

104. German Army Security Studies.--Before 1939, the Army High Command had no security organization of its own. Questions of security concerning Army systems were referred to the Codes and Ciphers Section of the German Defense Ministry. Huettenhain stated that he and Menzer, as members of the Codes and Ciphers Section, did a security study on the SZ 40 ("original model") and found that it could be solved in two days.[864] This led to its improved form.

In 1939, the Army High Command established its own Signal Security Agency (In 7/IV), which functioned as such until 1942. During the period of its activity, the Signal Security Agency (In 7/IV) examined the plugboard Enigma[865] from the point of view of security, and made security studies on two other cryptographs proposed for Army usage, the M 40 and SG 41.[866] The security study of the plugboard Enigma was occasioned by a suspicion roused during the Polish campaign in 1939 that the Poles were reading Enigma traffic.[867] Pietsch, Steinberg, and Bohm (mathematicians of In 7/IV) made security studies on the machine,

863 I 36 p 3

864 I 31 p 17

865 I 92 p 2

866 I 58 p 5. Buggish actually said "C-41" but doubless meant "SG-41." Both the M-40 and SG-41 are described from a cryptographic viewpoint in Volume 2 of this paper.

867 I 78 p 7

the results of which apparently set to rest any doubts about its security. The Army continued to use the system without change until Fricke (another mathematician of In 7/IV)[868] indicated that the Army's manner of using indicators led to an easy solution. At his recommendation, the indicator system was changed.[869]

The two machines proposed for Army use, the M-40 and SG-41, had been invented by Menzer, a member of the Signal Intelligence Agency of the Armed Forces (OKW/Chi). Security studies on the M-40 were made by Dr. Doering and Dr. Buggisch, mathematicians of In 7/IV[870] Dr. Buggisch stated that the studies proved the device to be moderately secure, but that it was never used because it was as bulky as the plugboard Enigma but could not print letters.[871] With regard to the SG-41, the studies made by In 7/IV showed it to be superior to the M-40, but Buggisch stated: "The Army hemmed and hawed and never did adopt it."[872]

In 1942, the responsibility for making security studies of German Army systems, and most of the personnel of In 7/IV who had worked on Army communications security testing, were transferred from In 7/IV to the Mathematical Section of In 7/VI. Pietsch, Steinberg, von Denffer, Hilburg, and Luzius were named among those transferred.[873]

The Mathematical Section of In 7/VI assigned security studies to two subsections: "7" and "13." Subsection "7" undertook the work on German hand systems; subsection "13," on German machine systems.[874] The first studies of subsection "7" on German hand systems proved that all hand systems currently used by the German Army were solvable. As a result, In 7/VI was ordered to collaborate with In 7/IV in the development of new systems for the Army.[875] Although In 7/VI would have preferred to establish this section within itself, where the preparation of systems would be done in close cooperation with cryptanalytic specialists, this point of view was not recognized by the Army and In 7/VI was ordered to send mathematicians back to In 7/IV. The mathematicians sent were Fricke, Jesse, and Kehren.[876] From that time on, subsection "7" confined itself to the study of hand systems handed to it by the Field Army. Mettig noted that the amateur systems with which the section dealt were very bad and betokened great ignorance on the part of the Field Army in regard to code and cipher security.[877]

Subsection "13," which was responsible for the security of

868 I 92 p 5
869 I 92 p 5; I 20 p 2
870 I 58 p 5
871 I 92 p 2
872 I 58 p 5
873 I 92 p 6
874 I 92 p 6
875 I 78 p 13
876 I 78 p 3

1987

German Army cryptographic machine systems, concentrated on security studies of the SFM T-52 teleprinters. SFM T-52a, b, and c were tested by Dr. Doering in the summer of 1942 and were shown to be easily solvable.[878] By the autumn of 1942, it was clear to the mathematicians of this subsection that SFM T-52c could not be made secure. Despite the warnings from the security unit, the Field Army continued to use SFM T-52c. They were particularly sure of it because they thought the land lines on which SFM T-52c messages passed could not be tapped by the enemy. Not until a cellar equipped to tap land lines was found in Paris in late 1942 did the Army consent to the improvement of the machine.[879] This improvement, the T-52d, was ready in early 1943 and was shown by Dr. Doering to be probably insecure. From his experiments with the T-52d evolved the T-52e, which was considered secure.[880]

Some investigation of the plugboard Enigma was carried on by subsection "13" although no definite conclusion was reached concerning its security. In 1943-44, definite proof was obtained from two Polish officers in a prison camp at Hamburg that the Poles had read the plugboard Enigma both before and for some time after the Polish campaign.[881] This proof corroborated the suspicions aroused at the time of the campaign in 1940. Two Army cryptanalysts, Pietsch and Doering, were sent to interrogate the Poles. Although the interrogations were said to have drawn a blank, it became evident that Polish cryptanalysts at Wicher had solved Enigma traffic, had gone to France after the Polish campaign and had continued their work there. Solution was said to have stopped sometime later. The mathematicians of subsection "13" believed that solution had ceased when the Field Army followed Fricke's indicator recommendations. The general result was that subsection "13" did not press the matter of Enigma security.

Subsection "13" had also been assisting in the design of Cipher Device 39 (Schluesselgeraet 39), an improved Enigma which was intended to employ a plugboard, changeable turnover rotors, pluggable reflecting wheels, and additional Hagelin-type drive wheels.[882] Buggisch stated these machines were his specialty. They were under construction at the Technische und Normalzeit firm at Frankfurt am Main at the time of the surrender.[883]

[878] I 58 p 2
[879] I 78 p 11
[880] I 78 p 12
[881] I 92 p 5
[882] I 58 p 6
[883] I 20 p 4

The responsibility for the security of German Army cryptographic systems remained with subsections "7" and "13" until November 1944, when it was turned over to the Signal Intelligence Agency of the Armed Forces (OKW/Chi). The Army then retained only the responsibility for seeing that the systems approved by OKW/Chi were properly used in the field.[884]

105. Attitude of the Field Army toward Security Studies.--The Field Army maintained an uncooperative attitude toward security studies made by the Mathematical Section of In 7/VI. Whenever the Field Army was asked to change a system, there was a storm of protest. All changes in methods were supposed to be enforced by the staff of the Army Communications Branch (Heeres Nachrichten Verbindungsabteilung, abbreviated HNV), and the nature of the results depended upon whether the officer at staff headquarters happened to know anything about cryptanalysis. Fricke said he usually did not.[885] Only with the greatest difficulty was the Field Army persuaded to change its methods.

One of the specific ways in which the Field Army consciously hampered progress in security studies was to refuse to furnish In 7/VI actual traffic. Fricke said that In 7/VI never knew how the Field Army actually used the systems which it approved. When In 7/VI asked for traffic for its studies, it was given specially prepared messages such as: "We are standing in Berlin and see the Polish infantry coming down the Frankfurt Allee."[886] However, the Field Army made a brief attempt in 1941 to provide the analysts with actual traffic. For this purpose a Signal Intelligence Regiment of the Replacement Army (Nachrichten Aufklaerung Abteilung/Chef der Heeresruestung und Befehlshaber des Ersatz Heeres, abbreviated NAA/Chef H Ruest u BdE) was formed. While two companies of this unit were to act as administrative units for personnel of In 7/VI, the third company was an intercept unit which worked in the field collecting material for the analysts. (Due to personnel shortage, however, this unit was dissolved in February 1942, and no subsequent attempt was made by the German Field Army to procure actual traffic for In 7/VI)[887]

As described in Paragraph 104, it was difficult to persuade the Field Army to accept as valid the security studies made by

884 D 68 pp 3-4

885 I 20 p 3

886 I 20 p 3

887 I 20 p 3

DOCID: 3486746

the cryptanalysts of In 7/VI. For instance, not until an entire cellar with excellent equipment for tapping land lines used by the T-52c was raided in Paris in early 1943, was the Army High Command persuaded that the security study made by In 7/VI had been valid.[888]

The attitude of the Field Army could be traced largely to the ignorance on all levels of matters pertaining to codes and cipher security. Fricke's remark that the staff officer of the HNV who controlled code and cipher methods usually knew nothing about cryptanalysis has already been mentioned. Mettig stated that the suggested systems handed to In 7/VI for scrutiny betrayed the lamentable ignorance of the Field Army.[889] Signal tables set up by the troops revealed serious cryptographic errors, such as the failure to change keywords for long periods.[890] In an attempt to correct this ignorance, In 7/VI gave lectures at the Army Signal School at Halle and issued instructions on code and cipher security. The situation, however, was never satisfactory. Buggisch aptly called it tragic-comic: When In 7/VI detected an insecurity, it was not able to achieve effective remedies; if In 7/VI wanted to install new devices, it had even more difficulties. The Army "hemmed and hawed" and never got around to acting.[891]

888 I 78 p 11
889 I 78
890 I 96
891 I 58 p 5

VOLUME 4

Chapter IX. Training of German Army Signal Troops

Paragraph

114. Training of Signal Recruits.--The Signal Intelligence Replacement and Training Battalion (Nachrichten Aufklaerungs Ersatz und Ausbildung Abteilung, abbreviated NAEUAA), which was located at Frankfurt/Main, was responsible for the training of German Army Signal recruits. It had control over Signal Intelligence Replacement and Training Companies in each Service Command (Wehrkreis) where basic training and some training in signal matters were given to the recruits.[895] In time of peace, basic training lasted for one year, signal training being taken up after the first three months. During the war, the time of basic training was shortened in order to place more troops more quickly in the field. Recruits were trained in direction finding, teletype operation, and simple field codes, and were then sent out into field units.[896] No special courses were conducted in the Replacement and Training Companies.

115. Training of Signal Technicians.--Most of the signal technicians were trained in specialist schools of various sorts. Schools for carrier frequency, switchboard operators, repair men, etc., were established by the Army and Division and Corps Signal Battalions and at Army Signal Depots.[897] Instructors were mainly non-commissioned officers who had had experience in the field.

116. Training of Specialists.--The Signal Interpreter Replacement and Training Battalion (Nachrichten Dolmetscher Ersatz

895 IF 250 p 2
896 IF 250 p 3
897 IF 250 p 3

194

und Ausbildungs Abteilung, abbreviated NDEUAA) was located at Halle/Saale.[898] This battalion was responsible for the training of signal interpreters who were to be employed in signal intercept units for radio and wireless monitoring. The battalion was divided into three companies: company one for Romance, company two for Slavic, and company three for Germanic languages. For matters of administration the battalion was divided into the following five platoons:[899]

1) cadre platoon (<u>Stammzug</u>) comprising cadre personnel, and instructors in military and intelligence technical matters.

2) instructor platoon (<u>Lehrzug</u>) comprising teachers and members of the instructor group.

3) training platoon (Ausbildungszug) comprising the students who were under instructions in some language.

4) alert platoon (<u>Marschzug</u>) comprising men who have passed their final examination and who are expecting to be sent into action.

5) pool (<u>Auffangkorporalschart</u>) comprising newcomers waiting for their entrance examination.

A rough estimate of the personnel shows that in 1944 there were about 350 to 400 men attending the various language classes. After the courses which lasted six weeks, the men were given a final examination. According to the results of this examination, they were assigned to one of the three following categories:[890]

S -- Speakers (<u>Sprachmittler</u>). These were people who spoke well and were able to make themselves understood, but who did not master the language in speaking and writing correctly.

U -- Translators (<u>Uebersetzer</u>). These were people who mastered the foreign language in writing, but were only fair in speaking.

D -- Interpreters (<u>Dolmetscher</u>). These were people who spoke and wrote the foreign language correctly and fluently and whose general education was up to a corresponding standard.

898 IF 105 p 5
899 IF 105 p 3
900 IF 105 p 5

Employment was assigned according to the category to which each person was assigned.

For persons of category "S," a special course in monitoring Allied radio communications was organized at Leipzig for English speaking personnel only. The course consisted of three weeks' daily instruction in the following subjects:[901]

1) USA and British organization of signal units
2) USA and British radio sets used at all levels
3) USA and British radio call signs
4) USA and British authorized abbreviations
5) USA and British message forms
6) USA and British fixed station and net operational methods
7) USA and British Army terminology

Each of the subjects was taught for one hour a day and had a brief examination. In most cases, the lectures were conducted in English to facilitate practice in this language.

117. Training of Signal Officers.--The Army Signal School at Halle (Heeres Nachrichten Schule, abbreviated HNS), conducted the course for officer candidates of the Signal Corps.[902] Emphasis here was in the first months evenly divided between technical and military subjects. The officer candidates were selected by their commanders in the field after having proved themselves in combat or in outstanding work in their specialty. All enlisted men were eligible, although the racial origin evidently played some part in the selection. One prisoner, for instance, states that he was not allowed to become an officer candidate because of a Jewish grandmother.[903]

After their selection, the men were given a four weeks course in tactics, Army regulations, customs, technical subjects, etc. Those who passed this preliminary course were sent to the Armed Forces Signal Troop School (Fuehrungs Nachrichtentruppen Schule, abbreviated FNS), where they were trained for three months in Signal Corps work.[904] From there they were sent into the field for a probation period as leaders of platoons. During this period of training, Colonel Grube states, many of the candidates lost their lives. A final three months at the Signal School at Halle brought with graduation the rank of Lieutenant. Failure

901 IF 131 p 4
902 IF 205 p 5
903 IF 127 p 1
904 IF 250 p 6

196

118. Training of German Army Cryptanalysts.--Nothing is known of the training of German Army cryptanalysts before 1939. Mettig states that when the Signal Intelligence Regiments (KONA) moved into the field in 1939, no cryptanalysts were available.[906] Colonel Radewig, the commander at that time of all intercept stations in the west, however, was able to procure a number of cryptanalysts from the Fixed Intercept Stations (Feste) around Berlin, and to this force he added a few mathematicians and linguists.[907] As a result, when the German offensive began in April 1940, the KONA's had a moderate supply of cryptanalytic personnel. The early years of the war, however, showed that many more cryptanalysts were needed. Provision to train these cryptanalysts was made by establishing a Training Section in In 7/VI under the leadership of Kuehn but Mettig stated that the work of the section was not fully exploited until 1942.[908] The section was located at Matthaikirchplatz 4 in Berlin until November 1943, when it was moved with the rest of the Agency to Jueterbog because of Allied bombings. In November 1944 the Training Section 7 of IN 7/VI became Section 5 of Group IV of the GdNA.[909] According to Graupe, the school consisted of about twenty officers with one hundred and twenty men, and about twelve women as stenographers.[910]

The course which lasted 10-12 weeks[911] is outlined in some detail in IF 122 pp 3-8. During the morning and for two or three afternoons a week, cryptography was studied from a syllabus. This syllabus included a brief history of cryptography, a general picture of the methods of encipherment, details of various means of encipherment and decipherment. During the remaining afternoons, the students evidently specialized in whatever field to which they were to be assigned. One prisoner of war, Gerd Coeler, states that during the afternoons he studied English military terms and abbreviations, studied the history and organization of the British Empire and the geography of England.[912] Karrenberg[913] outlines the course given for those who were specializing

905 IF 250 p 6
906 IF 78 p 4
907 I 78 p 4
908 I 78 p 7
909 IF 123 p 9
910 IF 127 p 2
911 IF 123 p 9
912 IF 122 p 2
913 I 166

197

in Russian cryptanalysis. Participants were selected from the personnel of the Signal Interpreter Replacement and Training Battalion who knew Russian. After the most capable interpreters had been selected they were given a course in Russian cryptography which included all types of Russian systems. For practice in this course actual Russian military texts were used by which the men were gradually accustomed to field problems.[914]

119. Evaluation of Signal Training.--The training of cryptanalysts by the Army appears to have been eminently successful. Through the classes of the Training Section at In 7/VI passed most of the men who later became outstanding in the field of cryptanalysis either in the KONAs or in the central agencies. Major Hentze, head of cryptanalysis at Paris (KONA 5) and later of Gruppe IV of GdNA; 1st Lt. Vauck, head of the Agents' section of In 7/VI; 1st Lt. Lueders, head of one of the subsections of the mathematical section of In 7/VI; and 1st Lt. Schubert, head of cryptanalysis at HLS Ost, were all graduated from this course.[915]

The training of signal troops in the field, however, appears to have been less successful. Attention is continuously drawn throughout the TICOM publications to the acute shortage in the Field Army of personnel who were well trained in signal intelligence operations. This was particularly true in the late years of the war when courses became more sketchy. The central agencies recognized this weakness and attempted to remedy it by publishing field manuals on security and having lectures given at the Signal School at Halle by members of In 7/VI. Despite these efforts, however, the Field Army remained, according to Fricke, pitifully ignorant of the principles of security. Ignorance undoubtedly lay at the bottom of the non-cooperative attitude of the Field Army in regard to the adoption of systems considered more secure than those in use by the Army. Conditions were aggravated at the end of the war by the necessity for sending all able-bodied men into the front line and by the general confusion of the Army. Very little training could be carried on by the Field Army during the late months since their schools were taken over by operating agencies. The Army Signal School at Halle, for example, had been used by In 7/IV since November 1943 for the preparation of Army keys; and after March 1945 it housed a considerable section of the Signal Intelligence Agency of the Armed Forces, including service personnel and male and female civilians. It may be safely stated that after 1944 little if any signal training was carried on by the Army.

[914] See Volume 4, Chapter VI for details of this course

[915] I 78 p 8

VOLUME 4

Chapter X. Liaison of the Signal Intelligence Service of the Army High Command with Other Signal Intelligence Services at Home and Abroad

Paragraph

106. Liaison with OKW/Chi.--The relations of the Signal Intelligence Agency of the Army High Command (OKH/GdNA and its predecessors) with the Signal Intelligence Agency of the Supreme Command of the Armed Forces (Oberkommando der Wehrmacht Chiffrier Stelle, abbreviated OKW/Chi) were conditioned by a number of important facts.

a. The office of the Chief Signal Officer, Armed Forces (Chef der Wehrmacht Nachrichtenverbindungen, abbreviated Chef WNV) and Chief Signal Officer Army (Chef des Heeres Nachrichtenverbindungswesens, abbreviated Chef HNW) were held jointly from August 1939 to the capitulation. The close relationship which evolved from this combined office is outlined by a German officer who was aide de camp to General Praun, Chef WNV and HNW from September 1944 until the capitulation.[920] As Chef WNV, General Praun (and his predecessors) was directly subordinated to General Jodl of the Armed Forces Operations Staff (Wehrmacht Fuehrungsstab, abbreviated WFST) and was responsible for all signal operations and policy from an inter-service point of view. As Chef HNW, General Praun was responsible for signal operations and policy within the Field Army, and in this capacity was subordinate to General Guderian, Chief of General Staff.[921]

[920] IF 108

[921] IF 108 p 2

b. The Signal Intelligence Service of the Army (GdNA and its predecessors) and the Signal Intelligence Service of the Armed Forces (OKW/Chi) stemmed from a common origin, the Codes and Ciphers Section of the German Defense Ministry. The Army High Command had set up its first Signal Intelligence Agency, the Intercept Control Station (Horchleitstelle), in 1933, by drawing a few trained cryptanalysts from the Codes and Ciphers Section of the German Defense Ministry. The Signal Intelligence Agency of the Supreme Command of the Armed Forces was the direct descendant of the Codes and Ciphers Section of the Defense Ministry and acquired its new name in 1939.[922]

The close inter-relationships of these three organizations is reflected in the relationships among the officers who controlled them. Colonel Boetzel, who ended the war as chief of the GdNA, had been from 1934 to 1939 head of the Codes and Ciphers Section of the Defense Ministry.[923] General Fellgiebel, who had been head of the Codes and Ciphers Section of the Defense Ministry from 1931-1932 held the office of Chief Signal Officer Army (Chef HNW) and Chief Signal Officer Armed Forces (Chef WNF) from 1939 until 20 July 1944.[924] Colonel Kettler who ended the war as head of the Signal Intelligence Agency of the Supreme Command of the Armed Forces (OKW/Chi) had been head of HLS Ost.[925] Lt. Col. Mettig, second in command of the OKW/Chi, had been head of OKH/In 7/VI from November 1941 to June 1943.[926]

Close collaboration of OKW/Chi and the Signal Intelligence Agency of the Army High Command (OKH/GdNA and its predecessors) can be traced in a number of recorded instances from 1939 to the capitulation. In 1939, Huettenhain, chief cryptanalyst of OKW/Chi, was sent by that organization to the Intercept Station of the Army at Frankfurt/Main to collaborate with the Army on the solution of a new French Army system.[927] The most cordial relationship between the organizations is manifest in his memoranda on his visit to Frankfurt/Main:[928]

> "When I was saying goodbye to the military head of the evaluation section of Army Group C at the termination of my attachment in FRANKFURT-ON-Main, the head of the evaluation section expressed his regret to me that he could not yet present me with some sign of outward

922 See Supra Chapter I

923 I 123 p 4

924 I 123 p 4

925 IF 123 p 3

926 I 78 p 2

927 See Supra, Chapter

928 D 60 pp 4-5

2004

recognition for work successfully carried out in FRANKFURT-On-MAIN. To that I replied that success attained was not due to the effort of an individual but was the result of development and common effort and that if outward recognition should reward this work, Herrn TRAPPE (Chi OKW), SCHMIDT (Chi OKW) and Professor Dr. Foppl (Chi OKW) should likewise remembered. The head of the project thereupon told me that these gentlemen would be similarly distinguished.

"In the course of the conversation, I said that for us the finest recognition was the knowledge that important intelligence, which could serve as a basis for the further conduct of the war, had been sent to G.H.Q. The head of the project replied that he quite understood this attitude but he would like to make military departments appreciate our work at the full value for up to now, they have shown little understanding of the difficulties of such work.

"At the same time, the head of the project requested me to convey his thanks to the Chiffrier Section OKW for the assistance given to the military deciphering section and remarked that in his opinion such a large decyphering task could not be done by OKH either now or in the near future."

In 1942, the Signal Intelligence Agency of the Supreme Command of the Armed Forces (OKW/Chi) sent a special Russian "party" to HLS Ost to collaborate with cryptanalysts there in the solution of a Russian 5-figure code. Prof. Dr. Novopaschenny, head of that party returned to Berlin in the autumn of 1943, but his cryptanalysts were absorbed into the unit at HLS Ost.[929]

OKW/Chi also collaborated with the Agents' section of OKH/In 7/VI in the solution of Russian agent traffic. The memoranda of Fenner, chief linguist of OKW/Chi, give a detailed picture of the nature of this collaboration.[930]

On 23 February 1943, Fenner's department was asked by Section III of the Armed Forces Radio Defense Corps (Fu III) to collaborate with the Agents' section of OKH/In 7/VI in work on certain Russian agents' traffic. By the end of March, OKH/In 7/VI had furnished Fenner's section with all traffic in that system intercepted since September 1941 so that a start was made on solution. Fundamental findings were communicated to In 7/VI which enabled its Agents' section to break into the system roughly at the same

[929] IF 123 p 3

[930] D 60 pp 16ff

time as did Fenner's group. After the initial break-in, however, it was agreed that In 7/VI should continue the work on this system while the Signal Intelligence Agency of the Armed Forces started work on another system. From then on, relations became somewhat strained because of the non-cooperative attitude of the Agents' section of In 7/VI in furnishing traffic to Fenner's section. The basic cooperation of the two departments, however, is noteworthy.

One of the most striking instances of cooperation between the Signal Intelligence Agency of the Supreme Command of the Armed Forces (OKW/Chi) and the Signal Intelligence Agency of the Army High Command (OKH/GdNA and its predecessors) is manifest in the work of the two agencies on Polish Resistance Movement Systems.[931] During the years 1943/44, the Agents' section of AgN/NA was able to intercept and solve the systems used by the Poles in their traffic with the Polish government in London. From this traffic the disposition of the Polish liberation troops as well as the friction between them and the Russians could be established. The traffic was considered so important that eight members of the Agents' section were transferred in the autumn of 1943 to the Polish section of the Signal Intelligence Agency of the Armed Forces (OKW/Chi) to work on the systems there. The clear text was published by the Signal Intelligence Agency of the Armed Forces in bulletins with extremely restricted distribution. The Signal Intelligence Agency of the Armed Forces also cooperated by intercepting this traffic at their own station at Lauf in order to be certain that it was completely covered. Speed in solving the traffic was obtained by having the messages sent to the IBM section of AgN/NA for sorting. The work on Polish traffic thus appears to have been as much a joint project as is possible for two separate agencies to attempt.

Long before the time of official "Chi-conferences" held by Lt. General Gimmler, Chief of the Armed Forces Communications Branch (Chef Amtsgruppe Wehrmachtnachrichten Verbindungen, abbreviated Chef AgWNV), the Army and the Armed Forces, Signal Intelligence Services worked together on security studies of German cryptographic machines and issued joint resolutions concerning their investigations. Among the papers of Dr. Huettenhain of OKW/Chi are memoranda describing this cooperation.[932] As early as December 1942, In 7/VI, OKW/CHI and Wa Pruef 7 proposed issuing a statement concerning improvements for the secret teletypewriter machine SFM T-52c to be submitted to the "big executive committee."[933] Although it is not known specifically what is meant by the "big executive committee," it is possible that it may have been composed

[931] I 115 p 9
[932] D 59
[933] D 59 p 6

298

of officials of these same organizations. Throughout 1943, General Thiele, who held the position of Chief of the Army Communications Branch (Chef Amtsgruppe Heeres Nachrichtenverbindungswesens, abbreviated Chef AgHNW) called conferences of representatives of the various services concerning matters of security. Buggisch, one of the mathematicians of In 7/VI, mentions conferences at which Drs. Stein and Hassenjaeger of OKW/Chi were present.[934] The minutes of one of these conferences (dated 13 December 1943) have been published.[935] It should be noted that the conference is said to have been called at the suggestion of In 7/IV, and was held in the office of that unit at Matthaikirchplatz 4, Berlin. Those who took part were Major Kempe, head of In 7/IV, Specialist Luehrs, Dr. Fricke, and Dr. Kehren, mathematicians of In 7/IV; Dr. Pietsch and Dr. Doering of AgN/NA; representatives of Wa Pruef 7; and Dr. Huettenhain, Dr. Stein, and 1st Lt. Hasenjaeger, mathematicians of OKW/Chi. From this evidence, it is clear that the "Chi-conferences" called by Lt. General Gimmler in 1944 were only a formal exteriorization of an already existing relationship. This is the reason that Buggisch of AgN NA and Huettenhain of OKW/Chi were able to minimize the efforts of Lt. General Gimmler.[936] Both observe that the conferences did not foster a closer relationship among the services -- the cooperation of Army and Armed Forces had been of the closest nature for many years, but the collaboration with other services was not improved.

At the formal "Chi-conferences" and at the official Army-Air-Naval conferences of 1944, the Armed forces could always depend upon the full cooperation of the Army. The completeness of this cooperation is illustrated by the fact that when OKW/Chi was ordered to take over the supervision of all security studies within the Armed Forces, the Army compiled by transferring to OKW/Chi all personnel of In 7/IV and of the security sections of the Mathematical Section of AgN NA.

In the field of machinery used for cryptanalytic and security studies, the Armed Forces and the Army appear to have informed each other fully concerning their respective developments although no exchange of machinery was made. As early as 1939/40, the mathematicians and former actuaries who had been drawn into In/7IV suggested the use of IBM machinery for statistical studies. This led to an extensive use of the machinery for security studies. When security studies were transferred from In 7/IV to In 7/VI in 1942, IBM machinery was developed by In 7/VI for both security

934 I 58 p 3

935 D 59 p 16

936 I 92 p 4; I 84 p 2

292

studies and cryptanalytic work. It is not known whether the Signal Intelligence Agency of the Armed Forces had its own IBM machines separate from those of the Army or not.[937] Mettig and Buggisch both state that it had no IBM machinery, but depended upon the IBM machines of the Signal Intelligence Agency of the Army. The preparation of three-letter codes for the use of the Army was done, for instance, by the IBM machines of the GdNA at the request of the Signal Intelligence Agency of the Armed Forces[938] In early 1945, the IBM section of GdNA was offered to the Signal Intelligence Agency of the Armed Forces (OKW/Chi); the transfer was never carried out, however, because of the turn of events.[939]

The relation of the Signal Intelligence Agency of the Supreme Command of the Armed Forces (OKW/Chi) and of the GdNA and its predecessors may be summarized as one of complete cooperation. Although the cryptanalytic problems of the two organizations were quite distinct, those of OKW/Chi dealing with diplomatic systems, of GdNA with Army systems, whenever joint problems were deal, with by the two agencies there was complete accord.

107. Liaison with the Navy.--The Signal Intelligence Agency of the Navy (Oberkommando des Marine, Seekriegsleitung, abbreviated OKM/4 SKL III) appeared to have little liaison with the Signal Intelligence Agency of the Army (GdNA and its predecessors). Tranow, the chief cryptanalyst of the Signal Intelligence Agency of the Navy, stated that the Navy cooperated with the Army until early 1944, but that thereafter the attempt at cooperation was given up since no results of value were obtained.[940]

The collaboration, where it existed, of the Signal Intelligence Agency of the Navy High Command with GdNA and its predecessors dealt principally with: the USA machine M-209, and IBM procedures.[941] In both instances, it so happened that the Navy received more from the Army than it gave.

a. Collaboration between OKM/4 SKL III and In 7/VI began in 1943 when In 7/VI passed over to the Signal Intelligence Agencies of the Navy and the Air Force the technique of recovering true settings from relative settings in M-209 solution. Thereafter, according to Lt. Muentz of OKM/4 SKL III there was considerable liaison between the three services in regard to M-209 and they exchanged all techniques.[942] Schulze, another

937 I 96 p 13; I 67 p 2
938 I 96 p 11
939 I 96 p 13
940 I 93 p 3
941 D 21 p 2
942 I 144 p 2

204

cryptanalyst in OKM/4 SKL III, stated that in his investigations of the M-209 he met Dr. Steinberg of In 7/VI and that they had a detailed conversation of the methods used by the German Army, Navy, and Air Force for solution of this system.[943] From these conversations he concluded that the Navy was superior in the matter of breaking into a message; the Army, in reconstructing the internal setting. This was mainly because the Army had more material to work on, and could depend upon having a few messages in depth every day, whereas the Navy never got traffic with identical settings. Schulze persuaded the Army to give the Navy some M-209 material in depth with which he could carry out experiments in OKM/4 SKL III to expedite the solution of the message.[944]

b. In regard to collaboration on IBM procedures, Tranow readily admitted that the Army first conceived the idea of using IBM machinery for cryptanalysis.[945] In March 1942, the Navy, Air Force, and Goering's Research Bureau (FA) visited the IBM section of In 7/VI in Berlin. "On this occasion," said Tranow, "I came to the conclusion that there were enormous possibilities in the IBM system for our work also." Tranow immediately set about to get some machinery for the Signal Intelligence Agency of the Navy, but found it difficult to obtain IBM machines at that time. From March to May or June 1942, the Signal Intelligence Service of the Navy sent work to the Naval Armaments Economic Section which was already using IBM machinery for statistical purposes. This Economic Section agreed to do the work on condition that Tranow furnish his own staff. Here again, Tranow had trouble, since the Signal Intelligence Agency of the Navy had very few IBM specialists in the ranks. He was forced to approach the Army and Air Force to obtain personnel in exchange for naval personnel of "equal value," as he is careful to point out. By May 1942, Tranow says, the Navy was able to carry out its own task.[946] According to Mettig, however, in June 1942, In 7/VI undertook a considerable volume of IBM work for the Signal Intelligence Agency of the Navy.[947] It seems reasonable to suppose that this is true, and that Tranow conveniently "forgot" this favor on the part of the Army. In September 1944, according to a Navy document, the Signal Intelligence Agency of the Navy was still "collaborating" with the Army on IBM procedure.

943 I 147 p 22

944 I 147 pp 22-23

945 I 146 p 17

946 I 146 p 17

947 I 78 p 12

As a matter of general policy, the Signal Intelligence Agency of the Navy High Command disapproved of indiscriminate exchange among the services. Lt. Muentz stated that the head of his section Franke, disapproved of any contact with other services, and maintained contact only with the Army on M-209 solution. Lt. Schubert of GdNA complained that he personally could not bring about closer relations between the two agencies.[948]

> "I endeavoured to achieve cooperation between the Army and Navy. This task was actually no concern of mine. A naval officer was detached for six weeks who looked at all Army systems originating in the west and east and I went to him to attempt some settlement. I tried to achieve collaboration but later events upset things. There are practically no points of contact between the Army and Navy."

108. Liaison with the Air Force.--Before the German Air Force established its own Signal Intelligence Agency (OKL/LN Abt 350, formerly Chi-stelle OBdL) in 1937 the Army fixed intercept stations (Feste) intercepted foreign Air Force traffic and worked on it at the Intercept Control Station (Horchleitstelle). According to Major Fiechtner of the German Air Force, however, the Army did not give air traffic so much attention as it did ground force traffic and the Air Force became increasingly dissatisfied with the Army's work. In 1935, the Air Force began the formation of its own signal intelligence service, although for three years close relations with the Army were maintained. Air Force employees underwent familiarization training at Army Fixed Intercept Stations and the Air Force's first intercept stations were set up according to Army prototypes. By 1939, the dependence of the Signal Intelligence Agency of the Air Force High Command (OKL/LN Abt 350, formerly Chi-stelle OBdL) on the Signal Intelligence Agency of the Army High Command (GdNA and its predecessors) was ended.[949]

During the succeeding period (1939-1945) relations of the Air Force and Army were particularly good in field operations. This was fostered by such means as unification of Army and Air Force signal regulations, a regular exchange of liaison officers, working personnel, equipment, reports, raw traffic, and cryptanalytic methods. A few outstanding examples of Army-Air Force collaboration have been selected from multitudinous instances on every battle front.

948 I 26 p 2

949 IF 181 pp 14-15

206

We know from the minutes of a Chi-conference held in October 1944 that the Army and Air Force attempted to coordinate their signal regulations. According to the notes of the minutes preserved among the papers of Huettenhain, Lt. General Gimmler, Chef AgWNV, stated that one special difficulty in signal communications was the fact that the diverse parts of the Armed Forces used different wireless and cipher phraseology. In response to this, Lt. Col. Schulze of the German Air Force stated that by means of far-reaching assimilation of Army and Air Force regulations, the difficulties arising in those services from different wireless and cipher phraseology would soon be overcome.[950] This attitude of cooperation between Army and Air Force is typical and extended to all echelons.

A regular exchange of liaison officers between Army and Air Force field units was maintained both on the eastern and western fronts. In the west, from 1942 an Air Force liaison officer had been stationed with NAAS 5 at St. Germain.[951] Major Hentze, CO of KONA 5, stated that the two units worked closely together and Hentze showed familiarity with the unit there, its complement, and its work.[952]

One of the chief duties of the Army liaison officer at an Air Force signal intelligence post was to keep the ground situation map up to date from Air Force reports.[953] Among other duties, the Air Force liaison officer at an Army signal intelligence post passed requests to the Air Force for support.[954]

Friendly liaison between commanders and men of units of the Air Force and Army which were closely associated in the field must not be overlooked as a source of contact. Col. Muegge and Col. Rosenkrantz form an excellent example of this type of relationship. When Col. Muegge was commander of the Signal Intelligence Regiment 4 (KONA 4) in Athens, Col. Rosenkrantz, an old friend of his, was commander of the Air Force Signal Intelligence Unit stationed there. When Col. Muegge was moved in 1943 to Italy as commander of Signal Intelligence Regiment 7 (KONA 7), Col. Rosenkrantz happened to be commander of the Air Force signal intelligence in Italy and the friendly relationships of their units continued.[955]

Much of the interchange of men and equipment between field units of the Air Force and Army was caused by the fact that the Army had very few long distance direction-finding sets, and

950 D 57 p 14
951 IF 180 p 24
952 I 113 p 8
953 I 130 p 10
954 I 107 p 3
955 I 18 pp 4-6

depended upon equipment and reports from the Air Force to compensate for this deficiency. Major Oeljeschlaeger of the Air Force stated that the Army Signal Intelligence Regiments willingly detached direction-finding parties to reinforce the Air Force effort and that the Air Force was always open to receive Army direction-finding requests.[956] Muegge told interrogators that as commander of KONA 7 in Italy he borrowed two Air Force Direction Finding sets with long and short wave receptive powers from Rosenkrantz's unit and 'forgot' to give them back.[957] NAA-11 in Finland relied on the excellent Direction Finding reports of the Air Force and stated that these reports were furnished directly to NAA-11 whenever they were requested.[958]

Intelligence reports of all sorts were exchanged at every level of field intelligence. Army Group Headquarters received from the local Air Force which served its area copies of the Air Force's daily situation report and fortnightly summary.[959] These fortnightly summaries were sent by the Army Group Headquarters to Jodl who stated that they were well illustrated with sketches and plans.[960] Among the lower echelons, reports, summaries, and experiences of value were constantly interchanged between units of the KONA and the correlative air signal intelligence units. Reports from the Air Force were of particular importance in the identification of enemy concentrations. Major Oeljeschlaeger of the German Air Force stated that the Air Force was always quicker off the mark than the Army mobile ground forces. The enemy could sneak up against German positions by imposing radio silence, but long before this the Air Force would have advised the Army commands of significant moves of Air Force ground units.[961]

An interchange of traffic and methods of solution was also constantly maintained between the two services. Newly established Air Force traffic was handed over to Air Force units when it was intercepted by the Army,[962] and from 1943 on an interchange of cryptanalytic methods on both western and eastern fronts was normal. On the western front, traffic and methods of solution for USA traffic M-94, M-209, TELWA[963] were exchanged between NAAS 5 and western Air Force signal intelligence units. After

956 I 41 p 3
957 I 18 p 4
958 I 106 p 4
959 I 130 p 11
960 I 143 p 6
961 I 41 p 3
962 I 130 p 15
963 I 112 pp 4-6

Section B of the Signal Intelligence Agency of the Air Force High Command (OKL/LN Abt 350) moved to Paris following the invasion, messages encoded in Slidex were decoded at Paris by Section B, of the Signal Intelligence Agency of the Commander in Chief of the Air Force, and by NAAS 5 at St. Germain and were exchanged daily in the form of written reports.[964] On the southeastern front there was also an exchange of cryptanalytic procedure. Muegge of KONA 4 contacted the deciphering unit of the Air Force unit in Athens for aid in the solution of RAF four-figure traffic. Although neither unit had any success collaboration was maintained.[965] On the eastern front common problems of the Air Force units and Army Signal Intelligence Regiments were continuously worked on together.[966] Collaboration of LN 353 and KONA 1 and 8 is specifically mentioned.[967]

The most striking instance of field collaboration is shown at the time of the Dieppe raid. The Air Force intercept company which was responsible for monitoring landing traffic had good line connections with German fighter defense and Army forces responsible for defense against landing operations. The Air Force unit maintained continuous contact with the Army units involved and exploited their findings for immediate action by Air and Army. The Army signal intelligence headquarters passed on this intelligence to the higher headquarters, thus maintaining an effective division of labor with outstanding results. The work at Dieppr was publicised in the German newspapers and Goering praised it in a speech.[968]

In summary, the Army and Air Force maintained in their field relations the close working relationship with an exchange of personnel equipment, reports, traffic and cryptanalytic methods. Relations between the central agencies are less well known, but appear to have been adequate for all that was necessary. Operative systems on both fronts, such as USA M-94, M-209, Slidex, and Russian systems, were worked on jointly by Army and Air Force units in the areas where the systems were used and methods of solution exchanged.

109. <u>Liaison with Foreign Office</u>.--Relations of the Signal Intelligence Agency of the Army High Command (GdNA and its predecessors) and the cryptanalytic section of the Foreign Office (Pers ZS) were not close. This is to be expected both from the nature of their separate commitments (the GdNA dealing exclusively

964 I 112 p 9
965 IF 190 p 7
966 I 26 p 2
967 I 130 p 15
968 I 109 p 5

with Army systems, the Foreign Office with diplomatic) and from the well-known unwillingness of the Foreign Office to share any information.

Buggisch, a mathematician of In 7/VI said that he worked at one time on the Swiss model of the Enigma with Kunze, one of the cryptanalysts of the Foreign Office, and on a 5-figure de Gaulle code in 1941 and 1942.[969] Further than this there is, to our knowledge, no record of any cooperation between the two agencies. Jodl, Chief of Operations of the Armed Forces, stated that he did not receive the products of the Foreign Office bureau which went directly to the Foreign Minister, Von Ribbentrop. He knew from military lectures that the Foreign Office had broken some political traffic, but his knowledge was not direct.[970]

110. Liaison with Goering's Research Bureau. Liaison between the Signal Intelligence Agency of the Army High Command (the GdNA and its predecessors) and Goering's Research Bureau (FA) was characterized in general by narrowness of approach and mutual animosity of feeling. This was true, apparently, at every level. Jodl, Chief of Operations of the Armed Forces, told interrogators that he knew little about the Research Bureau:

> "It was a large office and efficiently organized, but Goering's special affair."[971]

Items of special interest from the Research Bureau were passed to Jodl from Keitel, in a special folder and Jodl returned them after perusal. He himself received nothing directly from the Research Bureau. Likewise, Goering stated that he never received copies of Army decodes as such, and had no opinion of the ability of the "Army bureau."[972]

Between the GdNA and the Research Bureau, liaison was apparently poor. Buggisch of In 7/VI stated that this was because Mettig, head of In 7/VI from 1941 to 1943, was opposed to the Storm Trooper taint of the Research Bureau.[973] Sauerbier, a lesser light in the Research Bureau, claimed that the narrowness of the department heads of the Research Bureau affected relations of that organization with other bureaus including the GdNA.[974]

Whatever liaison was carried on by the Goering's Research

969 I 58 pp 5-6
970 I 143 p 5
971 I 143 p 5
972 I 143 p 16
973 I 64
974 I 162 p 4

210

209

Bureau was done by a single representative and never involved any exchange of visits of operational personnel. Klautsche, who was liaison officer for the Research Bureau after 1943, maintained an office at the Signal Intelligence Agency of the Armed Forces (OKW/Chi) and passed on material to the Navy, Air Force, and Army.[975] Besides actual contact with GdNA, Klautsche is said to have passed on intelligence material to the Army General Staff, Western Armies Branch, and Eastern Armies Branch.[976]

The lack of contact between personnel of the Research Bureau and the GdNA is very apparent from interrogations. Fricke, a prominent mathematician of In 7/VI who was later transferred to OKW/Chi, stated that he had never seen any personnel from the Research Bureau until the war was over and they turned up in prison camps.[977] Sauerbier of the Research Bureau said he did not know a single person in another cryptanalytic bureau.[978]

There are a few instances of cooperation between the Research Bureau and the In 7/VI, but Buggisch, an Army cryptanalyst, insists that these were very rare.[979] One of the outstanding instances of effective collaboration occurred when the Research Bureau was having difficulty with a Turkish diplomatic code. The problem of solution and reading was turned over to In 7/VI. Traffic was intercepted by KONA 4 in Athens and relayed to the Balkan section of In 7/VI where it was broken and read until the capitulation. Decoded messages were forwarded to the Research Bureau.[980]

Buggisch stated that there was an exchange of results between the Research Bureau and In 7/VI in connection with some work of the Research Bureau on a Russian secret teleprinter in 1943. The Research Bureau had analyzed the machine and recognized that it must resemble the German SZ 40. When the Russians altered their system, the Research Bureau communicated the results of its investigations to the Mathematical Section of In 7/VI and was given in regurn a report on the solution of a German secret teleprinter. No more details of the incident are known, but Buggisch emphasizes the fact that this exchange of results was a very rare occurrence.[981]

[976] I 54 p 4
[977] I 20 p 8
[978] I 162 p 4
[979] I 176 p 6
[980] IF 126 p 8
[981] I 176 p 6

Collaboration between the Research Bureau and the Agents' section of In 7/VI is hinted in the statement that Wenzel, a civil employee of the Research Bureau, was sent from the Research Bureau by the Radio Defense Corps (FU III) to the GdNA to work on Polish Resistance Movement Systems.[982] Nothing more is known concerning the incident from TICOM sources.

Evidence indicates that under pressure, Goering's Research Bureau resorted to the GdNA and its predecessors for help in intercept solution, and editing of difficult traffic, but that in general the Research Bureau held itself aloof and disaffected.

111. Liaison with Finland-- Liaison with Finland was always close, both at HLS Ost, and in the eastern field units. Formal liaison at HLS Ost was maintained by a Finnish liaison officer stationed there. This officer in 1942 was a Lt. Mikkoja,[983] and he was succeeded by 1st Lt. Ohn. Army traffic of Russia, Poland, Rumania, and Sweden was exchanged. The Finnish General Staff is said to have handed over to the Germans a copy of the Russian 5-figure codes which was used by the Russians in the first year of the war with Germany.[984] The Germans had a high opinion of Finnish cryptanalysis. Dettman of HLS Ost stated that he had visited Finland in 1942 and had exchanged technical letters ever since that time with the Finns.[985]

Liaison in the field is known in some detail from the reports of NAA-11 when it was in Finland.[986] NAA-11 kept a signal intelligence liaison officer stationed with the main Finnish signal intelligence unit at Sortavala. This liaison officer, whose name was Riemerschmidt, had a direct radio link to NAA-11. Although the Germans of NAA-11 never went to Sortavala themselves, small Finnish parties did visit NAA-11 from time to time.[987]

The liaison between NAA-11 and the Finns can be divided into several types: traffic liaison, cryptographic liaison and technical liaison.[988]

In the field of traffic liaison, NAA-11 is said to have varied its cryptographic priorities to give full attention to any special links requested by the Finns through Riemerschmidt. NAA-11 also aided the Finns in traffic analysis, in which the

[982] I 26 p 7

[983] I 21 p 2

[984] I 78

[985] I 116 p 10

[986] I 55 I 106

[987] I 106 p 4

[988] I 106 pp 3-4

212

Finns were admittedly weak. NAA-11's systematic work and its ability to grasp intelligence from the analysis of small amounts of traffic was of great benefit to the Finns. D/F operations were coordinated very closely between the Finns and NAA-11. Here, on the other hand, NAA-11 relied heavily on the Finns who had D/F sets with long range. According to Riemerschmidt, a liaison observer was stationed by the Germans with the Finnish stations at Mikkeli, Ylene, Kemi, and Rovanieme for the specific purposes of observing long range D/F.

In the cryptanalytic field, NAA-11 neither gave nor received straight intelligence from the Finns but cryptanalytic procedures were exchanged. The Finns gave the Germans some very valuable information on Russian 3- and 4-figure ciphers which they had succeeded in reading. It is amusing to note in connection that Riemerschmidt passed to NAA-11 some information and solution of traffic in the Russian RZ 1800 code which hae had received at Sortavala from HLS Ost and this reached NAA-11 faster than did the direction transmission from HLS Ost to NAA-11.

Technical liaison was also handled by Riemerschmidt and this proved far more helpful to the Finnish radio telegraph company than to NAA-11. Finnish equipment was mostly of German make, with some British and a few American receivers. The Germans gave the Finns a great deal of advice concerning the operation of the machines and on one occasion they put their own apparatus and men at the disposal of the Finns for an operation in a key sector during a Russian offensive.[989]

112. Liaison with Italy-- Liaison between Germany and Italy was negligible because of the German lack of confidence in the Italians. There could be no exchange of information, or intelligence when the Germans were so apprehensive of the Italin cipher department that they thought it not competent enough to institute changes in cipher procedures even if the Italians desired to do so.

This lack of confidence on the part of the Germans was based on long experience with Italian codes and ciphers. As early as 1941, Captain Dr. Fiala, head of the Italian section of In 7/VI, was sent to Rome to inform the Italians of their code and cipher weaknesses.[990] The Germans were particularly apprehensive at this time because they feared that movements of German troops around North Africa were being betrayed to the British by messages of the Italian wireless. Dr. Fiala's visit, however, does not seem to have impressed the Italians who were confident of their

[989] I 106 p 3

[990] I 78 p 11

233

own systems, and the Germans tried another scheme.[991] In 1942, the Italians were invited to visit the IBM section of In 7/VI to observe the use of these machines for cryptanalytic and security work. Captain Bigi, a cryptanalyst of the Italian army, was sent by the Italians for this purpose.[992] Upon his return to Italy, the Italians did set up an IBM section of their own, but it did not function efficiently and the Germans despaired of improving Italian cipher or cryptanalytic methods.[993] In late 1942, the Italian section of In 7/VI which had monitored Italian traffic was dissolved by order of Hitler.[994]

After Italy's defection to the Allies, the Italian section of In 7/VI was revived from June 1943 until November 1943 when it was again disbanded.[995] During this brief period, however, no relations with Italy were maintained.

113. Liaison with Japan.--According to all evidence, there was very little liaison between the Army and Japan. In 1943, two Japanese officers visited the HLS Ost at Loetzen for about half a day. According to Dettman 7 HLS Ost they were given a polite reception but shown very little of anything and were given no hints as to what solutions the Germans had reached on Russian traffic. The Japanese stated that they had solved the Russian OKK 6 and OKK 7 but just what help, if any, they gave the Germans on these systems is not mentioned.[996] Buggisch emphatically stated that he had never seen any Japanese around "in the flesh" and that he knew of no liaison with Japan.[997]

At the end of the war, the Germans had decided to send a cryptologic mission to Japan by submarine. Included among the officers were Major Opitz, a German intercept officer, Schubert, of HLS Ost, and Morgenroth, a Navy cryptanalyst. How little the mission knew of Japanese Signal Intelligence agencies is shown by the fact that they did not know whom they were to contact when they got there but were to ask the German Counter Intelligence in Japan for further instructions.[998] The last minute plan could not be carried out because of the precipitate end of the war.[999]

991 IF 1524; IF 1519
992 I 78 p 11
993 I 78 p 11
994 I 100 p 2
995 I 100 p 2
996 I 116 p 9
997 I 64 p 3
998 IF 108 p 12
999 I 48 p 3

Only one instance is remarked on in TICOM interrogations of exchange between the Japanese and Germans. This occurred, according to Barthel, in connection with an Army field cipher machine captured by the Japanese. Nothing more is known of the incident.[1000]

1000 IF 120 p 7

DOCID: 3486746

VOLUME 4

TAB A

AgN/NA (Amtsgruppe Nachrichten/Nachrichten Aufklaerung).--Department of Signals, Signal Intelligence. Name of cryptanalytic agency for non-Russian traffic 1943-1944 (successor to In 7/VI).
AHA (Allgemeines Heeres Amt.--General Army Office.
Air Signals Regiment.--Luftnachrichten Regiment (LN Regt).
Allgemeines Heeres Amt (AHA).--General Army Office.
Althans,_____, Corporal. Attached to NAAS 1.
AMTM. See Amtmann.
Amtmann (AMTM).--Specialist.
Amtsgruppe Nachrichten/Nachrichten Aufklaerung (AgN/NA).--Department of Signals, Signal Intelligence.
Andrae,_____, Lt. Col. Chief of Staff of Boetzel, Chief of Signal Intelligence Agency of Army High Command (OKH/GdNA).
Armed Forces Signal Troop School.--Fuehrungs Nachrichtentruppe Schule (FNS).
Army Communication Branch.--Heeres Nachrichten Verbindungsabteilung (HNV).
Army High Command.--Oberkommando des Heeres (OKH).
Army Ordnance, Development and Testing Group, Signals Branch.--Waffenpruefung (Wa Pruef).
Army Signal School.--Heeres Nachrichten Schule (HNS).
Army Signal Security Agency (1940-1942).--Inspectorate 7/IV (Inspektion 7/IV, abbreviated In 7/IV).
Arntz,_____, 1st Lieutenant. Aide-de-Camp to Praun. Chef WNV and Chef HNW.
Bailovic, Rudolf. Superior Governmental Councillor; former employee of Austrian Cryptanalytic Bureau; head of Balkan Section of In 7/VI; Specialist of Yugoslav systems of Tito and Mihailovic.
BANDWURM. Term used by the Germans to designate Russian Baudot letter "strip".
Barthel, Thomas. Member of KONA 7.
BAUDOT. A 32-character alphabet used in transmitting plain or enciphered teleprinter messages (corresponds to 26-letter Morse alphabet for hand-keying).
Befehlshaber Suedost.--Commanding Officer South-east.

216

Benold,_____, 1st Lieutenant. Commanding Officer of Close Range Signal Company (NAK Benold).
Berger, Georg, Inspector. In charge of documents in KONA 1.
Block,_____, Specialist. Head of Section 2, Group V, GdNA.
BLOCKNOT. Russian term, used by Germans to designate a one-time pad.
Boetzel,_____, Colonel. Chief of Signal Intelligence Agency of Army High Command (OKH/GdNA) 1944-1945. Had been Chief of Code and Cipher Section of German War Ministry 1934-1939.
Boscheinen, Heinz, Non-Commissioned Officer. Turkish Interpreter; Member of Bailovic's section at In 7/VI and also worked in Evaluation.
Breede,_____, Inspector (?). Member of British section of In 7/VI during 1941 and worked on Typex.
Buggisch, Otto, Dr. Cryptanalyst of In 7/VI.
Buschenhagen,_____, Lieutenant. Chief of Code and Cipher Section of German Defense Ministry 1919-1927.
Chef der Heeresruestung und Befehlshaber des Ersatzheeres.--Chief of Army Equipment and Commander of the Replacement Army (Chef H Ruest u BdE).
Chef der Wehrmacht Nachrichten Verbindungen (Chef/WNV).--Chief Signal Officer, Armed Forces.
Chef des Heeres Nachrichtenverbindungswesens (Chef/HNW).--Chief Signal Officer, Army.
Chef/GdNA (Chef/General der Nachrichten Aufklaerung).--Chief, Signal Intelligence Service.
Chef/General der Nachrichten Aufklaerung (Chef/GdNA).--Chief, Signal Intelligence Service.
Chef/HNW (Chef der Heeres Nachrichtenverbindungswensens.--Chief Signal Officer, Army.
Chef H Ruest u. BdE (Chef der Heeresruestung und Befehlshaber des Ersatzheeres.--Chief of Army Equipment and Commander of the Replacement Army.
Chef/WNV (Chef der Wehrmacht Nachrichten Verbindungen.--Chief Signal Officer, Armed Forces.
Chief of Army Equipment and Commander of the Replacement Army.--(Chef der Heeresruestung und Befehlshaber des Ersatzheeres (Chef H Ruest u. BdE).
Chief, Signal Intelligence Service.--Chef/General der Nachrichten Aufklaerung (Chef/GdNA).
Chief Signal Officer, Armed Forces.--Chef der Wehrmacht Nachrichten Verbindungen (Chef/WNV).
Chief Signal Officer, Army.--Chef der Heeres Nachrichtenverbindungswesens (Chef/HNW).
Chiffrierabteilung/Reichswehrministerium.--Code and Cipher Section/German Defense Ministry.

Chiffrier Stelle des Oberbefehlshabers der Luftwaffe (Chi-Stelle OBdL).--Signal Intelligence Agency of the Commander in Chief of the Air Force.

Chi-Stelle OBdL (Chiffrier Stelle des Oberbefehlshabers der Luftwaffe)--Signal Intelligence Agency of the Commander in Chief of the Air Force.

Close Range Signal Intelligence Company.--Nachrichten Nahaufklaerung Kompanie (NAK).

Close Range Signal Intelligence Platoon.--Nachrichten Nahaufklaerungszug (NAZ).

Code and Cipher Section/German Defense Ministry.--Chiffrierabteilung/Reichswehrministerium.

Combined Staffs Detailed Interrogation Center.--CSDIC.

Commander in Chief South.--Oberbefehlshaber Sued.

Commander in Chief West.--Oberbefehlshaber West.

Commanding Officer South-east.--Befehlshaber Suedost.

Control Station of Signal Intelligence--Leitstelle der Nachrichten Aufklaerung (LNA). Central evaluating agency of Army High Command 1942-1944.

Cryptanalytic Section of the German Foreign Office.--Sonderdienst des Referats Z in der Personalabteilung des Auswaertigen Amtes (Pers Z S).

CSDIC.--Combined Staffs Detailed Interrogation Center.

D-60. Miscellaneous papers from a file of RR Dr. Huettenhain of OKW/Chi. A TICOM publication.

Denffer, von. Mathematician in In 7/IV and In 7/VI.

Dettmann, Alex, 1st Lieutenant. Head of cryptanalysis at HLS Ost; later head of section 3, Group IV of GdNA. Specialty: Russian systems.

DF-18. "Russian Decryption in the Former German Army" by Dettmann and Samsonow. See T-805.

Doering, _____, Dr. Mathematician with In 7/VI, later GdNA. Specialty: Machine cipher, mathematical research.

Esterhazy, Paul, Count Wachtmeister. Member of Balkan section of In 7/VI.

Exter, Karl. Attached to NAA-11.

FA (Forschungsamt).--Goering's Research Bureau.

FAK (Nachrichten Fernaufklaerung Kompanie).--Long Range Signal Intelligence Company.

FAZ (Nachrichten Fernaufklaerungszug).--Long Range Signal Intelligence Platoon.

Feichtner, Ferdinand, Major. Commanding Officer of LN Regt 352 (German Air Force).

Fellgiebel, _____, General. Chief of Code and Cipher Section of German Defense Ministry 1931-1932; Chief Signal Officer of Army High Command and of Supreme Command of Armed Forces 1942-1944; Killed in July 1944 after attempt on Hitler's life.

218

Feste. 1923-1939: Abbreviation for Feste Horchstelle (Fixed Intercept Station); 1939-1945: Abbreviation for Feste Nachrichten Aufklaerungsstelle (Stationary Intercept company).
Feste Horchstelle (Feste).--Fixed Intercept Station.
Feste Nachrichten Aufklaerungsstelle (Feste).--Stationary Intercept Company.
FF (Funkfernschreib).--USA non-morse radio teletype.
Fiala,____, Captain. Head of Italian Section of In 7/VI during 1941-1942.
Fixed Intercept Station.--Feste Horchstelle (Feste).
FNS (Fuehrungs Nachrichtentruppen Schule).--Armed Forces Signal Troop School.
Forschungsamt (FA).--Goering's Research Bureau.
Fricke, Walter, Dr. Mathematician and cryptanalyst: In 7/VI 1941-1942; posted to In 7/IV in 1942; transferred in 1944 to OKW/Chi IIb. Specialty: Production of codes and ciphers, security studies of Army systems.
Fuehrungs Nachrichtentruppe Schule (FNS).--Armed Forces Signal Troop School.
Funkfernschreib (FF).--USA non-morse radio teletype.
Geheime Kommandosache (GKdoS).--Secret.
General Army Office.--Allgemeines Heeres Amt (AHA).
General der Nachrichten Aufklaerung. (GdNA).--Signal Intelligence Agency.
Gerlich, Wilhelm, Dr. Attached to NAAS 1 (of KONA 1). Specialty: Russian systems.
German Defense Ministry.--Reichswehrministerium.
German War Ministry.--Reichskriegsministerium.
Gimmler,____, Major General. Chief Armed Forces Communications.
GKdoS. See Geheime Kommandosache.
Goering's Research Bureau.--Forschungsamt (FA).
Gorzolla,____, Captain. Head of Group III, Signal Intelligence Agency of the Army High Command (OKH/GdNA).
Graul, Arno. Member of NAAS of KONA 1. Invented radio "fingerprinter."
Graupe,____, Corporal. Member of In 7/VI 1942-1943, and later member of FAK 624, NAAS 5 of KONA 5. Deserted in August 1944.
Habel,____, Captain. Successor to Seebohm as commanding officer of FAK 621 in North Africa. Captured February 1943.
HASSO (Horchauswertestelle Suedost).--Intercept Evaluation Station Southeast.
Hauptreferat.--Main Section.
Heeres Nachrichten Verbindungsabteilung (HNV).--Army Communication Branch.
Heeres Nachrichten Schule (HNS).--Army Signal School.

Heimann, Wilhelm, Corporal. Specialty: Russian procedure, call signs, and frequencies.
Hentze, Rudolf, Major Dr. Head of Group IV, Signal Intelligence Agency of the Army High Command (OKH/GdNA).
Herbrueggen,_____, Captain. Head of Personnel Section of In 7/VI in 1941.
Hertzer, Ernst, Major. Commanding Officer of KONA 1.
Hertzfeld, Heintz Wolfgang, Corporal. Member of Gruppe IV, GdNA; formerly member of British, Italian, Balkan sections In 7/VI.
Heudorf,_____, Corporal. Member of NAA 8.
Hilburg,_____, Corporal. Member of Mathematical Section of In 7/VI.
HLS (Horchleitstelle).--Intercept Control Station. Central cryptanalytic and evaluating agency 1933-1941.
HLS Ost (Horchleitstelle Ost).--Intercept Control Station East.
HNS (Heeres Nachrichten Schule).--Army Signal School.
HNV (Heeres Nachrichten Verbindungsabteilung).--Army Communications Branch.
Hoeh Kdr d NA (Hoeherer Kommandeur der Nachrichten Aufklaerung).--Senior Commander of Signal Intelligence.
Hoeherer Kommandeur der Nachrichten Aufklaerung (Hoeh Kdr d NA).--Senior Commander of Signal Intelligence.
Hoeppner,_____, Lt. Col. Commanding officer of KONA 8 in 1944.
Holetzko,_____, Captain. Member of LN Regt 353.
Horchauswertestelle Suedost (HASSO).--Intercept Evaluation Station Southeast.
Horchleitstelle (HLS).--Intercept Control Station. Central cryptanalytic and evaluating agency 1933-1941.
Horchleitstelle Ost (HLS Ost).--Intercept Control Station East.
Horchzug.--Intercept platoon.
Huettenhain, Erich, Dr. Cryptanalyst of Signal Intelligence Agency of Supreme Command of Armed Forces (OKW/Chi).
Huchting, Leonhard, Pfc. Attached to Feste 10.
I-2. "Interrogation of Dr. Huettenhain and Dr. Fricke at Flensburg, 21 May 1945." A TICOM publication.
I-3. "Uebersicht der Russischen Chi Verfahren (Nov. 1940-May 1945)." A TICOM publication.
I-7. "Statement of Major McIntosh on Uffz. Graul." A TICOM publication.
I-15. "Interrogation of Oblt. Schubert." A TICOM publication.
I-17. "Extracts of SHAEF Interrogations of Maj. Gen. Boner, Colonel Grube, Lt. Col. Mettig, and Major Rottler." A TICOM publication.
I-18. "Interrogations of Oberst Muegge, O.C. of NA 4 and NA 7 of German Army Sigint Service." A TICOM publication.

I-19 A-G. "Report on Interrogation of KONA 1 at Revin, France June 1945." A TICOM publication.

I-20. "Interrogation of Sonderfuehrer Dr. Fricke of OKW/Chi (Formerly of OKH/Chi)." A TICOM publication.

I-21. "Preliminary Interrogation of Oberst Kettler, RR Dr. Huettenhain, Sdf. Dr. Fricke and Oblt. Schubert (OKW/Chi), 15 June 1945." A TICOM publication.

I-23. "Interrogation of Major Ernst Hertzer, German Army Signals Intelligence Service (KONA 1)." A TICOM publication.

I-26. "Interrogation of Oblt. Schubert (OKH/Chef HNW/Gen.d.NA) on Russian Military and Agents' Systems." A TICOM publication.

I-30. "Report on Interrogation of Uffz. Karrenberg at Steeple Claydon on 7th July 1945 at 1100 a.m." A TICOM publication.

I-33. "Report on Traffic Analysis of BAUDOT Traffic by Capt. Jack Magilavy, A.U.S. and D.R. Uzielli, SIXTA." A TICOM publication.

I-36. "Translation of Paper Written by Reg. Rat. Dr. Huettenhain and Sonderfuehrer Dr. Fricke of OKW/Chi, Sections A.III and B.V." A TICOM publication.

I-45. "OKW/Chi Cryptanalytic Research on Enigma, Hagelin and Cipher Teleprinter Machines." A TICOM publication.

I-46. "Preliminary Report on Interrogation of Dr. Otto Buggisch (of OKH/Gen.d.NA) and Dr. Werner Liebknecht (employed by OKH and OKW as tester of cryptographic equipment) 23 June 1945." A TICOM publication.

I-48. "Report on Special Interrogation of Drs. Huettenhain and Fricke, Oberst Mettig, and Lt. Morgenroth carried out on 29th July 1945." A TICOM publication.

I-51. "Interrogation Report on Uffz. Herzfeld, Heintz Wolfgang, and Translation of a Paper he Wrote on the British War Office Code." A TICOM publication.

I-52. "Papers Written by Uffz. Herzfeld on Mihailovic and Tito Ciphers." A TICOM publication.

I-55. "Interrogation of Seven Members of NAA 11." A TICOM publication.

I-58. "Interrogation of Dr. Otto Buggisch of OKW/Chi." A TICOM publication.

I-59. "Interrogation of Uffz. Arno Graul at Revin." A TICOM publication.

I-60. "Further Interrogation of Oblt. Schubert of OKH/Chef HNW/Gen.d.NA." A TICOM publication.

I-62. "Field Interrogation of Paul Ratz of the German Army Signals Intelligence (1933-1945)." A TICOM publication.

I-66. "Paper by Dr. Otto Buggisch of OKH/In 7/VI and OKW/Chi on TYPEX." A TICOM publication.

I-67. "Paper by Dr. Otto Buggisch of OKH/In 7/VI and OKW/Chi on Cryptanalytic Machines." A TICOM publication.

I-68. "Consolidated Report Based on Two Interrogations of Oberst Randewig, of Hoeh. Wehrmachts Nafue z.b.V 700, carried out at C.S.D.I.C. on approx. 1 Aug. and 10 Aug. 1945." A TICOM publication.
I-69. "Summary of Cipher Information on Jugoslav Traffic Provided by Uffz. Herzfeld (Appendices to TICOM/I-52)." A TICOM publication.
I-72. "First Part of the Report by Wm. Buggisch on S.G. 41." A TICOM publication.
I-73. "Translated Version of Homework done by Wm. Buggisch." A TICOM publication.
I-74. "Interrogation Report on Obgefr. Keller, formerly Auswertestelle 4 and Nachrichten Aufklaerungskompanie 611." A TICOM publication.
I-75. "Interrogation Reports on German Field Sigint Personnel carried out at Buffer - Ltn. August Schroeder, Ltn. Starke, Obegefr. Heudorf, and Hptm. Holetzko." A TICOM publication.
I-76. "Interrogation Reports on Lehwald, Haupts, Klett and Lauerbach." Also I-76 Supplement (Diagrams). A TICOM publication.
I-78. "Interrogation of Oberstlt. Mettig on the History and Achievements of OKH/AHA/In 7/VI." A TICOM publication.
I-80. "P.O.W. Interrogation Report - Obgefr. Clement Schuck Insp. VII/6 (OKH)." A TICOM publication.
I-84. "Further Interrogation of R.R. Dr. Huettenhain and Sdf. Dr. Fricke of OKW/Chi." A TICOM publication.
I-86. "Interrogation of Oberstlt. Mettig of OKH and OKW/Chi on the higher direction of German cryptanalytic work." A TICOM-publication.
I-92. "Final Interrogation of the Wachtmeister Otto Buggisch (OKH/In 7/VI and OKW/Chi)." A TICOM publication.
I-96. "Interrogation of Oberstlt. Mettig on the Organisation and Activities of OKW/Chi." A TICOM publication.
I-98. "Interrogation of Oberst Randewig on German Deception Plans." A TICOM publication.
I-99. "Interrogation Report of Hptm. Herbert Roeder (Head of Gruppe VI, Gen.d.NA, OKH, 1944-45)." A TICOM publication.
I-100. "Report by Uffz. Herzfeld of NAAST 5 (Gen. d. NA) on the Work of the Italian Referat of In 7/VI." A TICOM publication.
I-106. "Final Interrogation Report on the Norway Party (NAA 11). A TICOM publication.
I-111. "Further Interrogation of Oberstlt. Mettig of OKW/Chi on 14th September 1945." A TICOM publication.
I-113. "Interrogation of Major Dr. Rudolf Hentze, Head of Gruppe IV (Cryptanalysis) General der Nachrichtenaufklaerung A TICOM publication.

I-115. "Further Interrogation of Oberstlt. Mettig of OKW/Chi on the German Wireless Security Service (Funküberwachung)." A TICOM Publication.

I-116. "Report of Interrogation of Ltn. Alex Dettmann and Oberwachtmeister Sergius Samsonow of OKH (Gen. d NA) at Oberursel, Germany, during August 1945." A TICOM publication.

I-118. "Joint Reports by Reg. Rat. Dr. Huettenhain and Sdf. Dr. Fricke, written at C.S.D.I.C. on or about 28th August 1945." A TICOM publication.

I-122. "Interrogation Report on Obergefreiter Hansa (OKH/Gen d. NA)." A TICOM publication.

I-125. "Interrogation Report on Anton Stock of OKH/Gen. d. NA." A TICOM publication.

I-127. "Interrogation of Oberstlt. Mettig of OKW/Chi." A TICOM publication.

I-128. "Deciphering Achievements of In 7/VI and OKW/Chi." A TICOM publication.

I-136. "Homework by Regierungsrat Dr. Huettenhain and Sdf. (Z) Dr. Fricke on Hagelin B.211." A TICOM publication.

I-137. "Final Report written by Wachtmeister Otto Buggisch of OKH/Chi and OKW/Chi." A TICOM publication.

I-142. "P/W Barthel's Account of German Work on British, American, Swedish, and French Machine Ciphers." A TICOM publication.

I-143. "Report on the Interrogation of Five Leading Germans at Nuremberg on 27th September 1945." A TICOM publication.

I-149. "Report by Uffz. Karrenberg and Colleagues on Allied Cypher Machines." A TICOM publication.

I-153. "Second Interrogation of Uffz. Karrenberg of OKH on the Baudot-Scrambler Machine ('Bandwurm')." A TICOM publication.

I-154. "Interrogation of Uffz. Rudolph Schneider of In 7/VI." A TICOM publication.

I-156. "Report of preliminary interrogation of Wilhelm Gerlich, AIC 1900, carried out by 3rd U.S. Army, 28th September 1945." A TICOM publication.

I-157. "Chart of Communications Within a Russian Army Drawn up by Uffz. Karrenberg." A TICOM publication.

I-160. "Homework by Sonderfuehrer Kuehn of Gen. d. NA on General Organisation and Work of French Referat." A TICOM publication.

I-161. "Further Statements on Typex by Huettenhain, Fricke, and Mettig." A TICOM publication.

I-164. "Homework by Kurt Sauerbier of RLM/Forschungsamt on Russian Agents' Traffic." A TICOM publication.
I-166. "Report by Uffz. Karrenberg on Russian Cryptographic Course." A TICOM publication.
I-167. "Report by the Karrenberg Party on the NKVD." A TICOM publication.
I-168. "Report by the Karrenberg Party on Miscellaneous Russian W/T." A TICOM publication.
I-169. "Report by Uffz. Karrenberg on the Bandwurm." A TICOM publication.
I-170. "Report on French and Greek Systems by Oberwachtmeister Dr. Otto Karl Winkler of OKH/FNAST 4." A TICOM publication.
I-171. "Report on Work on Russian Systems by Wachtmeister Berger of FNAST 6." A TICOM publication.
I-173. "Report by the Karrenberg Party on Russian W/T." A TICOM publication.
I-175. "Report by Alfred Pokorn of OKH/Chi on M.209." A TICOM publication.
I-176. "Homework by Wachtmeister Dr. Otto Buggisch of OKH/Chi and OKW/Chi." A TICOM publication.
I-178. "Homework by Hptm. Boedigheimer of IV/Nachr. Regiment 506." A TICOM publication.
I-179. "Homework by Obwm. Riel, of Stoerbefehlsstelle Balkan." A TICOM publication.
I-180. "Homework by Uffz. Keller of In 7/VI and WNV/Chi." A TICOM publication.
I-191. "Homework of Dr. Wilhelm Gerlich on Russian Systems." A TICOM publication.
IF-5. "Notes on Field Interrogation of Various German Army and Air Force Signal Intelligence Personnel on 18/20 May 1945." From TICOM.
IF-15. "Final Report of TICOM Team 1 on the Exploitation of Kaufbeuren and the Berchtesgaden area." From TICOM.
IF-40. "Final Report of TICOM Team 2." From TICOM.
IF-105. Two reports. First: Interrogation report on POW Heinz Boscheinen and Walter Kotschy. Second: Summary interrogation report. From Headquarters, 3rd US Army, SIS.
IF-107. "Interrogation of POW Werner K.H. Graupe regarding German Cryptographic Organization and Solution of Allied Codes."
IF-108. "Interrogation of Oblt Arntz." CSDIC (U.K.) SIR 1606.
IF-109. "Report on Information Obtained from Oblt Arntz. CSDIC (U.K.) SIR 1646.
IF-115. "Interrogation Report on Willy Grube." 6824 DIC (MIS) M.1185.
IF-117. "Interrogation Report on Willy Grube." 6824 DIC (MIS) M. 1190.
IF-120

IF-120 "First detailed Interrogation Report on Thomas Barthel." CSDIC/CMF/Y 40.
IF-122 "Third Detailed Interrogation Report on Gerd. Coeler." CSDIC/CMF/Y 38, 31 May 1945.
IF-123 "Consolidated Report on Information obtained from the following: Erdmann, Grubler, Hempel, Karrenberg, Schmitz, Susdowk." CSDIC (U.I.) SIR 1717.
IF-126 "Interrogation Report on Schwartze and Graupe." CSDIC (U.K.) SIR 1335.
IF-127 "Interrogation Report on Schwartze and Graupe." CSDIC (U.K.) SIR 1374.
IF-130 "Copy of MIS Dossier on Fellgiebel." From Captured German Army Official Dossier now in MIS Files, Pentagon.
IF-131 "Detailed Interrogation Report--Notes on Signal Intelligence (Monitoring)." 6824 DIC (MIS) M. 1080 18 March 1945.
IF-162 "Report on Preliminary Evaluation of German Equipment for interception of Russian Multichannel teletype circuits."
IF-171 "Report on Further Information obtained from Uffz. Kotschy and Uffz. Boscheinen both from Festungs art Abt. 1518, deserted Diffenbach." CSDIC (UK) SIR 1346.
IF-172 "Report on Further Information obtained from Uffz. Kotschy and Uffz. Boscheinen both Festungs art Abt 1518, deserted at Diffenbach 22 Nov. 1944." CSDIC (UK) SIR 1341 20 Dec. 1944.
IF-176 Seabourne Report, Vol. III. "Operation and Techniques of the Radio Defense Corps, German Wehrmacht."
IF-181 Seabourne Report, Vol. VI. "Origins of the Luftwaffe SIS and History of Its Operations in the West."
IF-190 "The Organization and History of the Cryptographic Service Within the German Army." CSDIC (UK) SIR 1704 8 July 1945.
IF-202 "Report on Information Obtained from PW Uffz Boscheinen, both of Fest Art Abt 1518, deserted at Diffenbach, 22 Nov. 44." CSDIC (UK) SIR 1326.
In 7/IV (Inspektion 7/IV, Inspectorate &/IV). Army Signal Security Agency 1940-1942; Army Agency for production of Army systems 1942-1944.
Inspektion 7/IV, Inspectorate 7/IV (In 7/IV). Army Signal Security Agency 1940-1942; Army Agency for Production of Ciphers 1942-1944.
Inspectorate 7/IV, Inspektion 7/IV (In 7/IV). Army Signal Security Agency 1940-1942; Army Agency for Production of Codes for Army 1942-44.

In 7/VI (Inspektion 7/VI, Inspectorate 7/VI). Central cryptanalytic agency of the German Army High Command 1941-1942. Central cryptanalytic agency of the German Army High Command for non-Russian traffic 1942-1943.

Inspektion 7/VI, Inspectorate 7/VI (In 7/VI). Central cryptanalytic agency of the Army High Command 1941-1942. Central cryptanalytic agency of the Army High Command for non-Russian traffic 1942-1943.

Inspectorate 7/VI, Inspektion 7/VI (In 7/VI). Central cryptanalytic agency of the Army High Command 1941-1942. Central cryptanalytic agency of the Army High Command for non-Russian traffic 1942-1943.

Intercept Control Station.--Horchleitstelle (HLS). Central cryptanalytic and evaluating agency of the Army High Command 1933-1941.

Intercept Control Station East.--Horchleitstelle Ost (HLS Ost).

Intercept Evaluation Station Southeast.--Horchauswertestelle Suedost (HASSO).

Jering, Karl, Tech. Sgt. Attached to Chi-Stelle / OBdL.

Jodl, Alfred, General. Chief of Armed Forces Operations Staff, OKW.

Karrenberg,_____, Corporal. Attached OKH/GdNA. Cryptographer on enciphered Baudot Traffic.

Kettler,_____, Col. Head of HLS Ost 1942; Chief of Signal Intelligence Agency of Supreme Command of the Armed Forces (OKW/Chi) 1942-1945.

Kneschke,_____. Head, section 2, Group IV, Signal Intelligence Agency of Army High Command (OKH/GdNA)

Koebe,_____, Lt. Chief of Understaff, Signal Intelligence Agency of the Army High Command (OKH/GdNA).

Koehler,_____, Technician. Head of linguistic section 1941-1945.

Kommandeur der Nachrichten Aufklaerung (KONA).--Signal Intelligence Regiment.

KONA (Kommandeur der Nachrichten Aufklaerung).--Signal Intelligence Regiment.

Kopp,_____, Col. Senior Commander of Signal Intelligence late 1944. Attached to C in C West.

Kotschy, Walter, Non Commissioned Officer. Hungarian Interpreter. Worked in Italian section of Afrika Korps. Trained in "encoding and decoding" at In 7/VI.

Kuehn,_____, Senior Inspector. Head of training section of In 7/VI 1941-1945 (later head of section 5, Group IV GdNA).

226

Kuehne, Hans Wolfgang, Technician. Head of French section In 7/VI from 1941 to Feb. 1945.
Lechner,_____, Major. Chief In 7/VI 1943; Commander KONA 6 1945.
Lenz. Waldemar, Doctor O/Funker. Member of French section In 7/VI; later in Paris. Involved in Schulze-Boysen Case.
Leitstelle der Nachrichten Aufklaerung (LNA).--Control Station of Signal Intelligence. Central evaluating agency of Army High Command 1942-1944.
Liebknecht,_____, Cryptanalyst in OKW/Chi.
Liedtke,_____, O/Insp. Head of English section of In 7/VI until 1943. Specialty: British codes.
LNA (Leitstelle der Nachrichten Aufklaerung).--Control Station of Signal Intelligence. Central evaluating agency of Army High Command 1942-1944.
LN Regt. (Luftnachrichten Regiment).--Air Signals Regiment.
Loeffler, Lt. Harry. Attached to Stationary Intercept Company 10 (Feste 10)
Long Range Signal Intelligence Company.--(Nachrichten Fernaufklaerung Kompanie (FAK).
Long Range Signal Intelligence Platoon.--(Nachrichten Fernaufklaerungszug (FAZ).
Lueders,_____, 1st Lt. Head of Mathematical section, sub-section 7 of In 7/VI.
Luftnachrichten Regiment (LN Regiment).--Air Signals Regiment.
Luzius,_____, Doctor Corporal. Mathematician in USA section of In 7/VI Specialty: M-209.
Main Section.--Hauptreferat.
Manaigo,_____, Corporal. Head of Italian section 1943, In 7/VI.
Mang,_____, Major. Organized In 7/VI in 1942; Chief In 7/VI 1941-1942.
Marquardt,_____, Captain. Commanding Officer NAAS 4. Head of Group 14, Sub Section 1a, of Signal Intelligence Agency of Army High Command.
Martini,_____,General. Chief Signal Officer of the Air Force.
Menzer,_____. Member of OKW/Chi.
Mettig,_____, Lt. Colonel. Signal Officer since 1933; Head, In 7/VI from November 1941 to June 1943; Second in command of OKW/Chi from December 1943 to April 1945.
Mje-Koja,_____, 1st Lt. Finnish liaison officer at Loetzen (HLS OST)
Moravec,_____, Lt. Adjutant to Boetzel, Chief of Signal Intelligence Agency of Army High Command (GdNA).

NAA (Nachrichten Aufklaerung Abteilung).--Signal Intelligence Battalion.
NAA/Chef H Ruest B d E (Nachrichten Aufklaerung Abteilung Chef der Heeresruestung u, Befehlshaber des Ersatzheeres).--Signal Intelligence Regiment of the Replacement Army.
NAAS (Nachrichten Aufklaerung Auswertestelle).-- Signal Intelligence Evaluation Center.
Nachrichten Aufklaerung Abteilung (NAA).-- Signal Intelligence Battalion.
Nachrichten Aufklaerung Abteilung/Chef der Heeresruestung u, Befehlshaber des Ersatzheeres (NAA/Chef H Ruest B d E).--Signal Intelligence Regiment of the Replacement Army.
Nachrichten Aufklaerung Auswertestelle (NAAS).--Signal Intelligence Evaluation Center.
Nachrichten Aufklaerungs Ersatz und Ausbildungs Abteilung (NAEuAA).-- Signal Intelligence Replacement and Training Battalion.
Nachrichten Dolmetscher Ersatz und Ausbildungs Abteilung (NDEuAA).--Signal Interpreter Replacement and Training Battalion.
Nachrichten Fernaufklaerung Kompanie (FAF).-- Long Range Signal Intelligence Company.
Nachrichten Fernaufklaerungszug (FAZ).--Long Range Signal Intelligence Platoon.
Nachrichten Nahaufklaerung Kompanie (NAK).--Close Range Signal Intelligence Company.
Nachrichten Nahaufklaerungszug (NAZ).--Close Range Signal Intelligence Platoon.
NAEuAA (Nachrichten Aufklaerungs Ersatz und Ausbildungs Abteilung).--Signal Intelligence Replacement and Training Battalion.
NAK (Nachrichten Nahaufklaerung Kompanie).--Close Range Signal Intelligence Company.
NAZ (Nachrichten Narhrichten Nahaufklaerungszug).--Close Range Signal Intelligence Platoon.
NDEuAA (Nachrichten Dolmetscher Ersatz und Ausbildungs Abteilung).--Signal Interpreter Replacement and Training Battalion.
NKVD (Narodni Kommissariat Vnutrinikh Del).--Peoples' Commissariat for Internal Affairs.

Novopaschenny, _____, Prof. Member of Signal Intelligence Agency of Supreme Command of Armed Forces (OKW/Chi) and of In 7/VI.

Oberbefehlshaber Sued.--Commander in Chief South.
Oberbefehlshaber West.--Commander in Chief West.
Oberkommando der Luftwaffe/General Nachrichten Fuehrer/Abteilung III (OKL/Gen Na Fue/III).--Signal Intelligence Service of the Air Force High Command.
Oberkommando des Heeres/Allgemeines Heeres Amt/Amtsgruppe Nachrichten/Nachrichten Aufklaerung (OKH/AHA/AgN/NA).--Signal Intelligence Department of Signals, General Army Office, Army High Command.
Oberkommando des Heeres (OKH).--Army High Command.
Oberkommando des Heeres/General der Nachrichten Aufklaerung (OKH/GdNA).--Signal Intelligence Agency of the Army High Command.
Oberkommando der Marine/Seekriegsleitung/III (OKM/SKL IV/III).--Signal Intelligence Agency of the Navy High Command.
Oberkommando der Wehrmacht/Chiffrierabteilung (OKW/Chi).--Signal Intelligence Agency of the Supreme Command of the Armed Forces.
Oberkommando der Wehrmacht, Wehrmacht Nachrichten Verbindungs Funküberwachung (OKW/WNV/FU).-- Radio Defense Corps_____.
Oeljeschlaeger, Franz, Major. Chief of Group II, Division III of the Chief Signal Office.
OHN, _____, 1st Lt. Finnish liaison officer at Loetzen (HLS Ost).
OKH (Oberkommando des Heeres).--Army High Command.
OKH/AHA/AgN/NA (Oberkommando des Heeres/Allgemeines Heeres Amt/Amtsgruppe Nachrichten/Nachrichten Aufklaerung).--Signal Intelligence Department of Signals, General Army Office, Army High Command.
OKH/GdNA (Oberkommando des Heeres. General der Nachrichten Aufklaerung).--Signal Intelligence Agency of the Army High Command.
OKL/Gen Na Fue/III (Oberkommando der Luftwaffe/General Nachrichten Fuehrer/Abteilung III).-- Signal Intelligence Service of the Air Force High Command.
OKM/SKL IV/III (Oberkommando der Marine/Seekriegsleitung/IV/III).--Signal Intelligence Agency of the Navy High Command.
OKW/Chi (Oberkommando der Wehrmacht/Chiffrier Abteilung).--Signal Intelligence Agency of the Supreme Command of the Armed Forces.

OKW/WNV/FU (Oberkommando der Wehrmacht, Wehrmacht Nachrichten Verbindungen Funküberwachung)--Radio Defense Corps of the Armed Forces High Command.
ORPO (Ordnungspolizei).--Regular Police
Ordnungspolizei (ORPO).--Regular Police
Oschmann,_____, Major. Chief of Code and Cipher Section of German Defense Ministry 1932-1934.
Osten-Sacken, von der, Baron Col. Head of HLS Ost 1942-1944. Implicated in plot on Hitler's life 20 July 1944 and committed suicide.
Pale, Erkki, Captain in Reserve. Chief of Finnish Crypt. Outfit at Sortanala.
Peilzug,_____. Direction Finding Platoon.
Peoples' Commissariat for Internal Affairs.--NKVD
Pers ZS (Sorderdienst des Referats Z in der Personal Abteilung des Auswaertigen Amtes).--Cryptanalytic Section of the Foreign Office.
Pietsch,_____. Baurat Dr. Sonderfuehrer, Head of Mathematical Section of In 7/VI (later Section 1 of Group IV, GdNA).
Praun,_____, General. Chief Signal Officer, Armed Forces, Chief Signal Officer Army 1944-1945 (Chef WNV Chef HNW).
Preuss,_____, 1st Lieutenant. Commanding Officer of Close Range Signal Company (NAK Preuss).
Radio Control Station.--Rundfunkueberwachungsstelle.
Radio Defense Corps of the Armed Forces High Command, (OKW/WNV/FU).--Oberkommando der Wehrmacht, Wehrmacht Nachrichten Verbindungs Funküberwachung.
Radio Intercept Station.--Wetterfunkempfangsstelle, (W-Stelle).
Randewig,_____, Col. Commander of Western Intercept Stations 1939 C.O. of Hoeh. Wehrmachts Nafue z.b. V 700.
Referat,_____. Section
Reichs Kriegsministerium.--War Ministry (term used during 1935-1938, later changed into Oberkommando der Wehrmacht).
Reichswehrministerium.--German Defense Ministry.
Rhinow,_____, Corporal. Member of Mathematical Section of In 7/VI.
Riemerschmidt,_____, 1st Lt. German Army liaison officer at RTK (Finnish Crypt. Outfit).
Roeder, Herbert, Captain. Head of Gruppe VI, Gen.d.NA, OKH, 1944-45.
Roessler, Capt. Chief Evaluator with KONA 1, Commanding Officer of NAAS 1.
Rohdan,_____, Pfc. Head of Swedish section of AgN/NA 1943.

DOCID: 3486746

Rundfunkueberwachungstelle.--Radio Control Station.
Samsonow, Sergius, Master Sergeant. Head of Section 3a of Group IV. Specialty: Russian Secret Police Systems (NKWD).
Sauerbier, Kurt. Member of FA. Worked on Russian Agents' Code.
Schenke, Specialist. Head of IBM section of In 7/VI 1942-1945.
Schmidt,_____, Captain. Commanding Officer of NAA 11, head of 'Norway Party'.
Schmidt,_____, Major. Head of Code and Cipher Section of German Defense Ministry 1927-1931.
Schubert,_____, 1st Lt. Expert on Russian and Polish Army and Agents' Codes and Ciphers.
Section.--Referat.
Seebohm,_____. Commander of FAK 621 in North Africa until capture July 1942.
Seemueller,_____, Lt. Col. C.O. of KONA 4 Feb. 1943-April 44.
Sendezug,_____. Communication Platoon.
Senior Commander of Signal Intelligence.--Hoeherer Kommandeur der Nachrichten Aufklaerung (Hoeh Kdr d NA).
Signal Intelligence, Department of Signals, General Army Office, Army High Command.--Oberkommando des Heeres/ Allgemeines Heeres Amt/Amtsgruppe Nachrichten/ Nachrichten Aufklaerung (OKH/AHA/AgN/NA).
Signal Intelligence Agency of the Army High Command.--Oberkommando des Heeres/General der Nachrichten Aufklaerung OKH/GdNA).
Signal Intelligence Agency of the Commander in Chief of the Air Force.--Chiffrierstelle des Oberbefehlshabers der Luftwaffe, abbreviated (Chi-Stelle, OBdL).
Signal Intelligence Agency of the Navy High Command.--Oberkommando der Marine/Seekriegsleitung IV/III (OKM/SKL/IV/III).
Signal Intelligence Agency of the Supreme Command of the Armed Forces.--Oberkommando der Wehrmacht/Chiffrier Abteilung (OKW/Chi).
Signal Intelligence Battalion.--Nachrichten Aufklaerung Abteilung (NAA).
Signal Intelligence Evaluation Center.--Nachrichten Aufklaerung Auswertestelle (NAAS).
Signal Intelligence Regiment.--Kommandeur der Nachrichten Aufklaerung (KONA).

DOCID: 3486746

Signal Intelligence Regiment of the Replacement Army.--Nachrichten Aufklaerung Abteilung/ Chef der Heeresruestung u. Befehlshaber des Ersatzheeres, (NAA/Chef H Ruest B d E).
Signal Intelligence Replacement and Training Battalion.--Nachrichten Aufklaerungs Ersatz und Ausbildungs Abteilung (NAE u AA).
Signal Intelligence Service of the Air Force High Command.--Oberkommando der Luftwaffe/ General Nachrichten Fuehrer/ Abteilung III (OKL/Gen Na Fue/III).
Signal Interpreter Replacement and Training Battalion.--Nachrichten Dolmetscher Ersatz und Ausbildungs Abteilung (NDE u AA).
Sonderdienst des Referats Z in der Personalabteilung des Auswaertigen Amtes (Pers ZS).--Cryptanalytic Section of the Foreign Office.
Specialist, See Amtmann (AMTM).
Starke,_____, Lt. Attached to NAK on the Eastern front.
State Police.--Ordnungspolizei(ORPO).
Stationary Intercept Company.--Feste Nachrichten Aufklaerungsstelle (Feste).
Steinberg, Dr. Technician. Mathematic section of In 7/VI; later section 1 of Group IV, GdNA; Worked on USA systems--M 94 and M 209.
T-805 "Russian Decryption in the Former German Army" by Dettmann and Samsonow. See: DF-18.
Thomas,_____, Pfc. Attached to NAAS 1.
USA non-morse radio teletype.--Funkfernschreib (FF).
Vaatz,_____, 1st Lt. German Air Force Liaison officer with Finnish Hq's at Mikkeli.
Vauck,_____,1st Lt. Head of Agents Section In 7/VI 1942-1945.
Waffen pruefung (Wa Pruef).--Army Ordnance, Signal Equipment Testing Laboratory.
Wa Pruef (Waffen Pruefung). Army Ordnance, Development and Testing Group, Signal Branch.
Wehrmacht Nachrichten Verbindungen/Funkueberwachung (WNV/FU).--Radio Defense Corps.
Wenzel,_____, Specialist. Attached to Forschungsamt (FA).
Wetterfunkempfangsstelle (W-Stelle).--Radio Intercept Station, (Weather).
W-Stelle (Wetterfunkempfangsstelle).-- Radio Intercept Station.
Winkler, Oscar, Corporal. Member of KONA 4.

DOCID: 3486746

TOP SECRET

GERMAN ARMY SIGNAL INTELLIGENCE SERVICE IN THE WEST

CHAIN OF COMMAND

SPRING 1944

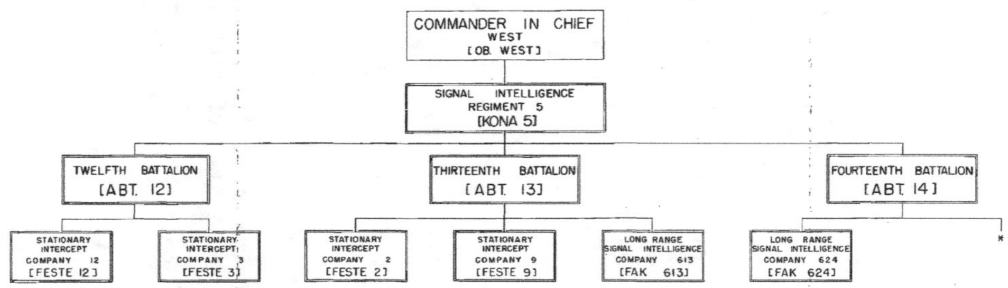

GERMAN ARMY SIGNAL INTELLIGENCE SERVICE IN THE WEST

CHAIN OF COMMAND

JANUARY 1945

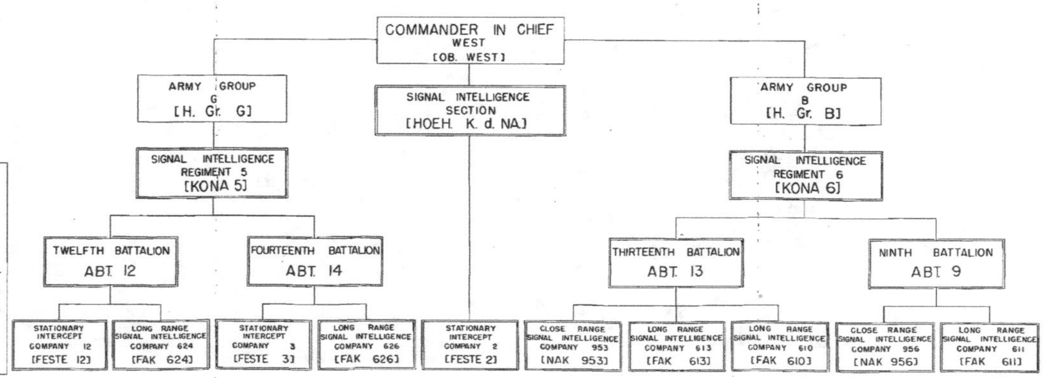

LEGEND

ABT.	–	ABTEILUNG
FAK	–	FERNAUFKLAERUNGSKOMPANIE
FESTE	–	FESTE HORCHSTELLE
H. Gr.	–	HEERESGRUPPE
HOEH. K. d. NA.	–	HOEHERER KOMMANDEUR DER NACHRICHTEN-AUFKLAERUNG
KONA	–	KOMMANDEUR DER NACHRICHTENAUFKLAERUNG
NAK	–	NAHAUFKLAERUNGSKOMPANIE
OB.	–	OBERBEFEHLSHABER
*		OTHER COMPANIES, IF ANY, NOT KNOWN

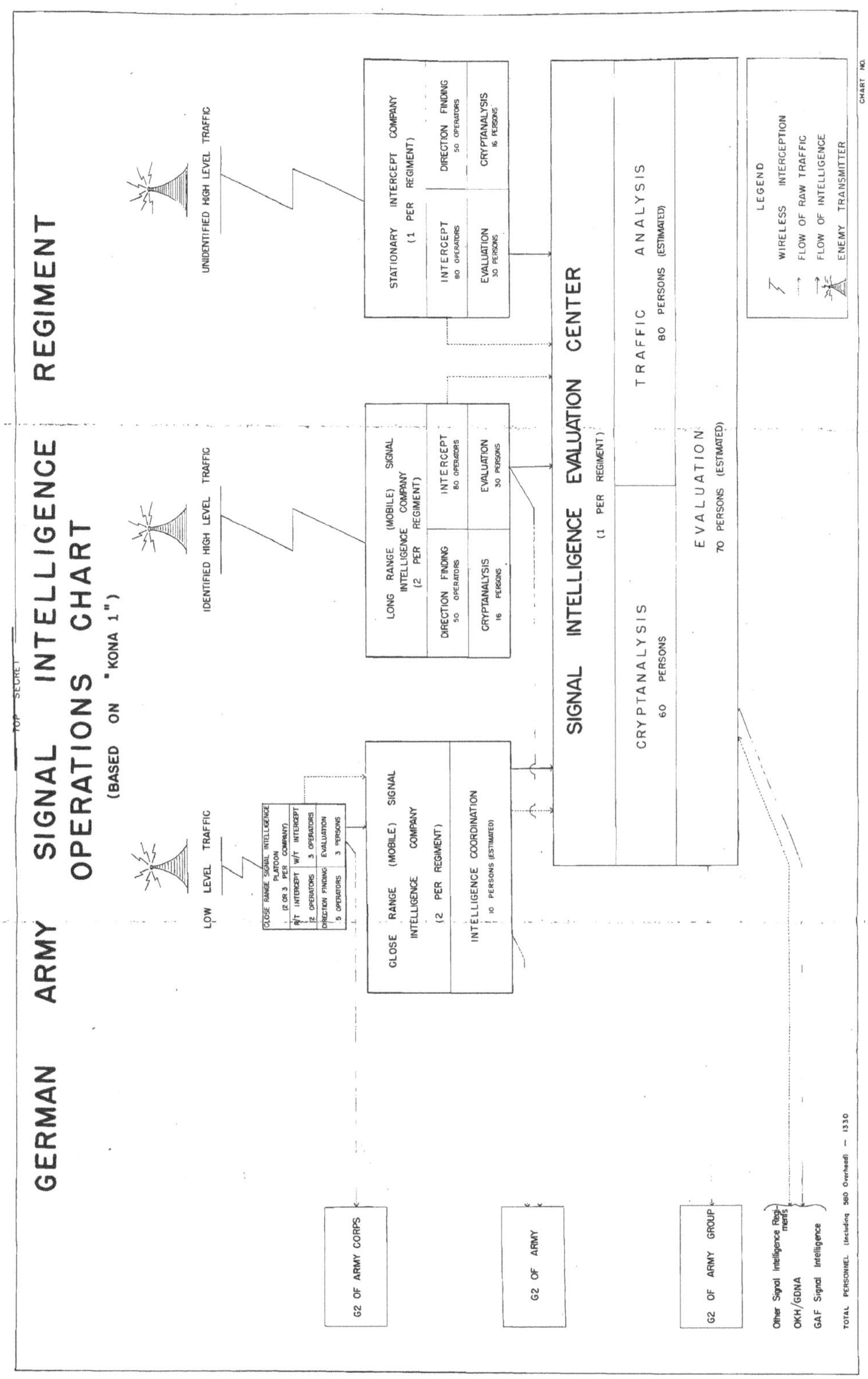
TOP SECRET
GERMAN ARMY SIGNAL INTELLIGENCE REGIMENT
OPERATIONS CHART
(BASED ON "KONA 1")
LOW LEVEL TRAFFIC
IDENTIFIED HIGH LEVEL TRAFFIC
UNIDENTIFIED HIGH LEVEL TRAFFIC
CLOSE RANGE SIGNAL INTELLIGENCE PLATOON (2 OR 3 PER COMPANY)
R/T INTERCEPT 2 OPERATORS
W/T INTERCEPT 3 OPERATORS
DIRECTION FINDING 5 OPERATORS
EVALUATION 3 PERSONS
CLOSE RANGE (MOBILE) SIGNAL INTELLIGENCE COMPANY (2 PER REGIMENT)
INTELLIGENCE COORDINATION 10 PERSONS (ESTIMATED)
LONG RANGE (MOBILE) SIGNAL INTELLIGENCE COMPANY (2 PER REGIMENT)
DIRECTION FINDING 50 OPERATORS
INTERCEPT 80 OPERATORS
CRYPTANALYSIS 16 PERSONS
EVALUATION 30 PERSONS
STATIONARY INTERCEPT COMPANY (1 PER REGIMENT)
INTERCEPT 80 OPERATORS
DIRECTION FINDING 50 OPERATORS
EVALUATION 30 PERSONS
CRYPTANALYSIS 16 PERSONS
SIGNAL INTELLIGENCE EVALUATION CENTER (1 PER REGIMENT)
CRYPTANALYSIS 60 PERSONS
TRAFFIC ANALYSIS 80 PERSONS (ESTIMATED)
EVALUATION 70 PERSONS (ESTIMATED)
G2 OF ARMY CORPS
G2 OF ARMY
G2 OF ARMY GROUP
Other Signal Intelligence Regiments
OKH/GDNA
GAF Signal Intelligence
TOTAL PERSONNEL (including 580 Overhead) — 1330
LEGEND
WIRELESS INTERCEPTION
FLOW OF RAW TRAFFIC
FLOW OF INTELLIGENCE
ENEMY TRANSMITTER
CHART NO.

DOCID: 3486746

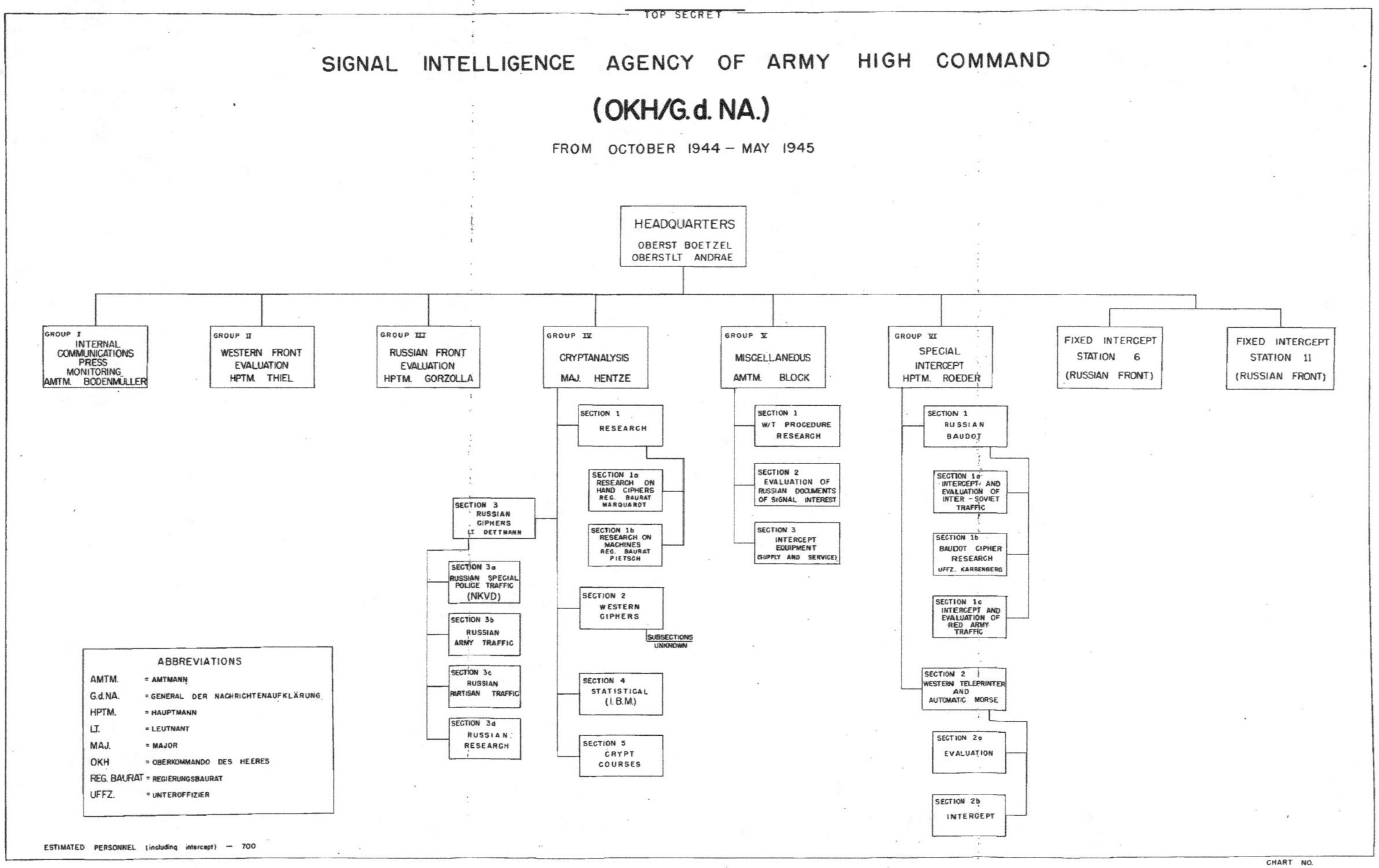

DOCID: 3486746

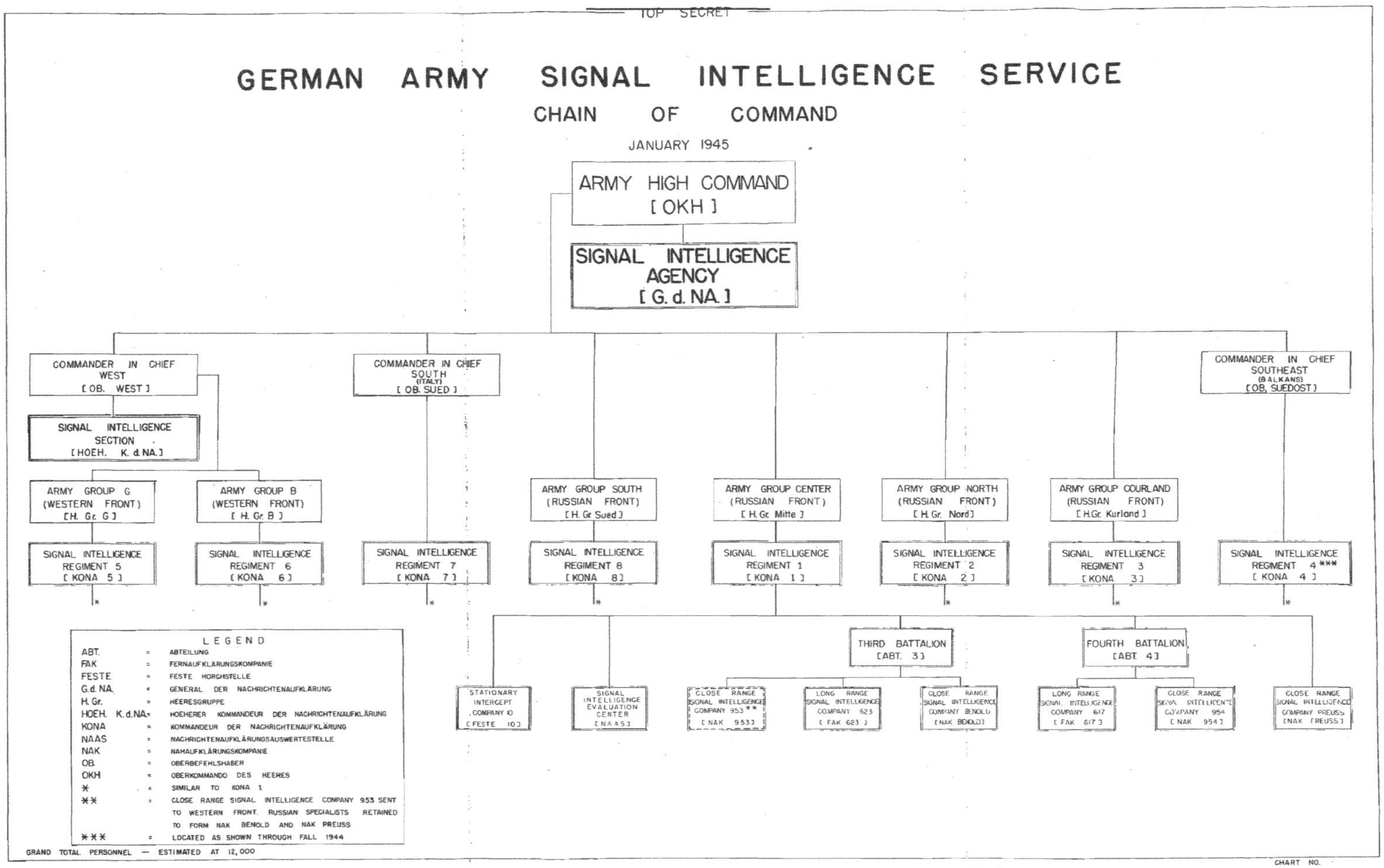

WNV/Fu/III (Wehrmacht Nachrichten Verbindungswesen Funkueberwachung III).--Radio Defense Corps.

Wollny, Oblt. Commanding Officer of Feste 6; formerly Commanding Officer of NAZ W of KONA 4.

Zillmann,_____, Senior Inspector. Head of British section of In 7/VI 1941.

Zipper,_____, Inspector. Head of section 1, Group V GdNA.

DOCID: 3560829

~~TOP SECRET CREAM~~

~~SECRET~~
By Authority of the
Commanding General
Initials Date
OCT 01 1946

ARMY SECURITY AGENCY

Washington, D. C.

EUROPEAN AXIS SIGNAL INTELLIGENCE IN WORLD WAR II

AS REVEALED BY "TICOM" INVESTIGATIONS

AND BY OTHER PRISONER OF WAR INTERROGATIONS

AND CAPTURED MATERIAL, PRINCIPALLY GERMAN

VOLUME 5--THE GERMAN AIR FORCE SIGNAL

INTELLIGENCE SERVICE

Prepared under the direction of the

CHIEF, ARMY SECURITY AGENCY

1 May 1946

WDGAS-14

~~TOP SECRET CREAM~~

VOLUME 5

The German Air Force Signal Intelligence Service

VOLUME 5

THE GERMAN AIR FORCE SIGNAL INTELLIGENCE SERVICE

Chapter I. The Service in General: Sources of Information Concerning It

Paragraph

1. Introduction.- This volume presents a discussion of the history, organization and operations of the German Air Force Signal Intelligence Service from its beginning in 1937 until the German capitulation in 1945.

The outstanding achievement of the German Air Force Signal Intelligence Service was its development of "signal intelligence without cryptanalysis."[1] The exploitation of every radio manifestation, which for the Germans included radar monitoring, the monitoring of beacons, the evaluation of tuning transmissions and chatter, highly efficient direction finding, radio telephone monitoring and traffic analysis, provided valuable strategic and tactical intelligence.

The Service was expanded from one officer and twenty civilians in 1937 to thirteen thousand persons in 1945, of which sixty-six hundred were in the West, four thousand in the East, and twenty-four hundred in the South.

2. Objectives.- The lightning advances of the Germans in 1939 had resulted in the German Air Force Signal Intelligence Service placing its main emphasis on radio telephone monitoring and tactical evaluation. During the quiet period after the fall of France, stress was placed on strategic evaluation in order to present a coherent picture of British Air Order of Battle and long range intentions. In addition, small units were located in the Balkans to provide intelligence of Russian deployment and intentions. Strategic evaluation continued throughout the war, but as allied raids were intensified in 1943 tactical evaluation again became important as a means of providing early warning of impending Allied raids. For this purpose an intricate system of reporting centers (Meldekopfe) and a central warning unit (Zentraler Gefechsstand fuer Funkauswetung) were established in 1944. The evaluation of the traffic of tactical air force units operating in conjunction with Allied ground armies was also stressed as the Germans were forced on the defense on all fronts.

[1] I 42 p 4

3. Detailed successes of Signal Intelligence.--The steps leading to the success of the German Air Force Signal Intelligence in their attack on Allied radio traffic will be treated in later chapters. A summary of that success will be indicated here by briefly sketching the results achieved against Russia, the United States, and Britain.

a. Russia.--Throughout the course of the war against Russia 85 per cent of the Morse ground-to-ground traffic of the Soviet Air Armies, Corps and Divisions and of the supporting ground organizations was deciphered. Ground-to-ground radio traffic (such as fighter control) consisting of simple word encodements was continuously solvable. The air-ground traffic of the Soviet long-range bomber formations, although only partially deciphered, permitted German traffic-analysts to chart Soviet air raids in time to give adequate warning. The great volume of information derived from message contents and from traffic analysis of the structure and functionings of the networks enabled the German Air Force Signal Intelligence Service in the East to present to its intelligence authorities an accurate and current listing of the Soviet Air Force order of battle on the three operational fronts, and of the deployment of the Russian ground forces to which the Soviet air forces served as an adjunct. Furthermore this information provided immediate and timely warning of air raids, route-tracking of bomber formations, as well as indicated long-range intentions of both Soviet ground and air forces, and provided information of supply and economic conditions.[2] Although up until the time of Stalingrad signal intelligence warnings had not been heeded, when the signal intelligence unit on the Southern Front correctly advised that the Russians had assembled 5 air armies in the Stalingrad sector, "sigint was held to be the main source of intelligence."[3]

b. United States.--The chief success against the United States Air Force was made possible by alert traffic analysis.

Although air-ground systems, used jointly by the Americans and British, were read in many cases (e.g. Bomber Code, REKOH, and SYKO), the effectiveness of cryptanalysis was definitely limited.

The Chief of the German Air Force Signal Intelligence Agency, Lt. Col. Friedrich, claimed that he had "no contents from ground-ground radio traffic;"[4] and interrogations showed that whatever success was achieved with M 209 was usually too late for exploitation.

Traffic analysis, however, was able to provide A-2 with a comprehensive and continuous picture of the battle order and deployment of the United States Air Force in Britain, later on the continent, and in the Mediterranean. Numerous predictions were also made of long-range air force intentions. Tactically, traffic analysis of "all radio manifestations" (which for the Germans included everything from radio signals to beacons) gave

[2] I 70 p 4

[3] I 41 p 7

[4] I 70 p 5

immediate ~~and~~ timely warning of American air raids. As a result of what Friedrich called "the reliance on good encipherment and neglect of supervision of American radio traffic... the almost continuous radio traffic in the air... and radio traffic beginning regularly and uniformly, always sent by routine procedure.."[5], the Germans were able to reconstruct in the West the organization and strength of the 8th United States Air Force (and its bomber and fighter commands), the 9th Air Force, and the Allied Expeditionary Air Force (consisting of the United States 9th Air Force, the 1st United States Tactical Air Force and the 2nd British Tactical Air Force). The United States 1st Tactical Air Force, Allied Air Transport Units and other air units were successfully monitored. Major long-range operations, such as the invasion and the break-through at Avranches were, with some degree of success, correctly forecast. Tactical monitoring of the United States air support parties "yielded much more information about Allied Army order of battle than did the regular army net works,"[6] since the air support parties acted in conjunction with specific ground units.

In the Mediterranean and Middle East the German Air Signals Regiment 352 was able to reconstruct with minute accuracy the dispositions and strength of the Allied Air Force -- the 9th Tactical Air Command (one Combat Mapping group, 4 fighter groups, and one medium bomber group), the 57th Medium Bomber Wing, the 5th, 47th, 49th, 55th, and 304th Heavy Bomber Wings, the 15th Fighter Command and the Mediterranean Air Transport Service.

The accurate reconstruction of Allied order of battle attests to the effectiveness of the German analysts. American A-2 evaluation of German signal intelligence operations directed against the United States 9th Air Force states that the portions of the German discussions "dealing with the operations and activities of the 9th Air Force reveal a full and complete knowledge on the part of the Luftwaffe Signal Intelligence Service... The success of (their) efforts and the degree to which (their) operations had been developed was an uncomfortable surprise... The information of the enemy was thorough, complete, and accurate in its broad aspects; there were minor discrepancies, inaccuracies, confusion; ... but, in general, it may be said that the Luftwaffe Signal Intelligence Service was a most scientific, professional and able organization, performing a valuable, meticulously complete, and reliable service for the enemy."[7] Operational strengths were in the main correctly estimated and the precision with which unit movements were followed is said to be truly impressive.

The success of the German Air Force Signal Intelligence in its analysis of American Air Force traffic was not exploited by the German operational units, which were sluggish in acting upon the information provided them. Friedrich complained that it was not his job to get the windmills (German fighters) airborne. It was up to him merely to give the warnings.

[5] I 70 p 5

[6] IF 182 p 83

[7] IF 177 p 24

3

In the Mediterranean, according to members of Air Signals Rgt. 352, "it was a course of bitter chagrin to the Luftwaffe Signal Intelligence Service that the German Command lacked the resources to translate its realistic intelligence into offensive action."[8]

c. Britain. - Royal Air Force systems produced the greatest amount of intelligence on air-ground circuits. SYKO, REKOH, Slidex and the Bomber Code were currently solved. Although the RAF 4-figure code was changed in November 1942 and thereafter proved most difficult for the Germans,[9] it had been read up to that time. Both on the strategic and tactical level, German Air Force Signal Intelligence achieved notable results on British Air Force traffic. In the West the Germans were able to reconstruct accurately the order of battle, deployment, strength, equipment, and intentions of the Royal Air Force, and through it, of the ground organization.[10] In order of battle, the following RAF units were continuously followed throughout the war: The 1st, 3rd, 4th, 5th, 6th, 8th, 91st, 92nd, 93rd, Bomber Groups; the 100th Group, the 9th, 10th, 11th, 12th, 13th, and 82nd Fighter Groups; the 15th, 16th, 17th, 18th, 19th Reconnaissance Groups of the Coastal Command; and units of the 2nd Tactical Air Force, and of the RAF Transport Command.

On the tactical level the monitoring of RAF VHF and centimeter radar transmission and navigational aids permitted the German Air Force Signal Intelligence Service "to accomplish the following:

(1) To give accurate, long and short interval, early warning of both daylight and night raids of heavy bomber formations;

(2) By continuously tracking heavy bomber formations to present to the fighter defense a lucid picture of the air situation, from the time of take-off to the landing of enemy formations; further,

(3) To interpret the picture of the air situation in such a manner as to predict the enemy's strength in formation, depth of penetration, targets, and deceptive tactics."[11]

In the Mediterranean area, German Air Force Signal Intelligence was able to chart RAF operations throughout the war. In the first years of the war German Air Force Signal Intelligence Service succeeded, by breaking "the most frequently used cryptographic systems ... to read the bulk of the messages intercepted."[12] The extensive use of radio communications (occasioned both by the geographical extent of the Mediterranean theater, and an insufficiency of wire communication facilities)[13]

[8] IF 185 p 24

[9] I 70 p 5

[10] IF 182 p 42

[11] IF 183 p 2

[12] IF 185 p 2

[13] IF 185 p 2

DOCID: 3560829

permitted a minutely accurate reconstruction of RAF order of battle, strength, equipment and intentions. German Air Force Signal Intelligence was able to follow RAF operations down to squadron level. The following units were monitored: the 206th and 225th Reconnaissance Squadrons, the 414th and 416th Night Fighter Squadrons, the 8th Fighter Group of the South African Air Force, the various units of the RAF Desert Air Force (MASAF), elements of the 90th Mediterranean Allied Photo Reconnaissance Wing, the RAF Mediterranean Allied Coastal Air Force (MACAF) and the various components of RAF Middle East, including the RAF Balkan Air Force, RAF Air Headquarters, Greece, Eastern Mediterranean, and Air Transport Command.

4. Administrative Difficulties.--The success of the Air Force analytic effort seems to have been achieved in spite of rather than because of the administration of the organization. Interminable disputes prevented the smooth functioning of the service. One of the issues frequently disputed was whether it was better for the Signal Intelligence Agency to be subordinated to the Chief Signal Officer (General Nachrichten Fuehrer, abb. Gen. Nafue), or to the A-2. Another subject of controversy was the separation of administrative from operational control, set out at least on paper, between the Senior Signal Intelligence Officer (Hoeherer Kommandeur der Funkaufklaerung, abb. Hoe Kmdr d Funkaufklrg) and the Signal Intelligence Agency. There were arguments over the exercise of the various types of control (administrative, tactical-operational, strategic-operational, etc.) over the units in the field, that is the Air Signal Regiments and the Air Signal Battalions (Luftnachrichten Regiments, abb. LN Regt, and Luftnachrichten Abteilungen, abb. LN Abt). The latter disputes involved the rival claims for the control of the Air Force Signal Intelligence, the centralized Signal Intelligence Agency, the decentralized local Air Forces (Luftflotten), the Senior Signal Intelligence Officer, and in the latter stages of the war, the Chief of the Air Raid Warning Service for Germany (Funkaufklaerungsfuehrer Reich, abb. FAF).

These claims, when they were settled at all, were resolved by compromise and appeasement. In general, the Signal Intelligence Service was subordinated to the Chief Signal Officer and not to the A-2, although the latter was the chief consumer of the intelligence product.

The control over the field regiments and battalions may be outlined as follows:

a. Administrative or service matters: Control was exercised by the Senior Air Signal Intelligence Officer (Hoe Kmdr d Lu FA) to whom the Commanders of the Air Signal Regiments and Battalions were subordinated.

b. Tactical matters (strategic movements and deployment): Control was exercised by the Signal Officer of the local air force (Luftflotte) to which the field unit was attached.

c. Operational matters: Control was exercised by the Signal Intelligence Agency (LN Abt-350 in the 1944 reorganization) of the Air Force (Oberbefehlshaber der luftwaffe, abb. Ob d L).

5. Sources of Information.- Several sources of information were used for this volume:

a. The TICOM interrogations of prisoners. (The I Reports)

b. A 13-volume report entitled "The Signal Intelligence Service of the German Luftwaffe" compiled by Col. J. G. Seabourne, chief of the Air Technical Intelligence Team of the USAAF. (IF 175 through IF 187)

c. Report of the British Air Ministry (A.D.I.(K)),[14] entitled "German Air Force Signals Intelligence in the War."

d. German documents captured by TICOM teams consisting of minutes of Signal Intelligence meetings, reports, etc., including filmed excerpts from the Supplementary Volume B to War Diary 2 (Division 1) (Anlagenband B. Zu Kriegstagebuch II [1 Abt]).

(1) TICOM, through its interrogations of prisoners, obtained a working picture of the German Air Force Signal Intelligence Service. Traffic analysts and cryptanalysts active in the Chi-Stelle and in the various field units explained the details of their operations. Chief among these were Lt. Col. Friedrich, head of the 3rd Division of the Office of the Chief Signal Officer (Gen. Nafue III) which dealt with signal intelligence, and at the same time Chief of Air Signal Battalion 350 (LN Abt. 350, The Signal Intelligence Agency). Specialist (Regierungsrat) Dr. Voegele, Chief Cryptanalyst of the German Air Force Signal Intelligence Service and specialist on Anglo-American systems, made a number of reports. Lt. Ludwig, chief evaluator on the Western front; Major Feichtner, Commanding Officer of Air Signals Regiment 352, which operated on the Mediterranean front; Captains Herold and Scheidl, 1st Lt. Werther and Chlubek; 2nd Lieutenants, Smolin and Rasch, all active on the Eastern front against Russia, and Major Oeljeschlaeger, of Friedrich's staff, provided reports of their respective activities.

(2) The 13-volume report prepared under the direction of Col. J. G. Seabourne, Chief of the Air Technical Team contains minutely detailed discussions by German Air Force Signal Intelligence Service personnel of the history and functions of their service. Col. Seabourne, who was "charged with the mission of securing and compiling data relative to the operations of the Luftwaffe Signal Intelligence Service in the course of World War II,"[15] was successful in obtaining elaborately illustrated expositions from German Air Force Signal Intelligence personnel. The reports are generally thorough, careful, and reflect the knowledge of the expert. The main subjects covered and the names of the chief reporters follow:

(a) History in General

Evolution of the Signal Intelligence Service 1914 - 1939	Major Feichtner
Origin of the German Air Force Signal Intelligence Service: The history and operations of the Chi-Stelle and of its various sections (Referate) which operated	T/Sgt Jering

[14] IF 189

[15] IF 177

with the Central Party at first but were later co-located with the field evaluation companies.

(b) Operations West

Subject	Author
History of operations	T/Sgt. Jering
Fighter warnings of Allied Strategic Bombings	T/Sgts. Watkinson and Jering
American Aircraft Warning Service and intelligence derived from Allied navigational aides, captured documents, and equipment.	Lt. Ludwig
Technical operations: Ludwig's studies consist of a detailed and documented account of the methods used to produce strategic intelligence on Allied order of battle and long-range intentions, and to give tactical intelligence on the operations of the American Air Support Parties and the British and Canadian tentacles (networks by which ground troops requested air support against German ground concentrations.)	Lt. Ludwig
Cryptanalysis of Western systems	Lt. Ludwig

(c) Operations East

Subject	Author
Organization and history in general from 1936-and particularly the story of the 1st Bn LN Regt 353	Col. Eick
Central Front operations Windels was CO of 2nd Bn, LN Regt 353	Major Windels
Southern Russian Front Herold was CO of the 3rd Bn, LN Regt 353	Capt. Herold
Strategic evaluation of Soviet Air Force traffic	Lt. Chlubek
Tactical Evaluation of traffic of Russian Long Range Bomber Force	Lt. Rasch
Russian Radio Procedure	Lt. von Lackum
Air Force R/T traffic	Lt. Mucke
Cryptanalysis of Soviet Systems	Lt. Chlubek

7

(d)	Operations South	
	History	Major Feichtner and T/Sgt. Jering, Lt. Lier, Major, Schultze, and Feldwebel Schlottman
	Technical operations of Ln Regt 352	
(e)	Organization of the Central Air Warning Service. Forster was Chief of the Reich Defense Signals Intelligence Service (Funkaufklaerungsfuehrer Reich, abb. FAF)	Col. Forster

In addition, miscellaneous studies and detailed biographies of various German Air Force Signal Intelligence Service personalities were included.

The TICOM and the Seabourne reports taken together present a comprehensive picture of the German Air Force Signal Intelligence Service. The many details and carefully executed diagrams contained in the Seabourne reports provide a wealth of material for further study. Liberal quotations from it will be found throughout this paper.

(3) The Air Ministry Report[16] consists of a series of reports comprising an account of the German Air Force Signals Intelligence Service from its beginnings, and describing the development of intercept, advance warning, route tracking and forecasting of air offenses, the breaking of Allied cryptographic systems in the West and in the North. It is pointed out, however, that further evidence from captured German Air Force documents has been helpful in supporting these interrogations. In general, the material is organized on the lines of the Seabourne report. A detailed description of the organization and operation of the unit operating in Norway (LN Abt. 355) is contained in the final portion of the Air Ministry Report.

(4) The above reports of German prisoners of war, obtained after the capitulation of Germany, are supplemented by various documents written during the course of the war. The most important of these, the War Diary, gives a complete Table of Organization for the Chief Signal Officer, (General Nachrichten Fuehrer, abbreviated Gen Nafue) and a description of duties for all offices under his control: particularly relevant for this paper are the sections on Gen Nafue I (allocation and employment of Signal Troops), Gen Nafue II (communications and cryptography), and Gen Nafue III (Signal Intelligence Service).

Minutes of various Supreme Commander of Armed Forces meetings which were attended by German Air Force Signals Intelligence Service personnel and copies of actual operational reports rendered from time to time prove a useful supplement to the interrogations and monographs.

[16] IF 189

DOCID: 3560829

Volume 5

Chapter II. Development of the German Air Force Signal Intelligence Service

Paragraph

6. January 1937 - September 1939.--On January 1, 1937 a Signal Intelligence Agency was established under the Air Ministry for the Commander in Chief of the German Air Force. It was called Chiffrier Stelle, Oberbefehlshaber der Luftwaffe (abbreviated Chi Stelle, OB d L). The Air Force was a new branch of the Armed Forces (Wehrmacht), legally in existence slightly more than a year. The Signal Intelligence Agency of the Commander in Chief of the Air Force (Chi Stelle OB d L) was the Air Force's first official entry into signal intelligence and consisted of but one officer and twenty civilians. Prior to the Chi Stelle's establishment, all intercept and evaluation of foreign air force traffic had been done by German Army signal intelligence units.

Fixed intercept stations were established during 1937 according to German Army prototypes and given the cover name of "Weather Radio Receiving Stations" (Wetterfunkempfangsstellen, abbreviated W-Stellen).[21] The intercept stations were supplemented by direction-finding stations which were called "Weather Research Stations" (Wetterforschungsstellen, abbreviated Wo-Stellen). In addition, mobile intercept platoons were established to operate in the field.[22] The platoons' original mission was the monitoring of German Air Force traffic for security purposes, but late in 1937 they were expanded into mobile Radio Intercept Companies (Luftnachrichten Funkhorchkompanin Mot) which collaborated with the fixed stations in the intercept of foreign air force traffic.[23]

21 IF 181 p 14; IF 189, 403, p 2

22 IF 189, 403 p 2

23 IF 189, 403, p 3

9

The intercepted material was passed to the Signal Intelligence Agency for analysis and evaluation after preliminary traffic analysis and cryptanalysis had been performed. The Agency completed the processing of the traffic and transmitted any intelligence derived from cryptanalysis or traffic analysis to the Commander in Chief of the Air Force, the Army, the Navy, and back down to local air force (Luftflotte) commanders. The Agency had the further duty of assigning broad intercept missions to the field units and publishing general orders for signal intelligence activities in general. [24]

It soon became evident that the intelligence needs of local air force commanders could be more quickly satisfied by having evaluation performed at lower levels than at the Signal Intelligence Agency. As a result field evaluation centers of company strength were established and given the cover name of "Weather Control Stations" (Wetterleitstellan, abbreviated W-Leit). [25]

In 1939, after several experiments at reorganization, the fixed and mobile signal intelligence units were combined into signal intelligence battalions, removed from the administrative control of Chi Stelle, and attached to Local Air Force Signal Regiments, in each case as the third battalion of what was primarily a communications regiment. Each signal intelligence battalion was composed of an evaluation unit, two mobile intercept companies and three fixed intercept stations. [26]

As a result of the above Signal Intelligence activities, it can be said that prior to the outbreak of war in September 1939 the German Air Force High Command had "a quite accurate picture of the air armament, deployment, and strength of foreign air forces, as well as their organization and expansion." [27]

7. <u>September 1939 to November 1944</u>.--The quick successes of the German Armed Forces in overrunning Poland in eighteen days in 1939, and France in a few weeks in the spring of 1940 denied the German Air Force Signal Intelligence Service an opportunity to distinguish itself. [28] As the British Air Ministry Summary states:

> "It is almost a truism that signal intelligence has its greatest value when the war is going badly and is of least importance when all is going well. Thus Germany's early lightning successes were a great handicap to the future development of its signals intelligence, for they rendered almost superfluous the help which it could have given if duly appreciated and developed. All that seemed necessary

24 IF 181

25 IF 181 p 16

26 IF 189, 403, p 4; IF 181 p 16

27 IF 180 p 4

was to listen to enemy R/T traffic while the German armies and the German Air Force were hammering their way way forward..." 29

However, in December 1939 the German Air Force Signal Intelligence Service demonstrated its value when it enabled German fighters to destroy a large Wellington formation over northern Germany by supplying the fighter command with the location, height, speed and size of the raiding force.[30] The result of this signal intelligence success was the realization that signal intelligence had an important place in Germany's air raid defenses.

With the stabilization of the Western front in 1940 and the opening of a campaign on the Eastern front in 1941, a great expansion of the German Air Force Signal Intelligence Service ensued. Because of the diverse fronts covered and the fundamental differences in their problems, the German Air Force Signal Intelligence Service field units operated as self-contained entities in the Western, Eastern, and Mediterranean sectors. Technical coordination existed between the individual specialist sections (Referate) of the Chi-Stelle, discussed in the next chapter, and the evaluation units (W-Leit) in the field.[31] The Chi-Stelle exercised operational control over the Evaluation Companies (W-Leit), handled field units' requests for personnel and special signal equipment, remained in constant touch with all signal intelligence problems in the field and was "accustomed to maintaining direct contact with the Leitstellen as well as with each individual outstation. This achieved the purpose of assuring a rapid exchange of fundamental intelligence within the Signal Intelligence domain. On the other hand, the General Staff was kept in the picture through the reports furnished by the Referate."[32]

As allied air raids became more frequent in 1942 and 1943 the tactical air raid warning aspect of signal intelligence was exploited. The evaluation centers with the field units flashed advance warning of allied heavy bomber raids to civilian and military authorities and carried on route tracking of the bombers for the benefit of German fighter control.[33] This tactical warning activity developed into an intricate system of tactical air raid warning centers which are described in detail in Chapter IV of this paper.

29 IF 189, 402, p 2

30 I 109 p 7

31 IF 180 p 6

32 IF 180 p 6

33 I 109 p 7

The development of airborne and navigational radar by the allies made necessary the creation of a radar observation service (Funkmessbeobachtungsdienst), and the radar jamming service (Funkstoerdienst). "Radar observation and jamming units were accordingly added to the existing wireless intelligence units in the West and South (in the summer of 1943). The radar control post (Funkleitstand) of the OB d L was created to correspond with the Chi-Stelle OB d L..." [34]

From the outbreak of war until the middle of 1944, operations of both the central and field units were sufficiently developed to provide a continuous flow of information to the Air Force High Command A-2. However, the many channels of tactical and operational command to which these units were subject and the growth and development of their work compelled a reorganization in the last stages of the war. This reorganization constitutes the most coherent form of the German Air Force Signal Intelligence Service, and is described immediately below (paragraphs 8 and 9) as the norm.

8. Reorganization on the Staff level in November 1944.-- The dynamics of signal intelligence operations make it difficult to find any point of rest at which an accurate statement of organization is possible. However, the several reorganizations of the entire service that occurred in 1944 to fill the needs arising throughout previous operations gave the service its final form.

In the spring of 1944, the first of these reorganizations took place. All signal intelligence units, including the Chi-Stelle which heretofore had been under the German Air Ministry [35] (i.e., Chi-Stelle OB d L) were placed under the tactical command of the Chief Signal Officer, 3rd Division (Gen Nafue III) in order to unify operations under a central command. [36]

This centralization in tactical matters and the decentralization in administrative affairs to the field command units, led to difficulties in guidance and supply. As a result, in the fall of 1944, after an abortive order by Goering to unify all German Air Force Signal Intelligence units through combining all listening, jamming, and radio traffic units as part of Air Signal Regiments [37], a new comprehensive organization was finally created. This new organization unified all home and field units into independent air signals regiments and battalions with numbers ranging from 350 to 359. Administration was centralized in a so-called Senior Signal Intelligence Officer (Hoehoerer kommandeur der Funkaufklaerung, abbreviated Hoehr Kdr d Funkaufklrg).

[34] IF 189, 403 p 5

[35] IF 180 p 5

[36] IF 189, 403 p 6

[37] No. 180-186 D 4 I 42

This final organization provided for centralized control in the Chief Signal Officer (General Nachrichten Fuehrer) instead of the A-2, or Air Ministry. Under the Chief of Staff of the Chief Signal Officer were three divisions: the first (Gen Nafue/I) supervised the assignment of air signals troops; the second (Gen Nafue/II) directed communications and German Air Force cryptography; and the third (Gen Nafue/III) directed signal intelligence, cryptanalysis, and security.

Gen Nafue/III had administrative control over the Chi-Stelle or Signal Intelligence Agency, and the commanding officer of Gen Nafue/III, Lt. Col. Friedrich, was also the commanding officer of the Chi-Stelle. Under the reorganization of November 1944 the Chi-Stelle was redesignated Air Signals Battalion 350 (Oberkommando der Luftwaffe, Luftnachrichten Abteilung 350, abbreviated "OKL/LN Abt 350").[38] Friedrich, in his position of dual command, regulated the planning for the entire German Air Force Signals Intelligence Service and "as the representative of the Chief Signal Officer remained the supreme authority until the very end on all Signal Intelligence Service matters of decisive importance" (Gen Nafue I, II, and III are described more fully in paragraph 5).[39] Nominally, however, the administration of the Signal Intelligence Service was placed in the hands of the old Signal Corps retainer, General Klemme, who was named Senior Signal Intelligence Officer (Hoehr Kmdr d Funkaufklrg). All signal intelligence matters pertaining to the defense of the Reich were placed in the hands of an Oberst Forster, who was named Chief of the Reich Signal Intelligence Air Radio Warning Agency (Funkaufklaerungsfuehrer Reich, FAF).

[38] This is designated "Signal Intelligence Agency of the Airforce High Command (OKL/LN Abt 350)" throughout other volumes of this report, as it was actually such an agency.

[39] IF 180 p 23

9. Reorganization of the Field Units in November 1944.-- The disposition and designation of the field units after the reorganization was as follows:

West: Air Signals Regiment 351 (LN Regt 351). This Regiment consisted of three battalions, and operated in conjunction with local Air Force 3.

Mediterranean and Middle East:

Air Signals Regiment 352 (LN Regt 352). This Regiment consisted of two battalions and operated with local Air Force 2.

East: Air Signal Regiment 353 (LN Regt 353). This Regiment consisted of three battalions. The first battalion operated with local Air Force 1 on the Northern Russian Front, the second, with local Air Force 6 on the Central Russian Front, and the third, with local Air Force 4 on the Southern Russian Front.

Scandinavia:

Air Signal Battalion 355 (LN Abt 355). This Battalion operated with local Air Force 5.

With the Reich:

Air Signal Battalions 356 and 357 were limited to advance warning and tactical operations, the former deriving its evaluations from "enemy" signals, the latter from the use of radar and navigational aids.

Air Signal Battalion 358 was concerned with training.

Air Signal Battalion 359 engaged in radar jamming and operated in conjunction with the Luftflotte Reich.

10. Staff Offices of the German Air Force Signal Intelligence Service and their Functions.--The information on the description of the T/O which follow are derived from Supplement B to War Diary #4, Division 1 of the Air Force High Command (Anlagenband B zum Kriegstagebuch 4 (I. ABT) vol 1.1. 45 bis 15.3.45) [40]

[40] Translation of this document is known as T-2558.

It should be emphasized that actual practice did not always reflect the T/O description of function.

a. Office of the Chief Signal Officer.--The responsibilities of the Chief Signal Officer, General Martini, included the following:

> "Regulation and direction of use of men and equipment in the Air Signals Troops; direction of operations and maintenance of signal communications of the Air Force; direction of use and operations of Air Security and Ground Installations for the Radio Navigation, Air Reporting (including Radar and Fighter-Control Service), Signals Intelligence, Radar Observation and Jamming Services..." The Chief Signal Officer "is responsible personally to the Reich Minister for Aviation and the Commander-in-Chief of the Air forces; organizationally and operationally to the Chief of General Staff of the Air Forces."

b. Chief of Staff, Office of the Chief Signal Officer.--Among the subordinates of the Chief Signal Officer was the Chief of Staff (Chef des Stabbes) Obslt. Morgenstern, who was charged with carrying into effect the duties of the Chief Signal Officer noted above. The execution of these duties followed three main lines of action:

"(1) Review of Air Signals Troops allocation and employment.

"(2) Preparation, construction, maintenance, and operation of all signals communications of the Air Force.

"(3) Operational planning and direction of the Air Security, Air Reporting (including radar), Signal Intelligence, Radar Observation and Jamming Service."

c. Divisions of the Office of the Chief Signal Officer.--The three duties of the Chief of Staff noted above were performed by three divisions (abteilungen) of the Office of the Chief Signal Officer. The organizational pattern consisted in a separation of each division into four or five functional groups, each of which was in tern subdivided into sections.

(1) Gen Nafue/I.

The first division, commanded by Major Franze, is described as a "specialist section of the Air Force, working over the allocations and employment of men and equipment..." and "therefore to be informed by the 2nd and 3rd Divisions on basic problems of allocation, employment of men and equipment, of operations, of signal intelligence and of jamming services.[41]

This division was organized into four groups. Group I directed Troop Allocation and Employment, supervised the General Signals Service, and published Organizational and Operational Regulation. Group II supervised Radio Navigation and the Air Security Service. Group III supervised Air Reporting (including radar) and the fighter-control service. Group IV was occupied with "Navy Liaison," which meant the review of signal questions arising between the Navy and the Air Force and cooperation between the two services in settling such questions. The specific duties of the various sections into which these groups were divided are set forth in detail in the War Diary.[42]

(2) The second division (Gen Nafue/II) controlled German Air Force signal communications and cryptography. The exact nature of the control is now known, but it was probably both operational and administrative. The second division was headed by Lt. Col. Dr. Schulze, and was divided into four groups (Gruppen). Group I did control planning for the second division. Group II supervised telephone service. Group III supervised teletype service. Group IV supervised communications and cryptography. By this is meant that it supervised the issue of cipher machines, cryptographic systems, and compiled and distributed keys. It did not make cryptographic security studies, which was the duty of Group IV of the third division.

The War Diary passage describing the work of Group IV illustrates the scope of Signal Intelligence activity of Gen Nafue/II. Pertinent excerpts from this description are therefore printed below.[43]

The areas of signal activity over which Group IV had supervision are of interest for their diversity. All the administrative functions are listed in full in the War Diary[44], and simply those pertinent are noted below. The largest of these sections, with the exception of the "Special Office," consisted of only four persons.

a. Section A.

Radio Operations and Cryptography

Direction and surveillance of all radio air security operations of the Air Force.

41 T 2558 p 17

42 T 2558

43 T 2558 pp 28-31

44 T 2558

Review of regulations affecting radio and air security and air reporting operations, and review of Air Force enciphering regulations (the latter carried out in cooperation with the units concerned in the Supreme Command Armed Forces, the Army High Command, and the Navy High Command).

Surveillance of tactical radio operations and radio deception measures.

Allocation of cryptographic systems under control of the Air Force.

Execution of radio practice and radio testing.

Publishing of operational directives for radio-operations-offices, and radio-control-offices of the Commander-in-Chief of the Air Forces.

(b) Distribution of literature on radio operations.

Section B.

Review of all operational codes of the Air Force, including the setting up of distribution lists, and review of requisitions necessary for the coordination of radio operations within the Armed Forces (effected in cooperation with the other branches of the Service).

Allocation and employment of flares and other signal devices (both ground and airborne) used in connection with Air Force activities (carried out in cooperation with the other branches and the Axis powers).

Section C.

Compilation and preparation of secret writing methods of all types, in cooperation with the agencies of other branches, and compilation of operational codes.

Distribution, shipping, and control of all secret writing devices and of operational codes.

Distribution and control of all cipher machines, with the exception of the enciphered teletype machine. Carried out in cooperation with Air Signal Ordnance Department.

Development of new enciphering procedures.

It should be emphasized that Section C's function was purely administrative and that the actual work outlined above, except for development of new enciphering procedures, was carried out by a "Special Office" having at least T/O parity with the other sections.

Section D.

Review of operational literature for Air Security Radio Operations.

Supervision of the setting up of radio beacons, plane recognition, and the allocation of call signs.

(3) Gen Nafue/III

The third division was the Signal Intelligence Service (Funkaufklaerung) of the Office of the Chief Signal Officer. As such, its primary function was the direction of all the analytic operations of the service, which were carried on by the Signal Intelligence Agency or Chi-Stelle (Chiffrier Stelle, Oberbefehshaber der Luftwaffe). In general, other matters, particularly those of organization, equipment, security, and personnel of this division were carried on by five different groups. Group I directed the total allocation, employment, and operations of signal intelligence and of the jamming services. Group II supervised the equipment and technical administration for intercept. Group III supervised equipment and technical administration for enemy radar monitoring and jamming (funkmessbeobachtungs und Funkstoerdienst). Group IV conducted security studies on German Air Force systems, issued security directives, and assisted in the development of new systems. Its duties, as described in the War Diary,[45] were performed by three sections:

(a) "Section A. Control of Cipher Systems and cipher equipment

Testing of keying-procedures in use in wire and wireless signal communications of the whole Air Force.

(i) for possible decipherment.
(ii) for areas of use and volume, density, and distribution of traffic.
(iii) for message form and content.

Requisitions for sampling check-up on German signal communications and evaluation of observations, in collaboration with the 2nd Division (i.e., Gen Nafue/II).

[45] T 2558 p 29

DOCID: 3560829

Directives for execution of camouflage and radio-deception measures in German communications operations (in cooperation with the 2nd Division).

Evaluation of decipherment results of German and enemy intercept services and working out of counter-measures.

Examination and testing of keying methods of Allied Powers' Air Force.

Cooperation with agencies of other branches.

(b) "Section B. Development of Keying Means and Keying Methods

Development of new keying means and procedures, in cooperation with the 2nd Division (Gen Nafue/II).

Working out of directives for special keys according to demands of the 2nd Division.

Cooperation on tactical-technical demands in development of keying equipment.

Use of enemy results for own development.

Cooperation with agencies of other branches.

(c) "Section C. Keying Directives

Cooperation on publication of Signal Operations instruction in cooperation with 2nd Division.

Cooperation on publication of keying directives for new encipherments, in cooperation with the 2nd Division."

Group V was concerned with Personnel.

(4) General Comments

Both by the above paper description and in actual practice, Group IV (Security) of the Third Division and Group IV (Cryptography) of the Second Division worked in close liaison. The frequent repetition of the phrase "in cooperation with the Second Division," appearing in the duties of the security section attest to this coordination of effort. Minutes of high-level meetings of OKW/Chi show the repeated attendance of both Lt. Col. Dr. Schulze, head of the Second Division and of Captain Forth, head of Group IV of the Third Division. [46] At these meetings, it was determined that OKW work "in close collaboration with the appropriate departments of the ... Air Force" in developing enciphering systems, but with respect to security, OKW/Chi is responsible for making "a security check" on all Air Force codes. [47]

It is frequently averred that the "production of keys is the affair of the separate branches of the Armed Forces" [48] and that guidance, alone, was furnished by OKW/Chi in devising keys. However, there appears to be some dispute about OKW's right to test Air Force systems. Practicing cryptanalysts of other services (Fricke and Huettenhain) declared [49] that there was no coordination of key testing, that each organization did its own and was under no obligation to submit its systems to OKW. However, Gen. Lt. Gimmler, Chief of Armed Forces Communications Branch, at a conference in November 1944 stated:

> "OKW/Chi is appointed as the only organization of the Wehrmacht for testing and checking all cipher systems used and proposed for use in the Reich."

In the description of the duties of both the cryptographic and security groups appear the phrases "radio disguise," "false transmissions," "directives for execution of camouflage and radio-deception measures in German communications operations." Friedrich had always forbidden wireless deception on the ground that "deception is worse than useless and inevitably betrays what it is meant to conceal." [50]

46 D 57

47 D 57 pp 7 8

48 D 55

49 I 84

50 I 13

DOCID: 3560829

VOLUME 5

Chapter III. The Chi-Stelle

11. Organization and Development.- This Chapter concerns the organization and development of the Signal Intelligence Agency of the Commander in Chief of the Air Force (Chiffrier Stelle, Oberbefehlshaber der Luftwaffe, abbreviated Chi-Stelle/OBdL, as of November 1944 Air Force High Command, Air Signal Battalion 350, Oberkommando der Luftwaffe, Luftnachrichten Abteilung 350, abbreviated OKL/LN ABT 350 and referred to throughout this volume as Chi-Stelle).

The Chi-Stelle of the Air Force was the most important of the units under the third Division of the Office of the Chief Signal Officer, (Gen Nafue/III) from a signal intelligence point of view. It was the highest authority for the German Air Force Signal Intelligence Service. Its functions are summarized by one German as follows: "It directed the activities of the listening service in accordance with the demands of the German Air Force Operations Staff and was responsible for the long-term evaluation of results and reporting to the latter; it also provided the means of collaboration with the other services."[51] From its origin in 1937 until 1940 it was located in Berlin; but right after "the start of the Polish campaign, the Chi-Stelle moved from Berlin to the Marstall, the riding academy of Frederick the Great in Potsdam-Wildpark. 'The Marstall' became a sort of second name for the Chi-Stelle, since it remained there until just before the German collapse."[52] It was divided into specialist sections (Referate), which reflected the geographical diversity of its interests. At the time of the collapse the principal sections were as follows: A. Staffing, allocation and employment of intercept sets; B. Evaluation West; B5. Evaluation of Allied transport and Ferry traffic; C. Evaluation Mediterranean; D. Evaluation East; E. Cryptanalysis.

[51] IF 190 No. 404 p 1

[52] IF 180 p 5

The bulk of the evaluation sections acted in close collaboration with the field evaluation companies attached to the Air Signals Regiments and Battalions and ultimately were co-located with them, since "it was considered more effective to have the long-term evaluation center close to the intercept units rather than close to the staffs which they have to feed."[53] For example, after the fall of France (1940), Ref. B moved from Potsdam-Marstall to Asnieres near Paris,[54] Section B5 moved in 1943 to Munich/Oberhaching (near an intercept station devoted to ferry traffic),[55 56] Section C, after a long stay at central headquarters, ultimately in early 1945 moved to Premstaetten, to join the evaluation company of Air Signals Regiment 352;[57] and Section D, directly after the beginning of the campaign against Russia, followed the General Staff to Zhitomir, then to Warsaw, and finally to Cottbus.[58] In every instance these sections were finally merged with evaluation companies of the field units, Section B with 25 Co of LN Regt 351, when both were co-located at

[53] IF 189 No. 404 p 1; I 109 p 27

[54] I 109 p 27

[55] IF 180 p 33

[56] B_5 appears to have achieved the status of an independent section on a parity with B. (See IF 189 404 p1, paragraph 1, and Ibid p 2 paragraph 6.) The other sections of Section B were:

- Liaison Officer with Army
- Liaison Detachment at PW camp
- Liaison Officer with Operations Staff
- B Immediate Evaluation
- B_1 RAF Bombrer Command
- B_2 8th U.S. Bomber Command
- B_3 Captured Material
- B_4 Fighter Formations
- B_6 RAF Coastal Command
- B_7 Master Index
- B_8 Combined Army and Air Force

[57] IF 180 p 35

[58] IF 180 p 14

DOCID: 3560829

Limburg after the Allied breakthrough at Avranches;[59] Section C with the 25 Co of LN Regt 352 at Premstaetten, after many delays;[60] and Section D with the 25 Co of LN Regt 353 at Cottbus.[61]

The cryptanalytic Section (Referat E) maintained a certain amount of centrality of operation with respect to Anglo-American solution, although the various field units were entrusted with the solution of lower grade systems, such as Bomber Codes, the Mediterranean U.S. M-209, SYKO etc.[62] All Soviet solution was shifted as far forward as possible because of the ease with which 85% of the systems were read, and even the sub-section of Section E. engaged on Russian Air Force Cryptanalysis (Section E.1) moved with the Eastern evaluation section (Section D) to the front. This decentralization is criticized in the Air Ministry Report[63] as follows: "...the crypto service should have been centralized; the output of a large centralized crypto service exceeds the sum total of the contributions of its individual members and is higher in quality." However, the operational needs for speedy solution made it mandatory for solution on the spot, where and when, it was needed. Moreover, the lack of homogeneity of traffic on both the Russian and Western fronts made it wise to decentralize the cryptanalytic operations.

a. Some opinions of the Chi-Stelle-- The evidence in the interrogations indicates that all did not run smoothly within the Chi-Stelle. According to the witnesses, who may well have been using the opportunity for their personal gripes as well as to impart information, there existed within the organization the familiar conflicts between the incompetence of favored officers and the unrecognized ability of progressive officers aware of the potentialities of signal intelligence. They indicate further that all the usual symptoms of an organization at odds with itself were manifest. Few of the personnel respected the ability of the others, these on the working level decried the weakness and indecisiveness of the commanding officers, commanding officers complained because of the division of responsibility and low morale continually hampered operations.

The Chi-Stelle, at the Marstall was said to have a "ministerial" aspect and a "relatively extravagant manner of existence."[64] Although Lt. Col. Friedrich, head of the service, was said to be a good replacement for the previous leaders, none of whom had "fully measured up to requirements,"[65] it later became clear, at least to Tech Sgt. Jering, a cryptanalyst of Chi-Stelle who had occasion to observe Friedrich

[59] I 109 p 27

[60] IF 184 p 53

[61] I 121 p 12

[62] I 112

[63] IF 189 No. 402 p 2

[64] IF 180 p 5

[65] IF 180 p 19

23

at work, that "the choice of an officer with no signal or intelligence training as chief of so highly specialized a service was not exactly a fortunate one." In describing one of the Sections, he commented upon "...the spirit of mental prostitution pervading the halls of the Marstall since the beginning of the war, nurturing a large class of previleged indolents who assiduluously opposed any change or innovation."[66] Of the same section Jering observed "the overall complexion of inefficiency...became worse during the last two years of the war as duty hours were lengthened, rations became slimmer, and air raids regularly interfered with the night's repose. Political sycophants, the threat of being sent to the front, which... would have been relished by no one, and the fear of transfer by way of disciplinary action, all served to suppress and curb men and women working twelve hours and more at a stretch..."[67] It should be observed that Jering himself may well have suffered the bitterness which frequently grows in a brilliant subordinate working under officers less acute then himself, and that therefore his remarks in no sense constitute a reliably objective account of this aspect of the organization.

The description of Lt. Col. Friedrich's personality and administration written by Major Ferdinand Feichtner, a man of outstanding reputation,[68] is a more objective appreciation:

> "When the then Major Friedrich of the General Staff took over command of the Chi-Stelle Ob. d. L. after a succession of predecessors as corrupt as they were incapable, everyone had for a time the impression that at last the right man was in the right place. By virtue of his close relation with the Luftwaffe High Command...the Chi-Stelle became for the first time a central and authoritative organism of command, over which no Luftwaffe A-2 could set himself any longer. Friedrich brought along new ideas and points of view to signal intelligence operations from his General Staff experience. He deserves most of the credit for the close liaison we enjoyed with the High Command. He gave the ideas and experiences of the specialists a hearing, backed them up without considering himself and accepted and acted on good suggestions that were offered to him. Unfortunately he failed to continue his high promise. I have the feeling that after 1942 the highly specialized departments of the signal intelligence service grew too much for him to keep up with, technically as well as from the view point of personnel. He often admitted that technical matters were fundementally incompatabile with his being, and as a General Staff Officer he had no Signal Corps training. But the worse

[66] IF 180 p 34

[67] IF 180 p 35

[68] IF 179 Foreward

24

feature of all was that he was unable to introduce any rational policy into the Signal Intelligence Service methods of assigning personnel. He never understood the situation enough to relieve the tension at the beginning of the war between the old civil servants, who had been in for years, and had become mostly parasitic growths, and the young blood which had just come in, and had proved itself worthy. The old guard had built an impregnable political stronghold for itself in the Marstall, and taken care of its own by giving them all the key positions. Another shortcoming was his failure to bring it about that this service, becoming ever more specialized, should be commanded by men who were familiar with these specialities. He was much more likely to depend on commanders who knew less of the actual interests of the radio intelligence service than he himself, but who had no idea whatever of the purpose and mission of the service which of course they, themselves, should have been duty-bound to represent and stand up for. Moreover he filled his staff with his own gravediggers, advisers who did not measure up to the responsibilities they held, either as people or specialists, but who nevertheless knew how to play up to their chief, whose mind was always on a thousand different things and who was fundamentally too good natured.

"A branch of the service which included the cream of German intelligence and which called for the highest degree of mental sharpness, technical ability, and knowledge of the world and the people in it, should have had a chief who was made differently from this professional soldier, whose horizon and ability never rose above the level of a good company clerk.

"Friedrich knew himself well enough to turn down the command of the signal intelligence division which was offered to him. His inability to make up his mind was at times most paralyzing to the dispatch of business. ...He always insisted in particular upon clear thinking and decision on the part of his subordinates, but whenever one sent him a teletype for an order, one would come back which was as cautious as the Delphic oracle, and always placed all responsibility on the recipient."[69]

The problem of the control of the Chi-Stelle by either the A-2 or the Chief Signal Officer was resolved by a four-sided organization: The Chief Signal Officer "was regarded as the supreme authority on all technical signal matters," A-2 was to provide "guidance of the intelligence activities of the Chi-Stelle," the newly-created Senior Air Signals Intelligence Service Officer (Gen. Klemme) had supreme administrative control over the Chi-Stelle and the field units, and

[69] IF 179 pp 53 - 54

DOCID: 3560829 the Signals Intelligence Service Chief for the Reich (FAF--Col. Forster) was given top authority in all matters relating to the defense of the Reich.

b. Relations with A-2 and the Chief Signal Officer:-- As seen in Chapter I the question of whether the Signal Intelligence Service should be subordinated to the Office of the Chief Signal Officer or to the A-2 was often debated.[70]

The main advantage of subordination to the Chief Signal Officer was "the increased facility with which signal communication could be provided and radio equipment allocated." The excellence of the communication system, which existed to the very end, was undoubtedly the result of this signal control. On the other hand, the close liaison between signal intelligence and signal security, which the Chief Signal Officer's control was also supposed to produce, "failed of realization, since in spite of the accurate knowledge of Allied mistakes in the field of radio and cryptographic procedure, as revealed by the work of Signals Intelligence Service, delinquencies of the same nature were either not corrected at all, or only partially so, by the Germans. There was an apparent lack of a qualified expert who might have evaluated the results of the Signals Intelligence Service with the end in view of improving the security of Luftwaffe radio communications."[71]

The chief argument in favor of subordination of the Chi-Stelle to A-2 was that all intelligence agencies would then be under a central administrative control. Actually, however, subordination to the Signal Officer rather than to the A-2, proved no bar to effective work, and relationships between the real specialist personnel of the Chi-Stelle and the higher intelligence authority which they served were good.[72] In the Chi-Stelle's work with A-2 the familiar difficulty was at first encountered that A-2, on the one hand, did not always recognize the value of signal intelligance; and, on the other, that Chi-Stelle's reports were written in Signal Intelligence terms, call signs, frequencies, etc., with A-2 being left to draw its own conclusions. In time however, "the evaluators learned to transform signal intelligence into an operational intelligence picture."[73] Once the evaluators were "imbued with tactical concepts, they sometimes turned to the other extreme, wishing to perform the A-2 function themselves, and arbitrarily mixing signal intelligence with intelligence from other sources... Only in the course of time was the happy medium found." The appointment of a liaison officer did not cure the dilemma, since, according to wont, a young man was chosen "well indoctrinated with drill regulations, but possessing very little signal intelligence experience. Unfortunately he became no more adept with time, had but slight tactical knowledge, and, in brief, did more harm than good. Although the specialist personnel of the Chi-Stelle became immediately aware of his deficiencies, nevertheless more than a year elapsed before a change took place."[74]

[70] IF 183 p 78

[71] Lt. Martin Ludwig of Chi-Stelle in IF 183 pp 78 - 79

[72] IF 183 p 80

[73] IF 183 p 80

[74] IF 183 p 81

DOCID: 3560829

c. Relations with the Field units:-- The creation in the Fall of 1944 of the post of Senior Signal Intelligence Officer (Hoeherer Kommandeur der Funkaufklaerung abbreviated Hoehr Kdr d Funkaufklrg) was intended to centralize the administration of the affairs of the Chi-Stelle and the field units. This centralization continued the "obscure relationships" at the highest headquarters and was the antithesis of what the field units required.

The centralization of administrative control "of the Signals Intelligence Service... in the hands of one of the many supernumerary Luftwaffe Signal Corps generals"[75] made the administrative problem of the field units more acute than ever. "In this case, also, the Chi-Stelle failed completely; since it had planned and supervised all Signals Intelligence Service operations from the beginning, it might easily have been the central administrative authority also."[76] The difficult situation confronting the Field units was eased by the cooperation of the local Air Forces. The local commanders of these often furnished quarters, rations and other services when the field units own supply service broke down.[77]

The various Sections of the Chi-Stelle exercised control of the Field units according to their location, ultimately working on the spot with these units. The organization and functioning of these sections will be treated below in the following paragraphs of this chapter.

d. Relations with the ZAF and FAF:-- As the strength of Allied air raids increased, tactical evaluation assumed an ever greater importance, and it became necessary to establish an agency which would summarize and integrate all the reports and information made available by the outlying tactical evaluation centers. This need was met by the creation of the Air Raid Warning Agency for the Reich (Zentraler Gefechtstand fur Funkauswertung, abbreviated ZAF) Treuenbrietzen. This unit, headed by Colonel Forster, was under the operational direction of the Chi-Stelle but administratively subordinate directly to Gen Nafue/III. In order to facilitate coordination between the all important ZAF and the other agencies affected by the information it disseminated a new position was created, and designated Chief of the Air Raid Warning Service for Germany (Funkaufklaerungsfuehrer Reich, abbreviated FAF) Col. Forster, head of the ZAF, filled this position also. In this capacity he was still under the Chi-Stelle for operational purposes, and acted as adviser to the Commanding General of Fighter Corps I.[78]

[75] IF 180 p 22

[76] IF 180 p 22

[77] I 130 p 4

[78] IF 181 p 62

27

12. Section A-- Staffing, Allocation and Employment-- This Section, which was closely connected with the office of the commanding officer, was divided into the following sub-sections: Operational Planning (planning for monitoring operations on all fronts, preparation of Tables of Organization and equipment and allocation of personnel to Signal Intelligence units); Personnel (routine personnel matters for entire Signal Intelligence); War Diary (a writing of detailed diary of the Signal Intelligence activities); Procurement (procurement of all special signal equipment for the Signal Intelligence Service); and Research (examination and repair of captured equipment).[79]

13. Section B--Evaluation West--[80] Section B was one of the best operational evaluation sections of the Chi-Stelle. Able personnel and intelligent administration permitted it to make significant contributions to German Air Force intelligence. Before the outbreak of the war, Section B was able to provide a comprehensive picture of RAF organization, locations, strengths, aircraft types, personnel and supply.[81] Its move to the Western front after the conquest of France served to intensify its activities.

The staff of Section B consisted initially of civil service personnel who had performed the same type of work in peace-time. A large number of soldiers--mostly university men, or business men versed in languages--were transferred to the section. As the civilians were drafted, despite their strenuous objections (since they usually received low ranks), distinctions between civilian and soldier tended to disappear. The soldiers became acquainted with their work and in many cases obtained better results than the civilians.

The wise policies of limiting personnel changes, training in signal intelligence and cutting down military duties to an absolute minimum promoted enthusiastic work.[82]

[79] IF 180 p 8

[80] This account is virtually a word-for-word repetition of the materials on Section B. See TICOM, I 109 pp 26 - 33, the Air Ministry Report, IF 189, No 404 and Volume V. of the Seabourne Report, IF 180 pp 27 - 32

[81] IF 180 p 9

[82] This was in sharp distinction to almost every other unit of German Air Force Signal Intelligence Service.

At the end of 1942 some of the male clerks and statisticians were replaced by women's auxiliaries (the Luftnachtrichten Helferinnen). The concensus is that although "these female auxiliaries were better than the soldiers, in work as assistants, on the other hand, attempts to employ women on independent work in evaluation, apart from a few exceptions were not successful."[83]

a. Organization-- "There were two diametrically opposed theories on the subject of the organization of the evaluation section. The first claimed that organization should be made to conform to the sources being covered; i.e. W/T evaluation, R/T activity evaluation, and D/F activity evaluation, and that all results should be dombined in a final evaluation."[84] This plan, which was not adopted for the Sections of the Chi-Stelle, was actually used in the evaluation companies in the field.[85]

"The second theory, which was proved superior for long-term evaluation in the West (and also in the South), favored an organization covering the setup of the enemy air force formations, i.e. RAF Bomber Command, VIIIth U.S. Bomber Command, AEAF, etc." Accordingly, Section B consisted of the following sub-sections:

B-1----Immediate Evaluation, Reception, Distribution, and routing of messages.

B-2----RAF Bomber Command, Strategic Evaluation

B-22---US. 8th Bomber Command, Strategic Evaluation

B-3----Captured equipment, material and navigational evaluation

B-4----Fighter Formations (RAF and 8th A.F. Fighter Commands, AEAF Fighters and Night Fighters). This unit was engaged in the evaluation of Tactical Air Force radio traffic.[86]

B-5----Originally USAAF outside Europe, and later ferry and transport traffic. (This sub-section became independent at the end of 1943, and is discussed below as a separate Section).

[83] I 109 p 27; IF 189 No 404 p 2

[84] IF 189 No 404 p 2

[85] The organization of the evaluation companies of the 1st, 2nd and 3rd Battalions of LN Regt 353 on the Russian front provides a good illustration of this type of organization. It is described later in this volume.

[86] IF 180 p 28

B-6----RAF Coastal Command, Strategic evaluation.

B-7----Master Index of Units and Locations.

B-8----Combined Army and Air Force. Traffic of the Air Support Parties and the tentacles; the 2nd Tactical Air Force, the U.S. 9th A.F., RAF ACC.

In addition a liaison detachment was stationed at the Air Prisoner of War Transit Camp (Durchgangslager Luft, abbreviated Dulag) at Oberursel.

Relations were also maintained between the head of Section B and a liaison officer of Army Signal Intelligence Regiment 5 (KONA 5) and a liaison officer of German Air Force Operations Staff I c (Intelligence).

b. Operations-- The chief tasks of Section B were the evaluation of "enemy" transmissions, control of intercept, and evaluation of captured material, equipment and navigational aids.

(1) Evaluation: Section B, in fulfilling its task of providing a long-term evaluation for the West, had to collate, evaluate, and check the results of the intercept units in the West and North. These units were in the West, Signal Intelligaace Regiment West (later LN Regt 351) and LN Abt. 357 after its withdrawal from LN Regt 351; and in the North, 3rd Battalion of LN Regt 5 (later LN Abt 355).

Section B based its evaluation judgments partly on the worked-out results of the Evaluation and Intercept companies and partly on the original operators' logs (day reports), especially for R/T traffic.

The principal materials at its disposal were:

> "1. The daily radio situation reports of the intercept or evaluation companies, which were mostly sent in by teletype, but sometimes also by radio or by courier.
>
> "2. The detailed composite reports of the intercept companies (appearing monthly), or the previously evaluated reports produced monthly by the Evaluation Companies.
>
> "3. Sometimes, especially for R/T evaluation, the original intercepts of the operators (day reports).
>
> "4. Other sources of information: P/W's statements, captured material, press and wireless (especially BBC) etc. These souces served to supplement or elucidate the section's own findings. Great care was taken to see that no Sigint information was mixed in with this. If recourse was had to other sources, these had to be named."[87]

[87] I 109 p 29

The following description of function appears:

"With the division of labor largely clarified, the specialists of section B had only to keep up to date and to clear up in cooperation with the Dulag and the relevant intercept unit any changes which occurred.

"If there appeared any new fields (e.g. appearance of the USAAF in Great Britain, setting up of 2nd TAF etc.) it was the task of Section B to encourage its advancement by using the best evaluators and to keep giving encouragement to the sigint units.

"In this connection, it proved advantageous not to have the personnel subordinated to LN. Regt West and thus to Luftflotte 3. In this way it was possible to announce all findings, and also to raise any necessary complaints, without regard for rank or appointment. On the other hand much duplication of work was caused by this peculiar position of Section B, and for this reason many people held the view, personnel of Section B included, that the best solution would be to incorporate the Section in the Regimental evaluation section (25/351). Quite a satisfactory solution of these questions was reached by their being later brought together in the same area at Limburg."[88]

(2) Control of intercept. "One of the most important functions of Section B was the control of listening activities. It was the Signal Intelligence Agency's practice for Evaluation to assign missions, and this was true of all the echelons of command. At the lower levels, the Evaluation Companies assigned missions to the intercept stations. The various Referate, in turn, controlled the intercept in their respective sectors. In such case "the necessary instructions were not issued directly by the Referat to the Companies but via the higher formation, for example, LN Regt West."[89] Such supervision was necessary since all the intercept stations tried to cover the frequencies which produced the greatest number of messages and therefore offered, at least superficially, the opportunity to produce the best results.

Section B had to see that not only the most productive frequencies but all frequencies important for obtaining a complete picture were monitored. In some instances pressure had to be put on intercept companies to keep them monitoring the many ground networks of the RAF and the USAAF because these frequencies were not productive of the sort of immediate action intelligence which it pleased the companies to pass to the flying units. None the less monitoring of these networks was demanded because they clearly showed the order of battle.

[88] I 109 p 29

[89] I 109 p 30

When a new line of traffic appeared, the intercept units often tried to keep to their accustomed monitoring program and to pass off new tasks to other intercept units. In these cases Section B always had to control interception according to the exigencies of the situation and often do the evaluation itself at first, and then pass it on to the evaluation company.

As will be seen in a later chapter the German theory of signal intelligence, which placed the prime emphasis on evaluation of "all enemy signals" and therefore imposed the exercise of intercept control in the evaluation sections, resulted in difficulties for the cryptanalysts.

(3) Evaluation of captured material, equipment and navigational aids (Section B-3).

All the sub-sections of Section B, with the exception of B-3, were engaged in long term evaluation. B-3 was organized to evaluate captured documents and material, including navigational aids, obtained from aircraft shot down. The increased Allied aircraft losses up to the period of the decline of the German air defense produced more and more of this captured material for signal intelligence.

The following were the main tasks of B-2:

"a. Clarification of Allied navigational aids through the evaluation of captured documents and equipment;

"b. Directing the monitoring of the radar intercept stations;

"c. Instruction of the intercept stations of the Signal Intelligence Service regarding information obtained from captured documents (frequencies, call-signs, codes, etc.);

"d. Examination of captured radio and navigational equipment, and informing signal intelligence units of the results of this examination."[90]

Accordingly, this sub-section was especially interested in the following secret and confidential documents and apparatus:

"1. X- or Q- group lists.
"2. Call-sign lists (R/T and W/T).
"3. Frequency lists (chiefly W/T).
"4. Bomber codes.
"5. Airfield lists giving exact data on station call-signs and frequencies, position of airfields, radio-beacons, etc. (especially frequently found in aircraft of VIII Bomber Command shot down).
"6. Note-books with important entries.
"7. Lists of radio-beacons and other navigational aids.

[90] IF 181 p 46

DOCID: 3560829

"8. Descriptions of apparatuses.
"9. Maps.
"10. Radio and navigational sets.
"11. Crystals from VHF-sets."[91]

As it came in, captured material was farwarded by those salvaging it to Dulag Oberursel. If aircraft were shot down near Signal Intelligence offices or stations, the officers and officials of the Signal Intelligence Service had the right to examine those things that interested them. In the Fall of 1944, this sub-section was withdrawn from Section B and subordinated to the Radar Control Post (Funkleitsland) at Potsdam-Eiche.[92]

The evaluation of captured documents relating to navigational aids, and the examination of equipment such as airborne search receivers, recognition devices and the navigational aids, was intended to suggest new procedures, determine whether a navigational aid would be useful to the German Air Force flying units, and whether the Allies were using German transmitters as navigational aids. Because these navigational devices were continually monitored by the Germans, intense interest was displayed in any of them that became available from capture.[93] The results of research into these navigational aids were published approximately each month in the Navigation Reports and passed to all interested units.

[91] IF 183 p 30

[92] IF 183 p 30

[93] The following pieces of equipment were listed: Group Radio Beacons; "Splasher" beacons (cover name "Orchestersessel"); J-Beams (cover-name "Rodelbahn"), the locations, frequencies, and recognition signals of which were all learned from captured documents; Circular Beacons (including "SE" beacons, airfield beacons, "Eureka" beacons, etc.); Hyperbole Navigation (G-Box); "Boomerang" procedure; "GH" procedure (cover name "Diskus"); Micro-H Systems (cover name "Schleuderball"); H2S" or "Magic Box" (British airborne search radar; cover name "Rotterdam", later "Laubfrosch", 2 cm. band); "H2X" ("Mickey", American airborne search radar; cover name "Meddo", 3 cm. band); IFF (airborne recognition devices; cover name "Flamme"); ASV apparatus (cover name "Eule"); "Weapon" (night fighter search radar; cover name "Grille"); night fighter warning devices ("Monica"), and Infra-red recognition devices.

Another task of B-3, in collaboration with salvage detachments, especially those of the Luftgaue, was to provide for the investigation of captured radio sets and crystals. Through many personal contacts with B-3, the salvage detachments were convinced of the importance of their work and cooperated whole-heartedly with the Signal Intelligence. After every investigation of a shot-down Allied aircraft, the salvage units teletyped the most significant results to the Signal Intelligence Service.

This type of report led to the following results:

"1. Comparison with existing documents, to see if R/T traffic from the approaching or shot-down aircraft had been picked up. If possible the squadron number was established from the call-signs. Comparison with squadron recognition markings.

"2. If the frequency-range of the formation in question was known, the gaps in that range could be filled in. An accurate knowledge of all frequency ranges is most important to long-term intelligence for setting up chains of subordination.

"3. Whenever questions were raised, Dulag Luft was informed, all briefing being passed via the Referat B liaison detachment at Dulag to the interrogating officers at Oberursel."

(4) Liaison with PW Transit Camp (Dulag Luft). The Liaison Detachment of Section B at the PW Transit Camp (Dulag Luft) at Oberursel was responsible for providing close cooperation between Signal Intelligence Service and PW interrogation. PW interrogation resulted in valuable information, particularly upon the numerical designation of units, details concerning enemy equipment, and the changes in enemy tactics.[94] It also expedited the evaluation of all captured material dealing with radio. Important findings such as new call-signs or frequencies were immediately reported by direct telephone line to Section B. The operations are described by Lt. Martin Ludwig in his article on liaison between Dulag Luft and Signals Intelligence Service[95] as follows:

"Signals Intelligence Service derived great benefits from the evaluation of captured material. All documents salvaged from Allied aircraft which had been shot down, crashed, or made emergency landings, were passed on directly to Dulag Luft by the salvaging unit (usually an air base headquarters). As long as communications within Germany remained relatively unimpaired (until the fall of 1944), captured material reached Dulag comparatively quickly. There it was assorted according to

[94] IF 183 p 84

[95] IF 183 pp 87 - 88

topic, and all documents pertaining to radio or radio navigation placed immediately at the disposal of the Signals Intelligence Service Liaison team. This team had on hand all lists of frequencies, call-signs, Q-groups, etc., and determined whether the captured documents contained any new intelligence, such as the call-signs and frequency of a newly occupied airfield. Any such new discoveries were immediately telephoned to Referat B. Later, the originals of all captured documents were sent to Referat B for detailed examination."

c. Reports.-- The most important units to which Section B had to report were:

(1) German Air Force, Operations Staff Intelligence
(2) Chief Signal Officer, Army High Command
(3) Naval High Command
(4) Army High Command
(5) Local Air Force
(6) Chi-Stelle Section C (for information of listening units in the South).
(7) Interrogation Centre (Oberursel).

In many cases (the Commander in Chief West, Local Air Force Command) and the evaluation unit of Signal Intelligence Regiment 5 at St. Germain received reports from Section B.

The following reports were issued by Section B:

Immediate reports (teletype or telephone) for important new facts, intentions to attack , changes of location, etc.

Radio Situation Reports, daily consolidated survey of the events of the preceding 24 hours.

10-Day Reports, concise reports on the long-term intelligence of the last ten days.

Monthly Consolidated Reports, detailed report with maps and diagrams, usually 50 to 60 typed pages in length.

Special reports, e.g. 'Army-Air Co-operation', 'Control of British Night Fighters', etc.

A chart of these routings shows the many headquarters serviced by the Section. (Chart 5-2)

14. Section B-5-- Allied Ferry and Transport Traffic--[96] In 1941 a section within Section B[97] was established to monitor America. This in turn, was divided into two subsections. One analyzed traffic which was concerned with the

[96]The text for the discussions on Section B-5 is taken, without change, from Tech Sergeant Jering's discussion of the Chi-Stelle contained in volume 5 of the Seabourne Report - IF 180 pp 32 - 34

[97]IF 180 pp 32 - 34

35

Army and Naval Air Forces of the United States which were then being built up hastily. This traffic was monitored insofar as it could be heard by Signals Intelligence Service stations in Germany, France, and Norway. This sub-section reached its peak at the turn of the year 1942-1943, when the fundamentally changed war situation dictated a more conservative use of radio receivers. The second sub-section worked on ferry service traffic on the North Atlantic route at first in connection with Atlantic reconnaissance traffic (Coastal Command). The South Atlantic route, as well as Pan-American Airways traffic in South America, was taken care of until 1942 by Section C. When the coverage of traffic from the United States proper was reduced, the afore-mentioned subsection of Section B took over the monitoring of this South Atlantic commitment from Section C.

The American ferry service increased in importance, and in the Middle of 1943 this "American" section was taken away from Section B. Reinforced with certain specialist personnel from Section C it was installed in Munich/Oberhaching as a separate Section (B5), in which the analysis of all ferry traffic was now combined. At the same time the large W/T intercept platoon located in Oberhaching, which administratively belonged to the Marstall battalion, took over the monitoring of all ferry traffic with the exception of that on the North Atlantic routes, which as previously, continued to be covered by the 16th Company of LNR 3 in Angers. The new Section evaluated all traffic and had the following responsibilities:

"a) The monitoring of the United States proper, which although it only touched the surface, still furnished an insight into the principal networks of the Army and Naval Air Forces, into training activity, air transport, defense zones, and the activation of new combat aviation units.

"b) The monitoring of the Atlantic ferry service. The Middle and Central Atlantic routes were monitored by the W/T platoon in Oberhaching and by Luftwaffe Signals Intelligence Service outstations in Spain, which operated under the cover name of "Purchasing Agencies"; the North Atlantic route was monitored by the 16th Co., LNR 3 and reports furnished to the Section.

"c) The monitoring of the American Air Transport Command by the platoon in Oberhaching.

"d) The monitoring of the RAF Transport Command, and of both American and RAF troop carrier commands. The greater part of this interception was also done in Oberhaching."

Airfield radio tower traffic (R/T on 6440 kcs.) was intercepted in Madrid, Montpellier and at various Signals Intelligence Service out-stations in the Balkans and Italy. This traffic was evaluated by Section B5, with the aid of extensive files.

The Section also had a small cryptanalytic team of its own, which deciphered intercepted messages on the spot.

Section B5 remained operational until the last weeks of the war, and was thus in a position to cover the British airborne landing at Bocholt. One week before the capture of Munich by the Americans its male personnel withdrew to the Alps, while its women auxiliaries were discharged.

15. Section C -- Evaluation South-- Section C has been described as the least capable of all the specialist units of the Chi-Stelle. Its commitment, the evaluation of Mediterranean traffic, was largely handled by the Air Signals Regiment in the South (LN Regt 352). Jering, apparently a chronically sour critic, observes of Section C. "During its entire career Section C produced not one special report; this in spite of the fact that activity in the South provided fertile material for such appreciations. ... The members of the Section buried themselves in the details of a highly specialized daily routine without anyone in the Marstall becoming much acquainted with the real problems facing the Signals Intelligence Service battalions in the South... In general, as clumsiness, distrust, and dodging of responsibility characterized the Chi-Stelle Command, so they marked the leadership of Section C. In order to keep its surplus of personnel occupied, ridiculous and unnecessary tasks, involving a labyrinth of paper work, were invented. As a result, all feeling for straight-forwardness and conscientiousness was lost. The majority of members of the Section, in spite of years of service in the Chi-Stelle, had never even seen a Signals Intelligence Service out-station. This reluctance to face realities naturally weakened the influence of the Section. In consequence its opinion in organizational matters carried but little weight, and for the most part it was limited to special problems of evaluation."[98]

a. Organization--[99] Section C, similarly to Section B, was organized into sections which corresponded to Allied units or activities (MATAF, 15th USAAF and 205 Group RAF, long range reconnaissance, radar reporting networks, transport and ferry service, and airfield radio tower traffic). In addition, two other sections, one devoted to press reports and prisoner of war intelligence, and the other to point-to-point networks, were especially successful. The two sections, in close cooperation with the other sections dealing with air-to-ground traffic, and making use of all collateral intelligence, collaborated in producing and maintaining a detailed organizational picture of MAAF which the Luftwaffe A-2 used to include in his monthly reports.

The following "sub-sections" were attached to Section C:

(1) Turkey

Three men revised and edited the material intercepted and evaluated by W-Leit Southeast, and prepared weekly and quarter-annual reports for the A-2.

(2) Sweden and Free France

Even the air forces of these countries were monitored in sketchy form by several out-stations and they provided the "raison d'etre" of several evaluators. Here also, reports were prepared for the A-2, sometimes monthly, sometimes less frequently. After the German withdrawal from France this section was united with Section B.

[98] IF 180 pp 34, 35, 36

[99] quoted from IF 180 pp 35-37

37

(3) Section C 2. This "sub-Section" was created in 1942, and was engaged in preparing a text-book on the radio and navigational procedures of the British, American and Russian Air Forces. This opus was given wide distribution, and all the larger Signals Intelligence Service units were given copies for the edification of Signals Intelligence Service personnel. Current supplements kept the work up to date. In the middle of 1944 the project was abandoned and the personnel transferred to Signals Intelligence Service out-stations.

b. Operations-- Each morning the teletyped material which had come in during the night from the two Signals Intelligence Service battalions in Italy and the Balkans, from the company in Montpellier, the Signals Intelligence Service stations in Spain, and later from the ZAF, as well as from those out-stations which were authorized direct communication with the Section, was assorted by the Chief of the Section and distributed to the appropriate sub-sections. Assembling and checking these reports with any data of their own, the sub-sections, in the course of the forenoon, prepared the daily report of the Section. After being edited by the evaluation officer, it formed the basis for the daily situation conference at which all controversial points were discussed. It was then mimeographed and around noon was ready for distribution. One copy was sent by courier to the General Staff, the others were mailed to the recipients.

The afternoon as a rule was devoted to the study of incoming reports and a review of the log sheets sent in from the units in the field; maps were prepared, and preliminary work done on the monthly report, the distribution of which corresponded in principle to that of Section B's reports. Correspondence with the regiments and battalions was taken care of, comments from the General Staff were studied and those relevant were passed on to the field units concerned.

16. Section D -- Evaluation East--[100] In peace-time this Section evaluated traffic intercepted from Russia, Czechoslovakia, Poland and the Balkan States, and kept the General Staff briefed on air activity in these countries through current reports. After the subjugation of these smaller countries, it concentrated entirely on the Soviet Union which had been considered of prime importance from the beginning. Owing to the different structure of the Signals Intelligence Service in the East, the frowth and development of this Section varied essentially from that of Section B and C. Whereas in the West and South cryptanalysis had to be abandoned to a certain extent, and the main emphasis from the beginning of the war was on traffic analysis and R/T evaluation, in the East the majority of enciphered messages could be read, which placed Signals Intelligence Service work on this Front in a quite different aspect. A further fundamental distinction was that in the West the enemy emerged

[100] quoted from IF 180 pp 13 - 16

practically each month with a new and revolutionary radio or radar technique, while the four years' struggle in the East brought relatively few technical innovations. To this was added the fact that during the course of the war each of the Russian air armies developed its own particular radio procedure, the individual evaluation of which, of necessity, had to be left to the Signals Intelligence Service battalions located on the various sectors of the Front which were specialists on this subject.

Thus Section D, more than any other Section, had to limit itself to a compilatory career. It began its activity in the Marstall, in the wake of German advances at the beginning of the campaign in the East (end of 1941) it moved to Niedersee in East Prussia. From here, in view of the large-scale operations planned on the southern sector for the spring of 1942, it followed the General Staff to Zhitomir, where it remained until May, 1943. The Russian advance caused its retreat to Warsaw, where, at the beginning of 1944 it set up a Meldekopf[101] which was incorporated into the Signals Intelligence Service defense system of the ZAF, (Central Air Raid Warning Unit). When, after the breakthrough at Minsk, the Russians began to threaten Warsaw, it moved again to Cottbus, south of Berlin. There, toward the end of 1944, it was merged with the regimental evaluation company of Signals Intelligence Service Regiment, East, which was formed at about that time.

a. Organization and Operations-- Only during the first two years of the war did the Section send its daily and fortnightly reports directly to the General Staff. At the end of 1942 a Signals Intelligence Service liaison team was established in the office of the A-2 to deal with signal intelligence originating in the East. The reports of Section D were almost unintelligible to a non-specialist, since they were crammed with technical data and terminology; hence they were edited and rewritten by this liaison team. Owing to the uncomplicated aspect of the work, the Section comprised only a few highly qualified men; in all there were only ten members. A rather large cryptanalysis platoon was attached to the Section. At its height the platoon consisted of about ninety men, but its importance dwindled appreciably in the last years of the war. The reason for this was that Russian cryptographic systems became ever more individual in character, and central treatment of them was found to be impractical.

There was also attached to the Section a large intercept platoon which monitored the point-to-point networks of the Russian rear defense zones. A Signals Intelligence Service company in Rzeszov, later Namslau, sent material intercepted to the Section by teletype; it was deciphered by the cryptanalysis platoon and the intelligence therein incorporated into the daily report. The second main source

101 "Reporting Center", further described in Chapter IV

of material for these reports were teletyped summaries from the three Signals Intelligence Service battalions in the East. From 1943 on, R/T traffic from Russian tactical aviation units increased in significance, even being important to final evaluation. During the latter years of the war it was particularly important on the northern sector where good land-line communication limited the use of W/T.

"Meldekopf Warsaw" consisted of a team of about ten men. Since Russian long-range bombers were active only at night, its personnel, radio operators and evaluators alike, was only occupied during the evening hours. If traffic was intercepted on any of the known bomber frequencies it was reported immediately to the ZAF as an early warning. Neither the radio discipline nor navigational ability of the Russian bomber crews was comparable to that of Allied crews in the West. Therefore, as a rule, the Meldekopf was able to report to the ZAF and to other appropriate headquarters, the exact strength, composition, and probable target of an enemy bomber formation. This information was usually determined, at the latest, while the Russian bombers were crossing the front lines.[102]

17. Section E -- Cryptanalysis-- The cryptanalytic Section (Section E) was formed within the Chi-Stelle after the creation of the German Air Force Signal Intelligence Service in 1938. At the outbreak of the war there were only 15 to 18 cryptanalysts. Fifty newly inducted enlisted man without the remotest training in cryptanalysis were then assigned to Section E by the Chief Signal Officer. The Section "expanded continuously, and toward the end of 1942 reached its peak strength of approximately 400 men." The subsequent release of physically-fit men to combat units and their replacement by women auxiliaries "caused cryptanalysis to suffer many a set-back."[103] Nevertheless, it is claimed that "even in January 1945 the Section could boast of having broken 35,000 messages in the West and 15,000 in the East..."[104]

a. Organization-- Section E was divided into two main units: E-1, which worked on Eastern systems, particularly Russia; and E-2 and E-3, which worked on Western systems, particularly British and American. Sub-section E-6 was engaged in IBM work.

The decentralization of cryptanalytic work, discussed above[105] was occasioned by the necessity of placing low-grade solution as far front as possible and the failure of the Air Force cryptanalysts to solve such high grade systems as SIGABA or the Russian one-time pads. It is stated that "new

[102] IF 180 pp 13 - 16

[103] IF 180 p 17

[104] IF 180 p 17

[105] Chapter II

DOCID: 3560829

difficult cryptanalytic problems were first explored by Section E in the Marstall. Later if the deciphering procedure was established in detail, a team of cryptanalysts familiar with the system, was sent to that Signals Intelligence Service battalion or company where the greatest amount of traffic in that particular system was being intercepted. Thus, eventually the personnel of Section E was scattered all over Europe." Cryptanalysis is discussed in more detail in Chapter V of this volume.[106]

18. The Radar Control Post (Funkleitstand)-- The Radar intercept control post (Funkleitstand), although an independent unit originally under the control of the Radar Service, finally was placed under the undivided jurisdiction of Gen Nafue III. In practice, "it was a Section for radar intercept"[107] and a type of Chi-Stelle for radar evaluation. The inter-relations between the Funkleitstand, Section B-3 (navigational aid evaluation), and the Central Command Post for Air-Raid Warning (ZAF) are difficult to ascertain. It has been stated that "the whole manner in which the radar intercept problem was treated is indicative of the confusion, bumptiousness and lack of coordination which prevailed in all higher headquarters in Germany during the last two years of the war."[108]

Friedrich stated that from pure traffic analysis of British radar service, the German radar monitoring service was enabled to ascertain or to establish:

"1. The mode of operation of ground sets. In cooperation with the listening service, it was possible to ascertain the areas in which interception by (or of) the enemy was not possible.

"2. Clarification of navigational aids to the extent that the English control systems became known (advance warning).

"3. Data for our own jamming service and technical hints for our own development of similar sets.

"4. Carrying out of route-tracking of formations in the air; in most cases from take-off until landing."[109]

The German Air Force Signals Intelligence Service early realized the potentialities of radar intercept evaluation and created radar intercept centers (Funkbefehlsstaende) at the individual field Signals Intelligence Service battalions, which "were intended to perform locally the same functions as the Radar Control Center (Funkleitstand) at Potsdam."[110]

[106] IF 180 p 17

[107] IF 180 p 39

[108] IF 180 pp 40, 41

[109] I 70 pp 6, 7

[110] IF 180 p 40

DOCID: 3560829

In 1944 the radar intercept centers were incorporated into the evaluation companies of their respective Signals Intelligence Service battalions, and radar intercept flash messages were sent directly to the reporting centers (Meldeköpfe), which were agencies collating all types of signal intelligence data relating to impending air-raids.

Volume 5

Chapter IV. Organization and Operation of the Field Units

Section A. Operations in the West

19. Organization of Field Units in the West-- The final German Air Force Signal Intelligence Service unit in the West, Air Signal Regiment 351, was the result of four years of continuous operation against Britain and eventually, the Western Allies. By the time the November 1944 reorganization took place, its activities had become mainly centered upon the tactical evaluation of Allied bombing operations. As a result of this emphasis, two "independent" battalions, Air Signals Battalion 356 (concerned with radar intercept in the Reich) and Air Signals Battalion 357 (concerned with intercept and evaluation of Allied bomber communications) were organized. To some degree, these two battalions were created from units which had been part of Air Signals Regiment West from which Air Signals Regiment 351 had been earlier derived.

Air Signals Regiment 351, also derived originally from Air Signals Regiment West, was organized into three battalions each of which had four to five companies. The first battalion (I/LN Regt 351) contained the regimental Evaluation company (25th Co LN Regt 351), the communications company (26th Co Regt 351) and two other service companies, the tactical reconnaissance company (1 Co Regt 351) and the signal repair company (2nd Co Regt 351). The second battalion (II/LN Regt 351) had a VHF (very high frequency, i.e. radio telephone) intercept and D/F company (7th Co Regt 351), which operated against the Tactical Air Force Fighter Command; two HF (high frequency, i.e., usual Morse channels) intercept companies (8th and 9th Cos, Regt 351), which operated against the French Air Force and the 1st U. S. Tactical Air Force; and a radar intercept company (10th Co, Regt 351).

The third battalion (III/LN Regt 351) had three HF intercept companies (12th, 13th, and 15th Cos Regt 351) which operated respectively against Allied transport units, Tactical Air Force and naval air raid warning service; a VHF (Very High Frequency) R/T intercept company (14th Co Regt 351), which operated against the Tactical Air Force Fighter Command; and a radar intercept company (16th Co Regt 351).

20. Intercept Missions of Field Units-- Intercept missions were assigned in the West by Section B of the Signal Intelligence Agency, which made the assignments to the Regiment (LN Regt 351) or to the evaluation company (originally W-Leit, later 25th Co. LN Regt 351).[111] Section B also directed search cover, including the employment of the search receivers and the identification of new traffic.[112] Search missions were allocated by assigning specific portions of the frequency spectrum to different sets. An operator with records of known and identified traffic could determine immediately whether traffic he intercepted was known. New traffic also appeared directly on or near frequencies regularly covered by the intercept companies. Whether picked up on search, or on fixed assignments, the newly discovered traffic was re-examined by the evaluation sections, identified, where possible, and put on further cover, where unidentified. Further monitoring disclosed whether it was practice or bona fide tactical traffic.[113]

21. Distribution of Reports by Field Units in the West-- Evaluation was performed at all possible levels: at the intercept stations by intercept platoons; at the battalions and regiment by evaluation companies; and finally, at the Chi-Stelle level by Section B, which worked with the field units. The intercept companies issued daily radio situation reports, which were transmitted to interested headquarters (including Section B) either by teletype, radio, or courier. Every month a detailed composite report was made by the intercept companies, and an evaluation report by the Evaluation companies.[114]

According to Jering,

> "Each SIS station and SIS company analyzed its allotted material with much flourish... Two reports went daily to the W-Leitstelle (the regimental evaluation unit) and to the pertinent Referat. The daily logs were sent by courier to the W-Leitstelle and to the Referat concerned, and there examined and evaluated. In spite of this duplication of work, the individual companies were allowed to operate independently, their independence varying with the ability of the company commander and the evaluators."[115]

[111] IF 181 p 28

[112] IF 183 p 60

[113] IF 183 p 61

[114] I 109

[115] IF 181 p 26

The development of tactical evaluation resulted in the routing of reports directly from the intercept stations and the intercept companies to the operational headquarters concerned.[116] The daily and monthly reports were then divided into "tactical and technical sections. The tactical included a description of enemy air activity from the Signal Intelligence point of view, while the technical part was a systematic compilation and identification of all intercepted traffic."[117]

The distribution of a typical report gives some clue to the recipients of the intelligence produced in the West. For instance, a report made by Evaluation Company 14/LN Regt 3, dated 28 April 1944, discussing "American Fighter and Fighter-Bomber Formations in England," covering the period from 8-18 April has a cover sheet reading as follows:[118]

"Distribution

I/GAF Listening Rgt, West	1
I/(Evaluation Co) GAF Listening Rgt. West	3
5/('Funkempfangs' Co.) " " "	2
3/(Interception Co) " " "	1
8/(" ") " " "	1
9/(" ") " " "	2
Listening Liaison Officer, Luftflotte 3, lc for attn Lt. Reser	1
" " " JK.II for atten Oblt. Z. Nieden	1
" " " Jd. 4 for atten Feld. Roeckerath	1
" " " Jd. 5 for atten Lt. Schwietzke	1
" " " Jafue 4 for atten Lt. Roschger	1
" " " Jafue 5 for atten Oblt Gruendl	1
" " " Jafue Brittany for atten Feldw. Ziemer	1
14/(Evaluation Co.) GAF Listening Rgt 3 (3 copies for VHF Platoon (mobile))	7
Copy for information to Main Crypt. Office, GAF Sec. B	25"

116 IF 181 p 35

117 IF 181 p 34

118 DF 10 pp 1 2

45

In the final stages of the Signal Intelligence operation in the West, when tactical evaluation was all important, Reports were routed by the various intercept and evaluation companies to the Reporting Centers (Meldeköpfe). These centers were the collating agencies for tactical intelligence concerning air raids, and functioned as instruments of liaison between Signal Intelligence Service and the Combat units. (They are described more fully in Paragraph 6, of this Chapter.) The units of the LN Regt 351 routed their reports to Reporting Center 2, the companies of LN Abt 357 (Bomber Intercept) routed theirs to Reporting Center 1, and the companies of LN Abt 356 (Radar Intercept) fed Reporting Center 3. In turn the Reporting Centers broadcast their evaluation and warning summaries to the Central Air Raid Warning Unit (the ZAF) and to various Army, Navy, and Air Force operational Commands.

22. Signal Communications of Field Units in the West-- In the middle of 1940 the wire channel system was in general as follows: Telephone or teletype lines connected each Signal Intelligence Service company and station with the Regimental Evaluation Company (W-Leit), and in turn linked the latter unit with the pertinent Chi-Stelle Section, the local Air Force (Luftflotte) headquarters, and the neighboring evaluation companies. Telephone or teletype lines also connected the Signal Intelligence companies and the Regimental Evaluation Companies with the German Air Force exchanges. The various Signal Intelligence companies and stations were linked to each other and to their outstations and D/F's by telephone. 119 As Germany's position deteriorated the communications systems were enlarged to accommodate the ever increasing flow of intelligence. In general, the communications channels between intercept station, D/F station, Evaluation Company, Chi-Stelle Section, and Air Force operational commands underwent continuous expansion. "The whole construction of the communications network was founded on the principle of passing on intercepted traffic as quickly as possible. A delay or more than two minutes could not be tolerated." 120 Major Ferdinand Feichtner's report describes the expansion of wire communications in the middle of 1942 as follows:

> In addition to the individual teletype lines with the companies, several telephone lines were available, most of them running from the switchboards of the evaluation companies to the intercept companies. Likewise there were one or two lines to the SIS liaison officers as headquarters.... (and) various direct lines from the companies to the SIS-liaison officers, the purpose of which was

119 IF 181 pp 27 28

120 IF 181 p 44

DOCID: 3560829

to achieve a minimum of delay.... This considerable expansion made necessary the building of large telephone centrals:

Exchange "Pirate"-------Meldekopf 1 of the 1st Battalion
Exchange "Breakwater"---Radar Intercept Center West of the 2nd Battalion
Exchange "Clairvoyant"--Evaluation Company of the 3rd Battalion, and also the regimental exchange

The regimental exchange finally comprised 5-7 FD 16's (switchboards) with about 150 trunk lines and 250-300 local drops.

In addition to the normal telephone centrals, in the case of the 8th Company and the 5th Company, D/F control communications had to be installed. The regimental teletype central had 6-8 lines to the Luftwaffe exchanges, in addition to lines to the companies and SIS-liaison officers. There were three teletype-cipher machines for top secret messages; and 8-10 for secret communications. Altogether, about 500-700 teletype messages were handled daily." [121]

The continued expansion of the Signal Intelligence Service and its orientation in the direction of preserving the Reich from air raids led to the formation of a Signal Intelligence Battalion attached to the German Home Defense Air Force. This, plus the assignment of Signal Intelligence liaison officers to the components of Fighter Wing (Jagdkorps) I "made numerous circuits necessary, both within Germany, and from Germany to the occupied territories. These wire requirements increased when the ZAF obtained an additional wire system." [122]

Major Feichtner describes an interesting practice made necessary by the intensified operations:

> "The extensive construction of D/F and radar intercept stations, both in Germany proper and in occupied territories, made it impossible for each of the Regiment's 176 out-stations and the 60 out-stations of the SIS-battalion Reich to have its own direct lines. For this reason the "Dante," or operational connection was introduced for the SIS. Upon use of the code-word "Dante" any conversation taking place over normal Luftwaffe circuits would be terminated and the line used for passing tactical reports for the duration of an air raid or other engagement. [123]

121 IF 181 pp 44 45

122 IF 181 p 54

123 IF 181 p 55

As for Radio Communications, Major Feichtner reports as follows:

"In the beginning of 1944 radio stations were set up by the regiment at out-stations, command posts and companies. Each company had:

a) A D/F Control network, or a radio link with its out-stations;
b) A radio link with its battalion;
c) A radio link with the pertinent Meldekopf.

The Meldeköpfe were included, either in the D/F control networks, or in the radio links between companies and out-stations. In this way it was provided that, in case of line trouble, all tactical reports would reach the Meldeköpf as quickly as possible, and from there would be broadcast as signal intelligence flash reports to interested headquarters. The code used by the Meldeköpf for these flash reports consisted of a code book of 1000 meanings. These encoded messages were reciphered with the appropriate cipher table and sent out on both long wave and short wave as 5-figure groups. The cipher systems of Meldeköpf 2 were held by the Army as far down as division."[124]

23. Strategic Evaluation by Field Units in the West-- In the description of actual operations it is frequently difficult to distinguish clearly between strategic and tactical evaluation, as some overlapping was inevitable. However, the two types of evaluation may be differentiated in terms of their objectives. The objectives of strategic evaluation for the Air Force Signal Intelligence were to establish the order of battle for the opposing Air Forces, to determine the order of battle and intentions of the Ground Forces as revealed through Air Force Communications, and to predict long-range intentions of the opposing Air Forces.

Each of these objectives was most carefully pursued, but the success was most remarkable in the establishment of the Allied Air order of battle. Through their thorough and highly skilled traffic analysis, the Germans obtained a continuous and highly accurate picture of the strength and disposition of the Allied Air Forces in Britain, in the Mediterranean, the Near East, and later, on the Continent. Frequently, the reconstruction was precise to the most minute detail, and call signs, frequencies and networks were in the vast majority of cases absolutely accurate.

[124] IF 181 pp 54-55

48

A great amount of material is available in the TICOM interrogations and in the Seabourne Report (especially Volume VII) documented by charts and diagrams showing the reconstructed order of battle of the RAF and the USAAF. Examples of these are annexed to show the meticulously careful work of the traffic analysts. (Charts 5-3, 5-4, 5-5, 5-6)

The establishment of the Ground Forces order of battle through analysis of Allied air traffic was of course more difficult. In the West, Air Force traffic ordinarily did not reveal the ground force organization. However, after the Invasion, when the Air Force was acting in direct support of ground operations, much information was disclosed of value to the Germans.

As for the prediction of long-range intentions of the opposing Air Forces, indications of coming events were frequently derived from strategic evaluation. The extent to which German Air Force Signal Intelligence was able to forecast the Dieppe raid, and the Invasion etc., has already been noted attention in the first chapter of this volume.

The degree to which information vital to the defense of the Reich was obtained through the Signal Intelligence activities in the West is illustrated by the following passage from an R/T report dated 4 April 1944 originated by the 5th ("Funkempfang ") Company, 3rd Battalion of Wireless I Intercept Regt West (later LN Regt 351):

> "Operations on the part of the USAAF against Reich territory, and operations against Western occupied territory during the period under review, were picked up again as from the first appearance of flying activity over England.
>
> "By thorough observation of, for the most part, very strong fighter protection, the direction of the attack may be ascertained, in spite of the deceptive course taken by the waves of bombers.
>
> "The change in call signs effected by the USAAF at the beginning of the month under review did not interfere with intelligence, and even within a few days it was possible to bring documents here completely up-to-date.
>
> "The D/F base line was again particularly effective. By endeavoring to follow all three bomber divisions very closely, it was possible, in addition to incursion into Reich territory, likewise to D/F the diversionary attacks against the occupied territory at the same time. It was, therefore, again possible to place the information available here at the disposal of the tactically important positions for the air defence of the Reich, up to three hours before the enemy formations crossed the coast of the Continent." 125

125 DF 11 p 4

24. Tactical Evaluation by Field Units in the West-- Tactical evaluation was far more important then strategic in the operations in the West. The primary purpose of tactical evaluation was to provide a prompt and efficient service warning of Allied air-raid incursions. The operational necessities of such a service demanded alert interception of all possible signal manifestations (signals, radar, beacons, noises and silences, *inter alia*), prompt and reliable evaluation, and immediate dissemination of the intelligence derived to the operational units and the defense organizations concerned.

The mass of available data regarding the organization and operations of this service and the results it achieved shows the outstanding success of this undertaking. If Germany was not able to counteract the attacks it was not the fault of signal intelligence which gave the warnings. So efficient was the operation that it won the attention of the very highest commands, and Goering was proud of the listening service.[126]

[126] The Germans tell a story, probably apocryphal but nevertheless significant, to this effect:

> Goering at first deprecated the possibility of deriving air raid warnings from traffic. However, on the occasion of one of the visits the Luftwaffe Chief made in the West, a master-sergeant (who wears two stars as his insignia--zwei Sterne) pleaded with Goering to listen in himself: "Please, Herr Reichsmarschall, if you would have the kindness yourself to listen..." Goering listened for half an hour, was astonished at the amount of talking that went on. Thereupon Goering turned to his officers and directed that the master-sergeant be promoted. However, there was no further enlisted rank he could receive. When the officers told Goering that, he said: "Make him a sergeant with three stars" ("Feldwebel mit drei Sternen"). New tables of organization, pay scales, allotments, etc., had to be devised to comply with the Reichsmarschall's request.

At his interrogation 127, he stated that Capt. Rueckheim (who commanded LN Abt 357 and who was instrumental in activating the Meldekopf organization) passed "him situation reports every evening at about 6 P.M. over a direct private line....even in the middle of the night, if operations were on, he could ring up Rueckheim and obtain the very latest information on the position; this enabled Goering to break in personally on the conduct of any operation at any time; for example, when his staff said that the raiders were going for Berlin, he might have more up to date intelligence direct from Rueckheim and could say 'No, they are going for Stettin.'"[128]

The realization that air force signal intelligence could produce tactical intelligence came as the result of a successful prediction of a Wellington raid in December 1939.[129] Anti-aircraft (flak) units had been relying on "ground observer service of the old type (visual and acoustic). It supplemented that service with its own troop units of ground observers, and later with its own radar."[130]

a. Organization:--As a unified command for route-tracking purposes became necessary, a new office was created, that of Chief of the Air Raid Warning Service for Germany (Funkaufklaerungsfuehrer Reich, abbreviated FAF). He was put under the Chi-Stelle for operational purposes, and acted as advisor to the Commanding General of the Fighter Corps (Jagdkorps), entrusted with the defense of Germany. The duties of the FAF are described by Col. Forster:

> "a) He was responsible for the tracking of the enemy's strategic air forces. He was directly under the Chief Signal Officer of the Luftwaffe (OKL, General Martini), who gave his commands and orders through the Chi-Stelle (Col. Friedrich). In the matter of military decisions the Funkaufklaerungsfuehrer Reich was subordinate to the Chief of the Signal Intelligence Service (General Klemme).
>
> "b) He was adviser to the Commanding General of Jagdkorps I, which was responsible for the Reich's defense. His command post (ZAF) was therefore near the command post of Jagdkorps I.
>
> "c) He was responsible for the functioning of the Signal Intelligence Service in the West; and
>
> "d) He was responsible for the direction of the entire jamming service within the area of Germany.) 131

127 I 143

128 I 143 pp 15.16

129 I 109 p 7

130 Col. Forster, head of FAF, IF 181 p 60

131 IF 181 p 63

b. The ZAF-- The central Reporting Center (Meldekopf) for Germany was known as the Central Air Raid Warning Unit (Zentraler Gefechtsstand Fuer Funkauswertung, abbreviated "ZAF"). It was located in Treuenbrietzen, near Berlin, and was the control and evaluation center for all tactical warnings significant in the defense of the Reich. It controlled for purposes of tactical operations all the Reporting Centers on all the fronts, but was most important in the German defense against British and American strategic long-range bombers. The ZAF was serviced by excellent signal communication from the field Reporting Centers. Circuits carrying tactical intelligence from the ZAF led to radar sites, Signal Intelligence liaison officers at tactical headquarters, field Reporting Centers and even out-stations.[132]

(1) Evaluation within ZAF

Evaluation within the ZAF meant primarily the tracking of enemy aircraft. All information from Signal Intelligence Wervice and collateral sources was plotted on special wall maps within the operations room, from which the minute-to-minute position of enemy bombers with their fighter cover could be determined at a glance. If a raid were being followed in the west, specialists on that area manned the operations room. (See chart 5-7) Ordinarily, this specialist personnel worked in the evaluation section[133], which, though of key importance, was small. Its work was mainly the collation of reports from the field. On the basis of these it issued a report on the air situation over Germany every twelve hours. A conference to brief all evaluators on the intentions and operations of the tactical units was held every evening at 1800 hours and was usually attended by Col. Forster, FAF.[134]

The command post for the jamming of all allied transmitters was located in the ZAF. This arrangement avoided the jamming of allied transmitters that were currently producing intelligence for the Germans.[135]

It must be emphasized that the ZAF did not reduce the importance of other Signal Intelligence activities. The combatting of heavy bomber incursions was such an important problem the Germans were simply forced to centralize tactical warnings in a special unit.

[132] IF 181 p 71

[133] IF 181 p 72

[134] IF 181 p 73

[135] IF 181 p 74

c. Reporting Center (Meldekopf) 1 -- Reporting Center 1, the oldest and most efficient of the tactical warning centers, operated against the Western allies.[136] Its operating technique served as a model for the Reporting Centers on all fronts, and this center will be briefly described as it is characteristic of all the others.

It was created originally in the summer of 1942 as a preparatory defense measure against the RAF, and was made up of officers, evaluators, and W/T operators from Signal Intelligence units in the West.[137] In its final form Reporting Center 1 exercised local tactical operational control of the Signal Intelligence units operating against strategic bombers based in Great Britain and later on the continent. This central was limited to tactical operations; and for administration the Signal Intelligence field units still were subordinated to local Signal Intelligence units.[138]

The tactical mission of Reporting Center 1 may be summed up as follows:

a. to give accurate early warning of the raids by heavy bombers;

b. by continuously tracking the heavy bombers, to present to German fighter units a clear picture of the air situation;

c. to interpret the air situation in such a way as to predict the strength and probable targets and tactics of allied bombers.[139]

In the final year of the war, Reporting Center 1 at Heiligenstadt[140] was part of the 1st Company of the Signal Intelligence field battalion, LN Abt-357. From this Battalion Reporting Center 1 received reports. It sent its own reports to the Air Force operational headquarters concerned, and to such naval units as Admiralty Deutsche Bucht, "E" Boat Command, Small Naval Forces Command and Naval D/F section Deutsche Bucht. (See chart 5-8)

The center developed into a War Room, with its own telephone exchange and radio station. Current tactical information was instantly plotted, and immediate reports flashed to ZAF and tactical units in the area. (See chart 5-9)[141]

136 IF 183 p 1

137 IF 183 p 1

138 IF 183 p 3

139 IF 183 p 2

140 IF 183 p 9

141 IF 183 p 9

During this time the 2nd Company of LN Abt-357 was committed to monitoring RAF training units, the 3rd Company to the bomber divisions of the Eighth USAAF, and the 4th Company to RAF Bomber Command. The battalion was augmented by a radar intercept company and a VHF R/T company as well as a D/F base line covering Western Germany.[142] The stations in the D/F base line were coordinated from the Reporting Center, a necessary measure if it was to supervise route tracking.[143]

Tactical evaluation sections were created within each intercept company. These sections maintained close contact with the Morse operators and passed the slightest sign of a bomber incursion back to the Reporting Center.[144]

d. Reporting Centers 2 and 3-- In the West there were two other Reporting Centers in addition to that just discussed. Reporting Center 2 was part of the 25th Company 1st Battalion of LN Regt 351, and number 3 was part of the 1st Company of LN Abt 356. The operations within these units resembled those within Reporting Center 1, with overall coordination exercised by the ZAF, and it would serve little purpose to detail activities within those units. Attention should be called, however, to the wide dissemination of reports made by Reporting Center 2. The reports sent by the various companies of the three battalions of LN Regt 351 which were sent to Reporting Center 2 besides being broadcast to the ZAF, were radioed to the following units:

Air Force:
- Air Staff West
- 14th, 15th, and 16th F (Fliegerdivisionen)
- 2, 28, 57, and 72 JG (Jagdkorps)
- 3rd and 4th Flak Korps.

(These fighter and anti-aircraft units could take operational counter-measures to the ensuing raid)

Army:
- Commander-in-Chief West
- Army Groups H, B, and D
- 25th, 7th, and 19th Armies
- 87th Army Corps (and five or six others)
- 5th Panzer Army
- 11th Panzer Division
- 1st Parachute Army

142 IF 183 p 7

143 IF 183 p 9

144 IF 183 p 8

Civilian Defense: Gauleiters of Wurzburg and Karlsruhe
Air Warning Services of INNsbruck, Munich, Nuernberg, Darmstadt, Halle
Navy "E" Boat Commander

Reporting Center 3, which received reports from LN Regt 356 (radar evaluation), reported to the Air Force operational units concerned with the defense of the Reich. (See chart 5-10)

In the final days of the war, the reports of the Reporting Centers regulated life within Germany as far as air raid precautions were concerned. The complete charts which follow picture in detail the routing and recipients of the information derived at the Reporting Centers. Technical Sergeant Gerd Watkinson of Reporting Center 1 writes that "never, once a report had been released to the effect that a night would be free of enemy aerial intrusion, did the personnel of the Meldekopf need to blush for a mistake in its calculation."[145]

[145] IF.183 p 11

VOLUME 5

Chapter IV Organization and Operations of the Field Units.

Section B. Operations in the East.

25. Development and geographical disposition of the field units-- The activation of LN Regt 353, the final signal intelligence unit in the East, was the last step in an evolution that had its beginning in 1936.[150]

In 1936, a fixed Radio Intercept Station was erected in Glindow, near Berlin. In 1937-1938, five more stations were erected at Breslau, Pilsnitz, Bromberg, Kobbelbude, and Hirschstaetten near Vienna. These field units were responsible for preliminary analysis and evaluation of Russian Air Force traffic, the final evaluation being done by the Chi-Stelle. The Chi-Stelle had operational control of the out-stations though administratively these were subordinated to the Signal Regiments of the Air Forces in whose area they operated. Stations at Hirschstaetten and Breslau were assigned to LN Regt 4, the rest to LN Regt 1. Signal Intelligence personnel considered this a bad arrangement as they were bound to two masters, and were constantly involved in jurisdictional disputes.

The monitoring of Russian radio traffic was extensive and complicated. Not only did each Russian Air Army have its own signal procedures and cryptographic systems, but the method used in the assignment of call signs and frequencies became ever more complex. This situation, added to the fact that the Air Forces resented the extra channel represented by the Chi-Stelle and were eager to obtain intelligence directly from the operating units, led to a reorganization in the summer of 1938. This reorganization saw the formation of collecting and evaluation agencies known as Wetter-Leitstellen (W-Leit), whose function was to issue interim reports to

[150] IF 186 pp 2-5

56

the local Air Forces and to expedite the flow of material to the Chi-Stelle. Cryptanalytic and evaluation personnel were drawn mainly from the fixed Radio Intercept stations and to a lesser degree from Chi-Stelle. A further step in organization was taken during the summer of 1939 when these collecting and evaluation centers (W-Leit) and the fixed and mobile Radio Intercept companies were formed administratively into Battalions. Each of these battalions was the third battalion in its respective Air Force Signal Regiment. Formerly the Signal Regiments had not dealt with intelligence matters.

At the outbreak of war with Poland, Section D of the Chi-Stelle exercised operational control over two groups of units administratively organized under two Air Signal Regiments. Under 3rd Battalion LN Regt 1, W-Leit-1 in Bernau controlled operationally the Signal Intelligence stations at Kobbelbude and Bromberg. (Later moved to Pilsnitz) Under the 3rd Battalion LN Regt 4, W-Leit-4 in Vienna controlled the fixed Radio Intercept stations at Breslau, Premstaetten (latter at Hirschstaetten) and Budapest plus the 10th Company, LN Regt 4. [151]

The years 1940 through 1942 saw modifications in the organization of Signal Intelligence units concerned with Russian traffic. There was of course a general shift in geographical disposition towards the East and accompanying changes of administrative control. The organization in the East remained fairly stable through 1943, but in 1944 an important reorganization of German Air Force Signal Intelligence units was effected. This took place in November of that year and consisted chiefly in the activation of LN Regt 353 to encompass all Signal Intelligence activities on the Eastern Front. The division of operational and administrative control was maintained. Section D of the Chi-Stelle still exercised operational control throughout the structure, while the Chief Signal Officer was administrative head through General Klemme, a purely administrative officer. At this time also, a Signal Intelligence regimental headquarters, with the 25th Co (evaluation), and the 12th Co (intercept) was activated in Cottbus. The balance of LNR-353 included three battalions as follows:[152]

"a. 1st Bn, LN Regt 353 (formerly 3rd Bn LN Regt 1) of four companies in East Prussia.

"b. 2nd Bn, LN Regt 353 (Signal Intelligence Bn East) of five companies in Poland.

"c. 3rd Bn, LN Regt 353 (3rd Bn LN Regt 4) of five companies in Austria.

151 IF 186 p 2 5

152 IF 186 p 6a

57

As the campaign in the East degenerated for the Germans, the Regimental Headquarters and its two companies retreated, arriving in Dresden in February 1945. From Dresden the headquarters moved on into the "Alpine Redoubt" where it was joined by the 2nd and 3rd Battalions in Wagrien. A 70-man platoon operated during the move. The 1st Battalion stayed in the North.

After Germany's capitulation the Regiment moved via Zell am See and Lake Chiem to the Luftwaffe concentration area in Aschbach in southern Bavaria. All personnel of the Headquarters, its companies and the 2nd and 3rd Battalions were discharged from there. The 1st Battalion fell into British hands at Luebeck in April 1945.[153]

26. Operations within the Battalions--The operations of LN Regt 353 in the East differed greatly from the operations of its sister units in the West. This difference in operating technique reflected the capabilities of the Soviet Union as compared with those of the Western Allies in the business of signal communication. German Air Force Signal Intelligence was designed to exploit Russian weaknesses as Soviet cryptographic and radio development was behind that of Britain and the United States. The Western Front was the sphere of the traffic analyst, but the Eastern units emphasized the cryptanalysis of Soviet ciphers.

The administrative and geographic changes of LN Regt 353 have been discussed. An examination of the three battalions (Abteilungen) and the organization of the four or five companies within each battalion follows.

The heart of the battalion was the evaluation company and its seven sections. In addition, the battalion included an operating and out-station company and two intercept companies. (See chart 5-11) In order to clarify the operation of a unit as complex as the battalion, this discussion will "start with the traffic" in the intercept company and out-station company and trace the course of the intercepted message until it emerges from Evaluation as intelligence.

a. Intercept Company-- Liaison between evaluation and intercept was very close. Operationally, the intercept company was subordinated to the T/A section of the evaluation company. The T/A section assigned the missions and reserved the right of direction over the watch officers in the intercept room. The CO of the intercept company was responsible for all intercept of Morse traffic, which was copied in the more or less permanent installation of the Battalion.[154] As far as possible, each intercept operator specialized in a particular circuit and learned the peculiarities of its operators.

153 IF 186 p 14

154 I 182 p 12

58

A D/F control station was located in the intercept room to take bearings on unknown stations, while the D/F section of the evaluation company stood ready to perform immediate plotting to assist intercept.[155]

b. Operating and Out-station Company-- The CO was responsible for the Battalion's signal communication and for the technical operation of the out-stations and D/F sites. Out-stations were usually maintained at fighter strips and were responsible for R/T intercept. Each R/T intercept operator had direct communication with the nearest D/F site and could switch over and have a fix taken.

Telephone and teletype circuits to higher headquarters, other battalions, and subordinate units were maintained where wire lines were possible. The company operated radio circuits to the out-stations, D/F sites, other battalions, and higher headquarters. The Germans never reached the ideal situation of having land lines between all D/F and intercept units, and radio was extensively used for D/F control.[156]

c. Evaluation Company-- The CO as head of all evaluation arranged a daily situation conference attended by the battalion commander and the heads of the seven evaluation sections. The conference coordinated the work of the entire unit based on the requests of the local Air Force (Luftflotte) and Wing (Fliegerkorps) serviced.[157] Evaluation was regional and only loosely aligned with the other battalions because of the large distances involved.[158]

How the Germans controlled the intercept units and processed the raw traffic into intelligence can best be made clear by brief comments on each of the seven evaluating sections.

(1) R/T (Radio Telephone) Evaluation--The R/T evaluation subsection was the final resting place for the R/T intercept copied in the out-stations. The out-stations had already issued immediate intelligence to flying formations, but it was the function of R/T evaluation to extract order of battle in the form of pilots' names, Russian unit designations, map grid information and all the miscellaneous bits and pieces to be gleaned from R/T.

On the technical side, the section worked out the relationship between frequency and call sign changes and checked this information with the traffic analysis subsection, as R/T and Morse circuits were often superimposed.[159]

[155] I 182 p 13

[156] I 182 p 9

[157] I 182 p 4

[158] I 42 p 2

[159] I 182 p. 5

(2) Long Range Bombers--This subsection was manned only when alerted by Soviet recce or weather aircraft or by the receipt of a Russian operational message. It was an integral part of the tactical warning system that will be described in the section on tactical operations against Soviet long range bombers.[160]

(3) Traffic Analysis-- The traffic analysis subsection exercised operational control over the Morse intercept companies and assisted their operation by reconstructing Russian radio networks, schedules and call signs. Each evaluator specialized in a particular Soviet air army. T/A passed a large amount of order of battle of Russian air armies to final evaluation. The section kept its own situation maps and records and through inference added to the overall intelligence picture.[161]

(4) D/F (Direction Finding) Evaluation-- The results of the field D/F sites were received by the D/F evaluation subsection daily. The results in the form of station locations were passed to the T/A section as an aid to T/A's reconstruction of Russian networks. Another function of the D/F Evaluation subsection should be noted here. In addition to its other tasks, it evaluated the results of radar monitoring done by two radar monitoring units (WIM-Truppe) attached to the 1st Battalion of LN Regt 353.[162] Soviet use of radar was never extensive, though it was used in the Leningrad area. The fact that the radar sites in this area communicated by R/T made it possible for German Signal Intelligence to warn German fighters that they had been apprehended by Russian radar.

(5) Cryptanalysis-- Incoming messages were registered and sorted according to whether or not they were currently readable. Traffic in systems as yet unbroken was referred to a research party. The balance was immediately decoded and the results passed to final evaluation.

The importance of the cryptanalytic subsection is illustrated by the number of persons it contained. Twice as many people worked in the cryptanalytic section as were in the other combined six sections of the evaluation company. Roughly 85 per cent of Russian traffic was readable. This weakness in Soviet cipher retarded the development of more advanced T/A methods in LN Regt 353. Evaluation received a wealth of message content material that made inference unnecessary.[163]

160 I 182 pp 5-6

161 I 182 p 6

162 I 163 p 3

163 I 182 p 7

60

(6) Weather Evaluation-- Meteorological messages went directly from the intercept operator to weather evaluation. Results of solved messages went directly to flying units and to the weather center at the Air Force High Command.[164]

(7) Final Evaluation-- The discussion of Final Evaluation has been purposely placed at the end of the break-down of the evaluation company as it was here that all the battalion's functions were brought together. Decoded messages from the cryptanalytic section were translated. Formations, names of people and units and their location and all other O B material were card indexed and coordinated with the results of T/A and R/T evaluation. Items of immediate importance were dispatched immediately, and a daily report to the local Air Force and the Wing was rendered that dealt with new order of battle, construction of new air fields, strength returns, fuel supplies, and new operational targets.[165]

The daily report to these two units followed roughly a 5-paragraph estimate of the situation as follows:

(a) New information on order of battle, airfield location, supply dump activity and RR activity. This section was teletyped in advance.
(b) Consideration of the air armies as to flying and ground units.
(c) Order of battle of the long-range bomber formations.
(d) Review of Black Sea or Baltic coastal units.
(e) Estimate of Russian home defense formations.

Semi-monthly reports followed the same form, but were much more detailed. Distribution was made to Air Force High Command, the Signal Intelligence Agency, Army Signal Intelligence, Air Force, Wing, and to subordinate units within LNR-353.[166]

27. The deployment of the Battalions-- LN Regt 353 was an Air Force unit, but its activities were often of tremendous help to the German Army. The Russians attached one air army to each army group in line with their conception of the use of air force.[167] Strategic moves of the Russian army groups were compromised by German signal intelligence activities against the accompanying air armies. The ground units would move up under radio silence, but it is extremely difficult to move aircraft without using transmitters, hence the radio activities of the aircraft would betray them.

164 I 182 p 8

165 I 182 p 5

166 I 107 pp 3 4

167 IF 187

61

The following order of battle will show how LN Regt 353 was deployed against the Russians:

a. 1st Battalion Northern Section in East Prussia monitored:
   Baltic Red Banner Fleet
   15th Air Army (2nd Baltic Front)
   3rd Air Army (1st Baltic Front)
   1st Air Army (3rd White Russian Front)
   4th Air Army
   16th Air Army (1st White Russian Front)
   15th Air Army (2nd White Russian Front)
   14th Air Army (2nd White Russian Front)
b. 2nd Battalion Central sector in Poland monitored:
   2nd Air Army (1st Ukranian Front)
   All Russian radio beacons
c. 3rd Battalion, southern sector in Austria:
   8th Air Army
   17th Air Army
   5th Air Army
   Russian Command networks
   18th Air Army (long range bombers)

The Germans were quick to improvise on all fronts. For instance, when the 1st Battalion found that the Russian 1st, 3rd, and 15th Air Armies and the Baltic Fleet Air Arm were using a disproportionate amount of R/T, its operations were adjusted to capitalize on this fact.[168] A detachment was put aboard the cruiser "Prinz Eugen" to monitor the Fleet Air Arm. Communication from the out-stations was speeded up to immediately exploit "hot" items The R/T in this sector often uncovered armoured and troop concentrations.

28. Strategic Results of LN Regt 353-- LN Regt 353 was a highly successful signal intelligence organization. Russian backwardness in communication technique was, of course, a significant factor in this success. The Soviets used their radios extensively, and they seemed to have difficulty constructing adequate wire lines. Furthermore, Russian R/T offered no great problem to the Germans as very little effort was made to disguise important information. As for Russian enciphered Morse traffic, as has been seen eighty-five per cent of this was read.

168 I 163 p 3

The networks of the flying formations, both air/ground and ground/ground, were most important for short time tactical intelligence, but the evaluation of this intercept did give some important strategic order of battle information, especially the deployment of units and personnel. Similarly, though long-range bomber circuits were studied mainly for tactical information, strategic moves and large air offensives were predicted sometimes days in advance. But networks of the ground organization of the Red Air Force were the most prolific sources of strategic intelligence, and solution of this traffic disclosed the deployment and intentions of the Red Air Force, its logistic set up, the condition of air fields and aircraft and provided a complete personality order of battle.[169]

Signal intelligence had much influence over the way in which the Germans used their air force. Because of the scarcity of fuel, the flying commands would not send up planes until intelligence gave them a target, as good intelligence cut out fuel consuming routine patrols.[170] In fact, the highest strategic intelligence levels were assisted by the insight into Russian economic, political, and morale conditions given to them by LN Regt 353.[171]

29. Operations against Long-range Bomber Force-- The Russian Long-range Bomber Force was independent of the Air Armies. Prior to 1945, it consisted of nine Corps directly controlled by the staff at Moscow. Early in this year, however, the force was reorganized as the 18th Air Army consisting of four corps.[172] Though a few four-engine PE-8's appeared at the end of the war as part of the Force, Soviet long-range bombers were strictly medium bombers by United States standards, consisting chiefly of IL-4's, IL-2's, B-25's, and A-20's. The 18th Air Army (the Long-Range Bomber Force) numbered about 1500 planes.[173]

The record of this long-range bomber force was not very impressive. Crews were poorly trained for large scale night operations, and the Soviets did not attempt daylight raids until just before Germany's collapse, when her resistance was broken. In general, the Moscow Command used its bomber force conservatively to preserve aircraft and crews. Sixty Russian bombers needed one hour under favorable weather conditions to take off and assemble for an operation. Take-off was scheduled for late afternoon and the lines were crossed at night-fall. R/T and Morse traffic was plentiful during take-off, assembly, and during the bombing run. Moreover, poor Russian navigation resulted in numerous requests for bearings and D/F fixes.[174]

169 I 134 pp 3 4

170 I 163 p 6

171 I 70 p 4

172 I 107 p 5

173 IF 187 p 33

174 IF 187 pp 35 36

LN Rgt 353's activities against the long-range bomber force was regional in its organization. As the raiding aircraft passed from one battalion region to another it was picked up and monitored until the mission was completed or until it passed into a third battalion's zone. Within the battalion, the long-range evaluation section coordinated the activities of D/F sites, out-stations and Morse receivers at the parent unit. The section was purposely located in the same room with the intercept operators at the battalion. (See chart 5-12)

The personnel of the long-range bomber evaluation section was alerted when advance warning of impending bomber operations was received. This advance warning could come from cryptanalysis or long-range bomber ground traffic, from the interception of a pre-operational "winds-aloft" weather message, or when Soviet weather or reconnaissance planes were sighted.[175] Upon being alerted, the section warned all out-stations of the impending Russian operation. The 20 or 25 known frequencies were passed out to all intercept units. As soon as activity was heard on a frequency, D/F was informed and a fix taken.[176]

Soviet bombers were usually first heard upon take-off. R/T and Morse air-ground traffic was plentiful on the Soviet side of the lines, which allowed D/F route tracking until radio silence was clamped down over German territory. The monitoring of ground control stations also helped in locating the bomber force.

Within the battalion evaluation section, the current location of the raiders was plotted on an illuminated map within sight of the intercept operators. Upon this map, all D/F results, reports from out-stations, and local intercept were plotted. There was no dearth of information to be posted. The Soviets gave away their position at times through careless use of R/T. Their air-ground Morse traffic was partially readable, and their D/F bearing activities furnished valuable data. The radar service was kept informed from minute to minute and as soon as the Soviets shut down radio silence, radar was in a position to take over.[177]

[175] D 8 p 7, I 82 p 6

[176] I 82 p 6

[177] IF 187

The Central Air Raid Warning Unit, last located at Treuenbrietzen, received current reports from each individual intercept unit on the eastern front. After evaluation, the information was flashed to the flying and flak units and to the Home Defense Air Force.[178]

30. Operations against the Air Armies-- The discussion of strategic intelligence activities emphasized the battalion's importance in the production of order of battle and other long-range intelligence. Very often the cryptanalysis and traffic analysis of the Morse traffic copied at the battalion accounted for immediate tactical warnings, but it was in the out-stations that the tactical R/R and D/F activities were carried on.

The out-stations were co-located with fighter and reconnaissance squadrons and groups, often in the same building as the aircraft reporting center of the headquarters of the formation they were serving. The procurement of personnel for these out-stations with the intelligence and language ability to be good R/T intercept operators was a serious problem. In spite of this difficulty, the Germans did very well with those they had.[179]

Ordinarily, fixed intercept schedules were not observed. Search receivers were employed and the tactical networks were scanned constantly. Only if the aircraft of the formation to which the out-station was attached took off on a mission, or enemy aircraft were heard in its sector, were particular frequencies covered. As soon as hostile aircraft were heard, D/F was informed and constant route tracking began, and as soon as the Russian bombers or fighter bombers were accurately located, German fighters were airborne. The results of German Radar served to amplify the findings of Signal Intelligence.[180]

The R/T networks of ground support liaison officers and even the R/T of armored units helped identify and locate targets for German fighter bombers.

[178] I 182 p 6

[179] I 182 pp 9-10

[180] I 182 p 11

31. Immediate Reports issued by LN Regt 353--
Immediate reports were issued whenever information was received on which direct action might be taken by German forces. They may be considered under three main subject headings:

a. Information on the activity of Long-range Bombers. This included warnings that bombers had taken off and D/F fixes on the aircraft in flight.

b. Information about railway activity, such as the arrival of trains with important freight at particular railway stations.

c. Requests for air support from liaison officers with the Red Army.

The most important recipient of these reports was the local Air Force. There were two direct land-lines between the Battalion and local Air Force headquarters, which were maintained throughout the many changes in location necessitated by the fluctuations in the land finding. Thus, it was never necessary to fall back on stand-by radio channels. Immediate reports were also passed to the regimental headquarters, which in turn was in close touch with the Air Force High Command and all the flying units.[181]

32 Results of the Operations of LN Regt 353-- The chief contribution made by LN Regt 353 to tactical operations on the Eastern Front was the constant supply of intelligence that made possible the economic and efficient use of German aircraft. With the shortage of aircraft capable of operating and with the shortage of fuel in particular, missions were usually flown by the formations in accordance with the decisions of the intercept service. Once German aircraft were airborne on a mission the ground control kept them constantly informed of the intentions and disposition of Russian fighters and bombers.

181
I 107 p 3

DOCID: 3560829

Volume 5

Chapter IV. Organization and Operation of the Field Units.

Section C. Operations in the South.

Paragraph

33. History from 1938 to August 1943-- The last Signal Intelligence unit operating in the southern sector, LN Regt 352, began in 1938 as a fixed station, W-Leit 13, in Oberhaching. This unit monitored French and English traffic from Africa. Section C of the Chi-Stelle (France) exercised complete control over W-Leit 13.

The war in the Mediterranean was well under way when a more or less comprehensive Signal Intelligence Service was created in the South under Section C, which was moved from France back to the Marstall. Signal Intelligence South included 9th Co, LN Regt 40 at Athens, and Signal Intelligence platoon from W-13 at Palermo, and a fixed station, W-Leit 14, at Vougliamend near Athens.[185]

During this early period, evaluation meant the deciphering and translation of allied traffic, and each Signal Intelligence unit did its own independent evaluation. The deciphered messages were sent immediately[186] to Section C, other Signal Intelligence organizations, and flying units. The A-2 of the flying unit did the actual evaluation.[187]

By the middle of 1941, the RAF had been reinforced and to offset the added British strength, local Air Force 2 was withdrawn from the eastern front and sent to Sicily. Within Air Force 2 were Wing 2 (Fliegerkorps II) in Messina, Wing 10 (Fliegerkorps X) In Heraklian, and the African Air Command. Each Wing, or Fliegerkorps, had a Signal Intelligence company and the Command had a platoon. W-Leit 2, an evaluation company, was attached to the local Air Force and became the center of Signal Intelligence activity within the local Air Force.[188]

[185] IF 184 p 1-5

[186] IF 184 p 6

[187] IF 184 p 6-7

[188] IF 184 p 8

Meanwhile, the 9th Company at Athens had become very active. This unit and its satellites were formed into one battalion and the W-Leit 2 and its subordinates into another. The new unit (the old 9th Company) became W-Leit 2, Southeast. Zones of operations were separated by a line drawn through Cape Passero, Malta and Tripoli. W-Leit 2 took everything west of the line and W-Leit 2 Southeast everything east. Lack of foresight and drive was responsible for the two units not being formed into a Regiment.[189]

The two W-Leit reserved the right of final evaluation. Their material came mainly from subordinate units that favored the interception of air-ground traffic and that had been successful in their cryptanalysis of point-to-point traffic, especially in the case of the RAF 4-figure code. W-Leit 2 organized its evaluation on the basis of fighter R/T, recce and bomber R/T, and air support traffic, while W-Leit Southeast's evaluation was based upon enemy units monitored (201 N C Group, 205 Group, 9th USAAF and Desert Air Force).[190] All units in the Mediterranean area overlapped as to the Allied units they monitored in order to service their own local headquarters with flash reports. The Signal Intelligence Agency failed miserably in coordinating their efforts.[191]

The steady degeneration of the war situation in the South for the Germans in 1943 made unification of the two units into a Regiment more and more urgent. The High Command's solution was the activation of a short-lived liaison unit at local Air Force (Luftflotte 2). This unit was intended to link the two Evaluation Centers (W-Leit) and the Chi-Stelle Section with the Air Force command in Italy and Greece. It was withdrawn after six months.

Section C of the Chi-Stelle began its most efficient operations in 1943. It had strengthened its control over the field battalions and acted as a final judge on policy matters. Technical experts were sent to the field whenever the field units needed help. Section C's best performance was on log analysis and T/A [192].

During 1943 many radar and VHF intercept out-stations were erected. The VHF stations were under W-Leit 2. These outstations carried the brunt of the operations, and thoroughly monitored the allied units operating against the German supply line from Sicily to the Africa Corps holed up in Tunisia.[193] During the same period, W-Leit Southeast began to concentrate more and more on T/A, route tracking, R/T, and radar evaluation. The RAF 4-figure cipher, which had been read continuously since March 1940, had become unreadable, entailing the shift in operational emphasis.

189 IF 184 p 8

190 IF 184 pp 16 17

191 IF 184 p 15

192 IF 184 p 26

193 IF 184 p 27

DOCID: 3560829

54 History August 1943 - October 1944-- The two Signal Intelligence units in the South continued to expand, but in different directions. W-Leit 2 was charged with monitoring the units operating against the Germans in Italy, while W-Leit Southeast covered the Adriatic coast, which was under threat of invasion. Both units were engaged in flight-tracking the missions flown by allied bombers which by now were based in Foggia.

Three days before the landing on Sicily, the evaluation company W-Leit 2 was flown from Taormina to Frascati, near Rome, and the rest of the unit followed close behind. While the unit was at Frascati, Italy's surrender caught it unaware. Just before it moved to Padua, it was so badly mauled in a raid by 170 B-24's that for a time the German Command could learn of the ground situation in Italy only through Allied air support messages, intercepted in Southern France.[194]

At Padua most of the key officers were relieved and replaced. After two months of moving and of being inoperative, W-Leit 2 set up shop, mainly as a tactical warning service. Among the tasks performed by this unit was the interception of the traffic of the medium bombers, which were engaged at this time in giving the roads and bridges in the German zone a going over. W-Leit 2 exceeded its commitments by contributing to the route-tracking of heavy bombers heading for Germany.[195]

W-Leit Southeast had for its mission the cover of frequencies heard in the Adriatic Area in general and the route-tracking of heavy bombers heading into the Balkans. Owing to the reverses in the fighting, the local Air Force in the Southeastern area moved from Athens to Salonika, taking the Signal Intelligence units along. In January 1944 W-Leit Southeast moved with the local Air Force near Belgrade. The unit set up a central Reporting Center for the Southeast connected to all units by direct land line. The outpost covered an area from Crimea to Crete and from Munich to Styria. There were seven companies in all.[196]

During this period W-Leit Southeast monitored R/T and Morse of the heavy bombers, but it became especially proficient in D/F'ing the IFF and panoramic devices aboard allied bombers.

The Reporting Centers and all units of W-Leit Southeast were of necessity highly mobile, and when the Russians broke through, the unit was moved and reestablished at Premstaetten.[197]

194 IF 184 p 42

195 IF 184 p.43

196 IF 184 p 49

197 IF 184 p 50

69

35. History October 1944-German Collapse-- After the retreats and reverses experienced in Italy, the Signal Intelligence units had to be rebuilt from the ground up. A new regiment, LN Regt 352, (See chart 5-13) was created, and this resulted in the combining of the two evaluation companies of the battalions (W-Leit 2 and W-Leit 2 Southeast) into a single regimental evaluation company (25th Company). Reporting Center (Meldekopf) 4 was immediately subordinated to regimental headquarters as the 26th Company. Furthermore, each of the two battalions comprised three radio intercept companies and one radar intercept company. All evaluation and technical direction was centrally located in the Evaluation Company at regimental headquarters.[198]

Although the final activation of LN Regt 352 was a good move, it resulted in no marked increase in signal intelligence efficiency in the South. Germany's battle lines were collapsing and communications within the country were in a sorry state. Early in 1945, the regimental staff, the evaluation company, and one intercept company moved to Attersee ahead of the Russians. When Vienna fell they were joined by Reporting Center 4 and the intercept companies from that area. Out-stations were withdrawn and the 2nd Battalion moved to Steinach-Puergg. All units under local Air Force 6 moved to the internment camp at Aschbach when Germany surrendered. The 1st Battalion was captured by the British at Canazei.

36. Intercept within LN Regt 352-- The receivers on hand and task assignments within LN Regt 352 illustrate the Regiments' deployment against the Allies in the South. The allocation was as follows: [199]

Allied air support units	65 receivers
Allied Radar Networks	30 receivers
Command Networks; Eastern Mediterranean and Balkans; transport and supply traffic	50 receivers
15th USAAF, 205 Group-RAF	25 receivers
VHF Air ground	35 receivers
HF D/F - sets	23 D/F's
Radar in 15 out-stations	100 receivers

198 IF-184 pp 69 70

199 IF-184 p 70

37. Evaluation within LN Regt 352-- A sharp distinction between tactical and strategic operations would be very difficult to draw in discussing evaluation in the South. In the early days, when German fortunes were ascendant, the emphasis in the Evaluation Companies (W-Leit) was upon cryptanalysis and the reconstruction of Allied order of battle. Gradually, as allied ciphers became more difficult and as Germany changed over to the defensive, tactical, short time warnings became the main Signal Intelligence commitment.

While during the early stages of the war German evaluation was limited to message content and elementary T/A, allied use of better cipher and more complex means of communication forced the Germans to adjust their evaluation methods accordingly.

By October 1944, when LN Regt 352 was activated, the Germans were using every signal manifestation to extract intelligence. The Morse point-to-point and air/ground traffic was D/F'd and evaluated, R/T in both HF and VHF ranges accounted for tactical warnings, the radio links between allied radar sites showed their activity against German aircraft, the actual monitoring of allied radar disclosed those areas not being covered, and the D/F ing of IFF and airborne radar was used to route-track allied bombers.[200]

The Germans in the South had more success against the US 15th AAF than against the RAF's 205 Group. British use of W/T, R/T and radiating devices was much more careful.[201] Major Ferdinand Feichtner, CO of LN Regt 352, summarized the operations against the 15th USAAF as follows:

a. Air Ground Morse

Prewarning of bomber flights was given by the tuning traffic. During the flight to the target the bombers sent short messages on a half hour schedule that could be D/F'd.

b. Air-Ground R/T

Interception of this traffic provided information concerning the flying units involved and their approximate strength during the take-off on an operation.

c. VHF Air/Air R/T

This traffic provided valuable information regarding the fighters accompanying the bombers. Continuous D/F ing was possible.

d. Meddo-Equipment

The D/F ing of Meddo was of assistance in locating bomber forces scattered over a large area.

e. IFF Device

The Americans did not shut off their IFF over German territory. The Germans used their radar unit Freya-D to make the device radiate. Measurements and tracking were possible up to 280 miles.

f. Meteorological Observation Planes

The cipher system used by the met recce planes could be read and their transmissions D/F'd. The interception of this traffic gave many advanced warnings of US bomber incursions.[202]

200 IF 126 p 17

201 IF 126 p 17

202 I 126 p 17-18

Reporting Center 4 was one and the same with 26th Company of LN Regt 352. In this unit, the tactical warnings from signal intelligence were coordinated with reports from the German radar and observation services. Immediate warnings were flashed to fighter units, Air Forces, and to civilian air raid defense officials. (See chart 5-14)

38. Communications within LN Regt 352-- LN Regt 352 maintained excellent signal communications despite frequent moves and general military reverses. Direct telephone lines were maintained between the Regiment and its units and to the local Air Forces and tactical units in its vicinity.[203] (See chart 5-15) Moreover, the regiment had its own private teletype system to all headquarters, the equipment being both plain text and enciphered (G-Schreiber) variety.[204] (See chart 5-16) A radio network was superimposed on the other means of communication, within which the Enigma was used for security.[205] (See chart 5-17)

39. Results of LN Regt 352-- The strategic importance of LN Regt 352 and the units that preceded it may be illustrated by the accompanying diagram from the Seabourne report. (See chart 5-18) The signal intelligence units in the South reconstructed the complete allied air order of battle from signal intelligence enemy traffic and kept it up to date.

On the tactical side the Signal Intelligence Service did a superb job of keeping the tactical units and civilian defense agencies informed of allied bomber attacks. Col. Hans Forster, FAF, Chief of the Air Raid Warning Service for Germany, stated that "suprises out of the South rarely occurred."[206]

[203] IF 184 p 71

[204] IF 184 p 72

[205] IF 184 p 73

[206] IF 181 p 69

Volume 5

Chapter IV. Organization and Operation of Field Units.

Section D. Operations in the North

40. History from 1940 to 1943-- In May 1940, soon after Norway was invaded, a group of signal intelligence personnel was sent from Husum to Oslo, Norway to set up the nucleus of signal intelligence activity in the North. The new unit, W-Leit 5, had as its mission evaluation and the supervision of any intercept units assigned to Norway. Its commitments were all Morse and R/T circuits of the RAF Coastal Command operating against the West Coast of Norway and all traffic originating in the North Sea area. The first intercept and D/F unit W-Stelle-25 was set up at Trondheim-Skatval during the same month.[210] W-Stelle 25 covered mainly the Morse and R/T of 18 Group Coastal Command. W-Stelle 25 moved to Stavanger at the end of August.

By the end of 1940, 3rd Battalion Air Signals Regiment 5 had been formed and included W-Leit 5 (an intercept unit), 9 LN Regt 5 at Noerland and W-Stelle 22 at Hussum in Schleswig Holstein. The 3rd Battalion of LN Regt 5 covered 15 and 18 Groups Coastal Command and the high frequency R/T of fighters based in Northern U.K. Beacons and Meteorological traffic were intercepted and Coastal Command Syko was read at Husum.[211]

When the fighter units of the RAF converted from HF to VHF R/T in April 1941, a very fruitful source of intelligence dried up on the Germans until they could be equipped with proper receivers. It developed that they never were.

By the end of the year all Signal Intelligence units were subordinated to LN Regt 5 and included 4 Adcock D/F's and 5 intercept installations.

Teletype lines were laid to Naval and German Air Force exchanges at Oslo as well as to Berlin, Hus..., and Noerland.[212]

An important development during 1942 was the organization of D/F Base Atlantic, a series of D/F stations at Bodo, Orlandet, Noerland, Husum in Germany, and Brest in France. The main function of the D/F base was the D/F ing of the aircraft of 15 Group Coastal Command on convoy escort and other units on anti-submarine patrol.

210 I 183 410/1945

211 I 183 410/1945 p 3

212 I 183 410/1945 p 4

73

The 2nd battalion of LN Regt 5 added the 8th intercept company in the fall of 1942. W-Leit 5 was redesignated 14/LN Regt 5 and W-22 became 15/LN Regt 2.

Intercept coverage was expanded to include all Morse and R/T in the North Sea, the Iceland bases and North Sea convoys, but operations in general were hampered by bad atmosphere.

The listening service in the North remained fairly stable throughout 1943. Excellent results were gained from D/F Base Atlantic, and coverage was extended to include the traffic of courier planes operating between Sweden and England.[213]

41. History from 1944 to 1945-- The year 1944 brought about a general reorganization of the entire German Air Force Signal Intelligence Service. The units in Norway were renamed as follows:

14/LN Regt 5 became 1/LN Abt 355
8/LN Regt 5 became 2/LN Abt 355
9/LN Regt 5 became 3/LN Abt 355
15/LN Regt 2 became 5/LN Abt 357

W-Stelle 10, the control station within Germany for Norwegian units was renamed Leitstelle der Funkaufklärung. A mobile radio intelligence unit was set up in Norway as an anti-invasion measure.[214]

2/LN Abt 355 was moved from Bardufoss to Holden because of poor reception.

D/F Base Atlantic lost its left wing when Brest fell to the allies, and its Svanik base when Northern Norway was evacuated.[215]

The VHF experiments that dated from 1941 were finally dropped for technical reasons. Good intelligence was gleaned from the Morse traffic of Coastal Command and US and British bomber units. R/T traffic was picked up when allied units approached the Norwegian coast.

An important source of intelligence on the North Sea convoys was the traffic of long range recce and carrier aircraft.[216]

42. Summation of activity in the North-- The German Air Force Signal Intelligence Service in Norway was a fairly successful organization when one considers the bad atmospherics in the region and the difficulty experienced by the units in the North in obtaining proper equipment.

No major land action or air offensive was ever carried out by the Allies in the North, so the German Signal Intelligence effort in the North was a side show in comparison with German signal intelligence operations on the Western and Eastern fronts.

[213] I 183 410/1945 p 6

[214] I 183 410/1945 p 7

[215] I 183 410/1945 p 8

[216] I 183 410/1945 p 8

VOLUME 5

Chapter V. Cryptanalysis

Paragraph

43. Introduction-- The central cryptanalytic bureau of the Air Force which both directed and carried on the cryptanalysis for that organization was Section E of the Signal Intelligence Agency (Chi-Stelle). The organization and functions of that section have already been described in Chapter III and will not be further treated here. This chapter describes rather the systems studied by the German Air Force cryptanalysts. It is divided into sections according to the countries whose systems are discussed. In each section, the systems studied will be listed, and briefly commented upon.

In general, the cryptanalysts appeared to feel their efforts did not receive the consideration they deserved. For instance, Specialist (Regierungs Rat Dr.) Voegele, Chief of the Cryptanalytic Section (Section E), declared that the primary object of intercept was traffic analysis and evaluation and that cryptanalysis was considered of secondary importance. He complained that he never was allowed any say in the allocation of the intercept tasks. He further found fault with the traffic which he did receive, pointing out that he frequently was passed eight or nine versions of the same message.[220] The denial to the cryptanalysts of a voice in directing coverage is noted by Technical Sergeant Jering of the Signal Intelligence Agency as well:

"A great difficulty which existed was that the Referat could exercise no definite influence on the number or location of intercept receivers covering

[220] I 112 p 5

traffic in which it was interested."[221]

In choosing the location of cryptanalytic units the Germans followed the principle of going as far forward as possible. On the Western Front and in the Mediterranean area immediately exploitable Allied systems such as the bomber code, the aircraft reporting code, SYKO and REKOH were worked on in the field battalions. On the Eastern Front the Battalions of Air Signals Regiment 353 carried on the current analysis of Russian 2, 3, and 4 figure systems.

All material impossible of solution in the field was returned to the Chi-Stelle for research. Thus, the Chi-Stelle carried on the analysis of United States strip systems, M-209 research, the recovery of the War Department Telegraph Code and research on the AM-2 (SIGABA). Russian 5-figure material which was incapable of solution in the field was studied by the Chi-Stelle.

44. Successes with U. S. Systems--

M-209 According to Voegele, the M-209 was first read in March or April 1944. The Germans averaged 6-8 days of currency each month on the Western Front, 1-2 days in the Mediterranean area. A "key chart" was captured in October 1944, giving the Germans 26-27 days of currency.

Voegele claimed 22 hours as his organization's best time on the complete solution of an M-209 system. The average time lag was 8-10 days due to the delay in receiving traffic. Eventually, the Air Force dropped the M-209 job, which was performed by the Army.[222]

Ludwig claimed that the M-209 traffic of the U. S. 8th Fighter Command (65th, 66th, and 67th wings), which carried administrative information and particulars about the Mustang fighter, was broken in February 1944 by the Army Signal Evaluation Center of Signal Intelligence Regiment 5 (NAAS 5) at St. Germaine, France. After the invasion, battle losses of the 101st Airborne Division were read. Ludwig also named the 9th Air Defense Command and 9th

221 IF 180 p 17

222 I 117 p 4

Engineer Command as units whose traffic was read. The reading of a XXIX TAC M-209 message helped tip-off an offensive in the Aachen area.[223]

The analysis of the M-209 was made more difficult when each army and command began using separate settings. Voegele's discussion on the German analysis of the M-209 included the following requisites for solution of the daily machine settings:

a. Two messages where part of the plain text could be asssumed and superimposed.

b. Message with mistakes later re-enciphered in correct system and key. 50 or 60 letters of decipherment were necessary to obtain a 12-hour setting.

The German Air Force's traffic totals for M-209 solution were about 100 per day in the West. The Mediterranean Area averaged 40 messages per day.[224]

Strip Systems

Section E west of the Chi-Stelle[225] read the Southern Route Strip System (indicator CENEB) as early as May 1942. Voegele described this as a 30 strip system. The introduction of a device increasing the security and a gradual reduction in traffic volume forced the discontinuance of work on this system. The Germans estimated 200 messages per day as the minimum requisite for solution of a strip cipher with channel elimination.[226] Voegele said it required two months to break a strip system using hand methods, but the eventual use of IBM machinery cut the time to from two to four weeks.[227]

The German solution of the CENEB strip cipher was very straightforward. They first found the 15 letter period and machined the traffic on this basis. A depth of 80 passages of parallel construction was needed to reconstruct the 100 strips, of which 30 were used each day.

[223] I 109 p 37

[224] IF 175 p 16

[225] See Chapter III

[226] IF 175 p 15, I 112 p 5

[227] I 119 p 3

A few messages were read 6 weeks after channel elimination was introduced in 1943, but the traffic fell off.[228]

A system with indicators XOGIB on the Southern Route could not be read.[229]

M-94

Section E West read an M-94 system with the indicator URSAL from the summer of 1942 until December 1943.[230]

REKOH

One day's Atlantic-Ferry-Route traffic of 60 messages was deciphered by the 16th Company, LN Regt 3 (later part of 3rd Battalion LN Regt 351). The evaluation section considered it unimportant and the project was dropped.[231]

Aircraft Reporting Code

In February 1944, the Aircraft Reporting Code was broken by 16th Company LN Regt 3 in Angers due to the large volume of traffic. Partial decipherment was possible with 150 messages per day.[232]

Aircraft Movement Code

The Aircraft Movement Code was solved and read currently after the fall of 1942. Variants, changes every 12 hours, and separate British and U.S. editions of systems made the problem increasingly difficult. When the code refused to yield to machine methods during the summer of 1944, the solution was considered no longer possible.[233]

8th Air Force and IX Bomber Command Codes

Lt. Ludwig of Chi-Stelle Section B (Evaluation West) claimed that the Bomber Code was nearly always solved by cryptanalysis when necessary. Very often the Chi-Stelle Section received copies from aircraft shot down at night and applied them to the next day's traffic. The fact that the codes were good from 1800 hours of one day until 1800 hours of the next day made for an ideal compromise situation.[234]

228 IF 175 p 15

229 I 119 p 5

230 I 112 p 5, IF 175 p 14, I 119 p 5

231 IF 175 p 16

232 IF 175 p 11

233 IF 175 p 12

234 I 109 p 38

DOCID: 3560829

War Department Telegraph Code — The one-part code feature of the War Department Telegraph code (indicator TELWA) greatly facilitated solution. The edition introduced in October 1943 had yielded 12,000 groups by May 1944 and was absolutely current after February 1945.[235]

DFC (Division Field Code) — DFC-17 was captured in the Mediterranean area and helped in the eventual solution of DFC's 19, 23, 28, and 29.[236]

US AAF "Q" Groups — The Germans placed no importance to the security of the "Q" groups. As with the Bomber Code, copies were recovered from shot down aircraft.[237]

Radio Teletype — Voegele spoke of a "6 letter indicator" teletype system between the USA and Africa from April to October 1944. The system was never read.[238]

Jones Template — The Germans never succeeded in solving the US Jones Template map grid system.[239]

Converter M-134-C (SIGABA) — Voegele of Section E and German Air Force Signal Intelligence Agency states categorically that the ABA was not broken.[240] Lt. Ludwig, Section B, whose knowledge was mainly hearsay, claimed army experts considered AM 2 (German designation for the ABA) breakable up to the end of the war, but he never heard of any success.

45. Successes with British Systems--

RAF Four-Figure — The RAF four figure system was an enciphered two part code used by the RAF for point-to-point communication between units and airfields. The descriptions of this code in the TICOM documents are given in much greater detail than for other

[235] I 112 p 5

[236] IF 175 p 16

[237] I 109 p 40

[238] I 112 p 5

[239] I 109 p 39

[240] I 112 p 4

systems; hence the code is more fully discussed here. The Germans began work on the system late in 1939 and were in a position to read the system with increasing ease from March 1940 until 1 November 1942, when a code book change resulted in reducing the amount of traffic read to fragments. Interception was stopped in the summer of 1944.[241]

Four figure traffic originating in Great Britain was worked on at Potsdam-Marstall without any success.[242] It was in the Mediterranean area that a small amount of work was done in September 1940 at Taormina, Sicily, and later at Athens. The German Air Force surmounted many difficulties during this period, going through two code book changes and encipherment changes at times every three to seven days. Traffic totals varied from 600 per day during the heaviest to 100 per day immediately before the Germans discontinued work on the problem. The knowledge gained from the four figure enciphered code formed the basis for evaluation for the rest of the war.[243]

The basic book of the RAF's enciphered code system was a one part code of 10,000 groups. The key "table" was a book of 100 pages, 20 lines on a page, and 5 four-digit key groups on a line. Each line had a four digit indicator and as there was no column coordinates, the encipherment always began at the beginning of the line. The line indicators were enciphered by a separate table of 100 groups and appeared as the second group of the enciphered message. The first two digits of the first group made up the control for the indicator encipherment; the third and fourth were nulls. The conversion from plain code to cipher was made by subtracting the code from the key.[244]

[241] IF 175 p 19

[242] I 109 p 35

[243] I 109 p 35

[244] I 112 p 10

DOCID: 3560829

Given sufficient traffic, the inherent weakness of this key system soon manifested itself. During the early stages of analysis, when the line indicators were not enciphered, overlapping messages could be identified.

On the 24th and 31st of December 1941, unenciphered messages were transmitted, compromising many groups in the basic book.

After the indicators were enciphered, stereotyped traffic made possible overlapping by external cipher "hits." The beginning groups of the overlapping messages were always some multiple of five apart, and setting up of the overlaps were facilitated by the fact that encipherment always began at the beginning of the line. The "hits" were indexed by machine, and their validity tested by the use of known high frequency differences in the code.[245]

Once the messages were overlapped, the highly stereotyped context made stripping the [illegible] easy.

The reconstruction of the indicator key had to wait until overlaps were set up. Every message that directly overlapped had the same underlying indicator. Therefore, by arbitrarily assigning 0000 as the value for the first plain indicator, all others that followed could be stripped on a relative basis and reduced to the same terms. The German relative table of indicator key was just as good for practical purposes as the British prime table.[246]

The delay between interception and deciphering was between two and fourteen days.[247]

<u>Syko Cards</u>

The Royal Air Force Naval Code was the basic book of an enciphered code system of which the Syko Card was the encipherment. A copy of the basic code was recovered from a Wellington shot down over Welhemshaven in September 1939. The British did not seriously alter the code for the duration of the war.

[245] I 112 p 10

[246] I 152

[247] IF 175 p 20

The daily reciprocal enciphering table was being reconstructed by February 1940. Messages on the daily table could be read by 1600-1700 hours. The introduction of several cards a day complicated the solution slightly, but 40 messages sufficed to solve a single card.

The traffic, which contained information concerning British and Axis convoys, submarines, naval vessels, and meteorological reports, averaged between 80 and 300 messages a day.[248]

Rekoh

Rekoh first appeared in 1942-1943 and was simply a non-reciprocal Syko. Slightly more traffic was necessary to accomplish solution than with Syko.[249]

Aircraft Reporting Code and UCO

The Aircraft Reporting Code replaced Syko and Rekoh in July 1943 and was used by reconnaissance planes in the West. 16th Company LN Regt 3 in Angers solved the system in February 1944.

ETA messages, frequency changes, and hourly barometric pressure broadcasts assisted the initial break-in.

The Aircraft Reporting Code had a particular importance in that it afforded a crib into UCO (the ground/air meteorological code). It was broken by cribbing the pressure reports from the Aircraft Reporting Code. The fixed Signal Intelligence station at Husum carried on this work. Lack of intercept in the last days confined solution to the met crib.[250]

Aircraft Movement Code

The Aircraft Movement Code was used on ferry flights from Tokoradi to India and totalled about 500 messages per day. The system was composed of pronounceable 5-letter code words, which were changed every 24 hours at first and later every 12 hours. W-Leit, Southeast, in Athens began work on it in the fall of 1942, and reading stopped in February 1944 when too many variants made solution impossible.[251]

[248] IF 175 p 18, I 109 p 36

[249] IF 175 p 19

[250] IF 175 p 22, I 112 p 3

[251] IF 175 p 21

DOCID: 3560829

Aircraft Movement Code (UK) — A three letter code with serial numbers in clear and repeated indicators passed between the UK and stations on the Belgian-French border. The Germans never solved it and assumed it to be an administrative or supply system.[252]

RAF 2-Letter Bomber Code — Pages of the Bomber Code, used jointly by RAF and USAAF, were obtained from a crashed aircraft in November or December 1942. Two weeks later the Germans were reading the system cryptanalytically. Traffic averaged 150-200 messages per day with 600 per day as high. 300 messages yielded 50-60% of the values. Letters and numbers from messages containing spellers or frequency information afforded the daily break-in.

The code changed daily at 0300 and could be broken during the US day raids and used to decode RAF traffic during the night operations. This conflicts with Lt. Ludwig's account.[253] Ludwig gives 1800 hours as the time the code was changed. The members of the US 8th Air Force were the day time unfortunates who had their traffic decoded on the basis of code values recovered during the RAF raid the previous night.[254]

Slidex — Slidex was a digraphic substitution system used in the army and air support networks. The coordinates of the substitution table changed daily, but offered no great problem to the German Air Force cryptanalysts.

The 3rd Battalion, Signal Intelligence Regiment West (later LN Regt 351) began work on Slidex in May 1943 at Bougival, near Paris. Much progress was made during the pre-invasion "Spartan" exercises in Britain, and by the time the Allies invaded, the Signal Intelligence Evaluation Center (NAAS 5 of the Army) of the Signal Intelligence Regiment 5 (Kona 5 of the Army) and 14/3 (W-Leit 3) had had sufficient experience to break the system operationally. The daily strips were recovered by 0700-0900 hours. The traffic averaged 15-40 messages per day.[255]

[252] I 112 p 3

[253] I 109 p 38

[254] IF 175 p 22

[255] I 109 p 38, IF 175 p 22

DOCID: 3560829

Government Telegraphic Code Work upon this system was begun by the Signal Intelligence Agency of the Supreme Command Armed Forces (OKW/Chi) in May 1939 and given to the Luftwaffe in August 1939. The traffic, containing mainly casualty and administrative information, averaged 200 messages per month. The Germans considered the system of small importance in the last years of the war.[256]

India Code The India Code was an unenciphered 4-letter code transmitted in 5-letter groups. Section E at least partially read this traffic until the end of the war.[257]

Inter-Departmental Cypher The basic book of this 4-digit enciphered code system was captured in Bergen, Norway in June 1940. Air attaches in the Near East, Portugal, Sweden and Switzerland used the system. Switzerland was always one table behind the others. Voegele, of Chi-Stelle Section E, received a photostat copy and began work on the system. Traffic was exchanged with OKM and OKW, the total volume being about 100 messages per month.

Two tables with indicator patterns CVCVC and VCVCV (where V = vowel and C = consonant) were used, and both were broken most successfully in 1940-41 when the tables changed quarterly. The date breaks occurred at intervals of between six weeks to two months.

Work on the Inter-Departmental Cipher was stopped in 1943 because the decodes were useless to evaluation.[258]

Bentley Code The Bentley Code was used by British Overseas Airways and was copied from South Africa, Southeast Africa, Egypt and Syria. During the war, about five hundred 5-letter groups beginning with Y were added. One encipherment for confidential administrative traffic was added during the winter of 1942-43. The solution was so simple that Voegele used it to train beginners in cryptanalysis, and the whole project was dropped in

[256] IF 175 p 18

[257] IF 175 p 18

[258] I 119 p 4, IF 175 p 21

DOCID: 3560829

1944 because Evaluation was no longer interested.[259]

Weather Systems The solution of enciphered meteorological messages was not the responsibility of the Chi-Stelle, but was undertaken to assist the weather service (the Signal Weather Monitoring Service or WENUEB). The Chi-Stelle solved the British Main Weather Code in April, 1940 and turned the keys over to WENUEB at Glindow, near Potsdam. In April 1942, the Signal Weather Monitoring Service received the solution of a five-figure Middle East weather cipher from W-Leit Southeast. Systems in the Atlantic Area carrying the indicators "Whist" and "Tooth" were worked on by the Signal Weather Monitoring Service without success.[260]

Miscellaneous Lt. Ludwig, of Chi-Stelle Section E, recalled the solution of a British single transposition cipher, involving a ten column rectangle. The system changed every Thursday at 2400 hours when the new key word was transmitted in the previous system;

The Germans had no success with double transposition despite notebooks captured at Leros and during the early days of the Normandy invasion. They did not find any messages of the same length in the same key.[261]

Typex Many attempts were made to get into this system, but work was discontinued as the Germans considered the TYPEX machine unbreakable.[262]

46. Cryptography of Soviet Systems-- Code in various forms with the transmitted text appearing as numbers was used almost exclusively by the Soviet Air Force.[263] Each Air Army did its own code compilation and had its own rules for use. Therefore, the following definitions of Soviet codes are extremely general and attempt only to describe types of codes, not specific systems:

[259] I 119 pp 4-5, IF 175 p 21

[260] I 112, 4(0) p 11; IF 175 p 23

[261] IF 175 p 24

[262] IF 175 p 24, I 119 p 5

[263] I 120 p 7

85

a. The table was a cryptographic device comprised of letters and words in a predetermined form, usually a square or rectangle with number coordinates. Security was enhanced by using variable coordinates that could be changed by the use of sliding strips or by the use of digraphic substitution enciphering tables.[264]

b. The code table (Signaltafel)

The code table was a highly specialized medium for use in air/ground communication. The vocabulary was highly stereotyped and limited to met reports, landing and take-off data, etc.

c. The code book was the principal cryptographic medium of the Soviet Air Force, especially in the ground organization. The Russians used all variations from small one-part books to two-part books with up to 30,000 values. Extra security could be gained with an additive encipherment of the basic code.[265]

47. Successes with Soviet Systems-- During the period 1937-1939, the Germans gained valuable experience during Soviet maneuvers. The traffic passed was mainly practice and dummy, but formed a foundation for later analysis. During the Soviet Occupation of Poland in September 1939 the Germans had almost 100 percent success with "OKK-5," a code system with a digraphic substitution encipherment, the most common Soviet Air system.

During the Finnish Campaign (1939 and 1940) the Germans concentrated their best cryptanalysts in Chi-Stelle Section E 1 (Russian cryptanalysis) and unbroken material went to the Chi-Stelle via teleprinter. During this period two and three figure Soviet traffic was completely broken, "OKK-5" was 95 per cent read, and considerable success was attained on the additive enciphered code system used by higher headquarters.[266]

The Soviets revamped their cryptographic setup after the Finnish Campaign. The Germans captured working directions to Soviet code and cipher officers that made only the barest reference to codes and ciphers being solved. The directions called for a general increase in cryptographic security.[267]

[264] I 120 p 10

[265] I 120 p 13

[266] I 120 p 38

[267] I 120 p 40

The "High Command of Soviet Cryptography" may not have admitted their compilation errors to subordinate code and cipher officers, but they did take strong measures to correct their mistakes. Regional methods of distribution instead of widely held systems, the shortening of effective periods, the abolition of one-part books, and the complication of enciphering technique were all introduced.

These changes did not bother the Germans too much. They were able to follow step by step the Russian modifications; as the changes were not too radical they "kept pace."[268]

1st Lt. W. Werther claims that a captured Soviet cipher machine was examined by the Signal Intelligence Agency in 1941-42. He did not, however, expand upon this.[269]

48. Standard operating procedure in dealing with Soviet Systems.--In the case of Soviet systems based on some form of the table, "statistical pictures" or frequency counts were first made. This procedure would usually reveal the size of the cipher unit (2, 3, or 4 figure). The next step was to deduce the number of tables involved and reduce the statistical picture down to the actual size of the table. This involved the elimination of indicator groups, "dummy" elements, and any clear numbers that appeared in the cipher text.

In the event a simple code table with coordinates was used, a simple book reconstruction job was in order.

The more complicated table systems, in which use was made of several tables with coordinates that were cyclically shifted or chosen from a 10 by 10 square, unique in its rows and columns (latin square), through the use of indicators, were solved by concentrating on each table as a separate entity. Naturally, those that stood out in the original frequency distributions were attacked first. Then, as solution of the tables progressed with relative page and row column designations, the designations were equated and the entire indicator, page and coordinate system could be reconstructed.

Some traffic could be read with these relative coordinates, but the reduction to prime values was very important. The shifting coordinates were often based on a latin square, or upon the cyclic variation of the same sequence or sequences.

[268] I 120 p 40

[269] I 120 p 43

87

The sooner this pattern could be isolated the sooner the entire system fell apart.[270]

The Soviets used 5-figure additive systems on high echelon circuits including some one time pads upon which the Germans did not waste any time. In the case of non-one time additives ("universal blocknots"), however, the situation was quite different. 1st Lt. Werther's account shows that the indicators were not enciphered. Overlaps were easily thrown together, flags of differences made up, columns equated, additive stripped and basic code recovered whenever sufficient traffic was available.[271]

49. Successes with systems of other nations.--

a. Lithuania: The Lithuanians used a grid system which was very insecure. Lithuanian traffic was read by Section E of the Chi-Stelle from 1938 until the Red Army entered Lithuania in the summer of 1939.

The Lithuanians used a ten by ten square in which the text was written out from left to right. A ten by ten grid with 25 cut-out cells was superimposed and the letters in the cells read off from left to right as cipher text. The grid was shifted four times to encompass the 100 letters in the underlying square. In the event a message was less than a hundred letters it was padded out by repeating the signature.[272]

b. Rumania: (1) 1st Lt. Werther worked on Rumanian Air Force Cipher material in Budapest in the Spring of 1939. He described it as a simple transposition system. A few days after he submitted a report that the system was about to break, he was recalled to the Chi-Stelle. Werther believes that the interference was deliberate and political. It is significant that the Hungarians later bought the system.[273] (2) Werther claimed that the Rumanian Police Cipher was so simple that the Germans considered it camouflaged treason. Exact information on German troop movements was transmitted in this system.[274]

[270] I 120 p 43

[271] I 120 p 53

[272] I 121 p 46

[273] I 121 p 8

[274] I 121 p 9

c. Yugoslavia: The Germans had no difficulty solving the Yugoslav Air Cipher and had currency on the system when the campaign against Yugoslavia started. The system was composed of lexicographic tables with 30 columns and 60 lines. The line and column coordinates were at first non-random and later random.[275]

d. France: Werther recalled a French code book enciphered with short periodic additives. Though it yielded very slowly to solution, the Germans read the system.[276]

e. Carpatho-Ukraine: Five letter monoalphabetic substitution messages were read in Budapest. The security of the cipher was nil.[277]

f. Poland: The German Air Force started work on Polish traffic a few weeks before Poland was invaded. A few take-off and landing reports were the only messages read.

1st Lt. Werther of LN Regt 353 saw a captured Polish two-part code book, which was made up of some 2000 values and was non-alphabetic.[278]

g. Czechoslovakia: Voegele began work on Czech material in 1937. Five letter air messages, of which a good bit were practice traffic, were read. A few tactical transposition messages were solved. Voegele believed the bulk of unsolved Czech material to be machine cipher.[279]

h. Spain: To the best of 1st Lt. Werther's knowledge the Spanish Reds transmitted their traffic almost exclusively in the clear.[280]

[275] I 121 p 9

[276] I 121 p 9

[277] I 121 p 8

[278] I 121 p 6

[279] I 121 p 7

[280] I 121 p 110

DOCID: 3560829

1. Turkish Air Force: Turkish systems fell in three categories: (1) Periodic substitution system which changed monthly and was broken in two hours. (2) Unenciphered alphabetic code book. (3) Single transposition enciphered weather reports.

Voegele considered Turkish material extremely simple. He never bothered with it but turned it over to subordinates.[281]

[281] I 119 p 5

90

VOLUME 5

Chapter VI Liaison

Paragraph

50. Introduction.-- The liaison of the German Air Force Signal Intelligence Service with other agencies engaged in signal intelligence activities was effective. The overall allocation of problems and spheres of activity was divergent and each service concentrated on its own commitments. At the high levels of command, the Supreme Command of the Armed Forces, the OKW, exercised a control over German security measures, but permitted each service of the Wehrmacht to work out its own techniques and policy in its signal intelligence work against foreign countries. Whenever problems overlapped between the services further down the chain of command, full technical information and intelligence was exchanged.

51 Relations with the Supreme Command of the Armed Forces, OKW.-- The relationship between OKW and the Air Force High Command, the OKL, was decided upon at a series of conferences held in Berlin in October and November 1944, presided over by the head of OKW/Chi and attended by representatives of the four services (OKW, OKH, and OKL).[285] The German Air Force operated independently of the Wehrmacht in matters of its intelligence activities against the Allies.

[285] D 57 p 10 p 15

Liaison was carried on at lower levels where necessary. Close cooperation existed between Gen Nafue II and security Group IV, Gen Nafue III of the Air Force and OKW in regard to German security and cryptography. On the upper level the head of cryptographic development at the Chi-Stelle of OKW worked in collaboration with the compilation departments of Army, Navy and Air Force. To test its own systems the Air Force maintained its own cryptanalytic security section in Gen Nafue III, but submitted its cryptographic materials to OKW/Chi for review.[286]

It is significant that Lt. Col. Friedrich, head of the Air Force Chi-Stelle, said during interrogation that he had never read one "activity report of OKW/Chi." In regard to any "very important signal materials" from OKW, Friedrich said he stopped reading them as they were of no interest to him.[287]

52. Relations with the Army High Command, OKH.-- Relations between OKL Signal Intelligence Service and the Army were on the whole quite good. The actual problems worked on by the two organizations were distinct, but results, reports and information were exchanged, and periodic meetings were held in order to discuss techniques and experience. Collaboration before suspected large Allied moves was especially close.

The 3rd Battalion of LN Regt 353 on Southern sector of Russian front collaborated with Signal Intelligence Regiments 1 and 8 (KONA 1 and 8) of the Army. Liaison officers were exchanged and evaluation closely coordinated. German Air Force Signal Intelligence Service often helped fill in the gaps through their work on the air armies when the Soviet land army observed radio silence.

[286] D 57 pp 7-8

[287] I 13 p 6

[288] I 126 p 14

The army employed a large number of search receivers. Any air frequencies were immediately passed to the Air Force, thereby saving the Air Force time-wasting search work.[289] In the West, LN Regt 351 fed its results to Commander-in-Chief of Army Group West.

53. Relations with the Navy High Command, OKM.-- In contrast to its relations with the army, the German Air Force Signal Intelligence Service had many actual problems in common with the signal intelligence service of the German navy. Both services attached a liaison officer to the Wing (Fliegerkorps) in Athens to coordinate the daily situation reports for the meetings of the general staff. Owing to his lack of experts, the admiral commanding German Naval Forces in the area turned over to the Air Force personnel and equipment for radar monitoring.[290]

The Navy was very much interested in the work 3rd Battalion of LN Regt 353 did on the air arm of the Soviet Black Sea Fleet. Accordingly, the Battalion kept the Navy informed on everything it received concerning the Red Navy. The Air Force Signal Intelligence was able to give the navy intelligence on the disposition of the some 180 planes of the Black Sea seaplane force. Of special importance was Russian air recce traffic, which when intercepted, constituted a warning of impending Soviet action against German convoys in the area.

Much the same situation existed in the northern sector. The 1st Battalion of LN Regt 353 put an R/T unit aboard the Prinz Eugen to monitor Soviet air units of the Baltic Fleet.

LN Abt 355 in Norway had direct wire lines to Naval Headquarters in Oslo, over which intercept information concerning RAF Coastal Command and Atlantic convoys was passed.[291]

289 I 130 p 15

290 I 126 p 14

291 I 187, #410

54. Relations with Weather Service (WENUEB).-- The monitoring of allied weather networks was not a primary commitment of German Air Force Signal Intelligence Service as the weather service (WENUEB) maintained its own intercept and analytic facilities. The German Air Force was, however, able to augment the weather service's coverage and analysis, and Signal Intelligence sources of weather information became increasingly important as Allied pressure cut down the activities of German weather recce aircraft.

A liaison officer (a technical sergeant) from the weather service was attached to Section B of the Chi-Stelle. This non-com made regular trips to the intercept units, instructing them in the significance of weather messages. He reported to the Chief Weather Officer on all weather frequencies not being covered by Signal Intelligence Service and any incidental weather intelligence.[292]

55. Relations with Goering's Research Bureau (Forschungsamt, abbreviated FA).-- The only contact between FA and the German Air Force Signal Intelligence Service seemed to be at periodic general meetings attended by representatives of all branches, although there was an occasional exchange of raw traffic between the two agencies.[293] Friedrich said that Voegele met with representatives of other agencies (FA included) to discuss cryptanalytics.

56. Relations with other Axis powers.--

a. Japan.-- Voegele, principal cryptanalyst of the German Air Force, visited Berlin twice in 1942 in an attempt to meet with Japanese Colonel Hayashi of the Japanese Military Mission in Berlin and discuss cryptographic matters. The meetings were prevented by Lt. Col. Kempf, of OKW/Chi.[294]

b. Finland.-- Lt. Col. Friedrich of German Air Force Signal Intelligence Service said that there was liaison with the Finns on Russian traffic and T/A. There was no liaison on matters of cryptanalysis. Detachments from German Air Force signal intelligence worked with the Finns at Mikkeli and Sortavala.[295]

[292] IF 183 p 90

[293] I 29 p 3

[294] I 119 p 17

[295] I 120 p 3

c. Italy.-- A very loose contact existed with the Italian Army Signal Intelligence Service. Unimportant frequencies of allied and Turkish air forces were exchanged. Personnel of German Air Force Signal Intelligence had a very low opinion of the Italian service.[296]

d. Hungary.-- Collaboration had existed with the Hungarians since before the war. The liaison consisted mainly in the exchange of radio intercept. The Hungarians had no capable cryptanalytic brains and lacked "reliability" in the eyes of the Germans.

The Hungarians attached an intercept company to the Eastern front in the Spring of 1942, but this was withdrawn after a year. In April 1944 a Hungarian intercept company was again attached within the framework of III Abt LN Regt 353. This company lasted until 5 January 1945, when it was withdrawn to a Hungarian collecting camp. The Germans considered it a good intercept unit.[297]

296 I 126 p 14

297 I 130 p 15

VOLUME 5

Chapter VII Critique of the Organization and Operations of the German Air Force Signal Intelligence Service.

57. Subordination to Chief Signal Officer rather than to A-2.-- The German Air Force Signal Intelligence Service was confronted with the same organization problems that the USA faced in the formation of a cohesive, efficient organization. It took five years of war, until October 1944, before the fairly unified service discussed in this paper as the norm emerged.

Both the A-2 and the Chief Signal Officer of the German Air Force desired control over signal intelligence. The German High Command subordinated the service to the Chief Signal Officer for operational reasons, although the A-2 was the chief recipient of its product. The High Command reasoned that the Signal Corps could better furnish personnel, equipment, and signal communication, and thought the A-2 lacked the technical know-how necessary to control the actual operations of signal intelligence units. Thus, the A-2 advised on intelligence matters but had no control over Signal Intelligence operations. Signal Intelligence reports to the A-2 had evolved gradually from technical discussions of circuits, new call signs, and such technicalities, to evaluated intelligence. German Air Force A-2's did not understand the purely Signal Corps technicalities, and this fact influenced the final decision in subordinating the signal intelligence service to the Chief Signal Officer. The decision to keep the signal intelligence service independent of the A-2 was a good one for them. Good intercept is all-important for the operations of any signal intelligence service. The effectiveness of the intercept service is determined by whether the enemy's transmitters can be heard, whether his operators are careless, and by many other strictly technical factors. Since all such technical questions of intercept are the province of the Office of the Chief Signal Officer, it would appear wise to subordinate the Sigmal Intelligence Service to that Office, rather than to the A-2. Signal Intelligence produces what is technically possible and not, except in a very general way, what the A-2 desires.

58. Centralization of operational and administrative control.--The final organization unified operational and administrative control within the signal intelligence structure at all levels of command. Lt. Col. Friedrich's dual capacity as head of Gen Nafue III and of the Signal Intelligence Agency (LN Abt 350) was the basis of this unification. Friedrich could bargain for equipment and other necessities from the Signal Corps while at the same time exercising operational control over the entire signal intelligence organization, although he did have a nominal superior in Gen. Klemme, Senior Signal Intelligence Officer. Col. Forster, Chief of the Air Raid Warning Service in Germany (FAF Reich) was head of tactical air raid warning operations, but he was subordinate to and received his orders through the Signal Intelligence Agency.

The experience of the German Air Force shows that its signal intelligence service had to be independent of outside control, equal and not subordinated to other intelligence agencies. This unity under Lt. Col. Friedrich, although not specifically provided for on paper, did in fact exist and was absolutely necessary for operating efficiency.

59. Organization of the Field Units.--In the final organization, all the field units were under the operational control of the Signal Intelligence Agency, which did not delegate its authority but moved its various sections to the field. On the Russian Front the ease with which the codes could be read, the large distances involved, and the difference in operating procedure within each Russian Air Army made it more practical to control the Battalions of LN Regt 353 locally. Sections E_1 and D split up and moved out to the headquarters of the three battalions, leaving a very small party at Chi-Stelle. On the fronts operating against the western allies the German Air Force decentralized T/A evaluation by putting Section B's evaluation personnel at the headquarters of the field units. A certain amount of centrality was maintained in the cryptanalysis of higher grade allied systems, due to the technical difficulties they presented.

97

The Germans found tactical evaluation to be a low echelon problem, to be attacked mainly by the field units. The individual intercept operator and field evaluator were in a position to supply much short time intelligence that would have been lost had traffic been immediately passed to higher echelons for evaluation. The production of strategic intelligence and the coordination of the intercept missions of the field units were performed by the personnel remaining at the Chi-Stelle at Potsdam, the traffic and operators' logs eventually found their way to this agency.

The distribution of control discussed in the three paragraphs above was the German Air Force solution to the problem of signal intelligence control, arrived at in the light of its particular experience. It would be wrong, however, to apply this organization uncritically to our own setup. Each country confronts different difficulties; each war presents a different geographical and communication problem.

60. <u>Advantages of a separate Air Force Signal Intelligence</u>-- The advantages or disadvantages of a distinct Air Force Signal Intelligence Service must be reviewed in any evaluation of the German Service. The organizations of the Wehrmacht called for a separate air arm, so when the Air Force found it needed signal intelligence it built up its own service without bothering with the details of signal intelligence control being centered in a single unit. It has been seen (Chapter I) that in the formation of its organization the Air Force followed the pattern already set by the Army.

<u>There were good reasons for a separate Air Force service.</u> Some of the problems of signal intelligence were strictly Air Force commitments. The most clear cut example of such a commitment is found in the operations against Allied strategic bombers. However, a similarly clear cut line of demarcation between Air Force and Army commitments could not be drawn in operations against tactical Air Forces which operated in conjunction with land forces. For example, in the case of Russia, the Air Armies were subordinated to Army Groups with which they had common communications channels. Furthermore, ground support units were linked with ground combat units by radio circuits. Again, in the West, the land forces and tactical Air Forces communicated on both air/ground and point-to-point circuits, and the commitments were not exclusively those of the Air Force.

These facts point to the wisdom in establishing a separate Air Force service to handle the problems which are of a peculiarly Air Force nature and indicate the necessity for signal intelligence units tailor-made for the intelligence needs of the Air Force. On the other hand, all the evidence underlines the necessity for a central, coordinating agency having overall control of signal intelligence matters, and making clear cut assignments on problems which inevitably overlap. The Germans in fact had machinery set up in OKW to answer this very need, but they did not use it, and cooperation between the branches of the Wehrmacht was difficult to achieve. Instead of overall control the Germans relied upon liaison at various working levels between the signal intelligence services of the Army, Navy, and Air Force. OKW, instead of functioning as an agency of overall coordination, restricted itself to the supervision of Wehrmacht cryptographic security and the ideal of the separate Air Force Signal Intelligence Service, subordinate to a central Signal Intelligence Agency controlling all the branches was never achieved.

61. Evaluation of German Air Force signal intelligence operations.--The Signal Intelligence Service of the Air Force achieved marked success in its operations in spite of the difficulties of organization. In the exploitation of every signal manifestation, the scrutiny of every phenomenon, the members of the service showed their advanced conception of signal intelligence.

On the Russian Front, methods remained rather elementary due to poor Soviet code and cipher security and primitive radio methods. In the west advanced cipher, communication, radio navigational and radar technique forced the Germans to rely on advanced T/A methods instead of cryptanalysis, and these they developed brilliantly.

The Germans exploited American mistakes to the utmost. Our heavy bomber raids were compromised by the tremendous volume of radio traffic that started before the raid and continued through take off and assembly, by the regularity with which routine reports were sent, and by the lax R/T discipline of the flying units. Even radio silence was significant, for if units remained absolutely quiet the Germans were alerted for an impending operation. Furthermore, American laxity in failing to switch off IFF over German territory made route tracking possible even when radio silence was observed, and Allied radar, both fixed and airborne, was carefully monitored. It is not surprising that the German estimate of U. S. security was that Americans relied too much on good cipher and did not practice sound radio discipline.

DOCID: 3560829

62. Recommendations-- The most important lesson to be learned from a study of the German Air Force Signal Intelligence Service is that we in the USA have been confronted with relatively simple signal intelligence problems. Cryptanalysis and T/A as we have known them, are not sufficient in tactical operations against an opponent as advanced as or more advanced than the USA in radio and cryptographic technique. The operational use by foreign countries of better codes and ciphers, better radio methods, and electronic devices of all kinds will make necessary our revising our conception of signal intelligence.

American security would benefit from an intense study of German Air Force signal intelligence operations, which have been reviewed only in outline in this volume. The successes claimed by POW's should be checked against our SOI's and operational records. Provision should be made to incorporate the lessons learned from these studies into the training programs of all units using radio and electronic equipment. From the examination of the materials upon which this volume is based, one fact stands out above all others: The German Air Force Signal Intelligence Service could not have been so successful in the West had American personnel been more security conscious.

APPENDIX

EARLY WARNING

By

Technical Sergeant Gerd Watkinson,
Duty Officer, Meldekopf 1, Luftwaffe SIS

[From IF-183 pp 12-32]

The problem of early warning became acute when the RAF began its heavy raids on Germany proper. It became even more urgent when the 8th USAAF joined the RAF Bomber Command in unrestricted aerial warfare against Germany, and the Luftwaffe limited itself for the most part to a defensive role. Reliable and timely early warning was to be one of the most important tasks of the Luftwaffe SIS.

The first attempts to obtain clues for advance warnings from enemy radio traffic hark back to bomber R/T traffic on 6440 kcs. ("Darky" frequency). From tuning traffic between ground stations and aircraft, and from early messages, the strength of RAF night intruder formations had been determined. In those days the number of bombers involved was no more than 80-100. Evaluation of this traffic was made easier by the separation of operational airfields and OTU bases. After 1943 the HF R/T traffic of combat units continually decreased, while that of the OTU's increased. For this reason, monitoring of the RAF Bomber Command R/T traffic yielded no fruitful results.

On the other hand, ever since 1943 the monitoring of American bomber R/T on HF frequencies gave very lucrative indications of impending air activity. During a later period, advanced warning had been given as early as the evening before daylight attacks of the 8th USAAF, simply on the basis of this R/T traffic. If, after normal daytime R/T traffic had come to an end, tuning and readability traffic, and W/T activity were renewed, then these observations were sent out by Meldekopf 1 as an early warning.

This type of advanced warning was facilitated by the fact that, at the end of 1943, the 8th USAAF introduced the use of special airfield frequencies in addition to the regular HF frequency of 6440 kcs. It remained, therefore, to determine the call-signs of the ground stations; the intercept operator needed only to have his receiver properly calibrated in order to identify the airfield in question. In the final period the efforts of the combat wings to give instructions to their formations on HF instead of VHF were realized. Perhaps it was due to reception conditions over England, which changed daily; at any rate, it was surprising how open and voluminous the HF traffic over England was, both during the assembly, and the approach flights to the target.

In the beginning of 1943, the first basic attempts were made to find possibilities for early warning in the air-to-ground W/T traffic. At that time a scrutiny of the radio traffic from the "Regional Control Stations" was begun. England was divided into fixed safety areas; the radio traffic for each zone was handled by a specified radio station, which was often a bomber airfield radio station as well. During the early afternoon hours a large number of unidentified call-signs would be heard in tuning traffic with those Regional Control Stations serving southern England; this would be followed, at night, by a rather large-scale raid on France, or over France into Germany. However, the experiment was a failure in the sense that the strength of an expected night attack could not be predicted from the number of call-signs heard communicating with these Regional Control Stations.

On the other hand, around this time a special phenomenon was noted by good SIS operators engaged in monitoring the enemy airfield D/F sections. Approximately one hour before the first enemy aircraft was plotted over the sea, certain, short whistling tones were heard, in varying intensity. In the case of a raid by approximately 250 bombers, 12-25 of these whistling tones were heard in short, chronological sequence. Specialists explained this phenomenon as the tuning of aircraft transmitters to zero beat. Thanks to these whistling signals, remarkable good advance warnings could be given from April to June, 1943. According to the D/F section, not only the strength, but also the probable area of attack could be predicted.

In addition short-interval early warning was guaranteed at all times through the interception of British H2S. The period in which the Meldekopf was able most accurately to predict raids was the summer and fall of 1943. When the whistling signals no longer occurred frequently enough to be reliable, monitoring of the radio station at Graveley Airfield (8 Pathfinder Group) furnished accurate clues. Gravely, one of the newer satellites of Wyton, was seldom heard by day. The radio station at every other bomber airfield sent its call-sign and the time, every 15 minutes for check purposes. Gravely was the only bomber airfield which sent its check signals only until noon, and then went off the air. If a mission were to be flown in the evening, the radio station would renew its checking transmissions in the late afternnoon, or at least long before take-off time.

Research conducted by the final evaluation section of Meldekopf 1 indicated that aircraft from Graveley took part in every enemy raid. Therefore, without incurring any risk, or considering the daily signal intelligence picture, an advance warning could be given on the basis of the resumption of quarter-hourly procedure at Graveley.

In the summer, new possibilities for early warning were explored, since it was known that the enemy was fond of changing his tactics suddenly. In addition to the continuous search for traffic on medium frequency, an effort was made to obtain a signal intelligence picture of all active squadrons, and to arrange the information according to the following pattern, in order to decide whether night attacks were impending or not:

Airfield	Number of aircraft heard	Number of tuning messages intercepted	Landings and peculiar messages

However, the evaluation of these tables was performed too superficially, and as a result no valuable intelligence was really gleaned from them. For this reason a small, select group of specialists was continually on the lookout for new methods of obtaining early warning.

First of all they proposed examining all the daytime radio traffic of the Pathfinder Group (8 Group). The reason for this was that no large-scale missions over Germany or the western occupied areas were flown without Pathfinders, which represented the brain of such an attack. If the radio traffic of this group yielded hints of an operation, then the method developed could be applied in the same way to the main body of the bombers. It so happened that the entire signal intelligence picture of 8 Group over the period of a month could be reconstructed relatively quickly, and hence the real work of evaluation could be started. The research proceeded on the theory that daytime radio traffic on non-operational days must be noticeably different in certain characteristics from traffic on days when no attacks followed. Thus, the radio traffic of all airfields of 8 Group was separated into different periods of the day, and subjected to a detailed examination. From this the following was determined:

On non-operational days, daytime radio traffic between aircraft and their airfields had no special peak. During the forenoon there was mostly identification and tuning traffic, with no special indication of haste on the part of the ground station. During the noon hours there was almost a complete lull in activity; the British partook generously of their noonday ease. In the afternoon tuning traffic began again, and now and then D/F traffic was heard. In scrutinizing the traffic of the airfield D/F sections, special attention was paid to those aircraft performing cross-country flights. Moreover, the W/T intercept companies which were entrusted with the monitoring of Bomber Command reported those Pathfinder aircraft call-signs which appeared in the traffic of other groups. After the traffic of the Conversion Unit at Wyton, which was quite voluminous, had been eliminated, there remained a good picture of the activity of the Pathfinders. The signal intelligence picture of this unit, on a day immediately preceding a night raid, looked approximately as follows:

In the morning there was lively tuning and recognition traffic, the peak being reached between 1000 and 1130 hours. The small amount of D/F traffic, appearing during the noonday hours was ascribed to ferry flights to and from the repair-shops. At noon came the "briefing-pause", and therefore very few Pathfinder aircraft were heard. To properly evaluate the noonday radio silence, an exact knowledge of weather conditions over the take-off areas was important. Therefore a weather map was made, and no source of information was ignored in building up the truest possible picture of the weather over the 8 Bomber Group bases (radio traffic between the ground stations of 8 Group and aircraft from other airfields; weather reports from training units flying over England, from deciphered bomber code messages, and from naval radio stations). The recall of British training units around noontime would be an unquestionable indication of an expected deterioration in the weather. Very frequently the signal intelligence picture would definitely indicate a raid, and then the sudden appearence of a bad-weather front would cause the mission to be cancelled.

In December practical utilization of the intelligence gained from the study of Pathfinder traffic was begun. Every evening an air situation report, such as the following, was broadcast:

Appreciation of the Air Situation, 1730 hours

In the forenoon, there was tuning activity on the part of all groups (both bomber and Pathfinder), but with no noticeable peak period. From noon on, cross-country flights by units of the Halifax Groups were observed, over the middle and western sectors of England, and over the Irish Sea.

In some instances flights of Pathfinder aircraft over the norther bases (6 Bomber Group) were observed. Pathfinder tuning traffic also came to a stop at noon. Training operations by the OTU's were carried out all day long, in all areas. Tuning traffic on medium frequency is normal, and shows no point of concentration.

Conclusion: No large-scale raid is intended.

This research was the impetus for a reorganization of the W/T intercept companies. In the same way as with the Pathfinders, a study was begun of the radio characteristics of the other groups. Daytime radio traffic was visually presented on large, glass blackboards by the use of appropriate symbols, and was posted hourly. On these blackboards were shown:

Air activity at a given airfield;
Tuning traffic from this airfield;
Volume of radio traffic with aircraft from other airfields.

When later the RAF also flew daylight missions, there was also included information as to which units had completed their missions.

A digest of this information, together with a record of the missions which followed, was kept in a diary, in order that every radio characteristic which seemed important to certain intercept problems could be referred to. This saved loss of time in thumbing through log sheets. To the blackboard picture was added a new board on which was noted those radio characteristics which could only be observed by the intercept operator (change of transmitter, increasing of signal strength, tuning to zero beat, change of radio operators, continuous notes, sending of V's, etc.). These characteristics were also tabulated and compared with those on the other blackboards.

This tiresome work was not done in vain. There emerged the facts that the Pathfinders of the minatory 5 Group tuned to the zero beat of their frequency long before their radio traffic over the target was heard, and that the same whistling tones could be heard from jamming aircraft of 100 Group, shortly after they took off from Foulsham. Also that the radio operators of 5 Bomber Group were changed frequently on non-operational days, while during a mission the same operator remained on the key.

The ever more frequent daylight raids of the RAF were predicted without difficulty. If, for example, 3 Bomber Group was to fly at noon, there was no tuning traffic during the morning. In short, an alerted group maintained radio silence.

105

Tuning traffic probably originated with the ground personnel rather than with the airborne radio operators. Perhaps it was also sent during repair-shop flights over an airfield, but this was not absolutely necessary. Perhaps it represented a certain playfulness on the part of radio repair sergeants who also wished to send a little radio traffic. The non-appearance of this tuning traffic became one of the most important clues for the Luftwaffe SIS in predicting a coming attack.

The following depicts the sequence of events in a night raid, showing how, in the latter years of the war, it could be identified by SIS, and advance warning given:

1700 hours: Lancaster units have been alerted for operations during the first half of the night. Whether Halifax squadrons are to be used also is not yet known. 5 Group commands special attention.

1800 hours: 100 Group has already taken off.

1825 hours: The first aircraft of 100 Group has been plotted; it reported damage. By means of many bearings its course is learned; it is flying over Dunkirk on a southeast course toward the Charleville area.

1825 hours: A bomber code message in the new setting, which is only valid for one night, is sent by an airfield of 1 Group; this means that the aircraft of 1 Group are already airborne, but their course is still unknown.

1900 hours: The monitoring of Allied aircraft reporting networks, carried out by Meldekopf 2, indicates a large enemy (British) formation in the Somme-Muendung area. At this point an advance warning is broadcast to all parties concerned.

1910 hours: An OTU aircraft attempts to home on an airfield of 5 Group and is turned away by the airfield D/F section (certain "Q"-signals). Therefore, the participation of 5 Group must be reckoned with. The HF and VHF D/F networks are alerted to monitor the frequencies of 5 Group.

1920 hours: An aircraft with a known operational call-sign requests a check bearing from the airfield D/F section of the Halifax units. Therefore, the Halifax units also warrant attention.

1935 hours: The Allied Air Raid-Reporting Service reports a second wave of aircraft. It is probable that on this night all groups are taking part in the raid.

1945 hours:	The first line bearing on a "Magic Box" (H2S) is reported. Since radar intercept is now bringing results, the course of the enemy units can now be checked, depending on the number of bearings. Once the course is accurately determined, night-fighters can be brought into play.
1950 hours:	A "Magic Box" is plotted over the Deutsche Bucht. Since no jamming aircraft fly into this area, it can only be a Mosquito flight or a mine-laying aircraft.
2000 hours:	The control stations of 4 and 6 Groups transmit "winds aloft" messages on a CQ call-up. From this it is known that the first wave consists of Halifax squadrons of 4 and 6 Groups, led by Pathfinders of 8 Group. The bomb-release signal can be expected within 20-30 minutes of the "winds aloft" messages, and therefore the f rmation will probably not intrude deep into Germany proper. Attention must now be given to the Boomerang-controlled Mosquitos of 100 Group.
2010 hours:	The first wave is plotted by radar intercept; course is toward the Rhine-Westphalia industrial district. The second wave is plotted for the first time in the Rheims area.
2020 hours:	A "winds aloft" message is heard on the 1 Group frequency; this time it is sent by the aircraft to the control station. 1 Group, therefore has penetrated deeper than the Halifax formation. This information allows identification to be given to previous "Magic Box" plots on this unit. Note: 100 Group usually flies in a wide formation, veiling the movements of other groups, and making it difficult to determine the course of individual units.
2025 hours:	The identification of all jamming aircraft which have been plotted is successfully completed, and their relative positions with respect to the individual units clarified; points of concentration of the jamming aircraft can now be reported.
2030 hours:	Zero beat tuning on the headquarters frequency of 5 Group is heard. Accordingly, fresh warning is given of activity on the part of this dangerous group whose course is still unknown.

2035 hours: The Boomerang-controlled target-markers for the Halifax formation are plotted. Special local warning is given to the area in which the attack is expected.

2037 hours: Interception of Pathfinder R/T traffic (VHF) on the "C" frequency of 8 Group; the aircraft are identified as Boomerang-controlled Mosquitos. A report to the ZAF states: Halifax formation will release bombs in few minutes.

2039 hours: "Winds aloft" messages are now sent by Pathfinders of 8 Group also. The contents are identical with those sent by 1 Group; thus, 8 Group are the Pathfinders for 1 Group. To what extent 8 Group is a part of the main bomber stream is, for the present, still not clear.

The report on the strength of the intruding formations states:

aa) Halifax formation approximately 380-450 aircraft (Lancasters of 6 Group have probably not accompanied them), led by Mosquitos.

bb) Lancaster formation heading toward Southwestern Germany with about 300 aircraft (to what extent 8 Group, except for its Pathfinders, is represented in the formation remains uncertain).

cc) 5 Group is active in undetermined strength; area of operations for the present unknown.

dd) Mosquito formation of 60-80 aircraft toward Berlin (target is only presumed, since Mosquitos regularly attack Berlin at this time of night).

2040 hours: 3 Group will probably not operate, since training activity is taking place on their airfields.

2050 hours: A small amount of training flight activity begins on two airfields of 5 Group. It is therefore presumed that specialized squadrons are carrying out a special mission.

2055 hours: OTU aircraft of 93 Group are recalled to their bases. Consequently there is probably a bad-weather front moving toward their airfields. The W/T companies are instructed to pay special attention to rerouting orders from the control stations of this group.

2115 hours: The control station of 8 Group sends a CQ message giving a report of winds aloft over the target. This indicates that the Lancaster formation will drop its bombs within the next half hour. The target area can then be determined by computing the distance that the Lancasters fly in the next half hour (their course being already known), and advance warning given.

2135 hours: The control station of 5 Group resumes its zero beat tuning. It might be for D/F purposes and 5 Group might be in the vicinity of the target.

2140 hours: Report from Jagddivision 7 target-markers over city X.

2140 hours: Aircraft of 1 Group send "winds aloft" messages for a section already flown through (for return flight purposes). The result is an SIS message stating: Lancaster formation has reached the target; no further penetration to the east.

2145 hours: The control station of 3 Group sends an order to a squadron from Waterbeach, diverting it to another airfield. Either the bad weather front has already reached the 3 Group bases, or Waterbeach must be kept open for aircraft returning from operations.

2145 hours: W/T Pathfinder traffic from the control station of 5 Group is intercepted. Accordingly, the special squadrons of the Group are in an area directly in front of the target. At the Maldekopf great excitement prevails; where are the aircraft? The possibility that they are over Germany is slight, because no flights were reported which have not been identified by SIS. After much telephoning to various tactical headquarters it is finally learned that a rather small bomber formation is approaching Bergen. Immediately an identification is made: these are the special squadrons of 5 Group. The first plot on a "master of ceremonies" of 5 Group confirms this assumption; the special squadron from Coningsby is flying over Southern Norway.

2150 hours: An aircraft of 8 Bomber Group sends the first report of results; it is plotted on its return flight from the area of city X in southwestern Germany. The return flight of the main bomber stream has therefore begun.

2150 hours: The Halifax airfields begin sending reports of weather over base. Landing conditions seem to be favorable in their area.

2153 hours: The first report of results is intercepted on the Coningsby airfiled frequency; it is immediately repeated on the Group frequency.

Note: The Pathfinder traffic of this group was especially interesting. The "masters of ceremonies" for the most part did not avail themselves of the three-letter code, and used plain text. 5 Bomber Group, which in other matters was generally acknowledged to be a well-trained unit, often employed new types of radio procedure car lessly. The introduction of "winds aloft" messages in December 1943 can be cited as an example. Instead of using the well-compiled code provided, messages were sent practically unencoded, or at least those parts were left unencoded which were most important to SIS. After several aircraft had measured the velocity of winds aloft on a certain section of the route, and passed this information on to their airfield, the headquarters then computed the probable wind velocity for that section of the route still to be flown, and transmitted this intelligence to its aircraft in flight. Since the code letters used for this purpose were easily broken, the headquarters actually revealed the intended depth of penetration of its bombers, and gave SIS an opportunity to determine the target in advance, to inform the Command between which degrees of longitude the bombers would change course, when they would drop their bombs, how many main waves there would be, etc. It was especially easy in the case of 6 Group to determine its division into various waves, because the Group headquarters sent a "winds aloft" message to each separate wave. The Pathfinders of 5 Group also used plain language when W/T traffic was first introduced; only later did they go over to the use of a special three-letter code which changed daily.

DOCID: 3560829

2155 hours: A bomber code message from the headquarters of 1 Group is deciphered and is found to contain re-routing instructions.

Note: Several times it happened that the bombers were called back by their control stations, shortly after passing over the English coast; in such a case certain aircraft receipted for the message. It was not determined to what extent the British had to authenticate unusual messages. Under certain circumstances the Luftwaffe SIS might have been able to send decoy orders to the bomber groups. However, such an attempt was forbidden by the Chi-Stelle, because it was afraid, by such a practice, of causing all Bomber Command W/T traffic to dry up.

Whatever further traffic was intercepted from the bomber formations on their outward flight could no longer be used tactically. Individual QDM's and reports of weather over bases pointed to landings; as a rule, flight-control traffic from the airfield D/F sections was of a minimum. Emergency calls from damaged aircraft served for purposes of statistics. Only if German long-range night fighters pursued the bombers on their return flight, did these messages have any tactical value.

By far the greater part of the effort was consciously directed to producing possibilities for early warning from the traffic of the RAF Bomber Command. All the possibilities uncovered were similarly applied to the monitoring of the 8th USAAF. However, in this case no such exertion, as following the British bombers required, was needed. The Americans were much more massive and primitive in their tactics, and can scarcely be said to have practiced restraint in their voluminous W/T and R/T traffic.

Long-interval advance warnings of raids by American bomber formations could usually be given as early as 2300 hours on the night before a daylight attack. The first indication of the raid proper was the interception of traffic from weather reconnaissance aircraft. The weather ships sent their reports to their home bases, as well as to certain prescribed headquarters. In this way they could be D/F'ed, and then it could be stated quite definitely into which areas the 8th USAAF would fly. Zero beat tuning was heard on the bomber division frequencies in the early morning hours preceding a raid. Next, the take-off of the individual units was monitored. During the assembly, which continued for as long as two hours, depending on the size of the raid, an exact picture of the composition and strength of the formations was obtained from VHF R/T traffic. A certain code-word then indicated that the bomber division was setting its course. Research work, as in the case of the RAF, was really not necessary; the Americans spoke of whatever they were doing quite openly.

The following is a description of the course of a typical American heavy bomber raid, and, as in the case of the example of an RAF raid, represents tactics during the latter years of the war:

2300 hours: Since R/T and W/T tuning traffic is being sent from 8th USAAF airfields, a raid must be intended for the next day.

0330 hours: A weather reconnaissance aircraft from Molesworth sends a message. A fix cannot be obtained from this one message.

0430 hours: Now weather ships of the 2nd and 3rd Bomber Divisions send messages; they are plotted over the assembly area in England.

0515 hours: A light jamming-screen appears over the southern portion of the North Sea, and off the eastern coast of England. At the samé time the first take-off messages are intercepted on W/T frequencies. The first operational call-signs are sent on the airfield W/T frequencies, an indication that no training flight, but rather a raid, is taking place.

0520 hours: A second weather reconnaissance aircraft of the 3rd Bomber Division is plotted while sending a message from a position over France. Inference: the 3rd Bomber Division, at least in part, will assemble over the continent (their assembly areas are learned from D/F-ing the radio beacons, as well as from captured documents).

0600 hours: Although it is known from the preceding W/T traffic, as well as from HF R/T messages, that the assembly is taking place, it is curious that still no VHF traffic is heard.

0620 hours: Individual aircraft are heard in tuning traffic with their ground stations (these tuning messages are especially frequent in the case of the 2nd and 3rd Bomber Divisions). Bearings indicate that they are heading toward the continent. A few formation leaders of the 2nd Bomber Division are now heard on VHF R/T, still over the assembly area in England, approximately over Cromer. With the exception of reconnaissance aircraft, there is still no sign of the 1st Bomber Division (the 1st Bomber Division, especially in the last period of the war, exercised exemplary restraint in its use of radio). A picture of the situation is now passed on to the people concerned: the 2nd and 3rd Bomber Divisions are assembling over the continent in considerable strength; of the 1st Bomber Division, which will also probably take part in this operation, nothing can yet be said as to when and where it will assemble.

0700 hours: A jamming screen is reported over the Belgium-Holland border area. It is not a reliable indication of a four-engined raid; it can just as well be a screen for a Marauder attack.
At the same time the first VHF traffic from the assembly area over France is intercepted. Callsigns of formation leaders and squadron colors are learned. The ZAF is given a preliminary picture of the expected strength while the division is still assembling. During the assembly, answers to questions concerning the stage of assembly are being given to interested headquarters; at the same time, the signal intelligence picture is being completed by calls to the SIS out-stations.

0730 hours: All the combat wings have now been D/F'ed; while, up to now, orders have been given principally on the wing frequencies, now the messages are sent on the division frequency. Therefore the assembly is nearing its final stage. Meanwhile the 1st Bomber Division has been heard in its assembly area over France, so that a comprehensive picture of the air situation can now be given; only the stage of assembly in the case of the 1st Bomber Division is still not known.

0740 hours: The first R/T traffic on the frequency of the fighter escort is heard; the approach flight must begin in the next few minutes.

0745 hours: The first message during the flight to the target is intercepted. It reads as follows: on time minus eight, on course, visibility three, too (time of origin) 0740.

At this point the defense is alerted. By D/F-ing these obligatory messages the exact position of the formation is learned. In the case of the 3rd Bomber Division, each combat wing commander has to send one of these messages; thus the Luftwaffe SIS can determine the strength of this division. Generally, its strength can be reported quite accurately to German tactical headquarters during the flight from the assembly area.

Early in 1944, some unit commanders of the 1st and 3rd Bomber Divisions even availed themselves of the MF D/F network, in order to orient themselves while still over the sea on their outward flight. It was quite obvious that practically nothing was being done to conceal the intentions of an attack.

Henceforth, continuous tracking is guaranteed by D/F-ing the abundant R/T and W/T traffic. A third prolific source is bearing on the "Mickey" equipment.

0800 hours: The first weather ships, reconnoitering the outward flight course, are heard on R/T, and appropriate D/F stations are detailed to monitor them continously. By following them, the route of the bombers can be accurately predicted.

There were days on which these weather reconnaissance aircraft could be plotted enroute to the target, two hours before the bomber formations left the assembly area. In the last period there was an increase in the number of cases where their messages were not sent through relaying aircraft on VHF, but on W/T. Special mention should be made of those weather ships of the 15th USAAF which revealed targets to the Luftwaffe SIS many hours before the raids actually began.

0900 hours: The first German fighters are mentioned in the bomber R/T traffic. Large-scale aerial battles were not frequently revealed in the signal intelligence picture; only in the case of several heavy raids on Berlin was there a plethora of reports

DOCID: 3560829

of attacks, of comments on the aggressiveness of German fighters, of curses from the unit commanders, and reprimands to their disorganized formations. The signal intelligence picture was not a very fruitful source of intelligence on Allied losses.

0930 hours: The reconnaissance aircraft report weather over the target (as a rule for several targets), and advise the bomber formation as to whether the bombing should be done visually, or by instrument.

0945 hours: The switching on of "Mickey" equipment indicates that the bombers are pivoting toward the target.

0950 hours: The formation leader of the first wave gives the order: "Bomb bays open" (clear text or code-word).

0953 hours: Wing after wing gives its bomb-release signal. Code-words occasionally used for this order varied according to the division.

1000 hours: The first reports of results are intercepted.

1100 hours: The first reports of weather over base are heard.

Note : Deciphering of bomber code messages presented no difficulties. They could be read with a depth of only three or four messages. The deciphering was facilitated by the fact that the most of the enciphered messages had been previously heard in plain language on R/T. Therefore it was only a problem of organization to collect this abundant material, and to concentrate it in the hands of the duty officer without any delay.

TAB A

VOLUME 5

Tab A

A Fu Luft (Aufklaerung Funk Luft?). See Air Radio Reconnaissance (Air Force Journal).

Air Force Administrative Area.--Luftgau.

Air Prisoner of War Transit Camp.--Durchgangslager Luft (Dulag)

Air Radio Reconnaissance (Air Force Journal).--Aufklaerung Funk Luft? (A Fu Luft).

Air Signal Battalion.--Luftnachrichten Abteilung (Ln Abt).

Air Signal Regiment.--Luftnachrichten Regiment (Ln Regt).

Air Warning Reporting Centers.--Meldekopf.

Albrecht, _____, 1st Lieutenant. Member of Group III, Division III of Chief Signal Office.

Anlagenband B zu Kriegstagebuch Nr. 4 (1. Abteilung) vom 1.1.45 bis 15.3.45.--Supplementary Volume B of War Diary No. 4 (Division 1) from 1 Jan. 45-15 March 45.

Anti-Aircraft Command.--Flakkorps.

Aufklaerung Funk Luft? (A Fu Luft).--See Air Radio Reconnaissance (Air Force Journal).

Becker, _____, 1st Lieutenant. Chief of Section B of the Signal Intelligence Agency (Chi Stelle) which was in charge of evaluation on the Western Front.

Beulmann, Franz, Major. Chief of Group I, Division III of the Chief Signal Office.

Bolich, _____, Specialist. Member of Group III, Division III of Chief Signal Office.

Bruehl, _____, Colonel. Chief of W-Leit 3 in Athens in July 1942

Camerlander, _____, Major. CO of LN Abt. 355 in Norway.

Central Air Raid Warning Unit.--Zentraler Gefechtsstand fuer Funkauswertung (ZAF).

Chef des Stabes, Generalnachrichten Fuehrer. See Chief of Staff to the Chief Signal Officer.

Chief of Staff to the Chief Signal Officer.--Chef des Stabes, Generalnachrichten Fuehrer.

Chief of the Air Raid Warning Service for Germany.--Funkaufklaerungsfuehrer Reich (FAF).

Chief Signal Office, Divisions I, II, III.--Generalnachrichten Fuehrer, Abteilung I, II, III (Gen Nafue/I, II, III).

Chief Signal Officer of the Air Force.--Generalnachrichten Fuehrer (Gen NaFue).

Chiffrier Stelle, Oberbefehlshaber der Luftwaffe (Chi-Stelle/OBdL). See Signal Intelligence Agency of the Commander in Chief of the Air Force.

Chi-Stelle/OBdL (Chiffrier Stelle, Oberbefehlshaber der Luftwaffe). See Signal Intelligence Agency of the Commander in Chief of the Air Force.

Chlubek, Gerd, 1st Lieutenant. Member of LNR-353. Cryptanalyst on Russian traffic.

Commander in Chief of the Air Force.--Oberbefehlshaber der Luftwaffe (OBdL).

D-8. Selected documents from War Diary #2 on Division 3 of Chief Signal Office.

Direction-Finding Stations (cover name: weather research stations).--Wetterforschungsstellen (Wo-Stellen).

Dulag (Durchgangslager Luft). See Air Prisoner of War Transit Camp.

Durchgangslager Luft (Dulag). See Air Prisoner of War Transit Camp.

Durr,_____, General. Inspector General of the German Air Force Signal Equipment.

Eick, Hans, Colonel. CO of LN Regt 353.

Etzer,_____, Specialist. Member of Group II, Division III of Chief Signal Office.

Evaluation Centers (cover name: Weather Control Stations).--Wetterleitstellen (W-Leit).

FAF (Funkaufklaerungsfuehrer Reich). See Chief of the Air Raid Warning Service for Germany.

Feichtner, Ferdinand, Major. CO of LN Regt 352.

Fighter Wing (in USAAF).--Jagdkorps.

Fischer,_____, Captain. Air Intelligence officer on Eastern Front. Specialist on Russian Air O/B.

Flakkorps. See Anti-Aircraft Command (in USAAF).

Fliegerkorps. See Wing (in USAAF).

Flight (in USAAF).--Staffel.

FMBSt (Funkmessbeobachtung-und Stoerdienst). See Radar Observation and Jamming Services.

Forster,_____, Colonel. Chief of Radio Air Warning Service.

Franz,_____, Major. Chief of Division I of the Chief Signal Office.

Friedrich,_____, Lt. Col. Chief of Division III of the Chief Signal Office (Signal Intelligence Service) and of the Chi-Stelle (Signal Intelligence Agency).

Friese,_____, 1st Lieutenant. Member of LN Regt 351.

Funkaufklaerungsfuehrer Reich (FAF). See Chief of the Air Raid Warning Service for Germany.

Funkbefehlsstand. See Radar Intercept Center.

Funkleitstand. See Radar Control Post.

Funkmessbeobachtung-und Stoerdienst (FMBSt). See Radar Observation and Jamming Services.

GAF SIS.--Oberkommando der Luftwaffe, Generalnachrichtenfuehrer/ III Abteilung (OKL/Gen Nafue/III).
Generalnachrichten Fuehrer (Gen Nafue). See Chief Signal Officer of the Air Force.
Generalnachrichten Fuehrer, Abteilung I, II, III (Gen Nafue/ I, II, III). See Chief Signal Office, Divisions I, II, III.
Gen Nafue (Generalnachrichten Fuehrer). See Chief Signal Officer of the Air Force.
Gen Nafue/I, II, III (Generalnachrichten Fuehrer I, II, III). See Chief Signal Office, Divisions I, II, III.
German Air Force High Command.--Oberkommando der Luftwaffe (OKL).
German Home Defense Air Force.--Luftflotte Reich.
Geschwader. See Group (in USAAF).
Goerner,_____, Corporal. Member of LN Regt 350.
Gosewisch,_____, Major General. Inspector General of the Luftwaffe Signal Corps.
Gromall,_____, Major. Worked on development of German Air Force signal equipment.
Group (in USAAF).--Geschwader.
Group of the Signal Intelligence Agency.--Gruppe.
Gruppe. See Group of the Signal Intelligence Agency.
Gruppe. See Squadron (in USAAF).
Henschke,_____, Lt. Gen. Director of Air Signal Replacement and Training Units.
Herold, Wadim, Captain. CO of III/LN Regt 353.
Hoeherer Kommandeur der Funkaufklaerung (Hoehr Kdr d Funkaufklrg). See Senior Signal Intelligence Officer.
Hoehr Kdr Funkaufklrg (Hoeherer Kommandeur der Funkaufklaerung). See Senior Signal Intelligence Officer.
Holetzke,_____, Captain. Member of I/LN Regt 353.
Horchabteilung. See Signal Intelligence Battalion.
Huebner, Erich, Captain. Chief of Section C of the Signal Intelligence Agency.
I-13. Composite Report on Two Interrogations of Oberstlt. Friedrich, Chief of the GAF Sigint Service. A TICOM publication.
I-41. Report on First Interrogation of Major Oeljeschlaeger Addendum: Interrogation of Major Beulmann. A TICOM publication.
I-65. Interrogations of Capt. Herold, LN Regt 353; 1st Lt. Werther, LN Regt 353; Lt. Ludwig, Chi-Stelle; and 1st Lt. Leichtle, LN Regt 351. A TICOM publication.
I-70. Paper on the German Air Force Signal Intelligence Service by Lt. Col. Friedrich, Chief of 3rd Division of Chief Signal Office and Chief of Chi-Stelle.

DOCID: 3560829

I-107. Preliminary interrogation of Obltn. Chlubek and Lt. Rasel both of III/LN Regt 353.

I-109. Translation of a Report by Lt. Ludwig of Chi Stelle Ob.d.L. (Bef.B) based on questions set for him at A.D.I.(K). A TICOM Publication.

I-112. Preliminary Interrogation of Specialist Dr. Ferdinand Voegele (Chi Stelle, Ob.d.L) and Major Ferdinand Feichtner (O.C. of LN Regt 352, etc.). A TICOM publication.

I-119. Further Interrogation of Reg. Rat. Voegele and Major Feichtner of GAF Sigint. A TICOM publication.

I-120. Translation of Homework by Obltn. W. Werther, Company Commander of 7/LN Rgt. 353, written on 12th August 1945 at A.D.I.(K). A TICOM publication.

I-121. Translation of Homework by Obltn. W. Werther, Company Commander of 7/LN Rgt. 353, written on 12th August 1945 at A.D.I.(K). A TICOM publication.

I-126. Homework by Major Feichtner, C.O. LN Regt. 352. A TICOM publication.

I-130. Homework by Hauptmann Herold, OC of LN Regt III/353. A TICOM publication.

I-133. Homework by Lt. Rasch of III/LN Regt-353. A TICOM publication.

I-134. Homework by 1st Lt. Chlubek of III/LN Regt 353. A TICOM publication.

I-135. Homework by Lt. Ludwig of the Chi Stelle Ob.D.L. A TICOM publication.

IF-175. Seabourne report, Vol. XIII. "Cryptanalysis within the Luftwaffe SIS." From Commanding General, 9th Air Force.

IF-176. Seabourne report, Vol. III. "Operations and Techniques of the Radio Defense Corps, German Wehrmacht." From Commanding General, 9th Air Force.

IF-177. Seabourne report, Vol. I. "Introduction and Report." From Commanding General, 9th Air Force.

IF-178. Seabourne report, Vol. II. "Biographies of Contributors." From Commanding General, 9th Air Force.

IF-179. Seabourne report, Vol. IV. "Biography of Major Ferdinand Feichtner." From Commanding General, 9th Air Force.

IF-180. Seabourne report, Vol. V. "The Chi-Stelle." From Commanding General, 9th Air Force.

IF-181. Seabourne report, Vol. VI. "Origins of the Luftwaffe SIS and History of Operations in the West." From Commanding General, 9th Air Force.

119

IF-182. Seabourne report, Vol. VII. "Technical Operations in the West." From Commanding General, 9th Air Force.
IF-183. Seabourne report, Vol. VIII. "Miscellaneous Studies." From Commanding General, 9th Air Force.
IF-184. Seabourne report, Vol. IX. "History of Operations in the South." From Commanding General, 9th Air Force.
IF-185. Seabourne report, Vol. X. "Technical Operations in the South Luftwaffe SIS." From Commanding General, 9th Air Force.
IF-186. Seabourne report, Vol. XI. "History of Operations in the East Luftwaffe SIS." From Commanding General, 9th Air Force.
IF-187. Seabourne report, Vol. XII. "Technical Operations in the East." From Commanding General, 9th Air Force.
IF-189. "GAF Signals Intelligence in the War." ADI (K). Report #402/1945.
Jagdkorps. See Fighter Wing (in USAAF).
Jering, Karl, T/Sgt. Member of Section C of the Signal Intelligence Agency.
Jordens,_____, Captain. Adminstrative CO of LN ABT 350 (Chi-Stelle as of the 1944 reorganization).
Kienitz,....., Colonel. Air Force Intelligence Officer. No other information available through TICOM.
Klemme,_____, General. Senior Signal Intelligence officer.
Klocke,_____, Dr. German Air Force Intelligence expert on Russian Air O.B.
Kriegstagebuch (KTB). See War Diary.
KTB (Kriegstagebuch). See War Diary.
Kupffer,_____, Major. Liaison officer to German Air Force Headquarters from Section D of the Signal Intelligence Agency. Outstanding authority on Russian Air O.B.
Kullman,_____, Major. Chief of Group III, Division III Chief Signal Office (radar monitoring and jamming.)
Leichtle, Georg, 1st Lieutenant. Member of Section A of the Signal Intelligence Agency.
Lier, Guenther, Lt. Member of LN Regt 352.
Ln Abt (Luftnachrichten Abteilung). See Air Signal Battalion.
Ln Helf (Luftnachrichten Helferin). See Women's Auxiliary (WA) (technical).
Ln Regt (Luftnachrichten Regiment). See Air Signal Regiment.
Loebell,_____, Major General. CO of Air Service Area (Luftgou) I.
Local Air Force.--Luftflotte.

DOCID: 3560829

1
Ludwig, Martin, Lt. Member of Section B of the Signal Intelligence Agency.
Luftlotte. See Local Air Force.
Luftflotte Reich.--German Home Defense Air Force.
Luftgau.--Air Force Administrative Area.
Luftnachrichten Abteilung (Ln Abt). See Air Signal Battalion.
Luftnachrichten Helferin (Ln Helf). See Women's Auxiliary (WA) (technical).
Luftnachrichten Regiment (Ln Regt). See Air Signal Regiment.
Majer, Karl, ____. Member of LN Regt 352.
Marks, ____, Lt. Once assigned to Signal Intelligence Agency.
Martini, ____, General. Chief Signal Officer of the German Air Force.
Meldekopf.--Air Warning Reporting Center.
Mooshake, Otto, Lt. Member of LN Regt 351.
Morgenstern, ____, Colonel. Chief of Staff to the Chief Signal Officer of the German Air Force.
Mucke, Helmut, Lt. Member of Regt. 353.
Naumann, ____, Senior Specialist. Chief of German Air Force Weather Service.
Nonnast, ____, Specialist. Chief of Group V, Division III of the Chief Signal Office (personnel).
Novopashni, ____, Prof. Member of Signal Intelligence Agency.
Oeljeschlaeger, Franz, Major. Chief of Group II, Division III of the Chief Signal Office.
OBdL (Oberbefehlshaber der Luftwaffe). See Commander in Chief of the Air Force.
Oberbefehlshaber der Luftwaffe (OBdL). See Commander in Chief of the Air Force.
Oberkommando der Luftwaffe (OKL). See High Command of the Air Force.
Oberkommando der Luftwaffe, Generalnachrichtenfuehrer, Abteilung III (OKL/Gen Nafue/III). See GAF SIS (German Air Force High Command, Signal Intelligence Service.
OKL (Oberkommando der Luftwaffe). See German Air Force High Command.
OKL/Gen Nafue/III (Oberkommando der Luftwaffe, Generalnachrichtenfuehrer Abteilung III). See GAF SIS (German Air Force High Command, Signal Intelligence Service).
Oberkommando der Wehrmacht Chiffrierabteilung (OKW/Chi). See Signal Intelligence Agency of the Supreme Command, Armed Forces.
OKW/Chi (Oberkommando der Wehrmacht Chiffrierabteilung). See Signal Intelligence Agency of the Supreme Command, Armed Forces.

121

Pick, Berthold, Lt. Asst. Chief, Section E of the Signal Intelligence Agency.
Porth,_____, Captain. Chief of Group IV, Division III of Chief Signal Office (cryptographic security).
Radar Control Post.--Funkleitstand.
Radar Intercept Center.--Funkbefehlsstand.
Radar Observation and Jamming Services.--Funkmessbeobachtung- und Stoerdienst (FMESt).
Radio Intercept Stations (cover name: Weather Radio Receiving Stations).--Wetterfunkempfangstellen (W-Stellen).
Rasch, Werner, Lt. Attached to 3rd Battalion, LN Regt 353.
Referat. See Section of the Signal Intelligence Agency.
Ristau,_____, Major, CO of LN Regt. 351.
Rueckheim,_____, Captain. CO of LN Abt 357.
Ruhling,_____, Captain. German Air Force Intelligence Specialist on Russian Air. O. B.
Sann,_____, Lt. Attached to LN Regt 353.
Schatz,_____, Corporal. Attached to LN Abt 350.
Scheidl,_____, Captain. CO of 1st Battalion of LN Regt 353.
Scheppelmann,_____, Corporal. Attached to LN Abt 350.
Schenerle, Erwin, Lt. Attached to LN Regt 351.
Schieferdecker,_____, Specialist. Member of Group IV, Division III of Chief Signal Office.
Schieran,_____, Specialist. Member of Group II, Division III of Chief Signal Office.
Schlottman, Gert, T/Sgt. Attached to LNR 352.
Schnippering,_____, Major. In charge of research on allied methods of communication.
Schulz,_____, Lt. Member of Group III, Division III of Chief Signal Office.
Schulz, Heinz, Lt. Attached to LN Regt 352.
Schulze,_____, Dr. Lt. Col. Chief of Division II of Chief Signal Office (communications and cryptography).
Section of the Signal Intelligence Agency.--Referat.
Senior Signal Intelligence Officer.--Hoeherer Kommandeur der Funkaufklaerung (Hoehr KDR d Funkaufklrg).
Siess,_____, Captain. Attached to LN Abt 350.
Signal Intelligence Agency of the Commander in Chief of the Air Force.--Chiffrier Stelle, Oberbefehlshaber der Luftwaffe (Chi-Stelle/OBdL).
Signal Intelligence Agency of the Supreme Command, Armed Forces.--Oberkommando der Wehrmacht Chiffrierabteilung (OKW/Chi).

Signal Intelligence Battalion.--Horchabteilung.
Squadron (in USAAF).--Gruppe.
Staffel. See Flight (in USAAF).
Stamm, Werner, T/Sgt. Attached to LN Regt 352.
Supplementary Volume B of War Diary No. 4 (Division I) from 1 Jan.-15 Mar 45.--Anlagenband B zu Kriegstagebuch Nr. 4 (1. Abteilung) vom 1.1.45 bis 15.3.45.
Trattner,_____, Captain. CO of LN Abt 356.
Truemena, Wilhelm, Sgt. Attached to LN Regt 353.
Voegele, Ferdinand, Specialist. Chief of Section E of the Signal Intelligence Agency and Principal cryptanalyst of the GAF.
Von Lackum,_____, Lt. Attached to LN Regt 353.
Von Lingen,_____, Lt. Cryptanalyst in Section E of the Signal Intelligence Agency.
War Diary.--Kriegstagebuch (KTB).
Watkinson, Gerd T/Sgt. Attached to LN Regt 351.
Werther, Waldemar, 1st Lt. Attached to the 7th Company, 2nd Battalion, LN Regt. 353. The most capable cryptanalyst on Russian Air Force cryptographic systems on the Eastern Front.
Wetterforschungsstellen (Wo-Stellen). See Direction-Finding Stations (cover name: weather research stations).
Wetterleitstellen (W-Leit). See Evaluation Centers (cover name: Weather Control Stations).
Wetterfunkempfanstellen (W-Stellen). See Radio Intercept Stations (cover name: Weather Radio Receiving Stations).
Windels, Hans, Major. CO of 2nd Battalion, LN Regt 353.
Wing (in USAAF).--Fliegerkorps.
Wisnikow,_____, Lt. Attached to Section E of the Signal Intelligence Agency.
W-Leit (Wetterleitstellen). See Evaluation Centers (cover name: Weather Control Stations).
Women's Auxiliary (WA) (technical).--Luftnachrichten (Ln Helf).
Wo-Stellen (Wetterforschungsstellen). See Direction-Finding Stations (cover name: weather research stations).
W-Stellen (Wetterfunkempfangstellen). See Radio Intercept Stations (cover name: Weather Radio Receiving Stations.
ZAF (Zentraler Gefechtsstand fuer Funkauswertung). See Central Air Raid Warning Unit.
Zentraler Gefechtsstand fuer Funkauswertung (ZAF). See Central Air Raid Warning Unit.
Zuerr,_____, Major General. Inspector General of German Air Force Signal Equipment.

DOCID: 3560829

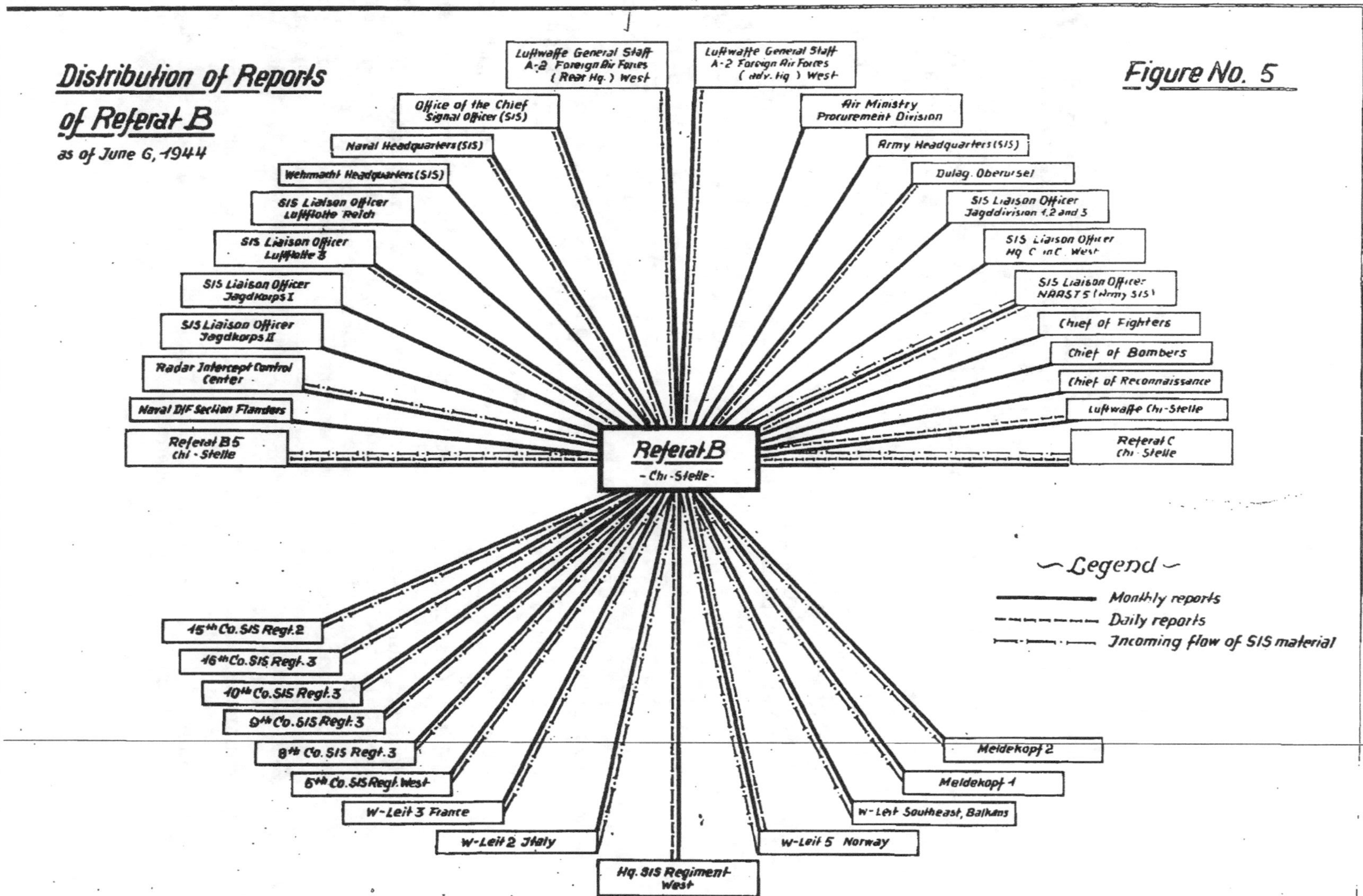

(CHART No. 5-2. From IF-180)

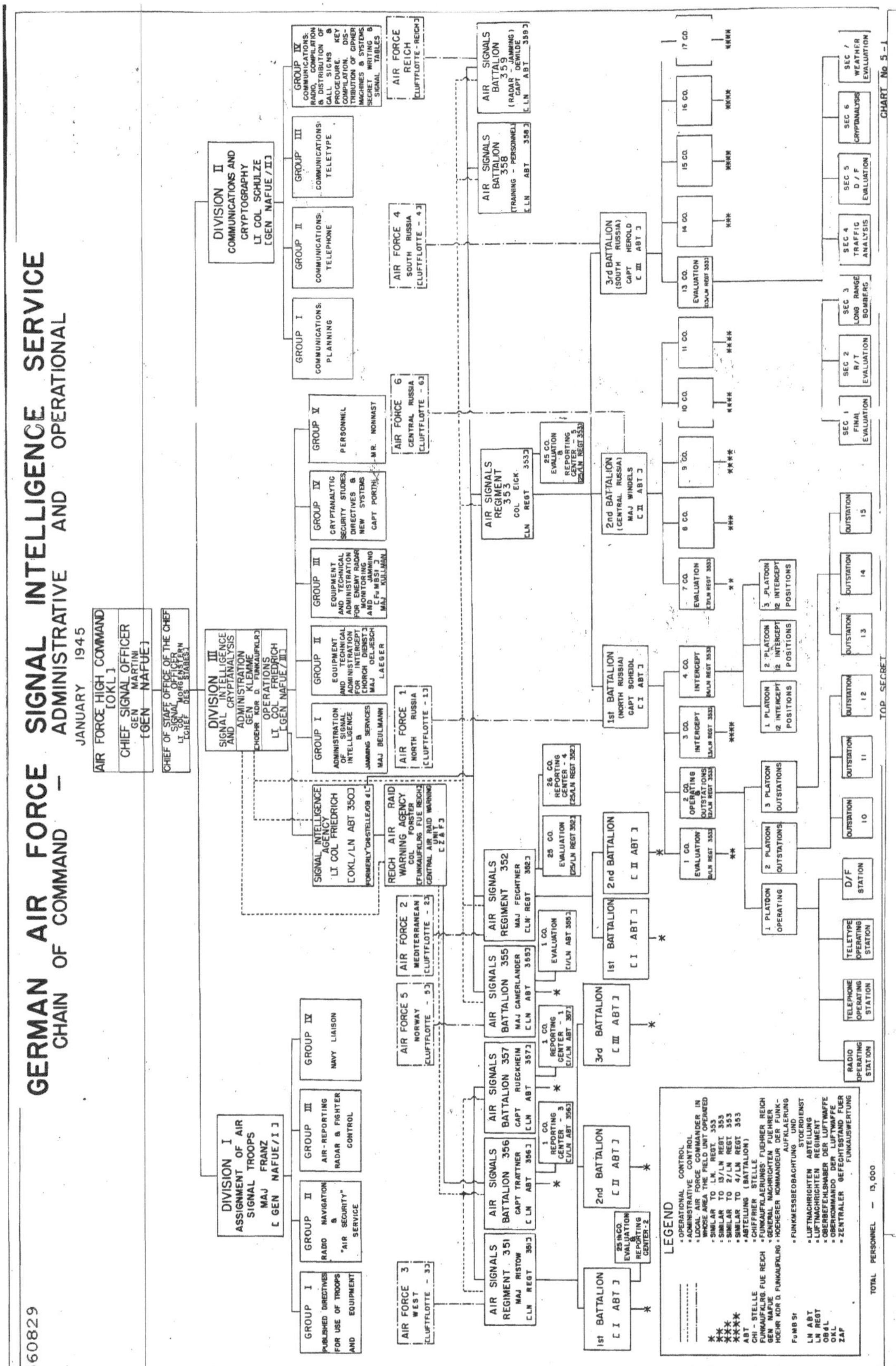
DOCID: 3560829
GERMAN AIR FORCE SIGNAL INTELLIGENCE SERVICE
CHAIN OF COMMAND — ADMINISTRATIVE AND OPERATIONAL
JANUARY 1945
AIR FORCE HIGH COMMAND [OKL]
CHIEF SIGNAL OFFICER GEN MARTINI [GEN NAFUE]
CHIEF OF STAFF OFFICE OF THE CHIEF SIGNAL OFFICER LT COL MORGENSTERN [CHEF DES STABES]
DIVISION I ASSIGNMENT OF AIR SIGNAL TROOPS MAJ FRANZ [GEN NAFUE/I]
GROUP I PUBLISHED DIRECTIVES FOR USE OF TROOPS AND EQUIPMENT
GROUP II RADIO NAVIGATION & "AIR SECURITY" SERVICE
GROUP III AIR-REPORTING RADAR & FIGHTER CONTROL
GROUP IV NAVY LIAISON
DIVISION III SIGNAL INTELLIGENCE AND CRYPTANALYSIS
ADMINISTRATION GEN KLEMME [HOEHR KDR D. FUNKAUFKLR]
OPERATIONS LT COL FRIEDRICH [GEN NAFUE/III]
SIGNAL INTELLIGENCE AGENCY LT COL FRIEDRICH [OKL/LN ABT 350] FORMERLY "CHI-STELLE/OB d L"
REICH AIR RAID WARNING AGENCY COL FORSTER [FUNKAUFKLRG FUE REICH] CENTRAL AIR RAID WARNING UNIT [Z & F]
GROUP I ADMINISTRATION OF SIGNAL INTELLIGENCE & JAMMING SERVICES MAJ BEULMANN
GROUP II EQUIPMENT AND TECHNICAL ADMINISTRATION FOR INTERCEPT [HORCH DIENST] MAJ OELJESCH LAEGER
GROUP III EQUIPMENT AND TECHNICAL ADMINISTRATION FOR ENEMY RADAR MONITORING AND JAMMING [FuMBSt] MAJ KULLMAN
GROUP IV CRYPTANALYTIC SECURITY STUDIES, DIRECTIVES & NEW SYSTEMS CAPT PORTH
GROUP V PERSONNEL MR. NONNAST
DIVISION II COMMUNICATIONS AND CRYPTOGRAPHY LT COL SCHULZE [GEN NAFUE/II]
GROUP I COMMUNICATIONS: PLANNING
GROUP II COMMUNICATIONS: TELEPHONE
GROUP III COMMUNICATIONS: TELETYPE
GROUP IV COMMUNICATIONS: RADIO, COMPILATION & DISTRIBUTION OF CALL SIGNS & PROCEDURE. KEY COMPILATION. DISTRIBUTION OF CIPHER MACHINES & SYSTEMS. SECRET WRITING & SIGNAL TABLES
AIR FORCE 3 WEST [LUFTFLOTTE - 3]
AIR FORCE 5 NORWAY [LUFTFLOTTE - 5]
AIR FORCE 2 MEDITERRANEAN [LUFTFLOTTE - 2]
AIR FORCE 1 NORTH RUSSIA [LUFTFLOTTE - 1]
AIR FORCE 6 CENTRAL RUSSIA [LUFTFLOTTE - 6]
AIR FORCE 4 SOUTH RUSSIA [LUFTFLOTTE - 4]
AIR FORCE REICH [LUFTFLOTTE - REICH]
AIR SIGNALS REGIMENT 351 MAJ RISTOW [LN REGT 351]
AIR SIGNALS BATTALION 356 CAPT TRATTNER [LN ABT 356]
AIR SIGNALS BATTALION 357 CAPT RUECKHEIM [LN ABT 357]
AIR SIGNALS BATTALION 355 MAJ CAMERLANDER [LN ABT 355]
AIR SIGNALS REGIMENT 352 MAJ FEICHTNER [LN REGT 352]
AIR SIGNALS REGIMENT 353 COL EICK [LN REGT 353]
AIR SIGNALS BATTALION 358 (TRAINING - PERSONNEL) [LN ABT 358]
AIR SIGNALS BATTALION 359 (RADAR - JAMMING) CAPT DEWILDE [LN ABT 359]
1 CO. REPORTING CENTER - 3 [1/LN ABT 356]
1 CO. REPORTING CENTER - 1 [1/LN ABT 357]
1 CO. EVALUATION [1/LN ABT 355]
25 CO. EVALUATION [25/LN REGT 352]
26 CO. REPORTING CENTER - 4 [26/LN REGT 352]
25 CO. EVALUATION & REPORTING CENTER - 5 [25/LN REGT 353]
1st BATTALION [I ABT]
25th CO. EVALUATION & REPORTING CENTER - 2
2nd BATTALION [II ABT]
3rd BATTALION [III ABT]
1st BATTALION [I ABT]
2nd BATTALION [II ABT]
1st BATTALION (NORTH RUSSIA) CAPT SCHEIDL [I ABT]
2nd BATTALION (CENTRAL RUSSIA) MAJ WINDELS [II ABT]
3rd BATTALION (SOUTH RUSSIA) CAPT HEROLD [III ABT]
1 CO. EVALUATION [1/LN REGT 353]
2 CO. OPERATING & OUTSTATIONS [2/LN REGT 353]
3 CO. INTERCEPT [3/LN REGT 353]
4 CO. INTERCEPT [4/LN REGT 353]
7 CO. EVALUATION [7/LN REGT 353]
8 CO.
9 CO.
10 CO.
11 CO.
13 CO. EVALUATION [13/LN REGT 353]
14 CO.
15 CO.
16 CO.
17 CO.
1 PLATOON OPERATING
2 PLATOON OUTSTATIONS
3 PLATOON OUTSTATIONS
1 PLATOON 12 INTERCEPT POSITIONS
2 PLATOON 12 INTERCEPT POSITIONS
3 PLATOON 12 INTERCEPT POSITIONS
RADIO OPERATING STATION
TELEPHONE OPERATING STATION
TELETYPE OPERATING STATION
D/F STATION
OUTSTATION 10
OUTSTATION 11
OUTSTATION 12
OUTSTATION 13
OUTSTATION 14
OUTSTATION 15
SEC 1 FINAL EVALUATION
SEC 2 R/T EVALUATION
SEC 3 LONG RANGE BOMBERS
SEC 4 TRAFFIC ANALYSIS
SEC 5 D/F EVALUATION
SEC 6 CRYPTANALYSIS
SEC 7 WEATHER EVALUATION
LEGEND
= OPERATIONAL CONTROL
= ADMINISTRATIVE CONTROL
= LOCAL AIR FORCE COMMANDER IN WHOSE AREA THE FIELD UNIT OPERATED
* = SIMILAR TO LN. REGT. 353
** = SIMILAR TO 13/LN REGT. 353
*** = SIMILAR TO 2/LN REGT. 353
**** = SIMILAR TO 4/LN REGT. 353
ABT = ABTEILUNG (BATTALION)
CHI - STELLE = CHIFFRIER STELLE
FUNKAUFKLRG. FUE REICH = FUNKAUFKLAERUNGS FUEHRER REICH
GEN NAFUE = GENERAL NACHRICHTEN FUEHRER
HOEHR KDR D. FUNKAUFKLRG = HOEHERER KOMMANDEUR DER FUNKAUFKLAERUNG
FuMB St = FUNKMESSBEOBACHTUNG UND STOERDIENST
LN ABT = LUFTNACHRICHTEN ABTEILUNG
LN REGT = LUFTNACHRICHTEN REGIMENT
ObdL = OBERBEFEHLSHABER DER LUFTWAFFE
OKL = OBERKOMMANDO DER LUFTWAFFE
ZAF = ZENTRALER GEFECHTSSTAND FUER FUNKAUSWERTUNG
TOTAL PERSONNEL — 13,000
TOP SECRET
CHART No 5-1

DOCID: 3560829

Organization and Strength of the 8th US Air Force
As of March 1945

Figure No 3

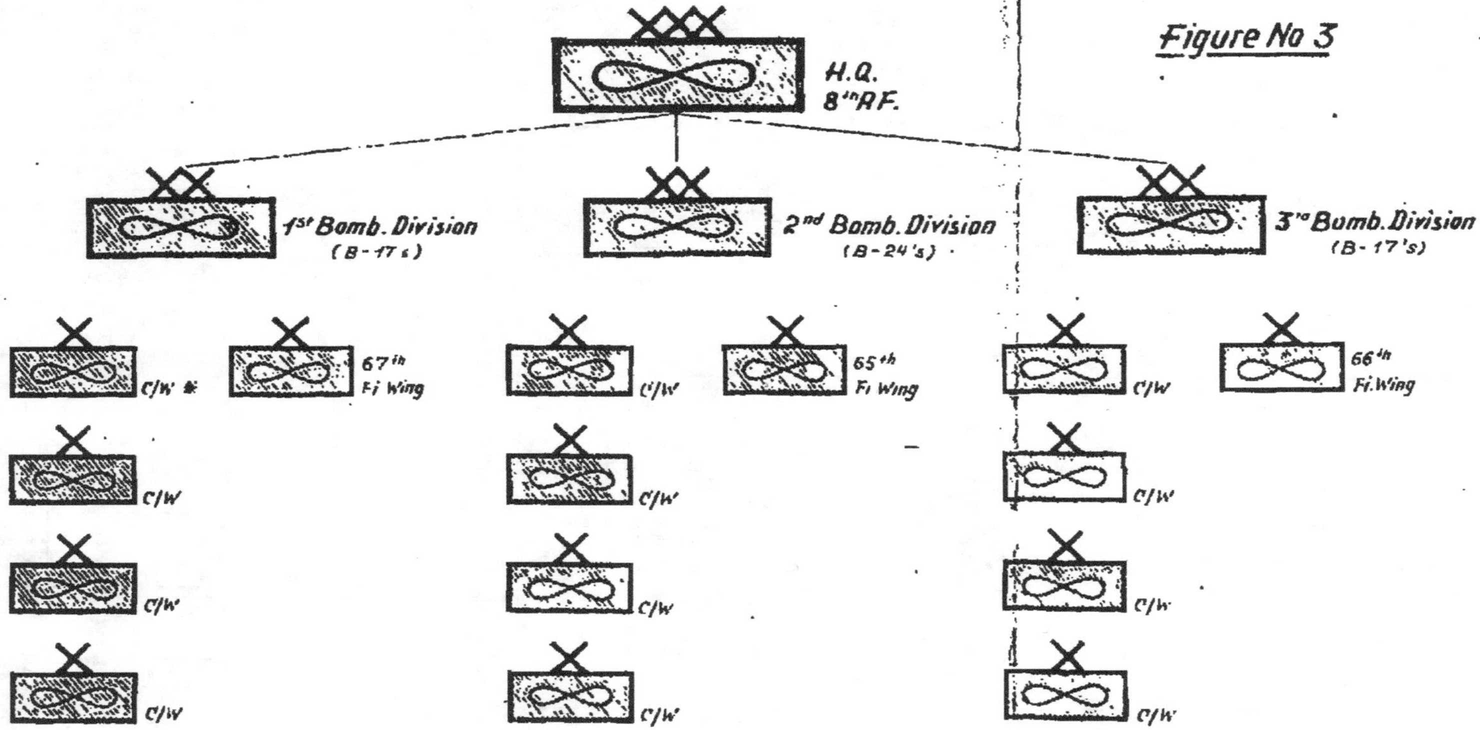

Total about 3300 Bombers (B-17's and B-24's) **and 1250 Fighters** (P-51's and some P-47's)

* C/W = Combat Wing

(CHART No. 5-4. From IF-182)

- 57a -

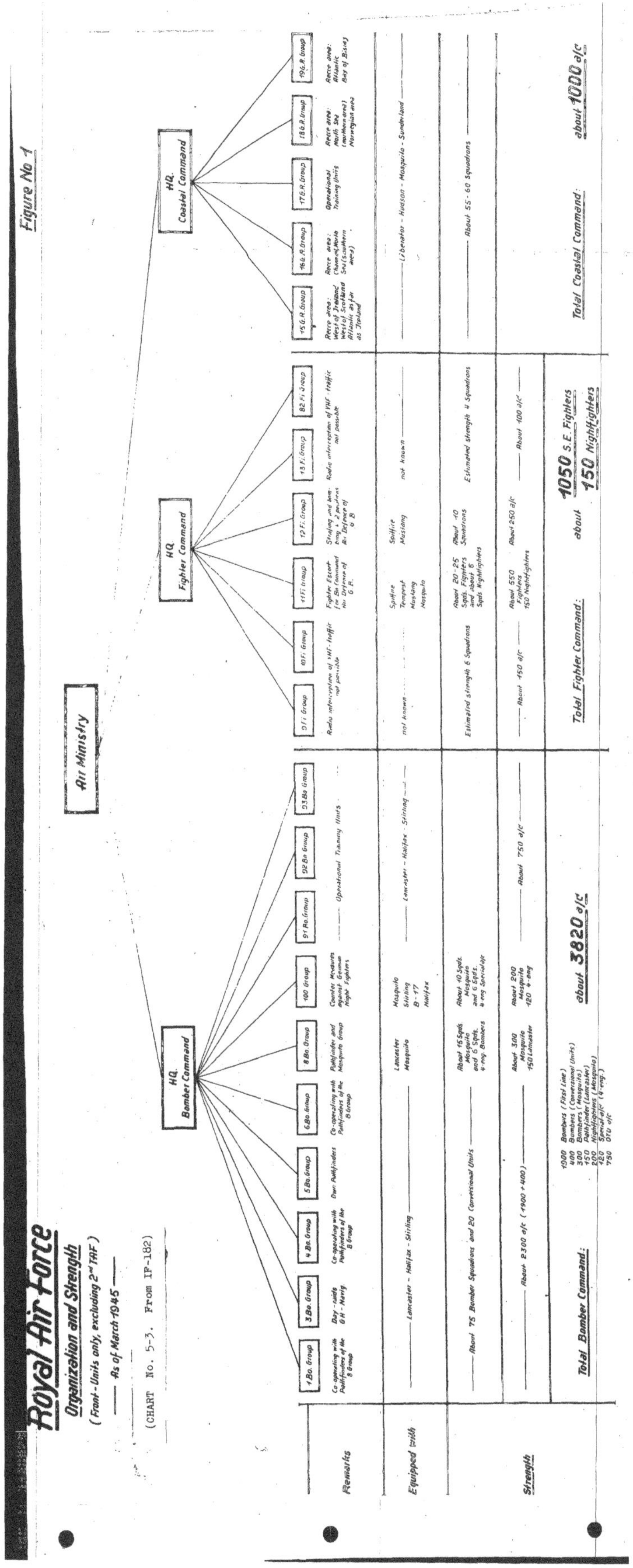
Figure No 1
Royal Air Force
Organization and Strength
(Front-Units only, excluding 2nd TAF)
As of March 1945
(CHART No. 5-3. From IF-182)
Air Ministry
HQ. Bomber Command
HQ. Fighter Command
HQ. Coastal Command
Remarks
Equipped with
Strength
1 Bo. Group
3 Bo. Group
4 Bo. Group
5 Bo. Group
6 Bo. Group
8 Bo. Group
100 Group
91 Bo. Group
92 Bo. Group
93 Bo. Group
Own Pathfinders
Operational Training Units
Lancaster - Halifax - Stirling
About 75 Bomber Squadrons and 20 Conversional Units
About 2300 a/c (1900 + 400)
About 750 a/c
Total Bomber Command:
about 3820 a/c
Total Fighter Command:
about 1050 S.E. Fighters
150 Nightfighters
Liberator - Hudson - Mosquito - Sunderland
About 55 - 60 Squadrons
Total Coastal Command:
about 1000 a/c

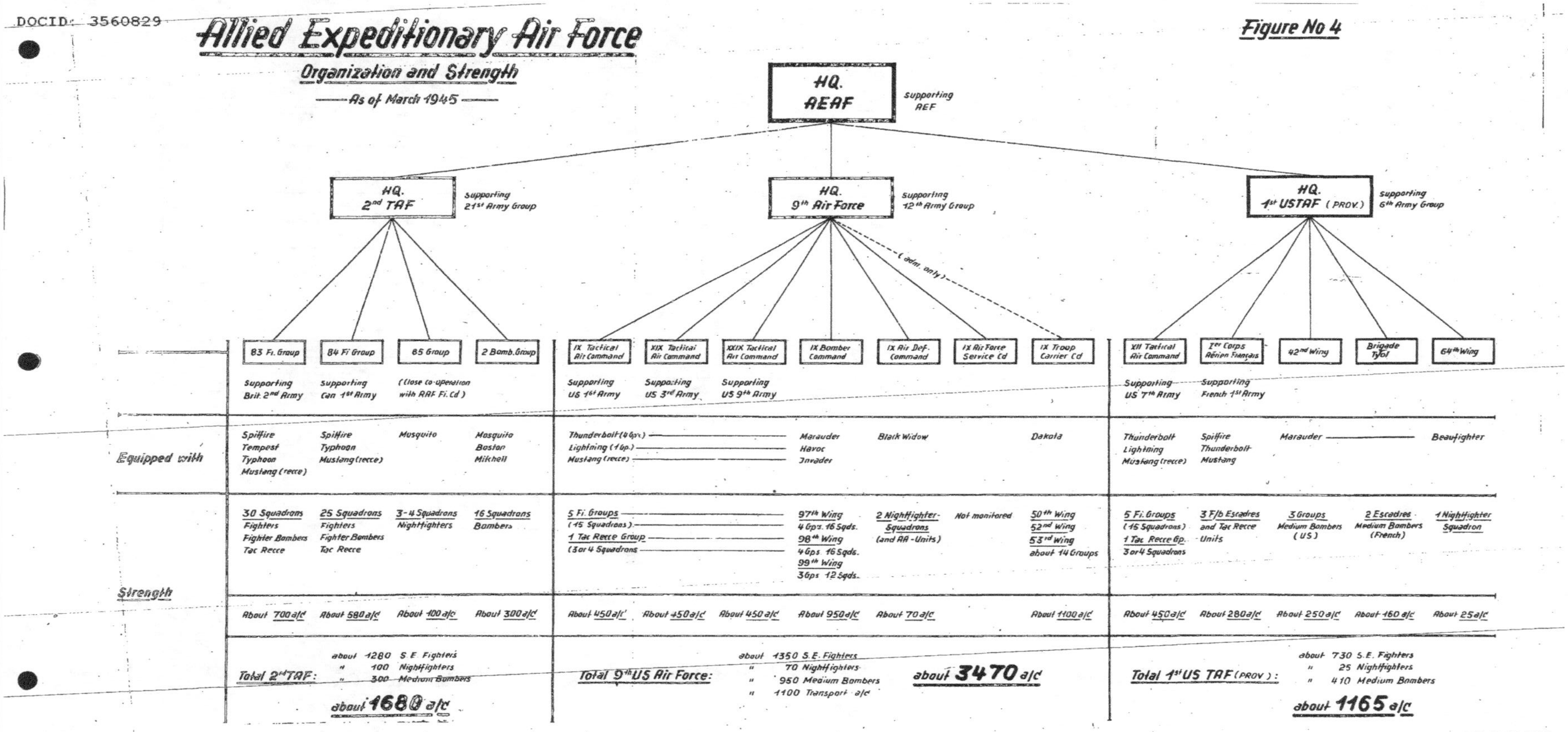
DOCID: 3560829
Allied Expeditionary Air Force
Organization and Strength
As of March 1945
Figure No 4
HQ. AEAF
Supporting AEF
HQ. 2nd TAF
Supporting 21st Army Group
HQ. 9th Air Force
Supporting 12th Army Group
HQ. 1st USTAF (PROV.)
Supporting 6th Army Group
(adm. only)
83 Fi. Group
84 Fi Group
85 Group
2 Bomb. Group
IX Tactical Air Command
XIX Tactical Air Command
XXIX Tactical Air Command
IX Bomber Command
IX Air Def. Command
IX Air Force Service Cd
IX Troop Carrier Cd
XII Tactical Air Command
1er Corps Aérien Français
42nd Wing
Brigade Tyjol
64th Wing
Supporting Brit. 2nd Army
Supporting Can 1st Army
(Close co-operation with RAF Fi. Cd)
Supporting US 1st Army
Supporting US 3rd Army
Supporting US 9th Army
Supporting US 7th Army
Supporting French 1st Army
Equipped with
Spitfire Tempest Typhoon Mustang (recce)
Spitfire Typhoon Mustang (recce)
Mosquito
Mosquito Boston Mitchell
Thunderbolt (4 Gps.) Lightning (1 Gp.) Mustang (recce)
Marauder Havoc Invader
Black Widow
Dakota
Thunderbolt Lightning Mustang (recce)
Spitfire Thunderbolt Mustang
Marauder
Beaufighter
30 Squadrons Fighters Fighter Bombers Tac Recce
25 Squadrons Fighters Fighter Bombers Tac Recce
3-4 Squadrons Nightfighters
16 Squadrons Bombers
5 Fi. Groups (15 Squadrons) 1 Tac Recce Group (3 or 4 Squadrons)
97th Wing 4 Gps. 16 Sqds. 98th Wing 4 Gps 16 Sqds. 99th Wing 3 Gps 12 Sqds.
2 Nightfighter-Squadrons (and AA-Units)
Not monitored
50th Wing 52nd Wing 53rd Wing about 14 Groups
5 Fi. Groups (15 Squadrons) 1 Tac Recce Gp. 3 or 4 Squadrons
3 F/b Escadres and Tac Recce Units
3 Groups Medium Bombers (US)
2 Escadres Medium Bombers (French)
1 Nightfighter Squadron
Strength
About 700 a/c
About 580 a/c
About 100 a/c
About 300 a/c
About 450 a/c
About 450 a/c
About 450 a/c
About 950 a/c
About 70 a/c
About 1100 a/c
About 450 a/c
About 280 a/c
About 250 a/c
About 160 a/c
About 25 a/c
Total 2nd TAF: about 1280 S.E. Fighters " 100 Nightfighters " 300 Medium Bombers
about 1680 a/c
Total 9th US Air Force: about 1350 S.E. Fighters " 70 Nightfighters " 950 Medium Bombers " 1100 Transport a/c
about 3470 a/c
Total 1st US TAF (PROV.): about 730 S.E. Fighters " 25 Nightfighters " 410 Medium Bombers
about 1165 a/c

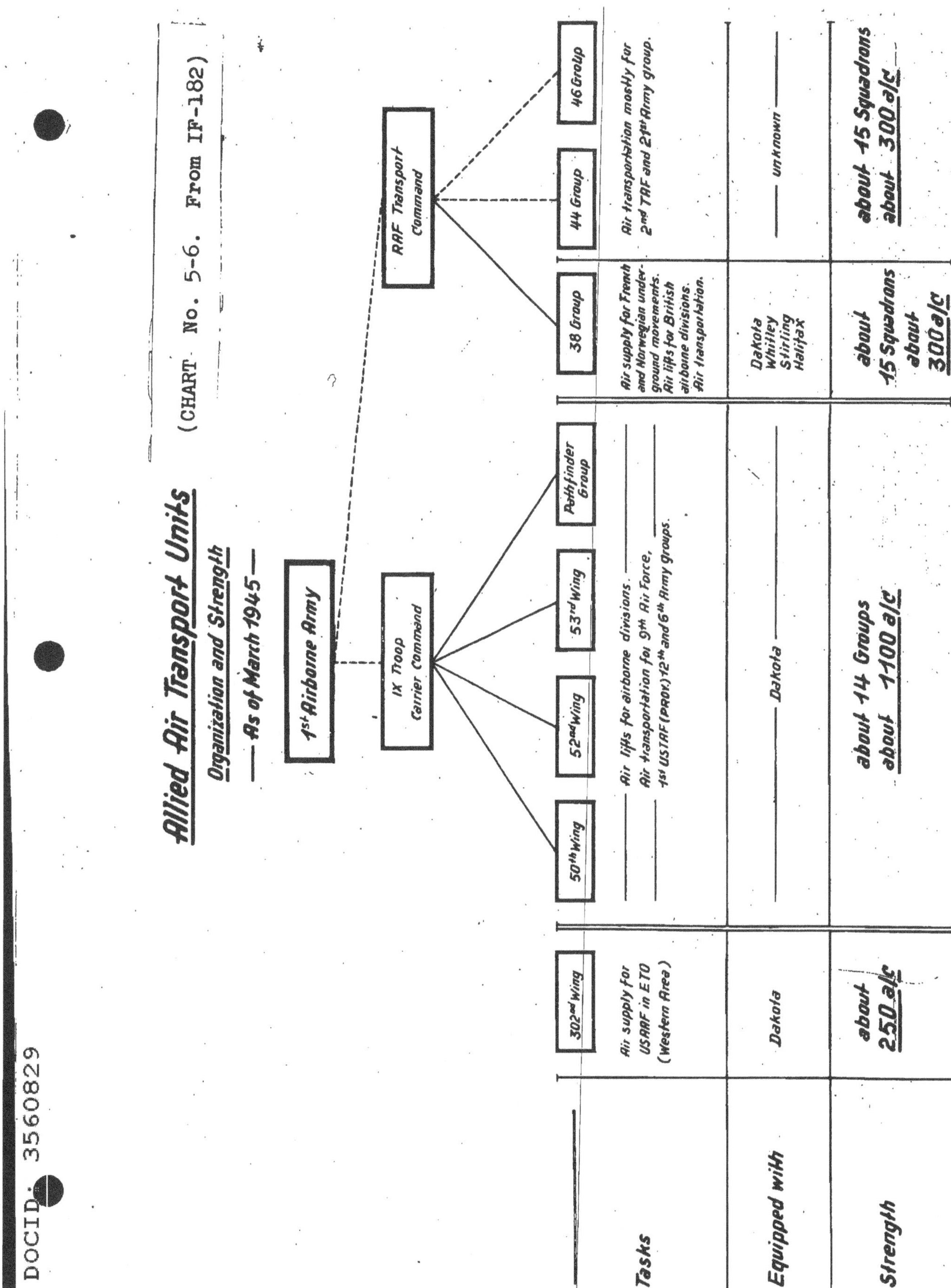
(CHART No. 5-6. From IF-182)
Allied Air Transport Units
Organization and Strength
As of March 1945
1st Airborne Army
IX Troop Carrier Command
RAF Transport Command
302nd Wing
50th Wing
52nd Wing
53rd Wing
Pathfinder Group
38 Group
44 Group
46 Group
Tasks
Air supply for USAAF in ETO (Western Area)
Air lifts for airborne divisions. Air transportation for 9th Air Force, 1st USTAF (PROV.) 12th and 6th Army groups.
Air supply for French and Norwegian underground movements. Air lifts for British airborne divisions. Air transportation.
Air transportation mostly for 2nd TAF and 21st Army group.
Equipped with
Dakota
Dakota
Dakota Whitley Stirling Halifax
unknown
Strength
about 250 a/c
about 14 Groups about 1100 a/c
about 15 Squadrons about 300 a/c
about 15 Squadrons about 300 a/c

Operations Room of the ZAF

(CHART No. 5-7. From IF-181)

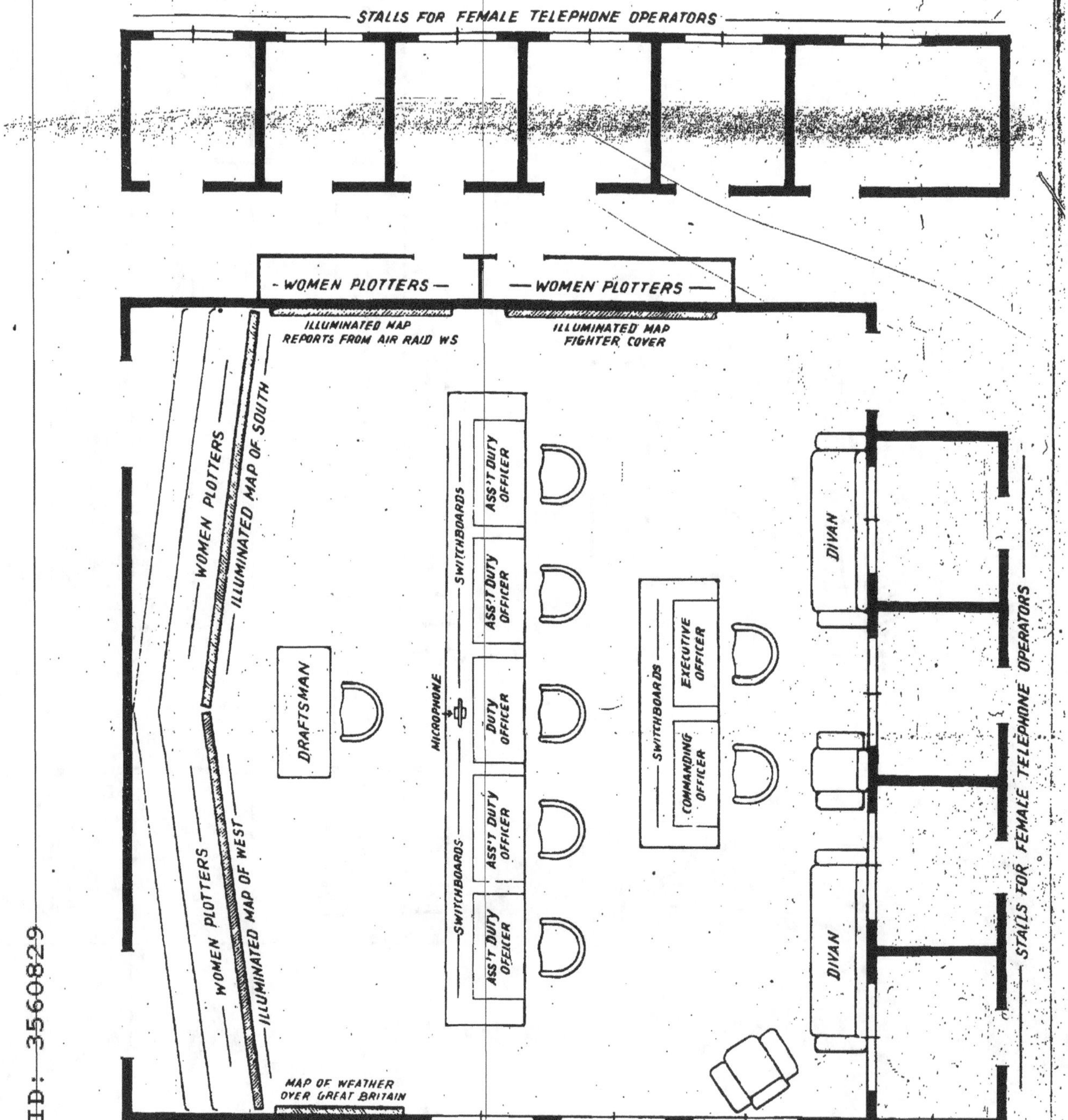

-70a-

DOCID: 3560829

(CHART No. 5-8. From IF-183)

Subscribers to SIS Broadcast of Meldekopf 1

(before the creation of the ZAF)

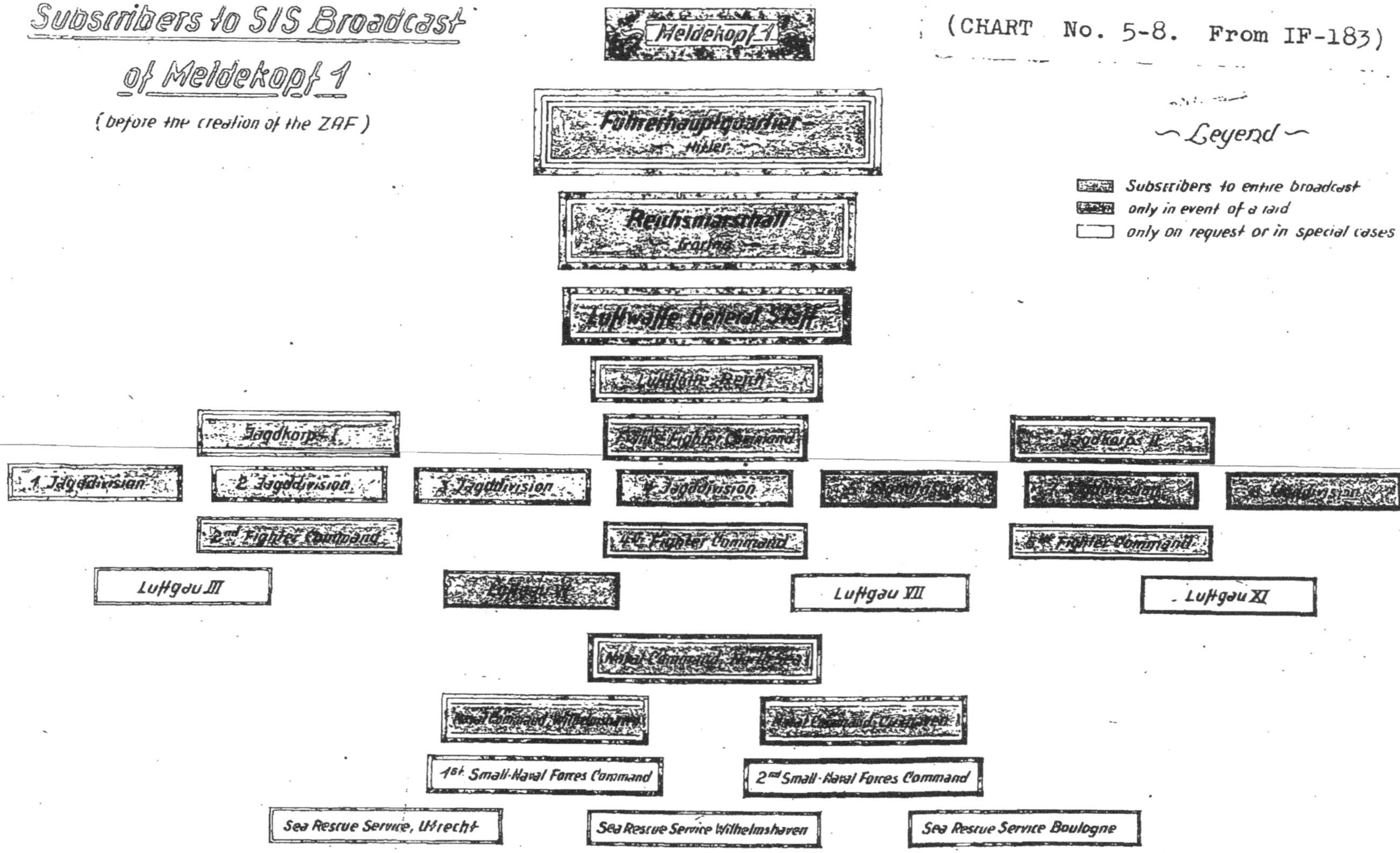

- 11a -

DOCID: 3560829

Operations Room of Meldekopf 1 — Heiligenstadt

~ November 1944 – March 1945 ~

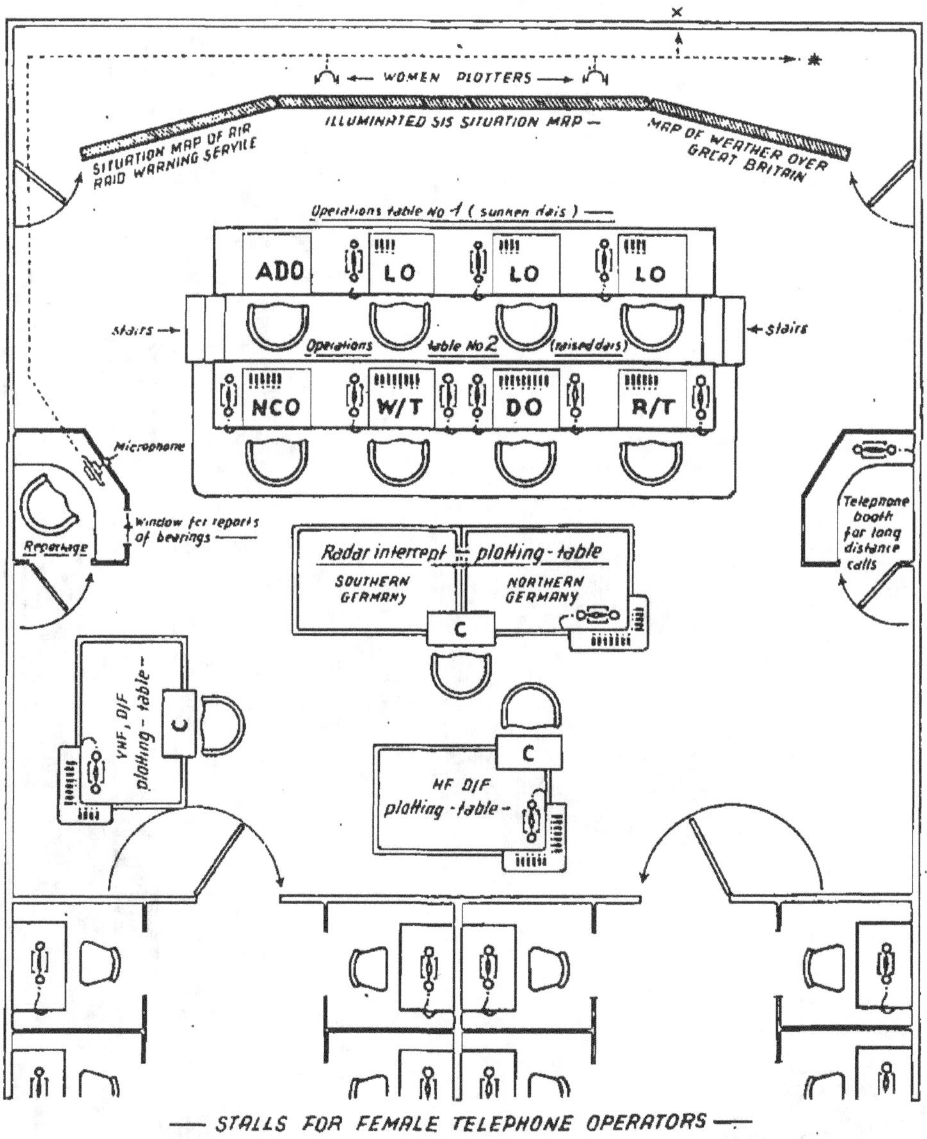

~ Legend ~

SYMBOLS:

- Switchboard
- Telephone
- C — Female Clerk
- ✱ —— SIS broadcast, W/T
- × —— SIS broadcast, telephone

ABBREVIATIONS:

ADO	Ass't duty officer
NCO	NCO in charge of wall maps
W/T	W/T specialist
R/T	R/T specialist
DO	Duty officer
LO	Liaison officers for various Hqs

(CHART No. 5-9. From IF-183)

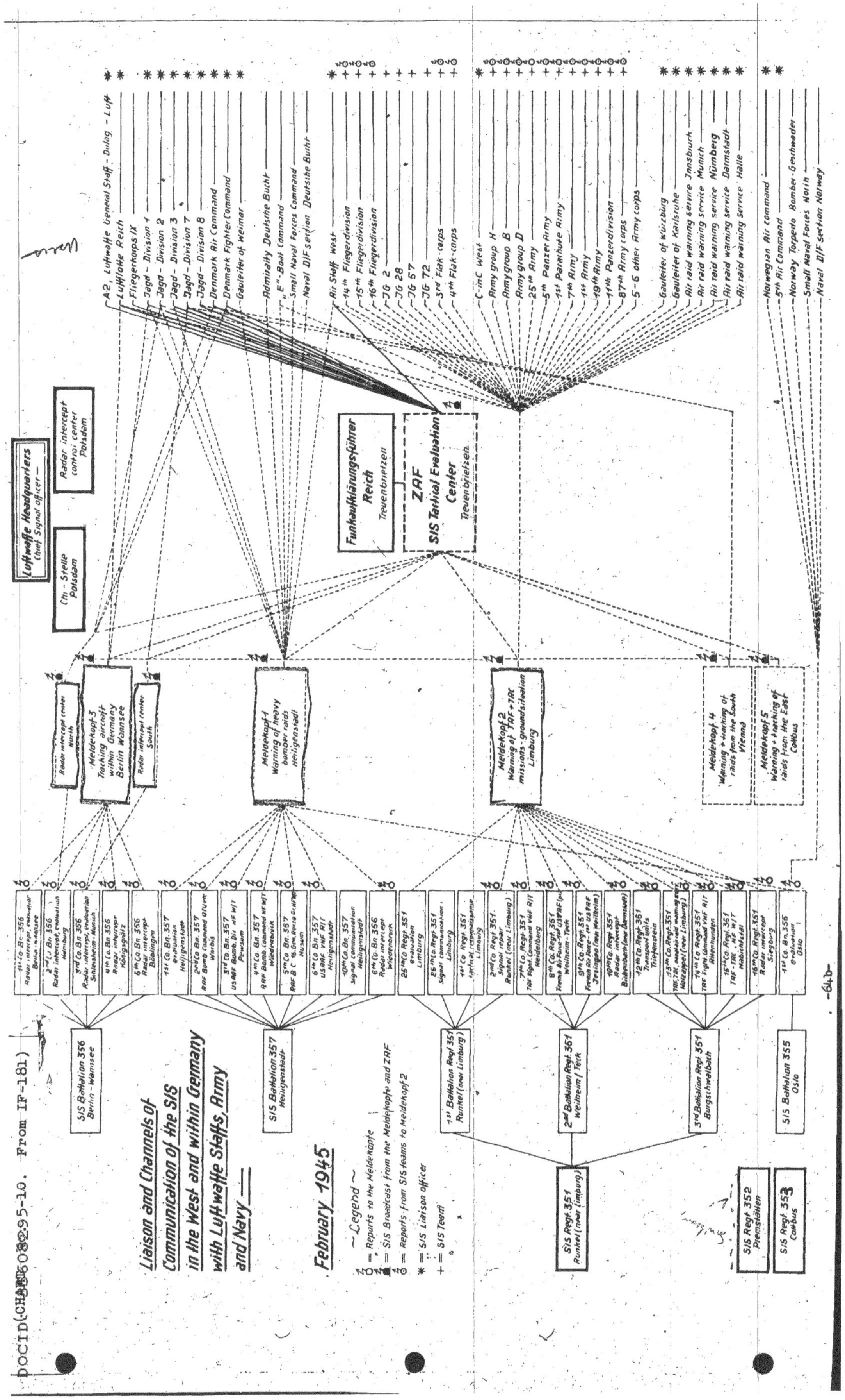
DOCID: 3560809
From IF-181
Liaison and Channels of Communication of the SIS in the West and within Germany with Luftwaffe Staffs, Army and Navy
February 1945
Luftwaffe Headquarters
Chief Signal officer
Chi - Stelle Potsdam
Radar intercept control center Potsdam
Funkaufklärungsführer Reich Treuenbrietzen
ZAF SIS Tactical Evaluation Center Treuenbrietzen
SIS Battalion 356 Berlin - Wannsee
SIS Battalion 357 Heiligenstadt
SIS Regt 351 Runkel (near Limburg)
SIS Battalion 355 Oslo
SIS Regt 352 Premslaffen
SIS Regt 353 Cotbus
-64b-

DOCID: 3560829

~~TOP SECRET "U"~~ TICOM/I-182

(CHART No. 5-11. From I-182)

Organisation of the Sigint Unit "I/353"

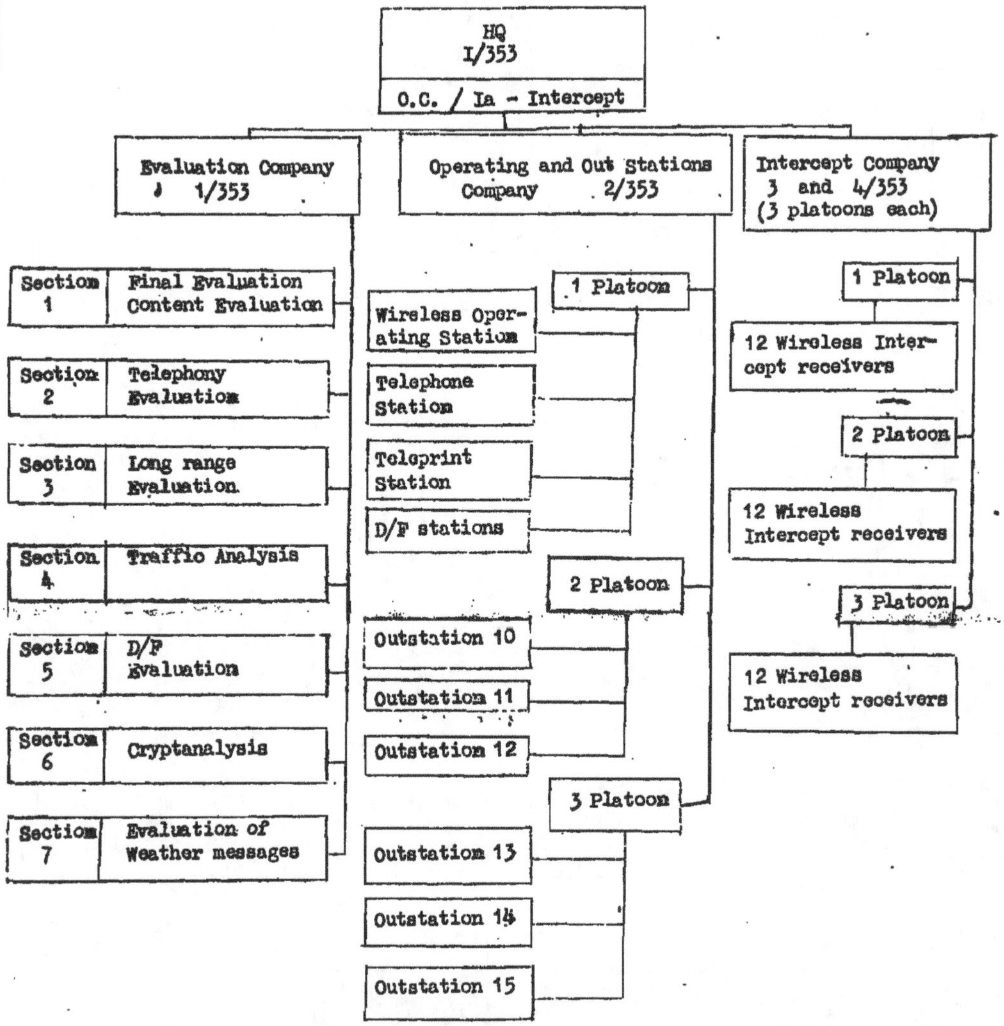

DOCID: 3560829

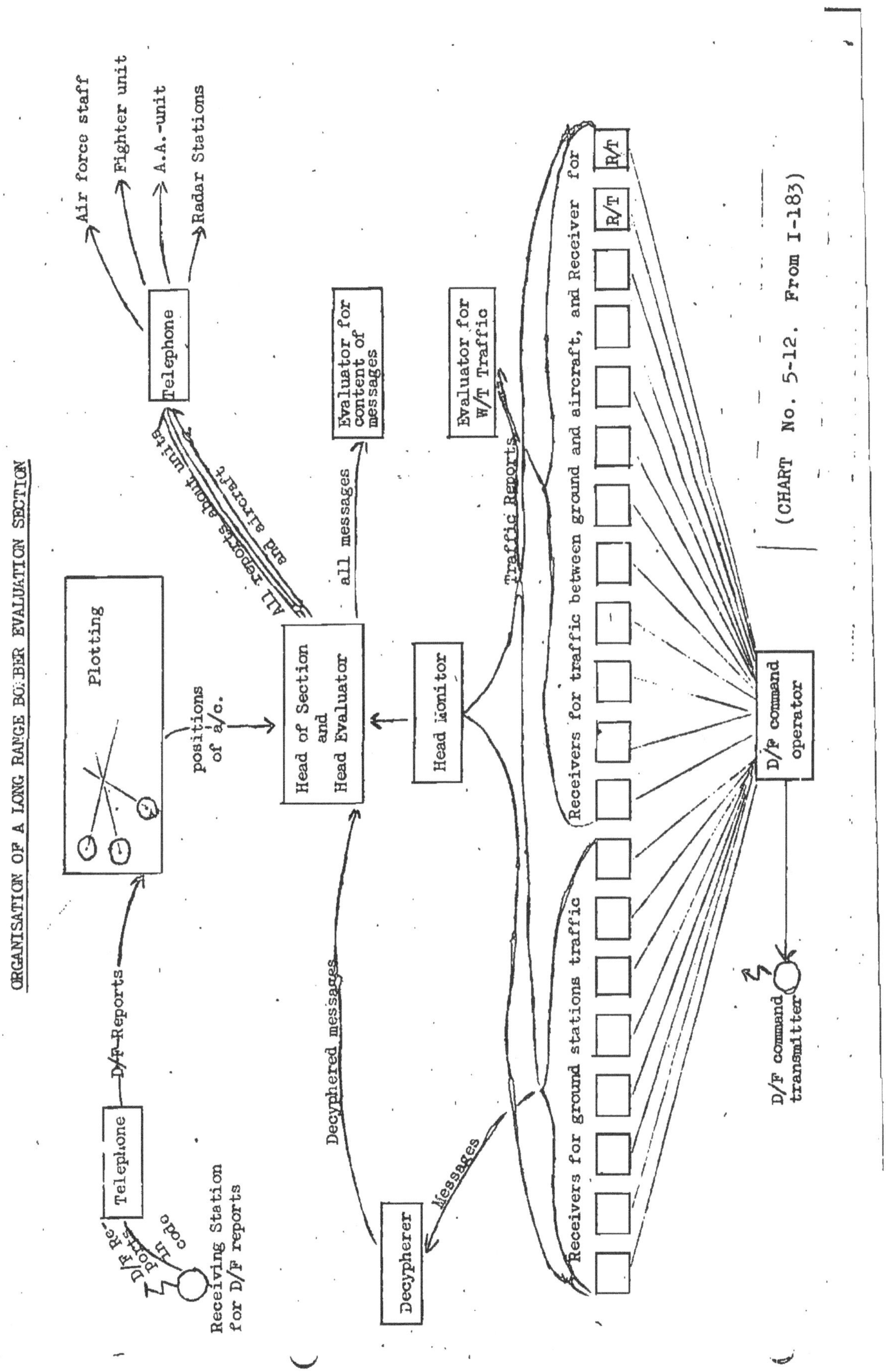

(CHART No. 5-12. From I-183)

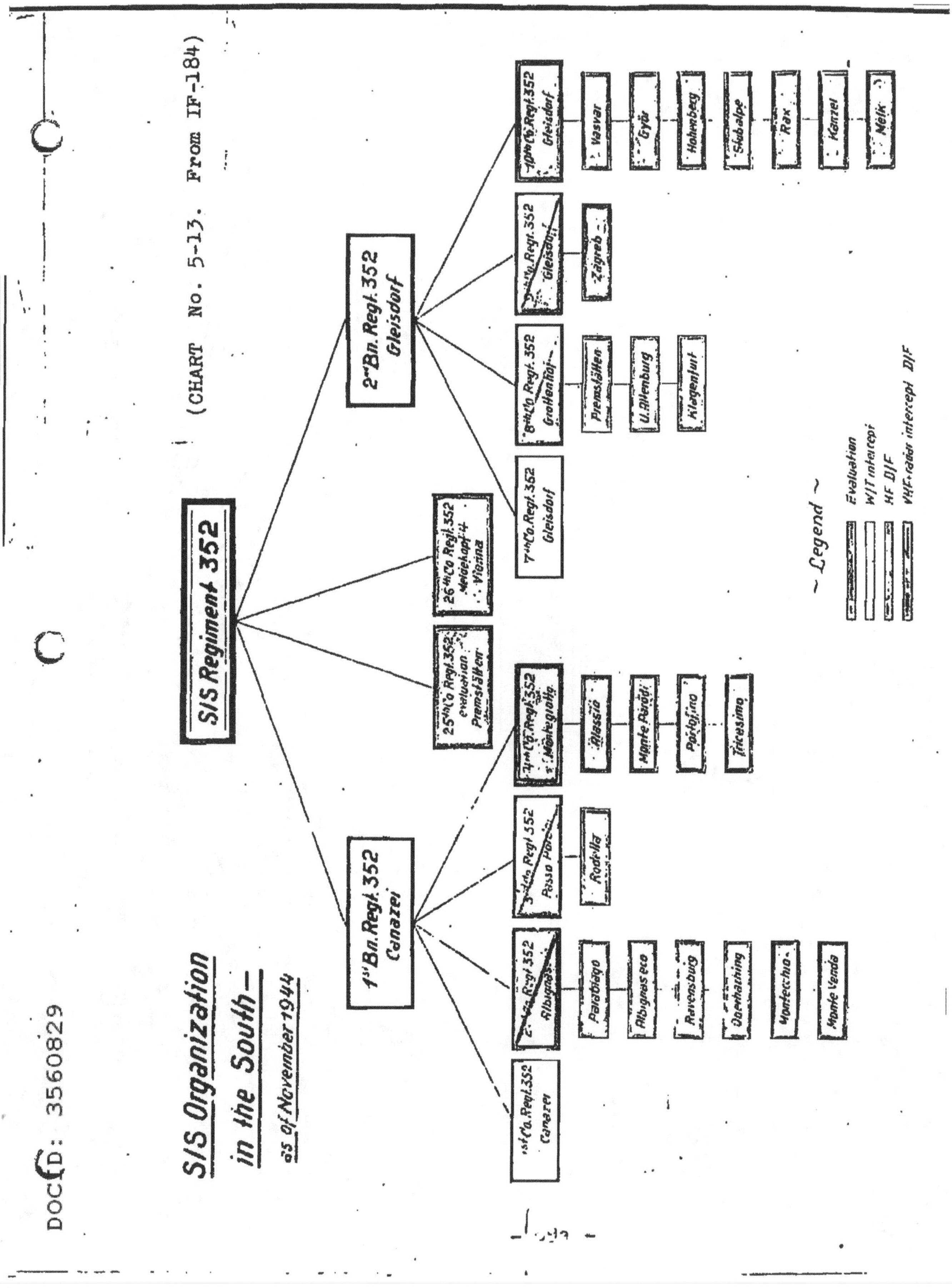
DOCID: 3560829
(CHART No. 5-13. From IF-184)
S/S Organization in the South—
as of November 1944
S/S Regiment 352
1st Bn. Regt. 352 Canazei
2nd Bn. Regt. 352 Gleisdorf
25th Co. Regt. 352 evaluation Premstätten
26th Co. Regt. 352 Meldekopf 4 Vienna
1st Co. Regt. 352 Canazei
2nd Co. Regt. 352 Albignasego
3rd Co. Regt. 352 Passo Pordoi
4th Co. Regt. 352 Montegiorgio
7th Co. Regt. 352 Gleisdorf
8th Co. Regt. 352 Grottenhof
9th Co. Regt. 352 Gleisdorf
10th Co. Regt. 352 Gleisdorf
Paradiso
Albignasego
Ravensburg
Oberhaching
Montecchio
Monte Venda
Rodella
Alassio
Monte Pardo
Portofino
Tricesimo
Premstätten
U. Hillenburg
Klagenfurt
Zagreb
Vasvar
Györ
Hohenberg
Stubalpe
Rax
Kanzel
Melk
~ Legend ~
Evaluation
W/T intercept
HF D/F
VHF + radar intercept D/F

DOCID: 3560829

(CHART No. 5-14. From IF-184)

Liaison and Channels of Communications of the SIS in the South — Fall of 1944 —

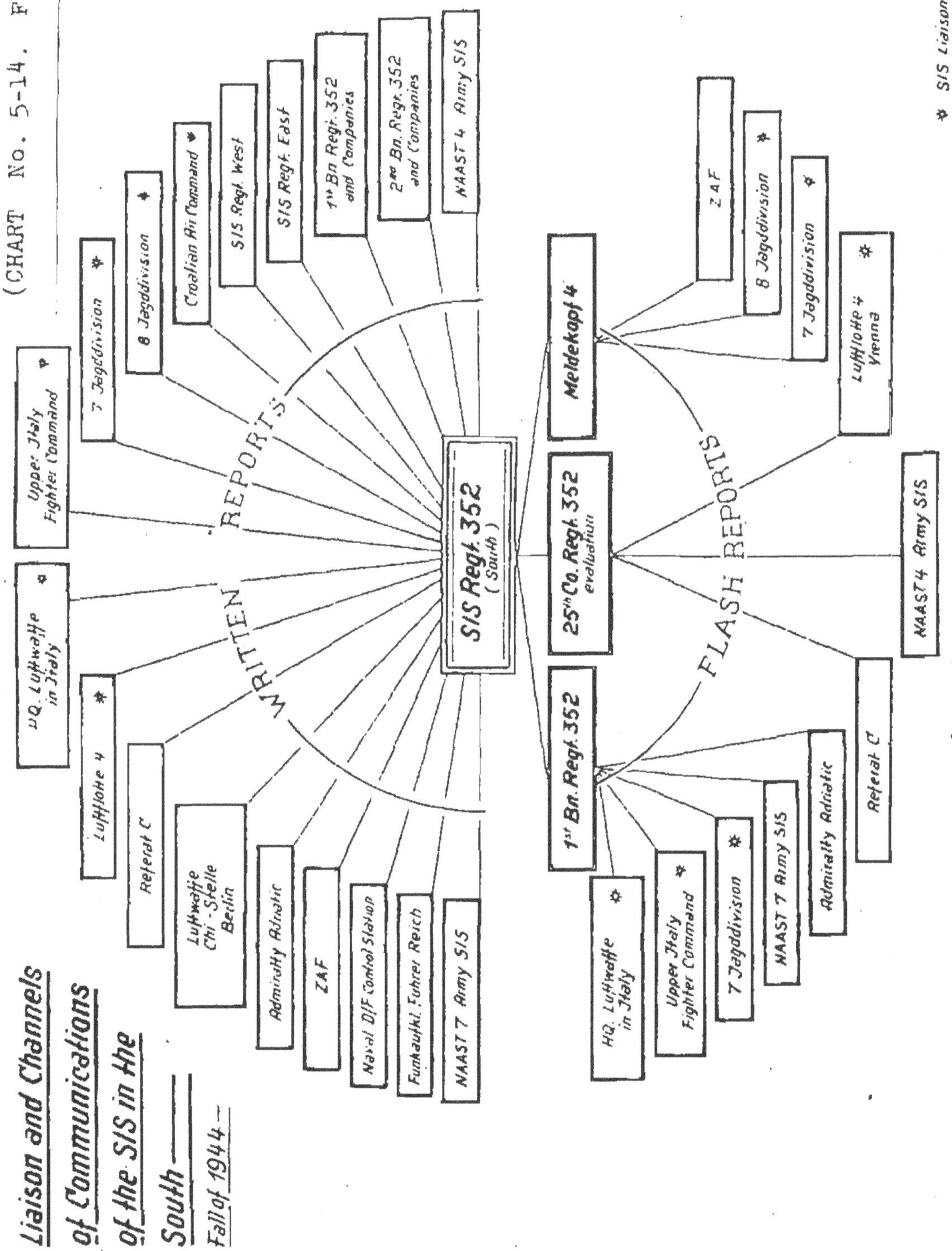

- 70 -

DOCID: 3560829

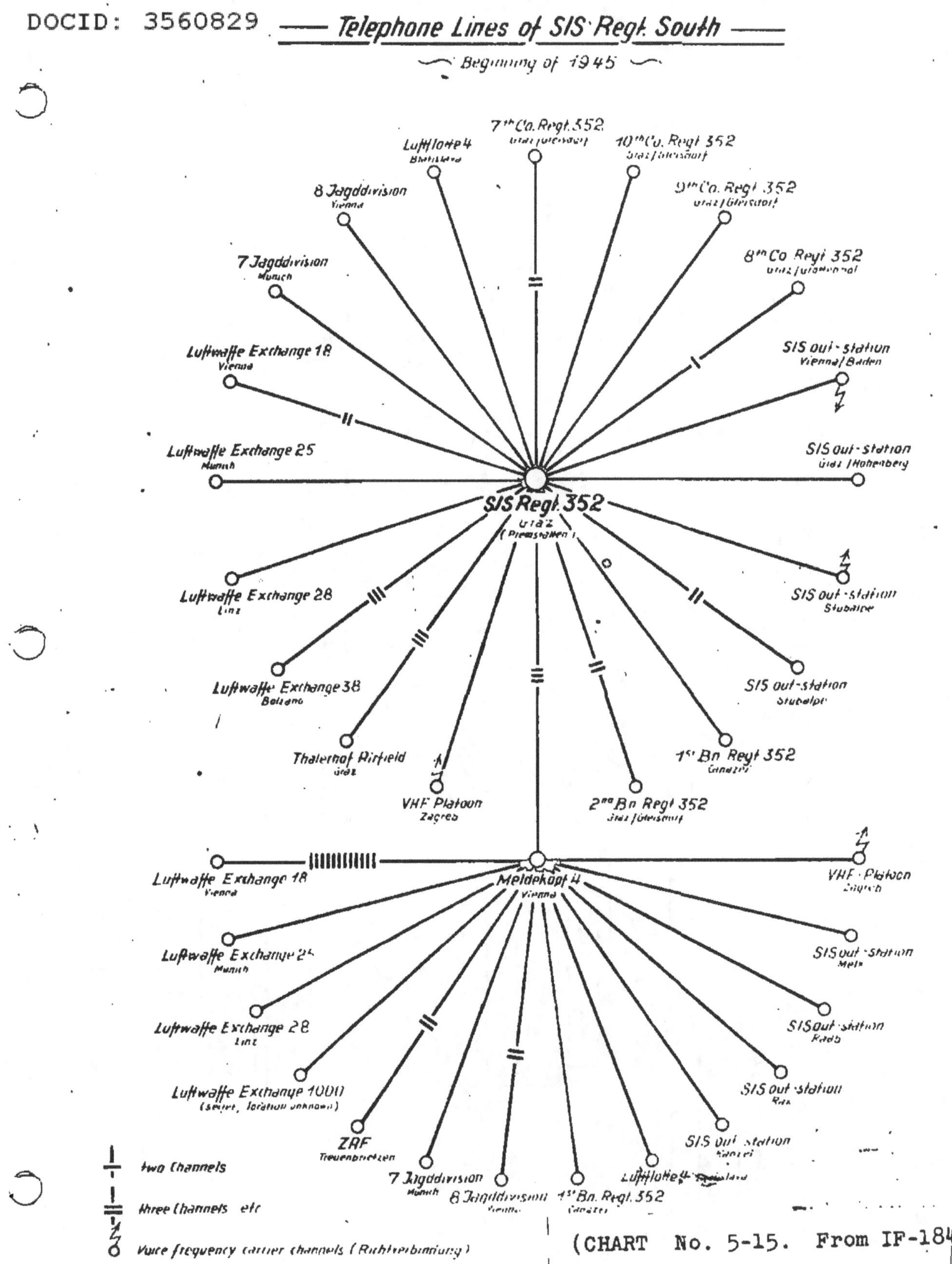

(CHART No. 5-15. From IF-184

- 71b -

Teletype Network of SIS Regt. South

Beginning of 1945

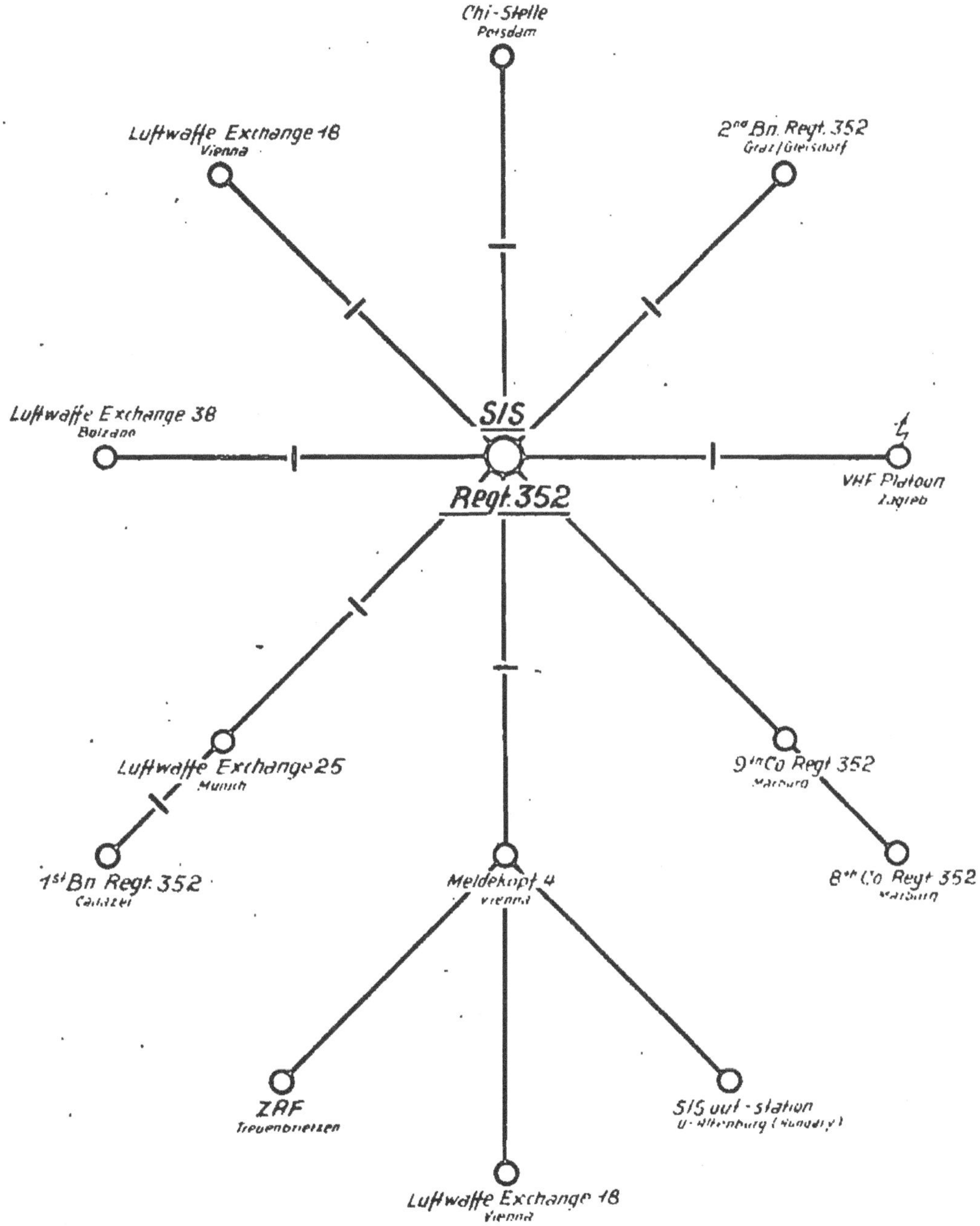

– Radio Teletype Carrier Channel (Richtverbindung)

– Teletype - Cipher Machine ("G" Schreiber)

(CHART No. 5-16. From IF-184)

- 72a -

DOCID: 3560829

SIS Radio Networks in the South

— Beginning of 1945 —

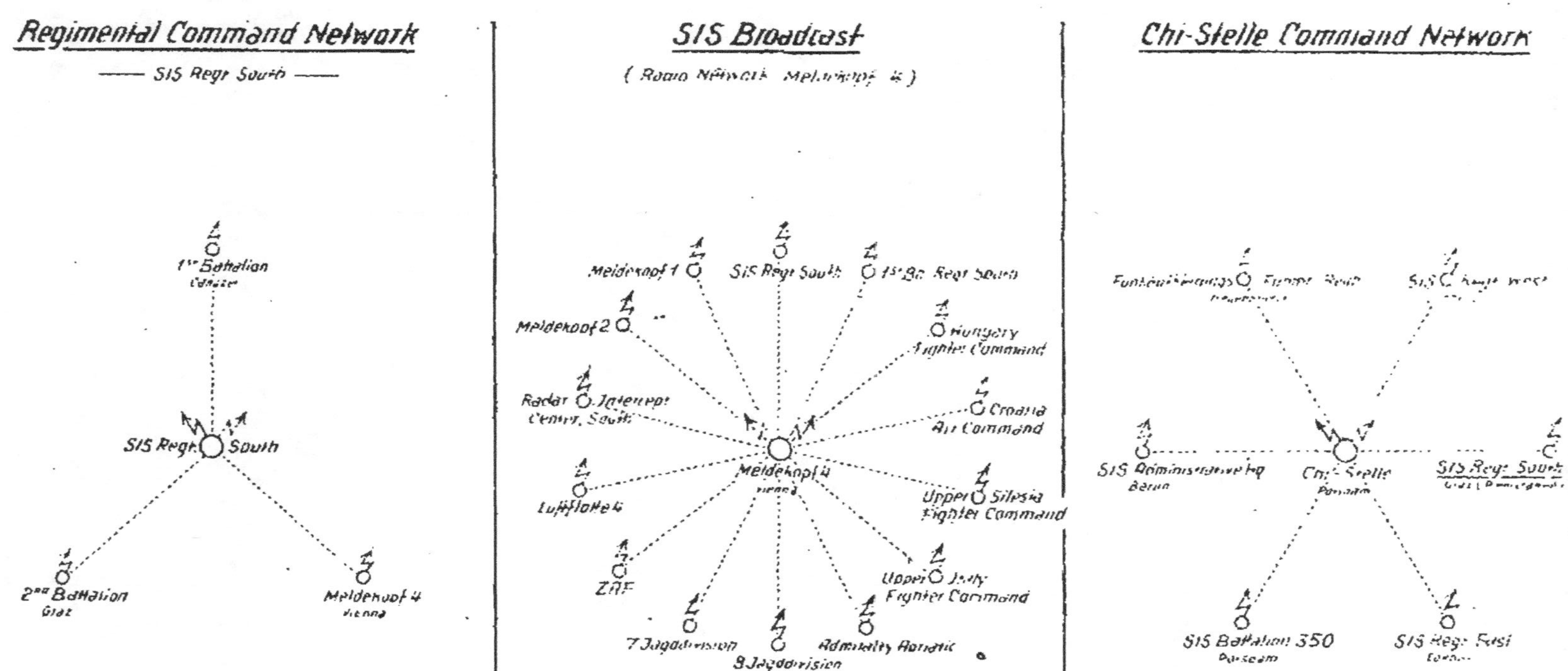

(CHART No. 5-17. From IF-184)

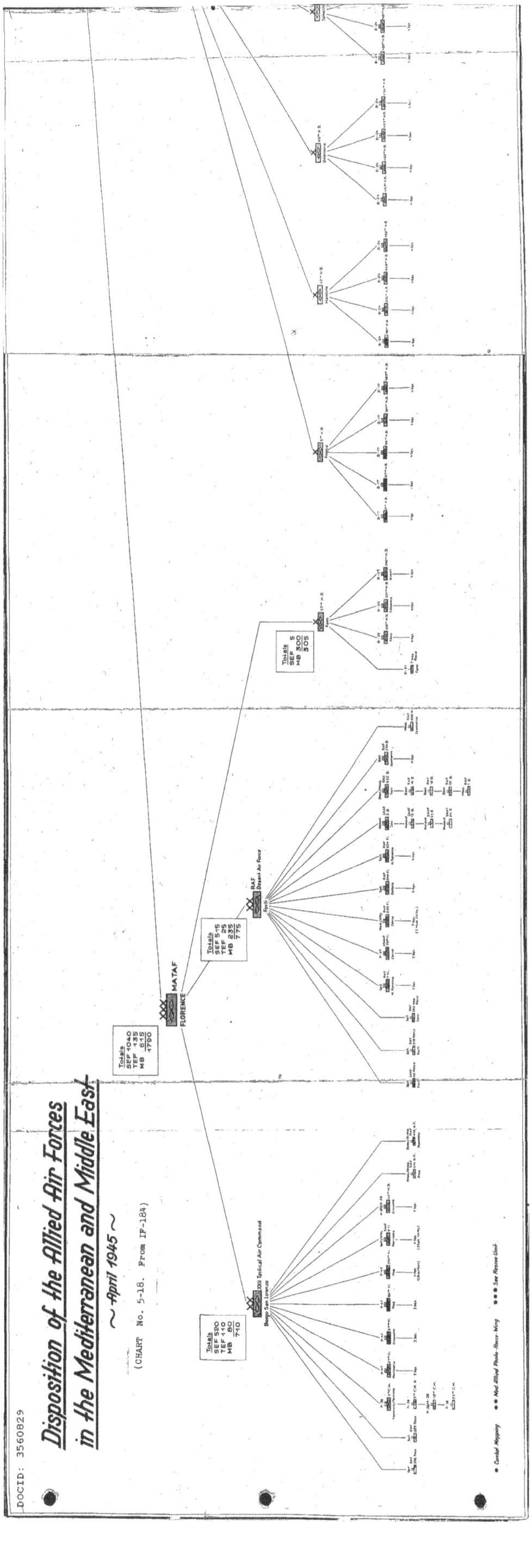
DOCID: 3560829
Disposition of the Allied Air Forces in the Mediterranean and Middle East
~April 1945~
(CHART No. 5-18. From IP-184)
Totals SEF 1040 TEF 135 MB 615 1790
MATAF
FLORENCE
Totals SEF 515 TEF 25 MB 235 775
RAF Desert Air Force
Forli
Totals SEF 5 MB 300 305
Fano
Totals SEF 520 TEF 110 MB 80 710
XXII Tactical Air Command
Borgo San Lorenzo

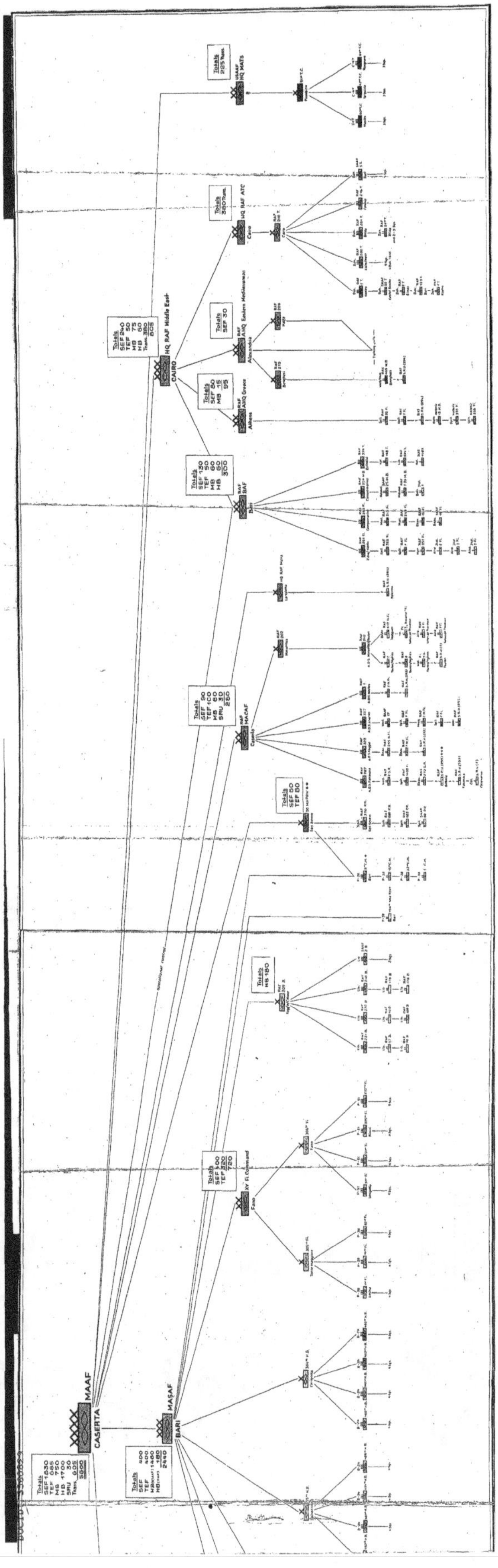
MAAF
CASERTA
MASAF
BARI
HQ RAF Middle East
CAIRO

: 3486663

TOP SECRET CREAM

ARMY SECURITY AGENCY

Washington, D. C.

EUROPEAN AXIS SIGNAL INTELLIGENCE IN WORLD WAR II AS REVEALED BY "TICOM" INVESTIGATIONS AND BY OTHER PRISONER OF WAR INTERROGATIONS AND CAPTURED MATERIAL, PRINCIPALLY GERMAN

VOLUME 6--THE FOREIGN OFFICE CRYPTANALYTIC SECTION

Prepared under the direction of the

CHIEF, ARMY SECURITY AGENCY

1 May 1946

WDGAS-14

S-4761
no. on yellow card
one on shelf

TOP SECRET CREAM

VOLUME 6

THE FOREIGN OFFICE CRYPTANALYTIC SECTION

DOCID: 3486663

VOLUME 6

THE FOREIGN OFFICE CRYPTANALYTIC SECTION (PER Z S)

Chapter I. History and Leading Personalities

1. Introduction.--A paper covering the genesis, history, and operations of the German Foreign Office Cryptanalytic Section can claim neither completeness nor absolute accuracy. The reasons for this deficiency are attributable to the paucity of data available as a basis for the paper.

In the first place, the existence of the Foreign Office Cryptanalytic Section (Pers Z S) while suspected, had never been definitely established until the Section was captured in April 1945. There was consequently little or no background information to assist the interrogators. Secondly, the exploitation of this specific target was the first major exploitation undertaken by TICOM. As such, it suffered from the general lack of experience found in new undertakings.

The interrogations, it is felt, were not extensive enough. So large was the field covered by the Pers Z S cryptanalytic effort -- over fifty countries during a period of twenty-five years -- that few interrogators were available who were competent to meet the German cryptanalysts on their own ground. Most of the interrogators and target officers were men who had not enjoyed any extensive experience on diplomatic systems; their work for some years had dealt with military problems. Faced with the necessity of conducting complete interrogations on subjects with which they were unfamiliar or on which, for security reasons, they could not openly appear to be well-informed, there were inevitably areas which were not completely covered. The interrogations, therefore, cover little more than those highlights which the Germans most readily recalled. Cryptanalysis was emphasized, while intelligence was almost completely neglected.

1

In May 1945, the TICOM principle of requiring prisoners to do extensive "homework," that is, write papers, as detailed as possible and in their own words, was not fully developed. The only Pers Z S report of this type, a most significant document from the cryptographic point of view, was issued with an apology for its preparation.[1]

There are equally serious deficiencies in the Pers Z S documents which were captured by TICOM. Little of the material had any currency; most of the documents antedated 1942. The records of the Turkish group and the records of the Mathematical-Cryptanalytical Subsection were alleged to have been and most probably had been completely destroyed prior to capture.

The account which follows, therefore, cannot pretend to be a complete statement as to the Pers Z S organization, its cryptanalytic effort, or its achievements. It is based entirely upon TICOM sources, and must therefore be regarded as a compilation of highlights, and a listing of certain clues which suggest facts and conclusions but do not document them.

2. German Foreign Office Organization for Cryptanalysis, Communications, and Security-- For many years the cryptanalytic activities of the German Foreign Office were concentrated in the "Special" (Cryptanalytic) Section, Z Branch, Personnel Bureau (Personal Z Sonderdienst, or Sonderdienst des Referats Z in der Personalabteilung des Auswaertigen Amtes). The section was generally called Pers Z S, an abbreviation of its short German title. It engaged in cryptanalysis of foreign diplomatic codes and ciphers. It did not work on military problems.[2]

Z Branch, referred to hereinafter as Pers Z, was headed by Minister (Gesandter) Selchow. Z Branch was latterly organized into four sections, one of which was the foregoing "Special" (or Cryptanalytic) Section (Sonderdienst, or Pers Z S). The Cryptographic Section (Chiffrierabteilung, or Chiffrierdienst, abbreviated Pers Z Chi), headed by Senior Specialist (Oberregierungsrat) Horst Hauthal, was engaged in the compilation and distribution of the codes and ciphers used by the Foreign Office. The Communications Section (Referat fuer Funkwesen, or Funkreferat, abbreviated as Pers Z F), headed by Senior Specialist (Oberregierungsrat) Ernst Hoffmann, handled the Foreign Office communications systems, including teletype circuits, telephone switchboards and radio links. The Administrative Section (Generalreferat, abbreviated Pers Z Gen), headed by Senior Specialist (Oberregierungsrat) Dr. Roy, handled personnel and administrative problems for the whole of Z Branch.[3]

[1] See I 89, Dr. Rohrbach's "Report on the American Strip Cipher"

[2] TICOM I 22 para 3

[3] I.1 p 14

DOCID: 3486663

3. History and Strength, 1919-1937-- The Foreign Office code and cipher work had originally been done in Bureau I (Abteilung I), the normal administrative bureau in a German governmental department. Its name at that time was probably the "Political Intelligence Bureau." As its cryptanalytic and cryptographic work expanded, it changed its name, taking the cover afforded by "Personnel Bureau."[4] Another source stated that the section was formerly known as the Cipher Section (Chiffrierabteilung), later concealed under the lengthy cover-name listed in Paragraph 2 above.[5] As late as 1925 the cryptographic activities and the cryptanalytic activities were unified under one head.[6]

It is not known when the Foreign Office started its cryptanalytic endeavors after the first World War. It is known that Zastrow, the Pers Z S expert on American systems, had seniority in the organization dating from December 1st, 1918. In any event, an uncautioned personnel list, dated May 1919, listed the names of [illegible] men and 11 women.[7] While the significance of the list is unknown, it does include the names of such well known personalities as Kasper, Kunze, Schauffler, Scherschmidt and Zastrow, all of whom were Pers Z S cryptanalysts in 1945. It is probably safe to assume that Foreign Office cryptanalytic efforts were well advanced before the conclusion of the peace treaty.

No documentary evidence is available on the strength of the organization during the period 1920-1937. In 1945 Paschke and Schauffler stated that, beginning with 20-30 people in 1918, the organization grew to a strength of approximately 50 in 1930.[8] This statement tends to support the view that the May 1919 list of 63 persons included more than cryptanalytic personnel, and was probably a list of Foreign Office cryptographic, communications and cryptanalytic personnel.

[4] I 1 p 14. A sentence in Document T56, Reports of the A Group, Page 52, gives a clue as to the section's former name: "The solution..(was)... achieved in the E Section of the Political Intelligence Bureau of the Foreign Office (E(entzifferungs??) abteilung der Politischen Nachrichtenstelle des Auswaertigen Amtes.

[5] I 22 para 3. Statement from Dr. Rohrbach. Since Dr. Rohrbach did not join Pers Z S until after the outbreak of war, the statement should be taken with reserve.

[6] DF 17 T3273 p 3

[7] DF 17 T3273

[8] I 22 para 125

3

4. Expansion, 1937-1939.--Captured documents show that the whole strength of Pers Z (including the four sections listed above in Par 1) came to 77 persons on November 1, 1937, and to 72 persons on July 1, 1938.[9] Unfortunately these lists did not give a detailed sectional breakdown. At least 20 persons were engaged in cryptographic work (compilation, security and message center), and it seems safe to deduce that the Cryptanalytic Section (Sonderdienst, or Pers Z S) did not dispose of a number greater than the estimate given above for the year 1930. Indeed, it could be assumed that the 1930 estimate of 50 persons was excessive. Data for the year 1939 tend to confirm this impression. Paschke and Kunze estimated the 1939 Pers Z S strength at 80-100 people.[10] A captured document gives a detailed breakdown of Pers Z S personnel as of December 1, 1939, showing a total strength of 92 persons.[11] Other documents show that 45 new appointments were made between September 1, 1939 and an unspecified date in November 1939.[12] Of these, 22 were regular appointments (Etatsstellen) and 23 were newly requested war service appointments (neuaufgeforderte Kriegsstellen). If the strength on December 1, 1939 were 92, and if 45 persons had been hired since September 1, 1939, then it seems reasonable to estimate the Pers Z S strength prior to the war as something less than 50 persons.

The available documents for the period 1937-1939 give the impression that all of Z Branch might have suffered from personnel shortages and inertia on the part of higher administrative authorities. The job descriptions (Begruendungen) accompanying the 1938 recommendations for promotion show that Dr. Kunze had been a specialist (Regierungsrat) since 1923, and that Paschke and Scherschmidt had held the same grade since 1927. Attention was drawn to the fact that:

> "Positions with comparable activities and responsibilities in other ministries are given the grade of Principal Specialist (Ministerialrat) or Senior Specialist (Oberregierungsrat). This in spite of the fact that the personnel concerned are usually younger and have had less time in grade."[13]

9 TF 24, Pers Z/1147, and 1938 personnel list

10 I-22, para 125

11 TF 24, Pers Z S Organization as of December 1, 1939

12 TF 24, Personnel list, dated November 1939

13 TF-24, 1938 Begruendungen. Such complaints are apt to be generic in governmental organization. No valid conclusions could be drawn without comparable data from other ministries.

The Cryptographic Section (Pers Z Chi) complained in the same year that it could no longer function efficiently without additional personnel.[14] Ten of its thirteen cryptographers were over fifty years of age, six of them over sixty. Night work represented too much of a strain for men of this age.

> "Due to the overloading of the Cryptographic Section, outgoing messages cannot be enciphered and checked with the necessary care. This regrettable state of affairs was most noticeable during May 1938, and September 1938, when the political atmosphere was at its tensest."

As of December 1, 1939, then, the Cryptanalytic Section (Pers Z S) had a strength of 92 persons. It was organized as follows:

LOCATION*	UNIT	STRENGTH	TOTAL
Luisenstift, under Dr. Schauffler	Schauffler's Group (Gruppe)	8	
	Paschke's Group	13	
	Scherschmidt's Group	10	
	Brandes' Group	11	
	Zastrow's Group	9	
	Karstien's Group	5	
	Kasper's Group	4	
	Hagen's Group	4	
	Records Group (Archiv)	4	
	Clerical Personnel	3	72
Jaegerstrasse 12 III, under Dr. Kunze	Special Group (Stosztrupp) [Mathematical cryptanalysis]	20	20
			92

* The exact location of Pers Z S prior to 1939 is unknown. In 1938 parts of the organization were housed at Wilhelmstrasse 75. In February 1939, unidentified elements were housed in the Koenigin Luise Stiftung, Berlin-Dahlem, Podbielski Allee 78. This location was called the "Luisenstift." Nothing is known as to the dates for occupation or evacuation of the quarters in Jaegerstrasse 12 III.

5. Further Wartime Expansion.--No detailed figures are available to cover the Z Branch expansion during the early war

[14] TF 24, Supplement to Pers Z/1400 of Nov 2, 1938

[15] TF 24, Personnel List dated October 1, 1940

5

years. By October 1, 1940, there were 290 employees in the entire branch, a three hundred per cent increase over the previously quoted figure of 72 for July 1, 1938.[15] On October 19, 1940 Pers Z S was stated to occupy quarters in three buildings, implying a further expansion over the 1939 figure.[16]

The last available statements as to total personnel are dated in January 1941.[17] At that time, Dr. Kunze reported he had 53 persons employed in the Jaegerstrasse, while Schauffler reported 88 persons at the Dahlem-Podbielski Allee location, a total personnel of 141.

In spite of the expansion, there is good evidence that the Pers Z S leaders still considered their personnel inadequate to cope with all problems. On November 26, 1940 (Schauffler?? - signature illegible) submitted a list of cryptanalytic problems ranging through seventeen countries, all of which were either completely neglected or insufficiently exploited due to personnel shortages.[18] He requested additional personnel to the number of 62, detailing the problems to which they would be assigned. In January 1941, Dr. Kunze requested 57 additional employees, 28 of whom would be employed on American and British problems, and Schauffler requested an additional increment of 17. Nothing is known from documentary sources as to whether or not these requests were favorably received.[19]

[15] TF 24, Personnel List dated October 1, 1940

[16] Berlin-Dahlem, Im Dol 2-6,5; the Luisenstift; and "some rooms" in the Ethnographic Museum (Museum fuer Voelkerkunde) at Prinz Albrecht and Koeniggraetzer Streets. These housing arrangements were to remain substantially unchanged until December 1943. The Jaegerstrasse quarters were in use as late as January 18, 1941.

[17] TF 24. Letters listing strength and requirements. One, dated January 18, 1941 is headed "Jaegerstrasse 12 III" and signed "K" (almost certainly Kunze). The other, headed "Dienststelle Podbielski Allee," is dated January 14, 1941 and signed by Schauffler.

[18] TF 24. Letter of Nov. 26, 1940.

[19] TF 24. Two letters, Pers Z/5705, dated November 12, 1941, and a letter from the Personnel Bureau of the Foreign Office, dated January 17, 1942, may be revealing. In the first letter, Minister (Gesandter) Selchow, head of Pers Z, requested the immediate allocation of 155 Labor Service Girls (Arbeitsmaiden) due to the "special haste incident to the execution of the Foreign Minister's new request ("wegen der besonderen Eile der Durchfuehrung der vom Herrn Reichsminister gestellten neuen Anforderung"). In the second letter, Principal Specialist (Legationsrat) Schwaeger, referring specifically to the Pers Z request for 313 regular employees, stated that the 1941 budgetary allocations had been exhausted. He cited the critical state of the labor market, and concluded that the request should be rephrased or rejustified on the ground that it was essential to the war effort ("aus kriegswichtigen Gruenden").

When the Section was captured in April 1945, its leaders stated that the peak in personnel was reached in 1945, when 180-200 persons were employed.[20] Another employee "thought" the total personnel was about 120.[21] Regardless of conflicting statements, it seems clear that Pers Z S never became a large organization, and that its personnel never exceeded two hundred in number.

6. <u>Organizational and Geographical Changes, 1943-1945</u>.--No major changes were made in the organization until December 1943. At that time, Berlin was partially evacuated on account of the

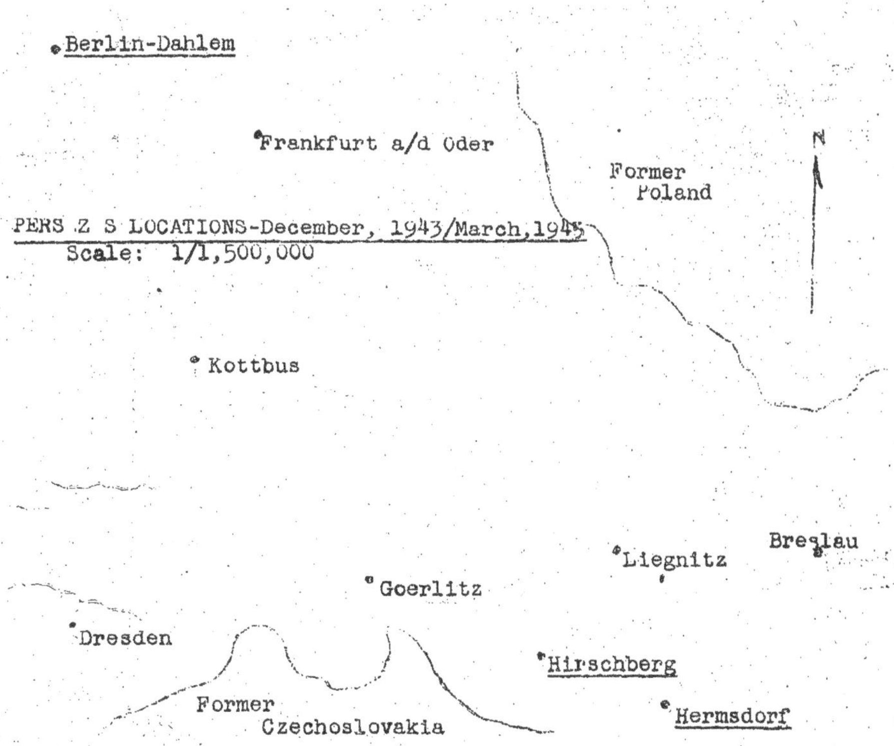

20 I 22, para 125

21 I 22, para 34

RAF bombings, and Pers Z S was split into one large group and two smaller groups. Dr. Schauffler and Dr. Paschke remained in Berlin-Dahlem, at Im Dol 2-6,5, with the main party (Stammabteilung). This party may have been reinforced by "parts of......Signal Intelligence Agency, Supreme Command of the Armed Forces (OKW/Chi)" which had been bombed out at the same time.[22] A part of Dr. Paschke's Subsection, under the leadership of Specialist (Regierungsrat) Dr. Karstien, went to Hirschberg in the Riesengebirge. The Mathematical-Cryptanalytic

PERS Z S LOCATIONS- April, 1945
Scale: 1 / 1,500,000

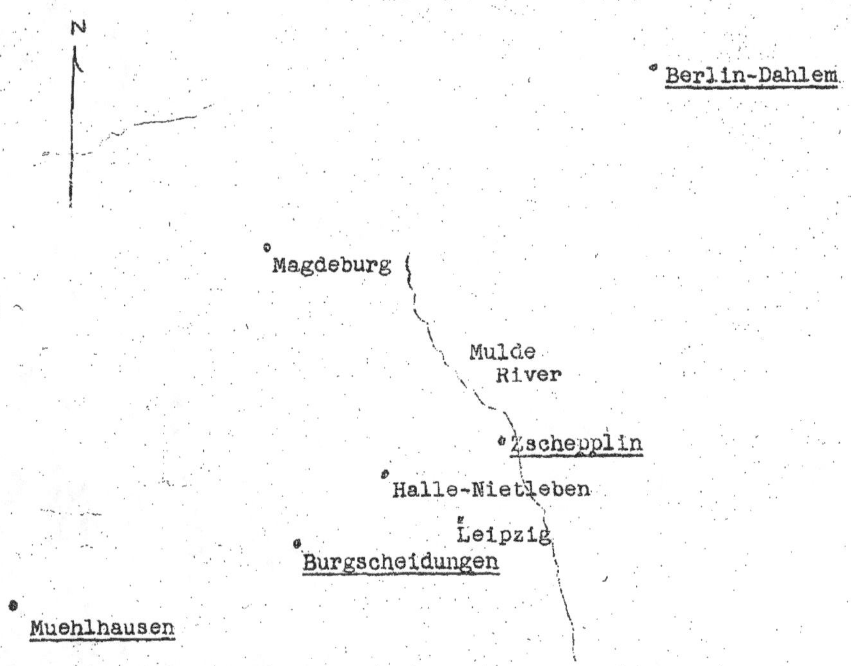

22 I-96, p 5. There is some evidence that there was an actual unification of certain Pers Z S-Signal Intelligence Agency of the Supreme Command of the Armed Forces (OKW/Chi) subsections after November 1943. For detailed discussion, see Chapter 4.

Subsection under Dr. Kunze, together with the I.B.M. machinery, was evacuated to Hermsdorf in Silesia. The three parties attempted to work as one, with a daily courier service linking all three locations.[23]

In February and March 1945, as the Russian advances became more threatening, the Hirschberg and Hermsdorf locations were evacuated. The Karstien group moved directly from Hirschberg to Burgscheidungen in the Unstrut area. They were joined there in April by Dr. Schauffler and some of the former Berlin-Dahlem group. Dr. Kunze's Mathematical-Cryptanalytic Subsection was split up, elements proceeding from Hermsdorf to Muehlhausen, and the majority, including the leaders, to Zschepplin. Dr. Paschke brought most of his subsection from Berlin to Zschepplin. An unidentified Pers Z S group went from Berlin to the Army-Air Force Signal School at Halle-Nietleben, later proceeding to Zschepplin.[24] No intercept traffic was received after March 1945. Some cryptanalytic work was continued on back material until the Burgscheidungen-Zschepplin areas were overrun in April 1945.

7. Important Personnel.--This paragraph consists of a compilation of data on some thirty Pers Z and Pers Z S personalities.

a. Z Branch (Pers Z) Personalities.

(1) Minister (Gesandter I Kl.) Selchow. Selchow was chief of Z Branch. Little is known of his background. Mention was made of the fact that he had engaged in similar work during World War I.[25] A personnel list, without a caption, dated May 1919, lists his name along with 62 others, presumptively in Foreign Office cryptographic or cryptanalytic activity.[26] The date of his appointment as head of Z Branch (Referat Z) is unknown. One source states that he had been head of the Branch since 1919.[27] He is listed as a Principal Foreign Office Specialist (Vortragender Legationsrat) on November 1, 1937.[28] He held the rank of Minister (Gesandte) in 1945. A document dated 1941 contains recommendations for the promotion of Senior Specialists (Oberregierungsraete) Paschke, Schauffler and

23 See Chart 6-1, and I-22, p 23

24 I 1, p 7

25 I 143, para 44

26 DF 17, T3273

27 I 1, p 17

28 TF 24, Personnel List of November 1 1937

Langlotz to Principal Foreign Office Specialists (Vortragende Legationsraete).[29] It might be deduced from this document that Selchow had been appointed Minister in 1940 or 1941.

But little more is known as to his ability. Statements from personnel in other cryptanalytic agencies imply that he was jealous and secretive about Z Branch (Referat Z) activities. His Pers Z S subordinates characterized him as "a competent administrator who knew little about cryptanalysis and was content to leave the specialists to run their affairs as it seemed best to them."[30]

Last reported in Salzburg in March 1945, he was not apprehended by TICOM.

(2) Senior Specialist (Oberregierungsrat) Dr. Roy. Dr. Roy was head of the Administrative Section (Pers Z Gen) in Z Branch. He is reported to have been with Z Branch since the early 1920's. Taken prisoner at Muehlhausen in April 1945, he was released as being of little importance to target teams and interrogators. I-206 ...

(3) Senior Specialist (Oberregierungsrat) Ernst Hoffmann. Hoffmann had seniority in Z Branch going back to 1919.[31] A Specialist (Regierungsrat) in July 1937, he was promoted to his last grade in 1940.[32] From 1940 he was head of the Communications Section (Referat fuer Funkwesen) in Z Branch, a section newly created at that time.[33] Nothing is known as to the fate of the section.

(4) Senior Specialist (Oberregierungsrat) Horst Hauthal. Hauthal was latterly head of the Cryptographic Section (Pers Z Chi) in Z Branch. His section remained in Berlin, and nothing is known as to its fate. A young man (born March 9, 1913), his rise in Z Branch was little short of meteoric when compared with the progress of his older colleagues. Joining Z Branch as a mathematician and cryptographer in January 1940, his promotion

29 TF 24, Anlage 1, Pers Z 5617/41

30 I 1, p 17

31 DF 17 T3273

32 TF 24, Anlage 1 to Pers Z 5617/41

33 TF 24, Pers Z 647/40 refers to Hoffmann as head of the "newly created subsection for radio communications problems ("Leiter des neugeschaffenen Referats fuer Funkwesen"). Job descriptions and personnel specifications show that Pers Z F disposed of telephone, teletype and messenger services, as well as radio.

DOCID: 3486663

to Senior Specialist (Oberregierungsrat) was achieved in less than five years.[34]

b. Pers Z S Personalities.

(1) Linguistic-Cryptanalytic Subsection

(a) Senior Specialist (Oberregierungsrat) Rudolf Schauffler. Although Schauffler was head of Pers Z S, it is not clear whether this title was more than nominal in 1945. The Pers Z S members listed him as head of a Subsection in 1945, while the 1937-1941 documents list him as head of the whole Section.[35] Latterly Paschke, a more forceful type and probably an abler administrator, appears to have usurped more and more of Schauffler's responsibilities.

Starting with Z Branch immediately after World War I, Schauffler had held the grade of Senior Specialist (Oberregierungsrat) since at least November 1, 1937, and was the senior cryptanalyst in the Section. In 1941 he had been recommended for the grade of Principal Foreign Office Specialist (Vortragender Legationsrat).[36]

Originally a mathematician, his main field of interest was theoretical research (Grundlagenforschung). To this end, he edited a private periodical ("Schriften des Sonderdienstes") which was concerned primarily with cryptologic methodology.[37] His language specialties were Japanese, and Chinese, which Pers Z S cryptanalytic group he headed. He also served as an adviser to the Foreign Office Cryptographic Section (Pers Z Chi) on security. Either he or Senior Specialist (Oberregierungsrat) Hauthal of the Cryptographic Section (Pers Z Chi) represented the Foreign Office in the Army-Air-Naval Security Coordinating Conferences.[38]

(b) Senior Specialist (Oberregierungsrat) Dr. Adolf Paschke. While junior in grade to Schauffler, Dr. Paschke during the latter years of the war became, with Schauffler, the joint head of Pers Z S. His nominal title was that of head of the Linguistic-Cryptanalytic Subsection.

Joining the Foreign Office group in 1919, he became a Specialist (Regierungsrat) in 1927 and a Senior Specialist (Oberregierungsrat) between 1937 and 1940. In 1941 he was recommended to the rank of Principal Foreign Office Specialist (Vortragender Legationsrat).[39]

[36] TF 24, Anlage 1, Pers Z 5617/41

[37] I 22, para 8

[38] I 84, para 11

[39] TF 24, Anlage 1, Pers Z 5617/41

Technically he was responsible for bookbuilders and translators, heading a subsection organized by countries and languages. He was also responsible for liaison with the armed forces. His language specialties were Italian, Greek and Russian, a group for which he assumed direct technical responsibility. A man of undoubted competence, possessing a strong personality and fierce energy, with good party connections, he probably had little difficulty in forging ahead of his more academically inclined colleagues.

(c) Technical Assistant (Willenschaftlicher Hilfsarbeiter) Karl Zastrow. From available information, Zastrow was the senior member of the Cryptanalytic Section, having entered service on December 1, 1918. A gifted analyst, he never advanced into the higher grades of officialdom. Pronouncedly absent-minded, it is doubtful if he were ever a capable administrator.

From available documents he appears to have headed the American and Scandinavian language group (Gruppe) under Dr. Paschke. However, by 1945 he was no longer head of this group, which was then directed by Dr. Hans-Kurt Mueller, with Zastrow as his deputy (Vertreter). He was the Pers Z S authority on American systems.[40]

(d) Senior-Specialist (Oberregierungsrat) Wilhelm Brandes. Dr. Brandes headed the group which, under Dr. Paschke's direction, exploited systems of Dutch, Swiss, Belgian or French origin. Having served with Dr. Paschke in World War I, he came to work for the Foreign Office in 1920.[41] He is listed as a Specialist (Regierungsrat) in October 1940, and was promoted to Senior Specialist (Oberregierungsrat) sometime between 1942 and 1945. A capable linguist and bookbuilder, he also had certain liaison functions for his own group.

(e) Senior Specialist (Oberregierungsrat) Dr. Herrmann Scherschmidt. Scherschmidt is listed as having been with the Foreign Office in May 1919.[42] Promoted to Specialist (Regièrungsrat) in 1927, he became a Senior Specialist (Oberregierungsrat) sometime between 1941 and 1945. Specializing in Slavonic and Near Eastern languages, he headed the Pers Z S Turkish group from 1934 to 1939. Thereafter he took over the Slavonic group until September 1943.[43] Desiring to return to Turkish at that time, he encountered personal difficulties in his old group

[40] I 22 p 24

[41] TF 24, Job Descriptions for 1938 Promotions (Begruendungen)

[42] DF 17 T3273

[43] I 63 p 2

and transferred to the Foreign Office Document Section (translations) until September 1944. He then reassumed his old post as head of the Turkish group (under Dr. Paschke), while Dr. Benzing, the previous head, shifted to Arabian and Iranian systems.

(f) Specialist (Regierungsrat) Dr. Hans-Heidrun Karstien. The exact date of Dr. Karstien's entry into Pers Z S is unknown, but it antedated the year 1930. In November 1937, he was an unclassified employee (Tarifangestellter) in Group X, then the highest pay grade. In November 1940, he was listed as a Specialist (Regierungsrat), a grade he held at war's end.

A specialist in Balkan languages (although he worked on Japanese and Chinese systems from 1930 till 1938), he worked under Dr. Paschke's direction, handling Bulgarian, Croatian, Polish, Slovakian and (Finnish?) work. When the Berlin group was split, in December 1943, Dr. Karstien was placed in charge of the party which went to Hirschberg. Proceeding to Burgscheidungen with his party when Hirschberg was threatened by the Russian advance, he was taken prisoner there in April 1945.

(g) Specialist (Regierungsrat) Dr. Johannes Benzing. Dr. Benzing joined Pers Z S on July 20, 1937. Born January 13, 1913 he was the youngest senior official (Beamter) in the Pers Z S Section. From available data, it seems clear that he was promoted to Specialist (Regierungsrat) sometime between 1941 and December 1943.[44]

A specialist on Near Eastern languages, he originally worked on Turkish under Dr. Scherschmidt. He headed this section from October 1939 until September 1944, when Dr. Scherschmidt returned from another Section of the Foreign Office. He was then placed in charge of work on systems belonging to Iran, Iraq, and Afghanistan.[45]

(h) Technical Assistant (Wissenschaftliche Hilfsarbeiterin) Dr. Ursula Hagen. As was indicated by Miss Friedrichs, it was difficult for women, no matter how able, to achieve proper recognition or seniority in Z Branch. Miss Hagen is a case in point. Born March 23, 1901, she entered Pers Z S on October 1, 1922. By 1939 (and through 1945) she was head of the group (under Dr. Paschke) which was responsible for work on England, Ireland, Spain, Portugal, and Latin American countries. In 1942 this

44 TF 24, Anlage 1 to Pers Z 5617/41

45 I 22, p 25

involved the supervision of twelve people.[46] Her grade and remuneration were never comparable to those of men with like seniority and similar responsibilities. She is last listed (February 1941) as a Technical Assistant (Wissenschaftliche Hilfsarbeiterin) Grade IV.[47] She was captured at Zschepplin in 1945, and evacuated to Marburg.

(i) Dr. Hans-Kurt Mueller. Little is known of Dr. Mueller's background or abilities. Born May 1, 1906, he went to work in Pers Z S on January 22, 1940. Specializing on American and Scandinavian systems, he is listed in December 1943 as Zastrow's deputy (Vertreter). By April 1945, due, no doubt, to superior administrative and organizational abilities, he is listed as the head of the group, with Zastrow as his deputy (Vertreter).[48] His last known pay grade was Technical Assistant (Wissenschaftlicher Hilfsarbeiter) Grade XII.

(j) Dr. Peter Olbricht. Dr. Olbricht, a former anthropologist with the Ethnographic Museum in Berlin, went to work for Pers Z S in December 1939. An Orientalist of some repute, he specialized on Chinese, Japanese and Manchukuoan systems, working under the direction of Dr. Schauffler. He was in the Hirschberg group from December 1943, and was eventually captured at Burgscheidungen.

(k) Miss Asta Friedrichs. While holding a position with low rank and seniority, Miss Friedrichs was one of the leading personalities in Pers Z S. She joined Pers Z S in September 19[illegible] after study at the Sorbonne and the American University in Sofia. She worked under Dr. Karstien, whose deputy (Vertreterin) she was, in the Slavonic group, specializing in Bulgarian.

(l) Miss Hildegarde Schrader. Miss Schrader joined Pers Z S in September 1939, as a specialist in French. By 1943 she was deputy to Dr. Brandes in the French-Belgian-Swiss section. When Dr. Brandes fell ill in 1944, she took over the leadership of the group, which was then in Hirschberg. She was captured at Burgscheidungen. Like Miss Friedrichs and Miss Hagen, she apparently never advanced beyond the grade of Technical Assistant (Wissenschaftliche Hilfsarbeiterin) Grade IV.

(m) Dr. Otfried Deubner. Dr. Deubner started his work with Pers Z S on July 7, 1940. By the end of the war he was

46 D 16, Report 4, p 6

47 TF 24, 1941 personnel list

48 I 22, p 25

assistant (Vertreter) to Dr. Paschke in the group which handled systems from the Vatican, Italy, Greece, and the USSR.[49] He was recommended for the grade of Specialist (Regierungsrat) in 1941 but apparently worked throughout the war as a Technical Assistant (Wissenschaftlicher Hilfsarbeiter) Grade III.

(2) Mathematical-Cryptanalytic Subsection.

(a) Senior Specialist (Oberregierungsrat) Dr. Werner Kunze. Like Paschke and Schauffler, Dr. Kunze was a cryptanalyst with 25 years of Pers Z S experience. A military cryptanalyst in World War I, he joined the Foreign Office in 1919.[50] The date of his promotion to Senior Specialist (Oberregierungsrat) is unknown, but it was previous to October 1, 1940.[51]

Kunze's Subsection, the Mathematical-Cryptanalytic Subsection, usually operated apart from the main Pers Z S party (Stammabteilung). Primarily a mathematician, Dr. Kunze's subsection consisted of linguist mathematicians and was also responsible for the Pers Z S I.B.M. machinery. They specialized in difficult systems, complex encipherments, and those problems which required a large expenditure of time and personnel, or the application of technical devices.[52] In December 1939, the group included 20 persons and was housed apart from Schauffler's Linguistic-Cryptanalytic Subsection. In December 1943, the Subsection was evacuated to Silesia (Hermsdorf). It came to Zschepplin in March 1945, where it remained until war's end.

(b) Prof. Dr. Hans Rohrbach. A professor of mathematics at the Charles University in Prague, Dr. Rohrbach divided his time equally between his teaching duties and work as a cryptanalyst. He started his work with Pers Z S early in 1940. An undated personnel list of that year shows him as "provisionally employed" (Kommissarisch beschaeftigt), with the assimilated grade of senior civil servent (hoeherer Beamter).[53] Possessing an excellent command of English, he had worked[54] on English, American, and Scandinavian, as well as Japanese systems.[54] By personality rather than seniority, he was one of the Pers Z S leaders. He was awarded the War Service Cross 2d Class (KVK II) in September 1944, probably for his work in the solution of the U.S. Diplomatic Strip System O-2.

[49] I 22, p 25

[50] DF 17, T3273

[51] TF 24, Handwritten Personnel List, dated October 1, 1940

[52] I 22, p 25

[53] TF 24, Undated Personnal List

[54] I 89 p 3

(c) Dr. habil. Helmut Grunsky. Born July 11, 1904, Dr. Grunsky went to work for Pers Z S in September 1939. Prior to that date, he had been teaching and doing mathematical research at the Prussian Academy of Sciences. He was a Technical Assistant Grade III (Wissenschaftlicher Hilfsarbeiter) in December 1940, and was recommended for promotion to Specialist (Regierungsrat) on March 5, 1941.[55] At that time he was listed as head of a "group" in the Subsection, a position he still held at the end of the war (Gruppenleiter, mathematischer Zweig).

(d) Dr. Hans Georg Krug. It is not known when Krug joined Pers Z S. It seems probable that he was one of the large group hired in early 1940. He is not listed on the Pers Z S personnel list of December 1, 1939, but his name is found among the 1941 recommendations for promotion, when he was recommended for the grade of Specialist (Regierungsrat). At war's end he was in charge of all the Pers Z S Hollerith installations.

(e) Dr. Erika Pannwitz. It is not known when Dr. Pannwitz joined Pers Z S. A mathematician, she was listed as the head of a group (Gruppenleiter) in April, 1945.[56]

(f) Klaus Schultz. Schultz joined Pers Z S shortly after the outbreak of war. A professional mathematician and statistician, he worked for the German Statistical Office (Statistisches Reichsamt) before the war.. He is listed as being with Dr. Kunze's subsection on December 1, 1939. His last known civil service grade is that of Technical Assistant Grade III (Wissenschaftlicher Hilfsarbeiter). It does not appear that his recommendation for promotion to Specialist (Regierungsrat) in 1941 was ever acted upon favorably. He is listed as the head of a group as early as March 5, 1941, and still held that post in April 1945.[57]

(g) Dr. Anneliese Huehnke. Mrs. Huehnke started work with Pers Z S on August 31, 1939. She is listed as the head of a group under Dr. Kunze on March 5, 1941. Never recommended for

55 TF 24, Recommendation for 1941 Promotions

56 TF 24, List of personnel submitted by Dr. Kunze April 1945.

57 TF 24, Anlage 1 to Pers Z 5617/41, and List of Personnel submitted by Dr. Kunze, April 1945.

DOCID: 3486663

promotion outside the grade of Technical Assistant (Wissenschaftliche Hilfsarbeiterin), she apparently ended the war in grade III.

(h) Dr. Karl Schroeter. Dr. Schroeter joined Pers Z S in the spring of 1941. A former lecturer in mathematical theory at the University of Muenster, he worked independently on Japanese additive and encipherment systems. He is listed as the head of a group under Dr. Kunze in the spring of 1945.

(3) Personnel on Loan from Signal Intelligence Agency, Supreme Command of the Armed Forces (OKW/Chi).

(a) Dr. Arthur Grosse (born February 8, 1910), Edgar Hierer (born March 22, 1916) and Kurt Rave were members of the Signal Intelligence Agency, Supreme Command of the Armed Forces (Okw/Chi) who were loaned to Pers Z S in December 1943, after the Signal Intelligence Agency Supreme Command of the Armed Forces (OKW/Chi) had been bombed out of its Berlin quarters. They worked on Japanese and Chinese problems. According to Dr. Rohrbach, they were "definitely lower grade personnel, and had come to be trained."[58] There is some evidence that Rave and Hierer were actually military personnel.[59]

(4) Missing Persons. Most of the key Pers Z S personnel were taken prisoner at Tschepplin or Burgscheidungen in April 1945. Dr. Scherschmidt was later located through P/W sources in a Heidelberg hospital. Other personnel, some of whom were known to have been with the organization in 1945, were never taken.

(a) Specialist (Regierungsrat) Dr.....Kasper. Dr. Kasper headed the Rumanian group in Dr. Paschke's Subsection. Listed as having been among the original May 1919 group, he became a Specialist (Regierungsrat) sometime prior to October 1, 1940.[60] When the Pers Z S Linguistic-Cryptanalytic Subsection was split in December 1943, he remained with the main body (Stammabteilung) in Berlin-Dahlem. He is not mentioned in the 1945 interrogations. It is not known whether he sought to elude capture by escape, or whether he was dead. His assistant (Vertreter), Wilhelm Menning, also not taken, was included in the Pers Z S personnel who went to Muehlhausen.

[58] I 22, para 50

[59] I 150, p 8

[60] TF 24, Personnel list of October 1, 1940

17

DOCID: 3486663

(b) Senior Specialist (Oberregierungsrat) Friedrich Niendorff. Niendorff, one of the original 1919 group, appears to have been the Pers Z S specialist on intelligence evaluation (Auswertung) and dissemination.[61] During the interrogations no specific queries were raised concerning his activities. It is possible that Niendorff was no longer with Pers Z S in 1945. However, he or his successor might have been able to throw some light on the intelligence value of the Cryptanalytic Section's achievements, and it is to be regretted that no attempt was made to probe further into his activities.

(c) Prof. Dr....Horn. Under Dr. Paschke's direction, Dr. Horn was responsible for the Pers Z S files (Archiv).[62] No specific information is available as to their scope, other than that they included personalities and place names from decodes, and were amplified from newspaper clippings. Dr. Horn was in the group which went to Muehlhausen, and was never taken prisoner.

[61] TF 24 Job Specifications for 1941 Promotions

[62] I 22 p 25

DOCID: 3486663

VOLUME 6

Chapter II. Intercept Control and Traffic Analysis

8. Sources of Intercept Material.- -Pers Z S had one small intercept station under its own control, called the Landhaus, in Dahlem. This station was used to cover priority links, such as Berlin-Ankara and Berlin-Lisbon.[65] Pers Z S was dependent for the bulk of its intercept upon the Signal Intelligence Agency of the Supreme Command of the Armed Forces (OKW/Chi), Goering's "Research" Bureau (FA), and the German Postoffice.

Traffic taken by the intercept stations of the Signal Intelligence Agency of the Supreme Command of the Armed Forces (OKW/Chi) at Lauf, Loerrach and Treuenbrietzen was forwarded by teletype, probably via OKW. An examination of message photocopies in the TICOM files shows that a large amount of intercept traffic was in fact received from these stations, as well as OKW/Chi/VIb, the section in the Signal Intelligence Agency of the Supreme Command of the Armed Forces (OKW/Chi) which specialized in the interception of the press, propaganda and news agency transmissions. Dr. Paschke stated that Pers Z S may have had traffic from the Signal Intelligence Agency of the Supreme Command Armed Forces (OKW/Chi) intercept stations in foreign countries, but since in most cases the traffic was recopied before it reached Pers Z S, there was no indication as to its origin.[66]

Traffic was also received from Goering's "Research" Bureau (FA). The intercept stations are unknown. At one time the traffic, both radio and telegraph, transmitted by the German Postoffice was forwarded to Pers Z S through the "Research" Bureau (FA). After the "Research" Bureau (FA) was bombed out, this traffic was received direct from the Postoffice.[67]

[65] I 22 Para 103

[66] I 22 Para 103

[67] I 22 Para 103

19

9. Intercept Control and Traffic Analysis.-- There was no mention of intercept control or traffic analysis in the interrogations or documents. There appears to have been an attempt to keep a check on traffic depths and the relative amount of garbled traffic.[68] In view of the fact that most of the Pers Z S intercept came from outside sources, and was taken on commercial and diplomatic links which used fixed frequencies and fixed call signs, it is doubtful if any serious efforts in traffic analysis would have been profitable.

[68] T2038, Report on Polish Systems as of January 1, 1941, referred to a Polish consular system which was unworkable, partly due to the poor condition of the intercept forwarded by the "Research" Bureau (FA). T2252, Report of the Italian Group for the Year 1940, mentioned that the Signal Intelligence Agency of the Supreme Command Armed Forces (OKW/Chi) intercept totals had increased markedly, and that many messages had been received which had not been taken by the "Research" Bureau (FA) intercept stations.

VOLUME 6

Chapter III. Cryptanalysis

10. General Pers Z S Organization for Cryptanalysis.-- As in many small organizations, the Pers Z S internal organization appears to have been established more in conformity with personal factors, than with any logical plan. In order properly to comprehend the section's organization for cryptanalysis, it is necessary first to understand the position of the three leaders within the organization.

From a professional point of view, Schauffler was the undoubted dean of the organization. Its head for twenty years, it seems probable (while never stated in so many words) that in the years just prior to 1945 he had less and less of the group's leadership. Dr. Paschke, wrapped in the mantle of his Italian successes, essentially a more forceful personality, and a party member, seems to have usurped (or been appointed to conduct)more and more of Schauffler's administrative functions. At no point, either in the interrogations or in the documents, is there a definite statement as to who was the constituted head of the organization in 1945. Perhaps there was none, but it seems probable that this role was played by Paschke while, in deference to Schauffler's seniority and prestige, no paper administrative changes were made. Kunze, the leading mathematical cryptanalyst of the group, appears only as the head of a subsection. With this equivocal situation as to leadership clearly in mind, it is possible to outline the Section's organization for cryptanalysis with some degree of understanding.

a. Mathematical and Linguistic Cryptanalysis. Chart 6-1, representing the Pers Z S organization as of April, 1945, is in most respects an ideal representation. In point of fact, there was in Pers Z S, in April 1945, very little which could be termed organization. There had not been ideal working conditions, with all elements of the Section located in the same building or same general area, since the evacuation of Berlin in November, 1943.

However, in spite of deviations from the sought-for norm or ideal, through all the vicissitudes of evacuation and re-evacuation, one cardinal organizational principle seems to have been retained: that mathematical cryptanalysis involving the initial solution of extremely difficult systems, the solution of complex encipherments and additives, and the application of machine techniques to these problems, should be kept separate from linguistic cryptanalysis, roughly defined as including current solution of known additive and enciphering systems, code-book reconstruction, translation and publication. This principle emerges clearly in Chart 6-1.[73] If Dr. Schauffler were placed in charge of a subsection enjoying primarily consultative and research functions, if Dr. Kunze were placed in charge of a subsection having mathematical-cryptanalytic activities, and if Dr. Paschke were placed in charge of linguistic-cryptanalytic activities, then a reasonably effective organization was possible.

b. Schauffler's Responsibilities. Schauffler's responsibilities, aside from some rather vague responsibilities as co-head of Pers Z S (with Paschke) embraced theoretical research on cryptanalytic methods and systems, publications, and consultation with the Cryptographic Section (Pers Z Chi) on the security of the Foreign Office code and cipher systems. His linguistic specialities were Japanese and Chinese, which linguistic group he headed, under Dr. Paschke.

[73] I 22, Appendix B. No conclusions can be drawn as to the general administrative efficiency of this division. In at least one instance (see T56, Pages 8,22), there seem to be differences of opinion between the mathematicians and the linguists as to the proper approach to a problem.

c. Paschke's Linguistic-Cryptanalytic Subsection. This Subsection consisted of a number of small linguistic groups, organized along semi-linguistic or semi-geographical lines. The group organization appears to have been fluid, varying according to the intelligence and cryptanalytic priorities. In general, it was organized into the following groups, with group heads as listed:

(1) Japan, China, Manchukuo....................Schauffler
(2) United States of America...................Zastrow
(3) France, Belguim, Switzerland, Holland......Brandes
(4) Italy, Greece, Vatican & USSR..............Paschke
(5) Turkey.....................................Scherschmidt
(6) Iran, Afhanistan,Arabic States.............Benzing
(7) Rumania....................................Kasper
(8) England and British Empire, Spain, Portugal & Latin-American..................Hagen
(9) Bulgaria, Croatia, Poland, Jugoslavia & Baltic States[74]........................Karstien

Personal considerations seem to have played an important part in the organization of the work groups. For example, Scherschmidt was in charge of work on Turkish from 1934 until 1939, and the work on Polish systems from 1939 until March 1943. Dr. Benzing took over his responsibilities on Turkish systems when Scherschmidt transferred to Polish. When Scherschmidt returned to Pers Z S in September 1944, he reassumed responsibility for Turkish, while Benzing took over a newly created group which worked on Iran, Afghanistan and other Arabic language systems.[75] Scherschmidt had originally been in charge of work on Bulgarian systems, but Dr. Karstien kept control of this work, as well as the remainder of the Slavonic languages (defined as Jugoslavian, Croatian, Polish and the Baltic States).

[74] I 22, Appendix A. Such was the fluidity of the organization after 1943 that no chart can properly show group heads and group organization for more than a short period. For example, Scherschmidt left Pers Z S from March 1943, until September 1944. Paschke headed the group which was responsible for Russian traffic, but, in point of fact, the traffic was never tackled. For these reasons, the listing given below will not correspond strictly to the organization given in Appendix A.

[75] I 63, page 2; I 103 page 3

23

d. Kunze's Mathematical-Cryptanalytic Subsection. The internal organization of Dr. Kunze's Mathematical-Cryptanalytic Subsection has never been precisely defined. A captured document, dated January 18, 1941, listed six work groups, whose responsibilities were, respectively, England, America, Japanese Diplomatic, Japanese Military, Greece, and study of German systems(eigene Verfahren). The list of group heads submitted by Dr. Kunze in April 1945, also included six names. However, it is doubtful if the division of responsibility in this subsection had remained constant for four years. From available evidence, it seems more probable that Dr. Kunze's Subsection had a loose internal organization which permitted full concentration of needed personnel on the most important problems as they arose.[76]

The Mathematical-Cryptanalytic Subsection had had its own IBM machinery since 1942. This machinery was used principally in solution of difficult additives and superencipherments, and not for bookbuilding purposes.

At the end of the war the installations included 20 punches, 10 sorters, 2 collators, 2 reproducers, 6 tabulators, one multiplier, and additional special machinery. The most useful special device was the so called "automaton", a rapid deciphering machine developed for use on the American Diplomatic Strip Cipher.[77] Another machine, a type of comparator (Spezialvergleicher), was developed to solve Japanese transposition ciphers by dragging the end of the message through the cipher text.[78]

[76] Five of the six group heads alone had worked on the solution of the U. S. Diplomatic Strip System 0-2. See I 89, page 3

[77] I 89

[78] I 22, Para 147

(e) War-Induced Geographical and Organizational Changes. In November, 1943, after the bombing of Berlin, the Pers Z S organization was split up into three groups. The main body (Stammabteilung Berlin-Dahlem), consisting of Schauffler, Paschke and most of the latter's Linguistic-Cryptanalytic Subsection, remained in Berlin. Dr. Karstien took a part of the Linguistic-Cryptanalytic Subsection to Hirschberg in the Riesengebirge. This group consisted of a part of Dr. Karstien's group (Bulgaria, Croatia and Poland, less Jugoslavia, which was left in Berlin under Schimmel), a Japanese-Chinese party under Dr. Olbricht, and Dr. Brandes' French language group (France, Belguim, Switzerland) under Miss Schrader, Dr. Brandes being ill at the time. This group engaged in code reconstruction, current solution of the more difficult additives and encipherments, and the translation of less urgent telegrams.[79] At the same time, Dr. Kunze's Mathematical-Cryptanalytic Subsection was moved to Hermsdorf in Silesia (Wilhelm Wander Schule). This organization, knit together by a daily courier service, remained unchanged until February 1945, when the various groups moved westward and southward to avoid the Russian advances.

11. General Summary of Cryptanalytic Successes.-- Considering the relatively small staff which Pers Z S had, the conclusion must be drawn that its cryptanalytic successes were considerable. Work was done on systems from approximately 50 countries. Of these 50 countries, apparently only three used diplomatic systems which completely defied successful cryptanalysis- Russia, Czechoslovakia, and Poland after 1942-1943. It is easy to scorn the Pers Z S inability to solve high grade machine systems, whether American SIGABA, English Type X, or Swedish Hagelin. Yet, with their small staff, they were able to read the Swiss Enigma for a short period of time, and to solve the Japanese "Red" machine.

As a diplomatic cryptanalytic agency, the investigator is forced to conclude that in its primary field, the solution of foreign diplomatic codes, the agency evidenced an extraordinary degree of competence. With the exception of Russian, substantial segments of the medium grade code systems used by the major powers were read. England, the United States, France, Italy (where the greatest success was achieved), China, Japan--many of their diplomatic codes and ciphers were read. With

[79] I 22, Appendix A

Turkey, Bulgaria, Belgium, Spain, Switzerland, Portugal and Poland (until 1942), nearly 100 per cent success was achieved. In the case of the Latin American countries, and the smaller European and Near-Eastern nations, complete success was apparently achievable, insofar as limitations of personnel and a relatively trivial message content might warrant. Had there been backing from von Ribbentrop, had there not been crippling jealousies at agency-head levels, there might have been even greater successes. For a more detailed consideration of the agency's cryptanalytic successes, see the breakdown by countries immediately following.

12. Detailed Listing of Cryptanalytic Successes by Countries.-

a. Argentina. Due to shortages of personnel and intercept difficulties, it does not seem probable that Pers Z S expended much effort on Argentine diplomatic systems. At least three main codes were known, one of which, a five-figure, one-part, 110,000 group system, usually enciphered by the addition or subtraction of a constant, was read almost without gaps. Two-hundred forty messages were decoded and published in 1942.[80]

b. Belgium. The Pers Z S cryptanalysts were familiar in 1945 with three readable Belgian codes. The main systems were four-figure, one-part or partially alphabetic codes, containing approximately 10,000 groups. They were usually enciphered with a daily changing unsystematic bigram substitution table. Three-hundred-seventy-three messages were published in 1942, a small proportion of the total intercepted and broken.[81]

c. Brazil. Prior to 1943, insofar as limitations of traffic depth and personnel permitted, the Pers Z S cryptanalysts seem to have read nearly all major Brazilian diplomatic codes. Three systems in particular seem to have been read almost without gaps: a five-figure, one-part, 165,000 group code (called "Bras. B1" by the Germans); a five-letter, partially alphabetic, 82,000 group code (called "Bras. B2"); and a five-figure, one-part, 100,000 group system (called "Bras. Z 1"). The basic book for "Bras. B2" was available in photostatic form. Traffic totals fell off sharply after the rupture of diplomatic relations in January, 1942, and it was not indicated whether the earlier successes were continued.[82]

80 I 172, para 17; D 16, Report # 4, Page 4

81 I 22, paras 156-159, D 54, Report # 8 Page 19

82 D 16 Report # 2 and Report # 4

DOCID: 3486663

d. Bulgaria. Bulgaria used two basic five-figure, 35,000-40,000 group code books. Both were one-part codes, repaginated for various links, usually used enciphered. Goering's "Research" Bureau (FA) had provided photocopies of the two books.[83] Senior Specialist (Oberregierungsrat) Scherschmidt stated that, from 1943, all major Bulgarian links were read.[84]

e. Canada (See United Kingdom)

f. Chile. Little information is available on successes with Chilean systems after 1942. The one-part, two/three/four-letter, 42,000 group code known as "Clave Solar" (Chilean name) was read at least until late 1942, and possibly until the end of the war.[85]

g. China. There is little direct information relative to Pers Z S successes with Chinese systems. The Chinese four-letter and four-figure codes were apparently read until 1930. Few details are available on the work done from 1930 until 1938. At that point, work was stopped, only to be taken up again early in 1941.

Interrogations showed that two three-letter codes, one military, and the other an attache system, were solved. Another three-letter system called "uti" was read in 1941-1942.[86] Documents, on the other hand, suggest a somewhat more extensive success. From available evidence, however, this cannot be verified.[87]

h. Czechoslovakia. It seems probable that Pers Z S did not work on Czech diplomatic systems. According to Dr. Karstien, the systems used were one-time pads and unbreakable.[88]

[83] T2038, Film 8, Report of the Polish-Bulgarian Group, August 13, 1941

[84] I 103, Para 3

[85] D16, Report # 4, Page 5. Miss Hagen, when interrogated in September, 1945, did not mention that the code had become unreadable. I 172, Para 16

[86] I 22, Paras. 59, 60, 180

[87] There is some evidence that all the Pers Z S work was not mentioned. The three systems mentioned in the text were unknown at ASA. However an examination of documents T197, 427, 1169, 1170, and 1172 suggests that there was some success in bookbreaking with HWM (Chinese name) a major diplomatic code.

[88] I 22, Para 71

i. Eire (Ireland). Considerable work was done on the Irish diplomatic links to Berlin. The Irish used the British Government Telegraph Code (GTC called "B-22" by the Germans), enciphered by the use of substitution alphabets. This code, a five-letter, one-part, 84,000 group system, had been captured at Bergen in 1940.[89]

j. England (See United Kingdom).

k. France. The Pers Z S success in solution of French diplomatic transmissions was considerable. Dr. Brandes stated in his 1941 report that approximately 75 per cent of French diplomatic transmissions were read.[90] Most diplomatic systems were four-figure, two-part codes, enciphered either through an additive system, or by bigram substitution tables. Many were compromised in 1940, and later, when they were deposited with the German Armistice Commission at Wiesbaden.

l. Great Britain (See United Kingdom).

m. Greece. According to Dr. Deubner, there were three main Greek diplomatic systems, all of which were read: an unenciphered five-letter code book (fifth letter for inflection only), carrying most of the traffic; an unenciphered four letter book, used mainly for traffic with Berne; and a four-figure book, used with bigram substitution, for traffic on the Moscow, Washington, Cairo and Ankara links.[91]

n. Holland (Netherlands). Little information is available relative to the Pers Z S work on Dutch systems. A 1939 report listed work on a four-letter, one-part code, and a figure code convertible to a letter basic book.[92]

o. Hungary. It is not known whether Pers Z S ever worked on Hungarian codes. In April, 1940, Dr. Paschke reported that he had discussed cooperation on Hungarian systems with Fenner and Seifert of the Signal Intelligence Agency of the Supreme Command Armed Forces (OKW/Chi). He recommended that Pers Z S attack the five-figure code designated as "U-3".[93]

[89] I 172, Para 11, and D 16, Reports #3 and #4

[90] D 54, Report # 5, Page 13

[91] I 22, Para 169. The reports from the Lehmann Group (Gruppe Lehmann) for 1939-1941 do not list such impressive successes, although they imply that shortages of personnel were a strong contributing factor. See T2052.

[92] T2050, Report on Dutch Systems, dated November 29, 1939

[93] T2043, Report of the Group Austria-Hungary, dated April,1940

p. Iran (Persia). Dr. Benzing stated that all the Iranian systems were read. The Iranians used three-letter, 12,000 - 13,000 group, one-part or reverse-alphabetic, enciphered code books.[94]

q. Italy. Work on Italian diplomatic codes was an outstanding Pers Z S achievement. From 1935 until late 1942, with lapses as new code books were introduced, Pers Z S apparently read all major Italian diplomatic codes. The 1940 reports from the Italian Group listed twelve codes, enciphered or unenciphered, all of which were read.[95] The work became increasingly difficult in 1942-1943, for the Italians introduced bigram substitution over the additive on the basic code books, "If the basic books had been changed, the traffic would have been impossible to read".[96] Some systems were read after the collapse in 1943. Mention was made of a Badoglio double transposition system which was never solved.[97] Dr. Paschke mentioned three Neo-Fascist systems which were read in the latter stages of the war.[98]

r. Japan. Pers Z S read the lower grade Japanese systems until 1934. After 1934 the Japanese went over increasingly to the use of a machine, ("JB-48", or the "Red" machine). This machine was solved in September 1938, and read currently until February, 1939, when the traffic became unreadable (the Germans failed to realize that a new machine, the "Purple" machine, had been introduced).[99] A major diplomatic code (known to the Germans as "JB-57) was solved at the end of 1941 and read currently for about two years. This was a two-four letter book, enciphered by a series of alphabets "and/ or" stencil transposition with nulls.[100] Some success was also achieved with other diplomatic systems, particularly "JB 64" (US JBA), a two/three letter code.

94 I 22, Para 166, and T2052, Report of the Lehmann Group, dated February 19, 1942

95 T2252, Report of the Italian Group for the Year 1940

96 I 22, Para 25

97 I 22, Para 168

98 I 22, Para 25

99 I 22, Para 19

100 I 22, Para 176

29

s. Jugoslavia. Neither interrogations nor captured documents shed much light on the Pers Z S work with Jugoslav systems. It is only known that some work was done on these systems after 1940-1941.[101]

t. Manchuria. Manchukuoan systems were handled by the group which worked on Japanese and Chinese systems. Little data is available on successes. A three-letter, Japanese-language code book, enciphered with a fifteen-place transposition was read. Shortages of personnel were always a limiting factor.[102]

u. Mexico. No information is available as to successes with Mexican systems after 1942. The principal codes, "Pomos", a one-part, five-letter code, and "Xepit", a similiar system, both enciphered by substitution alphabets, were read through 1942. The "Xepit" book was compromised in November, 1942, although it had been broken prior to compromise.[103]

v. Poland. Relatively little progress was made in solution after 1942. Dr. Karstien stated that Polish codes "were unbreakable in practice- there were too many of them, they required too much work".[104] The principal Polish diplomatic code (called "PD-1" by the Germans), an enciphered four-figure, two-part code, was broken in 1940 and read 100 per cent until October, 1942, when it went out of use.[105]

w. Portugal. A five-figure, partially alphabetic, 50,000 group book (called "302" by the Germans) was read with some success in 1941. Two other five-figure, partially alphabetic, 61,500 group books were compromised in December, 1942, when a basic book (called "205") was received from the Signal Intelligence Agency of the Supreme Command Armed Forces (OKW/Chi). After that time the traffic was read 100 per cent. The work done in the 1942-1945 period does not seem to have been covered in the interrogations.[106]

[101] T2038, Report on Jugoslavia at the beginning of the year 1941

[102] T76, Report of the Manchurian Group at the beginning of 1941

[103] D16, Report #4, Page 5

[104] I 22, Para 72

[105] I 63, Paras 5, 6

[106] D16, Reports #1, #2, #3, #4

DOCID: 3486663

x. Rumania. The Pers Z S work on Rumanian systems was not explored in the interrogations. Dr. Kasper and Menning, the head and deputy of the Rumanian group, respectively, were not captured. A one page report, signed by Kasper and dated 1940, listed seven known diplomatic systems (called "R11-R17" by the Germans), all five-figure codes, varying from 70,000 to 100,000 groups, and enciphered by means of ten-place substitution tables.[107] No statement was made as to successes in solution, but captured code book reconstructions indicate an approximate 5 to 10 per cent recovery on book groups.

y. Russia. Work on Russian diplomatic systems does not seem to have been a Pers Z S commitment. Dr. Kunze made it clear that Russian systems had been read up until 1927, but that no success had been achieved after that time. Presumptively he had reference to the introduction of one-time pads. Lt. Colonel Mettig of Signal Intelligence Agency of the Supreme Command Armed Forces (OKW/Chi) stated that "after a certain date" (which he could not remember), no Russian diplomatic traffic was attempted, either by his agency or Pers Z S.[108]

z. Scandinavia (Denmark, Norway, Sweden). Dr. Mueller, the nominal head of the Pers Z S Scandinavian group, stated that he had worked on Scandinavian systems for about three months in 1941. After that, all the work was transferred to the Signal Intelligence Agency of the Supreme Command Armed Forces (OKW/Chi).[109] On the other hand, Dr. Rohrbach stated he had investigated traffic thought to be Swedish Hagelin for three months in 1941, and again in August, 1944. There is no contradiction between the two statements, since Dr. Rohrbach worked in the Mathematical-Cryptanalytic Subsection and Dr. Mueller was in Dr. Paschke's Linguistic-Cryptanalytic Subsection.[110]

[107] D 54, T2050, Page 5 1940 Report of the Rumanian group

[108] I 22, Para 16; I 96, Page 14

[109] I 22, Para 182

[110] I 22, Para 48

31

aa. South Africa (See United Kingdom).

ab. Spain. Apparently little work was done on Spanish systems. In 1941 and 1942, the only years for which reports are available, work was done only on "04" (German name), a four-figure, partly alphabetic, 10,000 group code book. The book was partially recovered.[111]

ac. Switzerland. Generally speaking, all Swiss diplomatic systems were read except the Enigma cipher machine. That, too, was read for a time in 1941. The codes were chiefly three-letter books, usually bi-lingual, enciphered with a series of substitution tables. New wirings of the Enigma were solved by cribs every three months. Subsequent messages were recovered from message texts.[112]

ad. Thai (Siam). According to the 1941 and 1942 reports issed by Miss Hagen's group, the main Thailand Code was a one-part, five-figure, 110,000 group English language code, used both enciphered and unenciphered. It was read almost without gaps.[113]

ae. Turkey. Pers Z S started work on Turkish systems after the Montreux Conference in 1934. Most Turkish diplomatic traffic was read. Three codes were usually in use, changing at monthly intervals. In 1944-1945 the codes were chiefly one-part, with a cyclic additive, and were readily broken.[114]

af. United Kingdom (British Empire). The principal Pers Z S successes with Empire and British diplomatic systems were obtained on medium grade letter codes. The Government Telegraph Code (GTC- called "B22" by the Germans), used in communication with Canada, Australia (and also by Eire), and another Government Telegraph Code ("B23"), used solely for South African communications, were read. These were five-letter, one-part, 84,000 group codes, usually unenciphered.

[111] D16, Report #4, Page 4. "04" was the Spanish name also.

[112] I 22, Para 160, and D 54, Report # 8, Page 18

[113] D 16, Report # 3, Page 2

[114] I 22, Para 165; I 63

The former had been completely compromised at Bergen in 1940. The four-letter, two-part codes (called "B25", "B30" and "B31" by the Germans) had a more significant message content. "B25" and "B31" (the Foreign Office "R" Codes?) were considered most important by the Germans. The five-figure Interdepartmental Cipher, also compromised at Bergen, was worked on in 1941 and 1942, the bulk of the work being done by Goering's "Research" Bureau (FA).[115]

ag. United States of America. The Germans considered their main successes with American systems to have included the solution of the Grey Code (called "B3" by the Germans), the Brown Code ("B8"), and the State Department strip systems. The Grey Code had been in use since June 1918, and the Brown Code since 1938. Both systems were readable, the Brown Code having been compromised in 1941. The Strip System 0-1 was partially read in 1941, and the Strip System 0-2 was solved early in 1943.[116] The strip systems mentioned were not read currently, but only after a delay of months.

ah. Vatican. The 1940 Report of the Italian Group (Paschke) made it clear that while approximately 50 per cent of the Vatican traffic could be read, the traffic was not a major Pers Z S commitment. Reference was made to a one-part, three-letter code, enciphered by a transposition within the groups, and to a one-part figure code, enciphered by means of substitution alphabets and a sliding strip. Most of the book groups were secured from Goering's "Research" Bureau (FA).[117]

[115] D16, Reports #2, #3, #4; I 22, Paras 91-100; I 172 complete

[116] I 22, Para 24; DF 15, Reports of the A Group 1919-1942

[117] T2252, Report of the Italian Group for the year 1940

ai. Yugoslavia (See Jugoslavia).

aj. Latin America- Smaller States. Such was the security level of the systems used by the smaller Latin American states that only limitations of content, intercept and personnel prevented solution. Security levels varied from plain language (Nicaragua and Panama), to polyalphabetic substitution ciphers (Colombia and Venezuela), to enciphered codes (Bolivia and Peru). It does not appear from the 1941 and 1942 reports of Miss Hagen's group that the main Peruvian code was ever read, although lack of traffic depth and personnel shortages were important limiting factors. In 1941 a five-figure, 78,000 group Bolivian code, enciphered with a letter substitution table, could be read with some gaps.[118]

ak. Near Eastern Countries (excluding Iran and Turkey). Little work was done on systems originating in Afghanistan, Egypt, Iraq or Saudi Arabia. As was the case with the small Latin American states, traffic was usually inconsequential in content, lacking in depth, and there was never sufficient personnel to permit exploitation. Some work seems to have been done on Afghanistan, Abyssinia and Iraq.[119] The available personnel were almost invariably employed on Turkish and Iranian systems.[120]

al. Baltic States. There are no details on Pers Z S work with Finnish systems. Some work had apparently been done on Lettish and Lithuanian systems before these countries were incorporated into the USSR. Dr. Karstien stated that most Lettish and Lithuanian systems were transposition ciphers, singly or doubly enciphered, sometimes enciphered with a Vigenere substitution.[121]

[118] D16, Reports #2, #3, #4

[119] See work sheets and reconstructions in T1062, T1067, T1074, T1068, T1077

[120] I 22, Para 164

[121] I 22, Para 74

DOCID: 3486663

VOLUME 6

Chapter IV. Liaison and Collaboration with Other Cryptanalytic Agencies

13. Introduction.--

"Liaison with other German cryptographic units was bad... . The Signal Intelligence Agency of the Supreme Command Armed Forces (OKW/Chi) and Goering's "Research" Bureau (FA) also worked on diplomatic systems and the relations of all three stations were marked by jealousy rather than by cooperation".[126]

"There was... no overall coordination of policy for the various German cryptographic bureaus."[127]

[126] I 22, Introduction

[127] I 143, Para 51

Statements of this nature abound in the TICOM material. They imply a gross amount of duplication, strong personal jealousies, and occasional downright inefficiency. However, in many cases they do not represent informed opinion, and should therefore be treated with reserve. From the interrogations and the scanty documentary evidence available, it seems clear that the Pers Z S relationships with other cryptanalytic and cryptographic agencies do not lend themselves to generalization.

The amount of collaboration varied markedly from agency to agency. There is no mention of cooperation with the Army High Command (either with In 7/VI or OKH/LNA) after 1941-1942. Senior Specialist (Oberregierungsrat) Tranow of the Signal Intelligence Agency of the Naval High Command (OKM/4 SKL/III) apparently knew Dr. Schauffler. There was some personal antipathy between Senior Specialist (Oberregierungsrat) Voegele, the principal cryptanalyst in the Signal Intelligence Agency of the Air Force High Command (Chi Stelle, OBdL), and Dr. Kunze of Pers Z S. These agencies, however, had primary cryptanalytic interests of a military nature.

Liaison with Goering's "Research" Bureau (FA) appears to have been extensive. Intercept material was received from the "Research" Bureau (FA), and there was frequent cryptanalytic collaboration, including exchanges of recovered book groups and additives.

The collaboration with the Signal Intelligence Agency, Supreme Command of the Armed Forces (OKW/Chi), at least at lower administrative and technical levels, appears to have been the most extensive of all. Work was divided on various systems, personnel were exchanged on at least two occasions, and there is some evidence that elements of the Signal Intelligence Agency of the Supreme Command Armed Forces were actually housed with Pers Z S from November, 1943, until March, 1945. If collaboration with the Signal Intelligence Agency of the Supreme Command Armed Forces appears to have been good on cryptanalytic matters, the reverse was apparently the case where cryptographic matters and Foreign Office codes and ciphers were at stake. Dr. Huettenhain, chief cryptanalyst of the Signal Intelligence Agency of the Supreme Command Armed Forces (OKW/Chi) stated that:

> "OKW/Chi was never allowed to know the details of the ciphers used by the Foreign Office... . Even toward the end, when there was a further attempt to centralize security under OKW/Chi, the Foreign Office would not come into line. Selchow (Chief of Z Branch) strongly opposed it, preferring to remain independent".[128]

A detailed account of liaison activities follows.

14. Liaison with the Signal Intelligence Agency of the Army High Command (OKH/GdNA).-- As pointed out in the Introduction, there was little in the way of cooperation between Pers Z S and the Signal Intelligence Agency of the Army High Command and its predecessors. Dr. Otto Buggisch, formerly of the Army High Command Inspectorate 7/VI (In 7/VI), a pre-1944 agency, gives the only available information. Dr. Buggisch, worked in the French language group in the Army High Command Signal Intelligence Agency's Inspectorate 7/VI (In 7/VI) from November, 1941, until August, 1942. During this period he collaborated with Dr. Kunze of Pers Z S on a five figure DeGaulle code. He also worked with Dr. Kunze on the Swiss Enigma problem.[129] General Jodl, Chief of the Armed Forces Operations Staff, stated that he did not receive the Foreign Office decodes. However, he knew in a general way of the Pers Z S commitment and successes.[130]

This general lack of collaboration between Pers Z S and the Signal Intelligence Agency of the Army High Command (OKH/GdNA) does not, however, point to any lack of coordination on higher administrative levels, nor to jealousy and lack of cooperation between the two agencies. They had essentially two distinct and separate missions, one military and the other diplomatic. There was therefore little or no need for a detailed collaboration.

[128] I 31, Page 15

[129] I 58, Pages 5, 6

[130] I 143, Page 5

15. Liaison with the Signal Intelligence Agency of the Naval High Command (OKM/4 SKL/III).-- Like the Army, the Navy had little occasion to work with Pers Z S. Their respective problems and commitments were basically dissimiliar. Admiral Doenitz perhaps best summarized the situation when he said that he:

> "had no knowledge of the cryptanalytic bureaus maintained by the other services.... As for civil bureaus, he had never tried to find out, they were of no use to him."[131]

Senior Specialist (Oberregierungsrat) Tranow of the Signal Intelligence Agency of the Naval High Command (OKM 4/SKL/III) knew Schauffler of Pers Z S slightly. Schauffler had once given him some Japanese traffic for examination, but Tranow had never had time to study it.[132] Miss Hagen reported in 1942 that the English group had sent their results on British codes "B30" and "B31" to the naval agency, but had received nothing in return.[133] Uncooperative the Navy may have been, but the Pers Z S cryptanalysts were apt to be unaware of message content in terms of intelligence. The possibility that the "B30" and "B31" messages might have been of no interest to Naval intelligence apparently did not occur to Miss Hagen.

16. Relationships with the Signal Intelligence Agency of the Commander-in- Chief of the Air Force (Chi Stelle, OBdL).-- Like the Army and the Navy, the Air Force was primarily interested in messages emanating from its allied counterparts. Diplomatic traffic would probably have lain outside its scope of interest. There are, however, two examples of Pers Z S-Air Force collaboration in the signal intelligence field.

The first dates back to 1939. According to Dr. Schauffler, Dr. Kunze of Pers Z S was approached at that time by the "Luftwaffe" for assistance with British weather ciphers.[134] Nothing is known as to the extent or the success of the ensuing collaboration.

[131] I 143, Para 26

[132] I 147, Page 2

[133] I 172, Para 14

[134] I 22, Para 22. It is assumed that Schauffler meant the Commander-in-Chief of the Air Force (OBdL), rather than the "Research" Bureau (FA) in the Air Ministry.

The second instance of collaboration was noted by Dr. Huettenhain of the Signal Intelligence Agency of the Supreme Command Armed Forces (OKW/Chi). His letter of July 27, 1943, speaks for itself.[135]

"Three weeks ago a discussion was held in the Foreign Office between Oberregierungsrat Dr. Kunze (of Pers Z S), Regierungsrat Dr. Voegele (chief Air Force cryptanalyst).... Voegele declared his willingness to cooperate on the "AM10" (German name for a U. S. Strip System) and Dr. Kunze undertook to provide the necessary material.

"Voegele was held off for a fortnight. When he pressed for the production of the promised material, Dr. Kunze stated that he had changed his mind and would not provide the material, as Dr. Voegele had made disparaging remarks about his work... .

"Suggestion: LIV (unknown) or the head of OKW/Chi should arrange with Paschke for the already planned collaboration of Pers Z S with Chi Stelle OBdL actually to come into force. Should Pers Z S not consent, Chi will terminate the agreement with Pers Z S to get a free hand, so that Chi can collaborate with Air... ."

This incident is not mentioned in either the Pers Z S or the Voegele interrogations. It does suggest that the spirit of cooperation between Pers Z S and the Signal Intelligence Agency of the Commander-in-Chief of the Air Force (Chi Stelle, OBdL) was not all that it might have been.

[135] D 60, Page 5 It must be remembered that Pers Z S had solved the U. S. Diplomatic Strip System 0-2, and that the Air Force was interested in similiar systems (such as CENEB) used by the USAAF and not in "0-2" itself.

17. <u>Relationships with Goering's "Research" Bureau (FA)</u>.--

"Captain Oschmann...mentioned an utterance by his chief, Korvettenkapitaen Patzig, to the effect that all cryptanalytic connections with the Forschungsamt should be dropped, since cryptanalytic work did not belong in the province of the Forschungsamt."[136]

This unsigned letter, dated February 23, 1934, was probably written by Dr. Paschke. It was found in a file which dealt with Pers Z S-Reichswehr collaboration. It probably does not represent the then prevailing Pers Z S attitude, but it does constitute the first reference in the Pers Z S material to this new "third competitor", Goering's "Research" Bureau (the Forschungsamt, abbreviated FA).

The later material bearing on Pers Z S-"Research" Bureau relationships is fragmentary. It consists of scattered references in Pers Z S cryptanalytic reports, none later than 1942, and the interrogations made in 1945.

Goering is author for the statement that "the Foreign Office had continuously tried to interfere" (with the "Research" Bureau)[137] No dates are given and his statement may have been motivated by his antipathy to von Ribbentrop. He also said that "both agencies covered precisely the same field, and there was unfortunately almost complete duplication".[138] Dr. Paschke's statement that, in general, "there was less liaison with the "Research" Bureau than with the Signal Intelligence Agency of the Supreme Command Armed Forces (OKW/Chi)" seems to be the best summary.[139]

[136] DF 17, T3273, Letters on Proposed Foreign Office Defense Collaboration.

[137] I 143, Para 59

[138] I 143, Para 49

[139] I 22, Para 101

Pers Z S received a certain amount of its intercept from the "Research" Bureau. The names and locations of the intercept stations were unknown. Until November, 1943, when the "Research" Bureau was bombed out, it acted as the forwarding agency for traffic intercepted by the German Postoffice, both radio and cable-telegram traffic. Thereafter the Postoffice forwarded intercept material to Pers Z S direct.[140]

There is little evidence bearing on an official liaison. Seifert of the "Research" Bureau is author for the statement that intelligence produced by the "Research" Bureau was distributed to "all departments, including the Foreign Office... . At some of these departments we had liaison officers".[141] In another interrogation a Dr. Gerstmeyer is mentioned as the "Research" Bureau-Foreign Office Liaison Officer (Verbindungsmann).[142] Sauerbier of the "Research" Bureau stated that "liaison with the Foreign Office...was handled by a single representative, and never involved any exchange of visits by operations personnel".[143] Unfortunately, the interrogations do not state whether this liaison was cryptanalytic-technical, or of an intelligence dissemination nature. The latter assumption seems more probable. There is no statement as to whether Pers Z S itself was ever a direct beneficiary of this liaison.

From the Pers Z S side there is excellent, albeit scattered evidence that there was a technical liaison of sorts. Both the "Research" Bureau and Pers Z S were invited to attend as guests at the meetings of the unofficial Army-Air-Naval coordinating committee.[144] Dr. Paschke of Pers Z S evidently

[140] I 22, Para 103

[141] I 25, Page 2

[142] I 54, Page 4

[143] I 162, Page 4

[144] I 84, Para 11

knew Ministerial Director (Ministerialdirigent) Schroder of the "Research" Bureau. Senior Specialist (Oberregierungsrat) Brandes, head of the French language group in Dr. Paschke's Pers Z S Subsection, reported in 1940 that he was responsible for his group's liaison with the "Research" Bureau.[145] Goering's statement about "very close liaison with Pers Z S to avoid unnecessary duplication" takes on additional credibility when the information on technical liaison is examined in detail (See Sub. Para. a. following).

Out of this sketchy evidence, several very tentative conclusions may be formed for the period 1940-1942:

a. There was extensive duplication of effort between Pers Z S and Goering's "Research" Bureau (FA).

b. There was some sort of official liaison between Goering's "Research" Bureau and the "Foreign Office", exact nature and extent unknown.

c. On the technical level, there was apparently a fair amount of liaison. Where both agencies were working on the same problem, there was some exchange of information. Where solution was achieved, there were frequent exchanges of keys.

d. It is not known whether the situation outlined in Paras a-c above still held at the end of the war.

Detailed Listing of Pers Z S-FA Collaboration by Countries:

(1) Bulgaria.

A 1940 report from the Pers Z S Bulgarian Group stated that Goering's "Research" Bureau (FA) had furnished them with photocopies of two Bulgarian codes.[146]

[145] D 54, Report #5, Page 13. While Dr. Brandes had over twenty years of seniority in Pers Z S, it does not seem that his standing in the agency was sufficient to permit him to engage in liaison of the non-technical, policy-formational type.

[146] T 2038, Report on Bulgaria, January 1, 1940.

(2) England and the British Empire.

(a) The Interdepartmental Cipher, a Five-Figure System.

Miss Hagen, head of the Pers Z S English Group, has stated that "there was no liaison with the "Research" Bureau (FA) except on the subject of the Interdepartmental Ciphers." Pers Z S did not work on this cipher after the summer of 1942, but received sections of the additive sequences from the "Research" Bureau (FA).[147]

(b) Code B30

"In February, 1942, at the request of Senior Specialist (ORR) Waechter of the "Research" Bureau (FA), an attempt was made to establish contact with the "Research" Bureau (FA), which, did not get beyond a general exchange of ideas. The only concrete results were that the "Research" Bureau (FA) placed at our disposal a list of approximately 50 "B30" recovered groups."[148]

(c) Code B22

This code, called the Government Telegraph Code, was used by the Irish Government for diplomatic communications, with an encipherment by substitution alphabets. The "Research" Bureau (FA) solved the keys used on the Berlin and Madrid links in 1943. Pers Z S took over the keys from the "Research" Bureau in 1944.[149]

(3) France

(a) Code 19

Mention was made of the Pers Z S work in 1941 on a 10,000 group figure code designated as "19". The first solution was achieved by the "Research" Bureau, using captured tables, which were later turned over to Pers Z S.[150]

[147] I 172, Para 13, 14; D16, Reports #3 and #4

[148] D16, Report #4, Page 1

[149] I 172, Para 11

[150] D54, Report #8, Page 18

43

(4) Italy.

There was a fairly extensive Pers Z S "Research" Bureau (FA) cooperation, on Italian systems, at least through 1940. The "Research" Bureau intercept was made available to Pers Z S.[151] From April, 1939, through 1940 there was a regular exchange of encipherment tables. In September, 1940, and in November, 1940, there was a mutual exchange of book groups on two codes, namely "AR 38" and "RA 1".[152]

(5) Poland.

Two 1941 documents indicate that Pers Z S was receiving Polish intercept from the "Research" Bureau at that time, and that both were working on a secondary consular system, unnamed.[153]

(6) Scandinavia.

Dr. Mueller of Pers Z S stated that he "had some unofficial liaison with the people in the "Research" Bureau who were working on Scandinavian", but specifies no dates for this collaboration.[154]

(7) Spain.

The 1942 Pers Z S report from the Spanish Group mentioned several Spanish systems on which no work was done and added that"the "Research" Bureau held the opinion that machines were employed."[155]

(8) Switzerland.

(a) Swiss Enigma

In his 1941 report Dr. Brandes mentions solution of the Swiss Enigma. Apparently the "Research" Bureau furnished Pers Z S with a partial solution, which Dr. Kunze was able to complete. Thereafter there was an exchange of keys between the two agencies.[156]

[151] T 2252, Annual Report of the Italian Group for 1940.

[152] Ibid

[153] T 2038, Situation Report of the Polish Group, January 1, 1941

[154] I 22, Para 182

[155] Ibid, Page 4

[156] D54, Report # 8, Page 18

44

(b) Three-Letter Code.
The same report mentions a 2304 group, three-letter code in the same report. These tables were first solved by the "Research" Bureau, and later by Pers Z S.[157]

(9) Thailand.
At the beginning of 1942 the Thailand Code was turned over to the "Research" Bureau for copying.[158]

(10) Vatican.
While Pers Z S did some work on Vatican systems, the 1940 report indicates that most of the idents on Vatican systems were received from the "Research" Bureau.[159] Code values were exchanged in 1939 on an unidentified Vatican system.[160]

18. Liaison with the Signal Intelligence Agency of the Supreme Command Armed Forces (OKW/Chi).--
a. Cryptographic Cooperation.

> "Since the Army, with its military attachés, is dependent for transmission of its reports upon the cipher systems of the Foreign Office, it has a departmental interest in the security of diplomatic systems. It was suggested that close cooperation would be in the mutual interest... regarding breaches of security in the handling of ciphers."[161]

This statement, dated February 12, 1934, was taken from Dr. Paschke's notes. It documents the first known example of Pers Z-military cooperation looking toward an improved cipher security. It is not known whether the intent and doctrine stated here ever advanced beyond the discussion stage.

[157] Ibid

[158] D16, Report # 4, Page 3

[159] T2252, Annual Report of the Italian Group for 1940

[160] T 93

[161] DF 17, T3273, Page 3

The 1944-1945 picture shows strong Foreign Office (Pers Z) intransigeance in the matter of the Signal Intelligence Agency of the Supreme Command Armed Forces' (OKW/Chi) attempt to act as the senior German agency on all matters pertaining to security, and code and cipher compilation. In October, 1943, the Supreme Command of the German Armed Forces promulgated an order under which no code or cipher was to be employed in Germany without the prior consent of the Signal Intelligence Agency of the Supreme Command Armed Forces (OKW/Chi). In August, 1944, a special section (Gruppe IV) was created to coordinate the work of all departments in the armed forces which were interested in cipher matters.[162] From September, 1944, until January, 1945, special bi-weekly conferences on security were held under the chairmanship of Dr. Huettenhain of Signal Intelligence Agency of the Supreme Command Armed Forces (OKW/Chi). Their purpose was to achieve "unity among all German authorities using cipher systems", and out of them grew the unofficial Army-Navy-Air coordinating committee.[163] While Dr. Huettenhain could state with pride that the conference and the committee officially confirmed the preeminence of the Signal Intelligence Agency of the Supreme Command Armed Forces (OKW/Chi) as the main authority on cipher matters, it did not have any real powers. Recommendations could be made, but there was no obligation to comply. Furthermore, only service systems were covered.[164]

Foreign Office (Pers Z) representatives were invited to attend the meetings as guests. Usually Hauthal of the Cryptographic Section (Pers Z Chi) or Dr. Schauffler attended. Both Dr. Huettenhain and Lt. Col. Mettig stated that the Foreign Office went its own way in cipher security. Mettig is author of the statement that the Foreign Office "remained aloof and... would not cooperate, as it was not prepared to let other authorities see its ciphers".[165] Dr. Huettenhain's statement

[162] I 96, Page 13

[163] I 84, Page 4; I 176, Page 10

[164] I 84, Page 30

[165] I 96, Page 13

is requoted here:

> "OKW/Chi was never allowed to know the details of the ciphers used by the Foreign Office. He (Huettenhain) knew that one-time pads were used, and he had once met Schauffler and Hauthal. Even toward the end when there was a further attempt to centralize security under the Signal Intelligence Agency of the Supreme Command Armed Forces (OKW/Chi), the Foreign Office would not come into line. Selchow strongly opposed, it, preferring to remain independent."[166]

On the other hand, there is one instance of Foreign Office usage of equipment and systems furnished by the Signal Intelligence Agency of the Supreme Command Armed Forces (OKW/Chi). Dr. Schauffler noted that the Foreign Office used the Cipher Teleprinter (Geheimschreiber). The Signal Intelligence Agency of the Supreme Command Armed Forces (OKW/Chi) was responsible for the security of this device, having developed it and furnished it to the Foreign Office.[167]

b. Cryptanalytic Cooperation.

The Pers Z S/Signal Intelligence Agency of the Supreme Command Armed Forces (OKW/Chi) relationships in the cryptanalytic field contrast sharply with the collaboration, or lack of collaboration, in the cryptographic field. Both organizations considered diplomatic codes and ciphers as a primary commitment, with military attache systems as the exclusive province of the Signal Intelligence Agency of the Supreme Command Armed Froces (OKW/Chi). Since the Signal Intelligence Agency of the Supreme Command Armed Forces (OKW/Chi) was junior in the field to Pers Z S, a greater degree of jealousy and a lesser amount of cooperation might have been expected. However, from available sources it seems clear that

[166] I 31, Page 15

[167] I 22, Para 115

the cryptanalytic collaboration between the two agencies was the most extensive and probably the most successful of all the Pers Z S cooperation ventures. Duplication there was, and too much of it, but it is probable that this duplication was furthered by the attitude of jealous secrecy at the top of Pers Z, and a certain amount of lower-level resentment at the encroachments on a field which had once been exclusively in the possession of Pers Z S.[168]

Keitel, perhaps the most objective of the top leaders interviewed by TICOM (but also palpably uninformed on technical matters), characterized the Foreign Office as "extremely secretive and jealous about anything their bureau produced... . Von Ribbentrop always wanted to keep it strictly to himself."[169] Rave, Hierer and Grosse, who were on loan to Pers Z S from the Signal Intelligence Agency of the Supreme Command Armed Forces, (OKW/Chi) remarked on the duplication existing, and commented that Fenner and Paschke worked to avoid it. "Their efforts were not regarded with favor by Selchow", who thus appears again in the role of obstructionist.[170] Senior Specialist (Oberregierungsrat) Scherschmidt of Pers Z S, a veteran of 25 years cryptanalytic service, held a poor opinion of the Signal Intelligence Agency of the Supreme Command Armed Forces (OKW/Chi) translations in the Turkish field, and thought their results were disproportionate to the number of persons involved.[171] Dr. Rohrbach of Pers Z S was more than a little scornful toward the loaned personnel, characterizing them as having a lower level of capability that the regular Pers Z S members.[172]

[168] See DF 17, T3273

[169] I 143, Para 37

[170] I 22, Para 56

[171] I 103, Page 3

[172] I 22, Para 50

DOCID: 3486663

Assuming that some duplication and some personal jealousies did exist, the overall picture of the Pers Z S relationship with the Signal Intelligence Agency of the Supreme Command Armed Forces (OKW/Chi) is reasonably good. In the first place, Dr. Paschke and Principal Specialist (Ministerialrat) Fenner of the OKW Signal Intelligence Agency were old friends, both having been born in St. Petersburg.[173] By virtue of their positions these men were in a position to eliminate a substantial amount of duplication and friction. For example, when Pers Z S solved a new system which had a traffic content dealing with non-diplomatic matters, it was handed over to the Signal Intelligence Agency of the Supreme Command Armed Forces (OKW/Chi) for exploitation.[174] In 1940, after Pers Z S had worked on Scandinavian systems for three months, all Scandinavian work was transferred to the Signal Intelligence Agency of the Supreme Command Armed Forces (OKW/Chi).[175]

There were exchanges of personnel, the exact extent of which cannot be determined. Keitel is author of the statement that he "had put a few people at the disposal of von Ribbentrop... . at the outbreak of the war."[176] This group of people may well have worked on Chinese systems, for Schauffler mentioned that at the beginning of the war Chinese was taken up again, with the collaboration of the Signal Intelligence Agency of the Supreme Command Armed Forces (OKW/Chi), which supplied the personnel.[177] Rave, Hierer and Grosse of the Chinese Group were all Signal Intelligence Agency of the Supreme Command German Armed Forces (OKW/Chi) personnel, loaned to Pers Z S in December, 1943, to assist on Chinese

[173] I 172, Para 11. It is not intended to imply that Fenner and Paschke collaborated closely at all times. Questions of agency policy must have overridden friendship. For example, Fenner did not approve of contributions by Dr. Huettenhain to Dr. Schauffler's reports (I 31, Para 52). The military are also known to have engaged in a certain amount of cryptanalytic body-snatching. For example, a certain Dr. Rudolf Kochendoerfer, a leading mathematical cryptanalyst under Dr. Kunze in 1941, turns up as a corporal (Obergefreiter) in OKW/Chi in 1945 . I 176, Page 8

[174] I 22, Para 106

[175] I 22, Para 182

[176] I 143, Para 37

[177] I 22, Para 20

and Japanese traffic. Zastrow, the Pers Z S expert on U. S. systems was on one occasion loaned to the Signal Intelligence Agency of the Supreme Command Armed Forces (OKW/Chi) to work in their British-American group.[178]

As pointed out in the Introduction, there is some inconclusive evidence that parts of the Signal Intelligence Agency of the Supreme Command Armed Forces (OKW/Chi) may have been actually housed with Pers Z S. Keitel and Schauffler (cf. supra) mentioned a fairly extensive collaboration on Chinese at the beginning of the war. In his interrogation Rave might have implied that, in late 1943, after the RAF bombings of Berlin, the Chinese Section of the Signal Intelligence Agency of the Supreme Command Armed Forces (OKW/Chi) was at Im Dol, Dahlem, the Pers Z S address.[179]

Lt. Col. Mettig stated that, after the bombing,

> "Parts of OKW/Chi were accomodated with the Foreign Office... . Thus, in March, 1945, when OKW/Chi was moved to Halle-Nietleben, the equivalent parts of the Foreign Office accompanied it. These departments were thence to move to Eilenburg."[180]

Eilenburg is 10 miles from Zschepplin, the final location of a large part of the Pers Z S personnel. An unidentified part of Pers Z S was at Halle-Nietleben, and subsequently moved on to Zschepplin.[181] Since the senior member of the OKW/Chi group was 1st Lt. Adler, head of the Japanese Section, it might be assumed that the Pers Z S Japanese-Chinese section was the "party" mentioned.

[178] I 22, Para 84

[179] I 22, Para 52. "Rave had joined the OKW in October, 1941. He was first at Tirpitzufer 72-76 until it was bombed out, then at Im Dol, Dahlem." This same failure to dissociate Pers Z S and OKW/Chi is apparent in I 150, Page 8, where Uffz. Beyreuther mentioned Rave and Hierer as OKW/Chi members, both with military ranks.

[180] I 96, Page 5

[181] I-1, Page 7

In summation, it can be said that:

(1) The liaison between the Japanese-Chinese groups in Pers Z S and the Signal Intelligence Agency of the Supreme Command Armed Forces (OKW/Chi) appears to have been extraordinarily close.
(2) There is some evidence that, from November, 1943, until the end of the war, the two groups may have operated as one.

In other respects, the collaboration between the Signal Intelligence Agency of the Supreme Command Armed Forces (OKW/Chi) was also satisfactory. Certain problems were tackled on a cooperative basis, with a division of work. On the American State Department Strip Cipher ("O-2"), the Signal Intelligence Agency of the Supreme Command Armed Forces (OKW/Chi) worked on the point-to-point traffic, while Pers Z S worked on the circular traffic.[182] In the case of the Japanese "Red" Machine, Pers Z S worked on traffic from even days while the Signal Intelligence Agency of the Supreme Command Armed Forces (OKW/Chi) worked on odd days.[183] Results were exchanged. When the Signal Intelligence Agency of the Supreme Command Armed Forces (OKW/Chi) was bombed out in November, 1943, it seems to have made good use of the Pers Z S files until its own working material could be replaced. Tribute was paid by Colonel Kettler to the "good relations, both personal and professional, with the Foreign Office, which were then of great assistance."[184]

A detailed listing of known examples of Pers Z S collaboration with the Signal Intelligence Agency of the Supreme Command Armed Forces (OKW/Chi) follow .

[182] I 31, Para 52

[183] I 31, Para 53 It is worthy of noting that an identical "modus vivendi" was in effect from 1940 to 1942 between the U. S. Army and the U. S. Navy! This sort of "arrangement" was worked out in the U. S. by the "practical people" and not by the technical people concerned-- no doubt the German equivalent arrangement was worked out by the corresponding people!

[184] Zip/Sac, June 4, 1945, Page 3. OKW Activity Report for January 1, 1944, to June 25, 1944.

Detailed summary of cryptanalytic collaboration with the Signal Intelligence Agency of the Supreme Command Armed Forces (OKW/Chi):

(a) Brazil

BRAS B2.

This was a partially-alphabetic, five-letter, 82,400 group code. After Pers Z S had recovered about 2,200 groups, a copy of the original book was received from OKW/Chi.[185]

(b) England and the British Empire.

1. The Interdepartment Cipher, a five-figure system.

Pers Z S did not work on this system after the summer of 1942 or early 1943. However, OKW/Chi furnished a copy of the captured book and the solved additive sequences to Pers Z S.[186]

2. Code B30

This was a four-figure, two-part code. At the beginning of November, 1942, about 750 groups were turned over to OKW/Chi for copying. Idents were also furnished to Pers Z S by OKW/Chi.[187]

3. Code B31

This was another four-figure, two-part code (possibly the Foreign Office R Code of 1941 ?). In August, 1942, Pers Z S turned over about 1500 solved groups to OKW/Chi. Thereafter a regular exchange of solved groups was carried out between the two agencies.[188]

4. Code B22.

This was a five-figure, one-part code, known to the British as the Government Telegraph Code. It was also used by Eire for diplomatic transmissions. Pers Z S gave OKW/Chi all the Irish substitution and additive keys on this code.[189]

[185] D16 Report #2 p 3

[186] I 172, para 13; D 16, Report #2, p 1

[187] I 172, para 14; D 16, Report #4, p 2

[188] D 16, Report #4, p 2

[189] I 172, para 14

(c) Hungary.

In 1940 Dr. Paschke conferred with Fenner and Seifert of OKW/Chi with reference to initial Pers Z S work on Hungarian systems. It was agreed that Pers Z S should work on the system designated as "U3". It is not known whether or not any action was instituted.[190]

(d) Italy.

Pers Z S apparently considered itself the senior partner in the cooperative effort undertaken on Italian systems. The 1939-1940 reports from the Italian group mention that Pers Z S had broken the Italian diplomatic codes after OKW/Chi and the Austrian cryptanalytic organization had said the work was impossible, that OKW/Chi had no success when the exchanges of book groups and enciphering tables were terminated, etc.[191] The reports imply that Pers Z S considered its collaboration with Goering's "Research" Bureau more fruitful than that with OKW/Chi, although the OKW/Chi intercept was considered to be superior.[192] At the end of 1940 OKW/Chi and Pers Z S exchanged book groups on 4 codes, and there was a current exchange of solved encipherment tables.

There is little information covering the years 1941-1945, but Dr. Deubner's statement that "there was close cooperation with OKW/Chi" on Italian problems is probably correct.[193]

(e) Japan.

1. JB 57

JB 57 was a major Japanese diplomatic code. Toward the end of 1941, Pers Z S and OKW/Chi, working independently, solved the first daily keys.[194]

2. "Red" Machine.

Pers Z S worked on the even days, while OKW/Chi worked on the odd days.[195]

[190] T 2043, Film 9, Report of the Group Austria-Hungary, dated April 4, 1940

[191] See T2252

[192] T 2252, Annual Report of the Italian Group for the Year 1940

[193] I 22, Para 172

[194] D76, Film 41, 1941 Report of the Japan-Manchukuo-China Group.

[195] I 31, Para 53

(f) Mexico.

Xepit.

This five-letter code was compromised when OKW/Chi turned over a photocopy to Pers Z S on November 25, 1942. Pers Z S had broken it on the preceding day.[196]

(g) Portugal.

"205"

OKW/Chi gave Pers Z S a photocopy of this five-figure code book on December 14, 1942. Before the compromise, there had been a regular exchange of group meanings.[197]

(h) Russia.

There was no confirmed example of Pers Z S OKW/Chi collaboration on Russian systems. In February, 1934, there were Reichswehr-Pers Z S discussions on Russian military systems. Lt. Colonel Mettig stated that "after an unknown date" OKW/Chi did not work on Russian diplomatic traffic.[198]

(i) Turkey.

Rave, Hierer and Grosse said there had been "some co-operation on Turkish" early in 1943.[199]

[196] D16, Report #4, p 5

[197] D16, Report #4, p 3

[198] I 96, Para 14

[199] I 22, Para 56

DOCID: 3486663

(j) United States of America.

1. Code B6A

This five-letter code (called A1 by the State Department) was solved in September, 1939. A photocopy was received from OKW/Chi in 1941.[200]

2. Code B7

There is no direct mention of liaison on this system, but Pers Z S personnel appeared to be cognizant of the status of solution at other agencies, including OKW/Chi.[201]

3. Code B8

At the end of June, 1941, Pers Z S received a copy of this code (the Brown Code) from OKW/Chi.

4. "SV" (Diplomatic Strip System 01)

"In the summer of 1941 Pers Z S received from OKW/Chi a photocopy of the instructions for use , and 4 series of strips, which deciphered a number of messages." This appears to have been the Strip Device M-138A.[203] In the case of one (unidentified) U. S. Strip System, the Signal Intelligence Agency of the Supreme Command Armed Forces (OKW/Chi) worked on point to point traffic, while Pers Z S worked on circular traffic.[205]

19. Liaison with Foreign Cryptanalytic Agencies.-- All the Pers Z S personnel interrogated were unanimous in stating that they had never collaborated in any way with foreign (Finnish, Hungarian, Italian or Japanese) cryptanalysts. Pers Z S had never been visited by foreign cryptanalysts.

[200] DF 15, Introduction, p 4

[201] DF 15, pages 5, 6, 8

[202] DF 15, Introduction, p 4

[203] DF 15, p 5

[204] I 31, p 10. "SV" probably German abbreviation for Strip System (Streifenverfahren).

55

VOLUME 6

Chapter V. Intelligence

20. Summary and Conclusions.-- In summarizing the Pers Z S/Foreign Office organization for intelligence, as opposed to its organization for cryptanalysis, the following conclusions seem valid:

a. The question of intelligence output, and of organization for evaluation and dissemination, were neglected in the interrogations.

b. The personnel interrogated about this phase of their work, had either forgotten about the principal agency successes, or were apathetic and uninformed about the intelligence value of their activities.

c. No definite information is available as to the distribution of the Pers Z S decodes, their intelligence content, or their consideration and reception by higher authorities.

d. The organization seemed overly preoccupied with cryptanalysis as a science, and apparently did not think in terms of cryptanalysis as a prime source of intelligence.

21. Lack of Data on Intelligence in the Interrogations.-- The Pers Z S organization for intelligence, its evaluation and dissemination, seems to have been weak. From von Ribbentrop down, those interrogated could recall little important information which had been obtained from their work. Either there was little or no important intelligence in their decodes, or the material contained therein was never properly evaluated and fed back by higher authorities. The former impression must be erroneous.

An organization which read the Japanese "Red" machine and achieved nearly 100 per cent success on Italian diplomatic codes, must have produced some important intelligence results. The answer to the riddle must be sought elsewhere. It may have been the fault of internal organization (or lack of organization) for intelligence, or the attitude of the organization's leaders.[210]

One lead of potential significance was overlooked in the interrogations. Until September, 1941 (and probably later) there was a relatively high-ranking Pers Z S official, whose responsiblity was the evaluation of message content from an intelligence point of view. This was Technical Assistant (Wissenschaftlicher Hilfsarbeiter) Friedrich Niendorff, who had seniority in the organization dating from October, 1919.[211] There is no mention of Niendorff in the 1945 interrogations or personnel lists. In an organization which worked on the systems of some 50 countries and was invariably short of personnel, it is doubtful whether a separate evaluation group was overly desirable or efficient. However, had Niendorff been available, he might have been able to speak with some knowledge of the Sections's effectiveness as an intelligence agency. No attempt was made to cover the work done by Dr. Horn, who was in charge of cribs, files and personality lists (Archiv), and who presumably had some information along these lines.

22. Handling and Processing Intelligence.-- According to Miss Friedrichs, no intelligence was extracted from the material produced, except such as was necessary to continue reading the traffic.[212] Dr. Karstien, on the other hand, stated that the selection of material for publication was guided by considerations as to its possible intelligence value. This selection was made by the group head (Referent) on the basis of knowledge and experience.[213] Since Pers Z S apparently never had sufficient personnel to allow adequate cryptanalysis, it is probable that the group heads never had sufficient time to do a thorough analysis of the solved traffic.

[210] The interrogators also placed little emphasis on intelligence, and must share a part of the responsibility.

[211] See Anlage 2 to Pers Z 869/41 in TF 24

[212] I 22, Para 37

[213] I 22, Para 77

57

Miss Friedrichs and Scherschmidt apparently took pride in the careful standards of translation set up in the Section. Both commented on the rigid practices which prevailed in Pers Z S, in contrast to the looser practices prevalent with the Signal Intelligence Agency of the Supreme Command Armed Forces (OKW/Chi).[234] If the pride in careful translation evidenced by the above statements be taken in conjunction with Miss Friedrichs' statement as to work tempos, the impression could be drawn that care and precision in all phases of the work took precedence over considerations of urgency (intelligence?).[235]

Considering the emphasis laid by Schauffler and Rohrbach on the "Scientific" (wissenschaftliche) aspects of their work, and considering the strong academic tinge of the group as a whole, one may well wonder whether the Section as a whole had not fallen into that error of thought which may too easily dominate a cryptanalyst's work: viz., that cryptanalysis, an abstract science and the principal element in signal intelligence, may become an end in itself, and that the raison d'etre of cryptanalysis- the production of intelligence-may be obscured by these considerations.

a. Lack of Recognition by Higher Authorities.

This tendency can be magnified if cryptanalysts are not kept constantly aware of the meaning and signifance of their products, the importance of key messages, and the action taken by other authorities on the strength of cryptanalytic information. In this important respect the Pers Z S organization seems to have been deficient. Dr. Karstien's somewhat cynical statement that there was no official recognition of the work done by the organization is countered in part by Paschke's letter of commendation from von Weizsaecker for his Italian work, and the War Service Cross (KVK II) which was awarded to Dr. Rohrbach. These were probably isolated instances. Miss Friedrichs stated

[234] I 22, Para 38; I 103, Para 2. i.e. omitting corrupt groups or obscure passages.

[235] "There was no sense of urgency in the office, deciphered messages were not transmitted by teleprinter to their recipients." I 22, Para 37

58

that there had been no evidence of appreciation of the work done by the organization.

> "From time to time copies of messages issued had been returned to them bearing a stamp indicating they had been seen by the Fuehrer. Otherwise, no indication of the importance attached to their work had ever penetrated to the level at which she worked."[216]

If higher authorities did not tell the cryptanalysts that their work was of significant importance, it is not to be wondered that the technicians felt their work ignored and withdrew more and more into their own world of two-part codes and enciphering tables.

b. Attitude of the Pers Z S leaders.

Some responsiblity for the failure to disseminate internally information concerning successes must be assigned to the Pers Z S leaders. Selchow has already been characterized as a "competent administrator, who understood little about cryptography, and was content to let the heads of the subsections run their affairs as seemed best to them."[217] Paschke and Miss Hagen knew more about message content than did junior personnel.[218] Miss Friedrich stated that there was little encouragement given to the communication of results inside the organization by junior members, who were encouraged to mind their own business.[219] Apparently the Pers Z S leaders knew in a general way of their successes, but denied this information to the juniors who most needed the encouragement. It is possible of course, that there was little of great importance in the systems which Pers Z S read, but this seems scarcely credible. In all probability, the Pers Z S leaders were just not "intelligence-minded." They were cryptanalysts, they thought primarily in terms of cryptanalysis, and intelligence was to them a by-product of their work.

216 I 22, Para 36

217 I 22, Para 35

218 See I 22, Paras 107, 108, 110; I 27, Paras 3, 4.

219 I 22, Para 39

c. <u>Handling and Processing of Decodes</u>.

Information dealing with the assignment of missions is also limited. Instructions from von Ribbentrop were invariably of a general nature, and solely concerned with the subject matter of intelligence- Poland or the invasion. He did not concern himself with the details of systems. Selchow usually dealt direct with von Ribbentrop and did not go through Schroder or von Weizsaecker. To further confuse the issue of mission assignment, Miss Hagen stated that she received her instructions direct from the "Secretary" (Under-secretary Steengracht von Moyland).[221]

The distribution given to decodes is not known. The evidence is inconclusive even on the question of distribution within the Foreign Office. According to Dr. Paschke, von Ribbentrop "read only about 20-30 per cent of the material produced. His secretaries, Weber and von Loesch, selected these for him."[222] At one point in his interrogation von Ribbentrop stated that the selection of decodes for his own personal perusal was made by Inspector Schmidt. He saw between one and four items a day, or less.[223] His principal assistant, Steengracht von Moyland, or one of the secretaries, determined what distribution should be made outside the Ministry. Steengracht also drew his attention to certain other items.[224] If all these statements be taken at face value, at least five persons were involved in determining the distribution of decodes, with the consequent disadvantages of divided responsibility and possible loss of continuity.

Nor is it known where and how the Pers Z S intelligence was integrated into the total intelligence picture. All the top personalities interrogated at Nuernberg agreed that there was no central clearing house for intelligence at the top, and that this was unfortunate. There is some evidence that, due to the lack of high level coordination, the same decode might be passed to a ministry from two or three sources. Keitel did not

[220] I 172B, Par. 3

[221] I 172A, Para 18

[222] I 172B, Para 9

[223] I 143, Para 47

[224] I 143, Para 48

state whether or not he received all the Pers Z S decodes. Jodl knew in a general way of the Foreign Office achievements, but did not receive the Pers Z S output.[225] Where a message solved by the Signal Intelligence Agency of the Supreme Command Armed Forces (OKW/Chi) was not also in the hands of the Foreign Office, then a copy of the decode (VN) was passed to them.[226] Keitel also pointed out that the Foreign Office were

> "extremely secretive and jealous about anything their bureau produced. If, by any chance, Keitel produced direct to Hitler an OKW/Chi diplomatic decode and did not pass it via the Foreign Office, they became extremely annoyed. Actually, this happened very rarely."[227]

No mention is made of decodes exchanged between agencies for technical purposes, and decodes exchanged with agency heads to be used for intelligence purposes.

225 I 143, Para 6
226 I 143, Para 37
227 I 143, Para 37

VOLUME 6

Chapter VI. The Cryptographic Section of the German Foreign Office (Pers Z Chi)

23. History and Personnel.-- Little is known from TICOM sources concerning the history, strength and activities of the German Foreign Office Cryptographic Section (Chiffrierdienst des Referats Z in der Personalanteilung des Auswaertigen Amtes, abbreviated Pers Z Chi). It was responsible for the compilation, preparation and distribution of the codes and ciphers used by the German Foreign Office, as well as the cryptographic security of these systems. In the matter of security, senior personnel from the Cryptanalytic Section (Pers Z S) assisted the Cryptographic Section (Pers Z Chi) as consultants.[234] The Cryptographic Section was latterly (1943-1945) under the head of Senior Specialist (ORR) Horst Hauthal. Its previous head, a Senior Specialist (ORR) Langlotz, died in 1943.[235] At the end of the war, when Pers Z S was evacuated from Berlin, Pers Z Chi remained behind. No trace of the organization was found by TICOM personnel.

24. Cryptographic Work.-- Dr. Paschke, a consultant on cryptographic security, remarked that the Germans were convinced that their systems were cryptographically secure.[236]

[234] I 172B, Page 7; I 22, Para 8

[235] I 22, Para 70

[236] I 22, Para 118

62

It is possible that this attitude of complacency was responsible for some of the Anglo-American successes against Foreign Office systems. Pers Z Chi must have been responsible for the compilation of the "Deutsches Satzbuch" and the additive systems used for its encipherment, all of which were read by Anglo-American cryptanalysts. One of the additive systems was theoretically a "one-time pad" system, but was insecure because the additive used was predictable. This was the GEE additive (ASA trigraph) printed on the Number Printer (Numerierwerk) described in Volume 2 of this paper. An inspection of both recovered and captured daily key tables (Tagesschluessel) used in enciphering the indicators in the "Floradora" (ASA trigraph GEC) additive system indicates that these key tables may have been made up by a machine similiar to the Number Printer (Numerierwerk). There is no indication as to how the text additive itself was generated.

The Cryptographic Section seems to have been interested in improvements for the Enigma machine. In February, 1942, Schauffler and Hauthal discussed the construction of a new cipher machine with Willi Korn, chief engineer of the Enigma firm of Heimsoeth and Rincke, Berlin. It was to be called the Machine 42 (Maschine 42) and was in effect an Army plugboard Enigma with three additional rotors inserted in front of the plugboard. The machine never passed the theoretical development stage because of engineering and procurement difficulties.[237]

So far as is known from TICOM sources, the Foreign Office Cryptographic Section did not collaborate with any other German cryptographic agency. Schauffler and Hauthal attended the 1944-1945 meeting of the unofficial Army-Navy-Air coordinating committee on cryptographic security, which were held under the auspices of the Signal Intelligence Agency of the Supreme Command Armed Forces (OKW/Chi). A plugboard Enigma with a printing attachment, bearing the German Foreign Office label, has been captured, indicating that the military style Enigma was used for Foreign Office communications. It also used the military style cipher teleprinters.[238]

[237] T 5

[238] I 22, Para 115

63

TAB A

VOLUME 6

Tab A

Aler 1st Lt. Chief of Subsection V13 of OKW/Chi (Japan, China)

Administrative Section .See Pers Z Gen. Section responsible for personnel and administrative problems for all Foreign Office Z Branch, incl. Pers Z S, Pers Z Chi & Pers Z F.

ASA Army Security Agency (US)

Badoglio,Marshal .Prime Minister of Italian Government September, 1943-1945

Benzing, Dr. Johannes Specialist (RR).Cryptanalyst. Head of Pers Z S group for Near Eastern languages.

Beyreuther, Heinz,Sergeant (Uffz). Former cryptanalyst in Japanese Subsection at OKW/Chi

Brandes, Dr. Wilhelm,Senior Specialist (ORR). Cryptanalyst. Head of Pers Z S group for France, Belgium, Holland, Switzerland.

Buggisch, Dr. Otto,S/Sgt (Oberwachtmeister). Cryptanalyst. OKW/Chi. Formerly with Inspectorate 7/VI

Burgscheidungen. German village in Kreis Querfurt, Thuringia. Location of part of Pers Z S April/May, 1945.

Communications Section. See Pers Z F. Section in Z Branch, Foreign Office, which was responsible for Foreign Office communication networks, including telephone, teletype and radio. 1945 head was ORR Hoffmann (Funkreferat).

Cryptanalytic Section. See Pers Z S. Cryptanalytic Section in Z Branch of the German Foreign Office. (Sonderdienst des Referats Z in der Personalabteilung des Auswaertigen Amtes).

Cryptographic Section. See Pers Z Chi. Foreign Office Section in Z Branch responsible for preparation, compilation, distribution and security of Foreign Office codes and ciphers. 1945 head was ORR Hauthal (Chiffrierdienst des Referats Z in der Personalabteilung des Auswaertigen Amtes).

D16 Translations. "Annual Reports of the (Pers Z S) Group British Empire, Ireland, Thai, Portugal, Spain and Latin America." A TICOM Publication.

D54 Translations of various Z S reports dealing with work on French, Belgian, Dutch, Swiss and Rumanian systems).

DOCID: 3486663

Deubner, Dr. Otfried, Technical Asst. (WHA). Cryptanalyst. Deputy to Dr. Paschke in Pers Z S Italian-Greek-USSR group.

DF 17 "Miscellaneous Items from the Files of the German Foreign Office." A translation of T3273 and T165. A TICOM Publication.

Doenitz, Karl, Admiral. Head of German Admiralty. Briefly head of German govt. April/May/1945.

Fenner,....., Principle Specialist (Ministerialrat). Cryptanalyst. Head of Section IV of OKW/Chi.

Friedrichs, Miss Asta, Technical Asst. (WHA). Pers Z S cryptanalyst. Deputy to Dr. Karstien in Slavonic language section. Leading female personality in Pers Z S.

Gerstmeyer, Dr. Liaison Officer from Goering's "Research" Bureau (FA) to the Foreign Office.

Grosse, Sr.,Arthur. Pers Z S cryptanalyst, Chinese and Japanese language group. On loan to Pers Z S from OKW/Chi.

Grunsky, Dr. Helmut, Technical Asst. (WHA). Pers Z S cryptanalyst. Group head in Dr. Kunze's mathematical-cryptanalytic Subsection.

Hagen, Miss Ursula, Technical Asst. (WHA). Pers Z S Cryptanalyst. Head of language group England, Ireland, Spain, Portugal and Latin American countries.

Hauthal, Horst, Senior Specialist (ORR). Head of Pers Z Chi 1945.

Hermsdorf. Village in Silesia. Location of Pers Z S Mathematical-Cryptanalytic Subsection 12/43-3/45.

Hierer, Edgar. Minor Pers Z S cryptanalyst. On loan from OKW/Chi to Japanese-Chinese language group.

Hirschberg. Village in Riesengebirge. Location of part of Pers Z S 12/43-3/45.

Hoffmann, Ernst, Senior Specialist (ORR). Head of Pers Z F 1945.

Horn, Prof. Dr., Technical Asst. (WHA). In charge of Pers Z S files and records (Archiv) 1945. Not captured.

Huehnke, Miss Dr. Annelise, Technical Asst. (WHA). Pers Z S cryptanalyst. Group head in Mathematical-cryptanalytic Subsection.

Huettenhain, Dr. Erich. Chief cryptanalyst for OKW/Chi from 1937.

DOCID: 3486663

1-1. Final Report of TICOM Team 3 on the Exploitation of Burgscheidungen, dated June 8, 1945. Later canceled as I-1, and renumbered as a Team Report. A TICOM Publication.
1-22. "Interrogation of German Cryptographers of the Pers Z S Department of the Auswaertiges Amt." A TICOM Publication.
I-25. "Interrogation of Five Members of the RLM/Forschungsamt at Schloss Gluecksburg, near Flensburg, on 15th and 21st June 1945." A TICOM Publication.
I-27. "Preliminary Interrogations for Fraeulein Hagen, Head of the English Section of Pers Z S, Auswaertiges Amt." A TICOM Publication.
I-31. "Detailed Interrogations of Dr. Huettenhain, Formerly Head of Research Section of OKW/Chi, 18-21 June, 1945." A TICOM Publication.
I-54. "Second Interrogation of Five Members of the RLM/Forschungsamt." A TICOM Publication.
I-58. "Interrogation of Dr. Otto Buggisch of OKW/Chi." A TICOM Publication.
I-63. "Interrogation Report on ORR Herrmann Scherschmidt of Pers Z S Auswaertiges Amt." A TICOM Publication.
I-84. "Further Interrogation of RR Dr. Huettenhain and Sdf. Dr. Fricke of OKW/Chi." A TICOM Publication.
I-89. "Report by Dr. H. Rohrbach of Pers Z S on American Strip Cipher." A TICOM Publication.
I-96. "Interrogation of Oberstleutnant Mettig on the Organization and Activities of OKW/Chi." A TICOM Publication.
I-103. "Second Interrogation of Reg. Rat Herrmann Scherschmidt of Pers Z S Auswaertiges Amt on Turkish and Bulgarian systems." A TICOM Publication.
I-143. "Report on the Interrogation of Five Leading Germans at Nuremberg on 27 September, 1945 (Jodl, Keitel, Doenitz, Goering, von Ribbentrop)." A TICOM Publication.
I-147. "Detailed Interrogation of Members of OKM 4 SKL III at Flensburg." A TICOM Publication.
I-150. "Report by Uffz. Heinz Beyreuther on the Organization of OKW/Chi." A TICOM Publication.
I-162. "Report on Interrogation of Kurt Sauerbier of RLM/Forschungsamt held on 31 August, 1945." A TICOM Publication.

I-172. Interrogation of Hagen and Paschke of Pers Z S. A TICOM Publication.

Jodl, Alfred, General. Chief of the Armed Forces Operations Staff.

Karstien, Dr. Hans-Heidrun, Specialist (RR). Pers Z S cryptanalyst. Head of Slavonic language group.

Kasper, ... Dr., Specialist (RR). Pers Z S Cryptanalyst. Head of Rumanian language group. Not captured.

Keitel, Wilhelm, Field Marshal . Chief of Staff, Supreme Command Armed Forces (OKW).

Kettler, Hugo, Colonel. Chief of OKW/Chi 1943-1945.

Kochendoerfer, Dr. Rudolf, Corporal. Mathematical cryptanalyst, formerly with Pers Z S, latterly corporal with OKW/Chi.

Krug, Hans-Georg, Technical Asst. (WHA). I.B.M. machine expert in Pers Z S.

Kunze, Dr. Werner, Senior Specialist (ORR). Head of Mathematical-Cryptanalytic Subsection of Pers Z S.

Lehmann, Dr. Bruno. Cryptanalyst, Former head of Greek language group in Pers Z S.

von Loesch, Karl Heinrich. Secretary to Foreign Minister von Ribbentrop.

Menning, Wilhelm. Deputy head of Pers Z S Rumanian language group. Not captured.

Mettig, ..., Lt. Colonel. Second in command of OKW/Chi, 12/43-1945.

von Moyland. See Steengracht.

Muehlhausen. Location of elements of Pers Z S 1945.

Mueller, Dr. Hans-Kurt, Technical Asst. (WHA). Cryptanalyst. Head of Pers Z S American-Scandinavian group 1945.

Niendorff, Friedrich, Senior Specialist (ORR) In charge of Pers Z S intelligence evaluation 1941. Not captured.

Olbricht, Dr. Peter, Technical Asst. (WHA). Cryptanalyst, Pers Z S. Deputy head of Japanese-Chinese language group.

Oschmann, ..., Captain. Later Major. Head of Chiffrierabteilung in Reichswehrministerium 1932-34.

Pannwitz, Miss Dr. Erika, Technical Asst. (WHA). Cryptanalyst in Pers Z S. Group head in Mathematical-Cryptanalytic Subsection.

Paschke, Dr. Adolf, Senior Specialist (ORR). Pers Z S Cryptanalyst. Head of Linguistic-Cryptanalytic Subsection. Specialist in Italian.

Patzig, ..., Lt. Commander (Korvettenkapitaen). Unknown. Connected with Chiffierabteilung, Reichswehrministerium 1934.

Pers Z Chi. See Cryptographic Section, German Foreign Office.

Pers Z F. See Communications Section, German Foreign Office.

Pers Z Gen. German name unknown. Z Branch administrative Section, German Foreign Office.

Pers Z S. See Cryptanalytic Section, German Foreign Office.

Rave, Kurt. Minor Pers Z S cryptanalyst. Worked in Japanese-Chinese group. Loaned to Pers Z S by OKW/Chi.

Ribbentrop, Joachim von, Foreign Minister. German Foreign Office.

Rohrbach, Prof. Dr. Hans. Pers Z S cryptanalyst. Group leader in Mathematical-Cryptanalytic Subsection.

Roy, ..., Senior Specialist (ORR). Head of Pers Z Gen 1945.

Sauerbier, Kurt. Cryptanalyst, head of Section 9-c, Main Section IV (Agent systems) in Goering's "Research" Bureau.

Schauffler, Dr. Rudolf, Senior Specialist (ORR). Senior cryptanalyst and probable head of Pers Z S.

Scherschmidt, Dr. Hermann, Senior Specialist (ORR). Pers Z S cryptanalyst. Head of Turkish language group.

Schimmel, ... Pers Z S cryptanalyst. Head of Yugoslav group.

Schmidt,....., Inspector. Unknown. Probably Chief interpreter in German Foreign Office.

Schrader, Miss Hildegarde, Technical Asst. (WHA). Pers Z S cryptanalyst. Deputy head of French, Dutch, Belgian and Swiss group.

Schroder,....., Ministerial Director (Min. Dirigent). Head of main Section IV (Codes and Ciphers) in Goering's "Research" Bureau.

Schroeter, Dr. Karl, Technical Asst. (WHA). Pers Z S cryptanalyst. Group leader in Mathematical-Cryptanalytic Subsection.

Schultz, Klaus,Technical Asst. (WHA). Pers Z S cryptanalyst. Group leader in Mathematical Cryptanalytic Subsection.

Schwaeger, ..., Principle Specialist (ORR). Civil Servant, in charge of budget preparation in German Foreign Office.

68

Selchow, ..., Minister (Gesandte) Head of Z Branch (Cryptanalysis, Cryptography, Communications) in the German Foreign Office.

Steengracht von Moyland. Former ADC to von Ribbentrop. Succeeded von Weizsaecker as Undersecretary in the Foreign Office May 1, 1943.

T 56. Reports of the A Group. Reports and Studies by the American Group of the Cryptanalytic Section of the German Foreign Office 1919-1942.

T 76. Situation Report of the Manchurian Group Beginning 1941. Notes and Reports on Japanese Cipher Systems 1919-1941.

T 197. Unidentified Pers Z S Document covering work on Chinese.

T 427. Chinese 5/L Diplomatic Traffic (Film 10).

T 1062. Partially Reconstructed 3/1 code Afgh(anistan) 1.

T 1067. Afghanistan Traffic 1939-1944.

T 1068. Afghan Traffic 1939-1944.

T 1074. 1941 Traffic and Worksheets- Iraq.

T 1077. Washington - Addis Ababa Traffic, 1945.

T 1169. Chinese Diplomatic Traffic and Decodes.

T 1170. Old Material on HNM (abc)- Chinese.

T 1172. Chinese diplomatic traffic and explanation of system.

T 2038. Report on Polish Systems as of January 1, 1941. Report on the Polish-Bulgarian Group, dated Aug. 13, 1941. Report on Jugoslavia at Beginning of year 1941.

T 2043. Report of the Group-Austria-Hungary, dated April, 1940.

T 2050. See D 54.

T 2052. Various Reports from "Gruppe Lehmann," the Pers Z S Greek group 1939-1940-1941.

T 2252. Report of the Italian Group for the Year 1940.

T 3273. See D F 17.

Tranow,....., Senior Specialist (ORR). Principal GAF cryptanalyst in Signal Intelligence Agency of the Supreme Commander, German Air Forces.

Weber,...... Foreign Office Privy Councillor, Secretary to von Ribbentrop
Weizsaecker, Ernst von. Former Undersecretary in German Foreign Office. In 1943 appointed Minister to the Vatican.
Wilhelm Wander Schule. School building in Hermsdorf (Silesia), location of the Pers Z S Mathematical-Cryptanalytic Subsection 12/43- 3/45.
Sastrowo, Karl, Technical Asst. (WHA). Pers Z S cryptanalyst. Expert on U. S. systems.
Zschepplin. Village in the Delitsch-Eilenburg-Leipzig area. Location of part of Pers Z S April, 1945.

DOCID: 3486663

CAPTURED DOC & INTERROG NUMBERS B.TIB 2028

561

ADVATIS

BULLETIN NUMBER.

DOCID: 3486663

N-54-4

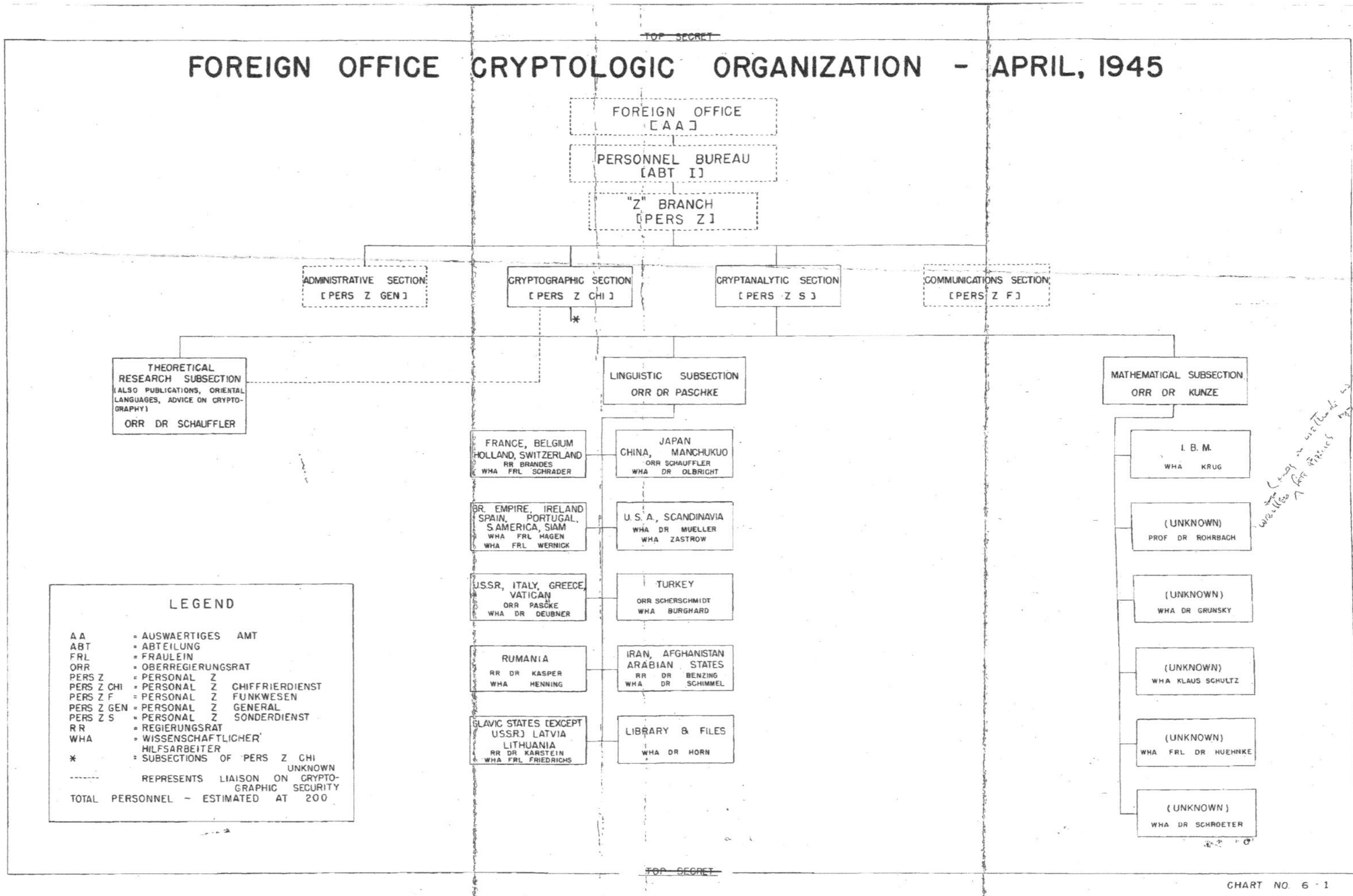
TOP SECRET
FOREIGN OFFICE CRYPTOLOGIC ORGANIZATION - APRIL, 1945
FOREIGN OFFICE [AA]
PERSONNEL BUREAU [ABT I]
"Z" BRANCH [PERS Z]
ADMINISTRATIVE SECTION [PERS Z GEN]
CRYPTOGRAPHIC SECTION [PERS Z CHI]
CRYPTANALYTIC SECTION [PERS Z S]
COMMUNICATIONS SECTION [PERS Z F]
THEORETICAL RESEARCH SUBSECTION (ALSO PUBLICATIONS, ORIENTAL LANGUAGES, ADVICE ON CRYPTOGRAPHY) ORR DR SCHAUFFLER
LINGUISTIC SUBSECTION ORR DR PASCHKE
MATHEMATICAL SUBSECTION ORR DR KUNZE
FRANCE, BELGIUM HOLLAND, SWITZERLAND RR BRANDES WHA FRL SCHRADER
JAPAN CHINA, MANCHUKUO ORR SCHAUFFLER WHA DR OLBRICHT
BR. EMPIRE, IRELAND SPAIN, PORTUGAL, S.AMERICA, SIAM WHA FRL HAGEN WHA FRL WERNICK
U.S.A., SCANDINAVIA WHA DR MUELLER WHA ZASTROW
USSR, ITALY, GREECE, VATICAN ORR PASCKE WHA DR DEUBNER
TURKEY ORR SCHERSCHMIDT WHA BURGHARD
RUMANIA RR DR KASPER WHA HENNING
IRAN, AFGHANISTAN ARABIAN STATES RR DR BENZING WHA DR SCHIMMEL
SLAVIC STATES [EXCEPT USSR] LATVIA LITHUANIA RR DR KARSTEIN WHA FRL FRIEDRICHS
LIBRARY & FILES WHA DR HORN
I. B. M. WHA KRUG
(UNKNOWN) PROF DR ROHRBACH
(UNKNOWN) WHA DR GRUNSKY
(UNKNOWN) WHA KLAUS SCHULTZ
(UNKNOWN) WHA FRL DR HUEHNKE
(UNKNOWN) WHA DR SCHROETER
LEGEND
AA = AUSWAERTIGES AMT
ABT = ABTEILUNG
FRL = FRAULEIN
ORR = OBERREGIERUNGSRAT
PERS Z = PERSONAL Z
PERS Z CHI = PERSONAL Z CHIFFRIERDIENST
PERS Z F = PERSONAL Z FUNKWESEN
PERS Z GEN = PERSONAL Z GENERAL
PERS Z S = PERSONAL Z SONDERDIENST
RR = REGIERUNGSRAT
WHA = WISSENSCHAFTLICHER HILFSARBEITER
* = SUBSECTIONS OF PERS Z CHI UNKNOWN
------- REPRESENTS LIAISON ON CRYPTOGRAPHIC SECURITY
TOTAL PERSONNEL - ESTIMATED AT 200
TOP SECRET
CHART NO. 6-1

DOCID: 3486670

~~TOP SECRET CREAM~~

ARMY SECURITY AGENCY

Washington, D. C.

EUROPEAN AXIS SIGNAL INTELLIGENCE IN WORLD WAR II AS REVEALED BY "TICOM" INVESTIGATIONS AND BY OTHER PRISONER OF WAR INTERROGATIONS AND CAPTURED MATERIAL, PRINCIPALLY GERMAN

VOLUME 7--GOERING'S "RESEARCH" BUREAU

Prepared under the direction of the

CHIEF, ARMY SECURITY AGENCY

1 May 1946

WDGAS-14

~~TOP SECRET CREAM~~

VOLUME 7

VOLUME I

Chapter I - Introduction

1. Short summary of the history, organization, and operations of the FA. Goering's Research Bureau, called "Goering's" by TICOM because of its final responsibility to Reichsmarschal Hermann Goering, was composed of about 2000 persons. The main office, under the direction of a Gottfried Schapper who held the civil service rank of a Ministerial Direktor, was divided into six main sections (Hauptabteilungen) indicated by Roman numerals, and fifteen sections (Abteilungen) indicated by arabic numerals. In addition there were one branch office and at least four Regional Offices besides an undetermined number of intercept stations. Main Section IV, of about 180 persons, was the cryptanalytic branch and handled that portion of the raw material (possibly 20%) which was in code or cipher. Goering's Research Bureau was charged with providing the Nazi state with reliable diplomatic, economic, and political information to be derived from monitoring all internal German telephone, telegraph, and wireless communications (including such communications from within Germany to foreign countries); foreign wireless communications of a commercial and diplomatic nature; foreign press and news broadcasts and speeches of politicians; and from the study of available newspapers and periodicals. To secure the raw materials for this project it operated its own intercept and monitoring service. The Research Bureau collaborated with the Abwehr and Gestapo in censoring all communications in Germany and in German occupied territory. The information produced was distributed in the form of finished reports (of various types) to Goering and Hitler and to the top Nazi officials and interested departments of the government. The home location of Goering's Research Bureau was Berlin, Charlottenburg 2, Schillerstrasse Nrs. 116-124

2. The discovery of the FA by TICOM. The Research Bureau appears to have been the Nazi Party Cryptanalytic Agency. The existence of this intelligence agency was unknown to British and American sources prior to its discovery by TICOM. TICOM Team 3 learned of the existence

DOCID: 3486670

of such an agency while questioning members of the Foreign Office Cryptanalytic Section at Burgscheidungen on 28 April 1945 and on 9 May 1945 Team 1 discovered the abandoned quarters of this organization in the barracks near the airfield at Kaufbeuren, 50 miles southwest of Munich. A file of administrative papers, including a directive, signed by Gottfried Schapper, the head of the bureau, were found which gave the organization at that time and served as a basis for further investigation.

3. Scope of this paper and indication of sources used. This report is an historical description of the RLM/FA and an evaluation of its operations. For convenience the abbreviation FA will be used in this paper whenever Goering's Research bureau is mentioned. (This is the standard reference used by the Germans themselves for the organization.) It will be seen that the FA was founded by Goering and protected under the cover name of Reich Air Ministry Research Bureau (Reichsluftfahrtministeriums/Forschungsamt) although the FA was actually not an operational division of the Air Ministry but was the Nazi Party rival of the military signal intelligence agencies. In Appendix I details of its cryptanalytic successes are given. Appendix II is a translation of the Kaufbeuren directive which sets forth the organization of the FA at the end of the war and indicates the content of other papers. Appendix III is an autobiography of Schapper, the last head of the FA. Tab A contains all known personnel of the FA, names of all other persons mentioned, identification of all places, terms, titles and abbreviations used, and a bibliography of references consulted in this paper. It is intended to present the details of its organization and to indicate the nature and success of its operations in as objective a manner as possible. The report is based on the various TICOM/Interrogation Reports[1] and as such is considerably subjective in that the interests of the interrogators and the opinions of the informants are reflected. Objective check of the statements elicited in the interrogations is possible from miscellaneous TICOM Documents

1. For convenience, these TICOM/Interrogations will be referred to as I in the footnotes.

2

which reveal details of cryptanalytic success and liaison with other agencies[2]; press reports[3], various non-TICOM Prisoner of War Interrogations[4], related entries in Intelligence reports[5], and in particular by various administrative memoranda found at Kaufbeuren[6]. Since the primary commitment of the TICOM Teams lay with German cryptanalysis their investigations properly covered German methods, successes, techniques, and equipment in that field. In the case of the FA, however, cryptanalysis was but one of several activities and, as the following pages will show, by no means the major

[2]Pers. ZS Yearly Report of British Empire Section for 1941 and 1942. D.Ic.Cf. Appendix I British systems.

[3]IF 188. Four stories based on telephone conversations between high German officials at the time of the Anschluss by an Associated Press reporter, Daniel De Luce, appeared on 4,5,6, and 7 November 1945 with a Berlin dateline. These stories not only revealed the extent of the telephone monitoring carried on by the FA but also indicated its success in reading a French diplomatic system at that time. An effort has been made to secure the original documents on which these stories were based. TICOM representatives in Europe, however, have reported 21 May 46 that the De Luce material "Did not indicate any French Code as having been broken nor did it give any information on cryptanalytic techniques nor did it indicate any successes with Allied Ciphers".

[4]Both the CSDIC (Combined Service Detailed Interrogation Center) and regular PW Interrogations have yielded considerable information and opinion on the Forschungsamt. Information so obtained must be carefully controlled with consideration of the informant's probable reliability. The opinion expressed is often tinged with jealousy or based on rumor and as such is of slight value even as gossip.

[5]The Weekly Intelligence Summary (Office of the Assistant Chief of Staff, G-2; Headquarters, United States Forces, European Theater) has reported on the FA (Number 12 of 4 October 1945), IF143, and referred to its wire-tapping activities (Number 15 of 25 October 1945), IF132.

[6]Ticom Document 240 (FILM 34).

one. It happened that the FA personnel available for questioning did not give the impression of having been exceptionally competent cryptanalysts. The grandiose claims made by Goering[7] and Schapper[8] are balanced by the generally low opinion of the FA appearing throughout the Interrogations. A final evaluation of the FA's cryptanalytic work lies somewhere between these extremes. Such presentation, with the FA cryptanalysis placed in terms of the overall operations of the FA, constitutes the following report.

[7] I. 108 and 143.

[8] Final Report of Team 1, Appendix 2, (I 15).

DOCID: 3486670

VOLUME 7

Chapter II - The History and Organization of the FA

A. The History of the FA.

4. The Founding of the FA. The establishment of the FA was brought about by Goering, himself, although the actual conception of the role of such an organization seems to be due to Schapper, the last head of the FA, and his predecessors, Schimpf and von Hesse. Independent statements by Goering[9] and by Schapper[10] are available which are in agreement on the details of the planning and founding of the FA. Confirmation and slight supplementation is found in the interrogations of ex-members of the FA and of individuals who had dealings with it[11].

[9] I 108 I 143 pp 12 ff.

[10] Final Report of Team 1, Appendix 2 (I 15)

[11] Members of the FA include senior specialist Dr. Martin Paetzel, specialist Otto Fingerhut, specialist Hoeckley Oden, Dr. Heinz Klautsche, principal specialist Seifert (I 25 and 54) and Lother Guenther (CSDIC, MU 500, HQ 7th Army, Ref. No. 708, 29 January 1945; I 46). Various members of the Foreign Office Cryptanalytic Section gave an outline of the organization of the FA (I 1) and Mettig (I 131) of the Signal Intelligence Agency of the Supreme Command of the Armed Forces was acquainted with its outline--Mettig to a surprising degree.

DOCID: 3486670

The first interrogation of Goering is of a general nature and is filled out by the second interrogation. The opinion of the Interrogators that Goering talked readily and reliably but had no mind for details appears to be correct in so far as his statements can be checked[12]. The first interrogation summarizes Goering's statements as follows:

> This name (Forschungsamt des Reichsluftfahrt Ministeriums-German Air Ministry Scientific Research Office) is merely camouflage as this office was not concerned with the Air Ministry in any way. It was conceived and founded by Goering in 1933 for the purpose of a central control over the collection and dissemination of vital information of military, commercial, and political nature. This information was obtained by the monitoring of all communications systems such as domestic and foreign radio, cables, etc.
>
> Previous to 1933 the Foreign Office had established a similar monitoring system, for intercepting wireless messages, and the police had monitored telephone conversations etc. but Goering wanted an organization of his own which could handle all phases under one central control. By various means he was able to obtain the services of some of the most able men in Germany for the construction and administration of this project. Goering was responsible authority, issued all directives, and dictated the policy. Under-Secretary Paul Koerner was second in command while the actual managing director was Ministerial Director [Gottfried] Schapper . . . .

[12] I 108, ii: "PW Goering cannot be considered a strictly truthful character when discussing personal relations, possessions, etc. and when an investigation of his income and fortune is made. At the same time he has been considerably shaken in his bloated belief in his own grandeur. He talks readily and, if is believed, reliably on questions about the Nazi state, personalities, the Air Corps, conduct of the war, etc. He is a drug addict. He has no mind for details and apparently considered such beneath him."

In fairness to Goering it should be noted that, according to an Associated Press story in the New York Times of 23 November 1945, Goering possesses the highest "I.Q." of the Nuremburg War Criminals (138!) and is assuming "leadership" in their deportment at the trials.

6

> The main office was situated in Berlin . . . . Employees were civilians, at least in the responsible positions but the total number of employees, distribution etc. were minor details with which source did not concern himself.
>
> The information was collected, decoded, classified and disseminated. All ministries were recipients of the finished product, receiving however, only that material which concerned their own particular province. . . . Goering's group was most successful due to the outstanding ability of his experts and technicians.[13]

This is expanded in the second interrogation where Goering is quoted to the effect:

> That Signals Intelligence had been of very great value, and particularly so as regards the product of the RLM/Forschungsamt. He had personally founded the FA in 1933; it had never in actual fact been a part of the Luftwaffe or of the RLM, but as some sort of camouflage was desirable for an organization of this nature it had been nominally attached to the German Air Ministry for the purpose of "cover". In 1933 he had discovered to his astonishment that no organization existed within the Reich to deal with cryptanalysis on anything approaching a broad general basis. In its early days the FA had covered all fields of traffic-- economic, political, diplomatic, private, military, etc.
>
> The work of the FA comprised two almost completely separate activities, firstly, that of telephone monitoring, and secondly that of interception and cryptanalysis. . . .
>
> He was very satisfied with the FA, which was a first class organization employing the very best cryptanalytic staff and with intercept arrangements for taking all available traffic. He thought that they were able to deal with 32 different languages. The virtues of the organization lay in the fact that they did not

[13] I 108 pp 2 and 3.

confine themselves to any particular field of intelligence and had no political axe to grind, nor ideology to follow; they were just given the technical requirements to intercept and break traffic and to disseminate intelligence.

He did not control the work programs of the cryptanalysts; they had a general directive to take everything and to read everything; further detailed direction was left to the head of the FA. If it was a question of needing additional staff they applied to State Secretary Koerner who also dealt with all of their higher administrative matters. The first head of the FA had been Kapitanleutnant Schimpf; he had been succeded by Prince Christoph von Hessen, who had eventually returned to the Luftwaffe; the post had then been taken over by Herr Schapper who had always belonged to the organization and who was probably the best technical man of them all. Goering used to visit them only once every year because the organization worked so well on its own. The high level channel of responsibility was from Schapper to Koerner and from him to the Reichsmarschall himself.[14]

Schapper, in the outline of the FA which he prepared for Team 1 at Augsburg on 1 June 1945, presents essentially the same facts as does Goering, although Schapper claims a greater role for himself:

The Forschungsamt.

1) Founded: April 1933

2) Reasons for the foundation: My work in the cipher bureau of the Reichswehr Ministry (1927-1933) had shown me the incompetence of the methods employed there so that I, with several of my colleagues, resigned from it and proposed to Goering the formation of an Intelligence Bureau for the Reich Government that should be free of departmental ties and extraneous influence.

[14] I 143 pp 12-13

3) Name: Goering consented, and only requested the camouflaging of the bureau under the name Reichsluftfahrtministerium-Forschungsamt. My request, that we should, however, be independent of the Air Ministry, was granted: the bureau became independent, with its own administration and establishment; it was also not subordinated to the Reich Air Ministry (Staatssekretär Milch), but allocated for supervision to Staatssekretär Koerner of the Prussian Ministry of State; finance was regulated directly from the (Prussian) treasury (Finanzhof).

4) The nature of the bureau: The bureau was consequently a civilian institution. For reasons of security a small number of its officials was put into German Air Force uniform as Armed Forces Officials for the duration of the war. This was done only with those officials who had to cooperate with outside authorities.

The research bureau restricted itself to intercepting and processing signals that could not [sic] be intercepted by technical means. . . .[15]

Schapper, as will be seen from his autobiography (AppendixIII), had served in an administrative capacity as a Signal Intelligence Officer during the first World War. His position in the Defense Ministry is not clear although he stated that it was administrative. His record as a Nazi is perhaps even more significant. He stated that he knew Goering well from the first World War. He was a member of the "National Society of Berlin to Rescue the Reich from the Revolution," and as such took part in the Kapp-Ludendorf putsch. Because of trouble with "communists" he migrated to Munich where he joined the Nazi Party in 1920, resigning after the 1923 Putsch but rejoining in 1931. From 1933 to 1937 or 1938 he admits to membership in the Allgemeine SS (General Elite Gaurd). All of these facts are significant for an understanding of the position of the FA and Schapper's role in it.

The statement of Seifert, Principal Specialist in charge of Evaluation in the FA, indicates that the first head of the FA, Schimpf, was also responsible for its formation:

[15]Schapper, IF 15 Appendix 2.

> The bureau was founded in 1933 at the instigation of a certain Kap.(?) Schimpf in order to provide diplomatic and commercial intelligence of an absolutely reliable kind by the monitoring of telephone, cable, and wireless links from the Reich outward and in the case of wireless from all countries, and to insure by the setting up of a new and independent organization the elimination of all bias which might have resulted from association with the old established ministries. The objective of the department was the production of a purely objective and scientific picture of the world-wide political and commercial situation.[16]

And again Seifert and Paetzel, Senior specialist in charge of Cryptanalytic Research for the FA:

> Q. When was the Forschungsamt founded?
> Seifert: In 1933
> Q. Who initiated it?
> Seifert: It was started by Korvetten Kapitän Schimpf who committed suicide.
> Q. Who was the driving force behind your organization?
> Seifert: It was started under the Air Ministry with the intention of its being an inter-service organization.
> Q. Where did Goering fit into the Organization?
> Seifert: The Fuehrer directed Goering to run this organization. I do not know more as I only joined at the end of 1933.
> Paetzel: I joined at the end of July 1933. The organization had then been running for two or three months.[17]

Still another interrogation may be cited which associates The FA with the Nazi Party:

> With the advent of the Nazis came the creation of the Forschungsamt which was directly responsible to Göring. This was placed under the command of a Kapitän-Leutnant Schimpf who had previously been Naval Liaison Officer

[16] I 54 p 3.

[17] I 25 p 3. It should be pointed out that the Air Ministry was established by a decree of 5 May 1933 (RGBl. I,p.241). The "two or three months" of Paetzel, and Schapper's "April" are not a discrepancy but furnish additional evidence that the FA was separate from the Air Ministry *ab initio*.

at OKH/Chi. Forschungsamt was really concerned with the interception of all communications - including telephones, telegraphs, postal correspondence, television (sic) and radio - which might help the Nazi Party to perfect its hold on life within Germany.[18]

5. Relations of the FA with other cryptologic agencies. From the reports cited above it seems clear that the FA was created by Goering at the suggestion of Schapper and Schimpf. (As Schimpf was the first head of the organization his influence with Goering was probably greater than that of Schapper.[19]) In spite of the cover name, the FA was not a part of the Air Ministry and the chain of command from Goering through Prussian State Secretary Koerner (rather than Milch of the Air Ministry) to the head of the FA emphasizes this independence. The first head was Kapitaen-Leutnant Schimpf, formerly liaison officer for the cipher section of the Defense Ministry (Reichswehrministerium/Referate G?) to the Navy cipher section, whose full name is unknown and who is reported to have committed suicide.[20] His successor was Prince Christoph von Hesse, who is only known as head of the FA.[21] Gottfried Schapper, the final head of the FA, became director in the fall of 1944. Both Lt. Col. Mettig and Dr. Huttenhain, Senior Specialist, of the Signal Intelligence Agency of the Supreme Command of the Armed Forces (OKW/Chi), refer to the recruiting of Defense Ministry cryptanalytic personnel by the FA and imply that this was the cause of some ill feeling between the two

[18] I 85 p 2 (This is a joint interrogation of Specialist Flicke, Technical Inspector Pokojewski, and Staff Inspector Hatz of the Signal Intelligence Agency of the Supreme Command of the Armed Forces.

[19] Schapper, IF 15, refers to "Goering, whom I knew well from the first world war." There is no evidence of Schimpf's relations with Goering.

[20] Seifert, I 25, says that he committed suicide. Goering, loc.cit., merely states that he died.

[21] Guenther, IF 46 p 3, states that Schapper's predecessor was "Prince von Hesse, who died in the fall of 1944" Goering, loc.cit., states that he returned to the Luftwaffe, and gives his Christian name.

organizations.[22] Schapper had served under Fenner, the head of the "Language Division" of the Signal Intelligence Agency of the Supreme Command of the Armed Forces (OKW/Chi, the successor of the Defense Ministry) and Seifert had also been a member of the senior organization although his position there is not known. The FA was the last entrant into the cryptanalytic field and it had the reputation of paying its employees "exceptionally well."[23]

Relations between the FA and the cipher section of the Defense Ministry and the Signal Intelligence Agency of the Supreme Command of the Armed Forces (OKW/Chi) were always strained. A letter of Dr. Paschke of the Foreign Office Cryptanalytic Section (Pers Z S) of 19 February 1934 is available which discusses plans for liaison between the cipher section of the Defense Ministry and the Foreign Office and specifically excludes the FA:

> On 19 II Capt Oschmann called on me to talk over with me technical details concerned in our (proposed) collaboration.

[22]Mettig, I 131 p 3: "The FA was a part of the Reichsluftfahrtministerium and was directly subordinate to Staatsekretaar Koerner, and through him, to Reichsmarschall Goering. The head of this department was Ministerialdirigent Tschapper (sic) who, prior to the establishment of the FA, had worked in OKW/Chi and served under Ministerialrat Fenner. Another former official of OKW in the FA was Regierungsrat Seifert. Collaboration between the FA and OKW/Chi was poor. This well may have been due to the personal differences between Ministerialrat Fenner and his former subordinate Tschapper." Huettenhain, I 21 p 1, refers to "some personnel transferred to the FA from OKW/Chi. This was not well received in the latter organization as they were regarded as people who has 'deserted the ship'". Also cf. Schapper's own statement, supra, that he left the service of the Defense Ministry because of his dissatisfaction with their antequated methods.

[23]Werther, I 121 p 12. Werther was company commander of 7 Ln REGT 353.

In the course of the conversation he mentioned an utterance by his chief, Corvette Capt. Patzig, to the effect that all cryptanalytic connections with the FA should be dropped since cryptanalytic work did not belong in the province of the FA.

Details of the collaboration were then drawn up in broad outline.

Berlin, 19 II 1934

Draft(The draft of the proposed collaboration then follows)

signed: Paschke[24]

There is no evidence that liaison on cryptanalytic matters was ever achieved between the two organizations. As will be shown below, however, the FA did supply the Supreme Command of the Armed Forces Signal Intelligence Agency with intercepted traffic and was represented on that agency's committee on cryptographic security. Huettenhain reveals that this lack of cooperation extended to the IBM machinery developed by the Signal Intelligence Agency of the Supreme Command of the Armed Forces (OKW/Chi) which was offered to the Signal Intelligence Agency of the Army High Command (OKH/GdNA), the Signal Intelligence Agency of the Air Force High Command (OKL/LN Abt 350), the Signal Intelligence Agency of the Navy High Command (OKM 4 SKL/III) but not to the FA:

> Owing to personal friction, political considerations (Nazi "taint"?) and other unsavory matters there was no liaison with the FA and they were not offered the machinery developed by OKW. Fenner was particularly prejudiced against Goering's party - in any case the general impression was that they achieved very little--they employed no mathematicians![25]

[24] DF 17. This is a translation by Dr Pettengill of T 3273, a series of letters by Paschke and other Foreign Office Cryptanalytic Section personnel.

[25] I 31 p 10. Actually Paetzel of the FA was a mathematician.

Mettig stated that the FA attempted to take over the radio broadcast monitoring carried out by the Signal Intelligence Agency of the Supreme Command of the Armed Forces (OKW/Chi)[26] and there were rumors that the "empire building" policy of the FA had resulted in an attempt by the FA to take over the entire agency after the disgrace of the Supreme Command of the Armed Forces (OKW) in the 20th of July 1944 plot.[27] (Himmler, Reichsfuehrer SS -Elite Gaurds- actually did take over the Signal Intelligence Agency of the Supreme Command of the Armed Forces (OKW/Chi) through Walter Schellenberg, the head of Amt VI of the Reich Main Security Office-Reichssicherheitshauptamt, RSHA).[28] The members of the FA who were interrogated gave no hint of any such intention on the part of the FA. There was necessary exchange of information on official keys and key changes used for inter communication between the FA and section X of the Signal Intelligence Agency of the Supreme Command of the Armed forces at least in 1945.[29] The FA was also reported to have received a copy of all traffic intercepted by all other agencies.[30]

For further details of the relations between the FA and the other cryptologic agencies the concluding chapter on liaison, under the specific agency, may be consulted. In general the best relationship existed with the Foreign Office Cryptanalytic Section but there is evidence of technical exchange with the Navy, Army, and Air Force Signal Intelligence Agencies. Finally, the relationship between the FA and the Abwehr (the German Intelligence Agency of the Supreme Command of the Armed Forces) and with the Gestapo can only be mentioned. The point of contact came

[26] I 131 p 3

[27] Mettig I 86 p 2

[28] I 86 P. 2. Cf. IF 164 and discussion in following paragraphs.

[29] Ticom Doc 240, Items 33,38,39,40,43 and 44, contain the messages from OKW/WNV/Chi to the FA with key changes for January through May 1945.

[30] I 82,p.5, Flicke, Pokojewski and Hatz of the Signal Intelligence Agency of the Supreme Command of the Armed Forces.

in the field of telephone monitoring. The official regulations for German war time censorship of all communications are available. In them the war time responsibility is given to the Abwehr but the peace time role of the FA and of the Gestapo are indicated and it is apparent that the monitoring stations of the FA continued in operation.[31] There is insufficient evidence, however, to show the location of FA telephone monitoring stations. It appears that they cooperated with the Abwehr Wehrkreis organization through out all of Germany and occupied territory. Evidence to be presented below shows that the Gestapo eventually took over the telephone monitoring of the Abwehr and of the FA in the middle of 1944. It is probable that the existing organization continued with the reports being routed to Amt IV of the Reich Main Security Office.[32] Finally, among the administrative papers found at Kaufbeuren was a handwritten rough draft of a letter which appears to have been a cover letter for material to be forwarded, possibly from FA-9, to the Stapoleit in Prague. The material was an undetermined number of "Czech messages". It is not known if these messages were read through cryptanalysis on the part of the FA but an additional instance of liaison between the FA and the police is afforded.[33] The messages were for the attention of a Herr Rummel.

31 Die Ueberwachung des Nachrichtenverkehrs im Kriege, TF 29. Ticom Document 240 contains various administrative memoranda of the FA, among them orders from Abwehr Wehrkries VIII (at Breslau) warning of an increase in Russian Agent activity with the approach of hostilities to Breslau. Also contained in these memoranda is indication that the telephone monitoring stations in Prussia and Poland were operating at the end of 1944. However, it should be noted that they were still controlled by the FA.

32 This is to be assumed from Goering's statement that the Gestapo took over telephone monitoring, confirmed by Goering and by Schellenberg, who differ only as to the date at which this occurred. Fuller discussion of this point is to be found in the following section which deals with the relations between the FA and the Reich Main Security Office. See also the discussion of the FA field stations in the section on the Operational Organization of the FA.

33 Ticom Document 240 item 42.

6. The FA as a Nazi organization. From consideration of the evidence it seems proper to regard the FA as the Nazi party signal intelligence agency and it seems reasonable to assume that it was created by the party to provide a counterpart for the various service Signal Intelligence Agencies and that of the Foreign Office on whose loyalty the Nazi's could not rely at the date the FA was erected (1933). This is supported not only by the definite suspicions expressed in the interrogations but by the history and organization of the FA. It has been seen that the original founding of the organization was due to friendship between Goering and Schapper, probably between Goering and Schimpf, and presumably between Goering and Prince von Hesse.[34] Besides the statement of Flicke et al, attributing the creation of the FA to the Nazis[35] there is support from Goering who relates the assignment of all telephone monitoring (within the Reich) to the FA by Hitler at the end of 1933;[36] reference to coordination by the Regular Police (Ordnungspolizei or Orpo) of telephone monitoring with the FA;[37] evidence that the Reich Main Security Office (RSHA) referred cryptanalytic problems to the FA;[38] and indication that Himmler tried to

[34]It is known that other members of the von Hesse family were friendly with Goering and other Nazis and held high diplomatic positons. CF IF 188.

[35]See above Para 4. (I 85).

[36]I 143 p 13.

[37]I 91 p 2 Robert Schlaka (General-Major), the chief of communications in the main office of the Ordnungspolizei, reported coordination with the FA in 1935-1937. Also see Sauerbier, I 162, for Orpo-FA liaison on Agents.

[38]I 54 p 4, the interrogation of five members of the FA captured at Flensburg, reports that: "None of the five knew anything about a cryptanalytic section of the Waffen SS. Seifert thought that there couldn't have been such a thing as he had seen intercepted cipher telegrams sent to them from the RSHA which RSHA had no facilities for deciphering. Paetzel, on the other hand, remarked somewhat dryly that from what he knew of the stubborn independence in this matter of the various services and the Foreign Office he would not be at all surprised if such a thing did in fact exist. However, he had no knowledge of it". Sauerbier, I 162 pp 3-4, states that the Ord-nungspolizei sent him Russian agent traffic. Werther, I 121 p 13, confused the FA and the Elite Guards and seemed to think that an Elite Guard Officer had attempted to recruit his services for a cryptanalytic agency headed by a former Naval officer (Schimpf?).

take over control of the FA.[39] (As will be shown, Himmler, through Schellenberg's arrangements with Koerner who controlled the FA finances in the Prussian State Ministry, had achieved some control of the FA in 1945). On 24 January 1945 the Gestapo (Amt IV of the Reich Main Security Office), sent an agents message to Section 9 of the FA(the section dealing with Slavonic languages) with a request that it be deciphered.[40] According to Mettig, the Signal Intelligence Agency of the Supreme command of the Armed Forces was originally a part of the Abwehr "Defense", actually the espionage and counter intelligence agency of the Defense Ministry, subsequently incorporated in the Supreme Command of the Armed Forces, and eventually taken over by Himmler):

> . . . . in the days of the Reichswehr, OKW/Chi was organistically part of the Abwehr and the liaison had been maintained. The directives given by Keitel's Office were very general, they were amplified and made more specific by Canaris and Hanson [heads of the Abwehr], who briefed the head of OKW/Chi. He then decided cryptanalytic details. After the 20th of July 1944 the Abwehr was taken over by the RSHA. [This chronology is not correct, see discussion below]. Briefing was then done by Schellenberg....At one time there was a row with the FA, provoked by the empire building policy of that body. The FA wished to take over OKW/Chi. It was emphasized that Schellenberg had no control over the FA and (perhaps for that reason) would have preferred to take over OKW/Chi himself. The RSHA or the SS did not maintain any cryptanalytic bureau of their own.[41]

The exact form which Schellenberg's control of the Signal Intelligence Agency of the Supreme Command of the Armed Forces (OKW/Chi) took is not certain and need not be gone into at any length here. As will be seen from the interrogation of Schellenberg given next, the acting heads of that agency expressed agreement with his views and appeared

39 Guenther, IF 46.

40 Ticom Document, Items 11 A & B, (Film 34).

41 I 86 p 2

to model their evacuation plans on his.[42] Schellenberg's evidence concerns both his efforts to take over the FA and to control the Signal Intelligence Agency of the Supreme Command of the Armed Forces:[43]

VIII. Deciphering.

24. The deciphering department of the OKW under Colonel Kettler supplied daily great quantities of deciphered messages which were called ever since the time of Ludendorff "V.N" (Verlaessliche Nachrichten). They were printed on thin white paper and carried a broad red edge. Schellenberg had established relations with the deciphering department at the OKW in 1942, because he wanted to exploit the experiences of the Wehrmacht both in "W/T Abwehr" as also in the development of German coding "methods" for his own use. Schellenberg made very early contact with General Fellgiebel, chief of the Wehrmachtnachrichtenverbindungen (in the OKW) as well as General Thiele, department chief under Fellgiebel. Both these men were killed in connection with the 20th of July. Schellenberg's relations with Theile were very good. They had come close to one another through their joint work in the Board of Directors of the Standard Electric company (the former American Holding company). Theile, after the arrest of Fellgiebel had become Fellgiebel's successor. In this capacity he wanted to bring a long discussed plan to fruition, i.e. unite all deciphering services of the Reich in one hand and to put them at the exclusive disposal of the Geheime Meldedienst for systematic interpretation and use.

25. Apart from the German Foreign Office which possessed an extensive deciphering service, the Forschungsamt was above all the organization which had not only

[42]For discussion of the relations of the Abwehr, the RSHA and the Signal Intelligence Agency of the Supreme Command of the Armed Forces see Vol. III Para. 2.

[43]IF 164. This is a long and rambling report of an interrogation of Walter Schellenberg, SS Brigadefuehrer in charge of Dept VI of the RSHA, SD Amt VI Ausland.

an extensive - one could almost say 100% - telephone monitoring service, but also a very large deciphering department. It also monitored normal broadcast services. (This was done too by the Foreign Office, the Propaganda Ministry, and the OKW!) The Forschungsamt also embraced an extensive press and publication interpretation department as well as one of the best existing archives. Schellenberg maintains that apart from the obvious reasons of saving personnel and other grounds of economy, the Amt Ausland together with the deciphering department of the Forschungsamt was really a domain of the Geheime Meldedienst. Schellenberg also saw that there was no need for the telephone monitoring service to be independent, but that it really belonged to the domain of Amt IV. Since 1942 Schellenberg insisted that Himmler should speak with Goering who had reserved the Forschungsamt as his purely personal field of work and to insist that he (Schellenberg) should take the Forschungsamt over.

26. Himmler always refused this. He declared that Goering would never do it as he believed that he would thereby make him (Himmler) and the SS too strong. Another very strange argument was added to this: Himmler said Goering should bear vis a vis Hitler the responsibility for all telephone monitoring, for if he, Himmler, would do this Hitler might suddenly conceive the idea that his own telephone conversations were overheard. Schellenberg thereupon acted independently. He needed the results both of the Forschungsamt as a whole and of the work of the deciphering department of the OKW. At the beginning of 1943 Schellenberg had come to a working agreement with Secretary of State Koerner (Prussian State Secretary, in charge of FA financial matters) and at the end of 1944 Koerner was prepared to concede to Schellenberg the Forschungsamt with the exception of the telephone monitoring, which since the middle of 1944 belonged to Amt IV. Sandberger and Rapp began in February 1945 to take the Forschungsamt over. Owing to the general development of the situation, however, this move did not take practical shape. After the arrest of Theile, a general, whose name Schellenberg has forgotten, was appointed chief of the Wehrmachtsnachrichtenverbinndungen. A general called Gimmler was put in charge of the Amtsgruppe (deciphering and W/T Abwehr). Colonel Kettler during

the time when Theile was in prison had continued to seek close contact with Schellenberg. Schellenberg put Kettler in touch with Dr Schmitz who entered and remained in close relationship with him. Kettler modelled his evacuation measures on those of Schellenberg because he had always thought, just as Gimmler had done, that Schellenberg by taking over the Forschungsamt would acquire decisive influence over the deciphering department.

A brief review of Nazi history with particular attention to the Elite Guards of Heinrich Himmler will clarify the position of the Reich Main Security Office of that organization and, it is hoped, indicate the integral role of the FA. The Reich Main Security Office (RSHA) was organized in 1936 as a single headquarters for the Party Security Service (Sicherheitspolizei, SIPO). The Security Service was in its origin a purely party organization. It was in fact the intelligence army of the Elite Guards whose origin and history are relevant. The Elite Guards were organized in 1925 to act as the bodyguard for the leading men of the Party. In 1929 Himmler was appointed by Hitler as Reichsfuehrer SS and under his guidance the SS (Elite Guards) grew into the watchdog of the whole Party and the formations controlled by it. In June of 1934 the Elite Guards served as the executive agency in the purge. At this time the Elite Guards were made independent of their parent body, the Storm Troops (Sturm Abteilung, SA), whose head, Röhm, was one of the leading victims. At this time it was decreed that the Security Service alone should be responsible for Party political intelligence. In June of 1936 Himmler was appointed as chief of German Police and reorganized the police services, organizing the Party security services in a single Main Office, the Reichssicherheithauptamt, paralelled by a similar main office for the regular police, the Ordnungspolizei (or ORPO - Constabulary), the Ordnungspolizeihauptamt.[44]

[44] The account given in the above paragraph is taken from IF 216 B, Sicherheitspolizei und Sicherheitsdienst, Ultra/Zip/Pal 4 of 1/1/44. For details of the Ordnungspolizei organization see in Tab A. Note that the Ordnungspolizei are not a Party organization and were independent of Kaltenbrunner and Schellenberg. This independence is seen in reported rivalry with both the Gestapo and the Abwehr and Radio Defense Corps (OKW/WFSt/Ag WNV/Fu III) in counter measures against Allied Agents (IF 176; and Volume 8 of these reports).

The RSHA, which now (April 1945) controls the whole German Secret Service for intelligence, sabotage, and security, both inside and outside Germany, is the GHQ of the Sipo and SD whose head, (Chef der Sipo und SD, abbreviated CDS), SS Obergrupenfuehrer Kaltenbrunner, reports directly to Himmler. Of the main German police, security, and special services, only the Orpo, or uniformed constabulary, is outside its control. The Sipo and SD between them comprise three services:

1)	Geheimestaatspolizei	(Gestapo)	- Sipo
2)	Kriminalpolizei	(Kripo)	
3)	Sicherheitsdienst	(SD)	

The SD is further subdivided into two departments, one collecting intelligence from outside the Reich, the other from inside Germany and occupied territory....The SD, both inside and outside Germany, is a fact finding department which takes no official action and tries to be as little known as possible.

The RSHA is divided into seven departments (Aemter) with the following official functions:

Amt I	Personnel
Amt II	Administration
Amt III	HQ of SD within the Reich
Amt IV	HQ of Gestapo
Amt V	HQ of Kripo
Amt VI	Foreign Intelligence (Amt Ausland, head, Schellenberg)[45]

As has been shown in the previous discussion, Amt VI took over the Abwehr, the intelligence agency of the Supreme Command of the German Armed Forces, in 1944. This control was strengthened by the 20th July 1944 plot which marked the failure of the military to throw off the increasing dominance of the Party and Himmler.

The FA was created in 1933 when the Party first came into political control of the Reich. The emphasis laid by Goering, Schapper, and others on the supply of reliable "political" intelligence seems to imply that the FA was

[45]If 216 The German Intelligence Service (Secret. SHAEF, Counterintelligence War Room, London: April, 1945) Paragraphs 5 and 6.

created because the Party could not rely on the existing Service and Foreign Office organizatinns. Goering received the responsibility for this organization while Himmler directed the Elite Gaurd. Schellenberg's testimony to Himmler's unwillingness to infringe upon Goering's field even in 1942; evidence of collaboration on cryptanalytic matters, coupled with the lack of evidence that the Elite Gaurd organization possessed a cryptologic unit of its own; and the importance placed on the FA in Schellenberg's plans for a glorified intelligence service after the Party had completed its domination of the Supreme Command of the Armed Forces Intelligence (OKW/ABWEHR) and Signal Intelligence Agencies (OKW/Chi) indicate the real position of the FA within the Nazi organization. Additional evidence of the close relationship between the Elite Gaurds and the FA may perhaps be inferred from Schapper's admission that he joined the Allgemeine SS (General Elite Gaurds as distinct from the Waffen SS, Armed Elite Gaurd) in 1933, the time at which he left the cipher section of the Defense Ministry and cooperated in the formation of the FA.[46]

7. Operations of the FA, April 1933 - May 1945. Only a sketchy outline of the FA's operational history can be drawn. It was created in April 1933 and by the end of that year had been assigned the task of monitoring all telephone circuits within the Reich. It is rumored to have been concerned in the "blood purge" of 30 June 1934.[47] At the time of the Anschluss (March 1938) the telephone monitoring and deciphering activities of the FA were in operation. A series of Associated Press despatches (!) reveal monitoring of the conversations of Goering with various German diplomats and officials in Austria. Apparently the FA prepared a special copy of these records and presented them to Goering. The file containing this material was found in the ruins of the Air Ministry and a newspaper "story" based on them. Also indicated in the newspaper columns was FA success in reading messages from the French foreign Office "to all ministers."[48] It is probable that these messages were not read through cryptanalysis as Goering refers to the ciphers of the French Foreign Office at the Quai d'Orsay having been

[46]See his "Curriculum Vitae" in Appendix 3.

[47]Flicke, Pokojewski, and Hatz, I 85 p 2.

[48]Cf note 3, Chapter 1, P. 3.

"obtained."[49] In September 1941 the FA produced a book containing the names of all foreign diplomats in Berlin, their partners in all conversations, and summaries of these conversations.[50] The FA continued its work on available diplomatic and commercial material and press broadcasts throughout the war. Operations were hampered by bombing. On 1 November 1943 and again on 7 July 1944 the Schillerstrasse quarters of the FA were heavily bombed and after each bombing a part of the FA was evacuated.[51] An administrative nucleus remained in Berlin at least until the closing of the Russian seige lines around that city.[52] The Berlin offices seem to have always included the administrative and personnel sections and during the last months of the war special arrangements in addition to the normal liaison channels were necessary. As is to be expected, the organization fluctuated considerably during the final months of the war and only the paper organization, learned from the administrative directives found at Kaufbeuren, can be described. The move to Breslau seems to have left Main Section I

[49] I 143 #74

[50] IF 143 p 1 This is an article from the Weekly Intelligence Summary #15, HQ, United States Forces European Theater containing information available from interrogation of a Major Johannes Gaenzer who was a member of Section III F of Abwehrstelle Berlin.

[51] Paetzel and Oden, I 25: "The whole establishment was completely destroyed by bombing (in November 1943)". Schapper, IF 15,p.22, stated that the FA moved to Breslau in December 1943. Guenther, IF 46, and Rentschler, IF 15, p 18, stated that the move to Breslau was forced by the bombing of 7 July. It appears, therefore, that after each bombing further evacuation was necessary. Sauerbier, I 162 p 4, stated that the move of Hauptabteilung IV to Breslau took place early in 1944 and remarked that working conditions in Breslau were poor and the work suffered in consequence.

[52] Ticom Document 240 contains various memoranda to and from administrative offices in Berlin. A special organization, the Zweigstelle or "Branch Office" Berlin was set up in March 1945. A special liaison and reporting center under the head of the Evaluation center, Seifert, was also set up at this time. Seifert and various personnel of the Branch Office escaped from the seige and were finally found with the Signal Intelligence Agency of the Navy High Command at Flensburg. (I 25, I 54, I 93 p 18).

and Schapper (or his predecessor, von Hesse) in Berlin. There is a directive dated 30 September 1944 at Breslau which is signed by Schroeder and is directed to all of the Main Sections except I.[53] The directive itself is of passing interest as it contains a memo from the Abwehroffizier of Wehrkreiskommando VIII warning of the danger of enemy agent activity with the approach of the Eastern front to Breslau.

Various directives are available concerning the evacuation of Breslau. Evacuation was completed and the various offices in that city were closed down as of 26 January 1945.[54] It seems from the evidence that the FA was organized into at least three Office-Branches (Amtesbereiche) in Berlin, Luebben (51°56"N 13°54"E, also the site of an FA intercept station) and Jueterbog, (51°59"N 13°40"E), the successor of the Amtesbereich Breslau. The Jueterbog branch was under the direction of Seifert and included Main Sections III, IV and V (Sections 4-13). It should be noted that Jueterbog was the last location of the FA known to the personnel of the Foreign Office Cryptanalytic Section.[55] As Jueterbog was also a location of the Signal Intelligence Agency of the Army High Command it is possible that information held by various Army personnel about the FA was gained at this time. Luebben was the location of Main Section II and was responsible for administration of the various out stations. As Main Section I is not specifically mentioned it is to be inferred that it remained in Berlin, especially as Section 1, charged with all security matters, is stated to be located there. Schapper, who signed the directives referred to above, dated them from Luebben. By early March a further movement of the FA had been effected and all of the Main Sections (less Section 15) had been reassembled at Kaufbeuren (47°53"N 10°37"E) with the organization indicated on the chart and from Kaufbeuren a small remnant of the FA moved on to Rosenheim (47°52"N 12°04"E)[56] Within this

[53] Ticom Document 240, item 37A.

[54] Ticom Document 240 items 22 and 29.

[55] I 1, p 18.

[56] IF 15, p.1. Kaufbeuren is approximately 50 miles southwest of Munich and Rosenheim is approximately 25 miles southeast of Munich. The air-line distance between Kaufbeuren and Rosenheim is roughly 75 miles.

period, either at the beginning of 1944 or the beginning of 1945, the telephone monitoring of the FA was given to the Gestapo (Amt IV of the Reich Main Security Office). However, the documents providing for the closing down of the Breslau outstations reveal that Telephone monitoring stations were then (January 1945) still controlled by the FA.[57] The Breslau/Kaufbeuren/Rosenheim party was under the direction of Schapper and this aprty remained the central body of the FA. A document found by Team 1 in the FA quarters at Kaufbeuren and signed by Schapper gives a reliable picture of the final organization of the FA.[58] The liaison officers responsible for passing FA materials to the other ministries remained in Berlin and a special section for Evaluation was set up under Seifert. A Berlin Branch Office and the Berlin Outstation also continued to function. Five members of the FA were transferred to OKM 4 SKL III (The Signal Intelligence Agency of The Navy High Command) on 16 May 1945 where they worked until arrested on 23 May 1945.[59] These five men were the departmental heads left in Berlin and it is obvious that a carefully coordinated split into both a northern and southern section of the FA had been arranged just as had been done for the Signal Intelligence Agency of the Supreme Command of the Armed Forces (OKW/Chi).[60] Rapp and and Sandberger, the two men named by Schellenberg as "taking over the FA" in February 1945, were last known by Schellenberg to have been in Flensburg and Marquardstein (near Rosenheim) respectively. However, this is not necessarily

57 Ticom Document 240 item 22. Schellenberg, IF 164, stated that all FA telephone monitoring was taken over in 1944. Schapper, IF 15, stated that it was in 1945.

58 Ticom Doc. 240, Item 34, A-D. This document is translated in appendix 2 of this report. It is clear from this directive that the Kaufbeuren group was the controlling body but it is also clear that special arrangements for continued service in Berlin had been made under the direction of Seifert and that an adequate functioning organization had remained there. As Rentschler is concerned in the directive found at Kaufbeuren and was one of the last to leave Schapper he was undoubtedly fully aware of the final organization and deliberately misled the interrogators.

59 I 25; I 54; I 93, P 18.

60 The interrogators of these five members of the FA also failed to discover that they had formed a special section left in Berlin. This point only becomes clear from the document found by Team 1.

due to any continuing connection with the FA. Rapp is stated to have been in charge of a "northern" section of Amt VI when the officer of the Reich Main Security Office (RSHA) were divided into northern and southern sections.[61] Sandberger was one of the key AMT VI officials and may be assumed to have accompanied the southern section.

The FA was originally located in Berlin, Charlottenburg 2, Schillerstrasse, 116/124, occupying a large building.[62] On moving to Breslau it took over the Hartlieb Barracks in Klettendorf.[63] At Kaufbeuren the FA was found by Ticom Team 1 to have been located in "six blocks" of a barracks near the Kaufbeuren airfield.[64] In the moves from Berlin the number of personnel decreased from the estimated 1500 to 2000 employed there.[65] Only some 450 persons continued on to Kaufbeuren and a mere 100 odd were left with Schapper at Rosenheim.[66] The administrative documents referred to previously contain evidence of a constant shuffling of personnel in the closing months of the war. A

[61] IF 164 p 35.

[62] IF 15 p 18, Guenther, IF 46 p 1.

[63] Guenther, IF 46, states that the FA occupied a "Flakkaserne" and the Pers Z.S. interrogees, I 1, state that the FA was in the Hartlieb Barracks.

D 21, the translation of a document giving distribution of work among the different cryptanalytic bureaus of the other German Armed Forces and Civil Departments, taken from a German Admiralty 4/SKL III folder entitled "Research Progress 1/12/43 - 1/11/44 "(Ticom Document No. T 519) gives as" #4 RLM/Forschungsamt at Breslau/Klettendorf: Cryptanalysis of diplomatic cyphers and GESTAPO matters. Collaboration with the Navy lately still only on fundamental questions of research." Ticom Document 240 item 32, Jueterbog, 2 January 1945 lists nine members of FA 9 who moved registered materials from "Klettendorf" to Jueterbog.

[64] IF 15 p 16.

[65] Rentschler, and Schapper, IF 15, and Seifert, I 54, give approximately the same figures.

[66] IF 15, I 54.

special section was created in Berlin to deal with the closing down of the Breslau Forschungsleitstelle and all members released for duty were to be immediately reported available to FA 3.[67] Administrative officers were shifted and trained evaluators were reassigned during the Kaufbeuren period but the details need not be given here. In addition various minor personnel were shifted from Kaufbeuren to Berlin.[68] The personnel of the FA were reputedly (enviously?) well paid.[69] At Kaufbeuren the personnel section was concerned with such matters as their soap ration and arrangement of laundering facilities in Kaufbeuren.[70]

[67] Ticom Document 240, Item 22.

[68] Ticom Document 240. See Appendix 2 for Summary of contents.

[69] Werther, I 121, p 12.

[70] Ticom Document 240 Item 23.

B. Operational Organization of the FA.

8. Organization of the Main Bureau. The following operational organization of the FA is intended to represent its structure while in Berlin. What historical changes can be determined will be indicated in the specific section involved. At the head was the Director (Ministerial Direktor) responsible for the management of all official business, and under him was the Main office at Berlin as well as the liaison offices, Regional Offices and intercept stations.[71] The main office was composed of six main sections, Hauptabteilung, which were subdivided into fifteen sections, Abteilung, which in turn were broken down into various sub-sections. As it was in the Hauptabteilung and Abteilung that the actual work of the FA was accomplished the best method of appraisal of its operations is to present the assignment, strength and history of each of these units with what little can be learned of their respective successes and personnel.

a. Hauptabteilung I - Administration: This main section was the administrative headquarters being charged with organization, established personnel and administration. At

[71]Schapper, IF 15. pp 20-22, IF 135.

28

the head was Principal Specialist Bergeren.[72] There were about 50 persons divided among two sections, Abteilung 1 with a Senior Specialist (ORR) Rosenhan at the head and Abteilung 2 under Senior Specialist (ORR) Kunsemueller. Section 1, the "Central Abteilung," was responsible for the official correspondence, the basic problems of personnel administration and budgetary matters, Civil Service Personnel (the higher officials, job descriptions etc.) and Security. This security included the guards, the electric eye system, passes and identification, and cover names and camouflage measures necessary to safeguard the secrecy of the organization and the nature of its work. The various administrative directives found at Kaufbeuren emanated from Main Section I or II in general. They typify the nature of the functions of the section. They range from an order concerning the drill of an FA Volksturm company at Kaufbeuren, through details of work shifts, Air Raid Precautions, and soap rations, to reissue of exhortasache (SECRET and TOP SECRET) classifications. This last memo, dated Berlin, 25 February 1945, declared that the Fuehrer had been greatly displeased to learn that Reuters (The British News Agency) had published a German SECRET paper.[73]

[72]No hard and fast hierarchy in the rank of German civil servants can be drawn. The three ranks most commonly referred to in the FA are Ministerial Rat or Principal Specialist (Min. Rat.), Oberregierungsrat or Senior Specialist (ORR), and Regierungsrat or Specialist (Reg. Rat.). Variations, as in the case of Oden, whose title is Reg. Rat. Dipl. Ing. -- Regierungsrat with Engineering Diploma, also occur. Schapper, as Ministerial Director, is above this hierarchy. Schroeder's Rank, Minister Dirigent, has no equivalent. A rather involved and not too relevant comparison to the P ratings of our own civil service is possible. Fenner, of The Signal Intelligence Agency of the Supreme Command of the Armed Forces (OKW/Chi), was both Min. Rat. and Oberst (Colonel). It would thus be possible to equate ORR with a Lt. Colonel and a Reg. Rat with Major. Civil Service here rates a Major as equal to a P-5.

[73]Ticom Document 240 item 45. The nature of the Reuters story is not known. For further examples of these directives see Appendix 2.

Section 2 was the Administrative section.[74]

b. Hauptabteilung II - Personnel: Personnel, presumably records etc, was the responsibility of this main section and its only section, Abteilung 3. Senior Specialist (ORR) Kempe was in charge of this section which consisted of from 80 to 100 persons.

c. Hauptabteilung III - Intercept: Senior Specialist (Min. Rat.) Breuer was in charge of this Main Section which was responsible for intercept, including intercept control and the actual intercept stations, and sorting and preliminary examination of the intercepted materials. The department was composed of about 200 persons and was divided into two sections. Section 4, under Specialist Popp, was responsible for all FA intercept. This included intercept control, determination of cover priorities, location of stations (described by Schapper as "employment of intercept forces") and actual administration of the intercept personnel. Section 5 was under Specialist Harrius who was relieved of duty and replaced by Specialist Dr Henke on 9 March.[75] This section served as a "message center" receiving

[74]Except where specifically cited as from other sources, this and the following paragraphs dealing with the organization of the FA are based on IF 15, 132, 135; I 25 and 54, and Ticom document 240. The statement of Schapper, which can be checked by the captured directive written by him and the interrogations of Seifert, Oden, Paetzel, Fingerhut and Klautachke-from which last the personnel strength figures are taken-are the most important and contain few if any contradictions. The interrogation of Rentschler, on the contrary, is incomplete and he appears to have consciously withheld or evaded giving information. The interrogation of Guenther is also incomplete but he appears to have been a minor worker and consequently poorly informed. The information taken from Weekly Intelligence Summary #12, IF 132, is often unique. So statements about the use of electric eyes and that Hauptabteilung IV developed codes and ciphers for the use of the FA are not indicated in the Ticom materials available. (IF 132 is based on the interrogations of Georg Schroeder and a "Report from Captured Personnel and Material Branch Military Intelligence Division," United States War Department, 25 June 1945, neither of which are in the possession of Ticom.)

[75]IF 135, Corrected as of 14 March. The 29 March order is available on Film 34 (Ticom Doc. 240).

30

all intercept and sorting and distributing it to the proper section of Main Section IV or Main Section V. This sorting does NOT appear to involve traffic analysis but is merely an identification of traffic type and a preliminary sort, as by language and system. Clear text material, including private and commercial messages, press broadcasts, the results of telephone monitoring and the like, were sent direct to Hauptabteilung V for evaluation. Code and cipher text was sorted as to type, e. g., military, diplomatic, and commercial. Military intercept was passed to The Signal Intelligence Agency of the Supreme Command of the Armed Forces (OKW/Chi) and diplomatic traffic was shared according to previous arrangement between the Foreign Office, The Signal Intelligence Agency of the Supreme Command of the Armed Forces (OKW/Chi) and the FA. (Rentschler states that this could be done by sorting on "the first group of the message which reveals the type.")[76] That material which was to be worked on by the FA was sent to the appropriate section of Hauptabteilung IV. According to Flicke, Pokojewski and Hatz the FA received duplicates of messages from all intercept sources and was the only agency to receive these facilities.[77]

d. Hauptabteilung IV - Codes and Ciphers: This Main Section of some 180 persons under Ministerial Dirigent Georg Schroeder was concerned with cryptanalysis of all codes and ciphers. Because of the preponderant interest of the Ticom teams in cryptanalytic activities most of the FA information obtainable from the Interrogations of working personnel is concerned with cryptanalysis. According to Kurt Sauerbier[78]

[76]Rentschler, IF 46.

[77]I 85 p 3.

[78]I 162: "Sauerbier is 41 years old, neat and anxious to impress. He joined the FA in its infancy in 1935 on the strength of a knowledge of Swedish and some English. He has no special mathematical training or qualifications and was an ordinary bank clerk in a Hamburg bank who was out of a job and heard that the FA was looking for men who knew languages. His poor manner of expression and the lack of conciseness and detail of his answers combined to give a total impression of distinctly mediocre ability and of an attitude typical of the entrenched civil servant, proud of his own little pew but seeing very little beyond it."

DOCID: 3486670

there were only about a dozen cryptanalytic personnel in the FA when he joined in 1935. Sauerbier took a short course in the fundamentals and then went to work on commercial code traffic. The head of the cryptanalytic section (which later became Hauptabteilung IV) was then, and remained, Principal Specialist (later Min. Dirig.) Schroeder. With the outbreak of the war the office was reorganized and this may have been the time at which the Hauptabteilungen were created. Late in 1943 various sections of the FA were forced to move to Breslau due to bomb damage to their Berlin quarters. Sauerbier has stated that the quarters in Breslau were inadequate and that production accordingly suffered.[79] We know that the Breslau Branch was under the direction of Schroeder as a directive from him to II,III,IV,V,1,2,3,4,5,6,7,8,9,10,11,12,13,14,15, and "AW Schule" (the School for Evaluators - Auswertungs Schule?") of 30 September 1944 is available. (The directive circulated a photocopy of a communication from the Breslau Abwehr Officer (Wehrkreiskommando VIII Abwehr) on the danger of Russian and Polish agents increasing their activity in Breslau).[80] From Breslau Main Section IV moved to Jueterbog where, with III and V, it came under the direction of Seifert. Schapper appears at Luebben[81] and Sauerbier and presumably additional personnel of IV returned to Berlin or fell casualties to the movement. The movement to Juеterbog was completed by 2 February 1945 as a letter of that date exists which names nine members of FA 9 who assisted in transporting classified materials from Breslau.[82] The date of the move to Kaufbeuren is not known nor or any details of the subsequent move to Rosenheim available. At Kaufbeuren the Main Sections, less FA 15, were reunited under Schapper. FA IV included sections 6,7,8, and 9 but by the end of March FA 6 does not appear on the routings of FA memoranda. Paetzel, deputy head of FA IV and head of FA 6 was at Kaufbeuren on 5 March but was taken prisoner at Flensburg with various fugitives from Berlin. His presence at Kaufbeuren

[79] I 162, p 4.

[80] Ticom Document 240, item 37.

[81] Ticom Document 240 items 22 and 29.

[82] Ticom Document 240 item 33.

32

in March is known from two directives concerned with air raid precautions, one originated by him and one naming him, Senior Specialist Waechter, Wenzel, and Schulze, Specialist Kroeger, and three other Specialists, Lehr, Kagelka, and von Stubenfauch who are otherwise unknown but may be assumed to be members of FA IV.[83]

Section 6 was a "Research" section. Paetzel stated that he:

> Was head of this Abteilung which came into existence only in 1941 and had fewer members than the others, in fact about 30. Whereas the other Abteilungen dealt with material which he described as "Aktuell", Abt. 6 worked on problems which could not be dealt with by the others currently and was also in the nature of a research section to work on new systems. They dealt in the main with diplomatic traffic of America, England, Japan, Free France, Spain and Spanish America. Their main machine success was with the Swiss Enigma as long as the same machine setting was used over a longish period. He also said that they had been able to break the Finnish Hagelin on a single message if they had 4,000 letters or more of text. He knew no details of the method as he had not worked on it himself. That had been done by RR Kroeger. They could also break it, of course, on a compromise. When asked if they had solved other machine systems, he replied that they had broken a Japanese system in '41 -'42 which was thought to be a machine system though their solution was not mechanical but employed simply paper strips. They had worked also on an American strip system where 30 out of a matrix of 50 strips were employed in a setting. This traffic was America-Europe but whether Washington-London or Washington-Paris was not known. Paetzel also described a Spanish additive system on which he had been working shortly before the end. The systems differed according to traffic link. Each link had 10 tables, with 100 four digit groups on each table. The indicator was the serial number (He did not know how it worked). It came in the 2nd or 3rd place and he believed that it was unenciphered as it caused no trouble. No other Spanish

[83] Ticom Document 240 item 30.

traffic was known to Paetzel; some links, however, had more tables than others.[84]

During the interrogation of the "Flensburg Contingent" of the FA, Oden, the "machine branch" representative (see Hauptabteilung VI) was questioned about IBM equipment. The question was answered, however, by Paetzel, who enumerated the following machines:

1 Alphabetic Tabulator
2 D.11 Calculating Tabulators
3 or 4 Sorters
1 Reproducer
"Many" Punchers[85]

They did not have a "Kartenmischer" [Collator]. It has been estimated that the equipment listed would have required ten to fifteen key punches. The personnel strength of the research section is sufficient to have operated this IBM equipment in conjunction with their other duties and the various statements about the compartmentization of the FA and the isolation of the cryptanalysts in particular support the assumption that IBM was not in a searate section.[86]

Schroeder is quoted to the effect that the FA developed its own codes and ciphers although no evidence of this is to be found in the available materials.[87] However, Kroeger, "[Cipher] machine specialist" of the research section is named as the representative to the Signal Intelligence Agency of the Supreme Command of the Armed Forces (OKW/Chi) Code and Cipher Committee set up by Theile and Gimmler with Huettenhain as chairman.[88]

[84] I 54 p 2.

[85] I 25 Passim.

[86] Sauerbier, I 162, states that the cryptanalytic section merely forwarded the untranslated text of its decodes to Evaluation and never heard what action or interpretation was taken on them. IF 132, presumably based on an interrogation of Schroeder which is not available to TICOM, also indicates this isolation, stating that the various sections were enveloped in extensive security regulations.

[87] IF 132

[88] Huttenhain and Fricke, I 84. It is stated that Kroeger was unable to attend all the meetings as the FA had moved to Breslau.

34

It is probable that the success with a Russian Teletype machine, attributed to the FA by Buggisch, although the information was admittedly second hand with him, was achieved in this section.[89] This is further supported by the fact that Sauerbier, who worked in the section dealing with Slavonic languages, did not know of any major Russian success and specifically mentions abandonment of work on a Russian Diplomatic system.

The exact history of Abteilung 6 is not clear. Paetzel states that the section came into existence in 1941. According to Rentschler it remained in Berlin.[90] Paetzel, however, names Kroeger as a member of the section and Huettenhain states that he was unable to attend the Code and Cipher Committee meetings regularly because of the move of the FA to Breslau.[91] The directive found at Kaufbeuren, moreover, carries Paetzel as head of Abteilung 6 and makes no indication that either he or the section were not at Kaufbeuren. Support for Rentschler's statement, none the less, comes from the fact that Paetzel was found at Flensburg with Seifert, Oden, Klautschke, and Fingerhut, all of whom were in the "northern section."[92]

Section 7, Overseas and Southwest, was under the direction of Senior Specialist Waechter and consisted of from 60 to 70 persons. Their work included USA, England, Latin America, Spain, Portugal, Turkey, Egypt, and the Far East. In the "Far East" besides Japanese and Chinese traffic Manchurian systems

89Buggisch quotes Doering and gives considerable information on the process involved. Even though second hand the story appears reliable I 64 p 2, I 176 p 6.

90IF 15 p 19.

91See I 84, of IF 132.

92Speculation over this point is unnecessary. It is clear that there was a special research section which worked on machine traffic and it is also clear that Kroeger was a machine specialist. Sauerbier, I 162, says that section IV moved to Breslau in 1944, working conditions were not good and the work suffered, and that all sections of the office were scattered after Breslau was evacuated.

DOCID: 3486670

were studied and evidence of work on a Thai system was found. Only one Japanese translator is known to have been available, Dr Erfurt, who also translated Chinese and Turkish. Senior Specialist Waechter is mentioned several times as the expert on American systems although this may have been partially due to a desire of Paetzel to avoid specific questioning. This section scored one of the more timely successes of the FA when it (or the predecessor of it in the pre-war FA) read Chamberlain's message to London for Hitler at the time of Munich. As responsible for English and United States systems, it also dealt with the messages of Harrison (U.S. Charge d'Affaire) from Berne and for cooperation with the Navy on British Interdepartmental cipher and various consular systems.

Section 8, West and South, under Senior Specialist Schulze, was composed of 30 to 40 persons. It worked on France, Belgium, Holland, Switzerland, Italy and Rumania. Major successes were achieved in the case of France. At the time of the Anschluss decodes were furnished Hitler (the code had apparently been "secured") which revealed that France would take no military action because of the refusal of England to back her. In the opinion of Rentschler Vichy systems were the easiest to break of all worked on by the FA. Rentschler, however, was not a cryptanalyst himself.

Section 9, East, Southeast, Middle and North, under Senior Specialist Wenzel, was composed of 60 to 70 people according to Paetzel but according to Sauerbier, who was a member of it, of 45 during the war. For the strength of FA 9 at Kaufbeuren a partial listing is possible based on a list of names, headed FA 9, with the signatures of those present or an indication of their transfer. This list is given in appendix 2. None of the names on this list are otherwise known nor has any check of these persons been made. The proportion of men to women is of interest (21 men - three with a Doctor's degree - and 12 women). Section 9 was divided into at least three sub-sections as Sauerbier was the head of Referat 9-C. This sub-section appears to have been a catch-all for assorted problems that did not fit into any other section. Its committments were: the diplomatic and consular traffic of Sweden, Denmark, and Norway; the commercial traffic or neutral countries; the ship traffic of Northern European countries; the secret messages of detained persons; Russian Agents Traffic. Among the successes with commercial codes claimed by Sauerbier are the code of INTABANK, a code of the Skoda Works, and Turkish shipping codes. 9-A is stated to have solved a Polish code and either 9-A or 9-B may be presumed to have dealt with the Russian commercial traffic received by Seifert.

Sauerbier's evaluation of the cryptanalytic section and its heads in particular is worth quoting, although it is not felt that his statements are to be taken at their face value:

> Sauerbier gives a general picture of a highly bureaucratic organization dominated by red tape and procedure, so that no department knew what the others were doing. Schroeder was old and fussy, liking quiet and disliking innovation. Paetzel was also very petty and academic in his outlook.
>
> This narrowness affected relations of the FA with the Auswaertiges Amt, OKW, and OKH. Liaison was handled by a single representative and never involved any exchange of visits by operations personnel. Sauerbier said he did not know one single person in any of the other organizations.
>
> Similarly there were no close relations between solution and evaluation work. The crypt sections simply did their work and handed the untranslated product over to the evaluation section without ever knowing what became of it thereafter.[93]

There is evidence that Sauerbier is either deliberately misleading his interrogators or was considerably misinformed. Lt. Schubert, the expert on Agent's traffic for the Russian Section of the Signal Intelligence Agency of the Army High Command, stated that "in January 1945 a RR Wenzel was sent to me from the FA by the WNV Fu III which was in charge of Agents systems to collaborate on Polish Resistance Movement traffic." Schubert knew that the FA had worked on Polish

[93] Sauerbier, I 162, p 4. These statements probably reflect more a "sour grapes" (or sour hops?) attitude of Sauerbier himself rather than an accurate picture of the Hauptabteilung. For fuller discussion and evaluation of the liaison between FA and the other agencies see below.

systems, but as far as he knew had not read any.[94] This is evidence not only of an exchange of working personnel but involves the head of Sauerbier's own section in connection with Sauerbier's self claimed specialty.[95] It further shows a coordination of cryptanalytic work on Agent's traffic by the authorized agency, The Radio Defence Corps (WNV FuIII), of the work of the FA and the Army High Command. Finally among the Kaufbeuren directives is a letter from the Reich main Security Office to FA 9 requesting that an agents message be deciphered.[96]

Details of all systems worked on by the FA with all TICOM references discovered are given in Appendix I and it was not felt necessary to duplicate this material in this organizational outline.

e. Hauptabteilung V - Evaluation: Principal Specialist Seifert, ~~the head of this Main Section~~, had 400 people under him, the greatest number in any of the sections of the "Bureau" proper. Seifert himself was captured at Flensburg and proved one of the most cooperative and talkative of the prisoners. The information releases of this section represented the finished product of the FA. Seifert was head of the temporary Jueterbog Branch and then became head of a reporting center in Berlin known by his name. He himself states that his presence at Flensburg was to organize the receipt of press and broadcast traffic. Senior Specialist Dr. Kurzbach, the head of Section 11, was alternate for Seifert in charge of V at Kaufbeuren. Seifert's statement of the objective of his department is as follows:

> The object of the department was the production of a purely objective and scientific picture of the world-wide political and commercial situation.

[94] I 26 p 7.

[95] I 164 is a study by Sauerbier of his special field, Russian Agent's Traffic.

[96] Ticom Doc. 240 Item 11.

The new material provided by its sources was forwarded after processing to the ministries concerned under three different categories viz.:

1) The individual items of current interest ("Aktuelle Meldungen").

2) Collected items on a given single subject ("zusammengafasste").

3) Consolidated reports ("Synthesen") e.g., Japanese-Russian relations.[97]

The bulletins of the FA were "Braun Meldungen"-Brown Reports (or the "Braunblaetter"-Brown Sheets). These were sent to the highest officials only; Keitel (Chief of Armed Forces), Jodl (Chief of Operations Staff), Goering, Ribbentrop (Foreign Minister), and Doenitz (Grand Admiral) admit having received them and they were of course also sent to Hitler himself.[98] Special reports with an even more restricted distribution were sent:

> . . . only to Goering and to Hitler; it depended on the subject and the existing circumstances, some of them might subsequently be passed by Hitler to the minister for Foreign Affairs. Typical examples were the Berlin-Rome telephone conversations between Mussolini and Ciano.

Hitler's view of the products of the FA was that they were very reliable; the material had to be presented factually to Hitler with no argument or appreciation, only the verbatim conversation or actual deciphered text. Editors were given very definite orders not to make guesses where there were gaps; if any portion were missing or was not clear, a row of dots had to be inserted and the appreciation, if any, inserted within parenthises. There was a special courier service with particular dispatch boxes of which only Goering, Hitler and Ribbentrop possessed the keys. The couriers had to travel in special motor cars and not in railway trains. All the reports had to be returned and sometimes there were difficulties because odd single sheets had been extracted and retained. In such cases a reminder was sent asking for the missing sheets. There were special

[97] I 54 p 3.

[98] I 143 p 15.

security regulations to prevent the reports being handed on from person to person.[99]

The best description of the routing of material to Hauptabteilung V and its processing there is given by Rentschler:

> Material which reached Main Abteilung V for evaluation came either from Abteilung 5 or Main Abteilung IV, depending upon whether it had been received in plain language or in code or cipher. Material from the decoding Abteilungen came to Abteilung V already translated while clear text material came as it was received except for Japanese and other non European languages which also were translated into German by experts ....
>
> Most of the material sent to Main Abteilung V was obtained from plain language sources; foreign radio, foreign press, telephone and telegraph messages to and from both foreign and occupied countries and internal communications. The quantity of decoded material varied with the various sections of Main Abteilung V; in Abteilung 11 perhaps 30% of the total was decoded traffic; 40% clear text, and another 30% came from radio broadcast and the press, in Abteilung 12 a considerably smaller percentage consisted of decoded material; in Abteilung 13 only about 7% or 8% of the total came from decodes.

[99] I 143 p 15. In regard to Hitler's opinion of Signal Intelligence, however, Ribbentrop, in the same interrogation (I 143) attributes a divergent view: "Ribbentrop, on being asked how valuable Signal Intelligence was to him and which countries provided the best material he hesitated for a long time; the value of this intelligence did not amount to very much -- Hitler had a queer, rather particular view about it -- he did not like this type of intelligence very much and said it was unreliable and often misleading; it was better to use one's own common sense. Ribbentrop said that occasionally a really important piece of intelligence was produced but even when pressed could not recollect a single specific example." Ribbentrop was described by the interrogators as highly suspecious and uncommunicative in distinction to Goering, who needed no prompting, and to Doenitz, Keitel and Jodl. See discussion of these points under FA Liaison below.

40

Most decoded traffic was read about 2-3 days after it was sent with some up to a week old. Apparently only Japanese traffic was read up to four or five weeks old. Rentschler professed almost complete ignorance of the workings of Hauptabteilung IV which was guarded by very rigid and strictly enforced security regulations.

On 31 May Rentschler was taken up on specific points of the previous days interrogation. Abteilungen 11-13 reported on an average 80 messages a day, including decodes and PL (Klärtext). They were given all texts, and then separated reportable from non-reportable. Abteilung 11, the one dealing with traffic of interest to the Foreign Office, reported perhaps 20-30 messages a day. This is interesting in view of Schapper's statement that this office put their main cryptographic effort on diplomatic ciphers.[100]

Goering thought that his organization had been able to deal with 32 different languages. His Interrogation revealed:

The virtues of the organization lay in the fact that they did not confine themselves to any particular field of intelligence and had no political axe to grind, nor ideology to follow; they were just given the technical requirements to intercept and break traffic and to disseminate intelligence. When they made an intelligence resume of some particular subject, for example that of aircraft production in the USA or the Yalta and Teheran conferences they produced an accurate factual account with no political bias. Reports such as these, often covering quite considerable periods, were frequently produced.

Goering's main principle had always been to keep the FA free from outside influences; Admiral Canaris, the Gestapo, and the Foreign Office had continually tried to interfere but he had managed to head them off. At one time the head of the FA had formed the idea that they should also deal with agent's traffic. Goering had found this out in about 1934 and had strictly forbidden any such action; such matters should be left to the concern of the Secret Service, and in any case the intelligence was generally unreliable.

[100] IF 15 pp 19-20

Goering said that the recipients of the daily bulletins, the "Brown Sheets" (Braunblätter) always emphasized the quality and reliability of the service. In 1940-1941 the selected file of reports which was passed to him daily contained as much as two hours reading. This report included intelligence from both types of FA; he was unable to say what proportion consisted of decodes. [However] The intelligence resulting from decoded telegrams was not always useful, they often consisted of absolute rubbish. The extent to which members of the diplomatic corps spread and retailed fantastic rumors was surprising. He himself had often made arrangements to have rumors planted and within a few days he observed them being passed on and spreading.

The work of the FA comprised two almost completely separate activities, firstly that of telephone monitoring, and secondly that of interception and cryptanalysis. As regards the first committment this had originally been limited to listening to telephone conversations to and from Foreign Embassies and those of important visiting foreigners -- in order to obtain political and economic intelligence. At a later date Hitler laid down that all telephone monitoring was to be Goering's responsibility, as far as he remembered this was at the end of 1933; hitherto internal telephone monitoring had been handled by the police. Inevitably the Reichspost were also concerned for a while since their cooperation and assistance were necessary for working out the technical side and for arranging special connections; the FA dispended with as much of this liaison as possible as soon as they found their feet. It was laid down that the post office had to obtain a specific permit from the FA if for any reason they wished to carry our monitoring themselves; later on, however, the Gestapo introduced themselves into the business and worked independently and without authorization from Goering, they worked clandestinely and for their own purposes; he thought it extremely probable that latterly all of his own telephone conversations had been monitored by them . . . .[101]

Hauptabteilung V was divided into four sections. Section 10, under the direction of Specialist Dr. Mews was named as "Information Dissemination" by Schapper's directive. According to Rentschler it served as the library, archives, and registration center, also confirmed by Fingerhut. Also according to Rentschler, it included five or six translators.[102] The files of the library have been described as:

> ... voluminous files of practically every type of information from every country. It maintained very complete cross-referense indices, recordings of intercepted phone and radio messages and transcriptions of public broadcasts of important world figures. In addition this section possessed a huge library of textbooks, maps, telephone directories, city plans, newspapers, and periodicals. All in all this section provided the material that all other sections needed in evaluating properly the messages intercepted by the field stations.[103]

This is a typically thorough example of the needs of the information section of any intelligence agency. Section 11, Foreign Policy Evaluation, under Senior Specialist Dr. Kurzbach (both Rentschler and Fingerhut were former members of this section) has left no specific record of its activities. Section 12, Economic Evaluation, was under Acting Head Brieschke. At Kaufbeuren, replaced on 20 March by Rautenkranz. Among the reports prepared by them were, in peace time, stock market "tips" based on examination of brokerage reports etc., which were used by the various

[101] I 143. The statements based on the interrogation in the document cited have been slightly rearranged in the above paragraph. Note that the date given by Goering for the taking over of all telephone monitoring by the FA would allow sufficient time for those monitoring activities to have been important in connection with the Blood Purge mentioned earlier in this paper as having been connected in some way with the FA.

[102] Fingerhut, I 54 p 3. Rentschler, IF 15 p 19.

[103] IF 132

43

German economic agencies in purchase and sale of foreign securities. Presumably these reports were utilized by the various individual members of the Nazi party receiving them (according to Guenther all Nazi Officials down to Gaulieter received FA reports) to their own profit. The head of this section is given by Rentschler as Dr. Rautenkranz but his name does not appear on the Kaufbeuren document. Section 13, Internal Affairs Evaluation, was under Specialist Rentschler. He states that he became head of the section in 1944 and that while still in Berlin it employed about 80 people. By the time the remnants of Hauptabteilung V reached Rosenheim, however, only 16 men and 4 girls were left in all of V. A special school for "Evaluators" in the headquarters and in the Aussenstellen was set up in 1943 under Specialist Heinz Fingerhut. He stressed, however, that this school did not train new personnel since they had no intake but indeed lost people to the armed forces, but existed mainly to provide refresher courses for Auswerter who by the nature of their work required a high degree of expert knowledge.[104]

f. Hauptabteilung VI, Technical. The Main Section was in charge of Senior Specialist Dipl. Ing. Stabenow. His alternate at Kaufbeuren was Senior Specialist Dr. Huppertsburg, the head of Section 14. This section, the only one shown, is called Technical by the Kaufbeuren document. Rentschler gives two section, 14 Development of Own Machines, and 15, Comparison and Evaluation of captured Machinery. Oden, however, a member of Main Section VI, gives the following description of his section:

> Hauptabteilung VI, O's own department, had two subsections, a) Preufung und Entwickling and b) Betrieb. He was the head of the latter subsection. He was thus responsible generally for the maintainence of all RLM/FA's communications but was not concerned at all with devising or developing new apparatus which was the

[104] I 54 p 3. Ticom Document 240 item 36 is the order transferring Specialist Dr. Rautenkranz from the School of the FA to FA 12 as head, effective 20 March 45 and also transfers Dr. Fingerhut to the Reporting Center Seifert. Item 37 includes a Schule AW (School of Evaluators?) in its routing.

44

> task of Abteilung a. When questioned about his connection with OKW on cipher security matters, he said that this was purely ad hoc. He was present only at discussions on the security of the T 52 and attended more by virtue of his previous employment with Siemens und Halske than by his present position with RLM/FA. They had no liaison with Wa Preuf VII except in connection with such apparatus as was supplied them by this body.[105]

As Oden remained in Berlin and Dr. Huppertsburg went to Kaufbeuren a reorganization in the course of which Abteilung 15 was dropped is a reasonably presumption. In his earlier interrogation Oden stated that he had joined the FA in 1936, having previously been an electrical engineer, and was responsible for the equipment of the intercept stations, their maintainence, and for certain personnel matters. In this interrogation he stated that some of the employees of Army Ordnance, Developing and Testing Group, Signals Branch had been classmates of his at school.[106] Both Huppertsberg and Oden are specifically mentioned by Boner of the German Air Force as concerned with telephone monitoring. Boner stated that the last known location of the telephone monitoring station, under Dr. Huppertsberg, was at Glueckstadt (Holstein) and that Oden would be able to give details.[107] There were approximately 200 persons employed in Hauptabteilung VI. It may be assumed that the FA, alone among the Signal Intelligence Agencies, ran its own communications. The communications of the Signal Intelligence Agency of the Supreme Command of the Armed Forces, (OKW/Chi) of the Airforce (OKL/Chi) and Navy (OKM 4 SKL/III) Signal Intelligence Services, of the Radio Defence Corps (OKW/WNV/FJ III), of the Abwehr, and of the Foreign Office were all run by section V of the Signal Intelligence Agency of the Supreme Command of the Armed Forces.[108] The absence of the FA in

[105] I 54 p 1.

[106] I 25 pp 4 and 8.

[107] I 17 p 3.

[108] DF 9, Activity report of the Signal Intelligence Agency of the Supreme Command of the Armed Forces for period 1 Jan 1944 through 28 June 1944.

this company is significant. It appears to reflect the antipathy of the Signal Intelligence Agency of the Supreme Command of the Armed Forces and the FA towards each other. Security of FA ciphers is thought to have been within the functions of section 6, which see.

Among the documents received by Ticom is a telephone directory containing names of members of the FA and of the Air Ministry as well as key officials in other government ministries.[109] The document appears to refer to the official (government) telephone net in Berlin. A tracing attached to the document shows direct telephone communications from Dr Huppertsburg (whose name appears) to Luebben, Constance, Cologne, Templin, Breslau and other known locations of FA installations on the one hand and to the Air Ministry and the Supreme Command of the Armed Forces (OKW) on the other. Through the switchboard of the Supreme Command of the Armed Forces connections could be made with the Army High Command (and its field telephone nets), The Reich Main Security Office, The Foreign Office, The Navy High Command, the Prussian State Ministry, the Reichspost and the Elite Gaurd Headquarters (SS Fuehrungshauptamt). Through the Air Ministry switchboard connections were possible with all branches of the Air Ministry and Air Force and a connection to Goering's estate at Karinhall is shown. Telephone numbers for all connections are given. (Some of the names of officials given in the directory will be discussed at the conclusion of this chapter). It may be assumed from the appearance of Dr Huppertsburg's name on the tracing that he was responsible for maintaining telephone communications for the FA.

9. War Time Expedients. The Branch Office Berlin and the Reporting Center Seifert. An administrative nucleus of undetermined strength was always maintained in Berlin in addition to various monitoring stations located there. The administrative documents captured at Kaufbeuren have revealed what is known of this administrative organization.

[109] D 22. The directory is said to be undated. It was found at Berchtesgaden by Ticom Team 1. All names appearing in the directory have been included in Tab A. In the case of members of the FA their inclusion in the directory is indicated by the citation of D 22 in the entry under their name.

DOCID: 3486670

A directive of 9 March 1945 signed by Schapper, set up the Branch Office Berlin (Zweigstelle Berlin).[110] Its functions appear to have duplicated those of FA I and II to a considerable extent and in addition the Branch Office Berlin would seem to have assimilated FA 15. Its functions were of an administrative nature, including security, correspondence administrative detail, personnel matters and, in addition, technical maintainence of equipment and communications. The head of the Branch Office Berlin was Senior Specialist Stabenow and he exercised administrative control over the Reporting Center Seifert and the various Liaison Offices. A member of FA 9, Dr Neuenhoff, otherwise unknown, was named as a requested liaison man between Branch Office Berlin and his section.[111] A Specialist Progich of the Luebben intercept station was also assigned additional duties as liasison man with the Branch Office.[112] Specialist Henke, named head of FA 5 on 9 March 1945, was assigned to the Branch Office Berlin on 20 March.[113] An example of the personnel work handled in Berlin is a request from FA 9 that Frau Helene Gertz, born Sponholz, be assigned to work in an intercept station. She is described as having a good knowledge of French and a reading knowledge of Russian. This request is addressed to Czwalinna at Marchstrasse 25 b on 27 March 1945 suggesting that the Branch Office Berlin was not, or was not all located in the Schillerstrasse.[114]

Even less is known of the Reporting Center Seifert (Dienststelle Seifert) than is known of the Branch Office Berlin. The directive setting up the Branch Office Berlin

110 Ticom Document 240 item 34.

111 Ticom Document 240 item 14.

112 Ticom Document 240 item 36.

113 Ticom Document 240 items 19 and 35.

114 Ticom Document 240 item 18.

also created the Reporting Center Seifert.[115] Seifert remained the head of Main Section V and had previously been the head of the Jueterbog Branch of the FA.[116] The administrative documents reveal the assignment of various persons to Seifert but there is no indication of the nature of their duties. On 13 April an Erna Lange (otherwise unknown) and Liselotte Brott of FA 9 were assigned to Seifert.[117] On 20 March 1945 Specialist DR. Fingerhut was assigned to the Reporting Center.[118]

10. The Liaison Offices of the FA. To assure liaison with other departments of the governmental agencies Liaison Officers to the various departments were set up. The officials charged with these responsibilities worked in the ministry to which they were assigned and were in telephonic communication with the FA (either with the Main Bureau, or, after it had evacuated Berlin, with the Branch Office Berlin). Liaison with the Foreign Office (AA) was directed by Dr. Gerstmeyer, that with the Supreme Command of the Armed Forces (OKW) by Dr. Klautschke; that with the Reich Main Security Office (RSHA) by Specialist with Engineering Diploma Scholz; that with the Propaganda Ministry (RMVP) by Herr Severitt; and that with the Economic Ministry and Ministry for War Production (RWiM) by Specialist Dr. Hilligardt.[119] Dr. Hilligardt was replaced on 1 April 1945 by Brieschke, who had previously served as head of FA 12, to which section Hilligardt was assigned although not in an administrative capacity.[120] Details of the nature of this liaison are known from the interrogation of Dr. Klautschke whose statement follows:

> Klautschke was the liaison officer (Verbindungs-nabb) to OKW and also OKM, OKL, and OKH. Although a member of the FA, he had his office in OKW. It was

115 Ticom Document 240 item 34.

116 Ticom Document 240 item 29.

117 Ticom Document 240 item 7.

118 Ticom Document 240 item 35.

119 Ticom Document 240 item 34.

120 Ticom Document 240 item 36.

48

his job to receive material from the FA and pass it on to the section concerned at OKW etc. At OKW he supplied Keitel and various departments, for example WFST/Amt Gr Ausl, Feldwirstchaftsamt, Attache Abteilung, Abwehr, and AWA. At OKM besides Doenitz he supplied 3SKL and Marineruestungsamt. At OKL Milch, LW Fuehrungsstab I C, Chef Technische L Ruest (Genamj. Diessing). At OKH General Staff, Fremde Heere West and Fremde Heere Ost.

There were similar liaison officers with the other ministries such as Dr. Hilligardt at Ruestungsministerium and Reichsqiratchaftministerium and Dr. Gerstmeyer with the Auswaertiges Amt.

His liaison duties were concerned solely with the passing of intelligence from FA to OKW etc. and of particular intelligence requests in the other direction. As far as he knew there was no liaison on cryptanalytic matters between the two. Certain raw material, however, which was not worked on at FA was passed regularly to OKW, for example military traffic. When asked if his connection with the OKW/ATT. Abt meant that the FA jandled attache ciphers he said no, that only the telephone conversations of their Allies' attaches in Berlin were concerned. These were mostly about their girl friends, and never contained anything of importance because the attaches knew they were monitored.[121]

This intercept traffic furnished by the FA to the Signal Intelligence Agency of the Supreme Command of the Armed Forces constituted about 1/3 of all intercept coming to their crypt section.[122]

[121] I 54 p 4.

[122] DF 9. An Activity Report of the Signal Intelligence Agency of the Supreme Command of the Armed Forces was captured in the Strub barracks near Berchtesgarden and contained this information. ZIP/SAC/ Paragraph 10, p 3.

11. The Intercept stations of the FA and its Regional Offices. The operational functions of the entire organization were carried out by intercept stations of five different types. These stations were known as Forschungsstellen and were categorized as follows:

A Stations	Telephone Intercept
B Stations	Wireless Intercept
C Stations	Radio Broadcast Monitoring
D Stations	Teletype and Telegraph Intercept
F Stations	Mail Censorship [123]

A listing of all places at which FA installations were or had been maintained with indication of the nature of such installations is included in Tab A in as far as such a list can be determined.

The A stations were scattered all through Germany and later in the occupied countries. These stations were equipped with one or two interceptor switchboards which enabled the operators to cut in on any conversation at any time. The tapping was done at the main telephone exchange of the post office and piped directly to the station, which was usually located in a private building. Included in the equipment of each listening post was a wiretype recorder, which could be brought into use whenever desired.

The operations of the A stations underwent a change with the advent of the war. Prior to September, 1939, the telephone intercept stations were most valuable in providing information from the many international lines then operating in Germany. Berlin, of course, had a huge A station to tap the conversations of the diplomatic corps. The capital station had a staff of more then a hundred people, including fifty to sixty interceptors. After war broke out, this source of information was completely eliminated and the A stations turned their attentions largely to the problems of war production bottlenecks, attitudes of various large industries, and other domestic affairs.

[123] IF 132 p 3. This information is presumably derived from Schroeder and possibly from other prisoners not available to Ticom.

The B stations were usually outside of towns at points of good wireless reception, not being faced with the problem of necessary proximity to telephone or cable lines. Radio messages were intercepted by short wave and then were relayed in written form to the headquarters of the FA. After war started, this type of intercept became increasingly important insofar as foreign information was concerned because of the end of telephonic communication from Germany to other countries.

Only one C station existed. This performed a pure monitoring service of public broadcasts from other countries. The three D stations were located at Berlin, Vienna, and Dortmund, the chief centers of cablegrams leaving Germany. The functions of the D stations were also greatly diminished after the outbreak of the war. The F stations were organized after Germany was at war and they were never very extensive in their operations. Censorship offices were operated by OKW and later by the RSHA. The F stations consisted of small groups attached to these censorship posts.

In addition to the stations operating in Germany, the FA was quick to set up operational units in occupied countries. In Holland and Poland, for example, A stations were installed by task forces operating with front line troops. In Vienna, an A station was functioning two days after the occupation. Both A and B offices were quickly established in the Balkans, in Belgium, and in the Baltic countries. In Danzig a station had been installed secretly even before the annexation. Mobile units were also used during the Polish campaign but they are reported to have been largely unsuccessful, chiefly because of lack of cooperation from the army.[124]

That the FA was concerned with postal censorship is confirmed by documentary evidence recently made available to TICOM.[125]

[124] Ibid. Part of this information is confirmed by interrogations available to Ticom. Guenther, IF 46, states that a special Giftkueche for tapping the conversations of Nazi officials was located in Berlin.

[125] TF 29, See pp 12, 38, and ANLAGE 9.

A German publication, Die Ueberwachung des Nachrichtenverkehrs im Kriege, which provides for the censorship organization to cover all forms of communication and gives full details of the duties and responsibilities, is available. These regulations make careful distinction between peace time, when the FA and the Gestapo are specifically named as active in censorship and time of war when all censorship functions devolve on Abteilung III of the Abwehr. The regulations provide considerable detail on liaison and cooperation between Abwehr III units and the FA and contain complete directions for forwarding all pertinent information obtained from censorship to all parties interested. These censorship regulations are undated but it is presumptive that they were drawn up before the war as the Abwehr is clearly distinguished from the Reich Main Security Office.

> Oden states that there were from 100 to 150 sets at the Templin and Luebben stations and from 20 to 30 at Cologne, Konstanz, Eutin, and Gols. Traffic was forwarded by cipher teleprinter, the T. 52, c,d, and e. The FA usually did not develop its own intercept equipment, using that of the Army, the Reichspost, or industry except in cases where they felt they were not getting what was wanted.[126]

Insight into the organization of the Regional Offices and Intercept Stations (Forschungsleitstellen and Forschungsstellen) has been derived from the administrative papers found at Kaufbeuren. In particular an order of 26 January 1945 closing down the Breslau Forschungsleitstelle is important.[127] Effective with close of business 26 January, the Forschungsleitstelle Breslau and its subordinate Forschungsstellen were closed. These Forschungsstellen were listed as follows.

Forschungsstelle	"A" Breslau with "D" functions.
Forschungsstelle	"B" Breslau-Deutsch Lissa
Forschungsstelle	"C" Breslau-Deutsch Lissa
Forschungsstelle	"A" Litzmannstadt (Lodz)
Forschungsstelle	"A" Kattowitz (Katowice)
Forschungsstelle	"A" Posen (Posnan)
Forschungsstelle	"B" Leba

[126] I 25 p 9.

[127] Ticom Document 240 item 22.

In addition, the Forschungstelle "A" Danzig was instructed to move as quickly as possible to Berlin and unite with the Forschungsleitstelle Berlin. The head of Forschungsleitstelle Breslau was relieved and Schmidt was appointed head of a "closing down section" of Forschungsleitstelle Breslau in Berlin and instructed to send all personnel released from duty to FA 3 for reassignment. (Specialist Niedermeyer, the relieved head of Forschungsleitstelle Breslau, was appointed chief of staff for the Jueterbog Branch of the FA on the same date and on 9 March he was made head of the Forschungsleitstelle Munich, entering on duty on 20 March).[128] The directive for the reorganization of the FA at Kaufbeuren of 9 March revealed the existence of four Forschungsleitstellen at that time.[129] These were:

Forschungsleitstelle Berlin	-	Specialist Thieme
Forschungsleitstelle Hamburg	-	Senior Specialist Kirbach
Forschungsleitstelle Vienna	-	Senior Specialist, engineering Diploma Fleischmann
Forschungsleitstelle Munich	-	Specialist Niedermeyer

As may be seen from the above, the FA regional offices were so located as to provide area coverage of Germany and of the occupied countries. The Breslau Forschungsleitstelle covered Eastern Germany and Poland, the Munich Forschungsleitstelle covered Southern Germany, the Vienna Forschungsleitstelle covered Austria, the Hamburg Forschungsleitstelle covered Western Germany (and possibly Denmark), and the Berlin Forschungsleitstelle covered Central Germany. This monitoring service, particularly the telephone monitoring ("A") stations), was probably chiefly involved in liaison with the Abwehr and (later) the Reich Main Security Office. Unfortunately no details of the channels for this liaison and cooperation are known. An order of 14 April 1945 gives evidence of the Copenhagen and Stettin Forschungstellen.[130] On this date the Copenhagen "A" Forschungstelle had moved from its former location to Nyropsgade 17/11 in Copenhagen. The new telephone number is given as Palae 9469 extensions 35, 8, 9, and 30

[128] Ticom Document 240 items 34 and 35.

[129] Ticom Document 240 item 34.

[130] Ticom Document 240 item 10.

DOCID: 3486670

and the "Armed Forces liaison telephone" is said to be unchanged. Palae is one of the central exchanges in Copenhagen. The same order stated that the Stettin "A" Forschungsstelle had moved to Griefwald, Banahoffstrasse 16/47, telephone Griefwald 3307, on 29 March. No strength figures for these regional offices, nor for the intercept stations, are available. A member of FA-9, Frau Helene Gerta, who was unwilling to remain at Kaufbeuren after the first of May, was suggested to the personnel section as suitable for employment at the Luebben intercept station. Her qualifications were said to include a knowledge of French and a reading knowledge of Russian.[131] The existence of a "D" station (telegraph and cable intercept) in Berlin is confirmed by a request from this Forschungsstelle for the forwarding address of FA-9 at Kaufbeuren. This request reveals that the Berlin station was designated D-2.[132]

12. Persons named as members of the FA or concerned with it but not assignable in its organization. Finally there remain to be mentioned several persons whose names have been associated with the FA but whose connection can not be definitely explained either with the above exposition of the history or of the organization. Such persons fall into two categories, apparent members of the FA and officials of other organizations recipients of FA material or concerned with its operations. The captured telephone directory of the FA is the chief source of the names involved. In this directory a "Becker" is carried as "RLM/FA/V/3" and a "Senior Specialist Boettger" is given as merely "RLM/FA" but their names are otherwise unknown. A man by the name of "Kell" is given as "Research Office A1/2 Berlin. Exploitation Center (RLM/FA/AWKopf)" and is presumably a member of the Berlin Forschungsleitstelle. One other man is named as a member of the FA in prisoner interrogations.[134] This is the former Austrian cryptanalyst, Rudolf Bailovic. Bailovic was a member of the Austrian Cipher Section before the Anschluss and refused to surrender the keys of his department to the Nazis at the time of the Anschluss. He was relegated to a minor position in the

[131] Ticom Document 240 item 18.

[132] Ticom Document 240 item 28.

[133] D 22, Ticom Doc. 249, found at Berchtesgaden.

[134] I 84, I 118, IF 126.

54

Austrian civil service but Generals Fellgiebel and Theile brought him to Germany to employ his services as a cryptanalyst. He is said to have worked for the FA for a few months when he quit the FA and was then employed with the Signal Intelligence Agency of the Army High Command and finally at the Signal Intelligence Agency of the Supreme Command of the Armed Forces as head of a section dealing with Balkan traffic. Towards the end of the war he is stated to have served more as an administrator than as a cryptanalyst. He is further said to have lived a quiet life with his wife,making no concealment of his strongly anti-Nazi views and refusing to wear German decorations when in uniform. In view of the attested strong anti-Nazi views of Bailovic it seems possible that his short association with the FA (where,incidentally,the nature of his duties are unknown) was due to the"Nazi taint" of Goering's organization. Finally the identity of one other of the members of the Reichswehrministeriums Cipher section who went over to the FA upon its creation has been discovered. In the correspondence of the Austrian Cipher Bureau, found among the archives of the Signal Intelligence Agency of the Supreme Command of the Armed Forces, is a letter from the well known Austrian cryptanalyst Andreas Figl written upon his retirement to his friends and collaborators in Germany.*The letter refers to members of the Reichswehrministerium(cipher section) who: " have aided in establishing todays collaboration:Messrs v. Buschenhagen and v. Rezniczek". A pencilled note after v. Rezniczek states "now with FA ".

In the second category of recipients of FA material are Koerner, Secretary of State in the Prussian State Ministry,who has been identified previously as controlling the FA finances;Principal Specialists Drape and Legler of the Prussian State Ministry and connected with the Four Year Plan; in the Air Ministry,Colonel Bokelburg,Group Leader of the Monitoring Department (RLM/Z.A./UEWA.), General der Flieger Bodenschatz,Head of the Office of Ministers, Lt.Gen. v. Doering,Group Head of the Equipment Department,Field Marshal Milch,Secretary of State for Air and Inspector General of the G.A.F.,and Colonel Simson,Commandant of the Air Ministry. In the Reichssicherheithauptamt Schellenberg is given as head of Amt IV and the names of Lt. General of Police SS Gruppenfuehrer Mueller (head of the Gestapo),Senior Specialist Bock,SS Obersturmbannfuehrer,Head of the State Police Central Office in Berlin,and"Krim.Komm" Ebeling,SS Obersturmfuehrer of the State Polce Central Office Section IV N. Two members of the Reichspost are also included in the directory, Postrat Hofmann ,head of "work connected with service matters"(RPZ/We-E),and Principal Specialist Wichmann,Head of the office of ministers and Department VII of the Reichspost.

* D 74, p. 17. This item was brought to the writers attention after the completion of the paper.As it is believed to be significant evidence it has been inserted here. Neither the name of v. Rezniczek nor D 74 appear in Tab A.

VOLUME 7

Chapter III - Evaluation of the FA

13. <u>Effectiveness of the FA and its liaison with other cryptologic and intelligence agencies in the opinions of various high Nazis</u>. The above outline of the organization and operations of the FA, taken in conjunction with Appendix I, the listing of FA cryptanalytic successes, is believed to be ample evidence for stating that the FA was a highly successful intelligence producing agency. These concluding remarks will attempt to evaluate its functions as appraised by the persons receiving its results and associated or working in rivalry with it.

From the account given above, it is obvious that the FA received a vast amount of material, processed it, and passed it on to all persons who could make use of it. The actual amount of cooperation between the FA and the Signal Intelligence Agency of the Supreme Command of the Armed Forces, the Signal Intelligence Agency of the Army High Command, the Signal Intelligence Agency of the Airforce High Command, the Signal Intelligence Agency of the Navy High Command, and the Cryptanalytic Section of the Foreign Office is difficult to estimate. The statements of individuals employed in the various agencies are remarkably defeatist in tone but this is little cause for wonder. FA personnel complain that they knew nothing of their operational counterparts in the other agencies and personnel in the other agencies raised the same complaint and charged that the FA was peculiarly exclusive and stand-offish in its relations with them. Yet examination of activity reports, yearly reports, captured work books, and memoranda reveal an active exchange between even the smallest operating sections of technical data, coordination and sharing of assignments, and exchange of personnel.

At the highest level of the Nazi Reich there was appreciation of the value of Signal Intelligence and at times a surprising knowledge of technical details and evaluation of the various agencies. General-oberst Jodl, Chief of Armed Forces Operations Staff, Grand Admiral Doenitz, Commander in Chief of the Navy and later Reichschancellor, Field Marshall Keitel, Chief of the Armed Forces, von Ribbentrop, Foreign Minister, and Field Marshall Goering were interrogated by Ticom.[135] Their testimony is summarized in the following paragraphs.

[135] I 143. The interrogators stated that "all the prisoners, with the exception of Ribbentrop, appeared willing to answer to the best of their ability the questions put to them. It was clear to the interrogators that the prisoners found the subject of signals intelligence a welcome relief in contrast to that of responsibility for war crimes. It must be borne in mind that these interrogations required a somewhat different handling from the previous norm of Ticom procedures. Because of the potential security danger inherent in the forthcoming war guilt trials, when these men will be publicly prosecuted and will speak from the box, it was impossible to exploit them to the full. Many significant "leads" thus had to be neglected by the interpreters."

a. Jodl recalled various specific successes, among them information derived from an American official in Cairo in 1942 whose messages were read by a German Army intercept unit in Italy which stopped when the key changed and messages from Harrison in Berne which he attributed to the FA. Jodl did not know the names of any cryptanalysts and was unwilling to discriminate between the work of the bureaus. He knew of the Foreign Office bureau and described the FA as large and efficiently organized but "Goering's special affair." He received copies of FA results which were selected for him from a larger amount of such FA reports by Keitel.

b. Keitel knew very little about the FA beyond the fact that it was "the third competitor" whose so-called Brown reports" he used to receive. He "was never able to fathom the special and rather mysterious selection which had been made specially for him; it appeared to him to be on an erratic and irrational basis." Keitel hoped that there had been adequate liaison and remarked that Goering and Ribbentrop had been completely against any suggestion of a combined intelligence agency (and admitted that he himself would have been reluctant to give up his own agencies).

c. Doenitz was much more familiar with the activity of the Navy Signal Intelligence Agency. He knew of such cryptanalytic details as "depth" and "key changes". He knew the names of several of the leaders of the Navy organization but denied receiving the reports of any other organization and knew very little about them.

d. Ribbentrop was described as the most difficult of the prisoners to "prime" for talking on the subject of signal intelligence. It was very hard to reduce the statements of his interrogation to coherent form. However, Ribbentrop stated that when he took over the Ministry of Foreign Affairs in 1938 he discovered that practically nothing existed in the way of a political intelligence organization and that nearly everything was in the hands of the Wehrmacht and SS (Armed Forces-Abwehr?-and Elite Gaurds). He stated that "this was unfortunate because everything went to Hitler and there was no clearing house." It seems clear that Ribbentrop was at first talking about "political intelligence" as something distinct from signal intelligence as the subsequent statements concern cryptanalysis and it may be assumed that he had discovered where the interests of his interrogators lay. He knew that "the Foreign Office Cryptanalytic Section Pers ZS was under Herr Selchow who had been engaged in this work during the first world war." He did not know the details of the organization but he stated that Selchow "liaised closely with the RLM/Forschungsamt, the organization which produced the 'Brown Reports. He saw between one and three of these Brown Report decodes everyday and remarked that in general the FA produced their decodes more quickly than the Foreign Office but their texts were far less clear and tended to be inaccurate." The FA "covered precisely the same field as Pers ZS and there was unfortunately almost complete duplication" which he believes he may have once tried to correct and also coordinate intelligence activities in general. He stated that Selchow maintained a "liaison on technical matters with OKW/Chi and probably compared notes with them" and believed that there was some sort of "technical exchange between OKW/Chi and the Forschungsamt". His reason for failing to achieve coordination of intelligence services is of interest: "as the system in force was for everyone to go privately and directly to Hitler it was scarcely worth trying." By comparison Keitel recalled that Ribbentrop was exceptionally jealous if anyone gave Hitler a diplomatic decode directly instead of passing it through the Foreign Office.

e. Goering was of course fulsome in his praises of the FA and has been cited in considerable detail for its history and accomplishments. He stated that he did not control the work program of the cryptanalysts and therefore should not be expected to know too much technical detail although he mentions the use of special cipher keys or a change of key when something important was happening. Specific examples recalled by Goering were the "messages of the American Minister in Berne" and the "Japanese Ambassador in Berlin reporting home." In the matter of liaison he stated that the FA did not deal with purely military traffic which was handled by the bureau of the Army, Navy and Air Force with whom the FA maintained liaison and exchanged intercepted traffic. He knew that the Foreign Office and the Signal Intelligence Agency of the Supreme Command of the Armed Forces also worked on civil ciphers and that there was a very close liaison with the Foreign Office to avoid unnecessary duplication.

DOCID: 3486670

f. Hitler's opinion of signal intelligence is mentioned by both Goering and Ribbentrop and the opinion expressed is completely divergent at first glance. Ribbentrop stated:

> Hitler had a queer, rather particular view about it-he did not like this type of intelligence very much and said it was unreliable and often misleading, it was better to use one's own common sense.

Goering, however, declared that:

> Hitler's view of the products of the Forschungsamt was that they were very reliable; the materials had to be presented factually to Hitler with no argument nor appreciation, only the verbatim conversation or actual text.

Goering's remarks came in a context where the telephone monitoring and broadcast monitoring activities of the FA were clearly in his mind. In connection with diplomatic decodes Goering had previously remarked that:

> The intelligence resulting from decoded telegrams was not always useful, they often consisted of absolute rubbish; the extent to which the members of the diplomatic corps spread and retailed fantastic rumors was surprising. He himself had often made arrangements to have rumors planted and within a few days he observed them being passed on and spreading.

Ribbentrop's remarks about the opinion of Hitler were immediately preceded by discussion of diplomatic decodes exclusively. It is likely that Hitler was familiar with FA results from the period before the war. Keitel refers to an unfortunate instance of Himmler passing a single message to Hitler withour collating it against other information and stated that Hitler had his own liaison officers to each agency in any case.

14. Extent of liaison at the operational level between the FA and other signal intelligence agencies. At the operational level it is possible to reconstruct a satisfactory picture of liaison and cooperation between the FA and the

60

other signal intelligence agencies. In many cases the personnel of the other agencies express opinions and prejudices or repeat rumors about the FA which can be positively refuted or revealed as prejudice and misinformation. Much of the evidence for FA success has been derived from the archives and records of the other organizations-no trace of the official archives of the FA has been found. The picture so reconstructed shows active and detailed cooperation, its details are set out in the following paragraphs and in the listing of FA successes in the appendix.

a. Liaison between the Signal Intelligence Agency of the Supreme Command of the Armed Forces (OKW/Chi) and the FA is known to have existed. A special liaison officer of the FA was assigned to the Supreme Command of the Armed Forces although not to the Signal Intelligence Agency. This man, known from the Kaufbeuren directive, was Dr. Klautschke, and he has himself testified on the form which his liaison took the form of passing intelligence to the Supreme Command and answering specific requests from them. He did not concern himself with cryptanalytic matters and states that liaison on these matters did not exist.[136] As has been amply documented in the sections of this paper dealing with the early history of the FA considerable ill feeling existed between the FA and Signal Intelligence Agency of the Supreme Command of the Armed Forces cryptanalysts. Instructions to exclude the FA from Foreign Office and Defense Ministery Cipher Section cooperation, references to ill feeling by Fenner for Schapper, and refusal of Signal Intelligence Agency of the Supreme Command of the Armed Forces IBM developments to the FA have been mentioned. All of these cases can be derived from the ill feeling between Schapper and Fenner. It seems clear that intercepted traffic was exchanged, indeed the Activity Report of the service organization, signed by Kettler, the head, shows that one third of all intercept received by the Signal Intelligence Agency of the Supreme Command of the Armed Forces came from the FA.[137] Mettig refers to attempts of the FA to take over the broadcast

[136] See above para. 5 and Cf I 54.

[137] DF 9

monitoring of the Signal Intelligence Agency of the Supreme Command of the Armed Forces.[138] The unwillingness of the Signal Intelligence Agency of the Supreme Command of the Armed Forces to give up their monitoring is understandable but in view of the interest and activity of the FA in this field it would seem that the duplication was unnecessary. In Security matters there was an effort at cooperation; Kroeger, the cipher machine cryptanalytic expert of the FA was a member of Huettenhains cipher security committee and Huettenhain knew enough of his activity to explain that he was unable to attend all meetings because his section had moved to Breslau. It should be noted that the FA, as running its own communications, was in a position to ignore Huettenhain and the willingness to have a permanent member of the committee may be accepted as a symptom of willingness to cooperate. Finally a typical example of ignorance of the FA may be cited. Fricke, of the Signal Intelligence Agency of the Supreme Command of the Armed Forces, was told that the FA employed over 2000 people and remarked: "For their deciphering they should have needed a handful. They must have had other work to do but what the devil could they have done with 2000 people!"[139]

b. As in the case of the Signal Intelligence Agency of the Supreme Command of the Armed Forces, cryptanalysts of the Signal Intelligence Agency of the Army High Command were not too well informed on the organization or operations of the FA. However, it is evident that considerably greater liaison existed between the FA and the Signal Intelligence Agency of the Army High Command than had existed between the FA and the Signal Intelligence Agency of the Supreme Command of the Armed Forces. This liaison took the form of actual division of tasks and sharing of personnel as well as liaison over IBM developments. What would appear to have been one of the most important cryptanalytic achievements of the FA is known only from the testimony of Buggisch of the Signal Intelligence Agency of the Army High Command who testifies (and the information was so important that two interrogations refer to the subject although in considerably less detail than might be

[138] I 131 p 3 See above para. 5.

[139] I 20.

desired) that the FA was able to break and read Russian teletype traffic.[140]

[140] I 64 p 2. "Buggisch heard in 1943 that the FA had claimed some success on a Russian teletype machine and had reconstructed the machine. It was a machine with a very long cycle being not prime but the product of several smaller cycles-like the SZ 42. Buggisch did not know the cycle of all of the individual wheels or any other details. He heard this from Doering who was then doing his research on the T 52 but liaison with FA was bad anyway (Major Mettig was particularly opposed to the SS taint) and the next he heard was that the traffic found by the FA had stopped. Buggisch remembered only that the cycle of one of the wheels was 37; the others he thought varied widely, from 30 to 80." This testimony is admittedly at second hand where it concerns the construction of the Russian machine. However, the indication that Mettig distrusted the FA because of an SS taint is of interest in evaluating his evidence quoted previously. Buggisch was questioned a second time on what specifically "were the results of the FA mentioned in connection with Russian cipher teleprinter" and his answer reveals additional liaison between the Signal Intelligence Agency of the Army High Command and the FA, I 176 p 6: "The FA (Forschungsamt) had analysed a Russian cipher teleprinter system in 1943 and recognized that it must have been based on a machine having certain similarities with the German SZ 40. After a short time the Russians altered the system. The FA then communicated its results to my unit and was given as a kind of recompense a report on the solution of a German cipher teleprinter. This was one of the very rare cases where FA and In 7/VI exchanged results. I did not study the FA results at that time, as I was not responsible for work on cipher teleprinters, and hence can give no details. At all events the Russian machine (just as in the German types SZ 40, SF 42, but in contrast to T 52 a,b,c, and d) gave only 32 different substitution alphabets, the succession of which became periodic only after an astronomically large number of steps. This succession was given by a system of pin wheels, the peripheries of which were prime to each other and at an estimate lay between 30 and 90. In any case there was no complicated mutual influence of the pin wheels on each other (as for example in the T 52 D)."

There is yet another example of FA liaison with the Signal Intelligence Agency of the Army High Command on Russia. Lt. Schubert, the officer in charge of the section of the Army High Command Signal Intelligence Service on the Eastern Front responsible for agent traffic, reported that the Radio Defence Corps (WNV/Fu) sent Specialist Wenzel of the FA to work with him on Polish Resistance Movement Traffic.[141] In the case of Turkish diplomatic traffic (the specific system is not known) complete cooperation is revealed. The FA gave the Signal Intelligence Agency of the Army High Command the mission of covering and reading all traffic. Traffic "was intercepted by Kona 4 and relayed to In 7/VI, referate of Bailovic."[142] Only decoded messages were furnished to the FA. The Signal Intelligence Agency of the Army High Command took the lead among the German agencies in the development and application of IBM machinery to cryptanalytic work. This machinery was made available to the other agencies. Tranow, of the Signal Intelligence Agency of the Navy High Command stated:

> About March 1942 we paid a visit, in conjunction with the German Air Force and the FA, to the OKH Hollerith department in Berlin, Victoriastrasse. . . .[143]

This is in marked contrast to the policy of the Signal Intelligence Agency of the Supreme Command of the Armed Forces reported by Huettenhain and cited above. Asomewhat peculiar reference to the effect of the creation of the FA on the cipher section of the Defence Ministry by personnel of the Signal Intelligence Agency of the Army High Command needs no discussion as it can not be determined whether the Defense Ministry or the Signal Intelligence Agency

[141] I 26 p 7. See also the discussion under Wenzel's section of Main Section IV above.

[142] IF 126 p 8. See further discussion of IF 126 in note 145 following.

[143] I 146.

of the Army High Command are involved and the meaning is ambiguous.[144] An equally unverified statement by two former members of the Signal Intelligence Agency of the Army High Command declared that:

> OKH In 7/VI worked for the FA in the field of diplomatic codes (for instance, they broke the Turkish code when the FA was having trouble with it.) FA received reports from the Signals Intelligence Evaluation section of the Army High Command from the Navy High Command, from the Armed Forces High Command and from the Foreign Office.[145]

[144] I 85 p 3. Flicke, Pokojewski, and Hatz:" b) the expansion of OKH/Chi. As a result of the situation created by the advent of the FA, General Schliecher, in the summer of 1933, began to lay plans for the expansion of OKH/Chi. This in volved the setting up of three new stations ... to cover Czechoslovakia and the Balkans. Progress was very slow .... By July 1939 the necessity for intercepting Czech traffic had ceased and it was decided to place the interception of diplomatic traffic under OKW, just created." It is barely possible that this reveals a division of labor under which the "OKH/Chi" group was to cover the Balkans diplomatic traffic while the FA concentrated on commercial traffic. This hypothesis might account for the Turkish diplomatic traffic handled by the Signal Intelligence Agency of the Army High Command although Rentschler, IF 15, claimed FA success with "high grade Turkish Diplomatic" but he cites no date. The only Czech commercial traffic of Skoda, claimed for 1935 by Sauerbier, IF 162. Such a division seems unlikely, however, and Paetzel, in I 25, mentions Bulgarian, Yugoslav, Hungarian and Greek traffic worked on by the FA.

[145] IF 105 B. This report, and IF 126, are based on interrogations of Heinz Boscheinen and Walter Kotschy. IF 105 B is a special PW interrogation carried out by a US Third Army Signals officer. The cover letter of this officer's

DOCID: 3486670

Finally, Dettman, and Samsonoff, the heads of the Russian referate on the Eastern Front for the Signal Intelligence

continuation of footnote 145.

report states that the original notes of the interrogation had been destroyed for security reasons. This interrogation took place on 29 November 1944. In the cover letter from Col. Bicher submitting the interrogation it was stated that the whereabouts of the prisoners was unknown but that they would be sought for further questioning. Actually Boscheinen and Kotschy were then (15 December) in the hands of CSDIC in the U. K., and the results of CSDIC interrogations were issued as SIR 1326 (equals IF 126) and SIR 1335 (equals IF 105). IF 126 is an interrogation of a general nature and corresponds essentially to the 29 November interrogation. What differences exist between IF 105 B and IF 126 are presumably due to misapprehension and condensation by the writer of the former. IF 105 is a "follow up" interrogation to IF 126 which concerns a training school for Turkish translators which seems to have been operated by the Abwehr or Mil. Amt. Unfortunately it was not at first recognized that IF 105 B was a separate document and it was thought to be a duplicate of one of the two CISCIC interrogations. It was accordingly mistakenly marked as a duplicate, and as a duplicate of IF 105 rather than of IF 126 which it does ressemble in material covered. References to both IF 126 and IF 105 B, have been corrected in the present volume and it is hoped that errors in citation arising from the faulty identification as a duplicate of IF 105 have been discovered elsewhere. Both IF 105 B and IF 126 discuss the Army High Command Signals Intelligence organization and the details of Kona 4 in particular. Both state that the Army High Command broke and read Turkish diplomatic for the FA. In both interrogations the FA is identified as being a part of the Air Ministry but it is confused with the Signals Intelligence Agency of the Air Force High Command. As there are references to agent activity in both interrogations it seems clear that the prisoners had confused the FA with either the Abwehr of the Mil. Amt. IF 126 states that the FA received and sent Evaluation reports to the Army High Command while IF 105 B states that the FA received them. In IF 126 a chart shows the FA receiving the results of telephone monitoring of a telephone intercept company of the Bulkan command as direct liaison while other reports to the FA go from Kona 4 through In 7/VI.

Agency of the Army High Command stated that there had been no relations with the FA after 1944 when the Signal Intelligence Agency of the Army High Command linked up with the Signal Intelligence Agency of the Supreme Command of the Armed Forces.[146]

c. The position of the FA and the Signal Intelligence Agency of the Airforce High Command under Goering should have facilitated an exchange between them. The absence, in the interrogations, of any reference to ill feeling between them indicates that such was the case. There are a few specific references to an exchange of technical information on specific problems. The functional division between them, however, precluded any need for constant liaison, the Signal Intelligence Agency of the Air Force High Command was concerned with air traffic which, as such, was no concern of the FA. The FA, on the contrary, did supply an undetermined amount of diplomatic and general intelligence to the Air Force High Command and to its Signal Intelligence Agency. The head of the Signal Intelligence Agency of the Air Force High Command, Friederich, stated:

> He did not work with them (the RLM/FA) except to the extent that Voegele (the chief cryptanalyst) sometimes met with cryptanalysts from this and other agencies to discuss general problems. The FA furnished the GAF

[146] I 116 p 2: "Subjects did not know whether RLM/FA worked on machine and/or Baudot traffic. OKH/Chi had no connections with the FA after 1944 when the former organization linked up with OKW/Chi. However, as a matter of opinion, they do not believe FA did." It is curious that Dettman and Samsonoff were ignorant of the Russian cipher teleprinter which the FA reported on and which was known to Buggisch. It is to be presumed that there had been relations between the two agencies prior to 1944 (Buggisch dated the teletype matter to 1943, it may be noted) from their statement that there were none after 1944. The lasting antipathy of the Signal Intelligence Agency of the Supreme Command of the Armed Forces to the FA again stopped any liaison, it appears.

> with appropriate traffic on occasion. We asked what was the function of the FA. He said its purpose was really hidden from the services, who were not allowed entry to the establishment. Only Voegele had any contact with them and that only with cryptanalysts....[147]

Voegele, the chief cryptanalyst of the Signal Intelligence Agency of the Air Force High Command, in "homework" he prepared for TICOM, referred to an exchange of additive for the (British) Inter Departmental Code with the Signal Intelligence Agency of the Supreme Command of the Armed Forces, the Signal Intelligence Agency of the Navy High Command, and the FA in 1940/42.[148] Zetsche (Hauptman in charge of Groupe A of Foreign Air Force West under Chef Ic) reported that the FA reports contained a great deal of significant information concerning economic and political matters. The reports from foreign broadcasts, as those of the BBC, were

[147] I 29 p 3. Friederich knew that they carried out monitoring of telephone and telegraph for Goering and the Nazis. He thought that Goering had founded it personally. "It was completely political, not military. When it worked on foreign systems it worked only on rear area traffic, such as industrial traffic it thought the Army might not be handling adequately. They worked particularly on inner Russian traffic. Asked if he could name any FA personnel he said they are always changing. There was a Min. Rat Schaper (with one P) who was not a soldier but a civilian official." Friederich appears to be well informed on the FA when compared to some other prisoners. His mention of inner Russian traffic is interesting, as Seiffert (I 25) stated that this was the outstanding FA success.

[148] I 112 p 9.

particularly important, especially for the period between the invasion and the collapse when they were often the only source of reliable information on the war situation.[149]

d. Liaison between the FA and the Signal Intelligence Agency of the Navy High Command is documented by references to the FA in Yearly Progress reports prepared by the Navy and by the interrogation of the chief Navy cryptanalyst, Tranow. As seen in the preceding paragraph, the FA and Air Force cooperated with the Navy on the British Inter-Departmental Cipher:

> I informed the FA, the OKW, and the GAF of the existence of this cipher in 1940 and the FA and the Navy worked on it. The OKW and the GAF restricted themselves rather to receiving the cypher data when worked out. The GAF did a little work on it, however, and passed any recovered keys on to us.

[149] I 159: "6. Of special interest and value were the broadcast links between the news agencies and their correspondents in the various capitals of the world. Of broadcasting stations, the B.B.C. and Swiss stations were considered the most reliable, Daventry in particular being appreciated for its figures concerning Allied sorties and losses. Indeed, during the period between the invasion and collapse, B.B.C. reports were often the only source of reliable information on the war situation. 7. Radio monitoring was done by OKW/Chi, its Naval counterpart, the Seehausdienst, and the FA, the results being sorted out and distributed by Ic/Luftwesen....9. Intelligence concerning foreign diplomatic exchanges was received from the FA (subordinated directly to Goering) through Ic/Luftwesen/Abwehr, and was given a restricted distribution. It consisted of intercepted Allied radio telegrams (e.g., London-Stockholm), ordinary radio reports (e.g., Atlantic Radio) and intercepted traffic between diplomats and ministers over certain links, e.g., Ankara-Moscow (Turk), Berne-Washington (American), and London-Washington (Poles). 10. The last mentioned source was of great value before and during the invasion and after the breaking off of German-Turkish relations. In general the FA reports contained a great deal of significant information concerning economic and political matters."

> The cypher went out of use in December 1942. That was the last of it. I believe it was afterwards still used occasionally at a few stations. I stopped work on it for the navy about the end or middle of December 1942. The FA continued to send us occasional results. In particular these consisted again and again of information about our U-boat losses and the British shipping losses etc.[150]

According to Tranow 2 to 3% of all Navy traffic came from the FA who supplied the German Navy with traffic from commercial links.[151] A Yearly Progress Report of the Signal Intelligence Agency of the Navy High Command refers to traffic in "Bentley's Code" which was supplied by the FA.[152] However, it should be noted that Tranow, when told by the interrogators that a number of messages dealing with North Russian convoy personnel matters were passed over commercial circuits, stated that the Navy had never seen them--"This material would have been done by the FA, if any such material was intercepted it was not passed to us."[153] Tranow did not mention receipt of reports based on broadcast monitoring. However, he did refer to "five FA men under Stabenow who had been doing press broadcast analysis" turning up at Flensburg after the war ended.[154] This presumably refers to Seifert, Paetzel Oden, Klautschke, and Fingerhut who were found and interrogated by Ticom at Flensburg where they were continuing to issue a "news bulletin" based on broadcasts

[150] I 147 p 11.

[151] I 93 p 18.

[152] D 17.

[153] I 93 p 18.

[154] I 93 p 18.

monitored there.[155]

e. The status of liaison between the FA and the Foreign Office Cryptanalytic Section is more fully known than that between any other of the agencies. Ribbentrop stated that Selchow, the director of the Foreign Office bureau, "Liaisoned closely" with the FA.[156] The extent of this liaison can be learned in detail in the chapter on liaison in the discussion of the Foreign Office Cryptanalytic Section (Volume VI) and in the appendix of FA successes at the end of this volume. As specific examples of the knowledge of the FA possessed by Foreign Office Personnel and of actual liaison a few instances will suffice here. The Foreign Office cryptanalysts from whom TICOM Team 1 first learned of the existence of the FA created an outline of the FA and knew the names of many of the section heads in Department IV (Hauptabteilung IV - Codes and Ciphers) with which they were immediately concerned.[157] The Yearly Report for 1942 of the Foreign Office, intearlia, reveals an exchange of code book recoveries. The name of Senior Specialist Waechter of the FA appears in this document, and the names of other FA personnel occur in reconstructed code books in the Foreign Office archives.[158] From this evidence

[155]Stabenow, from this evidence, seems to have been at Flensburg. He was the head of the Berlin Branch Office (see the Kaufbeuren directive) and could certainly have escaped from Berlin along with the other FA people. However, Ticom did not find and interrogate him. It is not known why this "lead" of Tranow's to his presence was not followed up.

[156]The interrogators of Ribbentrop (I 143) stated that he was the most poorly informed and hardest to extract information from of the high Nazi's questioned at Nuremburg. For this reason his statement that there was close liaison is apt to be disregarded. The evidence for liaison between the FA and Foreign Office, however, adequately bears out his statement and suggests that he was better informed on the matter than the interrogators had assumed.

[157]IF 15.

[158]D 16. Other examples are cited in the appendix with source reference.

the existence of technical cryptanalysis liaison between the FA and the other cryptologic agencies can not be denied and the categorical denial that technical liaison existed must be seriously questioned. Certainly there is good evidence for close liaison between the FA and the Foreign Office, Signal Intelligence Agency of the Airforce High Command, the Signal Intelligence Agency of the Navy High Command. Close cooperation with the Elite Gaurds and Abwehr is to be inferred. Only in the case of the Signal Intelligence Agency of the Supreme Command of the Armed Forces is there direct evidence that cryptanalytic liaison did not exist. Even here, however, there was liaison on security matters, an exchange of decodes,[159] interchange of intercepted traffic, and a definite agreement that the FA would not work on military traffic.[160]

15. Final Evaluation of the FA. The historical outline of the FA's operations revealed that their work continued even under the vicissitudes brought on by bombing and moving. Careful arrangements for dissemination of information existed and there is evidence that this exchange functioned at all levels. The FA undoubtedly had many faults as an intelligence agency but they seem to have been faults inherent in its history (the personalities involved, the Nazi taint, etc.,) and also occurring in other German intelligence agencies. Cryptanalysis supplied less than 20% of the information delivered by the FA, and the other 80% was considered so important that special arrangements were made for its continued production at Berlin and finally at Flensburg up to the very end. A shift in emphasis by the FA from telephone monitoring to commercial traffic and press and broadcast material is indicated through the course of its existence. The cryptanalytic element probably remained of constant importance throughout the history of the FA, with the press monitoring increasing towards the end of the war as other sources of readily available information diminished. Even at Kaufbeuren (when, according to Schellenberg, the FA

[159] Cf Goering, I 143, who said he "saw OKW/Chi decodes..." and Ribbentrop who "saw 2 or 3 Brown Reports a day.

[160] Cf Rentschler, IF 15.

should no longer have been concerned in telephone monitoring) the remains of a card index based on telephone conversations was found.[161] In the light of all the evidence available the FA must be recognized as a highly successful source of intelligence in the fullest sense of the word. So important was the intelligence produced that careful arrangements were made for furnishing it throughout the final stages of the war. The relationship between the FA and the Abwehr, Gestapo, and Police in general censorship operations and in counter-measures against agents can only be indicated. The FA does appear to have served the Abwehr, and so the Supreme Command of the Armed Forces, in telephone monitoring in Germany and in occupied territory, and it served the Elite Gaurds, the Reich Main Security Office, the Regular Police, and the Radio Defense Corps as a cryptanalytic agency for agent traffic. Any attempt to evaluate its ability in collecting and evaluating press broadcast and similar material is invidious due to the lack of information on the achievements of the other agencies performing this function, the Supreme Command of the Armed Forces, the Foreign Office (the Seehausdienst), and the Propaganda Ministry.

[161] IF 15 p 16 (appendix 2).

Appendix I.

Alphabetical Listing by Country of Systems Worked on by the FA.

This appendix presents the available information on the cryptanalytic phase of the FA's operations. Only eighty odd references to traffic worked on have been gleaned from the available material concerning the FA. Many of these references are vague and tend (especially when FA personnel were being questioned) to statements that traffic of such and such a country was only sorted according to link or that the diplomatic traffic of a country had been identified but not read. The archives and reports of the Cryptanalytic Section of the Foreign Office, of the Signal Intelligence Agency of the Navy High Command, and even the Signals Intelligence Agency of the Supreme Command of the Armed Forces reveal considerably more detail as to just which systems were worked on by the FA in liaison with the other German agencies. It should be noted that there is considerable evidence that the FA possessed copies of a surprising number of code books although there is no indication in Ticom Interrogations as to how the FA procured these items or even a hint that they were in the FA's possession. The following summary reveals six cases in which code books or ciphers were in the possession of the FA. In this appendix all available references to traffic worked on by the FA have been collected and the source indicated.

* * * *

American (United States) Systems

American Strip System.

Paetzel stated that "we attempted a strip system and read it here and there but not currently. We finally gave it up as it took too many personnel." He did not remember any of the originators. Traffic was America to Europe but whether Washington-London or Washington-Paris he did not recall. The system employed 30 out of a matrix of 50 strips in a setting. (I 25 p 3; I 54 passim). FA ability to read this system may have been due to liaison with the Foreign Office although there is no indication that such is the case.

American Five Figure System with Monoalphabetic and Bigram Substitution.

Paetzel stated that US plain systems were read and subsequently a US system consisting of a five letter book enciphered by monoalphabetic and bigram substitution. This system was not solved currently as they only read back material several months to a year old. The tables changed within the message and this change was shown by an indicator. The successor to this system was not broken because there was no indicator in the middle of the message to show where the tables changed. (I 25 p.3.)

American State Department System used by Harrison from Berne.

The messages of Harrison in Berne were mentioned as examples of signals intelligence by Jodl and Goering and by cryptanalysts of several agencies. These messages were sent in the compromised Brown code and Rentschler stated that they had been "read up until quite recently". (I 143, IF 15).

Joint American and British Systems.

Paetzel refers to FA success with American and British unenciphered codes but knew of no instance of an important message being sent in a low grade system. Rentschler knew that American and British commercial messages were read, some of which concerned ship movements. These were mainly concerned with individual ships; convoy information was not dealt with by his section (Evaluation). Tranow, of the Signal Intelligence Agency of the Navy High Command, referred to commercial messages supplied to the Navy by the FA. (I 25 p.4; IF 15; I 93).

Belgian Systems

Belgian Unenciphered books.

Paetzel stated that the Belgians used one book with and without substitution encipherment. It was read in both cases. (I 25 p.2.)

British Systems

British Consular Systems.

Rentschler stated that a message from the British consul at Cairo gave some information and Jodl recalls important information having been gained from this source. (The reference by Jodl is presumed to be to a FA decode.) In the Pers ZS Yearly Report for 1942, British Empire Section, there is reference to a statement by ORR Waechter of the FA of a fruitless attempt on a Teneriffe-Las Palmas Consular code. He also reported that a system used between Teneriffe and Las Palmas had been worked on by the FA in February 1942 which proved to be a case of transposed plain text. (IF 15, I 143, D 16).

British Diplomatic Systems.

Schroeder stated that Hitler delayed his discussions with the British Prime Minister, Chamberlain, during the Bad Godesburg [Munich] Conference for several hours while a message sent to London by the Prime Minister could be decoded. Seifert states that work on British Diplomatic cipher systems was useless and no success was obtained. "There was an occasional physical compromise. We captured clear text and a basic book in Norway but had no success with them cryptographically". He did not remember whether the clear text was ever available to Hauptabteilung V but did remember the basic books. In regard to low grade systems Seifert stated that un-enciphered books were attacked and read. Rentschler stated that second, third, and fourth grade British Diplomatic Codes could be read. (IF 132; I 25 p. 2; IF 15).

British Interdepartmental Cipher and/or Code.

Tranow, of the Signal Intelligence Agency of the Navy High Command, stated: "From the middle of 1942 results fell off because of less material. However, we continued to decipher a very good percentage of what material came in. The military situation had now changed. Russia had entered the war. Traffic with Ankara and Stockholm was very heavy but actual Navy traffic dropped considerably. I informed the FA, the OKW, and the GAF of the existence of this cipher in 1940 and the FA and the Navy worked on it. The OKW and the GAF restricted themselves rather to receiving the cypher data when worked out. The GAF did a little work on it, however, and passed any recovered keys to us. The cypher went out of force in December 1942. That was the last of it. I believe it was afterwards still used occasionally at a few stations. I stopped work on it at the Navy about the end or middle of December 1942. The FA continued to send occasional results. In particular these consisted again and again of information about our U-Boat losses and the British shipping losses etc. This was in the first months of 1943 up to the summer of that year. "Paetzel merely thought that the FA worked on Interdepartmental cipher. Voegele, chief of Section "E" of Chi Stelle (OKL/LN Abt 350) stated that there was an exchange of" recyphering book results for the Interdepartment Code [italics mine] with OKW, OKM, and the FA in 1940 up to 1942". The British Empire Section of the Pers ZS Yearly Report for 1942 stated that the work on this system was stopped in the summer of 1942 because the traffic received was slight and in consequence the additive sequences, which were received only late from the Ministry of Aviation (FA) revealed fragments of a text which was generally uninteresting. Miss Hagen, the head of the Pers ZS English Group, stated "there was no liaison with the FA except on the subject of the Interdepartmental Ciphers". (I 147; I 25 p.3; I 112 p. 9; D 16 reports 3 and 4; I 172 #13).

"Code 'B-30'".

The British Empire Section of the Pers ZS Yearly Report for 1942 refers to FA liaison in that year: "In February 1942, at the request of ORR Waechter of the FA, an attempt was made to establigh contact with the FA, which however, did not get beyond a general exchange of ideas. The only concrete results were that the FA placed at our disposal a list of approximately 50 'B-30' recovered groups". (D 16 report 4 page 1).

Bank of England Code.

Sauerbier states that a Bank of England Code was broken in 1941 (See INTABANK below. I 162).

Bulgarian Systems.

Bulgarian Codes.

Paetzel stated that Bulgarian systems were basically a few five digit-codes with repaginations or relineations. A 1940 report from the Pers ZS Bulgarian Group mentions that the FA had furnished them with photocopies of two Bulgarian codes. (I 25 p. 8; T 2038, Report of Bulgarian Group 1 January 1940). Ticom Doc. 240 (Film 34) has a list of Bulgarian material in the possession of the FA. It is not known whether this material was at Kaufbeuren or not. The list contained some twenty entries, including Dictionaries and Work Books, and was marked "To be Destroyed".

Chinese Systems

Chinese Traffic.

Chinese traffic was worked on at one time, according to Paetzel, but not towards the end. Some progress was made but nothing was read. (I 25 p. 7.)

Clandestine Traffic.

Clandestine Traffic of Detained Persons.

Clandestine traffic of detained persons, according to Sauerbier, was mostly scattered messages in individualistic systems which were rarely solved. (I 162.)

Czechoslovakia Systems.

Skoda Company Commercial Code.

According to Sauerbier one of the major undertakings in the prewar FA was the code used by the (Czech) Skoda firm to Iran and Iraq in 1935. This was concerned almost entirely with bridge building projects. (I 162.) Ticom Document 240 Item 42 is a cover letter for "Czech Messages" to be sent to the "Sta Poleit, Prag".

Danish Systems.

Danish Diplomatic Code.

Sauerbier said that about 50% of the traffic in the old Diplomatic code was read up until 1940. Nothing was solved thereafter except an occasional message in the old code on some minor commercial matter. (I 162.)

Ethiopian Systems.

Ethiopian Code.

Paetzel said that the FA had "done a little work on an Ethiopian Code". (I 25 p.8)

Finnish Systems.

Finnish Machine Ciphers.

Paetzel said that the FA at one time had cribs for the Finnish (or Swedish?) Hagelin and broke in. He subsequently stated that it was possible to break the Finnish Hagelin if they had 4,000 letters or more of text. (I 25, I 54).

French Systems.

French Diplomatic Ciphers.

Goering stated that "the ciphers of the French Foreign Office at the Quai d'Orsay had been obtained" but he did not remember the details nor give the date of this compromise. An Associated Press story, based on Goering's personal copy of his own telephone conversations at the time of the Ahschluss, indicates that the ciphers mentioned above may well have been a very high grade system. Goering was reasonably gaurded in his telephone conversation and the newspaper translation itself is not technically perfect from our specialized viewpoint. The conversations reveal Goering telephoning Hitler (in Austria to celebrate the triumphal of the Anschluss) that no action by France was to be feared because England had refused to back her in display of force. Goering assured Hitler that the information was certain because it was based on information from the Brown Reports taken from decoded telegrams of the French Foreign Office. The mention of the Brown Reports indicates that the FA was involved. The conversation was as follows: "Tell the Fuehrer that the Brown Reports have just come which are completely clear because they were seized [? Clear because the ciphers were "seized"??] . . . The French indeed wanted to go into action without any reservation and so pressed most hard on the British. I can send you all the decoded cables. And only because England declined the whole action has blown up . . . Today France tells its ministers in the various countries it can do nothing because England refused . . . " (I 143, IF 188).

French Code.

Pers ZS records referred to work in 1941 on a 10,000 group figure code designated as "19". The first solution was said to have been achieved by the FA using captured tables which were later turned over to Pers ZS. Dr. Brandes, the head of the French Language Section in Dr. Paschke's sub section of Pers.ZS, stated that he was responsible for liaison with the FA for the group. According to Seifert, the FA had success with all French unenciphered books ("This was particularly prodictive because the French used a large number of these books"). (D 54, p. 13, report 8, page 18; I 25 p. 2).

Vichy French Code.

Rentschler stated that the easiest system to break of all of those worked on by the FA was "French (Vichy period, De Gaule used Allied codes and consequently his diplomatic traffic is not read) since Vichy changed its code only about every four weeks. (IF 15). [This statement of Rentschler appears contradictory. It would be expected that Vichy codes would be available to the Germans without necessity for breaking, and the reference to "captured tables" in the paragraph above would support this belief. However, it may be that the FA and Foreign Office did not receive diplomatic codes or ciphers through the German Armistice commission which may not have been interested in such liaison.]

German Systems.

Commercial Codes.

Sauerbier said that in peacetime he was concerned almost entirely with commercial codes in the German language. This involved the traffic of German firms to foreign countries during the four year plan. (I 162.)

Greek Systems.

Greek Codes.

Paetzel said that just two Greek plain codes were read. (I 25, p. 8.)

Hagelin Machines.

Paetzel said that Hagelin messages were never broken because they were never long enough. He estimated that perhaps 5000 letters would be needed. However, in a second interrogation he contradicted himself in connection with Finnish and Swedish systems where he stated that cribs had been secured and the Hagelin read. He also stated that "it" could be read on 4000 letters. (I 25 p. 6; I 54.)

Hungarian Systems.

Additive System.

Paetzel stated that the Hungarians used an additive changing with the message which was not solved. (I 25, p. 8.)

Intabank System.

Intabank Code.

Sauerbier described the solution in 1944 of the code used by Intabank, the International Bank at Basle, as a major effort of the section. The code used was an old Bank of England code which had been solved in 1941. The pages were shuffled and an encipherment added but solution was achieved by the use of cribs and common form messages of which the best was a statement of the daily exchange rates between the various countries. The detail of the encipherment was as follows: the basic system was bigram substitution from a table different for each link and changing each three months. The text was divided into segments of three or four groups, and the plain text bigrams for encipherment were prearranged pairs as 1 and 15, 2 and 14, 6 and 10, etc. Very long depths and near-depths were produced on closely similar number values and this was the entry. The whole solution took about six months, starting with 1942-43 and working up to 1944. The interception of the traffic was not systematized at any time and Sauerbier did not believe that more than 50% of all the traffic was read as a result of the solution. (I 162).

Irish Systems.

Enciphered Code.

Paetzel said that FA/7 worked on Irish enciphered codes with considerable success up to the end of the war. Interrogation of Pers ZS prisoners referred to the Government Telegraph Code, which "was used by the Irish government for diplomatic communications, with an encipherment by two substitution alphabets. The FA solved the keys used on the Berlin and Madrid links in 1943. Pers ZS took over the keys from the FA in 1944. (I 54; I 172 p. 11.)

DOCID: 3486670

Italian Systems.

Enciphered code.

Rentschler claimed some success on high grade Italian diplomatic systems. The Annual Report of the Italian Group of Pers ZS for 1940 indicated a fairly extensive Pers ZS-FA cooperation on Italian systems. Intercept of the FA was made available to the Foreign Office and from 1939 through 1940 there was a regular exchange of encipherment tables. In September 1940 and in November 1940 there was a mutual exchange of book groups on two codes "AR 38 and RA 1". (IF 15, T2252.)

Japanese Systems.

Diplomatic Systems.

Rentschler claimed some success with Japanese diplomatic. Goering remembered that information was obtained from the Japanese ambassador in Berlin reporting home. Paetzel described a Japanese main diplomatic system which employed a code book enciphered by a combination of transposition and Raster. They were successful with this up until the last phase of the war. He also mentions a transposition with nulls over two and four letter code. This had a complicated indicator system. It was worked on in the middle of 1943 and again in January 1945 when it was believed to be the same system. (IF 15; I 143; I 25, p. 7; I 54.)

Machine System.

Paetzel stated that a Japanese system was broken in 1941-1942 which was thought to be a machine system although their solution was not mechanical but employed simply paper strips. (I 54).

Latin American Systems.

Paetzel stated that the FA "read all Mexican [traffic] and some smaller countries like Costa Rica, Paraguay, and Venezuela. They were usually periodic substitution but Mexico had codes." (I 25, p. 8.)

Manchurian Systems.

Paetzel said that Manchurian traffic was worked on but he knew nothing about it. (I 25, p. 7.)

82

DOCID: 3486670

Mexico - see Latin America.

Mihailovitch System.

Paetzel stated that the FA had success with Yugoslav traffic which he thinks was Mihailovitch. It was five digit or five letter with dinome substitution of the corresponding position of pairs of code groups. (I 25, pp 7-8).

Norwegian Systems.

Diplomatic Code.
Sauerbier said that an unenciphered five letter code was read completely up to 1940. Nothing was read after the Norwegian government moved to London. Sauerbier had a vague impression that they had gone over to a machine. (I 162).

Polish Systems.

Polish Diplomatic code.
The FA was interested in Polish systems between London and Washington, Berne, Cairo, and Jerusalem but had only sorted them by link. In describing the work of FA/9, Sauerbier only recalled the solution of a Polish diplomatic code in 1940-41. This he remembered as using one additive of specific length, which after 1943 became too long to produce depths, so after that date it was not solved. [This sounded to the Interrogator more like a Polish Home Office System than a Foreign Office system]. The Situation report of the Pers ZS Polish Group dated 1 January 1940, revealed that at that time both the FA and Pers ZS were working on a secondary consular system and that Pers ZS received Polish intercept from the FA. (I 22, I 162, T 2038.)

Polish Agents' Systems.
Seifert remembered traffic of Polish Agents in Czechoslovakia. Paetzel described these systems as numerous aperiodic systems employing many cover names but was unable (or unwilling?) to give any information about the key. Lt. Schubert, in charge of work on Agent Systems on the Eastern Front for the Signal Intelligence Agency of the Army High Command (OKH/In 7/VI) mentions Wenzel of the FA as an expert on Polish Resistance Movement traffic although he does not know if any of this traffic had been read by the FA. (I 25, I 54, I 26.)

DOCID: 3486670

Portuguese Systems.

Portuguese Codes.

Paetzel said that the "Portuguese were very conservative. They used a five digit code plus substitution. It was very, very simple." (I 25 p. 8.)

Russian Systems.

Diplomatic Code and Additive.

Sauerbier mentions "a few people who were engaged in a fruitless attack on Russian diplomatic traffic. This attack culminated in the belief that the system was a code with a non-repeating additive. (I 162.)

Commercial Systems.

Seifert mentions work by the FA on economic traffic passing between various points in Russia. "Our greatest success was obtained on internal Russian traffic which enabled us to discover the various bottlenecks in the Russian supply organization." Paetzel said that this traffic comprised several hundred messages a day and was clear text mixed with cover names and was used by industrial plants, foundries, armament works, plane factories and so on." (I 25, ppl-5)

Russian Teletype Traffic.

Buggisch (a specialist at both the Signal Intelligence Agency of the Supreme Command of the Armed Forces and at the Signal Intelligence Agency of the Army High Command on machines and Russian) "heard in 1943 that the FA had claimed some success on a Russian teletype machine and had reconstructed the machine. It was a machine with a very long cycle being not prime but the product of several smaller cycles-like the SZ 42." Buggisch did not know the cycle of all the individual wheels or any other details. He heard this from Doering "who was then doing his research on the T 52 but liaison with the FA was bad anyway (Mettig was particularly opposed to the SS taint) and the next Buggisch heard was that the traffic found by the FA had stopped. Buggisch remembered "only that the cycle of one of the wheels was 37; the others he thought varied widely, from 30 to 80." Buggisch was again questioned about this teletype machine success of the FA on what specifically were the "results of the FA mentioned in connection with the Russian cipher teleprinter and answered in written homework that: the FA had analysed a Russian cipher teleprinter system in 1943 and recognized that it must have been based on a machine having certain similarities with the German SZ 40. After a short time the Russians altered the system. The FA then communicated its results to my unit and were given as a kind of recompense a report on the solution of a German cipher teleprinter. This was one of the very rare cases where the FA and In 7/VI exchanged results. I did not study the FA results at that time as I was not responsible for work on cipher teleprinters, and hence can give no details. At all events the Russian machine (just as in the German types SZ 40, SZ 42 but in contrast to the T 52 a,b,c, and d) gave only 32 different substitution alphabets, the succession of which became periodic only after an astronomically large number of steps. This succession was given by a system of pin wheels, the peripheries of which were prime to each other at an estimate lay between 30 and 90. In any case there was no complicated mutual influence of the pin wheels on each other (as for example in the T 52 d)." (I 64 p. 2; I 176 p. 6)

Agent Traffic

Sauerbier, who worked on Russian Agent Systems for the Ordnungspolizei (Orpo) and wrote a lengthy paper on the type of systems involved, stated that he was approached by the Orpo in 1941 with a request for cryptographic advice on the systems used by the Russian agents. They gave him copies of systems that were captured with agents, and he grouped these by categories. Analysis was limited almost entirely to a study of characteristics and recognition signals with a view to advising on the possibility of a "Gegenspiel" [Counter-game--employing the agent after capture or pretending to be the agent.] This work was done first in Sauerbier's own time. Wenzel, his chief, opposed his involvement in it but was powerless to prevent it as the requests later came down through proper channels directed to Sauerbier. It was a one man job entirely with only occasional help of a girl file clerk. It generally took about one half of Sauerbier's time. He estimated that a total of 1500 different keys passed through his hands, mostly hand substitution systems, mostly in Russian but many in German (Sauerbier himself did not know any Russian). Of these only 4 or 5 were solved without a completely captured key. One of the achievements of which Sauerbier was proudest was the use of an ordinary book left behind by an agent to solve his traffic. Sauerbier was never concerned with radio procedures, but purely with the cipher systems used. He was able to give advice on the probable group to which an agent belonged and could then consult his records for an account of the success or failure of a particular technique of "Gegenspiel" against this group. (I 162; I 164.)

A possible additional example of FA "success" against the Russians was chanced upon after the completion of this paper and has been inserted here without evaluation. While going through an inventory of the various boxes of material recovered by TICOM from the Foreign Office Cryptanalytic Section (Pers ZS) the following item was noted : "Box 13, item 18. Green folding box containing: a) Pink folder marked 'Russisches Beutematerial (Ueber FA)' containing, (1) Photostats of Russian book of additive tables (including instructions for use), dated 1940. (2) Some photostats of 5 figure Russian traffic. (3) Blue folder containing photostats on ' Instruktion für die Behörden des NKWD zur Führung der Chiffre-Arbeit.'" This material is available as TICOM DOCUMENT 6 on Film 1.

Saudi Arabian Systems.

Saudi-Arabian Code.

When asked if the FA had done any work with Arabian codes, as Saudi-Arabian, Paetzel expressed surprise and asked if Saudi Arabia had a system of its own. (I 25 p. 8.)

Scandinavian Systems.

Dr Mueller of Pers ZS stated that he "had some unofficial liaison with the people in the FA who were working on Scandinavian" but specified no date for the collaboration. (I 22 #182.)

Spanish Systems.

Spanish Additive System.

Paetzel described a system of additives differing according to traffic link. Each link had ten tables, with 100 four digit groups on each table. The indicator (unenciphered) was the serial number and came in the second or third place. Paetzel stated that this was the most recent thing he had worked on personally. (I 25, p. 6.)

Spanish Code.

The Pers ZS Yearly Report for 1942 mentions a Spanish "04" Code which was not worked on by Pers ZS because of a lack of traffic. The FA worked on it and believed it was a machine system. It was a four digit code with 04 the indicator. (D 16, Report 4, p. 4 .)

Swedish Systems.

Swedish Consular Traffic.

Although Rentschler stated categorically that there was no success with Swedish systems Sauerbier mentions a 4 or 5 digit non alphabetic code especially used on the link between Stockholm and Tokyo. Almost all of the other links went over to machine in 1939 but Tokyo was unable to convert. The machine was Swedish made and was called the "KRYTAA". Sauerbier thinks it had 15 numbered wheels. [This sounded to the interrogator like a thoroughly garbled version of either the KRYHA or Hagelin machine. Sauerbier did not seem sensitive on the point or to be garbling deliberately]. He stated that none of the main consular links to Washington, London, or Paris were ever read nor was there any success with Swedish diplomatic in FA/9-C. (I 162.)

Swedish Hagelin.

Paetzel stated that they had this type of traffic. See the discussion under Finland for his statement that either the Swedish or Finnish Hagelin was broken and contrast Sauerbier immediately preceding. (I 25, p. 6; I 54.)

Swedish-Turkish Commercial.

Sauerbier stated that commercial traffic between Turkey and Sweden was attacked particularly and solved but yielded none of the expected information on shipping possibilities. [It is not clear whether this is Swedish or Turkish traffic.]

Swiss Systems.

Swiss Enigma Machine.

Paetzel stated that the Swiss Enigma was formerly broken for a while, but only when it was improperly used. The same internal settings were used for a long time. After the inner settings changed we did not have any more solution. At first we reconstructed the wheels from cribs and from the fact that the inner settings remained the same. In his 1941 Report Dr Brandes of Pers ZS mentions solution of the Swiss Enigma. Apparently the FA furnished Pers ZS with a partial solution which Dr Kunze was able to complete. Thereafter there was an exchange of keys between the two agencies. (I 25 p.3; D 54 report 8, p. 8.)

Swiss Three Letter Code.

The Pers ZS Yearly Report for 1941, Report Nr. 8, mentions a 2304 group, three letter code. Its tables were first solved by the FA and later by Pers ZS. (D 54 report 8)

Thailand Systems.

Thailand Code.

At the beginning of 1942 Pers ZS turned over a Thailand code to the FA to copy. (Pers ZS Yearly Report 1942, D 16, report 4, page 3.)

Turkish Systems.

Turkish Commercial-see Swedish-Turkish Commercial.

Turkish Diplomatic Systems.

Rentschler claimed some success with high grade Turkish diplomatic systems. Kotschy and Boscheinen stated that "OKH In 7/VI broke the Turkish Diplomatic Code when the FA was having difficulties with it" and subsequently stated that the FA turned over Turkish diplomatic to Kona 4 in the Balkans, receiving only decoded traffic from In 7/VI. (IF 15, IF 105B, IF 126.)

United States Systems-see American Systems.

Vatican Systems.

Vatican Code.

In a captured Pers ZS reconstruction of a Vatican Code Book the signature of a Fraulien Titschak appears with the date of August 1939 and a notation that she had copied out values at that time for the FA. (Fraulien Titschak was a member of the Foreign Office Cryptanalytic Bureau). The Annual Report of the Italian Group of Pers ZS for 1940 indicates that while Pers ZS did some work on Vatican systems most of the identifications on Vatican systems were received from the FA. (T 93, film F; T 2252.)

Yugoslavia Systems-see Mihailovitch.

APPENDIX II

Translation of a Forschungsamt directive signed by Schapper, found in the quarters occupied by the FA at Kaufbeuren on 9 May 1945 by Ticom Team 1. Ticom document 240 item 34, IF 135.)

GEHEIME REICHSSACHE
(Secret State Document)

1-29/45 gRs (14/3/45-in ink)* Kaufbeuren, 9 March 1945

to: I, II, III, IV, V, VI
1,2,3,4,5,6,7,8,9,10,11,12,13,14
Service Post Seifert
Branch Office Berlin
Ourstation Berlin
" Hamburg
" Vienna
" Munich
Liaison Office Foreign Office
" " Ministry of Economics
" " OKW
" " Reich Security Office
" " Propaganda Ministry

Subject: Organization; Present Reorganization of the Bureau and Branch Organization.

1. I have determined on the following organization of the Bureau:

Bureau Director:	Direction of Bureau Operations Ministerial Director Schapper
Main Section I: (Hauptabteilung)	Organization; secrecy; gaurds; security; official correspondence; Civil Service Personnel; basic problems of personnel administration and budgetary transactions.
i/c Section I (Abteilung)	Principal Specialist Bergeren Central Abteilung Gaurds; Security; Air Raid Defence;

*Crossed out in ink, apparently a correction as of 14 March.

89

	Organization; Correspondence; Secrecy; Camouflage, Special problems.
i/c	Senior Specialist Rosenhahn
Section 2	Administration
i/c	Principle Specialist Kunsemueller
Main Section II:	Personnel
i/c	Senior Specialist Kempe
Section 3	Personnel
i/c	Senior Specialist Kempe
Main Section III:	Interception, Sorting and Examination
i/c	Principal Specialist Breuer
Section 4	Interception
i/c	Specialist Popp
Section 5	Sorting
i/c	RR Dr. Henke
Main Section IV:	Codes and Ciphers
i/c	Minister Dirigent Schroeder
Section 6	Research
i/c	Senior Specialist Dr. Paetzel
Section 7	Overseas, Southwest
i/c	Senior Specialist Waechter
Section 8	West and South
i/c	Senior Specialist Schulze
Section 9	East, Southeast, Middle, North
i/c	Senior Specialist Wenzel
Main Section V:	Information collection and Evaluation
i/c	Principal Specialist Seifert While Principal Specialist Seifert heads the Service Post Seifert (as is mentioned below) Senior Specialist Dr. Kurzbach replaces him in Kaufbeuren.
Section 10	Information Dissemination
i/c	Specialist Dr. Mews

DOCID: 3486670

Section 11 i/c	Foreign Political Evaluation Principle Specialist Dr. Kurzbach
Section 12 i/c	Economic Evaluation Acting Head Brieschke
Section 13 i/c	Internal Affairs Evaluation Specialist Kentschler
Main Section VI: i/c	Technical Senior Specialist Dipl. Ing. Stabenow While Senior Specialist Dipl. Ing. Stabenow heads the Branch Office Berlin (see paragraph 2 below) he will be replaced at Kaufbeuren by Senior Specialist Dr. Huppertsberg
Section 14 i/c	Technical Senior Specialist Dr. Huppertsberg
Service Post Seifert in Berlin (Dienststelle Seifert) i/c	Information Head, Special instructions of the Bureau branches. Principal Specialist Seifert

2. Subordinate to the Bureau are:

a) The Branch Office Berlin (Zweigstelle Berlin) i/c — Senior Specialist Dipl. Ing. Stabenow

I have determined on the following organization of the Branch Office Berlin:

Work Section 1: (Arbeitsgebiet)	Security: ARP; Gaurds: Camouflaging ("Cover") of special correspondence; special assignments; Passes (Badges?) special supplies, courrier service.
i/c	Civil Servant Dr. Gerth
Work Section 2:	Administration

91

i/c	Specialist Henke
Work Section 3:	Personnel Administration
i/c	Specialist Czwalinna
Work Section 4:	Technical Development
i/c	Acting Head Specialist Truebenbach
Work Section 5:	Technical Maintenance
i/c	Specialist Oden

b) The Outstation Berlin of the Forschungsamt (Forschungsleitstelle)

i/c	Specialist Thieme

The Outstation Hamburg of the Forschungsamt

i/c	Senior Specialist Kirbach

The Outstation Vienna of the Forschungsamt

i/c	Senior Specialist Dipl. Ing. Fleischmann

The Outstation Munich of the Forschungsamt

i/c	Specialist Niedermeyer

c) The Liaison Office-Foreign Office (Verbudungstelle)

i/c	Civil Servant Dr. Gerstmeyer

The Liaison Office-OKW

i/c	Civil Servant Dr. Klautschke

The Liaison Office-Reich Security Office

i/c	Specialist Dipl. Ing. Scholz

The Liaison Office-Economic Ministry and Ministry for War Production

i/c	Specialist Dr. Hilligardt

The Liaison Office-Propaganda Ministry

i/c	Civil Servant Severitt

3. Postal Address

For the convenience of all concerned I give the following Postal address of the Forschungsamt:

For the Branch Office Berlin, Outstations Berlin and Hamburg, and the Liaison Offices:

Reichsluftfahrtministeriums-Forschungsamt
(1) Berlin-Charlottenburg 2
Schillerstrasse 116/124

For all higher offices:

Reichsluftfahrtministeriums-Forschungsamt
(13b) Kaufbeuren/Allg.

92

The courrier service between Berlin and Kaufbeuren continues, at this time it is the quickest possible connection.

4. Administrative Relation:
   a) The Reporting Center Seifert is administratively subordinate to the Branch Office Berlin.
   b) The Liaison Offices are administratively subordinate to the Branch Office Berlin.

5. Authority
   a) The head of the Reporting Center Seifert has essentially the authority of a Main Section head conformable to Standing Orders.
   b) The head of the Branch Office Berlin has essentially the authority of the head of an Outstation conformable to standing orders.

signed
Schapper
witnessed: Eulenberg
author

Description of Ticom Document 240 (Film 34)

Item	Date	Author	Place of origin	Contents
1	10/9/43	?	Berlin	List of equipment.
2	10/4/45	?	Kaufbeuren	List of destroyable Bulgarian Code books, Dictionaries, work sheets.
3 A-H	?	?	?	Faintly legibile hand written instructions for wiring, probably of a teletype machine.
4	?	?	?	Hand drawn chart showing floor plan of IBM room, presumably made by Ticom Team 1 at Kaufbeuren.
5 A-C	11/4/45	Schapper	Kaufbeuren	Instructions for forming an FA Völksturm company.
6	?	?	?	Names of five members of FA 9: Otto Lechner, Herman Plagens, Fritz Simon, Gottfried Gottschalk, Georg Krenzke.
7	13/4/45	?	Kaufbeuren	Notice of transfer of Liselotte Brott and Erna Lange to Seifert in Berlin.
8 A-B	17/4/45	Kempe	Kaufbeuren	Notice of drill schedule for FA Volksturm company.
9	?	?	?	Names of five members of FA 9: August Woisch, Juergen Deggau, Helmut Kuepper, Georg Matts, Walter Schubert.
10	10/4/45	?	Kaufbeuren	Notice of movement of two A Forschungsstellen. Copenhagen A station has moved from its previous address to Nyropsgade 17/11, telephone number Palae 9469 extension 35,8,9, and 30.

94

DOCID: 3486670

				The Wehrmacht liaison did not change (phone did not?). The A Station at Stettin moved on 29 March to Griefwald, Banahof Strasse, 16/47. Telephone Griefwald 3307.
11 A	24/1/45	Gestapo	Berlin	Letter from Amt IV A-5a of the Reich Main Security Office to the FA with an agents message to be deciphered.
11 B	25/1/45	FA	Berlin	Cover letter forwarding the above to Kaufbeuren.
12 ABC	7/4/45	Kuebbler Kempe	Kaufbeuren	Kuebbler, of FA 9 requests permission to stay overnight with his family at Hirschzell. The request is refused on the ground that his family, residents of Hamburg/Salle, should have evacuated to Saxony and Thuringia, not to South Bavaria.
13	6/4/45	Schapper	Kaufbeuren	Memoranda on interdepartment phone service.
14	7/4/45	?	Kaufbeuren	Request that Dr. Neuenhoff be appointed a special liaison man to Berlin for FA 9.
15	6/4/45	Schmidt	Kaufbeuren	Memo on laundry service with example of form to be filled out.
16	I L L E G I B L E			
17	?	?	?	List of personnel of FA 9, with signature or notation of transfer:

95

Arnold, Moritz
Brott, Liselotte
Degau, Juergen
Gertz, Helene
Grothe, Edity
Guelle, Otto
Gottschalk, Gottfried
Graudus, Alexander /Berlin
Jentsch, Julius 5.4.45 to Rubbler
Kiewadt, Ilse, transferred to FA 3.7.3
Kirstein, Karl
Krenzke, Georg
Kuebbler, Ferdinand
Dr. Kuepper, Helmut
Lade, Karl
Lechner, Otto
Dr. Ludwig, Helmut
Matys, Georg
Mayr, Margarete, signed for by Brett
Meinhard, Pauline
Nusbaum, Ingeborg
Dr. Plagens, Hermann
Remwerts-Lukjansky, Dimitri
Richter, Helga, signed for by Remwertz
Roth, Liselotte, 5.4.45 to Ruffler
Ruffler, Georg 5.4.45 to Berlin
Siemon, Fritz
Scheitinger, Josef
Schirajeff, Erika
Schubert, Walter
Steffens, Gerda
Thomas, Hildegard
Walger, Egon

18	27/3/45	Wenzel	Kaufbeuren	Note to Czwalinna, Berlin, Marchstrasse 25 b. Frau Helene Gertz, born Sponholz wants a transfer. A Forschungsstelle is suggested. She is good in French and reads Russian.

DOCID: 3486670

19	9/3/45	Schapper	Kaufbeuren	Order replacing RR Harrius with RR Dr. Henke as leader of FA 5.
20	20/3/45	Rosenhahn	Kaufbeuren	Memo showing official seal for 2nd quarter of year.
21	12/2/45	Schapper	Berlin	Note on transport for move from Breslau to Berlin.
22	A-D26/1/45	Schapper	Luebben	Order closing down the Forschungsleitstelle Breslau and its branches.
23	A-F 9/3/45	Bergeren	Kaufbeuren	Memo on laundry service. Gives soap ration for FA members.
24	A-B 2/3/45	Schapper	Kaufbeuren	Schapper circulates an order Hitler on papers of identification.
25	6/3/45	Kempe	Kaufbeuren	Order on military service and Volksturm drill.
26	5/3/45	Meyer	Kaufbeuren	Meyer, for FA 2, passes a notice on quarters for members of the FA.
27	5/3/45	Paetzel	Kaufbeuren	Memo to IV,7,8, and 9 on Air Raid Precautions.
28	A ?	?	Berlin	Handwritten note from Forschungsstelle D-2 wanting to know the correct address for FA 9.
	B 6/3/45	?	Kaufbeuren	FA-9 answers that its address is Kaufbeuren, Allg. 13 b.
29	A-C26/1/45	Schapper	Luebben	Order of Schapper setting up Berlin, Luebben and Jueterbog branches of the FA after the move from Breslau.

30 A-B	5/3/45	?	Kaufbeuren	Barely legible directive from FA IV to 7,8,9 on special air raid precautions, working schedules, evacuation of material. Names mentioned are: RR Lehr, RR Kagelka (?), RR von Stubenfauch, RR Kroeger, ORR Dr. Martin Paetzel, ORR Waechter, ORR Schulz, ORR Wenzel
31 A-B	31/1/45	Metzger	OKW/WNV/Chi	Teletype message addressed to RLM/FA for ORR Wenzel with cipher keys for February use.
32 A-B	1/3/45	Mayer	Kaufbeuren	Forwarding a memo on air raid precautions from a Major Esgele of the Kaufbeuren airfield.
33	2/2/45	?	Jueterbog	Memo from FA 9 to FA 3 stating that the following persons assisted in moving classified materials from Breslau to Jueterbog: Karl Kirstein, Alexander Graudes, Juergen Deggau, Erika Schirajeff, Georg Krenzke, Karl Lade, Fritz Simon, Otto Lechner, Egon Walger
34 A-D	9/3/45	Schapper	Kaufbeuren	Directive reorganizing the FA with the main bureau at Kaufbeuren, less FA 15.

98

DOCID: 3486670

				Setting up of a Berlin Branch Office and a Reporting Center under Seifert. Assignment of control of the Forschungsstellen and Liaison officers. (Translated as first part of this appendix. Note item 19, of the same day, which emends the above order.)
35	12/3/45	Schapper	Kaufbeuren	Order giving dates for entrance on duty of various officials named in item 34: RR Niedermeyer enters on duty at the Forsschungsleitstelle Munich on 20/3/45; RR Henke reports at the Branch Office Berlin on 1/4/45; and ORR Kunsemueller in Kaufbeuren on 10/4/45.
36	A-B20/3/45	Schapper	Kaufbeuren	Additional assignments and transfers of personnel: Item 34 is again emended with RR Dr. Rautenkranz transferred from the School of the FA to head of FA 12 as of 20 (corrected to 22) /3/45; Brieschke is releived as acting head of FA 12 and appointed Liaison Officer with the Ministry for War Production as of 1/4/45; RR Dr. Hilligardt is relieved as Liaison Officer to the Ministry for War Production and assigned to FA 1214145; RR Dr. Fingerhut is transferred to Seifert's Reporting Center in Berlin 22/3/45; RR Progich(?), while retaining his present position at the Waldlager, Luebben, is also a liaison official with the Berlin Branch Office.

DOCID: 3486670

37	A-C30/9/44	Schroeder	Breslau	Schroeder forwards a memo on agents (Polish and Russian, "Kundschafter, Spione, Saboteure") from the Abwehr Officer of Wehrkreis Kommando VIII. Photocopy was made by Schroeder and circulated.
38	13/1/45	Metzger	Dresden	OKW/WFSt/AgWNV/Chi III A sends official key for March to the FA. Signed by Major Metzger. Address of Metzger is Dresden N 31, Hindenburgkaserne.
39	3/2/45	Metzger	Dresden	Same as above, key for March, a new emergency key.
40	26/2/45	Metzger	Dresden	Same as 37, key for April.
41	28/3/45	?	Kaufbeuren	Hardly legible, is to FA 6,7,8,9 with FA 6 marked as for information.
42	23/3/45	?	?	Handwritten, not very legible, seems to refer to Stapoleit, Prag. Copies of Czech messages are to be sent to Herr Rummel of the Stapoliet at a Prague address.
43	1/2/45	Metzger	Dresden	A new cipher key for February from OKW/Chi.
44	26/3/45	Metzger	Halle/Salle	11 Cipher key for April, a new key.
45	A-C 4/4/45	Rosenhahn	Kaufbeuren	Memos on security circulated for information of FA departments. B refers to

100

DOCID: 3486670

				publication by Reuters of a matter with Secret classification and repeats Hitler's orders on handling Secret and Top Secret (C).
46 A-B	12/4/45	Bergeren	Kaufbeuren	Directive from Borman forbidding party members (Gauleiters) to try to correspond with old party friends in occupied (Allied occupied) territory, circulated by Bergeren.

101

Appendix III

Autobiography of Gottfried Schapper, last head of the FA. Prepared by Ticom and included as appendix 2 of IF 15.

Curriculum vitae of the former Ministerialdirektor Gottfried Schapper.

Born 16/12/1888 in Groszmoeringen, Kreis Stendal, son of the Evangelical Pastor, Dr. Karl Schapper.

Schools: Elementary school, Classical high school, matriculation certificate 1910.
1910 Fahnenjunker and Lieut. in Railway Regt No 2.
1913 Transferred to Signals.
1914-1918 In the First World War: O. C. Heavy W/T Station 15 in the west with AOK 5 (Crown Prince).
In the east with G.K.X., (Emmich)
" I Inf Div (Konta)
" 11th Bavarian Inf Div (Kneupel)
" AOK Linsingen
" Southeast (Balkans) with O.K. Mackensen as O. C. Deciphering Station Balkans.

1916-1917: O. C. Wireless Section High Command of the Army at GHQ and Director of the Cryptographic Bureau (Geheimwissenschaft 1. Abt.) of the High Command of the Army. (Interception, Deciphering, Intelligencing of all military and political signals interceptable by technical devices).
1918: Divisional Signals Commander with various divisions in the west.
1919: Discharged with rank of captain.
1919-1920: Married, fell into the hands of revolutionary swindlers, without work or food, harried by Communists, sold newspapers and other things on the streets, did odd jobs to ward off starvation.
1920: Secretary of the National Society of Berlin for Rescuing the Reich from the Revolution. Took part in the Kapp-Ludendorf Putsch. Persecuted by Communists, moved to Munich.
1920-1927: In Munich. Various jobs as business manager of National organizations, of clubs, businesses, and newspapers.
1920-1923: Member of the N.S.D.A.P. resigned after the Putsch of 1923.

102

1927-1933: In Berlin: Administrative officer and head of department in the cryptographic bureau of the Reichswehr Ministry. Resigned 1933, as I could not agree with the thoroughly incompetent methods of the cryptographic bureau, Therefore,
1933-April 1945 I went over to Goering, whom I knew well from the first world war; founding of the Forschungsamt (see my report on the Forschungsamt): head of sub-section, then head of section, and from 1944 director of this bureau.
1931: Joined the Nazi party and remained a simple member of it until April 1945.
1933-1937 or 38: Member of the Allgemeine SS, from which I resigned, as they refused to recognize my Christian philosophy of life.
1934: A Son was born to me.
1939-1945: Employment of the Forschungsamt in the second World War, under my direction, first as deputy head, then independently from 1944: at first in Berlin, after the bombings out, in Breslau and subsequently in Kaufbeuren.
April 1945: release and residence in Soellbrun-Niederwall near Rosenheim.
May: Arrested by CIC, interrogation in Rosenheim, imprisonment and interrogation in Salzburg, then captivity in Augsburg.

TAB A

VOLUME 7

Tab A

Abteilung. Section, Indicated by Arabic numerals.
Abwehr. Military Intelligence and counter espionage section of the Supreme Command of the Armed Forces. Taken over by RSHA in 1944.
Air Force High Command (Oberkommando der Luftwaffe q. v.).
Amt Ausland. Amt VI of RSHA q. v.
Arnold, Moritz. Member of FA-9 at Kaufbeuren.
Arbeits Gebiet. Work Section, Subdivision of Branch Office Beru.
Army High Command - see Oberkommando des Heeres.
Bailovic, Senior Specialist Rudolf. Bailovic is an Austrian and is reported to be violently anti-Nazi. He was a member of the Austrian cipher bureau (Austrian Chancellery Secret Section) and at the time of the Anschluss he refused to hand over the key of the secret cabinet. He therefore fell into disgrace and was relegated to an inferior position in the government. Fenner and Fellgiebel brought the best Austrian personnel to Germany and Bailovic was first given to the FA. No details of his stay there are known but he next appeared in the Signal Intelligence Agency of the Army High Command where he headed a Balkan section. Later he transferred to the Signal Intelligence Agency of the Supreme Command of the Armed Forces. Recently he has been employed more in an administrative capacity than as a cryptanalyst. He was said to have refused to wear any German medals while in uniform and lived quietly with his wife.
Becker, _____. Holder of an FA telephone number as a member of Main Section V-3, whatever that may be.
Bergeren, _____, Principal Specialist. Head of Main Section I of FA.
Berlin: The Main Bureau (April 1933-November 1943), the Service Post Seifert and the Forschungsleitstelle Berlin were located here. The Main Bureau was in Charlottenburg, a SW suburb of Berlin. The address was Berlin, Charlottenburg 2, Schillerstrasse Nrs 116/124.

104

DOCID: 3486670

In addition a telephone monitoring station (including a special "Poison Kitchen" for monitoring the conversations of Top Nazi officials), and two radio intercept stations at Templin and Luebben (q.v.) were located here. Forschungsstelle D02 was also in Berlin.

Bock, _____, Senior Specialist. SS Obersturmbannfuehrer, Head of State Police [Gestapo?] Central Office, Berlin.

Bodenschatz, _____, General der Flieger. Head of the Office of Ministers.

Boettger, _____, Senior Specialist. Given as a member of the FA and having an FA telephone number, otherwise unknown.

Bokelberg, _____, Col. Group leader of the Monitoring Department of the Air Ministry (RLM/S. A. UEWA.)

Boscheinen, Heinz: Non Commissioned Officer. Turkish Interpreter. Member of Bailovic's section of In 7/VI. Worked in Evaluation.

Branch Office Berlin.--Zweigstelle Berlin.

Brandes, Dr. Wilhelm, Senior Specialist (Oberregierungsrat), in charge of Language Groups France, Belguim, Holland, and Switzerland at the Foreign Office Cryptanalytic Section.

Breslau. 41'07"N 17' 00" E. Location of a Forschungsleitstelle and of a radio intercept station. After the 1943 bombing of the Berlin headquarters a part of the Main Bureau was located in the Hartlieb barracks in Klettendorf.

Breuer, _____, Principal Specialist. Head of Main Section III of FA.

Brieschke, Herr. Acting head of Section 12 at Kaufbeuren. On 20 March he was relieved as head of FA 12 and appointed Liaison Officer with the Economic Ministry and Ministry for War Production.

Brott, Liselotte. Member of FA 9 transferred to Seifert in Berlin.

Buggisch, Dr. Otto. Cryptanalyst of In 7/VI.

Burgscheidungen. Final location of the Foreign Office Cryptanalytic Section (Pers Z S). 51'13"N 11'47'E.

Canaris, Admiral. Head of the Abwehr, executed for involvement in 20th July Plot.

Charlottenburg: see Berlin.

Chi Stelle/Oberbefehlshaber der Luftwaffe.--Signal Intelligence Agency of the Commander In Chief of the Air Force. OBdL/Chi). Replaced in November 1944 by Signal Intelligence Agency of the Air Force High Command (OKL/LN Abt 350).

Cologne. 50' 56" N 06' 57" E. Location of a Forschungsstelle for radio intercept.

Constance. 57' 39" N 09' 10" E. Forschungsstelle, radio intercept.

Control Station for Signal Intelligence of the Army High Command - Oberkommando des Heeres Leitstelle der Nachrichtenaufklaerung. Became Signal Intelligence Agency of the Army High Command after November 1944.

Copenhagen 55' 41" N 12' 35" E. Site of an "AA" station, Nyropsgade 17/11, telephone Palae 9469, local 35, 8, 9, and 30.

Criminal Police. See Kriminalpolizei

CSDIC.-- Combined Service Detailed Interrogation Center.

D-16. -- ASA translations of yearly Progress reports of Pers Z S for 1927, 1941, and 1942.

D-17.-- OKM 4/ SKL III Yearly Progress report for 1/12/43-1/11/44.

D-21.-- Translation of OKM 4/SKL Research Progress report 1/12/43 - 1/11/44. T 519

D-22.--Translation (and chart) of telephone directory giving Forschungsamt numbers.

D-54.--Translations of Pers Z S reports on cipher systems of various countries.

Danzig. Forschungsstelle. 54' 21" N 18' 40" E.

Deggau, Juergen. Member of FA-9 at Kaufbeuren, assisted in transferring materials from Breslau to Jueterbog.

Dettmann, Alex, 1st Lt. Head of Cryptanalysis at HLS 057; later head of Section 3, Group IV, GdNA. Specialty: Russian systems.

Deutsch Lissa. 51' 08" N 16' 53" E. Town in Prussia between Breslau and Posnan. Site of a B and C station.

DF-9.--Activity Report of OKW/Chi, for period 1 Jan. 1944 through 28 June 1944, signed by Col Kettler.

DF-17.--Translation of T 3273, letter of Dr. Paschke and other Pers Z S personnel. Translated by Dr. Pettengill. (T-165).

Dienststelle Seifert.--Service Post Seifert.

Diessing, General Major (Brig. Gen.). Supplies FA information to Klautschke.

Dipl. Ing. Graduate Engineer.

Doenitz, Grand Admiral, Commander in chief of German Navy, Reich Chancellor.

Doering, Dr. Mathematician with In 7/VI, later GdNA. Specialty: machine cipher, mathematical research.

von Doering, _____, Lt. General. Group Head of Equipment department (D 22), Air Ministry.
Dortmund. Forschungsstelle for cable intercept. 51' 31" N 07' 27" E.
Drape, _____, MinRat. Prussian State Ministry and 4 Year Plan.
Ebelling. Krim Komm SS Obersturmfuehrer. State Police Central Office Section IV N.
Egert, Herr. Translator for Chinese, Turkish, Japanese mentioned as released 10/5/45.
Eulenberg. This name appears on the Kaufbeuren directive as the secretary who prepared it for Schapper's signature. Name is not legible.
Eutin. Forschungsstelle for radio intercept. 54' 09" N 10' 37" E.
FA. Forschungsamt q. v.
Fellgiebel, Lt. Gen. Erich. Chief Signal Officer of Army and Armed Forces High Commands from beginning of war until he was executed, 1944.
Fenner, _____, Principal Specialist. Chief of Section IV of OKW/Chi.
Fingerhut, Otto, Specialist. Member of the FA since 1937. He was employed in Main Section V and in 1942 became head of a school for Evaluators, giving refresher courses to members of the branch offices and station. In civil life he was Wissenschaftlicher Assistent at the University of Greifswald, a philologist in Scandinavian languages. He specialized on Italy, Russian, and the Far East in Main Section V. He was assigned to the Reporting Center Seifert on 20 March 1945.
Fleischmann, with Engineering Diploma. Senior Specialist, Head of the Forschungsleitstelle in Vienna.
Flensburg. 54' 56" N 09' 27" E. Final location of the Signal Intelligence Agency of the Navy High Command (OKM 4 SKL III).
Flicke, _____, Specialist. In charge of technical matters at OKW intercept station at Lauf.
Foreign Office Cryptanalytic Section (Pers Z S.)
Forschungsamt. The Goering controlled Nazi intelligence agency, responsible for radio, telephone and cable monitoring and cryptanalysis of encoded or enciphered messages.
Forschungsleitstelle. Outstation.
Fricke, Technician (Lieutenant Grade) Dr. Walther. Head of IIb, OKW/Chi: Development of systems, etc.
Fricke, _____, SS First Lt.: Liaison Officer, RSHA -OKW.

DOCID: 3486670

Friederich, Lt. Col. Chief of Division 7 of the Office of the Chief Signal Officer of the German Air Force and chief of the Chi Stelle (Chiffrierstelle) of the Oberbefehlshaber der Luftwaffe, which after November 1944 became LN Abt 350.
Gaenzer, Major Johannes. Member of Section IIIF (counter espionage and penetration) of Abwehrstelle Berlin.
GEHEIMESTAATSPOLIZEI, (Gestapo). Secret State Police. Part of the Sicherheitspolizei q.v.
General Leutnant.--Major General (Rank held by Schapper in Luftwaffe as head of FA).
Gerstmeyer, Dr. Liaison officer with the Foreign Office.
Gerth, Dr. Head of Section 1 of the Branch Office Berlin.
Gertz, Frau Helene, born Sponholz. Member of FA 9, had reading knowledge of French and German. Suggested for assignment to the Forschungsstelle Luebben.
Gestapo. Geheimestaatspolizei q.v.
Gimmler, Maj. Gen. Chief of Signal Equipment and Testing Branch (Wa Pruef 7), 1939-1943. Chief Signal Officer, Commander in Chief West, 1943-1945.
Glueckstadt (Holstein) Telephone monitoring. 53' 8" N 09" 25" E.
Goebbels, Dr. Paul. Propaganda Minister.
Goering, Hermann, Field Marshal. Commander in Chief of Air Force Air Minister.
Goering's Research Bureau.--Forschungsamt q.v.
Gols. Radio intercept station, near Vienna. 47' 51" N 16' 56" E.
Gottschalk, Gottfried. Member of FA-9 at Kaufbeuren.
Grauds, Alexander. Member of FA-9 at Kaufbeuren. Assisted in transferring material from Breslau to Jueterbog.
Greifswald. 54'41" N 13'23" E. The Stettin A station was evacuated to Greifswald in April 1945.
Grothe, Edith. Member of FA-9 at Kaufbeuren.
Guelle, Otto. Member of FA-9 at Kaufbeuren.
Guenther, Lothar. A member of the FA until some time towards the end of 1943 when he was drafted. Taken prisoner, his interrogation was one of the first sources of information on the FA (Interrogated 29 January 1945) although the information did not reach TICOM until later. Was a jurist in civil life. May have been a member of Main Section V.
Hamburg. 53' 33" N 10' 00" E. Forschungsleitstelle and a Forschungsstelle.

Hanson. A subordinate of Canaris in Abwehr, executed for involvement in 20th July plot.
Harrius, Dr. Head of Section 5 of the FA. The Kaufbeuren directive gives his name, which is crossed out in ink in a correction of 14 March 1945.
Hatz, Heinrich, Staff Director. In charge of administration, OKW intercept station at Lauf.
Haupt Abteilung. Main Section, indicated by Roman Numerals.
Henke, Dr. Named as alternate to Harrius in Section 5 of the FA, and carried as head of that section by the 14 March 1945 correction of the Kaufbeuren directive. On 1 April 1945 he was to report to the Branch Office Berlin.
von Hesse, Prince Christoph. The second head of the FA. He was succeeded by Schapper in 1944 at which time he either "died" (Schapper and Guenther) or "returned to the Air Force" (Goering).
High Command of the Armed Forces. See Oberkommando der Wehrmacht.
Hilligardt, Specialist, Dr. Liaison Officer with the Economic Ministry. Relieved by Brieschke on 20 March when Hilligardt was assigned to FA 12.
Himmler, Heinrich. Reichsfuehrer SS, Minister of the Interior, Head of the Elite Guard, Head of the Reserve Army. Chief of German Police, in which capacity he controlled both the regular police force, the Constabulary (ordnungspolizei through the Ordnungspolizei Hauptamt) but also the Security Police, Sicherheitsdienst and Sicherheitspolizei (SD and Sipo) through the Reich Main Security Office (Reichssicherheitshauptamt, RSHA) which took over the Abwehr into its Amt VI.
Hitler, Adolf. "Der Fuehrer."
Hofmann. Postrat, head of work connected with service matters. Reichspost.
Huettenhain, Senior Specialist Dr. Erich. Chief cryptanalyst for OKW/Chi from 1937.
Huppertsburg, Senior Specialist, Dr. Head of Section 14, alternate head of Main Section VI.
I-1 "Final reports of TICOM group 3 on final exploitation of BURGSCHEIDUNGEN." A TICOM publication.
I-17 "Extracts of SHAEF interrogations of Maj. Gen. Boner,. Col. Grube, Lt. Col. Mettig, Maj. Rottler". A TICOM publication.
I-20 "Interrogation of Sonderfuehrer Fricke of OKW/Chi, formerly of OKH/Chi at the OKM Signals School in Flensburg on 16-17 June 1945." A TICOM publication.

I-21 "Preliminary interrogation of Col. Kettler, R. R. Dr. Huettenhain, Sdf Dr. Fricke (OKW/Chi) and Lt. Schubert (OKH/Chi) at Schloss Glucksburg near Flensburg on 14 June 1945." A TICOM publication.

I-22 "Interrogation of German cryptographers of the Pers ZS of the Auswaertiges Amt in the U. K. at seven meetings during May 1945." A TICOM publication.

I-25 "Interrogation of five members of the FA at Schloss Glucksburg on 15 and 21 June 1945." A TICOM publication.

I-26 "Interrogation of 1st Lt. Schubert (OKH/Chef HNW/GendNA) on Russian military and agents systems at OKM Signals School, Flensburg on 17 June 1945." A TICOM publication.

I-29 "Third Interrogation of Lt. Col. Friedrich at Beaconsfield on 4 July 1945." A TICOM publication.

I-31 "Detailed interrogation of Dr. Huettenhain at Flensburg on 18 - 21 June 1945." A TICOM publication.

I-54 "Second interrogation of five members of the RLM/Forschungsamt at Dustbin Kransberg near Frankfurt on 28 July 1945." A TICOM publication.

I-64 "Answers by Buggisch of OKH/Chi to questions set by TICOM." A TICOM publication.

I-84 "Further interrogation of R. R. Dr. Huettenhain and Sdf. Dr. Fricke of OKW/Chi on questions set by Mr. Friedman." A TICOM publication.

I-85 "POW interrogation report on R. R. Flicke, Tech. Insp. Pokojewski, and Stabsintendant Hatz." A TICOM publication.

I-86 "Interrogation of Lt. Col. Mettig of OKH and OKW/Chi on the highest direction of German Cryptanalytic Work."

I-91 "Interrogation report on Maj. Gen. Robert Schlaka, chief of Communications of the Ordnungs Polizei. A TICOM publication.

I-93 "Detailed interrogation of members of OKM 4 SKL III at Flensburg." A TICOM publication.

I-108 "Interrogation of Goering on the RLM/Forschungsamt." A TICOM publication.

I-112 "Preliminary interrogation of Regierungserat Voegele and Major Feichner of the GAF Crypt. Bureau, (OKL)." A TICOM publication.

I-116 "Report of Interrogation of Lt. Dettman and Oberwachtmeister Samsonow of OKH (Gen d NA) at OOberursel, Germany, during August 1945." A TICOM publication.

DOCID: 3486670

I-121 "Translation of homework by Obltn W. Werther, company commander of 7/LN Regt. 353." A TICOM publication.
I-131 "Lt. Col. Mettig of OKW/Chi on Wa Pruef 7 and RLM/-Forschungsamt." A TICOM publication.
I-143 "Report on the interrogation of five leading Germans (Jodl, Doenitz, Keitel, Ribbentrop, and Goering) at Nuremberg on 27 Sept. 1945." A TICOM publication.
I-146 "Detailed interrogation of members of OKM 4/SKL III at Flensburg." A TICOM publication.
I-147 "Detailed interrogation of members of OKM 4/SKL III at Flensburg." A TICOM publication.
I-159 "Report on GAF intelligence based on interrogation of Hauptman Zetzche." A TICOM publication.
I-162 "Report on interrogation of Kurt Sauerbier 7 RLM/Forschungsamt, held on 31 August 1945." A TICOM publication.
I-164 "Homework by Kurt Sauerbier of RLM/Forschungsamt, on Russian Agents' Traffic." A TICOM publication.
I-172 "Interrogations of Hagen and Paschke of Pers ZS." A TICOM publication.
I-176 "Homework by Wachtmeister Dr. Otto Buggisch of OKH/Chi and OKW/Chi." A TICOM publication.
IF-15 Final Report of TICOM Team 1 on the exploitation of Kaufbeuren and the Berchtesgaden area. From TICOM.
IF-46 Interrogation of Lother Guenther, dated 29 January 1945. CSDIC, MC 500, Hq 7th Army, NR. 708.
IF-105 CSIDIK (U.K.) SIR 1326. Interrogation Report on POW Heinz Boscheinen and Walter Kotschy.--Continuation of IF 126, 105 B--summary of preliminary interrogation of these prisoners in the field. Received through Col. Bicher.
IF-126 CSIDIK (U.K.) SIR 1335. Interrogation report on Kotschy and Boscheinen.
IF-132 Das Forschungsamt des Luftfahrtminsteriums." Hq USFET. Weekly Intelligence Summary # 12, 4 Oct. 1945.
IF-135 Directive of Schapper setting up organization of FA at Kaufbeuren and the branches and outstations. Dated 9 March 1945.
IF-143 Weekly Intelligence Summary # 15 (25 Oct. 1945); (Office of the Assistant Chief of Staff, G-2; Headquarters United States Forces, European Theater), # 15 (25 Oct. 1945). This contains information on FA wire tapping given by a Major Johannes Gaenzer of Abwehrstelle Berlin/III F.

IF-164 Interrogation of Walter Schellenberg, Brigade Fuehrer and head of Amt VI of RSHA.
IF-188 Four Stories by Daniel DeLuce of Associated Press, Berlin, 4, 5, 6, and 7 November 1945 based on material found by him in the rubble of the Air Ministry.
IF-216 The German Intelligence Service. (SHAEF, Counter Intelligence war room; London; April 1945).
IF-216-B "Sicherheitspolizei und Sicherheitsdienst." Ultra/Zip/Pal 4, 1/1/44.
IF-255 Glossary of German administrative and political Terminology for use by officers and officials of the American Armed Forces of occupation (Hq 7th Army, APO 758).
IF-256 German-English Dictionary of German Administrative Terms. Civil affairs guide. War Department Pamphlet Nr. 31-16a, 3 July 1944.
IF-257 German Army and Air Force abbreviation, NU CX/MSS/S. 168
IN 7/VI Control Station of Signal Intelligence of the Army High Command, Inspectorate 7. After November 1944 this became the Signal Intelligence Agency of the Army High Command.
Inspectorate 7/VI Control Station of Signal Intelligence of the Army High Command, abb In 7/VI. Became Signal Intelligence Agency of the Army High Command after November 1944.
Jentsch, Julius. Member of FA-9 at Kaufbeuren. May have gone to Berlin with Ruffler.
Jodl, Alfred, Colonel General. General Oberst, Chief of armed forces operation staff.
Juterbog. 51'59"N 13'40"E. Temporary location of a branch of the FA in early 1945. Also a location of the Signal Intelligence Agency of the Army High Command.
Kagelka, Specialist. Member of FA IV?
Katowice (Kattowitz) 50'16"N 19'01"E. Site of an "A" station in Upper Silesia (Poland).
Kattowitz. See Katowice.
Kaufbeuren. 47'53"N 10'37"E. The Main Bureau was located in barracks at the Kaufbeuren airfield. The postal address was Kaufbeuren/Allgemeine.
Kaltenbrunner. Himmler's head of RSHA.
Keitel, Wilhelm, Field Marshal. Chief of the Armed Forces.
Kell, ____. Given as a member of the FA in the telephone directory: "Research Office A1/2 Berlin. Exploitation Center. (Rlm/FA/AW - Kopf)." This may mean he was in the Berlin Forschungsleitstelle.

112

Kempe, Specialist. Head of Main Section II and Section 3 of FA.
Kettler, Col. Hugo. Chief of OKW/Chi, 1943-1945.
Kiewadt, Ilse. Member of FA-9, transferred to FA 3 on 7 March 45.
Kirbach, Senior Specialist. Head of Forschungsleitstelle in Hamburg.
Kirstein, Karl. Member of FA-9 at Kaufbeuren, assisted in transferring material from Breslau to Jueterbog.
Klautschke, Specialist Dr. Heinz. Liaison Officer with the Supreme Command of the Armed Forces (OKW not just OKW/Chi). Stated that he had "university training in Economics and Politics."
Koenigsberg, 54'42"N 20'30"E. Forschungsstelle (IF-15).
Koeln. See Cologne.
Koerner, Dr. Paul. Prussian Secretary of State. Financial control of the FA. Reported to have negotiated with Schellenberg to hand over the FA to Schellenberg.
Konstanz. See Constance.
Kotschy, Walter. Noncommissioned officer. Hungarian Interpreter. Member of Italian Section of Afrika Korps. Trained in "encoding and decoding" at In 7/VI.
Krenzke, Georg. Member of FA 9 at Kaufbeuren. Assisted in moving documents from Breslau to Jueterbog.
Kriminalpolizei (Kripo). Criminal Police. Part of the Sicherheitspolizei q.v.
Kripo. Kriminalpolizei q.v.
Kroeger,_____, Specialist. Member of Section 6 of the FA "Machine" specialist of the FA, presumably cipher machines. Probably responsible for success with Russian Teleprinter. Stated to have broken Finnish Hagelin. A member of Huettenhain's Cipher Security Committee.
Kuebbler, Ferdinand. A member of FA 9 at Kaufbeuren. He requested permission to visit his family at night at Hirschzell but was refused on the grounds that his family, residents of Hamburg/Saale, should not have evacuated to Bavaria but to Saxony or Thuringia.
Kuepper, Dr. Helmut. Member of FA 9 at Kaufbeuren.
Kunsemueller,_____, Senior Specialist. In charge of Section 2 of the FA. Was to report in Kaufbeuren on 10 April 1945.
Kunze, Werner, Dr. Senior Specialist (Oberregierungsrat) head of Pers ZS mathematical cryptanalytic subsection.

Kurzbach, _____, Senior Specialist Dr. Head of Section 11 and alternate head of Main Section V of the FA. Was last seen in Kaufbeuren by Rentschler.

Lade, Karl. Member of FA-9 at Kaufbeuren, assisted in moving documents from Breslau to Jueterbog.

Lange, Eran. Member of FA transferred from Kaufbeuren to Berlin. Her previous section is unknown.

Leba (Pomerania). 54'45"N 17'33"E. Forschungsstelle.

Lechner, Otto. Member of FA 9, assisted in transferring material from Breslau to Jueterbog - was at Kaufbeuren.

Legler, MinRat. Prussian State Ministry and 4 Year Plan, D 22.

Lehr, _____, Specialist. Probably a member of FA IV.

Liaison Office. Verbindungsstelle.

Litzmannstadt. See Lodz.

Lodz (Litzmannstadt). 51'46"N 19'26"E. Poland. Site of an A Station.

Ludwig, Dr. Helmut. Member of FA-9 at Kaufbeuren.

Luebben/Spreewald. 51'56"N 13'54"E. Radio intercept Forschungsstelle, 65 kilometres south of Berlin.

Main Section. Hauptabteilung.

Marquardstein. 47'46"N 12'28"E. Near Rosenheim, location of Amt VI of RSHA at conclusion of hostilities.

Matys, Georg. Member of FA 9 at Kaufbeuren.

Mayr, Margareta. Member of FA 9 at Kaufbeuren.

Meinhard, Pauline. Member of FA-9 at Kaufbeuren.

Mettig, _____, Lt. Col. Second in command of OKW/Chi, Dec. 1943 to 1945.

Meyer, _____. Author of a memo on quarters for FA personnel at Kaufbeuren.

Mews, _____, Specialist Dr. Head of Section 10 of the FA, the library and archives. Was last seen in Kaufbeuren (Rentschler).

Milch, Erhard, Field Marshal. Secretary of State for Air and Inspector General of the G. A. F.

Ministerialdirektor - untranslated non TICOM definition is: director in a ministry, head of one or more divisions in a ministry. Schapper held this rank as head of the FA and claimed it was equivalent to General Leutnant Der Luftwaffe.

Ministerial Dirigent - untranslated German Civil Serivce Rank higher than Ministerial Rat (q.v.) and is possibly equivalent to Brigadier General or "P-8".

114

Ministerialrat abb Min Rat -- Principal Specialist (non TICOM translation is Superior Counsellor in a ministerial department (title of a Referent (Principal) in the first ministerial grade). This Civil Service Rank is approximately equivalent to Colonel or "P 7."
MinRat - Ministerialrat q. v.
Mueller. Lt. Gen. of Police, SS Gruppenfuehrer, Head of RSHA Section IV.
Muenchen. See Munich.
Munich. 48'08"N 11'35"E. Forschungsleitstelle and Forschungsstelle.
National Defense Forces. See Reichswehr.
National Ministry of Defense. See Reichswehrministerium.
National Ministry of War. Reichskriegsministerium q. v.
National Police. See Reichspolizei
Navy High Command. See Oberkommando der Kriegsmarine.
Neuenhoff, _____, Dr. Special Liaison man between FA-9 and Branch Office Berlin.
Niedermeyer, _____, Specialist. Head of Forschungsleitstelle Breslau to 26 January 1945 when he was relieved and appointed Chief of Staff for Seifert in Jueterbog. On 9 March he was appointed head of the Forschungsleitstelle Munich.
Nuernberg. See Nuremberg.
Nuremberg. 59'27"N 11'05"E. Forschungsstellen.
Nusbaum, Ingeborg. Member of FA 9 at Kaufbeuren.
Oberkommando der Kriegsmarine abb OKM - High Command of the Navy. (Combines military and administrative authority). Preceded (1889-1919) by Reichsmarineamt, (1920-1934) by Marineleitung in Reichswehrmi nisterium; under the Oberbefehlshaber der Kriegsmarine.
Oberkommando der Luftwaffe abb OKL - Airforce High Command. (See Reichsluftfahrtministerium).
Oberkommando der Marine 4 Seekriegsleitung/III. Signal Intelligence Agency of the Navy High Command.
Oberkommando des Heeres abb OKH - Army High Command or High Command of the Army. (under the Oberbefehlshaber des Heeres; organization based on Wehrgesetz and edict of 4 February 1938.
Oberkommando des Heeres General der Nachrichten Aufklaerung. Signal Intelligence Agency of the Army High Command.
Oberkommando des Heeres Leitstelle der Nachrichten Aufklaerung-- Signal Intelligence Agency of the Army High Command (prior to November 1944).

Oberkommando der Wehrmacht abb OKW - High Command of the Armed Forces or Supreme Command of the Armed Forces. (Formerly Reichskriegsministerium, 1935-1938, previously Reichswehrministerium, 1919-1934. The Reichskriegsministerium was dissolved by the decree of 4 February 1938. At the head of the OKW is the Chef des Oberkommandos der Wehrmacht subject to Hitler himself who is Oberster Befehlshaber der Wehrmacht in consequence of the laws of 6 March 1935 and of 21 May 1935.

Oberkommando der Wehrmacht Chiffrier Abteilung. Signal Intelligence Agency of the Supreme Command of the Armed Forces (OKW/Chi).

Oberregierungsrat, abb ORR - Senior Specialist (non TICOM definition is: Higher Government Counsellor of a Referent (Principal) in the second ministerial grade). Civil Service rank approximately equivalent to Lt. Col. or "P-6."

Oden, Specialist with engineering diploma, Hoeckley. Head of Section 15 of the FA and head of Section 5 of the Branch Office Berlin. Had been employed by Siemens und Halske and classmate of various members of Wa Pruef 7 and therefore collaborated on production of T 52 e.

OKH - Oberkommando des Heeres q.v.

OKH/Chi. Loose Terminology for: The Signals Intelligence Agency of the Army High Command, OKH/GdNA, Oberkommando des Heeres/ General der Nachrichten Aufklaerung, after Nov. 1944, prior to then Inspectorate 7/VI (abb In 7/VI), Control station of Signal Intelligence of the Army High Command (OKH/LNA).

OKH/GdNA. Abbreviation for the Signal Intelligence Agency of the Army High Command.

OKL - Oberkommando der Luftwaffe q.v.

OKL/Chi. Signal Intelligence Agency of the Airforce High Command. Properly OBdl/Chi or, after November 1944, OKL/LN Abt 350.

Sicherheitspolizei abb. Sipo - Security Police. One of the two main branches of the Police (Reichspolizei, q.v.) Organized in the Reichsicherheitshauptamt (RSHA) it included the Kriminalpolizei (Kripo) and Geheimestaatspolizei (Gestapo). The head of the RSHA was Kaltenbrunner who was responsible to Himmler.

Signal Equipment and Testing Branch (Wa Pruef 7) of OKH.

Signal Intelligence Agency of the Air Force High Command. Chi Stelle of the Oberbefehlshaber der Luftwaffe, which became Luftwaffe Nachrichten Abteilung 350 after November 1940.

116

OKM. See Oberkommando der Kriegsmarine.
OKM 4 SKL/III. Signal Intelligence Agency of the Navy High Command.
OKW. See Oberkommando der Wehrmacht.
OKW/Chi. See Signal Intelligence Agency of the Supreme Command of the Armed Forces.
OKW/WNV/FU. Radio Defense Corps qv.
Ordnungspolizei abb Orpo - Regular Police, Constabulary. Organized into a Main Office Constabulary, under the Chef der deutschen Polizei (Himmler). Constabulary is divided into five sections; Schutzpolizei (abb. Schupo, the Security Police, which is divided into Inspektionen or Administrative police, Abschnitte or Section police, Reviere or Precinct police, and Wasserschutzpolizei or Harbor police; Gendarmie (rural police); Technische Nothilfe (abb TN or Teno.-Office for Emergency Operation of Utilities); Feuerschutzpolizei (Fire Protection Police); and Verwaltungspolizei (who regulate traffic, public health etc). By regions the Constabulary has been subdivided into Landes-(regional), Kreis-(district), and Ortspolizei (local police).
Orpo. Ordnungspolizei, q.v.
ORR. Oberregierungsrat q.v.
Oschmann,____, Captain. Official of Defense Ministry Cipher Section.
Outstation.--Forschungsleitstelle.
Paetzel, Martin, Senior Specialist Dr. Head of Section 6 and alternate head of Main Section IV of the FA.
Paschke, Adolf, Dr., Senior Specialist. Co-head or head of Pers ZS and head of the Linguistic-Cryptanalytic Subsection. Also in charge of Wehrmacht liaison, (Foreign Office Cryptanalytic Section).
Patzig,____, Corvette Captain. Official at Defence Ministry, cipher section.
Pers ZS. Abbreviation for "Sonderdienst des Referats Z in der Personal Abteilung des Auswaertigen Amtes." The German Foreign Office Cryptanalytic Section.
Plagens, Dr. Hermann. Member of FA 9 at Kaufbeuren.
Pokojewski,Kurt, Technical Inspector. Subordinate to civilian in charge of OKW intercept station at Lauf; later became civilian in charge.
Polizei, Reichs. See Reichspolizei.
Popp,____, Specialist. Head of Section 4 of the FA.

Posen. See Posnan.
Posnan, (Posen). 52'25"N 16'58"E. Poland, site of an A station.
Principal Specialist. See Ministerial Rat.
Progich, _____, Specialist. A member of the intercept station at Luebben. He was also assigned liaison functions with the Branch Office Berlin.
Rapp, _____, SS Standartenfuehrer. Named by Schellenberg as working with Sandberger to take over the FA into Amt VI of RSHA in February 1945. Head of a Northern Section of Amt VI at Flensburg.
Rautenkranz, _____, Dr. A member of the Danzig Forschungsstelle. Last known as a prisoner in the 7th Army cage qt Augsburg but not questioned by TICOM. On 20 March 1945 he was transferred from the School (School for Evaluators) to head of FA-12.
Regierungsrat abb RR. Specialist (non TICOM definition is: Governmental Counsellor (title of a Referent (Principal) in the third ministerial grade). Civil Service rank approximately equivalent to Major or "P-5".
Regular Police. See Ordnungspolizei.
Reich Air Ministry Research Bureau. FA q.v.
Reich Main Security Office. The headquarters of Himmler, SIPO, and SD, (Security Police and Security Service) of the SS.
Reichskriegsministerium. German War Ministry (in charge of Army and Navy, 1935-1938, dissolved by decree of 4 February 1938(GBl.I,p.111); functions taken over by Oberkommando der Wehrmacht.)
Reichsluftfahrtministerium, abb. RLM. National Air Ministry, established by decree of 5 May 1933. In consequence of the reorganization of the Wehrmacht the Air Ministry is also the Oberbefehlshaber des Oberkommandos der Luftwaffe. Including Austria, the whole German territory is subdivided into Luftlottenkommandos and Luftgaukommandos.
Reichsluftfahrtsministerium/Forschungsamt. Forschungsamt q.v.
Reichspolizei. National Police. Established by edict of 17 June 1936 under Chef der deutschen Polizei within the jurisdiction of the Reichsinnenministerium. The whole police administration has been divided into Hauptamt Ordnungspolizei and Hauptamt Sicherheitspolizei (see Reichsicherheitspolizei). Himmler is Chef der deutschen Polizei.

Reichssicherheitshauptamt, abb. RSHA. Reich Main Security Office. Main Office of the Sicherheitspolizei, q. v.
Reichswehr. National Defense (Land and Naval) Forces. Term used after the first world war during the time the Defense Act of 23 March 1921, imposed by Versailles treaty, was in force (1919- 1935).
Reichswehrministerium. German Defense Ministry, in charge of army and navy (1919-1934). later called Reichskriegsministerium.
Remwettz-Lukjansky, Dimitri. Member of FA 9 at Kaufbeuren.
Rentschler, Specialist Erwin. Head of Section 13 of the FA, formerly a member of Section 11 as French expert. Joined the FA in 1934. Was interrogated by TICOM at Kaufbeuren.
von Ribbentrop, Joachim. Foreign Minister.
Richter, Helga. Member of FA 9 at Kaufbeuren.
Riga. 56'57"N 24'09"E. Forschungsstelle.
RLM. Reichsluftfahrtministerium q.v.
RLM/FA. Forschungsamt q.v.
Rohm, Ernst. Leader of SA, executed in "Blood Purge" 9 June 1934.
Rosenhahn,_____, Senior Specialist. Head of Section 1 of the FA.
Rosenheim. 57'52"N 12'08"E. Final location of the Main Bureau.
Roth, Liselotte. Member of FA 9 at Kaufbeuren. Probably went to Berlin with Ruffler on 5 April 1945.
RR. Regierungsrat q.v.
RSHA. Reichsicherheithauptamt q.v.
Ruffler, Georg. Member of FA 9 at Kaufbeuren. The notation, to Berlin with Ruffler, appears beside his name and that of several other members of FA 9 with the date of 5 April 1945.
SA. Storm Troops (Sturm Abteilung).
Samsonoff, M/Sgt. Sergins. Head of Section 32 of group IV of GdNA. Specialty. (Russian Secret Police Systems. NKVD).
Sandberger,_____. Head of Amt VI Kultur of RSHA and one of the key officials assigned job of taking over the FA in February 1945 by Schellenberg. Last known at Marquartstein near Rosemheim in charge of a southern section of Amt VI.
Sauerbier, Herr Kurt. In charge of sub-section C of Section 9 of FA. A specialist on Agent ciphers. Formerly a bank clerk, he joined the FA in 1935.
Schade. Head of Forschungsstelle in Danzig.

Schapper, Minister Director Gottfried. Head of the FA at the end of the war. Was associated with Schimpf, von Hesse and Goering in founding the FA. Had been in Signals Intelligence in World War I and a member of the cipher section of the Defense Ministry (predecessor of OKW/Chi) prior to founding of FA. Was third head of FA, holding rank equivalent to that of a General-leutnant of the German Air Force. Was interrogated by TICOM and furnished an outline of the FA, its history, and an autobiography (for which last see Appendix III).
Scheitinger, Josef. Member of FA 9 at Kaufbeuren.
Schellenberg, SS Brigadefuehrer Walter. Maj. Gen. of Police. Head of Amt VI of RSHA. Took over Abwehr as Mil. Amt of Amt VI, attempted to take over FA and did achieve control of it through an arrangement with Koerner. Also controlled OKW/Chi to some extent at the end.
Schimpf, Corvette Captain. First Head of FA, committed suicide. Had been liaison officer from Defense Ministry to the predecessor of OKM. Founded FA with Goering in 1933.
Schirajeff, Erika. Member of FA-9, assisted in moving documents from Breslau to Jueterbog. Last known at Kaufbeuren.
Schlaka, Robert, General Major. Chief of Communications in the Ordnungspolizei.
Schmidt, _____. Appointed head of the closing down section of the Forschungsleitstelle Breslau in Berlin on 26 January. A Schmidt is author of a memo on laundry service from FA I.
Schmitz, _____. Member of RSHA, Amt VI.
Scholz, _____, Specialist with engineering diploma. Liaison officer with the Reich Main Security Office.
Schroeder, Ministerialdirigent Georg. Head of Main Section IV of the FA.
Schubert, 1st Lt. Horst. GdNA specialist on Russian Agents' systems.
Schubert, Walter. A member of FA 9 at Kaufbeuren.
Schulze, Senior Specialist. Head of Section 8 of the FA.
SD. Sicherheitsdienst or Security Service. The Nazi Party secret police, formed out of the SS. It was organized with the RSHA and included with KRIPO and GESTAPO.
Section. Abteilung.
Security Police. See Sicherheitspolizei.
Security Service. See Sicherheitsdienst.
Secret State Police. Geheimestaatspolizei q.v.

Seifert, Principal Specialist Walter. Head of Main Section V and of the Reporting Center Seifert in Berlin. He came to the FA from the cipher section of the Defense Ministry in 1933. (He should not be confused with the Austrian Hofrat Seifert who was employed in OKW/Chi after the Anschluss.) Seifert had been head of the Juterbog Branch of the FA.

Seifert, Hofrat, Dr. Head of the Austrian Cipher Bureau. Came to OKW/Chi after the Anschluss where he was the Specialist on known codes and broke Polish, Turkish, Greek, and Vatican basic books. Head of Greek sub-section OKW/Chi: V 6. Do not confuse with Walter Seifert of the FA.

Senior Specialist. Oberregierungsrat q.v.

Severitt, Herr. Liaison Officer with Ministry of Information and Propaganda.

Sicherheitsdienst, Abb. SD. Security Service, part of the SS.

Signal Intelligence Agency of the Air Force High Command. Oberkommando der Luftwaffe Luftnachrichten Abteilung 350 (OKL/LN 350). Its predecessor was, prior to November 1944, OBdL/Chi Stelle.

Signal Intelligence Agency of the Army High Command. Oberkommando des Heeres/General der Nachrichten Aufklaerung. (OKH/GdNA) Its predecessor prior to November 1944 this was Inspectorate 7/VI of the Leitstelle der Nachrichten Aufklaerung of the Oberkommando des Heeres. (OKH/LNA/In 7/VI).

Signal Intelligence Agency of the Commander in Chief of the Air Force. Chi Stelle, Oberbefehlshaber der Luftwaffe.

Signal Intelligence Agency of the Navy High Command. Oberkommando der Marine 4 Seekriegsleitung III. abb. OKM 4 SKL/III.

Signal Intelligence Agency of the Supreme Command of the Armed Forces. (Oberkommando der Wehrmacht/Chiffrier Abteilung, abb. OKW/Chi). Formerly the Cipher section of the Defense Ministry.

Simon, Fritz. Member of FA 9 at Kaufbeuren assisted in moving documents from Breslau to Jueterbog.

Simson, ____, Col. Commandant of the Air Ministry D 22.

Sipo. See Sicherheitspolizei.

Sponholz. See Frau Helene Gertz.

Spreewald. See Luebben/Spreewald.

121

SS. Schutzstaffel-Elite Guard. The Armed SS (Waffen SS) and General SS, (Allgemeine SS). SS was responsible for the party security service, SD, and the RSHA.

Stabenow,_____, Senior Specialist. Head of Main Section VI of the FA. Head of the Branch Office Berlin. Possibly at Flensburg at the capitulation but not traced. (I 25, 54, 93, IF 135, D 22).

Steffens, Gerda. Member of FA 9 at Kaufbeuren.

Stettin. 53'25"N 14'34"E. Forschungsstelle.

von Stubenfauch,_____, Specialist. Member of FA IV?

Supreme Command of the Armed Forces. See Oberkommando der Wehrmacht. (This is the TICOM translation, official translation is High Command of the Armed Forces.)

Tallinn. 59'24"N 24'45"E. Forschungsstelle.

Templin. 53'07"N 13'30"E. Radio intercept Forschungsstelle. 70 kilometres north of Berlin.

TF 29. Die Ueberwachung des Nachrichtenverkehrs im Kriege. (The Supervision of Information Channels in War). German book containing regulations and organization for censorship of all communications. Responsibility given to Abwehr and cooperation of SS and SD and the FA, Deutsche Reichspost etc.

Thiele, Brig. Gen.: Chief of Staff to Chief Signal Officer of the Army.

Thieme,_____, Specialist. Head of Forschungsleitstelle Berlin.

Thomas, Hildegard. Member of FA 9 at Kaufbeuren.

TICOM. Target Intelligence Committee. Loosely used in this paper for the entire project, for the committee members, and for the publications. Activities and materials of that committee according to context.

T-240. This is the film (Film 34-16 millimetre) of the administrative directives found by Team 1 at Kaufbeuren. A summary of the contents, and complete translation of item 34 is given in appendix 2. Item 34 is also available as IF 135.

Tranow,_____, Principal Specialist. Head of English Cryptographic Section (III-F) of OKM 4 SKL/III.

Verbindungsstelle.--Liaison Office.

Vienna. 48'12"N 16'22"E. Forschungsleitstelle and Forschungsstelle.

DOCID: 3486670

Voegele, Ferdinand, RR, chief cryptanalyst and chief of Section E of the Chi Stelle of the Signal Intelligence Agency of the Air Force.
Waechter,_____, Senior Specialist. Head of Section 8 of the FA. Specialist on English and American systems concerning which he liaisoned with the cipher section of the Foreign Office.
Wa Pruef 7. Signal Equipment and Testing Branch of OKH.
Walger, Egon. Member of FA 9 at Kaufbeuren. Assisted in moving documents from Breslau to Jueterbog.
Wenzel,_____, Senior Specialist. Head of Section 9 of the FA.
Werther,_____. Company Commander of 7/LN Abt 353. Co CO of 7th Co 2nd Bttn Airforce Regiment 353.
Wichmann,_____, MinRat. Head of office of ministers and Department VII. Reichspost.
Wien. See Vienna.
Work Section. Arbeitsgebiet q.v.
Zetsche,_____. Captain in charge of Group A of Foreign Airforce West.
Zweigstelle Berlin. Branch Office Berlin.

ARMY SECURITY AGENCY

Washington, D. C.

EUROPEAN AXIS SIGNAL INTELLIGENCE IN WORLD WAR II
AS REVEALED BY "TICOM" INVESTIGATIONS
AND BY OTHER PRISONER OF WAR INTERROGATIONS
AND CAPTURED MATERIAL, PRINCIPALLY GERMAN

VOLUME 8--MISCELLANEOUS

Prepared under the direction of the

CHIEF, ARMY SECURITY AGENCY

1 May 1946

WDGAS-14

14255

VOLUME 8

Miscellaneous

DOCID: 3560798

VOLUME 8

Chapter I Italian Signal Intelligence Organizations

1. <u>Italian cryptology was centered in the Army and Navy Intelligence Services</u>.--Two organizations, which were primarily intelligence and not cryptologic bureaus, performed the major cryptological work for Italy before September 1943. These were:

a. Army Intelligence Service (Servizio Informazioni Militari, abbreviated S I M.)[1]

[1] S I M was subdivided into "offensive" and "defensive" branches. On November 1, 1941 the "offensive" branch which was concerned with all phases of intelligence against foreign powers, was detached, set up as an autonomous organization and called Servizio Informazioni Esercito (abbreviated S I E) (IF 1500, p 1) On June 15, 1943 S I E was absorbed back into S I M (IF 1500, p 9).

b. Navy Intelligence Service (Servizio Informazioni Speciali, abbreviated S I S.)

Each of the above had a cryptographic section, and each had a cryptanalytic section.[2]

There were also nine small signal intelligence field units attached to Italian Armies.[3]

Two ministries had minor cryptologic bureaus. The Ministry of Foreign Affairs Cryptographic Office (Ufficio Crittografico) prepared Italian diplomatic codes and ciphers. The Ministry of Interior Inspector General of the Political Police (Publica Sicurezza) scrutinized "communist" and "foreign agent" codes and ciphers.[4]

The Air Force Intelligence Service (Servicio Informazioni Aeronautica, abbreviated S I A) had no cryptanalytic section. It is not known whether it had any cryptographic section.

2. <u>Army Intelligence Service had eight sections.</u> Army Intelligence was under the Italian General Staff, and was commanded at one time by a Brigadier General Ame. It had eight main sections, of which three were directly concerned with cryptology, and only two were concerned with gathering military intelligence in the usual sense. The other three were evaluation, administration, and secretariat. On paper, therefore, cryptanalysis and cryptography were major functions of Army Intelligence.[5] The eight main branches and their functions were as follows:

a. The Secretariat Section operated the message center. It was first commanded by a Col. Nasta, who was later replaced by Col. Aldo Canale.[6]

b. The Organization of Agents and Army Intelligence section was responsible for espionage and the evaluation of intelligence produced by reconnaissance, interrogation of prisoners of war, and examination of captured documents. The

[2]IF-1500, p 1.

[3]IF-1520, p 2.

[4]IF-1502, p 2.

[5]See chart No. 8- 1.

[6]IF-1500, p 2.

2

Espionage Sub-section maintained field offices in occupied and neutral countries. Of particular interest is existence of an Argentine office whose activities were espionage against the United States.

The Army Intelligence Sub-section (also known as the I Sub-section) handled operational intelligence and its sections were attached to each Corps and Divisional Command. It was commanded successively by a Col. Pasquale and a Col. Gastaldi.[7]

c. The Evaluation Section collected and analyzed information gathered by the other sections and military attachés, and issued such information in the form of daily bulletins, weekly and monthly reports. Distribution was to the Minister of Foreign Affairs, the Minister of the Armed Forces and his Chiefs of Staff, and to the commanders of "main army units." The Evaluation Section also issued predictions on the political conduct of the war. The command officer was a Col. Pacinotti.[8]

d. The Monograph Section produced treatises relating to foreign nations and the general conduct of the war. The personnel consisted of young college professors who had an accurate historical knowledge of foreign countries.[9]

e. The Cryptography Section compiled and allocated ciphers to all army units. It also supervised printing of the most secret documents of the Army Intelligence Service, and provided linguists for all commands and units that required interpreters. This Branch was commanded by a Col. Piccinocchi.[10]

f. The Intercept Section was responsible for the interception of all commercial, military, and diplomatic traffic. It maintained its principal station at Forte Braschi, near Rome, and allotted one or two intercept companies to each army. It was under the command of a Col. Petrella.[11]

g. The Administration Section administered SIM personnel. It was also responsible for the securing and disbursement of funds.[12]

[7] IF-1500.

[8] IF-1500, p 4.

[9] IF-1500, p 5.

[10] IF-1500, p 5.

[11] IF-1500, p 5 - 6.

[12] IF-1500, p 6.

3

h. The Cryptanalytic Section attempted to break Allied Diplomatic, Army, and Commercial codes and ciphers.[13]

3. Cryptanalytic Section totaled approximately fifty persons. At the base only 25 cryptanalysts and 25 linguists and clerks made up the Army Intelligence Service Cryptanalytic Section.[14]

General Vittorio Gamba was in command from World War I to the Armistice. He experienced difficulty in procuring cryptanalysts after World War I[15] and the handicap was never overcome.[16]

The Section's other difficulties included a lack of funds and a lack of IBM equipment. At first IBM machines were used only at the office of the Watson Corporation (Italian IBM) in Rome. Another complication was the poor liaison with the Intercept Branch. All negotiations had to go through SIM headquarters.[17]

The Section never had Chinese and Japanese translators, and it always experienced difficulty in obtaining Russian, Turkish, and Arabic linguists.[18] All personnel, including the guards, wore civilian clothes.

Generally, the Section read only those diplomatic systems which had been in use for a long time. All statistical operations were accomplished by hand; it was not until the last stage of the war that IBM machines were used regularly. At the time of the Armistice, no general success had been achieved in breaking American and British diplomatic and military systems. Exceptions to this were: American military attaché systems involving traffic from Cairo, Basra, and Teheran in 1942; Berne, Madrid, and Lisbon traffic after November 1942; and the State Department "Brown" Code which had been compromised.[20]

[13] IF-1500, p 6.

[14] IF-1517, p 2.

[15] IF-1500.

[16] IF-1518.

[17] IF-1517, IF-1518, p 1.

[18] IF-1517, p 5.

[19] IF-1517, p 2.

[20] IF-1524, p 5; IF-1517, p 5.

The Cryptanalytic Section had three Sub-sections: Diplomatic, Military and Research, and Commercial. The allotment of personnel among the sections varied with the work load and current priorities; translators and typists were pooled.[21]

The Diplomatic Sub-section was subdivided into nine groups. Great Britain, Dominions, America, and Sweden were the responsibility of only one group, consisting of two cryptanalysts.[22]

The Military and Research Sub-section, consisting of five cryptanalysts, was divided into Military and Research units. The Military unit forwarded its results (via unknown channels) to the field cryptanalytic units and to those in Italian possessions. The Research unit was non-operational and was assigned the mission of making the initial break into systems. When the work reached an operational stage, the system was transferred to the Military unit. There was excellent liaison between them.[23]

The Research unit was handicapped by its late adoption of IBM methods. It did not have possession of any machines until late in the war. Until that time, such work as was done was processed at the offices of the Watson Corporation by employees of Watson who worked under the orders of SIM. With the acquisition of IBM machines, more ambitious projects were tackled.[24]

The Commercial unit, consisting of one cryptanalyst, was concerned with Italian commercial codes and ciphers. Its function was to censor Italian commercial traffic and to detect deviations from ordinary commercial code procedures. It was not concerned with foreign commercial codes.[25]

The Cryptanalytic Section received its traffic from the Intercept Section's four stationary intercept stations in Italy, and from its seven mobile units located in Italy, possessions, and occupied territory.[26]

[21]IF-1517, p 1-2.

[22]IF-1517, p 2.

[23]IF-1517, p 2, 6.

[24]IF-1518, p 1; IF-1519, p 1.

[25]IF-1517, p 2.

[26]IF-1517, p 2-3.

The final evaluation of the Cryptanalytic Section might be made in the words of General Gambà, the commanding officer. It was said to be of a "dilettante nature."[27]

4. Italian Army Field Signal Intelligence "Groups" combined cryptanalysis and interception. Evidently there existed in the Italian Army before June 1942 separate cryptanalytic field units and separate intercept units, assigned to the various Italian armies by the Army Intelligence Service (SIM). The organization and missions of these early units is not known. However, in June 1942 at Stalino Russia the Italian Eighth Army combined its cryptanalytic unit of ten officers and six non-commissioned officers with its intercept company, which had a strength of three hundred officers and men. Intercept functions were placed under the control of the cryptanalytic unit; heretofore, each group had been separately responsible to Eighth Army headquarters.

This so-called "Cryptanalytic Group" of the Eighth Army was directly responsible to the Eighth Army, and had no direct connection with the Army Intelligence Service (SIM) in Rome. The Germans later tried unsuccessfully to have this Group placed under their authority.[28]

The intercept unit of the Group maintained twenty-four receivers of which nine were fitted into mobile vans. Two mobile vans contained German direction finding sets. Difficulty was experienced in the operation of these units, due to poor instruction by the Germans.

The main contribution of the Cryptanalytic Group was intelligence derived from traffic analysis. Cryptanalysis was hampered by the inexperience of the cryptanalysts, ignorance of the Russian language, and lack of cooperation from the Germans, whereas intercept personnel were highly efficient and were able to identify individual Russian operators and discover changes of frequency. The result was an excellent evaluation of the Russian Order of Battle in that area. The Germans appear to have been surprised at the Italian ability to produce this intelligence.[29]

[27] IF-1518, p 1.

[28] IF-1520, p 2.

[29] IF-1520, p 2.

The success of the Eighth Army Group led to the formation of similar units. In June 1943, Lt. Col. Guido Emer, officer in charge of the Eighth Army Cryptanalytic Group, was ordered by the Army Intelligence Service (SIM) to organize a similar Group for each field army. The Groups were to be patterned after British and American units with special reference to the experience gained by the Eighth Army. Eight new Groups in all were set up for the 2nd, 4th, 5th, 6th, 7th, 10th and 11th Armies, and for the Italians in Rhodes.[30] The cryptanalytic element of a Group, "nucleo", contained from one to fifteen cryptanalytic officers assisted by non-commissioned officers who acted as translators and typists. The intercept unit varied in strength from a section to a company and a half. The resulting Groups never measured up to expectations, however, the 6th Army's Group was able to predict the landing in Sicily and there must have been minor successes.[31]

5. Italian Naval Intelligence Was streamlined. Italian Naval Intelligence, (Servizio Informazioni Speciali della Royal Marina, abbreviated SIS) was located in Rome and was directly responsible to the General Staff. It was organized into four branches, all of which had the common mission of discovering the enemy's power, organization, location, activities, and future plans. The four branches were set up on the basis of function and were as follows:

a. Intelligence Based on Radio Intercept - Branch B
b. Evaluation of Intelligence - Branch C
c. Intelligence Based on Espionage - Branch D
d. Counter-Intelligence - Branch E[32]

Branch B was subdivided into four subsections: Cryptanalytic, Intercept and Direction Finding, Security, and Clandestine Radio Intercept.

The Cryptanalytic Sub-section, located in Rome, was under the command of a Commandante De Monte.[33] It directed its efforts

[30] IF-1523

[31] IF-1520, p 3-5.

[32] IF-209

[33] IF-1527, p 1.

7

against British Naval and Air operational codes. Naval tactical codes and Air code enciphering tables were considered to be simple problems, despite the daily change in the case of the latter.[34] The Sub-section was also successful with a four-figure British Naval Code in 1941 and 1942. This system was not read after the landings in North Africa. A four-figure "Anglo-American Naval Code" was also read.[35]

The Intercept and Direction Finding Sub-section maintained seven principal intercept stations in Italy and its possessions. Six of these were linked together by teletype to facilitate operations particularly with respect to direction finding. The maintenance of one hundred and fifty watches daily, along with the traffic received from German intercept stations located outside of the Mediterranean, produced a daily average of three thousand messages.[36] This Sub-section also controlled intercept groups which were located on the flagships of all commands. These groups were under the command of a Navy Intelligence Service (SIS) officer who was supplied with material for the immediate decoding and interpretation of enemy traffic.[37]

The Security Sub-section had as its mission the cryptanalysis of Italian Naval Codes, Ciphers, and call signs. To maintain the inquiry on a purely cryptanalytic level, the Sub-section was kept in complete ignorance of Italian naval activity. If it was suspected that a system could be read, information was forwarded to the Communications Department of the General Staff. This information often contained suggestions for eliminating the danger.[38]

The Clandestine Radio Intercept Sub-section organized and controlled stations for Branch D. It is said that messages were relayed promptly to the Navy Intelligence Service (SIS).[39]

[34] IF 209

[35] IF-1527, p 2; See Chart 1 - 2.

[36] IF-209, p 6.

[37] IF-209, p 5.

[38] IF-209, p 10.

[39] IF-209, p 11.

Branch C evaluated all the intelligence produced by Branches B and D, except those of an immediate operational nature. It was organized on the basis of countries or groups of countries. It circulated translations among higher authorities and served as an information section for the other Branches.[40]

Branch D produced intelligence based on espionage. Initially, Branch D depended on ship captains and informers for information that was of doubtful value. Gradually it built up its own espionage centers in Europe, North Africa, and Asia Minor which were highly effective. Attempts at espionage in enemy countries failed. The main mission of these centers was to collect information of a naval nature. The secondary mission was to collect information of a political nature. Reports were relayed back to the Branch by means of clandestine stations set up by the Clandestine Radio Intercept Sub-section of Branch B. Aircraft flights were reported by fishing boats in the Mediterranean and Atlantic. Toward the end of the war, the Branch was given the task of sabotage.[41]

Branch E was responsible for counter-espionage. Branch E was originally divided into two sections; one dealt with military police functions; the other with counter-espionage. These activities were later combined in the form of centers. Eleven centers were set up in Italy. Five centers were maintained in occupied areas and North Africa. Branch E coordinated all activities relative to naval espionage and sabotage. It was reported that there was no successful act of sabotage against the Italian Navy.[42]

The Italian Air Force Intelligence Service (Servicio Informazioni Aeronautica, abbreviated SIA) relied on the Navy for cryptanalytic work during the whole war. The Navy carried out the intercept function as well, until 1941 when the Air Force set up its own intercept station. Intercepts from this station were sent to the Navy for solution.[43]

[40] IF-209, p 19.

[41] IF-209, p 17.

[42] IF-209, p 20.

[43] IF-209.

9

6. Italian-German liaison was marked by mutual distrust. Major De Witt, an Italian cryptanalyst, was of the opinion that poor liaison with the German Army Signal Intelligence Agency (OKH/GdNA and predecessors) was based on the German doctrine of taking a lot and giving nothing. This is a moot point when one considers what the Italians had to offer. In actuality, neither side ever expressed a willingness for complete cooperation.

Liaison on military traffic began in 1939 with an emphasis on French traffic. Major De Witt reported that the Italians and Germans were supposed to collaborate on the recovery of an enciphered code system which had a forty day period. There was great rivalry and no interchange of information was permitted by either side until the recovery had been completed.[44]

In 1942, the Italians learned from the Germans that certain Italian cipher systems (not named) were insecure. The Germans recommended the adoption of a Playfair cipher using ten tables. The Italian Army adopted the German suggestion for a short time and then dropped it. The Italian Cryptanalytic Section stated that it had found the recommended system to be insecure and expressed the fear that the Germans favored the system because they could read it.[45]

In January 1942, Capt. Augusto Bigi, a cryptanalyst, was sent to Berlin to investigate German cryptanalytic procedures, with special emphasis on IBM techniques. As a result of the mission's report to Army Intelligence Service (SIM), it was decided to undertake small scale experiments with IBM machines. With a view toward expansion of the use of IBM equipment, should the experiments prove successful, Capt. Bigi was again sent to Berlin in December 1942. The Germans did not allow Capt. Bigi to re-examine their installations and expressed a preference for sending a technician to consult with the Italians. This instance of non-cooperation is considered typical of the whole Italian-German relationship.[46]

Italians gave German liaison officers what purported to be true copies of their weekly summaries. But, in fact, these were edited and abridged documents, which contained nothing which was

[44]IF-1524, p 3.

[45]IF-1519, p 4; IF-1524, p 2.

[46]IF-1517, Appendix A, p 2.

contrary to the German view of the political and military situation. This was especially true with respect to reports dealing with Russia. The reason given by the Italians was that they wished to avoid an argument with the Germans.[47]

Further evidence of mutual distrust in the field of Italian-German liaison appears in the relationship between the Signal Intelligence Agency of the Navy High Command (OKM/4 Skl III) and the Italian Naval Intelligence Service (SIS).[48] Liaison began in 1933 on French systems, but was very slight from 1934 to 1937, at which time opinions were exchanged in regard to the security of Italian systems. In 1938, the Italians failed to elicit information regarding British Naval operational systems. The Germans did give information on the administrative system, but did not provide any information on the operational system until 1940. The Italians had made slight progress by that date and the subsequent exchange of information was mutually beneficial.

The lack of confidence in Italian cipher security influenced the Germans in their reluctance to provide the Italians with British Naval Cypher No. 3 (for convoys) until 1942. Collaboration on this system continued until the Badoglio revolution in July 1943. From that time on, liaison came to a gradual standstill, and all liaison ended in Sept. 1943.

The prevailing opinion among the Germans seemed to be that the Italians were temperamentally unsuited to cryptanalysis, and the German analysts appear to have been unwilling to initiate any action with the Italians without direct orders from above.[49]

7. Enemy Italian Cryptologic Activities did not terminate with the Armistice. The Military Intelligence service terminated its existence as a de jure organization with the signing of the Armistice. The personnel was subject to various pressures and fears which resulted in their scattering to the Allies, to Mussolini, to the Germans, or into hiding. The Germans took command of any remaining intelligence functions.[50]

[47] IF-1500, p 7.

[48] I-12.

[49] I-12.

[50] IF-1527, p 3.

The documents of the Cryptanalytic Branch of the Army Intelligence Service (SIM) were in part destroyed, but a great many were turned over to the Germans or taken into hiding against the day when the organization might be recreated. Capt. Bigi, a cryptanalyst, stated that he destroyed only old and obsolete documents.[51]

The successor to the Military Intelligence Service was the Defense Intelligence Service (Servizio Informazioni Difesa, abbreviated SID). It was under the direction of a Dr. Foschini. Organized in October 1943, it was successively located in Rome, Volta Mantovano, and Castiglioni delle Stivieri. Its organization paralleled that of the old Army Intelligence Service, and it was, in fact, a continuation of the previous organization.[52] It had available only twelve cryptanalysts for the task which had been too great for double that number. A further difficulty was its lack of intercept facilities. The Germans discouraged the development of intercept and are reported to have placed Dr. Foschini in a concentration camp because of his efforts to obtain intercept equipment. The only systems that were generally worked on were some of those that had previously been read by the Army Intelligence Service (SIM); namely, Turkish, Spanish, and Rumanian diplomatic codes and ciphers.[53] Occasionally a new system was broken.[54]

The cryptanalytic and intercept functions of the Defense Intelligence Service (SID) were reorganized in June 1944. All cryptanalytic and intercept activities were combined into the Intercept Section (Intercettazione Sezione) which was known as IN. The IN was subdivided into three "bureaus."[55]

a. The First Bureau consisted of naval personnel whose mission was to deal with tactical enemy air traffic and, to a small degree, naval traffic. This group had a short existence

[51]IF-1526, p 2-3; IF-1517, p 7; IF-1501.

[52]IF-1517, p 7.

[53]IF-1524, p 9; IF-1517.

[54]IF-1526.

[55]See Chart 8 - 1, IF-1524, p 8-9.

DOCID: 3560798

which terminated with the incorporation of its personnel into the Second Bureau in November 1944.[56]

b. The Second Bureau worked on diplomatic and military attaché codes and ciphers. The work was limited to systems already broken.

c. The Third Bureau confined its activities to the monitoring of press reports, particularly Reuters.[57]

8. TICOM has recovered Italian translations of decrypted traffic. TICOM has obtained the Italian translations of traffic decrypted by the Italian Defense Intelligence Service (SID) from late 1943 to early 1945. Notations indicated that the Republican Fascist Government had a particular interest in intelligence relating to conditions in liberated Italy; secondary importance was attached to messages dealing with conditions in its own territory. The decrypted traffic also revealed that messages of general intelligence value were read. Below are summaries of a few of the representative messages:

Worksheet 1111-Vatican to Lisbon 30 Dec. 1944-597 groups Portuguese message number 1.

Liberated Italy is economically devastated, expecially with regard to raw materials. It is at the mercy of the initiative of the liberators. Italians believe that the British are sincere in their desire actively to aid reconsturction. The public debt is 676 billion liras, three times national income, but the government is optimistic.

Worksheet 2925-Moscow to Paris 20 Feb. 1945-88 groups French message number 85.

Fourteen Frenchmen who escaped from German camps at Bleichhammer and Heydebreck report that they worked with 70,000 others on the production of synthetic benzine at plants in these localities. Annual production is estimated at 3,500,000 tons.

Worksheet 4525-Tokyo to Berne 23 Feb. 1945-266 groups Swiss message number 503.

The situation is critical in Japan. There is great popular apathy and misery. The Government would like to

[56] IF-1524, p 9.

[57] IF-1527, p 3; IF-1526, p 2; IF-1524, p 9.

evacuate Tokio, but it is unable to provide transport and lodging. The military fear the loss of Formosa and an invasion of Kyushu. A German defeat is believed inevitable, but it is hoped that the Germans will delay to the point of extermination. The press is very hostile to Russia, but the official attitude is very correct.

Worksheet 3330-Paris to Rio de Janeiro 1 March 1945-71 groups French message number 26.

It is reported from Montevideo that the Argentine is uncertain about entering the war. The militarists oppose this move and the United States has indicated that a mere declaration would be insufficient.

Worksheets 3333 and 3334-Washington to Paris 1 March 1945-74 and 57 groups French message numbers 94 and 191.

Argentina is suspected of being sympathetic not only to the German Government, but also to the Nazi ideology. Nazi technicians have been infiltrating into Argentina and now occupy prominent positions in the army and industry. It appears that the American Government, backed by the majority of public opinion, will not change its attitude toward Argentina unless the Argentine radically modifies its approving attitude toward Naziism.

Worksheet 2946-Paris to Rio de Janeiro 21 Feb. 1945-107 groups French message number 279, circular 22.

It is reported from Berne that Germany is suffering from a transportation crisis. The Reichsbahnen are no longer useful. Communications are generally destroyed. There is a coal shortage in Bohemia and Moravia and the Skoda works may have to shut down. Fuel oil is very limited in supply, and air raids and Russian advances have destroyed synthetic gasoline production. 200,000 workers are required to finish 15 synthetic gasoline plants by August 1945. It is believed that the construction plans are merely intended to give the impression of a will for indefinite resistance.

Worksheet 1513-Stockholm to Paris 17 Jan. 1945-89 groups French message number 9145

The Soviet Embassy is optimistic about the coming offensive against Berlin. Despite 200 German divisions in the East, the Red Army has numerical superiority and expects a decision early in 1945.

Worksheet 4535-Stockholm to Paris 28 March 1945-61 groups
French message number 149

In Switzerland it is estimated that Germany will fall in two weeks. The Nazi Government will not give up, but the armies will surrender.

Worksheet 3192-Stockholm to Paris 27 Feb. 1945-72 groups
French message number 71

Swedish correspondents in Berlin report a fatalistic attitude on the part of the populace. The people no longer mention Hitler. The executions of party officials, who deserted their posts, have been greeted with public satisfaction. The press has taken clever advantage of the mistakes in Allied propaganda. There is little probability of a popular revolt. It is believed that a revolution, if any, will have to come from the army.

Worksheet 933-Borovec to Zagreb 23 Aug. 1944-276 groups
Jugoslavian (Croatian) message number 1

The Bulgarian foreign minister has stated that Bulgaria joined the Axis to keep peace in the Balkans. Thrace and Macedonia were occupied because they were essentially Bulgarian areas and because foreigners would have occupied if Bulgaria hadn't. Bulgaria claims that she never made active war against the Allies, and that she wishes to keep good relations with Russia and the Balkans. In the case of Russia, the burden is on the Soviet to remain friendly with Bulgaria.

Worksheet 762-Bucharest to Moscow 5 Sept. 1944-206 groups
Rumanian message number 365

Rumania protests the treatment of her fleet by the Russians. The Red Navy has taken over Constanza and the Danube fleet. Serious incidents have occurred. Rumania asks that Russia be more cooperative and follow Molotov's stated policy of cooperation. Rumania disclaims any responsibility for U-boat activity in the Black Sea, placing the onus on Germany. Rumania wants peaceful cooperation.

Worksheet 1018-Tokyo to Lisbon 3 Dec. 1944-78 groups
Portuguese message number 47

Japan expects early Russian entry into the Asiatic war. This is considered inevitable due to Russia's interests in the Far East.

Worksheet 816-Vatican to Madrid 18 June 1944-179 groups Portuguese Message number . .

It is expected that Kesselring will give up soon. German collapse is attributable to destruction of communications and transportation. The zones of occupation of the Allies are predicted to be: 1) Great Britian-France, Belgium. Holland, Norway and Rhineland. 2) Russia-Germany, bounded by the Baltic, the Danube and Balkan areas. 3) United States- Central Germany, (Bavaria and Austria).[58]

9. <u>Italian cryptanalytic results</u>. Brigadier General Vittorio Gamba, the Director of SIM Cryptographic Section, had a very low opinion of Italian signal intelligence activities. Gamba attributes the Italians' poor showing to a lack of capable personnel and a lack of sufficient funds.[59] Gamba sums up successes against the USA and Britain as follows, "It is a fact that at the time of the Armistice no results had been attained in breaking the cypher systems of military and diplomatic traffic from England and the United States."[60] Gamba does claim that photostats of the US State Department's "Brown" Code[61] were available to the Italians and that SIM succeeded in solving a British diplomatic five figure code and an unenciphered two-part four-letter code.[62] More detailed information regarding Italian cryptanalytic successes may be found in Chart 1 - 2.

[58]T766-T772; T1546-T1581.

[59]IF-1518, p 1.

[60]IF-1500, p 6.

[61]IF-1518, p 4.

[62]IF-1518, p 2.

VOLUME 8

CHAPTER II

Hungarian Cryptologic Activities

1. Hungary's cryptanalytic bureau was organized for large scale efforts. The Hungarian cryptanalytic bureau (exact name not available from TICOM sources although it is called Abteilung X in I 193) was directly under the command of the Chief of the Hungarian General Staff. Until Russian advances in 1944 endangered the group, it was located in the Honved (Ministry of Defense) in Budapest.[68] Under the direction of General von Petrikovics,[69] the cryptanalytic bureau was organized into ten sections with a total of about fifty personnel:

a. Turkish Section
b. English and American Section (England, North and South America, and Egypt)
c. French Section (France and Colonies, Switzerland, Greece, Belgium, and Netherlands)
d. Russian Section (Bulgaria, Yugoslavia, Czechoslovakia, and Russia)
e. Rumanian Section
f. Swedish Section (Sweden and Norway)
g. Italian Section (Italy and Vatican City)
h. Spanish Section (Spain and Portugal)
i. ?
j. Japanese Section (Japan and China)[70]

[68] I-21, p 2; I-193, p 2.

[69] I-21, p 3.

[70] I-193, p 3.

The cryptanalytic bureau averaged 4 or 5 persons to each section.[71] The key section was the Turkish section, in which Lt. Titus Vass, called "the ace Hungarian cryptanalyst," worked. Emphasis was placed on Turkish traffic because of the intelligence derived concerning Allied affairs.[72] The Russian and French sections were considered the next most valuable, and it is reported that the main Russian diplomatic system was also read until it changed near the end of the war.[73] Another report indicates that the emphasis was on Italian, Rumanian, and Polish systems.[74]

From 40 to 100 messages were decoded each day. They were sent to a representative of Office Six of Reich Main Security Office (RSHA VI), to Regent Horthy, to the Chief of the General Staff, the Foreign Minister, and to the "Minister President."[75]

Conflicting estimates of the success of Hungarian cryptanalysis are reported in TICOM sources. It is stated that the Hungarians depended on the Germans for the solution of many systems.[76] However, the Reich Main Security Office's (RSHA) liaison officer in Hungary states that the most important cryptanalytic intelligence available to his group came from the Hungarians.[77] It has also been stated that the Germans received a great volume of results from the Hungarians, and this is attributed to the influence of Ronge who had been intelligence chief of the Austro-Hungarian Empire.[78] A total of approximately 90 code books belonging to the Hungarian cryptanalytic bureau have been captured, indicating that they successfully broke codes of the following twelve countries: Belgium, Bulgaria, Denmark, France, Greece, Italy, Netherlands, Portugal, Rumania, Croatia, Sweden, and the Vatican.[79]

[72] I-193, p 3.

[73] I-193, p 3.

[74] I-21, p 2.

[75] I-193, p 4.

[76] I-21, p 2.

[77] I-193, p 2.

[78] IF-141, p 2.

[79] A-27.

Among the documented failures of the Hungarians are the Secret and Confidential codes of American Military Attachés. Although these codes were compromised 100% by the Hungarians they were turned over to the Italian Army Intelligence Service (SIM) because the encipherment could not be broken by the Hungarians. The Italians were successful in breaking it.[80] A German officer of Section E 1 of the Signal Intelligence Agency of the Commander in Chief of the Air Force (Chi-Stelle, Ob d L, Section E) was assigned on the request of the Hungarians to break a Rumanian Air Force cipher. Just as this officer announced that he was on the threshold of solution, he was returned to his German unit because of political reasons, and the Hungarians were forced to buy this system from parties not stated, instead of solving it.[81]

2. Germans considered the Hungarian intercept organization inferior. Personnel of the Signal Intelligence Agency of the Commander in Chief of the Air Force (Chi-Stelle Ob d L), which maintained intercept stations in Hungary, reported that the Hungarian intercept service was worthless and that the Hungarian traffic analysis reports were useless. They also stated that the Hungarians were "cagey."[82]

3. Hungarian-German liaison began in the 1920's. In the 1920's, liaison on cryptanalytic matters began between the Hungarians and the predecessors of the Signal Intelligence Agency of the Supreme Command, Armed Forces (OKW/Chi).[83] This early liaison was close[84] and the Germans worked on systems

[80] IF-1524, p 4.

[81] I-121, p 8.

[82] I-130, I-65, I-29.

[83] I-21, p 2.

[84] Wheels for the Hungarian Enigma were wired by the firm of Konski and Krueger in Berlin. The Signal Intelligence Agency of the Supreme Command, Armed Forces(OKW/Chi) was unable to copy the wirings because Hungarian employees of the firm changed the wirings at night so that they would not conform to the records kept of the wiring. I-84.

requested by the Hungarians.[85] There was never an actual exchange of liaison officers by the German agency and the Hungarians. This was true even during the war. Communications were through the Hungarian Embassy and through occasional social visits.[86]

Liaison with other German agencies began at the start of the war when the Reich Main Security Office (RSHA) and the Signal Intelligence Agency of the Commander in Chief of the Air Force (Chi Stelle, Ob d L) set up offices in Budapest.[87]

The German Air Force set up a socalled "Weather Station" (cover name) in Budapest in 1938. This station intercepted and cryptanalyzed Rumanian and Jugoslav traffic. Initially, its personnel were in civilian clothes.[88] Liaison with the Hungarian intercept service was always poor and the Hungarians were always considered inferior.[89]

Liaison with the Reich Main Security Office (RSHA)[90] was marked by great respect for Hungarian cryptanalytic ability. The Hungarians passed all decodes on to this group, and the more urgent messages were radioed back to Berlin by the Reich Main Security Office (RSHA). When the Hungarian intelligence units retreated to Eastern Bavaria in 1944 with the approach of the Russians, their retreat was aided by the liaison officers of the Reich Main Security Office (RSHA). It is believed that the Hungarian records were hidden in Eastern Bavaria.[91] It is possible that the documents recovered by TICOM at Eggenfeld are the ones referred to.[92]

[85] I-21, p 2.

[86] I-21, p 2.

[87] I-193, p 2; I-130; I-65; I-29.

[88] I-130, I-65.

[89] I-29, I-130.

[90] In 1944 the Reich Main Security Office (RSHA) purchased a Turkish code from the Hungarians. Examination showed that it had originally been broken by the Signal Intelligence Agency of the Supreme Command Armed Forces (OKW/Chi) in 1943 and then had been turned over to the Hungarians. I-132.

[91] I-193, p 4.

[92] A-27.

Liaison with the Italians on cryptanalytic matters appears to have been very good. The Hungarians maintained liaison officers in Rome and made the results of their work available to the Italians.[93]

[93] IF-1500, p 7.

VOLUME 8

CHAPTER III

Finnish Signal Intelligence Organization

13. Finnish "Radio Intelligence Company" cryptanalyzed military, naval and diplomatic traffic. Finnish signal intelligence activities were a function of a Radio Intelligence Company (called Radio Telegraph Kompanie, abbreviated "RTK," by the Germans; Finnish name not given by TICOM sources) which was subordinate to the Finnish General Staff's military intelligence organization (name not known).[98] This Radio Intelligence Company apparently concerned itself with military, naval, and diplomatic traffic.[99] TICOM sources make no reference to any other cryptanalytic organization, or to any organization which dealt with Finnish cryptography.

The Radio Intelligence Company (RTK) consisted of a cryptanalytic unit, an intercept unit, and an evaluation unit. It was of battalion strength.[100] Its headquarters were at Sortavala. The cryptanalytic unit, under the command of Captain Erkki Pale, had a strength which was estimated to be of from 20 to 70

[98] I-106, p 3; I-31.

[99] I-31, I-12, I-16, I-142, I-78, I-120 and I-106.

[100] I-106, p 3.

cryptanalysts.[101] A Col. Hallama has been reported as head of the Finnish cipher section.[102]

Germans, interrogated by TICOM on the subject of Finnish cryptanalysis, unanimously agreed that the Finnish cryptanalysts were of the highest calibre and considered them an even match for their own analysts.[103]

14. <u>Finnish cryptanalysts were successful within the narrow definition of their mission.</u> The emphasis of Finnish cryptanalysis was placed on Russian traffic, particularly of a military and naval nature; secondary consideration was given to Polish, Swedish, Rumanian, and American traffic.[104]

The Finns succeeded in reconstructing the Russian five-figure code used during the first Russo-Finnish War. This book was given to the Germans by the Finnish General Staff.[105] The Russians were aware of the Finnish ability and issued instructions to their cipher officers which attributed Finnish successes to violations of security. It is interesting to note that the Russians did not admit the possibility of cryptanalysis of their systems, but they did emphasize the traffic analysis and monitoring aspects.[106] Other achievements against the Russians were the identification of the additive for a four-figure naval system[107] and the solution of a five figure "double substitution"[108] and the solution of three-figure and four-figure codes, especially Russian Secret Police Codes.[109]

[101] I-31, I-106 p 3, I-116.

[102] I-96.

[103] I-106 p 3, I-16, I-111, I-31, I-116.

[104] I-31, I-106 p 3.

[105] I-78.

[106] I-120 p 40.

[107] I-12 pp 14-15.

[108] I-16 p 2.

[109] I-106 pp 4-5, I-21 p 2.

DOCID: 3560798

Other instances of Finnish successes were: Reading of the American strip system, which the Germans called AM 10, and the reading of a Swedish diplomatic system which disclosed the fact that the M-94 was readable.[110]

15. Finnish intercept was well done, but the evaluation unit was not very competent. The intercept unit of the Radio Intelligence Company (RTK) consisted of a fixed station at company headquarters (approximately 200 men), four other fixed stations, and one motorized company.[111] Despite the age and variety of Finnish intercept and direction finding equipment, the Germans considered the Finnish intercept work to be of good quality and depended on the Finns for interception in the Baltic area and for long range direction finding.[112] The Russian security instructions, discussed in Paragraph 2 above, emphasized the ability of the Finnish intercept unit.[113]

The Germans considered the Finnish evaluation unit to be disorganized and attributed its incompetence to the emphasis placed on cryptanalysis. This unit consisted of about 20 persons.[114]

16. Finnish-German liaison was well organized and effective. Finnish-German liaison existed prior to 1939 and continued until Finland's final capitulation to Russia. The following German Signal Intelligence organizations maintained liaison with the Finns: Signal Intelligence Battalion 11 (NAA 11),[115] Control Station for Signal Intelligence (LNA),[116]

[110] I-31, I-142.

[111] I-106, p 3.

[112] I-16, I-106 p 4.

[113] I-120 p 40.

[114] I-116 p 10, I-106 p 3.

[115] I-106.

[116] I-106 p 3.

24

Signal Intelligence Agency of Army High Command (OKH/ G d NA),[117] Signal Intelligence Agency of Navy High Command (OKM/ 4 SKL/ III),[118] Signal Intelligence Agency of Supreme Command Armed Forces (OKW/Chi),[119] and the Reich Main Security Office (RSHA).[120]

Not only was there direct and large scale interchange of work on Russian systems,[121] but there was also interchange on such matters as the American strip system AM 10,[122] general intercept and direction finding problems,[123] and there is an instance where Finland turned over a translation of a Swedish message which stated that the M 94 was readable.[124]

Liaison consisted of courier service, regular meetings[125] and interchanges arranged by the Finnish General Staff.[126] For such purposes, Germany maintained headquarters (not named) at Tallinn, Esthonia; and there were also Germans in Finland at Kirkenes, Mikkeli, and Sortavala.[127]

At the conclusion of the Finnish-Russian War, the Signal Intelligence Agency of the Supreme Command Armed Forces (OKW/ Chi) invited the Finns to join it. No word was heard from the Finns after they crossed the Finnish-Swedish border.[128]

[117] I-21, I-111.

[118] I-12.

[119] I-12, I-31.

[120] I-193.

[121] I-12, I-31, I-16, I-106.

[122] I-31.

[123] I-106.

[124] I-142.

[125] It is observed that the Finns had one female representative at all these meetings I-31.

[126] I-31, I-78, I-12.

[127] I-12, I-106.

[128] I-96.

Liaison between Finland and Hungary is reported to have been close. The Germans assumed that the Hungarians who came to Berlin were on their way to Finland.[129]

17 Friendly Finnish-German relations did not preclude German cryptanalysis of Finnish systems. Although Senior Specialist Dr. Erich Huettenhain of the Signal Intelligence Agency of the Supreme Command Armed Forces (OKW/Chi) stated that no Finnish systems were read,[130] Abteilungen 9 and 6 of Hauptabteilung IV (Entzifferung) worked on Finnish traffic[131] and Abteilung 6 read at least one Finnish Hagelin message that was 4000 letters long.[132] It is also indicated that Goering's Research Bureau (FA) broke into "Finnish or Swedish" Hagelin messages several times on the basis of cribs.[133]

[129] I-21.

[130] I-31.

[131] I-31.

[132] I-54.

[133] I-25.

VOLUME 8

CHAPTER IV

Bulgarian Signal Intelligence

18. Bulgarian cryptanalytic ability is an unknown quantity. TICOM sources provide only a single reference to the Bulgarian cryptanalytic agency. In 1944, Group IV of the Signal Intelligence Agency of the Supreme Command Armed Forces (OKW/Chi) trained Bulgarians in a special course in cryptanalysis. Lt. Col. Mettig of that agency stated that General Staff Major Gentscheff, head of the Bulgarian cryptanalytic agency, was not enthusiastic about this course.[138]

19. Bulgarian-German liaison hardly existed. In or about 1940, the Signal Intelligence Agency of the Supreme Command Armed Forces (OKW/Chi) projected plans for the setting up of intercept stations in Bulgaria. Only one such station was completed. It is not known whether Bulgaria knew of this station. This station, which was located at Varna, was for the German Air Force. Under the cover name of "Kommando Nordland", this station employed 22 persons in civilian clothes. Five receivers were used to cover Syrian, Greek, and Mediterranean ferry flight traffic. No cryptanalysis was done; all enciphered traffic was sent back to the Signal Intelligence Agency of the Supreme Command, Armed Forces (OKW/Chi)[139]

[138] I-96, p 5.

[139] I-65, p 3.

VOLUME 8

CHAPTER V

Austrian Cipher Bureau

20. Austrian Cipher Bureau was small but active. The "Austrian Cipher Bureau"[144] was under the direction of Dr. Otto Klob until October 1935, when he was succeeded by Dr. Seifert. Its size and its relationship to other government bureaus is not known from TICOM reports.[145] The Cipher Bureau appeared to suffer from a shortage of personnel and from the many vacations provided by Austrian Civil Service. It must have been small, because a "catastrophic personnel shortage" was averted when three new members joined the organization in November 1935.[146]

The Austrian Cipher Bureau actively cryptanalyzed or intercepted the diplomatic traffic of the following countries: Belgium, Bulgaria, Czechoslovakia, France, Greece, Hungary, Italy, Jugoslavia, Poland, Rumania, Russia, Serbia (sic), Spain, Turkey, United Kingdom, and United States.[147] There is no evidence of cryptanalysis in naval or military traffic.

Although the major effort was expended on codes, there is some evidence of ability in the cryptanalysis of the Enigma Cipher Machine. The Austrians were asked by the Netherlands Government for an opinion on the security of the Enigma Cipher Machine. The Austrian Cipher Bureau rated it insecure on the

[144] so called in T 3614.

[145] T 84 I 118 T 3614.

[146] T 3614.

[147] T 3614 I 118, p 3.

basis of having read German messages enciphered by the Enigma.[148] The Enigma involved was probably the commercial type (without plugboard) as the incident occurred prior to 1938.[149]

21. Austrian Cipher Bureau was in close liaison with Germany. The closest possible liaison existed between the Austrian Cipher Bureau and the Signal Intelligence Agency of the Supreme Command, Armed Forces (OKW/Chi) and its predecessor, the Cipher Bureau of the German War Ministry.[150] This relationship was a secret held by only the highest officials. There was a constant interchange of traffic and results of cryptanalysis. The interchange was through the German Embassy in Vienna and a cipher system was used for secret messages between the two agencies. Social relationships were maintained. Secret assistance was given by the Germans to the Austriah Cipher Bureau in collecting evidence for treason trials. All of this took place at a time(1935, 1936,and 1937)when the world believed antagonism was apparent in the official relationships of Germany and Austria.[151]

When Anschluss was effected in 1938, four of the outstanding cryptanalysts of the Austrian Cipher Bureau, including its head, Dr. Seifert, became members of the German Signal Intelligence Agency of the Supreme Command, Armed Forces (OKW/Chi).[152]

Austrian liaison was not confined to the Germans. There is some evidence of liaison with the Dutch[153] and with the Hungarians regarding Serbian traffic.[154]

[148] I-142, p 4.

[149] I-78.

[150] I-118, p 3; T-3614.

[151] T-3614.

[152] T-3614; I-118, p 3; I-84.

[153] I-142, p 4.

[154] T-3614.

VOLUME 8

CHAPTER VI

Army Ordnance, Development and Testing Group, Signal Branch

22. Ordnance group developed German Army signal equipment. German Army signal equipment was developed and tested by the Army Ordnance, Development and Testing Group, Signal Branch (Chef der Heeresruestung und Befehlshaber des Ersatzheeres, Amtsgruppe fuer Entwicklung und Pruefung des Heereswaffenamts, Waffenpruefung, Abteilung 7, abbreviated Wa Pruef 7). This was one of twelve such branches for ordnance testing and development. It was itself broken down into seven groups, as follows:

Group I (Wa Pruef 7/I) procured raw materials and small equipment;

Group II (Wa Pruef 7/II) developed telephone and telegraph equipment and ciphony (ciphony was transferred to III in 1942).

Group III (Wa Pruef 7/III) developed radio communication equipment, teleprinter, facsimile and television equipment, ciphony and cipher devices.

Group IV (Wa Pruef 7/IV) developed radio intercept, direction finding and ciphony deciphering equipment.

Group V (Wa Pruef 7/V) developed permanent communications equipment for permanent installations.

Section VI (Wa Pruef 7, Referat VI) developed chemical and flare signal equipment.

Group VII (Wa Pruef 7/VII) developed radio remote control devices for rockets.[159]

[159] I-82, I-131.

23. Signal Branch was active in the engineering development of manual cipher machines.[160] The Development and Testing Group, Signal Branch (Wa Pruef 7) was entrusted with the engineering and development of many of the improvements on the Army Enigma. One of these was the variable notch rotor (Lueckenfuellerwalze) which was suggested by the Signal Intelligence Agency of the Supreme Command, Armed Forces (OKW/Chi).[161] To accommodate the new rotor, the Signal Branch (Wa Pruef 7) suggested that several positions of the "on-off" switch be omitted and that the keying pressure be changed to 1000 grams.[162] Signal Branch also developed printing attachments for both the Army and Navy Enigmas.[163]

The proposed new Enigma, SG 39, which was to combine motion features of the Hagelin machine with the Enigma cipher maze, was also engineered by the Signal Branch.[164]

Another of the Signal Branch's engineering and development problems was the SG 41, a keyboard Hagelin with interlocking motion. This device was suggested by Senior Inspector Menzer of the Signal Intelligence Agency, Supreme Command Armed Forces (OKW/Chi). The machine had two forms: the standard keyboard and the ten value keyboard for enciphering weather synoptics.[165]

Signal Branch (Wa Pruef 7) engineered other ideas of Senior Inspector Menzer. Among these were: production of an aluminum cipher grille ("Raster"),[166] which was abandoned in that form before being placed into use; the engineering and development of the "cipher box" (Schluesselkasten); and the "cipher disc" (Schluesselscheibe).[167] These last two items were developed

[160] Cipher and ciphony devices described in this and following paragraphs are more fully explained in Volume 2.

[161] I-57, p 7; D-59.

[162] D-59, p 22.

[163] D-59.

[164] D-59, p 22 p 26.

[165] I-72; D-59, p 16; I-57.

[166] D-59.

[167] I-96, 157.

simultaneously for the Reich Main Security Office (RSHA) as well as for the Army.[168]

There is no statement in the TICOM interrogations that the Signal Branch (Wa Pruef 7) had exclusive engineering control over the above developments, but indications are that it was perhaps the co-ordinator and controller wherever it joined with commercial firms in its work.

The same condition applies to teleprinters and ciphony, which are described below.

24. Signal Branch engineered teleprinter cipher devices. The teleprinter cipher attachments (Schluesselzusaetze) and the secret teleprinters (Schluesselfernschreibmaschinen)[169] were worked on by Signal Branch (Wa Pruef 7) for the Army. The major portion of this developmental work was under the direction of Dr. Werner Liebknecht.

A synchronizing device (Gleichlauf) to be used on teleprinter circuits to permit them to operate uninterruptedly for 24-hour periods, was also being considered by the Signal Branch (Wa Pruef 7)[170] in closest cooperation with Dr. Vierling of the Feuerstein laboratories.

25. Signal Branch was active in the development of ciphony. Signal Branch (Wa Pruef 7) was also engaged in development of German Army ciphony and the development of equipment for the interception and decipherment of enemy ciphony transmissions. This latter function was carried on mainly at its permanent intercept development station at Staats.[171] This installation was in a cave.

Work on German ciphony devices was carried on in cooperation with Dr. Oskar Vierling who directed the Feuerstein laboratory.[172]

[168] I-96.

[169] I-57, D-59.

[170] I-57, D-59.

[171] I-58.

[172] IF-15, See Volume 2, Chapter V.

None of the experiments reached the stage where complete security was believed to have been achieved. Types worked on included frequency inversion, which was abandoned in 1942, Time-Delay ("Tigerstedt"); the "Stepping Stones" (Bausteine), which were frequency scramblers;[173] and noise superimposition devices. For noise superimposition tests, a ciphony link was set up by direction of the Signal Branch between Athens, Crete, and Derna.[174] This link failed to produce satisfactory results.[175]

26. <u>Signal Branch tested Non-Morse intercept equipment.</u> Intercept equipment for Russian three-and nine-channel transmissions was designed.[176] Success was achieved in intercepting the Baudot link between Paris and Moscow.[177] Equipment was also designed for the intercept of American Baudot transmissions.[178] Study of captured French three-channel equipment was carried on at German stations at Berlin and Bordeaux, with an attempt to improve the equipment by the introduction of frequency modulation, but the design proved to be faulty. Some of the French equipment was later found stored by the Signal Branch at the Feuerstein Laboratory.[179]

[173] I-57, I-96.

[174] I-57.

[175] I-57.

[176] I-58, I-64.

[177] I-131, I-58.

[178] I-64.

[179] I-110.

VOLUME 8

CHAPTER VII

The Radio Defense Corps of the Armed Forces.

27. Radio Defense Corps attempted to locate Allied agents' radio transmitters. The Radio Defense Corps of the Armed Forces (Oberkommando der Wehrmacht, Wehrmacht Nachrichtenverbindung, Funkueberwachung, abbreviated OKW/WNV/Fu) had as its mission the following tasks:

a. To locate, primarily by direction finding, all high frequency and very high frequency transmitters of illicit traffic within Axis Europe.

b. To evaluate illicit transmissions in regard to their nationality, their relation to net or control stations, their schedules, their probable missions and their potential value as a source of intelligence or counter-intelligence.

c. To intercept illicit traffic where valuable to Inspectorate 7/VI (In 7/VI); or

d. To capture and destroy agents and their transmitters when the Reich Main Security Office (RSHA) did not do so; or

e. To capture and employ such agents and their transmitters for counter-intelligence.

Approximately 2500 persons were engaged in these activities. During World War II the Radio Defense Corps was successful in the following instances:

a. It predicted and spotted all attacks on the German "Colmar bridgehead", in January 1945, by traffic analysis of French agent traffic in that locality.

[184] This chapter is based on IF-176, IF-140-B and I-115.

DOCID: 3560798

b. It located and captured a large Russian spy net which was known as the "Schulze-Boysen" net.

c. It located, intercepted, and furnished information for the capture of a net carrying illicit Czechoslovakian traffic.

d. It located, intercepted, and occasionally broke up traffic nets of Marshal Tito's agents.

e. It located an Italian test transmitter said by the Italians to be proof against direction finding.

f. It provided men, equipment, and information to Luftwaffe night fighters for locating and destroying Allied airborne agent control stations.

g. It set up an IBM section for recording and traffic analysis of unknown traffic.

The Radio Defense Corps failed as follows:

a. It could not maintain effective control over illicit traffic originating in France.

b. It could not control the Mihailovitch-Cairo traffic.

c. It could not control illicit transmissions in Warsaw.

d. It did not maintain effective liaison with the Reich Main Security Office (RSHA).

e. It had almost no liaison with the Italians.

The Radio Defense Corps was of the opinion that it could have performed more effectively if the Supreme Command had allocated more personnel to it.

28. Radio Defense Corps easily located American agents' transmitters at the beginning of the war. The Radio Defense Corps held the following opinions of the ability of Allied agents:

a. United States: initially poor with marked improvement toward the end of the war.

b. Great Britain: generally one of the best and unbreakable at the end of the war due to new procedures and the general breakdown of the Radio Defense Corps.

c. France: medium quality but with a tremendous advantage derived from the cooperation of a great portion of the French population.

d. Poland: very good especially in respectto mobility of transmitters.

e. Russia: technically poor but with a massive organization that precluded all but superficial German counter measures.

35

DOCID: 3560798

According to the Radio Defense Corps, measures that could have been taken by agents to make the location and recognition of their transmitters most difficult were:

a. The camouflage of agent traffic as authorized traffic of the country in which the agent was operating.

b. The camouflage of the agent control station traffic as regular traffic normally issuing from the country of origin.

c. The frequent change of frequency and time of transmission.

d. The frequent change of the position of the transmitter.

Measures that could have made locating of very high frequency transmitters difficult and ineffectual include:

a. The operation of transmitters on 6 to 12 meters, only at locations close to the front.

b. The use in each net of two separate frequencies by control station and the agent.

c. The elimination of transmissions in clear.

d. The use of very low power outputs.

e. The instruction of agents in the proper use of equipment so that messages would be copied completely on the first transmission.

29. Radio Defense Corps was not alone in its field. There were other organizations whose work paralleled or interlocked with the Radio Defense Corps:

a. The Military Intelligence Radio Supervising Office (Abwehr, Abteilung III Funkueberwachung 3) did direction finding for military intelligence purposes.

b. The 3rd Battalion Air Signals Regiment 352 (LN Regt 352) and its predecessors cooperated in direction finding.

c. The Reich Main Security Office (RSHA) and the Secret Field Police (Sicherheitsdienst Kommando, abbreviated S D Kommando and Sicherheits Polizei, abbreviated SIPO) normally handled the arrest and interrogation of agents in such a way that the work of the Radio Defense Corps in counter-intelligence was hindered.

d. Cryptanalysis for the Radio Defense Corps was done by Inspectorate 7/VI (In 7/VI).

VOLUME 8

CHAPTER VIII

Laboratorium Feuerstein

30. History of Feuerstein Laboratory. One of the more fully exploited TICOM targets was the Laboratory Feuerstein which was located on a small mountain near Ebermannstadt in Upper Franconia some 15 miles from Bamberg and was owned and operated by Dr. Oskar Vierling. Since the laboratory and many of its projects have been described in considerable detail in special reports (In particular: I-43; E-7 to E-19)[189] and since evaluation and exploitation of the technical data in these reports is a matter for electronic engineers, the present chapter attempts merely a résumé of the history of the laboratory and a brief account of projects undertaken.

Essential to an understanding of the whole is the personality of the owner-director, Dr. Vierling. He was born in 1904 in Straubing and raised in a small town near Ebermannstadt. His parents were poor and after his local schooling he attended a school for mechanics in Nuernberg 1923/25. He then obtained a job as laboratory assistant in the National Office of Telegraph Technology in Berlin and after three years there joined the Heinrich Hertz Institute in 1928 to do oscillator research. During his ten years at the Institute he obtained his doctorate at the University of Berlin and contributed a number of papers on acoustics to reputable scientific journals. He also carried on private research for several concerns and was allowed to keep the income from his work.

In 1938 Dr. Vierling went to Hannover as director of high frequency and electro-acoustic research at the Technische Hochschule (graduate school of technology) there. Since the opportunities for advancement were slight, he proposed in 1939 joining the Siemens staff but was advised to start a private laboratory instead. This he did and Siemens paid a monthly retainer fee of 2000 marks for an option on all inventions. When this laboratory was bombed out, the site near Ebermannstadt was purchased, and Laboratorium Feuerstein (named for the mountain on which it sat) constructed. As Dr. Vierling's funds were inadequate he sought a loan from the German Army, but since the terms would have deprived him of real control, he sought and secured a bank loan which enabled him to complete the work. A small group remained in the vicinity of Hannover in charge of Dr. Sennheiser,[190] an associate who had purchased a part interest in that laboratory. From the time it opened in 1942 to the end of the war, the new laboratory at Feuerstein was subject to the usual "party" supervision.

For reasons of expediency, Dr. Vierling joined the "party" but seems to have been conspicuous by his failure to attend meetings and take any active part in party activities.[191] Close liaison was maintained with large manufacturing concerns which were to take over projects as soon as they reached production stage. Dr. Vierling claimed that his success in keeping his laboratory open was chiefly due to the fact that the larger concerns did not care to spend their time doing research on problems of a military nature with no peace-time applications. By standing well with the armed forces, Dr. Vierling seems to have been able to get high priorities despite his poor standing in the Party and even to have succeeded in doing a little work on the side on pet longrange projects not associated with the war.[192]

Shortly before the German collapse, Dr. Vierling was ordered to remove the speech privacy projects to the Bavarian Alps. Eventually a small laboratory was fitted up near Lofer in the Berchtesgaden area with Dr. Wilhem Göing[193] in charge but little was accomplished there. Dr. Vierling took the

[190] M-12.

[191] M-12, p 4.

[192] E-7.

[193] Göing was the Party representative at Feuerstein and documents were found showing that he was out for Vierling's scalp. M-12, p 4.

opportunity to rid himself of his ardent Nazis using the good excuse that they would be the most reliable persons to accompany the equipment south. He had also been ordered to destroy all other projects and equipment, but once the Nazis were gone he concealed much of his best equipment in the bombproof vault, screening it from inspectors by putting up a false wall, and hid a number of parts at various places in the vicinity. This done, he awaited developments.

When the laboratory was found by TICOM Team #4, it was being used as a German military hospital. When Dr. Vierling and some of his collaborators were found, they proved quite willing to tell about their work and to cooperate in restoring the laboratory to working condition and in reassembling dismantled projects. Under the direction of the TICOM investigators the available force of some 30 persons rushed work on selected projects and made new drawings to replace those destroyed. Dr. Vierling hoped this might help him keep his organization going during the transition period, feeling sure that he would later be able to employ his people on non-military research in acoustics.

The laboratory, consisting of a main building, two small special laboratories, Dr. Vierling's house, and some storage facilities, has been described in detail and photographed.[194] It is said to have been well built and admirably equipped.[195] Dr. Vierling said the investment in land, buildings, equipment and supplies amounted to 1,285,000 marks, equal in prewar exchange to $480,000.

As of Aug. 15, 1945, some 30 persons were engaged in work under TICOM direction. These included 10 engineers and physicists, 4 technicians, 6 mechanics, and 10 miscellaneous workers.[196] Apparently during the war a peak of 150 - 200 was

[194] E-7, E-17.

[195] Some notion of the adequacy of its equipment may be gained from the Appendices to E-7: App. b - instruments; App. c - sheet metal and forge shop tools; App. D - machine shop turning tools; App. E - 23 German scientific periodicals regularly received by the library; App. F - a list of Foreign periodicals Dr. Vierling would like to receive.

[196] See block diagram of Figure 5 apperded to E-7, and for some notes on five key men see E-7 App. G.

reached with many workers either over age or just out of school. Rules governing employment are interesting.[197] Wages seem to have been those usual for comparable work elsewhere in Germany while working conditions were superior. The staff seems to have worked in tolerable harmony.[198] A list of personnel is available in one of the TICOM publications.[199]

31. Special TICOM engineering team studied signal projects. When the hospital had been evacuated, and a special TICOM engineering team had assembled at Feuerstein late in July, the preliminary lists of projects were discussed, and certain groups of related projects were selected for intensive study. Dr. Vierling, who was quite willing to cooperate, started to clear out debris, recall key men, and reassemble equipment. The selected projects were set up, missing diagrams redrawn, and descriptions written. A decision by higher authority resulted on 16 August in the arrest of Dr. Vierling, the dispersal of his staff, and the dismantling of the laboratory, but in the time available much was accomplished. In the following paragraphs the major projects studied are enumerated without technical details.

a. Filter Design. Inasmuch as much of the work at Feuerstein depended for success upon accurate filters, and since Dr. Glubrecht, the expert in this field, seemed to have a knack with such designs, he was asked to design filters to meet difficult, though not impossible specifications, and to explain both his computations and his reasons for the selections he made. In this way the TICOM engineering team hoped to arrive at a reasonable estimate of the efficiency of his methods.[200] Standard type toroid coils and commercial condensers were used.

b. High Speed transmitters for agent's use. Four separate projects were involved:

197 E-18.

198 An exception was the case of Zappe who had been arrested for irregularities and disliked Dr. Vierling, cf. E-19, pp 5 and 10.

199 M-6.

200 E-12; E-7, p 43; M-4a m.

(1) an automatic high speed signal generator,
(2) a light weight transmitter,
(3) a carrier regenerator on the receiver, and
(4) a single side band demodulator.

When the dial of the signal generator was turned to any given letter a signal was generated and recorded on a steel wire or tape. This wire was run at high speed through the head of the transmitter (Taube) to make interception difficult, if not impossible. The carrier regenerator (Spitz) was originally designed to restore the suppressed carrier, while the single side band demodulator (Kaethe) received the intermediate frequency signal from an ordinary receiver (two instruments could be connected to demodulate two side bands independently). An interesting departure from American and British practice was that all filtering of carrier and side bands was at about 15 kc rather than at 100 kc.

Aside from the high speed, this equipment was intended to reduce tuning to a minimum, so that short messages might be sent with little risk of detection. It was said to be rather good.[201]

c. Speech Scramblers and associated equipment. The major speech scrambling project still under development at the end of the war was treated under three heads:

(1) A converter of the "Dudley" type consisting of an analyser and a synthesizer. The former measured certain features of speech and reported these measurements in the form of a small number of smoothly varying voltages which together constituted a running description of what was spoken into the microphone. The synthesizer used such a set of signal voltages to control an artificial speech reconstruction process resulting in a fair imitation of the original.

(2) Three fold wobbling the actual scrambling process, was the second step. As projected, the device would provide three stages of re-entrant band shifting, however, the device was only partially constructed.

(3) The wobbling called for a wobbling generator. A modified version of teleprinter cipher attachment SZ 42 was to supply the necessary key to render the whole secure.

[201] M-4a; E-8 pp. 8, 2 and 6; E-7 pp. 46, 48, 50.

41

Particular features proved of interest, but doubt was expressed by American engineers as to the practicability of the apparatus as a whole.[202]

d. Crystal controlled synchronization of cipher teleprinters (Gleichlauf).

Next to the speech scrambling devices, this seems to have attracted most attention. A quartz crystal 'mechanical' frequency generator [203] represented the first stage in this development. The synchronizating of two stations would be cut to a minimum since, once synchronized, both would run synchronously for 24 hours without resetting and send out enciphered space signals when no message was being transmitted. Such continuous transmission with adequate length of key would render it almost impossible for intercepters to determine where a message began or ended. The controlled synchronization would also overcome difficulties from interference and fading of signals and minimize the need for repetition of long parts of a message.

Intended for use with teleprinter cipher attachments of the SZ 42 type, the Gleichlauf project included, not merely development of the synchronizer, but also improvement in the cipher device itself, so that considerable information was obtained at Feuerstein respecting proposed changes in the Lorenz SZ machines.[204] Moreover, as above suggested, Dr. Vierling had visions of incorporating this principle in his speech scrambler. Rather full details were obtained.[205]

e. Teleprinter cipher attachments. In connection with the Gleichlauf problem several Lorenz cipher machines (SZ 38 and SZ 42) were turned over to Feuerstein for study. Vierling was to adapt them to the use of his synchronizer and also to improve the cipher mechanism and hence all Lorenz ideas in this connection were passed on to him. In consequence a fair picture of all contemplated changes could be secured.[206]

[202] Vocoder: E-10; E-7 p. 21; M-4a p. Three fold wobbler: E-11; E-7, p. 26; M-4a p. Gleichlauf: E-13; E-7, p. 37; M-4a n; I-43.

[203] M-4a h.

[204] E-14.

[205] I-43; E-13; E-14; E-7, p. 37; M-4a n.

[206] E-14.

32. Other Feuerstein projects were varied in nature. Feuerstein Laboratory projects of secondary importance to the TICOM engineering team were:

a. Acoustic torpedo: Feuerstein engineers (were used to) designed acoustic and filter components, AEG manufactured the torpedo.[207]

b. Schornsteinfeger, an anti-radar coating for submarines: depended on quarter (later eighth) wave length absorption.[208]

c. Nachtfee, a night fighter control system: based on phase modulation.[209]

d. Block circuit (wave trap) for intercept purposes. About the size of a matchbox, cheap and very efficient. Eliminated powerful, fixed stations thus permitting reception of weak signals. None found although produced in some number.[210]

e. Multiple frequency generation from one crystal: specially designed multi-vibrator circuits gave fully stable frequencies which were not harmonics of the basic crystal frequency. The model covered 80 spot frequencies with output of some 80 watts. Important to the Germans whose supply of crystals was limited.

f. Commercial radio receiver. High selectivity and sensitivity, used untuned IF and RF cirucits and replaced tuned circuits by filters. Sole tuning control was a tuned oscillator circuit. Essentially an efficient electrical band spread eliminating difficulty of HF tuning.

g. Voice frequency spectrograph. Two constructed for the laboratory with accuracy of 10-7.

h. Speech stretcher. Device permits recording on steel tape and reproducing at half (or double) speed without change of pitch. Valuable in increasing intelligibility of speech obscured by noise or high speed and where unknown dialects were involved.[211]

[207] Partial description in E-7, p. 54.

[208] Vierling stated that the only good protection was produced by IG.Farben. E-7, p. 55.

[209] See E-7, p. 54. USN got two complete sets.

[210] M-2.

[211] E-7, p. 36.

43

i. High output centimetric transmitter. Work was done at Hannover on a high output Magnetron transmitter and a continuous output of 2 kw had been attained. Vierling told of work at Erlangen on a Klystron transmitter giving a much higher output.

j. Electronic calculator. Would solve equations up to and including N^6; resolve equations to sine and cosine functions where N^0 is represented by a fundamental frequency whose amplitude is proportionate to the coefficient and the second and third harmonics, etc. The result was to be obtained instantaneously both as an Elysian figure and as a spot on a cathode ray tube.[212]

[212] E-7, p 50.

VOLUME 8

Chapter IX

Cryptologic Activities of the German Meteorological Service

33. German Meteorological Service was located in Berlin. The German Meteorological Service (Reich Wetterdienst) was located near Berlin at Glindow, Potsdam.[217] The Berlin headquarters, known as the Central Weather Service Group (Zentralwetterdienstgruppe), expanded during the war to include a secondary headquarters in Athens.[218] Little is reported in TICOM sources concerning the formal organization and size of the Service. It is reported that a cryptanalytic section was headed by a Senior Inspector Naumann who directed 10 specialists and 20 to 30 helpers.[219] The intercept and other functions of the Service were carried out by the Meteorological Intercept Control (Wetternachrictenueberwachung, abbreviated Wenueb) which was located at Glindow.[220] This group covered transmissions of German, German allied, and enemy weather reports.

An outstanding feature of the German Meteorological Service's organization was its close cooperation with the

[217] I-84, p 7.

[218] I-102, p 2.

[219] I-84, p 7.

[220] I-194, p 8.

German Air Force. Liaison extended down to the individual Luftflotten and to the various Signal Units of the German Air Force.[222] All German Air Force Signal Intelligence Units had standing orders to pass all weather information to the nearest weather station. This information was derived primarily from enemy planes in the area.[223] A weather evaluator was placed in Section B of the Chi/Stelle to expedite the handling of all weather data and messages and to see that the German Meteorological Service received all captured material relating to weather.[224] Cooperation with the German Air Force was hampered by poor communications during the early phases of the German campaigns in the Balkans and Russia.

Communications within the German Meteorological Service were normally by teleprinter networks in clear. This applied to communications within the occupied area in Russia. However, within German-allied areas such as Rumania, teleprinter traffic was enciphered.[225]

It may be inferred that weather reporting within the German framework was generally carried on in the usual manner. An example of the occasional unusual method is the dropping of parachutists behind the Russian lines for the purpose of sending back weather reports.[226]

34. Cryptographic Machines of the German Meteorological Service were those used by the German Army. For transmission of synoptics the German Meteorological Service originally used the international five-figure code with encipherment by means of substitution tables for the initial digraph and the final trigraph of each group. The period for each table was three hours. This system was dropped because the operators could not distinguish between clear code and the enciphered version;

[222] I-194.

[223] I-109.

[224] I-109.

[225] I-194, p 8.

[226] I-194, pp 10-11.

this resulted in security violations. To circumvent this difficulty, the five-figure group was represented as a six-figure group. The final digit of the first trigraph and the initial digit of the second trigraph represented the third digit of the original five-figure group. The six figures were then enciphered in the form of two trigraphs and transmitted as a six-figure group.

The substitution tables for the six-figure traffic were known as Siegfried tables. From 1943 on, Rumania, Hungary, and Bulgaria used the German six-figure system with a special set of substitution tables. Previous to this, an additive was used for the reports. Stations located at operational headquarters at the front used the six-figure system with a special set of tables. Earlier these front stations had used a "hand key" to obviate the need for distribution of tables.[227] Eventually, on the Eastern front the plugboard Enigma was used to encipher weather reports and cipher instructions of the German Meteorological Service.[228]

In 1943 and 1944, when the Germans became very active in Hungary, the reports (statements of general weather conditions, e. g., Fair and Warmer) were enciphered by use of a rectangle containing a limited vocabulary and three sets of sliding strips. The strips were used for a 3 or 4 month period. Regular synoptics were enciphered on the plugboard Enigma. This rectangle system was also used in 1943 by small airfields in the Crimea.[229]

One of the most common weather reporting systems was the Zenit Code. The Zenit Code was used originally in its form, but later its letter groups, and still later its figure groups, were enciphered. The Zenit Code was used by reconnaissance planes to report weather conditions over enemy territory. Allied air superiority forced the discontinuance of reports made while over enemy territory, and a time lag resulted when reports had to be delayed until the reconnaissance plans were again over German territory. As a supplement to the Zenit Code another code known as the Astra Figures was introduced.[230]

[227] I-194, pp 10-11.

[228] I-194, p 11.

[229] I-194, p 6.

[230] I-194, p 7.

Two other common systems for the encipherment of meteorological data were the Barbara Key, which was known to the Allies from 1939 on, but was not replaced until 1945, and the Raster, which was introduced in 1944. The Barbara Key is supposed to have been replaced by a new, and undescribed system prepared by Referat II B of Signal Intelligence Agency of the Supreme Command of the Armed Forces (OKW/Chi).[231]

The other machine beside the Enigma which has been mentioned for weather use was the Cipher Machine 41 a, Hagelin with interlocking motion, which was to have been used either with the standard keyboard or as a special model with 10 keys.[232] This may be the machine referred to as the replacement for the Enigma in January 1945 which gave the plain and cipher text on printed tapes.[233]

For telephonic communication of secret weather reports, cipher elements were limited to the cover name "FASAN", which indicated that the reports were weather, and the Group WIDDER, which preceded two 5 element groups which designated the station source. Encipherment of such reports took place only if the reports later went on the air.[234]

In regard to the German attitude toward the security of their own systems, the following statement of Dr. Walter Regula is of particular interest. "Russian military operations were faultlessly based on many years experience of climatic and weather conditions (it is thought) so that they did not need the current synoptics."[235] This statement was made relative to the question of whether the Russians worked on German weather systems.

35. German Meteorological Service successfully cryptanalyzed Russian Weather Systems. In 1939 and 1940, Germany stopped the circulation of reports and synoptics in clear.

[231] I-96, p 12.

[232] I-96.

[233] I-194.

[234] I-194.

[235] I-196.

This prompted similar action by the Russians. However, the Russians exchanged information concerning European Russia with Germany until the Germans discontinued because of the discovery that the Russians were giving the German information to the Allies.[236] Early Russian encipherment was by means of the "Copenhagen Cipher" with the later addition of additive tables.[237] In 1944 this system was worked on by the German Meteorological Service and by Regiment 353 using meteorological personnel.[238] Russian enciphering tables were captured early in the war and presented little difficulty.[239] Prior to the capture the Germans read only 2 or 3 days of each 3-week period.[240] The reconstructed and captured tables were used to read messages in Berlin, and then the messages were reenciphered and sent to all interested parties by radio. This sometimes resulted in a considerable time lag.[241] It soon became noticeable that the quality and quantity of Russian reports deteriorated. This gave rise to the belief that the Russians knew of the compromise.[242] The quality improved when the Russian front reached Hungary, but the cipher was so simple that front line units read the reports easily.[243]

The other major missions of the German Meteorological Service were concerned with British weather reports and reports from the Mediterranean area.[244] Although it has been stated that the British weather could be read once in a while,

[236] I-194, p 8.

[237] I-120.

[238] I-120.

[239] I-102.

[240] I-194.

[241] I-194.

[242] I-194.

[243] I-194.

[244] I-84.

the Signal Intelligence Agency of the Supreme Command of the Armed Forces (OKW/Chi) as a consultant was not able to break the British system introduced early in the war and the German Meteorological Service had no greater success.[245]

The fact that Canada, the United States, and Asiatic Russia did not encipher weather at the beginning of the war was of inestimable aid to Germany.[246] The Athens group was aided considerably by the fact that reports from Egypt and Sudan were not enciphered.[247] Further, the fact that reports from the Azores continued to be unenciphered for many months after the Allied occupation was of great assistance.[248]

It would appear that there was little interest in the United States reports. Little, if any, work was done on American systems, and most of the necessary information was obtained from the reports in clear sent by the Air Force.[249]

In 1941 and 1942, the Turkish weather systems were easily broken, but later changes made solution impossible.[250] It has been categorically stated that no attempts was made to read Japanese systems.[251]

The German Meteorological Service's success may be measured in part by the fact that in winter of 1942-1943 it had available almost all of the European and many non-European secret weather reports and synoptics in greater volume than all the data normally available in peacetime.[252] The intercept facilities of the German Meteorological Service were of added value in that they were able to predict the Allied air attacks from Southern Italy on Rumania and Hungary by evaluating the turning traffic over the various airfields.[253]

[245] I-102, I-84.

[246] I-194.

[247] I-102.

[248] I-194.

[249] I-84, I-102.

[250] I-194.

[251] I-84.

[252] I-194.

[253] I-194.

VOLUME 8

Chapter X Origin and Operations of TICOM

36. Origin of "TICOM".-- "TICOM" is the cover name for a joint combined "Target Intelligence Committee." This committee, formed in October, 1944, acted under the authority and on behalf of the Chairman, London Sigint Board (British), the Chief of Staff, ETOUSA, and the European Commander in Chief of the U. S. Navy (COMNAVEU).[258] As constituted, the Committee's operations were limited to the European Theater of Operations. TICOM was purely an Anglo-American organization[259] to exploit specifically the main German signal intelligence installations and organizations.

Four main general considerations were involved. First, in order to improve allied code and cipher security, it was essential for the Anglo-Americans to get data on German cryptanalytic successes with British and American systems. Second, it was also essential to capitalize on the German knowledge of Japanese systems. Third, it was desirable to exploit the research and planning undertaken by the Germans to improve their own cryptographic security. Lastly, it was imperative, after exploitation, to disperse personnel and destroy installations, thus preventing a re-emergence of the German cryptanalytic effort after the cessation of hostilities.

37. Mission and operations of "TICOM".-- The initial planning was done chiefly at Government Code and Cypher School in England. Detailed briefs were compiled covering the locations

[258] See directives attached as Appendices # 1-5 of this chapter; War Department, Chief of Staff, ltr of August 7, 1944; U. S. Navy, COMINCH, ltr 002577 of Sept. 5, 1944; CG, ETOUSA, ltr of October 9, 1944. (SHAEF/ISC/41); U. S. Navy, OP-20-G, Memo of September 15, 1944; SHAEF, Message S-84149, dated 15, 1945.

[259] I-1, dated October 14, 1944.

and personnel of the principal German cryptanalytic organizations. All available sources were used, including Ultra. Initial consideration was given to six targets, all of them then located in the Berlin area.[260] Priority I was given to the Signal Intelligence Agency of the Supreme Command of the Armed Forces (OKW/Chi), thought to be the principal diplomatic cryptanalytic agency. Priority II was assigned to three agencies: (1) Army Inspectorate 7/VI (OKH/In 7/VI), tentatively located in the Jueterbog area; (2) The Signal Intelligence Agency of the Air Force High Command (OKL/LN ABT/350), pin-pointed at Potsdam-Wildpark and (3) The Signal Intelligence Agency of the Navy High Command (OKM/4 SKL/III), then located at Eberswalde. Priority III was assigned to two other targets: (1) The Army High Command Signal Intelligence Control Station (OKH/Chef HNW/LNA), located at Zossen; and (2) the German Admiralty Headquarters ("Koralle") located in the Lanke area. It is notable that Goering's "Research Bureau" (FA) and the Foreign Office Cryptanalytic Section (Pers Z S) were either not known or not listed at the time. Neither were the changes in German army signal intelligence organization after October, 1944, properly outlined and evaluated.

All of the six priority organizations listed above were designated as Class B targets, that is, large Sigint installations to be exploited by TICOM specialists. The smaller sigint organizations which had operated with tactical commands (Class A Targets) were to be exploited in the same manner as other captured personnel and installations, with TICOM specialists available if requested.

Since the Class "B" targets listed above were located in the Berlin area, an area eventually to be occupied by Russian forces, initial consideration was given to a plan worked out in conjunction with T(arget)-Force, Berlin. This plan contemplated a simultaneous seizure and exploitation of the chief sigint centers through an air-borne action. Plans for this action were nearly completed in December, 1944. By February, 1945, it was clear that the proposed action was no longer feasible. The rapid Allied advances, the tactical, administrative and diplomatic problems involved, and the fact that most of the chief centers had either decentralized their activities, moved, or were preparing to move, were the decisive factors in the decision.

[260] I-1, Appendix

The ultimate action which TICOM took in regard to exploitation was based largely upon expediency. The exploitation plan, as revised in March, 1945, provided for six U. S.-British target exploitation teams. In the actual exploitation, team assignments were largely disregarded. Administrative questions and availability of personnel were the principal criteria used for assignments. Teams were dispatched to targets as they were overrun, notice being channeled back through the British Intelligence 21 Army Group, through Signal Intelligence Division (SID), ETOUSA, or through General Staff - Intelligence (GSI(s)), SHAEF. All six teams were eventually dispatched to targets.

Only two major German sigint centers were found reasonably intact and controlling the majority of their assigned personnel. Team #6, the first team sent out, left the United Kingdom in April, 1945, and operated in the Neumuenster-Ploen-Flensburg area. It succeeded in apprehending and isolating most of the key personnel in the Signal Intelligence Agency of the Navy High Command (OKM/4 SKL/III). Team #3 operated in the Halle-Weimar-Leipzig area from the end of April, 1945, until May 15, 1945. It succeeded in apprehending and evacuating most of the personnel and some of the documents belonging to the German Foreign Office Cryptanalytic Section (Pers Z S).

Due to circumstances beyond their control the other teams did not achieve similar success. Goering's "Research" Bureau (FA), the Signal Intelligence Agency of the Supreme Command of the Armed Forces (OKW/Chi), the army installations, and the Signal Intelligence Agency of the Air Force High Command (OKL/LN Abt-350) had all been partially dispersed out of Berlin due to the bombings. In March and April, 1945, these agencies had attempted to move southwards into the Munich-Salzburg area. As transportation became more and more chaotic, and as place after place was overrun by the Allied armies, most of the organizations seem to have disintegrated. Equipment and records were lost or destroyed, and personnel returned to their homes, or simply scattered at the approach of the allied armies.

Team #1, dispatched to the Berchtesgaden area to search for traces of the Signal Intelligence Agency of the Supreme Command of the Armed Forces (OKW/Chi), turned up the former headquarters of Goering's "Research" Bureau (FA and a handful of its personnel, secured the radio teleprinter communications train which had been attached to Field Marshal Kesselring's headquarters, and located a German unit designed to intercept Russian non-Morse (Baudot) traffic. Team #2, sent to the same general area with no specific mission, searched the Innsbruck area, and was eventually dispatched to the Pilsen area, where it took charge of and evacuated the key personnel in the Army Signal Intelligence Regiment (KONA #1) attached to Army Group Center. Team #4 left the United Kingdom in June, 1945, and proceeded to the vicinity of Ebermannstadt, where it exploited the Vierling Laboratory (speech scrambling development) at Unterstein. It also made an unsuccessful search for documents of the Signal Intelligence Agency of the Supreme Command of the Armed Forces (OKW/Chi) in the Schliersee area. Team #5, consisting of two officers only, supervised the diving operations in Schliersee which recovered many of the Cryptanalytic records belonging to the Signal Intelligence Agency of the Supreme Command of the Armed Forces (OKW/Chi).

38. Appraisal of the TICOM operation.--In appraising the TICOM operations, then, it can be said that the effort achieved partial success in its principal objective--the exploitation of all the principal German Sigint centers. Through the efforts of Teams #3 and #6, detailed information was secured on the organization and successes of the Naval and Foreign Office cryptanalytic organizations. The Signal Intelligence Agency of the Supreme Command of the Armed Forces (OKW/Chi) personnel who gave themselves up at Flensburg or were fished out of prisoner of war channels, together with the Schliersee documents, have produced a reasonably complete picture of the OKW/Chi organization, operations, and successes. Dr. Voegele, the chief cryptanalyst of the Signal Intelligence Agency of the Air Force High Command (OKL/LN ABT/350), was captured in the French area. His information, with that supplied by senior German Air Force signal officers and technical personnel at forward units, produced a good picture of the German Air Force Signal Intelligence Service and its cryptanalytic achievements (although much of the information was secured by agencies other than TICOM). The first definite information on Goering's "Research" Bureau came with the discovery of its former headquarters at Kaufbeuren A few of its personnel were taken, but its records and machinery were never located. The army organizations, with the notable exceptions of Nachrichten Aufklaerungs Abteilung 11 (NAA 11), in Norway, the German Signal Intelligence Regiment #1, Kommandeur der Nachrichten Aufklaerung #1 (KONA #1), and a handful of specialists, seem to have dissolved neatly into prisoner of war camps or the German countryside.

The TICOM organization continued to function until November 25, 1945, in order to register and distribute the documents captured.

DOCID: 3560798

WAR DEPARTMENT
THE CHIEF OF STAFF
WASHINGTON

August 7, 1944

Dear Eisenhower:

Following up my radio to you of August 7th concerning the organization of an American team to participate with the British Government Code and Cipher School in an investigation of German Signal Intelligence activities, I am enclosing a list of subjects for inquiry. The attached tab sets forth in itemized form the matters which we believe should receive primary attention. This schedule should be considered merely as a preliminary guide for the nature of the material uncovered in the early stages and in a large extent govern the course of the investigation.

Faithfully yours,

/s/ G. Marshall

G. Marshall

General D. D. Eisenhower,
Supreme Headquarters
Allied Expeditionary Force
London, England

Certified a true copy,

T. J. BETTS
Brigadier General

55

SCHEDULE OF SUBJECTS FOR INVESTIGATION

1. Complete cryptographic and cryptanalytic data on file at German centers, as well as equipment and operating instructions pertaining to the same.

2. Information as to the exchange of technical cryptographic and cryptanalytic knowledge between the Germans and other Axis powers, together with information on the cryptographic and cryptanalytic methods used by the latter so far as is known to the Germans.

3. Equipment used for intercept and direction finding purposes; special methods and apparatus for the rapid forwarding of raw material to cryptanalytic centers.

4. Methods and procedures employed in traffic analysis.

5. Methods and procedures employed in correlating and fusing information from traffic analysis and cryptanalysis.

6. Speech secrecy equipment, cryptographic facsimile encipherment, and all non-Morse cryptographic equipment as used both on wire lines and on radio circuits.

7. The chemical names as well as the military designations of all secret inks, the formula of the developers, details of the manufacture of micro-photographs, and all details of all methods, film and paper.

8. Radio and radar-jamming and anti-jamming equipment and techniques.

9. Complete information on the HS-293 and FX-1400 guided missiles, together with complete details of other similar remote control equipment.

Certified a true copy.

T. J. BETTS,
Brigadier General.

UNITED STATES FLEET
HQ OF THE COMMANDER IN CHIEF
NAVY DEPARTMENT
WASHINGTON, DC

FFI/A8

Serial: 002577 6 Sept. 44

TOP SECRET

From : Commander in Chief, U. S. Fleet

To : Commander, TWELFTH Fleet ,

Subj : Plan for Examination of German Radio Intelligence Organization

1. A combined British-United States plan is being evolved for the examination of the German radio intelligence organization immediately following the cessation of hostilities. The participation of the U. S. Navy in this project is to be conducted jointly with the U. S. Army.

2. Colonel George A. Bicher, AUS, now on duty at Supreme Headquarters, Allied Expeditionary Forces, has been directed by the Chief of Staff, U. S. Army, to assume direction of the U. S. Army participation in this project. Lieutenant Commander Robert B. Ely, III, USNR, now on duty in the Office of the Chief of Naval Operations, is being ordered to report to Commander, TWELFTH Fleet in order to assume direction of the U. S. Navy participation. Additional naval personnel will be assigned as necessary. It is the present intention not to order any naval officers senior to rank of commander to this project; therefore, all naval personnel will be under the immediate direction of Colonel Bicher.

3. Detailed instructions will be issued to Lieutenant Commander Ely prior to his departure from Washington.

4. It is desired that the naval party engaged in this project be afforded all facilities that will assist it in the accomplishment of its mission.

/s/ R. S. EDWARDS
Chief of Staff.

Copy to: CoS, U.S. Army (G-2)
Op-20-G

57

HEADQUARTERS
EUROPEAN THEATER OF OPERATIONS
OFFICE OF THE COMMANDING GENERAL

SHAEF/ISC/41 9 October, 1944

SUBJECT: Investigation of German Signal Intelligence Centers, Personnel and Equipment.

TO : Colonel George A BICHER,
Signal Intelligence Division,
OCSIGO, ETOUSA, APO 887.

1. The Chief of Staff, U. S. Army, in a letter to the Supreme Commander, Allied Expeditionary Force dated 7 August 1944, directed that an American organization participate jointly with the British in plans for a complete investigation of German Signal Intelligence Centers, personnel and equipment prior to and after cessation of hostilities.

2. As Director, Signal Intelligence Division, Office of the Chief Signal Officer, ETOUSA, you are directed by authority of the above mentioned letter, to effect the necessary liaison with the British authorities on this matter and to formulate plans to carry out the wishes of the Chief of Staff, U. S. Army, for presentation to this Haedquarters.

3. In this connection you are further advised that by letter of 6 September 1944, the Chief of Staff, U. S. Navy directed that the U. S. Navy join with the U. S. Army in this mission, and appointed Lieutenant Commander Robert B. Ely III, USNR, to assume direction of the U. S. Navy participation. By the terms of this letter Lieutenant Commander Ely and all other naval personnel will be under your immediate direction.

By command of General EISENHOWER:

T. J. BETTS,
Brigadier General.

58

CONFIDENTIAL
Op-20-G/ar

15 September 1944

MEMORANDUM

From: Assistant Director Naval Communications (OP-20-G).
TO : Lt. Comdr. R. B. Ely, USNR.

Subj: Instructions Concerning Special Duty.

Ref: (a) Letter of General Marshall to General Eisenhower of August 7, and enclosed list of subjects.
(b) COMINCH Serial 002577 of 6 Sept 1944.

1. In accordance with reference (b), you will be in charge of the naval participation in the plan covered by references (a) and (b), under the immediate direction of Colonel G. A. Bicher, AUS.

2. Op-20-G's interests in the plan include all of the items set out in the enclosure to reference (a), except paragraphs 8 and 9, with the following additions:

Item 2 We are likewise interested in any collaboration with neutral or non-belligerent powers.

Item 10 (new) Complete information as to devices, methods and procedures in handling transmitter and operator identification.

3. As soon as possible after arrival in U. K., confer with Colonel Bicher to cover the following points:

(a) the estimated number, location, and nature of targets.
(b) the anticipated changes in these targets.
(c) the existing arrangements for personnel and material to cover these targets.
(d) the kind and number of additional personnel which it appears should be provided by the U. S. Navy to assist in the conduct of this mission.

4. Upon conclusion, and, if necessary, during these conferences, full reports and recommendations should be sent to Op-20-G, employing CSP 1803 held by Commander TWELFTH Fleet.

59

5. Reports and recommendations thereafter will be made upon any changes in the basic plan being proposed which require the concurrence of the Director of Naval Communications, and upon such changes being made.

/s/ P. R. Kinney

P. R. KINNEY
Captain, U. S. Navy

S H A E F

Staff Message Control

OUTGOING MESSAGE

p r i o r i t y

TO: SIXTH ARMY GROUP FOR G-2, TWELFTH ARMY GROUP FOR G-2, EXFOR FOR GSI

FROM: SHAEF MAIN SIGNED SCAEF CITE: SHGBI

REF NO: S-84149 TOO: 051500B

1. Particularly desirable is special handling of German signal intelligence targets which may be overrun and captured with or without previous knowledge of their location. A signal intelligence target consists of:

(A) A center at which German codes and ciphers are produced or at which research is done on them, or

(B) A center at which cryptanalysis, interception and traffic analysis, or other activity to gain intelligence from non-German signals is carried out.

2. TICOM is a joint combined target intelligence committee organized to implement the desires of the Chief of Staff, US Army, the Commander in Chief, US Fleet, and the Chairman LONDON Sigint Board, and made responsible for the complete exploitation of German signal intelligence centers.

3. Upon location of such a target, it is desired that the custody of the target be released to the nearest Sigint Unit, who will seal it and establish a guard, notifying by fastest possible means thru Sigint channels the Director, SID, ETOUSA or Director War Station of the nature and extent of the target.

4. TICOM experts will be dispatched at the discretion of the Director, SID, ETOUSA or Director War Station for the purpose of exploiting the target, and they are hereby authorized

61

to take exclusive custody of the target, and to return any or all of its contents direct to such places as may be designated by them. On completion of their investigations the target will be released to the occupying force.

5. Instructions contained herein are to be applied to special targets as defined above and do not conflict with existing instructions for the passing back of captured Sigint documents and equipment from normal enemy message centers through Sigint channels.

6. It is desired that all units down to and including divisions and all Sigint units be notified of these instructions.

ORIGINATOR: G-2 AUTHENTICATION: T. J. BETTS, BRIG. GENERAL

INFORMATION: SGS
G-3
G-4
SIGNALS
OM ZONE
G-2 WAR DIARY
SHAEF FWD
SUMMARY
AG RECORDS

VOLUME 8

Chapter XI

The Chief Signal Officer of the Supreme Command of the Armed Forces and the Armed Forces Signal Communications Group

39. The Armed Forces Signal Communications Group as a subject of interest to TICOM. Determination of the authority or authorities responsible for direction and coordination of all Signal intelligence matters in the German Armed Forces is pertinent for an understanding of the relationships between the various service agencies studied by TICOM, the Signal Intelligence Agency of the Supreme Command of the Armed Forces (OKW/WFSt/AgWNV/Chi), the Radio Defense Corps (OKW/WFSt/Ag-WNV/Fu III), the Signal Intelligence Agency of the Army High Command (OKH/GdNA), the Signal Intelligence Agency of the Air Force High Command (OKL/LN Abt 350), and the Signal Intelligence Agency of the Navy High Command (OKM 4 SKL/III). The TICOM Interrogations only afford general statements that liaison did or did not exist (the implication generally is that liaison left much to be desired) although investigation of the work records and reconstruction of the operations of

the various agencies have indicated considerable exchange and cooperation. (In some instances better relations existed between individual service agencies and the two known non-service agencies, the Foreign Office Cryptanalytic Section (Pers ZS) and Goering's "Research" Bureau (FA)the Nazi Party radio intelligence and cryptanalytic agency) than existed among the service agencies themselves. An original German document giving the organization of the Armed Forces Signal Communications Group and indication of the duties and responsibilities of its components is available dated 28 September 1944.[270] The picture presented by this document is valid only for this date. Additional documents are available and have been used in the TICOM report on the Signal Intelligence Agency of the Supreme Command of the Armed Forces which shows the changes which were effected up to the end of the war.[271]

40. Provenance of Ticom information on the Armed Forces Signal Communications Group. This document was obtained from Lt. Col. Arntz, the aide of General Praun, the Chief Signal Officer (Chef WNV). Arntz had been the aide of Praun's predecessor, General Fellgiebel, who was executed for his part in the 20th of July plot. Arntz stated that Fellgiebel had informed him of the plot prior to the attempt on Hitler's life and for this reason Arntz, although undetected by the Gestapo, availed himself of an opportunity to inspect front-line divisions and surrendered near Remagen. He brought with him the documents cited and volunteered additional information in his various interrogations.[272]

[270] IF 163-C, "Anlage zu AgWNV/Z Ia Nr 2109/44 geh 28 Sept 44." IF 163-D, Appendix to Armed Forces Signal Communication, Operations Section Nr. 2109/44 Confidential dated 28 September 1944 is the translation.

[271] See Volume III Chart 1 showing the organization of the Signal Intelligence Agency of the Supreme Command of the Armed Forces. Cf. I 3 9, DF 8, 9, and 12.

[272] IF 163, parts A-E and IF 108. IF 163 is the field interrogation of Arntz and photostats of the documents he brought with him. IF 108 is the CSDIC (Combined Service Detailed Interrogation Center) interrogation.

DOCID: 3560798

41. Position of the Chief Signal Officer of the Supreme Command of the Armed Forces for coordinating signal and signal intelligence matters. One of the departmental divisions of the Armed Forces Operations Staff of the Supreme Command of the Armed Forces (Oberkommando der Wehrmacht/Wehrmacht Fuehrungsstab, abbreviated OKW/WFSt) was the Armed Forces Signal Communications Group (Amtsgruppe Wehrmacht Nachrichten Verbindung, abbreviated AgWNV). The Chief Signal Officer (Chef WNV) was the head of this department and at the same time held the office of Chief Signal Officer of the Army High Command (Chef des Heeres Nachrichtenwesens, abbreviated Chef HNW):

Chief Signal Officer, Supreme Command of the Armed Forces
(Chef WNV)
and
Chief Signal Officer of the Army High Command
(Chef HNW)
Lieutenant General Praun
(formerly Fellgiebel)

Armed Forces Signal Communication Group
(OKW/AgWNV)
Lieutenant General Gimmler
(formerly Thiele)

Army High Command Signal Communications Troops
(OKH/Kdr.FNT)
Colonel Ahrens

Signal Intelligence Agency of Army High Command
(OKH/GdNA)
Colonel Boetzel
(See Volume IV Chart 2)

Armed Forces Radio Security Section
(OKW/AgWNV/Fu)
Colonel Rosenkranz

Armed Forces Wire Communications
(OKW/AgWNV/KFA)
Colonel v. Knobelsdorff-Brenkerhoff

Signal Intelligence Agency of the Supreme Command of the Armed Forces
(OKW/AgWNV/Chi)
Colonel Kettler
[See Volume III Chart 1]

Armed Forces Signal Equipment
(OKW/AgWNV/GBN)
Colonel Dr. Inge. Grube

It is apparent that Praun was in a position to effect any necessary liaison between the Supreme Command of the Armed Forces Communications Group and the related Army High Command agencies. Keitel stated that Praun, in addition to his double function of working for both the Supreme Command of the Armed Forces and for the Army High Command, was also in close contact with the Navy High Command and with the Luftwaffe and drew personnel from them.[273] This presumably applies to Signals personnel in general rather than to Signal Intelligence personnel or even cryptanalysts. Arntz testified to the efforts of Praun, based on personal liaison, to improve relations with the Navy, Air Force, and Reserve Army in Signal Equipment matters and infers that the high position of Doenitz, Goering, and Himmler, the heads of these organizations, made any cooperation extremely difficult.[274]

42. Detailed description of the duties of the component sections of the Armed Forces Signal Communication Group based on a translated German document. The following description of the Armed Forces Signal Communications Group is based on translations of the organization order of 28 September 1944. The available translations have been checked against the German original and where necessary the German terms will be indicated.[275] The actual telephone numbers of the various agencies and even the home telephones of the departmental heads are given on the order but have not been reproduced here. All but the Radio Security Section were reached through the headquarters switchboard of the Supreme Command of the Armed Forces, it was reached through the switchboard "Dietrich". The order reads:

> Appendix to Armed Forces Signal Communications, Operations Section Nr 2109/44 Confidential (Geheime). 28 September 1944.
>
> Extract from the directives and work schedules for the Chief Signal Officer of the Supreme Command of the Armed Forces and the Chief of the Armed Forces Signal Communications Group and subordinate departments.

273 Keitel, Chief of Armed Forces High Command, I 143.

274 IF 108 p 2, paragraphs 10, 11, and 12.

275 The German original is IF 163-D, the document brought in by Arntz. This is translated verbatim in IF 163-C. Another version, which omits some of the Teutonic details, is IF 108, the CSDIC interrogation report on Lt. Col. Arntz circulated by the British.

Chef WNV 1). The Chief Signal Officer of the Supreme Command of the Armed Forces controls Armed Force Signal Commands. His permanent deputy is the Chief of the Armed Forces Signal Communication Group. . . . . .
Lt. Gen. Praun
Outer Office, Registry of Top Secret Correspondence.

AgWNV 2). Chief of the Armed Forces Signal Communications Group.
Lt. Gen. Gimmler
Outer Office, Duty Officer.

The Armed Forces Signal Communications Group includes:

Central Group	(Z-Zentral Gruppe)
Military Wire Communications	(KFA-Kriegsfernmeldeabteilung)
Chief of Signal Equipment	(GBN-Generalbevollmaechtigter Für Techn. Nachrichtenmittel)
Radio Security Section	(Fu-Abteilung Funkwesen)
Signal Intelligence Agency	(Chi-Chiffrier Abteilung)

The Armed Forces Signal Communication Group is the agency through which the Chief Signal Officer controls the Armed Force Signals Commands. The Signal Commands are authorized to carry on correspondence with the Armed Forces Signal Communications Group by virtue of their position in the chain of command.

AgWNV/Z 3) Central Group is the agency through which the Chief Signal Officer of the Supreme Command of the Armed Forces coordinates the control of the Armed Forces Signal Administration Group. Lt. Col. Trosken

Z Ia: Employment and Organization, Directives, Journal, Mobilization and Demobilization.
Major Adler

Z Ib: Personnel, Travel, Assignments, Transfers, peace-time and war-time T/O's and T/E's, furloughs, billets, alternate offices, regulations, gas and air defense. Major Proebster

Z Id: Administration, business, finance, transfer of foreign currency, pay classifications, illnesses and accidents of employees, group festivities, papers for official trips, ration cards for clothing and equipment, subsidies and assistance, furlough control. Civil Official (Amtsrat) Waak

Z Ie: Liaison office in the Post Office Department (RPM), business dealings with the Post Office by the Armed Forces in nonsignal technical matters, deferments from military service, special wire-communication personnel. Lt. Col. Neumann

Registry Office. Secretariat of Central Group, unclassified and Confidential letter registers. Neitzel (civilian)

AgWN V/KFA 4) Military Wire Communications Section, responsible for Armed Forces Wire Communications, organized into sub-sections (Stabs-referate). Col. v. Knobelsdorff-Brinkerhoff. Outer Office-Secret Letter Register

St/O: Internal department matters, personnel matters, correspondence concerning specialist personnel of the Post Office Department, procurement and employing personnel for special missions, motor vehicles and motor fuel. Major Brueggen

St/P: Planning and construction of channels for long and very long distance traffic (long distance cables, carrier frequencies, decimeter and radio teletype lines), large signal installations, installations and equipment for field headquarters, spare parts and supplies for carrier frequency and decimeter lines, employment of specialist personnel of the Post Office Department and the Long Distance Cable Company, Technical advice. KVR (War Official?) Pippart

St/F: Armed Forces Signal Officer at Hitler's Headquarters. Major Lohse

KFA I: Network layout according to tactical situation, gaurding of signal installations against air raid damage (jointly with St/P), arrangements for communications for special trains, special missions, agencies served outside the Armed Forces and allied (Axis) nations, employment of special units, basic problems of signal communications, traffic monitoring, priorities in signal traffic, official extensions in residences, administration of equipment. Major Magnussen

KFA II: Raw material control, procurement and supply, priorities for procurement and special construction projects, Long Distance Cable Planning Committee, financial planning for construction projects with government funds, depots for apparatus and technical installations ("LATE"), depots for telegraph construction material ("LYBZ").
Civil Official (Amtsrat) Keutel

KFA III: Wiring plans for all agencies served, card indexes and plans of special net works.
Lt. Col. Dr. Bethge

Secretariat: Confidential and Unclassified Register.
Civilian Schack

AgWNV/Fu 5) Radio Security Section. Col. Rosenkranz

Fu I: Organization and employment, basic radio regulations for Armed Forces and government Agencies, special radio connections, T/O's.
Major v. Laffert

Fu Ia: Radio traffic at field head quarters, officer personnel, detachments, journal, reports on activities, section orders, special certificates.
Capt. Pohmer

Fu Ia[1]: Employment and distribution of codes, Armed Forces code regulations, enlisted and civilian personnel, internal department matters.
Capt. Mushake

Fu Ib: Radio traffic control for Armed Forces and government agencies, general frequency distribution, control of broadcasting and sections, identification of hostile propaganda stations, wartime radio transmitting permits.
Civilian Mohr

Fu II: Procurement of equipment for Radio Counter-Intelligence, for OKW and government agencies, priorities, raw material allotments, procurement of motor vehicles, evaluation of equipment of agents.
Col. Fuchs

Fu III: THE RADIO DEFENSE CORPS. Supervision of Radio counter-intelligence cooperation with other counter-intelligence (Abwehr) organizations.[276] Major v. Barry

Secretariat: Secret, Confidential, and unclassified letter register, conducting of business transaction. Secretary Reinhardt

AgWNV/GBN 6) Chief of signal Equipment. Securing of signal equipment for Armed Forces and government agencies, control over development and manufacture, special missions.[277] Col. Dr. Inge Grube Outer Office, Secret Register.

GBN/A: Staff Specialist, internal department matters. Major Zellien.

GBN/B: Special Supply problems, particularly spare parts supply, equipment repair. Capt. Gorn

GBN/St: (Officer for special assignments), special missions, export, in-short-supply metals. Major Tuexen

GBN/I: Wire Communication equipment. Major Henkel

GBN/II: Radio and special communication equipment. Major Dipl. Ing. Gloeckner

GBN/III: Military economy and general economic matters (industrial matters, labor, raw materials, priorities). Major Doelitzsch

GBN/IV: Tube Office (wire and radio). Col. Baldus

[276]For a full discussion of the Radio Defense Corps see the write up of that organization. The field organization, its operations, liaison with the Abwehr and Reich Main Security Office and Italian Counter-Intelligence, and an evaluation of its techniques is available from the written report of a field commander of a counter-intelligence regiment in the West, Captain Wilhelm Kelch (IF 176) Discussion of the history of the Radio Defense Corps, personalities, cryptanalytic liaison, etcetera may be found in the interrogations of Arntz (IF 108 and IF 163) and of Mettig of the Signal Intelligence Agency of the Supreme Command of the Armed Forces, I 115. Also see I 21, 26, 162.

[277]It should be noted that a separate organization for development and supply of signal equipment existed in the Reserve Army under Himmler, the Army Ordnance Developing and Testing Group, Signal Branch. Arntz testified to Praun's difficulties in securing cooperation at so high a level.

GBN/Secretariat: Registry of Confidential and unclassified letters. Civilian Triphan ("Min. Reg.")

AgWNV/Chi 7) THE SIGNAL INTELLIGENCE AGENCY OF THE SUPREME COMMAND OF THE ARMED FORCES. Col. Kettler

Chi/Z: Personnel, internal department matters. Major Lober Secretariat

Chi/I: Organization, employment. Major Mettig

Chi/II: Evaluation of Radio messages. Lt. Col. Seyfarth

Chi/III: Reception of radio messages. Lt. Col. Kaehler

Technical radio specialist. Civilian Official (Reg Baurat) Salzbrunn

Chi/IV: Decoding (Cryptanalytic) Group. Principal Specialist Fenner

Chi/V: Wire Communications. Technical Inspector ("Techn.Obinsp.") (N) Buck

Chi/X: Special problems "X" in accordance with special instructions. Lt. Col. v. Kalchstein

43. Relation of the Armed Forces Signal Communications Group to the Amt Ausland und Abwehr of the Supreme Command of the Armed Forces and to the Reich Main Security Office. From the duties assigned to the various departments of the Armed Forces Signal Communications Group it will be seen that the Armed Forces Signal Communications Group was concerned with the signal communication phase of general censorship. The primary responsibility for wartime censorship was given to a separate division of the Supreme Command of the Armed Forces, the Amt Auslandnachrichten und Abwehr (Foreign Intelligence and Defense- the last specifically involving the employment of agents by the Germans and counter-intelligence measures against agents).[278]

[278] TF29, Die Ueberwachung des Nachrichtenverkehrs im Kriege, is the Secret regulations and duties of the German censorship organization. The issuing authority is not given nor is the date but the Abwehr is named as the responsible authority in the Supreme Command of the Armed Forces.

The functions of the Amt Ausland und Abwehr were taken over in early 1944 by Himmler in the Reich Main Security Office (RSHA). The functions were divided, responsibility for censorship and counter-intelligence being given to the Gestapo (Amt IV of RSHA) and the foreign intelligence functions going to Amt Ausland (Amt VI, under Schellenberg).[279] The Abwehr field organization was not disturbed in the reorganization, however, but was directed by the Reich Main Security Office. Various officials of the Abwehr were involved in the 20th of July Plot, e.g. Admiral Canaris and Col. Hanson, former heads of the Abwehr. Details of the censorship organization and of the Amt Ausland und Abwehr of the Supreme Command of the Armed Forces have not been investigated by TICOM.

[279] For details of the Abwehr see IF 216 A and B. For the organization of the Reich Main Security Office see the same documents and the interrogation of the head of Amt VI of RSHA, Schellenberg, IF 164. Some discussion of the relation of the Abwehr with the Signal Intelligence Agency of the Supreme Command of the Armed Forces is given in the volume on that agency, Volume III. The RSHA and the Abwehr are also discussed in connection with Goering's Research Bureau, Volume VII, paragraph 6.

VOLUME 8

Chapter XII. Physical Compromises

44. Introduction.--A part--probably a very small part--of the success of the Axis powers in dealing with foreign cryptographic systems was due to physical compromise of the systems. Unfortunately it is in most cases not possible to determine by what route the information reached Axis hands. A few cases are known to be of the "cloak-and-dagger" type, wherein a document was bought or stolen. More are cases of simple capture, either in action, or after the owner had fled, as at Dunkirk. But most of the instances of physical compromise known from TICOM sources are known only in the barest outlines: either a prisoner of war simply said, "We had a copy of such-and-such," or the copy itself was liberated by one of the TICOM teams.

45. United States Systems.--It has been stated that "the Germans, Hungarians, Italians, Finns and Japanese... all...had copies of most of the State Department codes and some of the strip systems... ." From "a source believed to be reliable" comes the report that the first American codes obtained by the Finns came from the United States Legation at Sofia. The Japanese had obtained these codes "at an unknown date early in the war" by bribing person or persons unknown. The Hungarian Intelligence Service was the middleman in this deal. According to the same source, the Japanese gave the American codes to the Russians, and these systems are also in the possession of the Swedes and French. In fact, American codes seem to have attained as catholic a distribution as American money. Systems involved in this complex of skulduggery are said to include State Department codes, Military Attaché Confidential Code No. 2, and strip ciphers.[285]

[285] IF-260.

The United States systems known from TICOM sources to have been physically compromised by European Axis powers are:

- The State Department A-1 Code;[286]
- The Brown Code;[287]
- A code called by the Germans "Z-3" or "Red";[288]
- A Military Attaché 5-letter code, no designation known, which the Italians received from the Hungarians;[289]
- "War Department Confidential Code No. 2", a Military Attaché system;[290]
- A Military Attaché 5-letter code called by the Germans "Mil I";[291]
- A Navy strip cipher which the Germans called "DUPYH" from the indicator.[292]

The State Department A-1 Code, called "B 6 a" by the Germans, was in 1941 in the hands of the Cryptanalytic Agency of the Supreme Command Armed Forces (OKW/Chi), which sent a photograph of it to the Foreign Office Cryptanalytic Section (Pers Z S).[293]

286 I-22 p 10; DF-15 p IV. The photostat itself was picked up by TICOM.

287 I-22 p 10; DF-15 p IV; IF-1524 p 9. See also IF-1518 pp 4-5. This photostat is in TICOMMA files as TF-10.

288 DF-15 p III.

289 IF-1524 p 4.

290 DF-15 p V.

291 DF-15 p 3.

292 I-93 p 9.

293 DF-15 p IV.

The Brown Code was likewise received by the Foreign Office Cryptanalytic Section (Pers Z S) from the Cryptanalytic Agency of the Supreme Command Armed Forces (OKW/Chi). This took place in June 1941;[294] but it is claimed that the code had already been broken before that.[295] This code was also in the hands of the Italians.[296]

The code which the Germans called "Z-3" or "Red" was a consular code of which the Germans say it was "solved, later captured and photographed due to lack of caution on the part of the Consul General at Frankfort a/M, but without instructions for encipherment, these instructions were captured later."[297]

The Military Attaché code received by the Italians from the Hungarians was one which the Hungarians had apparently tried unsuccessfully to strip. It went out of use in October 1942.[298]

The system called by the Germans "War Department Confidential Code No. 2" was in the possession of the German Foreign Office in photostat form; we do not know by what means it was obtained.[299]

The code which the Germans called "Mil I" was also in the possession of the German Foreign Office.[300]

Part of the Navy strip cipher "DUPYH" was in the possession of the German Navy, which claimed to have obtained the copy from the Japanese, who, according to the Germans, got it in 1942 from an unknown source.[301]

294 DF-15 p IV.

295 I-22 p 10.

296 IF-1524 p 9.

297 DF-15 p III

298 IF-1524 p 4.

299 DF-15 p V.

300 DF-15 p 3.

301 I-93 p 9.

46. Systems other than United States.--Two other codes of which the German Foreign Office Cryptanalytic Section (Pers Z S) received copies from the Cryptanalytic Agency of the Supreme Command Armed Forces (OKW/Chi) were a Brazilian diplomatic code (ASA trigraph BZD)[302] and a Portuguese diplomatic code. The latter was loaned in December 1942 for photographing, along with some of the substitution tables.[303]

Late in 1944 the Germans came into possession of a Manchurian codebook which had been stolen from the Manchurian Legation after the unreliable character in charge of it had failed to lock it up. A photostat was made and turned over to the Cryptanalytic Agency of the Supreme Command Armed Forces (OKW/Chi).[304]

On the subject of Rumanian codes the Italians were particularly boastful, claiming to have read all of them with the aid of photostatic copies.[305] They did not, however, reveal the source of all this bounty.

We know of two cases of physical compromise in connection with cipher machines, other than tactical capture of machines such as at Dunkirk and from downed planes. One was a "small cipher machine of Swedish origin" which had been "bought by the English" and was "in the possession of OKW"--we do not know how OKW got it. The Germans claimed to have read all messages from the Italian theater enciphered by this machine.[306]

The other was a Croatian Enigma machine which the Germans were able to compromise before it was ever used because a German firm made the machines and reported the wirings promptly to the German authorities. To be doubly sure, the Germans even bought one of the first keys used.[307]

[302] D-16, 1941 Report, p 3.

[303] D-16, 1942 Report, p 3.

[304] I-177 p 2.

[305] IF-1521 p 1.

[306] I-76 p 2.

[307] I-92 p 2.

Probably the simplest way to steal cryptographic material from someone is to walk into his office and pick it up. This was tried by the Germans--not on their enemies, to be sure, but on the Italians immediately after the armistice of 1943. Two German lieutenants walked into the Italian cipher office in Athens and began to pack up the material they saw lying about. But some Italian officers came in and "began shouting rather excitedly"--as well they might--so the Germans discreetly retreated--fetching along, however, what booty they had already collected. It turned out to include an enciphering table for use with the "Ellade" code.[308]

An example of how chicanery can double back upon itself and confound its perpetrator is the case of a Turkish code which the German Reich Main Security Office (RSHA) bought from the Hungarians and delivered to the Cryptanalytic Agency of the Supreme Command Armed Forces (OKW/Chi), which then discovered that the code was one which it had broken and given to the Hungarians over a year before.[309]

A breakdown by countries of the systems reported by German and Italian prisoners of war as having been physically compromised shows the following distribution:

France..........................	25 codes and ciphers
United Kingdom..................	9 codes and ciphers
Yugoslavia......................	4 codes and ciphers
Rumania and Turkey..............	4 codes each.
Russia..........................	2 codes
Belgium, Brazil, Bulgaria, Chile, Greece, Manchuria, Mexico, Poland, Portugal, Spain, and Uruguay..........................	1 code each

It will be noticed that the above list and the one in the last paragraph of this paper show French systems in the overwhelming majority. To what extent this can be ascribed to the "voluntary" relinquishment of codes after the fall of France, we cannot say; but it seems almost certain that the French defeat did swell the lists somewhat.

308 I-100 p 2.

309 I-132 p 2.

77

In addition to those compromises reported in prisoner of war interrogations, there are numerous ones known to TICOM only because the compromised material itself was picked up. It is in most cases impossible to determine the manner of capture of these systems, though in one instance the material did have a note attached giving the place of capture.[310] Especially when material was found among belongings of the Cryptanalytic Agency of the Supreme Command Armed Forces (OKW/Chi), there is no way of determining its origin; for it was specifically ordered that the three armed forces should place all captured material, on demand, at the disposal of this agency.[311]

An enumeration of the physically compromised systems known to TICOM only through samples follows:

France....................	68 codes and ciphers.
Greece....................	1 code.
Italy.....................	1 code.
Poland....................	3 codes.
Portugal..................	1 code.
Rumania...................	2 codes.
Yugoslavia................	1 code.

[310] T 477. The note was found with two of the three Polish Navy codes it mentions. It was addressed to the Signal Intelligence Agency of the German Navy High Command (OKM 4 SKL III), and signed Kempf, who was Chief of the Cryptanalytic Agency of the Supreme Command Armed Forces (OKW/Chi). Translated, it reads: "As enclosure, 3 Navy signal books captured in the cryptographic archives of the 2nd Dept. of the Polish General Staff (Pyry, 13 km south of the center of Warsaw) are being transferred for keeping."

[311] T 1620. The order is dated 1 Nov 1944.

VOLUME 8

TAB A

A 27. "List of Documents Received from Hungarian Crypt. Unit Eggenfelden." A TICOM document.
Abwehr.--Military Intelligence.
Adler, _____, Major. Chief of Section Ia of Central Group of Armed Forces Communication Group (Employment and Organization, Directive, Journal, Mobilization and Imobilization)
Ag WNV (Amtsgruppe Wehrmacht Nachrichten Verbindung).--Armed Forces Signal Communications Group.
Ahrnens, _____, Col. Commander of Signal Communication Groups under Army High Command (OKH/Kdr. FNT.
Air Force Intelligence Service.--Servicio Informazioni Aeronautica (SIA).
Ame, _____, Brigadier General. Head of Italian Army Intelligence Service.
Amtsgruppe Wehrmacht Nachrichten Verbindung (Ag WNV).--Armed Forces Signal Communications Group.
Armed Forces Operations Staff of the Supreme Command of the Armed Forces.--Oberkommando der Wehrmacht/Wehrmacht Fuehrungsstab (OKW/WFSt).
Armed Forces Signal Communications.--Wehrmachtnachrichtenverbindungen (WNV).
Armed Forces Signal Communications Group.--Amtsgruppe Wehrmacht Nachrichten Verbindung (Ag WNV).
Army High Command Signal Intelligence Control Station.--Oberkommando des Heeres/Chef des Heeres Nachrichten Wesens/ Leitstelle der Nachrichten Aufklärung (OKH/Chef HNW/LNA).
Army Ordnance, Development and Testing Group, Signal Branch.--Chef der Heeresruestung und Befehlshaber des Ersatzheeres, Amtsgruppe fuer Entwicklung und Pruefung des Heereswaffenamts, Waffen Pruefung, Abteilung 7 (Wa Pruef 7).
Army Signal Intelligence Regiment.--Kommandeur Der Nachrichten Aufklärung (KONA).
Arntz, _____, Lt. Col. Aide of Gen. Praun, Chief Signal Officer of Armed Forces.

79

Baldus,_____, Col. Chief of Section IV of Signal Equipment.
v. Barry,_____, Major. Chief of Section III of the Radio Security Section.
Bethge,_____, Lt. Col. Dr. Chief of Section III of Armed Forces Communications Group Wire Communication.
Biggi, Augusto, Capt. Italian cryptanalyst. Did liaison work with Germans regarding IBM machinery.
Brueggen,_____, Major. Chief of Subsection 0 of the Armed Forces Communications Group Wire Communication, Section 4.
Buck,_____, Technical Inspector. Chief of Chi/V of the Signal Intelligence Agency of the Supreme Command of the Armed Forces.
Canale, Aldo, Col. Chief of Secretariat Section of SIM. Succeeded Col. Nasta.
Canaris,_____, Admiral. Official of Abwehr, involved in July 20th plot.
Central Weather Group.--Zentralwetterdienstgruppe.
Chef der Heeresruestung und Befehlshaber des Ersatzheeres, Amtsgruppe fuer Entwicklung und Pruefung des Heereswaffenamts, Waffen Pruefung, Abteilung 7 (Wa Pruef 7).--Army Ordnance, Development and Testing Group, Signal Branch.
Chef des Heeres Nachrichten Wesens (Chef HNW).--Chief Signal Officer of the Army High Command.
Chef HNW (Chef des Heeres Nachrichten Wesens).--Chief Signal Officer of the Army High Command.
Chief Signal Officer of the Army High Command.--Chef des Heeres Nachrichten Wesens (Chef HNW).
Chiffrierstelle, Oberbefehlshaber der Luftwaffe (Chi-Stelle Ob d L).--Signal Intelligence Agency of the Commander in Chief of the Air Force.
Cipher Bureau of the German War Ministry. Predecessor to the Signal Intelligence Agency of the Supreme Command Armed Forces (OKW/Chi).
Chi-Stelle Ob d L (Chiffrierstelle, Oberbefehlshaber der Luftwaffe).--Signal Intelligence Agency of the Commander in Chief of the Air Force.
COMINCH.--Commander in Chief.
Combined Service Detailed Interrogation Center.--CSDIC.
COMNAVEU.--European Commander in Chief of United States Navy.
"Cryptanalytic Party" of the Eighth Army. Directly responsible to 8th Army, and had no direct connection with SIM.
Cryptanalytic Section of the German Foreign Office.--Sonderdienst des Referats Z in der Personal Abteilung des Auswaertigen Amtes (Pers Z S).
CSDIC.--Combined Service Detailed Interrogation Center.

D 16. "Translation of Annual Progress Reports by Pers ZS covering 1927, 1941, and 1942." A TICOM publication.
D 59. "Notes and Minutes of High-Level Meetings held at OKW/Chi--Cryptographic and Administrative. A TICOM Document.
DF 15. "Berichte der A Gruppe." American Systems worked on by Germans.
De Monte,_____, Commandante. Chief of the Cryptanalytic Sub-Section of SIS.
De Witt,_____, Major. Italian cryptanalyst.
Doelitzsch,_____, Major. Chief of Section III of Signal Equipment.
Doenitz, Karl, Grand Admiral Commander in Chief, German Navy; Reich Chancellor after Hitler's death.
E 7. "Final Report on the Technical Exploitation of the FEUERSTEIN LABORATORY (Director: Dr. Oskar Vierling) carried out by a Special Team under TICOM auspices." A TICOM publication.
E 8. "Detailed Feuerstein Technical Project Report. Reference No. 1 - Agents Transmitter "Taube", Single Sideband Demodulator "Kaethe" and Carrier Regenerator "Spitz"." A TICOM publication.
E 9. "Detailed Feuerstein Technical Project Report. Ref. No. 2; Little Baustein." A TICOM publication.
E 10. "Detailed Feuerstein Technical Project Report. Ref. No. 3: Artificial Speech and Encoding." A TICOM publication.
E 11. "Detailed Feuerstein Technical Project Report, Ref. No. 4: Three-fold Wobbulation and Mechanical Wobbulator Generators." A TICOM publication.
E 12. "Detailed Feuerstein Technical Project Report, Ref. No. 5: Filter Design and Construction." A TICOM publication.
E 13. "Detailed Feuerstein Technical Project Ref. No. 6: Synchronous Cipher System for Teletypewriters--Gleichlauf." A TICOM publication.
E 14. "Detailed Feuerstein Technical Project Report, Ref. No. 7: Investigation of SZ Cipher Machines at Feuerstein Laboratory." A TICOM publication.
E 15. "Detailed Feuerstein Technical Project Report, Ref. No. 8: Wave Analyser." A TICOM publication.
E 16. Detailed Feuerstein Technical Project Report, Ref. No. 9: Ein Neues Elektrisches Sprechgerät zur Nachbildung der Menschlichen Vokale von Karl Willy Wagner." A TICOM publication.

E 17. "Detailed Feuerstein Technical Project Report, Ref. No. 10: Feuerstein Laboratory Plans." A TICOM publication.
E 18. "Detailed Feuerstein Technical Project Report, Ref. No. 11: "Betriebsordnung" Laboratory Rules." A TICOM publication.
E 19. "Detailed Feuerstein Technical Project Report, Ref. No. 12: Technical Interrogation of Feuerstein Employees Dr. Fritz Sennheiser and Wolfgang Martini." A TICOM publication.
Emer, Guido, Lt. Col. Officer in charge of the 8th Army Cryptanalytic Party.
ETOUSA.--European Theater of Operations United States Army.
FA (Forschungsamt).--Goering's "Research" Bureau.
Fellgiebel, Erich, Lt. General. Chief Signal Officer of Army and Armed Forces High Commands from beginning of War until he was executed in 1944.
Fenner, _____, Principal Specialist. Chief of Chi/IV of the Signal Intelligence Agency of the Supreme Command of the Armed Forces.
Forschungsamt (FA).--Goering's Research Bureau.
Foschini, _____, Dr. Director of SID.
Fuchs, _____, Col. Chief of Section II of Radio Security Section.
Gamba, General Vittorio. Chief of Cryptanalytic Section from World War I to Armistice of World War II.
Gastaldo, _____, Col. Chief of Army Intelligence Subsection of SIM. Succeeded Col. Pasquale.
GCCS.--Government Code and Cypher School.
Geheime Staats Polizei (Gestapo).--German Secret State Police.
Gentscheff, Major I. G. Head of the Bulgarian cryptanalytic Agency.
German Meteorological Service.--Reich Wetterdients.
German Secret State Police.--Geheime Staats Polizei (Gestapo).
Gestapo (Geheime Staats Polizei).--German Secret State Police.
Gimmler, _____, Maj. Gen. Chief of Army Ordnance Development and Testing Group Signal Branch (Wa Pruef 7) 1939-1943. Chief Signal Officer to Commander in Chief West, 1943-1945. Chief of Armed Forces Communication Group (Chef Ag WNV).

Gloeckener, _____, Major, Graduate Engineer. Chief of Section II of Signal Equipment.

Goering, Hermann, Reichsmarschall. Commander in Chief of German Air Force, German Air Minister, etc.
Goerings's Research Bureau.--Forschungsamt (FA). One of the six principal German Cryptologic Organizations.
Gorn,_____, Capt. Chief of Section B of Signal Equipment.
Göing, Dr. Wilhem. Nazi Party representative at Feuerstein; in charge of a small laboratory near Lofer in the Berchtesgaden area.
Grube,_____, Col. Dr. Chief of Signal Equipment.
GSI.--General Staff Intelligence.
Hallama,_____, Col. Reported as head of the Finnish cipher section.
Hanson,_____, Col. Official of Abwehr, involved in July 20 plot.
Henkel,_____, Major. Chief of Section I of Signal Equipment.
Himmler, Heinrich. Reichsfuehrer SS, Minister of Interior, Chief of German Police.
Huettenhain, Senior Specialist Dr. Erich. Principal Cryptanalyst of the Signal Intelligence Agency of the Supreme Command, Armed Forces (OKW/Chi).
I 1. "Final Report on TICOM Team 3 on Final Exploitation of Burgscheidungen." A TICOM publication.
I 12. "Translation of the Preliminary Interrogation of O.R.R. Tranow of 4/SKL II/OICM, carried out at Flensburg on 24-25 May 1945 by TICOM Team 6. A TICOM publication.
I 16. Notes on Interrogation of Amsrat Schwabe and Obfkmstr. Warsecha on Russian Naval Cyphers. A TICOM publication.
I 21. Preliminary Interrogation of Oberst Kettler, R.R. Dr. Huettenhain, Sdf. Dr. Fricke and Oblt. Schubert (OKH/Chi).
I 22. "Interrogation of German Cryptographers of Pers ZS Department of Auswaertiges Amt." A TICOM publication.
I 25. "Interrogation of RLM/Forschungsamt Members: Dr. Paetzel, R. R. Fingerhut, R. R. Oden, Dr. Klautsche and Min. Rat. Seifert, at Schloss Gluecksburg on 15, 21 June 1945." A TICOM publication.
I 29. Third Interrogation of Oberstltn. Friedrich, Chief of the G.A.F. Signals Intelligence Service. A TICOM publication
I 31. Detailed Interrogations of Dr. Huettenhain formerly head of research section of OKW/Chi, 18th-21st June 1945. A TICOM publication.
I 43. Report Written by Vierling On:
a) Synchronising Device for Teleprinters (Gleichlauf)

83

b) Artificial Speech Apparatus
c) "Three-fold wobbling" process
d) Synchronising installation for producing the "wobble-frequencies"
e) Voice-Scrambling Apparatus (small BAUSTEIN)
A TICOM publication.

I 54. Second Interrogation of Five Members of the RLM/Forschungsamt. A TICOM publication.

I 57. Enciphering Devices worked on by Dr. Liebknecht at Wa Pruef 7. A TICOM publication.

I 58. Interrogation of Dr. Otto Buggisch of OKW/Chi. A TICOM publication.

I 64. Answers by Wm. Buggisch of OKH/Chi to Questions sent by TICOM. A TICOM publication.

I 65. Interrogation Report on Four Members of the G. A. F. Sigint Service. A TICOM publication.

I 72. First Part of the Report by Wm. Buggisch on S.G.41. A TICOM publication.

I 76. "Interrogation Reports on Lehwold, Haupts, Klett and Lauerbach." A TICOM publication.

I 78. Interrogation of Oberstlt. Mettig on the History and Achievements of OKH/AHA/In. 7/VI. A TICOM publication.

I 82. P.O.W. Interrogation Report-Dr. Werner Liebknecht of Wa Pruef 7 of the Heereswaffenamt. A TICOM publication.

I 84. Further Interrogation of R.R. Dr. Huettenhain and Sdf. Dr. Fricke of OKW/Chi. A TICOM publication.

I 92. "Final Interrogation of the Wachtmeister Otto Buggisch (OKH/In. 7/VI and OKW/Chi)." A TICOM publication.

I 93. "Detailed Interrogation of Members of OKM/4 SKL/III at Flensburg." A TICOM publication.

I 96. "Interrogation of Oberstlt. Mettig on the Organization and Activities of OKW/Chi." A TICOM publication.

I 100. "Report by Uffg. Herzfeld of NAAST 5 (Gen. d. NA) on the work of the Italian Referat of IM 7/VI." A TICOM publication.

I 102. "Interrogation Report on Dr. Sebastian of the German Met. Service on Allied Met. Systems." A TICOM publication.

I 105. "Interrogation report on Frau von Nida (wife of Major Wolfgang von Nida, onetime deputy Head of OKW/Chi)." A TICOM publication.

I 106. Final Interrogation Report on the Norway Party (NAA 11)." A TICOM publication.

I 109. "Translation of a Report by Lt. Ludwig of Chi Stelle Ob.d.L. (Ref.B) based on questions set for him at A.D.I.(K)." A TICOM publication.

I 110. "Information on Radio Communication Circuits operated in Conjunction with Feuerstein Laboratories." A TICOM publication.

I 111. "Further Interrogation of Oberstlt. Mettig of OKW/Chi on 14th September 1945. A TICOM publication.

I 115. "Further Interrogation of Oberstlt. Mettig of OKW/Chi on the German Wireless Security Service (Funküberwachung)." A TICOM publication.

I 116. "Report of Interrogation of Ltn. Alex Dettmann and Oberwachtmeister Sergius Samsonow of OKH (Gen.d.NA.) at Oberursel, Germany, during August 1945." A TICOM publication.

I 118. Joint Reports by Reg. Rat Dr. Huettenhain and Sdf. Dr. Fricke, written at C.S.D.I.C. on or about 28th August 1945. A TICOM publication.

I 120. "Translation of Homework by Obltn. W. Werther, Company Commander of 7/LN Rgt. 353, written on 12th August 1945 at A.D.I. (K)." A TICOM publication.

I 121. Translation of Homework by Obltn. W. Werther, Company Commander of 7/LN Rgt. 353, written on 12th August 1945 at A.D.I. (K)." A TICOM publication.

I 130. Homework by Hauptmann Herold, O.C. Ln. Regt. III/353. A TICOM publication.

I 131. Obstlt. Mettig of OKW/Chi on WA Pruef 7 and RLM/Forschungsamt. A TICOM publication.

I 132. Notes by Huettenhain and Fricke on OKW/Chi and the German I.S. A TICOM publication.

I 141. Interrogation of Amtsrat Schulze of 4 SKL III. A TICOM publication.

I 142. P/W Barthel's Account of German Work on British, American, Swedish, and French Machine Ciphers. A TICOM publication.

I 143. "Report on the Interrogation of Five Leading Germans at Nuernberg on 27th Sept. 1945." A TICOM publication.

I 177. "Interrogation of Kirfel on Far Eastern Systems." A TICOM publication.

I 193. "Interrogation of SS Obersturmbahnfuehrer Urban, Liaison Officer of RSHA/VI with the Crypto Bureau of Hungarian General Staff." A TICOM publication.

I 194. "Report by Dr. Regula on German Meteorological Intelligence Service." A TICOM publication.
IF 15. Final Report of TICOM Team 1 on the exploitation of Kaufbeuren and the Berchtesgaden area. From TICOM.
IF 108. "Interrogation of Oblt. Arntz." CSDIC (U.K) SIR 1606.
IF 140 B. German D/Fing in France. Nov. 13, 1945. War Dept. Strategic Services Unit.
IF 163. Photostatic copies of reports:(a) Statements by Arntz, 23 March 1945. (b) Organization and location of German Army Signal Intelligence Service in the West, 26 March 1945. (c) Appendix to Armed Forces Signal Administration, Operations Section, 28 Sept. 1944. (d) Translation of above appendix. (e) Employment, organization of the Signal Corps, 16 Jan. 1945. Hq. 12th Army.
IF 164. "Report on Interrogation of Walter Schellenberg."
IF 176. Seabourne Report. Vol III. "Operations and Techniques of the Radio Defense Corps, German Wehrmacht." From Commanding General, 9th Air Force.
IF 209. Italian Communications Intelligence. Report by Admiral Maugeri with U.S. Navy Introduction.
IF 260. Correspondence, MIS-OSS, on Finish Cryptanalytic Liaison with other Powers.
IF 1500. Italian Intelligence Service: Report on "Organization and Working of the Servizio Informazioni Esercito (S.I.E.) within the period 1/11/41--15/6/43." SCI/560/67 Oct. 18 1944.
IF 1501. First detailed interrogation report of Giuseppe SAMARUGHI. CSDIC/CMF/Y 29.
IF 1502. First detailed interrogation of Giuseppe DOSI. CSDIC (MAIN)/Y 16 21 Nov. 1944.
IF 1517. First detailed interrogation of Augusto BIGI, who worked in the Cryptographic Section of SIM before the Armistice and in SID afterward. CSDIC/CMF/Y 4. 8 Sept. 1944.
IF 1518. First detailed Interrogation of Vittorio Gamba, director of SIM Cryptographic Section until Armistice. CSDIC/CMF/Y 7. 16 Oct. 1944.
IF 1519. First detailed interrogation of Franco SCUILERI. CSDIC/CMF/Y 8.
IF 1520. First Detailed Interrogation og Guido EMER. CSDIC/CMF/Y 8. Oct 22 1944.
IF 1523. First Detailed Interrogation of Giovanni Gramola, pertaining to Turkish, French, British, and USA traffic. CSDIC (MAIN)/Y 24.

IF 1524. First Detailed Interrogation Report on Three SID Cryptographers -- de Witt, Biagi, Carlini. CSDIC/CMF/Y 32.
IF 1526. Second Detailed Interrogation Report on Five Italian SID Cryptographers -- de Witt, Biagi, Ulieni, Carlini, and Barbagallo. CSDIC/CMF/Y 35.
IF 1527. First Detailed Interrogation Report of Alberto Barbagallo, Italian Naval Cryptographer. CSDIC/CMF/Y 34.
Inspectorate 7/VI of Army High Command.--Oberkommando des Heeres/Inspektion 7/VI (OKH/In 7/VI).
Italian Army Intelligence Service.--Servizio Informazioni Militari (SIM).
Italian Defense Intelligence Service.--Servizio Informazioni Difesa (SID).
Italian Navy Intelligence Service.--Servizio Informazioni Speciali (SIS).
Kaehler,_____, Lt. Col. Chief of Chi/III of the Signal Intelligence Agency of the Supreme Command of the Armed Forces.
v. Kalckstein,_____, Lt. Col. Chief of Chi/X of the Signal Intelligence Agency of the Supreme Command of the Armed Forces.
Kettler,_____, Col. Chief of Signal Intelligence Agency of the Supreme Command of the Armed Forces.
Keutel,_____, Mr. Chief of Section II of Armed Forces Communications Group Wire Communication.
Klob, Otto, Dr. Director of Austrian Cipher Bureau until October, 1945.
von Knobelsdorff-Brenkerhoff, Col. Commander of Armed Forces Wire Communications (OKW/Ag WNV/KFA).
Kommandeur der Nachrichten Aufklärung (KONA).--Army Signal Intelligence Regiment.
KONA (Kommandeur der Nachrichten Aufklärung).--Army Signal Intelligence Regiment.
v. Laffert,_____, Major. Chief of Section I of the Radio Security Section.
Liebknecht, Werner, Graduate Engineer Dr. Chief of section IIIh of Army Ordnance, Development and Testing Group, Signal Branch (Wa Pruef 7), research agency for developing voice scramblers.
Lober,_____, Major. Chief of the Signal Intelligence Agency of the Supreme Command of the Armed Forces.
Lohse,_____, Major. Chief of Subsection F of the Armed Forces Communications Group Wire Communication, Section 4.
M 1. Vierling's Laboratory at Ebermannstadt. A TICOM publication.

M 2. Major Barlow's Report on Dr. Vierling's Laboratory. A TICOM publication.

M 4a. Full Preliminary Report of Investigation of Dr. Vierling's Laboratory "Feuerstein" -- by Major Heller. A TICOM publication.

M 6. Interim Report on Laboratorium Feuerstein -- by Lieuts. Howard and Tompkins, U.S.N.R. A TICOM publication.

M 12. CIOS Target Evaluation Report on Laboratorium Feuerstein, Ebermannstadt. A TICOM publication.

Magnussen,_____, Major. Chief of Section I of Armed Forces Communications Group Wire Communication.

Menzer,_____, Senior Inspector. Chief of Section IIc of Signal Intelligence Agency, Supreme Command Armed Forces (OKW/Chi) which dealt with the development of cipher machines.

Meteorological Intercept Control.--Wetternachrichtenueberwachung (Wenueb).

Mettig,_____, Lt. Col. Head of In 7/VI from Nov. 1941 to June 1943; Second in Command of OKW/Chi from Dec. 1943 to April 1945.

Military Intelligence.--Abwehr.

Mohr,_____, Mr. Chief of Section Ib of Radio Security Section.

Mushake,_____, Capt. Chief of Section Ial of Radio Security Section.

NAA (Nachrichten Aufklärungs Abteilung).--Signal Intelligence Regiment.

Nachrichten Aufklärungs Abteilung (NAA).--Signal Intelligence Regiment.

Nasta,_____, Col. Chief of Secretariat Section of SIM.

Naumann,_____, Senior Inspector. Chief of cryptanalytic section of German Meteorological Service.

Neitzel,_____, Mr. Chief of Registry Office.

Neumann,_____, Lt. Col. Head of Section Ie of Central Group of Armed Forces Communications Group.

Oberkommando der Luftwaffe/Luftnachrichten Abteilung 350 (OKL/LN ABT/350).--Signal Intelligence Agency of the Air Force High Command.

Oberkommando der Marine/4 Seekriegsleitung III (OKM/4 SKL/III).--Signal Intelligence Agency of the Navy High Command.

Oberkommando der Wehrmacht/Chiffrierabteilung (OKW/Chi).--Signal Intelligence Agency of the Supreme Command Armed Forces.

Oberkommando der Wehrmacht, Wehrmacht Nachrichtenverbindung, Funkueberwachung (OKW/WNV/Fu).--Radio Defense Corps of the Armed Forces.
Oberkommando der Wehrmacht/Wehrmacht Fuehrungsstab (OKW/WFSt).--Armed Forces Operations Staff of the Supreme Command of the Armed Forces.
Oberkommando des Heeres/Chef des Heeres Nachrichten Wesens/Leitstelle der Nachrichten Aufklärung (OKH/Chef HNW/LNA).--Army High Command Signal Intelligence Control Station.
Oberkommando des Heeres/General der Nachrichten Aufklaerung (OKH/GdNA).--Signal Intelligence Agency of the Army High Command.
Oberkommando des Heeres/Inspektion 7/IV (OKH/In 7/IV).--Signal Security Agency of the Army High Command.
Oberkommando des Heeres/Inspektion 7/VI (OKH/In 7/VI).--Inspectorate 7/VI of the Army High Command.
OKH/Chef HNW/LNA (Oberkommando des Heeres/Chef des Heeres Nachrichten Wesens/Leitstelle der Nachrichten Aufklärung.--Army High Command Signal Intelligence Control Station.
OKH/GdNA (Oberkommando des Heeres/General der Nachrichten Aufklaerung).--Signal Intelligence Agency of the Army High Command.
OKH/In 7/IV (Oberkommando des Heeres/Inspektion 7/IV).--Signal Security Agency of the Army High Command.
OKH/In 7/VI (Oberkommando des Heeres/Inspektion 7/VI).--Inspectorate 7/VI of the Army High Command.
OKL/LN Abt/350 (Oberkommando der Luftwaffe/Luftnachrichten Abteilung 350).--Signal Intelligence Agency of the Air Force High Command.
OKM/4 SKL/III (Oberkommando der Marine/4 Seekriegsleitung III).--Signal Intelligence Agency of the Navy High Command.
OKW/Chi (Oberkommando der Wehrmacht/Chiffrierabteilung).--Signal Intelligence Agency of the Supreme Command Armed Forces.
OKW/WFSt (Oberkommando der Wehrmacht/Wehrmacht Fuehrungsstab).--Armed Forces Operations Staff of the Supreme Command of the Armed Forces.
OKW/WNV/Fu (Oberkommando der Wehrmacht, Wehrmacht Nachrichtenverbindung, Funkueberwachung).--Radio Defense Corps of the Armed Forces.
Pale, Mikki, Captain. In command of cryptanalytic unit in Finland.
Pasquale, _____, Col. Chief of Army Intelligence Sub-section of SIM.
Pers Z S (Sonderdienst des Referats Z in der Personalabteilung des Auswaertigen Amtes). --Cryptanalytic Section of the German Foreign Office.

89

Col. Petrella. Chief of the Intercept Section of SIM.
Piccinocchi, Col. Chief of Cryptograhy Section of SIM.
Pippart,_____, Mr. Chief of Subsection P of the Armed Forces Communications Group Wire Communication, Section 4.
Pohmer,_____, Capt. Chief of Section Ia of Radio Security Section.
Proebster,_____, Major. Chief of Section Ib of Central Group of Armed Forces Communications Group.
Praun, Albert, Maj. Gen. Succeeded Fellgiebel as Chief Signal Officer of Armed Forces, 1944.
Proebster,_____, Major. Chief of Section Ib of Armed Forces Communication Group.
Radio Defense Corps of the Armed Forces.--Oberkommando der Wehrmacht, Wehrmacht Nachrichtenverbindung, Funkueberwachung, (OKW/WNV/Fu).
Radio Intelligence Company (called Radio Telegraph Kompanie, abbreviated RTK by Germans). The cryptanalytic organization of Finland. Called Abteilung X in I-193.
Radio Telegraph Kompanie. See Radio Intelligence Company.
Reinhardt,_____, Mr. Chief of Secretariat section of the Radio Security Section.
Ronge,_____. Chief cryptanalyst of the Austro-Hungarian Empire.
Rosenkranz,_____, Col. Chief of Radio Security Section.
RTK. See Radio Intelligence Company.
Salzbrunn,_____, Mr. In charge of a subsection of Chi/III of the Signal Intelligence Agency of the Supreme Command of the Armed Forces.
Schack,_____, Mr. Chief of Secretariat of Armed Forces Communications Group Wire Communication.
Secret Field Police.--Sicherheitsdienst Kommando, abbreviated (S D Kommando) and Sicherheits Polizei, (SIPO).
Servizio Informazioni Aeronautica (SIA).--Air Force Intelligence Service.
Servizio Informazioni Difesa (SID).--Italian Defense Intelligence Service.
Servizio Informazioni Militari (SIM).--Army Intelligence Service.
Servizio Informazioni Speciali (SIS).--Italian Navy Intelligence Service.
SIA (Servicio Informazioni Aeronautica).--Air Force Intelligence Service.
Seyfarth,_____, Lt. Col. Chief of Chi/II of the Signal Intelligence Agency of the Supreme Command of the Armed Forces.

90

S D Kommando. See Secret Field Police.
SHAEF.--Supreme Headquarters Allied Expeditionary Forces.
Sicherheitsdienst Kommando. See Secret Field Police.
Sicherheits Polizei. See Secret Field Police.
SID.--Signal Intelligence Division.
SID (Servizio Informazioni Difesa).--Italian Defense Intelligence Service.
Siefert, _____, Dr. Director of Austrian Cipher Bureau after 1935.
Signal Intelligence Agency of the Air Force High Command.--Oberkommando der Luftwaffe/Luftnachrichten Abteilung 350 (OKL/LN ABT/350).
Signal Intelligence Agency of the Army High Command.--Oberkommando des Heeres/General der Nachrichten Aufklaerung (OKH/GdNA).
Signal Intelligence Agency of the Commander in Chief of the Air Force.--Chiffrierstelle, Oberkommando der Luftwaffe (Chi-Stelle Ob d L).
Signal Intelligence Agency of the Navy High Command.--Oberkommando der Marine/4 Seekriegsleitung III (OKM/4 SKL/III).
Signal Intelligence Agency of the Supreme Command Armed Forces.--Oberkommando der Wehrmacht/Chiffrierabteilung (OKW/Chi).
Signal Intelligence Regiment.--Nachrichten Aufklärungs Abteilung (NAA).
Signal Security Agency of the Army High Command.--Oberkommando des Heeres/Inspektion 7/IV (In 7/IV).
SIM (Servizio Informazioni Militari).--Army Intelligence Service.
SIPO. See Secret Field Police.
SIS (Servizio Informazioni Speciali).--Italian Navy Intelligence Service.
Sonderdienst des Referats Z in der Personalabteilung des Auswaertigen Amtes (Pers ZS).--Cryptanalytic Section of the German Foreign Office.
T 84. "Hollaendische Verfahren."
T 477. "SZYFR Zasadniczy "Mar 2"." /Original copy of Polish 5-figure code book/.
T 1620. ES: P. 207. Army Signal Intelligence Organizations.
T 2649. Descriptions of inventions by Dr. Vierling.
T 3614. Records of Shipments from Austrian Cipher Bureau to Cipher Bureau of Reichswehr-Ministerium, Berlin. Also letters. (1934-1937).

91

TF 29. "Die Ueberwachung des Nachrichtenverkehrs im Kriege." German document containing instructions and Organization for all Censorship.

Thiele, Brig. Gen. Chief of Staff to Chief Signal Officer of Army.

TICOM. Target Intelligence Committee.

Trosken,_____, Lt. Col. Commander of the Central Group of the Armed Forces Communications Group.

Vass, Titus, Lt. "The ace Hungarian cryptanalyst." Worked in Turkish section.

Vierling, Oskar, Dr. Head of Feuerstein Laboratory, worked on German ciphony devices.

von Petrikovics,_____, General. Chief of the cryptanalytic bureau in Hungary.

Triphan,_____, Mr. Chief of Secretariat Section of Signal Equipment.

Tuexen,_____, Major. Chief of a Section of Signal Equipment.

Waak,_____, Civil Official. Chief of Section Id of Central Group of Armed Forces Communications Group.

Wa Pruef 7 (Chef der Heeresruestung und Befehlshaber des Ersatzheeres, Amtsgruppe fuer Entwicklung und Pruefung des Heereswaffenamts, Waffen Pruefung, Abteilung 7).--Army Ordnance, Development and Testing Group, Signal Branch.

Watson Corporation. Italian IBM Company.

Wehrmachtnachrichtenverbindungen (WNV).--Armed Forces Signal Communication.

Wenueb (Wetternachrichtenueberwachung).--Meteorological Intercept Control.

Wetternachrichtenueberwachung (Wenueb).--Meteorological Intercept Control.

WNV (Wehrmachtnachrichtenverbindungen).--Armed Forces Signal Communications.

Zappe,_____. Vierling employee.

Zellien,_____, Major. Chief of Section A of Signal Equipment.

Zentralwetterdienstgruppe.--Central Weather Group.

92

ITALIAN ARMY INTELLIGENCE ORGANIZATION

NOVEMBER, 1941 — SEPTEMBER, 1943

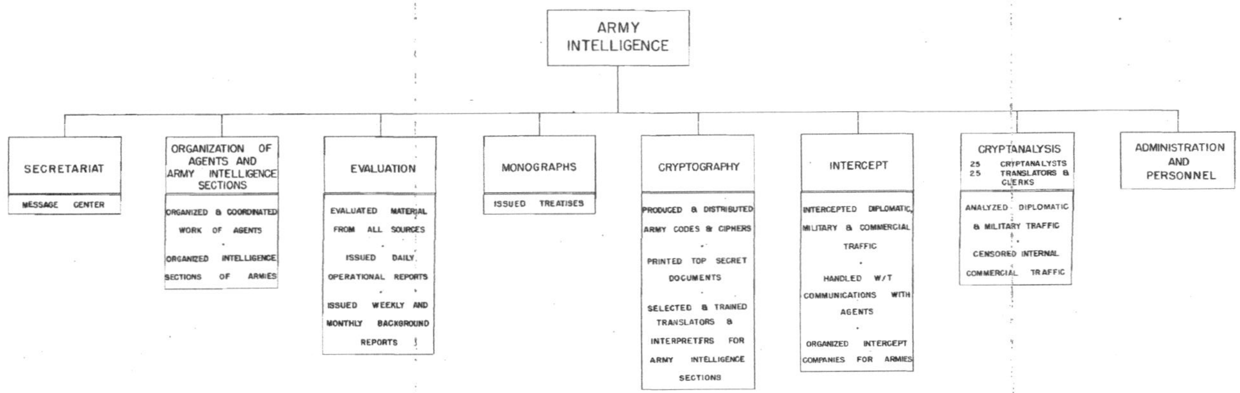

FASCIST/REPUBLICAN ITALIAN SIGNAL INTELLIGENCE ORGANIZATION

(FORMED FROM FORMER CRYPTANALYSIS AND INTERCEPT SECTIONS OF ARMY INTELLIGENCE)

SUMMER 1944 — MAY, 1945

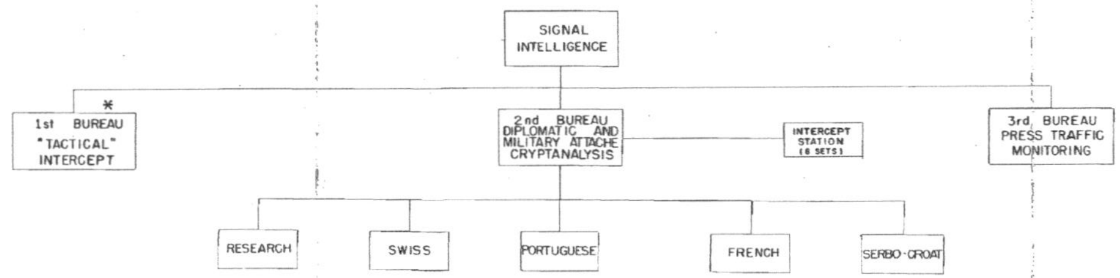

*CLOSED DOWN

ARMY SECURITY AGENCY

Washington, D. C.

EUROPEAN AXIS SIGNAL INTELLIGENCE IN WORLD WAR II AS REVEALED BY "TICOM" INVESTIGATIONS AND BY OTHER PRISONER OF WAR INTERROGATIONS AND CAPTURED MATERIAL, PRINCIPALLY GERMAN

VOLUME 9--GERMAN TRAFFIC ANALYSIS OF RUSSIAN COMMUNICATIONS

Prepared under the direction of the

CHIEF, ARMY SECURITY AGENCY

1 May 1946

WDGAS-14

TABLE OF CONTENTS

~~TOP SECRET CREAM~~

INTRODUCTION

The contents of this volume deal with German exploitation of Russian communications through Traffic Analysis. There is not as much source material available on Russia as there is on United States and England. The main interest of the interrogation officers normally was centered on gaining intelligence concerning American and British communications, and consequently, interest concerning German activity on the communications of other countries had to be of secondary importance. In addition, because of the conditions under which many of the interrogations were conducted--a number of them being made in active combat zones--there were oftentimes great difficulties encountered in carrying out even the necessary routine line of questioning. Even had there been ideal conditions under which to work it is probable that not much more intelligence could have been obtained on Russian communications because the German personnel who were engaged in that work were in the Russian zone of operations. Only a few of these fell into English or American hands--the Russians capturing the others. However, the material which is available does give a fairly adequate, though not complete, picture of Russian communications as seen by the German Traffic Analyst.

VOLUME 9

Chapter 1

SECURITY OF RUSSIAN COMMUNICATIONS

1. General Security.--Although the Russians monitored their own military communications for the more outstanding breaches of cryptographic and transmission security, company and secondary commands were very careless with their radio-telephone transmissions. Code cover names were rarely heard by German listening operators. However, many private conversations were intercepted as the Russians had a tendency to use radio-telephone facilities as an ordinary telephone. Also the Russian radio operators committed violations in security which greatly facilitated the work of the German Signal Intelligence.[1]

The Russian radio and radio-telephone operators habitually engaged in "operator chat". One instance of such conversations, and the subsequent value to German Signal Intelligence, occurred in January 1943 when the Germans learned that a British-American delegation was visiting the Russian Central front. In other instances the arrival of high-ranking officers was disclosed in private radio-telephone conversations as well as dates for planned offensives.[2]

Although their radio-telephone traffic was on a very low level of security, the morse and non-morse radio traffic of the Russian military forces reached a high degree of security during the later periods of the war. This appears

[1] I-75, p 4

[2] I-75, p 4

1

to have been due to the increased amount of radio training given the operators; the increased amount of traffic which they had to send; and the subsequent efficiency which came from practice.[3]

2. Security on Partisan Nets.--On the Russian Partisan radio nets good operators were employed and the Germans were unable to learn much about the operation and activity of these nets. In the winter of 1943 the Germans formed a detachment to trace the activity of the Partisan nets. These attempts however were unsuccessful owing to the fact that messages transmitted were very brief and there was only a short duration of radio activity when the nets were in operation.[4]

3. Army and Air Forces Nets.--The set-up of the Russian radio nets was a reflection of the organization of the Soviet Armed Forces. As radio facilities were used without restrictions, on account of inadequate line communications, traffic intercept and analysis, as a primary source of intelligence to the Germans, reached a high degree of efficiency. An insight into the makeup of the radio nets was facilitated by imperfect changes in the radio discipline.[5]

The air units of the Russian armies were forced, due to inadequate line communications, to exercise command from Air Army downwards by radio.[6]

In nets from division downwards in the Army composition radio-telephone channels were used for the passing in of communications in addition to the use of morse radio traffic. During the latter days of the war this use of radio-telephone increased. At the beginning of the war radio-telephone transmission in regard to opening of nets, message warning signals, and the use of the alphabet in spelling out names and code groups was carried out strictly in accordance with existing regulations. Such was not the case later: the traffic then

[3] I-75, p 4

[4] I-75, p 4

[5] I-70, p 4

[6] I-70, p 3

sometimes assuming a very free form. Radio-telephony was used for passing messages, fire orders for artillery, reports for the Air Warning Service, and also for general conversation between officers and commanders. The traffic consisted mostly of two-and-three-figure message-text, plain-text, and mixed figure-plain-text. Radio stations used cover names which were easily analyzed by the Germans. Call signs of these stations were mostly formed from the cover names of the stations. (Thus the call sign "MAP" was formed from the cover name of "MAPKA").[7]

In analyzing Russian traffic the Germans used all the data available: pad numbers, originators' serial numbers, call sign system composition, coordination and knowledge of map coordinates, any results obtained from decrypted materials, and any direction-finding information.[8]

[7] I-173, p 10

[8] I-19b, p 5

DOCID: 3633965

VOLUME 9

Chapter 2

GERMAN EXPLOITATION OF RUSSIAN COMMUNICATIONS

4. Russian Radio Procedure.--During the first days of the Russian-German war the speed of the transmitting operators was very low, but as time went on they developed their speed until at the end of the war the average speed attained was 16 to 18 words per minute. On some of the more important point-to-point radio nets the average speed was 25 words per minute.[9]

[9] IF-187, p 48

a. Procedure Signals.--The International "Q" and "Z" signal groups were used as procedure signals by the Russians. The Germans assumed that some of the Russian operators had been trained by the British because some well-known British abbreviations such as "ok", "pse", "for", "fm", "tks", etc., often were found in traffic. There was also a certain amount of amateur radio procedure used. In addition, as a separator between call signs the Russians used both "de" and "a". The letter "r" was used as a break between numbered groups in cipher text while a comma was used in clear-text messages. No break sign was used in the radio nets of higher headquarters, the only indication of a break sign being a pause after a word or code group had been completed. This was one radio characteristic which aided the German traffic analyst in identifying the traffic of higher Russian headquarters.[10]

b. Radio Discipline.--When Russian nets underwent call sign changes or frequency changes, the German intercept operators had little difficulty in identifying the nets since a lack of security in turning on of radio sets and checking of frequencies (known as "tuning") invariably permitted recognition of the changes in the nets.[11]

Security violations were often committed when work shifts were changed. An excellent example of the type of information thus made available to the Germans is to be found in the following intercepted message.

"This is Mishka, how did you sleep?"
"We could not decode the third group in your message number 25 of last evening."
"You must transmit it again."

Thus Mishka and his request not only gave the Germans the identity of the net but enabled them possibly to obtain a previously intercepted message in a new key if the second operator complied with the request to re-transmit the message.[12]

Some Russian operators furnished the Germans with a good insight into Russian morale by "griping" over the radio. Some of the operators were so obliging as to inform other operators of the new frequency which they would begin using at a specified time.[13]

[10] IF-187, p 48

[11] IF-187, p 49

[12] IF-187, p 49

[13] IF-187, p 49

5

Russian lapses in radio discipline often led to obtaining by the Germans of valuable intelligence. At one time the scarcity of traffic from a part of the Leningrad front led the German Signal Intelligence to think that the Russians were planning a new offensive. The German Signal Intelligence already knew the identity of Air Combat units which were based in that area. Therefore, when messages from the Finnish area were intercepted containing the names of escadrille leaders and instructions for future operations, it was established by the German Signal Intelligence that those units formerly located on the Leningrad front had moved to the Karelian front in Finland. This intelligence, which was subsequently proven correct, was obtained by the Germans although a complete change of call signs and frequencies had been made by the Russians.[14]

5. Special Traffic Characteristics.

a. Call Signs.--The following information concerning work which the Germans did on the Russian Call Sign Books was written by Uffz. (Non-commissioned officer) Wilhelm HEIMANN. The Russian call sign system, according to HEIMANN, is a continuation from a previously known system which the Germans had analyzed. The production of the call sign books was by the same method as had been used with the older system, but the manner of selection of the call signs by encipherment of the radio station basic numbers was different and new. This latter method was almost identical to the system used by the Germans after November 1944 when all the call sign systems used by the Germans were changed. HEIMANN thought perhaps the Russian method may have influenced the adoption of the same method by the Germans. One difference between the two methods was that while the Germans enciphered a call sign which was determined by the enciphered basic radio station number, the Russians merely used the enciphered basic number for determining directly the page, row, and column in the call sign book where the new call sign would be found. "Consequently", said HEIMANN, "the German system is unbreakable without, say, captured data; the Russian is quite breakable given sufficient call signs and day-to-day continuity."[15]

[14] IF-187, p 49.

[15] IF-19f, p 6.

When the Germans first began studying the Russian system of call signs their purpose was to establish the call sign books or systems (Unterlagen) from which call signs were taken; the method of selection of the call signs from the book; and the various groups of call sign users. The objective of the Germans in making the study was to determine, on the basis of the call signs used, the character and composition of any given radio net; to identify in that net the various formations; and to maintain continuity throughout call sign changes.[16]

The following methods and results of this study are given by HEIMANN:

"Call Sign Systems.

"There were found to be two tables (different) of call signs:

"TPR 43: a list of 1,200 words, the first three letters of which were used in keying traffic.

"Call Sign Books: each with 1,100 - 1,200 call signs, which were compiled of letters and figures in such a manner that (excepting compilers' errors) identical call signs could not occur.

"TPR 43 had 16 pages, 74 call signs per page, divided into three groups, each of 25 call signs. Each group had 5 lines, each with 5 call signs. (The above is based on captured documents.)

"A Call Sign Book contains 100 call signs, in 10 lines with 10 columns, on each of its 11 or 12 pages. (Confirmed also by captured documents.)

"From the numbering of captured documents the approximate scope of this material can be estimated at about 17 to 18 books. Up till now, about 12 or 13 books have been in use. Books were not compiled as complete books, but approximately 200 pages were first compiled and then split up into books. Each page contains 96 call signs beginning with 32 different characters, 3 call signs per character, and 4 call signs beginning with 2 other characters, 2 call signs per character.[17]

[16] IF-19f, p 1

[17] The translation here is very poor. What appears to be meant is: "Each page contains 100 call signs per page. 96 of these are 3-letter call signs which begin with 32 different possible characters. The remaining four call signs are 2-letter call signs and must begin with the remaining two letters of the Russian alphabet. The Russian alphabet with the English equivalents, together with the International Morse characters, are given on the next page.

7

DOCID: 3633965

RUSSIAN	ENGLISH	MORSE	RUSSIAN	ENGLISH	MORSE
А	A	.-	П	P	.--.
Б	B	-...	Р	R	.-.
В	V	.-- (W)	С	S	...
Г	G	--.	Т	T	-
Д	D	-..	У	OO	..-
Е, Э	E	.	Ф	F	..-.
Ж	ZH	...- (V)	Х	KH	.... (H)
З	Z	--..	Ц	TS	-.-. (C)
И	I	..	Ч	CH	---.
Й	I*	.--- (J)	Ш	SH	---- (Ö)
К	K	-.-	Щ	SHCH	--.- (Q)
Л	L	.-..	Ъ, Ь	HARD, SOFT SIGN	-..- (X)
М	M	--	Ы	YE	-.-- (Y)
Н	N	-.	Ю	YU	..-- (Ü)
О	O	---	Я	YA	.-.- (Ä)

* With another vowel.

8

"No call signs began with E, Z, R, U, SHCH ((Q)), and ∅. The 34 characters, therefore, used as beginners ((i.e., initial characters)) were:

"A, B, V ((W)), G, D, ZH ((V)), I, J, K, L, M, N, O, P, S, T, F, KH ((H)), TS ((C)), CH, SH, Y, X, IU, IA, 1, 2, 3, 4, 5, 6, 7, 8, 9.

"The unused beginners are obviously those likely to be confused with Russian International Call Signs, operating signals, etc.

"Since the 34 beginners would have yielded 3 x 34 = 102 call signs, 2 beginners in rotation were selected to form 2 call signs each.

"The affiliation of the books could thus be recognized by knowing which 2 initial characters on each page were those limited to form 2 call signs each.

"To keep check on the allocation of call signs to individual pages the compiler used a list in which the 34 initial characters each had two sheets, one extending from A to TS ((C)) and the other from CH to 9.[18]

"The compiler, having derived the call sign, say AAA, entered it in any position on the page which was then apportioned to one of the 17 or 18 books. The designation of its location, in terms of page and coordinates on that page, e.g., page 07, coordinates 23,[19] were then entered in the space for AAA. Some pages would then appear diagonally adjacent, while others would be vertically or horizontally adjacent.[20]

"The printed text of 11 or 12 pages was so arranged that two pages were printed on one side of a sheet of paper. Thus two pages were permanently associated.

"After some time these sheets, each of two pages, could be unbound and reshuffled so that a completely new arrangement of books resulted. Reshufflings of this type took place at the beginning of October 1944 and in the middle of February 1945.

"Manner of Selection."

"Formations working with TPR 43, especially from the division forward, were allotted a page by the chief signals

[18] See Figure 1, p 16

[19] Figure 2, p 16

[20] Figure 1, p 16

officer; selection was made according to the individual's fancy but often the page was used line by line. Such stereotyped usage led to the recognition of call signs."[21]

b. Russian Secret Police Nets.--The High Command nets of the Russian Secret Police (NKVD), often including the nets of regiments forward to battalion, entered the call sign selected from TPR 43 (either consecutively or at random) in 10 x 10 squares (100 call signs). By means of daily changing digit coordinates for the squares it was possible to issue a maximum of 100 call signs to a radio station provided with a 2-digit basic number. This system was valid for three months.

For example, consider a radio station with the basic number 31. The call sign for the first day is SHUF. The call sign for the second day is NASH, and the call sign for the 96th day is STA.[22]

For enciphering the 10's digits of the radio station basic number there were 6 vertical coordinate columns and for enciphering the 1's digits there were 6 horizontal coordinate rows, thus yielding 6 x 6 = 36 possible encipherments per month. The columns and rows changed monthly; the contents of the square changed quarterly.[23]

c. Air Force Ground Nets.--The nets of the Air Force Ground areas (RAB) entered the call sign selected consecutively from TPR 43 in similar squares and then used these squares, line by line, for 31 days. For the RAB which used this procedure the same call sign and meaning recurred every calendar month.[24]

For radio stations with call sign books 3-digit radio station numbers were issued. Thus up to 1,000 stations could make a daily change of call signs by means of one call sign book. The basic radio station number was changed daily by enciphering it by means of a simple substitution table which would then give the page in the call sign book; the vertical coordinate; and the horizontal coordinate. The intersection of these coordinates would then indicate the daily call sign.[25, 26]

[21] I-19f, p 2

[22] Figure 3

[23] I-19f, p 3

[24] I-19f, p 3

[25] Figure 4

[26] Figure 3

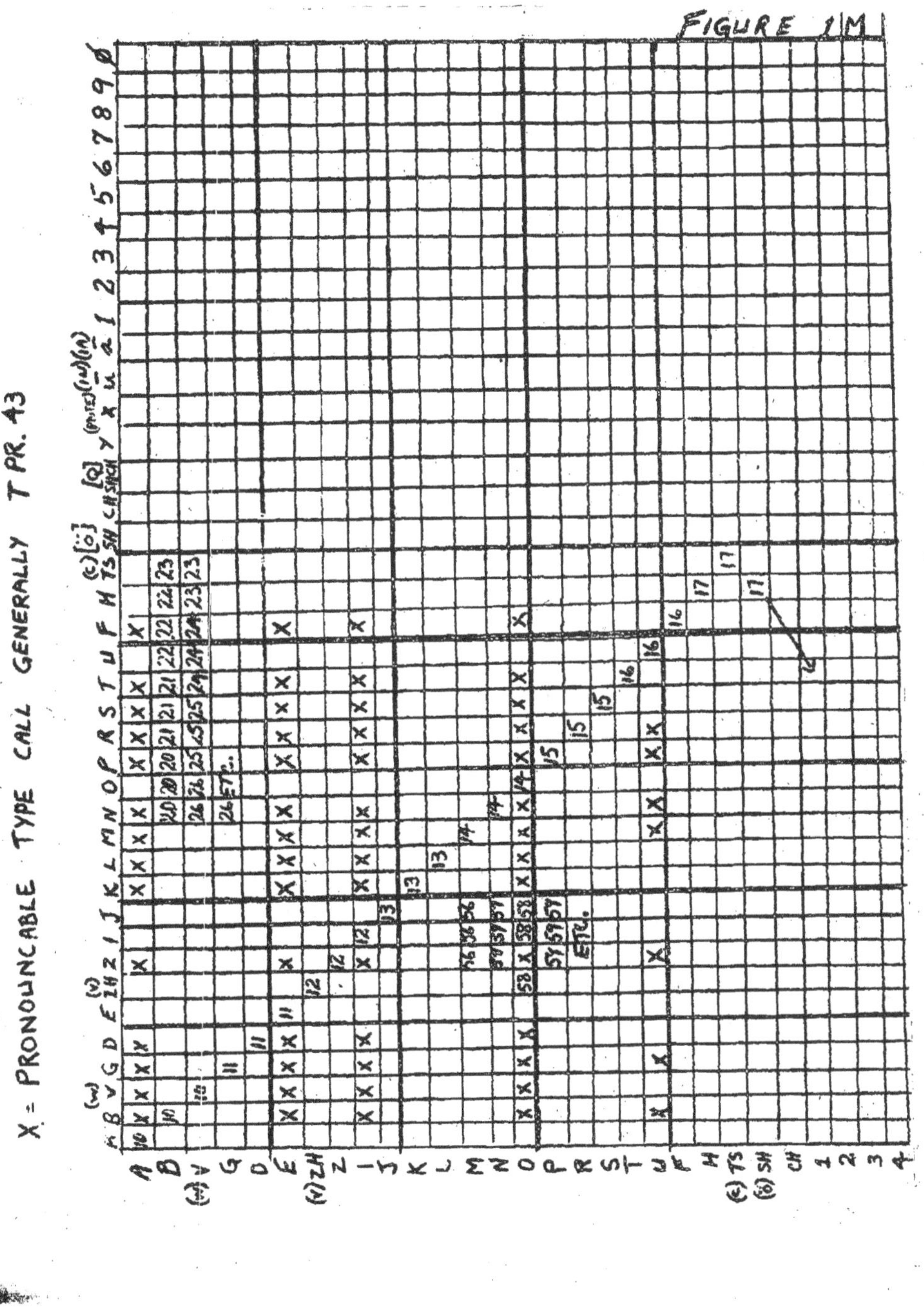
FIGURE 1M
X = PRONOUNCABLE TYPE CALL GENERALLY T PR. 43

DOCID: 3633965

FIGURE 2
PAGE IN CALL SIGN BOOK

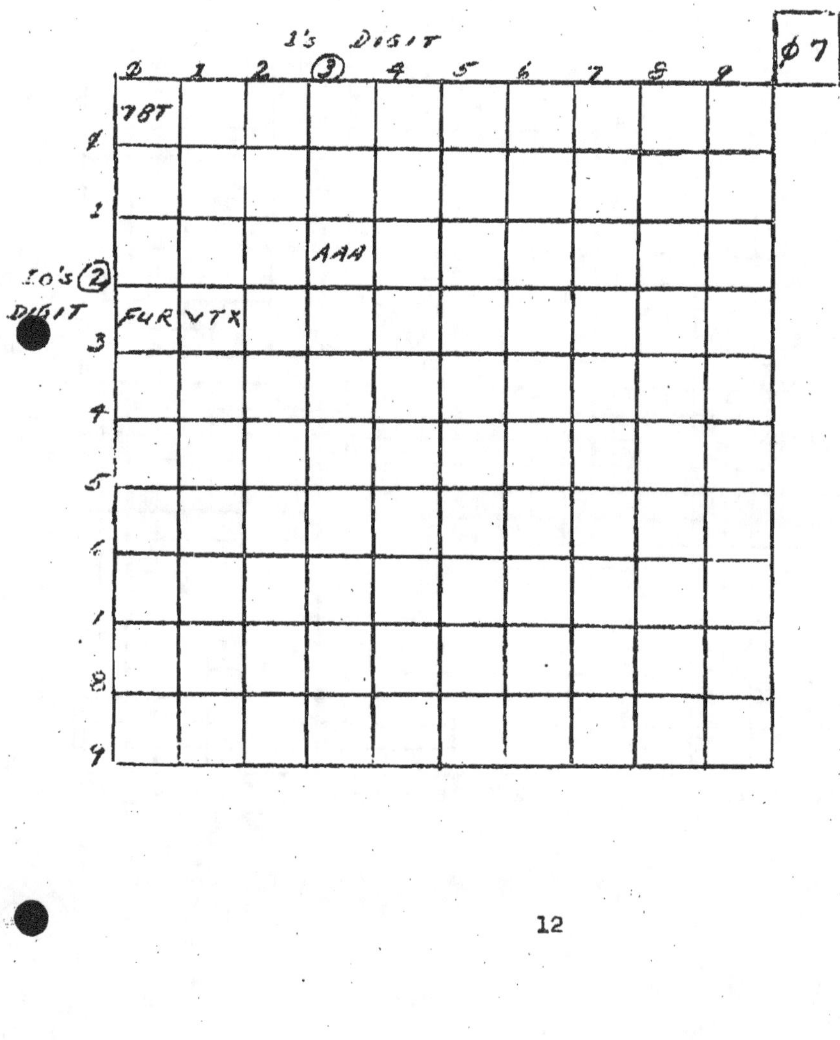

12

DOCID: 3633965

PAGE OF TPR 43 CALL SIGN BOOK

DAY OF MONTH

DAY OF MONTH

			2	17	96	3	1	9	8	5	
			61	1	7	8	9	1	Ø	7	
			3	48	10	7	3	5	1	9	
			9	5	6	BAC	FAL	DOM	SOM		
			Ø	3	1	POM	TUR	SHUF	LEN		
			4	7	3	MO3	STA	YOS	BOL		
			5	6	9	WOL	NKT				
			3	2	Ø						

Figure 3

1. Find day of month in 6 x 6 square in upper left hand corner.
2. Locate first digit (10's) of basic station number in vertical column in which day of month is located.
3. Locate second digit (1's) in horizontal row in which day of month is located.
4. Intersection of these coordinates gives call sign.

13

SUBSTITUTION TABLE FOR BASIC STATION NUMBER

Digits of basic radio Station number	Ø	1	2	3	4	5	6	7	8	9
100's digit substitution	5	7	2	6	Ø	8	1	3	9	4
10's digit substitution	6	4	5	2	7	3	Ø	8	9	1
1's digit substitution	2	8	4	6	Ø	7	5	3	1	9

Figure 4

1. Locate digits of basic radio station number at top.
2. Substitution for digit will be found in column underneath each digit according to 100's, 10's, or 1's position.
3. EXAMPLE: Radio station basic number = 587

   Substitution for first digit (5) in 100'th position is "8".

   Substitution for second digit (8) in 10's position is "9".

   Substitution for third digit (7) in 1's position is "3".

   Enciphered number is therefore 893 and gives:

   8 = page of book

   9 = vertical coordinate

   3 = horizontal coordinate.

The rows of 10 digits used in the substitution table (see Figure 4) were taken from a large table of 100 rows which were derived by cyclical substitution from 17 basic rows. The three rows of digits to be selected daily were found from a table which was valid for three months. This table consisted of a column indicating the day of the month. Opposite each day of the month were three columns. In each column was the number of the row which was to be selected from the large table of 100 rows. The table was 9 columns wide: the first 3 columns designating the first month; the second 3 columns the second month; and the last 3 columns the third month. The arrangement was such that in any one column no row of the 100 row table was repeated during the three months effective period.[27]

d. Groups of Call Sign Users.--The General Staff radio nets used their own call sign book up till about February 1945. After this date the call sign book was not identified by the Germans in other traffic. The High Command nets: i.e., the Front Armies and the Front Corps, used their own call sign book only from July 1944 until March 1945.

There were four call sign books for the Armies, Air Army, and Corps nets. The Armies of two or three widely separated fronts employed one call sign book jointly so that only by direction finding was it possible to establish on which front any particular Army was located. While the various groups of users had to be determined after every re-shuffling of the pages of the call sign books, this gave the Germans little trouble and often brought additional intelligence. For example, the last re-shuffling in April 1945 brought to light that the call sign books of the command nets contained an additional 11th page in place of the usual 10 pages "which was not affected by the enciphering process and served to select emergency call signs, which then were used as permanent call signs. The books of the Army nets even had two additional pages."[28]

e. Another German prisoner, Corp. HEUDORF, who was a radio and intercept operator on the Eastern front, also was interrogated on Russian use of call signs. He stated that until July 1944 the Germans knew the Russian call sign system

[27] I-19f, p 3

[28] I-19f, p 4

very well and were able to make predictions which were reliable. At the beginning of July 1944 the Russian radio nets maintained radio silence for seven weeks preceding the Russian offensive which took place in the late summer. When radio silence was lifted all the Russian call sign systems had been changed. From that time on it was very difficult for the Germans to have much success with the call sign systems. However by the end of May of 1945 HEUDORF stated that good progress had been made in solving the system.[29]

f. Five other German prisoners, Sgts. Erich KARRENBERG, Dietrich SUSCHOWK, SCHMITZ, HEMPEL, and Corp. GRUBLER, described the technique used by the Germans in identifying radio stations in the People's Commissariat for River Shipping (NKRF). They stated they had no particular difficulty in locating the stations

> "About 50% of the messages are not sent direct from the station of the sender to the recipient but are passed on, in some cases by way of three or four stations. For example, suppose that Saratov (RBUU) has some urgent messages for Moscow (RBFC). But the next traffic time between Saratov and Moscow is not until two hours later. However, Saratov has traffic at that moment with Kuibeshev (RBFR) and knows that because of its traffic schedule Kuibeshev will be working with Moscow immediately after it has finished with Saratov. So Saratov sends its messages to RBFR Kuibeshev:
>
> IZ RBUU 465 68 3/10 1200 MOSKWA A/P
> POLKOWNIKU PRONINU 465 143 476.....243/2
> GORBAOEW.[30]
>
> "On conclusion of the traffic RBFR acknowledges receipt of the messages to Saratov, calls Moscow and begins:
>
> IZ SARATOV 465 68 3/10 1200 MSK A/P
> PRONINU 465 143 476 ... ... 243/2
> GORBAOEW.
>
> "This shows clearly that RBUU is Saratov. Naturally one is not always so fortunate as to be able to follow such a pass-on in its entirety. A simple expedient is to collect signatures in conjunction

[29] I-75, p 8

[30] The message reads: FROM RBUU ... ...3/10 1200 hours Moscow. For Artillery Regiment, Lt. Col. PRONIN... ... Signed GORBAGEW.

with the call signs and places which come up with them. For example:

RBUU GORBAOEW SARATOV OEOERIN
OEOERIN GORBAOEW.

"If one has at least two names which come up together one can say certainly that the call sign and location have been identified. One name alone is not sufficient for identification, as in a large net there might easily be people with the same name working at different places."[31]

g. German personnel working on identification of Russian call signs, stations, and nets kept elaborate card indexes which contained all known and unknown call signs picked up on the entire Eastern front. These cards showed whether, and in what connection, the call sign had previously appeared. A cover name index was also kept which contained all the cover names that had been collected, and indicated the source and date of occurrence. With the assistance of these card indexes almost complete cover name tables for the Russian fronts were recovered.[32]

h. The call signs of all Russian ground stations were made up of three characters, either of letters, or letters and figures. An exception was the fixed 4-letter call sign used on several transport nets. For the greater part the call signs were taken from a call sign book used by the Russian Army after April 1944.

To form the call signs all the letters and the digits from 1 to 9 were used. However as in the case with the book TPR 43 the letters E, Z, R, U, SHCH((Q)) were not used as the first element of the call sign. Each page of the book contained 1,000 call signs. These call signs were changed at irregular intervals, sometimes daily and at other times at longer periods. When units and headquarters moved, a suffix was added to the call signs of the various echelons. Thus, "BEM"--rear echelon; "BEM-1"--advanced echelon.[33]

Call signs used by the Russian Army, Air Forces, and the

[31] I-168, p 7

[32] IF-187, p 2

[33] IF-187, p 50

Russian Secret Police (NKVD)[34] down to division nets had the general form of "XXB", where X could represent any letter of the roman alphabet or any digit from 1-9 (0 not being used), while B could only represent a letter. Letters of the Russian alphabet such as "IA" (.-.-), "IU"(..--), "CH"(---.), and "SH(----) were omitted for the purpose of camouflage since those letters only appeared in Russian morse traffic and thus call signs employing those morse characters would be recognized immediately as being Russian. Similiarly 0 was not used since the Russian operator always used the abbreviated form (-) which would have confused it with the letter T.[35]

The call signs were taken from a call sign book consisting of 26 pages, each page containing 35 x 35 or 1,225 items (the 26 letters of the roman alphabet plus the digits 1-9). The last element of the unenciphered station call sign indicated the page of the book (the 26 pages corresponding to the 26 letters of the roman alphabet); the first element of the call sign indicated the horizontal row of the designated page; and the second element indicated the vertical column. Call signs beginning with "SHCH (Q)" or "Z" were not used as these might be confused with the procedure signals of the International Q or Z code. One call sign block was kept for long periods of time, apparently for a year in most cases. It was assumed by the Germans that units of the Army, Air Force and the Secret Police (NKVD) all took their call signs from one block, for by this means the simultaneous appearance of the same call sign at different places was most easily avoided. Units which appeared in regimental nets down used call signs of the general form "BBB" in which "B" represented any letter of the Russian alphabet. These call signs were formed from the cover name allotted to the units. If, for instance, a

[34]The Russian Secret Police (NKVD) worked in conjunction with the Russian Armed Forces. The functions of the NKVD frontier troops were as follows:

a. Arrest of Army deserters.
b. Prevention of infiltration by enemy groups into rear areas.
c. Location and arrest of enemy agents dropped in rear areas.
d. Evacuation of civilians from battle zones.
e. Supervision of railroad traffic; guarding of railroad lines, traffic routes, bridges and industrial plants; close search of forests and villages for deserters and enemy agents.

[35]I-173, p 21

unit was allotted the cover name "SVJEZDA" for a certain time, it would use the call signs SVE, SZA, SED, etc., in its radio traffic. No changes might be made in the sequence of the letters. Call signs were chosen so that no confusion was possible. These call signs were changed at intervals of one day to a week, and occasionally were changed at the same time a new cryptographic system was placed in effect. However, there were exceptions to the above use of call signs. From time to time it was observed by the German operators and traffic analysts that some radio stations appeared whose call signs varied from each other only by the addition of a numeral. If these stations belonged to a division or higher echelon, then they were all in the same unit, but if the call signs appeared in a small unit the stations belonged to individual aircraft, tanks, etc., in communication with a ground station, leading tank, etc.[36]

The call signs of a few of the higher Secret Police (NKVD) units, and of the nets of the "Artillery Reserve of the Supreme Command" were, in some cases, made up of four elements. These were not taken from call sign blocks nor formed from cover names. In all internal state traffic of the People's Commissariat international call signs were used.[37]

i. Cover Names.--Cover names (simple in nature) were used frequently by the Russian military forces to cover or comouflage the identity of units, locations, proper names, airfields, etc., and could be found in various positions in messages. Examples of cover names which were common were ROSA and RUBIN.[38]

The German Signal Intelligence Regiment 353, which was on the Russian Northern front, reported it was easy to solve the simple code cover name system used by all the air units in that sector. Each air division had a code name which changed three times a month. Regiments used the basic divisional code name plus a figure suffix, the lowest regimental number having the lowest suffix. Aircraft had a basic code name according to type to which would be added the regimental suffix, and either a number or the pilot's name to indicate the individual

[36] I-173, p 21

[37] I-173, p 21

[38] IF-187, p 50

aircraft. Ground control stations with the armies in the field also had a basic code name with figure suffixes for subsidiary stations.[39]

j. Proper Names.--The use of proper names often led to the identity of particular Russian traffic. Statements of the capture of German prisoners, communiques, and press reports often served to confirm identifications which the Germans had previously made. Air base depots and airfield battalions used the names of unit commanders in the clear as a signature to messages or put the names in the actual message content in plainlanguage.[40]

k. Preambles.--Messages of the Antiaircraft Defense (Protivovosduschnaya oborona--PVO) units could be recognized from their preambles alone. Three 2-digit cover numbers and the abbreviation "VZD" (air--vozduch) were used in the preamble. At other times a 3-digit cover number followed by the abbreviation "MU" with "IJ" at the end of the message was to be found. The text of these messages usually contained 5-digit groups interspersed with 6-digit PVO grid references.[41]

l. Message Number Sequences.--Russian messages were numbered consecutively and these numbers could often be used to identify traffic. The message number was usually the last group in a message.

6. Methods and Results of German Traffic Analysis.--The analysis of Russian Army and Air Force traffic will be treated at the same time since the organizations of both were so closely tied together. The main purpose for the existence of the Russian Air Armies in the military command was for the support which they could give to the ground forces.[42]

The German traffic analysts worked hand in hand with the intercept operators on Russian traffic. The tasks of the traffic analysis section on the Southern Russian front were to record the radio characteristics of individual Air Armies, to identify the various radio nets and their inter-relationships, and to identify call signs and reconstruct call sign lists.[43]

[39] I-163

[40] IF-187, p 51

[41] IF-187, p 51

[42] IF-187, p 9

[43] IF-186, p 41

The successes on the Southern front and the information gained from sources other than cryptanalysis may be summed up as follows:

a. Knowledge of the Russian air situation.
b. Knowledge of the organization and order of battle of Russian Air Armies.
c. Knowledge of the strength of Russian units including types and armament of aircraft.
d. Knowledge of the location and occupation of airfields.
e. Knowledge of the movements and concentrations of Russian air and ground units.
f. Knowledge of operational intentions.
g. Knowledge of the amount and type of air transport.
h. Knowledge of the supply situation.
i. Knowledge of probable targets.[44]

Interrogation of members of the German Army Kona No. 1 (Kommandeur der Nachrichten Aufklaerung 1) brought to light some important facts concerning German successes in analyzing intercepted Russian traffic.[45] Kona 1 was engaged in the interception, analysis and evaluation of the Russian Army, Air, and Secret Police (NKVD) traffic on the southern half of the Russian front from June 1941 until May 1945. The Germans were able to obtain, as a result of this work, an accurate picture of the Russian order of battle. They were able, oftentimes, to predict the time and location of impending Russian offensives in sufficient time to be able to take advantage of such information. These results were achieved more by the close interrogation of all available sources of information (traffic analysis, evaluation, prisoner of war interrogation, captured documents, etc.) than by reading of enciphered or encoded traffic. However, there was considerable of the Russian low and medium grade traffic read. In the German command organization there existed considerable rivalry between the cryptanalytic and traffic analysis personnel on the relative merits of their respective units. This fact appears to have created definite disturbances as to which of the two units was the most valuable source of intelligence to the German High Command. It seems, from the overall picture presented by the interrogation of German personnel of the two units, that to the German Signal Intelligence the respective value of traffic analysis and of cryptanalysis was about three to one. This is due to two factors:

[44] IF-186, p 49

[45] I-19b, p 1

21

a. The general unreadability of Russian high grade traffic because of the extensive use of one-time pad systems.
b. The large amount of information that could be extracted from the generally low standard of Russian radio and cipher security, especially in respect to the use of call signs and radio frequencies and indicators.[46]

Russian security, from a cryptanalytic angle, was based almost entirely on the use of one-time pad systems for high level traffic and the use of a large number of code books and enciphering tables for medium and low level traffic.[47]

The main source of information to the traffic analyst came from the Russian use of call signs and indicator groups and from stereotyped direction-finding reports. On the basis of this information the German traffic analysts established a detailed and accurate order of battle of the Russian forces operating on the entire Eastern front. In addition they also gained information concerning Russian operational movements and intentions.[48]

The Russians had a habit of using the surnames of officers and pilots, for code and cover names. This was especially so in the Air Force. This type of information was considered very valuable by the Germans.

Quite often the information provided by the German Signal Intelligence units to the various German combat units went unheeded. For example, in the fall of 1941, when the Germans were attempting to effect a junction with the Finns at Tichvin, certain radio characteristics appeared in intercepted Russian traffic which had been noticed two weeks previously in traffic emanating from Siberia. This fact was evaluated by the German Signal Intelligence as an indication that Russian troops had been transferred in this short interval from Siberia to the sector north of Tichvin. The German Command maintained that such a thing was impossible, and therefore did not take any evasive action. Consequently, the Russians attacked in great force and won a decided victory. The

[46] I-196, p 1

[47] I-19b, p 1

[48] I-19b, p 19

junction with the Finns never took place. The railroad between Leningrad and Moscow was liberated by the Russians and the Germans were forced to take up positions on the Volchov front leaving the "hedgehog" redoubt at Demyansk to its fate.[49]

A clarification of the working organization of the Russian Air Force is advisable before considering the weak points in their transmission security. The Air Forces were an integral part of the Russian Army. Their operations were confined primarily to the tactical air support of ground operations. During operations actual command was by the ground force commanders, with the air commanders acting in an advisory capacity and having sole responsibility for the successful execution of missions. The structure of the Soviet Air organization emphasizes it as an instrument of the Army. Of some 12,000 Russian aircraft identified by the German Luftwaffe Signal Intelligence during the war (not counting long-range bombers which were in a separate organization) almost 10,000, or more than 80%, were fighters and fighter bombers. The remainder were bombers and operated mainly against front-line targets. At the end of the war there were 11 Russian Air Armies operating on the Eastern front. These were, from south to north, the 17th, 5th, 8th, 2nd, 6th, 16th, 4th, 1st, 3rd, 15th, and 7th Air Army. One Air Army was assigned to each Army Group to which it was operationally subordinate, and was then subdivided into Corps, Divisions, Regiments, and Escadrilles. Each Air Army had two to eight Corps, according to the importance of its work. At first these corps were mixed fighter, fighter-bomber, and bomber units. During the war, however, there was a tendency to change these mixed units into uniform corps, and by the end of the war there was only one mixed corps left on the East front: the VI Corps. Each corps was made up of two to three divisions; each division of two or three regiments; and each regiment of three escadrilles. Reconnaissance and artillery observation aircraft, as well as transport units, were sometimes organized into escadrilles, but usually they were regiments and were directly subordinate to the Air Army. Each Air Army also had one reconnaissance and one artillery observation regiment. In areas where preparations for a concentrated attack were being carried out the Air Armies were often reinforced by one or more of these regiments. By noting such reinforcements the Germans could recognize, at times, the intentions and probable plans of the Russians.[50]

[49] IF-186, p 16

[50] IF-187, p 9

DOCID: 3633965

<table>
<tr><th colspan="4">COMPARATIVE STRENGTH OF GERMAN AND ALLIED FORCES</th></tr>
<tr><th>GERMAN</th><th>AMERICAN</th><th>BRITISH</th><th>RUSSIAN</th></tr>
<tr><td>Staffel
9-12 planes</td><td>Flight
8-12 planes</td><td>Flight
8-12 planes</td><td>Escadrille
8-10 planes</td></tr>
<tr><td>Gruppe
(3 Staffeln)
27-30 planes</td><td>Squadron
20-30 planes</td><td>Squadron
20-30 planes</td><td>Regiment
about 30 planes</td></tr>
<tr><td>Geschwader
(3 Gruppen)
80-90 planes</td><td>Group
70-90 planes</td><td>Wing
70-90 planes</td><td rowspan="2">Division (2 or 3 Regiments, usually 3) 60-150 planes</td></tr>
<tr><td>Fliefü-Jafü
(2 Geschwader)
about 160 planes</td><td>Wing
210-360 planes</td><td rowspan="3">Group (number of planes depend on mission)</td></tr>
<tr><td>Flieger-Division
About 320 planes</td><td rowspan="2">Command (2 or more wings) 700-1,500 planes</td><td rowspan="2">Corps (2 or 3 Divisions) 120-450 planes</td></tr>
<tr><td>Flieger Korps
(2 or 3 Divisions)
About 600-900 planes</td></tr>
<tr><td>Luftflotte</td><td>Air Force</td><td>Command or Tactical Air Force</td><td>Air Army</td></tr>
</table>

Figure 5 [51]

[51] IF-187, p 9a

24

Lt. Werner RASCH, of the 353rd German Air Force Signal Intelligence Regiment in the East, gives the following account of the development and achievements of the Russian Long Range Bomber Forces (ADD--Avitsiya Dalneye Dyestviya).

"Soon after the outbreak of the Russian-German war, practically all of the Russian Long Range Bomber Force was destroyed, either by German attacks on Russian airfields, or in combat with German fighters. What was left of it was withdrawn from action. Marshall GOLOVANOV, chief of ADD, reorganized his forces with the intention of using them in night operations only, owing to the threat presented by the strong German flak defense. The first successful operations following the reorganization took place in the battle of Stalingrad ((September 1942 - February 1943)). From then on, ADD operations played an important part in all Russian offensives. The training for night operations was of long duration; at the end of the war each bomber regiment had crews which were still in a training status.

"The achievements of the ADD units were not very impressive. Crews were not trained for carrying out night attacks in close formation. In the latter days of the war 60 aircraft of a division need approximately one hour to assemble and take off, and even this was accomplished only under the most favorable navigational and meteorological conditions. In planning an attack, each division was allotted 20 minutes over the target; in that time it was intended that all aircraft of one division should have completed their mission and moved out to make room for the next division. Unless targets on the front itself were being raided, the front line was usually crossed before dark. This permitted the take-off to be made during daylight, and the first aircraft to take off were held in an assembly area in order that a close-flying formation be formed. Formations equipped with radio-telephone communications were again brought into close order by the leading aircraft of the regiments before going into the bomb run. Each regiment had several Pathfinder aircraft, which were flown by the most experienced crews, since the success of the mission depended upon their efforts. In addition to their flares, they usually carried a 1,000 pound bomb."[52]

[52] IF-187, p 30

7. Point-to-Point Nets.--These point-to-point nets of the Long Range Bomber Forces (ADD) alone were a sufficient basis on which the Germans could build up an accurate picture of the ADD organization. When the 18th Russian Air Army was reorganized the Germans immediately recognized such steps from traffic on these nets. The most profitable traffic in these nets, from an intelligence standpoint, came from units which were widely separated in the field as this necessitated the use of radio facilities for communication. In instances where the units were close together very little signal intelligence could be gained since there was slight need for radio transmissions.

From the intercept and analysis of traffic on these point-to-point nets, movements of the Russian Air Army units, locations and occupations of airfields, numbers of operational and unoperational aircraft, and locations of supply dumps could be determined. Traffic intercepted on these nets also gave the Germans considerable information regarding intended operations and offensives. One outstanding success along this line occurred when a Russian order to bomber units was intercepted by the Germans. The message ordered an attack on Shavli, Lithuania, where an entire German Panzer Army was immobilized due to a lack of sufficient fuel. The German Signal Intelligence Service reported the information to the Luftflotte which provided fighters to meet the Russian Long Range Bombers while German JU 52's dropped gasoline supplies to the encircled Panzer Army and enabled it to escape.[53]

8. Call Signs and Frequencies.--Three-character call signs were used in the radio nets between the Air Army and its Corps. They were changed once during the day and once at night, at which time the frequencies also were changed. Call signs were based on an arbitrary combination of letters and digits and were selected from a call sign list that changed monthly. The Germans were unable to determine whether any definite system was employed for the choosing of the call signs. They did notice, however, that during the course of a month a call sign used by a given radio station might be repeated without the succession of call signs which had followed at the time of the previous occurrence. Traffic between corps and divisions took place with a periodic change

[53] IF-187, p 36

of call signs, but on fixed frequencies. This fact aided the intercept tasks of the German Signal Intelligence. Frequencies used were in the 2,500-5,000 kilocycle band: i.e., the normal Russian military frequency band. The call sign systems and the time of change differed from corps to corps as there was no over-all unification in their communication systems, and this fact was a great aid to the German Signal Intelligence in identifying the various units. Each radio link had two different frequencies for use during the day and two different frequencies for use at night. The night frequencies lay in the 3,400-4,500 kilocycle band; the day frequencies between the 5,000-8,000 kilocycle band. As the seasons of the year advanced the day frequencies gradually moved up to a maximum of 10,000 kilocycles.[54]

9. Analysis of Characteristic Messages.--

a. Address and Signature Groups.-- Five-figure messages of the Russian Long Range Bomber units could not be decrypted by the German Signal Intelligence Service but they were able to extract a great deal of important information from the analysis of data found in the message numbers and delivery groups. In these messages the signature group was next to the last one before the message number group. This signature group was constant and served to identify the headquarters of the originator, each headquarters having a 3-digit designation. Two zeros inserted in front of the 3-digit signature designation completed the 5-figure group. Since no other Russian 5-figure traffic contained similar groups, this signature was the most essential characteristic for the identification of the traffic of the Long Range Bombers. The traffic was further identified by two address groups contained in the preamble of the messages. These address groups were likewise 3-digit groups, repeated periodically, one of them designating the unit and the other the section. In front of the address group appeared the symbol "ADR" (address). In front of the signature group appeared the symbol "SIG".[55]

b. Pre-arranged Message Forms.-- A very valuable source of intelligence was found in the pre-arranged message forms which all the Long Range Bomber units were required to send in to their commands. These messages contained data on regimental reports of locations, strength, and aircraft serviceability. One type of these pre-arranged message forms was "Form 1": a daily report sent by division to corps, containing regimental

[54] IF 187 p 37

[55] IF 187 p 38

strengths in personnel and aircraft. The text of the messages consisted of unenciphered numbers preceeded by a 2-digit null, resulting in a four or five digit group. The following is an example of such a message.

"12238 1350 1436 .... 2332 2430 2502 2629 2728 2801 2903 3002 3101."

After removing the first two nulls of each group the message can be interpreted as follows: (12)238 indicates the designation of the regiment whose strength is being reported: i.e., the 238th Regiment. The second group (13)50 contains data on personnel strength--the details of which were never definitely determined by the Germans. The last nine groups (2332 through 3101) refer to aircraft strength and must be read in units of three groups. After again removing the two nulls of each group, the first gives total number of planes; the second group the number of serviceable planes; and the third group the number of unserviceable planes. In this case (23)32, (24)30, (25)02 indicates there is 32 planes total; 30 serviceable, and 02 planes unserviceable. The second unit of three groups (i.e., groups 2629, 2728, & 2801) indicate the total number of aircraft on an airfield, and the number of serviceable and unserviceable planes. In this case there are a total of 29 planes, of which 28 are serviceable and 1 unserviceable. The last three groups (i.e., 2903, 3002, and 3101) refer to regimental aircraft which had landed at other airfields. In this case, a total of 3 planes, of which 2 are serviceable and 1 unserviceable.

Another pre-arranged message form, known as "Form 4," was sent every fifth day by division to corps, and by corps to Air Army. Here again the text of the message consisted of numbers in the clear slightly camouflaged by a two-digit null in front of each group. An example is as follows:

"22250 3246 4214 42685 5229 6203 7240 .... 1219"

By again removing the two nulls of each group the messages gives the following information:

(22)250 (32)46 (42)14 (42)685 (52)29 (62)03 (72)40 (12)19.

Message being reported by the 250th Regiment; located at 46, a grid system of coordinates not too difficult to solve (this system changed monthly); 14 aircraft type; 685 serviceable aircraft; 29 aircraft unserviceable; 03 and 40 give details of personnel strength which the Germans never could fully understand. The last group "19" indicates the number of crews ready for operations.

The two types of pre-arranged message forms given above were the two main sources of information for the German Signal Intelligence in gaining information of the organization, order of battle, location, and aircraft strength of the Russian Long Range Bomber Forces.[56]

c. Operations Reports.-- Reports of results of operations were also sent by corps to Air Army by pre-arranged message forms. These messages contained details as to the number of aircraft taking part in an attack, the target, time and altitude over the target, weight of bombs dropped according to type, results observed by flying personnel, details of German defenses, details of Russian losses, and observations of weather conditions. Quite often messages from corps to division containing operational orders were also intercepted. These messages contained details as to the target, the time of attack, and the altitude of attack, and often afforded ample time for German counter-measures to be effected. The division also reported to corps the number of aircraft to participate in the attack, as well as the time of take-off. This information provided the Germans with a valuable and reliable basis for route-tracking.[57]

d. Airfield Serviceability Reports.-- Corps were required to make daily reports on the serviceability of airfields being used by their regiments and divisions. Airfield locations were given by using a 6-digit grid reference system. The serviceability was indicated by constant 4-figure groups designating "serviceable," "partially serviceable," and "unserviceable." These reports afforded the German Air Force Signal Intelligence a good picture of Russian airfield serviceability and of any changes in location which might have taken place.

e. Orders for Use of Navigational Aids.--The headquarters of the Air Army transmitted messages to subordinate commands ordering the use of navigational aids for a particular day, and indicating the type of aid to be used. When these messages were intercepted it could be taken as a definite indication of a forthcoming operation. If no messages were intercepted it could be interpreted that no attack was to be anticipated during that day or that night.[58]

[56] IF-187, p 38

[57] IF-187, p 40

[58] IF-187, p 40

f. Weather Messages.--Weather messages were of great assistance to the German Signal Intelligence Service in identifying the geographical origin of other traffic intercepted on the same radio nets. These weather messages often mentioned in the clear the names and locations of Russian meteorological stations. Thus probable location of the radio station could be made.

The Russian weather messages could be recognized easily by the German Signal Intelligence Service because of message preamble characteristics, by random use of the letter "X" within the text, and by the absence of message number and delivery groups. In the early part of the war the Russians transmitted weather messages in the clear quite frequently. Later in the war all the messages were enciphered.

A large number of Russian weather messages were intercepted by the Germans. The contents of these messages, when decrypted, served two purposes. One purpose was to brief the German air crews on the weather conditions in Russia; the other purpose was to obtain advance warning of impending Russian operations. If a "winds aloft" message was intercepted by the Germans in the middle of the day, it could be taken as an indication of an impending air operation by the Russian corps transmitting the message.[59]

10. Air to Ground Traffic.--The assignment of call signs and frequencies used in air-to-ground radio traffic of the Long Range Bomber forces was performed individually by the corps signal officers and did not follow any uniform procedure throughout the entire Air Army. It was therefore a rather simple task, because of this lack of uniformity, for the German Signal Intelligence Service to identify the various individual corps by their call signs and frequencies. Each regiment, as well as each aircraft, was allotted two different frequencies: one for transmitting and one for receiving. The aircraft of each regiment were divided into two groups, each group transmitting on its own frequency. The frequencies of the ground stations, in general, lay between 2,500 and 3,000 kilocycles, while the frequencies of the aircraft were between 3,000 and 3,700 kilocycles. The aircraft of the IV Guards Corps of the 18th Air Army, whose units were equipped with American B-25 planes, and therefore had American radio sets, used frequencies between 1,800 and 2,500 kilocycles. Call signs on these air-to-ground nets remained in use for several months; the various call signs being repeated at irregular intervals of 5, 6, or 7 days. The

[59] IF-187, p 41

regimental ground stations used 2-or 3-letter call signs, while aircraft used 1-or 2-letter call signs with numerical suffixes. These suffixes referred to the pilot rather than to the aircraft, and were allocated by either the commanding regiment or commanding division. When the suffixes were allocated by the commanding regiment the numbers of the suffixes ran from 1 to 32; when allocated by the commanding division they ran from 1 to 100. The German Signal Intelligence Service could identify regiments after a short period of time because they also used special CQ call signs.[60]

a. Tuning and Take-off Traffic.--When the Russian bombers were assembling for the take-off on a mission the aircraft usually engaged in tuning traffic while still on the ground, and at the completion of tuning the traffic was usually terminated with a "QSA 4" or "QSA 5" procedure signal indicating what the signal strength of the radio set in the aircraft was. The tuning traffic furthermore was transmitted by one of the frequencies allotted for this purpose and was easily intercepted by the Germans. Thus, the beginning of an operation could be recognized immediately, because the end of the tuning traffic indicated that the take-off was to begin. In those divisions which had aircraft equipped with radio-telephone sets the noise of the engines being warmed up could be heard by the German operators, and this also served as an additional source of early warning. In the radio-telephone traffic, instead of using the complete call sign, only the numerical suffix was used.[61]

b. Direction-finding Traffic.--The navigational training of the Long Range Bomber Force crews was so poor that "QDM" and "QDR"[62] bearings constantly had to be given by the ground stations while the planes were enroute to the target. This fact aided the German Signal Intelligence Service in their route-tracking of the Russian Air Force because the Russians, instead of flying feint courses as did the Americans and British, usually flew a direct course to the target. Therefore, these direction-finding fixes sent by the ground stations could be taken as the actual course of the bombers and permitted the Germans to make a reasonably accurate target prediction. The direction-finding traffic between aircraft and ground stations did not possess any special characteristics as the bearings were given in the clear with little attempt at camouflage. The ground stations of the IV Guards Corps of the 18th Air Army used two nulls

[60] IF-187, p 41

[61] IF-187, p 42

[62] QDM requests magnetic course to steer with no wind.
QDR requests magnetic bearing in relation to station.

before a three-digit group indicating course bearings; e.g., 00252 indicating a course of 252 degrees. The I Guard Corps used the abbreviation "TRS" before giving bearings on the outward flight, and "OPM" before giving bearings on the return flight. Other corps transmitted the letter "W" three times before giving the course bearing on the outward flight and the letter "A" three times before giving the bearing on the return flight. These characteristics served to identify the type of traffic and unit.[63]

c. Tactical Traffic.--Over a long period of time German monitoring of bomber tactical traffic during approach flights resulted in the identification of the greater part of this type of traffic. The procedure signals used for this traffic differed with individual corps. In most cases the traffic consisted of 2 or 3-digit groups, sometimes enciphered and sometimes unenciphered. The III and IV Guards Corps were very free in their use of tactical traffic, their aircraft often reporting such data as take-offs, flight over the initial point (IPM), flight over the front, execution of mission, and observations over the targets. In such traffic the time was always given and this aided the German Signal Intelligence in its route-tracking. The ground stations also often transmitted data concerning the target or time of attack in cases where plans had to be changed after the planes had taken off. This data was very valuable to the Germans in determing the most favorable time to put their night fighters in the air for defense.[64]

11. Russian Air Service Command Traffic.--The largest unit of the Air Service Command was the District Air Base Depot (Rayon Aviazionnage Basirovaniya--RAB) and, in the case of the Naval Air Force, the Naval Air Base Depot (Morskaya Aviabasa--MAB). As a rule each Russian Air Army had three to five of these RAB's. In order to use to the fullest extent the intelligence which could be gained from an analysis of the daily reports sent by the airfield battalions to their District Air Base Depots it was necessary for the Germans to draw up as complete a Russian Air Service Command order of battle as possible. The reports contained details on number of serviceable and unserviceable aircraft in the tactical units. From such an order of battle the German Signal Intelligence Service of the Air Force was able

[63] IF-187, p 43

[64] IF-187, p 44

to corelate Russian airfields and tactical units, and to predict movements of tactical units on the basis of airfields under construction. The locations of the airfields could be readily determined from the contents of the radio traffic between battalions and RAB's, and from direction-finding of the sending stations. Reports on the building of new airfields were of special value to the Germans since these reports often revealed enemy intentions and permitted the Germans to prepare defensive action against intended Russian offensives. No offensive ever commenced without strong air support, which necessarily meant that airfields had to be located as near the active front as possible. The Russian Standard Operating Procedure called for aviation in direct support of the ground forces to be located at bases not more than 40 kilometers (24 miles) behind the front. On some occasions the air bases were so near the front that Russian planes on the ground were hit by German artillery. The number and location of airfields under construction was a very good indication of the time in which an offensive could be expected.[65]

Radio traffic involving movements of airfield battalions was also monitored closely by the Germans. ~~From this monitoring~~ they could obtain clues as to the direction in which the tactical units would later move. As an example, the reconquest of the Crimea by the Russians in the spring of 1944 liberated two Air Armies for further assignment. The German Command was naturally very much interested in where these units would go. In a few days the German Air Force Signal Intelligence Service had the answer. One airfield battalion had received an order to board a troop train in Simferopol. After the train departed the airfield battalion transmitted a message by radio to its District Air Base Depot at each stop along the way until it reached Gomel. It was obvious that the battalion would be followed by tactical units, if not by the whole Air Army. This assumption was confirmed a short time later when the entire 4th Russian Air Army moved from the Crimea to the Central front. The operational area of the second liberated Air Army--the 8th Air Army--was likewise quickly determined. A message from an airfield battalion was intercepted and read by the German Signal Intelligence Service. The message stated: "The headquarters for the 8th Air Army in Tarnopol are ready." In a very short time this Air Army moved from the Crimea to this new sector.[66]

[65] IF-187, p 21

[66] IF-187, p 23

a. Supply Traffic.--Valuable intelligence was obtained by the German Signal Intelligence from the interception of radio traffic which gave details on supplies of fuel, ammunition and other materials. Details of railway movements of supplies were transmitted by the District Air Base Depots to their subordinate airfield battalions. These messages contained information on the destination, number of railway cars being used, amount and type of supplies, and the scheduled time of arrival. When the trains arrived at their destination a message announcing their arrival was sent to the airfield battalions. As a result of the exploitation of this type of traffic the Germans were able to bomb successfully the stations soon after trainloads of fuel and ammunition had arrived. In the Southern sector a Service Command point-to-point radio net reported arrivals of replacement aircraft for the 17th, 5th, and 8th Air Armies. These replacement planes were ferried from the factories to the airfields. Tactical units down to regiment level receipted for these planes and supplies, and from interception of these strength reports the Germans were able to estimate the production and distribution rate of Russian planes. Current fuel and ammunition supplies at airfields were reported on pre-arranged-message forms transmitted by the air-field battalions. These messages, since fuel and ammunition supplies were always increased prior to an offensive, afforded the Germans a sound basis for predicting impending Russian offensives.[67]

b. Miscellaneous Air Service Command Traffic.--The Russian Air Service Command reported by radio on the achievements in salvaging German aircraft which had been shot down or which had been forced to land. These reports afforded the Germans with a source of information concerning their missing crews, and in many cases it was possible for the Germans to inform families that the crew members were alive and were Russian prisoners of war. Reports of interrogations of captured German military personnel were also often transmitted and intercepted by the Germans. In some cases as a result of the information contained in these reports, the German Command carried out court martial proceedings in absentia where the intercepted information carried sufficient proof that the German prisoners of war had revealed information of a secret nature. An Air Service Command of the 8th Russian Air Army on the southern front reported routes to be flown by aircraft in large-scale ground attacks, giving the time at which the attack would take place. For such

[67] IF-187, p 24

attacks the Russian Air Army usually ordered the placing of smoke markers in the frontal area on the day before the attack would take place. These smoke markers were used by the Russian planes as an orientation point, and not only indicated the proposed direction to be flown, but also corresponded to the direction the ground force would advance. After a study of these smoke signals the German Air Force Signal Intelligence learned that the signals were lit thirty minutes to an hour before the actual time of attack. Thus, when it was learned that smoke signals had been set out the German Signal Intelligence could usually inform the Air and Ground forces some twenty-four hours in advance of plans for a Russian offensive.[68]

12. Russian Air Raid Warning Service.--The Russian Air Raid Warning Service was monitored regularly by the Germans. From this source the following information was available:

a. Reports of German aircraft over Russian territory and their positions.

b. Reports of Russian and American aircraft over Russian territory.

In the case of flights made entirely over Russian territory the time of departure and airfield destination was included. In the case of flights which crossed the front into German territory the time of arrival at the front would be given. When observation of German aircraft was reported by the Russians it was possible for the German Signal Intelligence Service to warn the planes that the Russians knew their positions and to recommend a change of course or other evasive action. Reports on American aircraft often revealed information about the "shuttle" or "triangular" flights of the 8th and 15th U. S. Air Forces.[69]

13. German Monitoring and Analysis of Russian Naval Traffic.--The Russian Navy had its own Air Force which performed the following duties:

a. Protection of Russian Naval units and their bases.
b. Support of Naval operations.
c. Combat of enemy naval forces.

[68] IF-187, p 25

[69] IF-187, p 26

The German Air Force Signal Intelligence Service in the East monitored the air traffic of the Russian Naval Air Forces which were in a position to operate against the Germans. Those units monitored included the Black Sea Fleet Air Arm, the Baltic Fleet Air Arm, and the Arctic Fleet Air Arm. The amount of intelligence which the Germans were able to extract from this naval air traffic was due primarily to having solved the call sign encipherment table used by the Russian Naval units. This table "was foolishly kept in use for more than a year with the result that it was completely reconstructed by SIS." Not only the air units but also the naval units with which they operated could be identified by their call signs. Messages at the time of take-off which were transmitted by the Naval Air regiments and reconnaissance patrol reports could be read by the Germans in sufficient time to warn their convoys and submarines.[70]

Captain Wedim HEROLD, officer in charge of Ln. Regiment III/353 of the Signal Intelligence Agency of the Air Force High Command, gives the following information on traffic analysis performed by the Germans on Russian Naval traffic.

> "The Navy in the Southern Sector had the Black Sea Fleet of the Soviet Union as its monitoring area. As the Black Sea Fleet's code was unbroken, results could only be achieved by traffic and direction-finding evaluation. The navy was especially interested in the monitoring of Black Sea seaplane forces. The planes were monitored and the results passed to the German navy. The forces consisted of bomber, torpedo, fighter, and sea rescue units. Bases and strength were currently known.
>
> "The signal code of the reconnaissance aircraft could be read. The guiding of our own fighters by the listening service onto the reconnaissance aircraft on operations often brought us victories. The navy was especially interested in reconnaissance reports about our own ship movements, particularly for positions and courses of our own convoys, as after a report by the reconnaissance aircraft, attacks by aircraft or submarines could usually be reckoned with. The calling up of fighter protection, timely warning and changing of course often foiled the enemy's existing intentions of attack."[71]

[70] IF-187, p 16

[71] I-130, p 15

14. Advanced Warning Reports and Route-tracking.-- Advanced warning reports and route-tracking wrs often possible from the results of traffic analysis. The German Air Force Signal Intelligence Agency had more success than the German Army Signal Intelligence had against the Russians. One source of information from which the German Air Force Signal Intelligence were able to make use in giving timely warnings to the German Air Force came from the traffic of Russian Specialist Air Force Liaison officers who acted in an intermediary capacity between Army and Air Force for Army cooperation, close support, and tactical reconnaissance. These officers were known as "Flivos" (Fliegerverbindungsoffizier). The Flivos consistently transmitted messages which contained the starting time and course of the Russian Air units to which they were assigned. From the interception of these messages and the exploitation of the information derived therefrom, the German Air Force was able to destroy a large number of Russian planes. Assumptions of impending ground force operations could also be made noting an increase in local attacks or thrusts in the areas in which the Flivos were located. The Germans also had success in locating points of armored concentrations since orders asking for special air support would be transmitted by the Flivos. These requests for support originated at Army and Motorized Corps headquarters and came up on a point-to-point net between the Air Armies and their subordinate corps and independent divisions. As the cryptographic systems in which these messages were sent were being read by the German Signal Intelligence the German High Command was kept informed currently of those targets for which air support was requested. By the time operational instructions had been sent by the Russians to an Air Division by an Air Corps the German troops had ample time to take effective countermeasures. Thus these Flivos messages afforded the Germans an excellent means of making tactical evaluations of immediate value, especially when the reports contained Russian observations of German strong and weak points of defense. The reasons given by the German Signal Intelligence as to the usefulness of this traffic were: (a) because of the close cooperation between the Russian Air and Ground Forces, a heavy ground attack could be expected whenever strong air support was requested; (b) the Flivos reported their locations in these reports, thereby revealing the position of Russian Army and Corps headquarters at which the Flivos were located;

and (c) from ground situation reports transmitted by the Flivos several times a day, an accurate picture of the frontal sector of each Russian Army unit could be constructed.[72]

The German Air Force Signal Intelligence Agency furthermore claimed that from information obtained from the Flivos traffic the German High Command had full knowledge of the concentration of troops at Stalingrad. This information came when five entire Air Divisions moved into that area. The Germans had learned that whenever traffic revealed Flivos of five Air Divisions were present in any area it could be expected that the Armies of those divisions would appear there in a short time. The Germans furthermore claim they had information from the same source as to the plans of the Russians for the last drive upon Berlin, but were unable to do anything about the matter because of the serious condition in which their Armed Forces found themselves.[73]

a. Route-tracking Data Available from Messages.--When the German Signal Intelligence Service intercepted operation orders it was an easy task to track the course flown by Long Range Bomber Force formations. The only problems remaining were to identify the units participating in the formation, as several corps were quite often used in one raid, and to make necessary corrections if any new time was reported after the take-off of the predicted time of arrival over the targets. The 18th Air Army traffic of this type served to piece together the intelligence already derived from air-to-ground traffic, which at that stage was usually meaningless. The Russian Air Defense organizations also frequently transmitted notification of impending missions which gave data regarding the course to be flown over Russian territory. These messages, which were directed to the Russian Anti-air-craft Units, contained the number and types of planes as well as the location of the point of attack.[74]

b. Weather Reconnaissance.--In instances where the Germans did not intercept operational orders there still existed a possibility for predicting Russian bomber raids

[72] I-17; I-163; IF-186; IF-187

[73] I-17

[74] IF-187, p 44

from information derived from the interception of weather reconnaissance reports. These reports were usually carried out in the target area prior to an attack. From an analysis of these messages the Germans could usually predict whether or not a raid was soon to take place, as a raid generally occurred only if the ceiling over the target area was at least 3,000 meters and there was no more than 6 to 10% of cloud cover. Route tracking of the weather reconnaissance planes was aided because of the fact that they transmitted messages every 5 to 10 minutes, sometimes even reporting their position, and thus making direction-finding by the Germans unnecessary.[75]

c. Flash Reports.--Tactical intelligence resulting from the interception of Russian Long Range Bomber Forces (ADD) traffic was immediately enciphered and forwarded by wire to visual observational posts, to the Air Force, to the so-called "light division" for special missions in the German Army (Jagddivision), to the Anti-air-craft units, and to the Central Reporting Center for Defense of the Reich (Meldekopf). As a result of early warning through these flash reports German defensive preparations against an anticipated Russian night raid often took place during the morning preceeding the raid. As soon as the take-off of a bomber formation was established, a wire line from the Signal Intelligence Service evaluation company to fighter and Anti-air-craft unit headquarters was kept open, and all subsequent information currently reported to the stations. Another direct wire line was maintained to the nearest German Signal Intelligence Service radar intercept station. This station was kept informed of the course and altitude of the Russian bomber formation so that when radio silence was begun the radar station could take over the route-tracking.[76]

15. Intercept of Russian Radar.--Radar intercept on the Russian Eastern Front by the German Signal Intelligence Service brought only insignificent results since the Russians made little use of radar equipment. Very few details of Russian radar equipment are available. On several occasions, however, in traffic intercepted on point-to-point nets some mention of three types of equipments was found. These mentioned "RUS-1", "RUS-2" (Radio Ulavlivatel Samoletov), and "MRU"(Melki Radio Ulavlivatel). Several Russian prisoners

[75] IF-187, p 45

[76] IF-187, p 47

of war stated to German interrogators that intruder regiments of the Long Range Bomber Forces (ADD) used radar against German night fighters. However, the Germans never found any trace of any airborne radar equipment in the Russian planes which crashed or which were shot down. It was concluded by the German Signal Intelligence Service that the Russian prisoners only made the statements because of suggestions made by the interrogators rather than from any knowledge of such equipment because they knew the Germans and the Allies were using radar to a great extent and were only wishing their own forces were doing the same.[76] In the summer of 1943 the Germans did establish, from intercepted radio-telephone traffic, that the Russians were experimenting with ground radar to be used in their defense zones. Three or four German radar intercept teams were placed along the Eastern front and equipped with directionfinders. Intelligence obtained from these teams indicated that the Russians were making very little progress in the field of radar, and that their equipment was inferior to that of the Germans, British, and Americans. In the fall of 1944 the German Signal Intelligence further determined that on the Central Russian front, apart from several small radar sets apparently being used for anti-air-craft control, there was only one large installation which was near Warsaw. Further interception of Russian radio-telephone traffic later again indicated there were several other radar installations within the air defense zone, but the locations could never be established by German direction-finders.[77]

16. Russian Radio Counter-measures.--Very little information in reference to Russian use of radio counter-measures is to be found in TICOM materials. The Russians had a term (CYB) which denoted all types of varied camouflaged communications procedures, derived after 1942 by the Signals Officers for use at the front. The Russians apparently did not assume that their CYB-procedures would give 100% security. The procedures remained valid for indefinite periods, being changed either on the judgment of the Signals Officer who issued them, or when there was a suspicion of compromise.

[76] IF-187, p 29

[77] IF-187, p 70

Tactical codes, made up by field commanders.

In general, the CYB-procedures of the Russian Air Forces remained in use longer than those of the Army, since the Air Force procedures were employed behind the lines and were less exposed to physical compromise.[78]

17. German Use of Captured Russian Material.-- The German Signal Intelligence Service salvaged a large amount of material from Russian planes which were shot or forced to crash. However, the Germans did not gain much outstanding information from this material because they were already in possession of most of the important facts and information concerning Russian equipment. They were able to gain considerable information from the Standard Operating Instructions salvaged from planes. This included data on Russian codes, call signs, radio frequencies, maps, and grid-square enciphering systems.[79]

[78] I-116, p 3
[79] IF-187, p 71

VOLUME 2

Chapter 3

SUMMARY OF GERMAN SUCCESSES IN TRAFFIC ANALYSIS OF RUSSIAN COMMUNICATIONS

1. The Russians depended on the use of One-time Pad cryptographic systems for security of their high level traffic, and on code books and enciphering tables for their medium and low level traffic. The One-time Pads were not read by the Germans, but the medium and low level systems were read to a great extent.

2. The main source of information the German Traffic Analysts had came from exploitation of the Russian use of call signs, radio frequencies, message indicator groups, and direction-finding reports.

3. Another source of information came from the intelligence gained from reading pre-arranged message forms. The Russians used these forms extensively for reports. The Germans had little difficulty in reading such traffic.

4. There was very close cooperation between the German intercept operators and traffic analysts in the field. Integration of available information, such as traffic analysis results, evaluation of data, cryptanalysis, prisoner of war interrogations, captured documents, and other types of intelligence was carried out with excellent efficiency.

5. The Russian call sign systems were not as secure as the Russians believed. Given sufficient call sign traffic and day-to-day continuity the German Signal Intelligence Service was able to reconstruct the systems.

6. Some of the outstanding successes of German Traffic Analysis were:

a. A knowledge of the Russian Air Force order of battle and of battle situation.

b. A knowledge of the organization and order of battle of some Russian Army units.

c. A knowledge of strength, types, and armament of aircraft.

d. A knowledge of the location and occupation of airfields.

e. A knowledge of the movements and concentrations of Air and Ground Force units.

f. A knowledge of operational intentions.

g. A knowledge of the amount and type of air transport.

h. A knowledge of the Russian supply situation.

i. A knowledge of probable targets.

TAB A

VOLUME 9

TAB A

- ADD (Avitsiya Dalneye Dyestviya).--Russian Long Range Bomber.
ADR. Russian symbol for "adress" appearing in front of the address group in military messages.
Air.--Vozduch (Russian), abbreviated VZD.
Air Army. Russian equivalent to American Air Force, and British Command.
Air Liaison Officer.--German translation: Fliegerverbindungsoffizier, (FLIVO).
Antiaircraft Defense.--Protivovosduschnaya oborona (PVO).
Avitsiya Dalneye Dyestviya (ADD).--Russian Long Range Bomber Forces.
Corps (Air Force). 120-450 Russian planes (2 or 3 Divisions), partly equivalent to an American Wing.
CYB. A Russian term denoting all types of varied camouflaged communications procedure.
District Air Base.--Rayon Aviazionnage Basirovaniya (RAB). Largest unit of the Russian Air Service Command.
Division (Air Force) 60-150 Russian planes, unit classed between an American Group and Wing.
Escadrille. A flight of Russian planes, usually containing 8-10 planes.
Fliefü-Jafü. About 160 German planes (2 Geschwader), equivalent to American Wing.
Flieger-Division. About 320 German planes, classed between an American Wing and Command.
Flieger Korps. About 600-900 German planes (2 or 3 Divisions), partially equivalent to an American Command.
Flivo (Fliegerverbindungsoffizier).--German for Air Liaison Officer.
Fliegerverbindungsoffizier (Flivo).--German for Air Liaison Officer.
Geschwader. 70-90 German planes (3 Gruppen), equivalent to American Group, and British Wing.
Golovanov, Marshall. Russian commander of the Long Range Bomber Forces.
Grubler, Corp. A member of Gruppe VI, of the Signal Intelligence Agency of the Army High Command (OKH/Gen d. NA).

Gruppe. 27-30 German planes (3 Staffeln), equivalent to US and British squadron.
Heimann, Corporal William. A member of Kona 1, of the Signal Intelligence Agency of the Army High Command (OKH/Gen. d. NA).
Hempel, Sgt. Werner. A member of Gruppe VI, of the Signal Intelligence Agency of the Army High Command (OKH/Gen. d. NA). He was a Baudot intercept technician.
Herold, Captain Wadim. Officer in charge of Ln. Regiment III/353 of the Signal Intelligence Agency of the Air Force High Command (OKL/LN) in the East.
Heudorf, Corp. A member of Naa 8 (radio intelligence battalion) of the 3rd Panzer Army.
I-17. "Extracts of SHAEF Interrogation of the following German communications personnel: Maj. Gen. Boner, Col. Grube, Lt. Col. Mettig, Maj. Rottler." A TICOM publication.
I-19. (b) "30 reports written by Kona 1 personnel."
(f) "Report on traffic analysis of Russian wireless traffic." A TICOM publication.
I-70. "Paper on the German Sigint Service by Lt. Col. Friedrich." A TICOM publication.
I-75. "Interrogation reports on German field Sigint personnel carried out at Buffer. Lt. August Schroeder, Lt. Starke, Corp. Heudorf, Capt. Holetzko."
I-116. "Report on the interrogation of Lt. Alex Dettmann and Oberwachtmeister Sergius S[illegible] of OKH (Gen. d. NA)."
I-130. "Homework of Hauptmann Herold, O.C., Ln. Rgt. III/353." A TICOM publication.
I-163. "Report on interrogation of Hptm. Scheidl, Ltn. Sann, and Ltn. Smolin, all of I/LN. Rgt. 353 (East), on German Sigint activity against Russian Air Forces." A TICOM publication.
I-168. "Report by the Karrenberg party on miscellaneous Russian W/T." A TICOM publication.
I-173. "Report by the Karrenberg party on Russian W/T." A TICOM publication.
IF-187. Vol. XII, Seabourne Report. "Technical Operations in the East, Luftwaffe SIS."
IF-186. Vol. XI, Seabourne Report. "History of Operations in the East, Luftwaffe SIS."
IPM. Abbreviation for flight over initial point (Russian Air Force).
Jagddivision.--German "light" division.
JU 52. German Junker, transport plane.
Junker 52. German transport plane.

45

Karrenberg, Sgt. Erich. A member of Gruppe VI, Signal Intelligence Agency of the Army High Command (OKH/Gen. d. NA). Worked on Russian Baudot traffic.

Kona (Kommandeur der Nachrichten Aufklaerung) (Commander for Signal Intelligence). A Kona was the Signal Intelligence component in the German Army organization.

"Light" division.--German translation, Jagddivision.

Long Range Bomber Force.--Avitsiya Dalneye Dyestviya, (ADD).

Luftflotte. German equivalent to American Air Force and British Command.

MAB (Morskaya Aviabasa).--Russian words for Naval Air Base Depot; largest unit of the Russian Naval Air Force.

MAP. Call sign formed from the Russian cover name, MAPKA.

MAPKA. Russian cover name.

Meldekopf.--German word for "reporting center".

Melki Radio Ulavlivatel. A type of Russian radar.

Mishka. Russian radio operator's name as given in an example of a Russian radio message.

Morskaya Aviabasa (MAB).--Russian words for "Naval Air Base Depot." Largest unit in the Russian Naval Air Force.

MRU (Melki Radio Ulavlivatel).--A type of Russian Radar.

Narodni Kommissariat Vnutrinikh Del (NKVD).--Peoples' Commissariat for Internal Affairs.

Naval Air Base Depot.--Morskaya Aviabasa, (MAB). Largest unit in the Russian Naval Air Force.

NKRF.--Peoples' Commissariat for River Shipping.

NKVD (Narodni Kommissariat Vnutrinikh Del).--Peoples' Commissariat for Internal Affairs. A Russian Secret Police organization.

OPM. An abbreviation used by the Russian I Guards Corps before giving bearings on the return flight.

Partisan nets. Radio nets used by the Russian Partisans, a guerilla organization.

Peoples' Commissariat for Internal Affairs.--Narodni Kommissariat Vnutrinikh Del (NKVD). A Russian Secret Police organization.

Peoples' Commissariat for River Shipping.--NKRF

Protivovosduschnaya oborona (PVO).--Antiaircraft Defense (Russian).

PVO (Protivovosduschnaya oborona).--Antiaircraft Defense (Russian).

QDM.--Q-signal meaning a request for magnetic course to steer with no wind.

QDR.--Q-signal requesting magnetic bearing in relation to station.

QSA.--Q-signal meaning "What is the strength of my signal (1 to 5)?"
RAB (Rayon Aviazionnage Basirovaniya).--The largest unit of the Russian Air Service Command.
Radio Ulavlivatel Samoletov (RUS).--A type of Russian radar.
Rasch. Lt. Werner. A member of 353rd German Air Force Signal Intelligence Regiment in the East.
Rayon Aviazionnage Basirovaniya (RAB). District Air Base. Largest unit in the Russian Air Service Command.
Regiment (Russian Air Force). About 30 planes, equivalent to US and British squadron, German Gruppe.
Reporting center.--Meldekopf (German).
RUS (Radio Ulavlivatel Samoletov).--A type of Russian radar.
Schmitz, Sgt. A member of Gruppe VI, Signal Intelligence Agency of the Army High Command (OKH/Gen. d. NA).
Staffel. A flight of German planes, usually containing 9-12 planes.
Suschowk, Sgt. Dietrich. A member of Gruppe VI, Signal Intelligence Agency of the Army High Command (OKH/Gen. d. NA).
TPR 43.--A Russian Call Sign Book.
TRS.--An abbreviation used by the Russian I Guards Corps before giving bearings on an outward flight.
Uffz. (Unteroffizier).--In general, non-commissioned officer; as a specific title, corporal.
Vozduch (VZD).--Russian word for "air."
VZD (vozduch).--Russian word for "air."

www.ingramcontent.com/pod-product-compliance
Lightning Source LLC
LaVergne TN
LVHW080924210926
848485LV00004B/719